November 1-4, 2015
Seoul, South Korea

Association for
Computing Machinery

Advancing Computing as a Science & Profession

SenSys'15

Proceedings of the 13th ACM Conference on Embedded Networked Sensor Systems

Sponsored by:

ACM SIGARCH, ACM SIGBED, ACM SIGCOMM, ACM SIGMETRICS, ACM SIGMOBILE, and ACM SIGOPS

Supported by:

Golfzon, NSF, KAIST School of Computing, KAIST Center for Mobile Software Platform, KT, Naver Labs, Samsung Electronics, SK Telecom, Seoul Metropolitan Government, Korea Tourism Organization, Kyungpook Nat'l Univ. CSOS, and DGIST

Association for
Computing Machinery

Advancing Computing as a Science & Profession

The Association for Computing Machinery
2 Penn Plaza, Suite 701
New York, New York 10121-0701

ISBN: 978-1-4503-3631-4 (Digital)

ISBN: 978-1-4503-4102-8 (Print)

Additional copies may be ordered prepaid from:

ACM Order Department
PO Box 30777
New York, NY 10087-0777, USA

Phone: 1-800-342-6626 (USA and Canada)
+1-212-626-0500 (Global)
Fax: +1-212-944-1318
E-mail: acmhelp@acm.org
Hours of Operation: 8:30 am – 4:30 pm ET

Printed in the USA

General Chair's Welcome Message

On behalf of the organizing committee, it is my great pleasure to welcome you to the 13th ACM Conference on Embedded Networked Sensor Systems (SenSys 2015) in Seoul, Korea. This is the first time that the SenSys comes to Asia. Also, SenSys 2015 continues to be co-located with the ACM International Conference on Embedded Systems for Energy-Efficient Built Environments (BuildSys), to take place on November 4th and 5th following last year's success.

SenSys is a leading venue for publication and presentation of research results on systems issues in the area of embedded, networked sensors and sensor-enabled smart systems. This year's program has selected 27 exciting papers embracing a number of perspectives including energy, localization, systems, networking, information services and object/activity recognition. In addition to the regular full paper sessions, this year also sees a significantly expanded adjunct program, 26 demos and 34 posters. The workshop program has four workshops covering exciting topics in energy harvesting and energy-neutral sensing systems, context sensing and activity recognition, Internet of Things toward applications, real world wireless sensor networks. It also includes a Ph.D. Forum that provides a supportive environment for doctoral students to discuss their dissertation work. Last but not least, SenSys 2015 hosts two exciting keynote speakers: Professor Raj Rajkumar from CMU will provide a stimulating view on the challenges and opportunities of self-driving vehicles, and Dr. Hendrik F. Hamann from IBM will give an exciting talk on smarter solutions and physical analytics.

Putting together SenSys 2015 has been a huge team effort. I would like to thank many people for their tireless work, including the Local Arrangement Chairs JeongGil Ko, Jeongyeop Paek, and Jeonghoon Kang, Publicity Chairs Prabal Dutta, Koen Langendoen, and Insik Shin, Finance Chairs Sung-Ju Lee and Uichin Lee, Social Media Chair Eric Rozner, Registration Chair Sourav Kumar Dandapat, PC Local Organizer Niki Trigoni, Web administrators Chiwoo Cho and Sangwon Choi. A special thanks goes to the Student Travel Grants Chairs Young-Bae Ko, Raghu K. Ganti, and Taiwoo Park for the hard work acquiring funds and making it possible for dozens of students to come to SenSys 2015. I would like to acknowledge the tremendous efforts of the Technical Program Committee, including the chairs Cecilia Mascolo and Tarek Abdelzaher in particular, for making an outstanding technical program. In addition, I would like to thank Poster and Demo Chairs Rajesh Krishna BALAN, Inseok Hwang, and Seungwoo Kang, Doctoral Colloquium Chairs Nicholas Lane and Taiwoo Park, Workshop Chairs Marco Gruteser and Youngki Lee. A deep thanks goes to our Publication Chair Qin (Christine) Lv for managing and compiling all the details of the proceedings. I would like to thank Jie Liu and Kamin Whitehouse, the former and current Steering Committee Chairs. They have been very supportive in putting the conference together. Finally, I would like to express my deep gratitude to the sponsors of SenSys 2015.

I sincerely hope that this year's conference will provide you with a valuable opportunity to share ideas and experiences with researchers and practitioners from institutions around the world, and you will find it interesting, useful and enjoyable.

Junehwa Song
SenSys 2015 General Chair
Korea Advanced Institute of Science and Technology
South Korea

Program Co-Chairs' Welcome Message

It is our great pleasure to welcome you to the 13th ACM Conference on Embedded Networked Sensor Systems (SenSys 2015). We hope you enjoy this conference that attracts a diverse set of attendees from both academia and industry and is a leading venue for publications and idea exchange on networked sensing. SenSys this year introduces a highly selective, single-track program featuring systems issues of sensors and sensor-enabled smart systems, broadly defined. It provides an ideal venue to address research challenges facing the design, development, deployment, use, and fundamental limits of these systems.

The paper review process this year was highly selective. Out of 132 high quality submissions, only 27 were accepted for publication and presentation as full papers, yielding an acceptance rate around 20.45%. Submitted papers underwent a rigorous multistage review process. First, all submissions were checked for compliance and for general quality and topic match. Those not meeting conference criteria were administratively rejected without review. Papers surviving this stage were assigned three reviews in the first stage of the peer review process. At the conclusion of this stage, those papers that none of the reviewers recommended acceptance were rejected. The rest were assigned two additional reviews, thus totaling 5 reviews per paper. An online discussion phase then ensued, resulting in recommending 59 papers for discussion at the in-person physical PC meeting. At the conclusion of the PC meeting, a total of 27 papers were recommended for acceptance to the conference. All recommended papers were assigned shepherds to help ensure that the authors produce a final manuscript that satisfactorily addresses reviewer comments. All shepherded papers were ultimately accepted to the conference.

Our program this year covers an exciting set of topics including energy, localization, systems, networking, information services and object/activity recognition. It also includes a poster/demo session, a panel, and two distinguished keynote speakers: Professor Raj Rajkumar from CMU, and Dr. Hendrik Hamann from IBM Research.

Putting together the program of Sensys 2015 was a team effort. We would like to express our deepest gratitude to Prof. Junehwa Song, the General Chair, for organizing the team. We would also like to thank the authors for providing stellar contributions. We would like to express special thanks to the program committee members and shepherds who worked very hard in reviewing papers and providing suggestions for their improvement. We would also like to thank ACM and the other members of the organizing committee for all the logistical arrangements that made it possible to bring this program to the attendees. Last but not least, we would like to thank the attendees for your patronage of the conference and for making it a successful meeting place for multiple communities and a catalyst for discussions and creative exchange.

We hope that you will find this program interesting and thought-provoking and that the conference will provide you with a valuable opportunity to share ideas with other researchers and practitioners from institutions around the world.

Cecilia Mascolo
SenSys 2015 Program Co-Chairs
University of Cambridge, UK

Tarek Abdelzaher
SenSys 2015 Program Co-Chairs
University of Illinois at Urbana-Champaign, USA

Table of Contents

Session: Networking

Poster Session

Demo Session

Doctoral Symposium

Workshop Summaries

SenSys 2015 Conference Organization

General Chair: Junehwa Song *(KAIST, South Korea)*

Program Co-Chairs: Tarek Abdelzaher *(University of Illinois at Urbana-Champaign, USA)*
Cecilia Mascolo *(University of Cambridge, UK)*

Local Arrangements Co-Chairs: Jeonghoon Kang *(Korea Electronics Technology Institute, South Korea)*
JeongGil Ko *(Ajou University, South Korea)*
Jeongyeup Paek *(Chung-Ang University, South Korea)*

Finance Co-Chairs: Sung-Ju Lee *(KAIST, South Korea)*
Uichin Lee *(KAIST, South Korea)*

Social Media Chair: Eric Rozner *(IBM Research, USA)*

Publicity Co-Chairs: Prabal Dutta *(University of Michigan, USA)*
Koren Langendoen *(University of Delft, Netherland)*
Insik Shin *(KAIST, South Korea)*

Publication Chair: Qin (Christine) Lv *(University of Colorado Boulder, USA)*

Workshop Co-Chairs: Marco Gruteser *(Rutgers University, USA)*
Youngki Lee *(Singapore Management University, Singapore)*

Poster & Demo Co-Chairs: Rajesh Krishna BALAN *(Signapore Management University, Singapore)*
Inseok Hwang *(IBM Research, USA)*
Seungwoo Kang *(KOREATECH, South Korea)*

Doctoral Colloquium Co-Chairs: Nicholas Lane *(Bell Laboratories, UK)*
Taiwoo Park *(Michigan State University, USA)*

Student Travel Grant Co-Chairs: Yong-Bae Ko *(Ajou University, South Korea)*
Raghu K. Ganti *(IBM Research, USA)*
Taiwoo Park *(Michigan State University, USA)*

PC Local Organizer: Niki Trigoni *(University of Oxford, UK)*

Registration Chair: Sourav Kumar Dandapat *(KAIST, South Korea)*

Student Volunteer Chair: Hyung-Sin Kim *(Seoul National University, South Korea)*

Web Administrators: Chiwoo Cho *(KAIST, South Korea)*
Sangwon Choi *(KAIST, South Korea)*

Program Committee: Hojung Cha *(Yonsei University, South Korea)*
David Chu *(Microsoft Research, USA)*
Raghu K. Ganti *(IBM Research, USA)*
Marco Gruteser *(Rutgers University, USA)*
Rajesh K. Gupta *(University of California, San Diego, USA)*
Tian He *(University of Minnesota, USA)*
Wen Hu *(UNSW and NICTA, Australia)*
Polly Huang *(National Taiwan University, Taiwan)*
Fred Jiang *(Columbia University, USA)*
Bhaskar Krishnamachari *(University of Southern California, USA)*
Nicholas Lane *(Bell Laboratories, UK)*
Koen Langendoen *(University of Delft, Netherland)*
Akos Ledeczi *(Vanderbilt University, USA)*
Jie Liu *(Microsoft Research, USA)*
Archan Misra *(Singapore Management University, Singapore)*
Luca Mottola *(Politecnico di Milano, Italy)*
Amy L. Murphy *(Bruno Kessler Foundation, Italy)*
Lama Nachman *(Intel, USA)*
Gian Pietro Picco *(University of Trento, Italy)*
Kiran Rachuri *(Samsung US, USA)*
Kay Romer *(University of Graz, Austria)*
Anthony Rowe *(Carnegie Mellon University, USA)*
Silvia Santini *(Technische Universität Darmstadt, Germany)*
Lu Su *(University of Buffalo, USA)*
Sasu Tarkoma *(University of Helsinki, Finland)*
Niki Trigoni *(University of Oxford, UK)*
Kamin Whitehouse *(University of Virginia, USA)*

Advisory Committee: Jong-Deok Choi (*Samsung's Software R&D Center, South Korea*)
Seungryoul Maeng (*KAIST, South Korea*)
SangHyuk Son (*DGIST, South Korea*)

SenSys 2015 Sponsors & Supporters

Sponsors:

ACM Association for Computing Machinery

ACM SigArch, SigBed, SigComm, SigMetrics, SigMobile, SigOps

Gold Supporters:

GOLFZON New Experience

NSF

Silver Supporters:

KAIST School of Computing

Center for Mobile Software Platform

kt

NAVER LABS

SAMSUNG

SK telecom

SEOUL METROPOLITAN GOVERNMENT

KOREA TOURISM ORGANIZATION
www.visitkorea.or.kr

Bronze Supporters:

CSOS Center of Self-Organizing Software-Platform

DGIST 고신뢰CPS연구센터
Resilient Cyber-Physical Systems Research Center

Keynote Talk

Self-Driving Vehicles: The Challenges and Opportunities Ahead

Raj Rajkumar
George Westinghouse Professor
Department of Electrical and Computer Engineering, Carnegie Mellon University
Pittsburgh, PA, USA
rajkumar@cmu.edu

ABSTRACT

Self-driving vehicles seem to have become quite the rage in popular culture over the past 3 years or so. Jumpstarted by the DARPA Grand Challenges, the promise of self-driving vehicles does have the potential to revolutionize modern transportation. This talk will provide some insights on many basic questions that, however, still remain unanswered. What are the technological barriers? What can or cannot be sensed? Can vehicles recognize and comprehend as good as (or better than) humans? What role does connectivity play (if any)? Will the technology be affordable for the masses? How do issues like liability, insurance, regulations and societal acceptance impact deployment? The talk will be based on road experiences interspersed with some speculation.

Categories and Subject Descriptors

C.3 [**Special-purpose and Application-based Systems**]: Real-time and embedded systems

Keywords

Self-driving vehicles

SenSys '15, November 01-04, 2015, Seoul, Republic of Korea
ACM 978-1-4503-3631-4/15/11.
http://dx.doi.org/10.1145/2809695.2823464

BIO

Prof. Raj Rajkumar is the George Westinghouse Professor of Electrical & Computer Engineering and Robotics Institute at Carnegie Mellon University. At Carnegie Mellon, he directs National University Transportation Center on Safety, which is sponsored by the US Department of Transportation. He also directs the Real-Time and Multimedia Systems Laboratory (RTML), and co-directs the General Motors-Carnegie Mellon Connected and Autonomous Driving Collaborative Research Laboratory (CAD-CRL). Raj has served as the Program Chair and General Chair of six international ACM/IEEE conferences on real-time systems, wireless sensor networks, cyber-physical systems and multimedia computing/networking. He has authored one book, edited another book, holds three US patents, and has more than 150 publications in peer-reviewed forums. Eight of these publications have received Best Paper Awards. He has given several keynotes and distinguished lectures at several conferences and universities. He is an IEEE Fellow, and an ACM Distinguished Engineer. He has been given an Outstanding Technical Achievement and Leadership Award by the IEEE Technical Committee on Real-Time Systems. Prof Rajkumar's work has influenced many commercial operating systems. He was also the primary founder of Ottomatika Inc., a company that focused on delivering the core software intelligence for self-driving vehicles. Ottomatika was recently acquired by Delphi. His research interests include all aspects of cyber-physical systems.

http://www.ece.cmu.edu/~raj

Keynote Talk

Keynote Talk

From Sensors to Smarter Solutions with Physical Analytics

Hendrik F. Hamann
IBM T. J. Watson Research Center
Yorktown Heights, NY, USA
hendrikh@us.ibm.com

ABSTRACT

While in the past most information on the internet was generated by humans or computers, with the emergence of the Internet of Things, vast amount of data is now being created by sensors from devices, machines etc, which are placed in the physical world. Here we present a series of example applications enabled by such sensor data and what we call "Physical Analytics", which provides the underlying intelligence using a combination of physical and statistical models.

The smarter solutions, which are being presented in this talk, range from active energy management and optimization, environmental sensing and controls, precision agriculture to renewable energy forecasting. All these different applications have been built using a single platform, which is comprised of a set of "configurable" technologies components including ultra-low power sensing and communication, big data management technologies, numerical modeling for physical systems, machine learning based physical model blending, and physical analytics based automation and control.

Categories and Subject Descriptors

C.3 [**Special-purpose and Application-based Systems**]: Real-time and embedded systems

Keywords

Big data; IoT; Sensors; Controls

BIO

Dr. Hendrik F. Hamann is a Research Manager in the Physical Sciences Department at the IBM T.J. Watson Research Center, Yorktown Heights, NY. He received his PhD from the University of Goettingen in Germany. In 1995 he joined JILA (Joint institute between the University of Colorado and NIST) as a Research Associate in Boulder, Colorado. During his tenure at JILA he developed novel near-field optical microscopes to study single molecules at high spatial resolution. Since 2001 he is leading the Physical Analytics program in IBM Research, first as a Research Staff Member and currently as a Research Manager. Between 2005 and 2009 he worked on energy management all the way from the device level to large scale computing systems. His current research interest includes sensor networks, sensor-based physical modeling, renewable energy, precision agriculture, energy management and system physics. He has authored and co-authored more than 80 peer-reviewed scientific papers and holds over 90 patents and has over 70 pending patent applications. Dr. Hamann is an IBM Master Inventor and has served on governmental committees such as the National Academy of Sciences and as an industrial advisor to Universities. He is a member of the American Physical Society (APS), Optical Society of America (OSA), The Institute of Electrical and Electronics Engineers (IEEE) and the NY Academy of Sciences.

http://researcher.watson.ibm.com/researcher/view.php?person=us-hendrikh

SenSys '15, November 01-04, 2015, Seoul, Republic of Korea
ACM 978-1-4503-3631-4/15/11.
http://dx.doi.org/10.1145/2809695.2823463

Tragedy of the Coulombs: Federating Energy Storage for Tiny, Intermittently-Powered Sensors

Josiah Hester, Lanny Sitanayah, Jacob Sorber
School of Computing
Clemson University
{jhester, lsitana, jsorber}@clemson.edu

ABSTRACT

Untethered sensing devices have, for decades, powered all system components (processors, sensors, actuators, etc) from a single shared energy store (battery or capacitor). When designing batteryless sensors that are powered by harvested energy, this traditional approach results in devices that charge slowly and that are more error prone, inflexible, and inefficient than they could be.

This paper presents a novel federated approach to energy storage, called UFoP, that partitions and prioritizes harvested energy automatically into multiple isolated smaller energy stores (capacitors). UFoP simplifies task scheduling, enables efficient use of components with differing voltage requirements, and produces devices that charge more quickly under identical harvesting conditions than a traditional centralized approach. We have implemented a UFoP reference design and conducted extensive experimental evaluation, including a short deployment. Our experimental results using an MSP430-based prototype show that UFoP provides as much as 10% more computational availability, and as much as four times more radio availability than the centralized approach. For all applications and energy environments evaluated, UFoP harvested 0.7-10.2% more energy than the centralized equivalent; meaning UFoP adds zero energy overhead.

Categories and Subject Descriptors

C.3 [**Special-Purpose and Application-Based Systems**]: Microprocessor/microcomputer applications

General Terms

Reliability, Measurement, Performance

Keywords

Energy Harvesting; Federated Energy; Task Coupling; Capacitor; Embedded System

SenSys'15, November 1–4, 2015, Seoul, South Korea..

ACM 978-1-4503-3631-4/15/11 ...$15.00.
DOI: http://dx.doi.org/10.1145/2809695.2809707.

1. INTRODUCTION

Energy is the greatest single limiting factor in the design and effective operation of mobile sensors and other untethered computing devices. Reductions in power consumption and advances in energy harvesting are making long-term device deployments increasingly possible; however, harvested energy is often variable, scarce, and difficult to predict. Batteries are large and expensive. Batteries wear out, charge slowly, require special protection and charging circuitry, pose environmental risks, and fundamentally limit the lifetime and deployability of today's mobile computing devices.

These challenges have inspired a range of capacitor-based sensor devices [8, 9, 18, 20–22] that harvest energy, charge quickly, and can store only enough energy for short bursts of operation (a few seconds or even a few hundred milliseconds long). This new generation of tiny batteryless sensing devices will be cheaper, more durable, and more environmentally friendly than their battery powered predecessors. They will also have much tighter energy budgets and much more frequent power failures, two conditions that are poorly-supported by today's mobile hardware platforms, especially when it comes to storing and managing energy.

Traditional mobile devices store energy in a single common energy store (battery or capacitor) that is used to power all system components (*e.g.,* processors, sensors, radios and other peripherals) an approach that is simple to design and works well for devices with large batteries; however, when energy budgets are tight and failures frequent, each component's energy usage can significantly impact the availability of other components. For example, reading from a sensor may impact the device's ability to do computation. Power hungry operations, like transmitting a radio message, may cause the device to lose power entirely, becoming unavailable until the device can be recharged. Reasoning correctly about peripherals, consequent power consumption, and application priorities requires computational resources (for modeling and prediction) that transiently-powered devices cannot afford.

In this paper, we propose a new federated approach to storing harvested energy that relaxes the coupling between a tiny, intermittently powered device's individual components (or subsystems). Our approach, called UFoP (United Federation of Peripherals), uses individual per-peripheral energy stores and low-power control circuitry to isolate and prioritize individual peripherals. Federating energy storage allows power-hungry operations to proceed without sacrificing the device's immediate ability to use other peripherals, gather new data, process incoming data, and respond to incoming stimuli. This approach also simplifies the task of programming energy-aware logic—effectively replacing complex modeling of analog circuit behaviors with simple binary decisions based on whether or not a peripheral is available.

Listing 1: A conservative example program

```
when timer fires do { // Once every 1ms
  if can_sense_store_and_send? {
        while (!sample_buffer_full?) {
            collect_sample()
            sleep(1ms)
        }
        compute_and_store_mean()
        transmit_recent_means()
  }
    sleep()
}
```

Listing 2: A more optimistic program

```
when timer fires do { // Once every 1ms
  if can_sense? {
    collect_sample()
  }
  if sample_buffer_full? {
    compute_and_store_mean()
  }
  if can_send? && has_stored_means? {
    transmit_recent_means()
    }
    sleep()
}
```

Our initial implementation of the UFoP approach uses ultra-low-power comparators to control and prioritize the charging of individual energy stores, where the microcontroller gets the first priority. The main capacitor charges until it reaches 2.7 V, then the microcontroller turns on. When the input voltage reaches 3.1 V, the peripheral capacitors charge. In our experiments, we found that programs that use UFoP as the energy backbone had as much as 10% more computational availability, and as much as four times more radio availability than the centralized approach. Using UFoP, programs become more resilient, reducing low voltage events dramatically. Additionally, programs that use UFoP harvested more energy for all energy environments evaluated than programs using the traditional centralized energy storage approach.

While distributed energy storage has been employed in large-scale power systems [3], and hybrid storage systems have been used to improve the efficiency of battery charging [12, 15, 16], UFoP is, to the best of our knowledge, the first embedded system to employ federated energy storage, in a general way, to simplify management of individual system components.

2. CENTRALIZED ENERGY STORAGE

For half of a century, computing devices have used a centralized approach to power system components (processors, sensors, radios and other peripherals)—an approach that has reduced both device size and cost, and that, until now, has had no significant drawbacks. Whether power is supplied by a dedicated connection to wired infrastructure or by a battery that is regularly recharged, processors, memories, and peripherals all use a shared power supply and the nearly-universal assumption that power is unlimited and stable. System designers have, at times, made efforts to reduce power consumption and extend battery life, but they rarely consider whether the program's next action may impair the device's ability to perform additional functions.

However, when designing applications for batteryless and other transiently-powered mobile devices, supplying power to all components using a single centralized capacitor or battery reduces the system's flexibility and complicates programmer decision-making. The following challenges must be carefully considered by a system designer before developing an application using centralized energy storage:

Capacitor tuning: Capacitor size is a critical factor that defines how an energy-harvesting batteryless device will operate. Smaller capacitors charge quickly, but may not be able to store enough energy for more power-hungry tasks. Larger capacitors can store more energy, supporting longer bursts of computation and more power-intensive operations. Larger capacitors also charge more slowly, incur longer power outages, and waste more energy (leakage). A system designer can maximize device availability and up-time by selecting a capacitor that is just large enough to support the operations that the application needs to perform. When an application performs both energy-efficient tasks (*i.e.,* sampling lightweight sensors or performing simple data processing) and energy-intensive tasks (*i.e.,* wireless data transmissions), a centralized energy store must be large enough to support all operations—both heavy- and light-weight operations.

Task coupling: A common storage capacitor also produces a tight coupling between program tasks and system peripherals. Sampling a sensor, for example, will consume energy and may either leave insufficient energy for subsequent tasks or may cause the supply voltage to drop low enough that the device loses power altogether, and subsequent tasks must wait until more energy becomes available.

In order to illustrate these challenges, let's consider two simple programs described in Listings 1 and 2. Both programs gather sensor readings until a buffer is full, compute the mean of the readings, and wirelessly transmit a fixed number of recently computed means[1]. The first program (Listing 1) conservatively sleeps until it has harvested enough energy to an entire application cycle (collect, process, and transmit samples). The second (Listing 2) waits only until it has enough energy to complete the next task and then proceeds optimistically, assuming that enough energy will be harvested in the future to complete subsequent tasks.

Power failures are a constant concern for batteryless devices. When power failures do occur, computational state can be saved efficiently to nonvolatile memory (like FRAM) in case a power failure occurs between tasks or before a task completes. These checkpoints can be included explicitly by application developers or inserted automatically, using a system like Mementos [17]. Checkpoints allow some tasks to be resumed after a power failure; however, other tasks, like sampling a sensor or transmitting a radio packet, cannot be easily resumed due to timing and hardware constraints.

Consequently, the batteryless device that implements these example programs will need to determine, at runtime, when enough energy is stored on its capacitor to perform each desired task safely. A capacitor's stored energy can be estimated by measuring its voltage, and tasks can be safely run when that voltage exceeds a predetermined threshold (V_{safe}), which can be determined empirically or analytically based on the capacitance used, the time the task requires to complete (t_{task}), and the power needed while the task is executing. Figure 1 illustrates how this threshold is determined. If V_{safe} is chosen correctly, starting the task when the capacitor's voltage is higher than V_{safe} ensures that the task will always complete before the capacitor discharges to V_{fail}—the point at which essential

[1] A small number of previous means are transmitted to provide some redundancy in case a packet is lost.

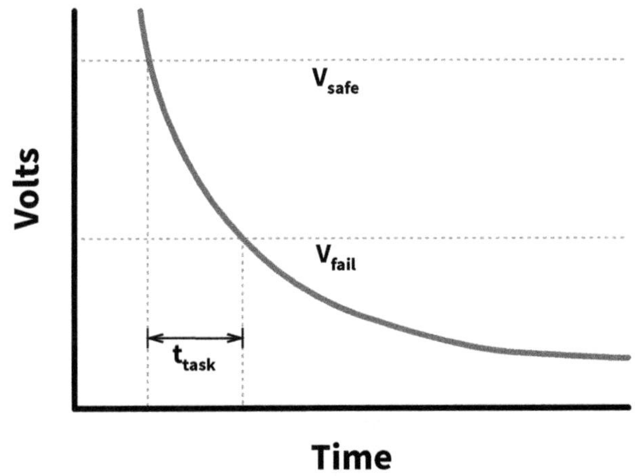

Figure 1: During task execution, capacitor discharge is sufficiently predictable to determine the voltage at which it is safe to begin executing it, in order to ensure that it will complete before a power failure.

hardware components—MCU, memory, sensors, radios, or other peripherals—turn off or become unusable.

Some tasks within a single application may take longer or consume more power than others, so a separate threshold, V_{safe}, will be needed for each individual task. System designers may optimistically try to execute a task before the safe threshold is reached, in the hope that future harvested energy will be sufficient to finish the task successfully. When energy is abundant, this gamble may allow the device to produce results more quickly. When harvested energy is insufficient, sub-threshold task execution will result in wasted effort and may result in avoidable power failures.

Software federation of the energy supply as described above can lead to close coupling of components. The top plot in Figure 2 shows the capacitor and microcontroller voltages over time for a solar-powered batteryless sensor node that gathers sensor data and transmits it wirelessly to a base station (see Listing 1). In this scenario, a control circuit waits to turn on the microcontroller until the capacitor charges to a voltage (*i.e.,* around 2.7 V) sufficient to initialize the processor and accomplish some computation, the control circuit then turns off the microcontroller when the voltage drops below 2 V[2] (when processing becomes unreliable for most microcontrollers). The chosen capacitor is large enough (195 µF) to power both data collection and radio transmission on a single charge, and the application waits until the voltage charges up high enough to ensure that the transmission completes most of the time.

In this scenario, each radio transmission causes the MCU voltage to drop dangerously close to (and occasionally cross) the 2 V point where the MCU becomes unstable. The larger capacitor also charges slowly, and leaks, meaning that time and energy is lost.

3. FEDERATING ENERGY

In light of the shortcomings of centralized energy storage, this paper argues for a different approach which stores harvested energy in multiple independent small capacitors, one for core processing functionality, and another for each peripheral. We call this federated approach UFoP (United Federation of Peripherals).

[2]The control circuit's hysteresis is adjustable. The thresholds used are those we have empirically found to work well, in practice.

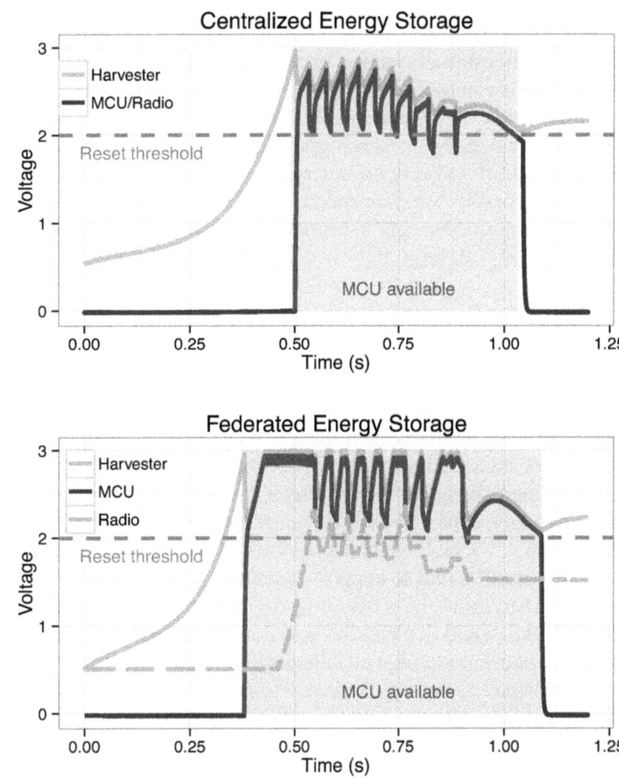

Figure 2: This figure shows a "sense-and-send" application using traditional centralized and our proposed federated energy storage approaches. Energy federation allows lightweight functionality (sensing and data processing in this example) to be available sooner.

By allowing the microcontroller, sensors, and radio to function independently, UFoP provides the following key benefits:

Useful work starts sooner: While some approaches have tried to mask volatility of the energy supply in software [2], the reality of capacitor based devices is that a smaller capacitor charges to an arbitrary voltage, faster than a larger one. A centralized approach may use software to mask volatility of the energy supply in order to simplify task management, but the energy store will still be unusable until it meets the necessary voltage for components to be turned on. By federating the energy storage, smaller capacitors charge more quickly, allowing lightweight tasks (some sensors and microcontroller operations) to be available while larger capacitors for radios and other power-hungry peripherals charge up. This can be seen in Figure 2 where the MCU becomes available hundreds of milliseconds before the centralized version.

Fewer power failures: Isolating each per-component capacitor prevents a power-hungry component from jeopardizing the whole system. For example, when the radio drains its dedicated capacitor's power to transmit messages, the device retains the ability (at least in the short term) to gather and process new data. UFoP prioritizes the charging of individual energy stores. In our current implementation, the microcontroller gets the first priority, while the priorities of sensors, radios, and other peripherals can be configured to suit individual applications. For example, the tight coupling present in the centralized approach shown in Figure 2 causes the supply voltage to dip below the reset threshold, endangering the device duty cycle. With UFoP, this problem occurs much less frequently.

Simpler application decisions: Each peripheral is available for use as soon as its capacitor is charged, and can be used independently of the charge state of other peripherals. When a peripheral is used and depletes its own energy, it becomes unavailable until it is recharged. This allows UFoP to "save up" energy for power-hungry tasks, like short bursts of radio communication, while allowing data collection and processing to continue. When using centralized storage, application decisions can be complicated—requiring designers to reason about the aggregate impact of multiple peripherals and tasks on a single capacitor. In contrast, a UFoP device can determine whether it can afford to use two peripherals (*e.g.,* a sensor and a radio), by simply checking their individual voltages.

Increased flexibility: UFoP devices provide more flexibility when combining peripherals with different energy requirements. For example, consider a sensor node that combines an MSP430 MCU as its computing core, a low-power sensor, and a more power-hungry radio. A larger capacitor will be needed in order to support the radio, which will charge much more slowly than a smaller capacitor that might be sufficient to support the other components for short bursts of operation. In a centralized energy architecture, radio transmissions would deplete the large common capacitor and may render the entire node unavailable while it recharges. In a UFoP device, the small capacitors dedicated to the core and sensor would charge more quickly, allowing the application to continue gathering and processing data, while waiting for the larger radio capacitor to charge. In both cases, data would be sent at roughly the same rate, but using UFoP the application would have more flexibility in deciding what to send.

Lower energy consumption: Not all system components require the same voltages to operate. UFoP allows individual component capacitors to be charged to the voltage required by that component, which often results in lower operating voltages and reduced per-component energy consumption.

Harvest more energy: When using UFoP, the energy harvester's voltage rises quickly (as the small microcontroller capacitor charges), but increases in harvester voltage is slow as power is diverted to charge peripherals. When UFoP's thresholds are set appropriately, the device spends more time in its most efficient voltage range and harvests more energy than the centralized equivalent.

3.1 UFoP Reference Design

Figure 3 shows a UFoP system that is integrated with two commonly used peripherals in sensing applications (*i.e.,* a sensor and a radio). The system consists of four main components: an energy harvester, charging controller, peripheral controller, and peripherals. The energy harvesting device harvests ambient energy and stores it in the first-stage capacitor. The charge controller is responsible for turning on and off the microcontroller and charging an array of peripheral capacitors. The peripheral controller turns on and off peripherals (sensor and radio), which are only available when their capacitors are charged.

Energy Harvesting: The UFoP system is powered by ambient sources. The energy harvester converts free energy from the environment (*e.g.,* solar, thermal, radio frequency (RF), and kinetic energy) into electrical energy (DC), which the harvester supplies to the rest of the system. From the harvester, the current flows to charge the first-stage capacitor that powers the microcontroller.

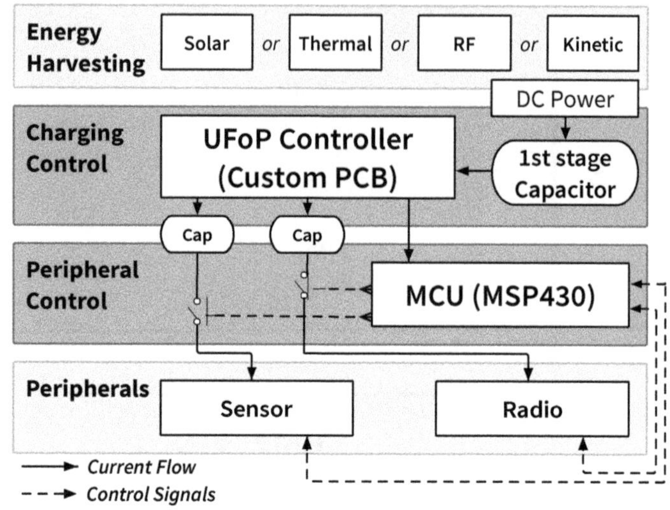

Figure 3: Overview of UFoP when integrated with a set of commonly used peripherals; a sensor, and a radio. A UFoP system is made up of four components: an energy harvester, charging controller, peripheral controller, and peripherals. The charge controller manages the charging of an array of capacitors (drawing from the first-stage capacitor) as well as turning on and off the MCU. The peripheral controller (an MSP430FR5739 in the current prototype) gates power to the peripherals, allowing peripherals to be completely off when not in use. Peripherals and the MCU communicate independently of the charging controller.

Charging Control: UFoP uses low-power control circuitry as charge controller to control and prioritize the charging of an array of capacitors as well as turning on and off the microcontroller. UFoP is designed with the microcontroller as a non-negotiable first power priority. A sensor without a microcontroller could not process data, and a radio without a microcontroller would have no signal to transmit. From an implementation perspective, this is ideal since the microcontroller can then be used to control the power flow to the peripherals. As sensors and radios can provide functionality regardless of the operation of other peripherals, subsequent priority values can be assigned based on system requirements. In our reference design, the first-stage capacitor charges until it reaches 2.7 V, then the microcontroller turns on. When the input voltage reaches 3.1 V, the current starts to flow into the peripheral capacitors.

Peripheral Control: The peripheral controller in the UFoP system can be any ultra-low-power microcontroller, like the FRAM based MSP430 processors. In our reference design, we use the MSP430FR5739 as peripheral controller; which only draws 81.4 μA/MHz in active mode. When the first-stage capacitor capacitor charges up to 2.7 V, the microcontroller turns on. The microcontroller gates power to the peripherals, allowing peripherals to be completely off when not in use. This control communication is independent from the charging control scheme. The switches in the peripheral controller are designed to open (disconnect) when the microcontroller loses its power and turns off, *i.e.,* when the main capacitor's voltage falls below 1.8 V. This design satisfies the MSP430FR5739 supply voltage requirements, *i.e.,* 1.8 V to 3.6 V. We built a thin software layer to manage the ADC polling, timers, and interrupt wake ups, for the MSP430 line of microcontrollers. This layer can easily be ported to other platforms, as the components and software practices are common among embedded systems.

Peripherals: Two of the most commonly used peripherals in sensing applications are sensor and radio. The type of the peripherals and the tasks they perform determine the size of the capacitors used. When an application uses a lightweight sensor and a radio, the size of the capacitor for the sensor should be a lot smaller than that for the radio. If the application requires intensive data transmission, the radio's capacitor size must be large enough to support the tasks. In the UFoP system, the peripherals are only available when their dedicated capacitors are charged.

3.2 Application Development Simplification

Federating energy storage changes how sensing applications are built. From the hardware point of view, sizing several capacitors appropriately to peripherals is much easier than sizing one capacitor to multiple peripherals and a microcontroller that could have different supply voltage requirements. For example, the MSP430 microcontroller works within the 1.8 – 3.6 V range, the CC2500 radio (a very common 2.4 GHz radio) works from 2.0 V to 3.9 V, and a humidity sensor used in our greenhouse monitoring application works from 3 V to 5 V. This combination makes it difficult for application developers to size a single capacitor and determine duty cycle. In this example, the radio and microcontroller could potentially never come online while waiting for the voltage to be sufficient for the humidity sensor to function. UFoP allows application developers to simplify this by sizing and dedicating each capacitor at a specific voltage to each peripheral.

From the software development point of view, UFoP allows a duty cycle when energy is scarce, and when it is abundant. That means UFoP lets the duty cycle scale up or down without hurting the average duty cycle performance. For example, in a classic "sense-and-send" application, the device can use a more powerful sensor when there is an abundance of energy, but performs only computations if there is very little energy. With UFoP, programmers have a more deterministic view of energy and task scheduling, allowing them to make better informed decisions during application development. In addition, UFoP simplifies applications by eliminating the need for complicated algorithms to predict when the peripherals become available.

4. IMPLEMENTATION

We have implemented a UFoP reference design on a custom printed circuit board. The prototype employs a variety of different hardware components. Two nano-power comparators are used per peripheral, that control the charging, and discharging of the peripheral capacitor. The current prototype supports two peripherals. An ICL7665 or MIC841 voltage monitor is used to monitor the first-stage capacitor, this monitor has a built in reference, and resistor defined hysteresis. The settable hysteresis allows a broad operating range for the microcontroller. Each of the comparators has a resistor divider defined trip point; the trip points and hysteresis are set in such a way that the microcontroller will always be on if the peripherals are charging.

Because UFoP is a hardware addition, some note must be taken of its size and cost. The current UFoP prototype measures 37.0 mm by 15.2 mm, with a low profile. The total cost of the prototype bill of materials, including all components, and PCB from a batch PCB supplier like OSH Park, amounts to less than $20 per device, further development could easily lower this cost. If the current prototype was produced at scales of a 1000, the price drops to less than $2 per device. Most of this cost would disappear in a custom silicon solution, which would also reduce the size and component count for a deployed sensor.

In addition to building the UFoP prototype, multiple systems were built or used in the evaluation. We used the energy environment emulator Ekho [10] to record and replay solar energy harvesting environments, as well as RF energy environments. Solar environments were generated by a programmatically controlled headlight focused on a solar panel. RF environments were generated from the harvester of a UMich Moo [24], which harvested RFID energy from the UHF band created by an Impinj Speedway RFID Reader. IV-surfaces were created by moving the reader back and forth across the front of the Umich Moo. The recorded IV-surfaces were later replayed in the lab using Ekho; which provided a realistic energy harvesting environment to test UFoP with. We plan to make all IV-surfaces we recorded freely available online at publication time. We also used an NI USB-6356 [11] and Measurement Computing USB-201 [4] data acquisition device (DAQ) for voltage and current measurements, as well as event counting. For all applications, we used MSP430FR5739 Launchpads as the main processing device.

We translated the programs described in Listings 1 and 2 into embedded C, running on the MSP430FR5739. Each program has two variants, one that is meant to run with UFoP functioning as the energy backbone, and one that runs with the traditional centralized energy approach. The federated and centralized variants are intentionally similar for both programs; the federated versions differ in that they dedicate an ADC per peripheral to monitor the energy storage levels of the radio and accelerometer supply voltages, in addition to the MCU energy storage levels. Both of these programs attempt to federate energy storage, one using UFoP, and one in software. We used these programs to evaluate the effectiveness of the federated energy approach in terms of availability, resiliency, and energy harvesting efficiency. We also developed federated and centralized versions of a greenhouse monitoring application, which is described in Section 6. These are similar in function to the above, but use a different set of peripherals. A basestation program was also created to listen for and log sensor readings during the greenhouse monitoring deployment.

All hardware designs, I–V surfaces, and software will be made freely available online at publication time.

5. EVALUATION

In this section, we evaluate the performance of sensing applications that use our UFoP reference design as an energy backbone. Specifically, we examine how federated and centralized variants of sense-and-send behave in solar and RF energy environments. We compare these two approaches and measure them in terms of availability, resiliency, and energy harvesting performance.

In our experiments, we found that programs that use UFoP as the energy backbone had as much as 10% more MCU availability, and as much as four times more radio availability than the centralized competitor. Using UFoP, programs become more resilient, reducing failures by 4.5*x* in some cases. Additionally, programs that use UFoP harvested 0.7-10.2% more energy, for all energy environments evaluated, than programs using a centralized energy storage approach; meaning UFoP adds zero energy overhead.

5.1 Methodology

To evaluate UFoP, we consider multiple programs, in a variety of energy environments, with the same hardware and peripherals, but interchanging the centralized and federated approach to energy storage. We use the following experimental setup to evaluate how UFoP contributes to the performance, in terms of availability, resilience, and energy efficiency of a tiny, capacitor-powered sensing system.

Program	I–V Surface	Availability					
		UFoP			Centralized		
		MCU (%)	*Radio (%)*	*Accel (%)*	*MCU (%)*	*Radio (%)*	*Accel (%)*
Optimistic	Solar	57.08	7.61	18.22	46.97	6.36	17.67
	RF High Energy	81.85	4.55	10.45	76.89	1.18	25.29
	RF Low Energy	86.58	1.23	9.43	75.69	0.64	20.93
Conservative	Solar	54.75	8.14	13.67	46.64	8.10	13.40
	RF High Energy	68.11	7.99	9.59	80.69	3.77	12.00
	RF Low Energy	74.23	4.67	5.70	74.97	2.66	8.09

Table 1: This table shows the percentage of time over the entire I–V surface that the peripherals and MCU were available, for both UFoP and centralized. For these results, the program described in Listing 2 (optimistic) and the program described in Listing 1 (conservative) were used, with the V_{safe} thresholds (as in, no radio transmission or power failures). For all three surfaces, using UFoP increases the availability of both the MCU (for computation) and the radio (for communication and data sending). UFoP does especially well on RF surfaces, where energy is scarce, since it does not have to wait to charge a much larger capacitor before it begins computation.

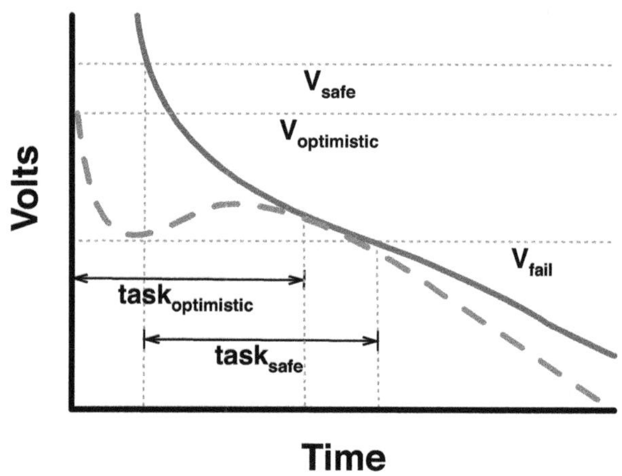

Figure 4: For our evaluation, two sets of thresholds were determined for each program variant. The first threshold, V_{safe} (the blue discharge curve), is set such that if no new energy is harvested, tasks started at this threshold are guaranteed to complete. The second threshold, $V_{optimistic}$ (represented by the red discharge curve), optimistically assumes new energy will be harvested to replenish the task capacitor during task execution.

Programs: We use the sense-and-send program variants described in Section 2 to provide points of comparison between UFoP and the centralized approach. The program described in Listing 2 we refer to as "optimistic" sense-and-send, the program described in Listing 1 we refer to as "conservative" sense-and-send. The program using UFoP monitors capacitor voltages, and gates energy flow to peripherals as needed. The centralized program attempts to federate energy storage in software, allocating from its single energy store when it becomes available at the required voltage.

Thresholds: Each program has certain voltage thresholds (V_{safe}) where the radio, sensor, and MCU turns on, as described previously in Figure 1. This threshold is the voltage on the capacitor that signifies there is enough energy to complete a task or set of tasks, such as sending a data packet over the radio. These thresholds are set in software for the radio and sensor, and hardware for the MCU. Thresholds are set differently for centralized, since the single capacitor must store enough energy to accomplish all tasks. We have two sets of voltage thresholds for each program, as shown in Figure 4. The first threshold, termed V_{safe} is the level that guarantees task completion. Setting the threshold above V_{safe} means a program will not get as many tasks done (but will never fail), while setting the threshold below V_{safe} will mean tasks are not guaranteed to complete. The second set of voltage thresholds is termed $V_{optimistic}$; the assumption is that new energy will be harvested to replace energy being used *during the task*, therefore these thresholds are set lower. Using the $V_{optimistic}$ set of thresholds does not guarantee task completion or zero power failures. These thresholds were gathered by manually executing programs with high and low thresholds over a solar I–V surface, effectively binary searching through all possible thresholds. V_{safe} and $V_{optimistic}$ thresholds were only gathered for the "optimistic" sense-and-send program. $V_{optimistic}$ thresholds were gathered for the "conservative" sense-and-send program.

Test Devices: Each of the applications were run on Texas Instruments MSP430FR5739 processors. These devices have low sleep currents (*i.e.,* 5.9 µA), multiple ADCs, and FRAM memory for checkpointing and data storage.

Peripherals: Each test device manages its own set of peripherals. Peripherals used are an MMA7361 triple-axis accelerometer, and a 315 MHz RF Transmitter (CDT-88). These peripheral types were chosen because they are ubiquitous in sensing applications.

Voltage Monitor Reference Designs: To compare the federated and centralized approach, we designed a supply voltage monitor, based on the ICL7665 and MIC841 (also used by our UFoP reference design) to act as the energy storage backbone for all centralized program executions. The ICL7665 or MIC841 charges a large capacitor bank, and turns on and off the MCU with hysteresis. The centralized supply voltage monitor and the UFoP reference design have the same amount of capacitance (energy storage) and many of the same components, however, the UFoP reference design federates its energy storage in hardware, while the centralized reference design federates energy sotrage in software. In the evaluation, we refer to the centralized voltage monitor device as the "centralized reference design."

I–V surfaces: To control the energy environment, we use an Ekho [10] device to record and emulate I–V surfaces. Ekho provides a repeatable energy environment which replaces the energy harvester as input to the energy storage approach. Without Ekho, it is very difficult to control for the energy environment in experiments. We recorded three eight-second I–V surfaces for our evaluation. The first surface was recorded from a solar panel harvesting energy from

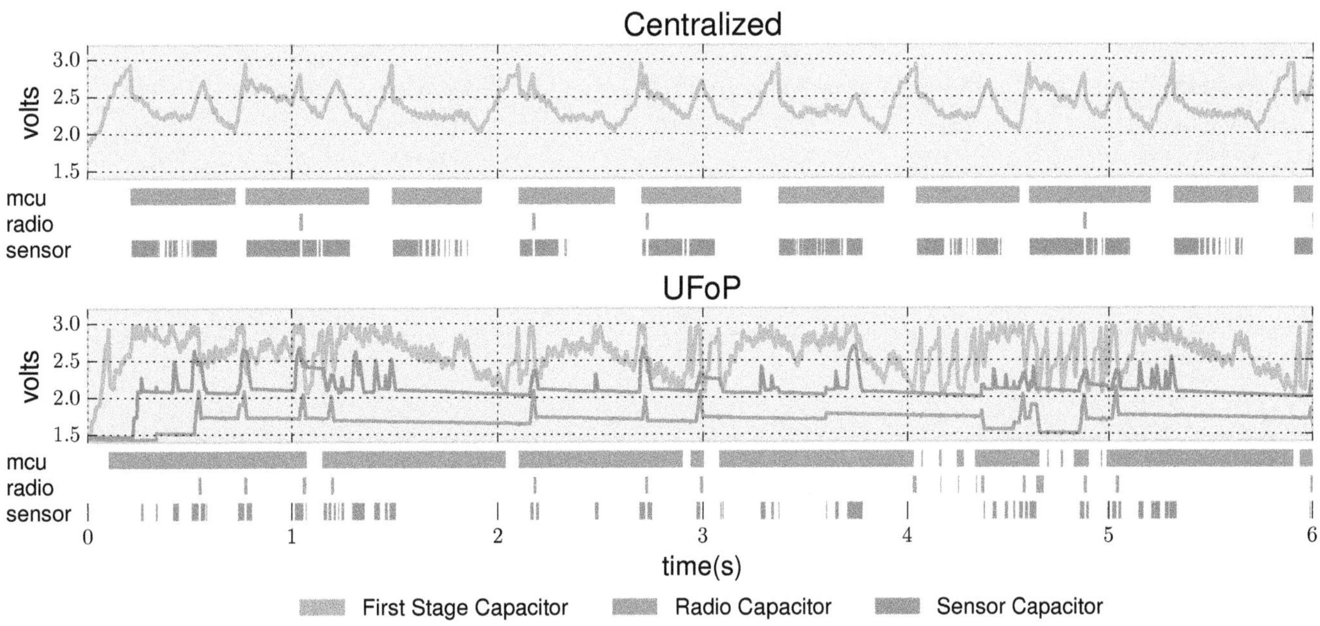

Figure 5: This figure compares the availability of the MCU, sensor, and radio when an MSP430FR5739 running the program described in Listing 2 executes across the I–V surface recorded from the RFID reader. The program was run multiple times using either the UFoP reference design or the centralized reference design, and the V_{safe} thresholds. Applications that use UFoP have significantly more MCU on-time, allowing more valuable computation, as well as significantly more sends over the radio. Because the radio can work with a lower supply voltage than the MCU, UFoP allows for more transmissions since the energy store is decoupled from the MCU. Sensor readings, while not as frequent as with centralized, are dispersed more evenly in time.

a car headlamp that turns on and off four times, creating a sinusoidal solar surface. This means the device under test goes through the entire life cycle; charge, deplete, recharge. The second and third I–V surfaces were recorded from the RF energy harvester on the Umich Moo, while it harvested from an Impinj Speedway RFID reader. The reader antenna was waved across the Moo at two distances to produce two surfaces, referred to as "RF High Energy" and "RF Low Energy" in the rest of the evaluation.

Taking these programs, thresholds, test devices, peripherals, supply voltage monitors, and I–V surfaces, we can assemble an experimental setup that will allow us to make fair comparisons between federated and centralized energy storage. By running each program variant (federated or centralized) in each recorded energy environment, we can attempt to answer these questions about UFoP:

- Does federating energy storage provide more sensing and computational availability? (5.2)
- Does federating energy storage make applications more resilient? (5.3)
- What is the effect of federating energy on energy harvesting efficiency as compared to the centralized approach? (5.4)
- What is the overhead of the federated energy approach? (5.5)

5.2 Availability

The percentage of availability of the MCU for computation, and peripherals for sensing or sending over an entire duty cycle, is a critical metric of evaluating performance of tiny energy harvesting systems. In this section, we evaluate the availability of both our test programs, when running on our UFoP reference design and the centralized reference design. We execute each of these programs, with both energy storage reference designs, ten times each, on all three of our recorded I–V surfaces. All of the optimistic sense-and-send programs use the V_{safe} thresholds, while the conservative sense-and-send programs use slightly "optimistic" thresholds. Using the Measurement Computing USB-201 [4] data acquisition device (DAQ), we recorded the voltage levels of all capacitors, the supply voltage of the MSP430FR5739 (the MCU), and the on and off times of the radio and accelerometer peripherals.

One set of program executions is shown in Figure 5. This figure shows the optimistic sense-and-send program executing across a surface generated by an RFID reader swiping over a Umich Moo. The three activity bars below each plot show when the MCU, the radio, and the accelerometer were in use. For this RF surface, UFoP provides more MCU on-time, and more radio transmissions. Because UFoP allows the application to use peripherals that do not have to exist at the MCU supply voltage, the UFoP program makes use of the lower voltage threshold of the radio to get extra work done in a low energy environment. Additionally, UFoP charges its capacitors faster, meaning that the MCU turns on sooner than the centralized version, this is shown in the bottom portion of Figure 5.

The results of all availability experiments are shown in Table 1. The percentage of time each component was being used is listed for both the centralized and federated approaches. For all cases, using UFoP shows improvement in availability. The most dramatic increase comes when using UFoP with low energy environments and peripherals that don't match the MCU supply voltage.

5.3 Resiliency

In this section, we evaluate the resiliency of our programs when using the UFoP reference design and the centralized reference de-

Program	Resiliency					
	UFoP			Centralized		
	-Threshold	*Low Voltage*	*Tx Fails*	*-Threshold*	*Low Voltage*	*Tx Fails*
Optimistic	-151 mV	6.2	3.5%	-130 mV	28.0	9.8%
Conservative	-93 mV	5.1	5.2%	-115 mV	34.6	16.3%

Table 2: This table shows the effect of over-estimating the harvestable energy. In the table, *-Threshold* is the voltage below the the V_{safe} threshold that was set when running programs for resiliency experiments. This threshold is used to determine when to turn on peripherals for the respective program listed on the left. These results are from execution over the solar I–V surface. The number of times the voltage on the microcontroller went below the minimum supply voltage and the percentage of radio transmission failures (because of MCU reset or peripheral reset) are shown. Poorly choosing voltage thresholds does not have as severe an effect when using UFoP, as with the traditional centralized approach.

sign. Resiliency is the measure of how tolerant an application is to voltage threshold miscalculation, task incompletion, and power failures (of the MCU or peripherals). While most application programmers try to get the equivalent of the V_{safe} threshold described in Section 5.1 to ensure no failures, it is very easy to miscalculate the required energy budget for a specific task, especially when it comes from a single supply. Being overly optimistic about potential energy to be harvested can result in failed radio transmission, corrupted memory, and low voltage events. A low voltage event, where the MCU voltage drops below the minimum supply voltage, does not necessarily mean the microcontroller is reset, but once it happens, the MCU begins to draw more current, memory usually becomes unwritable, and at worst the Supply Voltage Supervisor will trigger a brown out. Therefore it is a state best to avoid if possible.

To evaluate resiliency we executed both of our programs, using either of our energy storage reference designs, ten times each, on our recorded solar I–V surface. We lowered the turn-on voltage of the radio from the V_{safe} threshold by a percentage, to see what effect this optimism over energy harvesting would have. Since we did not have V_{safe} thresholds for the conservative sense-and-send program, we chose thresholds that ensured zero radio transmission failures or resets over the solar surface. Since these thresholds were not matched like the V_{safe} thresholds, the conservative results are illustrative of the effect of over estimating your energy harvesting. Using the DAQ, we recorded the voltage levels of all capacitors, the supply voltage of the MSP430FR5739 (the MCU), and the on and off times of the radio, and accelerometer peripherals. Using this data, we gathered for each execution, the number of times a low voltage event occurred and the percentage of radio transmission that failed.

Table 2 shows the results of this experiment. For the optimistic sense-and-send program, the lowered thresholds result in a dramatic increase in low voltage events, as well as a nearly 10% increase in transmission failures for centralized programs. The optimistic sense-and-send program that ran on the UFoP reference design had a much smaller failure rate. Power failures and low voltage events are inevitable for capacitor based sensing. UFoP reduces the number of low voltage events and failures by prioritizing the MCU and separating the peripherals energy storage. Using UFoP, the consequences of miscalculation of the energy harvesting potential of a future deployment environment becomes much less catastrophic.

5.4 Energy Harvesting Efficiency

Energy harvesters such as solar panels, piezoelectric ceramics, and thermal generators, do not supply a stable voltage to a sensor. The voltage on the harvester changes in response to the current draw of the sensor or vice-versa. This relationship between harvesting current and supply voltage can be described by an I–V curve. Energy harvesting over time can be described by a sequence of I–V curves; an I–V surface. Every I–V curve has a maximum power point (MPP) where the most energy can be harvested. Many systems attempt to track this point to increase energy harvesting efficiency. UFoP does not try to track the MPP, but because UFoP charges faster and keeps a more stable supply voltage, for some I–V surfaces, UFoP may harvest more energy by being closer to the MPP. This set of experiments seeks to compare the energy harvesting efficiency of the centralized and federated approach to energy storage, by observing the path that each approach traces across the same I–V surface. By keeping the same sensor combination, energy harvesting environment (I–V surface), and program, we can see the effect of the energy storage technique on efficiency.

The results of this experiment are shown in Table 3. For the energy harvesters used, the programs using the UFoP reference design generally harvested more energy than the centralized equivalent. UFoP will not always cause more energy to be harvested, however, if the voltage at the MPP of the particular I–V surface is close to the hardware set threshold voltage of UFoP, the stability of UFoP should provide more energy.

5.5 Overhead

Switching to a federated energy storage approach does come with overhead. This overhead comes from three places: 1) the addition of voltage monitoring hardware, which slightly increases the size, cost, and energy requirements, 2) the energy cost from polling voltage levels with the built-in ADC, and 3) software rewriting. We have not attempted to quantify the cost of software rewriting.

The biggest potential cost is the energy overhead; as UFoP is meant for energy harvesting systems, any energy spent on monitoring must be kept low. The active components that make up our reference design have a typical quiescent current draw of 2.7 µA. As a comparison, the centralized reference design has a quiescent draw of 1.5 µA. Despite the increase in overhead, the energy harvesting gains shown in Table 3 should offset the losses, and often give a net surplus of energy. Additionally, the larger capacitor used for the centralized approach has a larger leakage than the collection of smaller capacitors used in UFoP, causing some of the energy gains seen from using UFoP.

Most traditional centralized applications have some form of supply voltage monitoring through a dedicated ADC, interrupts on an input pin, or special hardware. UFoP has this same overhead, but multiplied by the number of peripheral capacitor voltages it has to monitor. The centralized reference design, over a one second period, expends 13.6 µJ polling, while the UFoP reference design expends 23.3 µJ over the same period. This extra energy cost can be reduced by polling fewer times, or using a low power or faster ADC. To reduce the polling overhead completely, an interrupt driven method

I–V surface	Energy Harvesting Comparison			
	UFoP		Centralized	
	mean (mJ)	*stddev* (mJ)	*mean* (mJ)	*stddev* (mJ)
Solar	11.49	0.05	11.41	0.06
RF High Energy	11.00	0.10	9.98	0.11
RF Low Energy	9.15	0.12	8.66	0.10

Table 3: This table shows the amount of energy harvested by the optimistic sense-and-send program on each of the I–V surfaces, for centralized and UFoP energy storage. The peripheral turn-on voltage was set to the V_{safe} threshold, such that no transmissions would fail, and no resets would occur. When using UFoP, the application harvests more energy for all I–V surfaces tested.

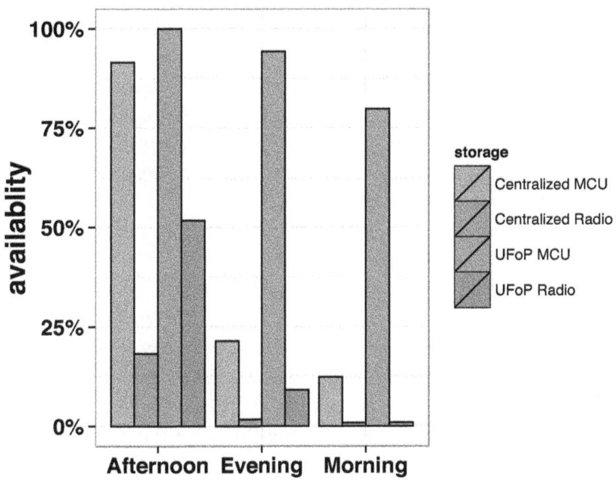

Figure 6: This figure shows the availability of the radio, and microcontroller, for both energy storage solutions, for the deployment. Three different time periods are shown; the afternoon, when the sun was brightest, the evening, when the sensors energy harvesting began to decrease dramatically, and the morning of the next day, when the energy harvesting begin to increase. Even though the centralized system and the UFoP system had the same amount of energy storage, the same harvester, and the same duty cycle, the UFoP sensor had more radio, and computational availability.

can be used. With this approach, UFoP can trigger a wakeup pin on the microcontroller when a peripheral capacitor has reached a logic level threshold. This form of voltage monitoring requires no extra energy beyond the sleep current of the microcontroller. If greater accuracy is required, the program can do an ADC check immediately after the interrupt wakes the microcontroller.

6. DEPLOYMENT

To evaluate UFoP in a real application scenario, we deployed a UFoP enabled greenhouse monitoring program for eighteen hours over two days, in a local greenhouse in late summer. We also deployed a centralized version on the same bed, as a comparison. Greenhouses waste a significant amount of water by overwatering plants. This happens because in large greenhouses, managers do not know the status of individual plant beds, and overwater to ensure plants do not die. This waste is significant for economic and sustainability reasons, as water is a finite and costly resource especially at large scales. Current commercial plant monitoring systems are little more than weather stations, these have dedicated power supplies, are too large or too expensive to be deployed densely, and can't move with the plants they monitor. Because of this, sensor data is usually very coarse, not localized, and often wrong (in the case of plants that were moved from bay to bay). Dense deployment of tiny, unobtrusive, energy harvesting, sensors has been suggested as one way to monitor large volumes of plants in a greenhouse. Equipping sensors with leaf wetness, temperature, and humidity sensors would provide all the information necessary for managers to make local decisions on water volume and plant health.

We developed an initial implementation of this greenhouse monitoring application with UFoP as an energy backbone. Two sensors derived from those discussed in Section 5.1 were built; one using our UFoP reference design, and one using the centralized reference design. Each sensor had two peripherals: a CC1101 transceiver for communication, and a resistive load that emulated a Decagon Devices LWS leaf wetness sensor, a standard sensor used in plant studies. The MSP430FR5739 was used as computational platform. Each sensor used a small solar panel (of the same model) for energy harvesting. To allow for data comparisons between the sensors, the panels were located as close as possible. Both sensors had the same amount of total energy storage in the form of SMD capacitors, and the same duty cycle. Both sensors periodically wakeup from a low power sleep mode, check the energy level(s) of the supply capacitor(s), and if high enough, sense and send a leaf wetness reading. A basestation was positioned inside the greenhouse to receive, and log, all sensor readings.

6.1 Choosing Capacitor Sizes

Choosing capacitors for both sensors required consideration of the duty cycle. Capacitors had to be large enough to support the peripherals, but not too large that they never charged to a high enough voltage. Before deployment, we profiled the distinct stages of the greenhouse monitoring duty cycle in terms of energy consumption, using an oscilloscope and current sensor. Each of these stages we matched to an adequately sized capacitor. The greenhouse monitoring program has three stages: "sense", "send", and "sleep". For each stage, we determined the minimum size of the capacitor, by looking at how much energy was used over time, for what voltage thresholds (we looked up voltage thresholds in device and peripheral datasheets). For example, the CC1101 transceiver when used during the "send" stage required 40ms at an average draw of 3mA to send a message, all with a supply voltage above 1.9V. A capacitor sized at 100 µF and charged to 3.2V stored enough energy at a high enough voltage to power the stage to completion.

The centralized version was equipped with the same amount of total energy storage as the UFoP enabled system, to keep the comparisons fair. Centralized thresholds were calculated in a similar fashion to UFoP. By summing the total energy required for all three stages, at the highest minimum voltage of all the components, the threshold voltage can be determined for the centralized variant.

While these capacitor size and voltage threshold calculations were done manually for this deployment, it is not hard to see how an automated system could size UFoP capacitors using simple peak detection techniques, developer or datasheet specified information about peripheral voltages, and energy harvesting information generated or gathered by an Ekho device.

6.2 Deployment Results and Discussion

An ARM microcontroller and light sensor was deployed with the sensors to unobtrusively record availability of the MCU, radio, and sensor over time. The amount of light on the solar panels was also recorded. Data was gathered for each sensor from 4pm, to 10am the following day. The UFoP equipped sensor outperformed the sensor with the centralized reference design in terms of MCU availability and radio availability as Figure 6 shows. The UFoP enabled sensor was able to harvest significantly more energy than the centralized version, especially during times when energy was scarce (evening and morning). In the morning, from 7-10am, the UFoP equipped sensors microcontroller was on for 79% of the time, while the centralized sensor's microcontroller was on for only 12% of the time. The amount of solar energy that was available to harvest, was not enough to charge the much larger capacitor on the centralized version, meaning that data was lost. In the evening, as the sun began to drop, the UFoP equipped system harvested enough energy for the radio to be broadcasting 9.6% of the time, while the centralized version was only able to broadcast 1.7% of the time. UFoP dramatically extended the amount of time the sensor was available compared to using a centralized energy approach.

This first implementation could be improved; in full sun both sensors were able to broadcast readings continuously, meaning that the solar panel used was too large. Greenhouse managers only need leaf wetness reports a few times an hour. By decreasing the size of the solar panel, sensors can be more densely deployed. Computational time was underutilized as well. UFoP allowed the sensor's MCU to be available even when there was very low sun, however, this computational time was not used. Future programs will use this time to calculate average leaf wetness readings, and calculate local statistics on plant status, freeing up computation on the basestation.

7. RELATED WORK

Currently in the literature there does not exist a federated approach that stores and manages harvested energy in hardware. However, in this section, we review state-of-the-art designs and implementations in energy harvesting and management for perpetual sensing systems.

Virtual battery [2] attempts to "virtualize" the available energy, allocating energy towards tasks. Virtual battery assumes a consistent voltage, power supply, and a known battery size. It does not consider how energy harvesting can change energy budgets. UFoP is designed to work with a volatile supply voltage, frequent power failures, unknown energy harvesting, and therefore unknown energy budget. The essential difference between these two systems is that virtual battery partitions available energy, while UFoP acts as a disruption tolerant energy manager, storing incoming harvested energy and notifying the application about changes in availability. To make a system like virtual battery work on intermittently powered devices, UFoP must first exist to hide the energy volatility. UFoP does simplify application development for intermittently powered devices in a similar way to virtual battery, in the sense that both systems inform the application what energy is available, however, UFoP manages this energy in real time and handles energy replacement. eShare [26] is another energy sharing system to balance energy supply and demand. The system's energy router consists of an array of ultra-capacitor with different levels of capacitances. Even though eShare can extend the network lifetime, this system can only be useful where power wiring is feasible.

Prometheus [12] uses two storage devices, *i.e.,* super-capacitor and lithium rechargeable battery. A solar panel charges the super-capacitor and when its voltage is higher than a threshold, it charges the battery. When the super-capacitor is exhausted, the battery is used. Heliomote [16] uses a solar panel and two AA type NiMH batteries. Energy harvesting occurs when the solar panel's output voltage is 0.7 V higher than that of the battery. When battery's voltage is higher than the solar panels, even though enough power may be available on the solar panel, a node can still draw current from the battery. Everlast [19] uses a solar panel and a super-capacitor. It charges a huge-sized super-capacitor (100 F) while tracking the Maximum Power Point (MPP) of its solar panel. AmbiMax [15] harvests energy from multiple ambient power sources (solar and wind) while performing Maximum Power Point Tracking (MPPT) on each of them. Each energy harvesting subsystem harvests energy and charges its own reservoir super-capacitors. The system is powered solely by the ambient sources when the reservoir capacitor array has a higher voltage at its terminal than a threshold. It draws power from the battery when the reservoir capacitor array's terminal voltage drops below the threshold.

Other related energy harvesting systems including TwinStar [28–30], EnHANTs [6, 7], SolarWISP [9] and the work of Yerva *et al.* [23]. TwinStar [28–30] is an add-on energy harvesting and management device, which uses ultra-capacitor as the only energy storage unit. It has a dual solar panel solution (a small boot solar panel and a big main panel to charge the ultra-capacitor). On top of the hardware, the controller maintains a high duty cycle when the voltage is high and a low duty cycle when the voltage is low. Energy-Harvesting Active Networked Tags (EnHANTs) [6,7] can be attached to objects that are traditionally not networked, such as books. The prototypes harvest indoor light energy using custom organic solar cells, communicate and form multihop networks using ultra-low-power Ultra-Wideband Impulse Radio (UWB-IR) transceivers. In [9], the authors add solar panel (SolarWISP) to WISP (RF-powered tag) for hybrid energy harvesting. SolarWISP increases effective communication range threefold and quadruples read rate. In [23], the authors propose to add a new tier in the sensor network architecture by using energy-harvesting leaf nodes, which can communicate with battery-powered branch nodes and wall-powered trunk nodes.

Software strategies for adaptive scheduling based on the dynamic energy supply are studied in [1, 13, 27]. DEOS [27] is a dynamic energy-oriented scheduling method that dynamically adjusts the execution of tasks based on the tasks' energy consumption and the system's real-time available energy. Dewdrop [1] is a CRFID runtime that makes effective use of harvested energy. It adapts a tag's duty cycle to match the harvested power to the sensing and computation cost of tasks. In [13], the authors propose mathematical models to predict the ideal battery size and the rate of availability of harvestable energy with an assumption that the energy consumed by a node is always less than or equal to the harvested energy. Mementos [17] is a software system that transforms general-purpose programs into interruptible computations that are protected from frequent power losses by automatic, energy-aware state checkpointing. At compile time, Mementos inserts function calls that estimate available energy. At run time, Mementos predicts power losses and saves program state to nonvolatile memory.

8. DISCUSSION

In our experiments, UFoP was able to improve the availability, resiliency, and energy harvesting efficiency of tiny sensor devices with capacitor-based energy storage. Based on our experimental results, we believe that UFoP is a step forward for perpetual sensing, potentially making long-term deployments for mobile and other untethered computing devices possible. However, ambient energy is still scarce in deployment and energy storage capacity is terminally limited. Therefore, even though UFoP is able to relax the short-term coupling between peripherals, power management is always an important issue to consider. In this section, we discuss software approaches to federating energy, UFoP's design limitations, design alternatives, and applications.

Software Energy Federation: An alternative approach to using UFoP is to attempt to federate energy in software, by balancing the peripherals voltage and energy requirements with the volatile energy supply. This approach is used by all centralized programs in Section 6 and Section 5. Federating (or virtualizing, as in Virtual Battery [2]) energy in software has the advantage of being reconfigurable; the duty cycle (and energy partitions) can be changed dynamically. Additionally, no new hardware is required. However, the cost of software complexity in adding a virtual layer must be considered, especially in resource constrained systems that harvests energy. Additionally, a software approach suffers from all the shortcomings (task coupling, slow charging, reduced MCU availability,) associated with a single energy store. Hardware federation, for the same energy supply, will always provide more availability, and resiliency, than a software federated approach.

Limitations: The current UFoP reference design has some limitations. Peripherals are susceptible to starvation since the peripheral capacitors start charging when the input voltage in the main capacitor reaches 3.1 V. This can happen when an application requires the microcontroller to run too much computation in a very low energy environment and thus the peripheral capacitors never have the chance to charge. The centralized system has the same starvation problem. Another cause of peripheral starvation is if the microcontroller has a higher active current draw than the one we currently use (81.4 μA). To overcome this limitation, an application developer can program, through software, the microcontroller to sleep for a brief period immediately after turning on.

The current UFoP reference design trades off speed for low quiescent energy consumption in the choice of its active components. Some of the comparators switch very slowly, meaning that high current peripherals may be able to draw too much from the first stage capacitor if no new energy is being harvested. This can be solved by limiting capacitor charging with a resistor or op-amp, or trading off low quiescent current for a faster switching peripheral gate comparator.

Another limitation of the current prototype is we cannot use the peripherals in the order we need if we change the behavior of an application during runtime. This issue can be handled with dynamic priority, allowing capacitors to be charged and used by different peripherals according to the application. We leave this for future work.

Applications: UFoP enables low power sensing applications that use a variety of peripherals, with different energy needs and voltage requirements. UFoP is most useful for perpetual, energy harvesting systems that aggregate multiple types of sensor data. We envisage UFoP being used in applications ranging from greenhouse monitoring, low power wearable devices (humans and animals), and any computational RFID application including but not limited to, inventory management, building monitoring, activity monitoring, and infrastructure monitoring.

9. FUTURE WORK

Currently, peripherals charge at the same rate, with no input from the application designer. Situations could be imagined where settable priorities would be wanted. Using a resistor on the charging line after the comparator that gates the peripheral capacitor could give a form of priority; the smaller the resistor the quicker the peripheral capacitor charges. Current languages and operating systems for programming embedded sensors [5, 14, 25] assume a stable power supply and a sufficiently large battery. With UFoP, some system components will not always be available when needed and thus some tasks will need to be postponed. We are currently developing a new programming language to ease building transiently-powered sensing applications using UFoP.

10. CONCLUSIONS

This paper presents UFoP, the first system for capacitor-based sensors that employs a federated approach to the storage and management of harvested energy. UFoP stores harvested energy in multiple independent small capacitors, one dedicated to each peripheral. It employs a charge controller that charges the capacitors while maintaining the supply voltage of the microcontroller. With UFoP, power-hungry tasks from a radio or a heavyweight sensor will not cause low voltage events that can potentially reset the microcontroller. In our experiments, we found that programs that use UFoP as the energy backbone had as much as 10% more computational availability, and as much as four times more radio availability than the centralized approach. Using UFoP, programs become dramatically more resilient, reducing low voltage events and radio transmission failure. Additionally, programs that use UFoP harvested more energy for all energy environments evaluated than programs using the traditional centralized energy storage approach; meaning that UFoP functions with zero overhead in many cases.

11. ACKNOWLEDGMENTS

The authors would like to thank the members of the PERSIST lab, for helpful discussions around UFoP deployments and experimentation. We also thank our shepherd Kay Römer, and our anonymous reviewers, for their helpful comments.

This research is based upon work supported by the National Science Foundation under grants ACI-1212680 and CNS-1453607. Any opinions, findings, and conclusions or recommendations expressed in this material are those of the authors and do not necessarily reflect the views of the National Science Foundation

12. REFERENCES

[1] M. Buettner, B. Greenstein, and D. Wetherall. Dewdrop: An Energy-Aware Runtime for Computational RFID. In *Proc. 8th USENIX Conf. Networked Systems Design and Implementation (NSDI'11)*, pages 197–210, Boston, MA, USA, Mar. 2011. ACM.

[2] Q. Cao, D. Fesehaye, N. Pham, Y. Sarwar, and T. Abdelzaher. Virtual Battery: An Energy Reserve Abstraction for Embedded Sensor Networks. In *Proc. 29th IEEE Real-Time Systems Symposium (RTSS'08)*, pages 1–11, Barcelona, Spain, Nov.–Dec. 2008. IEEE.

[3] J. A. Carr, J. C. Balda, and H. A. Mantooth. A Survey of Systems to Integrate Distributed Energy Resources and Energy Storage on the Utility Grid). In *Proc. IEEE Energy 2030 Conf. (ENERGY'08)*, pages 1–7, Atlanta, GA, USA, Nov. 2008. IEEE.

[4] M. Computing. Usb-201 data acquisition usb daq device 12-bit, 100 ks/s. `http://www.mccdaq.com/`

usb-data-acquisition/USB-201.aspx. [Online; accessed 30 March, 2015].

[5] A. Dunkels, B. Grönvall, and T. Voigt. Contiki—A Lightweight and Flexible Operating System for Tiny Networked Sensors. In *Proc. 1st IEEE Workshop on Embedded Networked Sensors (Emnets-I)*, Tampa, Florida, USA, Nov. 2004. IEEE Computer Society.

[6] M. Gorlatova, P. Kinget, I. Kymissis, D. Rubenstein, X. Wang, and G. Zussman. Energy Harvesting Active Networked Tags (EnHANTs) for Ubiquitous Object Networking. *IEEE Wireless Communications*, pages 18–25, Dec. 2010.

[7] M. Gorlatova, R. Margolies, J. Sarik, G. Stanje, J. Zhu, B. Vigraham, M. Szczodrak, L. Carloni, P. Kinget, I. Kymissis, and G. Zussman. Energy Harvesting Active Networked Tags (EnHANTs): Prototyping and Experimentation. Technical Report 2012-07-27, Electrical Engineering, Columbia University, New York, NY, USA, Jul. 2012.

[8] M. Gorlatova, R. Margolies, J. Sarik, G. Stanje, J. Zhu, B. Vigraham, M. Szczodrak, L. Carloni, P. Kinget, I. Kymissis, and G. Zussman. Prototyping Energy Harvesting Active Networked Tags (EnHANTs). In *Proc. 32nd IEEE Int'l Conf. Computer Communications (INFOCOM'13)*, pages 585–589, Turin, Italy, Apr. 2013. IEEE.

[9] J. Gummeson, S. S. Clark, K. Fu, and D. Ganesan. On the Limits of Effective Hybrid Micro-Energy Harvesting on Mobile CRFID Sensors. In *Proc. 8th Int'l Conf. Mobile Systems, Applications, and Services (MobiSys'10)*, pages 195–208, San Francisco, CA, USA, Jun. 2010. ACM.

[10] J. Hester, T. Scott, and J. Sorber. Ekho: Realistic and Repeatable Experimentation for Tiny Energy-Harvesting Sensors. In *Proc. 12th ACM Conf. Embedded Network Sensor Systems (SenSys'14)*, pages 1–15, Memphis, TN, USA, Nov. 2014. ACM.

[11] N. Instruments. Ni x series multifunction data acquisition. http://sine.ni.com/ds/app/doc/p/id/ds-163/lang/en. [Online; accessed 11 October, 2013].

[12] X. Jiang, J. Polastre, and D. Culler. Perpetual Environmentally Powered Sensor Networks. In *Proc. 4th Int'l Symp. Information Processing in Sensor Networks (IPSN'05)*, Los Angeles, CA, USA, Apr. 2005. ACM.

[13] A. Kansal, J. Hsu, S. Zahedi, and M. B. Srivastava. Power Management in Energy Harvesting Sensor Networks. *ACM Trans. Embedded Computing Systems (TECS)*, 6(4), Sept. 2007.

[14] P. Levis, S. Madden, J. Polastre, R. Szewczyk, K. Whitehouse, A. Woo, D. Gay, J. Hill, M. Welsh, E. Brewer, and D. Culler. TinyOS: An Operating System for Sensor Networks. In *Ambient Intelligence*. Springer Verlag, 2004.

[15] C. Park and P. H. Chou. AmbiMax: Autonomous Energy Harvesting Platform for Multi-Supply Wireless Sensor Nodes. In *Proc. 3rd Ann. IEEE Comm. Society Conf. Sensor, Mesh and Ad Hoc Communications and Networks (SECON'06)*, pages 168–177, Reston, VA, USA, Sept. 2006. IEEE.

[16] V. Raghunathan, A. Kansal, J. Hsu, J. Friedman, and M. Srivastava. Design Considerations for Solar Energy Harvesting Wireless Embedded Systems. In *Proc. 4th Int'l Symp. Information Processing in Sensor Networks (IPSN'05)*, pages 457–462, Los Angeles, CA, USA, Apr. 2005. ACM.

[17] B. Ransford, J. Sorber, and K. Fu. Mementos: System Support for Long-Running Computation on RFID-Scale Devices. In *Proc. 16th Int'l Conf. Architectural Support for Programming Languages and Operating Systems (ASPLOS'11)*, pages 159–170, Newport Beach, CA, USA, Mar. 2011. ACM.

[18] A. P. Sample, D. J. Yeager, P. S. Powledge, A. V. Mamishev, and J. R. Smith. Design of an RFID-Based Battery-Free Programmable Sensing Platform. *IEEE Trans. Instrumentation and Measurement*, 57(11):2608–2615, Nov. 2008.

[19] F. Simjee and P. H. Chou. Everlast: Long-life, Supercapacitor-operated Wireless Sensor Node. In *Proc. Int'l Symp. Low Power Electronics and Design (ISLPED'06)*, pages 197–202, Tegernsee, Germany, Oct. 2006. IEEE.

[20] S. Thomas, J. Teizer, and M. Reynolds. Electromagnetic Energy Harvesting for Sensing, Communication, and Actuation. In *Proc. 27th Int'l Symp. Automation and Robotics in Construction (ISARC'10)*, Bratislava, Slovakia, Jun. 2010. IAARC.

[21] Y. Yang, L. Wang, D. K. Noh, H. K. Le, and T. F. Abdelzaher. SolarStore: Enhancing Data Reliability in Solar-Powered Storage-Centric Sensor Networks. In *Proc. 7th Int'l Conf. Mobile Systems, Applications, and Services (MobiSys'09)*, pages 333–346, Krakow, Poland, Jun. 2009. ACM.

[22] D. Yeager, F. Zhang, A. Zarrasvand, N. T. George, T. Daniel, and B. P. Otis. A 9 μA, Addressable Gen2 Sensor Tag for Biosignal Acquisition. *IEEE Journal of Solid-State Circuits*, 45(10):2198–2209, Oct. 2010.

[23] L. Yerva, B. Campbell, A. Bansal, T. Schmid, and P. Dutta. Grafting Energy-Harvesting Leaves onto the Sensornet Tree. In *Proc. 11th Int'l Conf. Information Processing in Sensor Networks (IPSN'12)*, pages 197–208, Beijing, China, Apr. 2012. ACM.

[24] H. Zhang, J. Gummeson, B. Ransford, and K. Fu. Moo: A batteryless computational RFID and sensing platform. Technical Report UM-CS-2011-020, UMass Amherst Department of Computer Science, June 2011.

[25] R. Zhou and G. Xing. Nemo: A High-fidelity Noninvasive Power Meter System for Wireless Sensor Networks. In *Proc. 12th Int'l Conf. Information Processing in Sensor Networks (IPSN'13)*, pages 141–152, Philadelphia, USA, Apr. 2013. ACM.

[26] T. Zhu, Y. Gu, T. He, and Z. L. Zhang. eShare: A Capacitor-Driven Energy Storage and Sharing Network for Long-Term Operation. In *Proc. 8th ACM Conf. Embedded Networked Sensor Systems (SenSys'10)*, pages 239–252, Zurich, Switzerland, Nov. 2010. ACM.

[27] T. Zhu, A. Mohaisen, Y. Ping, and D. Towsley. DEOS: Dynamic Energy-Oriented Scheduling for Sustainable Wireless Sensor Networks. In *Proc. 31st Ann. IEEE Int'l Conf. Computer Communications (INFOCOM'12)*, pages 2363–2371, Orlando, Florida, US, Mar. 2012. IEEE.

[28] T. Zhu, Z. Zhong, Y. Gu, T. He, and Z. L. Zhang. Leakage-Aware Energy Synchronization for Wireless Sensor Networks. In *Proc. 7th Int'l Conf. Mobile Systems, Applications, and Services (MobiSys'09)*, pages 319–332, Krakow, Poland, Jun. 2009. ACM.

[29] T. Zhu, Z. Zhong, T. He, and Z. Zhang. Energy-Synchronized Computing for Sustainable Sensor Networks. *Ad Hoc Networks*, 11:1392–Ű1404, 2013.

[30] T. Zhu, Z. Zhong, T. He, and Z. L. Zhang. Feedback Control-Based Energy Management for Ubiquitous Sensor Networks. *IEICE Trans. Communications*, E93-B(11):2846–2854, 2010.

PowerBlade: A Low-Profile, True-Power, Plug-Through Energy Meter

Samuel DeBruin, Branden Ghena, Ye-Sheng Kuo, and Prabal Dutta
Electrical Engineering and Computer Science Department
University of Michigan
Ann Arbor, MI 48109
{sdebruin, brghena, samkuo, prabal}@umich.edu

ABSTRACT

We present PowerBlade, the smallest, lowest cost, and lowest power AC plug-load meter that measures real, reactive and apparent power, and reports this data, along with cumulative energy consumption, over an industry-standard Bluetooth Low Energy radio. Achieving this design point requires revisiting every aspect of conventional power meters: a new method of acquiring voltage; a non-invasive, planar method of current measurement; an efficient and accurate method of computing power from the voltage and current channels; a radio interface that leverages nearby smart phones to display data and report it to the cloud; and a retro power supply re-imagined with vastly lower current draw, allowing extreme miniaturization. PowerBlade occupies a mere 1" × 1" footprint, offers a $^1/_{16}$" profile, draws less than 180 mW itself, offers 1.13% error on unity power factor loads in the 2-1200 W range and slightly worse for non-linear and reactive loads, and costs $11 in modest quantities of about 1,000 units. This new design point enables affordable large-scale studies of plug-load energy usage—an area of growing national importance.

Categories and Subject Descriptors

B.4.2 [**HARDWARE**]: Input/Output and Data Communications—*Input/Output Devices*; C.3 [**COMPUTER-COMMUNICATION NETWORKS**]: Special-Purpose and Application-Based Systems

General Terms

Design, Experimentation, Measurement, Performance

Keywords

AC meter, Smart meter, Energy metering, Power metering, Plug-load metering, Data aggregation, Intermittent power, Wireless sensor

SenSys'15, November 01–04, 2015, Seoul, Republic of Korea
ACM 987-1-4503-3631-4/15/11.
http://dx.doi.org/10.1145/2809695.2809716

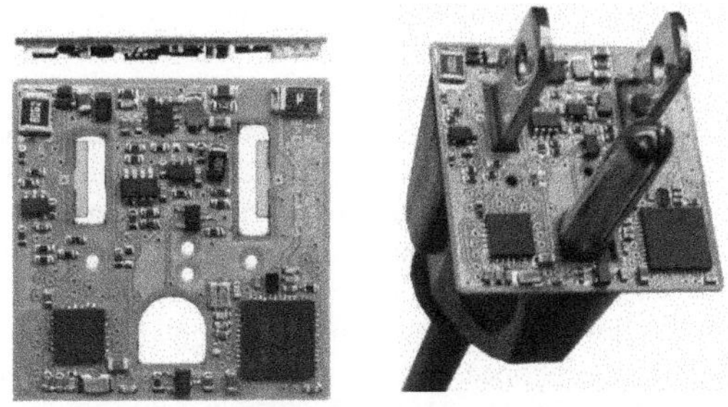

Figure 1: Profile, front, and perspective views of PowerBlade, a wireless power meter that measures real, reactive, and apparent power. PowerBlade's low profile and plug through form factor allow it to sit inconspicuously and unobtrusively between an electrical plug and an outlet, and its square-inch footprint spares adjacent outlets from being blocked. PowerBlade stores accumulated energy data locally and reports both instantaneous power and accumulated energy to a nearby smartphone or gateway over a Bluetooth Low Energy radio.

1. INTRODUCTION

Residential and commercial buildings in the US used 2,760 TWh of electrical energy in 2014 [19]. The majority of that usage comes from clearly obvious loads including HVAC, lighting, and appliances, however, approximately a 20% (and growing) share of electricity usage is due to "plug-loads," often called miscellaneous electrical loads (MELs) in industry terms [27]. These diverse loads, from televisions and computers to vending machines and box fans, represent the long-tail of electricity use. Understanding the characteristics of these loads requires insight into each device's individual consumption but the methods today are limited. As a result, ratepayers, regulators, and researchers lack the tools to *unobtrusively monitor* plug-load energy use with *high fidelity* and *low cost*.

To help address this problem, we present PowerBlade, a new power/energy meter that achieves a vastly smaller form factor than prior systems. PowerBlade occupies an unobtrusive and essentially two-dimensional volume, 1" × 1" × $^1/_{16}$", and meters loads plugged through it and into an outlet, as Figure 1 shows. Despite its small size, PowerBlade is a wireless true power meter, capable of metering real, reactive, and apparent power at kHz frequencies, aggregating these measurements into cumulative energy, and transmitting these data several times per second using a Bluetooth Low Energy (BLE) radio to a nearby smartphone or gateway. At a cost of $11 in modest quantities of 1,000 units, PowerBlade is the smallest and lowest cost AC plug-load meter with 1.13% accuracy over a 2-1200 W range for unity power factor loads, and slightly worse for non-linear and reactive loads. This small form factor, coupled with easy access to and transport of the meter data, may enable new applications.

Metering Device	Power Supply	Voltage	Current	True Power?	Data Output	Static Power	Volume
Kill-A-Watt [6]	Capacitor fed	Divider	Resistor	Yes	LCD	450 mW	14.0 in^3
Watts Up [17]	Capacitor fed	Divider	Resistor	Yes	LCD or USB	590 mW	31.9 in^3
Belkin Conserve Insight [3]	Capacitor fed	Divider	Resistor	Yes	LCD	440 mW	21.8 in^3
ACme-A [26]	Capacitor fed	Divider	Resistor	Yes	802.15.4	1000 mW	13.7 in^3
ACme-B [26]	Transformer	Divider	Hall effect	Yes	802.15.4	100 mW	13.7 in^3
Monjolo [23]	Energy harvest	None	Current Transformer	No	802.15.4	4 mW	7.8 in^3
Gemini [20]	Energy harvest	Virtual	Current Transformer	Yes	802.15.4	Not Published	
PowerBlade (this work)	Resistor fed	Divider	Magnetometer	Yes	BLE	80-176 mW†	0.07 in^3

Table 1: Comparison of various power meters. PowerBlade is the smallest, lowest power, wireless true power meter. †Depends on data rate.

PowerBlade provides an opportunity to think about power metering in a new way. Rather than metering every outlet in a building, PowerBlade is capable of metering every load, following the plug to any outlet with which it mates. This tight binding allows data to be collected about the plug-loads themselves rather than whatever happens to be plugged into an outlet, representing a paradigm shift from prior work that employed bulky power meters. Moreover, existing power meters do not make their data easily accessible to users, but using BLE allows PowerBlade's measurements to be received by unmodified smartphones. Section 2 provides a more detailed comparison of PowerBlade with existing power meters.

PowerBlade's small profile and literally plug-through design require revisiting nearly every aspect of power meter design. Since PowerBlade has no outlet of its own, it utilizes exposed conductive tabs built from rigid-flex PCB to make contact with the plug-through AC load. Traditional AC-DC power supplies require substantial volume to hold charge or dissipate power, owing to high load power, but PowerBlade draws less than 6 mW average power itself, allowing it to utilize a small and simple power supply. Conventional current sensing requires breaking the AC path with a sense resistor, encircling it with a current transformer, or monitoring the Hall effect in a plane parallel to the current flow, but these methods are not viable in the PowerBlade design. Rather, PowerBlade measures the magnetic field generated from the current passing through it using a wire-wound inductor optimally placed in the plane perpendicular to the flow of current. This magnetometer design allows the current waveform to be measured using commodity electronic components. These and other design concerns are described in detail in Section 3 and specific implementation choices are presented in Section 4.

PowerBlade offers accurate metering over a wide range of load powers. For resistive loads, such as incandescent bulbs, PowerBlade has an average error of 1.13% over the range of 2 W to 1200 W. We also test the meter on a range of common household loads including a toaster, refrigerator, Xbox, and WiFi router. Across these loads, PowerBlade has an average error of 6.5%. Section 5 provides a detailed evaluation of system accuracy, usability, and safety.

Despite PowerBlade's small size and high accuracy, we identify several opportunities for future improvements to the system. These include better synchronization between current and voltage channel acquisition, better calculation of power factor, securing the metered data, and providing timestamped and synchronized interval data at the 1, 15, or 60 minute intervals. We discuss these future improvements in Section 6.

With PowerBlade in hand, ratepayers, regulators, and researchers have an increased ability to understand plug-load usage patterns. Large-scale, long-term deployments in residential and commercial settings should lead to greater awareness of plug-load usage and plug-load trends—particularly growing energy waste due to high idle power—providing critical data to regulators for efficiency standards.

2. RELATED WORK

A true-power meter performs five distinct functions: (i) reduce the AC mains voltage to low DC voltages to power the meter itself, (ii) measure voltage, (iii) measure current, (iv) calculate power and energy, and (v) communicate these measurements. Scaling a power meter to PowerBlade's form factor requires revisiting each of these functions as they are all intimately tied to system form factor.

Table 1 presents a sampling of commercial and research meters, and key design choices along the five dimensions that these earlier devices embody. In this section, we survey these systems, noting the effect that these choices have on overall size and power draw. In particular, we survey three commercial meters—Kill-A-Watt [6], Watts Up [17], and Belkin Conserve Insight [3]—and three research meters—ACme [26] (two different versions), Monjolo [23], and Gemini [20]—alongside PowerBlade (this work).

2.1 AC-DC Power Supply

For a power meter to operate from the AC mains, it must rectify and step down the AC voltage to provide itself with low voltage DC. Half- or full-wave rectifiers are typically used for this purpose, and they can occupy a small volume using a single or multiple low-profile diodes. Voltage step-down, in contrast, requires more volume and is not blindly amenable to scaling. Moreover, step-down techniques often do not scale as DC power is reduced, requiring a minimum volume regardless of the DC power supplied, while energy harvesters often require bulky current transformers that are fundamentally unsuited to PowerBlade's form factor [20, 23].

Transformers are the most common step-down technique in "wall wart" power supplies and they are used in the ACme-B design [26]. They are inexpensive, efficient, and isolated devices but their volume does not scale linearly to the form factors needed in our case—the smallest AC transformer available from Coilcraft, for example, is approximately 0.31 in^3 [4], which would dominate our volume.

In capacitor-fed power supplies, a high voltage series capacitor drops the line voltage and limits current. Capacitor-fed power supplies are common in many AC power meters [3, 6, 17, 26] even though they do not provide isolation. Fortunately, however, their volume scales more directly with the load current they can supply. To source 10 to 100 mA, the capacitor must be high-valued (1-2 μF), and for high voltage rated capacitors this high value is only found in film capacitors. Such capacitors are often 0.5" on a side or larger. If, however, the supply must only source 10s to 100s of μA, the capacitor can be much smaller—high voltage 10-50 nF capacitors can be found in small, surface-mount ceramic packages.

PowerBlade eschews energy harvesters and transformers, due to scaling challenges, and instead embraces a capacitor-fed, Zener-regulated power supply. The key to making this design point viable is scaling the electronics power draw down to meet the limited supply.

2.2 Voltage Measurement

A true power meter must acquire time-synchronized voltage and current measurements and multiply them together to obtain power. The voltage channel is frequently obtained by intercepting the plug's prongs and using a voltage divider to obtain a scaled-down version of the voltage signal [3, 6, 17, 26]. Unfortunately, intercepting the power lines to obtain the voltage is not possible in a planar design. Other designs distribute the voltage and current measurements, and wirelessly recombine them, to obtain power [20, 28], while others do not use the voltage channel signal at all [23]. None of these these approaches are ideal for a plug-through meter. Taking distributed measurements requires at least two different devices which increases cost and makes deployment cumbersome, while only using the current channel leads to errors for non-unity power factors [20].

In contrast with the prior work, PowerBlade borrows an idea from the FlipIt plug-through USB charger [22] for its voltage acquisition. FlipIt uses spring-loaded wire contacts molded into a 0.066" thick piece of plastic through which a plug's prongs pass. PowerBlade improves upon this design by integrating the contacts directly into the PCB by employing a rigid-flex material which eliminates the molding, enabling the only meter design point that makes contact with the prongs without the need for an AC receptacle.

2.3 Current Measurement

Among the meters we survey, the most common methods for measuring current employ a sense resistor placed in series with the electrical path [3, 6, 17, 26], a Hall effect sensor placed co-planar to a current carrying conductor trace [26], and a current transformer (CT) that encircles the current carrying conductor [20, 23]. Unfortunately, none of these designs are suited to an essentially planar, plug-through form factor. Current sense resistors are inexpensive, accurate, and small, but they require the electrical path to be broken and an AC receptacle and prongs be used, making them unsuitable for our application. Hall effect sensors work by measuring the deflection of electrons in a conductor exposed to a magnetic field (like the one generated by a current). However, they require the magnetic field lines to be perpendicular to the plane of the sensing element which, in our case, is challenging since the magnetic field lines are co-planar with the circuit board; hence a Hall effect sensor would require a non-trivial third dimension.

In contrast with these methods of current sensing, PowerBlade uses an optimally-placed surface mount inductor to measure the variation in magnetic flux produced by a current carrying conductor, detectable as a voltage across the inductor's terminals. Used in this way, the inductor functions as a search coil (or inductive sensor) whose terminal voltage is proportional to the rate of change of the current over time. This approach requires signal integration to recover the original current signal. Using a small, surface mount inductor in this manner enables PowerBlade to maintain an essentially two-dimensional form factor—something that is difficult using conventional current sensing methods.

2.4 Power Calculation

There exist three common options for calculating power. The first is to use a power metering integrated circuit like the Analog Devices ADE7753 [1]. Three of the surveyed meters employ this or a similar chip [3, 17, 26]. These metering chips take as inputs current and voltage signals and provide as outputs real, reactive, and apparent power, as well as power factor, zero crossings, and other measurements. They provide accurate measurements but are costly in terms of area and power draw, consuming 0.3" × 0.3" × 0.08" PCB area and drawing 25 mW, respectively, placing them outside of acceptable area and power budgets for our application.

A second option employed by several meters in our survey is to calculate power from the acquired current and voltage in software running on an embedded microcontroller. This approach can be quite accurate but the accuracy is bounded by the sampling rate of the ADCs and the performance of the signal processing pipeline. PowerBlade employs this approach and uses a low power microcontroller to achieve an acceptably lower power draw.

In contrast with these approaches—hardware and software—the Monjolo design does not report true power [23]. A Monjolo power meter does not actually sample either the current or the voltage waveform. Rather, it uses a fixed V_{RMS} value and an approximation of the I_{RMS} value based on the activation interval of an energy harvesting sensor. With these data, Monjolo estimates apparent power, which is the per-cycle product of V_{RMS} and I_{RMS}, but not real or reactive power. Moreover, Monjolo exhibits high error for certain loads with significant harmonic content.

2.5 Data Communication

To be useful, a power meter must communicate its data to the outside world. How these data are communicated to users affects the meter size. All of the commercial meters we survey communicate their data to the user with an LCD display on the unit [3, 6, 17]. Of these three, the Kill-A-Watt and Watts Up have a readout physically located at the outlet while the Conserve Insight offers a readout on a five foot tether. Although a display improves data visibility, it also couples the size of the meter with the size of the screen, leading to a tension between making the meter smaller and making the screen larger. This tensions affects usability as more readable screens take up more space. In addition, data displayed solely on a screen cannot be easily recorded by the user for later use. Thus, LCD screens are not well-suited to the challenge of pervasive power metering.

Another communications option is wired, like USB or Ethernet, and one of the commercial meters we survey uses this method in addition to its LCD readout [17]. Although this offers an attractive low power, high-bandwidth link, the form factor ramifications are severe. The USB connection must be isolated from AC mains to be connected to a host computer, and this isolation requires substantial additional space that is unavailable in an essentially planar design.

Low power wireless radios allow the system to display or process data remotely, using a smartphone or computer. Unlike an LCD, radios require physically very little space in the meter. The radio-enabled meters we survey use 802.15.4, and ACme [26] uses a multi-hop mesh network, allowing data to propagate over potentially long distances. However, none of these meters allow users to connect directly using a smartphone. PowerBlade also employs a radio, but we chose a Bluetooth Low Energy radio which can directly leverage the rich interface available on nearby smartphones and will soon support IP connectivity and end-to-end networking [25].

2.6 Alternate Power Metering Methods

Fine-grained power data does not require individual load metering. This analysis explores devices that, similar to PowerBlade, meter consumption at the outlet where power is being drawn, but methods exist for acquiring this data without physical metering. Wu et al. demonstrate the ability to determine appliance on/off state through deployed sensors, and they use preexisting knowledge of the draw of each of these states to determine total power [30]. Further, ElectriSense [24] is able to determine device state simply by monitoring AC voltage at a single point and measuring the EMI generated by switched mode power supplies and propagated by the wiring throughout the building. Both options provide consumption information without the overhead of plug-load meters, but they also require prior knowledge of the systems to be measured.

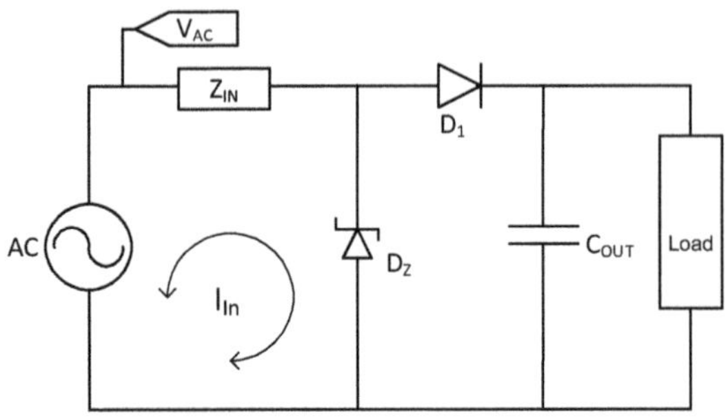

Figure 2: Zener regulated, half-wave rectified power supply. Z_{IN}, either a resistor or capacitor, is used to shunt the line voltage. D_1 is a rectifying diode. C_{OUT} is used to store charge between each positive half cycle of the AC wave. The maximum voltage exposed to the load is controlled by the Zener voltage of D_Z. On very low power loads, this supply can be made in a very small volume.

3. DESIGN

PowerBlade performs the same five functions as other power meters, but in a planar, plug-through form factor. This section examines the design space and tradeoffs in achieving this design point.

3.1 Power Supply

PowerBlade optimizes for size by using a power supply design that does not require an IC [21]. Figure 2 shows a Zener regulated, half-wave rectified power supply. This circuit offers a low component count, and only the shunt impedance, Z_{IN}, must be rated for AC voltage. The choice of Z_{IN} affects the final system's available power, overall volume, and idle power draw. In this study, we only examine components rated for the application: leads separated by at least the AC mains spark gap of 1.25 mm (package 1206 and larger). Resistors are further rated for the idle power dissipated (V_{AC}^2/R), and capacitors must be class X (AC rated "across the line") or above.

We note that this circuit is not isolated. Its ground is tied directly to the neutral line, which could be a possible safety issue when interacting with the circuit. Since the system is wireless, and is intended to be entirely packaged, this does not present a risk for the end user. More discussion on packaging is included in Section 5.2.4. One aspect of safety that does pertain here, however, is component count. In order to limit inrush current if Z_{IN} is a capacitor, it must be in series with a resistor. Further, when the system is de-powered the capacitor maintains its voltage. In order to prevent shock, an additional high-value bleed resistor must be placed in parallel with the capacitor. If Z_{IN} is a resistor, neither extra component is required. Although this is not explicitly included in the volume discussion below, it must be considered when selecting the final design.

Figure 3 shows the design space for Z_{IN} based on component volume and supplied current. A third parameter, not pictured, is idle power: the resistors add an idle power even when the load is not applied. This idle power scales directly with current supplied. Capacitors, however, do not affect idle power. The current draw follows Ohm's law ($I_{MAX} \approx V_{AC}/Z_{IN}$). Volume is calculated using components from DigiKey's electronic component database, and for resistors the smallest available component with the required power rating is shown.

This figure illustrates the fundamental tradeoffs for this simple supply: the volume occupied by the supply scales directly with the provided current. In other words, current is not free even though the system is attached to AC. Whether for resistors or capacitors, accommodating more current means moving to a larger package. Even within a given package, small variations are introduced, while small variations in value result in quantum jumps in volume.

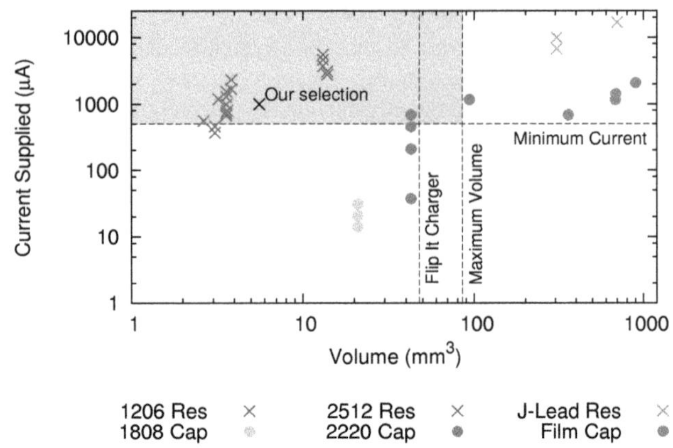

Figure 3: Selecting Z_{IN} based on volume occupied and current that can be supplied. If Z_{IN} is a resistor, lower resistance provides more current but also requires a larger size/package to dissipate the additional power. A capacitor does not increase idle power, and high capacitance (low impedance) provides more current but the extra capacitance requires a larger size/package. The resistors marked are the smallest available at the required power rating. There is a maximum volume that the system can occupy, as well as a minimum current required. The upper left quadrant, shaded, represents the viable design space for PowerBlade. Although any component in this quadrant is viable, there exist pareto-optimal points for volume, current, and idle power. We select a 1210 resistor, marked, back from the frontier to allow for tolerance as we develop the design.

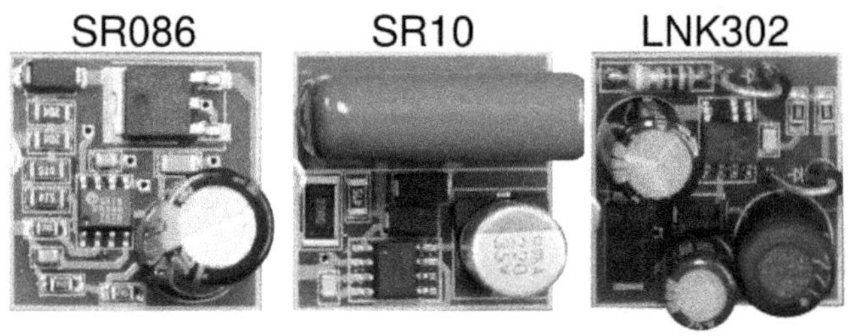

Figure 4: Low volume power supplies. Each supply is built within a 0.875 inch square. Large volume components are necessary for each supply and cannot be reduced significantly as load power decreases.

This relationship holds true for larger systems with increased power requirements. Figure 4 shows three low volume, direct rectification power supplies: the SR086 [13], the SR10 [14], and the LNK302 [9]. Each is dominated by one or more large components whose sizes scale with the current that can be supplied. The relationship is not limited to capacitors and resistors: although the SR10 uses a capacitor shunt similar to PowerBlade, the SR086 and LNK302 use a high-voltage transistor and inductor, respectively. All three of these supplies would exist in the far upper right of Figure 3, providing significantly higher current but requiring greater volume.

Figure 3 can be used to determine an approximate power point for the system. This can be used to select the remainder of the components, which in turn will yield a more precise minimum required current. The maximum volume and minimum current shown on the figure are for the final PowerBlade system. The range of acceptable volumes is determined experimentally on several NEMA outlets, with an additional dashed line representing an approximation of the Flip It USB charger's volume which also utilizes a very similar form factor and usage model.

The upper left quadrant of Figure 3, shaded, is the viable design space for PowerBlade. The pareto-optimal point for current is a 10 kΩ 2512 resistor that can supply 5.5 mA and requires 13.1 mm^3. The pareto-optimal point for volume is a 47 kΩ 1206 resistor that can supply 1.1 mA and requires 3.2 mm^3. These would add an idle power of 1.4 W and 300 mW, respectively. The pareto-optimal point for idle power is a 33 nF 2220 ceramic capacitor that can supply 684 µA and requires 42.8 mm^3, but adds no idle power. Our selection is also marked, a 1210 resistor selected away from the frontier to provide ample tolerance in power dissipation and design flexibility as we continue to develop the system. We selected a resistor just over our minimum current threshold to minimize idle power draw.

3.2 Voltage Sensing

Voltage sensing in this form factor requires a planar contact method, a voltage divider, and an ADC to acquire the voltage signal digitally. Of these, the method to contact AC voltage is the only requirement that cannot be solved with small, readily available components. We have identified two possibilities for contact: small spring loaded pins and flexible tabs built into the PCB itself.

A flexible tab built into the PCB bends to provide contact as the AC plug is inserted (this is the contact method shown in Figure 1). The benefit is easy manufacturing: the process of printing the circuit board provides the contact method. The tradeoff is in longevity. The flexible materials are not designed for elasticity, and after several insertions the flexible tab no longer provides a strong contact.

Another option is to mount a spring loaded pin sideways in the plane of the PCB. If the tip of the pin is rounded, the AC plug can slide past it as the spring-loaded pin applies contact. Such components are available off the shelf [10], and since they are designed to be compressed, they will maintain contact over more insertions than flexible tabs. The tradeoff is in the difficulty in manufacturing: mounting the pins is currently a manual procedure. We have yet to identify a process to reliably and repeatably mount the pin.

3.3 Current Sensing

Many existing current sensing techniques, like shunt resistors, are planar, but rely on interrupting an AC conductor, which PowerBlade cannot do. Instead, PowerBlade senses current non-intrusively by detecting the magnetic field surrounding an alternating current. As current passes through the AC prongs inserted through PowerBlade, the charge moving through each prong generates a magnetic field. Those fields add constructively between the prongs and destructively outside the prongs. Figure 5, generated by applying the Biot-Savart law, shows the relative strength and orientation of this magnetic field in the plane of PCB surrounding the prongs.

Two aspects of this figure guide the optimal placement of a sensor to measure this field. First, the magnitude of the field is on the order of 10-100 nT, which establishes bounds on the required transducer sensitivity. Second, although intuition might suggest that the constructive fields would be maximized directly between the prongs, the rapid decrease in field strength with distance from the conductor means the strongest signal is closest a prong.

Hall effect sensors and other vector magnetometers are capable of sensing this magnetic field, but packaged units cannot meet PowerBlade's form factor needs or power requirements. Many such devices also fail to meet the requirements of this system's design due to low sensitivity or low sampling rates. Instead, we observe that a surface mount wirewound inductor placed in the field can act as an inductive sensor or magnetometer. The alternating current in the wire causes a changing magnetic field which passes through the coils of the inductor and generates a voltage. A coil magnetometer used in this way is also known as a search coil [29].

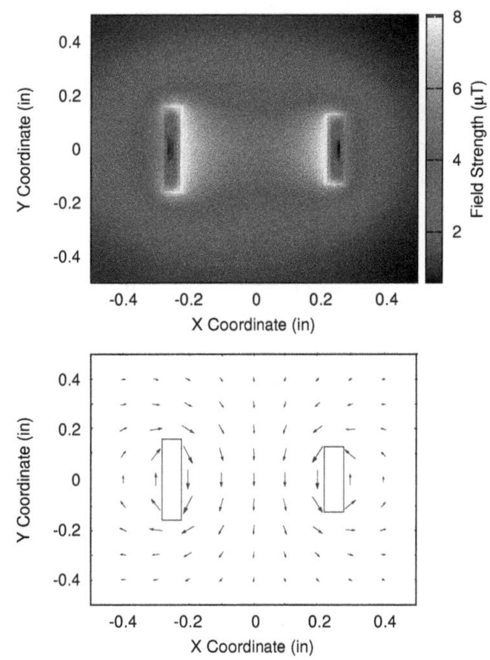

Figure 5: Superposition of magnetic fields around the prongs of an AC load plugged through PowerBlade. The top figure shows the relative magnitude of the field and the bottom shows the direction and relative magnitude, both with a 1 A constant current. The current flows in opposite directions in the prongs, so the fields add constructively between the prongs and destructively outside. Between the prongs, the field is largely oriented vertically. This model allows us to optimally position and orient a wirewound inductor in the field to maximize induced voltage.

$$V = -\mu N A \frac{dH}{dt} \tag{1}$$

The equation governing the voltage generated in the coil can be determined from Faraday's law of induction and is shown in Equation (1), where μ is the magnetic permeability, N is the number of turns in the coil, and A is the cross-sectional area of the coil. Note that voltage is proportional to the change in magnetic field strength over time. This means that voltage on the inductor is proportional to the change in current over time, rather than the current itself. The signal must be integrated to recover the original current waveform.

3.4 Power Calculation

If the form factor or power requirements prevent the use of a dedicated metering chip, as is the case for PowerBlade, then the only remaining option is to implement custom measurement software in a low power microcontroller. However, the choice of microcontroller must balance the fidelity of measurements with the availability of power. For example, a higher sampling rate will improve measurement accuracy, but it will also draw more power due to increased data conversion rate and more frequent processor wakeups. Similarly, the measurements themselves must be scaled from raw "ADC counts" to power statistics (W, VA, etc.) through various transfer functions that may require floating point arithmetic. The floating point operations could be performed on the PowerBlade unit itself, power and performance permitting, or they may be applied in the receiver. The particular operating point depends on a balance of many variables.

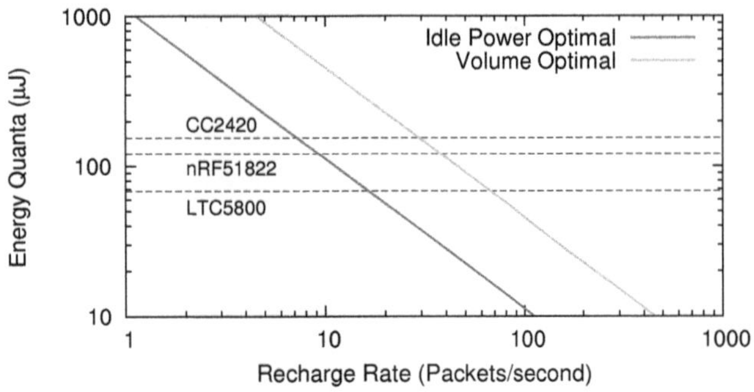

Figure 6: Maximum energy quanta vs recharge rate for two options for Z_{IN}. V_Z is fixed at 10 V. Both optimal volume and optimal idle power draw are shown, and increasing C_{OUT} results in a higher energy quanta at a slower recharge rate (upper left corner). The minimum energy to boot and send a packet is shown for three radio transceivers. For a given Z_{IN}, the maximum packet transmission rate for each transceiver lies at the intersection of the dotted line with the given curve.

3.5 Data Communication

Data communication often requires a continuous burst of power. For a wireless radio, this is the energy required to send a single packet, but even a display screen must display for a minimum duration to allow a human to read it. In some cases, the current required may be more than what is available, and if so, the power supply must store at least the energy required for a single such event (referred to here as energy quanta). How much energy is available is determined by three components from Figure 2: Z_{IN}, V_Z, and C_{OUT}.

Increasing C_{OUT} will increase the energy available, but at the expense of a slower recharge rate. Decreasing Z_{IN} results in greater current supply, which will increase both recharge rate and energy quanta (as additional current is available during the discharge event). Increasing V_Z will increase both energy quanta and recharge time, but will increase energy quanta more due to the quadratic term in energy calculation. Higher V_Z values are therefore preferred, but V_Z is also constrained by other components. Small options for C_{OUT} are commonly limited to 16 V, and many of the commercially available miniature buck converters offer significantly higher efficiencies in the 10-15 V range.

Figure 6 shows the recharge rate and energy quanta for two of the three pareto-optimal options for Z_{IN} from Section 3.1. The current optimal option is not shown; it could supply sufficient current to continuously operate certain radios but is undesirable due to its high idle power draw. V_Z is fixed at 10 V, and for a given curve, increasing C_{OUT} results in moving up and to the left. The range of capacitance shown for each curve (up to 22 µF) is readily available in a variety of small ceramic packages.

Also shown is the minimum energy required to boot and send a packet for three possible radios, the CC2420 [15], LTC5800 [8], and nRF51822 [11]. The measurement of the CC2420 was performed by Yerva et al. [31], the figure for the LTC5800 is available in its datasheet, and we measure the energy for the nRF51822 ourselves. The energy quanta figures need not be exact; their purpose is to drive the selection of a radio.

For a given radio and selection of Z_{IN}, the maximum recharge rate, in packets per second, is the intersection of the two lines. This can be used to determine the possible data rate or, if the required recharge rate is lower, Z_{IN} can be reduced from the optimal to reduce idle power. The latter is the case in PowerBlade.

Figure 7: PowerBlade PCB layout with key features labeled. Exact board dimensions are 1" × 1" × 0.066". The position of the sense inductor, placed close to the neutral prong, is marked.

Z_{IN} (Z)	Expected	Actual	Volume	Cost	Idle Power
22 nF (120 kΩ)	456 µA	451 µA	43.0 mm^3	$1.24	0 mW
33 nF (80 kΩ)	705 µA	740 µA	43.0 mm^3	$1.63	0 mW
56 nF (47 kΩ)	1161 µA	1137 µA	95.0 mm^3	$1.34	0 mW
100 kΩ	550 µA	538 µA	2.6 mm^3	$0.03	140 mW
80.6 kΩ	687 µA	658 µA	3.0 mm^3	$0.03	170 mW
75 kΩ	733 µA	716 µA	3.0 mm^3	$0.03	190 mW

Table 2: Expected and actual maximum current for various possible component choices for Z_{IN} in the supply in Figure 2. Also shown are the volume required and cost of each component, as well as its idle power draw when the system is connected to AC.

4. IMPLEMENTATION

This section describes how the components identified in Section 3 are integrated into a system in PowerBlade. This section also covers the steps required to operate the system as a true power meter, including how the wireless system is used and how the meter is calibrated.

4.1 Power Supply

We explore several components for Z_{IN} to evaluate their performance. Table 2 shows the expected maximum current from the supply and our experimentally measured actual current, as well as the volume, cost, and idle power that result from that component being selected. Resistors are able to deliver comparable current to that of capacitor shunts for a smaller volume and lower cost, but they increase idle power draw even when the load is powered off.

Although early versions of PowerBlade had footprints for both a 2220 package capacitor and 1210 package resistor, current designs optimize for size and cost by only providing space for the resistor. In addition to the significantly smaller size, the low cost of a resistor outweighs the cost added by its idle power. At $0.12 per kilowatt-hour, the 170 mW added by an 80 kΩ resistor would outweigh the cost of a 33 nF capacitor only after nine years of continuous operation. Current implementations use an 80.6 kΩ resistor, which leads to a design constraint for the rest of the system in that it must operate below a maximum average current of about 658 µA. Summing the power draw of the system and the idle power draw of the supply, this leads to an overall power draw of 176 mW for PowerBlade. Our present choices reflect the desire for frequent data transmissions supporting interactive use, but we note that higher Z_{IN} values are also possible with a concomitant reduction in data transmission rate.

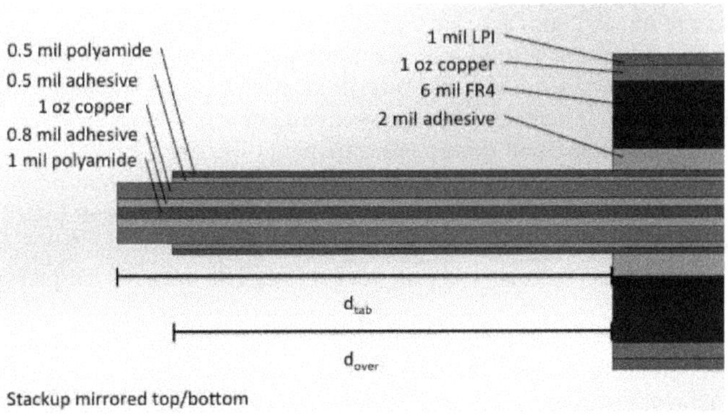

Figure 8: Cross-sectional layer stack-up in PowerBlade. Shown are the entire stack-up (right), as well as the stack-up of the tab itself (left) that contacts the AC plug. Using a rigid-flex PCB allows for easy manufacturing with multiple insertions.

The remainder of the components from Figure 2 are a 10 V Zener diode and 250 mA rectifier diode, both in a small SC-79 package, and a combined 55 µF from two parallel capacitors for C_{OUT}. We select a larger capacitance than the minimum required from Figure 6 to allow tolerance as we continue the design, and the added delay is only experienced when the unit is first powering on. The load will nominally see 8.9 V: the Zener voltage minus the rectifier forward voltage of 1.1 V. To regulate this output to 3.3 V we use a 3.3 V buck regulator, the Texas Instruments TPS62122 [16]. At the nominal input voltage of 8.9 V this regulator has an efficiency of 85-90%.

4.2 Contact

The single-PCB system shown in Figure 1 is a rigid-flex PCB—a stack-up of layers of both rigid and flexible materials with conductive copper layers sandwiched in between. For our proof of concept we select flexible tabs over spring loaded pins due to the ease in manufacturing. This method of circuit board construction maintains good contact for approximately 10-30 insertions, providing a pathway to a proof of concept, but we intend to continue to explore methods using spring loaded pins in future work.

Figure 8 shows a cross section of the flexible tabs. The innermost layers of the PCB are all flexible, the inner layers 2 and 3 of copper are fixed to a flexible polyimide core. These layers extend into the tabs to make contact with AC. They continue throughout the entire system, but are rigidized with FR4 material between this flexible core and the outer copper layers.

Extending only 5 layers into the tab provides insufficient support; the tabs bend on the first insertion and never return to form. Instead, we add an additional polyimide/adhesive pair on each side of the tab, with only the tip remaining exposed for contact. After exploring several options for d_{over}, we find that fully covering one side of the tab while exposing only the tip on the other side allows for maximum insertions. This requires loads be plugged through PowerBlade from back to front, but NEMA polarization means most loads already plug from this direction.

4.3 Measurement Amplifiers

Figure 9 shows the amplifier circuits used to measure voltage and current. PowerBlade measures line voltage directly through a voltage divider with a $V_{CC}/2$ offset to measure both positive and negative phases. $R_F = 4.99\ \text{k}\Omega$ and $R_{I1} = R_{I2} = 953\ \text{k}\Omega$, so V_{SENSE} can be approximated as Equation (2).

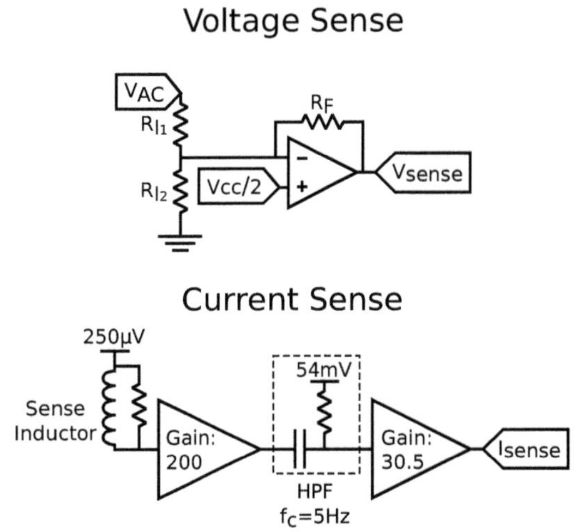

Figure 9: Voltage and current sensing circuits. Voltage sensing requires little volume, consisting of a voltage divider and amplifier with a $V_{CC}/2$ offset. Current sensing uses a horizontally wirewound inductor, amplified and filtered. The resulting signals V_{SENSE} and I_{SENSE} are measured by the MSP430.

$$V_{SENSE} \approx \frac{V_{CC}}{2} - 5.24 \times 10^{-3}\ V_{AC} \tag{2}$$

Based on these configurations, the voltage signal has a peak to peak amplitude of 1.79 V where the AC is 120 V_{RMS} (United States) and 3.28 V where the AC is 220 V_{RMS} (much of Europe and China).

PowerBlade measures the signal from the sense inductor in multiple stages. The inductor is referenced to 250 µV and amplified in two stages with a combined gain of about 6100x. Low frequency noise is removed with a high pass filter between the first and second stages, and this filter is referenced to 54 mV so the final signal is centered around $V_{CC}/2$.

$$I_{SENSE} \approx \frac{V_{CC}}{2} + \alpha \frac{dI}{dt} \tag{3}$$

Equation (3) describes the output of the current sense stage as a function of the derivative of the AC current, where α is a lumped parameter consisting of the characteristics of the coil, gain, signal distortions, and general uncertainty. After integration the current is represented by Equation (4), where β accounts for DC offsets in the system and integration offsets.

$$Current \approx \int \left(\frac{V_{CC}}{2} + \alpha \frac{dI}{dt} \right) dt \approx \alpha I + \beta \tag{4}$$

4.4 Calibrating PowerBlade

PowerBlade calibration requires two steps. The first step is to measure the scaling and offset values α and β, which must be done once per design. The second step is a device-specific calibration that accounts for slight variations between units.

To determine the scaling and offset values α and β, respectively, we measure the reported RMS current from PowerBlade for a range of resistive (unity power factor) loads. Figure 10 shows the RMS values of current reported as raw values. For the current system, these measurements are linear with an R^2 value of 0.999, and indicate an α of 40.85 and β of 25.0. Subtracting the offset β happens in PowerBlade, and for further testing, all units comprising a batch are programmed with this value.

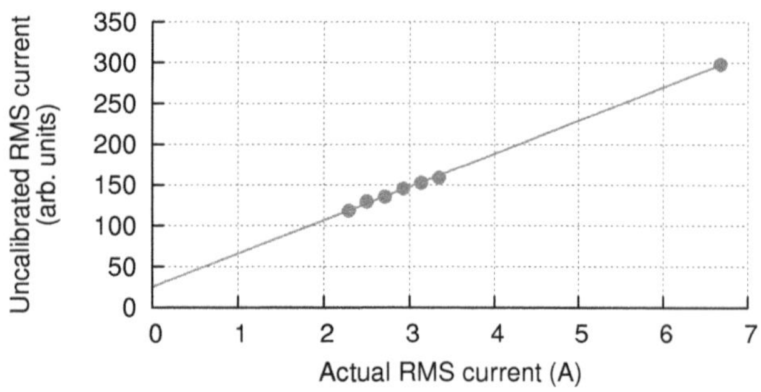

Figure 10: PowerBlade reported uncalibrated RMS current. These samples are used to calculate α and β from Equation (4) and allow us to refine our power calculations.

To reduce the computational burden on PowerBlade, we divide by α in the receiver, and for increased accuracy, each unit is calibrated again. We connect each PowerBlade in a batch to a 200 W load to compute a device-specific α, store that value in FRAM, and transmit it with each packet. We have observed a mean value for α across multiple units of 41.79, with a 95% confidence interval of 1.87.

Finally, after calibrating α for each device, we notice an exponential error not accounted for by the model. We experimentally determine the following correction $P = P_{RAW} - 6.6e^{-0.015P_{RAW}}$, where P_{RAW} is the power (in watts) after applying the α and β corrections, removes this error and yields the final power figures. The values of 6.6 and -0.015 are determined once per design.

4.5 Power Calculation

We save the overhead of a power metering IC by performing our power metering calculations on a MSP430FR5738. This chip is the master controller of the system and is the only component not automatically power gated at startup. It is selected due to its small size, power efficiency of 81.4 µA/MHz, and integrated 16 kB non-volatile FRAM, eliminating an external component.

To measure power, the MSP430 samples V_{SENSE} and I_{SENSE} at 2.52 kHz (42 samples per AC cycle). This frequency is both an even divisor of our timing clock (32,768 Hz) and an even multiple of the frequency to be sampled (60 Hz). Because I_{SENSE} is proportional to the derivative of current, the second measurement step integrates I_{SENSE} to obtain current (V_{SENSE} is a good representation of voltage). The integration is performed in software, but could be performed by hardware in the future. The final calculation step involves calculating power from voltage and current.

Because the MSP430 has real-time access to both voltage and current waveforms, it can function as a true power meter. Real power is determined by multiplying voltage and current at each point, and then averaging over the number of samples. Apparent power is determined by first calculating the root mean square voltage and current over a cycle, V_{RMS} and I_{RMS}, respectively, and then multiplying them. Knowledge of both real and apparent power allows the system to determine reactive power as well as the power factor of the load. Real power is also aggregated in the MSP430 to compute total watt-hours measured over time, and this number is stored in FRAM.

4.6 BLE Communication

Data are transmitted in broadcast-style BLE advertisement messages. The MSP430 first communicates to the nRF51822 via UART at 38,400 baud, and the nRF51822 repeats this data in the advertisement. The MSP430 sends UART data nominally at 1 Hz, and the nRF51822 sends advertisements at 5 Hz, so 4-5 identical packets are transmitted each second. This greatly increases the likelihood of reception, and does not dramatically affect the power draw.

In addition to a sequence identifier and information regarding versioning and scaling, each PowerBlade packet contains four fields: line voltage, instantaneous real power, instantaneous apparent power, and watt-hours. Real power and apparent power are 1-second averages, and can be used together to calculate power factor. Watt-hours is an over-time total, and in the event of zero packet loss watt-hours will, once scaled, also equal the integral of real power.

PowerBlade is robust against packet loss. The intended recipient of broadcast advertisements is either a smartphone or a fixed BLE receiver, but in the event of no receiver, only the resolution of the missed packet is lost. The overall watt-hours total remains an accurate reading in any received packet. Watt-hours is stored as a 32-bit number and can overflow. In the worst case with present calibration scaling values, measuring an 1,800 W load will lead to an overflow every 29 days. A 100 W load will overflow after 523 days of continuous measurement. Overflows are signaled in the advertisements so the true watt-hours reading can be recovered. If a receiver is not present for long periods of time, potential for data loss exists.

4.7 System Operation

Figure 11 shows the startup phase of PowerBlade and 7 s of steady-state operation. When the system first starts, there is only power to boot the MSP430; if more components are drawing power, the 3.3 V power rail will never enable and the system will lock up. Instead, MOSFETs separately power gate the sensing circuits and BLE radio. With only the MSP430 running, the capacitor charges, enables the 3.3 V rail, and eventually reaches a nominal 8.9 V.

When the MSP430 detects that the capacitor has charged to the nominal voltage it enables the sensing circuits, and these remain powered for as long as PowerBlade is powered. The MSP430 spends 1 s collecting measurements before enabling the nRF51822, which also remains powered for the duration of the trace. At this point the device has entered steady-state operation.

5. EVALUATION

We evaluate PowerBlade on the basis of accuracy in reporting real power for both a calibrated resistive AC load and an assortment of household loads. We also present benchmarks that affect the usability of the system, including PowerBlade's volume, cost, wireless performance, and safety of using the system.

5.1 Power Metering Accuracy

We evaluate PowerBlade's accuracy in two parts. First, we explore bench top accuracy, where we use PowerBlade to measure the power draw of a programmable AC load—the APS 3B012-12 [2]—set to unity power factor. This allows us to measure a large part of the metering range (up to 1200 W) in defined increments and in a controlled setting. Second, we use PowerBlade to measure the power draw of several household items. Although not an exhaustive list, this is representative of PowerBlade's target usage.

For the bench top accuracy, ground truth is provided by the 3B012-12 itself via its serial interface. For the household tests, ground truth is taken from two sources. On the low range, we use a professionally calibrated Power Line Meter (PLM) [5]. This device is limited to 480 W, however, so to measure larger loads we take ground truth from a Watts Up [17]. We report the Watts Up measurements over the low range as well, and it is clear that it is less accurate than the PLM (typical error of about 1.72%). The need to use two different meters for ground truth demonstrates the difficulty in creating a highly accurate whole-range metering solution. For each test we take 30 PowerBlade measurements, 30 ground truth measurements, and report the arithmetic mean and 95% confidence interval.

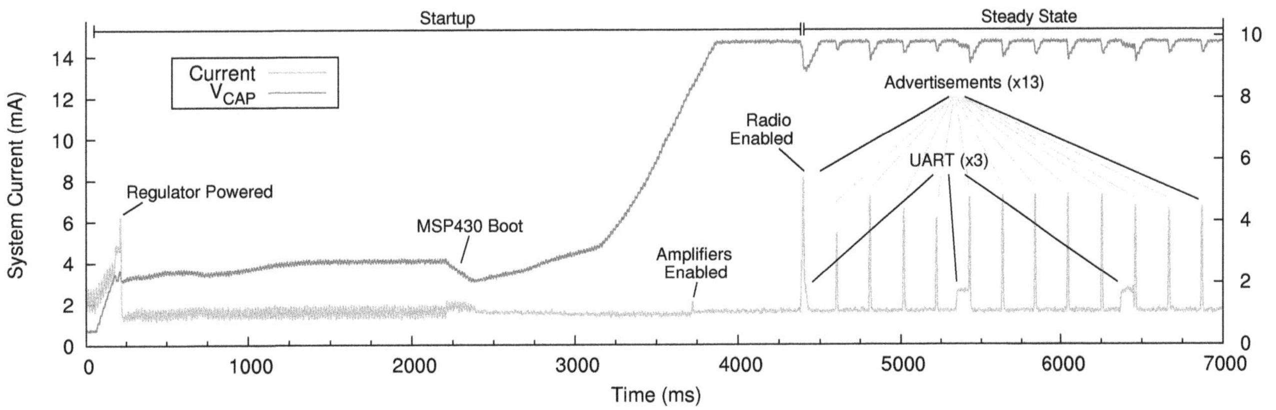

Figure 11: PowerBlade timing: storage capacitor voltage and 3.3 V regulator output current for the first 7 s of operation. At startup the measurement circuits and the nRF51822 are automatically disabled. For approximately 2 s the capacitors charge gradually, and around 2.25 s the MSP430 boots. When the MSP430 detects the capacitor has charged to the nominal voltage of 8.9 V it enables the voltage and current measurement circuits. For the first 1 s of the amplifiers being powered there is no data to transmit, so the nRF51822 is kept disabled. After 1 s of measurement the MSP430 enables the nRF51822 and sends data over UART. At this point the nRF51822 begins advertising data at 5 Hz for the remainder of operation and the MSP430 updates with new information over UART at 1 Hz. This results in up to five identical packets transmitted, which increases the likelihood of reception, and a sequence number transmitted with each packet denotes the duplicate.

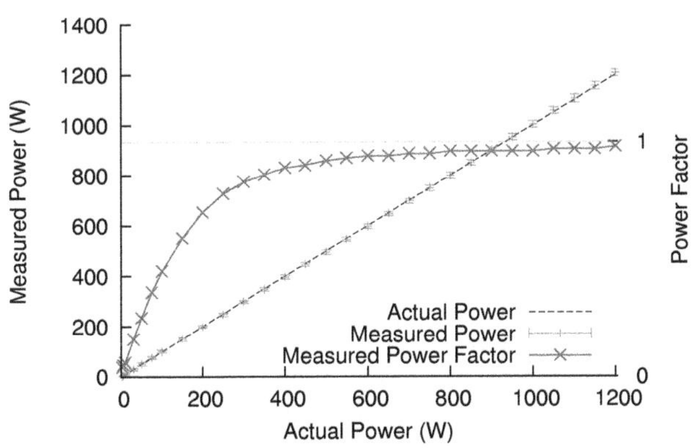

Figure 12: Metering accuracy for a variable resistive (power factor equals 1) load. Measured power vs actual power as well as measured power factor. Also shown are the 95% confidence intervals for real power. The minimum AC load for accurate metering is about 2 W and over the range from 2 W to 1200 W the average accuracy in real power is 1.13%. PowerBlade's metering and reporting system is accurate over a range of resistive loads.

5.1.1 *Resistive Loads*

Resistive loads with a unity power factor, which include incandescent lights and power-factor-corrected devices, exhibit a sinusoidal current waveform in-phase with voltage. To measure PowerBlade's accuracy in this simple but common case, we use an APS 3B012-12 programmable AC load set to a fixed unity power factor. Figure 12 shows the end-to-end accuracy for PowerBlade metering this resistive load. Displayed are the reported real power and power factor from PowerBlade, as well as the ground truth power up to the programmable load's maximum of 1200 W. Note that the true power factor is equal to one throughout the test.

We measure 29 wattages from 2.2 W to 1200 W: 50 W to 1200 W in increments of 50 as well as 2.2 W, 5 W, 10 W, and 75 W. For these measurements the average error is 2.3 W and the average percent error is 1.13%. At 2.2 W the error is 0.21 W (9.5%) and at 1200 W the error is 7.01 W (0.6%).

Device	**PF**	**Power**	**Watts Up Error**		**PowerBlade Error**	
150 W Bulb	1.00	162.17 W	1.22 W	(0.75%)	-0.99 W	(0.61%)
Fridge	1.00	108.22 W	-		-5.30 W	(4.90%)
Drill (Max)	0.99	235.21 W	1.69 W	(0.72%)	2.96 W	(1.26%)
Toaster	0.99	827.87 W	-		-22.11 W	(2.67%)
Vacuum	0.98	1246.96 W	-		15.24 W	(1.22%)
Microwave	0.92	1729.73 W	-		16.01 W	(0.93%)
Hot Air	0.83	305.54 W	0.88 W	(0.29%)	-1.93 W	(0.63%)
TV (Normal)	0.62	196.23 W	0.86 W	(0.44%)	-9.03 W	(4.60%)
50 W CFL	0.61	48.57 W	-1.08 W	(2.22%)	-9.51 W	(19.58%)
TV (Static Image)	0.61	129.51 W	-0.04 W	(0.03%)	-4.00 W	(3.09%)
Xbox	0.57	50.44 W	0.64 W	(1.27%)	-0.83 W	(1.65%)
MacBook	0.51	52.68 W	-0.41 W	(0.78%)	-4.49 W	(8.52%)
Blender	0.49	106.63 W	1.95 W	(1.83%)	36.97 W	(34.67%)
Router	0.46	9.11 W	0.22 W	(2.41%)	-0.62 W	(6.81%)
Drill (Low)	0.30	51.10 W	4.18 W	(8.18%)	20.40 W	(39.92%)

Table 3: Metering accuracy for a cross section of household devices. On this selection, the average percent error in real power is 6.5%. Although these devices produce more complex waveforms than a fully resistive load, PowerBlade remains acceptably accurate.

5.1.2 *Household Devices*

Resistive loads constitute a large fraction of household devices, but not all loads have sinusoidal current waveforms. Table 3 shows PowerBlade's accuracy for several devices found in a common household. For these devices, we simultaneously take a PowerBlade measurement, a Watts Up measurement and, if the load is below 480 W, a PLM measurement. If available, the PLM is used as ground truth. If not, the Watts Up is used. Although the fridge draws about 100 W, its start-up power tripped the 4 A fuse in the PLM, preventing PLM measurements for that load. For each device, we report its power and power factor, as well as PowerBlade's error and, if not used as ground truth, the Watts Up error for comparison.

This set of devices has a range of power from 9 W to 1730 W and a range of power factors from 0.30 to 1. The average absolute error for PowerBlade measurements of these devices is 10 W (4.3x higher than the resistive load), and the average percent error is 6.5% (5.8x higher). This error is dominated by two devices with highly inductive (low power factor) draws: the blender (PF=0.49) and the drill set to low power (PF=0.30). Each of these devices has an error of over 20 W and a percent error of over 30%, and excluding these two, the average absolute error drops to 7.2 W (3.1x the resistive load) and the average percent error drops to 4.3% (3.8x the resistive load). Correctly metering such devices is an area of future development.

The difficulty in measuring highly inductive loads, and further the difference in accuracy between the programmable load and the household devices, can be partially explained by examining the current waveforms. Figure 13 visualizes the current measurement process in PowerBlade for a few loads from Table 3. The known current signal, measured by a commercial current transformer [7], is shown along with I_{SENSE}, the signal output from PowerBlade's current amplifier (which, as described in Section 3.3, represents the derivative of the current waveform). Also shown is the post-integration representation of current. Voltage for each load is synchronized, and zero crossings of the common voltage are denoted by vertical lines.

Visible on the figure is the integral/derivative relationship between I_{SENSE} and known current, as well as the fidelity of the integrated signal to that known current. For devices with sinusoidal or otherwise smooth current waveforms, the integrated signal tracks well with known current. For other devices, however, high frequency components in the current waveform are suppressed by the integrator, resulting in increased error.

5.1.3 Watt-hour Accuracy

PowerBlade is designed to measure and report both instantaneous power and watt-hours, the sum over time that will be used by the utility company to levy charges. The figure of watt-hours also accounts for the possibility that one or multiple packets are not received: resolution is lost but watt-hours remains an accurate long-term measure. To evaluate PowerBlade's accuracy in reporting watt-hours, we take simultaneous measurements from the PLM, Watts Up, and PowerBlade for a television in normal viewing use. Figure 14 shows the measurements over time from Watts Up and PowerBlade as compared to the PLM.

After 15 minutes of normal television use, the PLM reported 49.07 Wh, the Watts Up reported 49.28 Wh (0.42% error), and PowerBlade reported 46.80 Wh (4.62% error). In instantaneous measurement trials the PowerBlade measurements for the television in full use were off by an average of 4.60%, the watt-hours figure of 4.62% error is consistent with the instantaneous readings.

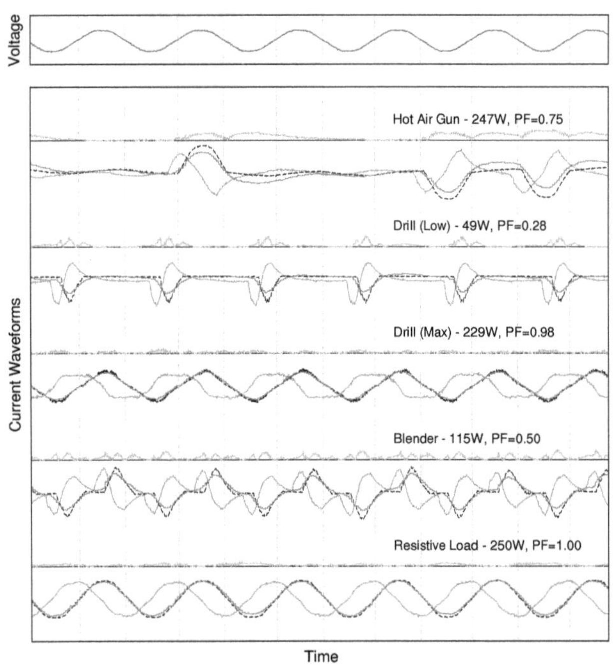

Figure 13: Current sensing fidelity. Output of current sense amplifier, I_{SENSE}, along with the internal representation of current, are shown for several household devices. Also shown is the true current waveform as measured by a commercial current transformer [7]. Visible is the derivative relationship between actual current and I_{SENSE}, as well as the distortions introduced by this sensing and integrating technique. This shows that PowerBlade's current sensing method reasonably captures the current waveform.

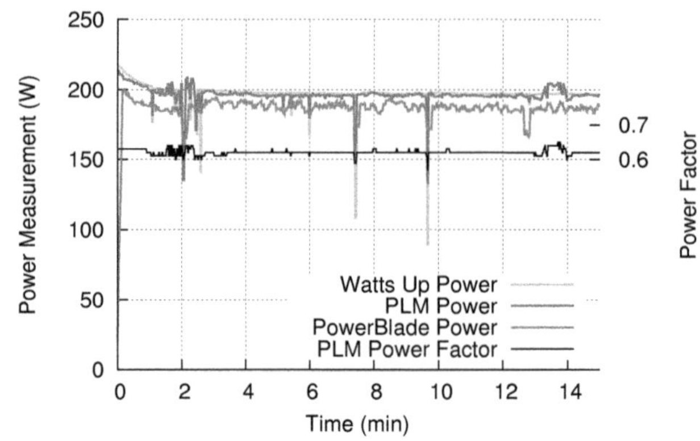

Figure 14: Metering accuracy over time for a television in use. Shown on the figure are reported power from the PLM (ground truth), Watts Up, and PowerBlade, as well as power factor reported from the PLM. At the end of 15 minutes the PLM reported 49.07 Wh, the WattsUp 49.28 Wh (0.42% error), and PowerBlade 46.80 Wh (4.62% error). This is consistent with PowerBlade's instantaneous error of 4.60% for the television in full use.

5.2 Usability Benchmarks

PowerBlade's accuracy makes it comparable to other power metering systems, but it is the usability of the system, and in particular the size, cost, and wireless communications, that most distinguish it. We also show through standard safety testing that PowerBlade is safe to use with the addition of an enclosure.

5.2.1 Volume

The defining characteristic of PowerBlade is its volume: the entire system is a single PCB. This circuit board is 1.0" on a side, and the PCB itself is 0.023" thick. The thickest component on the surface is the antenna at 0.043", so the combined total thickness of the system is 0.066". This is the same thickness as the pass-through section of the FlipIt charger, which is a certified commercial product.

5.2.2 Cost

The component breakdown in PowerBlade with costs is listed in Table 4. Prior to consumer use, PowerBlade needs an enclosure, but the system could be largely assembled for $10-$15 per unit. Although it is important to note the distinction between the cost of PowerBlade and the price of other systems, this is slightly less than the price of Kill-A-Watt ($23.99) and significantly less than the price of Watts Up ($130.95). The cost of $10-$15 for PowerBlade is also an un-optimized reporting of DigiKey pricing; the minimum viable cost would likely be much lower.

Component	Cost	Component	Cost
MSP430FR5738	$1.71	Sense inductor	$0.30
nRF51822	$1.66	Amplifiers	$2.51
Antenna, balun, & crystals	$1.70	MOSFETs	$0.12
Buck converter	$0.65	Other passives	$0.93
		PCB	$1.47
		Total	$11.05

Table 4: Cost for the PowerBlade system. The total system is roughly $11 in quantities of 1,000. We believe this represents an acceptable price point for effective plug-load metering deployments.

5.2.3 *Wireless Range*

We test the effectiveness of PowerBlade communications by measuring packet reception rates in three configurations of PowerBlade units. First we deploy and evaluate a single PowerBlade as a baseline. Next we place three PowerBlade units throughout a room as a more typical deployment case. Finally, we place three units on a single power strip and activate them simultaneously to test for possible packet collisions. We record both unique and total packets received per second. PowerBlade updates data at 1 Hz, and BLE packets are sent at 5 Hz, so nominally we should receive 1 unique and 5 total packets per second.

For each configuration we evaluate packet reception rate at three transmission distances, and perform the entire experiment both in an apartment and in a lab. The apartment consists of three rooms, with measurements taken in the same room, adjacent room, and two rooms away. Only a single other BLE device is active in the apartment. The lab consists of one room and hallways, and measurements are taken in the same room, immediately outside of the room in the hallway, and 20 m down the hallway from the room. The lab environment includes 16 non-PowerBlade BLE devices as well as numerous other devices active in the 2.4 GHz band.

Figure 15 shows the reception rate for each of these trials. In all cases, the unique reception rate is at or close to the nominal of 1 per second when in the same or adjacent rooms, but the total reception rate decreases from the same to the adjacent room. Further, the total reception rate is higher in the apartment than in the lab for both distances. Taken together these three results suggest that range and interference do effect BLE transmissions, but the redundancy in PowerBlade helps ensure reliable data communication.

The distant measurements show continued decline in total packets, but also a decrease in unique packets: 20% to 50% of the unique packets are not received at all (all five redundant packets were all dropped). This indicates that this distance—whether two rooms separated in a residential setting or 20 m down a hallaway in a university building—exceeds PowerBlade's usable range. We note that RF designs require some degree of lumped-parameter tuning to achieve maximum performance but PowerBlade's RF circuitry has not be tuned yet, so that may help explain these results.

5.2.4 *Safety*

PowerBlade is a prototype not designed for consumer use in its current form, but safety when using and deploying the system is still important. The UL safety standard that covers PowerBlade is UL 2735: Standard for Safety in Electric Utility Meters [18]. Although we do not have the resources at this time to perform an exhaustive safety evaluation, the enclosure requirements and single fault and mechanical tests in UL 2735 are good initial benchmarks for exploring the overall safety of the system.

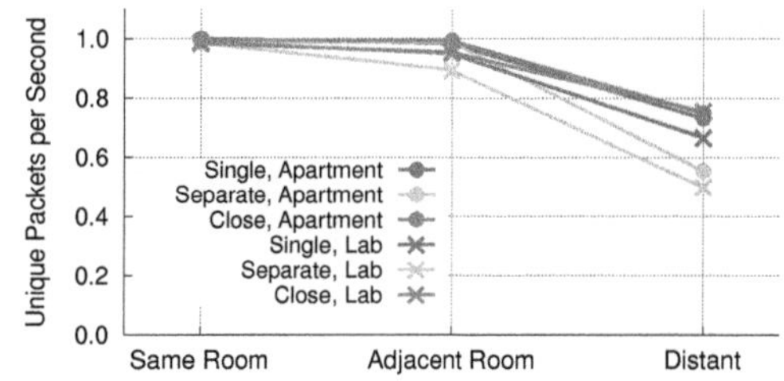

(a) Unique packets received per second

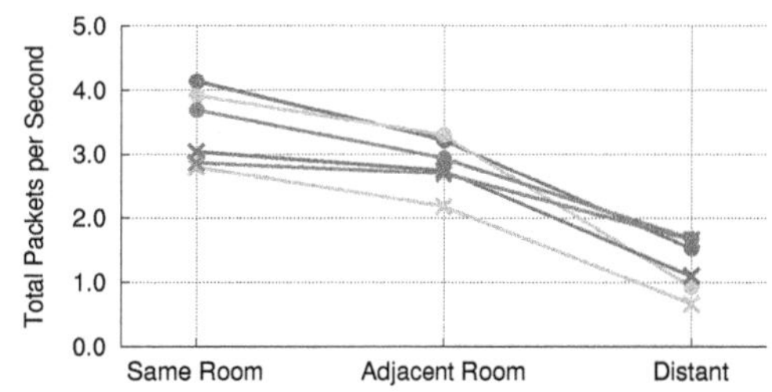

(b) Total packets received per second

Figure 15: Wireless reception rate for PowerBlade. Unique packets per second as well as total packets per second are recorded for each test. PowerBlade units are deployed singly, throughout a room, and adjacent on a power strip. The lab environment includes many other background sources of 2.4 GHz communications which may interfere with PowerBlade broadcasts. When in the same room as or adjacent room to a PowerBlade deployment, advertised power data is received once per second with a high probability.

The primary safety requirement is preventing electric shock by the unit. Figure 16 shows a PowerBlade unit after coating in a resistive material that protects the user from live parts. The resistive material does not noticeably affect wireless performance, and increases the total volume to 0.074 in^3 (12% increase). This currently requires a labor intensive application process, but for future builds we have identified a supplier capable of adding a heat-resistant overmolding in a scalable manufacturing process.

In addition to applying the conformal coating, we evaluate the system based on two sets of safety tests from UL 2735. The first is single fault testing for the electrical system, to determine if a failure in any one component could result in unsafe conditions. We identify three components that, in the event of a fault, will overload other components. In the power supply, Z_{IN} failing closed (short circuit) will expose the system to increased current, and D_Z failing open will no longer limit V_{CAP} to 9 V. In the voltage measurement circuit, R_{I1} failing closed (short circuit) will expose multiple components to 120 V. Circuit analysis indicates that Z_{IN} and R_{I1} failing open will result in no connection (no testing required). D_Z failing short will simply prevent charging, although we do test this condition.

As expected, shorting either Z_{IN} or R_{I1} results in secondary faults in other components. Shorting Z_{IN} results in open circuit faults in both D_1 and D_Z (D_1 is visibly damaged) but after 30 minutes there is no detectable change in temperature in the unit. Shorting R_{I1} results in open circuit faults and visible damage in both R_F and the voltage measurement amplifier. This test also results in a bright spark, audible pop, and momentary increase in temperature (to 33 degrees Celsius), but the temperature quickly decreases, and after 30 minutes there is no detectable ongoing change. Opening D_Z results in increasing V_{CAP} to 23 V, but the 3.3 V regulator continues to operate as normal and the system continues to function. Shorting D_Z results in no charging, but also no unsafe conditions.

Figure 16: Conformally coated PowerBlade. Shown are the unit after conformal coating has been applied, as well as the conformally coated unit attached to a load. Although this method requires a manual application process that is not manufacturable in large scale, it does protect the user from live parts. In the future an overmolding process will provide similar protection in a manufacturable way.

The second set of tests from UL 2735 is mechanical, to determine if the protective coating in Figure 16 can withstand real world conditions. Note that this conformal coating is a temporary solution; we use it to determine its effectiveness. The future overmolding technique will result in more durable protection. The conformally coated PowerBlade passes the static force and drop tests in UL 2735 without damage, but the impact test does destroy the unit and expose live parts. The live parts do not extend to the edge, however, and therefore do not present a safety hazard when the unit is plugged in.

6. DISCUSSION

In this section, we discuss some limitations of the current design, explore some possible workarounds, and propose some future directions for improvement. In particular, the accuracy could be further improved, the wireless system could be better utilized, and interval data could be collected with periodic timestamps.

6.1 Improving Accuracy

We identify two changes that could be taken in future designs to improve accuracy. First, the MSP430 microcontroller software algorithm that integrates I_{SENSE} to obtain the current waveform could be changed. Although the present implementation provides a usable signal, we believe a hardware implementation may better address baseline drift. Second, the acquisition of the current and voltage waveforms could be more tightly synchronized. For example, if the samples are acquired with a separation of 500 µs, that delay will introduce an measurement error of 6% on a 150 W resistive load. PowerBlade has a 22.2 µs delay between current and voltage sampling, but synchronous acquisition of the signals would be ideal.

Although error in real power is only 1.13% for the resistive loads and 6.5% for household devices, PowerBlade's error in power factor is often higher. Figure 12 shows the accuracy in power factor (which is actually accuracy in apparent power) decreases significantly at lower wattages. A similar effect is observed in the household loads. Real power is the metric used to assess utility charges, so we believe this to be the more important value, but we have yet to determine the source of the error in apparent power.

6.2 Wireless Communications

The advertisement-only communication model that PowerBlade employs presents two areas for improvement. First, any BLE receiver can eavesdrop on these broadcasts as the data are transmitted in clear-text, so data security is an obvious area of improvement. We have verified that a nearby smartphone can respond to a PowerBlade advertisement to open a BLE connection, showing that changes from the advertisement-only model are also possible.

6.3 Interval Metering

PowerBlade can store accumulated energy in non-volatile memory, allowing it to aggregate total load usage. However, this data is a scalar value representing total load since boot or since inception. PowerBlade could be much more useful if it could serve as a fine-grained interval meter, providing energy usage data broken down by periodic intervals—typically 1, 15, or 60 minutes in duration—that are synchronized in time with other meters and "wall" time as this allows better visibility into energy use over time.

To support interval metering, PowerBlade needs a reliable method of obtaining and keeping the time, likely a combination of a wireless time synchronization protocol and a real-time clock. The primary difficulty in adding a real-time clock (RTC) is limited long-term energy availability in this form factor. To that end, we have identified supercapacitors capable of storing sufficient energy to operate an RTC for extended periods [12]. We intend to explore the viability of interval metering in this form factor in future work.

7. CONCLUSIONS

The state-of-the-art in plug-load metering fails to provide consumers and corporations the detailed knowledge they need to understand and adjust their energy consumption patterns at a size, cost, power, and usability point that permits widespread adoption. While plug loads represent one of the faster growing segments of electrical loads, existing systems for measuring them remain too expensive, draw too much idle power, lack a wireless interface, and are often too large or too cumbersome to easily deploy.

To address the gap between emerging needs and existing solutions, we present PowerBlade, a new power/energy meter design that enables a new paradigm in metering by making the sensor so small and unobtrusive that it can be permanently attached to a plug rather than an outlet. PowerBlade accurately meters the power of a load in real-time and wirelessly transmits that data to nearby smartphones or gateways using a Bluetooth Low Energy radio. With a thickness of a mere $^1/_{16}$", PowerBlade is the first power meter that is truly plug-through. Realizing this diminutive form factor, however, requires revisiting all of the key design choices for a power meter.

In this paper, we introduce several new methods—voltage sensing, current sensing, and power supply miniaturization, among others—to realize a new metering design point. This design offers accuracy within 1.13% of ground truth on a resistive load and 6.5% on a selection of non-unity power factor household devices. Furthermore, we show that the system's volume, cost, wireless capability, and safety combine to make a usable and deployable system. With this new design in hand, researchers, ratepayers, and regulators will be able to inexpensively gain new insights into electricity usage patterns, hopefully yielding smarter and more energy-efficient choices.

8. ACKNOWLEDGMENTS

We thank our shepherd, Jie Liu, and the anonymous reviewers for their helpful feedback. This work was supported in part by the TerraSwarm Research Center, one of six centers supported by the STARnet phase of the Focus Center Research Program (FCRP) a Semiconductor Research Corporation program sponsored by MARCO and DARPA. This material is based upon work supported by the National Science Foundation under grant CNS-1350967, by the NSF/Intel Partnership on Cyber-Physical System (CPS) Security and Privacy under Award proposal title "Synergy: End-to-End Security for the Internet of Things, NSF proposal No. 1505684.", and by the Graduate Research Fellowship Program under grant number DGE-1256260. This work partially supported by generous gifts from Intel and Texas Instruments.

9. REFERENCES

[1] ADE7753 energy metering IC. http://www.analog.com/en/products/analog-to-digital-converters/integrated-special-purpose-converters/energy-metering-ics/ade7753.html.

[2] APS 3B series datasheet. http://www.adaptivepower.com/Resources/Documents/APS_3B%20Series_Datasheet-1014.pdf.

[3] Belkin conserve insight energy use monitor. https://www.belkin.com/conserve/insight/.

[4] Coilcraft flyback transformers Y8844-AL. http://www.coilcraft.com/pdfs/y8844.pdf.

[5] Electronic product design Inc. PLM-1. http://www.epd.com/power_meters.html#PLM-1.

[6] Kill-a-watt electricity use monitor. http://www.p3international.com/products/p4400.html.

[7] LEM TT 100-SD current transformer. http://www.lem.com/docs/products/tt100sd_e.pdf.

[8] Linear Technology LTC5800 wireless mote-on-chip. http://www.linear.com/product/LTC5800-WHM.

[9] LNK302 off-line switcher IC. http://www.mouser.com/ds/2/328/lnk302_304-306-179954.pdf.

[10] Mill-Max discrete spring loaded contacts. http://www.mill-max.com/assets/pdfs/024.pdf.

[11] Nordic Semiconductor Bluetooth Smart SoC. https://www.nordicsemi.com/eng/Products/Bluetooth-Smart-Bluetooth-low-energy/nRF51822.

[12] Panasonic electric double layer capacitors. http://media.digikey.com/pdf/Data%20Sheets/Panasonic%20Capacitors%20PDFs/EEC-EP0E333,EP0F333.pdf.

[13] SR086 adjustable off-line inductorless switching regulator. http://ww1.microchip.com/downloads/en/DeviceDoc/SR086%20D080613.pdf.

[14] SR10 capacitor-coupled, switched shunt, (CCSS) regulator. http://ww1.microchip.com/downloads/en/DeviceDoc/SR10%20B080613.pdf.

[15] Texas Instruments CC2420 RF transceiver. http://www.ti.com/product/cc2420.

[16] Texas Instruments TPS62122 step-down converter. http://www.ti.com/product/tps62122.

[17] Watts Up? Pro plug load meter. https://www.wattsupmeters.com/secure/products.php?pn=0.

[18] Standard for safety in electric utility meters. Technical Report UL2735, UL, May 2013.

[19] Electric power monthly with data for June 2015. Technical report, U.S. Energy Information Administration, aug 2015.

[20] B. Campbell and P. Dutta. Gemini: A non-invasive, energy-harvesting true power meter. In Real-Time Systems Symposium (RTSS), 2014 IEEE, pages 324–333. IEEE, 2014.

[21] R. Condit. Transformerless power supplies: Resistive and capacitive. http://ww1.microchip.com/downloads/en/AppNotes/00954A.pdf, 2004.

[22] B. Coxworth. Flipit lets you charge devices from outlets that are in use. http://www.gizmag.com/flipit-usb-charger/20024/, 2011.

[23] S. DeBruin, B. Campbell, and P. Dutta. Monjolo: An energy-harvesting energy meter architecture. In Proceedings of the 11th ACM Conference on Embedded Networked Sensor Systems, page 18. ACM, 2013.

[24] S. Gupta, M. S. Reynolds, and S. N. Patel. ElectriSense: single-point sensing using EMI for electrical event detection and classification in the home. In Proceedings of the 12th ACM international conference on Ubiquitous computing, pages 139–148. ACM, 2010.

[25] C. J. Hansen. Internetworking with Bluetooth Low Energy. GetMobile, 19(2), Apr 2015.

[26] X. Jiang, S. Dawson-Haggerty, P. Dutta, and D. Culler. Design and implementation of a high-fidelity AC metering network. In Information Processing in Sensor Networks, 2009. IPSN 2009. International Conference on, pages 253–264. IEEE, 2009.

[27] S. Kwatra, J. T. Amann, and H. M. Sachs. Miscellaneous energy loads in buildings. American Council for an Energy-Efficient Economy, 2013.

[28] T. Schmid, D. Culler, and P. Dutta. Meter any wire, anywhere by virtualizing the voltage channel. In Proceedings of the 2nd ACM Workshop on Embedded Sensing Systems for Energy-Efficiency in Building, pages 25–30. ACM, 2010.

[29] S. Tumanski. Induction coil sensors a review. Measurement Science and Technology, 18(3):R31, 2007.

[30] T. Wu and M. Srivastava. Low-cost appliance state sensing for energy disaggregation. In Proceedings of the Fourth ACM Workshop on Embedded Sensing Systems for Energy-Efficiency in Buildings, pages 53–55. ACM, 2012.

[31] L. Yerva, B. Campbell, A. Bansal, T. Schmid, and P. Dutta. Grafting energy-harvesting leaves onto the sensornet tree. In Proceedings of the 11th International Conference on Information Processing in Sensor Networks, IPSN '12, pages 197–208. ACM, 2012.

PowerForecaster: Predicting Smartphone Power Impact of Continuous Sensing Applications at Pre-installation Time

Chulhong Min[1], Youngki Lee[2], Chungkuk Yoo[1], Seungwoo Kang[3], Sangwon Choi[4], Pillsoon Park[5], Inseok Hwang[6], Younghyun Ju[7], Seungpyo Choi[1], Junehwa Song[1]

[1]School of Computing, KAIST, [2]School of Information Systems, Singapore Management University, [3]Computer Science and Engineering, KOREATECH, [4]Information and Electronics Research Institute, KAIST, [5]Division of Web Science Technology, KAIST, [6]IBM Research – Austin, [7]Naver Labs

[1,5]{chulhong, ckyoo, spchoi, pillsoon.park, junesong}@nclab.kaist.ac.kr, [2]youngkilee@smu.edu.sg, [3]swkang@koreatech.ac.kr, [4]sangwonc@kaist.ac.kr, [6]ihwang@us.ibm.com, [7]younghyun.ju@navercorp.com

ABSTRACT

Today's smartphone application (hereinafter 'app') markets miss a key piece of information, power consumption of apps. This causes a severe problem for continuous sensing apps as they consume significant power without users' awareness. Users have no choice but to repeatedly install one app after another and experience their power use. To break such an exhaustive cycle, we propose PowerForecaster, a system that provides users with power use of sensing apps at pre-installation time. Such advanced power estimation is extremely challenging since the power cost of a sensing app largely varies with users' physical activities and phone use patterns. We observe that the time for active sensing and processing of an app can vary up to three times with 27 people's sensor traces collected over three weeks. PowerForecaster adopts a novel power emulator that emulates the power use of a sensing app while reproducing users' physical activities and phone use patterns, achieving accurate, personalized power estimation. Our experiments with three commercial apps and two research prototypes show that PowerForecaster achieves 93.4% accuracy under 20 use cases. Also, we optimize the system to accelerate emulation speed and reduce overheads, and show the effectiveness of such optimization techniques.

Categories and Subject Descriptors

C.3 [**Special-Purpose and Application-based Systems**]: Real-time and embedded systems

Keywords

Power impact; Sensing applications; Pre-installation; Smartphone

1. INTRODUCTION

Today's smartphone app markets help users select desirable apps, providing diverse information such as features, screenshots, and user comments; however, they are missing a key piece of information: *power consumption* by an app. Users can only find out whether an app is power hungry after they install and use it. They count on such experiential perception to decide whether they keep the app or how long they use it. However, continuous

SenSys '15, November 1-4, 2015, Seoul, South Korea

DOI: http://dx.doi.org/10.1145/2809695.2809728

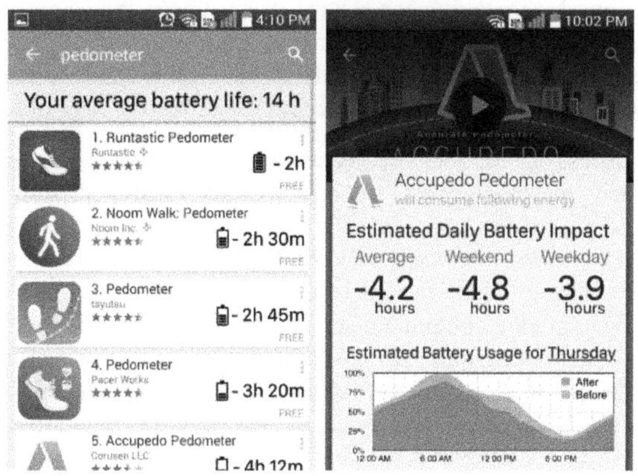

Figure 1. Power impact at pre-installation time

sensing apps [25][28] make such experiential power control no longer effective. They continuously drain battery in the background without a user's explicit awareness. For example, a pedometer app, Accupedo [1], consumes up to 200 mW of additional power, causing an early shutdown of a user's phone.

What if an app market provided the estimated power use of a sensing app? Given such information, users could make better informed decisions, even prior to installing the apps. Users are relieved of exhaustive trial and error, can decide judiciously to install a certain app, and may be less embarrassed with rapid battery depletion if they decide to accept the expected battery cost.

It is not straightforward to realize such a function in reality. A trivial way is for an app developer to post the average power of an app for common use cases. However, we noticed that such a reported power number would not be accurate for many individual users. The deviation mainly results from that the power use of a sensing app varies noticeably depending on users' physical activities, phone use, and other environmental factors. The error becomes even larger when the app applies various optimization techniques such as triggering power-hungry GPS with low-power accelerometers (See Section 2.2).

In this paper, we propose *PowerForecaster*, a system to provide an *instant*, *personalized* power estimation of a sensing app *at pre-installation time*. Figure 1 shows the two mockup screenshots that users would see in an app market when the system is integrated. PowerForecaster aims at enabling a number of unique user experiences. First, it provides power estimation at *pre-install time*, removing the hassle of installing and using apps one after another until users find power-efficient apps. Second, estimation is highly *personalized* to reflect an individual user's activity and phone use patterns, achieving higher estimation accuracies. Third, the system supports a wide variety of sensing apps without requiring any changes in the apps or additional information from developers.

To realize the unique features above, we take a *trace-driven emulation* approach. The key idea is (1) to pre-collect sensor and device usage traces on a user's real phone, which represent a user's physical activities and phone use patterns, respectively, and (2) to build a *power emulator* that assesses expected power use of a sensing app based on the pre-collected traces. The emulator executes the target sensing app over the sensor traces and tracks changes in the power states of key hardware components. At the end, it maps each power state into a power number and calculates total power consumption by aggregating all the power numbers caused by hardware use. In addition, it tracks the hardware use of other apps by replaying the device usage traces for accurate net power estimation. Note that a sensing app runs continuously and shares hardware with other apps. In this way, the system estimates power impact of the target app, accurately reflecting user behavior.

We address a number of technical challenges to make our approach feasible. Most importantly, we designed our own Android power emulator with significant extension to the original Android emulator to support various sensors, trace replay, and power tracking. The Android emulator [2] does not track power states of hardware components or emulate common sensor devices such as accelerometers. Moreover, it does not feed pre-collected sensor traces to the emulator, thereby precluding the possibility of emulation over users' real traces. Other existing emulators also [17][54] do not support power emulation of sensing apps.

We further optimize PowerForecaster to make its emulation fast and its collection of traces power efficient. First, it is needed to use longer user behavior traces for reliable power estimation, but this makes emulation very time consuming. The emulation by default takes as much time as the length of original traces. Advance emulation is challenging due to enormous combinations of users, sensing apps, and their version updates. PowerForecaster achieves fast emulation by (a) fast-forwarding replays in a way to capture changes in power states only and (b) parallelizing replays on multiple emulator instances. Our evaluation shows that it emulates 18-hour long traces within half of a minute, with a small error (6-7%). Second, it incurs nontrivial power overhead to collect sensor traces on a user's phone. From our empirical experiences, we developed a balanced duty-cycling policy to minimize necessary data collection while keeping power estimation accuracy high. Users do not need to repetitively collect sensor traces for various sensing apps. Instead, they collect traces for a day or two reflecting their behavior once and reuse them.

The contributions of this paper are summarized as follows. First, we show that continuous sensing apps' power use varies significantly depending on user behaviors, which motivates the need for personalized power estimation. Second, we premiere an accurate power estimation system for sensing apps, providing user-specific power estimation at pre-installation time. Third, we present our system optimization for fast estimation and energy-efficient trace collection. Finally, we demonstrate the accuracy and overheads of the system through extensive experiments.

2. MOTIVATION

2.1 Motivating Scenario

Krystal, a businesswoman in her 20s, intends to walk more when she commutes and meets her clients. She searches for a *pedometer* app to organize her walking and is happy to find a long list of apps on Google Play. She carefully selects and installs one with the claim by the developer: "*Consumes less than 5% of battery per day. Tested on a dozen popular phone models.*" However, she gets embarrassed finding her phone unexpectedly powered off in the afternoon. She gets upset, repeating installing and uninstalling one app after another. Positive comments on the battery efficiency were not consistent with her experiences. Even after a week, she could not find a satisfactory app. PowerForecaster addresses such discrepancies *in advance*. Figure 1 depicts what she would see for pedometer apps. For each, it shows the estimated decrement of *her own* phone's daily battery life *if she installed and used the app*. She can find the least battery consuming app suitable for her own daily life patterns without relying on doubtful claims and comments from developers and other users.

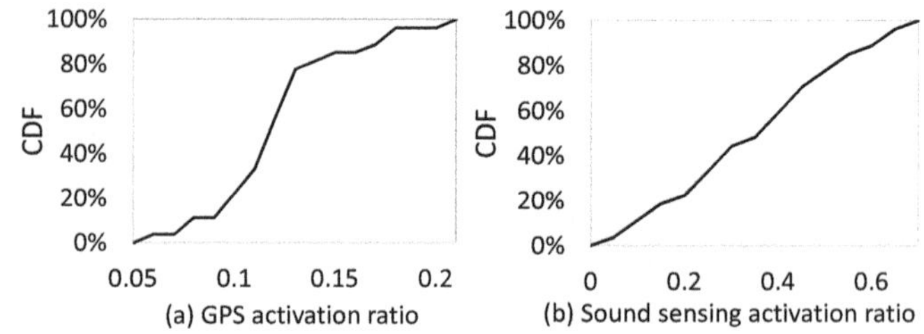

Figure 2. CDF of activation time ratio

2.2 Unveiling the Cause: User Behaviors

What causes such discrepancies between Krystal's experience and the developer's estimates or other users' experiences? It is mainly from diversity in individual user behavior, especially their physical activities and phone use. Users' different activities trigger different branches of logic in the same sensing app. For example, many apps adopt *conditional* sensing pipelines for power optimization, using low and high power sensors selectively [23][30][32]. Actual power use largely depends on how often and long the user's activities trigger the conditions. Different phone use patterns also affect *net power increase of a sensing app* as it *shares* hardware resources with other apps while running in the background [24]. For example, the app obtains already-triggered *wakelocks* at almost zero cost, a major power consumer otherwise.

We quantify the impact of user behavior on battery use with data traces from 27 people over two example sensing apps.

Data traces. We collected sensor and phone usage traces from 27 participants for three weeks (14 undergraduates, 7 company employees in their 20s-50s, 5 graduates in their 20s-30s, and 1 housewife in her 50s). We deployed a data-logging app on their phones. Data collection was set to 12 hours a day (from 10AM to 10PM), but actual collection time varied due to battery depletions. We analyzed data collected more than 8 hours a day.

Applications. We consider two sensing apps inspired by previous works: (1) *MyPath,* a location tracker [41] and (2) *ChatMon,* a conversation monitor [32]. MyPath records the GPS trace of a user every 10 sec. It triggers GPS only when the user is moving which is detected from cheaper accelerometer sensing. ChatMon monitors speakers and conversation turns by sound sensing and processing. Sound sensing is triggered only when the user is close to someone else, which is checked by Bluetooth scans every 2 min.

Effect of physical activities. We first computed the ratio of GPS activation time of MyPath to total execution time. Figure 2(a) shows the cumulative distribution of GPS activation time ratio.

The average ratio per user ranges from 5.7% to 20.2% (mean: 12%, SD: 3.2%). Assuming that MyPath runs 12 hours a day, the top user activates GPS 1.5 hours more than the bottom. We similarly show the ratio of sound sensing activation time of ChatMon, which monitors conversations with the top 5 frequently encountered people. Figure 2(b) shows the cumulative distribution of sound sensing activation time. The average ratio varied from 4.8% to 67.1% (mean: 34.9%, SD: 18.2%). The top user would activate 3.5 more hours of sound sensing than the average user, assuming that ChatMon runs 12 hours a day, which would cause a huge difference in users' power use.

Effect of phone uses. We further examined the effect of resource sharing by analyzing the net increase in CPU activation time caused by wakelocks ChatMon obtained. Here, we briefly discuss two different cases that show such sharing effect. First, two users, P6 and P13, showed similar activation time for sound sensing, but different net increase in CPU activation time. For both users, sound sensing was activated for 29% of the total duration. However, P6's CPU was solely activated by ChatMon for 15% of the total duration, while 22% was activated in case of P13. This difference comes from that P6 used his phone for other purposes for longer duration compared to P13, so P6's CPU was activated more already by other apps. Second, for the other case, P8, P15, and P16 showed similar sound sensing activation time, around 40%. However, they exhibited fairly different net increase in CPU activation time: 30%, 40%, and 33%, respectively. This indicates that phone use of individual users would affect net power consumption of a sensing app due to the sharing effect.

3. POWERFORECASTER DESIGN

3.1 Design Goals

Installation-free: PowerForecaster relieves tedious installation trials caused by sensing apps' unknown battery use. To this end, PowerForecaster needs to provide users with estimated battery consumption before they install and use the apps.

Accuracy: Power estimation should be accurate and reflect what users will experience when they actually use the apps. It needs to be tailored to reflect users' different behaviors.

Latency: Estimation needs to be performed in a short time to support on-the-fly requests from users.

Coverage: PowerForecaster aims at providing power estimation without modifying app binaries; any requirement to change the apps would significantly diminish its utility.

Overhead: PowerForecaster should minimize the overhead on users' mobile phones, especially to pre-collect various sensor traces and device usage traces required for power emulation.

3.2 Power Emulation Approach

We devise a *user behavior-aware power emulation* approach. The key idea is to reproduce the real execution environment of a target app and track its power use while replaying it over pre-collected traces of sensor and device usages. It has three advantages: (1) It accounts for major user-dependent variables, physical activities, and phone use patterns, which significantly affect the target app's power consumption. (2) It estimates power use of an app with no knowledge on its internal logic or prior power profiling required. The emulator tracks hardware use of the app by executing its executable with no need of its source code. (3) It considers shared hardware use with existing apps by reproducing their resource use.

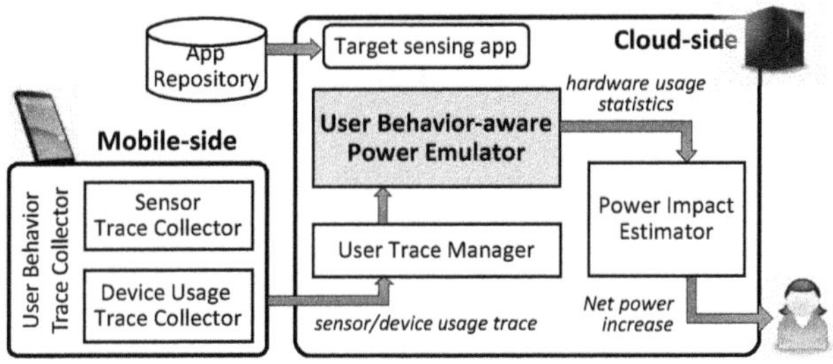

Figure 3. PowerForecaster architecture

There have been other approaches to estimate mobile apps' power use, but it is not trivial to apply them to the accurate estimation of sensing apps. *Development-time estimation,* direct measurement with a power meter or model-based schemes [42][56][57], hardly reflects individual user behavior, which largely affects sensing apps' power use. Another potential approach is *collaborative power estimation*. It shares power impact of sensing apps obtained from users who already used the app. The power numbers from the users with similar behaviors are provided to a potential user; a similar concept is proposed in [40] for energy diagnosis. However, this requires a large user base to find similar users due to plenty combinations of behavioral factors affecting power use of sensing apps. We believe PowerForecaster can complement this approach, as it works based on personal traces without a large user pool.

3.3 System Overview

PowerForecaster takes the executable of a target sensing app as an input and provides a personalized estimation of the target app's net power increase (mW) as an output. Later, the power numbers can be processed in various ways for user-friendly presentation (See Section 8 for examples). Figure 3 shows the architecture of PowerForecaster. It consists of two major components, a mobile-side trace collector and a cloud-side power emulator. Prior to power estimation requests, the mobile-side collector pre-collects user behavior traces (possibly for one weekday and one weekend reflecting user behavior). The traces are uploaded to and managed in the cloud server. Upon a request, the power emulator estimates power impact of a target app with the pre-collected traces.

Mobile-side: The mobile-side component collects user behavior traces in the background. The *sensor trace collector* collects a series of sensor data that captures users' physical activities. The *device usage trace collector* logs hardware component usages by existing apps, which are potentially sharable with a new sensing app. Not to interfere with usual phone use, the traces are uploaded to the cloud server only when the phone is on Wi-Fi and charging. The collected traces are used for various sensing apps in the future.

Cloud-side: Upon a power estimation request, the *user behavior-aware power emulator* executes the target app's executable and monitors its hardware usage. At the same time, it replays the sensor and device usage traces to reproduce the execution environments affecting the power impact of the app. As a result, the emulator obtains detailed hardware usage statistics including which, when, and how long hardware components are used. The *power impact estimator* computes the net power increase due to the app based on the cumulative statistics during the emulation.

3.4 System Scope and Limitations

It is extremely challenging to achieve all of our design goals for generic workloads and users. We clarify the scope and limitations of this study and our current system prototype.

Table 1. Sensor data, system call, and events

Sensor Type	Sensor Data	Related System Call	Related System Event
GPS	*longitude, latitude, altitude, speed, bearing*	gps_start(), gps_stop(), ...	GPS_EVENT_STARTED, GPS_EVENT_STOPPED,
Bluetooth	*name, address, bond state, type, UUIDs, RSSI*	startDiscoveryNative(), stopDiscoveryNative(), ...	ACTION_FOUND, ACTION_DISCOVERY _STARTED/_FINISHED
Wi-Fi	*BSSID, SSID, capabilities, frequency, level*	scan(), wifi_ctrl_recv()	SCAN_RESULTS _AVAILABLE_ACTION
Other sensors (accel. gyro, ...)	*values*	enableSensor(), disableSensor()	

Target apps: Our system focuses on continuous sensing apps that continuously run in the background, such as Google Fit [14], Accupedo [1], and NoomWalk [39]. Specifically, we focus on their autonomous sensing services that perform repetitive sensing tasks controlled by built-in sensing logics and programmatically detectable external events. We do not target conventional apps and sensing apps' UI activities, which are explicitly run and quit by users. The rationale behind this choice is that, for conventional apps, users retain controllability on how much they use the apps and thereby also on the apps' power use to some extent. For sensing apps, continuous sensing is a major drain on power. UI activities consume relatively less power as they are likely run for a short time compared to the whole operation time of sensing apps.

Tracked hardware components: For power estimation, our prototype considers hardware components commonly used by sensing apps: inertial sensors, GPS, Bluetooth and Wi-Fi scans, microphone, and CPU. (See Section 5.3 for details.) We have not yet considered other components such as display, network, or GPU, as those are used less commonly in sensing apps and contribute little to the overall power impact. Section 7 shows that our prototype estimates power use of various sensing apps with average error of 6.6%, considering aforementioned components. We understand that there are a few examples [53] using other components. Our emulation can further expand to consider such components by leveraging various power models proposed in [36][42]. For example, network power cost can be considered by tracking relevant factors such as packet transmission time and signal strength and by reproducing them in the emulator [36].

Selection of user traces: For accurate power estimation, it is important to collect user behavior traces that well reflect a user's common daily behavior. Of course, there could be daily variations of user behaviors, but literature has showed that user behaviors have patterns [8][13][34]. Our ultimate goal is to accurately predict the future power impact of a target app by considering routines and patterns of user behaviors. In this study, we focus on developing a power emulation system that precisely estimates net power increase of an app given proper behavioral traces. We leave capturing a user's routine as a future work.

Scalability to heterogeneous phones: It is well known that it is needed to build power models specific to individual phone models for accurate tracking of apps' power use. This raises a scalability issue, as a variety of phone models exist in today's market. Our system will face the same problem for its wider deployment as the core technique is based on pre-built power models. Note that our prototype incorporates power models for Nexus S and Nexus 5.

To be optimistic, a few phone models take considerable market share currently. Three popular iPhone models and top-10 Android

Table 2. Representative resource request APIs

Resource type	Request APIs	Parameters
CPU	*acquire*() / *release*() on WakeLock	timeout, ref. count
	setRepeating() / *cancel*() on AlarmManager	alarm type, trigger time, trigger interval
GPS	*requestLocationUpdates*() / *removeLocationUpdates*() on LocationManager	provider, minDelay, minDistance, criteria
Bluetooth	*startDiscovery*() / *stopDiscovery*() on BluetoothAdapter	
Other sensors (Accel., Gyro, ...)	*registerListener*() / *unregisterListener*() on SensorManager	sensor type, sampling rate

ones take 70%[1] and 33%[2] of iPhone and Android market share, respectively. Power modeling for those popular models will be feasible (even if manual measurements need to be involved). This possibly makes wide deployment of PowerForecaster feasible in practice, dealing with heterogeneous phones. For less-common models, we can consider other approaches. For example, most hardware chipset manufactures open up power profiles per different hardware states, and the profiles can be incorporated into PowerForecaster. In case such information is not available or the power consumption is not stable across the same phone models [6][57], we can leverage prior works to automatically self-construct power models for unknown phones [6][55]; these works achieve an accuracy of 90%-95%. Once power models are available, they can be easily incorporated into our system as we modularize it in a way to include new power models.

4. USER BEHAVIOR DATA COLLECTION

In this section, we explain what data are collected by the trace collector in detail. Section 5 describes how the collected data are used for power emulation.

Sensor trace: The *sensor trace collector* collects sensor data that reflect physical user behaviors. More specifically, it records three types of information. First, it records sensor data streams with timestamps from frequently used target sensors. Second, it records sensor-related system events notified from Android, e.g., *gps_event_started*. Such events are needed to ensure correct replays of sensing apps since many of them use these events as triggers to internal logic. Last, it hooks and logs the system calls and callbacks between the Android framework/kernel and the app. These are required to reproduce power states in sensor devices, as in users' real situations. For example, the time to activate GPS sensing largely depends on whether a user is outdoors or not. Recording GPS values alone is not sufficient to emulate such cold start, which subsequently affects the accuracy of power emulation. Table 1 shows sensor data, events, and system calls that we collect.

Device usage trace: Another important factor for accurate power emulation is to consider shared use of resources, as shown in Section 2.2. A naïve method is to *emulate other apps concurrently with a target sensing app* and accurately trace shared use of various hardware components. However, it requires heavy computation to emulate multiple apps concurrently. It is also challenging to log and replay realistic user inputs for foreground interactive apps. Thus, we take an approach to *record only the device usages of existing apps and estimate sharing effects* on the

[1] http://info.localytics.com/blog/more-iphone-6%E2%80%99s-being-sold-but-iphone-6-shows-stronger-user-engagement

[2] http://info.localytics.com/blog/android-device-samsung-maintains-dominance

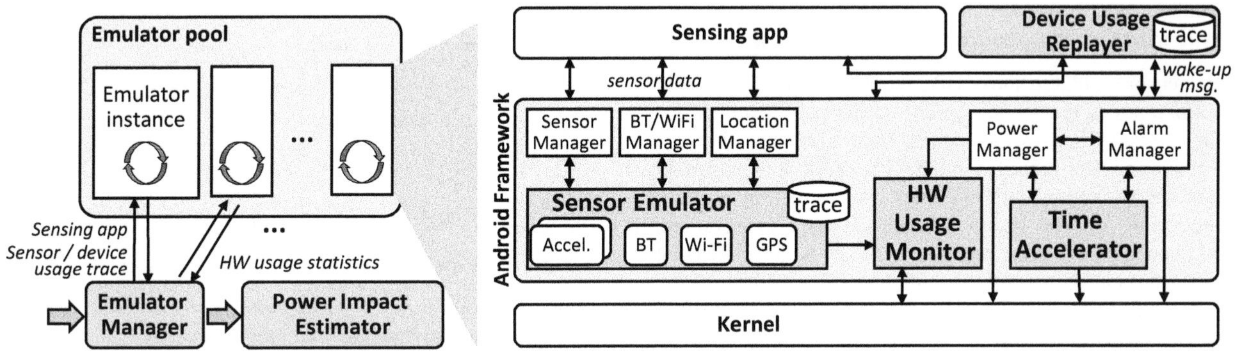

Figure 4. Architecture of user behavior-aware power emulator

emulation process. This enables to accurately account shared use of hardware with other apps without directly executing them.

The *device usage trace collector* records the requests from the existing apps to various hardware components, e.g., wakelocks for CPU, with timestamps. By replaying such requests while emulating the sensing app, it is possible to identify the shared accesses to various hardware components between the target sensing app and other apps. This can be reflected upon accounting the power impact of the target sensing app, resulting in more accurate estimation. Android exposes a narrow set of APIs that allows apps to request access to hardware such as sensors and CPUs. The collector logs a series of the API calls and parameters. Table 2 shows what our prototype collects in more detail.

5. USER BEHAVIOR-AWARE POWER EMULATION

Simply using existing mobile emulators [2][17][54], or their naïve extensions is not a feasible solution to emulate power use of sensing apps. Since their main goal is for testing and debugging of mobile apps, they do not support power monitoring during emulation. Also, they cannot reproduce a user's behavioral environments, which are essential for accurate power estimation. While there are simple sensor simulation tools, their functionality is highly limited for our purpose, as we will discuss in 5.1.

To address the issues, we develop a novel *user behavior-aware power emulator* by significantly extending the existing Android emulator. Figure 4 shows its architecture. Overall operation flow consists of the following three stages.

Pre-emulation stage: Upon a request, the *emulator manager* prepares the necessary inputs for emulation. It first obtains sensor and device usage traces from the *trace manager* as well as the executable of the target sensing app. It then initiates a set of power emulator instances in parallel to reduce the estimation latency (Section 6.1). Each instance installs the target app and receives a part of user traces from the emulator manager. Before executing the app, it replays pre-generated user interaction such as clicking a start button to bootstrap the app if necessary. It also adjusts its system clock to synchronize the time with the traces.

Power-emulation stage: After the preparation, the power emulator instance executes the target sensing app. While the app is running, the *sensor emulator* mimics the operation of sensors to fulfill the app's requests on sensor use by using the pre-collected sensor traces (Section 5.1). To consider the sharing effect, the *device usage replayer* reproduces the existing app's device use based on the device usage trace (Section 5.2). This allows the target app to execute as if it were running along with other apps. During the execution, the *hardware usage monitor* tracks system calls made to use hardware components such as sensors and CPU. At the end, it generates hardware usage statistics, a series of executed system calls along with corresponding timestamps.

Post-emulation stage: With the collected hardware usage statistics, the *power impact estimator* computes the net increase in power consumption by the target app (Section 5.3). For power estimation, we adopt a system call-based method using power profiles obtained by offline profiling [42]. We consider the following hardware components mainly used by sensing apps: *CPU, GPS, inertial sensors, microphone, Bluetooth/Wi-Fi scans.*

5.1 Sensor Emulation

The sensor emulator reproduces a user's physical behavior conditions by feeding the user's real sensor traces to the target app. For realistic emulation, it should feed sensor data at accurate timing and rate as the app demands. It should also emulate the hardware states of the corresponding sensor devices and account for power estimation afterwards.

Existing sensor data replay tools [12][51] do not meet our requirements. SensorSimulator [51] provides a custom library that relays pre-collected sensor data from a host PC to a mobile emulator. However, it requires app-side modification to use the library. ReRan [12] records and replays input events such as touch events and sensor data during the execution of an app for testing and debugging. While it does not require any modification of the app logic, the target app has to be executed during sensor data collection, which violates our pre-installation requirement. Also, both of them do not emulate the power state of sensor devices.

We develop a sensor emulator that mimics real sensor devices' operation and states. First, it provides apps with pre-collected sensor data while fulfilling their specific requests. Second, it replays sensor-related system events for correct app operations. Third, it tracks the changes in expected power states based on the sensor-related system call and callback logs to and from the kernel. The sensor emulator is located between the Android framework and the kernel, which is a middle layer that receives sensor data requests from multiple apps and interacts with the kernel. It hooks the sensor-related system calls from the framework to the kernel and provides sensor data using the collected trace.

Accelerometer, gyroscope, etc: The sensor emulator hooks all sensor activation and deactivation requests from the Android *SensorManager* to the kernel. To handle an activation request, it searches for sensor data corresponding to the request time from the collected trace and pushes them into the sensing app. Also, the sensor emulator performs a sampling of data in the sensor trace if necessary to meet the rate requirement of the sensing app.

GPS: The sensor emulator hooks GPS requests from the Android *LocationManager* to the kernel. Upon a request, it searches for GPS data corresponding to the request time and sends the data after the activation time recorded in the GPS traces. It is important to consider the activation time in a user's real situation, since it varies depending on the user environment (e.g., indoors and outdoors) even with the same request. It affects both the sensing app's execution and the power consumption of the GPS device. At times, there could be no GPS data exactly matching the request time since the GPS request interval of the app can be different from that used for the trace collection. The sensor emulator interpolates GPS data from two adjacent logs and uses them.

Bluetooth and Wi-Fi scan: The sensor emulator intercepts scan requests from the Android *BluetoothAdaptor* and *WifiManager*. Upon the request, it retrieves scan logs with a timestamp closest to the request time from the collected trace and forwards them to the apps. To ensure the apps' proper operation, it broadcasts relevant events, e.g., *bluetooth-discovery-finished*, *scan-results-available-action*, which are recorded in the trace along with scan results.

5.2 Device Usage Replay

The device usage replayer reproduces a user's phone use behavior to reflect the power-sharing effect in the emulation. The replayer runs in the background as an Android service simultaneously with the target sensing app. It uses the pre-collected device usage trace containing a list of time-stamped elements, (*timestamp*, *API function*, *parameter values*) as shown in Table 2. Based on the timestamp, the replayer calls the API with the parameter values.

Since API calls to access hardware components usually operate as a pair, e.g., *acquire()/release()*, both API calls should be contained in the trace for the accurate power estimation. However, one API call of the pair could be omitted at times because of duty-cycled data collection (Section 6.2) or the segmentation of device usage traces for parallel execution (Section 6.1). Before replaying the trace, the trace manager fills in the missing calls. For example, if there is only one *release()* in the given trace, it adds *acquire()* and set its timestamp to the beginning of the trace.

5.3 Estimation of Power Impact

During the emulation, the *hardware usage monitor* collects the hardware usage statistics, i.e., a collection of system calls made by the framework, and their timestamps. Sensor-related system calls are captured in the sensor emulator (See Table 1). To account for power use of the CPU, the hardware usage monitor intercepts wakelock requests, *acquire_wake_lock()* and *release_wake_lock()*, from the Android *PowerManager* to the kernel. Upon a request to acquire a wakelock, it also obtains CPU utilization of the target sensing app from */proc/stat* until a release request. We properly scale the CPU utilization to compensate for the different CPU performances between the server and the smartphone as in [36].

After the emulation, the *power impact estimator* computes the net power increase by the target app, $netP_{app}$ based on the hardware usage statistics. We compute $netP_{app}$ as follows:

$$netP_{app} = P^{D}_{with\_app} - P^{D}_{without\_app},$$

where D is the set of hardware components *app* uses and $P^{D}_{with\_app}$ and $P^{D}_{without\_app}$ are the power consumption of D with and without *app*, respectively. As noted earlier, our component set currently

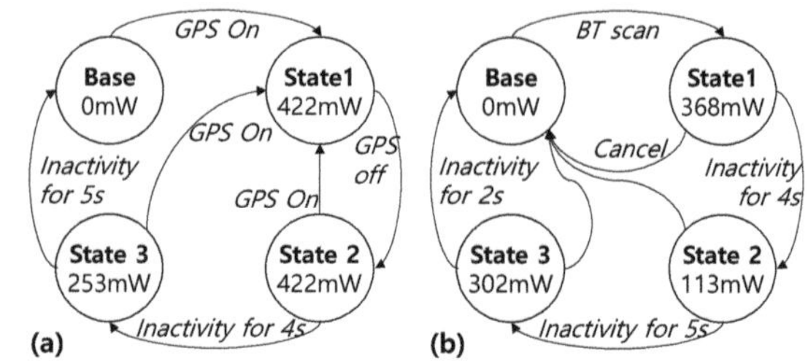

Figure 5. Power model of (a) GPS, (b) Bluetooth on Nexus S

supports *CPU, GPS, Bluetooth/Wi-Fi scans, microphone, accelerometer, gyroscope, and magnetometer.*

The power consumed by the aforementioned components is estimated with a system call-based power estimation [42]. We built a finite state machine (FSM)-based power model for each component based on associated system calls as in Figure 5. Then, we constructed an FSM for the entire device considering the sharing effect of system calls. The FSM-based power model facilitates to consider tail power state of hardware components and the sharing effect across system calls [42]. To make the power models, we profile the power states of the components for each system call using a power meter [38]. $P^{D}_{with\_app}$ is computed based on FSM models and hardware usage statistics made during the emulation. $P^{D}_{without\_app}$ is done similarly based on the hardware usage statistics after replaying the device usage trace only.

6. SYSTEM OPTIMIZATION

6.1 Acceleration of Emulation

A key challenge of emulation-based power estimation is a long execution time. Unlike typical apps, sensing apps operate closely tied to real-time clocks. They are governed by sampling rates, sensing intervals, and time window for data processing. Naïve emulation would take the same duration of sensor traces to replay. Powerful hardware may not necessarily reduce the emulation time for our workloads, e.g., reading accelerometer at 100Hz for 5 sec.

To address the challenge, we develop 3 acceleration mechanisms: *parallel execution*, *idle time skipping*, and *progressive estimation*. Figure 6 shows them for a commercial pedometer app, Accupedo [1]. We leverage unique characteristics of continuous sensing apps. First, they usually operate by repeating cycles. While the operations could be stateful within a cycle, they might be stateless in between. This implies the potential of parallel emulation. Second, sensing apps wakes up the device as little as possible to save energy; active periods are much shorter than idle periods. Accupedo wakes up every 10 sec to detect the user's movement with 20-ms accelerometer data and sleeps again if no movement. We can safely skip such long idle time to accelerate the emulation.

Parallel execution: Given an original long trace, the *emulator manager* splits it into shorter segments, e.g., 2-min-long each, and assigns a segment to each emulator instance. Each executes a target app independently, replaying sensor and device usage traces in an assigned segment. Upon completion, the hardware usage statistics from each instance are aggregated for total power estimation. A practical issue in parallel execution is to determine a proper length of a segment. It should be short enough to exploit parallelism, but long enough to include the stateful behavior in a cycle. Ideally, proper segment size depends on the apps' internal logic. Consider ChatMon detecting an encounter via BT scan every 2 min. The ideal segment size may be 2 min. Automatically identifying such sizes for each app is not trivial unless we know

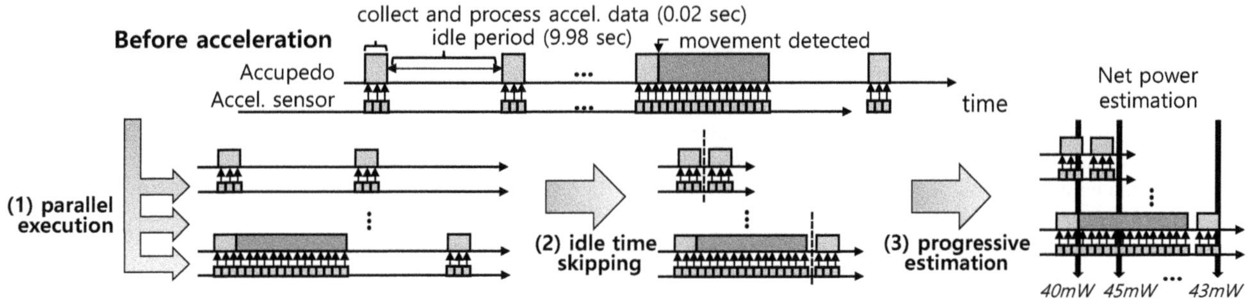

Figure 6. Acceleration mechanisms for sensing app emulation (with the Accupedo pedometer example)

the internal logic of the app in advance. In this paper, we use the same segment size for every app. We found that 2-min-long segments showed reasonable accuracy for all our example apps. An automatic solution might be possible, e.g., by analyzing repeated resource use patterns of a sensing app [33].

Idle time skipping: The *time accelerator* shortens emulation by skipping idle times of the device during the emulation. We regard idle time as a period for which all CPU wakelock requests are released. The time accelerator identifies the start and end of the idle time from the Android *PowerManager*, which manages all wakelocks. Upon detecting all wakelocks have been released (the start time), the time accelerator scans the alarm schedule in the Android *AlarmManager* until the very next alarm (the end time). It skips the idle time by setting the system clock to the end time.

Progressive estimation: Despite the significant reduction of emulation time by the techniques above, the final emulation time is bounded by the segment with the longest execution time. The execution time of a segment varies as idle time skipping is opportunistic upon user behavior. For more responsive service, we develop a progressive estimation. During the emulation, it estimates net power increase with interim results of emulation and progressively updates it. This technique does not reduce the execution time but reduces the first response time to the end user.

6.2 Energy-efficient Trace Collection

The trace collector collects sensor and device usage traces for power estimation of future sensing apps. The trace collection runs only for 1-2 days to reflect user behavior. Still, one might be concerned about the collector's power use, as it is desirable to collect raw sensor data at the highest rate for future generic use.

We applied a widely used duty-cycling technique to reduce power cost of the trace collector. The question is how far can we increase the cycle with minimal decrease of accuracy?. Figure 7 shows the estimation errors with respect to those without duty cycling and respective power overheads for various duty-cycles. We used two 18-hour-long traces of MyPath obtained from the real deployment experiments in Section 8 and set the active data collection duration to 2 min for a period; during the active collection, the sensor data is recorded based on the configuration of a full sensor set (Table 4). Based on the results, we use a 24-min duty-cycle period, i.e., the ratio of 1/12, where the power cost starts to saturate and the error is still below 10% even with the deviation. Such duty cycling is possible since a user's mobility, location and encounter tend to have temporal locality [8][13][34].

7. EVALUATION

We implemented PowerForecaster; on mobile-side, we developed the sensor trace collector as an Android service. We modified the

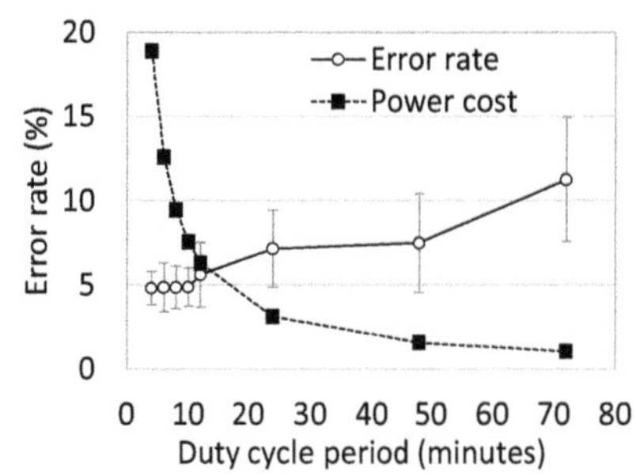

Figure 7. Effect of duty-cycling; bars represent standard deviation

Android system to track device usage and existing apps' hardware usage. On server-side, we developed the power emulator based on the Android emulator. We also made the user trace manager and power impact estimator in Java. PowerForecaster was evaluated for its accuracy, speed, and overhead for power emulation.

7.1 Evaluation Setup

We evaluated PowerForecaster under realistic settings with various apps and users with different behavioral characteristics.

Phones and servers: We used Nexus S (Android 4.1.2) and Nexus 5 (Android 4.4.4) phones for the experiments; we used Nexus S phones by default. For emulation, we arranged 12 desktop servers (with i7-2600k CPU and 16 GB RAM), where each server was configured to run one or more emulator instances in parallel. For a single power estimation request, the average CPU use was 5-10% per each emulator instance. We discuss the server-side resource use in more details in Section 7.3. We did not apply optimization techniques by default.

Sensing apps: We mainly used three sensing apps including a commercial pedometer app, *Accupedo* [1], and the two research apps we developed, *MyPath* and *ChatMon* described in Section 2. Section 7.2.2 describes the applicability of our system to two more commercial apps, *NoomWalk* [39] and *Pedometer2.0* [45]. The hardware components that the three commercial pedometer apps use in common are accelerometers and CPU. Note that, while diverse sensing apps have been proposed in a research domain, only a few types are commercialized, e.g., pedometers. To cover more diverse hardware usage, we selected MyPath and ChatMon. The former uses accelerometers, GPS, and CPU and the latter uses Bluetooth, a microphone, and CPU.

Comparison: For ground truth of the net power increase (mW) of a target sensing app, we used Monsoon power monitors [38]. It is obtained as the difference in power consumptions between when running a target sensing app with existing apps, and when running existing apps only. We made three alternatives that developers can potentially use to provide power impact of sensing apps:

Global-single measures the power using a power monitor while running the target app only, under a specific user behavior scenario, and provides it as an estimation result.
Global-average measures the power uses of the target app under multiple user behavior scenarios. It takes an average value to provide a representative estimation. Note that this does not consider the shared power use with other apps.
Global-single-shared measures the power while running both the target app and apps used in a specific user behavior scenario. Under this scenario, it provides an estimation taking into consideration the shared power use with other apps. Note that this baseline is equivalent to the ground truth of the chosen scenario.

User behavior scenario: For accuracy evaluation, we performed scenario-based experiments. We craft multiple one-hour scenarios with four parameters: mobility, encounter, indoor/outdoor status, and phone usage. We determine the parameter values and their combinations based on real user data described in Section 2. Table 3 summarizes the five scenarios used for our experiments. Figure 8 depicts detailed sequences of user activities and phone usages for *Scenario 4*. Other scenarios are made similarly.

Measurement and trace collection setup: For fair comparison, we need to ensure that the same user behaviors are applied while evaluating all the alternative techniques including the ground truth. We design a setup to easily conduct experiments over various alternatives. Figure 9 shows our setting with four phones (Phone A, B, C, and D) and three power monitors. First, Phone A and B are used for ground truth measurements; Phone A measures power consumption while running a target sensing app with existing apps. Phone B measures power while running existing apps only. The ground truth is calculated by subtracting power measurement of Phone A from that of B. For the PowerForecaster estimation, we configured Phone C to run existing apps and to collect sensor and device usage traces. Phone D measures power while running the target app only. *Global-single(ScenarioID)* and *Global-single-shared(ScenarioID)* use the power measured for a specific scenario while *Global-average* uses the average power measured across the five scenarios. An experimenter drove the cart with the phones and power monitors following each scenario. We used a script to run the same apps (web browser, video player, email client, and map) at the same timings.

7.2 Performance Analysis of PowerForecaster

7.2.1 Accuracy of Net Power Estimation

Figure 11 shows the power measurement with 3 sensing apps in 5 scenarios. Compared to the ground-truth, PowerForecaster accurately estimates net power increases by sensing apps. Average error rate is 6.6%: 5.3% for Accupedo, 6.8% for MyPath, and 7.7% for ChatMon, indicating that PowerForecaster closely traces the power use of the target sensing app. Even for the same app, its power consumptions vary across scenarios due to different user activities and phone usages. For ChatMon, the ground truth of the net power increase ranges from 29 mW to 227 mW.

The three alternatives show much lower accuracy. The average error rate of Global-average is 99% across all scenarios and apps. Global-single(Scenario4) shows an average error rate of 116%, indicating that it misestimates the app's power consumption by more than double compared to the ground truth. The average error rates for Global-single(Scenario2) and Global-single(Scenario3) are 59% and 128%, respectively. This indicates that the approach itself is likely to be error-prone regardless of the scenario since it

Table 3. Summary for five user behavior scenarios

ID	User	Activity	User behavior parameter			
			Moving	Indoor	Encounter	App usage
1	Graduate student (M, 30s)	Shopping alone	50 min	60 min	0 min	5 min
2	Undergraduate student (M, 20s)	Moving and class	10 min	45 min	15 min	20 min
3	Office worker (F, 30s)	Moving and lunch	20 min	40 min	60 min	15 min
4	Office worker (M, 20s)	Going out	30 min	30 min	40 min	30 min
5	Housewife (F, 50s)	Going out	30 min	30 min	40 min	1 min

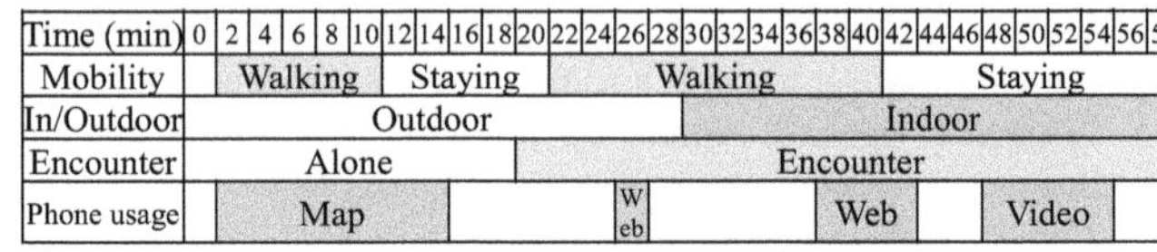

Figure 8. User behavior scenario 4

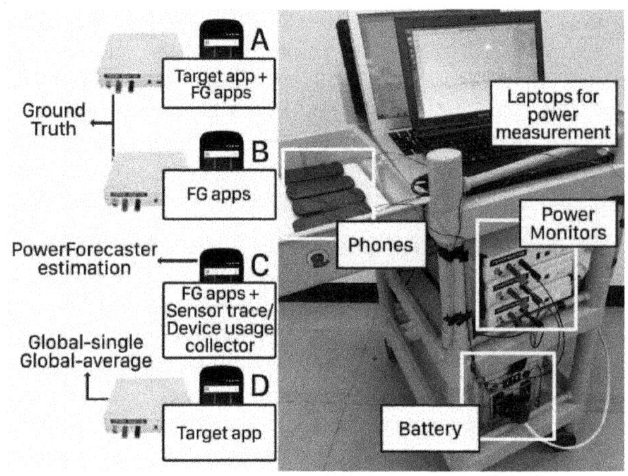

Figure 9. Experimental setup

estimates the power use of a target app based on the power measurement for a single specific scenario. Interestingly, even for Scenario 4, Global-single(Scenario4) shows high error rates (86% for Accupedo). This is because Global-single does not reflect the effect of resource sharing with existing app usage. Global-single-shared(Scenario4) which considers this sharing effect, produces an average error rate of 60%. The average error rates for Global-single-shared(Scenario2) and Global-single-shared(Scenario3) are 45% and 83%, respectively. Although the error is 0% for whichever scenario was chosen for this baseline, the average error depends on the differences in behavior modeled in other scenarios.

We analyze the characteristics for each scenario. For Accupedo, Scenario 1 shows the largest net power increase. Its movement duration (50 min) is the longest, consuming much power to process accelerometer data. However, little sharing effect due to short app usage (5 min) makes the largest impact. Scenario 2 is the opposite. Scenarios 4 and 5 reveal the resource sharing effect. They have the same movement behavior but different app usage time, 30 min and 1 min respectively. As a result, scenario 5 shows twice net power increase. MyPath shows a similar trend as it has accelerometer-based triggering. ChatMon exhibits different trends due to different sensing logic and user behavior affecting sensing operation. In scenario 1, there is no BT encounter and thus no audio processing. Accordingly, it shows the smallest net power increase. Scenario 3 has the longest time duration of encounter,

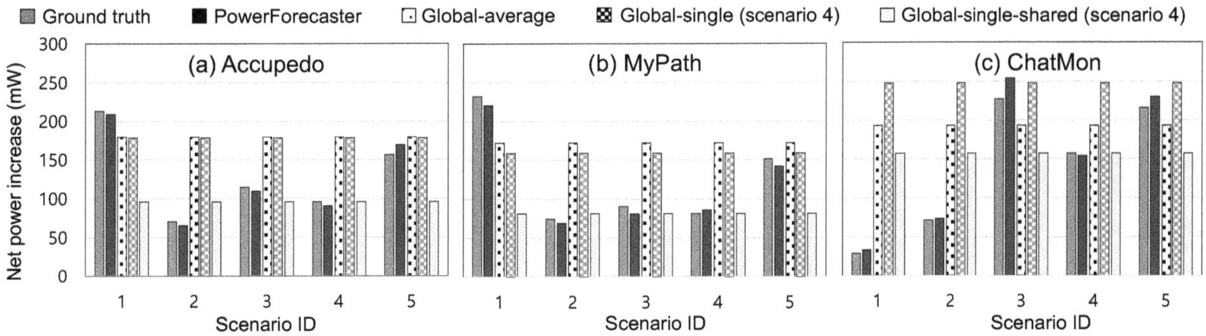

Figure 10. Accuracy of net power estimation by PowerForecaster

60 min., thereby performing sound processing for the entire time. Thus, it shows the largest net power increase. Although it has a greater encounter time of 20 min compared to Scenario 5, its net increase is similar to that of Scenario 5 due to resource sharing.

7.2.2 Testing with More Apps and Phones

We show the applicability of PowerForecaster to two more commercial pedometer apps, *NoomWalk* and *Pedometer2.0,* and a more device, Nexus 5. Figure 10(a) shows the results for Scenario 4. Our system accurately estimates the net power increase; the ground truth for NoomWalk and Pedometer2.0 is 9 mW and 103 mW while the estimations are 11 mW and 105 mW, respectively.

Next, we investigate the accuracy of PowerForecaster on Nexus 5 with Android 4.4.4. We built the power model for Nexus 5 and developed the PowerForecaster system based on Android 4.4.4. We conducted experiments with the three sensing apps: Accupedo, MyPath, and ChatMon with Scenario 4, Scenario 1, and Scenario 2, respectively. Figure 10(b) shows that PowerForecaster provides an accurate power estimation even with another phone with a different Android version. Average error rates of PowerForecaster and Global-single are 6% and 21%, respectively.

7.2.3 Effect of Emulation Acceleration

We evaluate the emulation acceleration in terms of time-accuracy tradeoff. For parallelism, we use 10, 5, 2, and 1 min segment sizes.

Parallel execution with idle time skipping: Figure 12 shows that the average error rate is still low when applying acceleration; in the figure, w/o skip means that only parallel execution is applied whereas w/ skip means that parallel execution and idle time skipping are all applied. Average error rates are 10.4% and 11.2%, respectively. While they are slightly higher than the those without acceleration, they are still reasonable. As expected, the segment size affects estimation accuracy. Accupedo shows less than or about 10% error rate overall, but the other two apps exhibit relatively large error rates for the 1-min segment. This is due to the characteristics of sensing logic of the apps. We briefly discuss the ChatMon case. For ChatMon, there are two conflicting factors affecting power estimation by parallel execution: the number of BT scans and the delay of sound sensing and processing. With 2-min intervals, ChatMon performs 30 BT scans for 1 hour. In parallel execution, however, the number can vary depending on the segment size. ChatMon is executed independently on each emulator and performs a BT scan when it starts. While the number of scans with 10- and 2-min segment is 30, it increases to 36 and 60 for 5- and 1-min segment, respectively, increasing the estimated power. At the same time, duration for sound processing can decrease in some segments, decreasing in estimated power. Sound processing is triggered only after ChatMon detects a BT

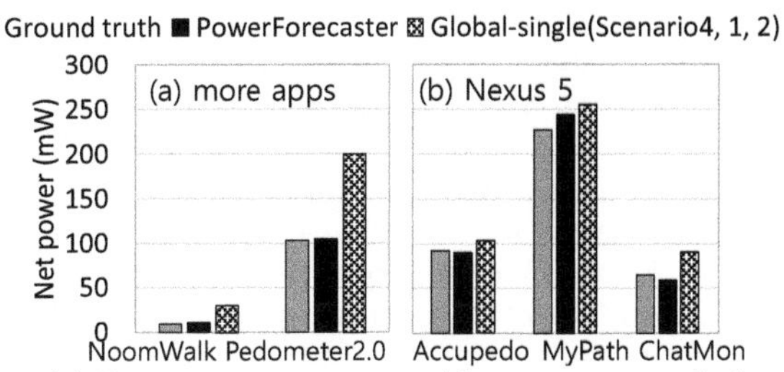

Figure 11. Power measurements with more apps and phones

encounter. Depending on the scenario, the two factors differently contribute to the increase or decrease of estimated power.

Figure 13 shows the CDF of elapsed time to complete emulation of the three sensing apps for all 5 scenarios when applying 2-min segments. For many segments, emulation is finished for less than 20 sec. While about 30% of segments show less than 10 sec of emulation time for Accupedo, the time for 70% of segments is less than 20 sec for MyPath. ChatMon has similar results to Accupedo.

Progressive estimation: Figure 14 shows the average error when applying 2-min segment parallel execution with idle time skipping. The average error quickly decreases within 10 sec for MyPath and Accupedo. MyPath shows 9% of error in 20 sec while Accupedo does 19%. After 30 sec, the error almost saturates. ChatMon takes relatively longer for saturation, i.e., 60 sec. Note that scenario 3 and 4 of ChatMon show saturation, less than 5% in 12 sec. ChatMon's high average error before saturating is attributed to the high error rate in Scenario 1. Its net power increase is very small compared to others, 28.9 mW. Thus, even a small difference in estimation such as 10 mW, results in a large error. An example of such difference is clearly shown in the first 10 sec, where the error rate unexpectedly increases as the estimation progresses. This is mainly due to ChatMon's logic which conducts a BT scan for the first 10 sec upon startup. Progressive estimation regards the power cost of the initial scan as representative of the whole scenario and thus overestimates the results compared to the small ground truth.

We summarize the results for the additional cases introduced in Section 7.2.2. When applying 2-min segment parallel execution with idle time skipping, our system shows 21% error (2 mW difference) for NoomWalk due to its lack of power use and 8% error for Pedometer2.0. For Nexus 5, the error rates are 2%, 5%, and 3% for Accupedo, MyPath, and ChatMon, respectively.

7.3 System Overhead

Mobile-side cost: We examine the mobile-side cost in terms of energy overhead and storage size. We omitted network cost since the trace upload is done only while the phone is on Wi-Fi and charged. We consider two sensor sets, a *basic* set with GPS, accelerometer, and Bluetooth, and a *full* set with all available

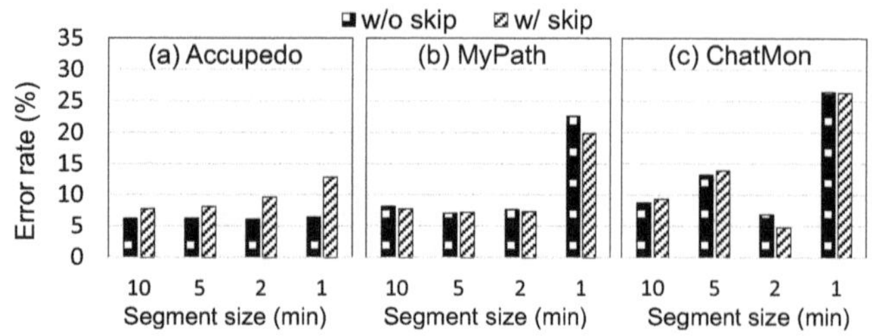

Figure 12. Effect of parallel execution and idle time skipping

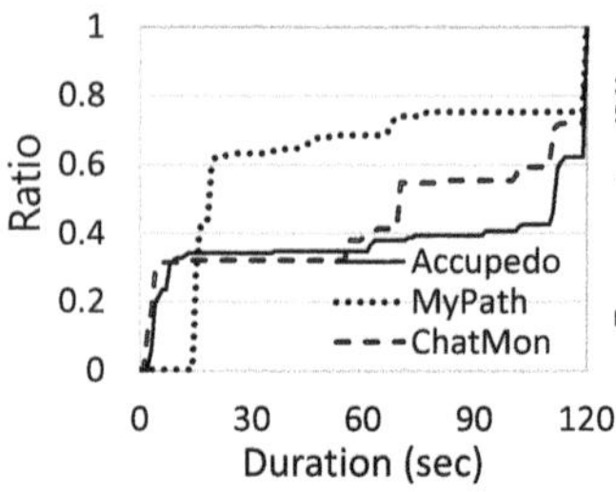

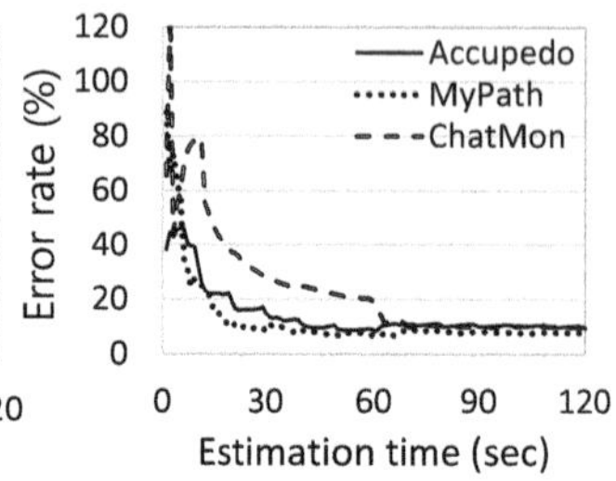

Figure 13. CDF of emulation time (left)
Figure 14. Effect of progressive estimation (right)

sensors. Table 4 shows the results calculated with 1/12 duty cycle, which we set from our empirical experience, as shown in Section 6.2; the expected battery-life decrease is computed assuming 15 hours of battery-life with the fully charged battery, 1500 mAh and 2300 mAh for Nexus S and Nexus 5, respectively. The overall power costs for both basic and full sensor collection were not significant. Even with a full set, the expected lifetime decrement on Nexus S is about an hour; while the cost to collect the sensor data within a cycle is large 390 mW, the average power is reduced to 32 mW due to duty cycling. The cost to collect device usages is negligible in terms of both power use and necessary storage. Note that one hour overhead occurred only a few times since the trace is collected once and used for various different apps.

Server-side cost: The major operations on the server-side are as follows. (1) Prior to a request, the emulator manager stores and manages user behavior traces. (2) Upon a request, it initiates power emulation on distributed phone emulators with the pre-segmented traces. (3) It collects the hardware usage statistics from the emulators and estimates the power impact. The costs of (1) and (3) are not significant. For (1), the network and storage cost is not large, as the maximum data size is about 35 MB for a single day of a user. For (3), the estimation takes less than one sec. For (2), the overhead to run a single emulator instance on our server is about 5% of CPU and 400 MB of memory. The major workload comes from simply emulating a virtual phone image even without foreground apps running; we observed that the extra workload for replaying the trace is quite marginal. We discuss the scalability issue for a worldwide service of PowerForecaster in Section 9.

8. REAL DEPLOYMENT EVALUATION

Experiment setup: We recruited 6 graduate students and 1 researcher(P1) on campus in Nov. 2014. We provided a Nexus S running our trace collector and had them use it as their primary phone. They installed their own SIM cards on the phone and the apps they usually use. Not to affect their usual phone use and corresponding power consumption, we provided another Nexus S to collect sensor data at the same time. To ensure the same user behaviors and environmental conditions for both phones, we taped them up to be carried together. For comprehensive analysis, we collected the full sensor data from 8 a.m. to 2 a.m. the next day.

Table 4 Mobile-side cost; accelerometer/light/proximity/magnetic (delay_fastest), gyroscope(delay_game), GPS/BT/3G/WiFi(1 min.)

Data	Storage (MB)	Avg. power (active period power) (mW),		Expected battery-life decrease (h)	
		Nexus S	Nexus 5	Nexus S	Nexus 5
device usage	0.24	< 1 (<1)	< 1 (<1)	-	-
sensor(basic)	11.1	23 (276)	25 (298)	0.8	0.5
sensor(full)	34.6	32 (390)	26 (314)	1.1	0.6

Each participant was compensated KRW 200,000 (USD 179). The experiments were conducted for two weeks. The first week was to collect prerequisite information to estimate power impact, including sensor traces, device usage traces, hardware usage statistics, and battery levels. When the second week started, each participant installed one of three sensing apps, Accupedo, MyPath, or ChatMon. The second week was to measure the decrease of the battery life when the participants used the designated app. For ChatMon, we recruited two students from the same project group and configured their ChatMons to detect each other.

User-friendly power impact estimation: For this study, we further process $netP_{app}$ in more user-friendly way. Specifically, we convert $netP_{app}$ to the expected decrease in the battery life (in hours) of the user's phone, by applying the following formula:

$$decrease(app) = battery\text{-}life_{without\_app} - battery\text{-}life_{with\_app}$$

$$= \frac{capacity}{P_{without\_app}} - \frac{capacity}{(P_{without\_app} + netP_{app})},$$

where $capacity$ is the phone's full battery capacity and $P_{without\_app}$ is the average power use of the phone before running the target sensing app. $netP_{app}$ is the net power increase of the app outputted by our emulator. For the user-friendly output, our collector logs phones' battery levels to estimate $battery\text{-}life_{without\_app}$. We use a simple method to calculate $battery\text{-}life_{without\_app}$: the reciprocal of the battery drain rate (%/h), computed by using the consecutive samples of <timestamp, battery level> as in [10][40].

Results: Table 5 shows the battery-life decrease of each sensing app for the 7 participants. The sensing apps reduced the phones' battery life by 12.1 hours on average. Interestingly, even a commercial app, Accupedo reduces battery life by 5.3-14.7 hours.

We investigate the estimation accuracy. We asked the participants to select two days during the first week, each with different IDs, on Table 6. Note that it is impossible to measure exact estimation accuracy without complete regeneration of a day's user behavior. Instead, we indirectly compare the estimated battery life with average battery life during the second week. For each selected day, Table 6 shows PowerForecaster's observed battery life and estimated future life, taking the user behavior on that day into the input. It also shows the actual second week battery life when the user used the sensing app. PowerForecaster estimates battery-life decreases with high accuracy even in uncontrolled real-life settings, over 90% for 10 cases out of 14. Even for Accupedo, a commercial app, accuracies were over 90% for all six cases.

There are few cases when the estimation was not accurate, e.g., for P5 with the trace 5-4. P5 mentioned he did not use the phone as usual, nor did he move much since it was a weekend day. P5's battery life was about 20 hours on average during the first week, but 33 hours in trace 5-4. This observation leads us to separately estimate power behaviors on weekends. We will extend PowerForecaster to make progressive classification of user's daily life patterns.

Table 5. Summary of real-deployment experiment

ID	Age	2nd-week sensing app	1st-week avg. battery life (h)	2nd-week avg. battery life (h)	Avg. battery life decrease (h)
P1	37	Accupedo	26.6	21.3	5.3
P2	26		49.6	34.8	14.7
P3	32		30.5	17.5	13.0
P4	32	MyPath	30.2	19.7	10.5
P5	23		19.0	15.3	3.7
P6	33	ChatMon	29.1	16.6	12.5
P7	24		39.3	14.8	24.5

Table 6. Estimation of battery life

ID	TraceID	Battery life (h)	Estimated (future) battery life (h)	2nd-week avg. battery life (h) / stdev
P1	1-4	24.5	**21.1**	**21.3** / 0.9
	1-6	26.2	**22.7**	
P2	2-5	50.0	**37.0**	**34.8** / 2.4
	2-7	47.5	**35.7**	
P3	3-4	24.6	**17.7**	**17.5** / 2.9
	3-7	22.4	**17.2**	
P4	4-1	33.2	**24.1**	**19.7** / 2.7
	4-7	24.8	**20.0**	
P5	5-4	33.6	**24.1**	**15.3** / 2.6
	5-5	17.7	**15.3**	
P6	6-1	24.5	**15.2**	**16.6** / 1.9
	6-5	45.6	**18.1**	
P7	7-2	41.3	**18.0**	**14.8** / 1.8
	7-3	42.7	**19.6**	

We also examine the estimation accuracy when applying all the optimization techniques. For 1/12 duty cycling, we picked out 2-min data every 24-min from sensor and device usage traces. We performed power emulation using the sampled traces with 2-min segment parallel execution and idle time skipping. Figure 15 shows the progressive estimation errors over time with trace 4-1 and 7-3, compared to the case using the whole trace without any acceleration techniques. Notably, with only 1/12 of the trace, PowerForecaster shows only 8.5% and 3.4% of errors, respectively. This is because the sampled data still represent the rest due to the context continuity. For the trace 4-1, our system reveals decreasing errors over time, 13% and 10% at 20 and 30 sec, respectively. For trace 7-3, it saturates to 3% after 5 sec.

Besides battery-life impact, PowerForecaster also provides in-depth analysis on future power behavior of sensing apps by using contextual information obtained from the sensor trace. Figure 16 shows the estimated power hotspots that P4 saw prior to use the MyPath app depending on the time and the location, respectively. While PowerForecaster basically targets end users, it can also be used to support developers to estimate battery-life impact of their apps in real-life situations. Based on behavior traces collected from diverse users, our system can provide the estimated impact of their apps over different users before the real deployment.

9. DISCUSSION

Daily variation of user behaviors: We focus on providing an accurate power impact estimate of a sensing app given users' behavioral traces of a specific day. However, it is arguable that the estimation for a past specific day can well represent the real power impact in the future. We believe that there are both possibilities and limitations here. The deployment study result in Section 8 shows that the estimation accuracy is reasonably good, which implies that there are likely to be similar behavioral patterns over

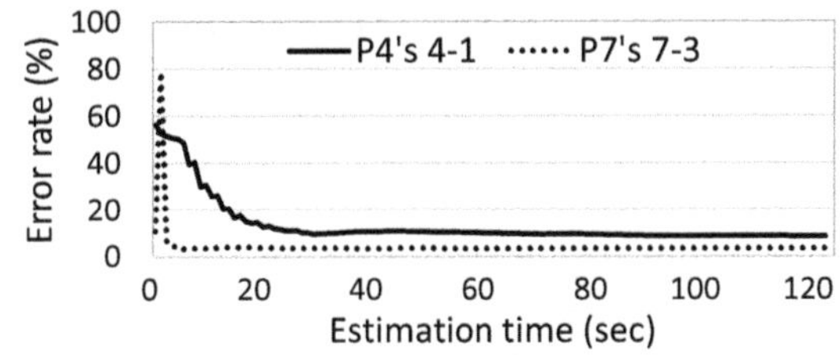

Figure 15 End-to-end performance with P4's 4-1 and P7's 7-3

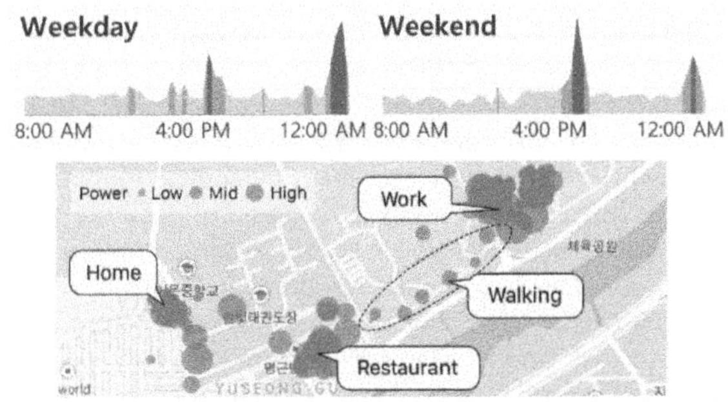

Figure 16 Expected power behavior of MyPath for P4

days. At the same time, there are also cases that exhibit large deviation from the estimate depending on users. From the results, it might be difficult to provide a single representative estimate of power impact based on one-day-long traces in the face of daily variations of behaviors. To address the problem, we can consider collecting user traces for several days (possibly periodically) and making an estimate in a more detailed form, e.g., a reasonable range instead of a single value or separate estimates for weekdays and weekends. While this can increase the mobile side cost, e.g., about an hour or less decrease in daily battery life for several days or a week, it might be a useful option for users who do not mind collecting traces for a longer period of time. Also, if it is possible, it may be able to recognize the behavioral patterns and model the user behaviors as studied in [8][13][34]. Such a model may allow us to estimate power impact of sensing apps more systematically.

Scalability: To complete a power forecasting request for a given user and a given sensing app, it takes about 30 seconds on average with a total of 45 parallel emulator instances running on two physical servers of the specifications aforementioned in Section 7.1. For the cost estimation, we used MyPath and an 18-hour-long trace from user P4 (see Section 8) under the optimization settings of 1/12 duty cycle and 2-min-long segmentation. To discuss the scalability for worldwide deployment, we attempt to estimate the volume of cloud infrastructure partly based on publicly available data and partly with our reasonable assumptions where no public data is available to the best of our knowledge. According to Google I/O 2015 [15], there are 50 billion app installations per year from 1 billion Android users. We do not know the number of sensing app installations out of those; we attempt to assume that 1 billion ones are for sensing apps. This guess is an aggressively high number based on (1) the fact that Google Fit, one of the most popular sensing apps, has been cumulatively installed about 5 million times (0.01% of 50 billion), and (2) the prospect that sensing apps will proliferate in the near future. Given these numbers, we expect about 2.8 million sensing app installations per day. The number of daily power forecasting requests may be higher than this; users may want to compare a few similar apps before installing one. We use 3 for a reasonable number of comparisons; it produces a total of 4 power forecasting requests, giving 11.2 million power forecasting requests per day worldwide.

Given the resources to complete a single request shown above, this worldwide workload could be handled by 7800 physical servers[3]. This would be reasonably practical, based on the existing server volume of today's commercial cloud such as 1 million servers in Microsoft datacenters[4].

Our estimation has a number of limitations. The true computing powers of a commercial cloud server are unknown. It lacks the notion of diurnal workload fluctuations, which may act adversely to the estimated server volume. The ever-growing popularity of sensing apps would also aggravate the scalability issue. On the contrary, a number of advanced strategies may be able to resolve the scalability issues. For example, (1) we can make the kernel ticks advance faster by modifying the Android emulator's kernel timer; it will further shorten the time to complete the processing of a given trace. (2) An emulator instance may be able to accommodate multiple target apps; this would be able to save a significant amount of computing resources as the major workload comes from emulating a phone image, rather than from running apps on top of it. (3) The service provider may predict an installation of a particular sensing app based on popularity or user profiles; making an estimation in advance by temporary surplus cloud resources would distribute the server-side peak loads.

Power estimation of advanced techniques for sensing apps: For power estimation of sensing apps, we currently focus on their repetitive sensing and subsequent data processing controlled by built-in logics. However, some apps could offload their heavy computation logics on the server to save energy [47][48]. To address such apps, it is required to track their network usage and estimate the corresponding power cost. We will extend our system to support power estimation of sensing apps' network usage. As in Section 3.4, a possible method would be to track network-relevant factors on a user's phone and reproduce them in the emulator [36]. Besides the cloud offloading, low power processors have been used for energy-efficient sensor data processing. Our system can be extended to handle such advanced architectures by building power models for low power processors and tracking their usages.

Privacy: To benefit from PowerForecaster, users are required to upload their sensor and device usage data into the cloud, which naturally raises privacy concerns. Optimistically, such concerns may be mitigated if a system provides sufficient utility [26]. Many users already upload their privacy-sensitive data such as location and photos to the cloud for better management and accessibility. However, to be conservative, privacy is a very subjective and sensitive issue [18]. To relieve the concern, our system will adopt proper solutions, e.g., allowing users to control the data type and granularity to upload as well as data collection period.

10. RELATED WORK

Continuous sensing apps and energy optimization: Recently, lots of continuous sensing apps have been proposed in a research domain [30][32][37][52]. In-depth exploration can be found in [25]. While much effort has been put toward developing an accurate recognition logic, they also adopt diverse optimization techniques to save battery. Also, many works propose common platforms for mobile sensing apps and system support for energy-efficient context sensing [5][11][19][20][21][22][29][31][46].

Power profiling and modeling: Power profiles and models are important baselines for energy optimization in mobile systems. There have been extensive efforts to build accurate models for the power consumption of mobile apps and phone H/W [6][7][36][42][43][55][56][57], on which the power model that we adopt for accurate power estimation is built. Similar to our emulation-based approach, WattsOn provides a tool to emulate apps' power use in development environments to support app developers [36]. Unlike our work, it targets interactive foreground apps and thus focuses on power emulation for display, CPU, and network. We, however, address the power impact of background sensing apps.

Energy diagnosis of running apps: Several works address energy diagnosis problems such as abnormal battery drain due to bugs and misconfigured apps [4][33][40][44]. They help users find the causes of undesirable battery drain and fix them. We complement these works with the expected power impact of continuous sensing apps before installing them, helping users make informed decision in advance.

Human battery interaction: Literatures on human-battery interaction for mobile users examined battery-charging behavior [9][49], user perception of battery interface [10][49], and change of user behavior by battery awareness [3]. However, since they mostly focus on conventional mobile apps, they did not address issues and concerns related to continuous sensing apps. As an early attempt, our previous study reported users' concerns about running continuous sensing apps [35]. Their different battery drain depending on user behavior could embarrass users due to disparities between users' anticipation of the near-future battery status and the actual outcome. It proposed a novel tool to provide user behavior-dependent battery drain information while running sensing apps, and showed its effectiveness. Unlike this work, PowerForecaster focuses on providing power impact of sensing apps at pre-installation time and thereby helps users make better informed decision in advance.

Mobile app testing: Recently, there have been research efforts to develop autonomous testing frameworks for mobile apps using mobile emulators [16][50][27]. They use a monkey tool to automate the execution of mobile apps by generating streams of user interface events and analyze runtime properties such as app crashes and page contents systematically on the emulator. Our system differs from those in two aspects. First, for the execution of sensing apps, we replay sensor data streams and sensor status, which are the major input of sensing apps. Second, we emulate the power state of sensor devices for the power impact estimation.

11. CONCLUSION

In this paper, we present *PowerForecaster*, a system that provides users with personalized power impact of continuous sensing apps prior to installation. We show that individual user behavior is a key to understand power impact of continuous sensing apps. We developed a novel user behavior-aware power emulator estimating power use by sensing apps based on user's real behavioral traces. We implemented and extensively evaluated the PowerForecaster prototype in terms of accuracy, speed, and system overhead.

12. ACKNOWLEDGMENTS

We thank our shepherd, Dr. Kiran Rachuri and anonymous reviewers for their valuable comments. This work was supported by the National Research Foundation of Korea(NRF) grant funded by the Korea government(MSIP) (No. 2011-0018120). The corresponding author is Seungwoo Kang.

[3] 2 servers × 0.5 min. × 5.6e+6 requests = 5.6e+6 server•min. = 3888 server•day.

[4] http://www.microsoft.com/en-us/server-cloud/cloud-os/global-datacenters.aspx

13. REFERENCES

[1] Accupedo. http://play.google.com/store/apps/details?id=com.corusen.accupedo.te

[2] Android emulator. http://developer.android.com/tools/help/emulator.html

[3] Athukorala, K., Lagerspetz, E., von Kügelgen, M., Jylhä, A., Oliner, A. J., Tarkoma, S., and Jacucci, G. How carat affects user behavior: implications for mobile battery awareness applications. In *Proceedings of the 32nd annual ACM conference on Human factors in computing systems* (CHI), 2014.

[4] Battery Doctor. http://ksmobile.com/product/battery-doctor.html

[5] Chu, D., Lane, N. D., Lai, T. T. T., Pang, C., Meng, X., Guo, Q., Li, F., and Zhao, F. Balancing energy, latency and accuracy for mobile sensor data classification. In *Proceedings of the 9th ACM Conference on Embedded Networked Sensor Systems* (SenSys), 2011.

[6] Dong, M., and Zhong, L. Self-constructive high-rate system energy modeling for battery-powered mobile systems. In *Proceedings of the 9th international conference on Mobile systems, applications, and services* (MobiSys), 2011.

[7] Dong, M., Lan, T., and Zhong, L. Rethink energy accounting with cooperative game theory. In *Proceedings of the 20th annual international conference on Mobile computing and networking* (MobiCom), 2014.

[8] Falaki, H., Mahajan, R., Kandula, S., Lymberopoulos, D., Govindan, R., and Estrin, D. Diversity in smartphone usage. In *Proceedings of the 8th international conference on Mobile systems, applications, and services* (MobiSys), 2010.

[9] Ferreira, D., Dey, A. K., and Kostakos, V. Understanding human-smartphone concerns: a study of battery life. In *Pervasive Computing*, 2011.

[10] Ferreira, D., Ferreira, E., Goncalves, J., Kostakos, V., and Dey, A. K. Revisiting human-battery interaction with an interactive battery interface. In *Proceedings of the 2013 ACM international joint conference on Pervasive and ubiquitous computing* (UbiComp), 2013..

[11] Georgiev, P., Lane, N. D., Rachuri, K. K., and Mascolo, C. DSP.Ear: Leveraging CO-Processor Support for Continuous Audio Sensing on Smartphones, In *Proceedings of the 12th ACM Conference on Embedded Networked Sensor Systems* (SenSys), 2014.

[12] Gomez, L., Neamtiu, I., Azim, T., and Millstein, T. Reran: Timing-and touch-sensitive record and replay for android. In *Proceedings of 35th International Conference on Software Engineering 2013* (ICSE), 2013.

[13] Gonzalez, M. C., Hidalgo, C. A., and Barabasi, A. L. (2008). Understanding individual human mobility patterns. *Nature, 453*(7196), 779-782.

[14] Google Fit, https://play.google.com/store/apps/details?id=com.google.android.apps.fitness

[15] Google I/O 2015, https://events.google.com/io2015

[16] Hao, S., Liu, B., Nath, S., Halfond, W. G. J., and Govindan, R. PUMA: Programmable UI-Automation for Large-Scale Dyanmic Analysis of Mobile Apps. In *Proceedings of the 12th international conference on Mobile systems, applications, and services (MobiSys)*, 2014.

[17] iOS simulator. https://developer.apple.com/library/ios/documentation/IDEs/Conceptual/iOS_Simulator_Guide/

[18] Itani, W., Kayssi, A., and Chehab, A. Privacy as a Service: Privacy-Aware Data Storage and Processing in Cloud Computing Architecture. In *Proceedings of the 8th IEEE International Conference on Dependable, Autonomic and Secure Computing* (DASC), 2009.

[19] Ju, Y., Lee, Y., Yu, J., Min, C., Shin, I., and Song, J. SymPhoney: a Coordinated Sensing Flow Execution Engine for Concurrnet Mobile Sensing Applications. In *Proceedings of the 10th ACM Conference on Embedded Networked Sensor Systems* (SenSys), 2012.

[20] Ju, Y., Min, C., Lee, Y., Yu, J., and Song, J. An Efficient Dataflow Execution Method for Mobile Context Monitoring Applications. In *Proceedings of the 11th IEEE International Conference on Pervasive Computing and Communications* (PerCom), 2013

[21] Kang, S., Lee, J., Jang, H., Lee, Y., Park, S., and Song, J. (2010). A scalable and energy-efficient context monitoring framework for mobile personal sensor networks. *IEEE Transactions on Mobile Computing, 9*(5), 686-702.

[22] Kang, S., Lee, Y., Min, C., Ju, Y., Park, T., Lee, J., Rhee, Y., and Song, J. Orchestrator: An active resource orchestration framework for mobile context monitoring in sensor-rich mobile environments. In *Proceedings of the 8th IEEE International Conference on Pervasive Computing and Communications* (PerCom), 2010

[23] Kim, D. H., Kim, Y., Estrin, D., and Srivastava, M. B. Sensloc: sensing everyday places and paths using less energy. In *Proceedings of the 8th ACM Conference on Embedded Networked Sensor Systems* (SenSys), 2010.

[24] Lane, N. D., Chon, Y., Zhou, L., Zhang, Y., Li, F., Kim, D., Ding, G., Zhao, F., and Cha, H. Piggyback CrowdSensing (PCS): energy efficient crowdsourcing of mobile sensor data by exploiting smartphone app opportunities. In *Proceedings of the 11th ACM Conference on Embedded Networked Sensor Systems* (SenSys), 2013.

[25] Lane, N. D., Miluzzo, E., Lu, H., Peebles, D., Choudhury, T., and Campbell, A. T. A survey of mobile phone sensing. *Communications Magazine, IEEE, 48*(9), 140-150.

[26] Lee, J. and Hoh, B. Sell Your Experiences: A Market Mechanism based Incentive for Participatory Sensing. In *Proceedings of the 8th IEEE International Conference on Pervasive Computing and Communications* (PerCom), 2010.

[27] Lee, K., Flinn, J., Giuli, T. J., Noble, B., and Peplin, C. AMC: Verifying User Interface Properties for Vehicular Applications. In *Proceedings of the 11th international conference on Mobile systems, applications, and services (MobiSys)*, 2013.

[28] Lee, Y., Iyengar, S. S., Min, C., Ju, Y., Kang, S., Park, T., Lee, J., Rhee, Y., and Song, J. (2012). Mobicon: a mobile context-monitoring platform. *Communications of the ACM*, 55(3), 54-65.

[29] Lee, Y., Ju, Y., Min, C., Kang, S., Hwang, I., and Song, J. CoMon: Cooperative Ambience Monitoring Platform with Continuity and Benefit Awareness. In *Proceedings of the 10th international conference on Mobile systems, applications, and services (MobiSys)*, 2012.

[30] Lee, Y., Min, C., Hwang, C., Lee, J., Hwang, I., Ju, Y., Yoo, C., Moon, M., Lee, U. and Song, J. Sociophone: Everyday

face-to-face interaction monitoring platform using multi-phone sensor fusion. In *Proceeding of the 11th annual international conference on Mobile systems, applications, and services* (MobiSys), 2013.

[31] Lu, H., Yang, J., Liu, Z., Lane, N. D., Choudhury, T., and Campbell, A. T. The Jigsaw continuous sensing engine for mobile phone applications. In *Proceedings of the 8th ACM Conference on Embedded Networked Sensor Systems* (SenSys), 2010.

[32] Luo, C., and Chan, M. C. SocialWeaver: collaborative inference of human conversation networks using smartphones. In *Proceedings of the 11th ACM Conference on Embedded Networked Sensor Systems* (SenSys), 2013.

[33] Ma, X., Huang, P., Jin, X., Wang, P., Park, S., Shen, D., Zhou, Y., Saul, L.K., and Voelker, G. M. eDoctor: Automatically Diagnosing Abnormal Battery Drain Issues on Smartphones. In *Proceedings of 10th USENIX Symposium on Networked Systems Design and Implementaton* (NSDI), 2013.

[34] Miklas, A. G., Gollu, K. K., Chan, K. K., Saroiu, S., Gummadi, K. P., and De Lara, E. Exploiting social interactions in mobile systems. In *Proceedings of the 9th international conference on ubiquitous computing* (UbiComp), 2007.

[35] Min, C., Yoo, C., Hwang, I., Kang, S., Lee, Y., Lee, S., Park, P., Lee, C., Choi, S., and Song, J. Sandra Helps You Learn: the More You Walk, the More Battery Your Phone Drains. In *Proceedings of the 2015 ACM international joint conference on Pervasive and ubiquitous computing* (UbiComp), 2015.

[36] Mittal, R., Kansal, A., and Chandra, R. Empowering developers to estimate app energy consumption. In *Proceedings of the 18th annual international conference on Mobile computing and networking* (MobiCom), 2012.

[37] Mohan, P., Padmanabhan, V. N., and Ramjee, R. Nericell: rich monitoring of road and traffic conditions using mobile smartphones. In *Proceedings of the 6th ACM conference on Embedded network sensor systems* (SenSys), 2008.

[38] Monsoon power monitor. http://msoon.com/LabEquipment/PowerMonitor/

[39] NoomWalk. http://play.google.com/store/apps/details?id=com.noom.walk

[40] Oliner, A. J., Iyer, A. P., Stoica, I., Lagerspetz, E., and Tarkoma, S. Carat: Collaborative energy diagnosis for mobile devices. In *Proceedings of the 11th ACM Conference on Embedded Networked Sensor Systems* (SenSys), 2013.

[41] Paek, J., Kim, J., and Govindan, R. Energy-efficient rate-adaptive GPS-based positioning for smartphones. In *Proceedings of the 8th international conference on Mobile systems, applications, and services* (MobiSys), 2010.

[42] Pathak, A., Hu, Y. C., and Zhang, M. Where is the energy spent inside my app?: fine grained energy accounting on smartphones with eprof. In *Proceedings of the 7th ACM european conference on Computer Systems* (EuroSys), 2012.

[43] Pathak, A., Hu, Y. C., Zhang, M., Bahl, P., and Wang, Y. M. Fine-grained power modeling for smartphones using system call tracing. In *Proceedings of the sixth conference on Computer systems* (EuroSys), 2011.

[44] Pathak, A., Jindal, A., Hu, Y. C., and Midkiff, S. P. What is keeping my phone awake?: characterizing and detecting no-sleep energy bugs in smartphone apps. In *Proceedings of the 10th international conference on Mobile systems, applications, and services* (MobiSys), 2012.

[45] Pedometer2.0, http://play.google.com/store/apps/details?id=com.csero.pedometer

[46] Ra, M., Priyantha, B., Kansal, A., and Liu, J. Improving Energy Efficiency of Personal Sensing Applications with Heterogeneous Multi-Processors. In *Proceedings of the 2012 ACM international joint conference on Pervasive and ubiquitous computing* (UbiComp), 2012.

[47] Rachuri, K. K., Efstratiou, C., Leontiadis, I., Mascolo, C., and Rentfrow, P. J. METIS: Exploring mobile phone sensing offloading for efficiently supporting social sensing applications. In *Proceedings of the 11th IEEE International Conference on Pervasive Computing and Communications* (PerCom), 2013.

[48] Rachuri, K. K., Mascolo, C., Musolesi, M., and Rentfrow P. J. SociableSense: Exploring the Trade-offs of Adaptive Sampling and Computation Offloading for Social Sensing. In *Proceeding of the 17th ACM Conference on Mobile Computing and Networking* (MobiCom), 2011.

[49] Rahmati, A., and Zhong, L. (2009). Human–battery interaction on mobile phones. *Pervasive and Mobile Computing, 5*(5), 465-477.

[50] Ravindranath, L., Nath, S., Padhye, J., and Balakrishnan, H. Automatic and Scalable Fault Detection for Mobile Applications. In *Proceedings of the 12th international conference on Mobile systems, applications, and services (MobiSys)*, 2014.

[51] Sensor Simulator, https://code.google.com/p/openintents/wiki/SensorSimulator

[52] Tan, W. T., Baker, M., Lee, B., and Samadani, R. The sound of silence. In *Proceedings of the 11th ACM Conference on Embedded Networked Sensor Systems* (SenSys), 2013.

[53] Tian, H., Ruogu Z., and Guoliang Xing. COBRA: color barcode streaming for smartphone systems. In *Proceedings of the 8th international conference on Mobile systems, applications, and services* (MobiSys), 2010.

[54] Windows phone 8.1 emulators. http://www.microsoft.com/en-us/download/details.aspx?id=44574

[55] Xu, F., Liu, Y., Li, Q., and Zhang, Y. V-edge: Fast Self-constructive Power Modeling of Smartphones Based on Battery Voltage Dynamics. In *Proceedings of the 10th USENIX SymPosium on Networked Systems Design and Implementation* (NSDI), 2013.

[56] Yoon, C., Kim, D., Jung, W., Kang, C., and Cha, H. AppScope: Application Energy Metering Framework for Android Smartphone Using Kernel Activity Monitoring. In *USENIX Annual Technical Conference,* 2012.

[57] Zhang, L., Tiwana, B., Qian, Z., Wang, Z., Dick, R. P., Mao, Z. M., and Yang, L. Accurate online power estimation and automatic battery behavior based power model generation for smartphones. In *Proceedings of the eighth IEEE/ACM/IFIP international conference on Hardware/software codesign and system synthesis*, 2010.

Zippy: On-Demand Network Flooding

Felix Sutton, Bernhard Buchli, Jan Beutel and Lothar Thiele
Computer Engineering and Networks Laboratory
ETH Zurich, Switzerland
{fsutton, bbuchli, beutel, thiele}@tik.ee.ethz.ch

ABSTRACT

In this paper, we tackle the challenge of rapidly disseminating rare events through a multi-hop network, while achieving unprecedented energy-efficiency. Contrary to state-of-the-art approaches, we circumvent the undesirable trade-offs associated with low-power duty-cycled protocols and backscatter technologies, and demonstrate a paradigm shift in low-power protocol design. We present ZIPPY, an on-demand flooding technique that provides robust asynchronous network wake-up, fine-grained per-hop synchronization and efficient data dissemination by leveraging low-complexity transmitter and receiver hardware. We are the first to demonstrate the on-demand flooding of rare events through a multi-hop network with end-to-end latencies of tens of milliseconds, while dissipating less than 10 microwatts during periods of inactivity. We present a prototype implementation of our proposed approach using a wireless sensor platform constructed from commercially available components. We extensively evaluate ZIPPY's performance in a laboratory setting and in an indoor testbed.

Categories and Subject Descriptors

C.2.1 [**Computer-Communication Networks**]: Network Architecture and Design—*wireless communication*

General Terms

Design, Experimentation, Performance

Keywords

Asynchronous rendezvous; on-demand; network flooding; time synchronization; wake-up radio; wake-up receiver; on-off keying; wireless sensor networks; cyber-physical systems

1. INTRODUCTION

Motivation. The past decade of wireless sensor network research has produced a plethora of robust and energy efficient protocols for disseminating *periodic* events through a network of resource-constrained motes arranged in a multi-hop topology. However, there are many real-world applications, such as industrial automation [13], structural health monitoring [19], medical alert systems [35], surveillance systems [43], and environmental monitoring [12], where events are not periodic, but occur only on *rare* occasions. Under this premise, state-of-the-art duty-cycled protocols are faced with an undesirable design trade-off between mote lifetime and end-to-end latency, and state-of-the-art backscatter technologies are limited by either the availability of infrastructure or low communication range. In this paper, we demonstrate a paradigm shift in low-power protocol design, where the aforementioned trade-offs are circumvented, thus enabling the rapid dissemination of rare events through a multi-hop network with unprecedented energy-efficiency.

Challenge. The key challenge is the dissemination of a rare event through a multi-hop network that is both rapid, *i.e.*, with low end-to-end latency, and energy efficient, *i.e.*, maximizes mote lifetime.

In order to exemplify the design trade-offs encountered when applying state-of-the-art techniques, we consider a concrete application scenario, whereby resource-constrained wireless gas sensors must rapidly alert a sink if the measured gas concentration exceeds a safe level. One approach is to apply a synchronous protocol, such as Glossy [8], to rapidly flood the event through the network to a sink. However, since the periodicity of the radio activity is directly linked to the end-to-end latency of the event, all motes in the multi-hop network must expend significant energy in order to achieve a low reporting latency of the event.

An alternative is to employ a Low-Power Listening [34] or Low-Power Probing [27] protocol. However, as demonstrated in [7], these duty-cycled protocols and their variants suffer the same undesirable design trade-off. That is, the need for low end-to-end latency increases the radio activity at each mote in the network, thereby reducing mote lifetime.

Yet another alternative is to employ backscatter technology where a dedicated [44] or ambient [24] high-power infrastructure provides motes with a medium for communication. However, such techniques are limited in their support for multi-hop connectivity as either the high-power infrastructure must be generated, ambient infrastructure may not always be available, or the achievable per-hop communication range is insufficient.

Proposed Approach. We present ZIPPY, a novel flooding technique that circumvents the aforementioned design trade-offs by leveraging low-complexity transmitter and receiver hardware. We exploit the ultra-low power dissipation

SenSys'15, November 1–4, 2015, Seoul, South Korea.
© 2015 ACM. ISBN 978-1-4503-3631-4/15/11 ...$15.00.
DOI: http://dx.doi.org/10.1145/2809695.2809705.

and unique timing properties of low-complexity radio hardware to perform on-demand flooding of rare events featuring end-to-end latencies on the order of milliseconds, while dissipating less than 10 microwatts during periods of inactivity. This level of energy efficiency makes it possible to support rare event dissemination for multiple years with low-capacity coin cell batteries.

ZIPPY combines four extensible components, which facilitate its adoption to a wide range of application domains. First, a robust *asynchronous network wake-up* ensures that all motes in the multi-hop network are awoken from a deep sleep state. Second, a novel *neighborhood synchronization* component achieves an average per-hop synchronization as low as $34\mu s$. Third, an efficient bit-level *data propagation* component supports the dissemination of event packets with near constant end-to-end latency. Finally, a *carrier frequency randomization* component ensures that the destructive interference associated with concurrent transmissions are mitigated during a ZIPPY flood.

Contributions. In this paper, we make the following contributions:

- We present a robust scheme for performing on-demand wake-up of a multi-hop network using low-complexity radio hardware.
- We introduce a novel technique for per-hop synchronization and flooding of an event packet through a multi-hop network.
- We introduce the design of an ultra-low power wireless sensor platform supporting ZIPPY, while dissipating less than 10 microwatts during periods of inactivity.
- We detail a prototype implementation of ZIPPY, and extensively evaluate its performance both with controlled laboratory experiments and within an indoor testbed.

The paper is structured as follows: Sec. 2 presents on-demand rendezvous using low-complexity radio hardware. Sec. 3 presents an overview of ZIPPY, followed by a detailed design and analysis of its operation in Sec. 4. A prototype implementation of ZIPPY and its extensive evaluation is provided in Sec. 5. Finally, we conclude with a discussion of related work in Sec. 6, and a summary of conclusions in Sec. 7.

2. ASYNCHRONOUS RENDEZVOUS

ZIPPY exploits an asynchronous rendezvous mechanism to facilitate on-demand network flooding. In this section, we study how a mote can achieve on-demand rendezvous with its one-hop neighbors using low-complexity radio hardware.

2.1 Background

One of the fundamental challenges of low-power wireless communication is how to support energy-efficient packet exchange between single-hop neighbors, while minimizing the energy consumed due to idle listening. Given two arbitrary wireless motes within range, packet exchange is only facilitated when both motes have their radios turned on at the same time, which is termed a rendezvous [23]. If a mote does not know when its neighbor wants to send a packet, it must expend energy by powering its wireless receiver in anticipation of packet exchange. This behavior is termed idle listening [5], and is a significant source of energy waste due to the high power dissipation of commonly used receivers.

Wireless sensor network research has primarily addressed the problem of idle listening in the *time* domain [39]. That is, by duty cycling the radio at the appropriate time, rendezvous between one-hop neighbors is supported, while also reducing the mote's average energy consumption. However, under such duty-cycled schemes, there exists a fundamental trade-off between energy efficiency and how often the motes rendezvous. Either the radio duty-cycle is increased to achieve a high rendezvous rate at the cost of higher energy consumption, or the radio duty-cycle is decreased to reduce energy consumption at the cost of a low rendezvous rate. In the case where on-demand rendezvous is desired, *e.g.*, to rapidly exchange a rare event, a design decision must be made between the energy efficiency of the mote, and the latency for the packet exchange.

An alternative approach is to address the problem of idle listening in the *power* domain. Instead of duty cycling the radio hardware, the power dissipation of the radio is such that it becomes feasible to have it always turned on. There are two variants of this approach, based on the dependency on *infrastructure*, or not.

Backscatter technologies are an *infrastructure*-based approach, where a high-power signal source, *i.e.*, either dedicated in the case of RFID tags [44] or ambient in the case of ambient backscatter [24], provides a medium in which passive RFID tags or backscatter-enabled devices can communicate by reflecting the incident signal. Whilst there has been significant advancements of this novel communication scheme [30], the infrastructure for dedicated backscatter consumes significant energy resources, while realistic signal powers of ambient sources, *e.g.*, from TV transmissions, are likely to constrain indoor non-line-of-sight communication links to only a few meters.

In this paper, we turn our attention to an *infrastructure-less* power domain solution to idle listening. Specifically, we use low-complexity receivers to decode transmissions from low-complexity transmitters. In contrast to backscatter technologies, the receiver is an always-on active circuit specifically designed for ultra-low power operation, while the transmitter is only used when there is data to transmit.

This particular approach has been proposed in the literature [14] more than a decade ago, with the low-complexity receivers referred to as wake-up radios or wake-up receivers. However, recent advances in ultra-low power electronics and the commercial availability of components have made it feasible to achieve always-on idle listening while dissipating on the order of a few microwatts. This is in stark contrast to the order of tens of milliwatts dissipated by commodity radio hardware typically integrated into wireless sensor platforms.

We next present how such ultra-low power receiver structures are realized in practice.

2.2 Asynchronous Mote Architecture

The key to achieving ultra-low power on-demand rendezvous lies in the complexity of the radio hardware and the modulation scheme. Embracing low-complexity digital modulation schemes, such as On-Off Keying (OOK), drastically simplifies the receiver and transmitter circuitry, *i.e.*, by reducing the number and specificity of components, which leads to a significant reduction in power dissipation. In particular, ultra-low power receiver designs, *i.e.*, exhibiting sub-microwatt power dissipation, have been demonstrated in the literature for the acoustic [41], radio frequency [33], and optical [18] spectra.

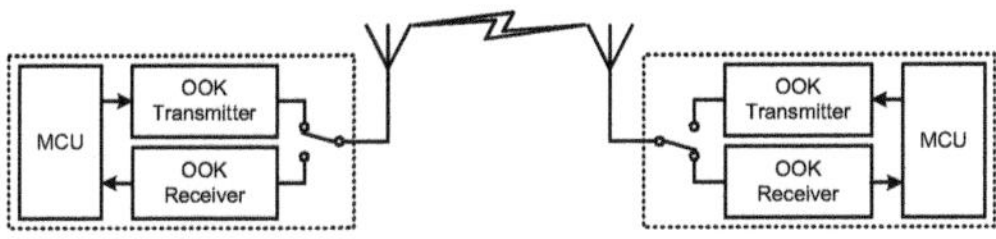

Figure 1: Proposed mote architecture with a microcontroller (MCU), OOK transmitter, and always-on ultra-low power OOK receiver.

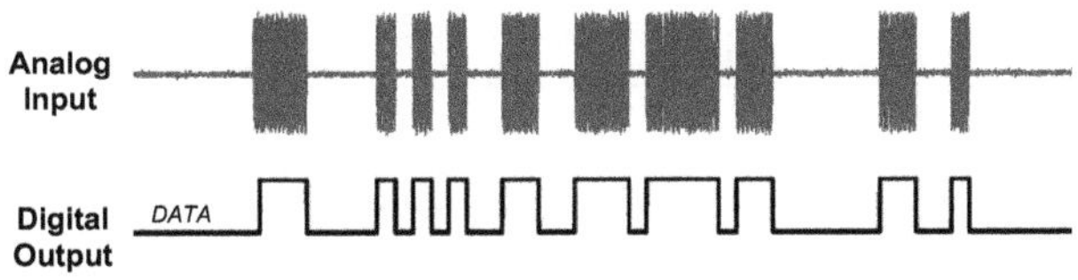

Figure 2: Example OOK signal at the input to the receiver and its corresponding demodulated output.

In this paper, we focus on low-complexity radio hardware for the ISM radio frequency band using the OOK digital modulation scheme. Fig. 1 illustrates the mote architecture assumed throughout this paper, where each mote consists of a microcontroller (MCU) provisioned with an OOK transmitter and an always-on OOK receiver. An RF switch controlled by the MCU selects the RF path from the antenna to either the input of the receiver, or the output of the transmitter. The OOK transmitter is designed such that its power dissipation is less than that of typical transceivers used for higher-complexity digital modulations, *e.g.*, the MAX7044 features a current drain of 14 mA compared to the CC430 which drains 29 mA with identical output transmission power. The OOK receiver is designed such that its power dissipation is on the order of microwatts, *i.e.*, several orders of magnitude below typical transceivers, thereby allowing always-on operation.

On-Off Keying is attributed as being the simplest of digital modulation schemes, where a 1 bit is represented by the presence of a carrier frequency over a bit period T_b, while a 0 bit is represented by the absence of a carrier frequency over a bit period T_b. Fig. 2 illustrates an example OOK-modulated bit sequence, both in its analog representation observed at the antenna of the OOK receiver, and its digital representation after decoding. The OOK receiver provides a single digital output, a *DATA* line, which is interfaced directly to the attached MCU for processing, which will be discussed next.

As illustrated in Fig. 2, the OOK receiver manipulates the digital level of the *DATA* line according to the envelope of the received OOK signal. Since the mote's MCU observes the state of the *DATA* line, it can perform two important functions, namely, *(i)* facilitate asynchronous rendezvous by the detection of the first rising edge of the *DATA* line, and *(ii)* decode an OOK modulated bit sequence by sampling the state of the *DATA* line within each bit period T_b. As discussed in Sec. 3, these two functions provided by the OOK receiver are pivotal to the operation of ZIPPY.

Despite the superior power-efficiency of low-complexity OOK receivers, they exhibit well-known practical limitations, as surveyed in [6]. We systematically evaluate the two most important limitations in Sec. 5.

We next describe how asynchronous rendezvous using low-complexity radio hardware is applied to a multi-hop network, while supporting tight per-hop time synchronization and energy efficient bit-level data dissemination.

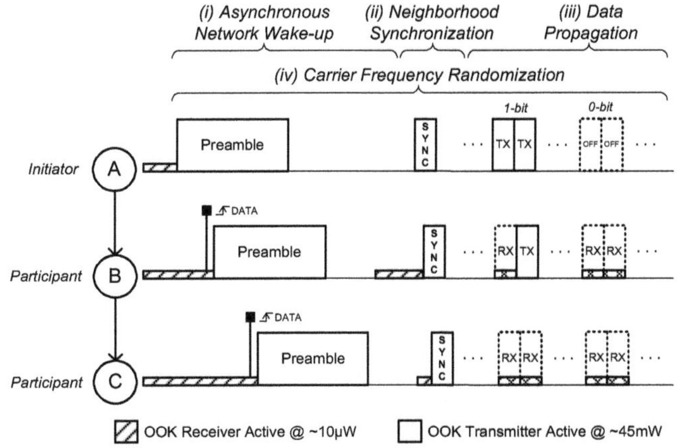

Figure 3: Overview of Zippy in an example 2-hop network, where the initiator mote has a rare event to disseminate through the multi-hop network.

3. OVERVIEW OF ZIPPY

In this section, we present an overview of ZIPPY, the first protocol to demonstrate the feasibility of on-demand multi-hop flooding using low-complexity radio hardware. Fig. 3 exemplifies the operation of ZIPPY, where an *initiator*, mote A, disseminates a rare event through a 2-hop network consisting of *participant* motes B and C. We next briefly describe the function of ZIPPY's four extensible components.

Asynchronous Network Wake-up. The initiator commences a ZIPPY flood by transmitting a preamble, *i.e.*, a sequence of 1 bits, using its low-complexity OOK transmitter. Since the OOK receiver at mote B is always on, the reception of the preamble will assert the receiver's *DATA* line, awaking its MCU from deep sleep. Mote B will then proceed to transmit a preamble so to wake-up its neighbor, mote C. The relaying of the preamble continues until all motes in the network are awake, and as a consequence, all motes achieve coarse-grained time synchronization, *i.e.*, on the order of milliseconds, to their nearest one-hop neighbors.

Neighborhood Synchronization. Shortly after the completion of the preamble transmission, the initiator transmits a single OOK 1 bit, termed the synchronization bit. Once the receiver of mote B detects the beginning of this bit, *i.e.*, by the rising edge of the receiver's *DATA* line, the mote immediately transmits a synchronization bit. The same process occurs at mote C. The time delay between the beginning of the synchronization bit transmission, and the instant it is detected at the MCU provides fine-grained per-hop time synchronization, *i.e.*, on the order of tens of microseconds.

Data Propagation. All motes now leverage the per-hop time synchronization in order to propagate a packet through the network with bit-level granularity. The packet is encoded using a repetition code, with the length of the code equal to the maximum hop count of the network. In the considered example, each bit of the packet is represented by two sub-bits, *i.e.*, a 1 is transmitted as 11 and a 0 is transmitted as 00. The initiator transmits all packet sub-bits, while each participant uses its OOK receiver to decode each sub-bit in sequence. If a sub-bit is decoded as a 1, the participant switches to its OOK transmitter and transmits any remaining 1 sub-bits, thereby propagating each bit to its neighbors.

Carrier Frequency Randomization. It is evident that transmissions during a ZIPPY flood will overlap. As shown in [40], the packet reception rate reduces as the number of concurrent transmissions increases. Furthermore, since we use low-complexity OOK receivers, we are not able to leverage the capture effect [20], which is associated with high-complexity receivers. Although it is shown in [2] that OOK receivers may be designed to exhibit the capture effect, the additional hardware increases the total power dissipation of the receiver, potentially negating the benefits of using it for asynchronous rendezvous. Therefore, during the execution of all aforementioned components of ZIPPY, we mitigate the impact of overlapping OOK transmissions by randomizing the carrier frequency used to represent OOK 1 bits.

While the mote architecture assumed throughout this paper targets the ultra-low power and low-complexity boundaries of the radio sub-system design space, we do not restrict the adoption of ZIPPY's four extensible components into existing motes and/or protocols. On the contrary, the fundamental components of ZIPPY may be combined to create innovative mote architectures and/or energy efficient extensions to established protocols. For example, asynchronous network wake-up and carrier frequency randomization provide a widely applicable and robust multi-hop wake-up service, while a state-of-the-art flooding protocol may benefit from the integration of asynchronous network wake-up, neighborhood synchronization and carrier frequency randomization components in order to reduce the energy footprint of disseminating rare events.

4. DESIGN AND ANALYSIS

We next present the design and analysis of ZIPPY's four extensible components. Where applicable, we characterize certain properties of the OOK receiver so to aid in the design and analysis of each component.

4.1 Asynchronous Network Wake-up

A precondition for communicating with all motes in a network is to ensure they are all turned on and listening, *i.e.*, the mote's MCU is active with a radio interface configured in receive mode. With the assistance of an always-on low-complexity OOK receiver integrated in each mote, the action of remotely waking-up a mote is achieved by the transmission of a preamble, *i.e.*, a fixed-length sequence of 1 bits. As introduced in Sec. 2, the always-on ultra-low power OOK receiver will detect the beginning of the preamble, activate its *DATA* line, and bring the attached MCU out of deep sleep using appropriate interrupt processing.

It follows that the fastest way to facilitate mote wake-up throughout an entire multi-hop network is to simply relay the preamble along each hop. That is, as soon as the *DATA* line is asserted by the OOK receiver, the attached MCU awakes from deep sleep, and proceeds to transmit the preamble. The duration of the preamble $T_{preamble}$ must therefore be longer than the time taken for the OOK receiver to detect the preamble and assert its *DATA* line. Fig. 4 illustrates the detailed timing relations between initiator and participant motes. In order to determine a suitable duration of the preamble, we must measure the delay T_{WAKE} from the beginning of the initiator's preamble transmission until the rising edge of the participant's *DATA* line. This timing characteristic is dependent on two factors: the OOK receiver hardware and the RF propagation effects. We next analyze

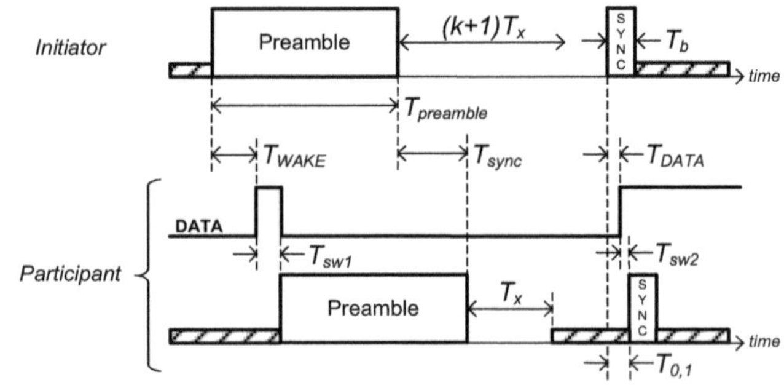

Figure 4: Timing diagram for Zippy's asynchronous network wake-up and neighborhood synchronization.

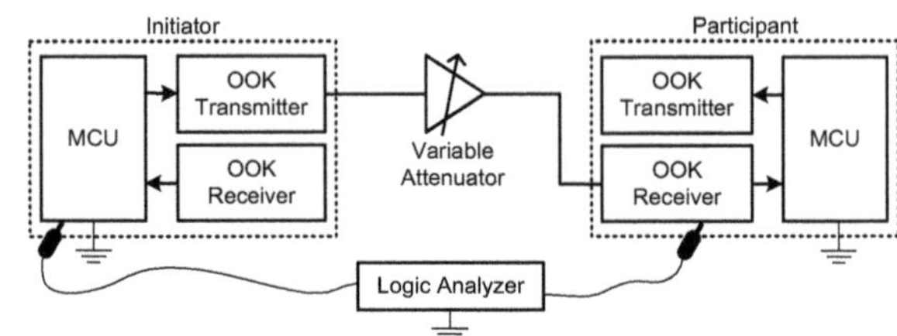

Figure 5: Experimental setup for the timing analysis of the OOK receiver's *DATA* line using a logic analyzer.

the timing properties of the OOK receiver used throughout this paper under ideal RF conditions in order to give a lower bound on the preamble length.

Using the experimental setup illustrated in Fig. 5, we measure the time taken for the receiver to assert its *DATA* line, T_{WAKE}, across the operating range of the receiver as controlled by a variable attenuator. A logic analyzer is used to measure the time between the start of the preamble transmission at the initiator's MCU, and the rising edge of the *DATA* line at the participant's OOK receiver. Fig. 6 plots the distribution of T_{WAKE} as the channel attenuation is varied such that the input signal power to the OOK receiver is between −31 dBm and −51 dBm.

The results indicate a very stable time distribution for T_{WAKE} across the operational range of the receiver. This is primarily due to the Automatic Gain Control (AGC) stage integrated in the OOK receiver detailed in Sec. 5.1. The AGC continuously adjusts a variable-gain amplifier to ensure that low input signals are able to be successfully decoded. Based on these experimental results, the preamble must be at least as long as the maximum observed T_{WAKE}, *i.e.*, $T_{preamble} > 370\,\mu s$.

Once the *DATA* line is asserted at a participant's MCU, the transmission of a preamble commences. The time taken to start the data radio transmission, T_{sw1}, is determined by the start-up time of the transmitter, and the software execution time needed to configure the hardware and appropriately fill the transmit buffer. This software delay can be made approximately constant, *e.g.*, the implementation detailed in Sec. 5.1 exhibits a T_{sw1} of approximately 350 μs.

At the end of the asynchronous network wake-up, the MCU of each wireless mote is awake, and has coarse-grained time synchronization to their nearest neighbor. Specifically, the per-hop synchronization, T_{sync}, is given by (1), where T_{prop} is the propagation delay of the carrier signal.

$$T_{sync} \geq T_{WAKE} + T_{sw1} + T_{prop} \tag{1}$$

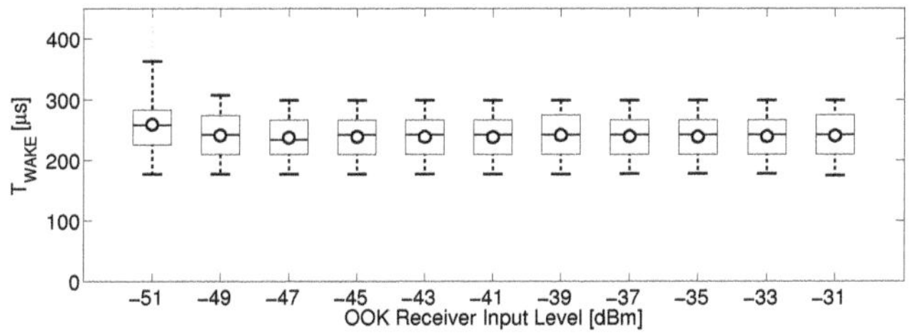

Figure 6: Delay to trigger the rising edge of the *DATA* line with respect to the receiver's input signal level.

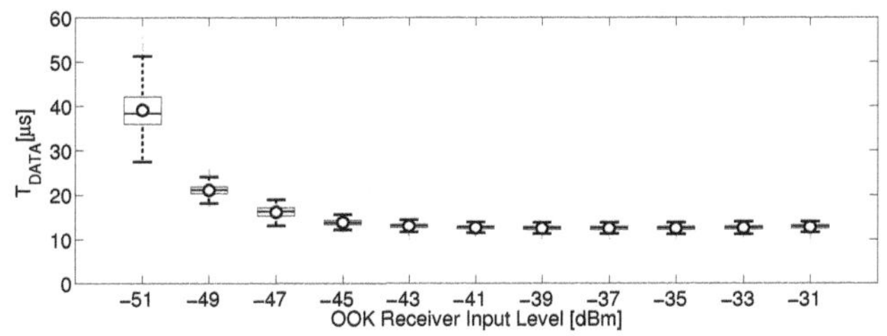

Figure 7: Delay to assert the *DATA* line in response to a neighbor's transmission of a 1 bit.

Based on the aforementioned characterization of the OOK receiver, the per-hop synchronization will be on the order of a millisecond. We next investigate how the per-hop time synchronization can be improved by further leveraging the timing properties of the low-complexity OOK receiver.

4.2 Neighborhood Synchronization

Since per-hop time synchronization is a prerequisite for rapid data dissemination through a multi-hop network, we aim to improve the per-hop time synchronization achieved by the asynchronous network wake-up. We take advantage of the fact that low-complexity OOK receivers decode on a bit-level, as opposed to a byte-wise or packet-wise reception offered by high-complexity receivers, *e.g.*, 802.15.4 compatible receivers. As introduced in Sec. 2, the OOK receiver provides a digital *DATA* line that represents the envelope of a received OOK signal. We now leverage the time it takes for the *DATA* line to assert, T_{DATA}, given that a neighboring mote has transmitted a 1 bit, in order to tightly synchronize motes to their neighbors. As indicated in Fig. 4, the delay T_{DATA} is expected to be smaller than T_{WAKE} since the receiver's AGC has settled to a steady state after the reception of the preamble.

Using the experimental setup illustrated in Fig. 5, we measure the time between the beginning of a 1 bit transmission from the initiator, until the rising edge of the participants *DATA* line using a logic analyzer. The time separating the preamble and the 1 bit transmissions is chosen to be longer than the receiver's AGC settling time. Fig. 7 illustrates the box plot of the delay T_{DATA}, as the OOK receiver's input signal level varies between −31 dBm and −51 dBm. We observe a statistically stable delay with an average of approximately 13µs for low and medium signal strengths. The average increases by a factor of three as the input signal power approaches the receiver's sensitivity level of −52 dBm, as evaluated in Sec. 5.1.1.

We leverage this advantageous timing property of the OOK receiver to achieve per-hop synchronization on the order of tens of microseconds. As illustrated in Fig. 4, once the asynchronous network wake-up is complete, the initiator transmits a synchronization bit, *i.e.*, a single 1 bit of duration T_b, using its OOK transmitter. The participant's OOK receiver will detect this bit, and assert its *DATA* line after an elapsed time of T_{DATA}. The participant's MCU then begins to transmit a synchronization bit using its OOK transmitter. The time to switch on the OOK transmitter, T_{sw2}, is a combination of hardware and software delays which are considered constant.

The relaying of the synchronization bit continues throughout the multi-hop network. In an ideal RF propagation environment, the time between the start of the synchronization bit transmission at hop i, and the start of the synchronization bit transmission at hop $i+1$ is at least $T_{i,i+1}$ seconds, as given by (2). The constant T_{prop} represents the carrier signal propagation time, which is considered negligible.

$$T_{i,i+1} \geq T_{data} + T_{sw2} + T_{prop} \quad (2)$$

The aforementioned neighborhood synchronization scheme has two caveats that necessitate further discussion. Firstly, once a participant has completed its carrier burst transmission, it must wait a minimum of T_x seconds before turning on its receiver in preparation for the relaying of the synchronization bit. If the receiver is turned on too early, the *DATA* line will activate in response to a neighbors preamble transmission, causing erroneous synchronization. Therefore, each participant must wait at least $T_x = \max(T_{WAKE}) + T_{sw1}$ seconds before reacting to the rising edge of its receiver's *DATA* line.

Secondly, the initiator must ensure that the synchronization bit is not transmitted before all motes within the multi-hop network have completed their preamble transmissions. Therefore, the initiator must know in advance the maximum number of hops the flood must propagate through. This poses no real practical limitation, as the maximum expected hop count can be estimated at the deployment time of the network. It follows that given a multi-hop network of k hops, the initiator must wait at least $(k+1)T_x$ seconds before transmitting the synchronization bit.

We show experimentally in Sec. 5 that a mean per-hop synchronization as low as 34µs is achievable in a 2-hop network, while only taking on the order of milliseconds to complete the ZIPPY flood.

4.3 Data Propagation

We next leverage the per-hop time synchronization in order to rapidly propagate a fixed length packet through a given multi-hop network. Since the OOK receiver provides bit-level granularity, we consider the bit-level propagation of a packet between single-hop participants.

The simplest method to propagate a bit through a multi-hop network is to transmit the bit as soon as it is received. This scheme is exemplified in Fig. 8(a), where the initiator transmits bit b_0, participant mote B receives the bit and transmits it in the next available bit period. This bit-level relaying continues throughout the multi-hop topology. Under this scheme, the initiator must know in advance the maximum hop count k of the network in order to determine when it can transmit the next bit b_1.

We therefore impose a structure where each bit consists of k sub-bits, where k is the maximum hop count of the network. All participant motes maintain a local counter j, which is initialized to zero. The counter represents the sub-

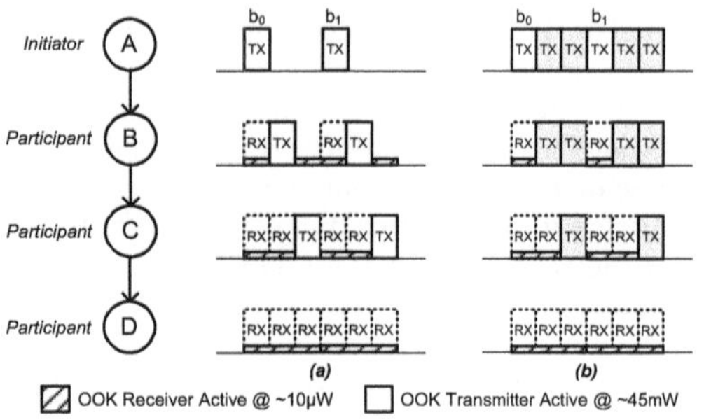

Figure 8: Bit-level propagation schemes using $k = 3$ sub-bits (a) without, and (b) with repetition.

bit, *i.e.*, between 0 and $k-1$, currently decoded by the participant. The counter is incremented by the participant at the end of each symbol boundary according to the following sequence:

$$j = (j+1) \bmod k \quad \forall j \in [0, k-1] \tag{3}$$

Once the sub-bit has been decoded, *i.e.*, the *DATA* line has been sampled and is deemed as either a 0 or a 1, the participant makes a decision on how to propagate the sub-bit based on the value of the counter j. If a sub-bit is decoded as a 0, the participant continues to listen for the next sub-bit. However, if a sub-bit is decoded as a 1, the participant will transmit a 1 during the next sub-bit if its counter value satisfies $j < k-1$. This behavior is illustrated in Fig. 8(a), where mote B decodes a 1 during sub-bit $j=0$, and therefore transmits a 1 in the next sub-bit. Similarly, mote C decodes a 1 during sub-bit $j=1$, and transmits a 1 in the next sub-bit. This scheme of bit-level data propagation ensures that all participants up to the kth hop have an opportunity to receive each bit transmitted by the initiator.

The reliability of this scheme can be further improved by *(i)* incorporating a repetition code for the initiator and allowing participants to transmit during empty sub-bits, and *(ii)* performing a majority vote sub-bit decoding at all participants. We next detail these two techniques, which are both incorporated into ZIPPY.

As illustrated in Fig. 8(b), the initiator of a ZIPPY flood employs a k-repetition code, whereby a single bit is transmitted repeated $k-1$ times. In order to leverage the transmission of the additional sub-bits from the initiator, each participant may propagate all remaining 1 sub-bits. That is, if a participant decodes the jth sub-bit as a 1, the remaining $k-j-1$ sub-bits are then transmitted as 1 bits. To exemplify the propagation scheme employed by ZIPPY, consider the example illustrated in Fig. 9, where initiator A transmits the first bit out of three, assuming a maximum hop count of $k=2$. Participant B will receive the first sub-bit as a 1, and then transmit during the remaining sub-bit, whereas participant C decodes the first sub-bit as a 0, and therefore refrains from transmission, and instead decodes the second sub-bit as a 1. This described scheme gives participants residing up to $k-1$ hops away from the initiator more than one chance at successfully decoding each bit.

Majority vote decoding, a scheme originally proposed in [37], is performed at each participant by sampling the *DATA* line of its OOK receiver n times per bit period T_b, where n is a positive odd integer. The sub-bit is decoded as a 1 if the *DATA* line was sampled high at least $\lceil \frac{n}{2} \rceil$ times, otherwise, the sub-bit is decoded as 0. Fig. 9 illustrates

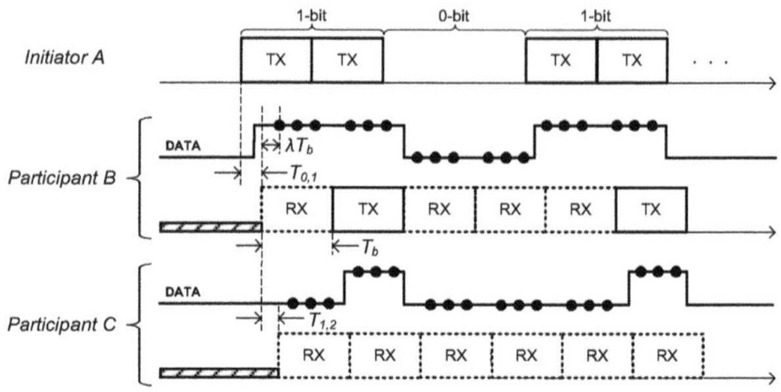

Figure 9: Bit-level propagation employed by Zippy with $n = 3$ majority vote sub-bit decoding.

the timing diagram for majority vote sub-bit decoding, with each sample per sub-bit separated by λT_b, where $\lambda = \frac{1}{n+1}$.

In order for the majority vote sub-bit decoding to function as intended, the sampling of the *DATA* line must not extend past the sub-bit boundary. This is prevented by ensuring the sub-bit period T_b is long enough, given the maximum per-hop synchronization delay $T_{i,i+1}$ experienced throughout the multi-hop network. This is analytically described by selecting the sub-bit period T_b such that the following inequality holds:

$$T_b > \frac{T_{i,i+1}}{\lambda} \quad \forall i \in [0, k-1] \tag{4}$$

It is evident that ZIPPY's data propagation is inherently biased toward 1 bits, since a 0 bit requires all k sub-bits to be decoded as 0, while a 1 bit requires only one of the k sub-bits to be decoded as 1. While this asymmetry may lead to packet corruption due to erroneous 1 bit propagation, ZIPPY leverages tight per-hop synchronization for aligning sub-bit boundaries, and majority sub-bit decoding for improved packet reception as evaluated in Sec. 4.4.

An important property of ZIPPY's data propagation scheme is that the end-to-end latency of a flood at each mote differs only by the small per-hop synchronization delays $T_{i,i+1}$. Specifically, the minimum end-to-end latency $L_{0,h}$ from the beginning of the initiator transmission until the participant at hop count h decodes the N_{data} bit packet, is given by:

$$L_{0,h} \geq T_{preamble} + (k+1)T_x + \sum_{i=0}^{h-1} T_{i,i+1} + (kN_{data}+1)T_b \tag{5}$$

We can therefore conclude that the theoretical minimum end-to-end latency $L_{0,h}$ increases linearly with the maximum hop count k, and with the number of packet bits N_{data}.

4.4 Carrier Frequency Randomization

We have so far only considered the operation of ZIPPY in a network of motes arranged in a line topology. We now extend its design to more realistic wireless networks where each hop may contain several participating motes.

The main challenge in extending ZIPPY into a dense network is interference. For example, when two motes simultaneously transmit an OOK-modulated 1 bit, the corresponding sinusoidal signals may constructively or destructively interfere at the antenna of the OOK receiver residing at the next hop. If the interference is constructive, then the receiver will decode the bit successfully without any adverse side effects. However, if the interference is destructive, the received signal level may be too low to be detected.

During a ZIPPY flood, destructive interference is undesirable as all aforementioned components may be affected.

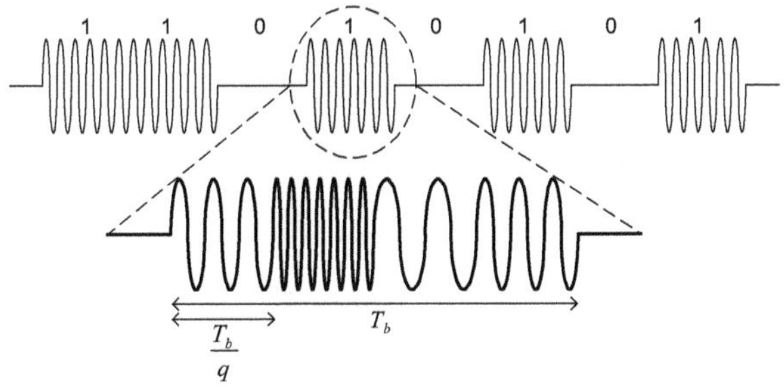

Figure 10: Example OOK transmission incorporating carrier frequency randomization with $q = 4$.

For example, destructive interference may result in a missed preamble reception, erroneous per-hop synchronization due to the late reception of the synchronization bit, or packet corruption due to erroneous decoding of sub-bits.

One solution to this problem is to avoid the interference by employing a collision avoidance mechanism, *e.g.*, Clear Channel Assessment (CCA) with random back-off. However, there are two severe problems that arise, making such mechanisms infeasible for ZIPPY. Firstly, the use of a random back-off would induce long delays between the relaying of each preamble. This will make it impossible to tightly bound the delay T_x, which is used by the initiator and all participants to correctly sequence the synchronization bit. Secondly, the induced delays of relaying the synchronization bit will drastically extend the per-hop synchronization bounds $T_{i,i+1}$, leading to an excessively long OOK bit period T_b in order to satisfy inequality (4) derived in Sec. 4.3.

Therefore, rather than trying to avoid collisions, ZIPPY embraces overlapping transmissions, but mitigates their effects by randomizing the carrier frequency used to generate OOK 1 sub-bits. Instead of transmitting each OOK 1 sub-bit using a single carrier frequency of duration T_b, each sub-bit is transmitted using a random sequence of $q > 1$ carrier frequencies, as depicted in Fig. 10. Since each mote randomly selects a different set of carrier frequencies per sub-bit, the probability of destructive interference during the entire sub-bit reduces.

In particular, each mote selects a carrier frequency $f = f_c + \beta\Delta$, at least q times per sub-bit period T_b, where f_c is the center carrier frequency, β is a discrete random variable uniformly distributed over a set of integers of size $M \geq 2$, and Δ is a minimum frequency offset. The parametrization of q, M, and Δ are dependent on the hardware of the OOK receiver, OOK transmitter, and the MCU used to control the two devices. Based on the developed prototype detailed in Sec. 5.1, together with extensive practical experiments, we support carrier frequency randomization with $q = 8$ random frequencies per sub-bit, with $M = 4$ random frequencies to choose from, centered about $f_c = 446.8\,\text{MHz}$, with each having a minimum offset of $\Delta = 135.41\,\text{kHz}$.

We next experimentally evaluate the effectiveness of carrier frequency randomization based on the aforementioned parameterization using the cabled setup as illustrated in Fig. 11(a). Using a 6-way RF power combiner, we combine the simultaneous transmissions of up to six participants, with the resultant signal cabled to an independent participant for decoding using its OOK receiver. An external signal generator is used to trigger the transmission of a randomly generated 32-bit packet from each of the attached participants. All participants share the same random

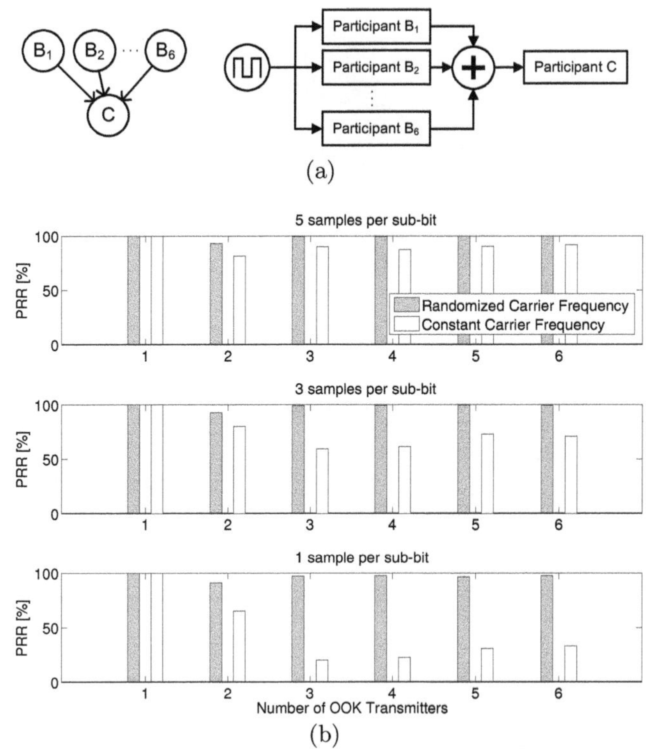

Figure 11: (a) Logical and physical experimental setup, and (b) results of evaluating carrier frequency randomization and majority vote sub-bit decoding.

seed, ensuring the packet is identical during each simultaneous transmission. Each participant randomly selects its own carrier frequency using a unique seed. An embedded CRC-8 within each packet is used to calculate the packet reception rate (PRR), with and without carrier frequency randomization enabled, and with and without majority vote sub-bit decoding. A total of a 1000 packets are generated for each test configuration. The transmission power of all participants is fixed at $-30\,\text{dBm}$. Shielded SMA cables interconnect all RF devices so to remove non-deterministic propagation effects.

The results of the experiment are illustrated in Fig. 11(b). As expected, a 100% PRR is achieved for a single transmitter, irrespective of the carrier frequency and majority decoding configuration. As the number of simultaneous transmitters is increased, the PRR drastically reduces when using a constant carrier frequency. This effect is slightly mitigated by increasing the number of samples per sub-bit from 1 to 5. In the case of only two simultaneous transmitters, we observed a slight reduction of PRR when using a randomized carrier frequency. Since it is a random process, we would expect the occasional bit error due to destructive interference. Nevertheless, the PRR remains higher than that achieved using a constant carrier frequency. In summary, carrier frequency randomization achieves almost 100% PRR with up to six simultaneous transmitters, thus making it a robust mechanism for ZIPPY to operate in dense networks.

5. EXPERIMENTAL EVALUATION

In this section, we present the design of a custom wireless sensor platform for the evaluation of ZIPPY. We first present the platform design, evaluate the sensitivity and false wake-up rate of its OOK receiver, and measure its total power

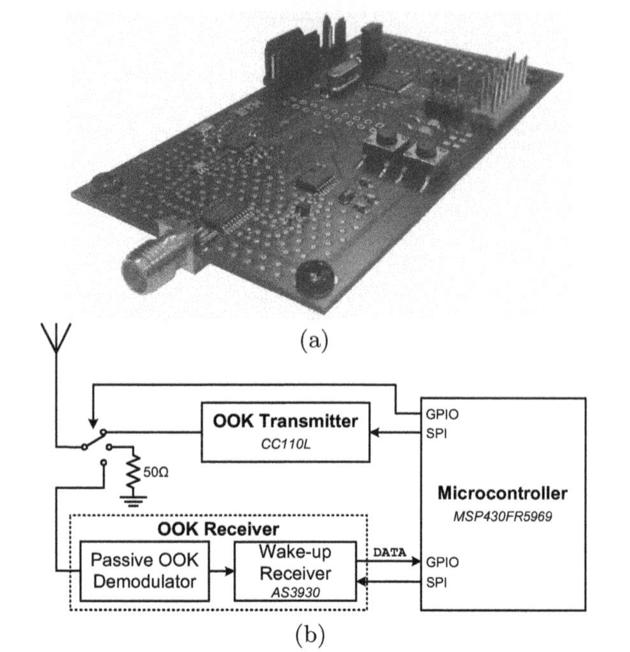

Figure 12: Prototype (a) and block diagram (b) of a wireless sensor platform supporting Zippy flooding.

dissipation. We then evaluate the performance of ZIPPY in a controlled laboratory setting and in an indoor testbed.

5.1 Prototype Wireless Sensor Platform

A prototype wireless sensor platform supporting ZIPPY is shown in Fig. 12(a), with its block diagram depicted in Fig. 12(b). The platform consists of a 16-bit MSP430FR5969 MCU interfaced to a CC110L transceiver, and an ultra-low power OOK receiver based on the AS3930 receiver. The antenna of the platform is connected to an ADG904 RF switch, which is controlled by the MCU. The antenna path can be fed into the OOK transmitter, the OOK receiver, or a 50Ω resistor. The components of the platform were selected based on their ultra-low quiescent supply current or ultra-low current drain during deep sleep mode.

OOK Receiver. The receiver is an adaptation of [11], where the impedance matching circuitry has been tuned for the 434 MHz ISM frequency band. The receiver consists of a passive OOK demodulator coupled with a commercially available AS3930 ASK receiver. We leveraged the *WAKE* line from the AS3930 to indicate the reception of a preamble, while the *DATA* line is used for detecting the synchronization bit and decoding packets. The OOK receiver supports a maximum data rate of 8.192 kbps, and features an ultra-low current drain of 2.7 μA measured at 3.0 V.

OOK Transmitter. In order to design a flexible wireless sensor platform for future research opportunities, we incorporated a multi-purpose wireless transceiver instead of a dedicated OOK transmitter module. Carrier frequency randomization is supported on the CC110L transceiver by configuring it for transmission using FSK-4 modulation. An OOK signal is produced by continuously generating random FSK-4 symbols, and using the antenna switch to generate either a 1 or a 0 sub-bit, as required. An OOK 1 sub-bit is produced by switching the antenna port to the CC110L transceiver for a period of T_b, while an OOK 0 sub-bit is produced by switching the antenna port to the 50Ω resistor for a period of T_b. A software-based pseudo-random number generator [26] is used to randomly select each FSK symbol from a uniform distribution, thus producing the desired randomization of the carrier frequency.

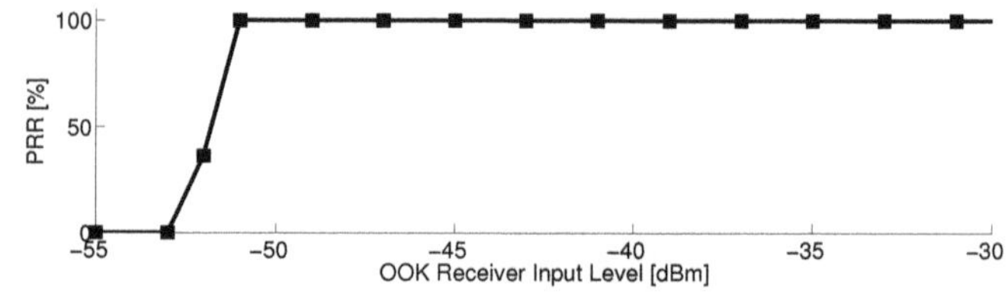

Figure 13: Sensitivity of the OOK receiver as measured experimentally with a variable attenuator.

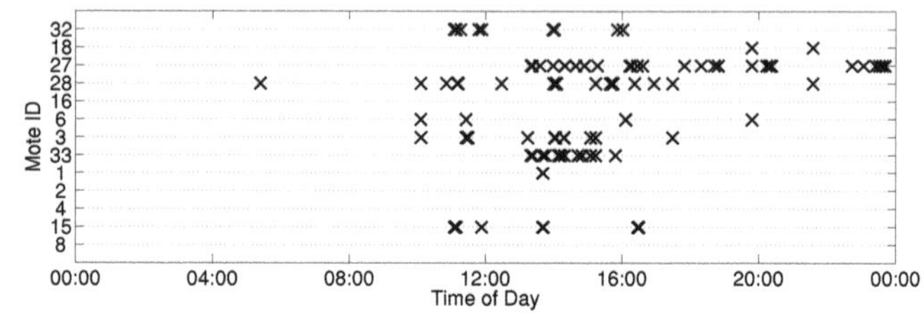

Figure 14: Sporadic false wake-ups observed during a 24 hour experiment on an indoor testbed.

5.1.1 Receiver Sensitivity

The sensitivity of a wireless receiver is defined as the minimum input signal power that supports successful decoding. While the receiver sensitivity has an influence on the overall reception range of the receiver, care must be taken not to infer reception range only from receiver sensitivity, as various techniques can be used to improve the RF link budget, *e.g.*, increasing the power of the transmitted signal and the use of high-gain antennas.

We measured the sensitivity of the OOK receiver using the setup described in Sec. 4.1, and illustrated in Fig. 5. By varying the attenuation between OOK transmitter and receiver, the sensitivity is determined by the minimum input signal level upon which the *DATA* line no longer asserts in the presence of an OOK 1 sub-bit transmission. As shown in Fig. 13, the receiver sensitivity of the OOK receiver is approximately −52 dBm. This sensitivity level is considered state-of-the-art compared to existing prototypes with a similar architectural design [10].

It is important to clarify that despite the apparent low sensitivity compared to high-complexity receivers, practical experiments have demonstrated ranges up to 15 meters non-line-of-sight in an office hallway, and up to 30 meters line-of-sight in an outdoor sports field. These experiments were carried out using quarter-wavelength omnidirectional monopole antennas with a ground plane of 25 cm^2, while being fixed 1.5 m above the ground.

5.1.2 False Wake-up Rate

Due to the low-complexity design of the OOK receiver, it is susceptible to external interference. In particular, we are interested in how often a false wake-up occurs, *i.e.*, when the *DATA* line asserts without an OOK preamble being transmitted. The receiver used in this work operates using subcarrier modulation [29], where a 434 MHz carrier produces the envelope of a 125 kHz carrier. While this design achieves

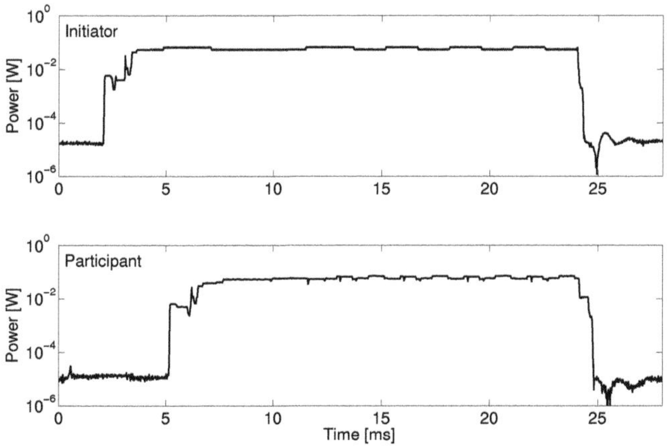

Figure 15: Power profile of initiator and participant motes during a Zippy flood.

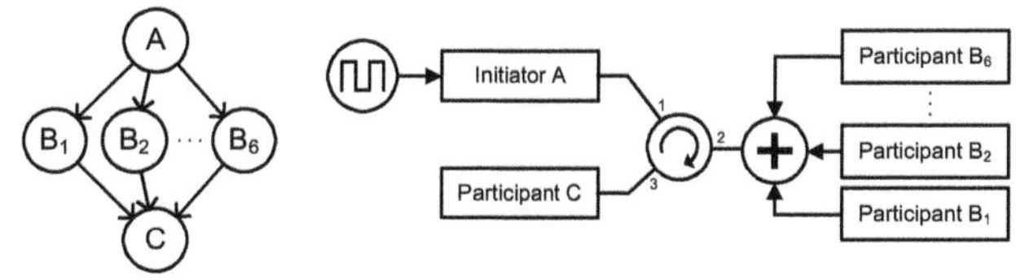

Figure 16: Logical (left) and physical (right) setup for the controlled laboratory experiments.

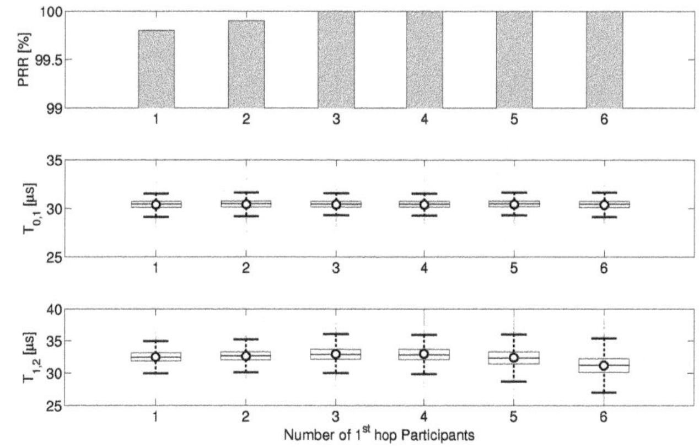

Figure 17: Packet reception rate and per-hop time synchronization of the cabled multi-hop network.

ultra-low power dissipation, it is susceptible to strong noise sources operating around the 125 kHz frequency, *e.g.*, from switch-mode power supplies, and devices operating in the 434 MHz ISM band, *e.g.*, other wireless modules.

In order to quantify the false wake-up rate of our prototype, we deployed 13 motes into an indoor office environment, as described in Sec. 5.3. During a period of 24 hours, we recorded each time a false wake-up occurred. The results of the experiment are shown in Fig. 14, where a cross indicates a false wake-up. In summary, four motes did not exhibit any false wake-ups, while mote 28 experienced the maximum of 3166 false wake-ups. With the exception of mote 27, the false wake-ups were predominantly recorded during office hours. The root cause for all the false wake-ups are not yet known, however, it is anticipated that RF shielding and common mode noise rejection circuitry may reduce some false wake-ups.

5.1.3 Active and Idle Power Dissipation

The power profiles of an initiator and a participant mote are depicted in Fig. 15, as measured using an Agilent N6705A DC Power Analyzer. The two platforms were supplied with 3.0 V, while having their on-board low-dropout regulators bypassed. The power profile begins with both motes in an idle listening mode, whereby the MCU resides in a deep sleep mode, *i.e.*, LPM4. During this time, the CC110L transceiver is in standby mode, the antenna switch is active, and the OOK receiver is active. The initiator and participant measured a total idle power dissipation of 9.6μW during periods of inactivity.

Once the initiator is triggered to begin a ZIPPY flood (parameterized with a maximum of $k = 2$ hops), *i.e.*, at approximately 2 ms into the power profile, the initiator begins to transmit the preamble, followed by the synchronization bit, and an 8-bit packet containing the bit sequence 0x55. The power dissipation during all OOK transmissions is approximately 70 mW, which concurs with the CC110L datasheet.

5.2 Controlled Multi-hop Experiments

We first evaluate ZIPPY in controlled laboratory experiments before extending the evaluation to an indoor testbed. The motivation for controlled experiments is two-fold, firstly, to provide a baseline timing analysis of the per-hop synchronization achieved by ZIPPY, and secondly to evaluate the robustness of ZIPPY in large, dense networks that would otherwise be infeasible to replicate in a testbed.

Experimental Setup. As illustrated in Fig. 16, a cabled 2-hop network is used to evaluate the timing and robustness of ZIPPY using a circulator. A circulator is a passive 3-port device that passes an RF signal between ports 1 and 2, but isolates the signal from port 3. Similarly, a signal may pass between port 2 and 3, but is isolated from port 1. Connecting a 6-port RF combiner at port 2 of the circulator enables the construction of sparse and dense 2-hop network topologies. A logic analyzer is connected to initiator A, and participants B_1 and C for the measurement of the per-hop time synchronization and evaluation of packet reception rate.

The initiator A starts the transmission of each ZIPPY flood according the the frequency of an external square-wave signal generator. Each flood consists of a 32-bit packet containing 24 randomly generated bits and an 8-bit CRC. ZIPPY is configured with $k = 3$ maximum hops, majority decoding with $n = 3$ samples per bit, and with carrier frequency randomization as described in Sec. 4.4. The transmission power of all motes is fixed at -30 dBm. The experiment begins with a single 1-hop participant, B_1, with all other combiner ports terminated with 50Ω SMA terminators. After the transmission of 1000 ZIPPY floods by initiator A, an additional 1-hop participant, up to a maximum of six, is connected to the cabled multi-hop network before restarting the experiment.

Results. The results of the controlled laboratory experiment are shown in Fig. 17. The robustness of ZIPPY is determined by the packet reception rate as measured at participant C. As more 1-hop participants are added, it is vital that the packet reception rate does not decrease. As we can see from Fig. 17, the packet reception rate remains at approximately 100% with up to six first-hop participants. This remarkable behavior is primarily attributed to the use of car-

Table 1: Zippy configuration used throughout all indoor testbed experiments.

Parameter	Description
$k = 2$ and 3 hops	Maximum hop count
$D = \frac{1}{T_b} = 1.364$ kbps	OOK receiver data rate
$N_{data} = 8$ and 16 bits	Packet length
$n = 3$ samples per sub-bit	Majority vote sub-bit decoding
$T_{preamble} = 1.4$ ms	Preamble duration
$T_x = 1.25$ ms	Participant wait delay

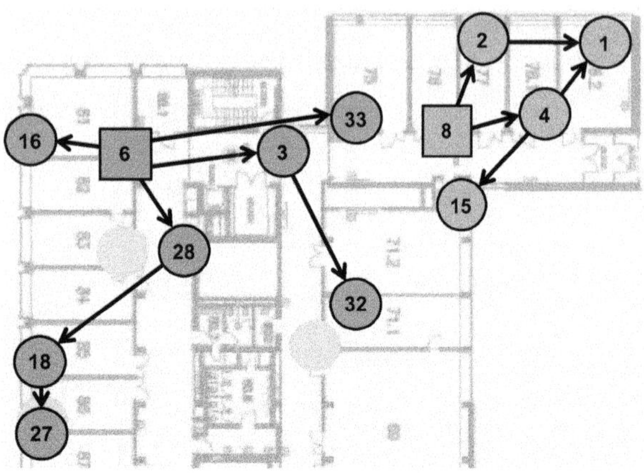

Figure 18: Indoor testbed deployment map, featuring large (left) and small (right) network topologies.

rier frequency randomization. As discussed in Sec. 4.4, the use of majority vote decoding slightly increases the packet reception rate under overlapping transmissions. This experimental result demonstrates an improvement on the packet reception rate achievable during concurrent OOK transmissions compared to using high-complexity receivers as presented in [40](Fig. 6), where simulations show that approximately 10% of all packets are corrupt when there is more than one concurrent transmission.

The per-hop time synchronization is determined by measuring the $T_{i,i+1}$ delay, as introduced in Sec. 4.2. The first-hop synchronization between the initiator A and participant B_1 is given by $T_{0,1}$, while the second-hop synchronization between participants B_1 and C is given by $T_{1,2}$. As shown in Fig. 17, the mean of the first-hop time synchronization is approximately 31 μs, and exhibits a very narrow distribution, irrespective of the number of additional participants. This result is not surprising, since the reception of the synchronization bit at B_1 is not affected by the reception of the synchronization bit by all other participants residing at the same hop. However, the mean of the second-hop time synchronization is slightly increased to approximately 33 μs, and has a wider distribution due to the colliding synchronization bit transmissions. As the number of 1-hop participants increases, the percentiles of the time distribution increase accordingly, however, the mean remains below 35 μs. This demonstrates that, under ideal conditions, ZIPPY provides fine-grained per-hop time synchronization, while also exhibiting robustness in sparse and dense network topologies due to carrier frequency randomization.

5.3 Testbed Multi-hop Experiments

We next evaluate ZIPPY's performance in an indoor testbed. **Experimental Setup.** We deployed a total of 13 prototype wireless sensor platforms into the FlockLab [21] indoor testbed, which is configured with fine-grained tracing capabilities [22]. The location of each deployed mote is depicted in Fig. 18. We configured the motes into two independent networks, a 2-hop network with a topology having more than one participant at the first hop, and a 3-hop network offering substantial spatial coverage. All motes were configured with carrier frequency randomization, as detailed in Sec. 4.4. Motes 8 and 6 were configured as the initiators for the small and large networks, respectively. All experiments were performed with 8- and 16-bit randomly generated packets. As discussed in Sec. 5.4, support for longer packets with ZIPPY is indeed feasible.

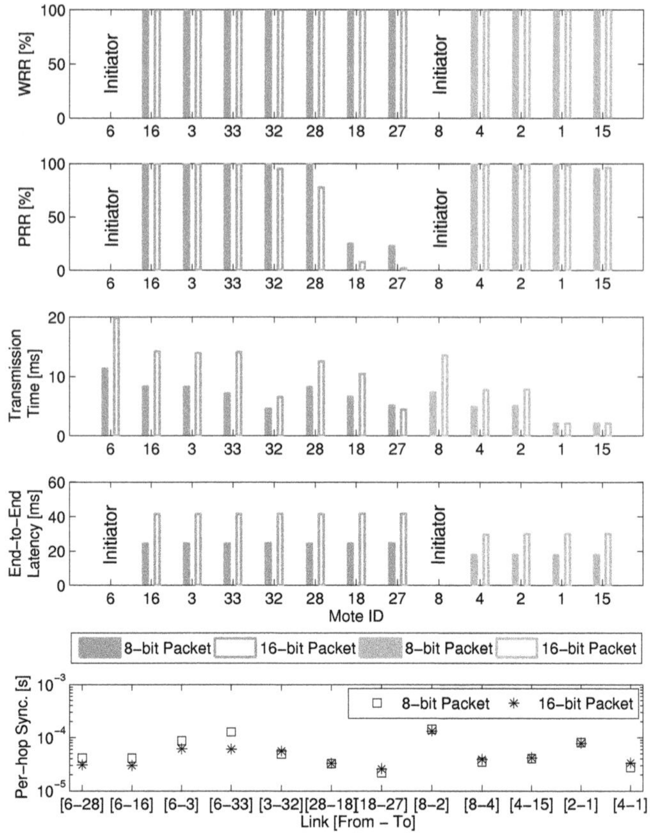

Figure 19: Results from indoor testbed experiments.

The experimental evaluation is based on the following four metrics: *(i) wake-up reception rate (WRR)* is the ratio of the number of motes that wake-up compared to the number of ZIPPY floods initiated, *(ii) packet reception rate (PRR)* is the ratio of the number of correctly received packets compared to the number of ZIPPY floods initiated, *(iii) transmission time* is the duration each mote had their OOK transmitter active per ZIPPY flood, *(iv) end-to-end latency* is the elapsed time between the start of the ZIPPY flood at the initiator until the end of the flood at each participant, and *(v) per-hop synchronization* is the mean time delay between the motes' nearest neighbor during all ZIPPY floods. We compute all metrics based on 500 ZIPPY floods using a static configuration, as listed in Table 1.

Results. The results of the testbed experiments are shown in Fig. 19, and are summarized as follows:

- We first observe a wake-up reception rate (WRR) of 100% for all motes deployed in the testbed. This is a remarkable result, given the challenging RF propagation environment imposed by the testbed: motes are separated by physical obstacles including thick concrete walls reinforced with steel, and metal piping affixed to the ceiling for plumbing, heating and ventilation. No false wake-ups were observed during the experiments.

- The packet reception rate (PRR) of the motes residing in the large network range from 1.8% (mote 27) up to 100% (motes 16, 3, and 33), while all motes residing in the small network exhibited a PPR exceeding 94.6%. The higher PRR in the small network is attributed to the improved link quality between motes, which exhibit shorter link distances and less physical obstruction compared to the large network topology.
- The transmission times are approximately equal for all motes having the same hop count. This is due to the way in which ZIPPY propagates each sub-bit of the packet. In addition to the preamble and synchronization bit transmissions, each initiator (motes 6 and 8) transmit all packet bits using a repetition code, as detailed in Sec. 4.3. As the hop count increases, the number of sub-bits to be propagated decreases, resulting in a decrease in transmission time per hop. For example, in the small network, mote 8 initiates the ZIPPY flood and takes 7.3 ms to transmit the preamble, synchronization bit, and an 8-bit packet, while motes 2 and 4, residing at the first hop, experience a transmission time of approximately 5.0 ms for the preamble, synchronization bit and only half of the packet sub-bits. Finally, the leaf motes, *i.e.*, motes 1 and 15, require a transmission time of only 2.0 ms, as they transmit only the preamble and synchronization bit. A maximum of 19.8 ms was observed by the initiator of the large network for the transmission of a 16-bit packet.
- The end-to-end latency is nearly constant for each network topology and evaluated packet length. Due to the way in which ZIPPY propagates sub-bits through the network, all participant motes complete a flood at approximately the same time, with small differences attributed to the per-hop time synchronization to their neighbors. The small and large networks exhibit average end-to-end latencies of 17.8 ms and 24.4 ms for the 8-bit packet, and 29.8 ms and 41.6 ms for the 16-bit packet, respectively.
- The mean per-hop synchronization ranges from 21.9 μs between motes 18 and 27, and 143.5 μs between motes 8 and 2. Apart from the link between motes 6 and 33, there are only slight differences between the 8-bit and 16-bit packet experiments. This is to be expected as the per-hop time synchronization is dependent on the reception of the synchronization bit and not on the length of the packet. It is important to highlight that the minimum per-hop synchronization observed is less than what was measured in the cabled experiments in Sec. 5.2. This is indeed feasible, as all links in the testbed are not perfectly isolated. For example, mote 27 may on occasion receive the synchronization bit transmitted from mote 28, while the data propagation is decoded from mote 18.

Comparative Analysis. We next compare the energy efficiency of ZIPPY in flooding on-demand events compared to state-of-the-art flooding protocols, such as Glossy [8]. We consider a static network topology with a maximum of $k = 3$ hops and with a packet length of 16-bits. As we have shown in the testbed experiments, ZIPPY can disseminate an event through a 3-hop network with an end-to-end latency of approximately 41.6 ms. If instead Glossy was used to disseminate on-demand events with a reporting latency comparable to ZIPPY, all motes must perform periodic Glossy floods each separated by at most 41.6 ms. Assuming the Glossy parameterization presented in [45] for the TelosB and CC2420 radio with a maximum number of transmissions $N = 2$, this corresponds to maximum transmission time of 1.9 ms per flood every 41.6 ms. In contrast, the ZIPPY prototype only needs a maximum transmission time of 19.8 ms once per event. Despite the specific radio-on time depending greatly on the specific mote hardware and the protocol software implementation, we can conclude that ZIPPY will consume less energy than periodic Glossy floods provided the average event inter-arrival time is greater than approximately 434 ms.

5.4 Protocol Limitations and Challenges

We next discuss limitations and challenges associated with the operation, implementation and evaluation of ZIPPY.

False Wake-up Detection. As discussed in Sec. 5.1.2, the always-on low-complexity OOK receiver is susceptible to false wake-ups. ZIPPY is designed such that a preamble is always transmitted once a wake-up is detected. Therefore in the worst-case scenario, if a false wake-up is detected at one mote, all motes in the network will erroneously participate in a ZIPPY flood. After the preamble has been erroneously relayed, two scenarios are possible, namely, *(i)* a synchronization bit is detected and an erroneous packet is decoded and delivered to a higher-layer application, or *(ii)* a synchronization bit is not detected causing a protocol timeout after an inactivity timer expires. Erroneous packets can be filtered at higher-layers using forward error correction, however, in either case, a false preamble detection results in the misuse of energy reserves, the impact of which depends greatly on the specific parameterization of ZIPPY.

Erroneous Synchronization. If a participant mote receives the synchronization bit too early due to a false wake-up, or too late due to poor RF propagation, subsequent transmissions may corrupt the reception of all other participants within its 1-hop neighborhood. The quantitative impact of erroneous synchronization has yet to be investigated, however, extensive tests suggest an adequate parameterization of the preamble length $T_{preamble}$ and participant wait delay T_x reduce the occurrence of this erroneous behavior.

Noise Resilience. The performance of modulation schemes in the presence of noise are characterized analytically by their bit error vs. signal to noise ratio (SNR) curve [31]. It is well known that higher-order modulation schemes, such as BPSK, exhibit a lower bit error probability for the same SNR compared to OOK modulation. Based on this analytical result, there are two approaches to improve the operation of ZIPPY's data propagation with respect to noise, namely, *(i)* increase the SNR at the input of the OOK receiver's decoder, or *(ii)* reduce the bit error by employing a higher-order modulation scheme.

The first approach seeks to increase the SNR of the receiver, thereby reducing the probability of bit error. This is achieved in practice by selecting an advanced OOK receiver incorporating a low noise amplifier, which is directly associated with an increase in power dissipation of the radio hardware. However, if the advanced receiver supports a sufficiently high data rate, ZIPPY's data propagation can operate with higher energy efficiency.

An alternative approach is to adopt a new modulation scheme that is more robust against noise, *i.e.*, where a lower

SNR is needed for the same probability of bit error. However, the challenge is to manage the adverse effects of simultaneous transmissions using a modulation scheme other than OOK. As introduced in Glossy [8], constructive interference can be leveraged to reliably disseminate packets through simultaneous transmissions using O-QPSK modulation.

Data Rate Reduction. The data rate of the OOK receiver had to be reduced to 1.364 kbps for the implementation of ZIPPY due to instability of the OOK demodulator output. We suspect that this is due to the dynamic operation of the AS3930's integrated AGC. Since the design of the AGC is not in the public domain, it is difficult to identify the root cause of this behavior. However, in principle, there are no limitations in operating ZIPPY at higher data rates using an appropriately designed AGC.

Packet Length Support. The packet length supported by ZIPPY is primarily dependent on the quality of the RF links between motes. As exemplified in Sec. 5.3, motes with poor RF connectivity, *e.g.*, motes 18 and 27 in the large network, will experience higher bit errors, resulting in a lower PRR as the packet length is increased. However, when motes have good RF connectivity, longer packet lengths may be supported with a high PRR. For example, in the small testbed network, ZIPPY has been shown to support a packet length of 64-bits with an average PRR of 96.7%.

Network Scalability. As shown in the experiments presented in Sec. 5.3, ZIPPY's end-to-end latency is approximately constant for a given network configuration, and increases linearly with respect to the maximum hop count k, and the number of packet bits N_{data}. Furthermore, the transmission time of the initiator is determined by the maximum hop count k, while the transmission time of participants decreases linearly with respect to its hop count. It is anticipated that the advantageous properties of carrier frequency randomization, as validated in Sec. 4.4, will also apply in large network deployments with appropriate parameterization. The validation of these network scaling properties remain a future research opportunity.

Antenna Ground Plane. The ground plane and placement of the antenna adversely impacted the range of the low-complexity OOK receiver. Since each FlockLab target slot has a defined physical footprint, the size of the antenna ground plane is therefore limited. Furthermore, by affixing the antennas close to thick reinforced concrete walls, as is the case for all indoor FlockLab targets, the antenna radiation pattern of each mote is altered. These two combined effects reduced the operation range of some links within the testbed deployment, necessitating the installation of larger antenna ground planes at selected FlockLab observers.

6. RELATED WORK

Asynchronous network wake-up was first proposed as part of the PTW [42] protocol, where each mote immediately transmits a preamble as soon as it is woken up by the reception of a preamble. The relaying of preambles has been recently extended in FLOOD-WUP [32] by leveraging the addressable wake-up mode supported by modern ultra-low power receivers. ZIPPY builds on their work by addressing the problem of motes simultaneously transmitting. Leveraging carrier frequency randomization, as introduced in this paper, provides a robust, rapid, and topology-independent asynchronous network wake-up. In addition, ZIPPY provides tight per-hop synchronization and data dissemination.

Several protocols employing ultra-low power receivers have been proposed in the literature, for example E2RMAC [15], WUR-MAC [25], and RTWAC [1], which provide single-hop packet transfer by leveraging an asynchronous rendezvous. While these protocols achieve improved end-to-end latency and energy efficiency compared to synchronous and pseudo-asynchronous protocols, they do not support asynchronous multi-hop data dissemination as demonstrated by ZIPPY. Furthermore, the aforementioned protocols have only been evaluated empirically through simulation, in contrast to the extensive indoor testbed deployment of ZIPPY.

RFID tags for asynchronous rendezvous in wireless sensor networks have been proposed in [16] using active tags, and in [3] using passive WISP [38] platforms. While simulations of RFID-enabled multi-hop communication indicate promising energy efficiencies [17], it is unclear if the power dissipation of the RFID reader, coupled with limited operational range, prohibits the realization of energy-efficient multi-hop data dissemination using RFID tags.

Ambient backscatter [24] is a novel communication paradigm, however, despite recent advancements of these passive receivers [30], the communication range of ambient backscatter devices is constrained by the power of the ambient signal source. Realistic signal powers of ambient sources, *e.g.*, from TV transmissions, are likely to constrain the communication range to only a few meters. In this work, we have demonstrated ZIPPY operating in an indoor testbed with challenging RF propagation conditions, achieving multi-hop connectivity with per-hop links of up to 10 meters.

Dual-radio wireless sensor platforms incorporating a high-powered transceiver and an ultra-low power receiver have been proposed in [4], [36], [28] and [9]. Although these prototype platforms support asynchronous rendezvous and single-hop data dissemination, they do not support carrier frequency randomization, and have not been experimentally evaluated in a testbed. We have shown experimentally using our prototype wireless sensor platform that carrier frequency randomization is a prerequisite for robust multi-hop data dissemination using low-complexity OOK receivers.

7. CONCLUSIONS

This paper is motivated by the need for rapid and energy efficient dissemination of rare events through multi-hop wireless networks. We present ZIPPY, a paradigm shift in protocol design, where the fundamental design trade-off between mote life-time and end-to-end latency is decoupled. ZIPPY supports on-demand multi-hop flooding with end-to-end latencies of tens of milliseconds, while dissipating less than ten microwatts during periods of inactivity. We detail the design, analysis and prototype implementation of ZIPPY, and extensively evaluate its performance in a laboratory setting and in an indoor testbed.

Acknowledgements. We thank Marco Zimmerling, our shepherd Kamin Whitehouse, and the anonymous reviewers for their valuable feedback, Roman Lim and Balz Maag for their FlockLab feature extensions and support, and Reto Da Forno for his power optimizations on the ZIPPY prototype. This work was scientifically evaluated by the SNSF and financed by the Swiss Confederation and by Nano-Tera.ch.

8. REFERENCES

[1] J. Ansari, D. Pankin, and P. Mähönen. Radio-triggered wake-ups with addressing capabilities for extremely low power sensor network applications. *International Journal of Wireless Information Networks*, 2009.

[2] D. Ash. A comparison between OOK/ASK and FSK modulation techniques for radio links. Technical report, RF Monolithics Inc, 1992.

[3] H. Ba, I. Demirkol, and W. Heinzelman. Feasibility and benefits of passive RFID wake-up radios for wireless sensor networks. In *Global Telecommunications Conference (GLOBECOM)*. IEEE, 2010.

[4] J. Brown, J. Finney, C. Efstratiou, B. Green, N. Davies, M. Lowton, and G. Kortuem. Network interrupts: supporting delay sensitive applications in low power wireless control networks. In *Proceedings of the 2nd ACM Workshop on Challenged Networks*. ACM, 2007.

[5] I. Demirkol, C. Ersoy, and F. Alagoz. MAC protocols for wireless sensor networks: a survey. *Communications Magazine, IEEE*, 2006.

[6] I. Demirkol, C. Ersoy, and E. Onur. Wake-up receivers for wireless sensor networks: benefits and challenges. *Wireless Communications, IEEE*, 2009.

[7] P. Dutta, M. Grimmer, A. Arora, S. Bibyk, and D. Culler. Design of a wireless sensor network platform for detecting rare, random, and ephemeral events. In *Proceedings of the 4th International Symposium on Information Processing in Sensor Networks (IPSN)*. IEEE, 2005.

[8] F. Ferrari, M. Zimmerling, L. Thiele, and O. Saukh. Efficient network flooding and time synchronization with glossy. In *Proceedings of the 10th International Conference on Information Processing in Sensor Networks (IPSN)*. IEEE, 2011.

[9] G. Gamm, S. Stoecklin, and L. Reindl. Wake-up receiver operating at 433 MHz. In *Proceedings of the 11th International Multi-Conference on Systems, Signals and Devices (SSD)*, 2014.

[10] G. U. Gamm and L. M. Reindl. Smart metering using distributed wake-up receivers. In *Proceedings of the IEEE International Instrumentation and Measurement Technology Conference (I2MTC)*. IEEE, 2012.

[11] G. U. Gamm, M. Sippel, M. Kostic, and L. M. Reindl. Low power wake-up receiver for wireless sensor nodes. In *Proceedings of the 6th International Conference on Intelligent Sensors, Sensor Networks and Information Processing (ISSNIP)*. IEEE, 2010.

[12] L. Girard, J. Beutel, S. Gruber, J. Hunziker, R. Lim, and S. Weber. A custom acoustic emission monitoring system for harsh environments: application to freezing-induced damage in alpine rock-walls. *Geoscientific Instrumentation, Methods and Data Systems Discussions*, 2012.

[13] W. Granzer, C. Reinisch, and W. Kastner. Future challenges for building automation: wireless and security. In *Proceedings of the IEEE International Symposium on Industrial Electronics (ISIE)*, 2010.

[14] C. Guo, L. C. Zhong, and J. M. Rabaey. Low power distributed MAC for ad hoc sensor radio networks. In *IEEE Global Telecommunications Conference*. IEEE, 2001.

[15] V. Jain, R. Biswas, and D. P. Agrawal. Energy-efficient and reliable medium access in sensor networks. In *IEEE International Symposium on a World of Wireless, Mobile and Multimedia Networks (WoWMoM)*. IEEE, 2007.

[16] R. Jurdak, A. Ruzzelli, and G. O'Hare. Radio sleep mode optimization in wireless sensor networks. *IEEE Transactions on Mobile Computing*, 2010.

[17] R. Jurdak, A. G. Ruzzelli, and G. M. O'Hare. Multi-hop RFID wake-up radio: design, evaluation and energy tradeoffs. In *Proceedings of the 17th International Conference on Computer, Communications and Networks (ICCCN)*. IEEE, 2008.

[18] G. Kim, Y. Lee, S. Bang, I. Lee, Y. Kim, D. Sylvester, and D. Blaauw. A 695pW standby power optical wake-up receiver for wireless sensor nodes. In *Custom Integrated Circuits Conference (CICC)*. IEEE, 2012.

[19] S. Kim, S. Pakzad, D. Culler, J. Demmel, G. Fenves, S. Glaser, and M. Turon. Health monitoring of civil infrastructures using wireless sensor networks. In *Proceedings of the 6th International Symposium on Information Processing in Sensor Networks (IPSN)*. IEEE, 2007.

[20] K. Leentvaar and J. Flint. The capture effect in FM receivers. *IEEE Transactions on Communications*, 1976.

[21] R. Lim, F. Ferrari, M. Zimmerling, C. Walser, P. Sommer, and J. Beutel. FlockLab: A testbed for distributed, synchronized tracing and profiling of wireless embedded systems. In *Proceedings of the 12th International Conference on Information Processing in Sensor Networks (IPSN)*. ACM, 2013.

[22] R. Lim, B. Maag, B. Dissler, J. Beutel, and L. Thiele. A testbed for fine-grained tracing of time sensitive behavior in wireless sensor networks. In *Local Computer Networks Workshops*, 2015.

[23] E.-Y. Lin, J. M. Rabaey, and A. Wolisz. Power-efficient rendez-vous schemes for dense wireless sensor networks. In *International Conference on Communications*. IEEE, 2004.

[24] V. Liu, A. Parks, V. Talla, S. Gollakota, D. Wetherall, and J. R. Smith. Ambient backscatter: wireless communication out of thin air. In *Proceedings of the ACM SIGCOMM Conference*. ACM, 2013.

[25] S. Mahlknecht and M. S. Durante. WUR-MAC: energy efficient wakeup receiver based MAC protocol. In *Proceedings of the 8th IFAC FET*, 2009.

[26] G. Marsaglia. The mother of all random generators, 1994.

[27] R. Musaloiu-E, C.-J. Liang, and A. Terzis. Koala: Ultra-low power data retrieval in wireless sensor networks. In *Proceedings of the 7th Conference on Information Processing in Sensor Networks (IPSN)*. IEEE, 2008.

[28] J. Oller, I. Demirkol, J. Casademont, and J. Paradells. Design, development, and performance evaluation of a low-cost, low-power wake-up radio system for wireless sensor networks. *ACM Transactions on Sensor Networks*, 2013.

[29] J. Oller, I. Demirkol, J. Casademont, J. Paradells, G. U. Gamm, and L. Reindl. Performance evaluation and comparative analysis of subcarrier modulation wake-up radio systems for energy-efficient wireless sensor networks. *Sensors*, 2013.

[30] A. N. Parks, A. Liu, S. Gollakota, and J. R. Smith. Turbocharging ambient backscatter communication. In *Proceedings of the 2014 ACM SIGCOMM Conference*. ACM, 2014.

[31] P. Z. Peebles Jr. *Digital communication systems.* Prentice-Hall, 1987.

[32] C. Petrioli, D. Spenza, P. Tommasino, and A. Trifiletti. A novel wake-up receiver with addressing capability for wireless sensor nodes. In *Proceedings of the International Conference on Distributed Computing in Sensor Systems (DCOSS)*, 2014.

[33] N. Pletcher, S. Gambini, and J. Rabaey. A 65 μW, 1.9 GHz RF to digital baseband wakeup receiver for wireless sensor nodes. In *Proceedings of the Custom Integrated Circuits Conference (CICC)*. IEEE, 2007.

[34] J. Polastre, J. Hill, and D. Culler. Versatile low power media access for wireless sensor networks. In *Proceedings of the 2nd International Conference on Embedded Networked Sensor Systems (SenSys)*. ACM, 2004.

[35] C. V. Pollack Jr. Wireless cardiac event alert monitoring is feasible and effective in the emergency department and adjacent waiting areas. *Critical Pathways in Cardiology*, 2009.

[36] T. Prabhakar, N. Soumya, P. Muralidharan, and H. Jamadagni. A Novel Wake-Up Radio WSN Mote. In *Proceedings of the Texas Instruments India Educators' Conference (TIIEC)*, 2013.

[37] I. Reed. A class of multiple-error-correcting codes and the decoding scheme. *Transactions of the IRE Professional Group on Information Theory*, 1954.

[38] A. Sample, D. Yeager, P. Powledge, A. Mamishev, and J. Smith. Design of an RFID-based battery-free programmable sensing platform. *IEEE Transactions on Instrumentation and Measurement*, 2008.

[39] C. Schurgers, V. Tsiatsis, S. Ganeriwal, and M. Srivastava. Optimizing sensor networks in the energy-latency-density design space. *IEEE Transactions on Mobile Computing*, 2002.

[40] M. Wilhelm, V. Lenders, and J. Schmitt. On the reception of concurrent transmissions in wireless sensor networks. *IEEE Transactions on Wireless Communications*, 2014.

[41] K. Yadav, I. Kymissis, and P. R. Kinget. A 4.4μW wake-up receiver using ultrasound data communications. In *VLSI Circuits (VLSIC), 2011 Symposium on*. IEEE, 2011.

[42] X. Yang and N. Vaidya. A wakeup scheme for sensor networks: Achieving balance between energy saving and end-to-end delay. In *Proceedings of the 10th Real-Time and Embedded Technology and Applications Symposium (RTAS)*. IEEE, 2004.

[43] P. Zappi, E. Farella, and L. Benini. Tracking motion direction and distance with pyroelectric IR sensors. *IEEE Sensors Journal*, 2010.

[44] P. Zhang, P. Hu, V. Pasikanti, and D. Ganesan. Ekhonet: high speed ultra low-power backscatter for next generation sensors. In *Proceedings of the 20th Annual International Conference on Mobile Computing and Networking (MobiCom)*. ACM, 2014.

[45] M. Zimmerling, P. Kumar, F. Ferrari, L. Mottola, and L. Thiele. Energy-efficient real-time communication in multi-hop low-power wireless networks. Technical report, TIK Report No. 356, 2015.

Rise of the Indoor Crowd: Reconstruction of Building Interior View via Mobile Crowdsourcing

Si Chen†, Muyuan Li†, Kui Ren†, Xinwen Fu‡, Chunming Qiao†

†Department of Computer Science and Engineering, SUNY at Buffalo

‡Department of Computer Science, University of Massachusetts Lowell

{schen23, muyuanli, kuiren, qiao}@buffalo.edu, xinwenfu@cs.uml.edu

ABSTRACT

Crowdsourcing is a technology with the potential to revolutionize large-scale data gathering in an extremely cost-effective manner. It provides an unprecedented means of collecting data from the physical world, particularly through the use of modern smartphones, which are equipped with high-resolution cameras and various micro-electrical sensors. In this paper, we address the critical task of reconstructing the indoor interior view of a building from crowdsourced data. We propose, design, and prototype IndoorCrowd2D, a smartphone-empowered crowdsourcing system for indoor scene reconstruction. We first formulate the problem via trackable models and then employ a divide and conquer approach to address the inherently incomplete, opportunistic, and noisy crowdsourced data. By utilizing the image information and sensory data in a coordinated way, our system demonstrates high result-accuracy, as well as allows a gradual build-up procedure of the hallway skeleton. Our evaluation result shows that IndoorCrowd2D achieves a precision around 85%, a 100% recall and a F-score around 95% for reconstructing college buildings from 1,151 datasets uploaded by 25 users. This reveals that our image and sensor hybrid method is more robust to overcome errors and outliers as compared to image-only method.

Categories and Subject Descriptors

H.3.4 [[**Information Storage and Retrieval**]: Systems and Software

General Terms

Algorithms; Design; Experimentation; Performance

Keywords

Crowdsourcing; indoor scene; panorama; multi-dimensional sensing

SenSys'15, November 1–4, 2015, Seoul, South Korea..

© 2015 ACM. ISBN 978-1-4503-3631-4/15/11 ...$15.00.

DOI: http://dx.doi.org/10.1145/2809695.2809702.

1. INTRODUCTION

The emerging technology has witnessed the birth of virtual tour applications that connect the physical and cyber world by enabling an immersive visual experience. The industrial state-of-the-art Google Street View [20] project provides 360 degree panoramic views along many public streets in the world, covering about 5 million miles of roads and more than 3,000 cities. However, unlike outdoor environment, only 91 indoor street view transit locations around the world are currently available from Google Map. The major obstacle to ubiquitous coverage is the complexity of the indoor environment [24]. As a result, existing outdoor street-view reconstruction techniques either cannot be directly applied to an indoor environment or become very costly.

Currently, indoor visualization has been studied by robotic and computer vision communities. One of the state-of-the-art solution is named simultaneous localization and mapping (SLAM) [13, 24, 44]. In [24], the authors present a SLAM-based human-operated backpack system which equipped with 2D laser scanners and inertial measurement units (IMU) to automatically reconstruct building interior view. Xiao and Furukawa [44] reconstruct the structure and interior view of world museums by jointly using several advanced computer vision algorithms and large-scale laser scanning 3D points. However, most of current SLAM-based indoor scene reconstruction techniques require specialize equipment to capture indoor scene and cannot be scaled well. Alternatively, some researches focus on utilizing image-based pose estimation techniques such as Structure from Motion (SfM) [1,36,37,40] and Multiview-stereo [17, 18] to process image collections and perceive spatial relationships of these images. However, indoor scenes are usually full of structurally similar and textureless objects, which violates assumptions of vision-based algorithms. Hence, these vision based solutions are usually unable to provide accurate spatial structure results at a large scale [14].

In this paper, we propose IndoorCrowd2D, a smartphone empowered system utilizing the power of the crowd for helping us reconstruct the building interior views at large scale and with low cost. Our system is able to provide immersive panoramic image viewing experience for building interior views with an effective scene navigation mechanism. It breaks away from established approaches to reconstruct indoor scenes, and explores an alternative architecture based on crowdsourcing and mobile-sensing. IndoorCrowd2D is expected to extend existing online map service to indoor environment at a large scale. Moreover, IndoorCrowd2D can enable a variety of applications including indoor navigation, localization and emergency management.

The power of crowdsourcing has been confirmed by the success of such projects as OpenStreetMap. It attracts more than one million contributors, and has achieved impressive accuracy in labeling approximately 21,107,200 miles of road across the world. Meanwhile, the ubiquity of smartphones and wearable devices facilitates extending the scale of such systems, liberating users from the need for a computer. Recent work has used crowdsourced smartphone inertial data to infer user trajectories and use them to reconstruct indoor digital map [2,9,21,27,34,49]. [19] takes one step further, both image and inertial data are used to generate an indoor floor plan.

To the best of our knowledge, we are the first to propose and implement a smartphone-based crowdsourcing system that explores the power of untrained users to generate building interactive panoramic maps at large scale following an open-source approach. Our system design focuses on indoor panoramic map generation. The final output of our system contains multiple panoramic images for visualizing the building interior view. We also provide a navigable hallway skeleton for each floor that enable users to easily navigate through a large scale indoor environment. Users can take an immersive virtual tour of a building by using an Internet browser.

We solve two major challenges within the IndoorCrowd2D design. Unlike the traditional indoor scene reconstruction technique, which utilizes professional equipment [13,20,24] to capture images in a pre-defined path, the image upload from the crowd are determined by many individual users. Therefore, the camera positions, view directions and camera moving trajectories are unknown in advance. This in turn creates a challenge when crowdsourcing and positioning indoor interior image at a large scale. To overcome the first challenge, we draw on multi-dimensional sensing. First, the inertial sensor inside smartphones combine with image data is utilized to track user movements. Then, we leverage multiple users' tracking information to re-establish the building hallway skeleton. Moreover, the output hallway skeleton offers an auxiliary information to help generating indoor scene panorama with the correct position. Regarding to the second challenge in our design, the crowdsourced data is inherently incomplete, opportunistic, and noisy. For instance, the image data is captured and uploaded by different users with a wide variety of mobile devices under various lighting conditions. Hence, our system should be robust and be able to handle heterogeneous, redundant, inaccurate and low-quality data. To solve this issue, IndoorCrowd2D employs a divide and conquer approach: i) the mobile application with a real-time data quality feedback mechanism is designed to guide users to provide good quality data. ii) a hierarchical processing pipeline at the cloud computing backend is designed to gradually filter out redundant and low-quality data. In addition, the building interior view reconstruction algorithm is engineered to guarantee a high accuracy and noise-tolerant performance. We summarize our contributions as follows:

- We formulate the problem via designing two trackable models, and also employ the divide and conquer approach to address the inherently incomplete and noisy crowdsourced data. Image information and sensory data are both unitized in a synergetic manner for the purpose of improving the results accuracy and allowing gradual building-up of the hallway skeleton. In particular, we design an aggregation algorithm, which utilize the visual information as "anchor point" to aggregate crowdsourced sensory data.

- We prototype the IndoorCrowd2D system by implementing a mobile application and a cloud computing backend. The mobile application offers the users a convenient method to capture the indoor interior view. Furthermore, the cloud computing backend is able to automatically generate the interactive panoramic maps.

- We evaluate the IndoorCrowd2D prototype in real-world scenarios. The performance of IndoorCrowd2D exhibits a significantly high recall, good precision and high F-measure. Based on our evaluation result, with approximately 425 crowdsourced datasets from 25 users, we can integrate the hallway skeleton and also generate the panoramas within it.

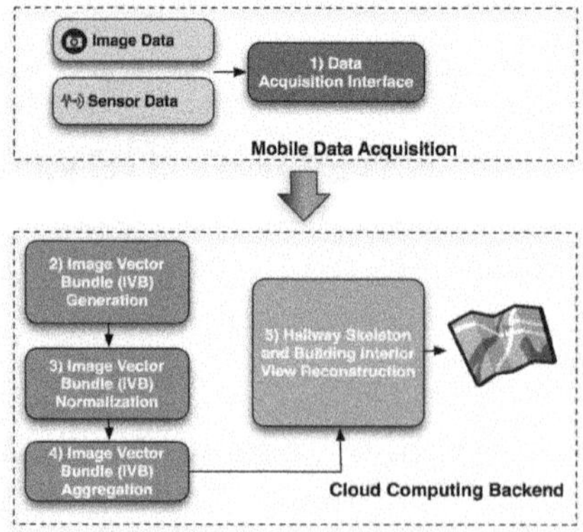

Figure 1: The architecture of IndoorCrowd2D.

The rest of this paper expands on each of these contributions, beginning with the design overview and system architecture (Section 2), followed by the system modeling (Section 3), design details (Section 4) and the implementation of a prototyped IndoorCrowd2D (Section 5). Experiments are conducted to assess this system (Section 6). After discussing the limitations of our system (Section 7), our work is compared with related works (Section 8). We summarize this paper in Section 9.

2. DESIGN OVERVIEW

IndoorCrowd2D is a smartphone-empowered crowdsourcing system for building interior view reconstruction. It leverages crowdsourced image and sensory data and does not rely on the priori that knowing any building interior information. The result of IndoorCrowd2D is an interactive panoramic map, which can be divided into two parts: i) indoor panoramic images and ii) building hallway skeleton. The first part aims at creating appealing panoramic images for visualizing the indoor interior view. The second part is built for providing an interactive navigation mechanism through these panoramas.

Compare with conventional approach, which hires volunteers to take pictures and logs the location and direction of each picture on the digital floor plan manually, it is very challenging to build up an accurate and complete interactive panoramic map by leveraging crowdsourced data only. This is because the crowdsourced individual user data are inherently opportunistic, incomplete, and noisy. Hence, we employ the divide and conquer approach, which is built upon two models: *indoor spatial model* (Section 3.1) and *indoor user trajectory model* (Section 3.2). The first model discretizes the continuous indoor space into grid matrix and represents it as unit cells in metric terms. The second model defines a special data structure named *image vector bundle*, which aims at providing accurate user movement information by combining both the sensory and the image data. Moreover, we apply a reduced Manhattan World assumption (RMW) [12] to simplify the structure of the hallway skeleton. In addition, this hallway skeleton structure is tailored for panoramic image navigation. Based on these two models, a complete building interior map is gradually discovered as long as sufficient crowdsourced data are collected.

As shown in Fig. 1, the architecture of the IndoorCrowd2D system consists of two components: an Android application runs on a mobile platform and a cloud computing backend. The mobile application is responsible for crowdsourced data acquisition. It allows users to shoot and upload building interior scenes annotated with synchronized sensory data including compass, gyroscope and accelerometer to the cloud. Then, the cloud processes multiple datasets simultaneously. For each dataset, the cloud first convert the sensory data and image data to an image vector bundle to represent the geospatial relationship among each consecutive image. Moreover, the cloud normalizes each image vector bundle based on the RMW assumption. For multiple user datasets, the cloud aggregates geospatially-similar image vector bundles together. Finally, our system completely reconstruct the indoor panoramic images, and also the hallway skeleton of the building.

Based on the flow of operations, we further divide the whole system into five modules, namely: 1) data acquisition interface (Section 4.1); 2) image vector bundle generation (Section 4.2); 3) image vector bundle normalization (Section 4.3); 4) image vector bundle aggregation (Section 4.4); 5) hallway skeleton and building interior view reconstruction (Section 4.5).

Since our approach does not require any professional equipments or special trainings, it alleviates the overhead of building interior view reconstruction compared to the conventional approach. Particularly, users are only involved in the data acquisition module. A typical use case could be: a user holds his/her smartphone, starts our mobile application, enters a room (our mobile application takes pictures automatically), walks around inside the room, then moves towards another room through a hallway. To save energy, our mobile application only captures the sensory data and the image data when user starts shooting. Also, it logs out the sensory data when user stops capturing the scene.

3. SYSTEM MODELING

3.1 Indoor Spatial Model

In IndoorCrowd2D, we design our own indoor spatial model to build the coordinates of the 2D indoor space. It represents the indoor environment by a homogeneous grid matrix, which reflects the accessibility of the indoor environment

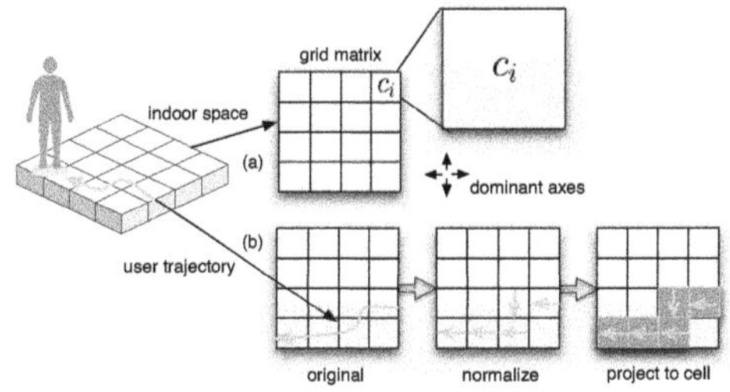

Figure 2: Indoor spatial model for IndoorCrowd2D

(shown in Fig. 2). Specifically, each cell contains a numerical value and is initialized as 0. It increased by 1 every time if a user trajectory is successfully projected to the cell grids. In addition, we store the user trajectory information to the cell for further processing. This model is tailored to IndoorCrowd2D because it provides trackable results and is applicable for our divide and conquer approach.

In order to initialize the grid matrix for each floor as well as preserve the structural and geometrical properties of the space at the same time, we introduce the reduced Manhattan World (RMW) assumption. According to the RMW assumption, we assume two perpendicular dominant axes are existed for each building floor. Also, each line segment (most corridors) inside the building floor is supposed to align with one of the two axes. Compare with predominant path-based space assumption that applied in [2, 19], the RMW assumption offers the following advantages in our building interior view reconstruction system: i) it produces clean, simple hallway skeleton as outputs, which is good enough for indoor panoramic map navigation. ii) it normalizes the orientation of each image, which benefits the reconstruction of the indoor interior views. Note that the RMW assumption may not suitable for some particular buildings, which are not predominantly rectangular (e.g. the Pentagon). However, according to [38], more than 90% of modern buildings are rectangular actually. We moreover discuss how to reconstruct non predominantly rectangular building and the possible impact of accuracy in Section 7.

Based on the RMW assumption, the grid matrix initialization process can be divided into two steps: First, we detect the dominant axes of the building (See Section 4.3). Second, we divide the indoor building space into a uniform square unit cells $C = \{c_{0,0}, c_{0,1}, .., c_{n,n}\}$ upon the detected dominant axes of the building. Then, we initialize each cell with value 0.

3.2 Indoor User Trajectory Model

We further put forward an indoor user trajectory model to provide accurate matches among the inherently incomplete, uncoordinated, and noisy user data. In this model, we propose to use a tailored image vector data structure to not only represent user movement inferred from the sensory data, but also include the corresponding image information. This proposed model takes an individual user trajectory, i.e., a sequence of captured images annotated with sensor data as the input. Next, it outputs a discretized image vector bundle, which is comprised of many image vectors and the geospatial information of these image vectors (shown in Fig. 3). Then, each image vector is mapped to a unit cell in the space model. The spatial relationships of the unit cells

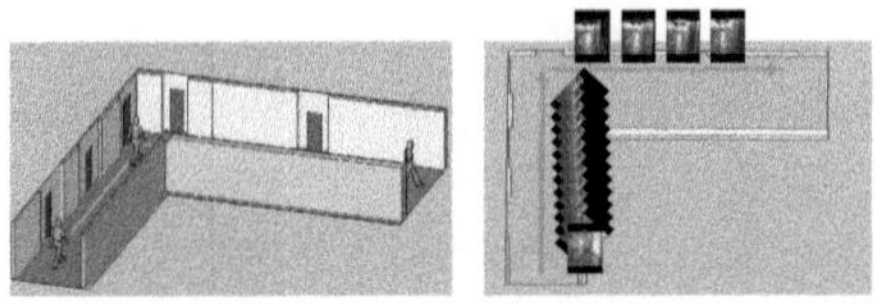

Figure 3: Indoor user trajectory model for IndoorCrowd2D

are further deduced from the image vectors. In general, our proposed models spontaneously allow the hallway skeleton to be built-up gradually.

We define the user trajectory by a sequence of image vectors $\boldsymbol{Z} = \{\vec{z}_1, \vec{z}_2, ..., \vec{z}_t, ..., \vec{z}_T\}$ represents the geospatial characteristics of user movement at each time t during the total track life T. We also refer $\boldsymbol{Z}^{\kappa}$ as an image vector bundle (IVB) generated by user with a reference number κ.

For each time step, we generate an image vector $\vec{z}$ by converting the raw sensor and the image data through image vector bundle generation algorithm (Section 4.2). Each of the image vectors $\vec{z}_t = [x^t, y^t, \vec{\psi}^t, \boldsymbol{I}^t, t]$ represents one user's movement, which include relative spatial location $[x, y]$, heading direction $\vec{\psi}$, image $\boldsymbol{I}$ at time t and timestamp. All the information is all extracted through the sensor data and camera visual tracking. Since a discretized indoor spatial model is applied, the normalization of each image vector $\vec{z}$ and the projection of the $\vec{z}$ to a cell $c_{i,j}$ are necessary.

3.3 Basic Elements of Building Interior View

In IndoorCrowd2D, we consider five basic elements of every building interior view, each of which defines a particular indoor scenario: corridor, room, wing, intersection, and open area (shown in Fig. 4). All of these elements have its own special visual or sensory features. We now briefly explain these basic elements: 1) Corridor, it is a narrow tract and usually have a long passageway. It is full of textureless walls and have various lightning conditions. The users' moving trajectories inside corridor are expected as a bidirectional flow; 2) Room, it is a portion of space separated by walls. An occupied room usually contains a few texture-rich man-made objects. The moving patterns of the user inside a room may differ a lot and may cover all locations where are reachable to the user. 3) Wing, it is a special corridor which one side is wall and the other side is transparent windows or open space. It usually contains more visual textures compare to corridor. However, the lightning conditions may various a lot due to the affect of sun-light. 4) Intersection, a place at which two or more corridors (or wings) cross. Users take turns at the intersection point and therefore create a unique moving pattern. 5) Open Area, an open space where it is like a room without walls (e.g. a lobby). Users could reach this place through nearly all possible directions. Therefore, the aggregated user trajectories could be complex at this place.

4. DESIGN DETAILS

4.1 Data Acquisition Interface Design

Data acquisition interface is designed for collecting images and sensory data from each user. In order to enhance the overall crowdsourced data quality from users, we design a

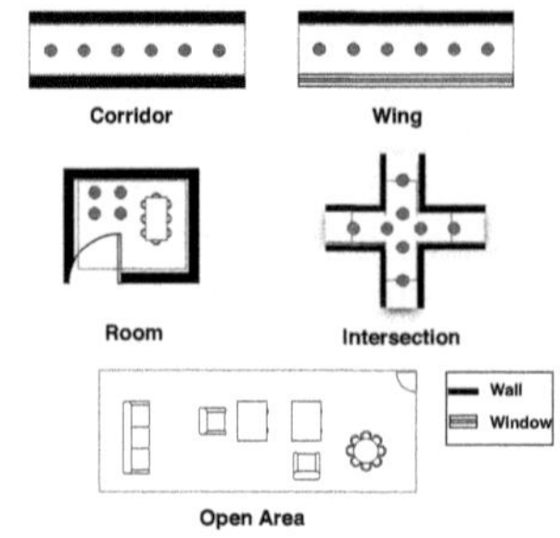

Figure 4: Basic elements of building interior view

mobile application that is deployed on user's smartphone. Compare to conventional approach that user requires to use specialize equipment, locate and logs the direction of each picture and walk through a pre-define path to capture the indoor scene, our application provides a much more handy data capture process. Indeed, we simplify the whole data capturing process and only require users to put minimal effort in capturing the indoor scene by using our mobile application. We further conduct a mobile application usability study in Section 6.

Proactive Data Collection. IndoorCrowd2D follows a proactive data collecting mechanism. Our application uses the smartphone's back camera to capture the indoor scene and does not require any other specialized equipment. Once start capturing, users can move freely and steadily holding the smartphone vertically or horizontally (landscape mode). Our mobile application automatically takes pictures for every t seconds and records the sensory data (accelerometer, gyroscope and compass) with the timestamp simultaneously.

Real-time Data Quality Feedback. In our smartphone application, we implement a real-time data quality feedback mechanism similar to [49] to guide the users to provide high quality data. While the user is capturing the scene, our application continues estimating the data quality metrics by processing the sensor data and the image data in real-time. The metrics are measured by the smartphone application include: i) linear acceleration, ii) angular acceleration and iii) the number of SURF [4] features in each picture. Moreover, the value of linear acceleration and angular acceleration can be directly read from mobile platform API, whereas, the number of SURF features should be obtained from the SURF feature detection algorithm by leveraging the OpenCV [7] library.

If the measured values of i) and ii) are beyond a certain threshold ($\vec{v}_h$, $\vec{\omega}_h$), it indicates that the user either moves or turns too fast. In this case, a hint appears on the screen to remind the user to slow down. If our application detects the number of features in iii) falls below a predefined threshold (τ_h), this exhibits that the user shoots feature-less objects, such as walls, and thereby, our application displays a hint that guides the user to record other places and avoids some feature-less objects.

Fig.5 shows the screen displays the SURF features of a image on the mobile platform in real-time.

4.2 Image Vector Bundle Generation

IndoorCrowd2D uses both the image and the sensor data to detect user motions and fuses these two orthogonal domains of data together to generate the image vector bun-

Figure 5: Detect SURF feature points of a image in real-time

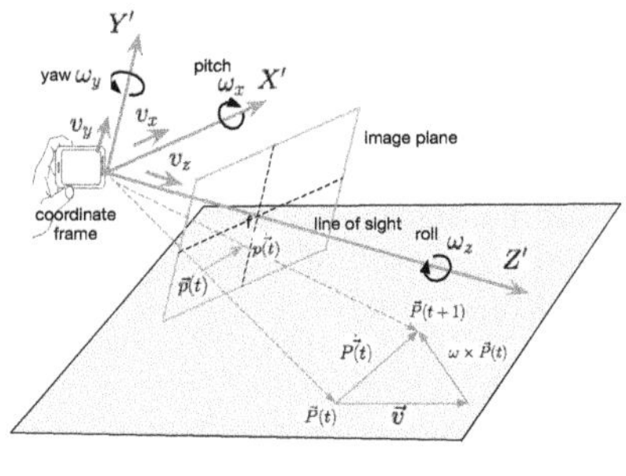

Figure 6: Optical flow model

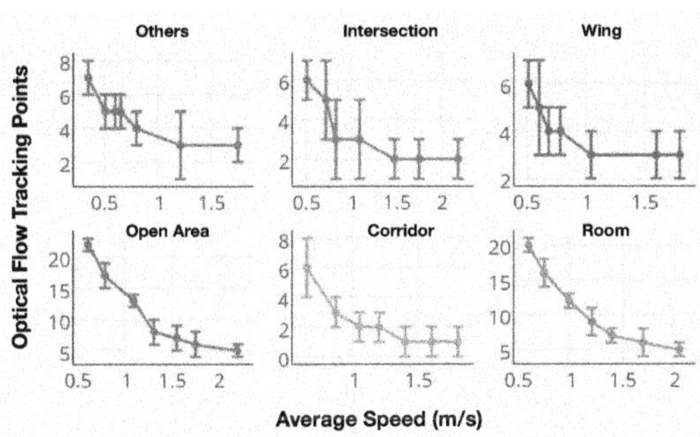

Figure 7: The relationship between user average speed and the number of optical flow tracking points

dle $\boldsymbol{Z}$. For each image vector $\vec{z}_t = [x^t, y^t, \vec{\psi}^t, \boldsymbol{I}^t, t] \in \boldsymbol{Z}$, the image data $\boldsymbol{I}^t$ and timestamp t are obtained directly from smartphone. The relative spatial location $[x^t, y^t]$ is initialized as 0 and calculated based on the difference of smartphone spatial location between the consecutive image vectors. The initial heading direction $\vec{\psi}^0 \in \vec{z}_0$, is acquired by the compass as long as the user starts capturing. As it is pointed out by [31], the compass is erroneous in indoor environment due to the higher magnetic inference in indoors than outdoors. Therefore, a compass calibration is necessary before starting the scene capturing. Note that the calibrated compass value is only applied to set the initial heading direction $\vec{\psi}^0$ of the user.

Relative Spatial Location Calculation. For each two consecutive image vector $\vec{z}_{t-1}$ and $\vec{z}_t$, the angle difference of heading direction between $\vec{\psi}^{t-1}$ and $\vec{\psi}^t$ is derived by the heading offset estimation method [31] and the reading of gyroscope [29, 42]. Furthermore, the distance $|z_{t-1}, z_t|$ is calculated by fusing the sensory data and the image data.

For the sensory data (accelerometer, gyroscope and compass), step counting method [29,48] is applied to measure the distance. For the image data, the relative speed of motion of the user between $\boldsymbol{I}^{t-1}$ and $\boldsymbol{I}^t$ is measured by using an optical flow model [25]. For a given pair of consecutive images $\boldsymbol{I}^{t-1}$ and $\boldsymbol{I}^t$ with the same or extremely similar indoor scenes, we can use the corresponding image feature movements (feature vectors) to estimate user velocity. The image feature is defined as some specific structures in a image. Fig. 6 illustrates the optical flow model used in the IndoorCrowd2D, which the smartphone held by a user moves in the ground-plane with the velocity $\vec{v} = (v_x, v_y, v_z)^t$ and the rotational velocity $\vec{\omega} = (\omega_x, \omega_y, \omega_z)^t$. Also, through using a perspective projection, the user movement trajectory $\dot{\vec{P}}(t)$ in the ground plane is expressed by the dynamics of the feature vector $\dot{\vec{p}}(t)$ in the image plane. Importantly, we require users holding their camera at the same height when applying the optical flow model. This criteria can be ensured by checking the relative angle change of the smartphone through gyroscope. Based on the optical flow model, the feature vector $\dot{\vec{p}}(t)$ is calculated using the iterative pyramidal Lucas-Kanade [6] method. The relationship between user average speed and the number of optical flow tracking points is shown in Fig. 7. According to the result, the optical flow based method provides auxiliary result when the user average speed is less than 1m/s.

Since the rotational velocity $\vec{\omega}$ can be directly acquired from the gyroscope sensor, the velocity of the feature vector $\vec{v}$ in the image plan can be simplified as:

$$\frac{\partial \dot{\vec{p}}(t)}{\partial t} = \vec{v} = \tilde{v}_x * \boldsymbol{i} + \tilde{v}_y * \boldsymbol{j} \tag{1}$$

Based on the equation (1), if the focal length of the smartphone camera f and the current distance H to the scene are given, we are able to calculate user velocity as:

$$\vec{v} = \vec{v}\frac{H}{f} \tag{2}$$

Next, the timestamp t is used to measure the time duration between every two consecutive images, and thereby, calculate the distance $|z_{t-1}, z_t|$. To merge the distance inferred from both sensory and image data, IndoorCrowd2D assigns a weight for each result and use the weighted linear combination method to achieve the merging purpose. Thus, the relative spatial location $[x^t, y^t]$ for $\vec{z}_t$ is easily acquired based on the distance $|z_{t-1}, z_t|$ and the heading direction $\vec{\psi}^t$.

Figure 8: (a). Contour of a building (b). Two dominant axes in red and blue picked up by the contour sample in cyan

4.3 Image Vector Bundle Normalization

After the image vector generation process, we further normalize the heading direction $\vec{\psi}^t$ for each image vector $\vec{z}_t \in \boldsymbol{Z}$ using the reduced Manhattan World (RMW) assumption. Under the RMW assumption, we assume that each building has two perpendicular dominant axes in 2D and each line segment (mostly corridors) inside the building is aligned to

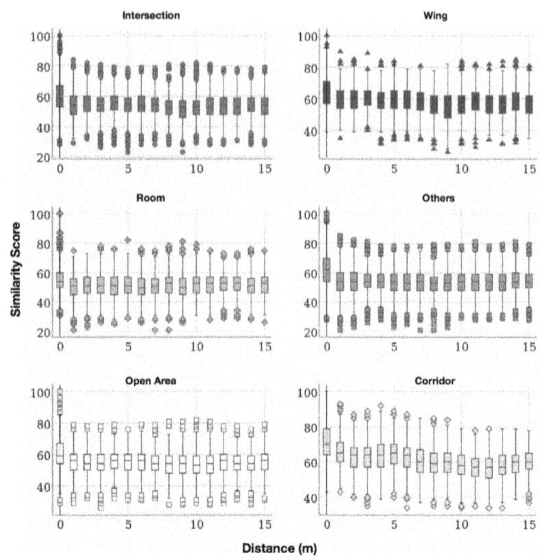

Figure 9: The relationship between image location and pHash similarity score (fixed walking direction).

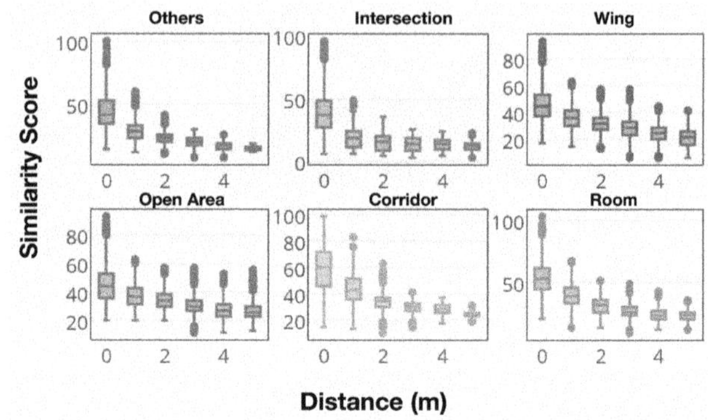

Figure 10: The relationship between image location and the similarity score of image feature matching (fixed walking direction).

one of the two axes. IndoorCrowd2D applies the following steps to detect the dominant axes of the building and align the user heading direction to one of the two dominant axes:

Dominant Axes Detection. We determine the two dominant axes by analyzing the building outlines that obtains directly from the Google Maps. This concept is identical to that in [39]. However [39] does not present an implementation and we hence conduct our own. First, we apply both the thresholding and the edge detection to the target image. Then, through utilizing the Canny Detector from the OpenCV, it extracts the contour of the building, which in the form of a series of clockwise vectors as illustrated in Fig. 8 (a). The next step is to normalize the vector directions to $0-90$ degrees, and also place those angles into a histogram. Through sampling the contour points every few pixels, the impact of short contours (contours only one pixel in length) is avoided. The average angle from the most frequent bins is taken as the direction of the first dominant axis, whereas the second dominant axis is perpendicular to the first dominant axis, as shown in Fig. 8 (b).

Normalize Heading Direction. we check the heading direction $\vec{\psi^t}$ for each image vector $\vec{z}_t$. As the gyroscope is accurate enough for detecting the change of the heading direction [29,42], it is sufficient to normalize the heading direction into four possible movement direction ($\uparrow, \rightarrow, \downarrow, \leftarrow$) in a two-dimensional space. For each image vector bundle $\boldsymbol{Z}$, the heading direction $\vec{\psi^t}$ is normalized by checking whether the value difference for each consecutive image vector is larger than 45 degrees.

4.4 Image Vector Bundle Aggregation

The image vector bundle aggregation module is designed to merge multiple image vector bundles. The main objective of the image vector bundle aggregation module is to achieve robust performance across a large variety of image vector bundles generated by different users, different smartphone models or various indoor environments. In order to decrease the complexity of its input, IndoorCrowd2D adapts a hierarchical approach wherein image vector bundle matching and merging take place in the following three steps.

pHash Filtering. The primary focus of the pHash algorithm [47] is calculating a fingerprint or hash of a particular image based upon the various visual features of its content, rather than processing the raw bits in the image. Unlike cryptographic hash functions such as SHA-1, in which small changes in input lead to drastically different hash values, pHash produces similar hash values if the visual features of the two images are similar. Thus, the similarity between two images is computed by calculating the Hamming distance between the two output fingerprints produced by pHash. pHash is very fast compared to other image similarity comparison methods, it only takes 65 seconds to hash 100 images. Fig. 9 shows the relationship between image location and pHash similarity score under different building interior scenes. The x-axis in this figure represents the linear distance between the shooting locations of the two images. According to the result, if we set the similarity score threshold properly, the pHash algorithm is able to reject most of the incorrect match but only preserve structurally identical indoor images (images shoot at the same indoor location).

Image Feature Extraction and Matching. To precisely match two image vector bundles, the SURF descriptors is selected for representing the points of interest on each image. We choose the SURF algorithm instead of SIFT because it is more robust, and its speed is sufficient for real-time processing, which is critical when dealing with crowd-sourced data. In our model, given a query image $\boldsymbol{I}^a \in \boldsymbol{Z}^A$ and a set of candidate images in $\boldsymbol{Z}^B$, we perform a match in the following manner: i) Construct a codebook of "visual features" through using the SURF algorithm; ii) Quantize these visual feature descriptors by the k-nearest neighbor (kNN) algorithm where $k = 2$; iii) Use Euclidean distance as a similarity metric for computing the number of good matches. The total process take around 1.5 seconds to match two images. Fig. 10 shows the correlation between distance and the similarity score of image feature matching. Similar to Fig. 9, the x-axis in this figure represents the linear distance between the shooting locations of the two images.The result exhibits that by using our kNN-based image feature matching algorithm, we are able to set a similarity threshold that only preserve the images, which belongs to the same location (distance less than 1m).

Longest Common Subsequence Image Vector Aggregation. Once a match between two images is detected, IndoorCrowd2D calculates the similarity scores of the two corresponding image vector bundles (IVBs) based on the longest common subsequence (LCS) metric. Let $\boldsymbol{Z}^A, \boldsymbol{Z}^B$ be the two IVBs with the length of i and j, respectively. Also, given that system metric is δ and matching threshold is ϵ, the LCS metric for the two IVBs is defined as follows:

$$L\left(\boldsymbol{Z}_i^A, \boldsymbol{Z}_j^B\right) = \begin{cases} 0, if\ i = 0\ or\ j = 0; \\ 1 + L(\boldsymbol{Z}_{i-1}^A, \boldsymbol{Z}_{j-1}^B), \\ \quad if\ d(\vec{z}_i^A, \vec{z}_j^B) \leq \epsilon\ and\ |i-j| < \delta; \\ max(L(\boldsymbol{Z}_i^A, \boldsymbol{Z}_{j-1}^B), L(\boldsymbol{Z}_{i-1}^A, \boldsymbol{Z}_j^B)), \\ \quad otherwise; \end{cases}$$

where parameter δ is used to control the maximum length difference between the two IVBs and ϵ represents the distance threshold. The similarity score SS for the two IVBs based on [50] is expressed as follows:

$$SS(\boldsymbol{Z}^A, \boldsymbol{Z}^B) = max_{f \in \mathscr{F}} \frac{L(\boldsymbol{Z}^A, f(\boldsymbol{Z}^B))}{min(i,j)} \qquad (3)$$

where $\mathscr{F}$ stands for a set of all possible translations. In our prototyped IndoorCrowd2D, if SS is larger than threshold ss_h, two IVBs can be merged into one larger IVB.

4.5 Hallway Skeleton and Building Interior View Reconstruction

In the last module, we leverage aggregated image vector bundles to generate the hallway skeleton and the indoor interior view. The hallway skeleton represents the topology of the hallway for navigation purpose. As it is mentioned before, IndoorCrowd2D selects an indoor spatial model to represent the environment. Hence, we need to further project our aggregated image vector bundles to the indoor space cell to reconstruct the hallway skeleton.The indoor interior view is generated separately by leveraging a δ-building interior view generation algorithm. This algorithm is a combination of several state-of-the-art panorama reconstruction algorithms. The end result of IndoorCrowd2D is an interactive building interior view reconstructed from the output results.

Reconstruct Hallway Skeleton. For each floor, we select the aggregated image vector bundles $\boldsymbol{Z}^{aggr}$ and project it to the indoor space matrix based on our indoor spatial model. The whole procedure is as the following: First of all, there is a homogeneous grid cell matrix to represent the indoor space, and also, each cell inside the matrix is initialize as number 0. Then, we map $\boldsymbol{Z}^{aggr}$ to the cell matrix by checking the relative spatial location $[x, y]$ of each image vector $\vec{z}_i \in \boldsymbol{Z}^{aggr}$. If there exists an image vector $\vec{z}_i$, which corresponds to a particular cell $c_{i,j}$, we therefore increase the value of $c_{i,j}$ by 1. We then store the reference number $[i, aggr]$ of image vector to $c_{i,j}$ The process is continuously repeated until all image vectors in the aggregated image vector bundle $\boldsymbol{Z}^{aggr}$ are projected to the indoor space matrix. Finally, the cells with value higher than a threshold h_{cell} (means this position is accessible) inside the indoor space matrix is chosen to represent the hallway skeleton.

δ-Building Interior View Generation. Up to this step, the hallway skeleton is completely generated. However, we also interested in the generation of a visually appealing building interior view. Therefore, we choose to use a cylindrical panorama, as such panorama present users with a more realistic representation of the indoor environment.

To generate a cylindrical panorama, the qualified images inside the aggregated image vector bundle Z^{aggr} have to satisfy with: i). the user's locations of these images should be as close as possible. ii). the viewing direction of these images should cover the scene in a wide angle (e.g. 360 degree for a 360-panorama). iii). every two images should have appropriate overlap part. For criteria i and ii, we use the reconstructed hallway skeleton for accurately selecting the candidate images. First, for a particular cell c_i inside the indoor space matrix, we check if it is accessible (the value is larger than h_{cell} if it's accessible). Second, if their exists more than one image vector $\vec{z}$ corresponding to c_i due to image vector aggregation, we then select images inside these image vectors as candidate images because they belongs to the same location, and therefore they should satisfy criteria i. Third, we check the normalized heading direction of these candidate images to make sure these images share the same or consecutive orientation values, which satisfies criteria ii. Finally, we send the images passed the check to a panorama reconstruct pipeline.

The panorama reconstruct pipeline performs incremental image stitching through a feature detector module, a feature matching module, and an inlier pair match estimation module to select the best matches (shown in Fig. 11 (a)). Although the shortcomings of our approach for image stitching include a slightly slower speed and a less accurate process comparing to state-of-the-art softwares (e.g., Autostich [8]), the results are more accessible dealing with non-overlap and textureless objects (criteria iii), which makes it particularly suitable for our crowdsourced image data.

Fig. 11 (a) exhibits the δ-building interior view generation process in a typical scenario. The output of RANSAC algorithm is a homography matrix, which establishes the number of features pairs that match closer than a predefined threshold. Once the homography matrix is computed, it is utilized to overlap the source image with the target image. In our scenario, however, the crowdsourced images may exhibit strong differences in light and white balance due to the same scene being captured from different perspectives and by different people. In order to obtain the good panorama images, it is necessary to perform images blending[8] first to smooth out the discontinuities between the two overlapping pictures before applying the homography matrix.

5. IMPLEMENTATION

The prototype of the IndoorCrowd2D system is composed of two parts: a data acquisition interface runs on Android mobile device and an indoor interior view pipeline deploys on a cloud.

For the data acquisition interface, we implement and test it on Android 4.0 KitKat. Three different smartphone models are chosen to test the compatibility, includes Google (LG) Nexus 5, Google (LG) Nexus 4, and SAMSUNG Galaxy Nexus. The reconstruction pipeline is implemented on Microsoft Azure platform using a network optimized A9 virtual machine (16 cores, 112 GB memory and Ubuntu Linux).

1)Mobile Application. Our mobile application enables the crowd to capture the building interior view. These user-generated-images can be further uploaded to cloud from user smartphones. For saving bandwidth, we pre-process the

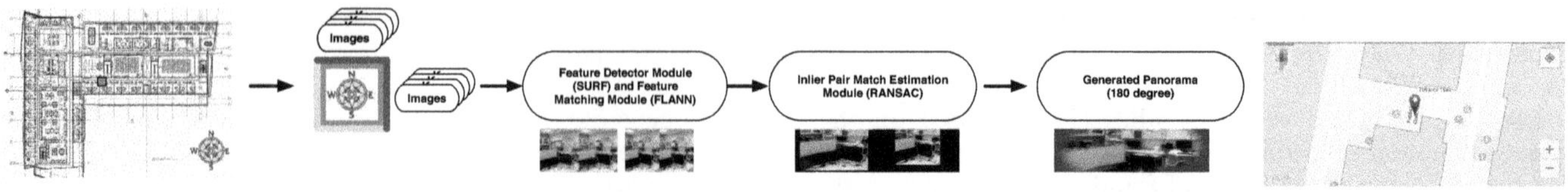

(a) (b)

Figure 11: (a) The δ-building interior view generation process in a room scenario, (b) Building location detection by dropping pinpoint

sensing data and filter out the redundant and low-quality part. The qualified datasets are zipped and separated into 5MB chunks for transmitting. The transmission only starts when Wi-Fi connections are available.

Real-time Data Quality Detection. To support on-board real-time image processing, we leverage an open-source OpenCV library to perform SURF feature extraction, and to process the extracted image and detect its quality further. To reduce the running time of the SURF feature detection, we tune the parameters to produce fewer SURF features per image. Note that this modification can reduce the feature detection accuracy. However, since we only need to judge if the numbers of features are fall below a threshold τ_{fea} (prevent user shooting feature-less object), the loss of accuracy does not affect our system.

Application Settings. We create a interactive setting interface to allow users input the building floor information. As shown in Fig.11 (b), once a user clicks the setting button, a pinpoint on the map appears to indicate their last known GPS location. These results may be inaccurate, which we address by allowing the user to drag and drop the pinpoint onto the correct map position. Note that we do not need users to provide very accurate location information, as this location information is only used for building detection. Our system works well as long as the pinpoint falls inside the outline of the target building. Once the user complete the previous step, a new screen will appear prompting the user to input their current floor number. Their input is then sent to the cloud along with building location data. Also, the input data is stored in our application. User does not need to re-input it unless he/she starts reconstruct a new building floor.

2)Cloud Computing Backend. The IndoorCrowd2D cloud computing backend is built upon Windows Azure virtual machine instances with Ubuntu Linux. Based on function, we can divide cloud computing backend into two layers: i) a communication layer which receives and stores the incoming crowdsourced image and sensory data. ii) a data processing layer to process received data and generate hallway skeleton and the interior views of the building.

Communication Layer. In this layer, we select an Tornado web server to receive crowdsourced data. The Tornado http server is a powerful, flexible web server. The mobile application send zipped data to Tornado web server in real-time through HTTP requests.

Data Processing Layer. Data processing layer process the crowdsourced data and output the final result. In the first step, our program first stores the received raw data into MongoDB. Then, our task scheduler (APScheduler) loads the data and send it to the hallway skeleton and the interior view reconstruct pipeline. Several function modules compose the pipeline and are all controlled by a task coordinator. Once the reconstruction is finished, the task scheduler stores the result back to the database and wait for new tasks. For visualizing the result, the WebGL technique is applied to create an interactive online GUI. It in charges of the user input and the result display (shown in Fig. 12). However, users can also ported our data to other online map services by using its API.

Figure 12: Screenshot for visualizing building interior view and hallway skeleton

6. PERFORMANCE EVALUATION

We evaluate our IndoorCrowd2D prototype in the following scenario: untrained and uncorrelated volunteers use our mobile application capturing indoor scenes in a typical college building to reconstruct the building interior and skeleton. We collect data on the college buildings at different times of day, and over a period of five months. Before conducting the experiment, 55,453 images of two different buildings (Teaching Building (TB) dataset and GYM dataset) from 1,151 datasets are successfully uploaded by 25 users. Some places were captured multiple times. Fig. 13 (a) shows the distribution of the basic elements inside the data.

6.1 Evaluation Methodologies

The ground truth hallway skeleton $\mathcal{S}_{true} = \{c_1, c_2, .., c_n\}$ is learned from the building floor map. Therefore, once we generate a building hallway skeleton $\mathcal{S}_{gen}$, the precision, recall, and F-measure of IndoorCrowd2D can be defined as follows:

$$precision = \frac{|\mathcal{S}_{gen} \bigcap \mathcal{S}_{true}|}{|\mathcal{S}_{gen}|} \tag{4}$$

$$recall = \frac{|\mathcal{S}_{gen} \bigcap \mathcal{S}_{true}|}{|\mathcal{S}_{true}|} \tag{5}$$

$$F - measure = 2 * \frac{precision * recall}{precision + recall} \tag{6}$$

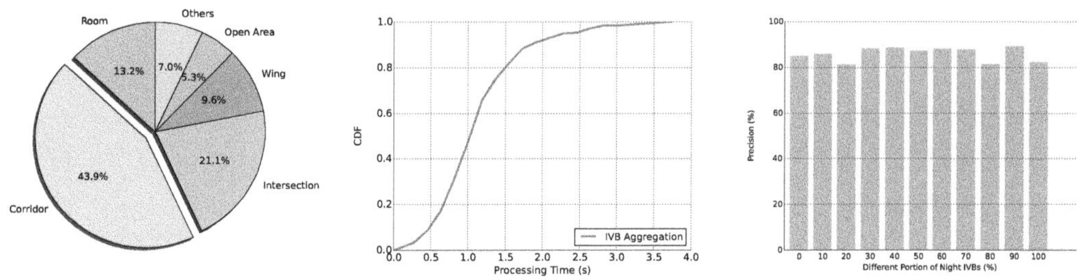

(a) The distribution of the crowdsourced building interior data (b) Building hallway skeleton reconstruct computational latency (c) Tolerance of various lightning conditions

Figure 13: IndoorCrowd2D performance evaluation for: (a) The distribution of the crowdsourced building interior data (b) Building hallway skeleton reconstruct computational latency (c) Tolerance of various lightning conditions

Note that, these performance metrics not only reveals the accuracy of the generated building hallway skeleton, but also affects the quality of panorama generation (because we use the hallway skeleton as the auxiliary information to help generate indoor panorama with the correct position).

For comparison purpose, we compute the precision, recall, and F-measure for both our method (with sensory and image data) and image only method (without sensory data). The image only approach is widely used in computer vision community. They assume the images are crowdsourced from the Internet. In this approach, the spatial relationship of each image is deduced by processing the visual information (e.g. through feature matching).

6.2 Evaluation Results

Hallway Skeleton Reconstruction Performance. As shown in Fig. 16, we compares the performance of IndoorCrowd2D with the image only approach. The precision, recall, and fall-out are computed over the entire set of pictures. The results exhibit that IndoorCrowd2D achieves a precision around 85%, a 100% recall and a F-score around 95% for the two datasets. We find that existing state-of-the-art vision algorithms still exist some drawbacks by further checking the results. In our crowdsourced test datasets, these computer vision algorithms tends to give incorrect results when encounter images of extreme distance/angle, feature-less objects (e.g. walls). According to the results, our image and sensor hybrid method is more robust to errors and outliers compare to the image only method.

Computational Latency. IndoorCrowds2D computational latency is highly dependent upon the time needed for the computer vision based image processing, especially the dominating subtask for aggregating two image vector bundles. Fig. 13 (b) plots the CDF graph of the single-threaded performance for matching two image vectors inside two different vector bundles $\boldsymbol{Z}$. Given that each image vector bundle contains around 20 image vectors in general, the performance of our system is comparable to the state-of-the-art.

Tolerance of Various Lightning Conditions. To test IndoorCrowd2D under varying lighting conditions, we manually select datasets that are captured from different periods of time in a day and categorize them into two groups: daylight datasets and night datasets by judging its images and timestamp. We keep the size of daylight dataset and night datasets equal.

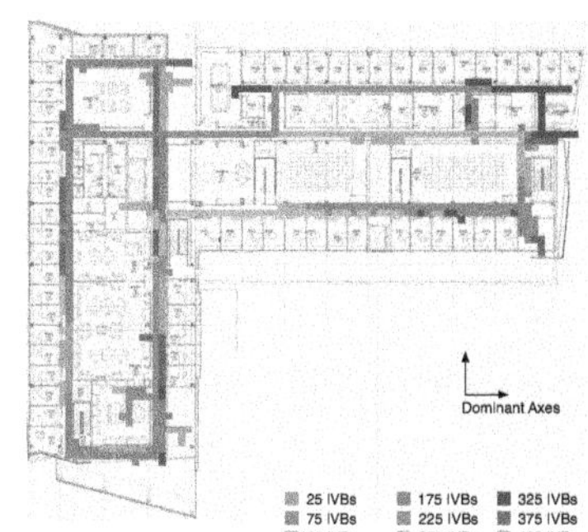

Figure 14: A typical gradually build-up scenario for IndoorCrowd2D (TB Dataset)

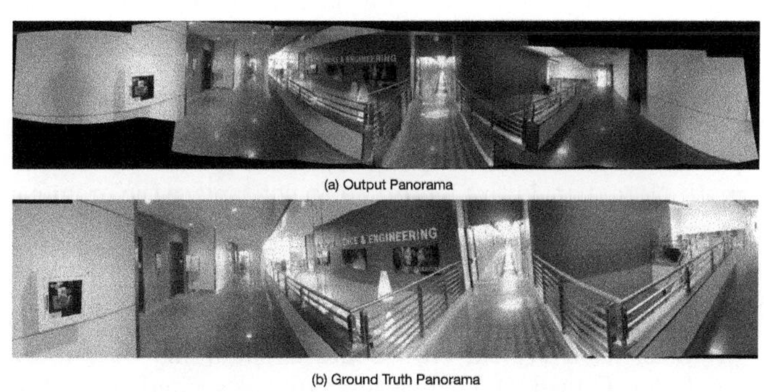

Figure 15: Quality comparison between the crowdsourced panorama (a) and the ground truth panorama (b). (TB Dataset)

We perform the following experiment: We randomly replace part of the daylight dataset, which is 10% of the dataset size in our experiment, with the same amount of night dataset. We keep doing this process and conducting the match on each newly generated dataset until the dataset becomes all-night. Fig. 13 (c) shows the skeleton precision with different portions of night IVB datasets. The result shows that the our building interior view reconstruction pipeline is robust to various lighting conditions.

Allowing Gradual Skeleton Build-up. Our building hallway skeleton reconstruction pipeline allows gradual

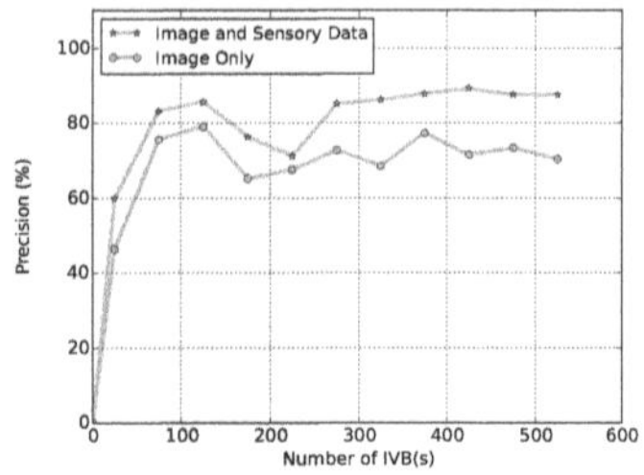

(a) Hallway skeleton precision for TB dataset

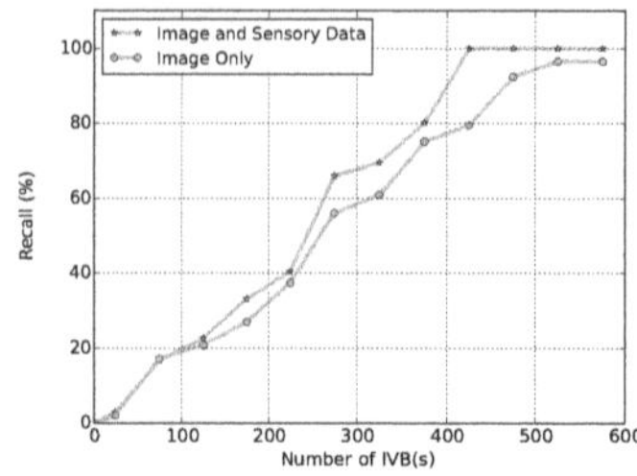

(b) Hallway skeleton recall for TB dataset

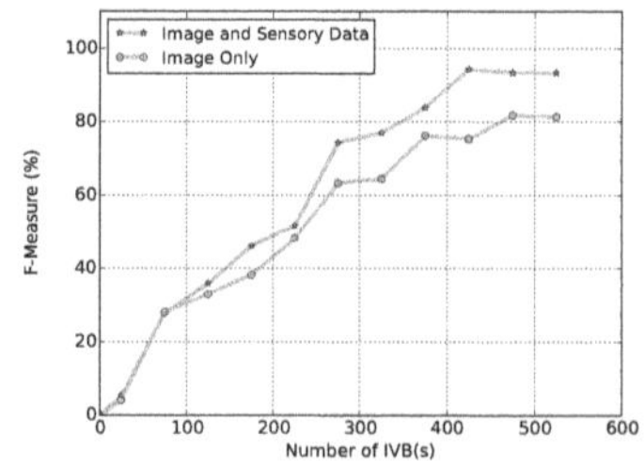

(c) Hallway skeleton F-measure for TB dataset

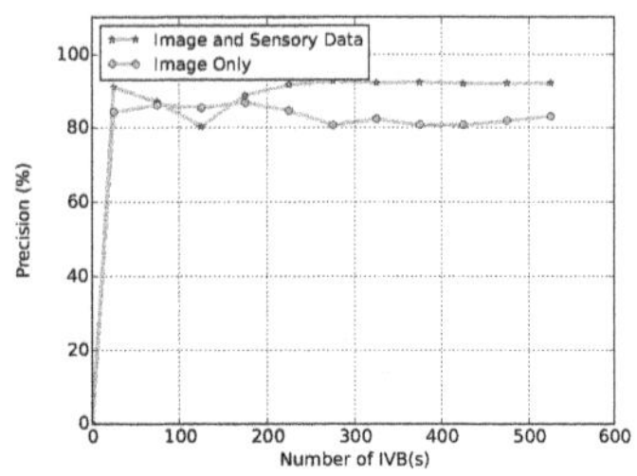

(d) Hallway skeleton precision for GYM dataset

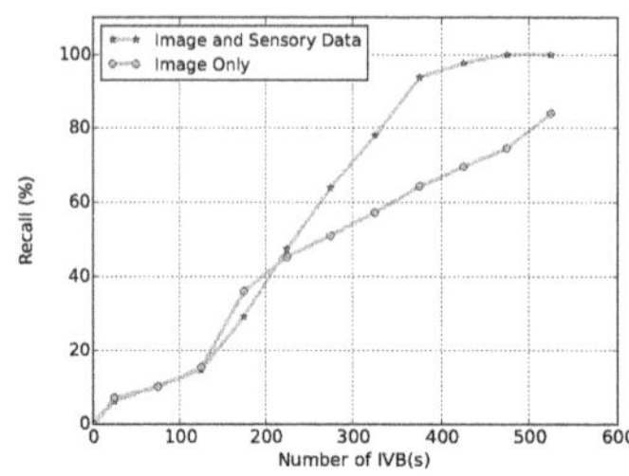

(e) Hallway skeleton recall for GYM dataset

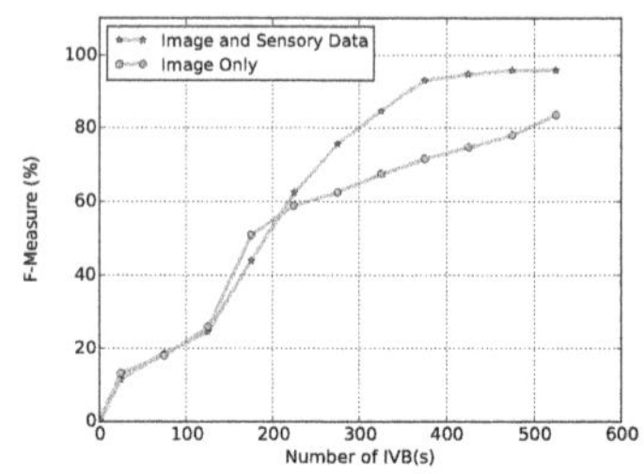

(f) Hallway skeleton F-measure for GYM dataset

Figure 16: IndoorCrowd2D performance evaluation (precision, recall, F-measure) for (a)-(c) TB dataset and (d)-(f) GYM dataset

build-up to save computational cost. IndoorCrowd2D automatically saves the previous reconstruction state when all the datasets are being processed. When new datasets arrive, it will restore the previous state and continue processing. Fig. 14 presents a typical gradually build-up process of the hallway skeleton construction, with new image vector bundles being added progressively. For the purpose of better visualization, we manually check each image inside the merged image vector bundles, and find its best possible position (by rotating it if possible) on the ground truth floor map. Note that, in this figure, we do not replace the previous longest skeleton with the newly generated one. Therefore, the final result shown in this figure is slightly different from the real data.

Quality Rank of the Resulting Panorama. Fig. 15 (a) presents a typical crowdsourced panorama output by the IndoorCrowd2D. Comparing with the ground truth, the output panorama preserve most of the details for an indoor scene. Thus, the overall quality of the crowdsourced panorama and the ground truth are evenly matched. However, since the crowdsourced image are taken by different users with different angles, and thereby, the resulting crowdsourced panorama inevitably containes some inconsistency and distortion parts.

Mobile Application Usability Study. 25 volunteers filled out a survey to evaluate the usability of our mobile application after they finished capturing the building interior. The survey contains two yes-no questions: a). "The usage instructions of the IndoorCrowd2D are easy to perform?" b). "Do you think the real-time feedback displays on the screen helps?" The results show that 80% of the volunteers agree on the first question and 88% of the volunteers agree on the second one. According to the results, the majority users believe that our mobile application alleviates the burden of building interior view reconstruction and encourages them to contribute high quality data.

7. DISCUSSIONS AND LIMITATIONS

Digital Floor Plan as A-priori Information. If the digital floor plan of a building is available as prior knowledge, then it can be utilized to detect the actual position of each room and corridor. In this case, we can adjust the image vector to the correct position by solving a non-linear least squares problem. We may for instance use the Ceres Solver to perform sensor data fusion, in order to estimate the image vectors' correct positions and orientations inside the building. Since we no longer rely on the Manhattan world assumption (we do not need to calculate the dominant axes), our system will thus be able to support non-predominantly rectangular buildings.

Reconstruct Building Skeleton for an Open-area. Unlike corridors and rooms, an open area such as a lobby may allow users to approach from different directions. Image vectors generated by different users will hence be aggregated in this area, due to our reliance on image features for matching pairs of image vectors. We state that IndoorCrowd2D is still able to provide reliable results in this special case due to the following reasons: As mentioned previously, for a particular location, if there exists more than one image, and these images share the same consecutive orientation values, a panorama will be generated by δ-building interior view generation algorithm. In an open-area, a 360° panorama would therefore be generated once sufficient key frames are gathered from all directions. The subsequent image vectors that captured the same open-area would then all be matched to the 360° panorama and converged into a point.

Reconstruct Multi-Floors in Single Round. IndoorCrowd2D requires users to input the number of floors they are on before they start capturing a scene. Once they input the correct floor number, we ask the user to stay on the same floor while capturing data. Towards the goal of enhancing the usability of IndoorCrowd2D, however, we plan to support 2.5D building interior and skeleton reconstruction in the future. According to [42], stairways can be detected by comparing the accelerometer patterns when the user is walking on stairs.

Non-predominantly Rectangular Buildings. As IndoorCrowd2D assumes there is not any prior-knowledge available about the building skeleton, we utilize the well established reduced Manhattan world assumption to compute the dominant axes for each building based on its outline. For reconstructing non-predominantly rectangular buildings, the key challenge is the dominant axes may differ from our output result. Hence, we need to leverage a digital floor plan to detect the actual position of the main skeleton of the building. In our future work, we plan to solve this problem by creating a system letting user providing building skeleton information.

Energy Consumption. IndoorCrowd2D mobile application runs on a user's smartphone. We measure the energy consumption of our mobile application by using the drop rate and the residual capacity of the battery. The result shows that our mobile application takes 1800 mW on average for capturing the scene in four minutes. The inertial sensor consumes about 35 mW when user capturing the environment. Photo shooting takes an average of 300 mW for continues shooting with a resolution setting of 640x480 and a time interval of 3s. However, unlike other mobile crowdsourcing systems, our mobile application does not require users to continues running a daemon process in the background. Hence, capturing several indoor locations should not constitute significant power consumption.

8. RELATED WORK

Indoor Smartphone Sensing. Recently, many researches focus on utilizing smartphone sensing technique to determine the status of a pedestrian in an indoor environment [3,10,11,23,29,31,39,42,43,46,49], such as heading direction, location and walking trajectory. For example, [11] jointly utilizes accelerometer, gyroscope and compass to obtain the user heading direction information. This method is limited due to error accumulation of the inertial sensors. Furthermore, [31] develops a system to accurately detect user heading direction by analyzing user walking in depth. Additionally, it is able to predict and reduce the magnetic interference of compass data. [32] utilizes camera picture combined with computer vision technique to detect the changes of heading direction by calculating the vanishing points. [39], similar to [32], leverages front camera pictures to calculate the building internal line-shape objects as a hint to detect user walking direction. For determine user location, the traditional way is using Wi-Fi fingerprint to locate the user. [29] applies collected user trajectory information to constrains the possible user location by physical walls and use the crowdsourced Wi-Fi data to establish a fingerprint database.

Digital Floor Plan Generation. There are many studies about the building floor plan generation, most of which focus primarily on the sensor data aggregation [2,19,35,41]. [2] uses crowdsourced data from smart phone sensors to automatically and transparently construct accurate motion traces. [19] utilizes both image and inertial data to infer the spatial information for an indoor environment and eventually generate an indoor floor plan. Our work differs from theirs is that our system aims to reconstruct visually appealing indoor interior view, instead of a floor plan. Therefore, we only rebuild a simple hallway skeleton leads to accurately locate reconstructed interior views and helps user navigate through these views.

Indoor Scene Reconstruction. Lately, several researches are focused on indoor and outdoor scene reconstruction [30]. [33] develops a smartphone application to let user capture a panorama of indoor scenes. Basically, users are able to label the edge of the room directly at the panorama. According to the labels, the application is capable to reconstruct room shapes based on the Manhattan World assumption. [22] proposed a set of key-frame selection algorithms based on crowdsourced sensor-rich videos to automatic generate outdoor panorama. In addition to 2D scene reconstruction, indoor 3D modeling is also a hot research topic. Some studies leverage professional equipments, such as depth sensors [45] and laser scanners [5,44] to reconstruct indoor scene. Other works like [13,26] uses Kinect, a commercial depth sensor to reconstruct 3D model. Recently, Google lunches the Project Tango [28] that contributes to a tablet for mobile 3D sensing. Although the output 3D models of these approaches are impressive, specialized equipments are unadoptable in our crowdsourcing setting. Moreover, the computer vision community develops several computer vision techniques to reconstruct 3D models directly from images [15,16]. They use some state-of-the-art 3D reconstruction techniques including Structure from Motion [1,36,37,40] and Multiview-stereo [17,18]. To enhance the result quality, an user-labelling sub-system is further developed in a recent work [45]. However, because these computer vision based 3D reconstruction algorithm still exists some drawbacks, the images used for 3D reconstruction need to be carefully selected [14]. Thus, these techniques are not suitable for our crowdsourced scenario.

9. CONCLUSION AND FUTURE WORK

We have described the design, implementation, and evaluation of IndoorCrowd2D – a novel crowdsourcing system empowered by off-the-shelf smartphones for building interior reconstructions. The prototype is readily deployable in real-world scenarios. As our future work, specific issues related to a crowdsourcing deployment, such as user recruitment, incentive mechanism and privacy preservation, will be further focused on. Once fully hardened, IndoorCrowd2D is expected to provide indoor panorama and geo-data for each individual floor of any building around the world. IndoorCrowd2D is expected to extend existing online map services to the indoor environments at an unprecedented scale, which is currently cost prohibitive. IndoorCrowd2D can also serve an important stepping stone towards the ultimate goal of economically-viable massive indoor 3D model reconstruction.

10. ACKNOWLEDGEMENT

We thank the helpful comments from Fan Ye and the anonymous reviewers. We are grateful to David Chu for shepherding our paper. This work was supported in part by US National Science Foundation under grants CNS-1421903, CNS-1318948, and CNS-1262275.

11. REFERENCES

[1] S. Agarwal, Y. Furukawa, N. Snavely, I. Simon, B. Curless, S. M. Seitz, and R. Szeliski. Building rome in a day. *Communications of the ACM*, 54(10):105–112, 2011.

[2] M. Alzantot and M. Youssef. Crowdinside: automatic construction of indoor floorplans. In *SIGSPATIAL GIS*, 2012.

[3] C. Arth, D. Wagner, M. Klopschitz, A. Irschara, and D. Schmalstieg. Wide area localization on mobile phones. In *ISMAR*, 2009.

[4] H. Bay, T. Tuytelaars, and L. Van Gool. Surf: Speeded up robust features. In *ECCV*, 2006.

[5] Y. Bok, Y. Hwang, and I. S. Kweon. Accurate motion estimation and high-precision 3d reconstruction by sensor fusion. In *Robotics and Automation*, 2007.

[6] J.-Y. Bouguet. Pyramidal implementation of the affine lucas kanade feature tracker description of the algorithm.

[7] G. Bradski. Opencv. *Dr. Dobb's Journal of Software Tools*, 2000.

[8] M. Brown and D. G. Lowe. Automatic panoramic image stitching using invariant features. *International Journal of Computer Vision*, 74(1):59–73, 2007.

[9] S. Chen, M. Li, K. Ren, and C. Qiao. Crowdmap: Accurate reconstruction of indoor floor plan from crowdsourced sensor-rich videos. In *ICDCS*, 2015.

[10] K. Chintalapudi, A. Padmanabha Iyer, and V. N. Padmanabhan. Indoor localization without the pain. In *Mobicom*, 2010.

[11] J. Chon and H. Cha. Lifemap: A smartphone-based context provider for location-based services. *IEEE Pervasive Computing*, (2):58–67, 2011.

[12] J. Coughlan and A. Yuille. Manhattan world: Compass direction from a single image by bayesian inference. In *ICCV*, 1999.

[13] M. F. Fallon, H. Johannsson, J. Brookshire, S. Teller, and J. J. Leonard. Sensor fusion for flexible human-portable building-scale mapping. In *IROS*, 2012.

[14] A. Furlan, S. Miller, D. G. Sorrenti, L. Fei-Fei, and S. Savarese. Free your camera: 3d indoor scene understanding from arbitrary camera motion. In *BMVC*, 2013.

[15] Y. Furukawa, B. Curless, S. M. Seitz, and R. Szeliski. Manhattan-world stereo. In *CVPR*, 2009.

[16] Y. Furukawa, B. Curless, S. M. Seitz, and R. szeliski. Reconstructing building interiors from images. In *ICCV*, 2009.

[17] Y. Furukawa, B. Curless, S. M. Seitz, and R. Szeliski. Towards internet-scale multi-view stereo. In *CVPR*, 2010.

[18] Y. Furukawa and J. Ponce. Accurate, dense, and robust multiview stereopsis. *PAMI*, 32(8):1362–1376, 2010.

[19] R. Gao, M. Zhao, T. Ye, F. Ye, Y. Wang, K. Bian, T. Wang, and X. Li. Jigsaw: Indoor floor plan reconstruction via mobile crowdsensing. In *MobiCom*, 2014.

[20] GoogleStreetView. https://www.google.com/maps/views/streetview.

[21] Y. Jiang et al. Hallway based automatic indoor floorplan construction using room fingerprints. In *Ubicomp*, 2013.

[22] S. H. Kim and others. Key frame selection algorithms for automatic generation of panoramic images from crowdsourced geo-tagged videos. In *WWGIS*. 2014.

[23] H. Liu, Y. Gan, J. Yang, S. Sidhom, Y. Wang, Y. Chen, and F. Ye. Push the limit of wifi based localization for smartphones. In *Mobicom*, 2012.

[24] T. Liu et al. Indoor localization and visualization using a human-operated backpack system. In *IPIN*, 2010.

[25] H. C. Longuet-Higgins and K. Prazdny. The interpretation of a moving retinal image. *Biological Sciences*, 208(1173):385–397, 1980.

[26] R. A. Newcombe et al. Kinectfusion: Real-time dense surface mapping and tracking. In *ISMAR*, 2011.

[27] D. Philipp et al. Mapgenie: Grammar-enhanced indoor map construction from crowd-sourced data. In *PerCom*, 2014.

[28] ProjectTango. https://www.google.com/atap/projecttango.

[29] A. Rai, K. K. Chintalapudi, V. N. Padmanabhan, and R. Sen. Zee: zero-effort crowdsourcing for indoor localization. In *Mobicom*, 2012.

[30] V. Raychoudhury, S. Shrivastav, S. Sandha, and J. Cao. Crowd-pan-360: Crowdsourcing based context-aware panoramic map generation for smartphone users. *Parallel and Distributed Systems, IEEE Transactions on*, 26(8):2208–2219, Aug 2015.

[31] N. Roy, H. Wang, and R. Roy Choudhury. I am a smartphone and i can tell my user's walking direction. In *Mobisys*, 2014.

[32] L. Ruotsalainen, H. Kuusniemi, and R. Chen. Heading change detection for indoor navigation with a smartphone camera. In *IPIN*, 2011.

[33] A. Sankar and S. Seitz. Capturing indoor scenes with smartphones. In *UIST*, 2012.

[34] G. Shen, Z. Chen, P. Zhang, T. Moscibroda, and Y. Zhang. Walkie-markie: indoor pathway mapping made easy. In *NSDI*, 2013.

[35] H. Shin, Y. Chon, and H. Cha. Unsupervised construction of an indoor floor plan using a smartphone. *ITSMC*, 2012.

[36] N. Snavely, S. M. Seitz, and R. szeliski. Photo tourism: exploring photo collections in 3d. *TOG*, 2006.

[37] N. Snavely, S. M. Seitz, and R. Szeliski. Modeling the world from internet photo collections. *IJCV*, 80(2):189–210, 2008.

[38] P. Steadman. Why are most buildings rectangular? *Architectural Research Quarterly*, 10(02):119–130, 2006.

[39] Z. Sun, S. Pan, Y.-C. Su, and P. Zhang. Headio: zero-configured heading acquisition for indoor mobile devices through multimodal context sensing. In *UbiComp*, 2013.

[40] P. Tanskanen, K. Kolev, L. Meier, F. Camposeco, O. Saurer, and M. Pollefeys. Live metric 3d reconstruction on mobile phones. In *ICCV*, 2013.

[41] TRXSystems. http://www.trxsystems.com/.

[42] H. Wang, S. Sen, A. Elgohary, M. Farid, M. Youssef, and R. R. Choudhury. No need to war-drive: unsupervised indoor localization. In *Mobisys*, 2012.

[43] C. Wu, Z. Yang, Y. Liu, and W. Xi. Will: Wireless indoor localization without site survey. *TPDS*, 24(4):839–848, 2013.

[44] J. Xiao and Y. Furukawa. Reconstructing the world's museums. In *ECCV*. 2012.

[45] J. Xiao, A. Owens, and A. Torralba. Sun3d: A database of big spaces reconstructed using sfm and object labels. In *ICCV*, 2013.

[46] J. Xiong and K. Jamieson. Arraytrack: a fine-grained indoor location system. In *Usenix NSDI*, 2013.

[47] C. Zauner. Implementation and benchmarking of perceptual image hash functions. 2010.

[48] X. Zhang, Z. Yang, C. Wu, W. Sun, and Y. Liu. Robust trajectory estimation for crowdsourcing-based mobile applications. 2013.

[49] Y. Zheng, G. Shen, L. Li, C. Zhao, M. Li, and F. Zhao. Travi-navi: Self-deployable indoor navigation system. In *Proceedings of the 20th annual international conference on Mobile computing and networking*, pages 471–482. ACM, 2014.

[50] Y. Zheng, X. Xie, and W.-Y. Ma. Mining interesting locations and travel sequences from gps trajectories. In *WWW*, 2009.

ALPS: A Bluetooth and Ultrasound Platform for Mapping and Localization

Patrick Lazik Niranjini Rajagopal Oliver Shih Bruno Sinopoli Anthony Rowe
Electrical and Computer Engineering Department
Carnegie Mellon University
{plazik,niranjir,oshih,brunos,agr}@ece.cmu.edu

Abstract

The proliferation of Bluetooth Low-Energy (BLE) chipsets on mobile devices has lead to a wide variety of user-installable tags and beacons designed for location-aware applications. In this paper, we present the *Acoustic Location Processing System (ALPS)*, a platform that augments BLE transmitters with ultrasound in a manner that improves ranging accuracy and can help users configure indoor localization systems with minimal effort. A user places three or more beacons in an environment and then walks through a calibration sequence with their mobile device where they touch key points in the environment like the floor and the corners of the room. This process automatically computes the room geometry as well as the precise beacon locations without needing auxiliary measurements. Once configured, the system can track a user's location referenced to a map.

The platform consists of time-synchronized ultrasonic transmitters that utilize the bandwidth just above the human hearing limit, where mobile devices are still sensitive and can detect ranging signals. To aid in the mapping process, the beacons perform inter-beacon ranging during setup. Each beacon includes a BLE radio that can identify and trigger the ultrasonic signals. By using differences in propagation characteristics between ultrasound and radio, the system can classify if beacons are within Line-Of-Sight (LOS) to the mobile phone. In cases where beacons are blocked, we show how the phone's inertial measurement sensors can be used to supplement localization data. We experimentally evaluate that our system can estimate three-dimensional beacon location with a Euclidean distance error of $16.1cm$, and can generate maps with room measurements with a two-dimensional Euclidean distance error of $19.8cm$. When tested in six different environments, we saw that the system can identify Non-Line-Of-Sight (NLOS) signals with over 80% accuracy and track a user's location to within less than $100cm$.

SenSys'15, November 1-4, 2015, Seoul, South Korea.
 ISBN 978-1-4503-3631-4/15/11...$15.00.
DOI: http://dx.doi.org/10.1145/2809695.2809727

1 Introduction

In order to improve indoor localization, low-cost beaconing systems like Gimbal [1] and iBeacon [2] allow users to instrument their environment. These devices typically perform approximate ranging using Received-Signal-Strength-Indicator (RSSI) values measured from short-range communication like Bluetooth Low Energy (BLE). BLE has gained traction in localization applications because unlike previous generations of Bluetooth, mobile devices can scan and rapidly detect tags without needing to be paired. The phone's operating systems can scan for tags in the background and selectively push notifications to an application when certain conditions are met. This ability of BLE to operate transparently while the phone is sleeping has enabled a number of location-aware services. For example, there are multiple BLE door locks available that periodically transmit proximity beacons to grant access if an authorized user is nearby. Unfortunately, BLE's ability to estimate distance (proximity) is based on radio signal strength that is affected by antenna type, orientation, environment specific path-loss and obstructions. This makes it difficult for BLE to act as a fine-grained localization source. Even if the ranging data is accurate, as demonstrated in [3], there are still significant barriers involved in setup and configuration of localization systems. It is extremely difficult for non-experts to create accurate maps of the environment and precisely survey beacon locations.

In this paper we present *ALPS*, a platform that augments BLE proximity beacons with ultrasonic transmitters in a manner that can help non-expert users quickly install and configure a precise and robust indoor localization system. A user simply installs three or more *ALPS* beacons in a space and then launches an app on their phone that interactively guides them through a configuration process. Once the space is configured, users can enter the space and the app will determine their location and can directly plot it relatively to a map of the area. As part of this training process, *ALPS* also characterizes the environment in terms of Line-Of-Sight (LOS) and Non-Line-of-Sight signal features such that it can filter out NLOS signals at run time.

The system consists of time synchronized beacons that transmit ultrasonic chirps similar to those described in [4] and [5]. These chirps are inaudible to humans, but are still detectable by most modern smartphones. The phone can use the Time-Difference-Of-Arrival (TDOA) of chirps to measure distances. As described in [5], if enough beacons are visible, a mobile phone can use TDOA to back compute the beacon transmit time in order to synchronize its clock with the infrastructure. Once synchronized it is possible to directly measure the Time-Of-Flight (TOF) for any new signals until the clocks drift apart. In contrast to previous work, *ALPS* uses BLE on each node to send relevant timing information. This both simplifies the design and allows for the entire ultrasonic bandwidth to be used exclusively for ranging. The approach from [4] was demonstrated to perform with an accuracy better than $2m$ at the IPSN 2014 localization competition [3]. These errors were significantly larger then what would be expected by TOF and likely a result of multi-path as well as incorrect beacon locations. Both of these sources of error are the key motivations for this work. Our updated approach of using BLE for data and the entire ultrasonic bandwidth for ranging improved performance to better than $30cm$ accuracy in the 2015 version of the competition. However, in both of these tests the receiver had sufficient beacons within LOS to perform TDOA ranging.

One major benefit of the evolving BLE ecosystems is that any user can rapidly deploy and annotate tags in a region of interest to build location-aware services. In some cases, the user can even define a location on a crowd-sourced map if an interior floor plan exists. *ALPS* takes this concept one step further and allows users to place three or more beacons in an area and then walk through a configuration process that generates a 3D map of the space with the precise location of each of the beacons. The approach is similar in nature to range-only Simultaneous Localization and Mapping (SLAM). An app on the smartphone guides the user through a process that allows the system to determine the dimensions of the room by placing the phone in key locations where it performs ranging measurements. Each beacon not only transmits BLE and ultrasound, but can also receive ultrasonic messages in order to perform inter-beacon ranging. The inter-node range information is required to solve the beacon mapping problem. Once the mapping process is complete, the system can leverage inertial measurements from new mobile users to precisely localize them in the space even if a subset of transmitters are obscured.

If the exact geometry of the beacons is known, a system needs three beacons in order to compute a two-dimensional location. If the geometry is not known, for example during installation, the system needs at least four beacons in order to perform the mapping operation. After profiling the ability to timestamp BLE packets, it was apparent that there is too much jitter in timing to use BLE as a precise starting point for the ultrasonic transmission (it is good enough to identify Time-Division-Multiple-Access (TDMA) slots). During the configuration phase we ask the user to hold their phone directly next to one of the beacons. We then use this beacon at zero-distance to synchronize with the infrastructure instead of requiring another beacon. The audio time synchronization during setup allows the user to use TOF ranging in order to localize the beacons and room anchor points in 3-dimensions. Time synchronization experiments on phones in [5] show that a smartphone can stay synchronized for tens of minutes before drift causes significant ranging error. Once the geometry is determined, users that enter the space can simply use TDOA (or TOF once synchronized to the infrastructure) and tracking to compute their locations.

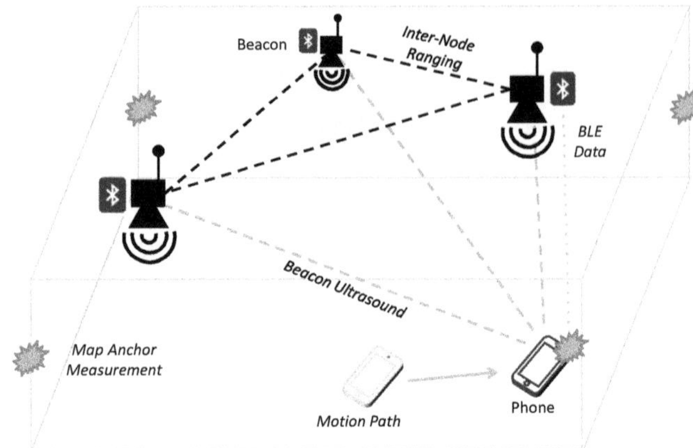

Figure 1. System overview

One of the major limitations of ultrasonic ranging systems is error due to interpreting NLOS or multi-path signals as LOS signals. As part of the configuration process, the system captures the signal strength of both BLE and ultrasonic transmissions along with the ultrasonic TOF data of each ultrasonic transmission. The user is asked to capture instances where the phone is in clear LOS of all beacons, as well as a few NLOS cases where beacons are obstructed. Using this data and the difference in multi-path attenuation properties of RF and ultrasound, the system is able to classify if a received signal is LOS or NLOS. When given direct LOS, ultrasonic ranging systems are highly accurate and can measure distances to less than $10cm$ of error. *ALPS* is able to ignore NLOS data and interpolate the true position using inertial measurement assisted tracking when beacons are blocked.

In summary, the contributions of this paper are (1) a hardware and software platform that augments BLE with ultrasonic transmissions for fine-grained localization, (2) a procedure that leverages this platform to help users automatically generate maps of the environment without any manual measuring and (3) an enhanced location tracking approach that uses machine learning to filter out NLOS signals when localizing users after the installation phase.

2 Related Work

Research on the topic of localization can be broadly classified into two main categories of range-based approaches [6, 7, 8, 9] and range-free approaches [10, 11, 12, 13]. Range-free approaches typically attempt to match either synthetic or naturally occurring signatures to a particular location or use tracking techniques like on-board inertial measurement data [14, 15, 16]. Range-based approaches use measured distances or angular estimates to known anchor points to compute a position. In this paper, we focus primarily on range-based technologies including Time-of-Arrival (TOA), TDOA, TOF and tracking approaches that use inertial data. For a more detailed general overview, we refer to [17]. Our approach uses TOF for setup and then uses TDOA with inertial tracking for run-time localization.

There is a large body of work in the mobile computing domain on TOF [18] systems that compute distances based on how long it takes for a signal to propagate from a sender to a receiver. For example, [19] and [20] both compute distances by measuring the Round-Trip-Time-of-Flight (RTOF) by recording a signal's departure and the return time divided by the propagation speed. This assumes that the receiver will retransmit a return signal within a fixed amount of time. BeepBeep [20] uses this approach on cellular phones to compute inter-device ranges. Even though smartphones are typically sensitive to ultrasonic sound, their speakers are highly directional in those frequencies, which lead [20] to use audible frequencies. The authors also focused on peer-to-peer ranging rather than infrastructure to device ranging.

TDOA systems can remove the requirement of knowing exactly when a signal was transmitted by using what is known as *pseudo-ranging*. Pseudo-ranging computes distances by looking at the relative differences between the arrival of several signals, assuming they were all transmitted simultaneously or at known offsets. As compared to TOA and TOF approaches, this requires one additional transmitter to allow the common distance from all broadcasting devices to be estimated. GPS [7] is the most popular example of this ranging approach. Similar approaches have been applied towards ultrasonic communication [21, 22, 4]. The Dolphin [21, 22] system adopts a pseudo-ranging approach using a $50kHz$ carrier with Direct-Sequence-Spread-Spectrum (DSSS) modulation. While extremely accurate, this approach requires custom hardware and is not applicable to standard smartphones. In [23], the authors expand upon Dolphin (while still requiring custom hardware) by adding a self-training deployment approach based on filtered motion within the space. This work in part inspired our inter-beacon ranging capability. In [24] the authors identify the location of a cellular phone in a car using ultrasonic pseudo-ranging from the car's audio speakers. This approach used fixed frequency tones in an extremely controlled environment where data transfer was not required.

In [4], we introduced an ultrasonic TDOA ranging approach that is able to perform ranging between speakers distributed in the environment and mobile devices. The system utilizes commercial tweeters and is evaluated on previous generations of smartphones with a wider frequency range above $20kHz$ than the current generation (iPhone 4 as opposed to 5-6). The approach also only supports pseudo-ranging and not TOF. Followup work [5] extended the approach with clock synchronization to enable TOF ranging and simplify the modulation scheme to accommodate newer phones with less available bandwidth above $20kHz$. We further extend upon this work by completely replacing the data communication component of the system with BLE such that the ultrasound is only used for ranging. We also focus on the configuration elements of the system by providing a mechanism to rapidly set up and map spaces. In the previous work, NLOS signals were a significant source of error. In this work, we show an approach to both detect NLOS signals as well as improve tracking in their presence by fusing inertial data from the phone's on-board sensors.

The radio and communications community has studied differentiating LOS and NLOS signals in depth. A survey of this work can be found in [25]. The most common approaches either use the coherence of the signal [26] or they look at the distribution of multiple consecutive signals for classification [27]. A recent approach that utilized features directly derived from RSS to identify and mitigate NLOS signals can also be found in [28]. As described in Section 4, we saw that the coherence of the ultrasound signal was more significantly influenced by the environment rather than the expected multi-path component of a NLOS signal. As suggested by [27], the distribution of LOS data has much less variance as compared to NLOS data, but in our case the data rate is so low that it would take tens of seconds to arrive at a reliable confidence interval. In contrast, we utilize environment specific training along with the fact that we have two significantly different transmission media to help classify LOS and NLOS from a single transmission.

The robotics community has developed multiple approaches for SLAM in indoor environments. Early work in SLAM required range and bearing measurements from the landmarks. Our system provides range information as well as inter-node ranges which can aid in mapping. [29] proposes techniques to localize connected nodes with noisy range measurements. [30] proposes utilizing a mobile node to map beacons that are sparsely connected. In this paper, we present a technique for mapping three transmitters with inter-node ranging in a single area. In case of larger spaces with connected rooms, varied number of nodes in each space, and sparse connectivity between the beacons, we can draw upon techniques from [30] and [29]. Finally, Google's project Tango and sensors like Occipital's Structure use depth sensors to scan and map 3D environments. We believe that our approach can help augment these techniques during the mapping process (improving both techniques) and then can be used for localization once the mapping is complete.

3 Architecture

A typical *ALPS* setup consists of three or more transmitters deployed in the target area as seen in Figure 1. Placement of the transmitters is flexible, however in our current implementation each beacon should be within LOS of each other and placed such that LOS coverage is maximized. In most deployments, this typically means mounting them to the ceiling. The transmitters are time synchronized using 802.15.4 radios that listen to periodic transmissions from a master node. The timing master node can be one of the installed beacons. Current closed-source BLE implementations limit access to the lower levels of the stack which makes it difficult to use BLE for tight timing.

3.1 Hardware

We developed an embedded hardware platform for our transmission infrastructure shown in Figure 2, which consists of the following main components: (1) An ultrasound transceiver board with an 802.15.4 radio shown in Figure 3(a), (2) a BLE daughter board shown in Figure 3(b), (3) a piezo bullet tweeter with attached omni-directional horn and (4) a battery pack for optional battery powered operation.

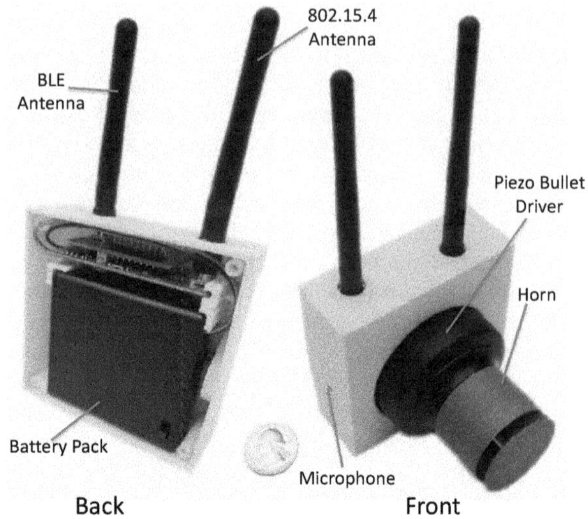

Figure 2. ALPS beacon

The ultrasound transceiver uses an Atmel Atmega256RFR2 SoC with an on-chip 802.15.4 radio. The CPU drives a Texas Instruments TLV320AIC3120 24-bit 192kHz audio codec via an I^2S interface, which we emulate using an SPI port and a timer output. The codec is connected to an Akustica AKU340 MEMS microphone for receiving ultrasound and includes an on-chip 1.6W (into 8 Ohms) class-D amplifier for driving the piezo tweeter. The system is able to achieve an audio sampling rate of 125kHz for playback and recording, which is limited by the clock speed of the microcontroller. This tightly coupled design allows for negligible end-to-end jitter from reception of an 802.15.4 packet to playback through the speaker of less than $20\mu s$.

The BLE daughter board shown in Figure 3(b) contains a TI CC2640 SoC with on-chip BLE radio and an ARM M3 core which attaches to the ultrasound transceiver board via two on-board connectors that supply it with power and connect I^2C and GPIO interfaces. BLE advertising transmissions can be triggered by the ultrasound transceiver through a GPIO interrupt to synchronize BLE and ultrasound packet transmission. The audio is produced by a low-cost ($< \$2.50$) Goldwood GT-400CD bullet piezo tweeter capable of producing sound well above our required frequency range of $20-21.5kHz$.

	Current (mA)	Power (mW)	Time (ms)	Energy (mJ)
100% Vol, Chirp	58.04	174.12	50	8.71
100% Vol, Tone	56.04	168.12	50	8.40
50% Vol, Chirp	33.31	99.30	50	4.97
50% Vol, Tone	32.77	98.31	50	4.97
BLE Idle	2.48	7.44	n/a	n/a
BLE Adv. 20ms	3.08	9.24	n/a	n/a

Table 1. Beacon power consumption

The power consumption of our prototype beacon is summarized in Table 1. The values for playback show the average power consumption of only the ultrasound transceiver board while continuously transmitting and the BLE numbers include the isolated BLE average power consumption. All currents were measured at a supply voltage of $3V$. Both boards draw a negligible amount of current ($< 800nA$ combined) when put into a deep-sleep mode. At 100% volume the beacon is capable of transmitting ultrasound signals to an off-the-shelf smartphone over a range of roughly $40m$. With ultrasound operating for 12h per day in a 7 slot TDMA schedule at half volume and BLE advertising continuously during these 12 hours, each beacon can operate from a 20AH lithium (Tadiran D-cell) battery for approximately 212.6 days. We believe that this can be optimized by a factor of 3-5x with more aggressive duty-cycling and improved BLE management. The audio efficiency could also be improved with a more efficient custom driver that resonates at our target frequencies.

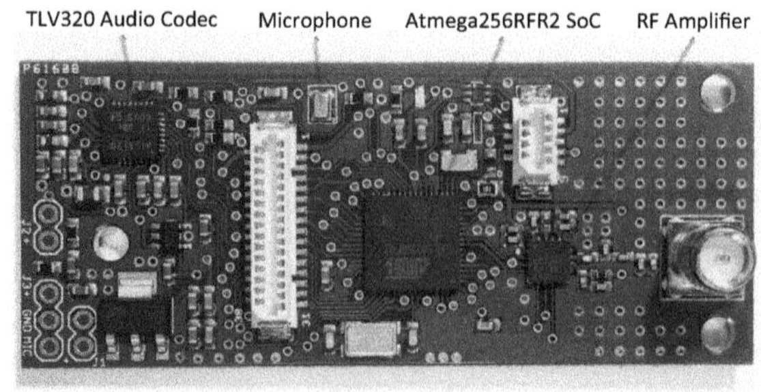

(a) MCU board

(b) MCU and BLE board

Figure 3. Ultrasonic beacon PCBs

3.2 Horn Design

In a typical loudspeaker, as the audio frequency increases, the spatial spread of the signal decreases, eventually forming a narrow beam. In our system, we ideally want an omnidirectional speaker that has a flat frequency response across the $18-24kHz$ frequency band that can uniformly deliver data without distortion. Since no such speaker was commercially available, we designed a custom transducer based on a multi-sector omni-directional horn design shown in Figure 2. This turned out to be a non-trivial effort that required significant experimentation.

We initially evaluated multiple commercial speakers in order to determine suitable driver components and geometries. In terms of frequency response, we found that ribbon tweeters had an excellent frequency response and horizontal dispersion pattern. Unfortunately, they require large magnets that are both heavy and expensive (\$50+). They also have a narrow vertical beam pattern. In certain scenarios,

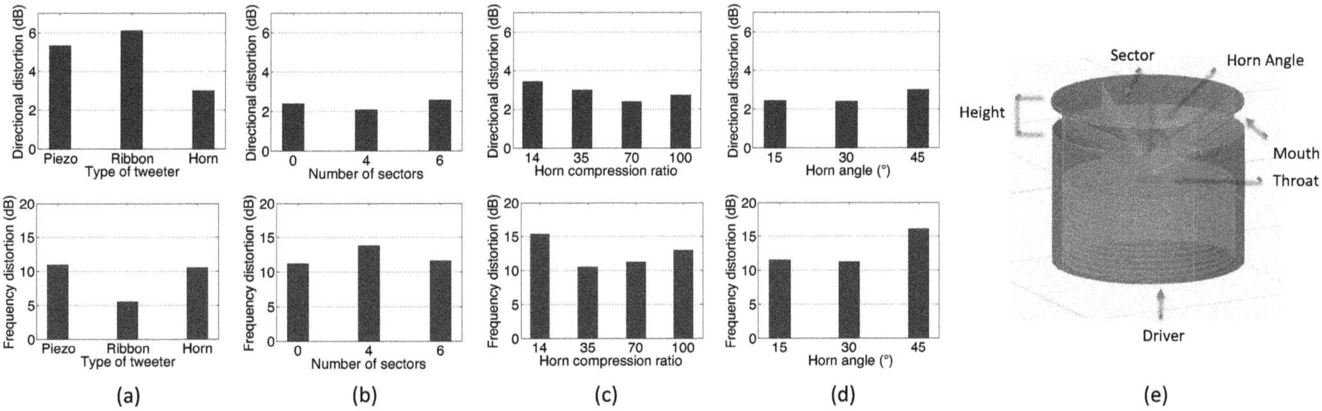

Figure 4. Low-cost piezo horn design evaluation

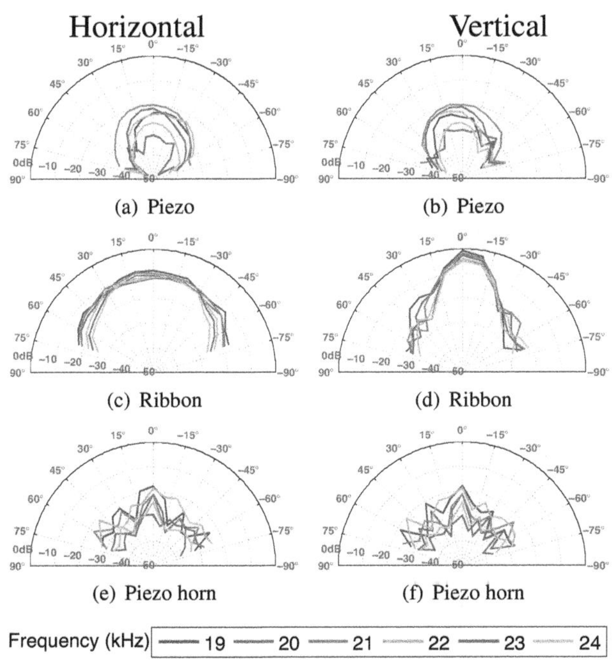

Figure 5. Ultrasonic beam patterns

they could be an ideal transducer but are too expensive for general purpose indoor localization applications. We also evaluated piezo electric tweeter elements since they are low-cost (< \$2.50) and have a reasonably linear frequency response. Unfortunately, without a horn to guide the signal, they are quite directional. The top two rows in Figure 5 show a comparison of the vertical and horizontal beam patterns of a ribbon tweeter and piezo driver.

The acoustic literature has many models that describe a wide variety of speaker designs [31]. Most of the common designs tend to be for audible frequencies and exhibit confined beam patterns. In order to design a custom horn, we initially modeled a cone based on standard horn equations. These models specify the width of the horn's mouth to be $4.76mm$ in diameter to support frequencies above $20kHz$. The resonant chamber needs to be at least 1 wavelength, or $1.6cm$ in length. The horn throat then needs to be sized in order to reduce distortion while having sufficient amplification. A point source (pin-hole speaker) would be ideal, except that the volume would be insufficient. Figure 4(e) shows the basic geometry of our omni-directional horn. In order to evaluate performance, we varied the horn angle, the height of the top of the horn and experimented with different numbers of internal sectors. Each horn variant was printed on an SLA 3D printer and then tested using a pan-tilt mechanism that allowed automatic frequency response measurements to be taken at different angles. We tested 12 different horn designs generating a vertical and horizontal frequency response plot measured using a swept sine deconvolution approach recorded on a measurement microphone.

We define two metrics to compare different speaker configurations. These metrics are computed from the gain values at different frequencies and directions, as seen in Figure 5. To measure the flatness of frequency response, we compute the frequency distortion. The frequency distortion of a speaker in a particular direction is the difference between the maximum and minimum gain in the frequency band of interest. We average this metric across all directions to compute the frequency distortion (lower plots in Figure 4(a-d)). To measure the deviation from omni-directionality for a speaker, we first find the gain in a particular direction by averaging the gain across the frequency band. We then compute the average deviation from the mean gain across all directions to arrive at the directional distortion (upper plots in Figure 4(a-d)). Both these metrics are averaged across the horizontal and vertical orientations for each speaker.

Frequency distortion as well as directional distortion both directly impact the SNR at the receiver. Frequency distortion will create a mismatch between the recorded signal and the template used during matched filtering, while directional distortion will vary the signal level with respect to the angle between the beacon and the receiver. A decrease in SNR increases timing jitter when determining the TOA of the received ultrasound transmissions, which in turn negatively impacts ranging and localization performance.

Since frequency response and amplitude can be compensated for through equalization and amplification (within reason), the most important factor is the directionality of the horn. Since the horn without sectors and the six sectored ver-

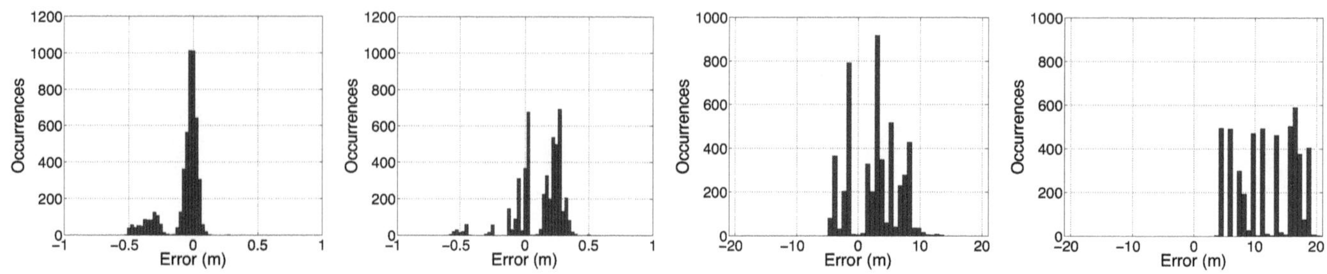

(a) Free space ultrasound ranging error (b) Corridor ultrasound ranging error (c) Free space iBeacon ranging error (d) Corridor iBeacon ranging error

Figure 6. Ultrasound and iBeacon ranging error in free space and corridor environments

sion with a 30° angle and a height of $10mm$ (compression ratio (throat area/mouth area) of 70) performed almost exactly the same in this respect, we selected the sectored version for increased mechanical stability. Figure 5(e) and Figure 5(f) show the beam pattern and frequency response across 140° of our final design.

3.3 Data and Ranging

In our previous work [4] and [5], we present two methods using ultrasonic chirps for modulating data and ranging information onto an ultrasound carrier. Similar to the system described in [5], we use TDMA to multiplex the transmission of our ultrasound transmitters over time and transmit ultrasonic chirps for precise ranging. Instead of encoding data using chirps, *ALPS* relies on BLE advertisement packets in an iBeacon compatible format to signal the current TDMA time slot. This eliminates the need for a complicated and more processing intensive demodulation step on the phone and makes the ultrasound signals shorter and more likely to be detected correctly. Receivers are also able to obtain BLE RSSI and iBeacon range measurements from these packets for detecting when a beacon is not within LOS.

Our ultrasound ranging signals consist of a $50ms$ up-chirp between $20kHz$ and $21.5kHz$ followed by a $50ms$ period of silence to wait for any reverberations to decay significantly. The silence duration as well as the volume is adjustable based on the room size and is determined during the configuration process. In the following time slot we broadcast an orthogonal $50ms$ down-chirp between $21.5kHz$ and $20kHz$ to further minimize possible interference from reverberation from the previous time slot and to allow the periods of silence between transmission to be kept to a minimum.

The primary requirements for a smartphone to be able to function as an ALPS receiver are that it is able to receive audio signals between at least $20-21.5kHz$ and delivers BLE advertisement packets to the application layer with low latency. In [32], the authors profile the frequency response of the microphones of 10 iOS and Android smart devices, and show that all of them provide adequate response in the $20-21.5kHz$ range.

In order to better understand the impact of the environment, we evaluated the ultrasound TOF and iBeacon ranging performance of our beacons in six different spaces. Figure 6 shows the ranging error in a free space and in a confined corridor setting. The data was collected by time synchronizing an iPhone 5S to the beacon by holding it directly at the speaker while it was playing evenly spaced $50ms$ chirp signals and then placing it at a known distance away from the beacon. The beacon would then transmit 500 additional periodic chirp signals per sampled distance after a known time delay, for which we calculated the measured distance based on the propagation time of the signal. We collected samples at 10 different beacon to receiver distances in every environment. 100 iBeacon distance samples were collected at the same time from the distance being reported in iOS. The iBeacon power level was calibrated by measuring its average RSSI at a 1m distance as recommended by Apple. For the free space case using ultrasound TOF a mean absolute ranging error of $8.9cm$ with 95% of the distance samples below $33.5cm$ in error was observed. The mean absolute ranging error for using iBeacon in this environment was $403.4cm$ with 95% of the distance samples below $845.6cm$ in error. For the corridor case a mean absolute ranging error of $17.9cm$ with 95% of the distance samples below $34.2cm$ in error was observed. The iBeacon distance measurements showed a mean absolute ranging error of $1209.9cm$ with 95% of the distance samples below $1861.3cm$ in error in this environment. We see that both BLE and ultrasound are negatively impacted by multi-path. This indicates that it is important to use the room geometry information to set transmit power.

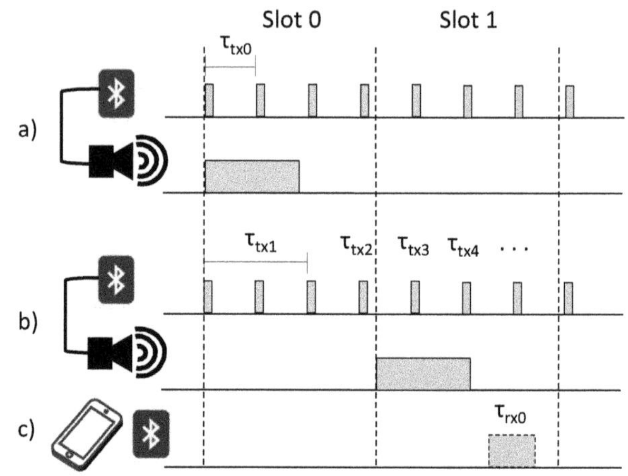

Figure 7. BLE timing data

In order to map received ultrasound transmissions to their respective transmitters, our beacons transmit periodic BLE advertisement packets that contain a counter value τ_{tx} indicating the time offset from the broadcast of the BLE advertisement packet to the beginning of the TDMA cycle shown

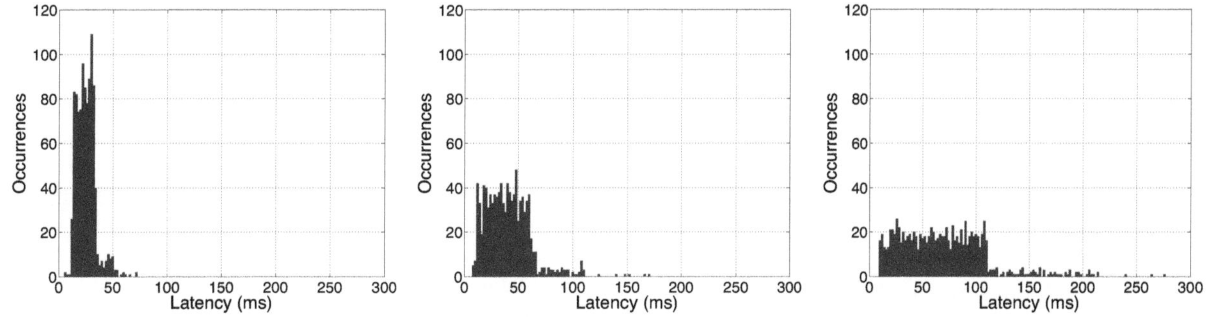

(a) 20ms advertisement interval (b) 50ms advertisement interval (c) 100ms advertisement interval

Figure 8. BLE advertisement packet reception latency

in Figure 7 (a), (b). Mobile receivers can synchronize to the TDMA cycle by timestamping the BLE packet reception τ_{rx} (Figure 7 (c)) and subtracting the received counter value from τ_{rx}. While BLE advertisement intervals can be as low as $20ms$, there is an indeterministic latency associated with receiving them in an application running on a smartphone. Typical smartphones such as the iPhone 5S do not allow low-level access to their BLE stack for accurate timestamping and also time-multiplex hardware resources between their WiFi, Bluetooth classic and BLE receivers, allowing them to only listen for BLE advertisements intermittently. On the iPhone 5S, received BLE advertisements are passed to the application roughly once a second, but it is unclear how often the phone receives BLE packets and how long it takes before they signal applications.

In order to evaluate the feasibility of time-synchronizing the phone to the TDMA cycle of the broadcasting infrastructure, we measured the latency between BLE advertisement packets and the audio input of an iPhone 5S. We set up a beacon to toggle a GPIO pin that was connected to the phone's microphone input when a new TDMA cycle started and simultaneously started broadcasting BLE advertisement packets containing τ_{tx}. The phone timestamped the reception of each BLE packet in the application and subtracted τ_{tx} to determine when the GPIO pin was toggled in its frame of reference. Simultaneously the phone was recording the GPIO trigger in an audio waveform, which was precisely timestamped to within $1ms$ using the technique detailed in [5]. Figure 8 shows the BLE advertisement packet reception latency for 20, 50 and $100ms$ advertisement intervals across 1000 packets. When set to a $20ms$ interval, we measured an average latency of $25.1ms$ with a maximum of $72.4ms$, which is well below our $100ms$ long TDMA slot length, hence allowing slot-accurate time synchronization via BLE. The less frequent intervals provided unacceptable worst-case latency of $169.3ms$ and $275.1ms$ (50 and $100ms$ intervals respectively).

3.4 Inter-beacon Ranging

In order to assist in determining the locations of the beacons, we require accurate direct inter-beacon measurements. Each beacon is equipped with a MEMS microphone connected to its audio codec which can stream audio to the network master node via 802.15.4. We implemented an inter-beacon TOF ranging procedure, where two beacons at a time listen for a trigger from the network master via 802.15.4, after which one of them transmits an ultrasonic ranging signal while the other records and streams the recording back to the network master for processing. The propagation time of the ultrasound signal can then simply be calculated from the received recording. Due to the higher sampling rate of the audio-codec (running at $125kHz$) and the direct RF time synchronization, this procedure provides range measurements with errors below $5cm$. We discuss how these measurements are used in Section 5.

4 Non-Line-of-Sight Filtering

A major source of error in TOF ranging systems is incorrect measurements due to NLOS signals. Failing to identify the NLOS signals can introduce estimation errors in ranging and thus seriously affect the localization performance. The identification of LOS/NLOS signals not only facilitates the process of selecting the right measurements, but also helps to further mitigate the ranging bias. Most of the identification techniques deal with the problem based on the range estimates or channel pulse response (CPR), but are often infeasible in real world since large amount of training data is required for characterization. The Cricket system [6] was one of the first efforts that noticed that the difference between two transmission media could be used to possibly infer NLOS transmissions. In Cricket, the frequency was quite high and the transmitters where highly directional, which likely made the correlation between RSSI distance and ultrasonic TOF more obvious. At lower frequencies, with chirp encoding and omni-directional transmitters, the ultrasound diffracts significantly more, making the distinction between LOS and NLOS more difficult.

In this section, we discuss the creation of a binary classifier for NLOS detection that is able to learn the characteristics of a space with relatively little training data. During our experiments, we collected 3600 samples of LOS data and 1200 samples of NLOS data from arbitrary locations in more then 6 environments. The unbalanced amount of LOS data and NLOS data are designed to model the real world scenario where LOS data is much easier to collect during the installation process. Since the rate of position updates is relatively low, we ideally want to find a set of features that can be extracted from a single measurement. The key insight to our approach is that we are able to detect ultrasonic TOF, ultrasonic RSSI and iBeacon RSSI, which are different in LOS and NLOS cases. In Table 2 we show classification accuracy

Features Set	Accuracy
$\{F_{us}\}$	0.644
$\{F_{iB}\}$	0.925
$\{F_{wave}\}$	0.767
$\{F_{delay}\}$	0.753
$\{F_{iB}, F_{wave}\}$	0.779
$\{F_{us}, F_{iB}\}$	0.965
$\{F_{delay}, F_{wave}\}$	0.787
$\{F_{us}, F_{iB}, F_{delay}\}$	0.959
$\{F_{us}, F_{iB}, F_{delay}, F_{wave}\}$	0.779

Table 2. Identification accuracy with multiple features

NLOS	Accuracy	FP	FN	Prec.	Recall
1%	0.805	0	0.195	1.00	0.805
4%	0.826	0	0.175	1.00	0.826
7%	0.837	0.007	0.156	0.992	0.843
10%	0.841	0.016	0.143	0.982	0.855

Table 3. Impact of training samples on F_{iB} and F_{us} performance

with different combinations of features, where F_{us} is the ratio of $RSSI_{us}$ to D_{iB}, F_{iB} is the ratio of $RSSI_{iB}$ to D_{iB}, F_{wav} is the normalized waveform of the received ultrasonic signal, and F_{delay} is the root mean square (RMS) delay spread of the ultrasonic signal. D_{iB} is the distance estimate returned by iBeacon, $RSSI_{us}$ and $RSSI_{iB}$ are RSSI values from ultrasonic and iBeacon respectively.

Based on the results in Table 2, we selected F_{us} and F_{iB} because they perform best with the least amount of training data. A Support Vector Machine (SVM) classifier is trained with 10-fold cross validation and grid search on selecting the best parameters in order to prevent over-fitting. Other features like the shape of the ultrasonic waveform performed poorly in our experiments.

In Table 3 we summarize the identification performance on our dataset while using 10% of the LOS data for training and varying the amount of NLOS data. We see that even with 1% of the NLOS data used for training, we are able to achieve 80% classification accuracy. In any one mapping collection cycle, this corresponds to about 300 LOS samples (which are easily captured while holding the phone in the open during the mapping phase) and 12 NLOS samples which the user is instructed to collect. However, we should note that most of classification error results from false negative (FN) instead of false positive (FP) due to the unbalanced data set, which can seriously decrease the performance of our localization algorithm. With an increased number of NLOS data samples in the training phase, we observe a slight increase in overall accuracy while FN probability greatly decreased as a trade-off with more data collection time.

As shown in Section 6, the ability to filter out NLOS measurements significantly increases overall localization performance.

5 User-Assisted Mapping

Any beacon-based localization system requires the location of the beacons with respect to the floor plan to provide meaningful location estimates. Most systems assume these beacon positions can be easily determined, but in practice this can be quite difficult. Errors in the position of the beacons can cause significant end-to-end localization errors. Generating beacon positions is a labor-intensive time-consuming process which involves either taking extensive range measurements to walls using laser rangers or employing other equipment like a robotic system with accurate motion control equipped with the ability to sense the signal from the beacons. What makes this process difficult is that the floor plan information itself may not be provided to the installer. We propose a semi-automatic mapping process where the installer deploys the beacons and walks around the room taking a few measurements to aid the mapping process.

The goal of the proposed mapping process is to (a) map the beacons with respect to the floor plan, and (b) generate the floor plan using landmarks such as the corners if it is not already available. This process can be performed by a non-expert user in a few minutes for a single area.

5.1 Procedure

The process for mapping three beacons in a single area is given below. The approach can be extended to more beacons in a single area and conceptually also multiple areas. Though not currently implemented, the app could potentially take existing floor plan images and determine anchor points within them. Our mobile app guides the user through these steps:

1. Deploy the three beacons such that they provide good coverage of the area and are in LOS of each other.
2. Hold the phone close to one of the beacons and select the *Sync* option in the app and wait for 10 seconds while the phone synchronizes to the beacons.
3. Identify three points on the floor such that all three beacons are visible from each point. Place the phone at each location, and select the *Floor reference point* option.
4. If the floor plan is not provided, walk around the room and go to each corner and select the *Corner reference point* option. This will compute line segments between the corner points.
5. Specify an origin and the orientation of the $x-y$ coordinate space. One way to do this is to select one of the corners as the origin and an adjacent corner to be on the x or y axis.

5.2 Algorithm

The basic principle of the 3-D mapping process is that we make use of the following three types of information to uniquely solve for the beacon positions (a) ultrasonic-based inter-node ranging (b) estimation of $z-plane$ using the three ground measurement points (c) user specified $x-y$ plane origin and orientation. The algorithm for mapping three beacons is as follows:

1. Given inter-node ranges r_{12}, r_{23}, r_{13} between the three beacons B_1, B_2, B_3, define a 3-D coordinate system $\mathbb{R}^3_a$ such that the three beacons are on the $z=0$ plane, B_1 is the the origin $[0,0,0]$, and B_2 is along the x axis $[r_{12},0,0]$. Coordinates of B_3 can be obtained as $[r_{13}\cos(\alpha), r_{13}\sin(\alpha), 0]$, where $\alpha = \arccos(\frac{r_{12}^2+r_{13}^2-r_{23}^2}{2r_{12}r_{13}})$

Figure 9. Panorama of automatically configured kitchen area using three beacons

2. Estimate the coordinates of the three ground measurement points with respect to the beacons in $\mathbb{R}_a^3$.
3. Define a new coordinate system $\mathbb{R}_b^3$ such that the plane that contains the three ground points is the new $z = 0$ plane in $\mathbb{R}_b^3$.
4. The $x-y$ plane of $\mathbb{R}_b^3$ can be defined by its origin and one of the axes. This can be chosen arbitrarily since we would re-assign the $x-y$ plane after generating the floor plan. In our implementation, we did the following: The projection of B_1 on the $x-y$ plane is assigned as the origin $(0,0,0)$ of $\mathbb{R}_b^3$. The projection of B_2 on this plane is assigned to lie on the y-axis of the new plane. The x-axis of $\mathbb{R}_b^3$ is found to be normal to the y and z axes.
5. Estimate the location of all the corner points in $\mathbb{R}_b^3$ using trilateration.
6. The $x-y$ coordinates of the required 2-D coordinate system are specified by the user during the calibration process. Either apply an affine transformation on $\mathbb{R}_b^3$ to get the final coordinate system, or for better accuracy, apply non-linear transformations to minimize error across all reference points if more than two reference points are available.

5.3 Evaluation

We evaluated our mapping process in half a dozen areas: a kitchen and lounge space, a lab, and in four office areas. The largest space in terms of area and number of corners was a lounge and kitchen space, as shown in Figure 9, with a total area of around 775 sq ft. and 10 corners. The generated map is shown in Figure 10. Note that this process requires all the corners to be in LOS of the three beacons. Some of the boundaries in Figure 10 were not physical walls but were either $1.5m$ tall partitions or were chosen to ensure all corners are in LOS. The results of the mapping process for the kitchen setup and averaged across all six experimental setups are shown in Table 4. Our system can determine three-dimensional beacon location with a Euclidean distance error of $16.1cm$ averaged over the three beacons, and can generate maps with room measurements with a two-dimensional Euclidean distance error of $19.8cm$ averaged over all the corners. We observe that while mapping the beacons, the overall error in the height is around $13.5cm$, while the error in the x or y coordinate is less than $4cm$. This is because the height

	Beacon Error (cm)				Corner Error (cm)	
Setup	**Avg.**	**x**	**y**	**z**	**Avg.**	**Max**
Kitchen	13.9	2.2	1.4	13.4	26.8	43.6
Lab	18.2	5.4	3.6	13.6	13.0	25.2
Office 1	17.5	4.6	3.5	15.0	10.7	13.9
Office 2	17.2	5.0	1.6	15.1	22.8	34.0
Office 3	15.5	2.3	1.7	11.1	18.9	40.9
Office 4	14.1	3.4	3.1	12.9	26.5	31.4
Overall	16.1	3.8	2.5	13.5	19.8	43.6

Table 4. Mapping error

of the beacons were within $1m$ of each other whereas they were well separated in the $x-y$ plane. Hence the height is more sensitive to errors.

6 Localization and Tracking

Once the beacons are mapped, they are capable of localizing a user in the region. During the mapping phase, as explained in Section 5.1, the user first places the mobile phone close to one of the beacons in order to synchronize with the infrastructure. However, we cannot expect this synchronization when the system is used for localization. In a 3D space with the beacons synchronized to each other, but not to the mobile phone, we must instead perform TDOA-based pseudo-ranging. In the presence of 3 beacons we cannot uniquely use trilateration to estimate the locations of the measurement points. We assume the height of the phone is between 0.9 and $1.2m$ and perform the multilateration. If there are regions where four or more beacons are located, we can adopt the technique in [5] to synchronize the phone to the beacons. This is done by first determining the phone's position using TDOA ranging and multilateration and then calculating the distance to at least one beacon. Since the ultrasound transmissions are periodic, the beginning of the TDMA cycle can be determined based on the distance to a beacon, the TOA of the transmission in the phone's recording buffer and the time slot of the transmission. Since the phone's ADC has a free running clock, we can synchronize it to the transmission cycle of the beacons by determining the sample in the recording buffer that corresponds to the beginning of the TDMA cycle. This then allows for TOF ranging to be used instead of TDOA. To solve for the location with only three beacons, we search through the region and find the 3D position that gives the minimum mean square error in TDOA for the obtained measurements. We can determine the bounds of the region in which we should perform this

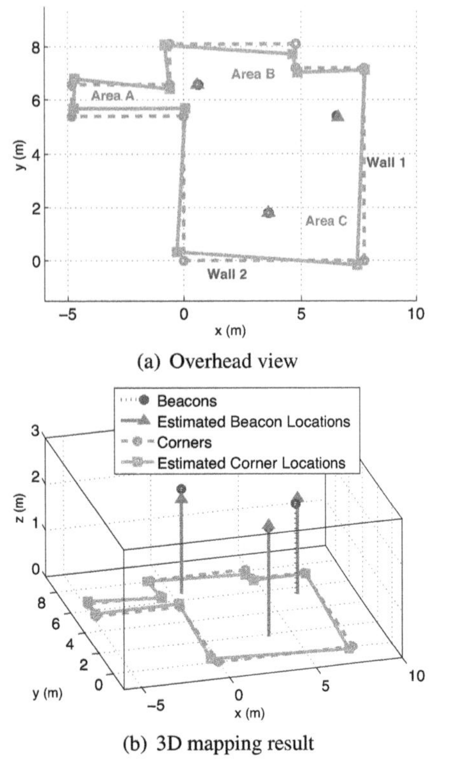

(a) Overhead view

(b) 3D mapping result

Figure 10. Kitchen area mapping output

search based on the set of beacons where we receive BLE data. We perform the search in an iterative manner, first on a $1m \times 1m$ grid, then $20cm \times 20cm$ and finally $2cm \times 2cm$ grid.

As can be seen in Figure 11(b), the system provides a localization accuracy within $30cm$ 90% of the time. However, in situations where the user blocks one or more transmitters while walking, or when a NLOS signal is detected, the system cannot update the location estimate. In these situations we make use of the Inertial Measurement Unit (IMU) sensors on the phone and a motion model to track the user and provide location updates as explained in the next section.

6.1 Implementation of Extended Kalman Filter (EKF) for Tracking

We implement an EKF to filter the location estimates of a mobile user by utilizing the phone's IMU sensors for tracking. For step count and direction we use the step count from the iPhone's accelerometer and the direction from the compass which already fuses the magnetometer with the rate gyros. The details of our process model and measurement model for the EKF are given below.

Our objective is the estimate the 2-D position (x_t, y_t) of the mobile device at time t. We define the state vector as:

$$X_t = \begin{bmatrix} x_t \\ y_t \end{bmatrix} \sim \mathcal{N}(\mu_t, \Sigma_t)$$

where μ_t is the expected value of X_t and Σ_t is the uncertainty in the state. The EKF generates estimates of μ_t and Σ_t based on the prediction from the previous state X_{t-1} and the process model, and then updates this estimate based on measurement Z_t and the measurement model. A time step of $t = 1$ is the time a person takes for one step while walking.

6.1.1 *Process Model*

The input u_t to this system is given by:

$$u_t = \begin{bmatrix} \Delta D_t \\ \theta_t \end{bmatrix}$$

with noise v_t such that:

$$v_t = \begin{bmatrix} v_t^D \\ v_t^\theta \end{bmatrix} \sim \mathcal{N}(0, M_t)$$

$$M_t = \begin{bmatrix} \sigma_D^2 & 0 \\ 0 & \sigma_\theta^2 \end{bmatrix}$$

ΔD_t is the step length of mobile device and θ_t is the heading. The step length and heading of the mobile device can be estimated from its IMU sensors and are used as input to the filter. σ_D^2 and σ_θ^2 are the variance in the step length and heading respectively. The focus of our work is not on implementing an accurate step length and heading estimation method, so for our model we conservatively assumed that $2\sigma_D$ is $10cm$ and $2\sigma_\theta$ as $45°$ (For a normal distribution 95.45% of the values lie within 2σ of the mean)

The process model is given by

$$\begin{bmatrix} x_t \\ y_t \end{bmatrix} = \begin{bmatrix} x_{t-1} \\ y_{t-1} \end{bmatrix} + \begin{bmatrix} (\Delta D_t + v_t^D)\cos(\theta_t + v_t^\theta) \\ (\Delta D_t + v_t^D)\sin(\theta_t + v_t^\theta) \end{bmatrix}$$

The process model is linearized and μ_t and Σ_t are updated as:

$$\mu_t = g(\mu_{t-1}, u_t)$$

$$\Sigma_t = G_t \Sigma_{t-1} G_t^T + R_t$$

where

$$g(\mu_{t-1}, u_t) = G_t \mu_{t-1} + \begin{bmatrix} \Delta D_t \cos(\theta_t) \\ \Delta D_t \sin(\theta_t) \end{bmatrix}$$

$$G_t = \begin{bmatrix} 1 & 0 \\ 0 & 1 \end{bmatrix}$$

$$R_t = V_t M_t V_t^T$$

$$V_t = \frac{\partial g(\mu_{t-1}, u_t)}{\partial u_t}$$

$$V_t = \begin{bmatrix} \cos(\theta_t) & -\Delta D_t \sin(\theta_t) \\ \sin(\theta_t) & \Delta D_t \cos(\theta_t) \end{bmatrix}$$

6.1.2 *Measurement Model*

Though the actual measurements from our system are the TDOA values from the set of visible transmitters, these can not be directly used with an EKF due to the linear approximation of the TDOA equations. Instead, we first estimate the position using the TDOA measurements, and use this estimate as our measurement. Our measurement model is given by:

$$Z_t = \begin{bmatrix} x_t \\ y_t \end{bmatrix} + w_t$$

$$w_t \sim \mathcal{N}(0, Q_t)$$

where $Z_t = [\hat{x}_t, \hat{y}_t]^T$ is obtained by multilateration. From Figure 11, we observe that 90% of the range errors are less than

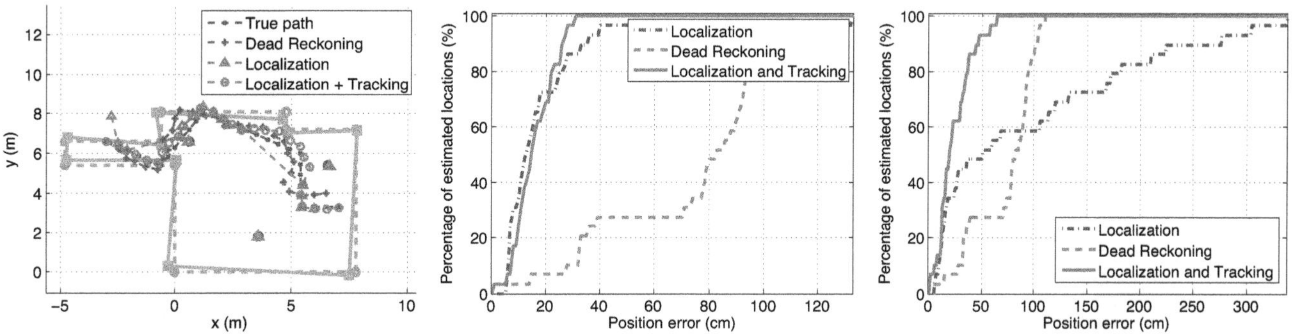

(a) Tracking path (b) CDF without obstacles (c) CDF with obstacles

Figure 11. Tracking performance in the kitchen with and without obstructions. Note scale of x-axis.

$30cm$. We assume that the errors in the $\hat{x}_t$ and $\hat{y}_t$ are uncorrelated and assign $Q_t = \sigma_z I$ where $\sigma_z = 30cm$

In case one or more transmitters are blocked, or if the phone identifies that one of the signals from the beacons is a NLOS signal, it does not update its measurement Z_t. In this case, we assign $Q_t = \sigma_n I$ where σ_n is a large number, such that the filtering effectively updates the estimate of the location based purely on tracking.

6.2 Evaluation

We evaluated the accuracy of our system, and the localization and tracking algorithm in the same 6 experimental environments where we performed the beacon mapping. We used the map that was generated by our mapping process. In each test a user held an iPhone 5S and took approximately 30 steps in the area. We collected data from the compass and read step values. Ultrasonic measurements from the beacons were also collected at every step. We analyzed the data offline using Matlab. Results from our largest scenario (the kitchen area) are presented in Figure 11. The *Localization* line refers to position estimated based on only the ranges from the beacons, the *Pedestrian Dead Reckoning* line refers to position estimates purely based on the IMU sensors and the motion model, the *Localization and Tracking* line refers to the output of the EKF explained above. Figure 11(b) shows that tracking does not improve the accuracy much as compared to using only localization since the localization is much more accurate (error less than $30cm$ 90% of the time) than the estimates from the motion model. We then simulated situations when the user blocks one transmitter by removing some of the range measurements from a beacon in the data-set. The *Localization* line in Figure 11(a) shows the localization estimates under this case. The location does not update when insufficient measurements are received. We observe that in such cases the system benefits from tracking, as seen in Figure 11(c), and the error is less than $50cm$ 90% of the time.

7 Limitations

While promising, there are still a number of open challenges with respect to *ALPS*. Users are required to install three beacons per LOS location. If the beacons share the same height then z-axis resolution will be limited. The NLOS detection system is still environment dependent and it can be difficult to capture a comprehensive data set. All beacons require LOS in order to accurately determine their distances as part of the setup process. The proposed mapping process works for a single space covered by three beacons. In the future, we intend to look at using tracking of the mobile device as part of the mapping process to link multiple regions, possibly connected by corridors or separated by walls or doors. The power requirement of the ultrasonic transmitters is still relatively high compared to BLE-only solutions, which require larger packaging or more frequent battery replacement. This approach also requires two radios in order to synchronize and communicate with mobile phones. We believe that BLE alone could provide synchronization between beacons in the future. Another consideration is that the system transmits in a frequency range that is audible to animals. We believe that the duration, duty-cycle and volume of the system can be set low enough that the impact on animals would be minimal. Some motion detectors already operate at this frequency.

8 Conclusions

In order for indoor localization systems to gain traction, they need to be precise and simple to install. This paper presents a platform called *ALPS* that uses a combination of ultrasound and BLE to rapidly bootstrap precise localization in small and medium sized areas. After placing three or more beacons on the ceiling of an area, the devices communicate with each other and a phone app walks the user through a calibration and mapping process. In our experiments, users were able to map room corners and the beacon positions with an average error of $19.8cm$ and $16.1cm$ respectively, without having to manually measure any distances. They would simply capture key locations by placing their phone as instructed by an app. Once the map has been generated, the system can perform precise localization using TDOA data from ultrasonic transmitters that utilize bandwidth just above the human hearing range, but can still be detected by modern smartphones. When beacons are blocked, the system is able to continue estimating positions based on inertial data from the phone as well as filter out NLOS signals using an SVM classifier that looks at the ratios between BLE RSSI, ultrasonic RSSI and ultrasonic TOF. We designed and evaluated a stand-alone hardware platform that is able to broadcast time synchronized ultrasonic signals along with BLE packets.

9 Acknowledgements

This research was funded in part by the Bosch Research and Technology Center in Pittsburgh and TerraSwarm, one of six centers of STARnet, a Semiconductor Research Corporation program sponsored by MARCO and DARPA.

10 References

[1] Gimbal: http://www.gimbal.com/ (viewed 2/13/2015).

[2] iBeacon: https://developer.apple.com/ibeacon/ (viewed 2/13/2015).

[3] Dimitrios Lymberopoulos, Domenico Giustiniano, Vincent Lenders, Maurizio Rea, Andreas Marcaletti, et al. A realistic evaluation and comparison of indoor location technologies: Experiences and lessons learned. In *Proceedings of the 13th International Symposium on Information Processing in Sensor Networks*, IPSN '14, 2015.

[4] Patrick Lazik and Anthony Rowe. Indoor pseudo-ranging of mobile devices using ultrasonic chirps. In *Proceedings of the 10th ACM Conference on Embedded Network Sensor Systems*, SenSys '12, pages 99–112, Toronto, Ontario, Canada, 2012. ACM.

[5] Patrick Lazik, Niranjini Rajagopal, Bruno Sinopoli, and Anthony Rowe. Ultrasonic time synchronization and ranging on smartphones. In *21st IEEE Real-Time and Embedded Technology and Applications Symposium*, RTAS '14, 2014.

[6] Nissanka B. Priyantha, Anit Chakraborty, and Hari Balakrishnan. The cricket location-support system. In *Proceedings of the 6th Annual International Conference on Mobile Computing and Networking (Mobicom '00)*, pages 32–43, New York, NY, USA, 2000. ACM.

[7] B.W. Parkinson and S.W. Gilbert. Navstar: Global positioning system - ten years later. *Proceedings of the IEEE*, 71(10):1177 – 1186, oct. 1983.

[8] Gaetano Borriello, Alan Liu, Tony Offer, Christopher Palistrant, and Richard Sharp. Walrus: wireless acoustic location with room-level resolution using ultrasound. In *Proceedings of the 3rd International Conference on Mobile Systems, Applications, and Services (MobiSys '05)*, pages 191–203, New York, NY, USA, 2005. ACM.

[9] Kamin Whitehouse, Chris Karlof, Alec Woo, Fred Jiang, and David Culler. The effects of ranging noise on multihop localization: An empirical study. In *Proceedings of the 4th International Symposium on Information Processing in Sensor Networks*, IPSN '05, Piscataway, NJ, USA, 2005. IEEE Press.

[10] P. Bahl and V.N. Padmanabhan. Radar: an in-building rf-based user location and tracking system. In *Proceedings of the 19th Annual Joint Conference of the IEEE Computer and Communications Societies (INFOCOM '00)*, volume 2, pages 775 –784, 2000.

[11] A. Ward, A. Jones, and A. Hopper. A new location technique for the active office. *IEEE Personal Communications*, 4(5):42 –47, oct 1997.

[12] Konrad Lorincz and Matt Welsh. Motetrack: a robust, decentralized approach to rf-based location tracking. In *Proceedings of the 1st International Conference on Location- and Context-Awareness (LoCA'05)*, pages 63–82, Berlin, Heidelberg, 2005. Springer-Verlag.

[13] Stephen P. Tarzia, Peter A. Dinda, Robert P. Dick, and Gokhan Memik. Indoor localization without infrastructure using the acoustic background spectrum. In *Proceedings of the 9th International Conference on Mobile Systems, Applications, and Services (MobiSys '11)*, pages 155–168, New York, NY, USA, 2011. ACM.

[14] Zhuoling Xiao, Hongkai Wen, Andrew Markham, and Niki Trigoni. Lightweight map matching for indoor localisation using conditional random fields. In *Proceedings of the 13th International Symposium on Information Processing in Sensor Networks*, IPSN '14, pages 131–142, Piscataway, NJ, USA, 2014. IEEE Press.

[15] Anshul Rai, Krishna Kant Chintalapudi, Venkata N. Padmanabhan, and Rijurekha Sen. Zee: Zero-effort crowdsourcing for indoor localization. In *Proceedings of the 18th Annual International Conference on Mobile Computing and Networking*, Mobicom '12, pages 293–304, New York, NY, USA, 2012. ACM.

[16] Pengfei Zhou, Mo Li, and Guobin Shen. Use it free: Instantly knowing your phone attitude. In *Proceedings of the 20th Annual International Conference on Mobile Computing and Networking*, MobiCom '14, pages 605–616, New York, NY, USA, 2014. ACM.

[17] Isaac Amundson and Xenofon D. Koutsoukos. A survey on localization for mobile wireless sensor networks. In *Proceedings of the 2nd International Conference on Mobile Entity Localization and Tracking in GPS-less Environments (MELT '09)*, pages 235–254, Berlin, Heidelberg, 2009. Springer-Verlag.

[18] Kaveh Pahlavan, Xinrong Li, Mika Ylianttila, Ranvir Chana, and Matti Latva-aho. An overview of wireless indoor geolocation techniques and systems. In *Proceedings of the IFIP-TC6/European Commission International Workshop on Mobile and Wireless Communication Networks (NETWORKING '00)*, pages 1–13, London, UK, UK, 2000. Springer-Verlag.

[19] Zheng Sun, R. Farley, T. Kaleas, J. Ellis, and K. Chikkappa. Cortina: Collaborative context-aware indoor positioning employing rss and rtof techniques. In *IEEE International Conference on Pervasive Computing and Communications Workshops (PERCOM '11 Workshops)*, pages 340 –343, march 2011.

[20] Chunyi Peng, Guobin Shen, Zheng Han, Yongguang Zhang, Yanlin Li, and Kun Tan. A beepbeep ranging system on mobile phones. In *Proceedings of the 5th International Conference on Embedded Networked Sensor Systems (SenSys '07)*, pages 397–398, New York, NY, USA, 2007. ACM.

[21] Mike Hazas and Andy Ward. A novel broadband ultrasonic location system. In *Proceedings of the 4th International Conference on Ubiquitous Computing (UbiComp '02)*, pages 264–280, London, UK, UK, 2002. Springer-Verlag.

[22] Mike Hazas and Andy Ward. A high performance privacy-oriented location system. In *Proceedings of the 1st IEEE International Conference on Pervasive Computing and Communications (PERCOM '03)*, pages 216–223, Washington, DC, USA, 2003. IEEE Computer Society.

[23] Michael McCarthy, Paul Duff, Henk L. Muller, and Cliff Randell. Accessible ultrasonic positioning. *IEEE Pervasive Computing*, 5(4):86–93, October 2006.

[24] Jie Yang, Simon Sidhom, Gayathri Chandrasekaran, Tam Vu, Hongbo Liu, Nicolae Cecan, Yingying Chen, Marco Gruteser, and Richard P. Martin. Detecting driver phone use leveraging car speakers. In *Proceedings of the 17th Annual International Conference on Mobile Computing and Networking (MobiCom '11)*, pages 97–108, New York, NY, USA, 2011. ACM.

[25] M.P. Wylie and J. Holtzman. The non-line of sight problem in mobile location estimation. In *Universal Personal Communications, 1996. Record., 1996 5th IEEE International Conference on*, volume 2, pages 827–831 vol.2, Sep 1996.

[26] C. Tepedelenlioglu and G.B. Giannakis. On velocity estimation and correlation properties of narrow-band mobile communication channels. *Vehicular Technology, IEEE Transactions on*, 50(4):1039–1052, Jul 2001.

[27] S. Venkatraman and J. Caffery. statistical approach to non-line-of-sight bs identification. In *Wireless Personal Multimedia Communications, 2002. The 5th International Symposium on*, volume 1, pages 296–300 vol.1, Oct 2002.

[28] Zhuoling Xiao, Hongkai Wen, Andrew Markham, Niki Trigoni, Phil Blunsom, and Jeff Frolik. Non-line-of-sight identification and mitigation using received signal strength. *Wireless Communications, IEEE Transactions on*, 14(3):1689–1702, 2015.

[29] David Moore, John Leonard, Daniela Rus, and Seth Teller. Robust distributed network localization with noisy range measurements. In *Proceedings of the 2nd international conference on Embedded networked sensor systems*, pages 50–61. ACM, 2004.

[30] Joseph Djugash, Sanjiv Singh, George Kantor, and Wei Zhang. Range-only slam for robots operating cooperatively with sensor networks. In *Robotics and Automation, 2006. ICRA 2006. Proceedings 2006 IEEE International Conference on*, pages 2078–2084. IEEE, 2006.

[31] L.L. Beranek. *Acoustics*. McGraw-Hill electrical and electronic engineering series. McGraw-Hill, 1954.

[32] Hyewon Lee, Tae Hyun Kim, Jun Won Choi, and Sunghyun Choi. Chirp signal-based aerial acoustic communication for smart devices. In *Computer Communications (INFOCOM), 2015 IEEE Conference on*, pages 2407–2415, April 2015.

iMoon: Using Smartphones for Image-based Indoor Navigation

Jiang Dong Yu Xiao Marius Noreikis Zhonghong Ou Antti Ylä-Jääski
{jiang.dong, yu.xiao, marius.noreikis, zhonghong.ou, antti.yla-jaaski}@aalto.fi
Aalto University
Espoo, Finland

ABSTRACT

The adoption of indoor navigation for smartphones has been relatively slow in the past years, although it would be direly needed in complex indoor areas. The primary barriers for its adoption include the lack of fine-grained and up-to-date indoor maps and the potential deployment and maintenance cost. In this paper we investigate the feasibility of utilizing crowdsourced data for building a smartphone-based indoor navigation system, focusing on the technical challenges caused by the varying quality of crowdsourced data. We developed *iMoon*, an indoor navigation system based on sensor-enriched 3D models of indoor environment, and evaluated its performance via a field study in a public building covering around 1,100 m^2.

iMoon builds 3D models of indoor environment from crowdsourced 2D photos, and compiles a navigation mesh from the generated 3D models. Depending on the input for 3D modelling, indoor pedestrian paths may be partly missing from the output. *iMoon* solves this issue by integrating into navigation mesh the pedestrian paths recognized from crowdsourced user motion trajectories. With photo-based 3D models, *iMoon* supports image-based localization that identifies user's position and facing direction with photos, and provides visual navigation instructions that show when and where to turn. To reduce response delay while maintaining the accuracy of localization, *iMoon* partitions 3D models based on the density of 3D points, and selects partitions for image-based localization using Wi-Fi fingerprints. According to our experimental results, *iMoon* works properly, and our solution of indoor localization achieves competitive performance compared with traditional approaches: in most cases, a user can be located within an average of 3.85 seconds with a location error of less than 2 meters and a facing direction error of less than 6 degrees.

Categories and Subject Descriptors

C.2.4 [**Computer-Communication Networks**]: Distributed Systems

SenSys'15, November 1–4, 2015, Seoul, South Korea.
ACM 978-1-4503-3631-4/15/11.
DOI: http://dx.doi.org/10.1145/2809695.2809722 .

Keywords

Indoor mapping; Indoor navigation; 3D modelling; Mobile crowdsensing

1. INTRODUCTION

Indoor navigation systems for smartphones would be direly needed in complex indoor environments such as airports, shopping malls and museums. Unfortunately, the adoption rate of indoor navigation systems is still very low, even though initial efforts into deploying them were taken several decades ago. There are multiple reasons for the slow progress. First of all, indoor navigation requires fine-grained and up-to-date indoor maps that provide sufficient information for calculating navigation routes and instructions. Although floor plans are widely available in public places like shopping malls and airports, most of them lack details, or have not been kept up to date. Therefore, they can rarely be used directly for indoor navigation. Secondly, even in the case where accurate indoor maps do exist, most systems rely on pre-scanned radio maps or pre-installed hardware [13, 17] for localization, which are expensive to put into use and cumbersome to maintain. Thus, we saw it worthwhile to investigate whether we could develop an alternative indoor navigation method that would not need pre-created indoor maps, pre-scanned radio maps or pre-installed hardware. Inspired by the success of mobile crowdsensing applications [24] such as Waze social GPS maps & traffic[1] and OpenSignal[2], we came to the conclusion that mobile crowdsensing might be the key for creating such a system. The indoor navigation system *iMoon* was born out of this investigative work.

iMoon is based on sensor-enriched 3D models that are created and constantly maintained using crowdsourced photos and sensor data collected from smartphones. The system can be bootstrapped in a new location by taking photos and collecting sensor data in random spots in the location. Furthermore, photos publicly available from the Internet can also be used. Our previous work [8] demonstrates that it is feasible to build initial 3D models for places of interests, e.g., Rock Church in Helsinki, for indoor localization purpose, by using photos downloaded from Flickr. As *iMoon* users[3] enter the location, move around, and navigate using the app, the system constantly updates the 3D models with

[1] https://www.waze.com/
[2] http://opensignal.com/
[3] A demo video of *iMoon* mobile app is available on YouTube: `https://youtu.be/sNvf7N_s59c`

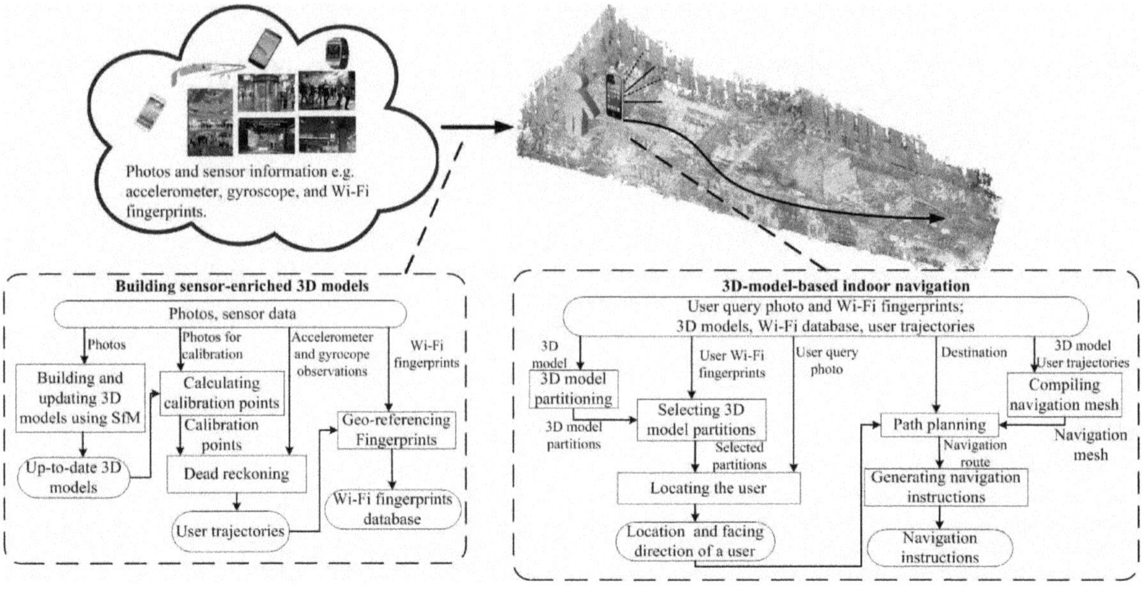

Figure 1: Overview of *iMoon*, a mobile crowdsensing-based indoor navigation system for smartphones.

new photos and sensor data collected from the users' devices. In practice, the more the system is used in a location, the more accurate it will get.

iMoon utilizes several existing techniques as building blocks. The primary contribution of *iMoon* is that it provides a whole-system solution for mobile crowdsensing-based indoor navigation, and addresses several technical challenges that are caused by the varying quality of crowdsourced data.

Firstly, *iMoon* takes crowdsourced photos as the input to build 3D models (in the form of 3D point clouds) of the indoor space of interest using Structure-from-Motion (SfM)[4] techniques [10, 30, 32], and then creates navigation meshes for path planning based on the obstacle information extracted from the 3D models. Because the crowdsourced photos are taken using different devices at random locations, the generated 3D models may not cover every corner of the space, and may include denser points in certain areas than others. As a result, the pedestrian path information needed for calculating navigation routes may be partially missing from the navigation meshes. To tackle this problem, we propose to track user trajectories using motion sensors available on smartphones, and integrate the pedestrian paths extracted from the crowdsourced user trajectories into the navigation meshes.

Secondly, with 3D SfM models, *iMoon* provides image-based localization that identifies user's position and facing direction using the photos taken in situ. The problem with this approach is that the response time increases significantly as the sizes of the 3D models increase, because location is determined by matching the 2D features in the query photo against the 3D points contained in the 3D models. To enable fast localization, *iMoon* employs model partitioning based on the density of 3D points, and selects partitions for feature matching based on Wi-Fi fingerprinting. Experimental results demonstrate good performance for this partitioning scheme.

In this paper we present the design, implementation and thorough evaluation of *iMoon*. The contributions of this paper are summarized as follows:

1) We address several technical challenges to enable *iMoon*: we combine the pedestrian paths recognized from crowdsourced user trajectories to complement the incomplete ones extracted from crowdsourced 3D models of indoor environment; we speed up the localization process by density-based model partitioning and fingerprint-based partition selection for compute-intensive operations.

2) We develop algorithms to generate simple, yet intuitive sets of choreographed visual navigation instructions to benefit people with difficulties in reading maps.

3) We implement a prototype of *iMoon* to evaluate its feasibility and performance. Experimental results demonstrate that *iMoon* works properly and has good performance. According to our experiments carried out in a real building covering around 1,100 m^2, using a 3D point cloud generated from 2,197 photos, in most cases, *iMoon* can locate a user within 4 seconds, with a location error of less than 2 meters and a facing direction error of less than 6 degrees.

It is worth noting that the response delay can further be shortened by offloading computation to more powerful machines. In addition, the *iMoon* client can be run on wearable devices like Google Glasses to provide better user experience, especially for people with visual impairment.

2. SYSTEM OVERVIEW

We argue that a good indoor navigation system should fulfill the following requirements: (1) it should be able to locate the users precisely and efficiently; (2) it should supply the users with flexible navigation routes and user-friendly navigation instructions. To date, when people are talking about indoor navigation, it is usually assumed that fine-grained and up-to-date indoor maps already exist for navigation purpose. In reality, however, such maps are not yet

[4]SfM itself refers to the process of simultaneously computing a 3D point cloud (the structure) representing the pictured scene and the camera pose per each image (the motion).

widely available. Furthermore, today's navigation instructions are mostly in texts or texts-converted voice, which are problematic for people having difficulties in reading maps.

The *iMoon* indoor navigation system fulfils the aforementioned requirements. The system is based on a client/server architecture. The client serves two purposes: (1) collecting photos and sensor data (i.e., accelerometer, gyroscope and Wi-Fi fingerprints) to assist the server to build 3D models for indoor environment; (2) providing localization results and navigation instructions to the users.

Accordingly, as illustrated in Figure 1, the server provides two main functions: (1) building sensor-enriched 3D models, (2) and providing navigation services based on the 3D models. These functions are explained briefly below, while more details will be given in Section 3 and Section 4, respectively.

Building sensor-enriched 3D models. Firstly, *iMoon* builds an initial 3D model from the crowdsourced photos using SfM techniques. The 3D model will be updated constantly by newly collected photos, either from the Internet or from the *iMoon* clients. Secondly, *iMoon* detects user trajectories and adds them to the 3D model. In practice, sensor data including accelerometer and gyroscope readings are used as the base for detecting user trajectories. These trajectories are automatically calibrated by the photos taken on the way. Thirdly, the Wi-Fi fingerprints collected along the user trajectories are automatically geo-referenced and added to the 3D model to enable fast localization.

3D-model-based indoor navigation. iMoon combines image-based localization with fingerprint-based approach for fast localization. The 3D model is partitioned into multiple smaller models based on the density of 3D points during an offline process. A localization request includes a photo and, if available, a group of Wi-Fi fingerprints collected in situ. These Wi-Fi fingerprints are used to match with the geo-referenced Wi-Fi fingerprint database. Once coarse locations are found, the model partitions that contain these positions are selected for executing image-based localization. After the source and the destination are identified, *iMoon* calculates navigation routes based on navigation meshes using path finding algorithms. The navigation meshes are first compiled from the obstacle information extracted from the 3D models, and then modified by adding the pedestrian paths extracted from crowdsourced user trajectories. For each selected navigation route, *iMoon* creates navigation instructions using textual and visual information contained in the 3D models.

3. BUILDING SENSOR-ENRICHED 3D MODELS OF INDOOR ENVIRONMENTS

This section describes how we utilize crowdsourced data in building sensor-enriched 3D models for indoor environments. The 3D models are later used for implementing indoor navigation. In Section 3.1, we describe how we apply SfM techniques to build and update 3D models, taking crowdsourced photos as input. After that, in Section 3.2, we explain how we utilize the motion sensors available on smartphones in detecting user trajectories, and in enriching the 3D models with crowdsourced user trajectories. Additionally, we add the Wi-Fi fingerprints collected along user trajectories to the 3D models (see Section 3.3).

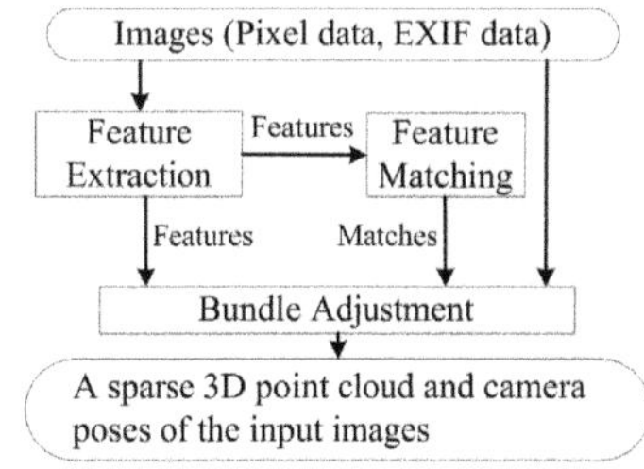

Figure 2: The pipeline of generating sparse 3D point clouds from 2D photos using SfM techniques.

3.1 Initializing and Updating SfM-based 3D Models

iMoon applies SfM techniques to build sparse 3D point clouds from unordered 2D photos. As illustrated in Figure 2, a typical SfM pipeline includes 3 steps: feature extraction, feature matching, and bundle adjustment. Firstly, highly distinctive and invariant features are extracted from images using algorithms like Scale-Invariant Feature Transform (SIFT) [18]. After that, the SfM pipeline tries to match features between photo pairs. Some photos are automatically dropped if they do not have enough common matches with others. Finally, the matches are input for the bundle adjustment step that jointly produces optimal estimates of camera poses and locations of 3D points.

iMoon implements the SfM pipeline based on VisualSFM [2, 32], a state-of-the-art SfM tool chain. VisualSFM integrates SiftGPU [1] and parallel bundle adjustment [33] to accelerate the feature extraction and feature matching processes. The output of the pipeline includes a sparse 3D point cloud and a list of estimated camera poses. In detail, a sparse 3D point cloud is a set of data points in a 3D coordinate system. Each 3D point is represented as a tuple consisting of the 3D coordinates (location), color, and a list (showing what images and which features in these images have been used for reconstructing the particular point). For each input image, there is a camera pose included in the output. A camera pose is described with the 3D coordinates of the camera position, focal length, and rotation.

Our previous work [8] has demonstrated an opportunity to create initial 3D models of certain indoor environments from publicly available Internet photos. As it is very likely that there exist insufficient number of photos at the beginning to cover every corner of the space and to contain all the details (e.g., obstacles), in the design of *iMoon*, we choose to constantly update models with new arrivals of photos.

We extend VisualSfM to support automatic model update as described below. First, if the new photos provide more details of an area already covered by the latest 3D models, the new photos will be registered to the latest models based on feature matching. Second, if the new photos reflect changes in indoor scenes, or cover an area that has not been included in the latest 3D models yet, these photos cannot be directly registered to the latest models. In this case, *iMoon* will first create 3D models from the new photos and then try to merge them with the existing ones. For the first case (i.e., photos reflecting changes), *iMoon* will calculate the field of view for each of the new photos, and then apply a ray tracing algorithm to detect which points from the previous models lie inside the field of view. The detected points will then be removed from the latest 3D models. In case there are insufficient common features between models (i.e., covering different areas), these models will remain disconnected. Potential solutions to the fragmentation issue will be discussed in Section 6.

3.2 Detecting User Trajectories using Motion Sensors

The *iMoon* client collects accelerometer and gyroscope readings from smartphones as users traverse in indoor environments. Based on these readings, the *iMoon* server calculates user trajectories based on dead reckoning [15], and uses photos taken on the way for trajectory calibration. The process of automatically detecting and calibrating user trajectories is implemented through two steps.

Firstly, the *iMoon* server obtains the camera position of each photo taken on the way based on the image-based localization method, which will be described in Section 4.1. The camera positions are set to be the calibration points.

Secondly, between every two successive calibration points, the *iMoon* server computes a trace based on step count, heading offset, and stride length. Steps are counted based on accelerometer data [15], while the heading offset between two steps is calculated from gyroscope readings. The stride length is first set to its default value, e.g., 0.7 meter, and then updated according to the accumulated walking distance and step count. The position after each step is reckoned based on the previous position and the accumulated heading offset. The calculated trace will be calibrated based on the locations of the two calibration points [31].

Given a set of user trajectories, *iMoon* discovers pedestrian paths by selecting the paths that have been covered by a minimum number of trajectories. By default we set the number to 2. Each pedestrian path is represented as a sequence of points. These paths are integrated into the 3D point clouds while compiling navigation meshes. More details about compiling navigation meshes will be presented in Section 4.2.

3.3 Geo-referencing Wi-Fi Fingerprints

The *iMoon* client collects Wi-Fi fingerprints while capturing accelerometer and gyroscope data along user trajectories. Based on time stamps, these Wi-Fi fingerprints can be easily geo-referenced and attached to the 3D point clouds after the user trajectories have been automatically calibrated. The geo-referenced Wi-Fi fingerprints are stored in a database which will be used for fingerprint-based 3D model partition selection, as described in Section 4.1.

4. 3D-MODEL-BASED INDOOR NAVIGATION

After building the sensor-enriched 3D models as described in Section 3, we continue to discuss how indoor navigation can be conducted in this section. We first describe indoor localization in Section 4.1; then we present how navigation meshes can be compiled in Section 4.2; in Section 4.3, we state how we create user-friendly navigation instructions.

4.1 Indoor Localization

Given a query photo, the image-based localization is expected to return the location where the photo is taken and the direction in which the camera is facing. A straightforward method is to register the query image into the 3D point clouds based on feature matching. In theory, the feature matching is conducted between the query image and each of the images used for building the point clouds. If enough matches[5] can be found, the features provided by the query image will be added to the point clouds, and a camera pose of the input will be returned.

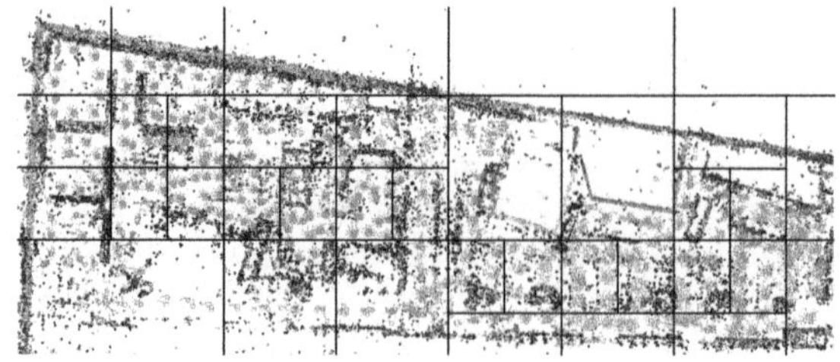

Figure 3: An example of density-based point cloud partitioning. Each partition includes points corresponding to features extracted from no more than 100 photos. Both the width and length of each partition are larger than 5 meters. The camera positions are marked as green dots in the figure.

Algorithm 1 Pseudo code of indoor localization algorithm implemented in *iMoon*

Input: User's query photo: U_{photo}, Wi-Fi Fingerprints: U_{Wi-Fi}
Output: User's location: U_{loc}, User's facing direction: U_{dir}

```
//Apply k-NN to get a set of coarse locations based on Wi-Fi fingerprints
//DB_{Wi-Fi}: Database of geo-referenced Wi-Fi fingerprints
L_coarse = k-NN(U_{Wi-Fi}, DB_{Wi-Fi});
//Select model partitions based on coarse locations
Partitions= SelectPartition(L_coarse);
//Find photos taken near the coarse locations from the selected partitions
Photos_nearby = SearchPhoto(L_coarse, Partitions);
//Identify user's location and facing direction based on feature matching between U_photo and each photo in Photos_nearby.
[U_loc, U_dir] = StartSfMInParallel(U_photo, Partitions, Photos_nearby);
```

The size of a 3D point cloud, in terms of the number of 3D points, increases with the number of photos involved. It results in consuming more resources to load the point cloud into memory or to go through each point in the point cloud. To lower the memory consumption and to enable parallel processing, *iMoon* partitions a point cloud into smaller sub-clouds, and execute feature matching operations only on selected partitions.

Density-based Model Partitioning. *iMoon* partitions a 3D point cloud into smaller ones following two rules. First, each partition includes 3D points that are created based on the image features extracted from a limited number of photos. Second, the area covered by each partition should not be too small. In practice, we define the minimum length and width of the area covered by each partition. An example is visualized in Figure 3.

Fingerprint-based Partition Selection. *iMoon* selects partitions for feature matching as described in Algorithm 1. It first applies K-Nearest Neighbour algorithm (k-NN) to acquire a set of coarse locations based on Wi-

[5]By default, VisualSFM set the minimum number of common features between two matched images to be 15.

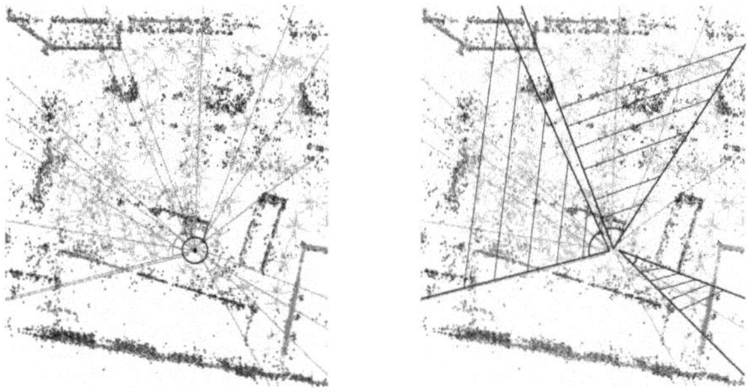

(a) (b)

Figure 4: An example of photo selection. (a) After a coarse location (black dot at the center) is acquired, 7 photos within the radius (i.e., the green dots within the black circle) are checked. The red points represent the 3D points covered by these photos. The field of view of an image is represented by two lines and an arc between them. (b) 3 out of the 7 checked photos (marked with black) are selected for feature matching based on camera position and facing direction.

Fi fingerprinting. After that, *iMoon* selects the partitions that cover these coarse locations, and then searches within the selected partitions for photos that are taken close to the coarse locations. In practice, the search space is defined by radius. To minimize the processing time while maintaining the performance, *iMoon* chooses a subset of photos within each radius as candidates for feature matching with the query photo. The candidates are chosen as described below. If the search result contains more than one photo taken from the same location and having the same facing direction, only one of these photos is selected. In case too few photos are returned, the radius will be increased to find more photos satisfying the requirements. Figure 4a and 4b depicts an example of photo selection based on the rules mentioned above.

Identifying Location and Facing Direction. After a set of candidate photos are returned, *iMoon* executes feature matching between each candidate photo and the query photo. The processing of photo pairs are conducted in parallel. If enough matches are found, the estimates of camera position and rotation will be returned. The facing direction of a camera is derived from the estimated camera rotation. It's possible that several positions and rotations are returned, since several partitions were selected during the previous fingerprinting step and more than two of them contain enough common features for registering the query photo. In practice, the location of the user is estimated as the midpoint among all the returned camera positions, and the user's facing direction is defined by averaging the camera angle offsets.

4.2 Compiling Navigation Meshes

After locating the end user, we need to calculate a navigation path for her, for which a navigation mesh is fundamental. Given a 3D point cloud of indoor environment, some points may represent obstacles, e.g., tables, chairs and walls. *iMoon* compiles a navigation mesh from a point cloud by extracting obstacles from these points, treating the rest of the blank areas as traversable areas. It is implemented through the following four steps.

1) *iMoon* filters out the points related to floor and ceiling by simply removing the points with the z-axis value, which represents the height, lower or higher than certain thresholds. In our experiment, we set the threshold to be 10 cm for the floor and 2 m for the ceiling. The rest of 3D points are projected directly onto the ground plane to acquire a 2D point set.

2) When there are user trajectories available, pedestrian paths will be extracted from these trajectories. A pedestrian path includes a sequence of points. Assuming that there are no obstacles like walls and tables along the path, all the points along the path can be removed from the 2D point set obtained in the previous step. As the path width is undefined, we assume that points included in a path always stay on the central line of the path. Thus *iMoon* also removes the neighbouring points that are close to the central line. In practice, we set the distance threshold to be 25 cm, assuming that the minimum path width is 50 cm.

3) *iMoon* applies the algorithm proposed by Duckham [9] to generate non-convex polygons out of the 2D points derived in the previous step. The basic idea of the algorithm is to wrap a set of points with a polygon, specifying which points belong to the outline and which lie inside the polygon. One polygon represents one obstacle. Accordingly, all the 2D points must be divided into groups, with each group corresponding to one obstacle. In practice, *iMoon* groups the points if the distance between any two points is less than a threshold, e.g., 50 cm.

4) After extracting the shape contours, *iMoon* extrudes all 2D shapes towards the z-axis to form solid meshes. The generated navigation meshes are saved in a Wavefront Object (.obj) file.

4.3 Generating Navigation Instructions

Based on the navigation meshes described in Section 4.2, *iMoon* implements an A* like path finding algorithm using RecastDetour library[6]. For each navigation path, *iMoon* generates turn-by-turn navigation instructions for users. As shown in Figure 5, an instruction comprises three parts: 1) a photo that shows the place where the given instruction is valid, 2) a piece of text that tells the user to go straight or make a turn and approximately how many meters to go until the next waypoint, and 3) an arrow sign that indicates which path to take next.

The photo is selected from the photo set used as input for 3D modelling. The selected photo is expected to cover the waypoint and to be clear enough to understand the surroundings. In our prototype, the photo is selected based on the following four steps.

1) Search for the 3D point that is closest to the 3D location of the waypoint in question, and find all the photos that contain features corresponding to this point. If less than N photos (N is set to 5 by default) are found, skip 2).

2) Sort the photos selected in 1) by the distance between the camera position and the waypoint, and for the next step select the first N photos with the shortest distances.

3) Sort the selected photos by the relative rotation regarding the navigation route. Its purpose is to find the photos that are taken facing the closest angle as the user will traverse the path. Thus, the best angle is facing the same way

[6]https://github.com/memononen/recastnavigation

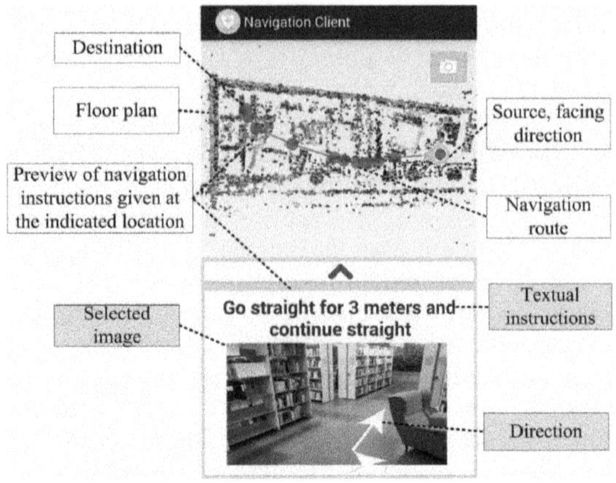

Figure 5: A screenshot of the *iMoon* Android app in navigation mode. The upper part includes a mini map with the color information of each 3D point reserved. The navigation route (blue line) drawn on the map includes 3 waypoints between the source and the destination. The lower part gives a preview of the navigation instructions when the user arrives at the waypoint marked by a red dotted circle. The current position and facing direction of the user (in green) are updated on the move. In addition to the textual instruction, the selected image shows the expected view, and the arrow indicates the path to take.

as the user walks. After sorting, we take the first M photos (M is set to 3 by default) for the next step.

4) Sort the photos selected in 3) by the distance between the 3D point (defined in the first step) projection on the photo and the center of the photo. The photo with the closest center to the 3D point (thus also to the waypoint) is selected to form the navigation instruction that is given at the waypoint.

Once *iMoon* obtains a suitable photo, it draws directional arrows on it and renders textual instructions. Assume that the current location of a user is L_C, and the direction of the user is denoted by a vector $\vec{a}$. There will be 2 arrows drawn on the image: between L_C and an upcoming waypoint L_W (the one that was used to find the navigation photo), and between L_W and the next waypoint L_{W2}. Since the model building step extracted rotation matrices for each input image, *iMoon* calculate 2D projections of L_C, L_W and L_{W2}, and draw arrow shapes on the selected image by connecting these points. We denote the vector from L_C to L_W by $\vec{b}$, and the one from L_W to L_{W2} by $\vec{c}$. *iMoon* generates two textual instructions based on the angle between $\vec{a}$ and $\vec{b}$, and that between $\vec{b}$ and $\vec{c}$, respectively. According to the value of the angle, denoted by $\angle A$, *iMoon* provides textual instructions as defined in Eq. (1).

$$\text{Text} = \begin{cases} \text{'Go straight'}, & -T \leq \angle A \leq T \\ \text{'Turn left'}, & 180^\circ + T < \angle A < 360^\circ - T \\ \text{'Turn right'}, & T < \angle A < 180^\circ - T \\ \text{'Go back'}, & 180^\circ - T \leq \angle A \leq 180^\circ + T \end{cases} \quad (1)$$

where T is a threshold in degrees (set to 15° by default). The instruction also contains the information about the distance between L_C and L_W.

Data Set	Content	Usage	Dates
A	2,197 photos , 119 user trajectories, 4,239 Wi-Fi fingerprints	Building initial 3D models	Aug. 2014
B	355 photos, 31 user trajectories, 1,181 Wi-Fi fingerprints	Updating 3D models	Sep. 2014 - Mar. 2015
C	2,552 photos, 5,420 Wi-Fi fingerprints (Set A ∪ B)	Analyzing the quality of the generated 3D models	Aug. 2014 - Mar. 2015
D	2,220 groups of photos and Wi-Fi fingerprints	Performance evaluation of indoor localization	Sept.- Oct. 2014

Table 1: Summary of the data sets collected during our field study.

5. EVALUATION

We implemented a prototype of *iMoon* to evaluate the feasibility of building an indoor navigation system using crowdsourced photos and sensor data. Since August, 2014, we have been carrying out a field study on the ground floor of the computer science building in our campus (referred to as **CS hall** in the rest of the paper). According to the field study, the functionalities of *iMoon* have proved to work properly. Therefore, we will focus on the performance evaluation of *iMoon*, and will introduce in this section the methodology, the experimental data sets, and the experimental results, including a short summary of feasibility study.

5.1 Methodology

iMoon can be used for locating users, calculating navigation routes, and providing turn-by-turn navigation instructions. Performance of *iMoon* depends on the performance of the localization, the accuracy of the navigation meshes used for path planning, and the accuracy of the navigation instructions. Because the navigation meshes are generated from the sensor-enriched 3D models (cf. Section 3), the accuracy of the navigation meshes is determined by the quality of the 3D models in use. Similarly, the accuracy of the navigation instructions depends on the accuracy of the estimates of user's position and facing direction, which also relies on the quality of the 3D models. Therefore, for performance evaluation of *iMoon*, we focus on the quality of the 3D models and evaluate it using the following metrics: the accuracy of the indoor layout extracted from the 3D models, and the performance of the 3D-model-based indoor localization.

We aim at answering the following questions based on performance measurement: What kind of crowdsourced data is desired for building high-quality 3D models of indoor environments for the purpose of indoor navigation? Does *iMoon* outperform the state-of-the-art indoor localization techniques? What is the impact of the input for 3D modelling on the localization performance?

5.2 Data Collection

We collected data in the CS hall, which is approximately 1,100 m^2, covering a library, a cafeteria, and a corridor connecting over ten lecture rooms and offices. During weekdays,

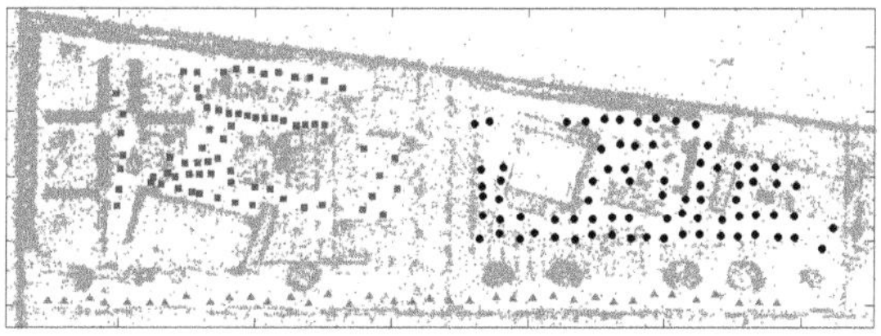

Figure 6: 185 measurement points where data set D was collected. They were distributed in the cafe (black circle), corridor (red triangle) and library (blue square).

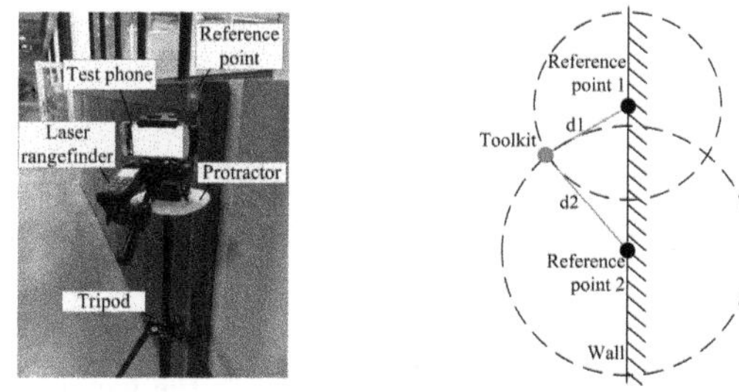

(a) (b)

Figure 7: Evaluation toolkit. The left-hand figure shows a self-built toolkit that consists of a laser rangefinder, a protractor, an Android phone running *iMoon* mobile app, and a tripod as a stand. The right-hand figure demonstrates how trilateration is applied to determine the location of the toolkit based on measurements of the distance to each reference point.

more than 500 students and staffs visit the CS hall on daily basis. The indoor scenes of the cafeteria change frequently due to promotions and decorations. During the field study, the construction work of a new food store started in March, 2015. Our data sets, as summarized in Table 1, include the data collected both before and after these changes occurred.

To bootstrap the system, we recruited 5 volunteers in August, 2014 and asked them to collect photos in the CS hall. The volunteers can choose by themselves where to take photos. For each location they chose, they were requested to take 5 to 10 photos with the camera facing different directions. Meanwhile, the *iMoon* mobile app was configured to record Wi-Fi fingerprints and the readings of accelerometer and gyroscope while the volunteers were walking in the CS hall. The data collection started immediately after the first photo was taken, and can be stopped manually. Over a period of 3 weeks, the volunteers collected in total 2,197 photos and 4,239 groups of Wi-Fi fingerprints along 119 walking traces (referred to as **data set A** in Table 1).

After the system was initialized with the data set A, the volunteers were invited to test the indoor navigation services. During the trial period, another 355 photos and 1,181 Wi-Fi fingerprints along 31 walking traces were collected (referred to as **data set B**) till March 2015. Accordingly, the 3D models available at the end of March 2015 were built from the union of the data set A and B (referred to as **data set C**).

During September and October 2014, we collected **data set D** for the performance evaluation of indoor localization[7]. The data set D includes 2,220 photos taken from 185 measurement points in the CS hall. As shown in Figure 6, the measurement points are distributed evenly across the walkable area in the hall.

We used a self-built toolkit, as shown in Figure 7a, to obtain the ground truths corresponding to the data set D. At each measurement point, we took photos and collected Wi-Fi fingerprints using the Android phone placed on the tripod. After taking one photo, the camera was rotated horizontally by 30 degrees before taking another one. More specifically, before taking the first photo at each measurement point, the camera was facing the same direction defined as the baseline direction. After that, the camera was rotated by 30 degrees to take the next photo. We repeated the process until the camera was facing the baseline direction again. At each measurement point, we collected 12 photos. Additionally, we used a laser rangefinder to measure the distance to each reference point. Given the measurements from the distance and locations of the reference points, we calculated the actual location of the camera based on trilateration, as illustrated in Figure 7b. For each photo, the actual location and the facing direction of the camera was recorded and used as the ground truth for accuracy analysis.

[7]Note that the 3D models built from the data set A were used for performance analysis in this case.

5.3 Accuracy of Navigation Mesh

We built an initial 3D model of the CS hall using data set A in August 2014. Following the SfM pipeline described in Section 3.1, the initial 3D model (as shown in Fig. 8b), which includes 253,839 3D points, was successfully built from 1,968 (out of 2,197) photos in data set A. Based on the generated 3D models and the user trajectories included in data set A, *iMoon* compiled a navigation mesh as described in Section 4.2. The navigation mesh is visualized in Figure 9a. For comparison, a navigation mesh generated from the initial 3D model only is also shown in Figure 9a. We can see that the pedestrian paths, especially the one along the corridor, are better reconstructed when user trajectories are used for compiling navigation meshes.

From September 2014, the initial models have been updated constantly using the photos in data set B. As illustrated in Figure 8b and 8c, the 3D models have been successfully updated to reflect a significant change of indoor layout caused by the ongoing construction work of a Subway store. The actual indoor scenes before and after the construction work started are shown in Figure 8e and 8f, respectively.

Compared with the official floor plan released in 2008 (c.f. Figure 8a), the 3D models generated by *iMoon* well reconstruct the outline of the CS hall. To evaluate the accuracy of the reconstructed outline, we calculated the Euclidean distances of walls surrounding the CS hall based on the 3D models, and measured the ground truth using a laser rangefinder. After that, we calculated the distance error as defined in [23]. Specifically, the distance error for a correctly detected segment is defined as the average distance between the detected segment and its associated ground truth segment. The overall distance error, denoted by E_D, is calculated below.

$$E_D = \sum_{i=1}^{N}[length(s_i)E_d(s_i)] / \sum_{i=1}^{N} length(s_i), \qquad (2)$$

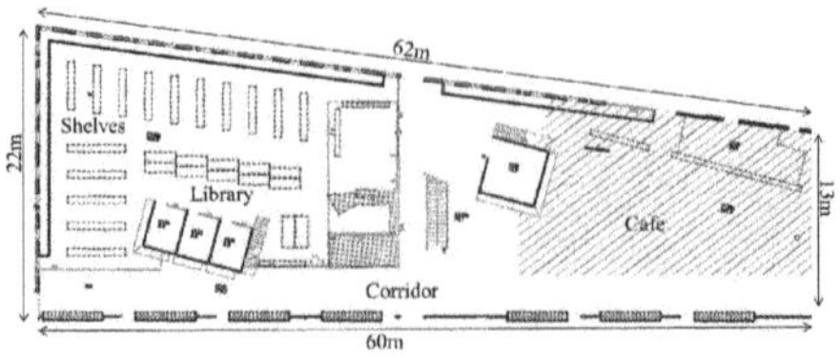

(a) Official floor plan updated in 2008.

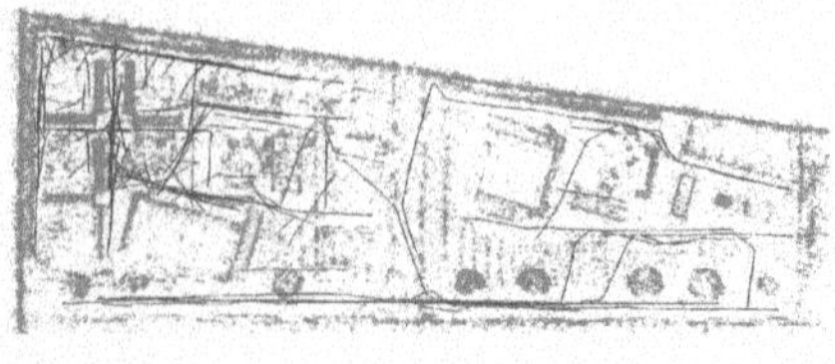

(b) A 2D view of the initial 3D model built in August, 2014. The blue lines marked on the figure indicate the walking traces of the volunteers.

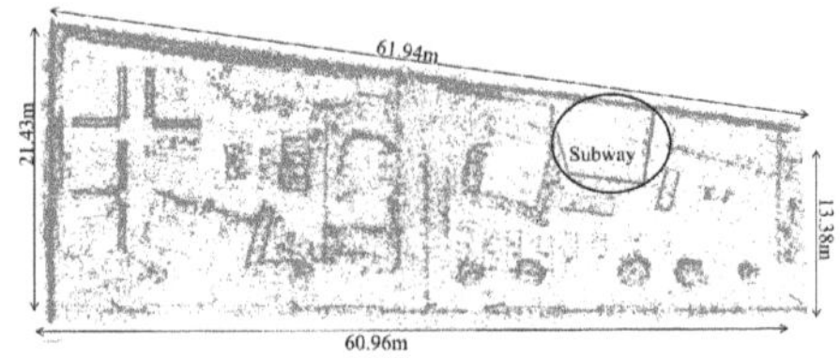

(c) A 2D view of the 3D model updated in March, 2015.

(d) A bird view of the library in the CS hall in November, 2014.

(e) No Subway store existed in the CS hall in November, 2014.

(f) A new Subway store was under construction in March, 2015.

Figure 8: Comparison of the generated 3D models with the actual layout of the CS hall.

(a) Two navigation meshes of the library area. The grey solid polygons represent the one compiled from the initial 3D model only, while the black hollow polygons correspond to the one utilizing also the user trajectories in data set A.

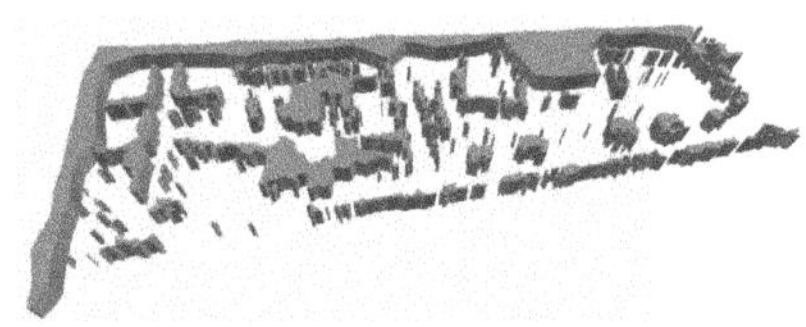

(b) The navigation mesh of the CS hall updated in March, 2015.

Figure 9: Navigation meshes generated from 3D models.

where N is a number of correctly detected segments, and $E_d(s_i)$ is the distance error for a correctly detected segment s_i. According to the results, *iMoon* is able to reconstruct the outline of the CS hall with an overall distance error of 0.502 meters.

Based on the 3D models built in March, 2015, *iMoon* compiles a navigation mesh including 215 obstacles. The navigation mesh is visualized in Figure 9b. We calculate the average location error of obstacles according to Eq. (3). Denote the coordinates of an obstacle in the mesh by (x_i, y_i), and its actual coordinates by (X_i, Y_i), the average location error of obstacles, denoted by $E_{obstacles}$, can be calculated as

$$E_{obstacles} = \sum_{i=1}^{N} \sqrt{(x_i - X_i)^2 + (y_i - Y_i)^2}/N \quad (3)$$

where N is the number of obstacles. For the navigation mesh generated from the 3D models available in March, 2015, its average location error is 0.78 meters, which indicates a reasonably high accuracy of the navigation mesh.

Our experiment results have shown that the data set A, which includes 2,197 photos collected from locations that are nearly evenly distributed in the area, is enough to build a 3D model of the CS hall with reasonably good quality. Concerning the complexity of indoor structure and the diversity of indoor scenes, the number of photos needed for building a good-quality 3D model varies with indoor environments. Furthermore, the quality of 3D models depends also on the manner of data collection, including where to take photos and what to be captured by the photos.

To analyze the impact of data collection, we sampled the photos in data set C in 5 different ways, and compared the results of the 3D models built from each subset accordingly. The 3D models created from all the photos in data set C was used as the baseline. First, we grouped the photos by location and facing direction, and then evenly selected 50% of the photos. The set of sampled photos is referred to as **Sample 1**. Similarly, we evenly sampled 25% of the photos from data set C to form **Sample 2**. Compared with the data set C, the photos in Sample 1 and Sample 2 were taken with lower density but still trying to cover the whole space. To emulate the data collection in a more random manner, we also built **Sample 3** an **Sample 4** by selecting 50% and 25% of photos from data set C randomly, regardless of location or facing direction. In principle, in order to use as few photos as possible for building 3D models while maintaining the performance of localization, the input photos are expected to have as little overlap as possible while having sufficient common features to be matched. Depending on various factors such as the settings of the cameras and the texture of the walls, it is not possible to tell exactly how many photos are needed. For comparison, we manually selected 20% of the photos from data set C by removing photos that captured similar scenes. The selected photos form **Sample 5**.

The number of 3D points generated from the 5 samples are listed in Figure 10. From the figure we can observe that as less photos are used for 3D modelling, the output 3D models are more prone to be fragmented, which is clearly illustrated in cases where Samples 2, 3, and 4 are used as

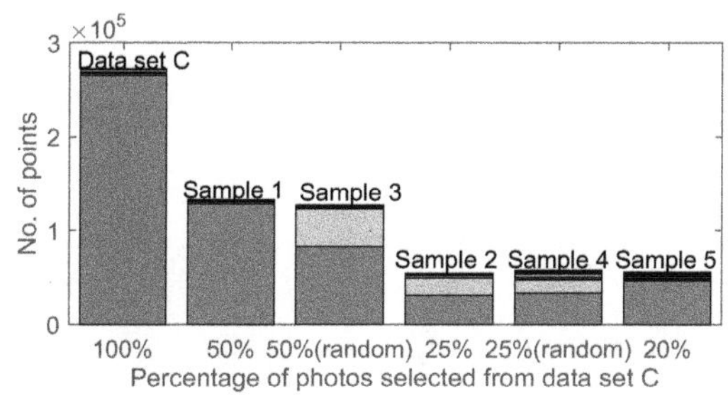

Figure 10: Comparison of the number of 3D points included in the 3D models built from different samples. The different color in each bar represents the number of points included in each fragment of the 3D model in question.

Area	No. Measurement Points	No.of Photos	Hit rate		
			Image	**Wi-Fi**	*iMoon*
Cafe	78	936	91%	100%	91%
Corridor	37	444	100%	100%	100%
Library	70	840	98.6%	100%	97.1%
Total	185	2,220	95.7%	100%	95.1%

Table 2: Comparison of hit rate between image-based localization, Wi-Fi fingerprinting and the localization algorithm implemented in *iMoon*.

(a) (b) (c)

Figure 11: Examples of non-matching inputs (a) (b) and a matching input (c) from one measurement point located in the corridor.

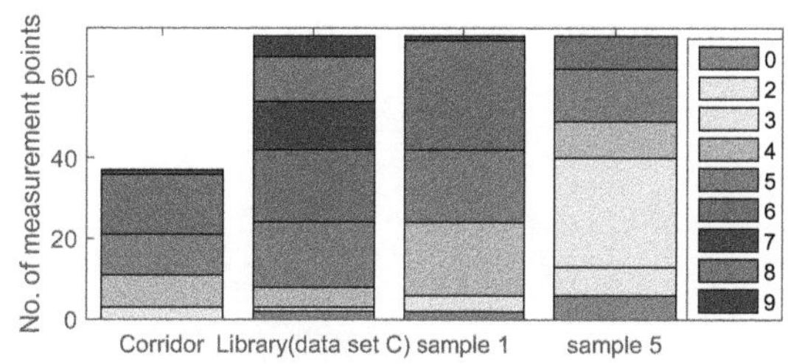

Figure 12: The numbers of measurement points where the indicated amount of matching inputs are identified at each point. Samples 1 and 5 are subsets of data set C in the library. Each color represents the number of matching inputs at a certain measurement point. For example, there are 15 (out of 37) measurement points in the corridor. At each of these points 6 matching inputs can be found.

input. On the other hand, the 3D models built from Sample 1 remain almost as intact as the ones from data set C, from fragmentation perspective. Compared with the largest 3D models generated from Samples 3 and 4, the biggest 3D model created from Sample 5 contains more 3D points. This is because the scenes captured by different photos in Sample 5 are expected to have less overlaps. The impact on the density of 3D points will be discussed in Section 5.4.3.

5.4 Performance of 3D-model-based Indoor Localization

We measured the performance of indoor localization with four metrics, namely, hit rate, location error, direction error, and response delay. **Hit rate** refers to the percentage of measurement points that can be located. When there is a hit, the accuracy of the result is measured with **location error**, and **direction error** if the result includes also user's facing direction. The location error calculates the distance between the estimated location of the measurement point and the ground truth, while the direction error measures the angle offset from the actual facing direction. Additionally, **response delay** measures how much time it takes for the server to return the result. Note that the response delay of indoor localization depends on the computation complexity of the localization algorithm under test, as well as the computing power of the computing infrastructure in use.

iMoon combines Wi-Fi fingerprinting with image-based localization to achieve fast while accurate indoor localization. To provide an objective comparison with the state-of-the-art, we provided a reference implementation of the image-based localization (abbreviated as **Image**). The reference implementation of **Image** applies Breadth-first Search (BFS) to select candidates for feature matching, and tries to search through the whole 3D point cloud instead of selected partitions to get the best possible result. Both *iMoon* and the reference implementation of **Image** were tested with the 3D models built from the photos in data set A. In addition, to provide a comparison with the Wi-Fi fingerprinting based approaches, we utilized the Wi-Fi fingerprints included in data set A to implement a standalone Wi-Fi fingerprinting solution (abbreviated as **Wi-Fi**). We then used data set D to test the performance of both *iMoon* and **Wi-Fi**. The experimental results are presented in the following subsections.

5.4.1 Hit Rate

If a valid location can be returned by the localization algorithm, we consider the input as a **matching input** for the algorithm; otherwise, it is considered as a non-matching input. In data set D, 12 photos and the associated Wi-Fi fingerprints were collected from each measurement point. If at least one of the 12 groups of data was considered as matching input, we count the corresponding measurement point as a locatable point. The hit rate is calculated as the number of locatable points divided by the total number of measurements points.

In Table 2 we compare the hit rate among *iMoon*, **Wi-Fi**, and **Image**. In general, the hit rate is reasonably high in all the three cases. Compared with **Wi-Fi**, the two image-based schemes (i.e., *iMoon* and **Image**) fail to locate around 5% of the measurement points. This is because of the changes of indoor scenes occurred after the initial 3D model was built. Compared with the corridor, the layout of the cafeteria and the library changed more frequently, which explains the relatively low hit rates in such areas. Furthermore, **Image** also achieves slightly higher hit rate than *iMoon*. This is because *iMoon* only selects a subset of model partitions for feature matching in order to lower the

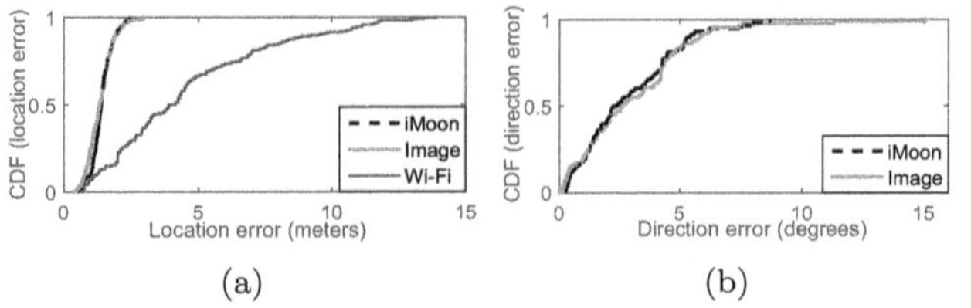

Figure 13: Comparison of (a) location error and (b) direction error between *iMoon*, **Image**, and **Wi-Fi**. Note that **Wi-Fi** does not return user's facing direction.

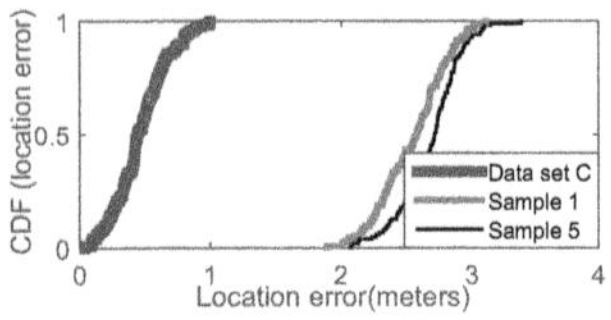

Figure 14: Comparison of location error between scenarios where the 3D models were built from data set C, Sample 1, and Sample 5, respectively.

response delay. The partitions filtered out by Wi-Fi fingerprints in *iMoon* may contain feature matches with the query photo.

Photos taken by different users at the same place may cover different scenes, due to the user's facing direction and the configurations of the camera such as focal length. If the photo includes mostly the texture-less scenes, e.g., white walls, it is very likely that not enough distinguishable features can be used for feature matching. Thus, most likely, these photos will become non-matching inputs. Because our measurement points are distributed evenly in the CS hall and 12 photos facing different direction were taken at each point, it is inevitable that a certain number of photos were taken with the camera facing texture-less scenes. Two examples are shown in Figure 11a and 11b. Those photos provide much less features compared with the example of matching input shown in Figure 11c. This also explains why the experiment in the library has higher percentage of measurement points with more matching inputs than in the corridor, as shown in Figure 12. In practice, if the first photo taken by a user is a non-matching input, *iMoon* will request the user to face a different direction and then take a new photo for another try. When people try to locate themselves, they will very possibly take photos of distinguishable scenes instead of plain walls. Thus, the number of matching inputs can be expected to be higher in real cases.

5.4.2 Accuracy

As explained previously, we collected ground truth of locations and facing directions using own developed toolkit, and evaluated the accuracy of indoor localization based on the ground truth and the estimated location and facing direction (if available). As shown in Figure 13a and 13b, the accuracy of *iMoon* is very close to that of **Image**. In both cases, for at least 90% of the valid inputs, the location error is less than 2 meters, while the direction error is less than 6 degrees. Similar to the hit rate (cf. Table 2), the accuracy of **Image** is slightly different from that of *iMoon*, due to the pre-filtering of model partitions used in *iMoon*.

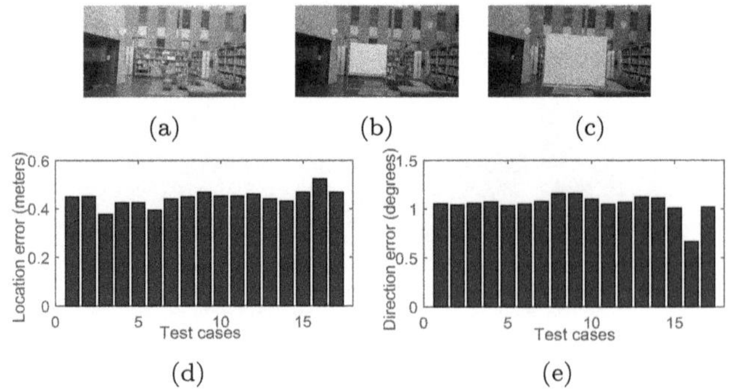

Figure 15: Location and facing direction errors in the cases where a whiteboard was brought into the scene and then moved towards the camera.

The result of **Wi-Fi** does not include an estimate of the facing direction. The location error of **Wi-Fi** is less than 5 meters in approximately 70% of the test cases and less than 10 meters in 90% of cases. Obviously, the accuracy of **Wi-Fi** is relatively low, compared with the image-based approaches. On the other hand, because the hit rate of **Wi-Fi** is higher, it is reasonable to fall back to the coarse locations provided by Wi-Fi fingerprinting, when the system fails to obtain a more accurate location based on photos.

5.4.3 Robustness

To investigate the impact of the input for 3D modelling on the accuracy of localization, we chose the 3D models built from **data set C** as a reference, and built another two models from **Samples 1** and **5**, respectively, for comparison. We chose the library as the testing environment, and selected the related photos from **data set D** for test.

As illustrated in Figure 14, the system achieves higher accuracy with the reference model than the ones built from Samples 1 or 5[8]. Recall that more test data become matching inputs with a denser point cloud, as shown in Figure 12. Hence, we can conclude that the positioning accuracy increases with the density of the point cloud. Nevertheless, the density does not increase if less photos are used for building the point cloud.

Objects like whiteboards and chairs may appear (disappear) or move around frequently in the building after the 3D models are built. Additionally, people may accidentally show up in front of the camera when photos are taken for localization. To evaluate how the localization accuracy is affected, we conducted a set of tests where we brought a whiteboard to the library and moved it towards our camera slowly, trying to block the whole camera view gradually. We took 18 photos from the same location while the whiteboard was moving as described in Figure 15a – 15c. After that, we used *iMoon* to locate the camera with each of these photos. With 17 out of the 18 photos, *iMoon* successfully identified the location with comparable accuracy, as shown in Figure 15d and 15e. *iMoon* failed to locate the camera only when the photo captured nothing more than the whiteboard. The localization accuracy remained at the same level as far as the location was successfully identified.

[8]The indoor navigation system performs better than average in the library, because the scenes in the library are more distinguishable than the corridor for example. That is why the results in Figure 14 are better than the ones shown in Figure 13a.

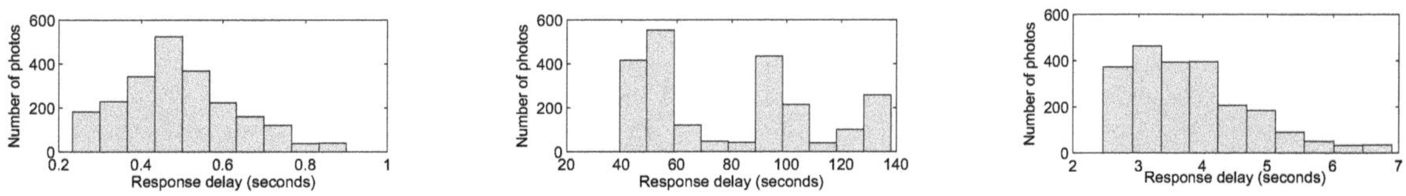

(a) Wi-Fi Fingerprinting (b) Image-based localization (c) iMoon

Figure 16: Comparison of response delay between indoor localization algorithms using the data set D as test data set.

5.4.4 Response Delay

We deployed *iMoon* on a server equipped with an Intel Xeon processor E5-2650 (8-core, 2.6GHz), 64GB RAM, and a Tesla K20C GPU. We measured the response delay using data set D as input, and compared the results between *iMoon*, **Wi-Fi**, and **Image**. Note that the testing data set includes both matching and non-matching inputs from the perspective of localization.

Figure 16a shows that the response delay of **Wi-Fi** is less than 0.6 s for 87% of the input. For **Image**, as presented in Figure 16b, it takes more than 40 s to generate a response (including the time spent in loading the 3D models). The loading time increases with the size of 3D models. According to our experiment, the loading time can be ignored for a 3D model built from less than 300 photos. However, it takes as long as 35 s to load a 3D model built from 2,000 photos. Excluding the loading time, 41% of the tests take around 15 s to complete the process of feature matching and camera pose estimation, while the rest of the tests take longer time due to selecting more images for matching.

iMoon supports 3D model partitioning and fingerprint-based partition selection. As shown in Figure 16c, the response delay, including loading time, is decreased to 4 s for 73% of the tests when each model partition contains features extracted from less than 100 photos. The response delay excluding the loading time is on average 3.85 s with standard deviation of 1.5 s. Note that the response delay can be further decreased by utilizing more powerful machines.

5.5 Summary

From the experiments and analysis presented above, we can reach the conclusion that it is feasible to build a 3D-model-based indoor navigation system with reasonably high performance, using only the photos and sensor data collected from smartphones. The quality of 3D models, nevertheless, is affected by multiple factors, including the number of photos used for generating the 3D models, and the coverage and the facing direction of the input photos. Although the coverage of crowdsourced photos may be limited to certain areas of interest, with more and more photos becoming available, there is an increasing chance of producing high-quality 3D models for the purpose of indoor navigation. Furthermore, the accuracy and response delay of *iMoon* are decent and acceptable compared to the state-of-the-art.

6. DISCUSSION AND FUTURE WORK

Varying quality of crowdsourced data. Although crowdsourcing provides a relatively cheap way of collecting data, there is always an uncertainty in the quality of the available data. In other words, it is hard to know in advance how much data contributed by the crowd is actually usable. For example, in places of interest, people are usually much more interested in taking photos of landmarks rather than ordinary scenes like white walls. This can be observed from photos available on Internet photo sharing websites like Flickr and Instagram. As a result, the crowdsourced photos may not cover every corner of the space of interest, which means the 3D models generated from the crowdsourced photos may have "holes" in them and some models may be disconnected from each other, causing the fragmentation issue. Although *iMoon* can still provide indoor navigation with slightly compromised accuracy using "non-perfect" 3D models, it is worth investigating incentive schemes that would encourage and guide users to provide data for fixing the "holes". Developing such an incentive scheme is part of our future work. We will also investigate the feasibility of utilizing crowdsourced user trajectories for connecting 3D models in order to solve the fragmentation issue. We believe that with these new features, *iMoon* will be able to provide increasingly better service.

Tracking user trajectories using non-perfect maps. In navigation mode, once the initial location is identified, *iMoon* starts tracing users using the motion sensors on smartphones, whereas for the purpose of trace calibration users are still requested to take photos while making turns. It is possible to track users based on the sensor data only. An example solution is particle filtering based dead reckoning [15, 25]. The challenge to such solution comes from the fact that the navigation meshes built from crowdsourced data may not be complete or 100% accurate. This issue should be taken into account while applying the existing algorithms for indoor navigation based on crowdsourced maps.

Combination of latency-constrained and compute-intensive operations. Generally, building 3D models requires heavy computation. Compared with 3D modelling, calculating locations or generating navigation instructions demands less computing power, whereas it is much more sensitive to delay. To meet the requirements of low latency and computing power, we propose to deploy *iMoon* in a hybrid cloud infrastructure. For example, the initial 3D models are first generated on public clouds, like Amazone EC2, which have more computing power, and then transferred to a private cloud that is much closer to the end users. After that, the real-time navigation services will be provisioned from the local cloud, e.g., a cloudlet [28] or a Nokia RACS server.

Measurement of user experience. In the future, we will deploy *iMoon* using hybrid cloud infrastructure in more dynamic environments such as shopping malls, and evaluate the performance of *iMoon* in realistic scenarios. We plan to conduct a survey between test users and ask them to score the system from the perspective of user experience, including the accuracy, response delay and user-friendliness of the services.

Utilizing text and sign information from crowdsourced images. We plan to extend our system to support descriptive search, e.g., by place name or room number. Photos taken from indoor environment usually contain signs and descriptive texts, it makes sense to utilize such information for place search to improve usability. We plan to apply sign recognition and optical character recognition techniques to extract information from the input photos. If a sign or word is detected from a photo, we can first acquire pixel coordinates of the sign/word in the photo. Then, a set of features can be extracted from the photo. By comparing the coordinates of each feature point with the photos of the recognized sign/word, the closest feature point to the sign/word can be found and set as the location of the sign/word in question.

7. RELATED WORK

3D-Model-based Indoor Mapping. 3D modelling has been widely used for indoor mapping. Conventionally, 3D models for indoor mapping are generated from the data captured by laser scanners and/or depth cameras through war-driving. For example, the system presented in [23] obtained 3D point cloud of indoor environment from laser scanners positioned in multiple locations, and extracted 2D floor plan from the 3D point cloud. KinectFusion [21] implemented real-time 3D surface reconstruction of room-sized scenes based on the depth data streamed from a moving Kinect sensor. The recently developed SLAM (Simultaneous Localization and Mapping) based indoor mapping tools, such as Google Cartographer and Xsens Scannect [6], are equipped with inertial measurement units in addition to laser scanners and depth cameras. The Cartographer-like backpack systems can automatically create floor plans when the backpacker-wearers walk inside the buildings.

Differently from SLAM, SfM techniques enable 3D modelling of indoor and outdoor environments using unordered 2D photos. These photos can be taken by ordinary devices like smartphone cameras. Based on SfM, Agarwal et al. [3] constructed 3D models of Rome city from 150K photos found from Internet photo sharing sites. Furukawa et al. [11] used SfM and multi-view stereo for reconstructing and visualizing an entire house interior. Previous work has also tried to solve the technical issues, such as the disconnection of the photo-based 3D point clouds [20] and the connection of wall segments based on motion sensor data [12]. *iMoon* also adopts SfM for 3D modeling of indoor environments. Depending on the input, the generated 3D models may not contain all the pedestrian path information. *iMoon* solves this issue by complementing the 3D models with crowdsourced user trajectories.

Indoor Localization and Navigation. Previous work has proposed to utilize fingerprints of Wi-Fi [4], magnetic field [7], Bluetooth [5] for finding locations in indoor environments. Fingerprinting-based approaches require a training data set comprising measurements at known locations in the space of interest. Since labelling fingerprints is labour-intensive, Zee [25] proposed automatic inferencing of location based on the combination of inertial sensor information and the constraints imposed by the map. The inertial sensor information was collected while simultaneously performing Wi-Fi scans. Similarly, Nguyen et al. [22] applied dead reckoning approach to track users in indoor environment. Due to the error accumulation of the dead reckoning approach, Nguyen et al. utilized active learning for automatically identifying strategically important locations which should be labelled manually. Rather than manually labelling Wi-Fi fingerprints, *iMoon* utilizes random photos taken along user trajectories for automatic calibration, utilizing the feature of image-based localization.

Image-based localization system with the use of 3D SfM model allows users to locate themselves by simply taking photos from where they are. Photos are localized with high accuracy based on image feature matching and camera pose estimation. However, this process is slow due to heavy computation. To accelerate this process, Lu et al. [19] proposed to use the visual words and the approximate nearest neighbour methods. Similarly, Sattler et al. [27] proposed a framework for efficient 2D-to-3D matching based on visual vocabulary quantization and a prioritized correspondence search. Differently from the previous work, *iMoon* utilizes Wi-Fi fingerprints instead of image features for reducing the search space, taking the advantage of fast response of Wi-Fi fingerprinting and high accuracy of image-based localization.

In addition to location, a walking direction of user is also useful for creating and updating navigation instruction. Google Project Tango development kit[9] combines 3D motion tracking with depth sensing to allow mobile devices to know where it is and how it moves through the space. *Walk-Compass* [26] detected the walking direction within a few steps using sensors available on smartphones, while Husen et al. [14] employed a dense Wi-Fi infrastructure to determine the orientation. In our work, user's facing direction is considered to be the same as the facing direction of the smartphone camera, and is obtained from the camera pose provided by image-based localization.

Regarding navigation instructions, a conventional 2D map based navigation system provides instructions including abstract paths [29] and texts [16]. With image-based 3D models, *iMoon* is able to generate navigation instructions that include visual hints. In practice, *iMoon* shows what the user is expecting to see in front by selecting photos from the input of 3D models based on user's position and facing direction.

8. CONCLUSION

We presented *iMoon*, a low-cost and whole-system solution for indoor navigation in this paper. *iMoon* is partially built on top of several existing techniques, e.g., SfM and fingerprinting. Nonetheless, *iMoon* brings new functions and addresses several technical challenges to enable mobile crowdsensing-based indoor navigation. It utilizes crowdsourced photos to build the 3D models of the indoor space of interest, and detects pedestrian paths from crowdsourced user trajectories. It also enables fast localization by taking advantage of the high hit-rate and low response delay of Wi-Fi fingerprinting. The new elements introduced into *iMoon* make it functional and perform well, as demonstrated in the field study. *iMoon* would be a good primer for any system considering providing indoor navigation services based on crowdsourced photos and sensor data.

9. ACKNOWLEDGMENTS

We thank the anonymous reviewers and Prof. Xiaofan Jiang for their insightful comments and suggestions. We thank our group members and volunteers, Emil Kreutzman, Iivari Äikäs, Teemu Kämäräinen, Morteza Neishaboori and Yinan Zong. This work was supported by the Academy of Finland, grant number 278207 and 268096.

[9]https://www.google.com/atap/project-tango/

10. REFERENCES

[1] Siftgpu: A gpu implementation of scale invariant feature transform (sift). http://cs.unc.edu/ ccwu/siftgpu/.

[2] Visualsfm : A visual structure from motion system. http://ccwu.me/vsfm/.

[3] S. Agarwal, Y. Furukawa, N. Snavely, I. Simon, B. Curless, S. M. Seitz, and R. Szeliski. Building rome in a day. *ACM Commun.*, 54(10):105–112, 2011.

[4] P. Bahl and V. Padmanabhan. Radar: an in-building rf-based user location and tracking system. In *Proc. of INFOCOM 2000*, pages 775–784.

[5] L. Chen, L. Pei, H. Kuusniemi, Y. Chen, T. Kroger, and R. Chen. Bayesian fusion for indoor positioning using bluetooth fingerprints. *Wireless Personal Commun.*, 70(4):1735–1745, 2013.

[6] J. C. Chow. *Multi-Sensor Integration for Indoor 3D Reconstruction.* PhD thesis, University of Calgary, 2014.

[7] J. Chung, M. Donahoe, C. Schmandt, I.-J. Kim, P. Razavai, and M. Wiseman. Indoor location sensing using geo-magnetism. In *Proc. of MobiSys'11*, pages 141–154, New York, NY, USA.

[8] J. Dong, Y. Xiao, Z. Ou, and A. Ylä-Jääski. Utilizing internet photos for indoor mapping and localization – opportunities and challenges. In *Proc. of SmartCity'15*, pages 1–6, Hong Kong, China.

[9] M. Duckham, L. Kulik, M. Worboys, and A. Galton. Efficient generation of simple polygons for characterizing the shape of a set of points in the plane. *Pattern Recogn.*, 41(10):3224–3236, 2008.

[10] J.-M. Frahm, P. Fite-Georgel, D. Gallup, T. Johnson, R. Raguram, C. Wu, Y.-H. Jen, E. Dunn, B. Clipp, S. Lazebnik, and M. Pollefeys. Building rome on a cloudless day. In *Proc. of ECCV'10*, pages 368–381, Berlin, Heidelberg.

[11] Y. Furukawa, B. Curless, S. M. Seitz, and R. Szeliski. Reconstructing building interiors from images. In *Proc. of ICCV'09*, Kyoto, Japan.

[12] R. Gao, M. Zhao, T. Ye, F. Ye, Y. Wang, K. Bian, T. Wang, and X. Li. Jigsaw: Indoor floor plan reconstruction via mobile crowdsensing. In *Proc. of MobiCom'14*, pages 249–260, New York, NY, USA.

[13] Y. Gu, A. Lo, and I. Niemegeers. A survey of indoor positioning systems for wireless personal networks. *IEEE Commun. Surveys Tuts*, 11:13–32, 2009.

[14] M. N. Husen and S. Lee. Indoor human localization with orientation using wifi fingerprinting. In *Proc. of ICUIMC'14*, pages 109:1–109:6, New York, NY, USA.

[15] F. Li, C. Zhao, G. Ding, J. Gong, C. Liu, and F. Zhao. A reliable and accurate indoor localization method using phone inertial sensors. In *Proc. of UbiComp'12*, pages 421–430, New York, NY, USA.

[16] J. Link, P. Smith, N. Viol, and K. Wehrle. Footpath: Accurate map-based indoor navigation using smartphones. In *Proc. of IPIN'11*, pages 1–8, Guimaraes, Portugal.

[17] H. Liu, H. Darabi, P. Banerjee, and J. Liu. Survey of wireless indoor positioning techniques and systems. *IEEE Trans. Syst., Man, Cybern.*, 37(6):1067–1080, 2007.

[18] D. G. Lowe. Distinctive image features from scale-invariant keypoints. *Int. J. Comput. Vision*, 60(2):91–110, 2004.

[19] G. Lu and C. Kambhamettu. Image-based indoor localization system based on 3d sfm model. In *Proc. of SPIE*, Intelligent Robots and Computer Vision, 2014.

[20] R. Martin-Brualla, Y. He, B. C. Russell, and S. M. Seitz. The 3d jigsaw puzzle: Mapping large indoor spaces. In *Proc. of ECCV'14*, pages 1–16. Zurich, Switzerland.

[21] R. A. Newcombe, S. Izadi, O. Hilliges, D. Molyneaux, D. Kim, A. J. Davison, P. Kohi, J. Shotton, S. Hodges, and A. Fitzgibbon. Kinectfusion: Real-time dense surface mapping and tracking. In *Proc. of ISMAR'11*, pages 127–136, Basel, Switzerland.

[22] L. T. Nguyen and J. Zhang. Wi-fi fingerprinting through active learning using smartphones. In *Proc. of UbiComp'13 Adjunct*, pages 969–976, New York, NY, USA.

[23] B. E. Okorn, X. Xiong, B. Akinci, and D. Huber. Toward automated modeling of floor plans. In *Proc. of 3DPVT'10*, Paris, France.

[24] Z. Ou, J. Dong, S. Dong, J. Wu, A. Yla-Jaaski, P. Hui, R. Wang, and A. Min. Utilize signal traces from others? a crowdsourcing perspective of energy saving in cellular data communication. *IEEE Trans. Mobile Comput.*, 14(1):194–207, 2015.

[25] A. Rai, K. K. Chintalapudi, V. N. Padmanabhan, and R. Sen. Zee: Zero-effort crowdsourcing for indoor localization. In *Proc. of Mobicom'12*, pages 293–304, New York, NY, USA.

[26] N. Roy, H. Wang, and R. Roy Choudhury. I am a smartphone and i can tell my user's walking direction. In *Proc. of MobiSys'14*, pages 329–342, New York, NY, USA.

[27] T. Sattler, B. Leibe, and L. Kobbelt. Fast image-based localization using direct 2d-to-3d matching. In *Proc. of ICCV'11*, pages 667–674, Barcelona, Spain.

[28] M. Satyanarayanan, P. Bahl, R. Caceres, and N. Davies. The case for vm-based cloudlets in mobile computing. *IEEE Pervasive Comput.*, 8(4):14–23, 2009.

[29] A. Serra, D. Carboni, and V. Marotto. Indoor pedestrian navigation system using a modern smartphone. In *Proc. of MobileHCI'10*, pages 397–398, New York, NY, USA.

[30] N. Snavely, I. Simon, M. Goesele, R. Szeliski, and S. Seitz. Scene reconstruction and visualization from community photo collections. *Proc. of the IEEE*, 98(8):1370–1390, 2010.

[31] H. Wang, S. Sen, A. Elgohary, M. Farid, M. Youssef, and R. R. Choudhury. No need to war-drive: Unsupervised indoor localization. In *Proc. of MobiSys'12*, pages 197–210, New York, NY, USA.

[32] C. Wu. Towards linear-time incremental structure from motion. In *Proc. of 3DV'13*, pages 127–134, Seattle, USA.

[33] C. Wu, S. Agarwal, B. Curless, and S. M. Seitz. Multicore bundle adjustment. In *Proc. of CVPR'11*, pages 3057–3064, Washington, DC, USA.

VeTrack: Real Time Vehicle Tracking in Uninstrumented Indoor Environments

Mingmin Zhao[1], Tao Ye[1], Ruipeng Gao[1], Fan Ye[2], Yizhou Wang[1], Guojie Luo[1]
[1]EECS School, Peking University, Beijing 100871, China
[2]ECE Department, Stony Brook University, Stony Brook, NY 11794, USA
{zhaomingmin, pkuyetao, gaoruipeng, Yizhou.Wang, gluo}@pku.edu.cn, fan.ye@stonybrook.edu

ABSTRACT

Although location awareness and turn-by-turn instructions are prevalent outdoors due to GPS, we are back into the darkness in uninstrumented indoor environments such as underground parking structures. We get confused, disoriented when driving in these mazes, and frequently forget where we parked, ending up circling back and forth upon return. In this paper, we propose VeTrack, a smartphone-only system that tracks the vehicle's location in real time using the phone's inertial sensors. It does not require any environment instrumentation or cloud backend. It uses a novel "shadow" tracing method to accurately estimate the vehicle's trajectories despite arbitrary phone/vehicle poses and frequent disturbances. We develop algorithms in a Sequential Monte Carlo framework to represent vehicle states probabilistically, and harness constraints by the garage map and detected landmarks to robustly infer the vehicle location. We also find landmark (e.g., speed bumps, turns) recognition methods reliable against noises, disturbances from bumpy rides and even hand-held movements. We implement a highly efficient prototype and conduct extensive experiments in multiple parking structures of different sizes and structures, with multiple vehicles and drivers. We find that VeTrack can estimate the vehicle's real time location with almost negligible latency, with error of $2 \sim 4$ parking spaces at 80-percentile.

Categories and Subject Descriptors

C.2.4 [**Computer-Communication Networks**]: Distributed Systems—*Distributed Applications*; C.3 [**Special-Purpose and Application-based Systems**]: Real-time and embedded systems

Keywords

Vehicle real time tracking; indoor environments

1. INTRODUCTION

Thanks to decades of efforts in GPS systems and devices, drivers know their locations at any time outdoors. The location awareness enables drivers to make proper decisions and gives them a sense of "control." However, whenever we drive into indoor environments such as underground parking garages, or multi-level parking structures where GPS signals can hardly penetrate, we lose this location awareness. Not only do we get confused, disoriented in maze-like structures, frequently we do not even remember where we park the car, ending up circling back and forth searching for the vehicle.

Providing real time vehicle tracking capability indoors will satisfy the fundamental and constant cognitive needs of drivers to orient themselves relative to a large and unfamiliar environment. Knowing where they are generates a sense of control and induces calmness psychologically, both greatly enhancing the driving experience. In smart parking systems where free parking space information is available, real time tracking will enable turn-by-turn instructions guiding drivers to those spaces, or at least areas where more spaces are likely available. The final parking location recorded can also be used to direct the driver back upon return, avoiding any back and forth search.

However, real time vehicle tracking indoors is far from straightforward. First, mainstream indoor localization technology leverages RF signals such as WiFi [7, 45] and cellular [28], which can be sparse, intermittent or simply nonexistent in many uninstrumented environments. Instrumenting the environment [4, 5] unfortunately is not always feasible: the acquisition, installation and maintenance of sensors require significant time, financial costs and human efforts; simply wiring legacy environments can be a major undertaking. The lack of radio signals also means lack of Internet connectivity: no cloud service is reachable and all sensing/computing have to happen locally.

In this paper, we propose VeTrack, a real time vehicle tracking system that utilizes inertial sensors in the smartphone to provide accurate vehicle location. It does not rely on GPS/RF signals, or any additional sensors instrumenting the environment. All sensing and computation occur in the phone and no cloud backend is needed. A driver simply starts the VeTrack application before entering a parking structure, then VeTrack will track the vehicle movements, estimate and display its location in a garage map in real time, and record the final parking location, which can be used by the driver later to find the vehicle.

Such an inertial and phone-only solution entails a series of non-trivial challenges. First, many different scenarios exist for the phone *pose* (i.e., relative orientation between its coordinate system to that of the vehicle), which is needed to transform phone movements into vehicle movements. The phone may be placed in arbitrary positions - lying flat on a

SenSys'15, November 1–4, 2015, Seoul, South Korea..
© 2015 ACM. ISBN 978-1-4503-3631-4/15/11 ...$15.00.
DOI: http://dx.doi.org/10.1145/2809695.2809726.

surface, slanted into a cup holder. The vehicle may drive on a non-horizontal, sloped surface; it may not go straight up or down the slope (e.g., slanted parking spaces). Furthermore, unpredictable human or road condition disturbances (e.g., moved together with the driver's pants' pockets, or picked up from a cupholder; speed bumps or jerky driving jolting the phone) may change the phone pose frequently. Despite all these different scenarios and disturbances, the phone's pose must be reliably and quickly estimated.

Second, due to the lack of periodic acceleration patterns like a person's walking [23, 26, 33], the traveling distance of a vehicle cannot be easily estimated. Although landmarks (e.g., speed bumps, turns) causing unique inertial data patterns can calibrate the location [39], distinguishing such patterns from other movements robustly (e.g., driver picking up and then laying down the phone), and recognizing them reliably despite different parking structures, vehicles and drivers, remain open questions.

Finally, we have to balance the conflict between tracking accuracy and latency. Delaying the location determination allows more time for computation and sensing, thus higher tracking accuracy. However, this delay inevitably increases tracking latency, which adversely impacts real time performance and user experience. How to develop efficient tracking algorithms to achieve both reasonable accuracy and acceptable latency, while using resources only on the phone, is another great challenge.

VeTrack consists of several components to deal with the above challenges to achieve accurate, real time tracking. First, we propose a novel *"shadow trajectory"* tracing method that greatly simplifies phone pose estimation and vehicle movements computation. It can handle slopes and slanted driving on slopes; it is highly robust to inevitable noises, and can quickly re-estimate the pose after each disturbance. We devise robust landmark detection algorithms that can reliably distinguish landmarks from disturbances (e.g., drivers picking up the phone) causing seemingly similar inertial patterns. Based on the vehicle movements and detected landmarks, we develop a highly robust yet efficient probabilistic framework to track a vehicle's location.

In summary, we make the following contributions:

- We develop a novel robust and efficient "shadow trajectory" tracing method. Unlike existing methods [17, 40, 46] that track the 3-axis relative angles between the phone and vehicle, it only tracks a single heading direction difference. To the best of our knowledge, it is the first that can handle slopes and slanted driving on slopes, and re-estimates a changed pose almost instantaneously.

- We design states and algorithms in a Sequential Monte Carlo framework that leverages constraints from garage maps and detected landmarks to reliably infer a vehicle's location. It uses probability distributions to represent a vehicle's states. We further propose a one-dimensional *skeleton road* model to reduce the vehicle state complexity, and a prediction-rollback mechanism to cut down tracking latency, both by one order of magnitude to enable real time tracking.

- We propose robust landmark detection algorithms to recognize commonly encountered landmarks. They can reliably distinguish true landmarks from disturbances that exhibit similar inertial data patterns.

- We implement a prototype and conduct extensive experiments with different parking structures, vehicles and drivers. We find that it can track the vehicle in real time against even disturbances such as drivers picking up the phone. It has almost negligible tracking latency, 10° pose and $2 \sim 4$ parking spaces' location errors at 80-percentile, which are sufficient for most real time driving and parked vehicle finding.

Next, we give a brief overview (Section 2), describe the shadow trajectory tracing (Section 3), Sequential Monte Carlo algorithm design and the simplified road skeleton model (Section 4), landmark detection algorithms and prediction-rollback (Section 5). We report evaluation (Section 6), review related work (Section 7). After a discussion of limitations (Section 8), we conclude the paper.

2. DESIGN OVERVIEW

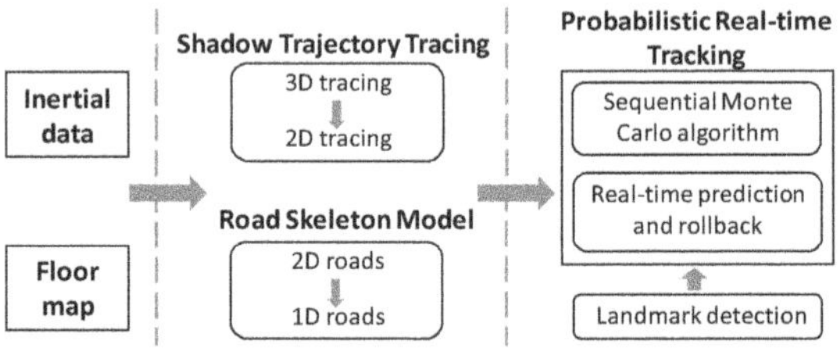

Figure 1: Shadow trajectory tracing simplifies 3D vehicle tracing into 2D shadow tracing while road skeleton model further reduces 2D tracing into 1D. VeTrack represents vehicle states probabilistically and uses Sequential Monte Carlo framework for robust tracking. It uses landmark detection to calibrate vehicle states and prediction/rollback for minimum latency.

VeTrack utilizes smartphone inertial data and garage floor maps (assumed already available). The two components of shadow trajectory tracing and skeleton road model simplify the problem, while the probabilistic framework utilizes landmark detection results and prediction/rollback mechanism for robust and real time tracking (Figure 1). Shadow trajectory tracing tracks the shadow of the vehicle on 2D plane instead of the vehicle in 3D space; the road skeleton model abstracts 2D strip roads into 1D line segments to remove inconsequential details while keeping the basic shape and topology.

To deal with noises and disturbances in data, VeTrack explicitly represents the states of vehicles (e.g., locations) with probabilities and we develop algorithms in Sequential Monte Carlo framework for robust tracking. They leverage landmark detection results to help calibrate the vehicle locations to where such landmarks exist, and the prediction/rollback mechanism to generate instantaneous landmark recognition results without waiting for completely passing of landmarks.

3. TRAJECTORY TRACING

3.1 Conventional Approach

The standard approach to infer a vehicle's current location $\overrightarrow{x}(t)$ is double integration of acceleration: $\overrightarrow{x}(t) = \iint \overrightarrow{a}(t)dt$. This requires the vehicle's acceleration in the global coordinate system G be estimated, and is usually done in three steps in existing work [17, 40, 46].

Assume the 3 axes of the vehicle's coordinate system are X^V, Y^V and Z^V. First the gravity direction is obtained using mobile OS APIs [1] that use low-pass Butterworth filters to remove high frequency components caused by rotation and translation movements [47]. It is assumed to be the direction of Z^V in the phone's coordinate system (i.e., vehicles moving on level ground).

Next the gravity direction component is deducted to obtain the acceleration on the horizontal plane. The direction of maximum acceleration (caused by vehicle accelerating or decelerating) is estimated as Y^V (i.e., forward direction). Finally, X^V is determined as the cross product of Y^V and Z^V using the right-hand rule. The X^V, Y^V and Z^V directions in the phone's coordinate system give a transformation matrix that converts the phone's acceleration into that of the vehicle.

However, during investigation we find several limitations: First, when a vehicle is on a slope (straight up/down or slanted), the direction of gravity is no longer the Z-axis of the vehicle. Second, accelerometers are highly noisy and susceptible to various disturbances from driving dynamics and road conditions. Thus the direction of the maximum horizontal acceleration may not always be the Y-axis. In experiments we find that it has around 40° errors at 80-percentile (Section 6.2). Finally, to reliably detect the direction of maximum horizontal acceleration, a changed phone pose must remain the same at least 4s [46], which may be impossible when frequent disturbances exist.

3.2 Shadow Trajectory Tracing

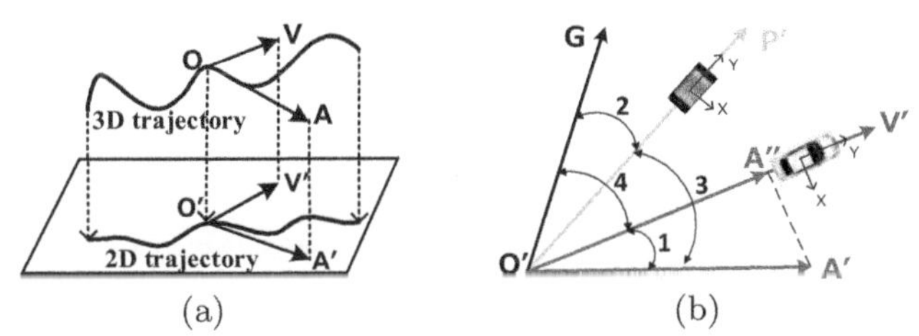

Figure 2: (a) Intuition: points O and O' are the positions of the vehicle and its shadow. $\overrightarrow{OV}$ and $\overrightarrow{OA}$ are the velocity and acceleration of vehicle in the 3D space. V' and A' are the projection of V and A onto the 2D ground. (b) Illustration of the method to estimate $\angle 1$ from $\angle 2$, $\angle 3$ and $\angle 4$.

To overcome the above limitations, we propose a "shadow" trajectory tracing method that traces the movement of the vehicle's *shadow* projected onto the 2D horizontal plane (Figure 2(a)). Points O and O' represent the positions of the vehicle and its shadow. $\overrightarrow{OV}$ and $\overrightarrow{OA}$ are the velocity and acceleration of the vehicle in 3D space. V' and A' are the projection of V and A onto the 2D ground. It can be shown easily that $\overrightarrow{O'V'}$ and $\overrightarrow{O'A'}$ are the velocity and acceleration of the shadow. This is simply because the projection eliminates the vertical direction component but preserves those on the horizontal plane, thus the shadow and vehicle have the same horizontal acceleration, and thus the same 2D plane velocity and coordinates.

We use another method to trace the shadow location. Instead of direct double integrating on the original acceleration vector ($\overrightarrow{\boldsymbol{x}}(t) = \iint \overrightarrow{\boldsymbol{a}}(t)dt$), we use the moving direction of the shadow (unit length vector $\overrightarrow{\boldsymbol{T}}(t)$) and its speed amplitude $s(t)$: $\overrightarrow{\boldsymbol{x}}(t) = \int \overrightarrow{\boldsymbol{T}}(t) \cdot s(t)dt$, where $s(t)$ can be computed as $\int a(t)dt$, integration of the acceleration amplitude along moving direction. Although there are still two integrations, the impact of vertical direction noises is eliminated due to the projection, and the moving direction $\overrightarrow{\boldsymbol{T}}(t)$ can be measured reliably by gyroscope and maps (i.e., forward/backward along pathways only). Thus our method achieves better accuracy and robustness than the conventional approach.

We need to estimate three variables in this method (Figure 2(b)): 1) the shadow's moving direction $\overrightarrow{O'V'}$ (i.e., $\overrightarrow{\boldsymbol{T}}(t)$) in the global coordinate system. 2) the horizontal (i.e., shadow's) acceleration $\overrightarrow{O'A'}$. 3) angle $\angle V'O'A'$ ($\angle 1$), the angle between the horizontal acceleration vector and vehicle's shadow's heading (i.e., moving) direction; this is used to project the shadow's acceleration along the vehicle moving direction $\overrightarrow{O'V'}$ to get tangential acceleration amplitude $|\overrightarrow{O'A''}|$(i.e., $s(t)$).

Next we explain how to estimate them in three steps.

1) When the vehicle is driving straight, the shadow's moving direction is approximated by the direction of the road, which can be obtained from the garage map and the current location estimation. When the vehicle is turning around a corner, VeTrack accumulates the gyroscope's "yaw" (around gravity direction) to modify the heading direction until the vehicle goes straight again. We develop robust algorithms to distinguish straight driving from turning and disturbances (Section 5).

2) From existing mobile OS APIs [1], the gravity direction can be detected. We deduct the gravity direction component from the phone's acceleration vector to obtain the horizontal acceleration vector $\overrightarrow{O'A'}$.

3) Figure 2(b) illustrates how to calculate $\angle 1$ ($\angle V'O'A'$): $\angle 1 = \angle 2 + \angle 3 - \angle 4$ (i.e.,$\angle V'O'A' = \angle GO'P' + \angle P'O'A' - \angle GO'V'$). $\overrightarrow{O'G}, \overrightarrow{O'P'}, \overrightarrow{O'V'}$ are the Y-axes of the global, phone's shadow's and vehicle's shadow's coordinate system. 3.1) $\angle 2$ is the phone's shadow's heading direction in the global coordinate system. Its relative changes can be obtained reliably from the gyroscope's "yaw", and we use a distribution around the compass' reading upon entering the garage to initialize it. Because the Sequential Monte Carlo framework can calibrate and quickly reduce the error (Section 4), an accurate initial direction is not necessary. 3.2) $\angle 3$ is essentially the horizontal acceleration direction in the phone's shadow's coordinate system, which is already obtained in step 2). 3.3) $\angle 4$ is the vehicle's shadow's moving direction in the global coordinate system, already obtained in step 1).

Shadow trajectory tracing and 3D tracing are theoretically equivalent when there are no noises. However, shadow tracing needs much less variables and is subject to less noises. 1) Shadow tracing does not need to track variables in the vertical dimension (e.g., altitude, angle, speed and acceleration). All of them are subject to noises and require more complexity to estimate. 2) On the horizontal plane, the moving direction can be estimated accurately based on the prior knowledge of road directions (Section 4.4). The distance is computed using the acceleration amplitude along the moving direction. Thus inertial noises perpendicular to the moving direction do not impact the distance estimation. 3) Shadow tracing uses gyroscopes to estimate pose, while conventional 3D tracing uses accelerometers that are more susceptible to external disturbances. Therefore, shadow tracing is much less complex, subject to less noises, and thus achieves better accuracy and higher robustness.

During experiments, we find that: our shadow tracing method can handle arbitrary phone and vehicle poses and the vehicle can go straight up/down or slanted on a slope. It has much smaller errors ($5 \sim 10^{\circ}$ at 80-percentile) and better robustness. It also re-estimates a changed phone pose almost instantaneously because gyroscopes have little latency; thus it can handle frequent disturbances.

4. REAL TIME TRACKING

4.1 Intuition

The basic idea to locate the vehicle is to leverage two types of constraints imposed by the map, namely paths and landmarks. Given a trajectory estimated from inertial data (Figure 3), there are only a few paths on the map that can accommodate the trajectory. Each detected landmark (e.g., a speed bump or turn) can pinpoint the vehicle to a few possible locations. Jointly considering the two constraints can further reduce the uncertainty and limit the possible placement of the trajectory, thus revealing the vehicle location. We will first describe the tracking design here, then landmark detection in Section 5.

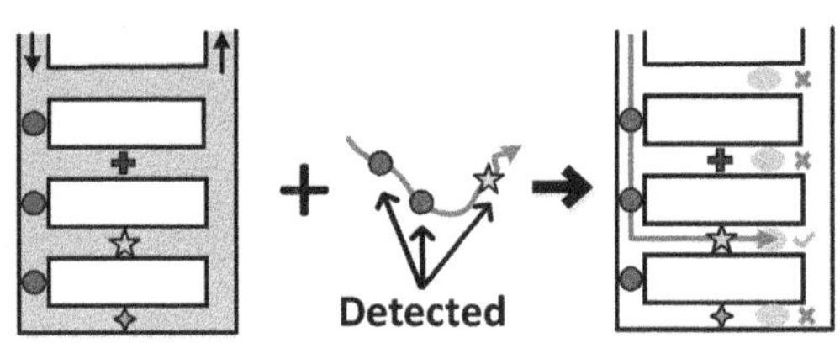

Figure 3: Using both map constraints and detected landmarks can narrow down the possible placement of the trajectory more quickly.

To achieve robust and real time tracking, we need to address a dual challenge. First, the inertial data have significant noises and disturbances. Smartphones do not possess speedometer or odometer to directly measure the velocity or distance; they are obtained from acceleration integration, which is known to generate cubic error accumulation [39]. External disturbances (e.g., hand-held movements or road conditions) causing sudden and drastic changes may not be completely separated from vehicle movements. Together they make it impossible to obtain accurate trajectories from inertial data only. Second, the requirement of low latency tracking demands efficient algorithms that can run on resource-limited phones. We have to minimize computational complexity so no cloud backend is needed.

To achieve robustness, we use probability distributions to explicitly represent vehicle states (e.g., location and speed) and the Sequential Monte Carlo (SMC) method to maintain the states. This is inspired by probabilistic robotics [35]: instead of a single "best guess", the probability distributions cover the whole space of possible hypotheses about vehicle locations, and use evidences from sensing data to validate the likelihoods of these hypotheses. This results in much better robustness to noises in data. To achieve efficiency, we use a 1D *"skeleton road"* model that abstracts paths into one dimensional line segments. We find this dramatically reduces the size of vehicle states. Thus the number of hypotheses is cut by almost one order of magnitude, which is critical to achieve real time tracking on resource limited phones. Next we will describe the road skeleton model and the detailed SMC design.

4.2 Road Skeleton Model

The road skeleton model greatly simplifies the representation of garage maps. It abstracts away inconsequential details and keeps only the essential aspects important to tracking. Thus it helps reduce computational overheads in the probabilistic framework. We assume that garage maps are available (e.g., from operators), while how to construct them is beyond the scope of this paper.

Given a map of 3D multi-level parking structure, we represent each level by projecting its map onto a 2D horizontal plane perpendicular to the gravity direction. Thus the vehicle location can be represented by a number indicating the current level, and a 2D coordinate for its location on this level. To accommodate changes when a vehicle moves across adjacent levels, we introduce "virtual boundaries" in the middle of the ramp connecting two levels. As shown in Fig.4(b), a vehicle crossing the dash line of the virtual boundary between levels will be assigned a different level number. This kind of 2D representation suits the needs for shadow tracing while retaining the essential topology and shape for tracking.

Note that we call it 2D representation because the floor level remains unchanged and does not need detection most of the time. It is updated only when the vehicle crosses virtual boundaries between levels. Its estimation is also much simpler and easier than accurate 2D tracking, where most challenges exist.

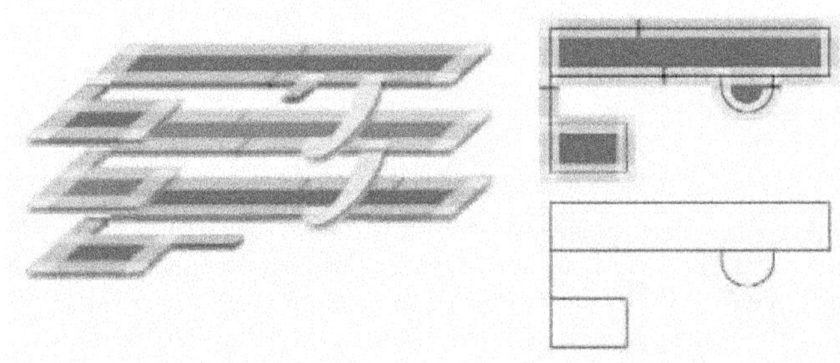

Figure 4: (a) shows the 3D floor plans of a multi-level parking structure. A vehicle enters the entrance on the floor B1, goes down to other two levels crossing the virtual boundaries. (b) shows the 2D projection of Floor B2 in (a). (c) shows the 1D road skeleton model of (b). Points on (c) represent landmarks, corresponding to bumps and corners in (a) and (b).

The key insight for the skeleton model is that the road width is not necessary for tracking vehicle locations. Since the paths are usually narrow enough for only one vehicle in each direction, the vehicle location has little freedom in the width direction. Thus we simplify the road representation with their medial axis, and roads become 1D line segments without any width (Fig.4(c)).

Compared to a straightforward 2D strip representation of roads, the skeleton model reduces the freedom of vehicle location by one dimension, thus greatly cutting down the state space size in the probabilistic framework and resulting in one order of magnitude less complexity.

4.3 Probabilistic Tracking Framework

The tracking problem is formulated as a Sequential Monte Carlo (SMC) problem, specifically, the particle filtering framework [21]. The vehicle states (e.g., location, speed) at time t are represented by a multi-dimensional random variable $s(t)$. Each hypothesis (with concrete values for each dimension of $s(t)$) is called a "particle" and a collection of J particles $\{s_t^{(j)}\}_{j=1}^J$ are used to represent the distribution of possible vehicle states at time t.

The framework operates on discrete time $\{1, ..., t-1, t, ...\}$ and repeat three steps for each time slot. Without loss of generality, we assume J particles $\{s_{t-1}^{(j)}\}_{j=1}^J$ already exist at $t-1$ and describe the progress from $t-1$ to t.

State update predicts the set of states $\{\hat{s}_t^{(j)}\}_{j=1}^J$ at time t based on two known inputs, the previous state $\{s_{t-1}^{(j)}\}_{j=1}^J$ and most recent movement m_t such as the speed, acceleration that govern the movement of the vehicle. For example, given the previous location and most recent speed, one can predict a vehicle's next location. To capture uncertainties in movement and previous states, a random noise is added to the estimated location. Thus J predictions $\{\hat{s}_t^{(j)}\}_{j=1}^J$ are generated.

Weight update uses measurements z_t made at time t to examine how much evidence exists for each prediction, so as to adjust the weights of particles $\{\hat{s}_t^{(j)}\}_{j=1}^J$. The likelihood $p(z_t|s_t)$, how likely the measurement z_t would happen given state s_t, is the evidence. A prediction $\hat{s}_t^{(j)}$ with a higher likelihood $p(z_t|s_t = \hat{s}_t^{(j)})$ will receive a proportionally higher weight $w_t^{(j)} = w_{t-1}^{(j)} p(z_t|s_t = \hat{s}_t^{(j)})$. Then all weights are normalized to ensure that $\{w_t^{(j)}\}_{j=1}^J$ sum to 1.

Resampling draws J particles from the current state prediction set $\{\hat{s}_t^{(j)}\}_{j=1}^J$ with probabilities proportional to their weights $\{w_t^{(j)}\}_{j=1}^J$, thus creating the new state set $\{s_t^{(j)}\}_{j=1}^J$ to replace the old set $\{s_{t-1}^{(j)}\}_{j=1}^J$. Then the next iteration starts.

Note that the above is only a framework. The critical task is the detailed design of particle states, update, resampling procedures. Thus we cannot simply copy what has been done in related work, and have to carefully design algorithms tailored to our specific problem.

4.4 Tracking Algorithms

4.4.1 State and Initialization

Our particle state is a collection of factors that can impact the vehicle tracking. Since the number of particles grows exponentially with the dimensionality of the state, we select most related factors to reduce the complexity while still preserving tracking accuracy. Our particle states include:

- level number k,
- position on 2D floor plane $X = (x, y)$,
- speed of the vehicle v,
- α/β, phone/vehicle shadows' 2D heading directions.

The first dimension k is introduced for multi-level structures. Position of the vehicle is represented as a 2D coordinate $X = (x, y)$ for convenience. In reality, due to the 1D skeleton road model, the position actually has only one degree of freedom. This greatly reduces the number of particles needed.

Initialization of particles: We use certain prior knowledge to initialize the particles' state. The last GPS location before entering the parking structure is used to infer the entrance, thus the level number k and 2D entrance location (x, y). The vehicle speed v is assumed to start from zero. The vehicle heading direction β is approximated by the direction of the entrance path segment, and the phone heading direction α is drawn from a distribution based on the compass reading before entering the garage. As shown later (Section 6), the phone's heading direction can be calibrated to within 15°, showing strong robustness against compass errors known to be non-trivial [37].

4.4.2 State Update

For a particle with state $(k_{t-1}, x_{t-1}, y_{t-1}, v_{t-1}, \alpha_{t-1}, \beta_{t-1})$, we create a prediction $(\hat{k_t}, \hat{x_t}, \hat{y_t}, \hat{v_t}, \hat{\alpha_t}, \hat{\beta_t})$ given movement $m_t = (a_x, a_y, \omega_z)$ where a_x, a_y and ω_z are X, Y-axis accelerations and Z-axis angular speed in the coordinate system of the phone's shadow.

First, $(\hat{x_t}, \hat{y_t})$ is updated as follow:

$$\hat{x_t} = x_{t-1} + v_{t-1}\Delta t \cdot \cos\beta_{t-1} + \epsilon_x, \tag{1}$$

$$\hat{y_t} = y_{t-1} + v_{t-1}\Delta t \cdot \sin\beta_{t-1} + \epsilon_y, \tag{2}$$

where ϵ_x, ϵ_y are Gaussian noises. If $(\hat{x_t}, \hat{y_t})$ is no longer on the skeleton, we project it back to the skeleton. Level number $\hat{k_t}$ is updated when a particle passes through a virtual boundary around the floor-connecting-ramp, otherwise $\hat{k_t} = k_{t-1}$.

Next, velocity v_t is updated as follow:

$$\hat{a_t} = a_y \cdot \cos\gamma_t - a_x \cdot \sin\gamma_t + \epsilon_a, \tag{3}$$

$$\hat{v_t} = v_{t-1} + a_t \cdot \Delta t + \epsilon_v, \tag{4}$$

where γ_t is the angle between the Y axes of the two shadows' coordinate systems and ϵ_a, ϵ_v are Gaussian noises.

Finally, α_t and β_t are updated as follows:

$$\hat{\alpha_t} = \alpha_{t-1} + \omega_z\Delta t + \epsilon_\alpha, \tag{5}$$

$$\hat{\beta_t} = \begin{cases} \beta_{t-1} + \omega_z\Delta t + \epsilon_\beta, & \text{if } turn = True; \\ \text{road direction at } (k_t, x_t, y_t), & \text{otherwise.} \end{cases} \tag{6}$$

where $\epsilon_\alpha, \epsilon_\beta$ are random Gaussian noises. The above allows the phone to change its angle α to accommodate occasional hand-held or jolting movements, while such movements will not alter the vehicle's angle β if the vehicle is known to travel straight.

4.4.3 Weight Update

Weight update uses detected landmarks and floor plan constraints to recalculate the "importance" of the current particle states. The basic idea is to penalize particles that behave inconsistently given the floor plan constraints. For example, since a vehicle cannot travel perpendicularly to path direction, a particle with velocity orthogonal to the road direction will be penalized. It will have much smaller weights and less likely to be drawn during resampling.

We compute the weight w_t as

$$w_t := w_{t-1} \prod_{i=0}^{2} w_{ti}, \tag{7}$$

Each w_{ti} is described as follows.

- **Constraints imposed by the map.** We define $w_{t0} = cos^2(\beta_t - \beta_{t-1})$. It is designed to penalize particles that have a drastic change in the vehicle heading direction, since during most of the time a vehicle does not make dramatic turns.
- **Detected landmarks.** When an i-th type landmark [1] is detected, w_{ti} of the current state is updated as $\mathcal{N}(D_i(x_t, y_t); 0, \sigma_i^2)$ where $D_i(x_t, y_t)$ is the distance to the closest landmark of the same type and σ_i^2 is a parameter controlling the scale of the distance. If no landmark is detected, $w_{ti} = 1$. This method penalizes the predicted states far away from detected landmarks.

Finally all weights are normalized so they sum up to 1.

4.4.4 Resampling

A replacement particle is selected from the predicted particle set $\{\hat{s}_t^{(j)}\}_{j=1}^J$ where each particle $\hat{s}_t^{(j)}$ has probability $w_t^{(j)}$ being selected. This is repeated J times and J particles are selected to form the new state set $\{s_t^{(j)}\}_{j=1}^J$. Then the next iteration starts.

5. LANDMARK DETECTION

A parking structure usually has a limited number of landmarks (e.g., speed bumps and turns), and their locations can be marked on a garage map. When a vehicle passes over a landmark, it causes distinctive inertial data patterns, which can be recognized to calibrate the vehicle's location.

However, realizing accurate and realtime landmark detection is not trivial because: 1) road conditions and hand movements impose disturbances on inertial sensor readings; and 2) to minimize delay, landmark recognition results are needed based on partial data before the vehicle completely passes a landmark. We present landmark detection algorithms robust to noises and hand movements, and a prediction and rollback mechanism for instantaneous landmark detection.

5.1 Types of Landmarks

Speed bumps generate jolts, hence acceleration fluctuations in the Z-axis when a vehicle passes over. Note that drainage trench covers, fire shutter bottom supports may also cause similar jolting patterns. We include them as "bumps" as well in the garage map.

Many factors can cause ambiguities in bump detection. For example, Figure 5 shows the acceleration signal along the Z-axis as a vehicle starts and passes over four bumps along a straight road. The first tremor in the left green box (around $10 \sim 17s$ marked with "J") is caused by the vehicle's starting acceleration. It lasts longer but with smaller magnitude compared to those caused by the bumps (in red boxes marked "$B1$"-"$B4$"). The tremor in the right green box (around 60s marked "M") is due to the user's action - holding the phone in hand, then uplifting the phone to check the location. They generate vertical acceleration that may be confused with those by bumps.

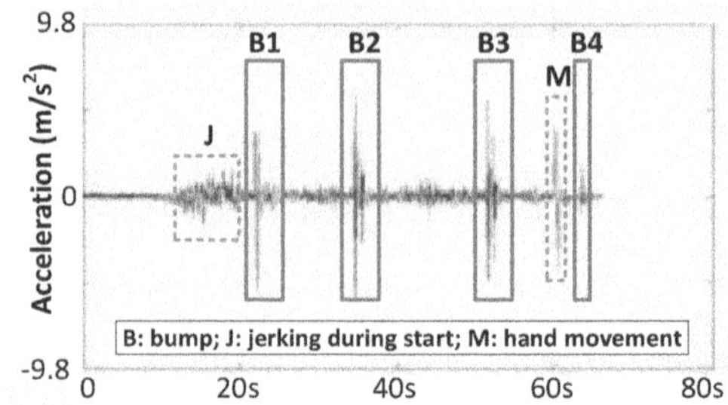

Figure 5: Acceleration along the Z-axis. There are starting acceleration (J), four bumps (B1-B4) and one hand movement (M) along the trajectory.

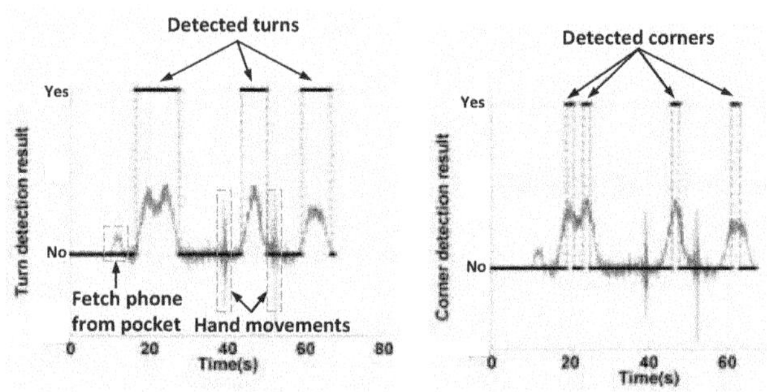

(a) Turn detection (b) Corner detection

Figure 6: Turn and corner detection. (a) Three turn periods are correctly detected, even there are several different hand movements. (b) 4 corners are correctly separated, even when only 3 turned are detected.

Turns are defined as durations in which a vehicle continuously changes its driving direction, usually around road corners. They can be detected from the gyroscope readings of angular velocities around the gravity direction (i.e., "yaw"). During turns a vehicle's direction differs from the road direction. Its direction changes in such periods are accumulated to track the vehicle's heading direction.

There exists work [46] using simple thresholding on turning angles to detect turns. However, we find they cannot reliably distinguish vehicle turns from hand movements (e.g., putting the phone on adjacent seat and picking it up to check the location).

Corners. A turn may span over an extended period, from its start to the end. The corner where two road segments join can be used to precisely calibrate the vehicle's location. The main challenge is consecutive turns: they might be detected as a single one, hence missing some corners. For example, in Figure 6(a), the first two turns may be detected as only one turn period.

We observe that when a vehicle passes at a corner, its angular velocity usually is at a local maxima, corresponding to the maximum turn of the steering wheel. To identify corners precisely, we use a sliding window to find local maxima of angular velocities within each turning period. Each local maxima is marked as a corner. Figure 6(b) shows that

[1]We use only bump and corner here because their locations are precise; turns are used in vehicle angle β update in Eqn 6.

the left most two consecutive corners within the same turn period are properly separated.

5.2 Feature and Classification Algorithm

We use machine learning techniques to recognize bumps and turns. Corners are detected within turns using the above local maxima searching. The critical issue is what features should be used. Although one may feed the raw signal directly to these algorithms, it is usually much more efficient to design succinct, distinctive features from raw signals.

For bumps, we divide acceleration along the Z-axis into 2-second windows sliding at 0.2s intervals. This window size is chosen empirically such that both front and rear wheels can cross the bump for complete bump-passing. For turns, we use gyroscope angular velocities around the vertical direction, and divide the signal the same way. We observe that smaller windows lead to drastic accuracy drop, while larger ones incurs more delay.

We observe that there are two kinds of common hand movements that may be confused with bumps or turns: 1) hold the phone in hand, and occasionally uplift it to check the location; 2) put the phone in pockets/nearby seat, pick up the phone to check the location and then lay it down. The first causes a jitter in Z-axis acceleration, and might be confused with bumps; the second also has Z-axis gyroscope changes, and might be confused with turns.

We have tried a number of different feature designs, both time-domain and frequency-domain, to help distinguish such ambiguities. We list five feature sets which are found to have considerable accuracy and low computation complexity (detailed performance in Section 6).

(1) **STAT35** (35 dimensions): we equally divide one window into 5 segments, and compute a 7-dimensional feature [29] from each segment, including the mean, maximum, second maximum, minimum, and second minimum absolute values, the standard deviation and the root-mean-square.

(2) **DSTAT35** (70 dimensions): In addition to STAT35, we also generate a "differential signal" (i.e., the difference between two consecutive readings) from the raw signal, and extract a similar 7-dimensional feature from each of its 5 segments.

(3) **FFT5** (5 dimensions): we do FFT on the raw signal in the whole window, and use the coefficients of the first five harmonics as a 5-dimensional feature.

(4) **S7FFT5** (35 dimensions): in addition to FFT5, we also extract the same 5 coefficients from each of two half-size windows, and four quarter-size windows. Thus we obtain 35 dimensions from 7 windows.

(5) **DFFT5** (10 dimensions): the first five FFT coefficients of both raw and differential signals.

We explore a few most common machine learning algorithms, Logistic Regression (LR) [9] and Support Vector Machine (SVM) [9]. After feature extraction, we manually label the data for training. We find that SVM has higher accuracy with slight more complexity than LR, while both can run fast enough on the phone. So we finally decide to use SVM in experiments. We find it has bump and turn detection accuracies (percentage of correctly labeled samples) around 93% (details in Section 6.2).

We have also tried some threshold-based methods on temporal [14] and frequency domain [22] features, but find it is impossible to set universally effective thresholds, and the frequency power densities by hand movements can be very similar to those of landmarks. Thus they are not sufficiently robust.

5.3 Prediction and Rollback

The reliability of landmark detection depends on the "completeness" of the signal. If the window covers the full duration of passing a landmark, more numbers of distinctive features can be extracted, and the detection would be more reliable. In reality, this may not always be possible. The landmark detection is repeated at certain intervals, but many intervals may not be precisely aligned with complete landmark-passing durations. One naive solution is to wait until the passing has completed. Thus more features can be extracted for reliable detection. However, this inevitably increases tracking latency and causes jitters in location estimation and display, adversely impacting user experience.

We use a simple prediction technique to make decisions based on data from such partial durations. To identify whether a car is passing a landmark at time t, assume that the signal spanning from $t-\tau$ to $t+\tau$ covering the full 2τ landmark-passing duration is needed for best results. At any time t, we use data in window $[t-2\tau, t]$ to do the detection. The results are used by the real time tracking component to estimate the vehicle location. At time $t+\tau$, the data of full landmark-passing duration become available. We classify data in $[t-\tau, t+\tau]$ and verify if the prediction made at t is correct. Nothing needs to be done if it is. If it was wrong, we rollback all the states in the tracking component to t, and repeat the computation with the correct detection to re-estimate the location.

This simple technique is based on the observation that most of the time the vehicle is driving straight and landmarks are rare events. Thus the prediction remains correct most of the time (i.e., during straight driving), and mistakes/rollbacks happen only occasionally (i.e., when a landmark is encountered). From our experiments, rollbacks happen in a small fraction ($\sim$ 10%) of the time. Thus we ensure low latency most of the time because there is no waiting, while preserving detection accuracy through occasional rollback, which incurs more computation but is found to have acceptable latency (0.1 $\sim$ 0.3s) (Section 6).

6. PERFORMANCE EVALUATION

6.1 Methodology

We implement VeTrack on iOS 6/7/8 so it can run on iPhone 4/4s/5/5s/6. Our code contains a combination of C, C++ for algorithms and Objective C for sensor and GUI operations. A sensor data collector sends continuous data to landmark detectors to produce detection results. Then the real time tracking component uses such output to estimate the vehicle's location, which is displayed on the screen. The initialization (e.g, loading map data) takes less than 0.5 second. Sensors are sampled at 50Hz and the particle states are evolved at the same intervals ($20ms$). Since each landmark lasts for many $20ms$-intervals, the detectors classify the landmark state once every 10 samples (i.e., every 0.2 second), which reduces computing burden.

We conduct experiments in three underground parking lots: a $250m \times 90m$ one in an office building, a $180m \times 50m$ one in a university campus and a 3-level $120m \times 80m$ one in a shopping mall (floor plans shown in Figure 7). There are 298, 79, 423 parking spots, 19, 12, 10 bumps, 10, 11, 27 turns and 4, 2, 6 slopes, respectively.

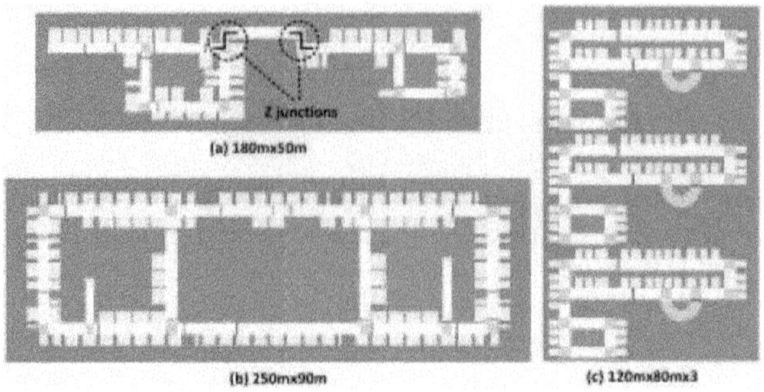

Figure 7: Floor maps of three underground parking lots: (a) university campus: $180m \times 50m$ with 79 parking spots, 12 bumps and 11 turns. (b) office building: $250m \times 90m$ with 298 parking spots, 19 bumps and 10 turns. (c) shopping mall: 3-level $120m \times 80m$ with 423 parking spots, 10 bumps and 27 turns. The chosen parking spots and entrance are marked for each lot.

For each parking lot, we collect 20 separate trajectories each starting from the entrance to one of the parking spots (shown in Figure 7) for inertial sensor data at different poses. The average driving time for trajectories is 2~3 minutes, and the longest one 4.5 minutes. Exemplar trajectories to five test spots are illustrated in Figure 8.

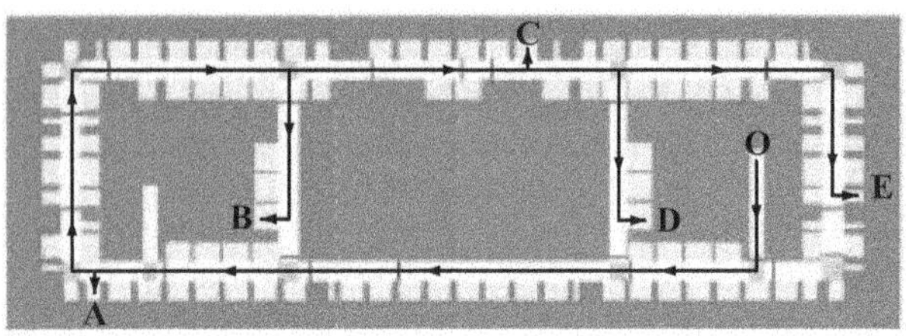

Figure 8: Driving trajectories and test spots. Each trajectory begins at the entrance O and ends at one of the test spots (A to E).

For all three lots, we use a mould to hold 4 iPhones with 4 different poses: horizontal, lean, vertical and box (Figure 9(a)). To further test the performance and robustness of our system, we use 4 more iPhones for the challenging 3-level parking lot with one in driver's right pants' pocket, one in a bag on a seat and two held in hand. The one in pocket is subject to continuous gas/brake pedal actions by the driver, while the one in bag to vehicle movements. Once in a while, one hand-held phone is picked up and put down on the user's thigh, causing Z-axis accelerations similar to those by bumps; the other is picked up from and laid down to adjacent seat, causing Z-axis angular changes similar as those by turns. These 8 poses hopefully cover all common driving scenarios. The UI of VeTrack is shown in Figure 9(b).

We use video to obtain the ground truth of vehicle location over time. During the course of driving, one person holds an iPad parallel to the vehicle's heading direction to record videos from the passenger window. After driving, we manually examine the video frame by frame to find when the vehicle passed distinctive objects (e.g., pillars) with known locations on the map. Such frames have those objects in the middle of the image, thus the error is bounded by 0.5 vehicle length and usually much better.

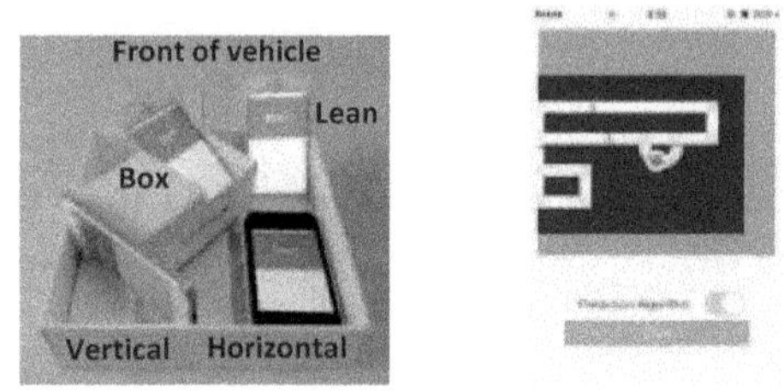

(a) (b)

Figure 9: Mould and VeTrack UI.

To align inertial data and video collected from different devices temporally, we first synchronize the time on all the iPhones and iPad. Then different people holding different devices will start the data collecting/recording applications at the same time. These operations establish the correspondence of data in the time series of different devices.

6.2 Evaluation of Individual Components

Landmark classification accuracy. To train landmark detectors and test their performance, we use recorded videos to find encountered landmarks and label their locations on the whole trajectory. Then we use sliding windows to generate labeled segments of sensor readings. Note that disturbances caused by hand movements are labeled as non-bump and non-turn because they should not be confused with bumps or turns. In total we generate 14739 segments for bump detector and 57962 segments for turn detector.

We evaluate classification accuracy (percentage of test samples correctly classified) of six different sets of features (described in Section 5). We randomly choose 50% of the whole dataset to train the SVM classifier and others to test the performance. We repeat it 20 times and report the average performance in Table 1. It shows that they all have high accuracy around 90%. We decide to use DFFT5 with relatively high accuracies (93.0% and 92.5% for bump and turn) and low complexity in further evaluation.

Table 1: Accuracies of different feature sets.

	dimension	bump	turn
STAT35	35	92.7%	92.8%
DSTAT35	70	92.6%	93.4%
FFT5	5	91.8%	92.2%
S7FFT5	35	92.5%	92.6%
DFFT5 (chosen)	10	93.0%	92.5%

We repeat the test across different garages: using the data from one as training and another as testing. In reality, we can only obtain data from a limited number of garages for training, at least initially. Thus this test critically examines whether high accuracies are possible for vast numbers of unknown garages. Table 2 shows the cross-test accuracies of bump and turn detection, respectively. Each row represents training data and column test data. We observe that the accuracies are around, and some well above 90%. This encouraging evidence shows that it is very possible to retain the accuracy when training data are available from only limited numbers of garages.

Precision and recall of landmark detection.

After training landmark detectors, we further test their precision (ratio of true detections among all detected land-

Table 2: Cross-test of bump/turn detection (%)

train/test	office	campus	mall
office	95.5/93.6	91.9/95.6	90.1/90.3
campus	93.7/94.1	93.9/96.3	88.5/90.8
mall	94.1/92.3	90.6/94.6	91.5/91.0

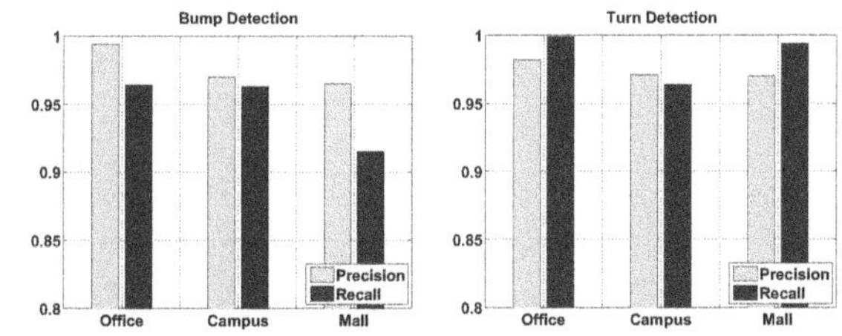

(a) (b)

Figure 10: Precision and recall of bump and turn detection in three different garages.

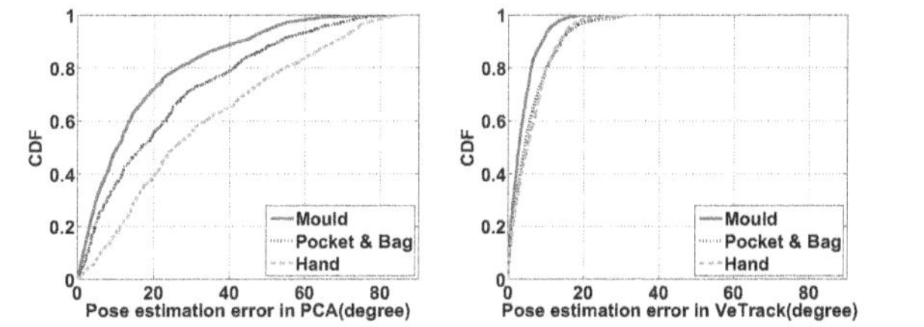

(a) (b)

Figure 11: CDFs of pose estimation error: (a) 3D method. (b) Our 2D method.

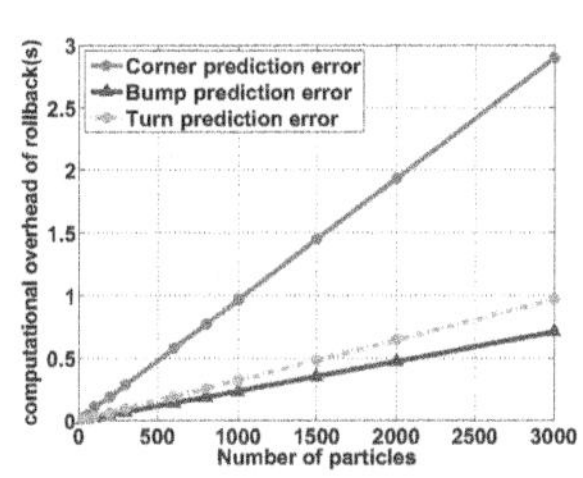

Figure 12: Latency by different rollback types and numbers of particles.

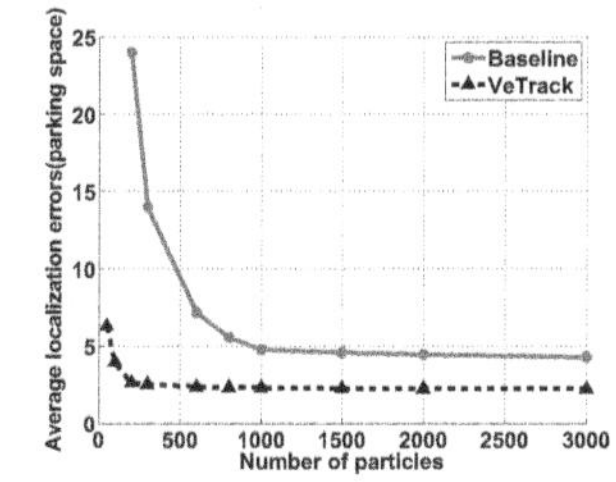

Figure 13: Tracking error by numbers of particles.

marks) and recall (ratio of true detections to groundtruth number of such landmarks) over whole traces. They tell how likely the detector makes mistakes (high precision means less chances for mistakes), and how close all groundtruth ones are detected (high recall means more real ones are detected). An ideal detector would have 100% precision and recall.

The precision and recall of bump and turn detection are shown in Figure 10. Both prediction and recall of bump detection are over 91% and those of turn are over 96%. Turn detection has better performance because it uses features from more reliable gyroscope data. We also find that poses in the mould has the best performance because they have the least disturbances; those in pocket and bag are better than in those in hand because they do not experience disturbances from hand movements.

Accuracy of shadow tracing. The performance of trajectory tracing highly depends on the accuracy of phone pose estimation (relative orientation between the phone and vehicle's coordinate systems). We compare its accuracy in 3D and 2D tracing methods. Similar to other work [17, 40], we use principle component analysis (PCA) in 3D method to find the maximum acceleration direction as Y-axis. To obtain the ground truth, we fix a phone to the vehicle and align its axes to those of the vehicle. The error is defined as the angle between the estimated and ground truth Y-axis of the phone. For fair comparison, we project the 3D pose to horizontal plane before calculating its error.

The CDFs of errors (Figure 11) show that: 1) Our 2D method is more accurate, with the 90-percentile error at $10 \sim 15^o$ while that of the 3D method is around $50^o \sim 70^o$, which in reality would make accurate tracking impossible. 2) The 2D method is more robust to disturbances in unstable poses such as pocket/bag and hand-held, whereas the 3D method has much larger errors for the latter two. This shows that our shadow tracing is indeed much more practical for real driving conditions. In addition, we find that the PCA needs a window of 4s for unchanged pose, while the 2D method is almost instantaneous.

6.3 Realtime Tracking Latency

Realtime tracking latency is the time the tracking component needs to finish computing the location after obtaining sensor data at t. When there are prediction mistakes, it also includes latencies for detecting mistakes, rollback and re-computing of the current location. This is measured on iPhone 4s, a relatively slower model. As shown in Table 3, landmark detection for bump, turn and corner each cost $\sim$ 0.2ms. In almost $\sim$ 90% of time where predictions are correct, one round of tracking is computed within 1.7ms. The 2.3ms computing finishes within the 20ms particle state update interval, causing no real time delay. For about $\sim$ 10% of time, recovering for bump, turn and corner errors (each $\sim$3%) take 64ms, 47ms and 193ms. The worst case is less than $0.2s$, hardly noticeable to human users.

Table 3: Realtime Tracking Latency.

	bump	turn	corner
landmark detection	0.21ms	0.22ms	0.22ms
90% realtime tracking		1.7ms	
10% rollback	47ms	64ms	193ms

Figure 12 shows the latency as a function of number of particles, each curve for one different type of wrong predictions resulting in rollback. All curves grows linearly, simply because of the linear overhead to update more particles. Note that the difference between latencies of different curves is caused by different sizes of rollback windows (1s, 1s and 3s for bump, turn and corner detection errors, respectively). Although bump and turn detection have the same rollback window sizes, recovering turn errors has slightly higher computation overhead. In experiments we find that $100 \sim 200$ particles can already achieve high accuracy, which incurs only $0.05 \sim 0.2s$) latency. Such disruptions are minimal and not always perceptible by users.

6.4 Tracking Location Errors

Parking location errors. The final parking location is important because drivers use it to find the vehicle upon return. We use the number of parking spaces between the real and estimated locations as the metric, since the search

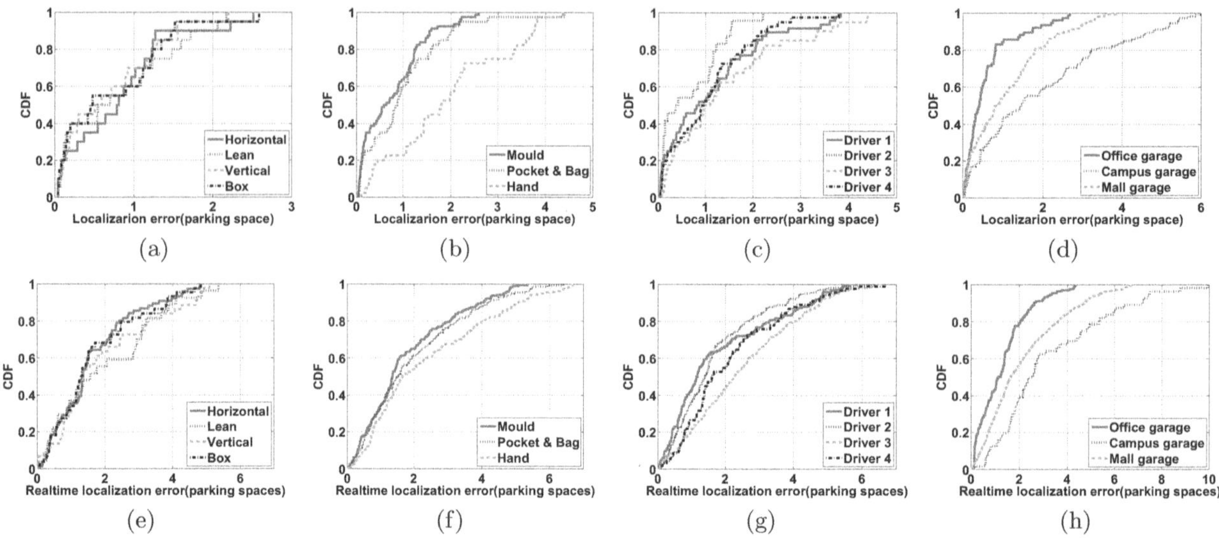

Figure 14: Final parking location errors (1st row) and realtime tracking location errors (2nd row). (a)(e) 4 phones in the mould. (b)(f) in mould, pocket&bag, and hands. (c)(g) different drivers. (d)(h) different garages.

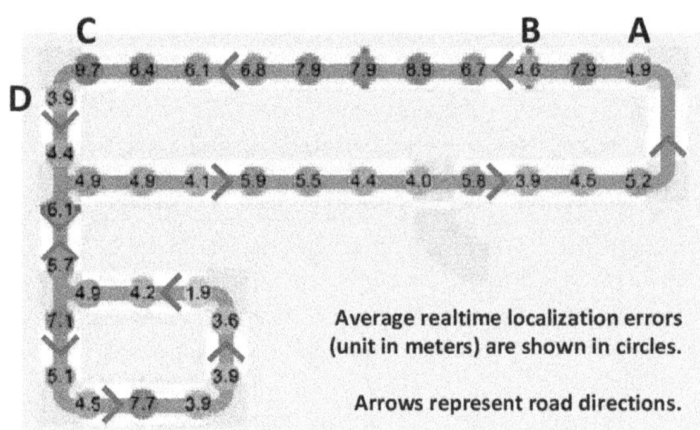

Figure 15: Average realtime tracking errors on different garage locations.

effort depends more on how many vehicles to examine, not the absolute distance.

In order to compare all 8 poses, we show the results in the mall garage. Figure 14(a) shows the 4 phones in the mould. They have relatively small errors: all four poses have similar performance, with 90-percentile error less than 2 parking spaces. The maximum error is less than 3 parking spaces, which is sufficient for remote keys to trigger a honk to locate the car.

Figure 14(b) shows results for different pose categories. Poses in the mould category achieve the best performance, i.e., $\sim$ 2 parking spaces at 90-percentile, with maximum error of 3 parking spaces. Those in the pocket or bag endure small disturbances thus achieve performance that is a little worse than mould category, i.e., $\sim$ 2 parking spaces at 90-percentile, with maximum error of 4 parking spaces. Those in hand have largest errors, i.e., $\sim$ 4 parking spaces at 90-percentile, with maximum error of 5 parking spaces. These larger errors are due to hand disturbances causing more incorrect landmark detections.

We also evaluate the impact of different drivers. Figure 14(c) shows those of two taxi drivers (1 and 3) driving cabs and two volunteer drivers (2 and 4) driving their own cars. The results do not differ too much among different drivers; all have 1.5 $\sim$ 3 parking space errors at 80-percentile, while the maximum error of 5 parking spaces is from a taxi driver who drives very aggressively, which causes more incorrect detections.

Finally we evaluate impact of the type of parking garage. The 90-percentile errors are around 2,3 and 5 parking spaces, respectively, and maximum errors are 3, 5 and 6 parking spaces, respectively. The difference is caused by different structures. The office garage has best results because it has regular shapes (7(b)) and smooth paved surfaces which minimize road disturbances. The campus garage is the worst because of its irregular shape (7(a)), especially the "Z"-junction of two consecutive turns where many drives take a shortcut instead of two 90-degree turns.

Real time location error. We present the CDFs of real time tracking error in the second row of Figure 14, arranged the same as the first row. The trends are similar in general, but real time errors are generally 50 $\sim$ 100% larger than corresponding parking errors. For example, Figure 14(e) shows all 4 poses in the mould have 90-percentile error around 4 parking spaces. The maximum error is $\sim$ 5 parking spaces. While those in Figure 14(a) are 2 and 3 parking spaces. Figure 14(f) shows that poses in the mould have the least errors, while those in hand have largest errors, the same trend as Figure 14(b) while all errors are about 60% larger than those in Figure 14(b). Figure 14(g) and (h) are similar as well.

This is because: 1) For final parking location we penalize particles still having non-negligible speeds after the vehicle has stopped. Thus remaining particles are those that have correctly "guessed" the vehicle states. 2) Real time errors include many locations in the middle of long straight driving, where no landmarks are available for calibration. Such locations tend to have larger errors. 3) The vehicle location has much larger uncertainty at the beginning. Thus relatively greater errors are included in real time results. But final location is usually after multiple calibrations, thus better accuracy.

Spatial distribution of real time tracking errors on a garage map with 3 bumps and 8 turns is shown in Figure 15. Each circle has a number, the error averaged over different traces and poses for that location. We observe that in general the error grows on straight paths, and is reduced after encountering landmarks (e.g., from 4.9m after a corner A, growing to 7.9m then reduced to 4.6m after a bump B; 9.7m at C before a corner to $3.9m$ at D).

The number of particles also impact tracking accuracy. We compare VeTrack with a straightforward baseline that uses 3D tracing and 2D road strips, without two critical components of 2D tracing and 1D roads, Figure 13 shows results for the mall. VeTrack's average localization error quickly converges to $\sim$ 2.5 parking spaces when there are 200 particles (the office and campus garages need only 100 $\sim$ 150 particles). More particles do not further decrease the error because they are still subject to landmark detection mistakes. The baseline needs about 1000 particles to stabilize, and it is around 5 parking spaces. This shows that VeTrack needs about one order of magnitude less particles, thus ensuring efficient computing for real time tracking on the phone; it also has better accuracy because of the two critical components.

7. RELATED WORK

Phone pose estimation. Existing work [17, 24, 40] estimates the 3D pose of the phone. The latest one, A^3 [47], detects high confidence compass and accelerometer measurements to calibrate accumulative gyroscope errors. The typical approach [40] in vehicular applications is to use the gravity direction as the Z-axis of the vehicle, assuming it is on level ground; gyroscope is used to determine whether the vehicle is driving straight; and the direction of maximum acceleration is assumed to be the Y-axis of the vehicle. As explained in Section 3, it cannot handle vehicles on a slope, and the direction of maximum acceleration may not be vehicle forwarding direction. The estimation also requires long time of unchanged pose, unsuitable under frequent disturbances.

Landmark detection. Distinctive data patterns in different sensing modalities of smartphones have been exploited for purposes including indoor localization [6, 32, 39]. Similarly, VeTrack detects distinctive inertial sensor patterns by road conditions (e.g., bumps and turns) to calibrate the location estimation. Its algorithms are designed specifically for robustness against noises and disturbances on inertial data from indoor driving.

Robotic localization. SLAM is a popular technique for a robot to acquire a map of its environment while simultaneously localizing itself in this map [25]. It has been adapted for indoor localization leveraging WiFi signals [15]. Unlike SLAM, VeTrack assumes the map is available and determines the vehicle location. This is equivalent to robot localization which finds the pose of a robot relative to a given map [35].

Earlier work on robot localization uses Kalman Filters [38] and Markov localization [35]. More recent Sequential Monte Carlo (SMC) [16, 36] uses a set of samples (i.e., "particles") drawn from a probability distribution to represent the position. The samples evolve over time based on the action model and measurements [35].

VeTrack uses the same SMC approach. But SMC is only a framework: what states are needed to model the dynamics of the physical system, what algorithms are needed to update such states, are all problem dependent. Also smartphone inertial data have significant noises and disturbances; they do not have high precision sensors such as laser rangers, high definition cameras, wheels that can provide accurate measurements for robots. Thus the state/weight initialization and update have to be carefully designed to produce reasonable results despite low quality data.

Dead-reckoning. Dead reckoning is a well explored approach that estimates the future location of a moving object (e.g., ground vehicle, robot or aircraft [3, 8, 20]) based on its past position and speed. Compared with them, VeTrack does not have special, high precision sensors (e.g., odometer in robotics or radar [27] for ground vehicles), while the required accuracy is much higher than that of aviation.

Dead reckoning has been used for indoor localization using smartphones equipped with multiple inertial sensors [12, 30]. Its main problem is fast error accumulation due to inertial data noises and a lot of work has attempted to mitigate the accumulation. Foot-mounted sensors have been shown effective in reducing the error [31, 42]. Smartphones are more difficult because their poses are unknown and can change. Some outdoor localization work (e.g., CompAcc [13]) employs periodic GPS measurements to recalibrate the location. UnLoc [39] replaces GPS with virtual indoor landmarks with unique sensor data patterns for calibration.

To prevent the error accumulation, VeTrack simultaneously harnesses constraints imposed by the map and environment landmarks. Landmark locations most likely remain unchanged for months or even years. The 2D pose estimation handles unknown and possibly changing phone poses. Their output provide calibration opportunities in the SMC framework to minimize error accumulation.

Estimation of vehicle states. There have been many research efforts using smartphones' embedded sensors to monitor the states of vehicles (e.g. dangerous driving alert [23], car speaker [43] and CarSafe [44]); inspect the road anomaly or conditions (e.g., Pothole Patrol [14]); and detect traffic accidents (Nericell [24] and WreckWatch [41]). The vehicle speed is a critical input in many such applications. While it is easy to calculate the speed using GPS outdoors [19, 34], the signal can be weak or even unavailable for indoor parking lots. Some alternative solutions leverage the phone's signal strength to estimate the vehicle speed [10, 11]. VeTrack uses inertial data only, thus it works without any RF signal or extra sensor instrumentation.

There have been autonomous parking system prototypes where a vehicle can sense the environment, detect available spots and finally park itself (e.g., CoCar [2]). Such systems usually leverage high precision cameras, laser rangers and advanced computer vision techniques, which are not feasible within the much constrained hardware of commodity smartphones.

8. DISCUSSION

Uncertainty in starting locations and speed. During the initialization of particles, we assume the location is at entrance and the speed zero. However, when the VeTrack app starts, the car may have already entered the garage. Thus the start of the trace may not be the entrance and the velocity not zero. This assumption can be easily removed by sampling from an empirical distribution to set the initial location and velocity. We do need more particles to represent the distribution, but the constraints imposed by paths and landmarks will quickly narrow down the possible locations of the vehicle. In one experiment we tried a speed distribution between $0 - 10m/s$ and 3000 particles. We find that after $2 - 3$ landmarks the location estimation quickly converges and the system can still achieve high accuracy. Basically when enough landmarks exist, the uncertainty can still be reduced and vehicle location determined.

Unsupervised feature learning. We design certain features manually for machine learning techniques. However, those features might not be the optimal under all circumstances; more efficient features specific to different environment may exist. We plan to investigate unsupervised feature learning [18] to automatically devise features for better performance and generality.

Stationary or reverse conditions. There are certain movement patterns not yet considered in this work: when the parking lot is congested, the vehicle may exhibit stop-and-go movements with long stationary periods; drivers may back up the vehicle into parking spaces. We plan to add stationary and reverse detection algorithms so that these conditions can be properly recognized and handled within the real time tracking component.

Simultaneous disturbances and landmarks. In our experiments disturbances such as hand-held movements happen only during straight driving but not bumps or turns. This is a reasonable assumption for a single driver that is most likely focusing on driving through these landmarks, and will not have the extra cognitive bandwidth to pick up the phone and look. However, if the phone is held by a passenger, hand-held movements could happen any time, even with small probabilities. We will investigate what impact this may have on VeTrack and further improve the robustness of our detection algorithms.

Other types of landmarks. In VeTrack, we mainly use bumps and turns as landmarks to recalibrate the location of vehicles. However, other types of landmarks (e.g., spots with RF signals or special magnetic fields) could also be incorporated. Whenever available, they provide additional constraints and calibration opportunities that limit the possible locations of the vehicle and would further improve the accuracy. It's just unfortunate that in the three underground parking structures we experimented, no RF signal were available. This is because the functional areas of those buildings (e.g., office, malls) are usually above ground. Thus no WiFi APs are deployed underground. We acknowledge although this is not uncommon in big Asian cities due to high population density, in other parts of the world (e.g., North America) above-ground parking structures can take advantage of WiFi signals wherever available.

Generalization of techniques. The real time tracking problem itself is quite specific. However the shadow trajectory tracing and 2D phone pose estimation techniques are essential to model and infer vehicle dynamics where arbitrary phone pose or special driving conditions (e.g., slopes or even slanted driving on slopes) exist. Thus the benefits are general to phone-vehicular applications, not just underground navigation.

Landmark mapping. Garage maps may not necessarily have landmark locations measured and marked. In reality we did not find this too much an overhead. Within half an hour we were able to manually measure their locations and mark them on maps. Because this is a one-time effort with long-lasting benefits, we believe it is worthwhile.

More varieties in different factors. The performance of VeTrack may depend on many factors, including the structures of parking lots, drivers, vehicle and phone make/models. We intentionally choose parking structures of three different building types (office, campus and mall), with several drivers and vehicle make/models. For example, the one in the mall has circular connecting ramps which are common for multi-level parking structures. We find that the yaw reading from gyroscope can reliably tell the turned angle and thus the location on such cylinder ramps.

Although we have tried our best to extend these factors, they are not exhaustive due to our limited resources and manpower. Nevertheless, we believe the most challenging part is the accurate 2D tracking of vehicle location, which we have designed multiple techniques and addressed extensively. We plan to conduct more comprehensive experiments in more types of parking structures, drivers, vehicle and phone make/models to identify potential limits and improve the design.

9. CONCLUSIONS

In this paper we describe VeTrack which tracks a vehicle's location in real time and records its final parking location. It does not depend on GPS or WiFi signals which may be unavailable, or additional sensors to instrument the indoor environment. VeTrack uses only inertial data, and all sensing/computing happen locally on the phone. It uses a novel shadow trajectory tracing method to convert smartphone movements to vehicle ones. It also detects landmarks such as speed bumps and turns robustly. A probabilistic framework estimates its location under constraints from detected landmarks and garage maps. It also utilizes a 1D skeleton road model to greatly reduce the computing complexity.

Prototype experiments in three parking structures and with several drivers, vehicle make/models have shown that VeTrack can track the vehicle location around a few parking spaces, with negligible latency most of the time. Thus it provides critical indoor location for universal location awareness of drivers. Currently VeTrack still has quite some limitations, such as manual feature design, simultaneous disturbances as discussed previously. We plan to further investigate along these directions to make it mature and practical in the real world.

Acknowledgments

We thank the anonymous reviewers for their constructive critique, and our shepherd Marco Gruteser for his valuable feedback and advice, all of which have helped us greatly improve this paper. We also thank Kaigui Bian for his input during early investigation of the work. This work is supported in part by NSF CNS-1513719, NSFC 61231010 and Beijing Municipal NSF 4142022.

10. REFERENCES

[1] Apple Developer Center. https://developer.apple.com/.
[2] CoCar: Autonomous Parking in an Underground Parking Garage. https://www.youtube.com/watch?v=G4XYMbtH758.
[3] Inertial navigation system, Wikipedia. https://en.wikipedia.org/wiki/Inertial_navigation_system.
[4] Parking sensors mesh network. http://www.streetline.com/parking-analytics/parking-sensors-mesh-network/.
[5] SFpark. http://sfpark.org/how-it-works/the-sensors/.

[6] M. Azizyan, I. Constandache, and R. Roy Choudhury. Surroundsense: Mobile phone localization via ambience fingerprinting. In *Proceedings of the 15th Annual International Conference on Mobile Computing and Networking*, MobiCom '09, pages 261–272, New York, NY, USA, 2009. ACM.

[7] P. Bahl and V. N. Padmanabhan. RADAR: An in-building RF-based user location and tracking system. In *IEEE INFOCOM*, 2000.

[8] D. M. Bevly and B. Parkinson. Cascaded kalman filters for accurate estimation of multiple biases, dead-reckoning navigation, and full state feedback control of ground vehicles. *Control Systems Technology, IEEE Transactions on*, 15(2):199–208, 2007.

[9] C. M. Bishop et al. *Pattern recognition and machine learning*, volume 1. springer New York, 2006.

[10] G. Chandrasekaran, T. Vu, A. Varshavsky, M. Gruteser, R. Martin, J. Yang, and Y. Chen. Tracking vehicular speed variations by warping mobile phone signal strengths. In *Pervasive Computing and Communications (PerCom), 2011 IEEE International Conference on*, pages 213–221, March 2011.

[11] G. Chandrasekaran, T. Vu, A. Varshavsky, M. Gruteser, R. P. Martin, J. Yang, and Y. Chen. Vehicular speed estimation using received signal strength from mobile phones. In *Proceedings of the 12th ACM International Conference on Ubiquitous Computing*, Ubicomp '10, pages 237–240, New York, NY, USA, 2010. ACM.

[12] I. Constandache, X. Bao, M. Azizyan, and R. R. Choudhury. Did you see bob?: Human localization using mobile phones. In *Proceedings of the Sixteenth Annual International Conference on Mobile Computing and Networking*, MobiCom '10, pages 149–160, New York, NY, USA, 2010. ACM.

[13] I. Constandache, R. Choudhury, and I. Rhee. Towards mobile phone localization without war-driving. In *INFOCOM, 2010 Proceedings IEEE*, pages 1–9, 2010.

[14] J. Eriksson, L. Girod, B. Hull, R. Newton, S. Madden, and H. Balakrishnan. The pothole patrol: Using a mobile sensor network for road surface monitoring. In *Proceedings of the 6th International Conference on Mobile Systems, Applications, and Services*, MobiSys '08, pages 29–39, New York, NY, USA, 2008. ACM.

[15] B. Ferris, D. Fox, and N. D. Lawrence. Wifi-slam using gaussian process latent variable models. In *IJCAI*, volume 7, pages 2480–2485, 2007.

[16] D. Fox, W. Burgard, F. Dellaert, and S. Thrun. Monte carlo localization: Efficient position estimation for mobile robots. *AAAI/IAAI*, 1999:343–349, 1999.

[17] H. Han, J. Yu, H. Zhu, Y. Chen, J. Yang, Y. Zhu, G. Xue, and M. Li. Senspeed: Sensing driving conditions to estimate vehicle speed in urban environments.

[18] G. Hinton, S. Osindero, and Y.-W. Teh. A fast learning algorithm for deep belief nets. *Neural computation*, 18(7):1527–1554, 2006.

[19] B. Hoh, M. Gruteser, R. Herring, J. Ban, D. Work, J.-C. Herrera, A. M. Bayen, M. Annavaram, and Q. Jacobson. Virtual trip lines for distributed privacy-preserving traffic monitoring. In *Proceedings of the 6th International Conference on Mobile Systems, Applications, and Services*, MobiSys '08, pages 15–28, New York, NY, USA, 2008. ACM.

[20] Y. Kanayama, Y. Kimura, F. Miyazaki, and T. Noguchi. A stable tracking control method for an autonomous mobile robot. In *Robotics and Automation, 1990. Proceedings., 1990 IEEE International Conference on*, pages 384–389 vol.1, May 1990.

[21] K. Kanazawa, D. Koller, and S. Russell. Stochastic simulation algorithms for dynamic probabilistic networks. In *Proceedings of the Eleventh conference on Uncertainty in artificial intelligence*, pages 346–351. Morgan Kaufmann Publishers Inc., 1995.

[22] K. Li, M. Lu, F. Lu, Q. Lv, L. Shang, and D. Maksimovic. Personalized driving behavior monitoring and analysis for emerging hybrid vehicles. *Pervasive Computing*, 2012.

[23] J. Lindqvist and J. Hong. Undistracted driving: A mobile phone that doesn't distract. In *Proceedings of the 12th Workshop on Mobile Computing Systems and Applications*, HotMobile '11, pages 70–75, New York, NY, USA, 2011. ACM.

[24] P. Mohan, V. N. Padmanabhan, and R. Ramjee. Nericell: Using mobile smartphones for rich monitoring of road and traffic conditions. In *Proceedings of the 6th ACM Conference on Embedded Network Sensor Systems*, SenSys '08, pages 357–358, New York, NY, USA, 2008. ACM.

[25] M. Montemerlo, S. Thrun, D. Koller, and B. Wegbreit. Fastslam: A factored solution to the simultaneous localization and mapping problem. In *AAAI/IAAI*, pages 593–598, 2002.

[26] S. Nawaz, C. Efstratiou, and C. Mascolo. Parksense: A smartphone based sensing system for on-street parking. In *Proceedings of the 19th Annual International Conference on Mobile Computing & Networking*, MobiCom '13, pages 75–86, New York, NY, USA, 2013. ACM.

[27] D. H. Nguyen, J. H. Kay, B. J. Orchard, and R. H. Whiting. Classification and tracking of moving ground vehicles. *Lincoln Laboratory Journal*, 13(2):275–308, 2002.

[28] V. Otsason, A. Varshavsky, A. LaMarca, and E. De Lara. Accurate gsm indoor localization. In *UbiComp 2005: Ubiquitous Computing*, pages 141–158. Springer, 2005.

[29] S. Preece, J. Goulermas, L. Kenney, and D. Howard. A comparison of feature extraction methods for the classification of dynamic activities from accelerometer data.

[30] A. Rai, K. K. Chintalapudi, V. N. Padmanabhan, and R. Sen. Zee: Zero-effort crowdsourcing for indoor localization. In *Proceedings of the 18th Annual International Conference on Mobile Computing and Networking*, Mobicom '12, pages 293–304, New York, NY, USA, 2012. ACM.

[31] P. Robertson, M. Angermann, and B. Krach. Simultaneous localization and mapping for pedestrians using only foot-mounted inertial sensors. In *Proceedings of the 11th International Conference on Ubiquitous Computing*, Ubicomp '09, pages 93–96, New York, NY, USA, 2009. ACM.

[32] S. P. Tarzia, P. A. Dinda, R. P. Dick, and G. Memik. Indoor localization without infrastructure using the

acoustic background spectrum. In *Proceedings of the 9th International Conference on Mobile Systems, Applications, and Services*, MobiSys '11, pages 155–168, New York, NY, USA, 2011. ACM.

[33] A. Thiagarajan, J. Biagioni, T. Gerlich, and J. Eriksson. Cooperative transit tracking using smart-phones. In *Proceedings of the 8th ACM Conference on Embedded Networked Sensor Systems*, SenSys '10, pages 85–98, New York, NY, USA, 2010. ACM.

[34] A. Thiagarajan, L. Ravindranath, K. LaCurts, S. Madden, H. Balakrishnan, S. Toledo, and J. Eriksson. Vtrack: Accurate, energy-aware road traffic delay estimation using mobile phones. In *Proceedings of the 7th ACM Conference on Embedded Networked Sensor Systems*, SenSys '09, pages 85–98, New York, NY, USA, 2009. ACM.

[35] S. Thrun, W. Burgard, D. Fox, et al. *Probabilistic robotics*, volume 1. MIT press Cambridge, 2005.

[36] S. Thrun, D. Fox, W. Burgard, and F. Dellaert. Robust monte carlo localization for mobile robots. *Artificial intelligence*, 128(1):99–141, 2001.

[37] Y. Tian, R. Gao, K. Bian, F. Ye, T. Wang, Y. Wang, and X. Li. Towards ubiquitous indoor localization service leveraging environmental physical features. 2014.

[38] E. A. Wan and R. Van Der Merwe. The unscented kalman filter for nonlinear estimation. In *Adaptive Systems for Signal Processing, Communications, and Control Symposium 2000. AS-SPCC. The IEEE 2000*, pages 153–158. IEEE, 2000.

[39] H. Wang, S. Sen, A. Elgohary, M. Farid, M. Youssef, and R. R. Choudhury. No need to war-drive: Unsupervised indoor localization. In *Proceedings of the 10th International Conference on Mobile Systems, Applications, and Services*, MobiSys '12, pages 197–210, New York, NY, USA, 2012. ACM.

[40] Y. Wang, J. Yang, H. Liu, Y. Chen, M. Gruteser, and R. P. Martin. Sensing vehicle dynamics for determining driver phone use. In *Proceeding of the 11th annual international conference on Mobile systems, applications, and services*, pages 41–54. ACM, 2013.

[41] J. White, C. Thompson, H. Turner, B. Dougherty, and D. C. Schmidt. Wreckwatch: Automatic traffic accident detection and notification with smartphones. *Mob. Netw. Appl.*, 16(3):285–303, June 2011.

[42] O. Woodman and R. Harle. Pedestrian localisation for indoor environments. In *Proceedings of the 10th International Conference on Ubiquitous Computing*, UbiComp '08, pages 114–123, New York, NY, USA, 2008. ACM.

[43] J. Yang, S. Sidhom, G. Chandrasekaran, T. Vu, H. Liu, N. Cecan, Y. Chen, M. Gruteser, and R. P. Martin. Detecting driver phone use leveraging car speakers. In *Proceedings of the 17th Annual International Conference on Mobile Computing and Networking*, MobiCom '11, pages 97–108, New York, NY, USA, 2011. ACM.

[44] C.-W. You, N. D. Lane, F. Chen, R. Wang, Z. Chen, T. J. Bao, M. Montes-de Oca, Y. Cheng, M. Lin, L. Torresani, and A. T. Campbell. Carsafe app: Alerting drowsy and distracted drivers using dual cameras on smartphones. In *Proceeding of the 11th Annual International Conference on Mobile Systems, Applications, and Services*, MobiSys '13, pages 461–462, New York, NY, USA, 2013. ACM.

[45] M. Youssef and A. Agrawala. The horus wlan location determination system. In *ACM MobiSys*, 2005.

[46] M. Zhao, R. Gao, J. Zhu, T. Ye, F. Ye, Y. Wang, K. Bian, G. Luo, and M. Zhang. Veloc: finding your car in the parking lot. In *Proceedings of the 12th ACM Conference on Embedded Network Sensor Systems*, pages 346–347. ACM, 2014.

[47] P. Zhou, M. Li, and G. Shen. Use it free: Instantly knowing your phone attitude. In *Proceedings of the 20th annual international conference on Mobile computing and networking*, pages 605–616. ACM, 2014.

ShopMiner: Mining Customer Shopping Behavior in Physical Clothing Stores with COTS RFID Devices

Longfei Shangguan*§, Zimu Zhou†§, Xiaolong Zheng*, Lei Yang*, Yunhao Liu*, Jinsong Han‡
*Tsinghua IoT Center and School of Software, Tsinghua University
†CSE Department, Hong Kong University of Science and Technology
‡School of Electronic and Information Engineering, Xi'an Jiaotong University
Email: {longfei, xiaolong, young, yunhao}@greenorbs.com,
zzhouad@cse.ust.hk, hanjinsong@mail.xjtu.edu.cn

Abstract

Shopping behavior data are of great importance to understand the effectiveness of marketing and merchandising efforts. Online clothing stores are capable capturing customer shopping behavior by analyzing the click stream and customer shopping carts. Retailers with physical clothing stores, however, still lack effective methods to identify comprehensive shopping behaviors. In this paper, we show that backscatter signals of passive RFID tags can be exploited to detect and record how customers browse stores, which items of clothes they pay attention to, and which items of clothes they usually match with. The intuition is that the phase readings of tags attached on desired items will demonstrate distinct yet stable patterns in the time-series when customers look at, pick up or turn over desired items. We design ShopMiner, a framework that harnesses these unique spatial-temporal correlations of time-series phase readings to detect comprehensive shopping behaviors. We have implemented a prototype of ShopMiner with a COTS RFID reader and four antennas, and tested its effectiveness in two typical indoor environments. Empirical studies from two-week shopping-like data show that ShopMiner could achieve high accuracy and efficiency in customer shopping behavior identification.

Categories and Subject Descriptors

H.4 [**Information Systems Applications**]: Miscellaneous

Keywords

Shopping behavior, RFID, Backscatter communication

1. INTRODUCTION

Shopping behavior analysis is of great importance to understand the effectiveness of marketing and merchandising efforts [2, 18]. With deep shopping behavior data, retailers can capture customers' flavors, test new arrivals, and adjust marketing strategy to optimize brand profitability. Mining customer shopping behavior in online stores is easily achievable by analyzing the click streams and customer shopping carts [3, 10, 11]. However, retailers with physical stores still lack effective methods to identify comprehensive customer behaviors. The only information readily available to retailers is the sales history, which fails to reflecting customer behaviors before they check out, like how customers browse the store, which products they show interest in, and what products they match against. Therefore, it is essential to explore new ways to capture customer behaviors in physical stores.

Previous efforts have exploited video cameras to monitor customer shopping behaviors in clothing stores [22, 23, 24]. However, such methods require densely deployed cameras to capture human actions, and complicated computer vision to recognize and analyze arm motions. Furthermore, video-based methods are susceptible to non-line-of-sight (NLOS) visual channels in crowded clothing stores where people frequently move around to pick up or try on clothes. Another brunch of methods tracks customer routes in stores, with the goal of mining hot zones and popular products [17, 31]. For example, the more people traverse along a route, the higher attentions the items around this route gain. Unfortunately, these approaches fail to provide high-fidelity information that is specifically relevant to shopping behaviors, like product browsing, pick-up actions and clothes trying-on.

RFIDs are emerging as an essential component of Cyber Physical Systems (CPS). Many well-known garment manufacturers (*e.g.*, Abercrombie & Fitch, Calvin Klein, Decathlon) adopt passive RFIDs for sales tracking and anti-counterfeiting [30]. We envision the adoption of RFIDs will sweep the clothing market in near future, and in this paper, we explore the feasibility of mining customer behavior in physical clothing stores with RFID devices. By carefully analyzing the customer shopping process in clothing stores (Section 2), we abstract three basic behavior mining functionalities essential to retailers: discovering popular category, identifying hot items and excavating correlated items.

- **Popular category** represents the clothes frequently *viewed* by customers.Since customers pay more views on items that meet their tastes, popular category data reveal customers' flavor, hence providing valuable information to retailers' trading strategy.

SenSys'15, November 1–4, 2015, Seoul, South Korea..
© 2015 ACM. ISBN 978-1-4503-3631-4/15/11 ...$15.00.
DOI: http://dx.doi.org/10.1145/2809695.2809710
§: co-primary author.

- **Hot items** are the clothes frequently *picked up* or *turned over* by customers. Hot items reveal whether customers show deeper interest in items after their first glance.
- **Correlated items** are the clothes that are frequently matched with or tried on together, which can facilitate retailers to infer customer shopping habits and adopt bundle-selling strategies to boost profit.

These comprehensive shopping data reflect *what items the customers browse, which items they show interest in, and which items they match with.* By jointly analyzing these three kinds of shopping data with readily available sales history, the physical retailer can acquire much deeper business value. For example, popular items with little trying-on (*i.e.*, not hot) may indicate the designs of these items are not run of the mill, while the hot item with unsatisfying sales volume may suggests an unacceptable price, which indicates sales promotion or discount should be taken.

In this paper, we present ShopMiner that enables customer shopping behavior sensing using commercial off-the-shelf (COTS) RFID devices. The basic principle is that the phase readings of tags attached on desired items demonstrate distinct yet stable patterns when customers look at, pick up, turn over, or match desired items. These patterns are viable for an accurate shopping behavior mining service in clothing stores. Specifically, customers are likely to stand still for a while in front of attractive items, and hence block the wireless links between reader antennas and attractive items. Therefore, the phase reading of popular tags show a distinct pattern from those unpopular ones (*i.e.*, not viewed by customers). Similarly, the phase reading of hot tags will change dramatically when customers pick them up or turn them over, *e.g.*, observing pictures on the face/real side. The correlated items are brought together by one customer, thus experiencing a similar moving trail and temporal phase changes.

ShopMiner's design harnesses these unique spatial-temporal phase reading correlations. The key techniques of ShopMiner are a novel foreground/background segmentation scheme for popular category detection, a robust statistical model for hot item identification, and a clustering algorithm for correlated items excavation. We implement ShopMiner on COTS RFID devices including an ImpinJ R420 reader, four Yeon antennas model YAP-100CP and a set of Alien UHF passive tags. We test ShopMiner's performance in two scenarios. Experimental results show that ShopMiner can detect popular items with a True Positive Rate (TPR) of 92%, identify hot items with an accuracy of 94% and 87% for pick-up and turn-over, respectively, and achieve over 85% accuracy for correlate item excavation in multiple users case.

Contributions. (1) ShopMiner is a unified sensing framework. Although some previous works have explored RFID-based shopping behavior sensing [5, 16], none have incorporated the three key factors that are essential to retailers, *i.e.*, what items the customers browse, which items they show interest in, and which items they match with. (2) As a long-term running system, ShopMiner considers both computational intensity and storage overhead. We design a hierarchical architecture and a set of efficient algorithms for multistage customer behavior detection. (3) We implement ShopMiner on COTS RFID devices, and conduct comprehensive experiments in two shopping-like scenarios. Empirical studies show that ShopMiner achieves over 90% TPR for customer behavior detection.

(a) (b) (c) (d)

Figure 1: (a): hanging out and staying still in front of the interested item; (b), (c): browsing the interested item; (d): matching and trying items on in the fitting room;

Roadmap. The rest of paper is organized as follows. Section 2 presents the scope of ShopMiner. We present the detailed design of ShopMiner in Section 3 and the system implementation in Section 4. In Section 5, we interpret the experiment methodology, followed by detailed performance evaluation. Section 6 reviews related work, Section 7 discusses the limitations and we conclude in Section 8.

2. SCOPE

We envision ShopMiner can be deployed in clothing stores to monitor customer behaviors during shopping without body instrument. Figure 1 shows the typical shopping process in clothing stores before customers check out. It contains the following steps: browsing items and standing still in front of the attractive items; examining interested items by picking them up or turning them over; unsling desired items and trying them on in fitting rooms. These three steps contain comprehensive data and can help to optimize the retailer strategies. For example, by counting which items are mostly viewed by customers, the retailer could find those popular categories; by identifying and counting which items are picked up or turned over, the retailer could find those hot items; while by detecting which items are frequently picked up together or matched with, the retailer could find implicit correlation among clothes hence adopting tie-in promotion.

3. DESIGN

In this section, we elaborate on the design and the processing flow of ShopMiner. Throughout this paper we assume each piece of clothes is attached with a passive tag.

3.1 Discovering Popular Category

Popular items are the clothes frequently viewed by customers. The more times an item is viewed by customers, the higher attention it gains. Such information may serve as the baseline to examine the success of new products. In addition, it can also capture the flavor changing of customers and further help to optimize the product designing.

3.1.1 Shadowing effect of human body

We explore RF signal changes of multiple tag-to-antenna links to discover those popular categories. As Figure 2(a) shows, when a customer stands still in front of an item, his/her body naturally blocks the line-of-sight (LOS) link between the reader antenna and the focused item. Accord-

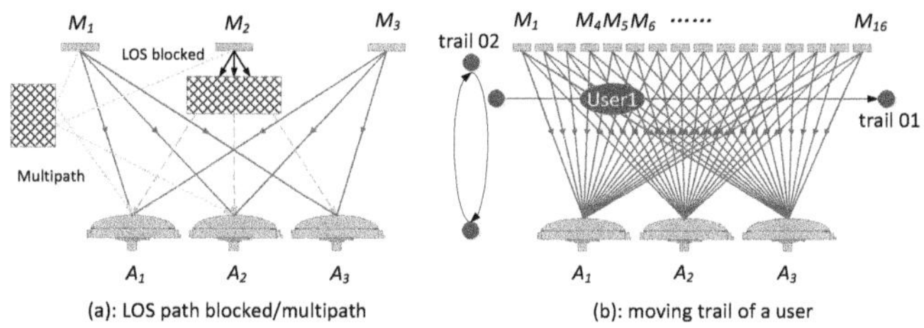

Figure 2: Illustration of popular zone discovering

ingly, the links that pass through the human body will, on average, experience higher shadowing losses [15].

As an illustrative measurement, we deploy 48 backscatter links in an office environment. The link topology is shown in Figure 2(b). We use a commercial RFID reader ImpinJ R420 with three directional antennas as the power source and the receiver to interrogate RFIDs. The antenna is placed 3 meters away from the items and 1.2 meters above the floor. We conduct the following measurement. One volunteer hangs out along the trail 01, stands still for about 8s to browse item 04, and then leaves away. We collect the phase trend along each link and explore their temporal dynamics.

Figure 3 plots the phase measurements of four tags in this measurement study, namely tag 04, 05, 06 and 07. In accordance with our analysis, we find that during the first 4s, the phase patterns of these four tags maintain in a different yet stable level, indicating a relative steady link state. Within the period of 4s to 12s, the phase trend of tag 04 changes to another stable level, manifesting that a blocker stands still in front of tag 04 and blocks its LOS link. During the last 6 seconds, the phase patterns of tag 05, 06 and 07 change sequentially, indicating that a blocker leaves away and blocks these tags' LOS paths sequentially. The measurement result shows that the body shadowing effect holds potential for non-invasive popular category discovery.

3.1.2 Noise statistics

The wireless propagation channel is affected by both the body shadowing and the ambient dynamics. As an example in Figure 2(a), people stand near the clothing rack will create a new signal propagation path, leading to multi-path effect. In multi-path environments, small changes of a few multipath components, even outside of the backscatter communication area can impact the measured phase.

To model the multi-path effect on the phase dynamics, we ask three volunteers to walk back and forth along trail 01 and 02 for 10min. Over 20,000 phase readings are recorded from 48 backscatter links. We randomly choose five tags and explore their temporal dynamics. As Figure 4 shows, the phase values fluctuate continuously and form a Gaussian-like distribution. We further test the distribution of the five tags' phases against the standard Gaussian distribution. The linearity of the points on the Q-Q plot, as shown in Figure 5, demonstrates that the data are normally distributed.

In a nutshell, both the body shadowing and the multipath effect will introduce temporal phase dynamics. The phase dynamics exerted by the multipath effect is relatively slight and follows Gaussian distribution, whereas the phase value changes significantly when the LOS path is blocked.

3.1.3 Detection scheme

To capture the items in popular category (termed as popular items), we are inspired by the foreground detection prob-

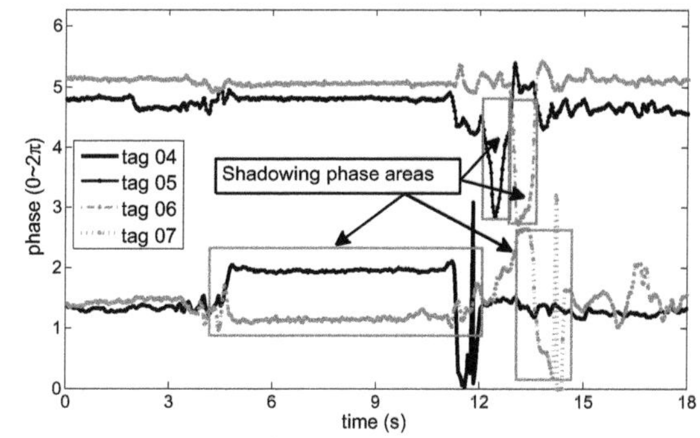

Figure 3: Illustration of phase trends of four tags

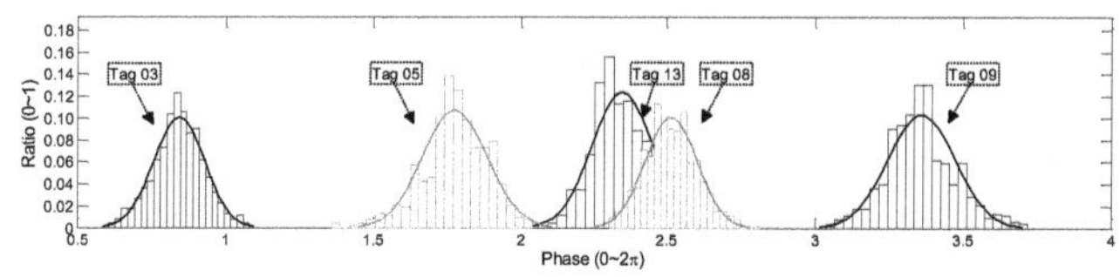

Figure 4: phase value distribution of five tags

lem in image processing. This problem aims to capture the foreground pixels that show significantly different values between contiguous image frames. In the context of ShopMiner, we need to distinguish the popular items that show remarkable phase changing from the temporal phase trend. The similarity between the two problems motivate us to design a foreground detection based scheme for popular items discovery. Without loss of generality, time is partitioned into consecutive windows.

Composing phase frame: ShopMiner first splits the phase trend into multiple phase frames. Each frame contains $m \times d$ pixels. m is the number of tags in the reading zone and d is the frame length. The pixel value $r_{i,j}$ is the phase reading of the ith tag (t_i) collected within the jth window (w_j). Since each tag will be interrogated multiple times within one window, their average value is regarded as the phase measurement of this tag in this window. We vary parameter settings and set $|w|$ and d to 0.02s and 50, which empirically balance computational efficiency and detection granularity.

Foreground detection: After splitting phase trend into frames, ShopMiner analyzes pixel values in each frame line-by-line. Pixel values that do not fit the background distribution are considered foreground. Notice that the phase distribution of each tag shows a distinct Gaussian-like distribution. Hence, we create m Gaussian models, each corresponding to one tag. ShopMiner then examines each pixel by comparing its value against the corresponding distribution. Specifically, given a pixel value $r_{i,j}$, let $N_i(\mu_i, \sigma_i^2)$ be the Gaussian model of tag i. ShopMiner formulates the following hypothesis test with H_0 foreground and H_1 background:

$$\begin{cases} H_0 : r_{i,j} \notin (\mu_i \pm \frac{\sigma_i}{\sqrt{k_i}} \cdot z_{\alpha/2}) \\ H_1 : r_{i,j} \in (\mu_i \pm \frac{\sigma_i}{\sqrt{k_i}} \cdot z_{\alpha/2}) \end{cases} \quad (1)$$

where $0 < \alpha < 1$, and k_i is the sample size. $(\mu_i \pm \frac{\sigma_i}{\sqrt{k_i}} \cdot z_{\alpha/2})$ stands for the confidence region with the confidence level $(1 - \alpha)$. For example, H_1 under $\alpha = 0.05$ indicates that the pixel (i, j) is foreground with 95% probability.

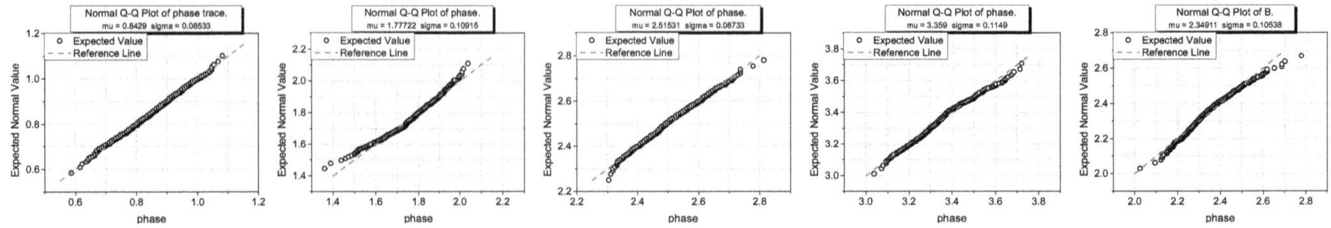

(a) tag 03 (b) tag 05 (c) tag 08 (d) tag 09 (e) tag 13

Figure 5: QQ Plot of sample data versus standard normal

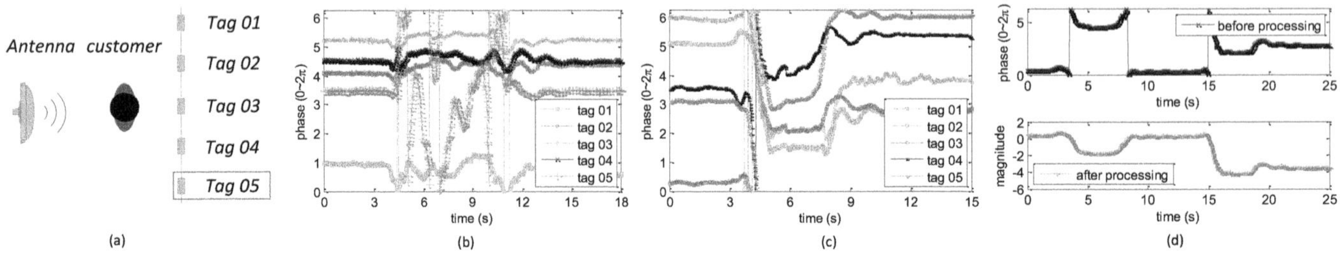

Figure 6: (a): the sketch of experiment field; (b): pick-up case; (c): turn-over case; (d): the phase trend before/after de-periodicity;

Detecting popular category: In one frame, if the majority part of pixels in row i are detected as foreground (*i.e.*, >80%), then it is highly possible that all links between tag t_i and reader antennas are blocked by human body. To this end, ShopMiner formulates the following hypothesis test with H_0 popular category items and H_1 unpopular category items:

$$\begin{cases} H_0 : s_i \geq \theta \\ H_1 : s_i < \theta \end{cases} \tag{2}$$

where s_i is the number of consecutive frames that the tag t_i's links are blocked by human body. θ denotes a pre-defined threshold. The rationale behind this detection scheme is that since customers naturally stand still for a while in front of popular items, the LOS links between these tags and antennas will retain blocked for some time. Such a threshold-based method prunes those tags whose LOS links are unintentionally blocked by customers. Since the threshold is primarily determined by the signal variations incurred by human blockage of the LOS path, it is mainly affected by the link distance and is robust to ambient factors e.g. shop sizes, layouts and reader placements. According to our experiments, within the effective range of RFID readers (around 6m), a fixed threshold yields satisfactory detection performance and a pre-trained threshold can scale to other shops without per-shop calibration.

Model training and updating: To precisely detect the foreground, it is essential to have an accurate Gaussian model for each tag. Initially, the parameters of m Gaussian models are computed when there are few or no customers in the shop (*e.g.*, before the opening or after the closing). Then pixel values of the background parts are inserted into the model and the model parameters get updated. By doing so, the model parameters are updated continuously, and hence adapt to the temporal environment dynamics.

ShopMiner is immune to the spatial disorder of items. This is because each clothing item is associated with a unique RFID tag and ShopMiner can pinpoint which item of clothing is actually blocked by referring the tag ID.

3.2 Identifying Hot Items

Hot items are those with greater interests to customers. The traditional way to identify hot items, *e.g.* the sales history, only considers the purchased items as hot, and provides partial information for retailer strategy changing. ShopMiner identifies the hot items by exploiting the phase changing caused by customer behaviors. Specifically, it detects and counts the following customer actions:

(1): *Turn-over action*: A customer observes an interested item by turning it over from the side-view to the front-view.

(2): *Pick-up action*: A customer takes a close look at an interested item by picking it up from the clothing rack.

These two actions indicate different levels of human interest on items, and hence should be identified separately. It is understandable that customers often turn over the attractive item at first glance, and pick it up for a close browsing when they show greater interest to this item. Hence in ShopMiner, we detect and identify these two actions separately.

3.2.1 Exploiting the similarity of pick-up and turn-over for action detection

We assume that customers will pick up or turn over one interested item every time. Both the turn-over and the pick-up actions will alter the item state from stationary to kinetic. Consequently, the kinetic item will experience fierce phase changing that naturally separates them apart from other stationary items. As an illustrative experiment, we place five items of clothes on a rack and ask one volunteer to mimic the customer. In the first experiment, the volunteer is required to pick up item 05, have a close browsing, and then put it back. In the second experiment, the volunteer is required to turn over item 05 to see its front-face, hold it for a while and then loose her grasp. The phase trends of the five items are shown in Figure 6(b) and Figure 6(c), respectively.

We first look at the pick-up action. As Figure 6(b) shows, initially the phase trends of these five tags all remain stable. When the volunteer picks up item 05 at 4th second, the phase trend of this item jumps abruptly until the vol-

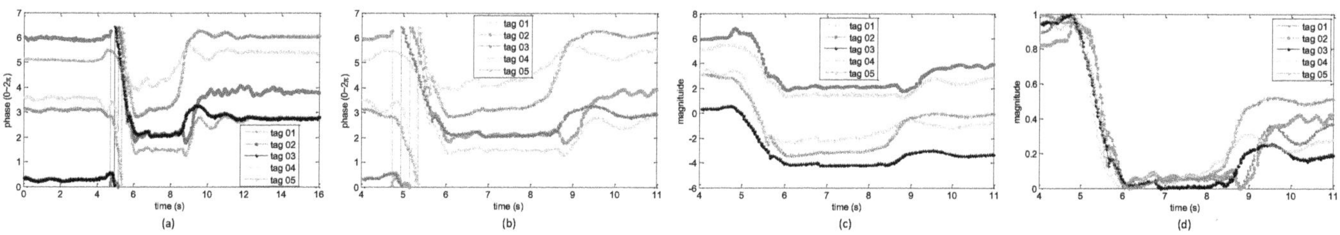

Figure 7: (a): the original phase trends; (b): after segmentation; (c): after de-periodicity; (d): after normalization;

unteer put it back at the 12th second. Similarly, as shown in Figure 6(c), when the volunteer turns over the item 05 at the 4th second, the phase trend of this tag changes significantly. The phase trend then keeps stable during the period of [4s, 8s], indicating that it is held steadily by the volunteer. As the volunteer looses her grasp, the item will rapidly recover to its original position, leading to a fierce phase changing. The measurement indicates that it is possible to detect pick-up and turn-over actions by observing the phase trend of tags. That is, identifying whether a period of phase changing occurs.

3.2.2 *Exploiting the dissimilarity of pick-up and turn-over for action identification*

In clothing stores, it is common to see that clothes are hung compactly to each other on the rack, with their side-views facing to customers (Figure 1). Consequently, when the customer picks up one item to have a close browsing, the nearby items will be struck unintentionally, hence experiencing a slight shaking. As a result, the phase trends of these items will demonstrate a minor yet different variation tendency to the desired item (like tag 01, 02 ,03 and 04 in Figure 6(b)). In contrast, when the customer turns over one item (say item 05) to see its front face, the items around this item will be forced to turn over as well, hence experiencing a similar motion trail as item 05. As a result, the phase trends of these items will show a similar tendency to tag 05 (like tag 01, 02 ,03 and 04 in Figure 6(c)). Therefore, it is viable to distinguish turn-over and pick-up actions by jointly considering the phase trend of nearby tags, *i.e.*, comparing the similarity of their phase trends.

3.2.3 *Identification scheme*

Based on above analysis, we first design a segmentation-based pick-up/turn-over detection scheme. This scheme exploits the similarity of pick-up and turn-over actions, and can accurately report the occurrence of these two actions. Then a peer-assisted identification scheme is put forward to further distinguish these two actions.

Segmentation-based detection: ShopMiner performs segmentation on the phase trend to detect whether a pick-up or turn-over action occurs. Denote the phase trend as $S = (s_i) \in R^{1\times N}$, where N is the discrete time point. Within each window, we categorize phase values into multiple bins, and get the discrete probability distribution function (PDF) of phase values within each window. Given two consecutive windows w_i and w_j, let P and Q be their PDFs. We computes the *KL-divergence* of these two PDFs as follows:

$$D_{KL}(P||Q) = \sum_i P(i) \cdot ln\frac{P(i)}{Q(i)} \quad (3)$$

The *KL-divergence* describes the similarity of phase trends within two consecutive windows. We denote the period when there is a pick-up or turn-over action as *motion period.* The remaining period is denoted as *silent period.* Within the silent period, the phase value will maintain in a relative stable level. Hence the KL-divergence of two consecutive windows within the silent period should be small. In contrast, if at least one window is within the motion period, the PDF of these two windows should be significantly different, which leads to a large KL-divergence value. ShopMiner checks $D_{KL}(P||Q)$ to detect whether the current window is within the silent period. After finding all windows within the silent interval, we can extract the motion interval accordingly. Consequently, a tag with a motion interval indicates a pick-up or turn-over action occurs.

Improving the granularity: the segmentation-based scheme can successfully detect the pick-up and turn-over actions due to its sensitivity to phase dynamics. However, since both the pick-up and turn-over actions will introduce phase turbulence to nearby items. The phase trend of these items may vary as well and hence will be detected by the segmentation-based scheme. To demonstrate this, we invite one volunteer to perform take-up and turn-over actions on the clothing rack for 200 times, and we find that the false alarm rate breaks 40%. To improve the detection granularity, we exploit the statistical feature of the phase trend. It contains two steps: de-periodicity and variance comparison.

De-periodicity: The phase value reported by the reader API is a periodic function ranging from 0 to 2π. As a result, when the phase value decreases to 0, it will jump to 2π, and then decreases as usual (Figure 6(d)). We term this abrupt phase changing phenomenon as a phase hop. In ShopMiner, we adopt the method in [16] to handle the phase hop problem. The general idea is to add or subtract 2π on the phase value when the phase hop occurs. The phase trend before/after de-periodicity is shown in Figure 6(d).

Variance comparison: Suppose m tags are detected in the segmentation step. For each tag i, we denote its phase samples within the motion period as $S_i = (s_j) \in R^{1\times N_i}$. N_i is the length of the sample group, and may vary from tag to tag due to the multi-path self-interference [38] and random access principle of ALOHA protocol. We thus split each sample group into N frames. The frame length is set to 0.1s. Since multiple samples may locate within a frame, we computes their average (denoted as s'_j), and use it as the phase value of this frame. Then we compute the variance of S_i as follows:

$$Var(S_i) = \frac{1}{N}\sum_{j=1}^{N}(s'_j - \mu)^2 \quad (4)$$

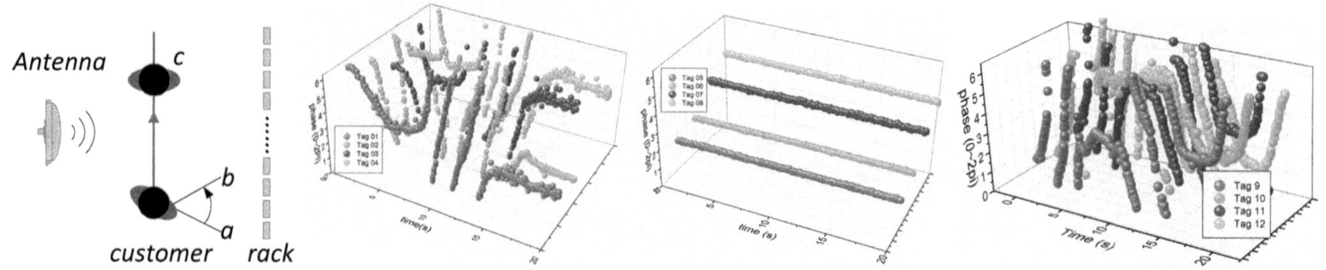

(a) (b) (c) (d)

Figure 8: (a): the customer moving trail; (b): the phase trends of correlated items; (c): the phase trends of stationary tags nearby; (d): the phase trends of another group of correlated items;

After computing the variance of each tag, the one with the highest variance is denoted as the desired tag. The rationale is as follows: the motion of nearby items is indirectly driven by the human action. The driven power will be absorbed by clothes and diminishes rapidly as it prolongs. As a result, the desired item will experience much higher turbulence than the undesired ones, and hence show a larger variance.

Peer-assisted Identification: After finding out the desired tag, the next step is to distinguish the customer action, *i.e.*, pick-up or turn-over. Recall that the phase trend of nearby tags would demonstrate a similar variation for turn-over, yet behave differently for pick-up. Hence we exploit this dissimilarity for action identification. Specifically, for each of the m phase trends, we zoom out the local dissimilarity of phase samples by normalizing this phase trend (Figure 7(d)). After the normalization, we splice these m phase trends consequently into a single phase trend, say $S = (s_j) \in R^{1\times N}$. Then autocorrelation is performed on S:

$$\chi(m,\tau) = \frac{\sum_{k=0}^{k=\tau-1}[s_{m+k} - \mu(m,\tau)][s_{m+k+\tau} - \mu(m+\tau,\tau)]}{\tau\cdot\sigma(m,\tau)\cdot\sigma(m+\tau,\tau)} \tag{5}$$

where $\mu(k,\tau)$ and $\sigma(k,\tau)$ are the mean and standard deviation of the phase samples $< s_k, s_{k+1}, ..., s_{k+\tau-1} >$, respectively. In our case, τ equals to the number of data samples within the motion period, and is known a prior. Generally, the phase trend S, if connected by k similar phase trends, should behave like a periodic signal, hence demonstrating a higher auto-correlation value. Therefore, we can ascertain whether the motion period is caused by turn-over by checking the autocorrelation coefficient as follows:

- if $\chi(m,\tau) \geq \delta$, then *action* = *turn-over*;
- if $\chi(m,\tau) < \delta$, then *action* = *pick-up*;

We test various thresholds over 1,000 experiments in our shopping-like scenario, and find a unified threshold $\delta = 0.65$ optimal for our case. This threshold is impacted by the layout of shops as well as link distance, hence should be calibrated for different shops. Note that reordering the item, which occurs frequently in retail stores, does not impact the detection performance, since ShopMiner does not rely on any sequence or position information of items for pick-up/turn-over detection.

3.3 Excavating Correlated Items

Our correlation analysis aims to find the items that are usually tried on together, *e.g.*, dress shirt and tie are usually

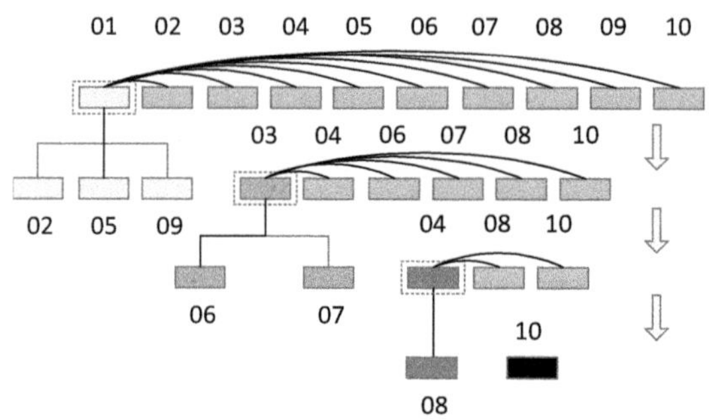

Figure 9: sketch of clustering procedure

tie-in together, while people buying suit pants often consider about the dress shoes. Previous effort [5] proposed an RSS-based localization technique for correlated item discovery, based on an intuition that correlated items held by the same person should be in close proximity. However, after scrutinizing this method in real-world applications, we find that such a method is error-prone due to the following two reasons. On the one hand, items around the customer may also be in close proximity to the items in hand, and hence will be mistaken as correlated items. On the other hand, the ambient environment of clothing stores is fast-changing. Customers block/generate signal propagation paths dynamically, hence dampening the resolution of localization-based scheme.

3.3.1 Spatial-temporal correlation of signal features

ShopMiner explores the spatial-temporal correlation of phase trends to discover those correlated items. The observation is that correlated items, either in hand or in the shopping bag, follow a similar moving pattern with the customer, hence experiencing consistent temporal signal changing.

As an illustrative measurement, a customer is asked to carry four pieces of clothes in hand and walks to the fitting room. The walking trail is shown in Figure 8(a). Figure 8(b) illustrates the temporal phase trend of these four items. All these four phase trends demonstrate a similar temporal pattern. Specifically, when the volunteer rotates from a to b, because the distance between the tag and antenna first increases and then decreases, the phase trend thus shows a symmetric profile. As the customer walks to c, the phase trend changes repeatedly within $[0, 2\pi)$ and finally maintains in a stable value when the customer reaches c and stays for a while. On the other hand, comparing Figure 8(b) with Figure 8(c) and Figure 8(d), the tags within different category have diverse temporal phase profiles, which naturally separate them apart. The measurement validates the feasibility of using phase trend similarity for correlated item discovery.

3.3.2 *Clustering correlated items*

Given a set of phase trends $(x_1, x_2, ..., x_n)$, our goal is to partition the n phase trends into m (m is unknown a prior and $m \leq n$) sets $\mathbf{S} = \{S_1, S_2, ..., S_m\}$, such that the within-cluster sum of squares is minimized:

$$\underset{\mathbf{S}}{\operatorname{argmin}} \sum_{k=1}^{m} \sum_{i,j \in S_k} \mathcal{T}(x_i, x_j) \quad (6)$$

where $\mathcal{T}(x_i, x_j)$ is the distance between x_i and x_j. To solve this optimization problem, we design a heuristic algorithm which iteratively partitions tags into different categories.

We give a toy example to explain this algorithm. Figure 9 shows a running case where ten tags need to be classified. In the first iteration, the algorithm randomly picks one tag as the pivot (*e.g.*, tag 01 in the example), and computes the distance between its profile with the remaining. Tags that are with sufficiently close proximity with the pivot are clustered together. The algorithm then randomly chooses another pivot and repeats this process on the unclassified tags until the within-cluster sum of squares is minimized. Once the algorithm terminates, we achieve the corresponding tag set.

Distance metric $\mathcal{T}(x_i, x_j)$: in designing the distance metric, we are facing two crucial issues: the first is the *phase trend inconsistency*, which means that phase trends are with different length due to the fragile backscatter links and multi-path effect. The second issue is the *interrogation time inconsistency*, which indicates the phase values are sampled in different time slots due to the random access character of ALOHA protocol. To address these issues, we use the Dynamic Time Warping (DTW) metric [33] to measure the distance of phase trends. This metric allows two time series that are similar but locally out of phase to align in a non-linear manner, hence naturally addressing both the phase profile inconsistency and interrogation time inconsistency.

Addressing phase scaling challenge: a practical challenge arises when we try to directly apply DTW to compare phase trends: phase scaling due to the different position of tags. The phase value is proportional to the tag-to-antenna distance, which may vary a little bit from tag to tag within the same category. As we can see from Figure 8(b), *V-shapes* within these four tags are the scaled version to each other. This scaling problem could degrade the performance of DTW. To address this challenge, we employ a variant of the DTW algorithm called Derivative Dynamic Time Warping (DDTW) [9], which exploits the same principle of DTW yet uses the derivative of phase values as the input data. DDTW can overcome the phase value difference in the Y-axis by working with the derivatives of phases where only the slope of phase matters and not the absolute values.

4. IMPLEMENTATION

In this section, we present the details of system implementation, and address several deployment issues.

4.1 Methodology

Hardware: we build a prototype using COTS UHF RFID devices. Each item of clothes is attached with an Alien

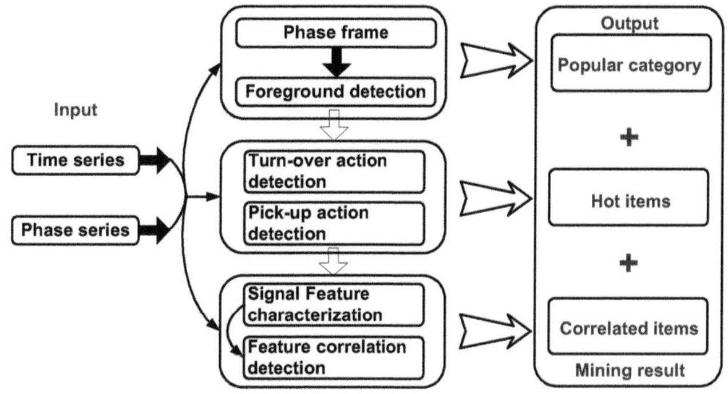

Figure 10: Workflow of ShopMiner

passive RFID tag model AZ-9634. An ImpinJ reader R420 and several Yeon antennas model YAP-100CP work as the receiver to energize these passive tags and collect readings. The reader is connected to a local server via an Ethernet cable. To minimize the influence of network latency, we time-stamp each tag reading by the reader's local clock.

Software: we implement the software component of our system in Java. Figure 10 shows the workflow of our ShopMiner system. At the lowest level is the data collection module, which is integrated with the Octane SDK and continuously interrogates the nearby tags to capture the phase readings, at a rate about 340 readings per second. The tag readings are grouped according to the tag ID (96bit or 128bit identifier) and stored in the local database. Initially, the data processing module fetches out the phase reading, and feeds them into the popular category discovery module. After discovering the popular items, ShopMiner collects their tag IDs and performs pick-up/turn-over detection on these tags. ShopMiner finally clusters these hot items to excavate the correlated items. The software runs on a Lenovo PC with an Intel Core i7-4600U 2.10GHz CPU and 8GB RAM.

4.2 Deployment issues

One deployment issue is to minimize the population of items for correlation analysis. In a large garment store, everyday hundreds of items would be picked up or turned over frequently. While the majority part of these items will be placed back directly without any trying on [32]. Essentially, these items do not belong to any category of correlated items, and hence could be filtered out a prior. In ShopMiner, only the tags satisfying the following two conditions will be considered as candidates for correlation analysis: 1): this item has been picked up or turned over; 2): this item is sequentially identified by different RFID readers (indicating the item is in motion). Such heuristic prunes a large portion of uncorrelated items and boosts the efficiency of correlation analysis.

Another deployment issue is to minimize data storage. In our system, the RFID reader periodically interrogates tags. Hence the acquired data accumulates gradually. Figure 11 shows a snapshot of the data volume augmentation when the RFID reader monitors 5 items in front. The data volume increases linearly with the time and rapidly accumulates to over 10Mb at the end of the 30th second. Suppose the system monitors 100 items in a small clothing stores. Then each hour it will generate at least 24G volume of data, which is intolerable for practical deployment. To reduce the data storage overhead, ShopMiner runs the popular cat-

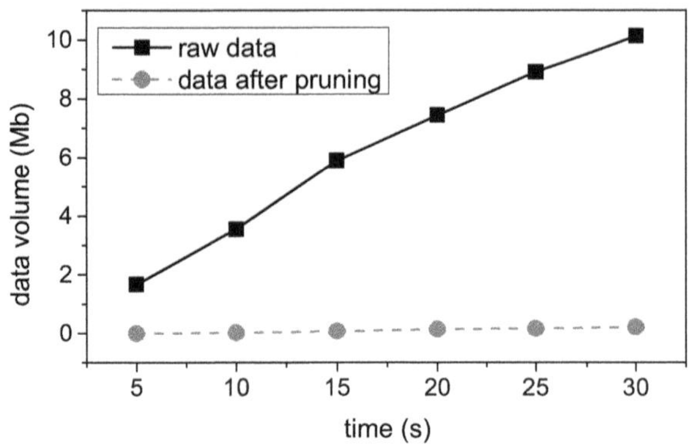

Figure 11: the snapshot of data storage in ShopMiner

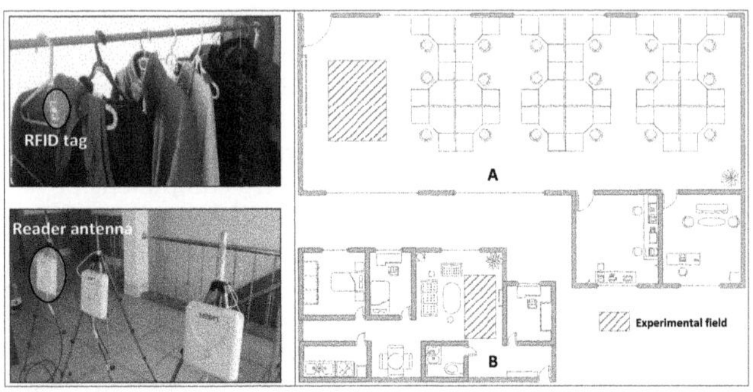

Figure 12: Deployment of the prototype in the office/home environment

egory discovery module and hot item identification module in a real-time manner. Only those hot items will be taken into account and their data will be stored in the database for offline correlation analysis. We call this process as early data pruning. As Figure 11 shows, after the early pruning, ShopMiner introduces significantly lower storage overhead, which accumulates to 0.2Mb at the end of the 30th second. From a long-term view, the data volume would accumulate to about 480Mb of a one-hour monitoring duration for 100 tags, which is negligible compared to one-hour raw data volume. We admit that for large-scale shops, tag populations would be high and hence the data volume would accumulate rapidly. For this case, we recommend to perform offline correlation analysis each hour and discard accumulated data after each round of data analysis.

5. EVALUATION

In this section, we introduce the experiment scenario and detail the system performance. We keep two places of decimal of the experimental result throughout the evaluation part.

5.1 Scenario

We evaluate the performance of ShopMiner in two typical indoor environments: (a) an office room of $26\times14\ m^2$ and (b) a twin-bedroom apartment of $13\times9\ m^2$. The layouts of these two rooms are shown in Figure 12. The office environment mimics the large-scale shopping square (*e.g.*, H&M, Zara, Abercrombie & Fitch, etc.). We recruit 10+ volunteers to mimic customers that browse commodities here. The apartment environment mimics little clothing stores (*e.g.*, private

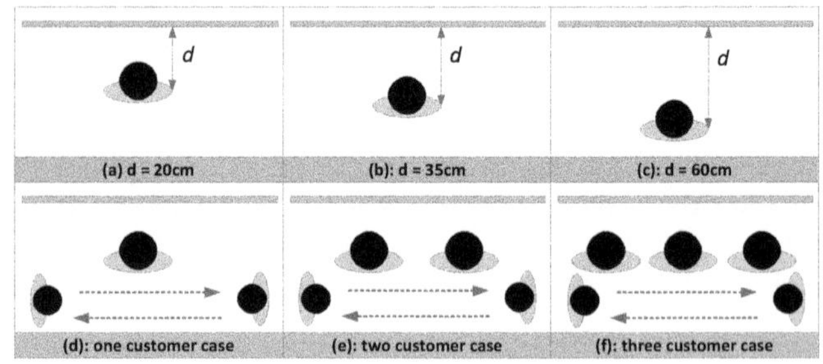

Figure 13: Illustration of testing scenarios: including three item-to-customer distance settings ((a), (b), (c)) and three different number of customer settings ((d), (e), (f))

clothing stores), where less than 5 customers are asked to hang out there. In each testing environment, we hang 20 pieces of clothes on a clothing rack. The clothing rack is with 2 meters long and 1.4 meters high. The space of adjacent clothes is about 5cm. It should be noticed that the shopping behaviors studied in this work are general motions that the customer will perform in all kinds of retail stores, hence our scheme could adapt to other types of display configurations such as supermarket, stationary store *etc.*. The location of the clothing rack is denoted as the dashed squires in Figure 12. To evaluate the robustness of ShopMiner, we also test its performance with different item-to-customer distance and different number of nearby customers (shown in Figure 13).

5.2 Popular category discovery

We first examine the impact of different parameter settings on the performance of popular category discovery. Then we test the system performance with a focus on its detection granularity and robustness. Granularity represents the minimum number of items that ShopMiner can detect when the customer stand still in front of an interested item. Robustness reflects the ability to resist outer changes without a significant decline in granularity.

5.2.1 Parameter configuration

Impact of confidence level (1-α): The confidence level (Equation 1) plays a key role in popular category discovery, and cannot be configured arbitrarily. To explore a proper confidence level, we vary α from 0.01 to 0.2, and calculate the true positive rates (TPR) and true negative rates (T-NR) of ShopMiner. TPR represents the fraction of cases where ShopMiner correctly identifies body shadowing events among all body shadowing events. TNR represents the fraction of cases where ShopMiner correctly identifies non-body shadowing events among all non-body shadowing events. We plot the TPR and TNR under various confidence level settings in Figure 14. ShopMiner achieves balanced TPR and TNR over 91% using a confidence level of 0.86. We thus use this threshold in the following experiments.

Impact of threshold θ: We further investigate the influence of threshold θ (Equation 2) on the system performance. In practice, if θ is too large, then ShopMiner will mistaken the browsing event as non-browsing case. For example, one customer stands still for a short time to browse the interested item, and then leaves away. On the contrary, if θ is too small, then ShopMiner will mistaken a large portion of

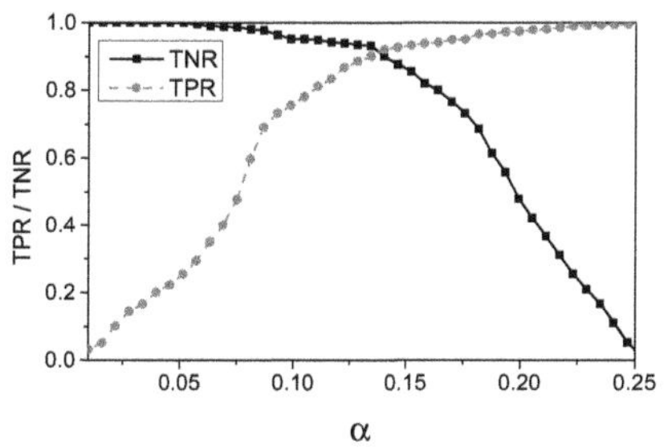

Figure 14: Impact of confidence level

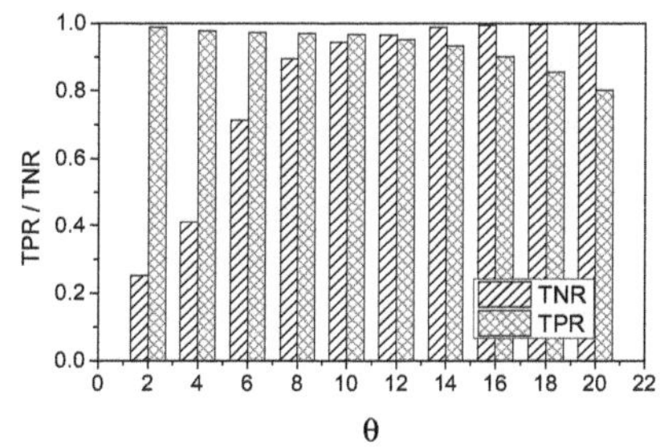

Figure 15: Impact of threshold γ

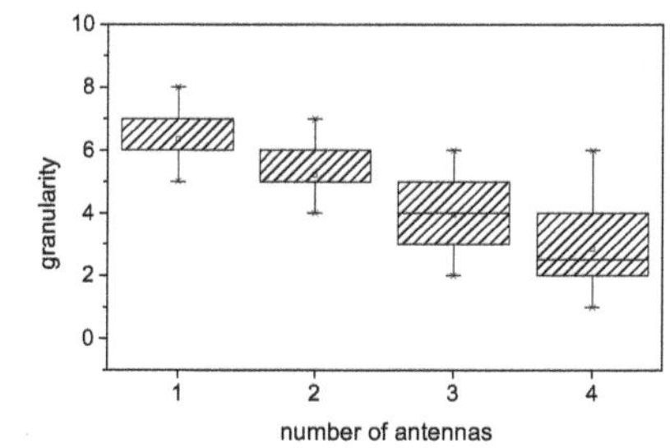

Figure 16: Impact of different number of antennas

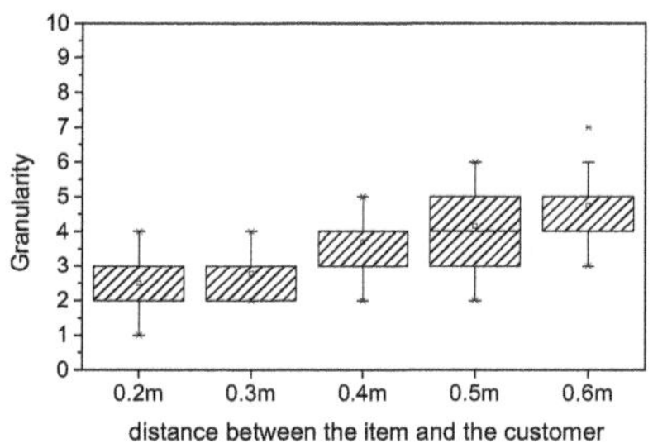

Figure 17: Impact of item-to-customer distance

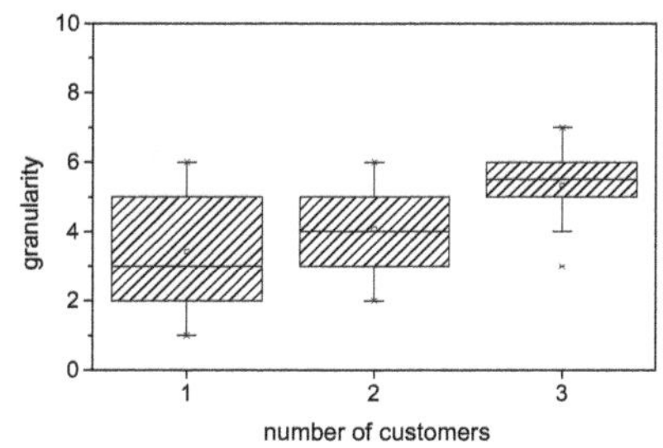

Figure 18: Impact of multiple customers

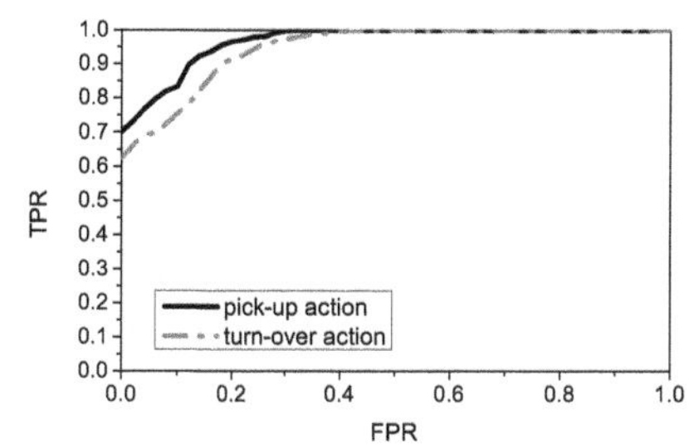

Figure 19: ROC curve

non-browsing events as browsing event. *e.g.*, customer walks slowly around the cloth rack and unintentionally blocks the LOS path between clothes and the antenna. We define the TPR as the fraction of cases where ShopMiner correctly identifies browsing event among all body browsing events; and TNR is the fraction of cases where ShopMiner correctly identifies non-browsing event among all non-browsing events. Figure 15 plots the TPR and TNR under a range of threshold settings. ShopMiner achieves a balanced TPR and TNR of over 92% using a threshold of 12s. We will use this threshold in the subsequent evaluations.

5.2.2 Overall Performance

Granularity: We vary the number of reader antennas and observe the granularity changing. In this experiment, a customer browses clothes and stands still in front of the interested ones (*i.e.*, popular category). The distance between the customer moving trail and the clothing rack is 0.3m. We repeat the experiment 50 times under each antenna setting. Figure 16 depicts the relationship between the number of antennas and the detection granularity. The detection granularity is about 6 pieces of clothes on average with only one reader antenna. With more antennas, the detection granularity improves significantly and finally achieves 3.2 pieces of clothing on average when the reader antenna added to 4. Although such granularity fails to precisely reveal the specific item that the customer is browsing, it can remarkably narrow down the scope of candidates. Furthermore, as items with the same style are often hung closely together, hence such granularity can guarantee that ShopMiner identifies those clustered popular category of clothes. Based on the experiment result, we use four antennas in the following experiments.

Robustness: We first vary the distance between the clothing item and the customer (termed as item-to-customer distance) d from 0.2m to 0.6m, and examine how this distance affect the detection granularity. The antenna is put 2 meters away from the clothing rack. Figure 17 shows the result. As this figure indicates, the detection granularity decreases moderately as we expand the distance between the item and the customer. Specifically, when the customer is with close proximity to clothing items, *e.g.*, $d = 0.2m$ or $0.3m$, the detection granularity maintains in a similar and fine-grained level, with the granularity of 2.5 and 2.9 pieces of clothes on average. As we increase d to 0.6m, the detection granularity drops to about 5 pieces of clothes on average. This may be because the customer blocks more LOS paths between the undesired items and the antenna, hence leading to much coarser detection granularity.

We also test the granularity of ShopMiner in multiple customer cases. In this trail of experiments, we arrange different number of customers to browse clothes simultaneously. The distance between the clothing rack and the customer is set to 0.3m. Figure 18 shows the detection granularity changing when different number of customers browse clothes simultaneously. As expected, when there is only one customer, ShopMiner achieves a relative good result, with a detection granularity of 3.2 pieces of clothes on average. As more customers get enrolled, *e.g.*, n = 3, the detection granularity drops slightly to 5.3 pieces of clothes on average. This may be because more people will naturally block more LOS paths and introduce much complex multi-path reflections.

Summary: from the experiment result we can see that ShopMiner can detect the popular item with a TPR of 92%. The detection granularity degrades slightly with the variation of tag-to-antenna distance and number of customers. Besides, the result also indicates that the granularity can be improved by deploying more reader antennas.

5.3 Hot item identification

We test the accuracy and robustness of the hot item identification scheme based on the following metric: TPR and

Table 1: Confusion matrix of action identification

Ground-truth	Predicted	
	Turn over	Pick up
Turn over	187	13
Pick up	9	191

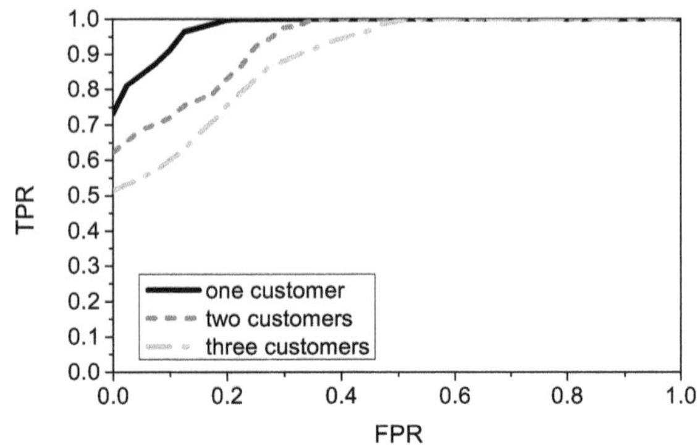

Figure 20: Impact of multiple customers

FPR. TPR is defined as the proportion of cases where ShopMiner successfully detects the pick-up and turn-over actions among all pick-up and turn-over actions performed by the customer. FPR is defined as the proportion of cases where ShopMiner mistakes other actions as pick-up or turn-over actions over all non-pick-up and non-turn-over actions.

Accuracy: In this trail of experiments, we ask a volunteer to randomly pick up or turn over different clothing items 20 times. Other customers hang out around the clothing rack to generate multi-path propagation interferences. The experiment is conducted 20 times in total in two testing scenarios by 10 different customers. The ground-truth is captured by a video camera. We summarize the detection result by plotting the Receiver Operating Characteristic (ROC) curves in Figure 19. As the result indicates, ShopMiner achieves a better detection accuracy in pick-up case than that in turn-over case. Specifically, we can see that ShopMiner acquires a balanced detection accuracy of 94% with a FPR of 13% for the pick-up case, and that of 87% with a FPR of 16% for the turn-over case. The primary reason of this performance gap may be because the phase turbulence of the desired item is much more significant than that of nearby items (unintentionally stricken by the desired item) in pick-up case, whereas the phase turbulence of the desired one is relatively similar to other nearby items in turn-over case.

We further investigate the identification accuracy of ShopMiner. The confusion matrix is shown in Table 1. Each row here denotes the actual activity performed by the volunteer and each column represents the activity recognized by ShopMiner. Each element in the matrix corresponds to the fraction of actions in the row that were regarded as the activity in the column. As the result shows, ShopMiner achieves a true positive rate of 94% and 96% for turn-over and pick-up action, respectively. The turn-over action is misclassified as pick-up action with 7% probability, while the pick-up action is often misclassified as turn-over action with 5% probability. The result clearly demonstrates that the auto-correlation based detection scheme can successfully distinguish pick-up and turn-over actions with high accuracy.

Robustness: To quantify the robustness of the detection scheme, we test its performance in multi-person cases and plot the ROC curves in Figure 20. As the result indicates, with one customer, ShopMiner achieves a balanced detection accuracy of 92% with a FPR of 13%. The detection accuracy decreases slightly with more customers, yet ShopMiner still achieves an accuracy of 85% with a FPR of 22% with three customers. This is expected since multiple customers will introduce complex signal propagation environment, which further introduces phase disturbance to each item.

Table 2: Confusion matrix of action identification

Ground-truth	Predicted					
	Turn over			Pick up		
	1	2	3	1	2	3
Turn over	187	184	178	13	16	22
Pick up	9	10	13	191	190	187

We further investigate the multi-person impact on the identification accuracy. Table 2 shows the identification result. As the confusion matrix indicates, the misclassification rate rises moderately with the increase of customer population. Specifically, when there are two customers performing pick-up or turn-over actions in front of the same clothing rack, ShopMiner achieves preeminent performance, with an average misclassification rate of 8% and 5% for turn-over and pick-up, respectively. This index increases slightly for the three customer case, and finally peaks 11% and 7% for the four customer case. This may be because when multiple customers turn over clothes on the same clothing rack, the clothes nearby the desired ones will be pushed by multiple customers. As a result, their phase trends will change irregularly in some cases, hence degrading the identification performance. Nevertheless, ShopMiner still achieves 89% and 94% TPR, demonstrating its potential for real deployment.

Summary: the result shows that ShopMiner achieves an overall detection accuracy of 94% and 87% for pick-up and turn-over cases, respectively. The TPR of action identification is 96% and 94% for pick-up and turn-over actions, respectively. Besides, the result also indicates that ShopMiner is insensitive to the variation of customer populations.

5.4 Correlated item excavation

We evaluate the performance of our iterative correlation detection scheme using the metric *Detection accuracy*. The detection accuracy is defined as the proportion of cases where ShopMiner correctly identifies correlated items over all correlated items.

Accuracy: We examine the detection accuracy under different number of correlated items. In this trail of experiments, we arrange one customer to bring different number of correlated items and hang out around the reader's reading zone. The experiment is conducted 200 times by 10 different customers. We then use different distance metric (DTW and DDTW) for correlated item detection. Figure 21 shows the detection accuracies. As is shown, the detection accuracies using different distance metrics both decrease slightly with the increase of the number of correlated items. Specifically, when there are few customers (*e.g.*, 1 or 2), the detection accuracy of ShopMiner retains around 91% and 83% for the DDTW and DTW distance metrics, respectively. With more customers, the performance gap of ShopMiner under different distance metrics becomes more significant, and finally peaks at 10%. It manifests that DDTW metric significantly improves the detection accuracy.

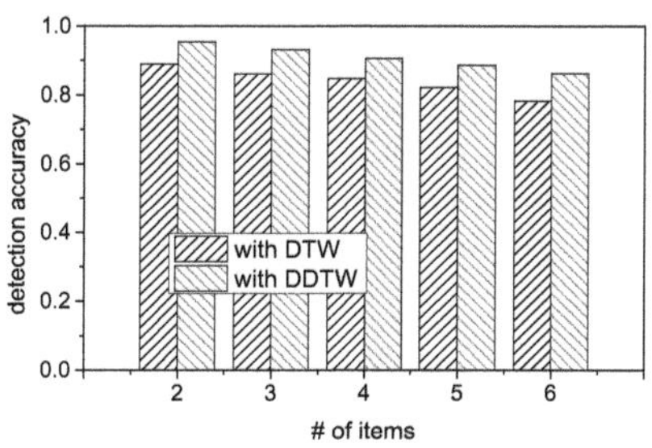

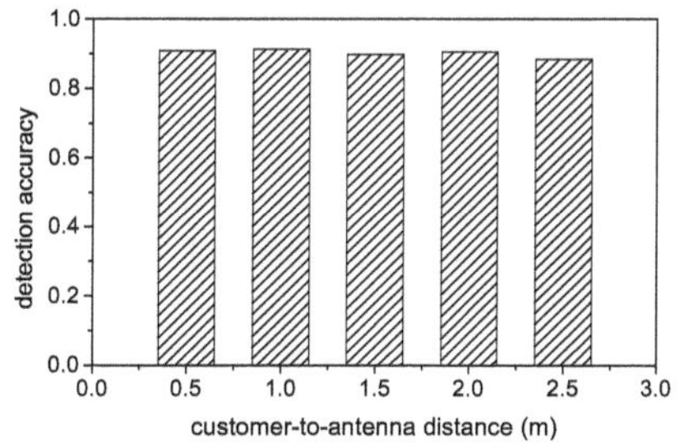

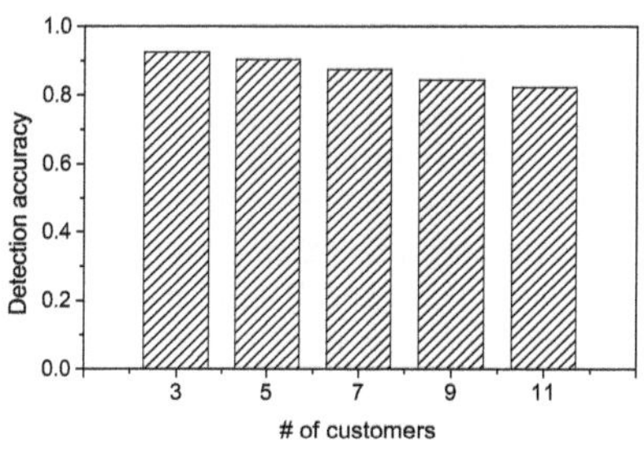

Figure 21: # of items vs. detection accuracy

Figure 22: Impact of customer-to-antenna distance

Figure 23: Impact of customer populations

Robustness: We investigate the impact of the customer-to-antenna distance on the detection accuracy. As shown in Figure 22, the distance between the customer and the antenna has little impact on the detection accuracy. Specifically, when the customer stands close to the antenna, *e.g.*, 0.5m or 1m away, the detection accuracy retains above 90%. The detection performance then degrades slightly to over 88% when the customer is 2m away from the antenna. Hence with the increase of the distance between the customer and the antenna, there is no significant performance degradation. This result shows that our correlation detection scheme is insensitive to the customer-to-antenna distance.

We further examine the impact of customer population on the detection accuracy. In this trail of experiment, we arrange different number of customers to walk around, with each customer bringing different number of clothes. As shown in Figure 23, ShopMiner achieves an overall accuracy of 92% when there are three customers. The detection accuracy then decreases slightly with more customers. However, ShopMiner still achieves an detection accuracy over 85% with 11 volunteers. This result shows that ShopMiner is robust to customer population changes.

Summary: Experimental result shows that ShopMiner achieves an overall detection accuracy of over 93% with one customer, and that of over 85% with six customers. The result also indicates that ShopMiner is insensitive to the number of customers and the antenna-to-customer distance.

6. RELATED WORKS

Offline shopping behavior mining: Despite the academic and commercial success in online shopping data acquisition, relative few efforts have been paid on the offline shopping data acquisition. You *et al.* [37] discussed the usage of mobile phones to monitor shopping time at physical stores. Hagan *et al.* [20] proposed a solution on offline customer behavior collection by mounting the data collection device in the shopping cart. Kanda *et al.* [7] designed a sensor network based shopping behavior analysis system in retail stores, with the goal of tracking and clustering consumer locations, and further inferring the hot items. These solutions fail to provide high-fidelity information on offline shopping behaviors, such as how customers browse stores, and what items they show interest.

Wearable sensor based activity recognition: It is natural to use wearable sensors for human activity recognition. JigSaw [19] continuously monitored and classified user activities and infers context like walking, cycling and running. Swimmaster [1] provided a fine-grained assessment of swimming by extracting swimming parameters such as velocity, arm strokes, body balance, and body rotation. Researchers also employed wearable sensors for other kinds of human activity detection, such as smoking [21] and sleeping [4, 6].

Some research also explored detecting offline shopping behaviors with smart devices. Lee *et al.* [12] presented a smartphone based customer shopping behavior modeling framework, which aims to examine the impact of six kind of human activities on customer behaviors. Rallapalli *et al.* [26] proposed a solution on tracking physical browsing by customers in retail stores using the inertial sensors on smart glasses. Sen *et al.* [27] explored the possibility of using smartphone sensing data to detect pre-defined shopping activities in physical retail stores. These works can provide certain customer activity recognition services. However, these schemes require each user to wear a special hardware, which is burdensome and may degrade the shopping experience.

WiFi-based posture recognition: Researchers also exploit WiFi signal changes for device-free human activity sensing. WiSee [25] leveraged wireless signals to enable human gesture recognitions. AllSee [8] provided a gesture-recognition scheme that can operate on battery-free wireless devices. WiHear [34] designed a novel signal processing technique to detect human speaking from WiFi signals. E-eyes [35] extracted the CSI information from 802.11 symbols for in-home human activity sensing, like washing, watching, brushing teeth. While these techniques relieve users from wearable sensors, they suffer from environment dynamics, and hence cannot be deployed in physical stores for customer behavior monitoring.

RFID-based human/object sensing: Previous research also explored the signal changes of RFID tags for human or object sensing. OTrack [28] exploited the spatial-temporal correlation of RSS signals to track the tag order in baggage sorting system. STPP [29] designed a phase profiling technique for the relative localization of rfid tags in 2D space. Togoram [36] tracked mobile RFID tags within centimeter level accuracy by using the SAR and hologram technique. Our work is inspired by the above works in phase based tag motion detection. However, our focus is on leveraging the phase pattern to infer customer behaviors, rather than capturing the tag's position. CBID [5] and Tagbooth [16] are the most related works to ours. CBID [5] exploited the Doppler effect on human actions to detect customer behavior in shopping malls. Tagbooth [16] used the RSSI patterns to detect and identify the pick-up motions in physical retail stores. Our work differs from these two works in two aspects. On the one hand, our system incorporates three key factors that are essential to retailers, i.e., what items the customers browse, which items they show interest in, and which items they match with. In contrast, CBID and Tagbooth could only observe and detect pick-up motions and infer those correlated items. On the other hand, our system solely adopts the phase patterns to mining the customer shopping behavior, whereas CBID and Tagbooth mainly rely on RSSI and doppler shift for customer behavior identification.

7. DISCUSSION

This section talks about the practical deployment issues.

Distinguishing employee/customer: the current ShopMiner prototype mostly aims at clothing stores in a self-service/supermarket mode, where few employees are expected to continuously put products back in shelves and where customers are free to pick up and try on the items as wished. For retail stores with employees guiding customers or frequently putting products back in place, ShopMiner may experience severe interference since ShopMiner is unable to distinguish employees and customers via RF signals. A partial solution is to ask each employee to attach an RFID tag with special ID so that ShopMiner can simply discard the phase readings if the special ID is detected.

Deployment Cost for Full Coverage: mainstream commercial RFID readers can now support 4 antennas with each antenna effectively covering an area of 4m x 4m square. Hence the retailer can monitor nearly an area of nearly 60^2 with one reader, which costs less than 1000 USD. In addition, retailers are more interested in the shopping behaviors of some items (e.g. new products) than others (e.g. items on sale). Therefore, full radio coverage might be necessary only for certain important regions in the stores. According to our survey on a local clothing stores in Xi'an, another practical deployment concern comes from the placement of the readers, whether the four-antenna readers of relatively large size can be fixed on walls or ceilings without violating the decoration styles of the stores.

Impact of Crowded Stores: in our clothing store like evaluation, ShopMiner retains satisfactory performance (detection granularity of 5.3 pieces of items, hot item identification accuracy of 85%, and correlated item identification accuracy of 92%) when monitoring 3 customers browsing 1 rack simultaneously using 1 reader. According to our survey on two local clothing stores in Xi'an, it is sufficient to support 3-5 customers per rack most of the time, especially for those expecting pleasant user experience. In our clothing store like evaluation, ShopMiner retains satisfactory performance when monitoring 3 customers browsing one rack simultaneously. As customers standing still or walking in the shops close to the rack can partially alter the multipath propagations of the target customer, the phase profiles will experience slight fluctuations. Consequently, ShopMiner only mis-detects a customer when other customers occasionally block the LOS path of the target customer. However, since close presence of many customers can severely affect the RF signals and create complex multipath propagation environments of the targeted customer, the performance of ShopMiner can degrade dramatically in crowded stores, e.g. when it is Christmas sale.

Extending Beyond Clothing Stores: on one hand, the current ShopMiner prototype can be extended to some types of retail stores e.g. bookstores, where the items are of similar material, and are relatively tidily placed. On the other hand, RFID tags attached on metal products can experience severe radio interference, which can lead to failure of ShopMiner. It is also difficult to even attach an RFID tag on certain products, e.g. fruits. Hence the current version of ShopMiner may be inapplicable in computer stores and part of the grocery stores.

8. CONCLUSION

In this paper, we present the design, implementation and evaluation of ShopMiner, a RFID-based customer shopping behavior mining system works in physical clothing stores. By attaching each clothing item with a RFID tag, ShopMiner could "see" and detect how customers browse the stores, which category of items they show interest, and which items they match with. Such comprehensive shopping behavior data could benefit retailers in capturing customers' flavors, testing new arrivals, and further optimizing their commercial strategies. We examine the accuracy and robustness of ShopMiner in various testing scenarios. The preliminary result shows that ShopMiner could achieve high accuracy and efficiency in customer shopping behavior identification, hence hold potential for practical deployment.

9. ACKNOWLEDGEMENT

We would like to thank the anonymous reviewers and our shepherd, Ms.Lama Nachman, for providing valuable comments. This work is supported in part by the NSFC Major Program 61190110, the national high technology research and development program of China (863 Program) under Grant No.2013AA014601, NSFC General Program NO.61572282 and No.61572396, Hong Kong RGC Grant HKUST16207714, and China Postdoctoral Science Foundation funded project under NO. 2015M570100.

10. REFERENCES

[1] M. Bächlin, K. Förster, and G. Tröster. Swimmaster: A wearable assistant for swimmer. In *Proceedings of the 11th International Conference on Ubiquitous Computing*, UbiComp '09, pages 215–224, 2009.

[2] D. R. Bell and J. M. Lattin. Shopping behavior and consumer preference for store price format: Why "large basket" shoppers prefer edlp. *Marketing Science*, 17:66–88, 1998.

[3] Y. H. Cho, J. K. Kim, and S. H. Kim. A personalized recommender system based on web usage mining and decision tree induction. *Expert systems with Applications*, 23(3):329–342, 2002.

[4] W. Gu, Z. Yang, L. Shangguan, W. Sun, K. Jin, and Y. Liu. Intelligent sleep stage mining service with smartphones. In *Proceedings of the 2014 ACM International Joint Conference on Pervasive and Ubiquitous Computing*, UbiComp '14, pages 649–660, 2014.

[5] J. Han, H. Ding, C. Qian, D. Ma, W. Xi, Z. Wang, Z. Jiang, and L. Shangguan. Cbid: A customer behavior identification system using passive tags. In *Proceedings of the 2014 IEEE 22Nd International Conference on Network Protocols*, ICNP '14, pages 47–58, 2014.

[6] T. Hao, G. Xing, and G. Zhou. isleep: Unobtrusive sleep quality monitoring using smartphones. In

Proceedings of the 11th ACM Conference on Embedded Networked Sensor Systems, SenSys '13, pages 4:1–4:14, 2013.

[7] T. Kanda, D. F. Glas, M. Shiomi, H. Ishiguro, and N. Hagita. Who will be the customer?: A social robot that anticipates people's behavior from their trajectories. In *Proceedings of the 10th International Conference on Ubiquitous Computing*, UbiComp '08, pages 380–389, 2008.

[8] B. Kellogg, V. Talla, and S. Gollakota. Bringing gesture recognition to all devices. In *Proceedings of the 11th USENIX Conference on Networked Systems Design and Implementation*, NSDI'14, pages 303–316, 2014.

[9] E. J. Keogh and M. J. Pazzani. Derivative dynamic time warping. In *SDM*, pages 5–7, 2001.

[10] R. Kohavi, N. J. Rothleder, and E. Simoudis. Emerging trends in business analytics. *Communications of the ACM*, 45:45–48, 2002.

[11] J. Lee, M. Podlaseck, E. Schonberg, and R. Hoch. Visualization and analysis of clickstream data of online stores for understanding web merchandising. In *Applications of Data Mining to Electronic Commerce*, pages 59–84. 2001.

[12] S. Lee, C. Min, C. Yoo, and J. Song. Understanding customer malling behavior in an urban shopping mall using smartphones. In *Proceedings of the 2013 ACM Conference on Pervasive and Ubiquitous Computing Adjunct Publication*, UbiComp '13 Adjunct, 2013.

[13] Z. Li, W. Chen, C. Li, M. Li, X.-Y. Li, and Y. Liu. Flight: Clock calibration using fluorescent lighting. In *Proceedings of the 18th Annual International Conference on Mobile Computing and Networking*, Mobicom '12, 2012.

[14] Z. Li, W. Du, Y. Zheng, M. Li, and D. Wu. From rateless to hopless. In *Proceedings of the 16th ACM International Symposium on Mobile Ad Hoc Networking and Computing*, MobiHoc '15, 2015.

[15] Z. Li, Y. Xie, M. Li, and K. Jamieson. Recitation: Rehearsing wireless packet reception in software. In *Proceedings of the 21th Annual International Conference on Mobile Computing and Networking*, Mobicom '15, 2015.

[16] T. Liu, L. Yang, X.-Y. Li, H. Huang, and Y. Liu. Tagbooth: Deep shopping data acquisition powered by rfid tags. In *Proceedings IEEE Conference on Computer Communications*, INFOCOM'15, 2015.

[17] Y. Liu, Y. Zhao, L. Chen, J. Pei, and J. Han. Mining frequent trajectory patterns for activity monitoring using radio frequency tag arrays. *IEEE Transactions on Parallel and Distributed Systems*, 23(11):2138–2149, 2012.

[18] G. L. Lohse, S. Bellman, and E. J. Johnson. Consumer buying behavior on the internet: Findings from panel data. *Journal of interactive Marketing*, 14:15–29, 2000.

[19] H. Lu, J. Yang, Z. Liu, N. D. Lane, T. Choudhury, and A. T. Campbell. The jigsaw continuous sensing engine for mobile phone applications. In *Proceedings of the 8th ACM Conference on Embedded Networked Sensor Systems*, SenSys'10, pages 71–84, 2010.

[20] T. P. O'hagan and C. E. Lewis. Shopping cart mounted portable data collection device with tethered dataform reader, 1998. US Patent 5,821,513.

[21] A. Parate, M.-C. Chiu, C. Chadowitz, D. Ganesan, and E. Kalogerakis. Risq: recognizing smoking gestures with inertial sensors on a wristband. In *Proceedings of the 12th annual international conference on Mobile systems, applications, and services*, MobiSys'14, pages 149–161, 2014.

[22] E. M. Pereira, J. S. Cardoso, and R. Morla. Motion flow tracking in unconstrained videos for retail scenario. In *Pattern Recognition and Image Analysis*, pages 340–349. 2013.

[23] M. Popa, A. K. Koc, L. J. Rothkrantz, C. Shan, and P. Wiggers. Kinect sensing of shopping related actions. In *Constructing Ambient Intelligence*, pages 91–100. 2012.

[24] M. Popa, L. Rothkrantz, Z. Yang, P. Wiggers, R. Braspenning, and C. Shan. Analysis of shopping behavior based on surveillance system. In *Proceedings of IEEE International Conference on Systems Man and Cybernetics*, SMC'10, pages 2512–2519, 2010.

[25] Q. Pu, S. Gupta, S. Gollakota, and S. Patel. Whole-home gesture recognition using wireless signals. In *Proceedings of the 19th annual international conference on Mobile computing & networking*, MobiCom'13, pages 27–38, 2013.

[26] S. Rallapalli, A. Ganesan, K. Chintalapudi, V. N. Padmanabhan, and L. Qiu. Enabling physical analytics in retail stores using smart glasses. In *Proceedings of the 20th Annual International Conference on Mobile Computing and Networking*, MobiCom '14, 2014.

[27] S. Sen, D. Chakraborty, V. Subbaraju, D. Banerjee, A. Misra, N. Banerjee, and S. Mittal. Accommodating user diversity for in-store shopping behavior recognition. In *Proceedings of the 2014 ACM International Symposium on Wearable Computers*, ISWC '14, 2014.

[28] L. Shangguan, Z. Li, Z. Yang, M. Li, and Y. Liu. Otrack: Order tracking for luggage in mobile rfid systems. In *Proceedings IEEE Conference on Computer Communications*, INFOCOM'13, pages 3066–3074, 2013.

[29] L. Shangguan, Z. Yang, A. X. Liu, Z. Zhou, and Y. Liu. Relative localization of rfid tags using spatial-temporal phase profiling. In *12th USENIX Symposium on Networked Systems Design and Implementation*, NSDI'15, pages 251–263, 2015.

[30] T. Staake, F. Thiesse, and E. Fleisch. Extending the epc network: the potential of rfid in anti-counterfeiting. In *Proceedings of the 2005 ACM symposium on Applied computing*, pages 1607–1612, 2005.

[31] L.-A. Tang, Y. Zheng, J. Yuan, J. Han, A. Leung, C.-C. Hung, and W.-C. Peng. On discovery of traveling companions from streaming trajectories. In *Proceedings of 28th International Conference on Data Engineering*, ICDE'12, pages 186–197, 2012.

[32] M. Uzan. Consumers online and offline shopping behavior. 2014.

[33] T. K. Vintsyuk. Speech discrimination by dynamic programming. *Cybernetics and Systems Analysis*, 4(1):52–57, 1968.

[34] G. Wang, Y. Zou, Z. Zhou, K. Wu, and L. M. Ni. We can hear you with wi-fi! In *Proceedings of the 20th annual international conference on Mobile computing and networking*, MobiCom'14, pages 593–604, 2014.

[35] Y. Wang, J. Liu, Y. Chen, M. Gruteser, J. Yang, and H. Liu. E-eyes: device-free location-oriented activity identification using fine-grained wifi signatures. In *Proceedings of the 20th annual international conference on Mobile computing and networking*, MobiCom'14, pages 617–628, 2014.

[36] L. Yang, Y. Chen, X.-Y. Li, C. Xiao, M. Li, and Y. Liu. Tagoram: real-time tracking of mobile rfid tags to high precision using cots devices. In *Proceedings of the 20th annual international conference on Mobile computing and networking*, MobiCom'14, pages 237–248, 2014.

[37] C.-W. You, C.-C. Wei, Y.-L. Chen, H.-H. Chu, and M.-S. Chen. Using mobile phones to monitor shopping time at physical stores. *Proceedings of IEEE Pervasive Computing*, 10(2):37–43, 2011.

[38] P. Zhang, J. Gummeson, and D. Ganesan. Blink: A high throughput link layer for backscatter communication. In *Proceedings of the 10th international conference on Mobile systems, applications, and services*, MobiSys'12, pages 99–112, 2012.

Smart Devices are Different: Assessing and Mitigating Mobile Sensing Heterogeneities for Activity Recognition

Allan Stisen[‡], Henrik Blunck[‡], Sourav Bhattacharya[*], Thor Siiger Prentow[‡],
Mikkel Baun Kjærgaard[‡], Anind Dey[†], Tobias Sonne[‡], and Mads Møller Jensen[‡]
[‡]Department of Computer Science, Aarhus University, Denmark
[*]Bell Laboratories, Dublin, Ireland
[†]Carnegie Mellon University, USA
{allans, blunck, prentow, mikkelbk, tsonne, mmjensen}@cs.au.dk
sourav.bhattacharya@bell-labs.com, anind@cs.cmu.edu

ABSTRACT

The widespread presence of motion sensors on users' personal mobile devices has spawned a growing research interest in human activity recognition (HAR). However, when deployed at a large-scale, e.g., on multiple devices, the performance of a HAR system is often significantly lower than in reported research results. This is due to variations in training and test device hardware and their operating system characteristics among others. In this paper, we systematically investigate sensor-, device- and workload-specific heterogeneities using 36 smartphones and smartwatches, consisting of 13 different device models from four manufacturers. Furthermore, we conduct experiments with nine users and investigate popular feature representation and classification techniques in HAR research. Our results indicate that on-device sensor and sensor handling heterogeneities impair HAR performances significantly. Moreover, the impairments vary significantly across devices and depends on the type of recognition technique used. We systematically evaluate the effect of mobile sensing heterogeneities on HAR and propose a novel clustering-based mitigation technique suitable for large-scale deployment of HAR, where heterogeneity of devices and their usage scenarios are intrinsic.

Keywords

Mobile Sensing, Activity Recognition

Categories and Subject Descriptors

I.5.2 [**Pattern Recognition**]: Design Methodology; I.5.4 [**Pattern Recognition**]: Signal processing

1. INTRODUCTION

Off-the-shelf modern smartphones readily support an increasingly rich set of embedded sensors such as accelerometer, gyroscope, compass, WiFi, NFC and GPS [30, 45]. This growing ubiquity of sensor rich mobile devices in our everyday lives provides a unique opportunity to unobtrusively capture contextual information from the underlying human behavior in real-time. This growth has also led to an easier development, deployment and a wide proliferation of publicly available mobile sensing applications. Novel mobile sensing applications have also opened up new possibilities for mobile sensing research.

Among the sensors available on mobile consumer device platforms, the accelerometer is one of the earliest and most ubiquitous. The accelerometer has gained immense popularity in HAR research as it allows recognizing a wide variety of human activities, while having a relatively small energy footprint [8]. Accelerometer-based HAR has been deployed in a large number of domains including smart homes [5, 32, 38], health care [31, 37], daily activity tracking [29], fitness tracking [16], fall detection of elderly people [18] and transportation mode detection [9, 24, 42]. Other motion-related sensors, such as compass and gyroscope, are becoming increasingly common-place and often used for assisting and complementing the accelerometer. Motion sensors can be further paired with sensors, e.g., GPS, GSM, WiFi, and barometer, especially for recognizing tasks beyond basic HAR.

Although, a large body of motion sensor-based HAR research exists, real-world performance variations across, e.g., device manufacturers, models, OS types, and CPU load conditions, have been largely overlooked and not been evaluated rigorously yet. When a HAR system is deployed 'in the wild', i.e., across heterogeneous devices and usage situations, recognition performances are often significantly lower than what is suggested in previous research, as noted, e.g., by Amft [2] and Blunck *et al.* [13]. While device placement and orientation and differences in how users perform physical activities have been noted and mitigations for the adverse effects on HAR have been proposed, heterogeneities across devices and their configurations have not been studied rigorously. In this paper, we aim to bridge this gap in HAR research by systematically studying various heterogeneities in motion sensor-based sensing, their impact on HAR, and propose mitigation solutions. Below we elaborate on three major types of heterogeneities, which yield impairments of HAR.

Sensor Biases (SB): To keep the overall cost low, mobile devices are often equipped with low cost sensors, which are often poorly calibrated, inaccurate, and of limited granularity and range, compared to dedicated sensors for HAR, e.g., a dedicated standalone Inertial Measurement Unit (IMU). Furthermore, sensor biases may shift over time through everyday device usage, e.g., accidental device dropping might increase sensor biases.

Sampling Rate Heterogeneity (SRH): As of 2014, on the Android platform alone there are more than 18,000 distinct smartphone models [36]. Often popular smartphones vary in terms of the default and

SenSys'15, November 1–4, 2015, Seoul, South Korea..
 ISBN 978-1-4503-3631-4/15/11 ...$15.00.
DOI: http://dx.doi.org/10.1145/2809695.2809718.

supported sampling frequencies for accelerometer and other sensors. To highlight this in Table 1 we summarize the supported maximum accelerometer sampling frequency across 36 devices, spanning over 13 device models, used in our experiments.

Sampling Rate Instability (SRI): A number of factors, including delays in OS level timestamp attachment to sensor measurements and instantaneous I/O load, affect both the actual as well as the reported sampling rate of sensors on a device. For example, heavy multitasking and I/O load on mobile devices, as exhibited in typical usage scenarios, often lead to unstable sampling rates as the mobile OS frequently fails to attach accurate timestamp information as the measurements arrive. Unpredictability (and inevitability) of such loads makes the multitasking impairments challenging in HAR. Further irregularities in sampling rate may be introduced by modern sensing strategies. For example APIs supporting continuous sensing on the mobile platforms often rely heavily on dynamic duty-cycling to lower the overall power consumption [8].

In this paper, we empirically quantify the above heterogeneities, experimentally evaluate their effects on the HAR performance, and discuss mitigation of these impairments. In the following, we summarize the main contributions of our work:

- We present several sources of intrinsic heterogeneities in mobile sensing, focusing on accelerometer sensors. We conduct an extensive analysis of such heterogeneities using 31 smartphones, 4 smartwatches and 1 tablet, representing 13 different models from 4 manufacturers, running variants of Android and iOS, respectively (see Section 3).
- We systematically study the influence of these heterogeneities on HAR performance by conducting a case study using nine users, each carrying 2 instances of 3 smartphone and 2 smartwatch models. We report the effects of heterogeneities on various feature representation techniques and classifiers popular within HAR research considering a number of cross-validation techniques (see Section 4).
- We propose a novel clustering-based approach as a mitigation technique to improve HAR performance in the presence of heterogeneities (see Section 5).

2. RELATED WORK

Within the field of ubiquitous computing research, sampling rate unpredictability when using motion sensors on smartphones is a known issue: For example, Lane et al. [30] report that for Nokia Symbian and Maemo phones, accelerometers would return samples unpredictably to an application at $25-38$ Hz and Bieber et al. [11] report that such variations can change during normal phone usage, e.g., while making and receiving calls. Using interpolation in pre-processing as a mitigation technique, the authors reported an accuracy of 95% for distinguishing activities such as 'walking', 'running', 'jumping', 'biking' and 'driving' on the phone. However, they did not report on the impact that the impairments, and the proposed mitigations, had on the overall activity recognition performance. Albert et al. [1] show that the accelerometer sampling rate on T-mobile G1 phones running Android varies between $15-25$ Hz. The authors also use interpolation as a potential solution without studying its impact in detail.

Various research investigates motion sensor biases. Among early works, Lötters et al. proposed an online calibration method to mitigate accelerometer drift and offset over a long period of time [33]. The proposed method relies on the fact that under *quasi static* conditions, a measurement vector from a tri-axial accelerometer should equal $1g$. The online approach requires a few minutes to carry out and results in a post-procedure bias of $0.03g$, without requiring explicit orientation information. Gulmammadov also studied the accelerometer bias drifts, in the domain of aerospace engineering, and modeled bias as a combination of time and temperature dependent variables [22]. By conducting a set of experiments in a controlled laboratory setting the author reported that 99% of the drifts could be eliminated. Batista et al. also proposed a calibration technique, based on time-varying Kalman filtering and gravity estimation, for estimating biases observed on *micro-electrical-mechanical-systems* accelerometers (tri-axial) [7]. Through a set of simulation experiments using a *motion rate table* the authors show good performance of their approach. Sensor biases are prevalent not only for accelerometers but also for other sensing modalities: For example, Barthold et al. studied the influence of heavy magnetic environments and motion on gyroscope-based orientation estimations [6]. The authors also point out that offline sensor calibration techniques are hindered by that the sensor heterogeneities, e.g., biases and offsets, are often dependent on time and temperature, thereby limiting the applicability of such calibration techniques. Within the robotics community, calibration of IMUs via sensor fusion has been investigated, utilizing cameras and multiple sensors modalities, e.g., gyroscopes, magnetometers and accelerometers [26]. Banos et al. report on translating—across several sensor modalities—HAR from one sensor platform domain to another one, e.g., from a Kinect to an IMU [4]. Such methods could be used to align and potentially calibrate sensors to mitigate device heterogeneities.

In regards to the heterogeneities as discussed herein, a number of observations have been made in regards to the challenges these yield for real-world deployments: Amft [2] notes that HAR performances are often overly optimistic and that significant performance impairments may occur when utilized 'in the wild'. Blunck et al. [13] give a taxonomy of device-, user- and project-specific heterogeneities and sketch challenges for mobile app development and deployment projects. They further note that the recent rapid evolution of smartphone technologies increases these challenges.

Within the HAR community, usage heterogeneities in regards to device orientation and on-body placement have been thoroughly investigated. The severe HAR accuracy impairments these can cause have been investigated, initially for on-body-sensors but increasingly also for phones [3, 6, 9, 17, 25, 28, 44, 46]. For usage heterogeneity, various mitigation techniques for HAR have been proposed, e.g., body motion approximations aimed at on-body sensor setups [28], gravity vector estimation techniques for smartphones [25], as well as the training of several classifiers each associated with an individual phone orientation and/or placement, often combined with algorithms for identifying this context information from given data samples [17, 46].

To the best of our knowledge, this paper is the first to rigorously assess both the heterogeneities as described in Section 1 in regards to challenges and impairments they come with, as well as potential mitigations of these for HAR, using a wide range of smart device models.

3. HETEROGENEITIES IN ACCELEROMETER-BASED SENSING

To systematically study heterogeneities in mobile sensing, in this section we report results from a number of static and non-static experiments focusing on accelerometer data from 36 mobile devices covering Android and iOS smartphones and several Android smartwatches. The details of the devices used in our study are listed in Table 1.

3.1 Sensor Biases (SB)

As with any motion sensors, accelerometer models (and instances) differ in precision, resolution, and range, and often suffer from various biases. Initial calibration is often done by the manufacturers using linear models, considering gains and offsets on each of the three accelerometer axes.

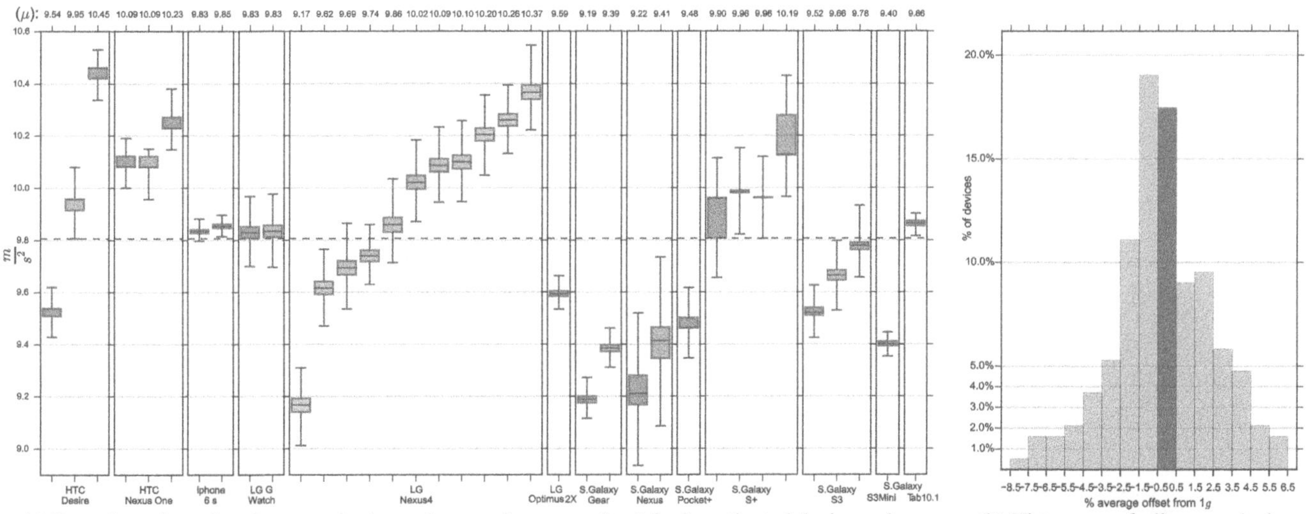

(a) Box plots of acceleration magnitudes and respective means (top) for investigated devices when lying on the back, with the whiskers indicating min/max values.

(b) Histogram of all mean deviations from Zero-g-offset.

Figure 1: Accelerometer biases of mobile devices in six different orientations under static conditions.

	#	Release	Max. sampling rate (Hz)
Smartwatch			
LG G	2	2014	200
Samsung Galaxy Gear	2	2013	100
Smartphone			
Apple iPhone 6	2	2014	100
Samsung Galaxy Pocket+	1	2013	100
Samsung Galaxy S3 mini	1	2012	100
Samsung Galaxy S3 mini	2	2012	100
LG Nexus 4	11	2012	200
Samsung Galaxy S3*	3	2012	150
Samsung Galaxy Nexus	2	2011	125
Samsung Galaxy S+	4	2011	50
LG Optimus 2X	1	2011	100
HTC Desire	3	2010	50
HTC Nexus One	3	2010	25
Tablet			
Samsung Galaxy Tab 10.1	1	2011	100

Table 1: Device models used in our experiments with number of instances used, year of release and accelerometer sampling rate; models selected for HAR investigation marked by an asterisk.

However, small errors may exist including rotation of the accelerometer package relative to the circuit board and misalignment of the circuit board to the final product. Errors can also be introduced during the soldering and final assembly process. Furthermore, if a device experiences shock, e.g., falling on the ground, the sensor can be misaligned causing unwanted biases.

In our first experiment we measure the *Zero-g-Offset* of devices, i.e., the bias observed when a device lies still on a flat surface (quasi static) and is exposed to only gravity, i.e., to an acceleration of $1g \quad 9\ 81m\ s^2$. To measure Zero-g-Offsets, we collect data from all devices listed in Table 1 for a timespan of one minute while all devices lie still on their back side.[1] Subsequently, we repeat this procedure by cycling through all six sides of the devices, thereby generating six minutes of data per device. All the devices have previously been used in various user-centric research projects, and thus, to some extent, have experienced real life usage scenarios covering a wide range of domains and applications. We also collected ground truth using a highly accurate standalone IMU, an xsens MTx, to detect presence of any unwanted external forces. The mean and standard deviation of the IMU measurements were $=9\ 82m\ s^2$ and $\chi{=}0\ 008$, respectively, when averaged over the entire data collection period. Figure 1(a) shows box plots, i.e., five point summaries (showing min, Q_1 (first quartile), median, Q_3 (third quartile) and max), of the gravity (under quasi static conditions) observed on individual devices. The respective mean readings are given at the top of the figure.

Interestingly, Figure 1(a) highlights not only the (often large) biases for different devices, but also the measurement volatility for some of them (see, e.g., the Samsung Galaxy Nexuses), and that biases and volatility may differ even for the devices of the same model (prominently for, e.g., the Galaxy S+ phones). Figure 1(a) is in line with a recent work stating that smartphones are often well distinguishable by their accelerometer fingerprint, which the authors define via its biases and variations [19]. Note, that for all of the six orientations, similar biases and volatilities were observed. To highlight the significance of the Zero-g-Offsets of the devices, Figure 10(b) shows a histogram of the mean deviations of estimated gravities from $1g$ across individual experiments, i.e., for six orientations per device, using a bin width of $0\ 01g$ (1%). Averaged offset biases, i.e., deviations, span from $\quad 8\ 5\%$ to $+7\ 5\%$ of g (i.e., $\quad 0\ 83m\ s^2$ to $0\ 74m\ s^2$). The figure also indicates a near Gaussian distribution of the biases across all devices with a mean of $9\ 76m\ s^2$. The absolute deviation, averaged over all runs was found to be $0\ 35m\ s^2$.

Overall, the biases for some tested devices correspond in magnitude to the acceleration as experienced during a train commute. Thus, for a HAR system these biases may easily lead to confusing activities or occupational states.

3.2 Sampling Rate Heterogeneity (SRH)

The maximum sampling rate supported by a mobile device varies significantly across device models and manufacturers. E.g., for the 14 device models investigated we observed 5 different maximal accelerometer sampling rates(see Table 1). With the heterogeneity among sampling rates for training and test devices come challenges for the HAR system design. One naive solution is to train an activity recognition system individually for each sampling rate to be encountered. Unfortunately, this

[1]Devices were configured to record accelerometer measurements on the local file system with their respective maximum sampling rate.

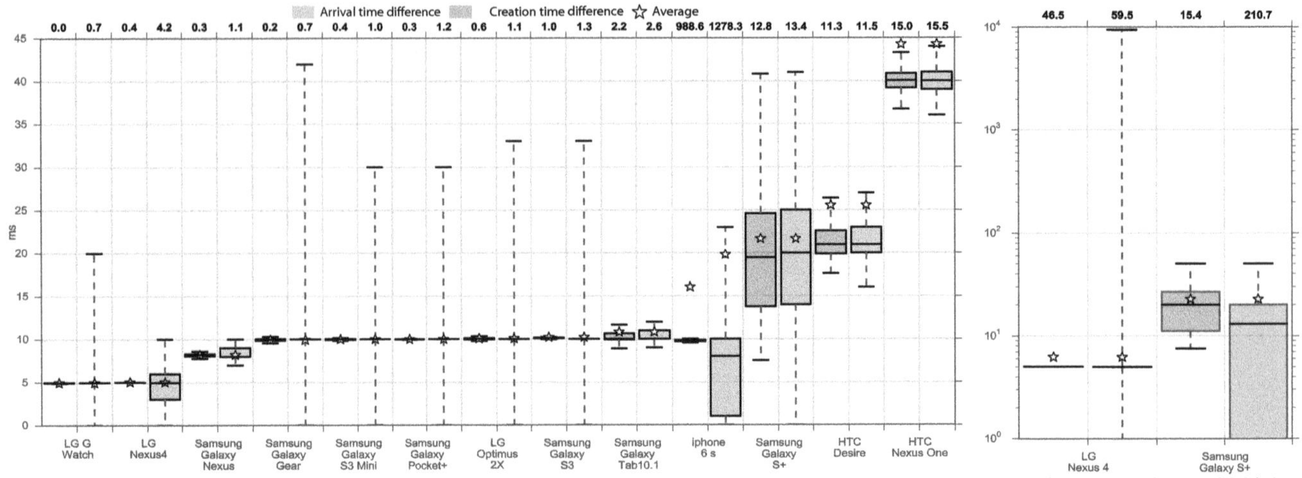

(a) Timespans between consecutive samples as estimated using using creation time (blue) and arrival time (green).

(b) Timespans when under high CPU load (y-axis in log-scale).

Figure 2: Variations in timespans between consecutive samples as estimated using using creation time (blue) and arrival time (green): shown in box plots, with whiskers at 1 5 IQR with outliers removed, and with standard deviation figures (top), for **accelerometer** readings.

solution does not scale because ground truth data collection becomes time consuming and costly [9]. As an alternative, sub- or super-sampling is often used as a pre-processing technique before training or applying a HAR system. We investigate the effects of sub- and super-sampling on HAR in Section 5—since, to the best of our knowledge, a systematic study of these has not been published yet.

3.3 Sampling Rate Instability (SRI)

Contrary to the sampling rate heterogeneity across devices, sampling rate instability is a phenomenon specific to a device. We define sampling rate stability as the regularity of the timespan between successive measurements. On most mobile platforms, there are two common ways to obtain timestamps for sensor measurements: using (i) *creation time*, i.e., the timestamp that the OS or device driver attaches to the sensor measurement and (ii) *arrival time*, i.e., the time when the measurement is received and time stamped by the application code. Ideally, the difference between these two timestamps should be close to zero and constant. This is often not the case for two reasons: Firstly, a small delay exists between the actual recording of a measurement on the chip and it being communicated to various applications. Secondly, the creation timestamp is often not guaranteed to be in the prescribed time format; instead the only guarantee is that the timestamps are monotonic. In this paper we use Network Time Protocol (NTP) to record arrival times, to synchronize with other devices, as well as for activity labeling.

To illustrate the sampling rate instability problem, Figure 2(a) shows for all device models listed in Table 1 tukey box plots for the timespans between consecutive samples—according to creation (blue) and arrival time (green), respectively. Furthermore, the whiskers in the box plots represent here the 1 5 IQR (interquartile range); outliers, i.e., samples outside the 1 5 IQR, are removed for better readability. Stars indicate the average timespan between consecutive samples—which for many devices is set far apart from the median, indicating the there exist not overly many, but long-timespan outliers. For each device model, the timespans aggregated in the box plot are those observed in the Zero-*g*-offset experiment. For most device models, the median timespan is reasonably close to the expected timespan, according to the sampling rates listed in Table 1. Thus, the figure also illustrates the sampling rate heterogeneity (SRH) for the devices listed. Furthermore, it is visible from both the plots, and more so from the standard deviations, that instabilities between measurements are larger for arrival time than for creation time (prominently, e.g., for LG Nexus 4)—and the same holds for the time span ranges.

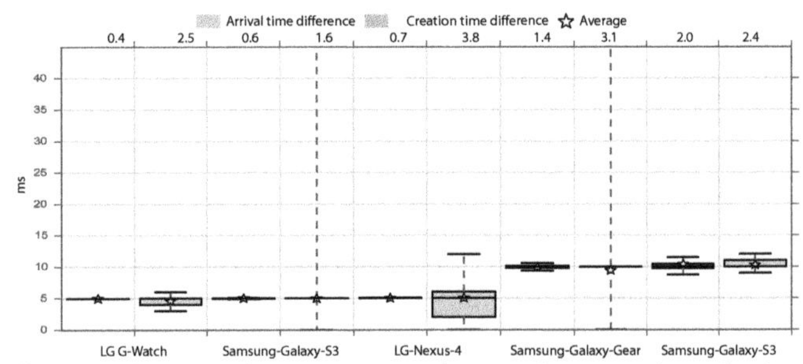

Figure 3: Timespans between consecutive samples—as estimated using using creation time (blue) and arrival time (green); shown in box plots, with whiskers at 1 5 IQR, with outliers removed, and with standard deviation figures (top), for **gyroscope** readings.

The phenomena generalize beyond accelerometer readings. For example, Figure 3 shows results for gyroscope in place of accelerometer readings. The general picture is the same as in Figure 2(a), and also the characteristics for individual devices are similar as well—although the Samsung Galaxy Gear and S3 devices seemingly exhibit even more and larger arrival time outliers, stemming again from some measurements being received in 'bursts'.

Another interesting anomaly is revealed for the iPhone accelerometer data: As the operating systems occasionally decides to suspend the sensing app used (seemingly, often after the phone has been still for several minutes), few very long timespans are introduced, which lead to very high standard deviations. As it turned out, this feature of iOS made it also hard to compare fairly the iPhones' HAR performance with other device models, and we thus decided to not use the data collected with iPhones in the analysis of the HAR experiments to be presented.

Multitasking Effects (ME)

Modern smartphones support running a large number of applications each of which may cause high CPU loads for extended periods of time. The OS often prioritizes among various running tasks and in doing so may affect the sensor sampling of one or several HAR applications

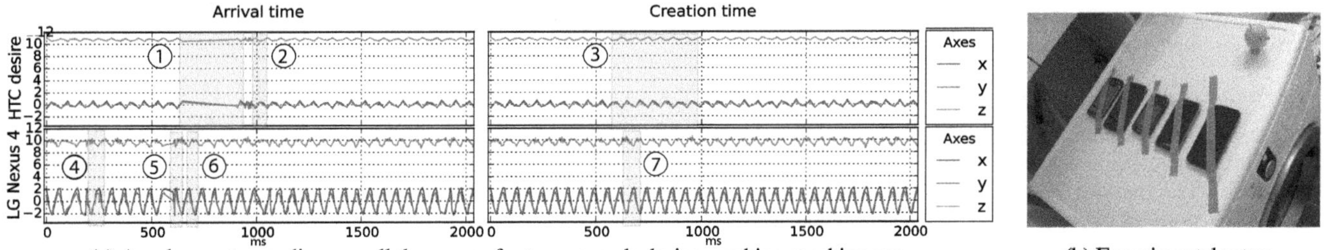

(a) Accelerometer readings on all three axes for two seconds during washing machine run. (b) Experimental setup.

Figure 4: Effects of heterogeneities on accelerometer readings from phones lying on a running washing machine.

running on the device. To study the multitasking effects on sensor sampling we run a benchmarking application, inducing high loads, on four phones (two instances each of LG Nexus 4 and Samsung Galaxy S Plus) for 4 minutes, while they are configured to sample accelerometer readings at the device's maximum rate. Figure 2(b) shows box plots of the timespans between measurements recorded on the devices (creation and arrival time) under such heavy CPU load. Note that the figure's y-axis yields a logarithmic scale to accommodate the large outliers. The median timespan rises from 5 $2ms$ to 9 $2ms$, almost twice the intended timespan, c.f. Figure 2(a), and that the longest timespans between measurements experienced are over $1s$. As also in the experiment with no additional loads, the range of timespan is lower for creation time than for arrival time for both the device models. Interestingly, for Samsung Galaxy S Plus phones the average timespan between measurements for arrival time (33 $2ms$) is almost twice that for creation time (17 $7ms$). Thus, our experiments indicate that high CPU load impact actual sampling rates and instability very differently across devices models even if they run the same OS version and the same concurrent programs.

3.4 Heterogeneity Effects in Non-static Scenarios

Mostly, to illustrate the impacts of heterogeneities more visually and intuitively, we conducted another experiment, in a dynamic scenario yielding regular, i.e., stable and periodic movement. To this end, we taped several devices on top of a washing machine and recorded data during a regular washing program, see Figure 4(b). Figure 4(a) shows examples of the resulting accelerometer measurements during a two second exampled period. These measurements are given with timestamps according to their arrival time (left) and their creation time (right), respectively. Overall, the periodicity of the accelerometer measurements is clearly visible. However, the measurements show various anomalies, which are related to the heterogeneities described above. For both example devices measurement outages according to their arrival time are observed as measurements are delivered in bulks, see, e.g., the readings highlighted in green and marked (1), (2), (5) and (6). Whereas, the creation timestamps reveal that the measurements were instead taking almost equidistantly in time, e.g., compare (3) to (1) and (2). However, they may not always be collected equidistantly: (7) shows some variations in timespan between samples, smaller though than indicated by arrival time, at (5) and (6). Overall, the plots clearly illustrate some of the pitfalls in mobile sensing, and these may be harmful for HAR, especially when the use case renders it crucial to sensitively recognize and timestamp, e.g., short events, and/or starts or stops of, or breaks during activities.

4. IMPACTS OF HETEROGENEITIES ON HAR

In the following, we analyze the effect of various sensing heterogeneities, as detailed and investigated in Section 3, on the performances of HAR systems, using results from a case study.

4.1 HAR Case Study

We follow Bulling et al.'s exposition of HAR systems using supervised learning approach, which is composed of a sequence of signal processing and machine learning techniques, coined *activity recognition chain* (ARC) [15]. A typical ARC for HAR is composed of five stages: (i) *data collection*, (ii) *pre-processing*, (iii) *segmentation*, (iv) *feature extraction* and (v) *classification*. Although, accelerometer heterogeneities impact throughout the entire stages of an ARC, their effect is significant on the feature extraction stage. Accordingly, we study the impact of heterogeneities on three popular feature types in HAR research: (i) *time-domain*, (ii) *frequency-domain* features [20], and (iii) features extracted from *empirical cumulative distribution functions* (ECDF) [23].

Data Collection

In our case study, we consider the HAR task of detecting, and distinguishing among, six different user activities: 'Biking', 'Sitting', 'Standing', 'Walking', 'Stair Up' and 'Stair down'. Although simple, the selected activity classes (or a subset of them) have been investigated prominently in a large number of HAR publications [10, 11, 14, 27, 29, 41, 47]. We consider example data[2] gathered by nine users (age range 25 30 years). All users followed a scripted set of activities while carrying eight smartphones (2 instances of LG Nexus 4, Samsung Galaxy S+ and Samsung Galaxy S3 and S3 mini) and four smart watches (2 instances of LG G and Samsung Galaxy Gear). All eight smartphones were kept in a tight pouch and carried by the users around their waist, whereas two smart watches were worn on each arm. Each participant conducted five minutes of each activity, which ensured a near equal data distribution among activity classes (for each user and device).

Based on the results presented in the previous section, eight phones from two different manufacturers were selected to investigate diverse sensing scenarios. These smartphone models yielded different maximum sampling frequencies: 200 Hz for LG Nexus 4, 150 Hz for the Samsung Galaxy S3, 100 Hz for Samsung Galaxy S3 mini and 50 Hz for Samsung Galaxy S plus, approximately. The smart watches also varied in the supported maximum sampling rate, e.g., 200 Hz for LG G and 100 Hz for Samsung Galaxy Gear (see Figure 2(a)). Furthermore, the devices exhibit different accelerometer biases and gains.

To further minimize external factors affecting heterogeneities in accelerometer sensing, the data collection for the case study was carried out while keeping the CPU load of all phones minimal, i.e., only running the data collection application. Furthermore, we fixed also for each activity two environments and routes where the activity was to be executed. We then divided the user pool into two groups, each of which used the exact same environment and routes for their activities, respectively.

We limited our experiments to not consider explicitly differences in on-body placements and instead we will discuss these in Section 6. Consequently, we will compare data only among devices with simi-

[2] The data set has been made publicly available at **http://tinyurl.com/pxele7w**

lar on-body placements; in particular, we will analyze HAR results separately for smartphones and for smartwatches, respectively.

Pre-processing and Segmentation

For the scope of the evaluation of the effect of sensing heterogeneity on HAR in this section, we do not perform any preprocessing steps. We will though discuss pre-processing techniques for mitigation purposes in Section 5. Whenever timestamps are used in computations on the sensor measurements, e.g., frame extractions at the later stages of the ARC, we use creation time. In line with the standard approaches [9, 40], we employ a sliding window approach that overcomes the need for explicit semantic segmentations, which is a non-trivial task. In this work, we select a fixed window length of 2 seconds, with 50% overlap between two successive windows. Due to presence of heterogeneity in sensing, our measurement windows contain a variable number of measurements.

Feature Extraction

For evaluating the sensing heterogeneities on HAR for different features, we chose popular features and group them into several types. For the selection of popular time-domain and frequency domain features, we relied on the extensive survey on HAR techniques by Figo *et al.* [20].[3] These features are based on expert's knowledge, specific to the activity recognition domain, and have been used in a number of HAR systems. All the time-domain features, except the correlation-based features, are computed using motion sensor measurements from each axis x, y, z, and from the resulting reading magnitude, i.e., $\sqrt{x^2+y^2+z^2}$. The correlation features are computed by considering all possible pairwise combinations among the three axes.

The frequency features used in our experiments include the normalized spectral coefficients in the range from 0 to 20 Hz (or the maximum frequency available in the signal), with bin width of 0.5 Hz (i.e., 40 features in total), the entropy of the coefficients, the dominating frequency and its normalized magnitude, the normalized sum of the coefficients, and the discrete component.

ECDF features, on the other hand, do not depend on domain knowledge and are computed following the work of Hammerla et al. [23]. However, the ECDF features require setting a parameter value, namely the number of bins used in the inverse function computation. In our experiments we use 30 bins, which was previously shown to perform well in real world activity recognition tasks [23].

Furthermore we investigate the use of Principal Component Analysis (PCA). PCA is a popular dimensionality reduction technique within the field of machine learning and statistics [12]. PCA archives data compression by projecting data onto a linear orthogonal subspace such that the variance in the projected data is maximized. Contrary to the feature-engineering approaches popular within the HAR research, PCA can be used to learn features from sensor measurements in an unsupervised manner [9, 39].

Classification and Performance Metric

To evaluate the impact of heterogeneity on HAR performances we consider four popular classifiers used in activity recognition research, namely nearest neighbor classifier with $k = 5$, $C4.5$ decision tree, support vector machines (SVM) with linear kernels, and random forest classifier. We adopt the F_1-score, which is the harmonic mean of precision and recall, as our primary evaluation metric:

$$F_1\text{-score} = \frac{2 \cdot \text{precision} \cdot \text{recall}}{\text{precision} + \text{recall}}$$

[3]More specifically, we used all time- and frequency domain features, as listed in Table 2 and 3 of [20], respectively, with the exception of the cross-time/frequency-domain Wavelet feature.

Moreover, in line with standard practices in HAR research [9, 43], we report the weighted average of the individual F_1-scores of all classes, which is more resilient to class imbalances in the test dataset, i.e.:

$$\text{Avg. } F_1\text{-score} = \frac{\sum_{i=1}^{c} w_i \cdot F_1^i\text{-score}}{\sum_{i=1}^{c} w_i}$$

where, F_1^i-score is the F_1-score of the ith class and w_i is the number of samples of class i in the test dataset. Lastly, we perform statistical testing to measure variations in recognition performances using the McNemar χ^2-tests with Yates' correction [35].

4.2 HAR Performance Evaluation

To assess impacts of accelerometer heterogeneities on HAR, we perform a number of evaluations in different modes. These modes differ in how training vs. test are generated and separated from each other.

We present recognition performance in terms of F_1-scores in a sequence of figures, starting with Figure 5. Figure 5 shows in different colors the F_1-scores obtained by eight different training/test data definitions, explained further below, using smartphone data only. In particular, we will use the figure to quantify how drastically performance is reduced when the training was agnostic of the specific devices used in the test data. Results are shown in three plots, in each of which is used just one of the three main feature types considered, namely ECDF, frequency-, and time-domain features, respectively. In each of three plots, results are given individually for applying one of four learner types considered, namely C4.5 decision tree, linear support vector machines, K-nearest neighbor, and random forest ensemble learner.

Comparing evaluation modes: The first two training vs. test data generation are very traditional within machine learning and activity recognition, respectively:

Random 10-fold stratified cross validation (CV) randomly assigns one out of 10 folds to each data item. In each of the 10 folds over which performance is averaged afterwards, test data is recruited as the data items labeled with just one number out of 1 to 10. Within activity recognition (and generally with high-frequent time series data input) this evaluation usually leads to overfitting, and thus to overly optimistic recognition performance estimates: for time series, a random labeling implies that for each test data item there will very likely be several training data items which are very close by temporally—and thus very similar, as they sample almost the exact same situation as the test data item. Thus, as expected, the scores for 10-fold CV are the best for each feature type and learner combination considered.

Leave-one-user-out cross validation mode tests in each fold with data from one user, and trains with data from all others; scores are averaged over folds, i.e., test users. This mode provides realistic performance, and results lower than for 10-fold CV are expected, as body, movement, and general execution of the scripted activities will differ among users.

The following four evaluation modes assess the impact of heterogeneities as they are expected in 'in the wild' scenarios: In the *leave-one-model-out cross validation* training data is used from all considered phone models, but one, saved for test data and thus yet unknown to the HAR system. The *one-model* evaluation mode resembles training with only one phone model (as done in many HAR publications)—but testing is done with all the variety of the other considered phone types. As such, this mode resembles a typical low-effort real-world deployment scenario. Cross validation then averages over the training phone models selected. In a variant of this mode, in the *one-model-leave-one-user-out* mode, additionally one user's data is used for testing, but not for training. Cross-

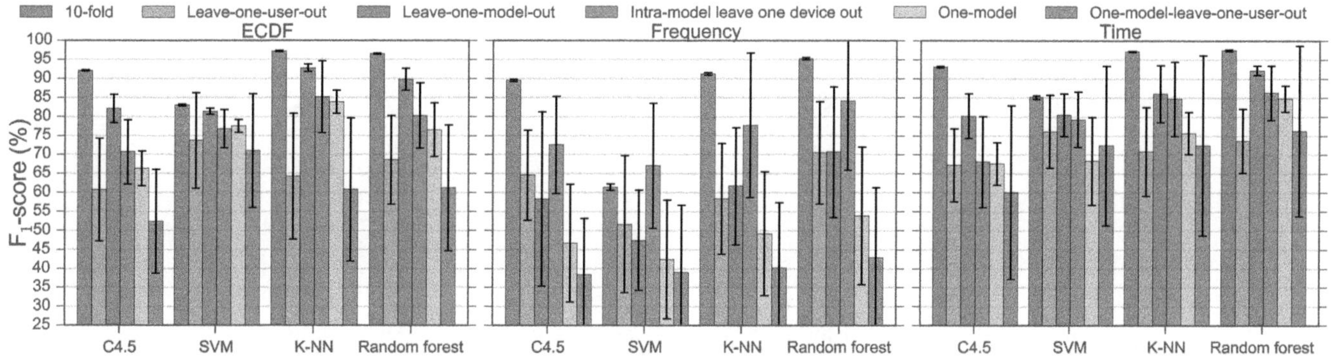

Figure 5: Comparing activity recognition performances on **smartphones** across three feature types (ECDF, Frequency and Time domain), across four classifiers, and across various cross-validation evaluation modes. The error bars represent the standard deviations across folds.

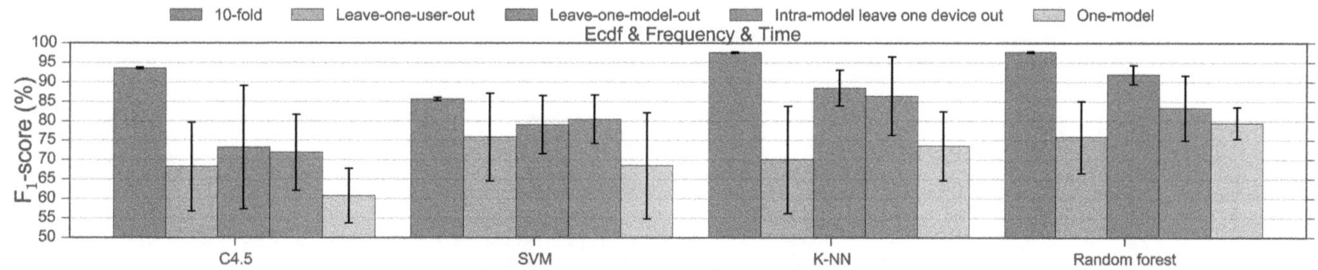

Figure 6: Comparing activity recognition performances on **smartphones** using three feature types (ECDF, Frequency and Time domain) **combined**, across four learner types, and across various cross-validation evaluation modes. The error bars represent the standard deviations across folds.

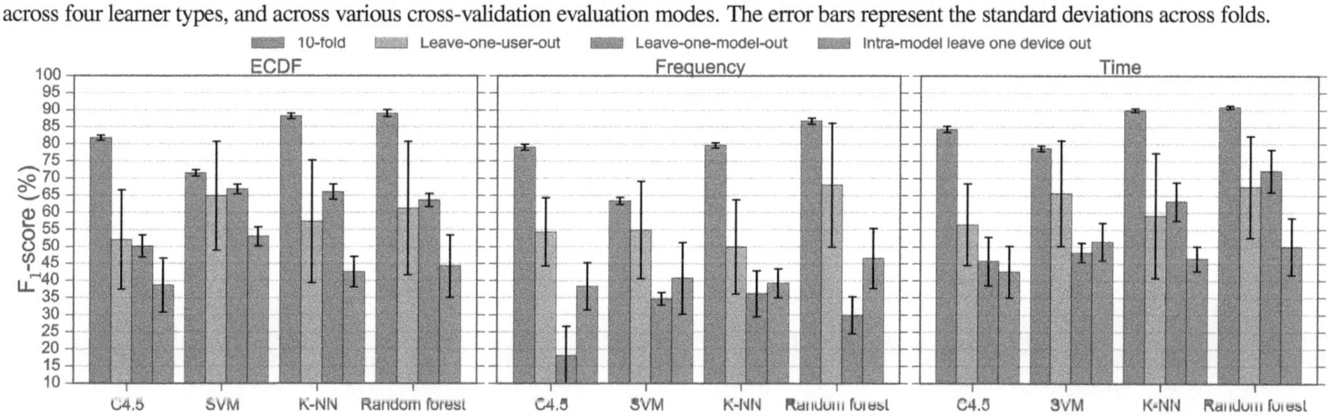

Figure 7: Comparing activity recognition performances on **smartwatches** across three feature types (ECDF, Frequency and Time domain), across four classifiers, and across various cross-validation evaluation modes. The error bars represent the standard deviations across folds.

validation than occurs by cycling through training phone model and test user. From the latter results one can assess the breakdown in F_1-score when training only with one device (56.4%, averaged over all learner and feature types) in comparison to the leave-one-use-out mode (66.7%).

Conversely, in *intra-model-leave-one-device-out cross validation* mode the test model is known to HAR system (and has been trained for specifically) but the particular test phone instance of the model is yet unknown. Despite that, classification with only the model's data yields significantly higher F_1-scores (on average: 77.7%) than for the *one-model* mode. Generally, the comparison of 'intra-model' scores over 'one-model' scores provides an estimate of the benefits of training classifiers specifically for individual phone models, i.e., up to 30 percentage points for some learner and feature types combinations. Such training of a classifier for each phone model individually is infeasible for most app deployment scenarios, and thus in Section 5 we will propose a more feasible training scheme requiring less training devices—via clustering of devices yielding similar characteristics.

Comparing features and learner types: We compare now the performances shown in Figure 5 across the three considered feature types. Complementing, in Figure 6 shows the performance when all three types are used together. From the figures, the combination yields higher scores (for all evaluation modes) than when using any of the three types alone. Using the features types alone, all offer similar scores when evaluated using the traditional *10-fold* or *leave-one-user-out* evaluation—but the frequency-domain features are impacted by far the most by the heterogeneities. Next, for the time features we see that the *leave-one-user-out* mode yields the lowest results compared to other modes. Furthermore, for the tree based learners (random forest and C4.5), the *leave-one-model-out* validations yield higher scores than the intra-model based mode. Thus, the time features are not impacted as much by the sensor heterogeneities as by the variance in the activities across users. Whereas, in contrast to the frequency domain features, sampling rate variability has less of an impact compared to the sensor biases. For the SVM and k-nn the heterogeneities seem to impact equally on the HAR system's score, as the results are quite similar for all but the *10-fold* and *leave-one-user-out* cross validation.

The effect of learner choice is more significant in the presence of heterogeneities. Specifically, ensemble learners do well, likely due to

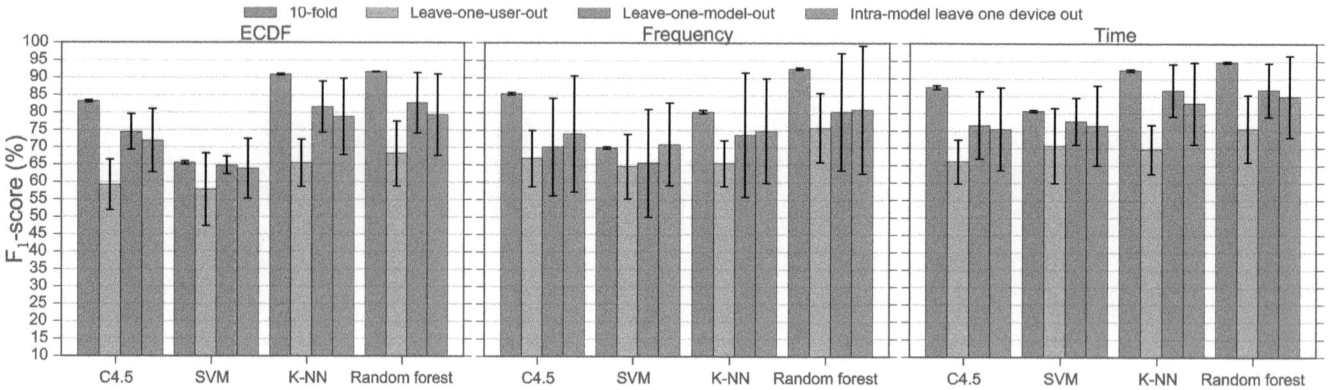

Figure 8: Comparing activity recognition performances on **smartphones** across three feature types (ECDF, Frequency and Time domain), across four classifiers, and across various cross-validation evaluation modes, when using **gyroscope** in place of accelerometer sensor data. The error bars represent the standard deviations across folds.

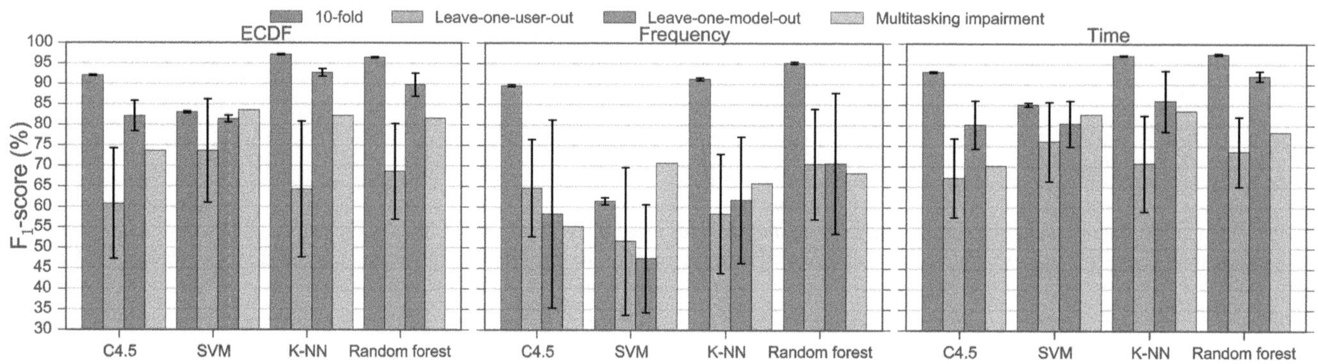

Figure 9: Comparing activity recognition performances on **smartphones** across three feature types (ECDF, Frequency and Time domain), across four classifiers, using the 10-fold, leave-one-user-out,leave-one-model-out and **multitasking-impairment** cross validations. The error bars represent the standard deviations across folds.

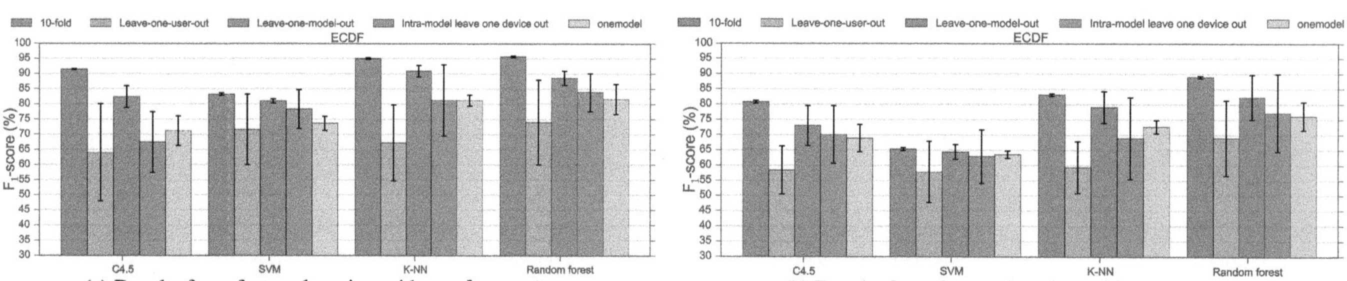

(a) Results from feature learning with **accelerometers**

(b) Results from feature learning with **gyroscopes**

Figure 10: Comparing activity recognition performances on **smartphones** across three feature types (ECDF, Frequency and Time domain), across four classifiers, and across various cross-validation evaluation modes, when using **PCA feature-learning**. The error bars represent the standard deviations across folds.

their ability to abstract from (and not overfit to) characteristics particular to the used devices. For the machine-generated ECDF features the picture is different though: performance across learners is more similar, and the k-nn learner outperforms the random forest. In addition, we see for the ECDF and Time domain features that both the leave-one-user-and-model-out yields lower scores than the leave-one-user-out across all learners, whereas for the frequency features it is all learners except the k-nn. This shows that the combined effect of user variance and the sensor heterogeneity impacts the learners more than the effects individually.

Comparing smartphones and smartwatches: As the sensor orientation, position, and dynamics of human arm movements are significantly different between our smartphone and smartwatch data, we repeated the evaluations discussed above for smartwatches in place of smartphones, see Figure 7: compared to the phones' scores, the relative smartwatch HAR scores across learner and feature types are generally impacted in a similar manner; only the absolute impairment levels are somewhat worse than for the phones. The latter observation may though be foremost due to the higher complexity in experienced user motion (which increases the challenge to tell apart the scripted activity types).

Comparing accelerometer vs. gyroscope data: As an indication of the generalizability of the results to other sensing setups, we used the gyroscope data in place of the accelerometer data, see Figure 8: The resulting relative performance across evaluation mode, feature, and learner types is very similar to that of accelerometer data. In absolute performance, the accelerometer scores are slightly higher (and, not shown, slightly lower than for fusing accelerometer and gyroscope data) which fits the intuition that the accelerometer yields somewhat higher amounts of motion clues and information, especially since the features used, while well applicable to gyroscope data, were designed for accelerometer data.

Comparing single- vs. multitasking: We also evaluated the impairments on HAR caused by multitasking: To this end, we trained using single-tasking data, and tested using multitasking-impaired data, see

Figure 9. The impairments are most severe for frequency features—due the unstable sampling frequencies during heavy multitasking.

Comparing with PCA-based feature learning Finally, we consider PCA based feature learning by constructing a feature space retaining 95% of the energy in the data. The results of the PCA experiments are given in Figure 10. PCA suffers from the blind normalization problem [23, 39] and the ECDF feature learning help to overcome it—thus, in Figure 10 these features show the best performance: Especially for easily overfitting learners, such as the C4.5, the results for, e.g., the one-model mode are improved over those without PCA, c.f. Figure 5. For other feature types, PCA application proves harmful, lowering the performance results. Additionally, the dimensionality reduction achieved by PCA helps to run the inference task faster, which helps to improve the overall energy consumption to a low level on resource constraint devices.

Summary of results: The evaluations show that heterogeneities can cause severe performance breakdowns in real-world scenarios, especially when compared to standard evaluation modes, such as the overly optimistic *10-fold* cross-validation, yielding an average F_1-score of 91 0%, or even the more realistic *leave-one-user-out* cross-validation, yielding 66.7%, especially if training is undertaken with only one device model (yielding 56 4% when additionally leaving one-user-out in training). When instead training with diverse (here: all but one investigated model), performances are much improved, and impairments for not training with the one test model are lower than for not training with the test user. Overall, breakdowns are most significant i) for frequency-domain features–and especially when the phone is multitasking heavily, c.f. Figure 9, and ii) when learners are used that are prone to overfitting, such as the C4.5 tree learner. In such learning configurations, the use of PCA may improve performance, see Figure 10. Generally, claims made in this summary still apply when using smartwatches instead of -phones, see Figure 7, and when using gyroscope instead of accelerometer data, see Figure 8.

5. METHODS FOR MITIGATION OF HETEROGENEITY EFFECTS

In the following, we investigate several candidate techniques for mitigating the impairments caused by heterogeneities, as described in the previous section. These candidate techniques pervade several stages of the activity recognition chain (ARC). As the two primary mitigation approaches, we will evaluate first a clustering of devices for similar devices, resulting in a classifier for each identified cluster. Secondly, we investigate the re-sampling of the sensor data from all devices to a common identical sampling rate, resulting also in equidistantly spaced samples for all devices after the preprocessing step. Finally, we also analyze in more detail the respective performance, of various combinations of mitigation techniques with various feature and leaner types, partially in order to arrive at favorable combinations to recommend.

5.1 Sensor Heterogeneity Based Clustering

The comparison of the recognition performance in Figure 5 of *one-model* vs. *intra-model-leave-one-device-out* mode reveals the advantage of training classifiers for similar devices—here: for devices of the same model. However, training for each device model individually comes with great costs and is thus not a practical deployable solution due to the vast amount of different device models. Furthermore, as presented in Section 4.3, also the sensor bias may vary greatly for devices of the same model, and such biases also impact the HAR system's performance—which is not taken into account with device model-based learners. We thus explore a less costly approach to account for diverse devices, based on clustering devices w.r.t. their respective heterogeneities: We train for each identified cluster a targeted classifier, in order to account account

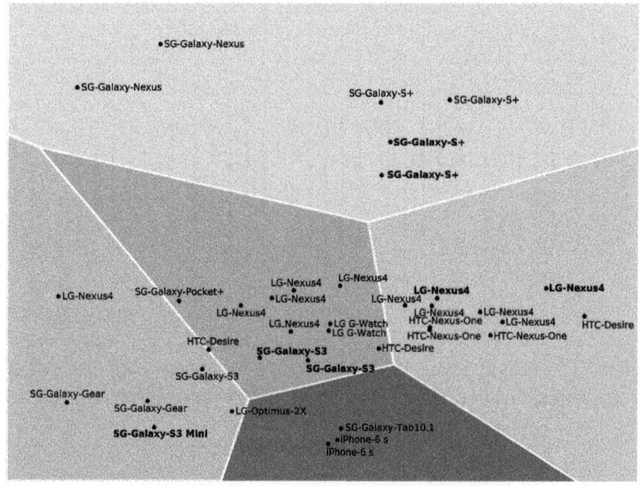

Figure 11: Device instances, clustered by features representing characteristic device heterogeneities. Here shown for the PCA-determined two most significant features, namely sensor bias and sampling frequency stability while devices are lying still on their back. Bold labels mark devices used later for the HAR impact investigation, and white crosses mark cluster centroids.

for devices' individual bias characteristics as well as for model characteristics such as default sampling rate. To this end, we chose an affinity propagation clustering algorithm [21]. Figure 11 visualizes the resulting clusters and the clustered devices in the feature space spanned by the following two features: median sensor bias, and standard deviation of sampling frequency. The respective feature data is taken from the static experiment described in Section 3. In Figure 12 we present results for employing clustering of devices using the two features as above as well as the standard deviation of the sensor bias and of the median sampling frequency. For the 36 devices, of in total 13 different models, the clustering algorithm chosen generated 5 distinct clusters. The cluster-based approach is evaluated in various *intra-cluster*-based modes in Figure 12—which use classifiers built specifically from the training data of a test device's device cluster. Visibly, modes such as *intra-cluster-leave-one-user-out* show significantly higher F_1-scores than for training with only one device model, c.f. Figure 5. Secondly, performance is also higher than when training with data from all devices (green), at 69.1% vs. 66.7%.[4] Furthermore, the *intra-cluster-leave-one-user-and-device-out* results indicate that training classifiers for whole device clusters is as accurate as the for real-world deployments much more laborious and thus less realistic alternative of training classifiers for each individual phone model: When comparing to the *intra-model-leave-one-user-and-device-out* modes, the F_1-score averaged over all feature and learner types is even higher, at 64.2% vs. 61.7%.[5]

5.2 Interpolation

In the following, we investigate interpolation as a means to mitigate the heterogeneities in sampling rates across device models, and to improve the performances shown in Figures 5 and following. Specifically, we interpolate via down- or up-sampling of input sensor data to a common target rate of choice for all devices, varying the interpolation methods and target rates. Unifying to a common target rate, as a pre-processing step within ARC for HAR, ensures that i) each time window of data fed

[4] When excluding from the training the data from the test device's cluster (red), performance drops vary and are especially steep for frequency features and for learners prone to overfitting such as C4.5.

[5] Note though, that the respective results suffer from the limits of our data collection: for two out of the three clusters, we can train only with one phone, and thus the learning is prone to overfitting.

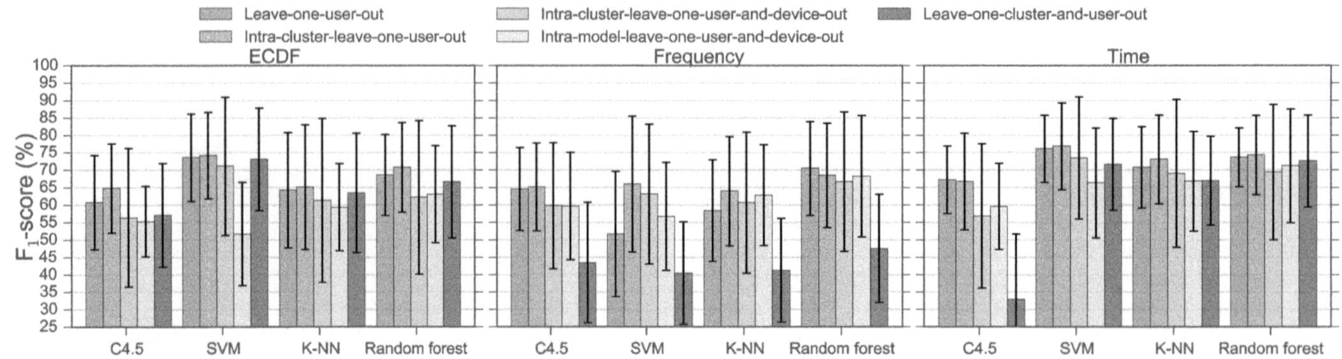

Figure 12: Activity recognition performance using *leave-one-user-out* as a baseline and variants thereof where classifying a test instance uses a classifier trained specifically for the cluster (resp. the model) a respective test device belongs to. The error bars represent the standard deviations across folds.

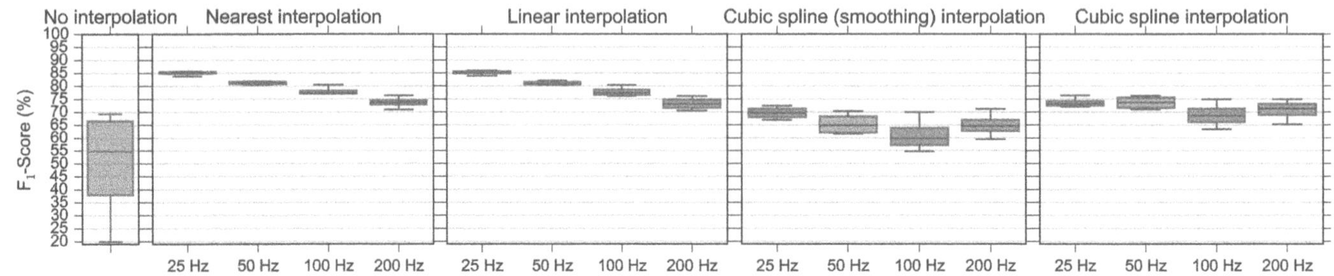

Figure 13: Activity recognition performance using the solely frequency domain features and using the SVM learner; for various interpolation methods and target rates, and using the *leave-one-model-out* cross validation.

into the ARC segment step contains the same number of (interpolated) samples, and ii) that all samples in each data window are equidistantly separated in time.

Interpolation techniques: The following four interpolation schemes were used as part of the preprocessing stage:

Nearest: The interpolation value at time t is set to be the value of the one of the input samples that is closest in time to t.

Linear interpolator: The value at time t is the piecewise-linear interpolation, i.e. the linear interpolation between the input samples adjacent to t in the sequence of input sample timestamps.

Cubic Splines: uses cubic splines, i.e., piecewise polynomial interpolation of degree 3 with continuous first and second derivative.

Smoothed cubic splines: Splines as above but subject to a positive smoothing factor s, which reduces the number of interpolated input samples in favor of fulfilling a smoothness condition: $\,_{i=1}^{m}(y[i]$ $spl(x[i]))^2 \quad s$, where m is the number of input samples considered, and s is 0 2 m.

The target sample rates which have been evaluated in this case study were the following: 25, 50, 100, and 200 Hz. In Figure 13 we present results for all combinations of these interpolation methods and target sampling rates. The results were obtained using *leave-one-model-out* cross validation and using learner and feature type pairing which was most impaired by sampling rate heterogeneities and instabilities, c.f. Figure 5, namely frequency features and SVM. Clearly, generally interpolation can improve the HAR accuracy: Highest gains (for median accuracy: from 55% to ca. 86%) are achieved for low target rates, and for nearest and linear interpolation. Interestingly, for more complex interpolation methods (i.e. for cubic but also other ones) less gains (or, for less impaired feature/learner combinations, even negative gains) result, and also no clear trend favoring lower target rates can be seen. Both is likely explained by that complex interpolations may introduce noise and artifacts in the data—which impedes learners, as they may learn from artificially introduced characteristics instead of from those present in the actual sensor data. This factor likely also explains why down-sampling yields higher gains than up-sampling: Also up-sampling is prone to introduce artifacts in the data, while down-sampling is likely to just preserve the real data's characteristics.

This holds at least for most HAR-typical activity types—as those chosen for our experiments—because their characteristics are rather low-frequent; thus, these characteristics are likely to preserved when down-sampling to 25 Hz. Note though that this may not hold for more exotic HAR tasks and strategies, e.g. for distinguishing (riding in) fossil-fueled from electric vehicles by way of recognizing the characteristic engine vibrations in the former cars.

Impact on Sampling Frequency Heterogeneities

The results presented in Section4 revealed that the differences in sampling frequencies across device models impairs HAR performance, and we now evaluated to which extent these impairments can be mitigated via interpolation. Applying down-sampling to 25Hz in pre-processing, yields results shown in 14(b), here for *leave-one-model-out* cross validations, as used also in Figure 13. In the figure, (**), (*) indicate when improvements were statistically significant at levels $p < 0\ 01$ and $p < 0\ 05$, respectively. Conversely, red asterisks are shown instead, if interpolation significantly impairs the performance.

Overall, the impact of the interpolation shows mixed results across learners, feature types and to some extent interpolation methods. Furthermore, in line with Figure 13, linear and nearest interpolation perform better than the spline interpolation variants.

For **frequency features**, interpolation significantly ($p < 0\ 001$) increased the original performance (labeled 'No interpolation') across all learners and interpolation methods—up to more than 30 percentage points in case of using the SVM learner. Interpolation is though far less helpful for other feature types: For **time domain features** nearest and linear interpolation still improve performance, but spline interpolation impairs it. For **ECDF features**, interpolation has little to no positive effect and in most cases will impair the performance.

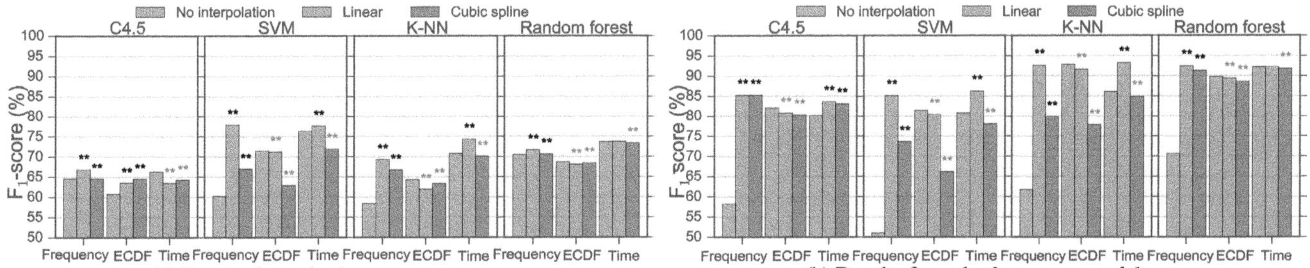

(a) Results from the *leave-one-user-out* (b) Results from the *leave-one-model-out*

Figure 14: Activity recognition performance across all devices using *leave-one-user-out* and *leave-one-model-out* cross validations. (**),(*), for the following significance levels $p < 0~01$, $p < 0~05$ comparing interpolated with 25 Hz sampling frequency and non-interpolated data.

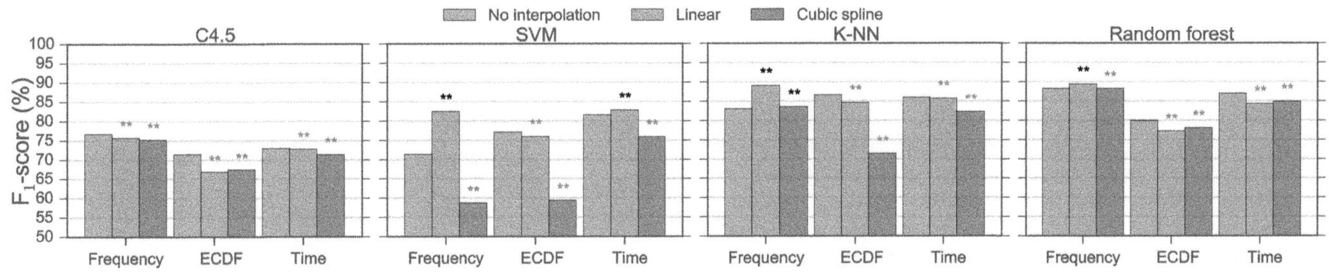

Figure 15: Activity recognition performance using *Intra-cluster-leave-one-device-out* evaluating learners trained with clusters of similar devices. (**),(*), for the following significance levels $p < 0~01$, $p < 0~05$ comparing interpolated with 25 Hz sampling frequency and non-interpolated data.

For comparison, Figure 14(a) evaluates the same interpolation options as shown in Figure 14(b) but for the *leave-one-user-out* evaluation mode. Here, since training has seen the devices used in testing, unlike in Figure 14(b), interpolation has lost most of its positive effects, even when applied for frequency features. Note that the interpolation methods nearest (resp. smoothed cubic splines) are not shown in the figure, but perform very similar to linear (resp. cubic spline) interpolation.

5.3 Combining Interpolation and Clustering

We have also studied the impact of interpolating when combined with clustering devices with similar heterogeneities. These results are reported in Figure 15, and—similar to Figure 14(a)—only in a few instances the interpolation actually improves the HAR performance, e.g., for frequency features in SVM, K-NN and random forest ($p < 0~001$). This poor performance is likely due to that the clusters take into account the sampling frequencies and respective instabilities, and thus devices with similar frequencies and instabilities are in the same cluster and the potential benefits from employing sample rate conversion via interpolation is lowered.

Overall, the results in Figure 14 and 15 indicate that interpolation, and specifically down-sampling, is most useful in case of heterogeneous sampling frequencies w.r.t. training vs. test data. Furthermore, results indicate that interpolation can mitigate the impairments caused by differing sampling frequencies, but not the issues of sampling instabilities. Further evidence of the latter is given by running training with multi-tasking impaired devices, c.f. Section 3: Here, the effects of interpolation on performance are not better (and largely even worse) then when training with non-impaired devices, indicating that instabilities are not mitigated by interpolation.

Summary of results: The evaluations in this section provide evidence that training classifiers specifically for clusters of devices with similar characteristics increases HAR performance cost-effectively. Furthermore, interpolation, specifically down-sampling, can improve HAR performance—specifically when frequency features are used, and when training and test devices differ in sampling frequency. If the latter is already mitigated, e.g., by a clustering based approach, interpolation is only recommendable for pre-processing for frequency-domain features, but should rather not be employed for time-domain or ECDF features.

6. DISCUSSION

In this section we discuss the generalizability of the presented results across new and next-generation classes of devices, as well as further motion and other sensors in place of or additional to accelerometer and gyroscope. Finally, we also discuss assumptions and limitations of the evaluation presented here.

Device Types and Evolution

A natural question to ask is whether the various heterogeneities across devices diminish as the user device technology evolves. Indeed, the results presented here seem to indicate a trend: Newer and more expensive models are likely to yield lower biases; in regards to sensor biases, this trend may though also be caused by the longer wear and tear that the tested instances of older model were exposed to compared to devices of newer models.

An initial intuition of ours that was clearly not backed by the results was that smartwatches, being of smaller form factor and with more limited resources than smartphones, would exhibit far larger sensor biases and sampling instabilities, especially under high CPU load. On the other hand, smaller devices are expected to be more single-purpose-build and less required to fulfill a wide range of tasks. Thus, less multitasking impairments may be expected in real-world use. While biases and instabilities were not stronger, in the actual activity recognition performance smartwatches though showed lower performance than the selected smartphones, c.f. Figure 5 and 7. The results are not conclusive though, in regards to whether that may be attributed to harmful heterogeneities or rather to the difference in learning settings, as the on-body placement is vastly different from the task to learn from the smartphones' data, which were residing in a hip-mounted pouch.

A natural extension of the study is to extend the type of investigated user devices further, beyond tablets, smartphones and -watches and to other, popular or emerging mobile devices, specifically wearables, such as smart earphones and wristbands. Such investigation may be fruitful, as our results on the hypothesis that smaller, less powerful devices suffer more from heterogeneity or its impacts on HAR performance were inconclusive when comparing smartphones with -watches, see above.

A similar extension is to obtain and compare with more results from devices running other OS. While we provide some results for iOS devices, the automatic-sleep phenomena, c.f. Section 3, hindered a fair comparison with other devices in the HAR evaluations. We undertook a preliminary investigation, collecting data from Android but also some iPhones of some 50 CS students in a setup as described in Section 3. The results showed that the frequency irregularities are of similar magnitude than for the average over the investigated Android phones.. Similarly, also the quality of and biases within the acceleration measurement sets themselves were comparable to those stated in Section 3, with deviation from 1G of up to a $\pm 2.5\%$, and an average standard deviation of 0.039G.

Feature types

In this paper we have shown that the performance of three feature types, i.e., time-domain, frequency-domain and ECDF features, have greatly varying performances in HAR in the presence of sensor heterogeneities. Furthermore, the frequency features, without preprocessing, have been shown to be most vulnerable in heterogeneous settings. Thus, based on this case study, especially ECDF but also time features are strongly recommended for HAR when sensor heterogeneities are present.

However, other domains of HAR uses domain specific knowledge to look for specific frequencies, e.g., for detecting freezing of gait in patients with Parkinson's disease [34]. Thus, interchanging features might not be an applicable strategy in all use cases, as it was in our case study. For these instances, based on our case study we have shown that preprocessing the signal with simple interpolation methods will significantly increase the performance, when sensor heterogeneities are present.

Sensor Types

Another extension of the study presented here is to consider popular in-device sensor types other than the accelerometer and gyroscope. Regarding issues with heterogeneities of sampling frequencies across devices, and regarding irregularities of sampling frequency, a natural expectation is that it will affect sampling from other in-device sensors equally as the thoroughly investigated accelerometer sensor. Our results for investigating the gyroscope support this hypothesis. On the other hand, we expect these impairments to be less severe on HAR for sensors which sample at significantly lower frequency or for which high-frequency sampling and sampling stability is less crucial, e.g. for location sensors or for the magnetometer when used to obtain mere device orientation.

Furthermore, our evaluation of sensor biases focused largely on static setups. Regarding varying and mediocre quality of sensing, other sensor types have varying characteristics. Additionally, for some sensors, such as the magnetometer or GNSS-based location sensors, the heterogeneities induced by the user's current environment are much more severe: While the accelerometer is biased only to a small extent, specifically by the ambient temperature, a magnetometer is heavily biased by magnetic inference as induced by, e.g., building elements and installations, or motor vehicles. Furthermore, for many sensors, biases such as gain and offset are typically temperature dependent [26], and, e.g., during the stress test of the phones, c.f. Section 3 the temperatures were noticeable hotter, and the authors are unaware whether the phones have built-in control of temperature dependent calibration. Thus, during the stress test the phones' biases and offsets may have changed due to the higher temperature.

Combined Mitigating of Further Heterogeneities

Beyond the device-centric heterogeneities focused on in this paper, see Section 1, further heterogeneity types are present in most real-world HAR scenarios [2, 13], prominent among which are device orientation and on-body placement. Several of the mitigation techniques for the latter, see Section 2, follow a divide&conquer approach via training classifiers for similar configurations (e.g., w.r.t. placement and orientation) as does our clustering technique (applied for device characteristics). The same concept can be applied to both these dimensions (and to even more) simultaneously—whereas the number of classifiers to be trained then grows exponentially with the dimensions, i.e. heterogeneity types, considered. Also the estimation (and the thereby facilitated 'subtraction') of the gravity vector from acceleration data could be combined with the mitigation techniques described herein, as a pre-processing step.

7. CONCLUSIONS

In this paper, we have presented and analyzed heterogeneities present in the motion sensor output of common smartphones, -watches and tablets. We furthermore analyzed the impairments these heterogeneities cause for human activity recognition tasks. To this end, we presented results from several experiments investigating datasets, which are made public, involving in total 36 devices.

The investigation presented identifies and analyses the following three sensor heterogeneity categories, focusing on accelerometer and gyroscope sensors: Firstly sensor biases, which for some investigated devices showed in stillness deviation of 8% deviation from the sole exerted force, gravity—a bias large enough to account for the acceleration of a fast train. Secondly, severe sampling instabilities occur on many investigated devices, especially when these are running other tasks, which yield high loads. Finally, also the heterogeneous nominal sampling rates of different devices yield a big challenge for activity recognition on device models not yet seen in the training phase. Furthermore, we have investigated, using a case study, the impairments these heterogeneities yield for human activity recognition, as well as several techniques for mitigating these. As mitigation techniques in the form of preprocessing methods we investigated various interpolation schemes and low-pass filtering, as well as the clustering of devices according to their heterogeneity characteristics—which then allows to train classifiers targeted at individual device clusters. Additionally, we evaluate both impairments and mitigation effects for different feature types, namely time domain, frequency domain and ECDF features, and four learner types, namely C4.5 trees, SVMs, k-NN learners, and random forests. The impairments in the case study were significant, lowering the recognition accuracy in our case study by up to a third for some choices of feature and learner types, most notably for frequency-domain features. The mitigation techniques were shown to regain much of these heterogeneity-caused accuracy losses. Finally, we have discussed implications and potential extensions of the presented work.

8. ACKNOWLEDGEMENTS

This work has been supported by the Danish Advanced Technology Foundation under J.nr. 076-2011- 3., and by The Danish Council for Strategic Research as part of the EcoSense project (11-115331). Parts of this work were done during stays of the first author at Carnegie Melon, US, and of the second author at the University of Münster, Germany.

Furthermore, We would like to thank the reviewers and especially our sheperd Lama Nachman for their helpful suggestions and comments.

9. REFERENCES

[1] M. V. Albert, S. Toledo, M. Shapiro, and K. Kording. Using mobile phones for activity recognition in parkinson's patients. *Frontiers in neurology*, 3, 2012.

[2] O. Amft. On the need for quality standards in activity recognition using ubiquitous sensors. In *How To Do Good Research In Activity Recognition. Workshop in conjunction with Pervasive*, 2010.

[3] S. A. Antos, M. V. Albert, and K. P. Kording. Hand, belt, pocket or bag: Practical activity tracking with mobile phones. *Journal of Neuroscience Methods*, 231:22 – 30, 2014.

[4] O. Banos, A. Calatroni, M. Damas, H. Pomares, I. Rojas, H. Sagha, J. del R Millán, G. Troster, R. Chavarriaga, and D. Roggen. Kinect= imu? learning mimo signal mappings to automatically translate activity recognition systems across sensor modalities. In *IEEE Int. Symp. Wearable Computers (ISWC)*, 2012.

[5] L. Bao and S. S. Intille. Activity recognition from user-annotated acceleration data. In *2nd Intl. Conf. Pervasive Computing (Pervasive)*, pages 1–17, 2004.

[6] C. Barthold, K. Subbu, and R. Dantu. Evaluation of gyroscope-embedded mobile phones. In *IEEE Intl. Conf. Systems, Man, and Cybernetics (SMC)*, Oct 2011.

[7] P. Batista, C. Silvestre, P. Oliveira, and B. Cardeira. Accelerometer calibration and dynamic bias and gravity estimation: Analysis, design, and experimental evaluation. *IEEE Trans. Control Systems Technology*, 19(1):1128–1137, 2011.

[8] S. Bhattacharya, H. Blunck, M. Kjærgaard, and P. Nurmi. Robust and energy-efficient trajectory tracking for mobile devices. *IEEE Trans. Mobile Computing (TMC)*, 14(2):430–443, 2015.

[9] S. Bhattacharya, P. Nurmi, N. Hammerla, and T. Plötz. Using unlabeled data in a sparse-coding framework for human activity recognition. *Pervasive and Mobile Computing*, 15(0):242–262, 2014.

[10] G. Bieber, P. Koldrack, C. Sablowski, C. Peter, and B. Urban. Mobile physical activity recognition of stand-up and sit-down transitions for user behavior analysis. In *Intl. Conf. Pervasive Technologies Related to Assistive Environments (PETRA)*. ACM, 2010.

[11] G. Bieber, J. Voskamp, and B. Urban. Activity recognition for everyday life on mobile phones. In *Universal Access in Human-Computer Interaction (UAHCI)*. Springer, 2009.

[12] C. M. Bishop. *Pattern Recognition and Machine Learning*. Springer, 2006.

[13] H. Blunck, N. O. Bouvin, T. Franke, K. Grønbæk, M. B. Kjærgaard, P. Lukowicz, and M. Wüstenberg. On heterogeneity in mobile sensing applications aiming at representative data collection. In *UbiComp '13 Adjunct*, pages 1087–1098. ACM, 2013.

[14] T. Brezmes, J.-L. Gorricho, and J. Cotrina. Activity recognition from accelerometer data on a mobile phone. In *Intl. Work-Conf. Artificial Neural Networks (IWANN)*. Springer, 2009.

[15] A. Bulling, U. Blanke, and B. Schiele. A tutorial on human activity recognition using body-worn inertial sensors. *Computing Surveys (CSUR*, 46(3), 2014.

[16] F. Buttussi and L. Chittaro. Mopet: A context-aware and user-adaptive wearable system for fitness training. *Artificial Intelligence in Medicine*, 42(2):153 – 163, 2008.

[17] Y. Chen, Z. Zhao, S. Wang, and Z. Chen. Extreme learning machine-based device displacement free activity recognition model. *Soft Computing*, 16(9), 2012.

[18] J. Dai, X. Bai, Z. Yang, Z. Shen, and D. Xuan. Mobile phone-based pervasive fall detection. *Personal Ubiquitous Comput.*, 14(7), 2010.

[19] S. Dey, N. Roy, W. Xu, R. R. Choudhury, and S. Nelakuditi. Accelprint: Imperfections of accelerometers make smartphones trackable. *Network and Distributed System Security Symp. (NDSS)*, 2014.

[20] D. Figo, P. C. Diniz, D. R. Ferreira, and J. M. P. Cardoso. Preprocessing techniques for context recognition from accelerometer data. *Personal and Ubiquitous Computing*, 14(7):645–662, 2010.

[21] B. J. Frey and D. Dueck. Clustering by passing messages between data points. *science*, 315(5814):972–976, 2007.

[22] F. Gulmammadov. Analysis, modeling and compensation of bias drift in mems inertial sensors. IEEE 4th Intl. Conf. Recent Advances in Space Technologies (RAST), June 2009.

[23] N. Y. Hammerla, R. Kirkham, P. Andras, and T. Ploetz. On preserving statistical characteristics of accelerometry data using their empirical cumulative distribution. In *ISWC*. ACM, 2013.

[24] S. Hemminki, P. Nurmi, and S. Tarkoma. Accelerometer-based transportation mode detection on smartphones. In *11th ACM Conf. Embedded Networked Sensor Systems (SenSys)*, 2013.

[25] A. Henpraserttae, S. Thiemjarus, and S. Marukatat. Accurate activity recognition using a mobile phone regardless of device orientation and location. In *IEEE Body Sensor Networks Conference (BSN)*, 2011.

[26] J. D. Hol. *Sensor fusion and calibration of inertial sensors, vision, Ultra-Wideband and GPS*. PhD thesis, Linköping University, Sweden, 2011.

[27] Y. Kawahara, H. Kurasawa, and H. Morikawa. Recognizing User Context Using Mobile Handsets with Acceleration Sensors. In *IEEE Intl. Conf. Portable Information Devices (PORTABLE)*, pages 1–5, 2007.

[28] K. Kunze and P. Lukowicz. Dealing with sensor displacement in motion-based onbody activity recognition systems. In *ACM Intl. Joint Conf. on Pervasive and Ubiquitous Computing (UbiComp)*, pages 20–29. ACM, 2008.

[29] J. R. Kwapisz, G. M. Weiss, and S. A. Moore. Activity recognition using cell phone accelerometers. In *SIGKDD Explorations Newsletter*. ACM, 2011.

[30] N. Lane, E. Miluzzo, H. Lu, D. Peebles, T. Choudhury, and A. Campbell. A survey of mobile phone sensing. *Communications Magazine, IEEE*, 48(9), 2010.

[31] J. Lester, T. Choudhury, and G. Borriello. A practical approach to recognizing physical activities. In *4th Intl. Conf. Pervasive Computing (Pervasive)*, 2006.

[32] B. Logan, J. Healey, M. Philipose, E. M. Tapia, and S. Intille. A long-term evaluation of sensing modalities for activity recognition. In *Proceedings of the 10th international conference on Ubiquitous computing (UbiComp)*, 2007.

[33] J. C. Lötters, J. Schipper, P. H. Veltink, W. Olthuis, and P. Bergveld. Procedure for in-use calibration of triaxial accelerometers in medical applications. *Sensors and Actuators A: Physical*, 68(1-3):221–228, 1998.

[34] S. Mazilu, M. Hardegger, Z. Zhu, D. Roggen, G. Troster, M. Plotnik, and J. M. Hausdorff. Online detection of freezing of gait with smartphones and machine learning techniques. In *IEEE Intl. Conf. Pervasive Computing Technologies for Healthcare (PervasiveHealth)*, pages 123–130. IEEE, 2012.

[35] Q. McNemar. Note on the sampling error of the difference between correlated proportions or percentages. *Psychometrika*, 12(2):153–157, 1947.

[36] OpenSignal. Android Fragmentation Visualized. **`http://opensignal.com/reports/2014/android-fragmentation/`**, 2014. Accessed 17-Mar-2015.

[37] J. Pärkkä, M. Ermes, P. Korpipää, J. Mäntyjärvi, J. Peltola, and I. Korhonen. Activity classification using realistic data from wearable sensors. *Biomedicine*, 10(1):119–128, 2006.

[38] C. Pham and P. Olivier. Slice&dice: Recognizing food preparation activities using embedded accelerometers. In *Intl. Conf. Ambient Intelligent (AmI)*, 2009.

[39] T. Plötz, N. Y. Hammerla, and P. Olivier. Feature learning for activity recognition in ubiquitous computing. In *Intl. Joint Conf. Artificial Intelligence (IJCAI)*, volume 22, page 1729, 2011.

[40] T. Plötz, P. Moynihan, C. Pham, and P. Olivier. Activity recognition and healthier food preparation. In *Activity Recognition in Pervasive Intelligent Environments*. Atlantis Press, 2011.

[41] S. J. Preece, J. Y. Goulermas, L. P. J. Kenney, and D. Howard. A comparison of feature extraction methods for the classification of dynamic activities from accelerometer data. *IEEE Trans. Biomedical Engineering*, 56(3):871–879, 2009.

[42] S. Reddy, M. Mun, J. Burke, D. Estrin, M. Hansen, and M. Srivastava. Using mobile phones to determine transportation modes. *ACM Trans. Sen. Netw.*, 6(2):13:1–13:27, 2010.

[43] H. Sagha, S. Digumarti, J. del R Millan, R. Chavarriaga, A. Calatroni, D. Roggen, and G. Tröster. Benchmarking classification techniques using the Opportunity human activity dataset. In *IEEE Intl. Conf. Systems, Man, and Cybernetics (SMC)*, 2011.

[44] P. Siirtola and J. Röning. Recognizing human activities user-independently on smartphones based on accelerometer data. *Intl. Journ. Interactive Multimedia and Artificial Intelligence*, 1(5), 2012.

[45] X. Su, H. Tong, and P. Ji. Activity recognition with smartphone sensors. *Tsinghua Science and Technology*, 19(3):235–249, 2014.

[46] L. Sun, D. Zhang, B. Li, B. Guo, and S. Li. Activity recognition on an accelerometer embedded mobile phone with varying positions and orientations. In *Ubiquitous intelligence and computing (UIC)*. Springer, 2010.

[47] J. Yang. Toward physical activity diary: motion recognition using simple acceleration features with mobile phones. In *1st Intl. Workshop Interactive Multimedia for Consumer Electronics*, pages 1–10. ACM, 2009.

FEMO: A Platform for Free-weight Exercise Monitoring with RFIDs

Han Ding*, Longfei Shangguan†, Zheng Yang‡, Jinsong Han*,
Zimu Zhou†, Panlong Yang§, Wei Xi*, Jizhong Zhao*
*Xi'an Jiaotong University
†Hong Kong University of Science and Technology
‡Tsinghua University
§PLA University of Science and Technology
{dinghanxjtu,shanggdlk,hmilyyz,zhouzimu.hk,panlongyang,weixi.cs}@gmail.com,
{hanjinsong,zjz}@mail.xjtu.edu.cn

ABSTRACT

Regular free-weight exercise helps to strengthen the body's natural movements and stabilize muscles that are important to strength, balance, and posture of human beings. Prior works have exploited wearable sensors or RF signal changes (*e.g.*, WiFi and Blue-tooth) for activity sensing, recognition and counting *etc.*. However, none of them have incorporate three key factors necessary for a practical free-weight exercise monitoring system: recognizing free-weight activities on site, assessing their qualities, and providing useful feedbacks to the bodybuilder promptly. Our FEMO system responds to these demands, providing an integrated free-weight exercise monitoring service that incorporates all the essential functionalities mentioned above. FEMO achieves this by attaching passive RFID tags on the dumbbells and leveraging the Doppler shift profile of the reflected backscatter signals for on-site free-weight activity recognition and assessment. The rationale behind FEMO is 1): since each free-weight activity owns unique arm motions, the corresponding Doppler shift profile should be distinguishable to each other and serves as a reliable signature for each activity. 2): the Doppler profile of each activity has a strong spatial-temporal correlation that implicitly reflects the quality of each performed activity. We implement FEMO with COTS RFID devices and conduct a two-week experiment. The preliminary result from 15 volunteers demonstrates that FEMO can be applied to a variety of free-weight activities and users, and provide valuable feedbacks for activity alignment.

Keywords

activity recognition and assessment; RFID

SenSys'15, November 1–4, 2015, Seoul, South Korea..
© 2015 ACM. ISBN 978-1-4503-3631-4/15/11 ...$15.00.
DOI: http://dx.doi.org/10.1145/2809695.2809708.

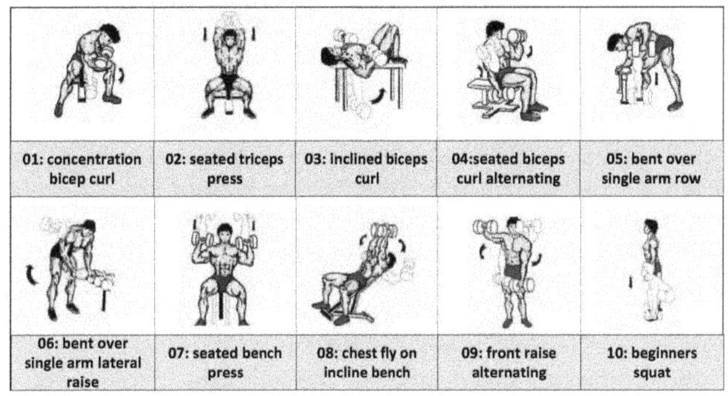

Figure 1: Sketches of the tested free-weight activities

1. INTRODUCTION

Free-weight exercise is indispensable in a balanced exercise program and provides numerous health benefits. It helps to stabilize bones and muscles that are relevant to strength, balance and posture, and contributes to weight loss and overall health [20]. Some researches recommend free-weight training twice a week for adults [2], even for those who walk or run regularly. Moreover, some individuals may prefer free-weight exercises to aerobic exercises as the main fitness activities simply for lifestyle or convenience reasons.

Monitoring and evaluation supports are crucial for free-weight exercises. Compared with aerobic exercises *e.g.* running, people are more vulnerable to inefficient training or even accidental injuries in free-weight training. Stretching or warping muscles improperly, *e.g.*, to the wrong direction or at a high speed, can lead to strains and tears. Timely guidance is also important for exercise safety and quality since people might forget their progress, skip essential steps, or miscount a sequence.

Despite academic and commercial success in aerobic exercise monitoring [10, 11, 12, 16, 43], there is a void in automatic free-weight exercise monitoring and evaluation. A personal trainer is still by far the most common solution to free-weight training monitoring, which incurs high recruitment costs [1]. Unlike aerobic exercises where speed, distance and terrain are essential, the quality of free-weight training is mostly defined by repetitions, durations and activity sets. Existing schemes on general activity recognition [8, 25] and aerobic exercise tracking [12, 16] fail to capture such high-fidelity information for free-weight exercises. Some pioneer work explored inertial sensors *e.g.* accelerometer and gyroscope, for free-weight training monitoring [9, 28], yet these techniques cannot reliably handle the variety of arm motion patterns and diverse training paces. Furthermore, they also require body-worn sensors to function, which poses inconvenience and might cause unwanted motion changes during training. A promising alternative is to leverage wireless signals for device-free activity sensing. Recent research has explored the feasibility of WiFi signals for gesture and activity recognition [27, 30, 41], yet either involves customized hardware (*e.g.*, software radios [30] and directional antennas [27]) or targets at location-aware activities [41], thus unsuitable for ubiquitous free-weight exercise tracking.

In this paper, we design FEMO, an automatic, non-invasive and light-weight Free-weight Exercise MOnitoring system. We enable non-invasive free-weight exercise monitoring by attaching passive Radio Frequency IDentification (RFID) tags on assisted instruments (*e.g.* dumbbells) during training, and analyzing signals backscattered from tags during exercises. Attaching passive RFID tags on instruments like a dumbbell poses minimum overhead due to their negligible weight and size. FEMO works by analyzing the Doppler shifts extracted from the backscattered signals. It automatically recognizes, counts, and assesses the exercises on-site and in real time. The detailed assessment feedbacks are also displayed on FEMO's UI module to assist activity rectification.

The design of FEMO involves the following challenges:

(1) How to detect and extract accurate Doppler shifts from backscatter signals? Doppler shifts are accessible from commercial RFID readers via a standard API. However, the raw Doppler measurements are too noisy to precisely portray the tag movements (*i.e.* dumbbell trails).

We address this problem by transforming the received phases from backscatter signals into the corresponding Doppler shifts (§3.1). FEMO tracks this Doppler stream and segments the Doppler shifts of each activity performed even at diverse paces (§3.2).

(2) How to recognize free-weight exercises on-site? Traditional activity recognition schemes rely on sophisticated feature selection and complex classification techniques for accurate recognition, which incur a large computational latency and are sensitive to training data.

FEMO addresses this problem by analyzing the temporal patterns of RF signals affected by body movements. Our observation is that each free-weight activity is a unique combination of basic arm motions. These combined arm motions exhibit unique yet stable Doppler shift profiles in the temporal domain, producing light-weight and robust features for activity recognition. We detail this idea and optimize the recognition process in §3.3.

(3) How to assess user performances? Since FEMO aims to provide useful feedbacks to users as guidance for improper activity rectification, it is important to quantify the quality of each performed activity.

In FEMO, we define a set of metrics evaluating the quality of activities during free-weight exercises from both the local and global views. An assessment framework is proposed to evaluate both the activity details and the activity consistency within each training group.

We implement FEMO as a framework consisting of four core modules: Doppler value pre-processing, activity segmentation, activity recognition and activity assessment. We prototype FEMO on commodity hardware including a Commercial Off-The-Shelf (COTS) RFID reader, a directional antenna, and two passive RFID tags attached to the dumbbells. It runs on a central server and processes the tag reading stream in pipeline. It also provides an interface to other applications such as activity counting and training process tracker, where they can obtain the current activity primitives from FEMO via programming interfaces. We evaluate the performance of FEMO on free-weight training data collected in two weeks from 15 volunteers. The data cover 1,534 minutes of exercises, with 4,500 repetitions of 10 representative exercises. Results demonstrate that FEMO can be applied to various representative free-weight activities, and provide valuable feedbacks to users, especially beginners.

We summarize the contributions of this paper as follows:

- We introduce the first passive RFID-based system for free-weight exercise monitoring. This system enables on-site activity recognition and assessment, and provides rich feedbacks to the user for activity rectification. Different from prior works that only coarsely recognize to which type the activity is belonging, our FEMO system can provide fine-grained measurements on the activity by using the subtle Doppler values retrieved from COTS passive RFID devices.

- We present a set of algorithms to effectively extract free-weight exercise information from backscatter signals. Specifically, our algorithms enable 1) extracting minute Doppler shifting from noisy tag readings reported by commercial RFID readers; 2) segmenting the Doppler streaming such that each segment contains an intact activity; 3) assessing the exercise performance and providing useful feedbacks to the bodybuilder.

- Last but not the least, we establish a proof-of-concept prototype and conduct two-weeks experiments. Results demonstrate the effectiveness of our system. It can detect ten typical free-weight activities with an average accuracy of 90.4%, and facilitate rectifying irregular exercise behaviors, especially for fitness novices.

2. OVERVIEW

This section briefly introduces the taxonomy of the targeted free-weight activities and the overall work-flow of FEMO.

2.1 Taxonomy of Free-weight Activities

In this paper, we focus on ten common and representative free-weight activities, which can train different parts of the muscle groups. We choose these popular activities based on a two-week questionnaire investigation on fitness enthusiasts in our university. Similar to [9], we categorize these activities into different groups based on the muscle groups desired to be trained. Figure 1 illustrates ten free-weight activities of interests, which will be used to demonstrate our work throughout this paper.

2.2 FEMO Work-flow

Figure 2 presents the work-flow of FEMO. It contains four major steps: preprocessing, activity segmenting, activity recognition, and activity assessment.

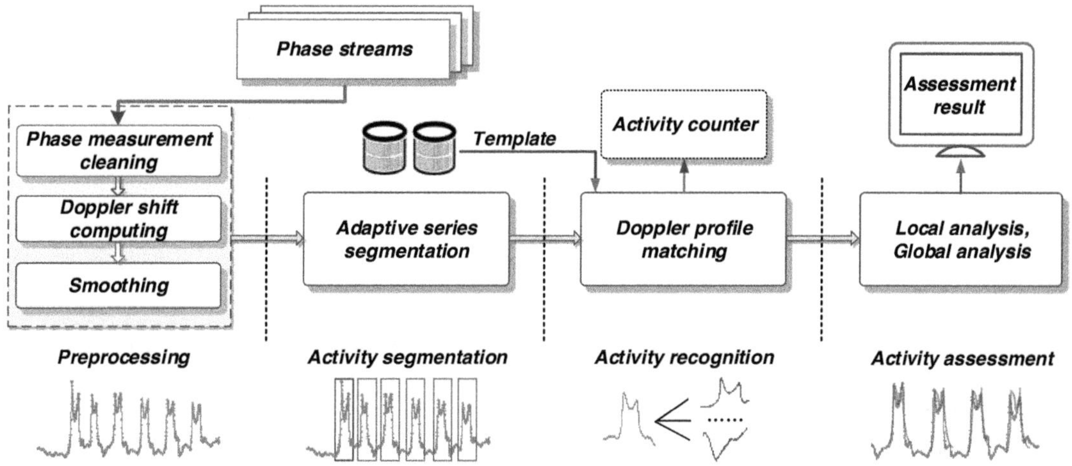

Figure 2: An overview of FEMO's work-flow

The first step is preprocessing, where the system purifies the raw phase readings and computes the Doppler shifts. In this step, FEMO first mitigates the noisy phase readings introduced by the hardware heterogeneity of the reader and the inconsistency of tag orientations. FEMO then computes the Doppler values and finally employs a moving-average filter to smooth the Doppler values.

The second step is to segment the Doppler stream, such that each segment contains a single free-weight activity. A main challenge lies in the heterogeneity of Doppler profiles with respect to different activities. We find that the state-of-the-art, *e.g.*, threshold-based filters [9, 10] or peak detection schemes [14], fails to segment the activity precisely. In FEMO, we exploit the stochastic characteristics of Doppler values and design a KL-divergence based segmentation algorithm. This algorithm works efficiently and adapts to various free-weight activities and users.

The third step is to recognize each activity from the Doppler segment. Towards accurate and prompt recognition, we build up a body movement model and observe that each activity has a unique yet stable combination of arm motion trails. Based on this observation, we employ the Doppler profile as the feature of each activity and design a fingerprint based activity recognition scheme. To improve the recognition efficiency, we leverage the motion order of arms to prune the unqualified matching candidates in advance.

The final step is to measure the quality of each activity and provide valuable feedbacks to users. In FEMO, we assess each activity from both the local and global views. Local analysis concentrates on the activity details by comparing the proposed features against the standard ones. The global analysis focuses on the consistency of each group of activities by measuring the smoothness and continuity of activities within each group. The assessment results are displayed on the end-user interface to assist activity rectification.

3. SYSTEM DESIGN

This section details the FEMO design and highlights the challenges, key observations, and core techniques behind the activity segmentation, recognition and assessment of FEMO.

3.1 Data Acquisition and Preprocessing

Standard Doppler API: Commercial RFID readers offer a standard API to retrieve Doppler shifts. However, according to our initial experiments, we find that the reported Doppler values fail to precisely depict the free-weight activity. As an example, we perform the *Bent over single arm lateral raise* ten times in front of an ImpinJ R420 reader. Figure 3 plots the Doppler values reported by the standard API. Ideally, the Doppler values should be close to zero when the user keeps still, yet increase positively (negatively) as the dumbbell moves towards (away from) the reader. Since the activity is repeated ten times, the Doppler shifts should show a consistent pattern. However, from Figure 3, we find that the reported Doppler values change irregularly over the whole process. The results indicate that neither the tag's approaching nor the opposite movement to the reader results in a clear positive or negative peak. Even worse, it is difficult to recognize the repetitive pattern from the collected Doppler readings. The technical report released by Impinj states that the reader estimates the Doppler shift of a tag through the time duration and phase difference of a single tag packet. Thus, the inaccurate Doppler may be related to both the time disalignment and phase noise. Hence we seek other methods to acquire precise Doppler values.

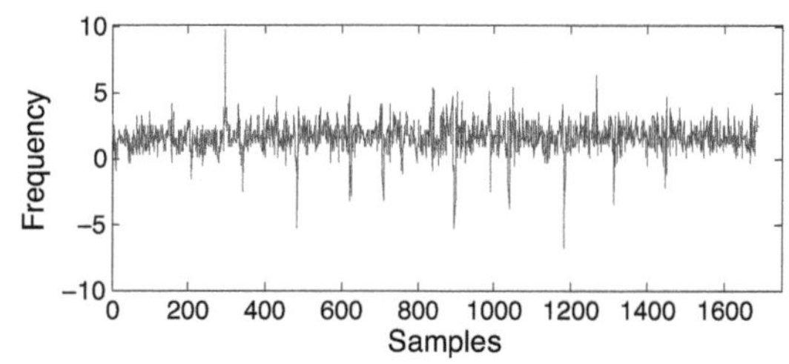

Figure 3: Doppler phase shifting acquired from the API

RF phase measurement: Instead of directly using the Doppler shifts from the API, we deduce the Doppler shifts from the phase measurement reported by the commercial reader. The phase value of an RF signal θ describes the offset of the received signal from the original one before transmission, ranging from 0 to 2π.

$$\begin{cases} \theta = (2\pi\frac{2l}{\lambda} + \mu) \mod 2\pi \\ \mu = \theta_{Tx} + \theta_{Rx} + \theta_{TAG} \end{cases} \tag{1}$$

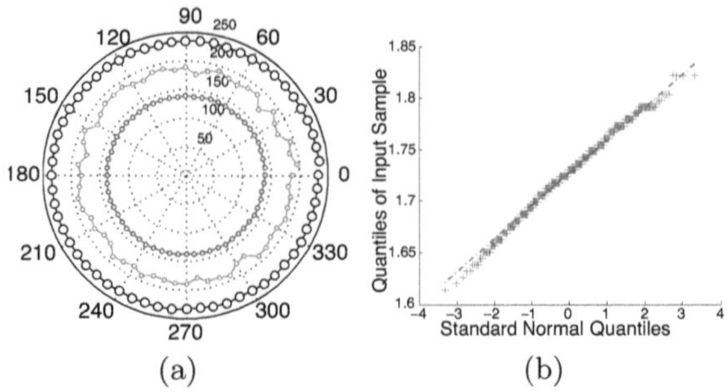

Figure 4: (a) Phase measurements under different tag orientations (b) QQ Plot of sample data versus standard normal distribution

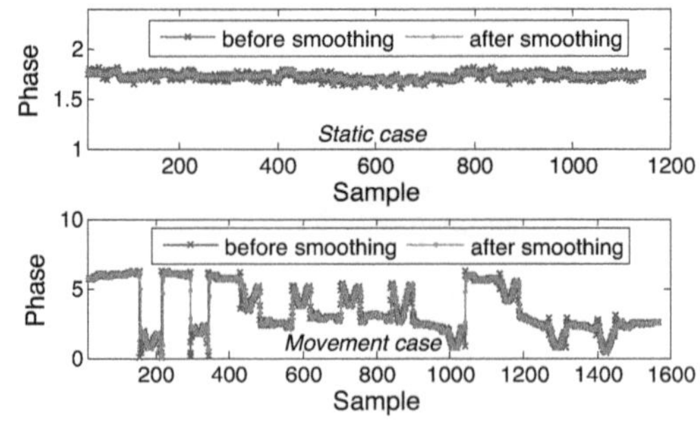

Figure 5: Phase measurements before/after smoothing under static/movement cases

where l is the distance between the antenna and the tag, λ is the wavelength, and μ is the system noise. Due to the imperfect manufacture, the reader's transmit circuits (θ_{Tx}), the receiver circuits (θ_{Rx}), and the tag's reflection characteristics (θ_{TAG}) will introduce additional phase rotations, *i.e.*, noises, to the phase measurement.

3.1.1 Preprocessing

Phase measurement smoothing: To deduce precise Doppler shifts, it is crucial to minimize the phase noise. We change the tag orientation with respect to the antenna with a step of 6° and examine how sensitive the phase measurement is to tag orientations. The antenna is set to be 2m away from the tag. Figure 4(a) shows the raw phase measurements when the tag rotates 2π (marked as red points). We find that due to the inherent circuit noise, the phase values fluctuate continuously and randomly. We further test the distribution of these measurements against the standard Gaussian distribution (shown in Figure 4(b)). The linearity of the points on the Q-Q plot suggests that the data are normally distributed, with a standard deviation of 0.0332 radian. Based on this observation, we model the phase measurement θ as a Gaussian random variable $\mathcal{N}(\mu, 0.0332)$. We then utilize the standard Kalman Filter [17] to smooth the phase values. We test various lookback window sizes, and empirically set it as 10 which optimizes the smoothing performance.

Figure 5 shows the phase measurement before/after smoothing in both the static and movement cases. The difference indicates that the Kalman filter effectively enhances the stability of phase measurements of static tags. For the moving-tag case, we can see that the phase values change steadily after filtering. Yet they still retain a clear profile of each free-weight activity.

Deducing Doppler shifts: Doppler shifts are generated due to the relative movement between a sender and a receiver, *e.g.*, the stationary reader and the moving tag. Suppose at time t_i and t_{i+1}, the reader receives two consecutive signals from the moving tag, with the phase readings θ_i and θ_{i+1}. Let v be the tag's moving speed within the period of $[t_i, t_{i+1}]$. v can be regarded as a constant due to the short interval between two consecutive tag readings. Hence the distance (d) that the tag moves equals to $v \cdot (t_{i+1} - t_i)$. On the other hand, we know that the signal in the backscatter communication traverses 2 times of d. Thus we have:

$$2v \cdot (t_{i+1} - t_i) = \lambda \cdot (\frac{\theta_{i+1} - \theta_i}{2\pi}) \tag{2}$$

The Doppler shift can be further expressed as:

$$f = \frac{v}{\lambda} = \frac{\theta_{i+1} - \theta_i}{4\pi \cdot (t_{i+1} - t_i)} \tag{3}$$

Figure 6(b) shows the phase-deduced Doppler shifts. The measurements are collected when a volunteer performs *Bent-over lateral raise* ten times. Compared with the noisy Doppler values reported by the API (Figure 6(a)), the deduced Doppler values clearly show ten repetitive patterns.

Despite the high resolution, from Figure 6(b) we find that the deduced doppler value still fluctuates over time. This is because the time interval between any two consecutive readings may vary due to the random access mechanism of ALOHA protocol [32]. Such non-uniform time intervals lead to Doppler fluctuations and jitters that overwhelm the original appearance of each activity. Therefore, after computing the Doppler value, we apply a moving average filter over the last n readings (n=10 in FEMO) to smooth the Doppler values. Figure 6(c) shows the final results.

3.2 Activity Segmentation

The activity segmentation module identifies Doppler segments that are likely to contain a complete free-weight activity. We define each segment as $\kappa_i = (t_s : t_e)$, with start time t_s and end time t_e within the Doppler stream. The segmentation yields a set of segments K, with each containing a free-weight activity: $K = \{\kappa_1, \kappa_2, ..., \kappa_m\}$.

There has been extensive efforts on activity segmentation [8]. Most of them assume that each activity will exhibit a clear peak in the received signal stream. Thus by comparing each signal strength with a static threshold, the activity segments will be located accordingly. However, such a solution is unsuitable for FEMO as a free-weight activity usually contains multiple peaks within an activity period. The one-peak detection scheme may split one activity into multiple segments.

3.2.1 Key observations

In FEMO, the activity segmentation scheme is based on the fact that people tend to take a short rest after each activity to control the training pace. We term such a short rest as a *resting interval.* The resting intervals have small Doppler values, which naturally separate the activities. Thus by extracting the start and end times of each resting interval, we can acquire each activity segment accordingly. Nevertheless, a simple threshold still fails since people may adjust poses slightly within the resting intervals, leading to sharp Doppler peaks in the resting intervals. Such Doppler peaks can exceed the threshold and incur incorrect segments.

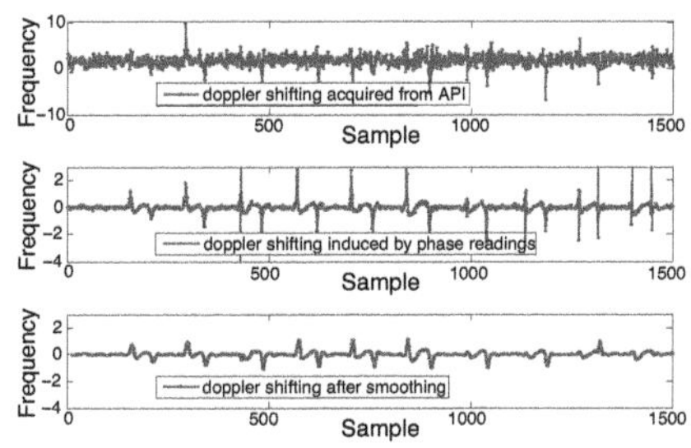

Figure 6: Doppler shift of 10 consecutive *Bent-over lateral raise*

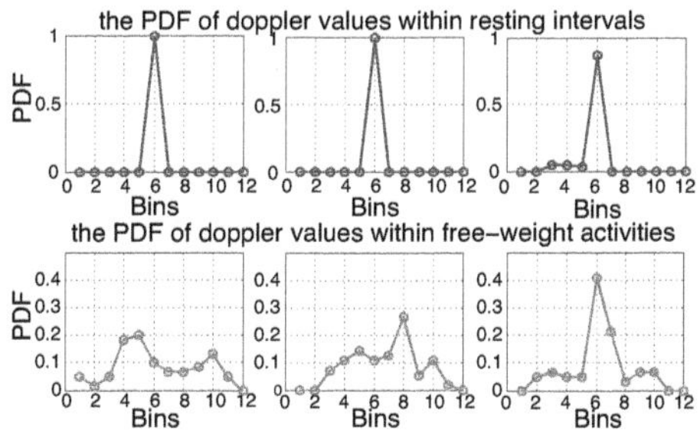

Figure 7: PDF of doppler values within different windows

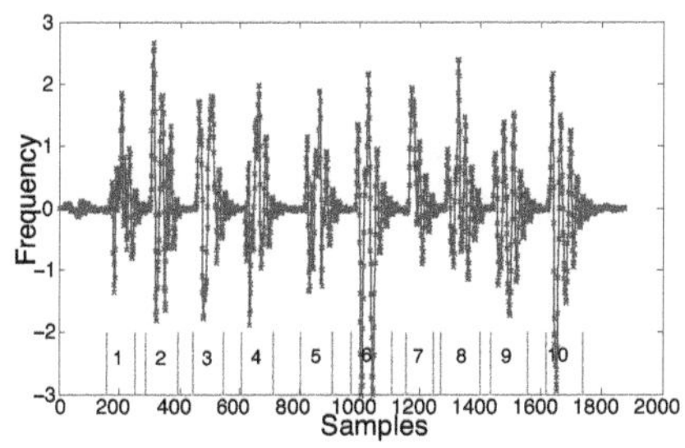

Figure 8: Segmentation result of 10 activity performing

Our segmentation scheme leverages two insights:

- The sharp Doppler values usually take a small portion of the whole data within the resting interval.
- Except for the sharp Doppler values incurred by the pose adjustment, the remaining Doppler readings within the resting interval are relatively small and stable.

Thus if we split a resting interval into multiple consecutive windows, the distribution of Doppler values within each window should be similar. Conversely, the Doppler values outside the resting interval corresponds to the free-weight activity. These values change rapidly and show a completely different distribution from those in the resting interval.

3.2.2 Segmentation scheme

The above analysis leads us to an adaptive segmentation scheme based on the KL divergence [34]. Denote the Doppler stream as $S = (s_i) \in \mathbb{R}^{1\times N}$, where N is the number of discrete time points $t_1, ..., t_N$ at which the Doppler values are sampled. For each w consecutive Doppler values, we group them into a window. Within each window, we further categorize the Doppler values into multiple bins. The bin size is empirically set as 0.35. Then we can get the discrete probability distribution function (PDF) of Doppler values within each window. Given two consecutive windows w_i and w_j, let P and Q be their PDF, respectively. The KL divergence of Q from P is defined as:

$$D_{KL}(P||Q) = \sum_i P(i) \cdot ln\frac{P(i)}{Q(i)} \qquad (4)$$

The KL divergence measures the information loss when Q is used to approximate P. In FEMO, there are three cases:

1. both windows are within the resting interval;
2. both windows are within the activity period;
3. one is within the resting interval and another is within the activity period;

In the first case, $D_{KL}(P||Q)$ will be close to zero due to the similar probability distributions within these two windows (Figure 7(a)). In the latter two cases, $D_{KL}(P||Q)$ will be significantly larger than zero as the distribution varies sharply among these two windows (Figure 7(b)). Hence by checking $D_{KL}(P||Q)$, we can ascertain whether the current window is within the resting interval or not. After finding all windows within the resting interval, we can extract the activity segment accordingly. Figure 8 shows the segmentation result over a Doppler stream, we see that all of these ten activities are correctly identified. We also notice the Doppler profile of each activity is completely contained in the corresponding segment, indicating accurate and robust segmentation.

3.3 Activity Recognition

The activity recognition module aims to identify the free-weight activity within each segment. Many previous works focus on building a robust activity recognition system [9, 10, 29, 30, 41]. The main principle is to extract unique features for the activity from the input signals, and train a classifier to distinguish each unlabelled activity. However, this method has two major drawbacks. First, the system performance is sensitive to the training set. If the training set is small or biased, the classifier will suffer from low recognition accuracy. Although a larger training set may lead to a more accurate classifier, it will incur a higher overhead (*e.g.*, time and cost for collecting the ground-truth) on system realization and deployment. Second, such a method suffers from higher latency. To get a better performance, researchers leverage advanced graphic model (*e.g.*, Hidden Markov Model (HMM) and Conditional Random Field (CRF)) to explore the transition between consecutive activities. These model based enhancements, however, usually incur much higher computational overhead as they require a large amount of training data to determine the parameters of their models before deployment. Moreover, they will involve the states of previous activities when recognizing the current activity, which is also very computationally costly. We are motivated to design our activity recognition scheme balancing accuracy and overhead.

3.3.1 Fingerprint Matching

We find that each free-weight activity can be considered as a combination of different arm motions. For various free-weight activities, each arm motion presents a unique motion trail, generating unique Doppler profiles. Figure 9 demonstrates the effectiveness of Doppler profile. The two upper subfigures verify the stability of Doppler profiles while the uppermost and the lowermost ones confirm that the Doppler profiles disperse in different free-weight activities. Hence, the Doppler profile can discriminate the free-weight activities and act as a reliable signature.

FEMO compares the profile in each segment against the standard to identify free-weight activities. Hence we need to evaluate the similarity between two Doppler profiles. We argue that the Euclidean-distance metric is unsuitable since activity segments may vary in length due to personal

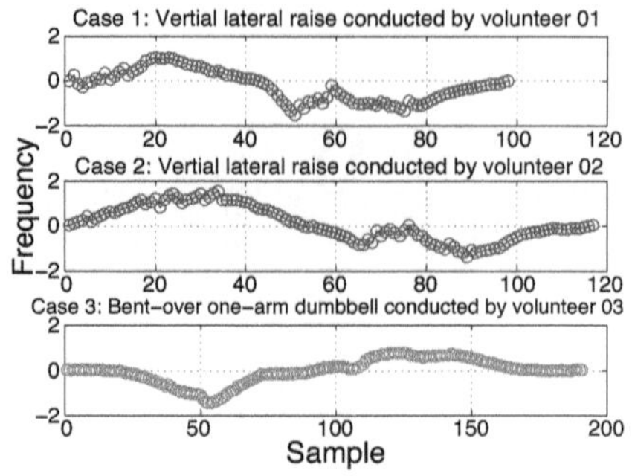

Figure 9: Doppler profiles of gym activities

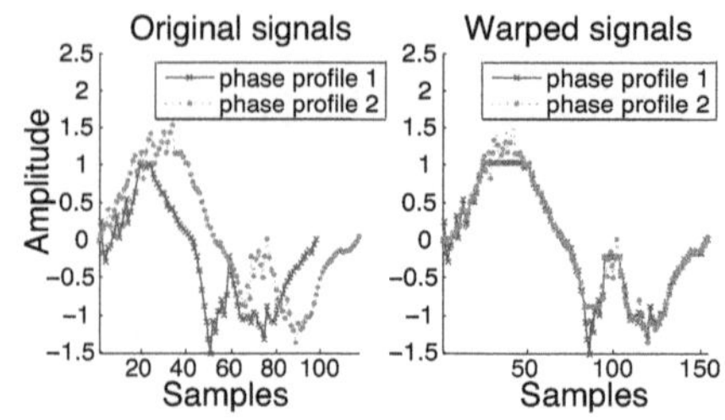

Figure 10: Original and warped signals

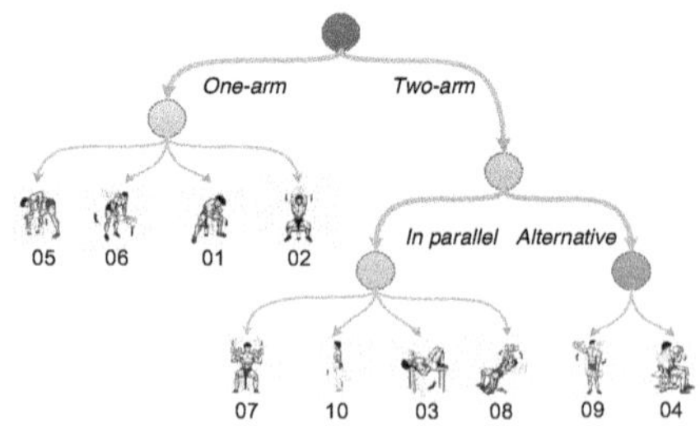

Figure 11: The pipeline of activity recognition

preferences, physical characters (weight, height) and other reasons.

FEMO uses *Dynamic Time Warping* (DTW) [35] to compute the similarity between two Doppler profiles. The benefits are twofold. On one hand, DTW compares two profiles with different lengths. On the other hand, DTW automatically compresses or stretches a sequence to minimize the distance between two sequences, thus focusing on the shape similarity rather than the absolute values. Figure 10 shows the Doppler profiles of bent-over one-arm dumbbell that are aligned with DTW. We observe that Doppler profile 1 is stretched and shifted to match with Doppler profile 2.

3.3.2 Hierarchical activity recognition framework

Directly using DTW for activity recognition is costly. The complexity of DTW is $O(mn)$, indicating a large overhead for long Doppler profiles, especially when we have to compare one Doppler profile against all candidates in the database. To reduce the computational overhead, we design a hierarchical activity recognition framework based on two observations on the arm motion pattern:

1. The free-weight activity involves either a single arm motion or two arm motions.
2. For the two arm motion activities, they are either conducted in parallel or alternatively.

Figure 11 shows the decision-tree based recognition scheme. At the first level, FEMO classifies the candidate by detecting whether the current activity is a single arm activity or not. This process can be achieved by checking whether the attached two tags on the dumbbells are detected together. If yes, FEMO further classifies the candidate by checking whether the current two-arm activity is performed alternatively or not. This process can be done by examining the concurrency of activities within these two doppler streams. Specifically, let t_o and t_l be the overlapping duration and the longest time duration of two activity segments, respectively. If $t_o \geq \beta \cdot t_l$, FEMO ascertains these two motions are conducted in parallel. With above pruning process, we can shrink the candidate group to no more than half its original size.

In our implementation, we set β as $\frac{2}{3}$ by default. Identifying the tag ID takes $O(1)$ time, while judging the concurrency of two activities is achievable in $O(1)$ time. These two simple operations help to prune the unqualified profiles in an early stage of activity recognition, thereby improving the computational efficiency. After the activity recognition, all activities will be labelled and stored for activity assessment.

3.4 Activity Assessment

The activity assessment aims to characterize the *quality* of the exercise and provides feedback to users. We first measure the quality for each individual activity by comparing its characteristics against the standard ones. Note that free-weight activities are often grouped where each group contains a set of repetitive activities. Activity consistency within an activity group is also essential to the gym training [18]. Hence we assess the quality of activities from two perspectives, *i.e.*, the *local view* and *global view*, to reflect both the offset of each individual activity from the standard and the inconsistency of a activity group.

3.4.1 Local Analysis

Local analysis evaluates the quality of each activity by concentrating on its *duration* and *intensity*, which are two general criteria for evaluating the free-weight activities.

Duration: It measures how long an activity is performed by the user. The duration of an activity is critical to the free-weight training [3]. A longer duration indicates a slower arm motion, which potentially corresponds to an ineffective muscle workout. If the duration is too short, the muscle will be stretched or warped fiercely, leading to an excessive muscle workout. Either case degrades the effectiveness of gym training. In order to improve the training efficiency, FEMO measures the difference of the durations between each conducted activity and the standard. Let d_i be the duration of activity i, d_s be the duration of the corresponding standard activity. FEMO computes their difference $d_i - d_s$ and reports the result to the user at the end of each activity group.

Intensity: Intensity is another important metric to evaluate the quality of free-weight activities. It reflects the energy of the arm motions expended by an activity [39]. It is understandable that a high quality activity should show a similar energy trend to the standard. Adapting this idea to the doppler domain, it then becomes much clear that we measure the similarity between their doppler segments. Specifically, Let $A = \{a_1, a_2, ..., a_m\} \in \mathbb{R}^{1\times m}$ be the doppler segment of the desired activity, $B = \{b_1, b_2, ..., b_n\} \in \mathbb{R}^{1\times n}$ be the corresponding standard activity. In FEMO, we first align these two doppler segments by DTW to address the potential inconsistency of segment length. After that, we compute their similarity using Euclidean distance metric. A shorter distance between two doppler segments indicates a higher similarity, and hence a higher performance of this activity.

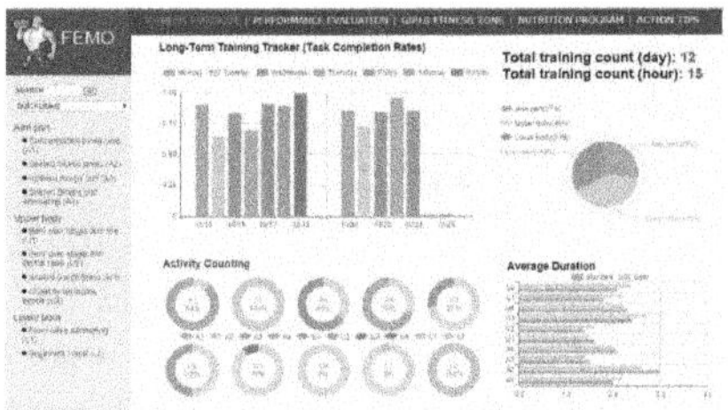

Figure 12: Training tracker service

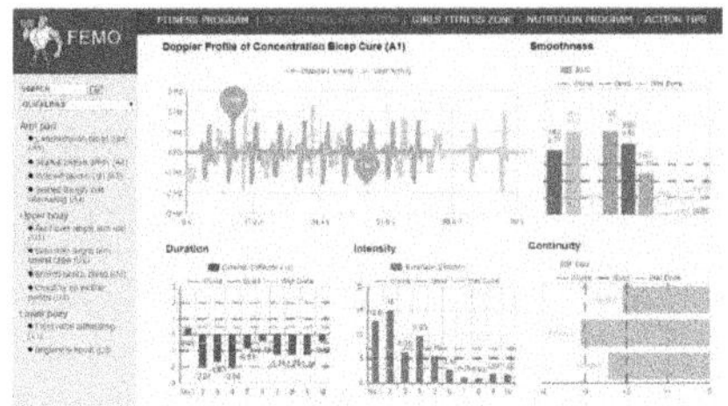

Figure 13: Performance assessment

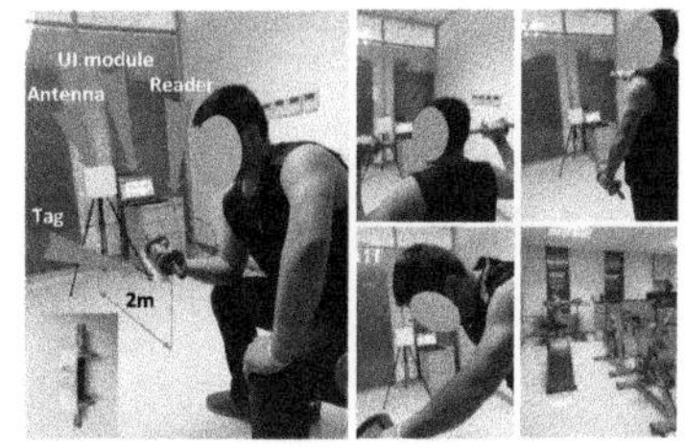

Figure 14: Experiment scenario

3.4.2 *Global Analysis*

Global analysis aims at monitoring how well each group of activities are performed, with an emphasis on unveiling the abnormal activity pattern and irregular resting intervals within each activity group. This part concentrates on two kinds of characteristics: *smoothness* and *continuity*.

Smoothness: Smoothness reflects how similar each activity is to the remaining activities within an activity group. Dumbbells also require more balance and more muscular control than others, such as the training with barbells or machines, and balance is crucial for optimal performance [6]. Smoothness can well reflect the balance by measuring the similarity of exercises in a group. A larger similarity indicates more regular arm actions, corresponding to effective muscle trainings. To evaluate the smoothness of an activity, we employ the discrete PDFs of all the Doppler values within an activity segment as the proposed features. Specifically, let $PDF(A) = \{p_i\}_{i=1}^{m}$ be the PDF of the activity segment A, where p_i represents the ith bin value. Since the Doppler value induced is at the granularity of 0.3 Hz, the number of bins to calculate the discrete probability distribution function is also set to the granularity of 0.3 Hz. In our measurements, we find that the fluctuation range of most Doppler values is around 6 Hz, we therefore set the number of bins to 20. To compare the similarity between two activities, we employ the Earth Mover's Distance (EMD) [33]. EMD measures the dissimilarity between two discrete probability distribution function $PDF(A) - \{p_i\}_{i=1}^{m}$ and $PDF(B) - \{q_j\}_{j=1}^{n}$. It is the minimal effort required to transform one histogram into another.

Continuity: Continuity depicts the consistency of resting intervals within an activity group. For efficient training, the users should pace themselves throughout the exercises [7]. A higher consistency of resting intervals indicates that the user has a good motion pace control, *i.e.*, a regular muscle stretching/warping pace. Ideally, within an activity group, the resting intervals should be consistent with each other. However, even a professional gymnasium trainer may fail to keep strictly consistent resting intervals. Thus we model the resting interval of the standard activity group as a standard normal random variable. To evaluate the continuity of activities performed within an activity group, we investigate the statistical characteristic of resting intervals and employ kurtosis as a metric. The coefficient of kurtosis is a measurement on the degree of peakedness in a variable distribution. Specifically, let $R = \{r_i\}_{i=1}^{m}$ be the vector of resting intervals within an activity group. The kurtosis can be computed as follows:

$$\beta_2 = \frac{\sum_{i=1}^{m}(r_i - \mu)^4}{(\sum_{i=1}^{m}(r_i - \mu)^2)^2} - 3 = \frac{\mu^4}{\sigma^4} - 3 \qquad (5)$$

where μ and δ are the mean value and standard deviation of the resting interval vector. As larger β_2 value indicates a concentrated distribution of resting intervals, therefore a better continuity of activities that the user performs.

4. SYSTEM IMPLEMENTATION

This section presents both the hardware composition and software realization of FEMO.

Hardware: We implement a prototype of FEMO on COTS UHF RFID devices, including an ImpinJ reader Model R420, a Laird antenna model A9028R0NF (with a gain of 8dbi), and a set of passive RFID tags. As the metal dumbbell will block the magnetic waves, we place the tag on a plastic form, which is further attached to the dumbbell. The reader is connected to a backend PC via an Ethernet cable and continuously reports the signal features backscattered from tags, including RSSIs, phase angles, and Doppler shifts. We time-stamp each tag reading by using the reader's local clock in order to eliminate the influence of network latency.

Software: The software of FEMO is fully implemented in C#. It comprises of three components: data collection module, data analysis module and UI module. The data collection module is integrated with the Octane SDK, an extension of the LLRP Toolkit, which supports continuous tag interrogation at a rate of 340 readings/s. The data analysis module is responsible for recognizing and assessing the quality of each performed activity. The assessment results are displayed on a web-based UI module. The software runs on a Lenovo PC with an Intel Core i7-4600U 2.10GHz CPU and 8GB RAM.

UI module: FEMO currently provides two services to the bodybuilder: training tracker service and activity performance assessment service. Figure 12 shows the UI page of the training tracker service. This service aims to provide daily training statistics to the bodybuilder, including the accumulative training summary and daily activity summary. The former one records the training frequency, workout and duration of the bodybuilder. The latter one reports the amount of activities and average duration of each activity. In this way, FEMO provides the raw training data to the bodybuilder. Figure 13 illustrates the UI page of the activity performance assessment service. This service offers the quantitative performance assessment on each activity in the daily training. The user can visualize his doppler profiles of the current activity group against the standard template for evaluating his activity performance. The service also offers quantitative reports on the quality of the selected activity group against the standard template, such as the smoothness of each activity and duration/intensity differences from standard template, within each activity group. Based on the

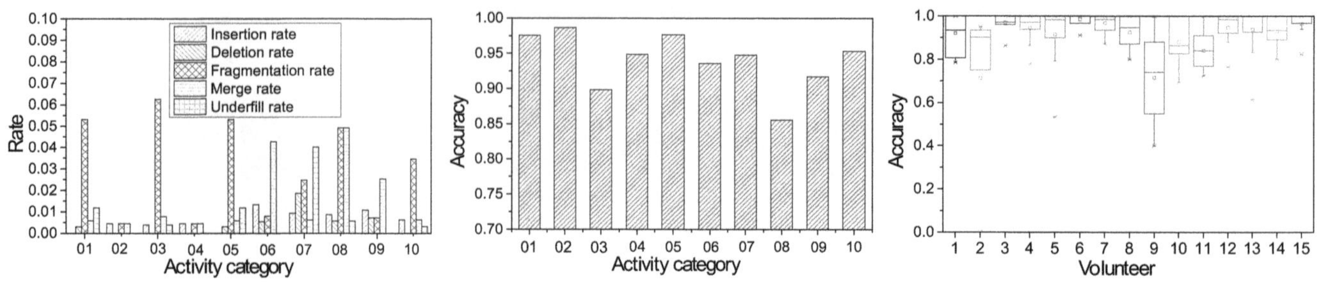

(a) Fine-grained result over 10 activities (b) Accuracy over 10 activities (c) Accuracy over 15 people

Figure 15: Evaluation result of activity segmentation scheme

comparison, the user obtains a thorough summary on the continuity of activity groups. Although our current FEMO prototype only has fundamental functions, *e.g.*, the visualized quality report for daily activities and logging data along the overall training process, we plan to integrate more advanced functionalities in our future work, such as the customized training reminder and intelligent training advisor.

5. SYSTEM EVALUATION

In this section, we conduct extensive experiments and evaluate the performance of FEMO in terms of accuracy, effectiveness, and overhead.

5.1 Experiment setups

The experiment scenario is shown in Figure 14. We attach two Impinj H47 passive tags on a pair of dumbbells. Each dumbbell weighs 2.5kg. Note that the H47 passive tag is a non-metal mount tag hence does not work on metal surfaces, we thus mount it on a foam plastics that is attached on the dumbbell. The foam plastics sufficiently isolates the tag from the metal. To conduct a comprehensive evaluation, we design a training workout with the ten free-weight activities. In this workout, each activity is required to be performed with three groups of ten repetitions. Then we recruit 15 volunteers (vary in age, gender, height, and weight) to follow this workout and track their training process during two weeks. The total duration of the training is 1,534 minutes, with over 4,500 repetitions in total. The 15 volunteers are diverse in weight, height and exercise frequency. Among them, some ones are our acquaintances, and others are not. To obtain standard templates, we recruit one gym trainer who has over 5 years experience and let him perform this workout under the same settings as the other volunteers. In addition, to get the mostly effective assessment of his training, we recommend the trainer to stand at a constant place during his free-weight exercises.

5.2 Activity segmentation

5.2.1 Evaluation metric

We evaluate the activity segmentation scheme based on six metrics [8]: insertion rate, deletion rate, fragmentation rate, merge rate, underfill rate and accuracy. The former five metrics are used to examine the segmentation robustness while the last is to examine the overall segmentation accuracy. The detailed explanation of these metrics are as follows:

- **Insertion rate**: The proportion of cases that FEMO detects an activity within the resting interval. It examines how resilient FEMO is to noisy Doppler peaks within resting intervals.
- **Deletion rate**: The proportion of cases that FEMO misses one activity. It examines how sensitive FEMO is to weak Doppler changes incurred by gym activity.
- **Fragmentation rate**: The proportion of cases that FEMO splits a single activity into multiple ones. It evaluates the ability of FEMO in processing complicated or incoherent activities.
- **Merge rate**: The proportion of cases that FEMO merges multiple activities into a single one. It evaluates FEMO's ability in segmenting the activity with high training pace (*i.e.*, with tiny resting intervals).
- **Underfill rate**: The proportion of cases that the segmented activity is incomplete. It examines whether our method is capable to accurately while completely excavate the entire doppler profile for an activity.
- **Accuracy**: $\frac{\#\ of\ correctly\ detected\ activity}{\#of\ activities\ that\ are\ performed}$. It examines the overall performance of FEMO on activity segmentation.

5.2.2 Evaluation result

Fine-grained segmentation performance: Figure 15(a) shows the fine-grained performance of the segmentation scheme. In particular, the insertion rate is zero for activity 01 and 05. This value then increases steadily to around 0.005 for activities 02, 03, 04 and 10. Finally, it almost reaches 0.015 for activities 06, 07, and 08, which occupies ignorable portion of all the segments. For all activities, the insertion rate is extremely low. *This result indicates that our method is resilient to those doppler peaks within the resting interval.*

After checking the deletion rate, we find that it is also extremely small (below 0.01) for all the desired activities except activity 07. This is because that people usually raise the dumbbells up slowly when performing activity 07, leading to minor Doppler values. Such minor changes, in some cases, may be incorrectly put in resting intervals. Nevertheless, FEMO still controls the deletion rate below 0.02 for activity 07. *This result clearly demonstrates that FEMO is sensitive to Doppler changes incurred by the gym activity.*

As the bar chart in Figure 15(a) shows, FEMO achieves diverse fragmentation rate for different activities. The fragmentation rate is relatively small for activities 02, 04, 06 and 09, *i.e.* below 0.01 on average. It then triples for activities 07 and 10, and further quintuples for activities 01, 03, 05 and 08. This is because activities 01, 03, 05 and

08 contain a reciprocating motion, and people tend to keep a stable posture for a while within these activities. Despite the high disparity, we observe that the overall fragmentation rate for ten activities is below 0.065. *This result shows that the probability of segmenting one activity to multiple ones is very small.*

In Figure 15(a), we also notice a gap between the maximum and minimum merge rates. This is due to the diverse training pace on different gym activities. For example, in our experiment, we find that the resting interval is relative longer for activity 01, 02 and 03, which results in a lower merge rate. While for activity 06, 08 and 09, people tend to take a short rest after performing the activity. Such a short rest leads to activity omissions, yielding a relative larger merge rate. Although the gap exists, it is still relative small (approximate to 0.05) and FEMO can achieve a merge rate of below 0.065 in the worst case. *Therefore, we can conclude that our method scales well to different training paces.*

Figure 15(a) also shows the underfill rate of FEMO. We find that FEMO can precisely capture the entire Doppler profile of activity 02, 04, 06 and 09. Then the underfill rate increases slightly for more complex free-weight activities (*e.g.*, activity 01, 03, 05 and 08). The highest underfill rate is 0.04 for activity 08, indicating FEMO can precisely capture the entire doppler profile of this activity with a success rate of 0.96. *This result clearly states that our method can accurately excavate the entire doppler profile for each activity.*

Accuracy w.r.t Activity diversity: Figure 15(b) plots the result of overall segmentation accuracy with respect to different activities. The performance of the segmentation result can be categorized into three groups. The first group contains activities 01, 02, 05, and 10, where FEMO achieves a segmentation accuracy over 0.95. In the second group, FEMO achieves a segmentation accuracy between 0.9 and 0.95. This group contains activities 04, 06, 07, and 09. While the last group contains activities 03 and 08. For this group, FEMO achieves an accuracy between 0.85 and 0.9. The first two categories together cover eight out of ten activities, indicating that FEMO can achieve a high accuracy (*i.e.*, > 0.9) for the major activities. As for the last group, although the segmentation accuracy reduces, it is still above 0.85. *Therefore, we can conclude that FEMO is robust to activity diversity and can achieve desirable segmentation accuracy.*

Accuracy w.r.t Human diversity: In this experiment, we examine the effect of human diversity on the segmentation accuracy. For each volunteer, we compute the segmentation accuracy on different activities and get the overall accuracy distribution. The result is shown in Figure 15(c). The overall segmentation accuracy for the 15 volunteers maintains in a high level. Specifically, the median accuracy is above 0.9 for 12 volunteers. For the remaining 3 volunteers (volunteer 9, 10, and 11), we can see that FEMO achieves a relative inferior performance, with an accuracy of 0.83 on average. Interestingly, based on the physical characteristic records of volunteers, we find that all the three volunteers seldom go to the gym. As a result, the lack of exercise of these volunteers may lead to non-standard behaviors, thus lowering the segmentation accuracy of FEMO. We further investigate the fine-grained segmentation accuracy distribution of each volunteer. We can see that as shown in Figure 15(c), those who take exercise regularly (*e.g.*, volunteer 3, 4, 6 and 12), the box is relatively short, suggesting that the segmentation accuracy of overall activities has a high level similarity with each other. While for those sedentary group (*e.g.*, volunteer 9, 10 and 11), we can see that the box of accuracy distribution is comparatively tall, indicating that FEMO holds different accuracy performance on different kinds of activities.

Actual	Predicted label									
label	A 01	A 02	A 03	A 04	A 05	A 06	A 07	A 08	A 09	A 10
A 01	0.89	0.03	0	0	0.03	0.05	0	0	0	0
A 02	0.01	0.89	0	0	0.05	0.05	0	0	0	0
A 03	0	0	0.88	0	0	0	0.07	0.04	0	0.01
A 04	0	0	0	0.93	0	0	0	0	0.07	0
A 05	0.02	0.02	0	0	0.94	0.02	0	0	0	0
A 06	0.06	0.02	0	0	0.03	0.90	0	0	0	0
A 07	0	0	0.04	0	0	0	0.89	0.03	0	0.04
A 08	0	0	0.03	0	0	0	0.03	0.93	0	0.01
A 09	0	0	0	0.16	0	0	0	0	0.84	0
A 10	0	0	0.01	0	0	0	0.02	0.02	0	0.95

Figure 16: Confusion matrix of activity recognition

5.3 Evaluation on activity recognition

5.3.1 Evaluation metric

It is possible that the activity recognition system can miss, confuse, or falsely detect activities that did not occur. Thus, in evaluating our activity recognition scheme, we employ the following three metrics:

Precision P: $\frac{TP}{TP+FP}$, where TP and FP represent the true positives and the false positives. Precision is the fraction of correctly recognized activities that are relevant to all the recognized activities.

Recall R: $\frac{TP}{TP+FN}$, where FN is the false negatives. Recall is the fraction of the correctly recognized activities that are relevant to all this kind of activities.

False Positive rate FPR: The proportion of cases that FEMO mistakes an activity for other activities.

5.3.2 Evaluation result

Overall Accuracy on different activities: Figure 16 shows the confusion matrix for the 10 free-weight activities across 15 volunteers. Each row denotes the actual activity performed and each column represents the activity recognized by FEMO. Each element in the matrix represents the fraction of activities in the row that were regarded as the activity in the column. As is shown, the average accuracy is 0.90 with a standard deviation of 0.03 for 10 gym activities. This shows that we can extract rich information about free-weight activities from the Doppler profiles. *The result clearly shows that FEMO achieves a high and stable activity recognition performance, due to its efficient Doppler profile extraction scheme and robust profile matching algorithm.*

Examine the fine-grained performance: In this experiment, we examine the the precision, recall and false positive rate of the recognition performance. The result is shown in Figure 17. FEMO achieves an average precision of 0.90 with a standard deviation of 0.04. This result demonstrates that FEMO substantially returns more actual labels to the activity than error labels. As Figure 17 shows, although the recall fluctuates over different activities, it still maintains a high level for all of these 10 activities, achieving a mean value of 0.91 with a standard deviation of 0.03. This result

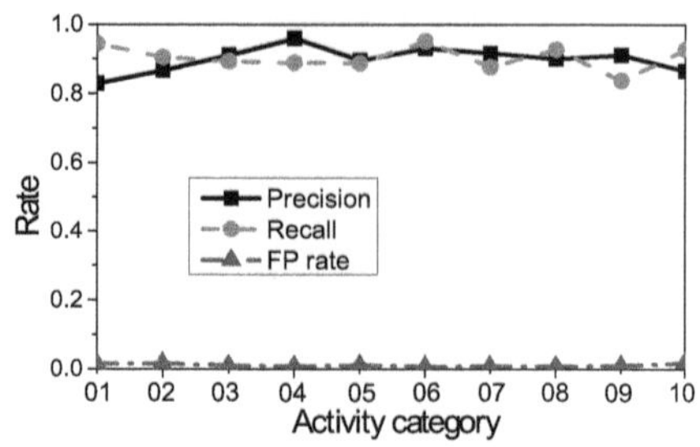

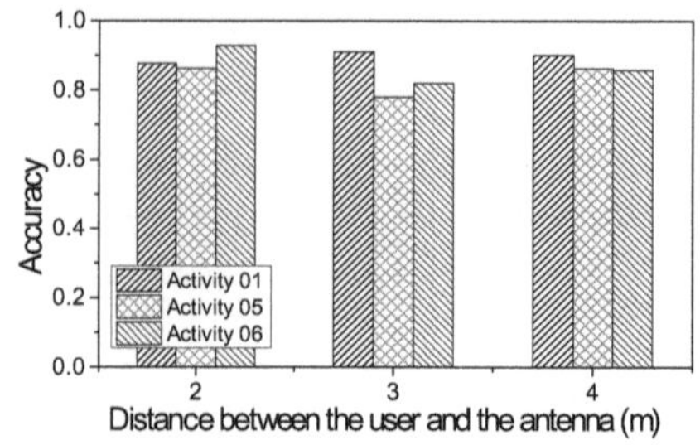

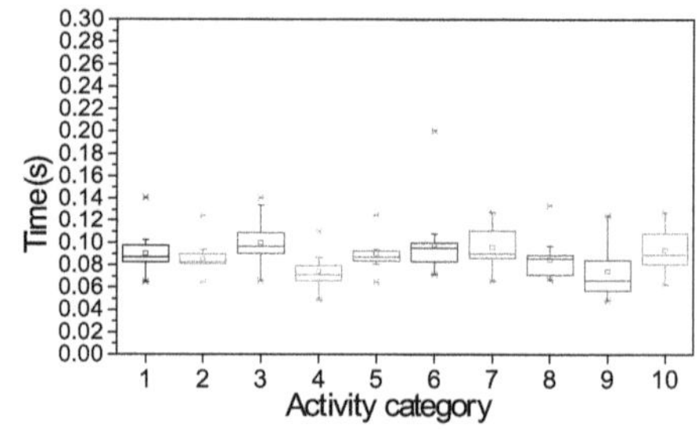

Figure 17: Precision, Recall and FP

Figure 18: Accuracy over different antenna-to-user distances

Figure 19: Computational latency

demonstrates that FEMO can recognize all of these 10 activities with high accuracy. *In a nutshell, the high precision and recall achieved by FEMO manifests that our recognition scheme scales well to different activities.*

We then examine the *FPR* of the recognition result. A higher *FPR* implies a great portion of other activities that are mistakenly classified as the targeting activity. As a result, people may ignore the system's notifications and eventually abandon the system. Figure 17 shows the *FPR* cross 10 activities. We observe that FEMO achieves an average FP rate of 0.011 with a standard deviation of 0.004. Such a low FP rate suggests that FEMO rarely takes other activities as the targeted activity. Therefore, we can trust the activity recognition result with high confidence.

Impact of antenna-to-user distance: we further examine the impact of antenna-to-user distance on the activity recognition. In this trail of experiments, we ask three volunteers to perform activities under different antenna-to-user distance settings. Each activity is performed 30 times by each volunteer. For each activity, we average the recognition accuracy of these volunteers. We randomly pick out three activities and show their recognition accuracy in Figure 18. As the result indicates, when the user is with close proximity to the antenna, the recognition accuracy of these three activities all maintain in a high level. As we expand the user-to-antenna distance, the recognition accuracy changes moderately. *This result clearly demonstrates that our recognition scheme is insensitive to the user-to-antenna distance.*

5.4 Evaluation on activity assessment

FEMO can show the user the detailed assessment information about *Duration*, *Intensity*, *Smoothness*, and *Continuity* of his/her exercises. Then, to evaluate the activity assessment service, we survey the 15 volunteers to get qualitative feedback on the effectiveness and practicability of our system objectively based on their true experience. This includes the user satisfaction and attractive feature. For each aspect, the volunteer is required to give a score between 1 (lowest) to 5 (highest). And we treat these scores as the evaluation for our activity assessment module.

Overall feedbacks: Table 1 shows the overall feedback on FEMO. Participants consider that FEMO could help to reach the training goal with an average satisfaction score of 4.5, the standard deviation is 0.6. The potential to motivate regular training achieves a score of 4.7 on average, with std=0.4. Besides, participates also show high interest (4.6) to use FEMO for monitoring their free-weight training process. Overall, the feedback confirms that FEMO can help to reach training goals faster, motivate the training, and attract participants for long-term use.

Feedback item	Rating	std
could help to reach the training goal	4.5	0.6
could help to rectify the irregular motion	4.7	0.4
would continue using it	4.6	0.6

Table 1: feedback on FEMO after two weeks training

Attractive services: Table 2 shows the ratings on different services provided by FEMO. In the result, the most attractive services that the participants agree with is the accumulative training summary and the local assessment. These two services are scored 4.7. The global assessment is also attractive, achieving a score of 4.6. Although the daily activity summary is less attractive compared with the others, it still achieves a pretty high score (4.3 with std=0.4). Therefore, from above results we believe that FEMO really provides valuable feedback to the user.

5.5 System Overhead

Recognition Latency: FEMO should provide timely activity recognition such that the statistical information of the training process can be displayed promptly. We measure the recognition latency of each activity as the duration from the time point that bodybuilder finishes this activity to the time point the recognition result is shown in the UI module. For each kind of activities, we randomly choose 20 repetitions from 15 volunteers and record their recognition latency. The distribution of the recognition latency for each kind of activities is shown in Figure 19. It shows that FEMO achieves a recognition latency of 0.09s on average for these 10 activities. *Therefore, we can conclude that FEMO can provide on-site activity recognition result.*

Storage overhead: the RFID reader in FEMO periodically interrogates with tags to sense the body motion. The acquired data is thereby accumulated gradually. To examine the storage overhead of FEMO, we give a snapshot of storage augmenting when a volunteer performs activity 03. The result is shown in Figure 20. For comparison, we also plot the accumulated raw data within the same period acquired from the reader before the FEMO processing. We observe that the storage overhead of the raw data stream increases linearly with the time. It rapidly accumulates to over 7.5Mb at the end of the 30th second. Since conducting a workout commonly takes over one hour, recording this whole training process may incur about 1Gb storage overhead. In contrast, we can see that FEMO incurs significantly lower storage overhead, which accumulates to 0.33Mb at the end of the 30th second. From a long-term view, FEMO would accumulate about 40Mb of a one-hour training procedure,

Service item	Rating	std
accumulative training summary	4.7	0.3
daily activity summary	4.3	0.4
global assessment	4.6	0.5
local assessment	4.7	0.4

Table 2: Service assessment after two weeks training

which is negligible compared to one-hour video based recording. *Therefore, we can conclude that as a long-term running system, FEMO is much storage-efficient.*

6. CASE STUDY

We deploy our FEMO system into a small fitness room in our lab. As the bottom-right figure shown in Figure 14, there are other equipments coexisting, such as treadmills and pedalling machines. We conduct experiments in this scenario and test the robustness of FEMO.

In this trail of experiments, we ask three volunteers to perform activities under various conditions. The first group of experiments (Condition #1) are conducted in normal environment, *e.g.*, relatively constant surroundings. In the second group of experiments (Condition #2), the volunteers perform their dumbbell activities with some other trainers running on the treadmills concurrently. During the third group of experiments (Condition #3), a disturber walks across the line of sight between the reader antenna and the volunteer frequently. We pick out three one-arm activities as the examples. Every volunteer performs each activity 30 times under each condition. The segmentation and the recognition accuracy are shown in Figure 21 and Figure 22. From the results we can see that the segmentation accuracy scales well under various conditions. On the other hand, the recognition accuracy has a significant reduction under condition #3. It tells that when the line of sight from the reader antenna to the user is frequently blocked, the Doppler profile will change and become hardly recognizable. However, both segmentation and recognition accuracy (say 0.93 and 0.87) under condition #2 are slightly influenced, which supports the deployment of FEMO in a real gym in the future.

7. DISCUSSION AND FUTURE WORKS

7.1 Discussion

This section discusses limitations and practical deployment issues.

(1) **Impact of Item Placement**: In a real gym, there exists various objects or fitness equipments, and they are considered as obstacles to FEMO. These obstacles (some of them are in the metal material) have slight impact on the accuracy of FEMO, as long as they do not exactly block the line of sight from the reader antenna to the user (tag). In common scenarios, the obstacles may reflect or absorb some signals, resulting in the reduction of signal energy. But they have negligible inference to the Doppler profile as well as our solutions.

(2) **Deployment Cost for Full Coverage**: The current Impinj reader we adopted is not particulary cheap. However, passive RFID technology is promising to be widely spread in the near future. And Impinj reader is a mainstream COTS device, which supports the extension and application of FEMO.

(3) **Scaling to Reader Diversity**: The impinj reader offers a standard API to retrieve Doppler values, but they are not accurate. If we use other devices that can report accurate Doppler shift, FEMO can skip the signal preprocessing and utilize subsequent modules to monitor free-weight activities directly. Thus, FEMO works well with current readers that report low-quality Doppler shift readings, and will perform much better and more efficient if using those readers with high-quality Doppler shift reporting.

(4) **Handling Unknown Activities**: In this paper, we evaluate 10 popular free-weight activities. It is possible for users to perform incomplete actions during the exercises due to *e.g.* fatigue, which may lead to unknown Doppler profiles. In the current prototype, we filter out these unknown Doppler profiles by comparing their DTW distance with a pre-calibrated threshold. Similarly, other activities, such as picking up or putting down dumbbells, can also be filtered. Only those qualified profiles (*i.e.*, DTW distance below the threshold) are counted.

(5) **All-time Accessibility**: In FEMO, we require the user to do exercise within the interrogation zone of the antenna so that the tag can be interrogated interruptedly during the exercise. It is possible to relax this constraint on user location via boosting the transmitting power and optimizing the antenna position. It is also viable to extend the coverage of the reader by using multiple antennas to ensure all-time accessibility of tags even if the user is out of the interrogation zone of one or several antennas.

(6) **Extending to Multiple Users**: In the current prototype, we only evaluate FEMO in single-user cases. We envision FEMO can be extended to multi-user case via multiple antennas or distributed MIMO technology, *e.g.* each antenna separately monitors one user. As part of our on-going studies, we also leverage multiple antennas to monitor synchronized sports like group dancing training and computer-supported cooperative working.

7.2 Future Works

(1) **Scaling to non-stop activities**: We admit that our proposed segmentation algorithm is based on the fact that people tend to take a short rest after each activity to control the training pace. When adopting the algorithm to deal with non-stop activities, the segmentation accuracy will degrade to a certain extent. We will design a more robust algorithm in our future work.

(2) **Quantitative metric for activity assessment**: In the current prototype, we take the data collected from one gym trainer with 5-year experience as the standard templates. To further improve the effectiveness and availability of FEMO and provide more accurate assessment result, we would extend the standard templates to suit different users, *e.g.*, recruiting more professional trainers or coaches (varying in gender, height, weight, *etc.*) to provide the standard activity templates. Thus, FEMO can choose appropriate templates for the user based on his/her personal information when he/she first uses FEMO. Also, to improve the design of assessment criteria so as to further improve the availability of FEMO, we would consult these coaches to give more professional advices or acquire qualitative feedbacks from focus groups.

8. RELATED WORK

The design of FEMO is closely related to the following research categories.

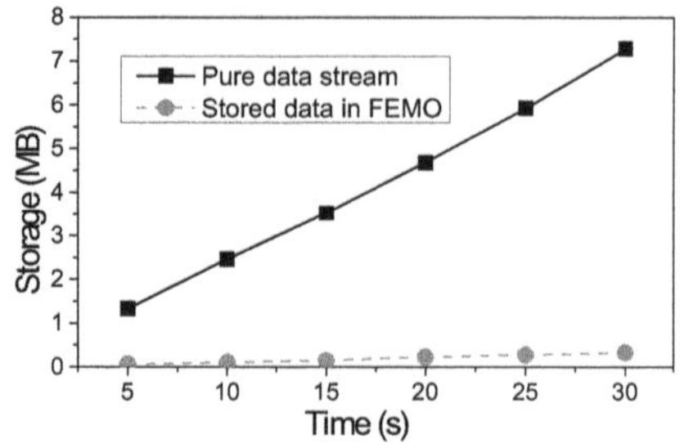

Figure 20: Storage overhead

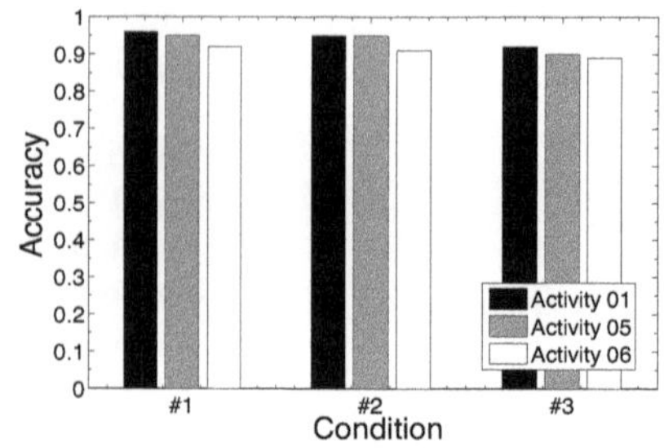

Figure 21: Segmentation accuracy over various conditions

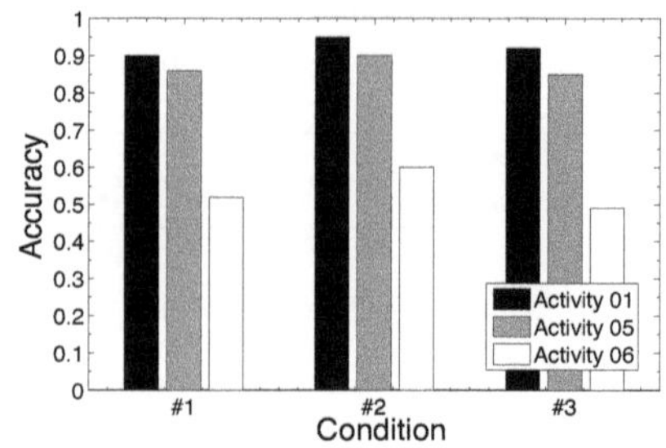

Figure 22: Recognition accuracy over various conditions

Activity Recognition: There is a large body of works on human activity recognition. Based on different processing patterns, the works in this domain can be broadly divided into two categories. The first category of works leverage dedicated sensors, *e.g.*, the gyroscope and accelerometer, for human activity recognition. These works build upon the fact that the sensor can provide rich information reflecting the gesture recognition. UbiFit Garden [10] infers the body movement via a on-body sensing module, and displays the result on the mobile terminal to encourage individuals' training enthusiasm. RistQ [29] leverages the accelerations from a wrist strap to detect and recognize smoking gestures. Chang *et al.* [9] also use accelerometer sensors embedded in a glove to recognize and track the free-weight exercises in the gym. Although these proposals have demonstrated an inspiring power in activity recognition, the requirement of wearing some dedicated sensors is usually cumbersome or unsuitable for gym activity recognition. Besides, the performance of these sensor based schemes is sensitive to the hardware characteristics (*e.g.*, the sampling rate or computational capacity), which limits the wide adoption in practice.

Another brunch of activity recognition solutions exploit the change of wireless signals incurred by the human's actions. RF-IDraw [40] can infer a human's writing by tracking a passive RFID tag attached to his/her pen. E-eyes [41] leverages WiFi signals to recognize the in-home activity of human beings. In particular, there are many prior works detecting movements by resorting to Doppler effect [5, 19, 37, 38]. Their common insight is that the Doppler shift generated from the non-rigid-body motions of humans contains valuable information related to the human movement. The authors in [5, 37] extract certain features from the Doppler shift to distinguish among humans, animals, and vehicles. The work proposed in [19] can classify seven human activities (such as the running, walking, etc.) by extracting Doppler features from the signals collected by a 2.4GHz Doppler radar. By deploying Doppler sensors on the wall or tables, the work proposed in [26] can sense daily human activities using the Doppler effect in 24GHz microwaves. WiSee [30] exploits the Doppler effect of WiFi signals caused by the body reflection to infer nine typical human motions. Similar to our work, these approaches are device-free such that users are released from wearing or carrying any devices. However, they either adopt dedicated hardware (*e.g.*, Software defined radio, Doppler radar, *etc.*) or require complicated signal processing procedure, introducing a high deployment cost or huge computational overhead. Moreover, they have to rely on high-frequency signals (such as 2.4GHz, 24GHz), in which cases the Doppler change induced by human motions are obvious and easy to track. Our work releases this constraint in that we realize the accurate activity recognition and assessment by using a much lower frequency spectrum, *i.e.*, 860MHz $\sim$ 960MHz, which is adopted by COTS passive RFID devices. Within this spectrum, the Doppler changes are subtle and vulnerable to noises [22]. In addition, we enable the on-site activity recognition and assessment by adopting several efficient techniques, *e.g.*, DTW, and provide rich feedbacks to the user for assessments.

Context-awareness Sensing: Recent advances in lightweighted sensors [23] and signal processing techniques have witnessed the prosperity of context-awareness sensing. CrossNavi [36] enables the crossroad navigation for the blind with the calibration of built-in sensors on commodity phones. SurroundSense [4] exploits built-in sensors on smartphones to characterize ambient features for logical localization. Similarly, SoundSense [24] analyzes the characteristics of sound events via a mobile phone to recognize the context around the user. The sound characteristics are further used for monitoring the face-to-face interaction [21], non-speech body sound recognition [31], speaker counting [42], and sleep quality monitoring [15, 13]. These works can provide partial indication on human environment, thereby enhancing the activity recognition performance.

9. CONCLUSION

In this paper, we present the design, implementation and evaluation of FEMO, a passive RFID based free-weight activity monitoring system. FEMO attaches passive RFID tags to the training devices, *i.e.*, dumbbell in this work, and leverages the backscattered signal for on-site activity recognition and assessment. The result of extensive experiments collected from 15 volunteers demonstrates that FEMO can be applied to a variety of free-weight activities, providing valuable feedbacks for users' activity rectification.

10. ACKNOWLEDGEMENTS

This work was supported in part by National Basic Research Program of China (973 Program) under Grant No. 2015CB351705, NSFC under Grant No. 61572396, 61373175, and 61402359; the Natural Science Basic Research Plan in Shaanxi Province of China under Grant No. 2014JQ832; the Specialized Research Fund for the Doctoral Program of Higher Education under Grant No. 20130201120016. We thank the valuable comments from our shepherd Dr. Tian He and anonymous reviewers.

11. REFERENCES

[1] Are Personal Trainers Worth the Price. http://www.telegraph.co.uk/health/dietandfitness.html.

[2] Centers for Disease Control and Prevention. Physical activity recommendations for adults. cdc.gov/physicalactivity/everyone/guidelines/adults.html.

[3] Learn How to Slim and Strengthen Your Midsection with the Best Core Exercises. http://www.askthetrainer.com/best-core-exercises/.

[4] M. Azizyan, I. Constandache, and R. Roy Choudhury. SurroundSense: Mobile Phone Localization via Ambience Fingerprinting. In *Proceedings of ACM MobiSys*, 2009.

[5] I. Bilik, J. Tabrikian, and A. Cohen. GMM-based Target Classification for Ground Surveillance Doppler Radar. *IEEE Transactions on Aerospace and Electronic Systems*, 42(1):267–278, 2006.

[6] Dumbbells, Barbells, and Kettlebells. http://www.bodybuilding.com/fun/grapgym9.htm.

[7] A Simple Protocol for Testing Your Work Capacity. http://breakingmuscle.com/strength-conditioning/a-simple-protocol-for-testing-your-work-capacity.

[8] A. Bulling, U. Blanke, and B. Schiele. A Tutorial on Human Activity Recognition using Body-worn Inertial Sensors. *ACM Computing Surveys*, 46(3):33, 2014.

[9] K.-H. Chang, M. Y. Chen, and J. Canny. Tracking Free-weight Exercises. In *Proceedings of ACM UbiComp*, 2007.

[10] S. Consolvo, D. W. McDonald, T. Toscos, M. Y. Chen, J. Froehlich, B. Harrison, P. Klasnja, A. LaMarca, L. LeGrand, R. Libby, et al. Activity Sensing in the Wild: A Field Trial of Ubifit Garden. In *Proceedings of ACM CHI*, 2008.

[11] S. B. Eisenman, E. Miluzzo, N. D. Lane, R. A. Peterson, G.-S. Ahn, and A. T. Campbell. Bikenet: A mobile sensing system for cyclist experience mapping. *ACM Transactions on Sensor Networks*, 6(1):6, 2009.

[12] Fitbit. https://www.fitbit.com/.

[13] W. Gu, Z. Yang, L. Shangguan, W. Sun, K. Jin, and Y. Liu. Intelligent Sleep Stage Mining Service with Smartphones. In *Proceedings of ACM UbiComp*, 2014.

[14] N. Y. Hammerla, T. Plötz, P. Andras, and P. Olivier. Assessing Motor Performance with PCA. In *Proceedings of IWFAR*, 2011.

[15] T. Hao, G. Xing, and G. Zhou. iSleep: Unobtrusive Sleep Quality Monitoring using Smartphones. In *Proceedings of ACM MobiSys*, 2013.

[16] iOS 8 HealthKit. http://www.apple.com/ios/whats-new/health/.

[17] R. E. Kalman. A new Approach to Linear Filtering and Prediction Problems. *Journal of Fluids Engineering*, 82(1):35–45, 1960.

[18] C. Kennedy-Armbruster and M. Yoke. *Methods of Group Exercise Instruction.* Human Kinetics, 2014.

[19] Y. Kim and H. Ling. Human Activity Classification Based on Micro-Doppler Signatures Using a Support Vector Machine. *IEEE Transactions on Geoscience and Remote Sensing*, 47(5):1328–1337, 2009.

[20] J. Kruger, H. M. Blanck, and C. Gillespie. Dietary and physical activity behaviors among adults successful at weight loss maintenance. *International Journal of Behavioral Nutrition and Physical Activity*, 3(1):17, 2006.

[21] Y. Lee, C. Min, C. Hwang, J. Lee, I. Hwang, Y. Ju, C. Yoo, M. Moon, U. Lee, and J. Song. Sociophone: Everyday Face-to-face Interaction Monitoring Platform using Multi-phone Sensor Fusion. In *Proceeding of ACM MobiSys*, 2013.

[22] H. Li, Y. Can, and P. S. Alanson. IDSense: A Human Object Interaction Detection System Based on Passive UHF RFID. In *Proceedings of ACM CHI*, 2015.

[23] Z. Li, W. Chen, C. Li, M. Li, X.-y. Li, and Y. Liu. FLIGHT: Clock Calibration Using Fluorescent Lighting. In *Proceedings of ACM MobiCom*, 2012.

[24] H. Lu, W. Pan, N. D. Lane, T. Choudhury, and A. T. Campbell. SoundSense: Scalable Sound Sensing for People-centric Applications on Mobile Phones. In *Proceedings of ACM MobiSys*, 2009.

[25] H. Lu, J. Yang, Z. Liu, N. D. Lane, T. Choudhury, and A. T. Campbell. The Jigsaw Continuous Sensing Engine for Mobile Phone Applications. In *Proceedings of ACM SenSys*, 2010.

[26] S. Masatoshi and M. Kurato. Activity Recognition Using Radio Doppler Effect for Human Monitoring Service. *Journal of Information Processing*, 20(2):396–405, 2012.

[27] P. Melgarejo, X. Zhang, P. Ramanathan, and D. Chu. Leveraging Directional Antenna Capabilities for Fine-grained Gesture Recognition. In *Proceedings of ACM UbiComp*, 2014.

[28] D. Morris, T. S. Saponas, A. Guillory, and I. Kelner. RecoFit: Using a Wearable Sensor to Find, Recognize, and Count Repetitive Exercises. In *Proceedings of ACM CHI*, 2014.

[29] A. Parate, M.-C. Chiu, C. Chadowitz, D. Ganesan, and E. Kalogerakis. RisQ: Recognizing Smoking Gestures with Inertial Sensors on A Wristband. In *Proceedings of ACM MobiSys*, 2014.

[30] Q. Pu, S. Gupta, S. Gollakota, and S. Patel. Whole-home Gesture Recognition using Wireless Signals. In *Proceedings of ACM MobiCom*, 2013.

[31] T. Rahman, A. T. Adams, M. Zhang, E. Cherry, B. Zhou, H. Peng, and T. Choudhury. BodyBeat: A Mobile System for Sensing Non-speech Body Sounds. In *Proceedings of ACM MobiSys*, 2014.

[32] L. G. Roberts. ALOHA Packet System with and Without Slots and Capture. *ACM SIGCOMM Computer Communnications Review*, 5(2):28–42, 1975.

[33] Y. Rubner, C. Tomasi, and L. J. Guibas. The Earth Mover's Distance as a Metric for Image Retrieval. *International Journal of Computer Vision*, 40(2):99–121, 2000.

[34] R. A. L. S. Kullback. On Information and Sufficiency. *Annals of Mathematical Statistics*, 1951.

[35] S. Salvador and P. Chan. Toward Accurate Dynamic Time Warping in Linear Time and Space. *Intelligent Data Analysis*, 11(5):561–580, 2007.

[36] L. Shangguan, Z. Yang, Z. Zhou, X. Zheng, C. Wu, and Y. Liu. CrossNavi: Enabling Real-time Crossroad

Navigation for the Blind with Commodity Phones. In *Proceedings of ACM UbiComp*, 2014.

[37] A. Stove and S. Sykes. A Doppler-based Automatic Target Classifier for a Battlefield Surveillance Radar. In *Proceedings of IEEE RADAR*, 2002.

[38] D. A. Tesch, E. L. Berz, and F. P. Hessel. RFID Indoor Localization based on Doppler Effect. In *Proceedings of IEEE ISQED*, 2015.

[39] How to measure exercise intensity. `http://www.weightwatchers.com/util/art/index_art.aspx?tabnum=1&art_id=20971`.

[40] J. Wang, D. Vasisht, and D. Katabi. RF-IDraw: Virtual Touch Screen in the Air Using RF Signals. In *Proceedings of ACM SIGCOMM*, 2014.

[41] Y. Wang, J. Liu, Y. Chen, M. Gruteser, J. Yang, and H. Liu. E-eyes: Device-free Location-oriented Activity Identification using Fine-grained WiFi Signatures. In *Proceedings of ACM MobiCom*, 2014.

[42] C. Xu, S. Li, G. Liu, Y. Zhang, E. Miluzzo, Y.-F. Chen, J. Li, and B. Firner. Crowd++: Unsupervised Speaker Count with Smartphones. In *Proceedings of ACM UbiComp*, 2013.

[43] A. Zhan, M. Chang, Y. Chen, and A. Terzis. Accurate caloric expenditure of bicyclists using cellphones. In *Proceedings of ACM SenSys*, 2012.

Glimpse: Continuous, Real-Time Object Recognition on Mobile Devices

Tiffany Yu-Han Chen
MIT CSAIL
yuhan@csail.mit.edu

Lenin Ravindranath
Microsoft Research
lenin@microsoft.com

Shuo Deng
MIT CSAIL
shuodeng@csail.mit.edu

Paramvir Bahl
Microsoft Research
bahl@microsoft.com

Hari Balakrishnan
MIT CSAIL
hari@csail.mit.edu

ABSTRACT

Glimpse is a continuous, real-time object recognition system for camera-equipped mobile devices. Glimpse captures full-motion video, locates objects of interest, recognizes and labels them, and tracks them from frame to frame for the user. Because the algorithms for object recognition entail significant computation, Glimpse runs them on server machines. When the latency between the server and mobile device is higher than a frame-time, this approach lowers object-recognition accuracy. To regain accuracy, Glimpse uses an *active cache* of video frames on the mobile device. A subset of the frames in the active cache are used to track objects on the mobile, using (stale) hints about objects that arrive from the server from time to time. To reduce network bandwidth usage, Glimpse computes *trigger frames* to send to the server for recognizing and labeling. Experiments with Android smartphones and Google Glass over Verizon, AT&T, and a campus Wi-Fi network show that with hardware face detection support (available on many mobile devices), Glimpse achieves precision between 96.4% to 99.8% for continuous face recognition, which improves over a scheme performing hardware face detection and server-side recognition without Glimpse's techniques by between 1.8-2.5×. The improvement in precision for face recognition without hardware detection is between 1.6-5.5×. For road sign recognition, which does not have a hardware detector, Glimpse achieves precision between 75% and 80%; without Glimpse, continuous detection is non-functional (0.2%-1.9% precision).

Categories and Subject Descriptors

D.4.7 [**Operating Systems**]: Organization and Design—*Real-time systems and embedded systems; Interactive systems*

Keywords

mobile computing; wearable computing; cloud computing; caching; Google Glass

SenSys'15, November 1–4, 2015, Seoul, South Korea.
© 2015 ACM. ISBN 978-1-4503-3631-4/15/11 $15.00
DOI: http://dx.doi.org/10.1145/2809695.2809711.

Figure 1: Offloading every frame to a server reduces trackability (right): the stop sign's location is wrong.

1. INTRODUCTION

Cameras of good quality are now available on almost every handheld and wearable mobile device. The high resolution of these cameras coupled with pervasive wireless connectivity makes it feasible to develop continuous, real-time object recognition applications. These applications *locate* objects in a video stream and *label* them with information associated with the objects. For example, an application that helps a user assemble furniture can pinpoint and label each piece [53, 6], a driver assistance application that locates and labels road signs can improve driver safety [28], a tourist application that recognizes landmarks and buildings can improve user experience, and so on. Researchers have also proposed applications of object recognition for smart homes [45, 42] and perceptual user interfaces [54, 36].

To support these applications, the object recognition system must provide high *trackability*, i.e., it should be able to locate an object accurately and label it with an identifier. Achieving high trackability in real-time on mobile devices is challenging because the required computer-vision algorithms are computationally intensive and must run at the real-time rate of 30 frames per second (see §2.3). Hardware support for face detection (locating a face) is available today, but labeling a face scales with the size of the corpus of faces, and is infeasible on a mobile device.

For these reasons, object recognition tasks must be offloaded to more powerful servers. Offloading is a well-known idea [13, 23, 22], but in the context of continuous recognition, it must be applied with care because wireless network latencies are too high. For example, if it takes 700 milliseconds to transfer a frame and recognize its objects at a server (measured time on an LTE network), when the results arrive they will be over 20 frames old, and the located object may

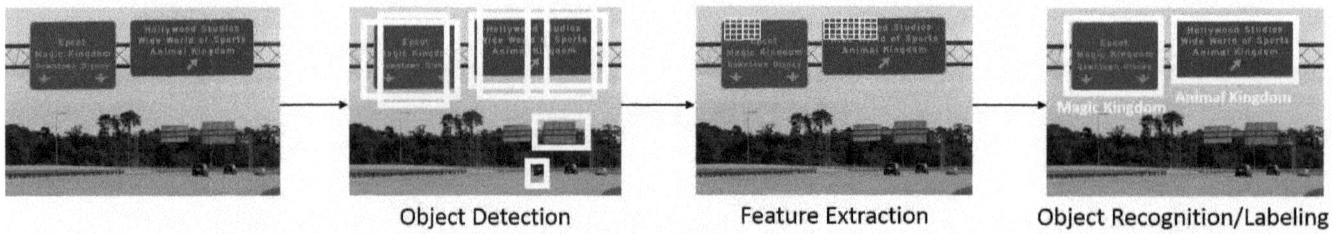

Figure 2: The three computationally-intensive stages of the object recognition pipeline.

no longer be at the reported position. An example is shown in Figure 1: the user sees incorrect results.

This paper presents the design, implementation, and evaluation of Glimpse, a continuous, real-time object recognition system that achieves high trackability, while reducing the amount of network bandwidth consumed relative to alternative designs. Glimpse achieves high trackability by maintaining an *active cache* of frames on the mobile device, and computing over the cached frames using the stale hints that arrive from the server to get an estimate of an object's location in the current frame. Because tracking an object through every cached frame takes too long, the active cache subsamples frames using the rate of change between scenes, the network delay, and the device capability.

Glimpse reduces bandwidth consumption by strategically sending only certain *trigger frames* to the server to obtain object recognition hints. Trigger frames are ones for which the server's answer is likely to differ from the local tracking.

Glimpse occupies an interesting point in the design space of possible ways to split computation between the server and mobile. The server does the hard work of recognition and labeling, sending back both labeled objects and features to use in the mobile's active cache, but this information is always a little stale. The mobile tracks the objects locally using the active cache, not going through every cached frame, and whenever a response for a past frame arrives from the server, it "catches up" to the current frame and processes subsequent frames in real time.

The active cache and trigger frames are generic techniques that may be applied to a wide range of real-time, vision-based systems. Advances in computing hardware and vision algorithms are likely to change the placement of components in a system like Glimpse in the future. For instance, today, there is no hardware support on mobile devices for detection of objects other than faces, but that may change in the future. As long as the processing delay is significantly higher than the time between subsequent frames (33 ms), the results will be stale by the time it is shown to the user. The active cache will hide this latency from the user, while trigger frames reduce the number of frames that must be processed. We discuss the generality of these techniques in §9.

We have implemented Glimpse for recognizing road signs and faces and have conducted experiments with Android smartphones and Google Glass. We evaluate two versions of Glimpse, sw and hw. In both versions, object recognition (labeling) runs on the server. In the sw version, object detection for road signs and faces run on the server as well, whereas in the hw version (implemented only for faces), detection runs in mobile hardware.

Our main experimental results are:

1. Over campus Wi-Fi, Verizon LTE, and AT&T's LTE, Glimpse (hw) achieves precision between 96.4% to 99.8% for face recognition. By contrast, a scheme that performs hardware face detection and server-side recognition without Glimpse's techniques achieves precision between about 38.4% and 56.5%; the improvement with Glimpse (hw) is between 1.8-2.5×. These improvements are due to the active cache.
2. The improvement in precision for face recognition without hardware (sw) is between 1.6-5.5×. For road sign recognition, which does not have a hardware detector, the improvement is enormous: 42× for Wi-Fi and 375× for Verizon LTE (road sign recognition does not work in the baseline here). Again, the active cache is responsible for these improvements.
3. Trigger frames reduce the bandwidth by up to 2.3× and consumes 25-35% less energy compared to using the active cache alone, while retaining the same accuracy.

A video demonstration of Glimpse is at the URL, `http://people.csail.mit.edu/yuhan/glimpse`.

2. BACKGROUND AND DESIGN

This section describes the object recognition pipeline and tracking, and Glimpse's challenges and architecture.

2.1 Object recognition pipeline

The recognition pipeline for objects or faces, which runs on a video frame, consists of three stages: *detection*, *feature extraction*, and *recognition* (Figure 2).

Detection: This stage searches the frame for objects of interest and locates them with bounding boxes, but without labels. The object detector uses distinctive characteristics of objects such as a closed boundary for cars, a prominent color contrast from the background for road signs, and region differences for faces (the eyes are darker than the cheeks).

Feature extraction: This stage processes the content inside the bounding box computed by the detector to extract features that represent the object, using methods like the scale-invariant feature transform (SIFT) [34, 12] and speeded-up robust features (SURF) [7, 12].

Recognition/Labeling: This stage recognizes the object and assigns a label to it using a machine-learning classifier trained offline using a database of labeled object images. The training phase extracts feature vectors as mentioned above, after which it constructs a model such as a Support Vector Machine [18]. Online, it uses the trained model to convert feature vectors into a label.

2.2 Object tracking

The goal of object tracking is to follow a moving object from one frame to the next in a video stream. Glimpse

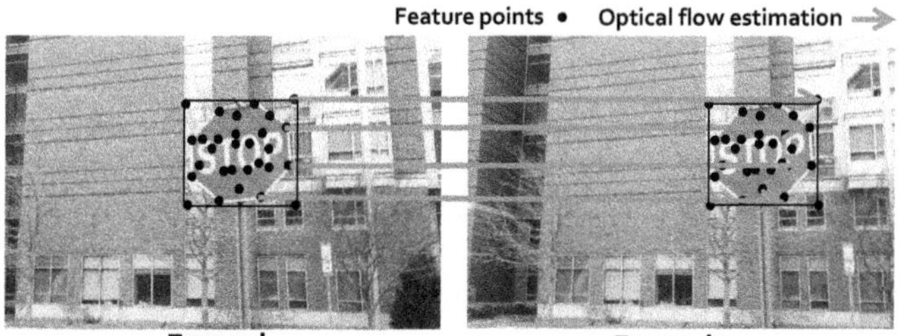

Figure 3: Extracting feature points on a road sign in frame i, computing the optical flow for each of the points, and locating the points in frame $i+1$.

Scheme	Device-only	Offload to Server (Wi-Fi)
Road sign recognition	11.32 J	0.54 J
Face recognition	5.16 J	0.44 J

Table 1: Energy consumption of the object recognition pipeline for a single frame on a Samsung Galaxy Nexus.

uses the Lucas-Kanade tracking algorithm [35], which maps the location of the object from one frame to the next in two steps: (1) extract feature points representing the moving object [49], and (2) estimate where those feature points could be in the second frame to locate the object. For the first step, one can reuse the feature points and the bounding box obtained in the *feature extraction* and *detection* stages. Alternatively, one could apply algorithms such as *good features to track* [49], SIFT [34], or SURF [7] to locate corners and prominent points in the moving object. These features points are then tracked across frames using optical flow techniques [8, 24], which compute the velocity of points between frames.

The result of the tracking stage is a set of successfully tracked feature points in the second frame. Figure 3 shows an example of extracted feature points on a road sign, and the result of tracking. In general, object tracking is a faster operation compared to the recognition pipeline.

2.3 Challenges and approach

We ran the various recognition and tracking tasks described above on different platforms and measured their performance. Table 2 shows the results for Google Glass, a smartphone, and a server machine. We found that all stages showed significant processing time differences between the server and the mobile device. For example, running object detection on the device can be 11-21× slower than running it on a typical server machine; feature extraction can be 18× slower, and recognition can be 14× slower.

The increased processing time also leads to increased energy consumption. Table 1 compares the energy consumption for processing a single frame on the device and offloading. The energy consumed by executing the entire pipeline on the device is 12-21× more compared to energy consumed when each frame is offloaded to the server.

The feature extraction and the recognition stage have a large memory requirement. Beyond a point, the trained model will be too big to fit in a mobile device's memory. In addition, maintaining and updating the database of labeled objects is best done on the server.

Recently, some mobile device manufacturers have incorporated face detection in hardware [1]. The facility significantly reduces detection time by 6×, from 1129 ms to 175 ms (Table 2 rows 5 and 6). Feature extraction and recognition, however, are still expensive operations that are best executed on the server. Moreover, there are no hardware detectors for other objects other than faces on devices today.

Finally, we note that object tracking is fast on the mobile device (last row of Table 2).

These results demonstrate the importance of offloading object recognition tasks to the servers. Offloading, however, presents a key challenge: network delivery and server processing latency, which could be several hundred milliseconds (or more) for individual frames. Sending every frame to the server would significantly degrade trackability (Figure 1).

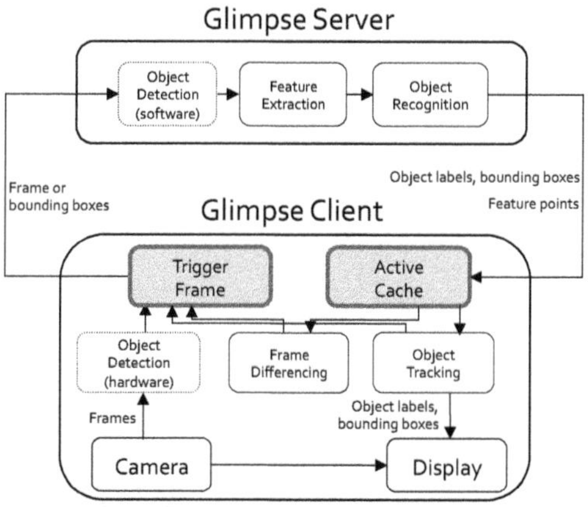

Figure 4: Glimpse Architecture. We explain active cache in §3 and trigger frame in §4.

Figure 4 shows the processing architecture of Glimpse. The Glimpse client runs on the mobile device, receives and stores frames captured by the device's camera, and sends *trigger frames* to the server. The server runs the stages of the recognition pipeline on each frame it receives, producing bounding boxes with labels as well as *feature points* for each recognized object. The client uses the feature points in its tracking phase through the *active cache*, processing only a carefully selected subset of frames to track, adjusting the bounding boxes to the current frame (§3), thereby hiding the network latency from the user. It continuously annotates the user display with the tracked bounding boxes and object labels.

The key aspects of Glimpse are its active cache and trigger frames, which are described in the next two sections.

3. ACTIVE CACHE

The active cache addresses the following problem: how to locate moving object(s) on the mobile device when it takes many frame-times to obtain information, which turns out to be stale, about the object(s) from the server?

Our approach tracks objects on the mobile device by computing the optical flow [8, 24] of features between the *processed* frame for which results are obtained from the server and the *current* frame viewed by the user. To aid this tracking, in addition to returning labels and bounding boxes, the server also returns the feature points for recognized objects in the *processed* frame. Tracking these feature points will allow us to move the bounding box to the correct location in the *current* frame. Unfortunately, this solution only works if the displacement of the object is small between the frames.

Stage	Google Glass Execution Time (ms)	Mobile Client Execution Time (ms)	Server Execution Time (ms)	Model Memory Usage (MB)	Settings
Road Sign Detection [2]	-	2353 ± 242.4	110 ± 32.1	-	Server uses 4 cores.
Road Sign Feature Extraction	-	1327.73 ± 102.4	69 ± 15.2	0.21/object	Using convolutional neural networks with the BVLC GoogleNet model [29, 26, 51]. Server uses a GPU.
Road Sign Recognition	793.3 ± 102	162.1 ± 73.2	11 ± 1.6	0.03/object	Using linear SVM [18] to classify 1K objects with 4K features. Server uses a GPU.
OpenCV Face Detection	3130.18 ± 800.1	2263.71 ± 478.15	197.77 ± 10.56	0.89	Using the frontal face classifier [56, 55]; the minimum size of the detected face is 30×30 pixels.
FaceSDK Face Detection	-	1129 ± 239.5	92.26 ± 21.79	0.12	Mobile client: Nokia Lumia 928.
Hardware-based Face Detection [4]	-	174.6 ± 70.0	-	-	Mobile client: HTC One M8.
Facial Feature Extraction	309.8 ± 101.2	84.55 ± 25.57	19 ± 3.15	35	Extracting 57K features around 27 landmarks [9, 10].
Face Recognition	2912.3 ± 448	537.8 ± 224.1	41.13 ± 3.11	1.25/object	Using linear SVM to classify 224 objects with 57K features.
Tracking	43.22 ± 9.1	37.7 ± 11.5	1.2 ± 0.4	0	Lucas-Kanade tracking with 3 pyramid levels and 30 feature points [35].

Table 2: Performance of object detection, feature extraction, recognition, and tracking. Unless stated otherwise, the Mobile Client is a Samsung Galaxy Nexus Android smartphone and Server is a Intel Core i7 with 3.6GHz, 4-core CPU. The performance is averaged across 1293 frames with resolution 640 × 480.

The performance of tracking degrades as the displacement increases. Figure 5 shows an example. When the user's view is changing, objects move within hundreds of milliseconds. Hence running merely one object tracking from the *processed* frame to the *current* frame is insufficient to achieve good accuracy (we give experimental results in §7).

To accurately find the location of objects in the *current* frame, Glimpse maintains an active cache of intermediate frames; it runs object tracking through a subset of the cache.

This approach works because tracking works when the object displacement is small, which is generally the case in consecutive frames. The active cache stores all the subsequent frames from the frame that gets transmitted to the server for processing. When the mobile device receives the recognition results from the server, it runs object tracking from the processed frame, through the cached frames, to catch up with the current frame.

Unfortunately, it is not practical to run through *all* the cached frames. Object tracking for a frame takes over 30 ms on today's mobile platforms (see Table 2). Tracking through every frame in the cache does not allow us to catch up to the frame being viewed. For example, suppose we send *frame 1* to the server and the end-to-end delay to obtain results from the server is 1 second. At 30 frames per second, we would have cached 33 frames. Because it takes 38 ms to track an object on a mobile device, we need at least 1140 ms to run through all the cached frames. By the time we produce a result for *frame 30*, the user is already viewing *frame 64*, rendering the results stale. Note that we cannot start object tracking on the cached frames before we obtain results from the server because we need the bounding boxes and feature points for tracking.

Therefore, we have to speed up the processing of cached frames to catch up with the current frame as fast as possible. Discarding frames will speed-up the computation, but might sacrifice trackability. Glimpse uses an adaptive subsampling strategy that takes the observed delay, the device's capabilities, and the changes of the scene into consideration. The method subsamples frames without compromising trackability by solving two problems:

1. How many frames to select from the active cache?
2. Which frames to select?

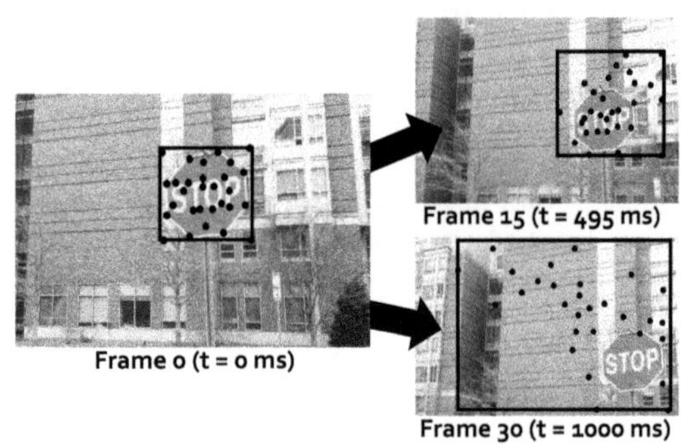

Figure 5: Tracking performance degrades as the displacement of the object increases.

3.1 How many frames to select?

Let f_i be the ith frame captured by the camera. If we send f_i to the server for recognition, we store subsequent frames in the active cache. Assuming the results come back when the client is viewing frame $f_{i+(n-1)}$, we will have cached n frames (f_i to $f_{i+(n-1)}$) in that duration. Our goal is to pick l out of n frames, or $p = l/n$ fraction of frames so that we can catch up without sacrificing tracking performance. A smaller p allows us to swiftly catch up to the current frame, but might degrade performance since we discard many frames; a bigger p ensures reliable tracking, but it takes more time and we would be left with stale results.

The selection of p depends on two factors: (i) the end-to-end processing delay of a frame (i.e., the value of n), and (ii) the execution time e of the tracking algorithm on the client. The lower the mobile's computation capability, the larger the value of e, so p must be small. When the network

Figure 6: Frame differencing.

delay is low, n is small, and we can select a larger p without degrading trackability.

For any given platform, using a set of videos tagged with ground truth, we simulate different n, e, and p, and pick the p that maximizes trackability. In our experiments, when e is 30 ms or more, $p = 0.1$ works the best for different values of n. But when e is 20 ms or less, the best p depends on n (§7.2). At runtime, we measure e for every tracking call and maintain an average. We directly find n as the number of cached frames. We query a model stored locally with e and n to get p.

3.2 Which frames to select?

Given a sequence of frames $F = \{f_i, ..., f_{i+(n-1)}\}$ stored in the cache and a fraction p, we select $l = p * n$ frames from the cache for tracking. A straightforward approach is to pick l frames at regular intervals, but this method does not give us the best results when objects are moving across frames. For instance, if the object only starts moving after frame $f_{i+(n/2)}$, we can skip frames in the first half.

The selected l frames should capture as much movement as possible, and not have much redundancy between each other. To solve this problem, we first need a metric to characterize movement between two frames. This metric must be easy to compute, lest we lose the benefit of iterating through only a subset of frames.

Glimpse uses a lightweight *frame differencing* function to calculate the "movement" between two frames (Figure 6). First, we convert the frame to grayscale and compute the absolute difference of pixel values $a_{i,j}(x, y)$ for every pixel (x, y) between frame i and frame j, and consider it significant if it exceeds a threshold:

$$a_{i,j}(x, y) = |f_i(x, y) - f_j(x, y)| \quad (1)$$

$$d_{i,j}(x, y) = \begin{cases} 1 & a_{i,j}(x, y) > \phi \\ 0 & otherwise \end{cases} \quad (2)$$

Based on our experiments, we pick $\phi = 35$, a value sensitive enough to capture scene movements and robust to changes caused by noise. We then compute the frame difference (movement metric) $d_{i,j}$ between frame i and frame j as:

$$d_{i,j} = \sum_{x,y} d_{i,j}(x, y), d_{i,j} \geq 0 \quad (3)$$

Computing $d_{i,j}$ is linear in the size of the frame, taking only a few milliseconds on a mobile device; it can be computed when the frame is inserted into the active cache.

Using the frame difference metric, the frame selection problem can now be redefined as follows: given a sequence of frame differences $D = \{d_{i,i+1}, ..., d_{i+(n-2),i+(n-1)}\}$, divide D into $(l + 1)$ partitions, such that the maximum sum over all the partitions is minimized. This is a *linear partition* problem, which can be solved with a dynamic program in $O(ln^2)$ time, by defining $H[n, l]$ as the optimum value of a partition arrangement with n frame differences and l partitions:

$$H[n, l] = \min_{j=i}^{i+n}(\max\{H[j, l-1], \sum_{k=j}^{i+n} d_{k,k+1}\}) \quad (4)$$

Figure 7: Tracked feature points deviate due to changes in the angle of the object.

4. TRIGGER FRAMES

Unlike existing systems [20, 14, 22] that need to send every frame (or as many as the network can handle) to the server, Glimpse reduces bandwidth consumption by sending only certain *trigger frames* to the server to obtain the object recognition hints.

The Glimpse client uses three techniques:

1. It monitors tracking performance and sends frames to the server when the local tracking is about to fail.
2. It sends frames to the server when there is a significant change in the scene.
3. If the scene is constantly changing, it avoids sending too many frames by keeping track of the number of frames in flight.

Detecting tracking failure.

As shown in Figure 7, the tracked feature points would deviate from their correct location and degrade trackability performance as the size, angle, or appearance of the objects changes. When tracking degrades, the client sends a frame to the server to get a new set of feature points to track.

To measure the tracking performance, we make the following observation: since all tracked points are on the same object, when an object moves between frames, the moving distance of those points between frames should be similar. Therefore, we can quantify the tracking performance by measuring these distances between frames. We use the standard deviation of distance of all tracked points between two frames. The larger the standard deviation, the higher the possibility that tracking is failing. We use a threshold of ω_{std} to identify trigger frames, set using experiments to balance between getting new features in a timely way and not sending too many frames.

Detecting scene changes.

In addition to monitoring tracking performance of recognized objects, we should also identify trigger frames when new objects come into the scene. However, it is too expensive to run object detection on the client. To detect if the scene has changed, Glimpse uses the frame differencing technique described in §3.2. We use the formula in Equation 3 to quantify how much the frame has changed from the previously transmitted frame. When the number of "significantly different pixels" between the current frame and the previously transmitted frame is greater than a threshold, ϕ_{motion}, we identify it as a trigger frame.

Limiting the number of frames in flight.

When the scene is constantly changing, the above heuristics could trigger many frames to be sent to the server, causing a network or server bottleneck and also increasing energy consumption. Glimpse limits the number of in-flight frames sent to the server for which results are pending. When there are already i_{max} frames in flight, and we identify a trigger frame, the client waits to receive the results for a frame before sending the next frame[1]. Our experiments show that, having $i_{max} = 1$ frame strikes a good balance between accuracy and resources consumed for various network types (§7).

5. IMPLEMENTATION

We have implemented the Glimpse client for Android smartphones and Google Glass. We also ported the client to Linux for evaluating Glimpse in a controlled setting (§6).

Glimpse Client: The Android implementation of Glimpse uses the OpenCV library (version 2.4.10) [40] written in C/C++ on top of JNI. To speed up the computation, except the dynamic program for frame selection, all the core functions are written in C++, and are invoked using JNI. On Google Glass, running frame differencing on a 640×480 frame using Java takes 220 ms, compared to only 32 ms using C++. We use a separate thread for receiving camera frames and a separate thread for computation (§7.4 describes the detailed energy/overhead measurements). For object tracking, we use the Lucas-Kanade function [35] provided in OpenCV with the default parameters. We declare an object has disappeared if its bounding box is too small (15×15 pixels for road signs [47], and 25×25 pixels for faces), or we do not have enough feature points to draw the bounding box (i.e., the number of feature points is fewer than 4). OpenCV returns frames captured from the camera in both RGB and grayscale format. Because object tracking does not require a color image, we store the frame as a grayscale image in the active cache. We use 640×480 frames and compress each frame into a JPEG image (quality level = 70) before transmission. Each frame is sent using HTTP POST request with multi-part/form-data content type.

Glimpse Server: The server implements the road sign recognition pipeline and the face recognition pipeline (§2.1).

For road signs, we first detect them using boundary, shape, and color [2]. We speed up detection by parallelizing the image processing with four cores. For feature extraction, we train a convolutional neural network model [26, 29] (BVLC GoogleNet Model [51]) using labeled road signs to obtain the computer-crafted features. For classification, we train a SVM classifier with a linear kernel [18] using the features extracted in the previous step. To enable road sign tracking, we use the *good features to track* [49] and return 30 feature points (the top 26 features and the 4 corners of the bounding box) to the client for tracking.

For face detection at the server, we use the Viola-Jones object detector [56, 55] to determine the locations of faces in the frame. In our implementation, we use the Microsoft Face SDK Viola-Jones detector (C#) because it is faster than the OpenCV implementation (Table 2), and generates fewer false positives. For feature extraction, we first locate 27 semantic facial landmarks such as eyes, nose, and mouth in a facial image using a boosted shape regression [9]. We then build the features by extracting multi-scale patches centered at facial landmarks [10] and describe each patch with the local binary pattern (LBP) descriptor. Similar to classifying road signs, we also train a linear SVM model for classifying faces. For face tracking, we return feature points for the 27 landmarks and the four corners of the bounding box computed during the detection and feature extraction stage.

To train the road sign feature extraction and classification models, we use a subset (50%) of the labeled road signs in our dataset (§6). To train the face classification model, we use a training dataset with 224 subjects, with 20 to 40 images for each face. 211 out of the 224 subjects are public figures and the images are collected from the web with URLs from PubFig [30] and CFW [62]. For the subjects featured in our video dataset (§6), we collected images from their Facebook pages. When the server starts, it reads the detection, feature extraction, and classification models from disk into memory for faster processing.

If the client cannot reach the server to send a *trigger frame* because of network failures, we continue to retry periodically. In the mean time, if we are able to track objects locally, we continue tracking them. Currently, Glimpse does not support completely disconnected operation. It informs the user that the service is disconnected and stops annotating objects. To support disconnected operation, we could implement a lightweight, less-accurate object recognition pipeline locally with a small set of features, trained on a few objects. When the client gets disconnected from the server, we could run the local object recognition pipeline. Note that because the local processing will still be computationally expensive with a high response latency, the active cache and trigger frames will remain important.

6. EVALUATION

We evaluated Glimpse using real-world data and trace-driven emulation. Emulation allows us to compare Glimpse with other schemes under reproducible conditions. We also ran Glimpse on Android smartphones and Google Glass to measure its resource consumption.

6.1 Data Collection

We collected two datasets to capture different scenarios, and to evaluate Glimpse's ability to recognize and track different objects. For ground truth, we manually inspected every frame, assigned labels, and marked the objects of interest with bounding boxes. Labeling the video frames is a cumbersome manual process; to the best of our knowledge, we are not aware of any publicly available labeled mobile video dataset.

1. **Face Dataset:** We recorded 26 videos with an Android smartphone. The videos are at 30 frames per second at a resolution of 640×480 pixels per frame. The length of each video ranged from 10 seconds to 16 minutes. Scenarios in the video include shopping with friends, chatting in a restaurant, and waiting at a subway station. In all, we have collected and curated 30 minutes of video, with 54,020 frames and 35,824 (non-distinct) faces.
2. **Road Sign Dataset:** We downloaded 4 walking videos recorded with Google Glass on YouTube. Two videos are from the United States, one from England, and

[1]We always send the current frame to the server even if the identified trigger frame was in the past.

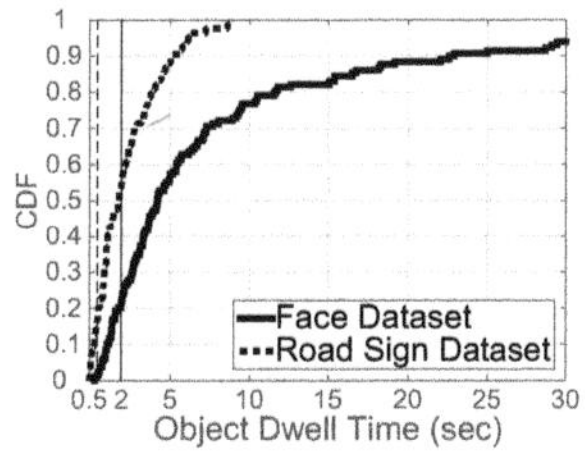

(a) The CDF of the dwell time of each object.

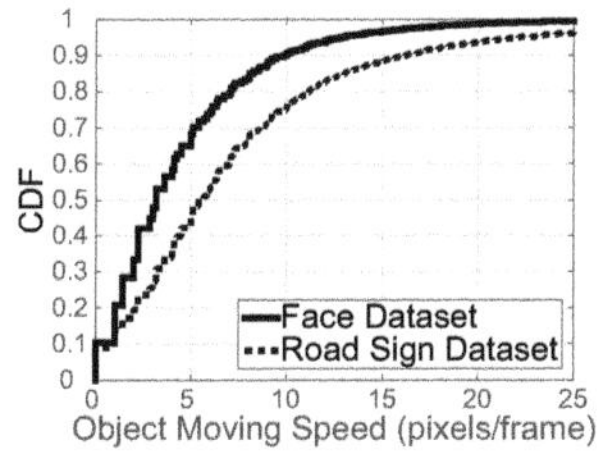

(b) The CDF of object moving speed.

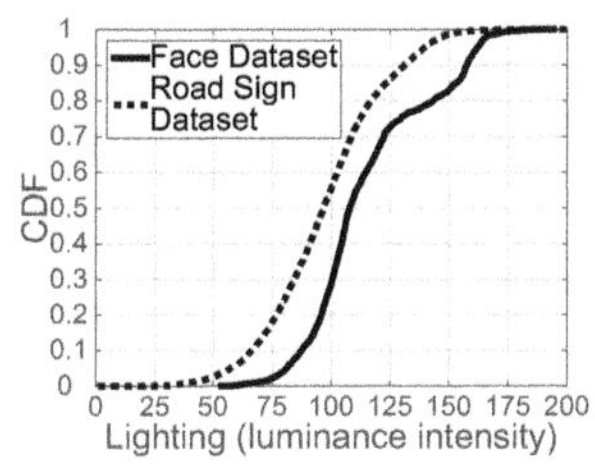

(c) The CDF of luminance intensity of frames.

Figure 8: Dataset characteristics.

one from China. In total, we have 35 minutes of video, with 63,003 frames and 5,424 labeled road signs.

Figure 8(a) shows the CDF of dwell time of each object for the two datasets. The dwell time is the total time an object continuously appears in the view of the camera. In the road sign dataset, 50% of the road signs have a dwell time less than 2 seconds, and 90% of the road signs are less than 5 seconds. In the face dataset, 50% of the faces have a dwell time less than 5 seconds, and 90% of the faces are less than 20 seconds. Figure 8(b) shows the CDF of movement of objects between successive frames (in pixels per frame). Our datasets contain objects moving at various speeds. In the road sign dataset, 90% of the signs move less than 15 pixels between two successive frames (the inter-frame time is 33.33 ms). In the face dataset, 90% of the objects move less than 10 pixels.

Figure 8(c) shows the CDF of luminance intensity (0 - 255) of each frame; a smaller value indicates a darker frame. Our dataset contains varied lighting conditions (luminance intensity between 50 to 160). Note that mobile cameras automatically adjust their aperture to avoid excessively bright or dark images.

6.2 Experimental Setup

To conduct comparative and reproducible experiments, we built an emulation framework with a Linux machine running the Glimpse Client, and a Windows machine running the Glimpse Server. The client stores all the 30 recorded videos locally. To simulate a camera feed, each video frame has a timestamp indicating when it should be processed by the client.

We connect the client and server with a crossover Ethernet cable. To emulate different types of networks, we run the Mahimahi tool [37] on the client. Mahimahi takes network measurement traces as input, and delays each packet delivery time based on the per packet delay in the input trace. In our evaluation, we use wireless network traces described in two recent papers [59, 16], which included Wi-Fi, Verizon Wireless's LTE, and AT&T's LTE network. In addition to controlling the network, we also simulate the compute delays for tracking and frame differencing using micro-benchmarks collected from smartphones and Google Glass hardware.

6.3 Evaluation Metrics

To evaluate Glimpse's trackability, we use *intersection over union (IOU)* [14] as the measure. The IOU of object i is defined as

$$IOU_i = \frac{area\,|O_i \cap G_i|}{area\,|O_i \cup G_i|}, \tag{5}$$

where O_i is the bounding box of the detected object, and G_i is the bounding box of object i's ground truth. We consider the object to be *successfully tracked* if $IOU_i > 50\%$ [14] (i.e., accurately located), *and* the label matches the ground truth.

To quantify Glimpse's performance across large number of video frames, we define the following metrics:

- **Precision (%)**, defined as the ratio of the number of objects successfully tracked to the total number of objects detected by the scheme.
- **Recall (%)**, defined as the ratio of the number of objects successfully tracked to the total number of objects in the ground truth.
- **F1 score (%)**, defined as the harmonic mean of precision and recall.
- **Bandwidth Usage (Kbits/s)**, measured as the total number of kilobits transmitted per second between the client and server.

We normalize both precision and recall for each evaluated scheme using the best precision (93%) and the best recall (96%) we can achieve. We obtain the best results when there are no network and server delays and when the client tracks every frame. The trackability in this ideal condition is less than 100% because our ground truth misses a few objects that object tracking is able to correctly track, and object tracking misses a few objects that we are able to correctly tag as ground truth (e.g., objects that are too small). With this normalization, we are able to measure the performance of Glimpse's techniques independent of imperfections in the vision algorithms or labeling.

7. RESULTS

To evaluate Glimpse, we compare it to the following schemes to measure the benefits of the techniques in Glimpse:

- **Server only:** In this scheme, there is no tracking at the client. The client sends frames to the server and outputs the responses as they arrive. We evaluated different server-only schemes, changing the maximum number of frames in flight, and present results for 1 frame and 30 frames in flight (the results for other values are in between these two).
- **No active cache:** Here, the client tracks between the frame sent to the server (*processed* frame) and the *current* frame, without an active cache. It sends a new frame to the server once we receive a response for the previous frame.
- **Active cache only (no trigger frame):** Here, the client maintains an active cache and tracks through frames using our dynamic programming (DP) algo-

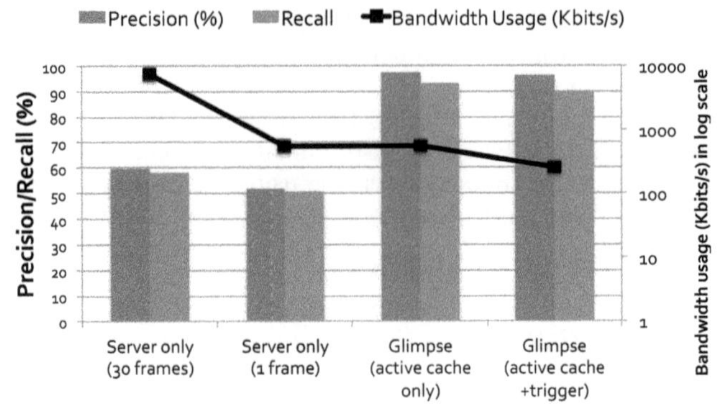

Figure 9: Performance of Glimpse on Wi-Fi for tracking faces. The end-to-end delay (the latency from mobile to server and obtain a response) is 425-455 ms in all schemes, except for 30 frames in flight (542.2 ms).

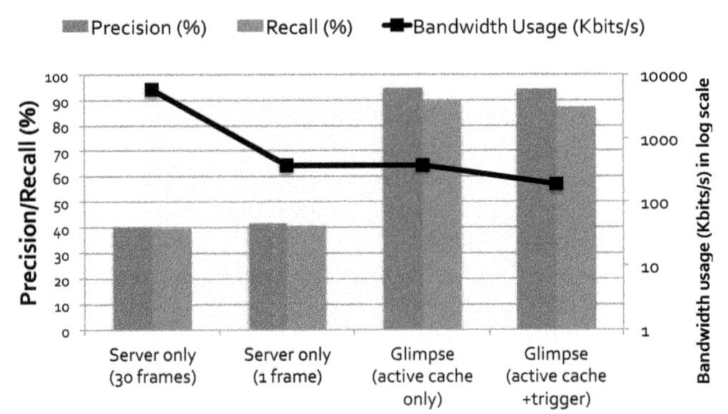

Figure 10: Performance of Glimpse on Verizon's LTE for tracking faces. The end-to-end delay is 656-721 ms in all schemes, except for 30 frames in flight (1102.5 ms).

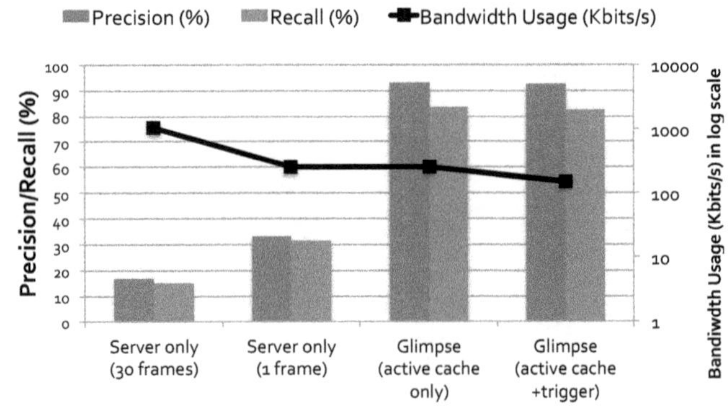

Figure 11: Performance of Glimpse on AT&T's LTE for tracking faces. The end-to-end delay is 927-1041.2 ms in all schemes, except for 30 frames in flight (7391.7 ms).

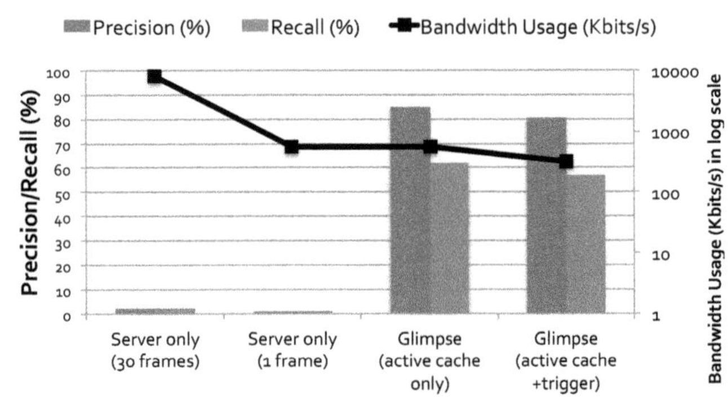

Figure 12: Performance of Glimpse on Wi-Fi for tracking road signs. The end-to-end delay is 510-548 ms in all schemes, except for 30 frames in flight (683.1 ms).

rithm, but there are no trigger frames. The client sends a new frame to the server after receiving response for the previous frame.

In §7.1 we show the end-to-end performance of Glimpse and how it compares to other schemes. In §7.2 and §7.3, we show the benefits of the active cache and trigger frames, respectively. Finally, we evaluate the energy consumption and overhead in §7.4.

7.1 End-to-end performance

We use the network conditions as described in §6.2. Figures 9, 10, and 11, show the end-to-end performance for face recognition on Wi-Fi, Verizon, and AT&T's LTE networks, respectively. Figures 12 and 13 show the end-to-end performance for road sign recognition on Wi-Fi and Verizon's LTE. On the AT&T's LTE network, the network latencies are too high to do real-time road sign recognition. The dwell times of road signs are short (Figure 8), and in most cases, the object moves out of the frame before we get a response from the server.

Significant improvement in precision and recall: Under all network conditions, Glimpse significantly improves the trackability (precision and recall) compared to *Server-only* schemes [22]. The improvement is more prominent as the network delay increases. Even in the fastest network, Wi-Fi, Glimpse improves trackability by 1.8× for face recognition. In the slowest network (AT&T's LTE network), Glimpse achieves a precision of 92.3% (vs. 33%), a recall of 82.6% (vs. 31.8%), an improvement of a factor of 2.8×. For fast moving objects such as road signs (Figures 12 and 13), the improvement is even more significant. Glimpse improves trackability by 71× to 114×; without Glimpse, continuous recognition is non-functional (under 1% precision and recall) for the *Server-only* schemes.

Glimpse's recall decreases as the network delay increases because the dwell time of certain objects become shorter than the end-to-end delay, and hence we miss them. Further, the recall is lower for the road sign recognition compared to face recognition because of the dwell time of road signs are much shorter than that of faces (Figure 8). In Glimpse, when a new object appears in the scene, we identify a trigger frame, but we miss tracking the object till we get a response about that object from the server. Since Glimpse allows only one outstanding frame in flight (§7.3), in the worst case, the discovery overhead could be two round trips worth of frames. When dwell times of objects are longer, we use local tracking to continuously locate the object; but when the dwell time is short (as in the road sign's case), we incur the discovery overhead more often, reducing the recall. If we eliminate the discovery overhead from the recall calculation, the recall increases to 78% on Wi-Fi and 50.2% on Verizon's LTE.

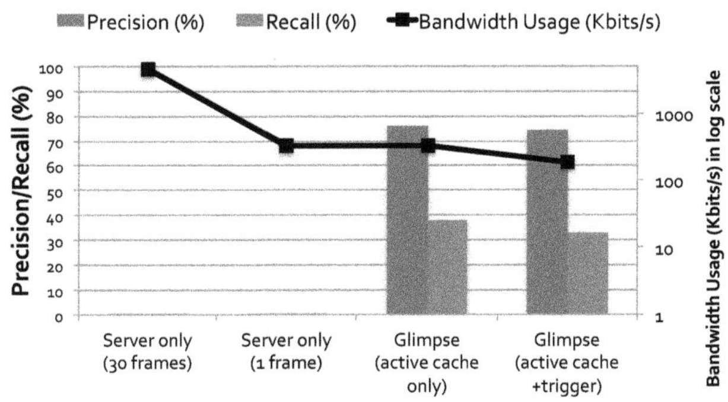

Figure 13: Performance of Glimpse on Verizon's LTE for tracking road signs. The end-to-end delay is 901.1-963.2 ms in all schemes, except for 30 frames in flight (1765.2 ms).

Networks	Schemes	Precision (%)	Recall (%)	Bandwidth Usage (Kbits/s)
Wi-Fi	Server only	56.5	52.2	616.1
	Server only (1 frame in flight)	54.7	52	52.5
	Glimpse	**99.8**	**92.1**	**28.9**
Verizon's LTE	Server only	50.8	47.4	605.2
	Server only (1 frame in flight)	47	44.3	40.2
	Glimpse	**99.4**	**90.7**	**25**
AT&T's LTE	Server only	38.4	31.6	335.8
	Server only (1 frame in flight)	41.3	39	32.1
	Glimpse	**96.4**	**85.5**	**20.7**

Table 3: Glimpse with face detection in hardware.

Significant bandwidth reduction: Figures 9, 10, 11, 12, and 13 also show the bandwidth usage for various schemes. Trigger frames reduce the amount of bandwidth used without compromising precision or recall compared to using only the active cache.

7.1.1 *Face detection in hardware*

As mentioned in §2.3, some mobile devices [1] are now equipped with face detection hardware. Even with face detection at the client, the recognition operation still needs to be offloaded to the server. If Glimpse's goal is to only detect faces, the face detection hardware can help us reduce the amount of the data transmitted to the server. Instead of sending the entire frame, we can send only the bounding box of faces. Even in this case, Glimpse needs to hide the latency of face detection at the client and the latency introduced by the network and the server.

To show that active cache and trigger frames are beneficial irrespective of where detection happens, we evaluated Glimpse on the face dataset with face detection done on the client. Table 3 shows the results. The baseline scheme sends only the detected faces to the server instead of the entire trigger frame. Glimpse considers the current frame as a trigger frame if (1) tracking fails, or (2) the face detection hardware detects a new face that the system does not recognize.

We measure the hardware face detection latency using the Android FaceDetectionListener [4] API on a HTC One M8 and incorporate it into our emulator. The face detection latency is listed in Table 2, and the number we get is similar to the one reported in [11].

Without Glimpse, even with the face detection hardware, the trackability is poor, and the bandwidth usage remains high since the device does not have the capability to recognize the face, and needs to send all the detected regions to the server for recognition. Glimpse improves the trackability by 1.8× to 2.3×. Since Glimpse tracks the face on the client, face detection hardware helps us detect when new faces appear, reducing the bandwidth usage.

These results demonstrate that regardless of where processing happens, if the processing incurs a latency, Glimpse hides it effectively using its *active cache.* Similarly, *trigger frames* enables the system to reduce the number of frames actually processed thereby saving resources.

Datasets	Networks	Glimpse (active cache only) F1 score (%)	No active cache F1 score (%)
Road Sign	Wi-Fi	71.4	48.5
	Verizon's LTE	50.9	26.1
Face	Wi-Fi	95.1	87.2
	Verizon's LTE	91.9	82.1
	AT&T's LTE	88	78.1

Table 4: The F1 score of Glimpse (active cache only) vs. without maintaining an active cache.

7.2 Benefits of the active cache

Table 4 shows that maintaining an active cache improves the trackability, compared to the *No active cache* scheme, which does tracking without a cache.

The performance of *No active cache* degrades as the network delay increases because it becomes harder to track the object without going through intermediate frames.

For the road sign video, on Wi-Fi, the *No active cache* approach achieves 48.5% F1 score comparing to 71.4% with the active cache, which is an 1.4× gain. For the face video, we also improve the F1 score by up to 12% (AT&T's LTE).

The benefits of the active cache stem from our ability to pick the right frames for tracking. As we show next, simply tracking through all frames in the cache can lead to poor performance.

7.2.1 *Picking a subset of frames from the active cache*

As discussed in §3.1, object tracking on the client takes tens of milliseconds. By the time the client processes all the frames in the cache, depending on the end-to-end delay, the final tracking result could be stale as hundred of milliseconds would have elapsed.

The fraction of frames that can be processed depends on the execution time of object tracking e, and the number of frames in the cache n. Figure 14 shows the F1 score (y-axis) when we change the fraction of frames picked (x-axis) for different n (lines) and different e (sub-graphs). When e is 30 ms, and n is 30 frames, if we were to pick every frame in the cache for tracking, the F1 score is less than 30%. Similarly, if we do not pick any intermediate frame, the F1 score is less than 65%.

Figure 14 shows that the best fraction depends on e and n. In our experiments, e was between 30 ms and 40 ms; hence, we chose 0.1 (independent of n). As hardware capabilities improve, e will decrease, and the fraction to choose will change with n.

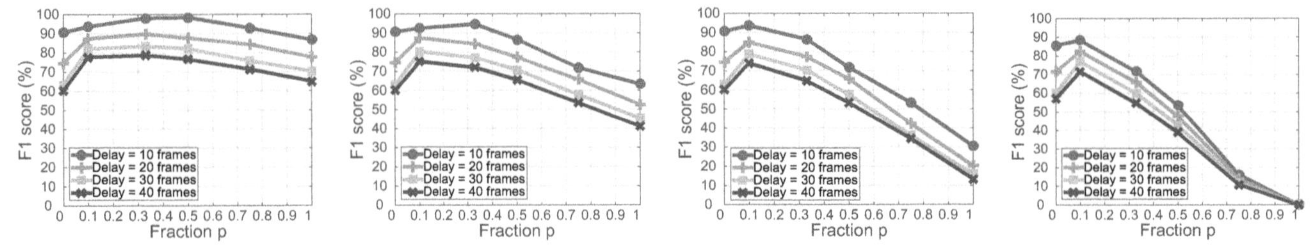

(a) $e = 10$ ms. (b) $e = 20$ ms. (c) $e = 30$ ms. (d) $e = 40$ ms.

Figure 14: Performance of tracking based on the fraction of frames picked from the active cache using both datasets.

Network	DP-based F1 score (%)	Fixed-interval F1 score (%)
Wi-Fi	82.2 ± 7.5	73.3 ± 12.4
Verizon's 3G	77 ± 9.4	59 ± 11.7

Table 5: F1 score for hard videos in the dataset. For this experiment, we selected 50% of all videos that had the worst F1 score. For Wi-Fi, we use both the face and road sign datasets. For Verizon's 3G network, we use only the face dataset.

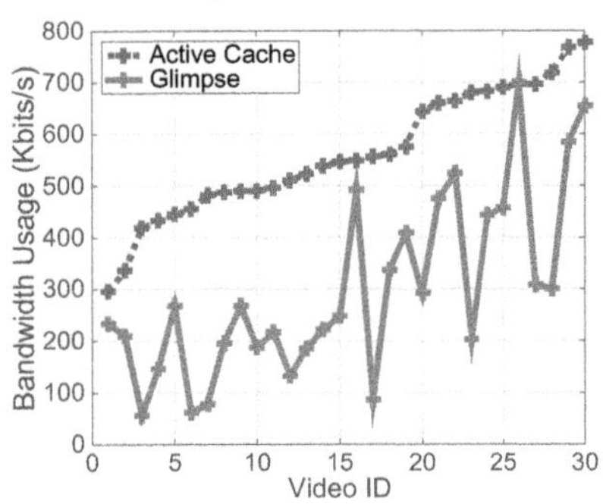

Figure 15: Bandwidth usage of each video by Glimpse and the *Active cache* scheme without trigger frames. The *Active cache* line is sorted by bandwidth usage. The Glimpse line shows the bandwidth usage of the corresponding video.

7.2.2 Dynamic programming to pick frames

What is the benefit of the dynamic programming algorithm (§3.2) for frame selection compared to a scheme that simply selects one out of every k frames regularly? Given the fraction of frames to pick from the active cache, we use a dynamic programming approach to capture the object movement instead of picking frames at a regular interval.

We found that for every video in our dataset, the dynamic programming algorithm performs equal to or better than selecting frames at regular intervals. The gain is small for videos with little movement (for them it is immaterial which frames we choose), but high-motion videos are a different story. The aggregate improvement in precision and recall across all videos is only around 4%, but our approach outperforms the fixed-interval scheme on scenarios where there is a lot of movement. Table 5 shows the F1 score for the hard videos in our dataset. For this experiment, we selected 50% of the videos that had the worst F1 score. On these hard cases, the dynamic programming method improves the F1 score by about 12-31% on average depending on the network type.

7.3 Benefits of trigger frames

Under all network conditions (figures in §7.1), *trigger frames* reduce bandwidth by at least 1.5× (2.3× in the worse case) compared to the *Active cache only* scheme, without appreciably reducing precision or recall. We save a factor of 31.3× compared to naively sending every frame to the server.

Figure 15 shows the bandwidth usage for each video. It compares the scheme without trigger frames and Glimpse with trigger frames. Glimpse consistently reduces the bandwidth usage. For certain videos, Glimpse provides as much as 6× savings. By transmitting less data to the server, Glimpse also saves energy in the mobile device compared to a scheme without trigger frames. We describe the energy measurements in detail in §7.4.

The bandwidth savings stem from Glimpse's ability to locally track objects without going to the server, and its ability to accurately identify tracking failure and scene changes. We evaluate the importance of both detecting tracking failure and detecting new objects (frame differencing) to identify trigger frames. We compare Glimpse's performance with a scheme that identifies trigger frames only by frame differencing. Though the bandwidth consumed reduces by 53%, the precision and recall also reduce by up to 12%. We get similar performance degradation if we detect only tracking failure without identifying new objects. Hence, detecting both tracking failure and new objects are crucial for identifying *trigger frames.*

We also evaluate the impact of various thresholds used to trigger frames. Figure 16 shows the F1 score and bandwidth usage for varying values of these thresholds. As ω_{std}, the standard deviation of feature point distance, increases, Glimpse becomes more tolerable to deviation of feature points. The number of trigger frames decreases, reducing bandwidth usage, but trackability also decreases because of imminent tracking failures. Similarly, as ϕ_{motion} increases, Glimpse becomes less sensitive to new objects, and we get fewer trigger frames. The bandwidth usage decreases, but the trackability decreases as well because we start missing objects. We pick $\omega_{std} = 0.5$ and $\phi_{motion} = 153600$ (half the number of pixels in a frame) to strike a balance between bandwidth usage and accuracy. Also, allowing more frames in flight has no impact on accuracy, but almost doubles the bandwidth usage. Hence, we use $i_{max} = 1$ in practice.

7.4 Energy consumption

We evaluate the energy consumption of Glimpse by measuring the energy consumption of its components and scaling them in proportion to their usage. We use a Samsung

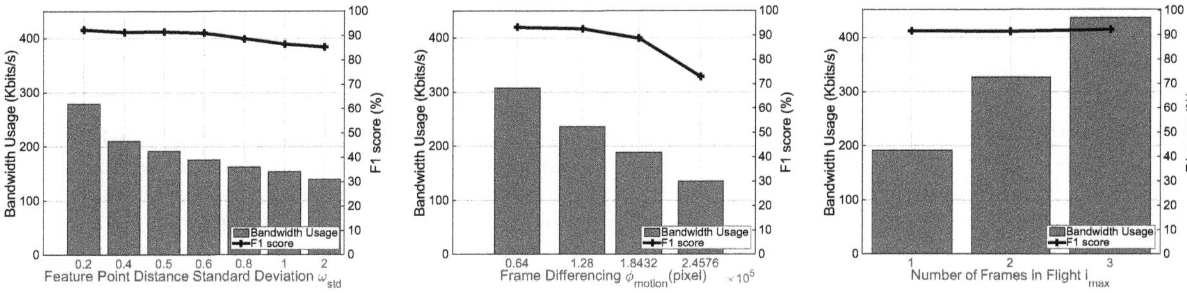

(a) ω_{std}, the standard deviation of feature point distance.

(b) ϕ_{motion}, the frame difference threshold.

(c) i_{max}, the number of frames in flight.

Figure 16: Bandwidth usage and F1 score for various parameters on identifying trigger frames for the face dataset. We see the same trends for the road sign dataset.

Mode	Power (mW)	Current (mA)	Battery Life (h)
Sleep	56	15.1	122.5
Idle	1009.2	272.9	6.8
Screen on + Frame Capturing	2124.6	574.2	3.2
Verizon's LTE uplink (Active)	2928.2	791.4	2.3
Verizon's LTE downlink (Active)	1737	496.3	3.7
Verizon's LTE (Idle)	1324.6	358	5.2
Wi-Fi uplink	1871.5	506	3.7
Wi-Fi downlink	1289.9	347.8	5.3

Table 6: Energy measurement for various operations on the Samsung Galaxy Nexus with an 1850 mAh battery.

Component	Execution Time (ms)
Frame differencing	7
Active cache (DP frame selection)	1.7
Tracking failure detection	< 1
Tracking	37.7

Table 7: Average execution time of each of Glimpse's components on the Samsung Galaxy Nexus.

Galaxy Nexus smartphone with a 1.2 GHz dual-core ARM processor, 1 GB RAM, and a 1850 mAh battery. The CPU has four operating frequencies: 350, 700, 920, and 1200 MHz.

Table 6 shows the energy consumption for various operations on the smartphone. Without any computation, capturing frames from the camera with the screen turned on consumes 2124.6 mW, and the CPU runs at 350 MHz. When Glimpse is running, it uses two cores, and the CPU raises its frequency to one of the three higher settings, consuming an average of 2947 mW. Transmitting a frame via LTE consumes a total of 2928.2 mW and in Verizon's LTE, the radio tail length [15] is around 10.2 secs. Transmitting one frame on Wi-Fi consumes 1871.5 mW on average. Table 7 shows the average execution time of Glimpse's components. Based on our trace-level emulation, we model the expected energy consumption for running Glimpse.

Table 8 shows the expected battery life when running Glimpse. Compared to a scheme that sends 1 frame every RTT (1 frame in flight), Glimpse improves the battery life by 35% on Wi-Fi and 25% on LTE. For Google Glass (Wi-Fi), based on the energy measurement numbers reported in [33], compared to a scheme that sends 1 frame every RTT, Glimpse can improve the battery life by 24%.

Network	Glimpse battery life time (h)	1 frame/RTT battery life time (h)
Wi-Fi	1.9 ± 0.1	1.4
Verizon's LTE	1.5 ± 0.1	1.2

Table 8: Estimated battery life time.

8. RELATED WORK

We discuss prior work on network latency hiding, object recognition, and mobile computation offloading.

Network latency hiding: Latency hiding techniques have been widely used as a method for hiding state inconsistencies between distributed nodes. It has been used to mitigate the effects of network latency and provide smooth user experiences in many distributed interactive applications, including remote display [31, 43] and multi-player network games [5, 57]. A common form of latency hiding technique is *dead reckoning*, where clients simulate the states of other hosts using speculation; incorrectly predicted states are rolled back when the actual ones arrive from the hosts.

Glimpse has similar goals, but object movements in video are harder to predict. The results obtained from the server are stale and cannot be directly shown to the user; we need to carefully correct the results to provide a smooth user experience. To the best of our knowledge, Glimpse is the first work that successfully hides network and server latency for object recognition applications.

Object recognition: Object recognition identifies and locates objects in an image. There is a huge body of work on object recognition in the computer vision community, and state-of-the-art methods [52, 10, 21, 19, 32, 3] achieve high precision. Unfortunately, these techniques have significant computation and memory needs, and in practice, realizing them on a mobile platform is difficult. Glimpse can use any of these algorithms, and apply its latency hiding mechanism to hide the processing latency. Besides, much of the advances come from the use of improved object features, which can be easily incorporated into Glimpse for object tracking.

Other work focuses on enabling object recognition on mobile devices with a client-server design. For example, some papers [25, 27] deploy a recognition system that allows clients to upload images to the server for object classification. Other papers [20, 14] provide continuous object recognition on mobile devices by running the tracker on the mobile client, and the recognition on a server. Another paper [58] proposes a location-aware face recognition framework that uses location information as a hint to reduce the search space of the recognition algorithm. However, these papers consider neither the impact of network and server processing latency on the performance of the system, nor the bandwidth and energy consumed.

Recently, there has been work focusing on optimizing computer vision algorithms to make them usable on mobile devices. For example, Shen et al. [48] optimize the projection matrix for the Sparse Representation Classification (SRC) and implement a fast and robust face recognition system on the mobile device. Glimpse's techniques are orthogonal and can be useful even for these client-only systems to hide the processing delay and reduce the amount of resources consumed.

Object tracking and scene change detection: There are many existing tracking algorithms [60, 17] and scene change detection techniques [39, 63]. Glimpse's active cache can use these tracking methods for catching up with the current frame; similarly, trigger frames can be sent using any of these scene change detection algorithms. Most of these techniques require substantial computational resources, and are not suitable for applications on mobile devices with real-time requirements. We use the Lucas-Kanade tracking [35] and frame differencing for their simplicity, fast execution, and limited resource requirements.

Mobile computation offloading: Resource limitations on mobile devices and the need for responsiveness for compute- and bandwidth-intensive interactive applications have given rise to the idea of delegating work to nearby computers, called "cloudlets" [46], which are one wireless hop away from the mobile device. Gabriel [22, 23] is a system that uses cloudlets for face and object recognition. These cloudlets run the object recognition pipeline and the client ships every frame to the cloudlet. In contrast, Glimpse does not require an extra cloudlet infrastructure, and is readily deployable. Also, the use of cloudlets can still benefit from techniques used in Glimpse to hide the processing latency of compute-intensive recognition tasks (and the network delay in the last hop) and save cloudlet resources by processing only selected frames.

Several systems deal with network variability and device heterogeneity by dynamically determining the most suitable division of work between the cloud and client. Wishbone [38] shows how to take a data-flow graph of operators and partition them across sensor nodes and the cloud using static profiling to determine a good split. MAUI [13] optimizes the energy consumption for interactive applications using an adaptive pipeline partitioning. Its profiler gathers runtime information and finds the optimal partitioning by solving a linear program. Cloud-Vision [50] extends the idea of code partitioning to server farms and aims to minimize the response time given heterogeneous communication latencies and server compute power. Odessa [41] makes offloading and parallelism decisions using runtime profiling with the goal of reducing the total execution delay. Glimpse is complementary to the above systems. Glimpse's goal is to hide the processing delay irrespective of where the delay occurs and reduce the number of frames processed.

9. DISCUSSION

Generality of Glimpse: Active cache and trigger frames are generic techniques that can be applied to other vision-based applications. The active cache technique can be applied to any vision application that has real-time constraints. For example, a surveillance control system [61] or video analysis application that tracks objects such as cars needs to hide the recognition delay to track the location of objects in real time. The trigger frame technique can be applied to any vision processing system to reduce the resources consumed.

Limitations of Glimpse: Glimpse can have reduced performance when the detected object does not show prominent contrast from the background, and does not have enough salient feature points to enable reliable tracking. Advances in object tracking can be easily incorporated into Glimpse.

Lighting conditions can affect the performance of vision algorithms used in Glimpse. Our dataset covers a reasonably wide range of lighting conditions and we do not notice any performance degradation – for the face dataset, under the Wi-Fi network, the F1 score for the brightest and the darkest videos are 98% and 97%, respectively. However, we believe that performance can degrade in extremely low-light conditions. Advances in cameras and vision algorithms can help improve the performance of Glimpse in these scenarios.

Currently, Glimpse uses a fixed frame differencing threshold (§4) for trigger frames. Our experiments show that a single threshold works well for a wide range of face and road sign recognition scenarios. It is possible that a single threshold might be suboptimal when we include more recognition scenarios, requiring an adaptive threshold [44].

Future work: One direction for future work is to incorporate on-board inertial sensors such as accelerometers and gyroscopes to improve the performance of Glimpse. Inertial sensors can identity and quantity movement and can help tracking and trigger frame selection. However, inertial sensors only capture the movement of the device and the user, but not the objects that the user is observing. Therefore, a vision-based trigger frame approach would still be required.

10. CONCLUSION

We presented Glimpse, a continuous, real-time object recognition system for mobile devices and wearables. Glimpse captures full-motion video from the camera, recognizes objects, and annotates the images with bounding boxes and labels. Because the vision algorithms for object recognition entail significant computation, Glimpse uses a distributed architecture with the object recognition pipeline running at the server. To hide the processing latencies, Glimpse uses an active cache of video frames on the client and performs object tracking on a subset of frames to correct the stale results obtained from the processing pipeline. To save resources, Glimpse locally tracks objects, and identifies trigger frames by efficiently detecting tracking failure and scene changes. Experiments with Glimpse shows that it achieves high precision and recall, saves bandwidth, and significantly outperforms other schemes.

11. ACKNOWLEDGMENTS

We thank the industrial partners of the MIT Center for Wireless Networks and Mobile Computing (Wireless@MIT) for their support. We also thank the volunteers who helped gather our datasets.

12. REFERENCES

[1] iPhone 6 Face Detection. https://www.apple.com/iphone-6/cameras/.

[2] Road sign detection and shape reconstruction using gielis curves. https://sites.google.com/site/mcvibot2011sep/home.

[3] DeepFace: Closing the Gap to Human-Level Performance in Face Verification. In *CVPR*, 2014.

[4] Android camera.facedetectionlistener. http://developer.android.com/reference/android/hardware/Camera.FaceDetectionListener.html.

[5] J. Aronson. Dead reckoning: Latency hiding for networked games. http://www.gamasutra.com/view/feature/131638/dead_reckoning_latency_hiding_for_.php, 1997.

[6] R. Azuma. A survey of augmented reality, 1997.

[7] H. Bay, A. Ess, T. Tuytelaars, and L. Van Gool. Speeded-up robust features (surf). In *CVIU*, 2008.

[8] S. S. Beauchemin and J. L. Barron. The computation of optical flow. In *CSUR*, 1995.

[9] X. Cao, Y. Wei, F. Wen, and J. Sun. Face alignment by explicit shape regression. In *CVPR*, 2012.

[10] D. Chen, X. Cao, F. Wen, and J. Sun. Blessing of dimensionality: High-dimensional feature and its efficient compression for face verification. In *CVPR*, 2013.

[11] J. Cho, S. Mirzaei, J. Oberg, and R. Kastner. Fpga-based face detection system using haar classifiers. In *FPGA*, 2009.

[12] A. Collet Romea, M. Martinez Torres, and S. Srinivasa. The moped framework: Object recognition and pose estimation for manipulation. In *IJRR*, 2011.

[13] E. Cuervo, A. Balasubramanian, D. Cho, A. Wolman, S. Saroiu, R. Chandra, and P. Bahl. MAUI: Making smartphones last longer with code offload. In *MobiSys*, 2010.

[14] M. Dantone, L. Bossard, T. Quack, and L. Van Gool. Augmented faces. In *ICCVW*, 2011.

[15] S. Deng and H. Balakrishnan. Traffic-Aware Techniques to Reduce 3G/LTE Wireless Energy Consumption. In *CoNEXT*, 2012.

[16] S. Deng, R. Netravali, A. Sivaraman, and H. Balakrishnan. WiFi, LTE, or Both? Measuring Multi-Homed Wireless Internet Performance. In *IMC*, 2014.

[17] D. Exner, E. Bruns, D. Kurz, A. Grundhofer, and O. Bimber. Fast and robust camshift tracking. In *CVPRW*, 2010.

[18] R.-E. Fan, K.-W. Chang, C.-J. Hsieh, X.-R. Wang, and C.-J. Lin. LIBLINEAR: A Library for Large Linear Classification. In *JMLR*, 2008.

[19] V. Ferrari, L. Fevrier, C. Schmid, and F. Jurie. Groups of adjacent contour segments for object detection. In *Pattern Analysis and Machine Intelligence, IEEE Transactions on*, 2008.

[20] S. Gammeter, A. Gassmann, L. Bossard, T. Quack, and L. Van Gool. Server-side object recognition and client-side object tracking for mobile augmented reality. In *CVPRW*, 2010.

[21] R. B. Girshick, P. F. Felzenszwalb, and D. McAllester. Discriminatively trained deformable part models, release 5. http://people.cs.uchicago.edu/ rbg/latent-release5/.

[22] K. Ha, Z. Chen, W. Hu, W. Richter, P. Pillai, and M. Satyanarayanan. Towards wearable cognitive assistance. In *MobiSys*, 2014.

[23] K. Ha, P. Pillai, W. Richter, Y. Abe, and M. Satyanarayanan. Just-in-time provisioning for cyber foraging. In *MobiSys*, 2013.

[24] B. K. P. Horn and B. G. Schunck. Determining optical flow. In *MIT Technical Report*, 1981.

[25] N. Ismail and M. I. M. Sabri. Mobile to server face recognition: A system overview. *World Academy of Science, Engineering and Technology*, 2010.

[26] Y. Jia, E. Shelhamer, J. Donahue, S. Karayev, J. Long, R. Girshick, S. Guadarrama, and T. Darrell. Caffe: Convolutional architecture for fast feature embedding. *arXiv preprint arXiv:1408.5093*, 2014.

[27] B. Kehoe, A. Matsukawa, S. Candido, J. Kuffner, and K. Goldberg. Cloud-based robot grasping with the google object recognition engine. In *ICRA*, 2013.

[28] R. Klette, J. Ahn, R. Haeusler, S. Herman, J. Huang, W. Khan, S. Manoharan, S. Morales, J. Morris, R. Nicolescu, F. Ren, K. Schauwecker, and X. Yang. Advance in vision-based driver assistance. In *ICETCE*, 2011.

[29] A. Krizhevsky, I. Sutskever, and G. E. Hinton. Imagenet classification with deep convolutional neural networks. In *NIPS*. 2012.

[30] N. Kumar, A. Berg, P. Belhumeur, and S. Nayar. Attribute and simile classifiers for face verification. In *ICCV*, 2009.

[31] J. R. Lange, P. A. Dinda, and S. Rossoff. Experiences with client-based speculative remote display. In *ATC*, 2008.

[32] B. Leibe, A. Leonardis, and B. Schiele. Combined object categorization and segmentation with an implicit shape model. In *ECCV*, 2004.

[33] R. LiKamWa, Z. Wang, A. Carroll, F. X. Lin, and L. Zhong. Draining our glass: An energy and heat characterization of google glass. In *CoRR*, 2014.

[34] D. G. Lowe. Distinctive image features from scale-invariant keypoints. In *IJCV*, 2004.

[35] B. D. Lucas and T. Kanade. An iterative image registration technique with an application to stereo vision. In *IJCAI*, 1981.

[36] A. Mayberry, P. Hu, B. Marlin, C. Salthouse, and D. Ganesan. iShadow: Design of a Wearable, Real-time Mobile Gaze Tracker. In *MobiSys*, 2014.

[37] R. Netravali, A. Sivaraman, K. Winstein, S. Das, A. Goyal, and H. Balakrishnan. Mahimahi: A lightweight toolkit for reproducible web measurement (demo). In *SIGCOMM*, 2014.

[38] R. Newton, S. Toledo, L. Girod, H. Balakrishnan, and S. Madden. Wishbone: ProïñĄle-based Partitioning for Sensornet Applications. In *NSDI*, 2009.

[39] C.-W. Ngo, Y.-F. Ma, and H.-J. Zhang. Video summarization and scene detection by graph modeling. *IEEE Trans. Cir. and Sys. for Video Technol.*, 2005.

[40] Opencv4android. http://opencv.org/platforms/android.html.

[41] M.-R. Ra, A. Sheth, L. Mummert, P. Pillai, D. Wetherall, and R. Govindan. Odessa: Enabling interactive perception applications on mobile devices. In *MobiSys*, 2011.

[42] S. Rallapalli, A. Ganesan, K. Chintalapudi, V. Padmanabhan, and L. Qiu. Enabling physical analytics in retail stores using smart glasses. In *Mobicom*, 2014.

[43] T. Richardson, Q. Stafford-Fraser, K. Wood, and A. Hopper. Virtual network computing. In *Internet Computing, IEEE*, 1998.

[44] P. Rosin and T. Ellis. Image difference threshold strategies and shadow detection. In *BMVC*, 1995.

[45] A. Sankaranarayanan, A. Veeraraghavan, and R. Chellappa. Object detection, tracking and recognition for multiple smart cameras. *Proceedings of the IEEE*, 2008.

[46] M. Satyanarayanan, P. Bahl, R. Caceres, and N. Davies. The Case for VM-Based Cloudlets in Mobile Computing. *Pervasive Computing, IEEE*, 2009.

[47] J. Schmidhuber. Multi-column deep neural networks for image classification. In *CVPR*, 2012.

[48] Y. Shen, W. Hu, M. Yang, B. Wei, S. Lucey, and C. T. Chou. Face recognition on smartphones via optimised sparse representation classification. In *IPSN*, 2014.

[49] J. Shi and C. Tomasi. Good features to track. In *CVPR*, 1994.

[50] T. Soyata, R. Muraleedharan, C. Funai, M. Kwon, and W. Heinzelman. Cloud-vision: Real-time face recognition using a mobile-cloudlet-cloud acceleration architecture. In *ISCC*, 2012.

[51] C. Szegedy, W. Liu, Y. Jia, P. Sermanet, S. Reed, D. Anguelov, D. Erhan, V. Vanhoucke, and A. Rabinovich. Going deeper with convolutions. In *CoRR*, 2014.

[52] C. Szegedy, A. Toshev, and D. Erhan. Deep neural networks for object detection. In *NIPS*. 2013.

[53] G. Takacs, Y. Xiong, R. Grzeszczuk, V. Chandrasekhar, W. chao Chen, K. Pulli, N. Gelfand, T. Bismpigiannis, and B. Girod. Outdoors augmented reality on mobile phone using loxel-based visual feature organization. In *MIR*, 2008.

[54] V. Vaitukaitis and A. Bulling. Eye gesture recognition on portable devices. In *UbiComp*, 2012.

[55] P. Viola and M. Jones. Rapid object detection using a boosted cascade of simple features. In *CVPR*, 2001.

[56] P. Viola and M. J. Jones. Robust real-time face detection. In *IJCV*, 2004.

[57] A. I. Wang, M. Jarrett, and E. Sorteberg. Experiences from implementing a mobile multiplayer real-time game for wireless networks with high latency. *Int. J. Comput. Games Technol.*, 2009.

[58] Z. Wang, J. Yan, C. Pang, D. Chu, and H. Aghajan. Who is here: Location aware face recognition. In *PhoneSense*, 2012.

[59] K. Winstein, A. Sivaraman, and H. Balakrishnan. Stochastic forecasts achieve high throughput and low delay over cellular networks. In *NSDI*, 2013.

[60] K. Zhang, L. Zhang, and M.-H. Yang. Real-time compressive tracking. In *ECCV*, 2012.

[61] T. Zhang, A. Chowdhery, P. Bahl, K. Jamieson, and S. Banerjee. The design and implementation of a wireless video surveillance system. In *MobiCom*, 2015.

[62] X. Zhang, L. Zhang, X.-J. Wang, and H.-Y. Shum. Finding celebrities in billions of web images. *IEEE Transactions on Multimedia*, 2012.

[63] Y. Zhuang, Y. Rui, T. Huang, and S. Mehrotra. Adaptive key frame extraction using unsupervised clustering. In *ICIP*, 1998.

Truth Discovery on Crowd Sensing of Correlated Entities

Chuishi Meng[1], Wenjun Jiang[1], Yaliang Li[1], Jing Gao[1], Lu Su[1], Hu Ding[1], Yun Cheng[2]
[1]SUNY Buffalo, Buffalo, NY USA [2]Air Scientific, Beijing, China
{chuishim,wenjunji,yaliangl,jing,lusu,huding}@buffalo.edu,chengyun.hit@gmail.com

ABSTRACT

With the popular usage of mobile devices and smartphones, crowd sensing becomes pervasive in real life when human acts as sensors to report their observations about entities. For the same entity, users may report conflicting information, and thus it is important to identify the true information and the reliable users. This task, referred to as truth discovery, has recently attracted much attention. Existing work typically assumes independence among entities. However, correlations among entities are commonly observed in many applications. Such correlation information is crucial in the truth discovery task. When entities are not observed by enough reliable users, it is impossible to obtain true information. In such cases, it is important to propagate trustworthy information from correlated entities that have been observed by reliable users. We formulate the task of truth discovery on correlated entities as an optimization problem in which both truths and user reliability are modeled as variables. The correlation among entities adds to the difficulty of solving this problem. In light of the challenge, we propose both sequential and parallel solutions. In the sequential solution, we partition entities into disjoint independent sets and derive iterative approaches based on block coordinate descent. In the parallel solution, we adapt the solution to MapReduce programming model, which can be executed on Hadoop clusters. Experiments on real-world crowd sensing applications show the advantages of the proposed method on discovering truths from conflicting information reported on correlated entities.

Categories and Subject Descriptors

H.4 [**Information Systems Applications**]: Miscellaneous

General Terms

Algorithms, Human Factors, Performance

SenSys'15, November 1-4, 2015, Seoul, South Korea.
© 2015 ACM. ISBN 978-1-4503-3631-4/15/11 ...$15.00.
DOI: http://dx.doi.org/10.1145/10.1145/2809695.2809715.

Keywords

Crowd Sensing; Truth Discovery; Correlation

1. INTRODUCTION

Crowd sensing has emerged as a new way of gathering information about entities by collecting observations from humans. With the ubiquitous mobile sensing devices (e.g., smartphones), it becomes easier and easier for the population to sense and share the information they perceived. Specifically, users can report certain conditions of their environment, such as traffic conditions, broken public utilities, gas prices, weather conditions and air quality, to central servers. On the central server, user-contributed information is aggregated to obtain useful information. Much attention is now contributed to the development of crowd sensing systems for various application domains [4, 7, 14, 21, 32, 38].

An important task in the crowd sensing system is the aggregation of user-contributed information. Users may provide conflicting and noisy information on the same entity, and then how to discover the true information (i.e., the truth) among these conflicting observations is the key question. Especially when most users report false information, the true information is unable to be discovered by voting or averaging. Intuitively, we should trust information from reliable users, i.e., users who often report true information. However, users' reliability degrees are not known *a priori.* To tackle the challenge of discovering both true information and user reliability, truth discovery methods [26, 27, 28, 44, 47] have been proposed based on the principle that reliable users tend to report true information and truth should be reported by many reliable users.

Although truth discovery techniques can be applied to crowd sensing applications to extract true information, existing methods do not take into consideration the correlations among entities in truth discovery. In fact, correlations exist ubiquitously among entities. For example, nearby segments of the same road may share similar traffic conditions, locations in the same area may have similar weather conditions, and a station may have similar gas prices during a short period. Such correlation information can greatly benefit the truth discovery process—information obtained from reliable sources can be propagated over all correlated entities, such that the aggregated information is more trustworthy. Especially, taking correlations into consideration will be more helpful when the coverage rate is low, i.e., users only provide observations for a small portion of the entities. In such cases, many entities may receive observations from unreliable users, and thus reliable information borrowed from correlated entities is important. In contrast, if we regard entities as independent ones and ignore their correlations, the truths on entities that are not observed by reliable users cannot be discovered.

In this paper, we propose an effective truth discovery framework for crowd sensing of correlated entities. In the crowd sensing systems, users make their observations on some entities among a set of correlated entities, and report the observations to a central server via smartphones. We propose an approach that jointly infers user reliability and truths among correlated entities. We formulate the task as an optimization problem, in which truths and user reliability are unknown variables, and correlations are modeled as regularization terms. The regularization terms make the optimization difficult to solve due to the correlations among unknown variables. To tackle this challenge, we propose to partition the variables into disjoint independent sets, and conduct block coordinate descent to iteratively update truths and user reliabilities. To process large-scale data, we further propose a parallel solution implemented on Hadoop cluster. Experiments on three crowd sensing applications show the effectiveness and efficiency of the proposed approaches.

In summary, we make the following contributions:

- We propose an effective optimization-based framework to solve the problem of truth discovery for crowd sensing of correlated entities. The proposed objective function measures the differences between the user-input observations and the unknown truths, and integrates users' reliabilities as unknown weights. The correlation regularization terms punish the deviations in the truths between correlated entities.
- To tackle the challenge introduced by the regularization terms, we propose to partition entities into disjoint independent sets, and then develop an iterative solution based on block coordinate descent with convergence guarantee. We introduce an approach that partition entities into disjoint independent sets for general cases, and propose effective ways to construct disjoint independent sets for the crowd sensing task with spatial and temporal correlations.
- We further propose a MapReduce based solution for the truth discovery of correlated entities. This is implemented on a Hadoop cluster and we show its ability of processing large-scale data.
- We conduct experiments on three crowd sensing datasets, i.e., air quality sensing, gas price inference and weather condition estimation datasets. Results demonstrate that the proposed approaches outperform existing methods in discovering true information for correlated entities.

The rest of the paper is organized as follows. We describe the system overview in Section 2. The proposed optimization framework and solutions are detailed in Section 3. In Section 4, we describe the proposed parallel solution based on MapReduce model. Evaluations are shown in Section 5. We review the related work in Section 6 and conclude the paper in Section 7.

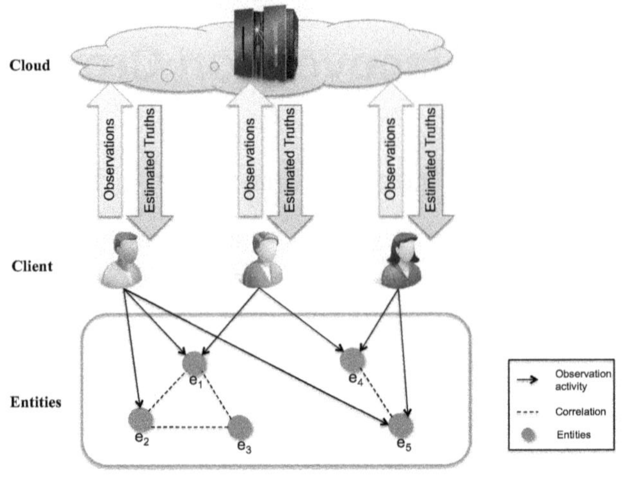

Figure 1: System Framework

2. SYSTEM OVERVIEW

In this section, we introduce the problem setting and the problem formulation. We start with some definitions.

DEFINITION 1. *An* entity *is a thing or phenomenon which can be observed by crowd users; a* user *is a crowd sensing participant who contributes information about the entities; and an* observation *is the information perceived by a particular user on a particular entity.*

For example, the temperature at a particular location and time is an entity for a weather reporting application. Each participant is a user, and the temperature observed and reported by a user at a location and time is an observation.

DEFINITION 2. *A* truth *is the true value of an entity. A user's* weight *is the reliability degree of the information provided by the user.*

Note here truths and user weights are unknown, and they are the expected output. Correlations between entities are considered: If two entities are correlated, their truths should be close to each other. Consider the aforementioned example. The truth is the real temperature on a particular location and time, and a weight is assigned to a user which indicates how likely the observations reported by him/her are reliable, i.e., how close they are to the truths. Then the problem we try to solve is to estimate both truths and user weights given the observations collected from users.

With these definitions, we now describe the crowd sensing system. Figure 1 shows the framework of this system. Users make observations on entities, and upload their observations to the cloud server via smartphones. On the server side, the proposed truth discovery method is conducted to derive both truths and user weights. In the following, we discuss details about the processes at the user and server sides respectively. **Client**. On the client side, each user provides observations about entities, and uploads them to the server. The entities can be actively or passively observed, and the users may make the observations by themselves or report the observations with the help of sensors. Take WeatherSignal[1] as an example. It is a crowd sensing application which can

[1]http://weathersignal.com

not only automatically collect temperature, pressure data via sensors integrated in users' smartphones, but also allow users to manually report the weather conditions.

Server. On the server side, once observations are collected from users, the proposed truth discovery method will be conducted. The reliability degree of each user is calculated, together with the estimated truths for entities. As discussed, correlation information among entities is important, and thus it is taken into consideration in the proposed algorithm which will be detailed in Section 3.

3. TRUTH DISCOVERY ON CORRELATED ENTITIES

In this section, we describe the proposed truth discovery algorithm on correlated entities. The optimization framework and its solution are discussed. We then propose the parallel solution based on MapReduce model in Section 4.

3.1 Proposed Framework

We first define the mathematical notations for the problem. Each entity is indexed with i, and e_i denotes the i-th entity. Each user is indexed with k. An observation is represented as $x_i^{(k)}$ which indicates that it is observed by user k on entity e_i. All the observations made by user k is represented as $\mathcal{X}^{(k)}$. The truth for entity e_i is denoted as $x_i^{(*)}$, and the truths of all the entities are defined as $\mathcal{X}^{(*)}$. The weight for user k is w_k, and the collection of all the user weights is $\mathcal{W}$. Table 1 summarizes the important notations used in this paper. With these notations, we can formally define the problem as follows.

Problem Definition. Suppose there are N entities and K users. The input are observations $\{\mathcal{X}^{(1)}, \mathcal{X}^{(2)}, \cdots, \mathcal{X}^{(K)}\}$ collected from all the K users and the pairwise correlations among entities. Let $N(i)$ denote the set of entities which have correlations with entity e_i. The expected output are the truths $\mathcal{X}^{(*)}$ and the user weights $\mathcal{W}$.

The intuitions behind the proposed method are that truths should be close to the observations given by the reliable users, and correlated entities should have similar true values. Based on these intuitions, we formulate the following optimization problem:

$$\min_{\mathcal{X}^{(*)},\mathcal{W}} f(\mathcal{X}^{(*)},\mathcal{W}) = \sum_{i=1}^{N}\Big\{\sum_{k=1}^{K} w_k||x_i^{(*)} - x_i^{(k)}||^2 + \alpha \sum_{i' \in N(i)} S(i,i')||x_{i'}^{(*)} - x_i^{(*)}||^2\Big\} \quad (1)$$

$$\text{s.t.} \quad \sum_{k=1}^{K} \exp(-w_k) = 1$$

Here α is a hyper parameter that balances between the two terms in the objective function. $S(i,i')$ is a similarity function which captures the correlation degree of two entities. Note here the design of this similarity function depends on the specific application since entity correlations have different properties in different applications. For example, one way of modeling the similarity under spatial correlation is Gaussian kernel, $S(i,i') = \exp(-d^2(i,i')/\sigma^2)$. Here $d(i,i')$ is the Euclidean distance of two entities and σ is a scaling parameter that controls how fast the similarity decreases as the distance increases. In general, the Gaussian kernel is a measure of similarity between entity i and i'. It evaluates to 1 if the two input values are identical, and approaches 0 as they move further apart.

The objective function $f(\mathcal{X}^{(*)},\mathcal{W})$ in Eq(1) captures the intuitions we have mentioned. The first term $\sum_{i=1}^{N}\sum_{k=1}^{K} w_k||x_i^{(*)} - x_i^{(k)}||^2$ aims at minimizing the disagreement between observations and truths, among which the disagreement on entities from the users with higher reliability degrees (i.e. w_k) are weighed higher. This means that higher penalties are given to more reliable users if their observations deviate from the corresponding truths. The second term in the objective function $\sum_{i=1}^{N}\sum_{i' \in N(i)} S(i,i')||x_{i'}^{(*)} - x_i^{(*)}||^2$ models the other principle, i.e., the truth of an entity should be close to the truths of the entities it has correlation relationships with. In addition, the similarity function ensures that more attention should be paid to the entities with correlation degrees. By this objective function, we ensure that 1) the truths are picked from information contributed by reliable users and 2) correlated entities have similar truths.

The constraint in Eq(1) is used to restrict the range of weights, otherwise the weight may go to negative infinity.

In sum, with the proposed framework in Eq(1), we search for the values for two sets of variables, i.e. truths $\mathcal{X}^{(*)}$ and user weights $\mathcal{W}$, by minimizing the objective function $f(\mathcal{X}^{(*)},\mathcal{W})$ under the constraint.

For an optimization problem with two sets of variables, it is natural to use block coordinate descent approach [3] to solve the problem. The idea is to iteratively update one set of variables while fixing the other one. However, due to the existence of the regularization term, it is non-trivial to solve Eq(1) as variables are correlated. In order to tackle this challenge, we first construct disjoint independent sets of entities based on their correlation relationships. Here, an independent set is a set of entities among which no correlations exist. For example, entities shown in Figure 1 can form three disjoint independent sets. There are five entities which are denoted as nodes in the graph, and the links indicate the correlations. As can be seen, e_1, e_2, e_3 are correlated with each other, and e_4, e_5 are correlated. The three independent sets are thus $\{e_1, e_4\}$, $\{e_2, e_5\}$ and $\{e_3\}$, in which entities within each set are not correlated. The methods to construct disjoint independent sets will be discussed in Section 3.3.

Here, we assume that independent sets are obtained. We denote j as the index for an independent set. We use $\mathcal{I} = \bigcup_{j=1}^{J} \mathcal{I}_j$ to denote the set containing all the entities, and $\mathcal{I}_j$ denotes the j-th subset. As truths are defined for entities, the collection of truths $\mathcal{X}^{(*)}$ can thus be divided into subsets based on independent sets, i.e., $\mathcal{X}^{(*)} = \{\mathcal{X}_1^{(*)}, \mathcal{X}_2^{(*)}, \cdots, \mathcal{X}_J^{(*)}\}$.

Based on the disjoint independent sets, Eq(1) can be rewritten as follows:

$$\min_{\mathcal{X}^{(*)},\mathcal{W}} f(\mathcal{X}^{(*)},\mathcal{W}) = \sum_{\mathcal{I}_j \subset \mathcal{I}}\sum_{i \in \mathcal{I}_j}\Big\{\sum_{k=1}^{K} w_k||x_i^{(*)} - x_i^{(k)}||^2 + \alpha \sum_{i' \in N(i)} S(i,i')||x_i^{(*)} - x_{i'}^{(*)}||^2\Big\} \quad (2)$$

$$\text{s.t.} \quad \sum_{k=1}^{K} \exp(-w_k) = 1$$

Table 1: Frequently Used Notations

Symbol	Definition
K	number of users
k	index of users
w_k	weight of user k
$\mathcal{W}$	the set contains all user weights
N	number of entities
i	index of entities
e_i	the i_{th} entity
$\mathcal{I}$	the set contains all entities
$\mathcal{I}_j$	the j_{th} independent set of entities
J	number of independent sets
$x_i^{(*)}$	the true value of entity i
$x_i^{(k)}$	observation provided by user k on entity i
$\mathcal{X}^{(*)}$	the set of true values of all entities
$\mathcal{X}_j^{(*)}$	the set of true values of entities from independent set j
$N(i)$	entities which have correlation with entity i
$S(i,i')$	the similarity degree between two entities
$\mathcal{Y}$	the set of all variables

Comparing Eq(1) and Eq(2), the outer-most summation over entities in Eq(1) is decomposed into the summation over all independent sets which is further decomposed into summations over entities within one set. By this means, we are able to solve the problem with the solution proposed in the next section.

3.2 Proposed Solution

In Eq(2), user weights $\mathcal{W}$ and truths $\mathcal{X}_1^{(*)}, \mathcal{X}_2^{(*)}, \cdots, \mathcal{X}_J^{(*)}$ should be learned simultaneously to minimize the objective function. In order to achieve this goal, block coordinate descent approach [3] is utilized to iteratively update the values of one set while fixing the values of others until convergence. There are two cases at each iteration: One is to update user weights $\mathcal{W}$ while fixing all the sets of truths $\{\mathcal{X}_1^{(*)}, \mathcal{X}_2^{(*)}, \cdots, \mathcal{X}_J^{(*)}\}$, the other is to update one set of truths $\mathcal{X}_j^{(*)}$ while fixing user weights and all the other sets of truths $\{\mathcal{W}, \mathcal{X}_1^{(*)}, \cdots, \mathcal{X}_{j-1}^{(*)}, \mathcal{X}_{j+1}^{(*)}, \cdots, \mathcal{X}_J^{(*)}\}$. We discuss the details of the two cases as follows.

Update $\mathcal{W}$ while fixing $\{\mathcal{X}_1^{(*)}, \mathcal{X}_2^{(*)}, \cdots, \mathcal{X}_J^{(*)}\}$: In this case, all sets of truths are fixed, then user weights $\mathcal{W}$ can be computed based on the difference between the truths and the observations made by the user:

$$\mathcal{W} \leftarrow \arg\min_{\mathcal{W}} f(\mathcal{X}^{(*)}, \mathcal{W}) \quad \text{s.t.} \quad \sum_{k=1}^{K} \exp(-w_k) = 1. \qquad (3)$$

We can solve this optimization problem based on Lagrange multipliers approach. The Lagrangian of Eq(2) is given as:

$$L(\{w_k\}_{k=1}^K, \lambda) = \sum_{\mathcal{I}_j \subset \mathcal{I}} \sum_{i \in \mathcal{I}_j} \Big\{ \sum_{k=1}^{K} w_k ||x_i^{(*)} - x_i^{(k)}||^2$$
$$+\alpha \sum_{i' \in N(i)} S(i,i')||x_i^{(*)} - x_{i'}^{(*)}||^2 \Big\} + \lambda(\sum_{k=1}^{K} \exp(-w_k) - 1),$$

where λ is a Lagrange multiplier. Let the partial derivative of Lagrangian with respect to w_k be 0, we get:

$$\sum_{\mathcal{I}_j \subset \mathcal{I}} \sum_{i \in \mathcal{I}_j} ||x_i^{(*)} - x_i^{(k)}||^2 = \lambda \exp(-w_k). \qquad (4)$$

From the constraint that $\sum_{k=1}^{K} \exp(-w_k) = 1$, we can derive that

Algorithm 1 Truth Discovery on Correlated Entities

Input: Observations from K users: $\{\mathcal{X}^{(1)}, \ldots, \mathcal{X}^{(K)}\}$.
Output: Truths $\mathcal{X}^{(*)} = \{x_i^{(*)}\}_{i=1}^N$, user weights $\mathcal{W} = \{w_k\}_{k=1}^K$.

```
Initialize the truths X^(*);
for i ← 1 to N do
    Construct a correlation graph G_corr in which an edge
    denotes the existence of correlation between the two nodes;
end for
Partition entities into disjoint independent sets {I_1, ..., I_J}
in G_corr;
repeat
    Update user weights W according to Eq(6) to infer user
    reliability degrees based on the estimated truths;
    for j ← 1 to J do
        for i ∈ I_J do
            Update the truth of the i_th entity x_i^(*) from the
            set I_J according to Eq(8) based on the current estimates of
            user weights;
        end for
    end for
until Convergence criterion is satisfied;
return X^(*) and W.
```

$$\lambda = \sum_{k=1}^{K} \sum_{\mathcal{I}_j \subset \mathcal{I}} \sum_{i \in \mathcal{I}_j} ||x_i^{(*)} - x_i^{(k)}||^2. \qquad (5)$$

We can then derive the update rule for each user's weight by plugging Eq(5) into Eq(4):

$$w_k = -\log \left(\frac{\sum_{\mathcal{I}_j \subset \mathcal{I}} \sum_{i \in \mathcal{I}_j} ||x_i^{(*)} - x_i^{(k)}||^2}{\sum_{\mathcal{I}_j \subset \mathcal{I}} \sum_{i \in \mathcal{I}_j} \sum_{k'=1}^{K} ||x_i^{(*)} - x_i^{(k')})||^2} \right), \qquad (6)$$

where k' denotes the index of a user. This update rule shows that a user's weight is higher when his observations are more often close to the truths.

Update $\mathcal{X}_j^{(*)}$ while fixing $\{\mathcal{W}, \mathcal{X}_1^{(*)}, \cdots, \mathcal{X}_{j-1}^{(*)}, \mathcal{X}_{j+1}^{(*)}, \cdots, \mathcal{X}_J^{(*)}\}$: In this case, user weights $\mathcal{W}$ are fixed, and the sets of truths are also fixed except $\mathcal{X}_j^{(*)}$. We update the truth for each entity in $\mathcal{X}_j^{(*)}$ by minimizing the objective function:

$$\mathcal{X}_j^{(*)} \leftarrow \arg\min_{\mathcal{X}_j^{(*)}} f(\mathcal{X}^{(*)}, \mathcal{W}). \qquad (7)$$

Let the derivative of Eq(2) be 0 with respect to $x_i^{(*)}$, then for each $i \in \mathcal{I}_j$, or equivalently for each $x_i^{(*)} \in \mathcal{X}_j^{(*)}$, we have the following update rule:

$$x_i^{(*)} = \frac{\sum_{k=1}^{K} w_k x_i^{(k)} + \alpha \sum_{i' \in N(i)} S(i,i') x_{i'}^{(*)}}{\sum_{k=1}^{K} w_k + \alpha \sum_{i' \in N(i)} S(i,i')} \qquad (8)$$

At this step, we can solve for $x_i^{(*)}$ with Eq(8) because the correlated variables are separated into disjoint independent sets. Specifically, we only update truths from independent set $\mathcal{X}_j^{(*)}$, which means that their correlated entities are not in this set, but in the other sets. Note that we have already fixed the truths of the other sets, and thus they are constants. As shown in Eq(8), $x_i^{(*)}$ is updated by averaging over the observed values weighted by user weights $\sum_{k=1}^{K} w_k x_i^{(k)}$ and the values of its correlated entities $\sum_{i' \in N(i)} x_{i'}^{(*)}$.

The proposed method is summarized in Algorithm 1. Disjoint independent sets $\{\mathcal{I}_1, \cdots, \mathcal{I}_J\}$ are first constructed according to the correlation information among entities (to be discussed in the following section). Then the algorithm iteratively updates user weights and truths based on Eq(6) and Eq(8) until convergence criterion is satisfied.

3.3 Construction of Disjoint Independent Sets

As discussed in Section 3.1, disjoint independent sets of entities should first be formed before the iterative solution can be used to solve Eq(1). Therefore, how to partition entities into disjoint independent sets is an important step. In this section, we first discuss how to form disjoint independent sets for any general cases in Section 3.3.1. Special cases of dealing with spatial and temporal correlations are discussed in Section 3.3.2 and Section 3.3.3 respectively.

3.3.1 *General Cases*

We can form a correlation graph based on the pairwise correlations among entities. In the graph, each vertex represents an entity and two vertices have an edge if they are correlated (i.e., two vertices are associated). Then the task of partitioning entities into disjoint independent sets is equivalent to the vertex coloring problem on the correlation graph. A vertex coloring is an assignment of colors to each vertex of a graph such that no edge connects two identically colored vertices. The problem of finding minimum number of colors for a given graph, i.e. minimum vertex coloring, is an NP-complete problem. However, some heuristic algorithms have been proposed, which are efficient and can produce good solutions in practice. We adopt the well-known Dsatur algorithm [5] to find disjoint independent sets in our task.

The procedure is described as follows. We first define the *saturation degree* of a vertex as the number of different independent sets that are covered by the associated vertices. The main idea is to iteratively select the vertex (entity) with the maximal saturation degree and put the selected entity into the corresponding independent set. The algorithm starts by arranging the vertices by a decreasing order of degrees, and the vertex with the maximal degree is put into independent set 1. After the initialization, an iterative process is performed to put entities into independent sets. During each iteration, the entity with the maximal saturation degree is chosen. In the tie case, we can break the tie by choosing the entity with the maximal degree. Then the selected entity is put into the independent set with the smallest index. This process continues until all the entities are processed.

In sum, given any correlation graph, we are able to construct disjoint independent sets by applying the aforementioned method. However, this step may still be time consuming especially when there are a large amount of entities. Fortunately, efficient methods can be applied to certain types of correlations, such as temporal and spatial correlations. In the following, we present the proposed approaches of independent set construction for these two special cases, which have only $O(1)$ time complexity.

3.3.2 *Temporal Correlations*

In many real-world applications, temporal correlations exist among entities. Examples include weather conditions (e.g., temperature, humidity) and air quality measures (e.g., PM2.5, NO_x). Temporal correlation is a local correlation and it typically exists only within a certain time window, i.e., the values of entities within a small time window are similar. This property enables us to develop a more efficient way to construct disjoint independent sets.

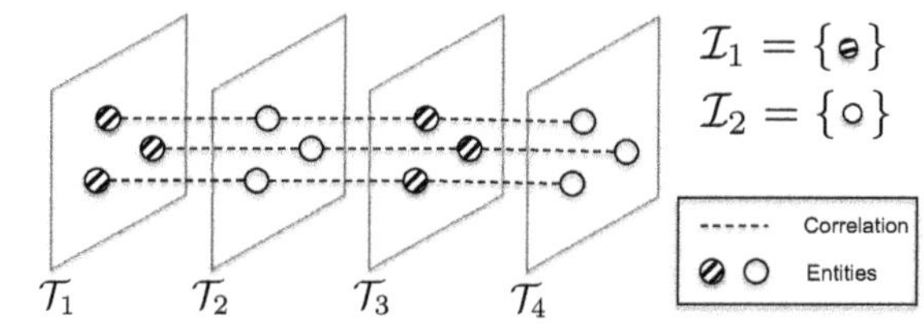

Figure 2: Separating entities based on temporal correlation when $p = 1$

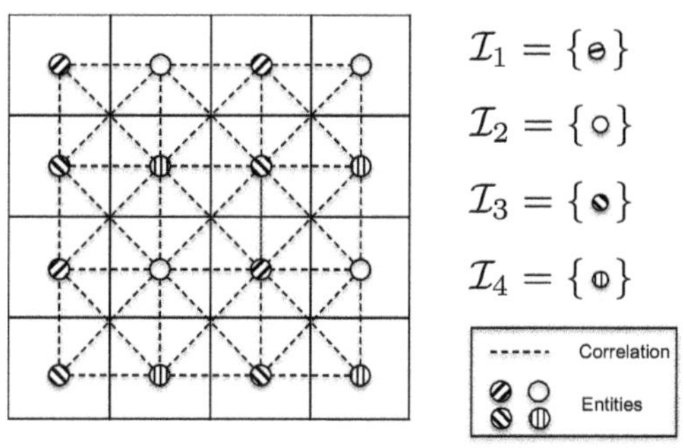

Figure 3: Separating entities based on spatial correlation

Let $\mathcal{T}_i$ denote the collection of entities in the i-th time slot, and $\mathcal{I}_i$ denote the i-th independent set. Without loss of generality, we assume that temporal correlations exist within $p+1$ consecutive time slots, i.e., entities correlate with all those from previous p time slots. We also assume that there are $(p+1)(Q+1)$ time slots in total. Then $p+1$ disjoint independent sets can be formed as follows. In each set, there are $Q+1$ time slots:

$$\left\{ \mathcal{I}_i = \bigcup_{q=0}^{Q} \mathcal{T}_{i+(p+1)q} \right\}_{i=1}^{p+1}.$$

Specifically, when $p = 1$, we only consider the temporal correlations among two consecutive time slots, i.e., entities only correlate with those from the previous time slot. In this case, all entities in odd-numbered time slots $\mathcal{I}_1$ and even-numbered time slots $\mathcal{I}_2$ can form two disjoint independent sets. An example is shown in Figure 2 in which we have four time slots $\{\mathcal{T}_1, \mathcal{T}_2, \mathcal{T}_3, \mathcal{T}_4\}$. Then two disjoint independent sets can be formed as $\mathcal{I}_1 = \{\mathcal{T}_1, \mathcal{T}_3\}$ and $\mathcal{I}_2 = \{\mathcal{T}_2, \mathcal{T}_4\}$.

3.3.3 *Spatial Correlations*

Spatial correlations are another type of correlations that widely exist in real world. For example, gas prices among gas stations and weather conditions within certain geographical areas are usually very similar. Spatial correlation is also a local property which allows the design of an efficient method of disjoint independent set construction. Specifically, entities distributed on a gridded map can be separated into four disjoint independent sets. Let $e_{(i,j)}$ be the entity on the i-th row and j-th column of the gridded map, and let $p = \{1, 2, \cdots, P\}$ and $q = \{1, 2, \cdots, Q\}$ be the indices. Four independent sets can be constructed as follows:

$$\mathcal{I}_1 = \left\{ e_{(2p,2q-1)} \right\}_{p=1,q=1}^{P,Q}, \mathcal{I}_2 = \left\{ e_{(2p-1,2q-1)} \right\}_{p=1,q=1}^{P,Q},$$
$$\mathcal{I}_3 = \left\{ e_{(2p-1,2q)} \right\}_{p=1,q=1}^{P,Q}, \mathcal{I}_4 = \left\{ e_{(2p,2q)} \right\}_{p=1,q=1}^{P,Q}.$$

They are formed in a way that entities in even rows and odd columns form independent set $\mathcal{I}_1$, those in odd rows and odd columns form $\mathcal{I}_2$, those in odd rows and even columns form $\mathcal{I}_3$ and those in even rows and even columns form $\mathcal{I}_4$. Figure 3 illustrate an example of the four disjoint independent sets constructed on a gridded map. As can be seen, entities in each set are not correlated with the others in the same set.

3.4 Convergence Analysis

Here, we formally prove the convergence of the proposed iterative approach shown in Algorithm 1 by the following theorem.

THEOREM 1. *The iterations shown in Algorithm 1 converge and the solution is a stationary point of the optimization problem in Eq(2).*

PROOF. We can simplify the optimization problem as follows when variables are represented as $\mathcal{Y} = \{\mathcal{W}, \mathcal{X}_1^{(*)}, \mathcal{X}_2^{(*)}, \cdots, \mathcal{X}_J^{(*)}\}$

$$\begin{aligned} &\text{minimize} \quad f(y) \\ &\text{s.t.} \quad y \in \mathcal{Y} \end{aligned} \tag{9}$$

Suppose for each $y_i \in \mathcal{Y}_i$,

$$f(y_1, \cdots, y_{i-1}, \xi, y_{i+1}, \cdots, y_m)$$

viewed as a function of ξ, attains a unique minimum $\bar{\xi}$ over Y_i. Let $\{y^k\}$ be the sequence generated by the following updating rule

$$y_i^{k+1} \leftarrow \arg\min_{\xi \in Y_i} f(y_1^{k+1}, \cdots, y_{i-1}^{k+1}, \xi, y_{i+1}^k, \cdots, y_m^k)$$

According to the proof for block coordinate descent in [3], every limit point of $\{y^k\}$ is a stationary point if the above conditions hold.

In the following, we only need to prove that Algorithm 1 satisfies the conditions. Specifically, we need to prove that each iteration generates a unique minimum for the updated variables. This is proved based on the two cases of updates:

Case One: This is to update $\mathcal{W}$ while fixing $\{\mathcal{X}_1^{(*)}, \mathcal{X}_2^{(*)}, \cdots, \mathcal{X}_J^{(*)}\}$. In order to show the convexity of Eq(2), we introduce another variable t_k, so that $t_k = \exp(-w_k)$. Then Eq(2) can be expressed in terms of t_k as follows:

$$\begin{aligned} \min_{\{t_k\}_{k=1}^K} f(t_k) = &\sum_{\mathcal{I}_j \subset \mathcal{I}} \sum_{i \in \mathcal{I}_j} \left\{ \sum_{k=1}^{K} -\log(t_k)||x_i^{(*)} - x_i^{(k)}||^2 \right. \\ &\left. +\alpha \sum_{i' \in N(i)} ||x_i^{(*)} - x_{i'}^{(*)}||^2 \right\} \\ \text{s.t.} \quad &\sum_{k=1}^{K} t_k = 1 \end{aligned} \tag{10}$$

The objective function of Eq(10) is a linear combination of negative logarithm functions and constants, and thus it is convex. In addition, the constraint is linear in t_k, which is affine. Therefore, Eq(2) is convex while fixing all the truths, such that a unique minimum for w_k can be achieved with the update rule in Eq(6).

Case Two: This is to update $\mathcal{X}_i^{(*)}$ while fixing $\{\mathcal{W}, \mathcal{X}_1^{(*)}, \cdots, \mathcal{X}_{i-1}^{(*)}, \mathcal{X}_{i+1}^{(*)}, \cdots, \mathcal{X}_J^{(*)}\}$. When fixing user weights $\mathcal{W}$, Eq(2) is a summation of quadratic functions with respect to $x_i^{(*)}$. It is convex since these quadratic functions are convex and summation operation preserves convexity. As a consequence, a unique minimum for $x_i^{(*)}$ can be achieved with the update rule in Eq(8).

Therefore, this proves the convergence of the proposed method. □

3.5 Time Complexity

We analyze the time complexity of the proposed method by analyzing each iteration's running time. Assume there are K users and N entities. The user weight update step costs $O(KN)$ time because for each user we calculate the square error between its observations and truths. In the truth update step, for each entity we calculate the weighted sum of observations from K users, the sum of correlated values and the sum of K users' weights. Totally it also needs $O(KN)$ time. Therefore, the time complexity is linear with respect to the number of observations.

4. MAPREDUCE IMPLEMENTATION

Crowd sensing applications usually have a large amount of participants who may generate a large amount of observations. To conduct truth discovery on this "big data", we hope to take advantage of cloud computing techniques to process large-scale data in parallel. Among parallel programming models, MapReduce [11] is widely adopted for many data mining tasks on large-scale data. In this section, we describe our design of a MapReduce model based parallel algorithm on Hadoop platform.

A typical MapReduce model contains two phases: 1) the map phase reads the input data, and converts it into key-value pairs; 2) the reduce phase takes the key-value pairs generated from the map phase as input, and performs the needed operations on them. For the proposed truth discovery task, the objective is to adapt Algorithm 1 to a parallel version. However, this is a non-trivial task. The challenge is that truths are updated according to Eq(8) with respect to each independent set. This requires us to fix all the other variables while updating those within one independent set. Obviously, this prevents us from deriving an efficient parallel process to compute truths all at once.

In order to solve this problem, we design a MapReduce algorithm based on asynchronous parallel coordinate descent. The proposed method iteratively calculates user weights and truths. During each iteration, the input data include observations from all K users $\{\mathcal{X}^{(k)}\}_{k=1}^K$, truths and user weights estimated from the last iteration (at iteration t)—$\mathcal{X}^{(t)(*)} = \{x_i^{(t)(*)}\}_{i=1}^N$ and $\mathcal{W}^{(t)} = \{w_k^{(t)}\}_{k=1}^K$. The outputs are truths and user weights calculated in the current iteration (at iteration $t+1$). The proposed method is shown in Algorithm 2. In the following, we will describe the details of the functions used in the proposed MapReduce truth discovery algorithm.

Input Data Format. The input data is formatted as tuples of three elements: the ID of an entity (denote as i), the ID of a user (denote as k) and the observation by the k-th user

Algorithm 2 MapReduce Implementation

Input: Data from K users: $\{\mathcal{X}^{(1)}, \ldots, \mathcal{X}^{(K)}\}$.
Truths at iteration t: $\mathcal{X}^{(t)(*)} = \{x_i^{(t)(*)}\}_{i=1}^{N}$
User weights at iteration t: $\mathcal{W}^{(t)} = \{w_k^{(t)}\}_{k=1}^{K}$
Output: Truths at iteration $t+1$: $\mathcal{X}^{(t+1)(*)}$
User weights at iteration $t+1$: $\mathcal{W}^{(t+1)}$

function MAP(Key id, Value v)
  $(i, x_i^{(k)}, k) \leftarrow v$;
  $observ\_error \leftarrow (x_i^{(k)} - x_i^{(t)(*)})^2$;
  EMIT($-k$, $observ\_error$);
  EMIT(i, $(x_i^{(k)}, k)$);
end function

function COMBINE(Key id, Value[] v)
  if $id > 0$ **then**
    $combined\_value = null$;
    for $v_i \in v$ **do**
      Append v_i to $combined\_value$;
    end for
  end if
  if $id < 0$ **then**
    $combined\_value = 0$;
    for $v_i \in v$ **do**
      $combined\_value = combined\_value + v_i$;
    end for
  end if
  EMIT(id, $combined\_value$);
end function

function REDUCE(Key id, Value[] v)
  if $id > 0$ **then**
    $[x_i^{(k)}, k] \leftarrow v$;
    Calculate $x_{id}^{(t+1)(*)}$ according to Eq(8);
    EMIT(id, $x_{id}^{(*)(t+1)}$);
  end if
  if $id < 0$ **then**
    $id \leftarrow -id$;
    Calculate nominator of $w_{id}^{(t+1)}$ according to Eq(6);
    EMIT($-id$, $w_{id}^{(t+1)}$);
  end if
end function

Calculate $w_{id}^{(t+1)}$ according to Eq(6);
return $\mathcal{X}^{(t+1)(*)} = \{x_i^{(t+1)(*)}\}_{i=1}^{N}$ and $\mathcal{W}^{(t+1)} = \{w_k^{(t+1)}\}_{k=1}^{K}$.

for the i-th entity (denote as $x_i^{(k)}$). In this way, the input is represented in the form of $(i, x_i^{(k)}, k)$.

Map Function. The input to the Map function is a collection of tuples. The Map function pre-processes input tuples and outputs key-value pairs to be used in the Reduce function. In order for Reduce function to calculate truths, one output key-value pair includes entity id i (i.e., the key) and $(x_i^{(k)}, k)$ (i.e., the observed value together with its user id). Also, in order for Reduce function to calculate user weights, the Map function pre-calculates the squared observation error based on the observation $x_i^{(k)}$ and the truth estimated from the last iteration $x_i^{(t)(*)}$. Then another key-value pair is emitted, which is user id k (i.e., the key) and the observation error (i.e., the value). Here we use a positive index as the emitted entity id, and a negative one as the emitted user id. This helps the Reduce function to distinguish between these two types.

Reduce Function. The Reduce function takes the key-value pairs emitted from the Map function as input. Truths and user weights are calculated and emitted as outputs. Upon receiving key-value pairs with positive keys, the Reduce function calculates the truths according to Eq(8). Each output tuple includes entity id and the calculated truth for this entity. If the Reduce function receives key-value pairs with negative keys, the nominator in the user weight calculation (Eq(6)) is calculated and emitted. Final user weights will be derived in the wrapper function.

Combine Function. Since the number of entities and users can be quite large, the overhead from the communication and sorting operations may dominate the running time. In order to reduce this kind of overhead, a Combine function is designed. It works in a similar way with the Reduce function. For key-value pairs with positive keys, the combiner will return local summation over the observation errors with the key. As for key-value pairs with negative keys, the combiner will just append the value and output the key-value pair.

Wrapper Function. A wrapper function is designed to control the iterative procedure. This function first initializes the truths as the mean of the observations provided by different users, and initializes user weights as $\frac{1}{K}$. Then the initial values and input data are fed to the Map function. Truths can be directly collected from the output of the Reduce function and user weights can be derived according to Eq(6) with the returned values from the Reduce function. We repeat the whole process until the estimated truths converge or after a certain number of iterations.

5. EVALUATIONS

In this section, we report the experimental results on datasets from three real-world crowd sensing applications, i.e., air quality sensing, gas price inference and weather condition estimation datasets. The results demonstrate that the proposed method outperforms state-of-the-art truth discovery methods because it incorporates correlations among entities into the model. The experiment setup is discussed in Section 5.1. Results are discussed in Section 5.2, Sections 5.3 and 5.4. Running time of the proposed method on Hadoop cluster is presented in Section 5.5.

5.1 Experiment setup

In this section, we present the performance measures and discuss the baseline methods which are compared in the experiments.

5.1.1 Performance Measures

In the experiments, the inputs for all methods are observations about entities given by different users. The outputs are the estimated truths and user weights. For each dataset, we have the ground truths, i.e., the actual true values of entities. However, they are not used by the proposed approach or the baselines, but are only used for evaluation. Note that all datasets contain continuous data, and thus we adopt the following measures to evaluate the performance.

- *Mean Absolute Distance* (*MAD*) measures the overall absolute distance between each method's outputs and

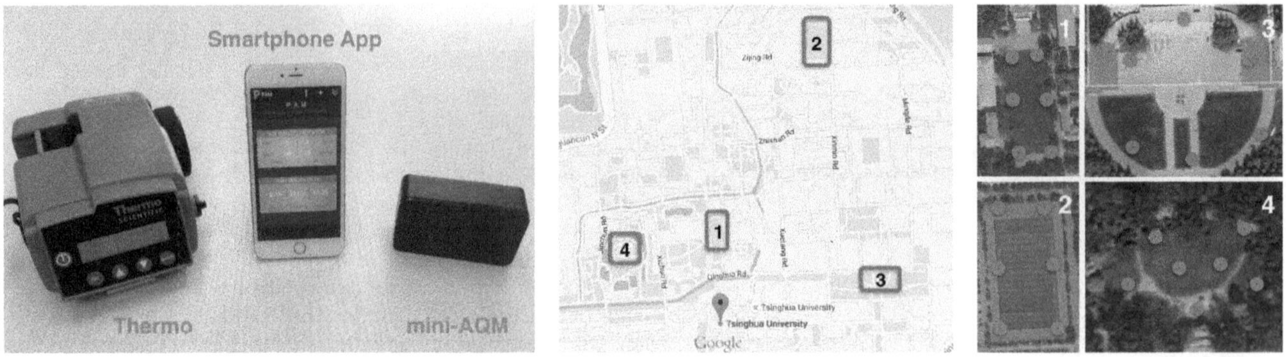

(a) Air Quality Sensing Devices (b) Areas for Sensing (c) Locations for Sensing

Figure 4: Air quality sensing devices and locations. (a) shows the mini-AQM, its smartphone App and the thermo. The mini-AQM is portable and carried by participants. Thermo is the device for collecting ground truths. (b) shows the four areas designated for air quality sensing at Tsinghua University. (c) shows the locations designated for sensing in each area.

the ground truths, which is computed by averaging the absolute difference over all the entities.

- *Root Mean Square Error (RMSE)* is computed by taking the root of the mean squared differences between each method's outputs and the ground truths.

MAD and *RMSE* both measure the differences between outputs compared with ground truths. The lower the measure, the closer the method's outputs to the ground truths, and the better it performs. *RMSE* emphasizes on larger errors compared with *MAD*.

5.1.2 Baseline Methods

In the experiment, the proposed Truth Discovery method on correlated entities is denoted as TD-corr. We compare it with the following state-of-the-art truth discovery methods which are designed to work on continuous data:

Gaussian Truth Model (GTM) is a Bayesian model that solves the problem of truth discovery on continuous data. Conflict Resolution on Heterogeneous data (CRH) is a framework that infers the truths from multiple sources with different data types, such as continuous and categorical data. Confidence-Aware Truth Discovery (CATD) is proposed to detect truths from multi-source data with long-tail phenomenon. Besides these truth discovery approaches, simple averaging methods, such as Mean and Median, are also compared.

We implement all the baselines and set the parameters as suggested in the corresponding papers. All the experiments are conducted on a Windows machine with 8G RAM, Intel Core i7 processor.

5.2 Experiments on Air Quality Sensing System

Air quality monitoring has drawn great attention these days, since people are suffering from deteriorated air quality over the past years, especially for cities in developing countries such as Beijing and New Delhi. In this experiment, we target the sensing of particulate matter with diameter less than 2.5 micron (PM2.5) with mini-AQM – a portable air quality sensing device designed for personal use [1, 7], as shown in Figure 4(a). The readings of mini-AQM are uploaded automatically into the server and can be checked on users' smartphone App as well. We have 14 participants equipped with mini-AQMs and let them conduct sensing tasks in 4 areas at Tsinghua University (Figure 4(b)). These areas are selected to represent different types of environments. Within each area, there are 6 or 7 locations (Figure 4(c)). The participants perform air quality sensing on all locations of each area within one hour. The PM2.5 values of the locations within one area are correlated, since the areas are limited in scale and the time window is short. The collected data have 25 entities and each entity represents the PM2.5 value of one location. The ground truths are collected with Thermo [2] (Figure 4(a)), an accurate but expensive sensing device.

5.2.1 Experimental Results

Performance w.r.t users' coverage rate. The results on this air quality sensing dataset are summarized in Table 2 measured by MAD and RMSE. To inspect the results visually, we also show the results in Figure 5. As users may not have observations for all the entities in many real-world applications, we conduct experiments on different coverage rates of users. The rate is defined as the percentage of entities that are observed by the user. For example, the coverage rate of 1.0 means that the user provides observations for all entities, and the coverage rate of 0.2 means that the user only provides observations for 20% of entities. We compare the performance of all the approaches when the coverage rate varies from 0.1 to 1.0.

As shown in Table 2 and Figure 5, TD-corr outperforms all the baselines under any coverage rate, as the MAD and RMSE of TD-corr are the lowest. These results demonstrate the advantage of the proposed approach which incorporates important correlation information in truth discovery. Note here CATD performs worse compared with other truth discovery methods. The reason is that CATD is designed for data with long tail effect and is not suitable for this data.

Another observation from Table 2 and Figure 5 is that the improvement over the baselines increases when the coverage rate decreases. For example, when the coverage rate is 0.8, TD-corr performs 25% better than the best baseline, and when the coverage rates are 0.4 and 0.2, TD-corr per-

Table 2: Performance Comparison on Air Quality Sensing System w.r.t Varying Coverage Rate

	Coverage Rate									
	0.2		0.4		0.6		0.8		1.0	
Method	MAD	RMSE	MAD	RMSE	MAD	RMSE	MAD	RMSE	MAD	RMSE
TD-corr	**6.2442**	**7.5426**	**5.5579**	**6.7327**	**4.3506**	**4.9962**	**3.8850**	**4.3650**	**3.5830**	**3.9234**
CRH	20.8943	43.2959	11.2952	18.3067	6.7254	8.9643	5.1653	6.5588	3.6809	4.6713
CATD	26.6218	46.4943	23.4346	30.6744	26.1897	31.2542	29.3994	33.7851	31.6699	35.6129
GTM	21.2988	42.2436	14.3768	25.7079	7.0405	10.5310	5.6053	7.5208	4.1867	5.2125
Mean	25.2916	48.0523	23.3865	39.2801	18.6068	29.5817	17.6935	27.0485	17.3739	25.0735
Median	21.6812	43.7129	14.2530	27.8183	7.2927	10.0167	6.1827	7.5137	5.6931	6.7028

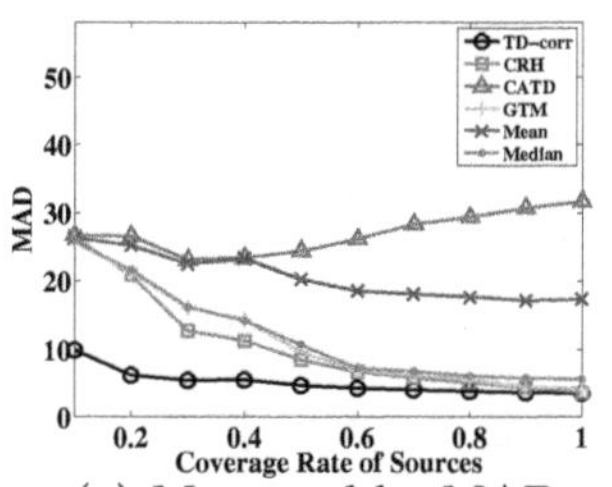

(a) Measured by MAD

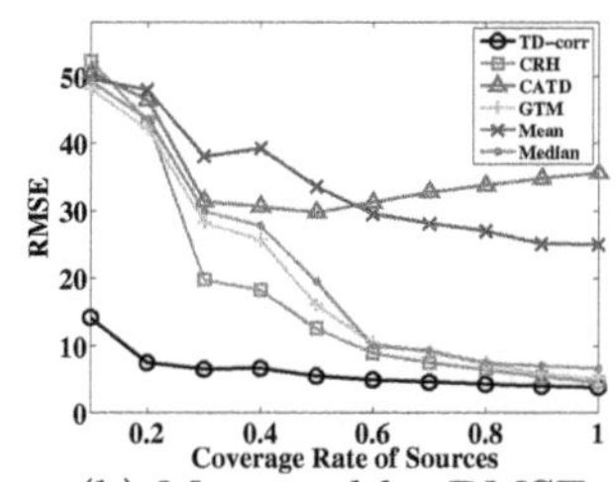

(b) Measured by RMSE

Figure 5: Performance Comparison on Air Quality Sensing System w.r.t Varying Coverage Rate

forms 51% and 70% better than the best baseline respectively. The reason is that when the coverage rate is lower, the number of entities observed by reliable users also decreases. Thus, there will be more entities receiving observations mostly from unreliable users, or even worse, receiving all the observations from unreliable users. The baseline methods purely infer truths by integrating over those unreliable observations, and thus their estimates are biased. In contrast, the proposed method is able to discover the truths because it takes correlated entities into consideration. Then information observed by reliable users can be propagated to entities that are not observed by reliable users and helps infer the truths of those entities.

5.3 Experiments on Gas Price Inference

An interesting crowd sensing application is to solicit gas price reports from crowd users and aggregate their answers to get correct gas prices. In this application, each user reports the observed gas prices for some gas stations to the server—some may report true values but some of the reported information may be wrong. The server then conducts truth discovery to identify the true price for each station.

To conduct this experiment, we first collect gas prices of 2175 gas stations from the GasBuddy website[2], which are treated as the ground truths. The data are collected from 48 cities across the whole US continent for one day. Correlations exist among gas stations within the same city. The observations of users with different reliability degrees are generated by adding different levels of Gaussian noise upon the ground truths. There are 2175 entities in the dataset. We conduct each experiment for 10 times and report the average results.

[2]http://www.gasbuddy.com

5.3.1 Experimental Results

Performance w.r.t users' coverage rate. The results with 30 users are summarized in Table 3 and Figure 6 measured by MAD and RMSE. Compared with the experiments on the air quality dataset, similar results can be observed. The proposed method outperforms the baselines especially when the coverage rate is low.

Performance w.r.t number of users. Figure 7 demonstrates the performance when varying the number of users from 10 to 100. The results show the following: 1) TD-corr performs better than the baselines on the data with any number of users. The incorporation of correlation information leads to a better estimation of truths. 2) The improvement is more significant when there are fewer users. The reason is when the number of users is smaller, there are more entities receiving observations mainly from less reliable users, and the estimated truths would be biased towards unreliable reports. The proposed method's advantage in propagating reliable information over correlated entities is thus clearly shown.

Correlation accuracy. Here we show that the proposed approach indeed takes correlation among entities in the estimation of truths. We define the measure of correlation accuracy as follows. We measure the similarity between entities based on the estimated truths, and regard two entities as correlated ones if their distance passes a threshold. We then compare the correlations derived from the estimated truths and the ground-truth correlations. Then the correlation accuracy is defined as the percentage of correlations that are the same as the ground truths. Figure 8 shows the correlation accuracy under different thresholds (0.01, 0.03, 0.05, 0.07, 0.09, 0.1, 0.2, 0.3). Figure 8(a) and Figure 8(b) show the results when coverage rates are 20% and 80% respectively. It can be seen that TD-corr captures the correlation information better than the baselines under any setting, and its correlation accuracy can reach a high value even when the threshold is low, such as 0.05 or 0.07.

5.4 Experiments on Weather Condition Estimation

Another interesting crowd sensing application is to collect and aggregate weather conditions reported by users. User can report weather information, such as temperature, pressure, humidity. Data can be acquired with integrated sensors in smartphones or manually input by users. The truth discovery approach can then be conducted on the collected noisy data to identify the true weather conditions. In order to emulate this application, we collect weather forecast data from three weather forecast platforms (Wunder-

Table 3: Performance Comparison on Gas Price Inference w.r.t Varying Coverage Rate

	Coverage Rate									
	0.2		0.4		0.6		0.8		1.0	
Method	MAD	RMSE	MAD	RMSE	MAD	RMSE	MAD	RMSE	MAD	RMSE
TD-corr	**0.0727**	**0.0963**	**0.0725**	**0.0941**	**0.0713**	**0.0917**	**0.0713**	**0.0912**	**0.0685**	**0.0867**
CRH	0.2881	0.3714	0.1959	0.2475	0.1563	0.1968	0.1370	0.1720	0.1191	0.1488
CATD	0.2766	0.3574	0.1854	0.2344	0.1469	0.1850	0.1280	0.1610	0.1120	0.1400
GTM	0.2770	0.3582	0.1856	0.2348	0.1471	0.1852	0.1281	0.1610	0.1120	0.1400
Mean	0.2994	0.3851	0.2051	0.2590	0.1645	0.2071	0.1442	0.1810	0.1256	0.1570
Median	0.3272	0.4204	0.2299	0.2912	0.1853	0.2337	0.1640	0.2064	0.1415	0.1772

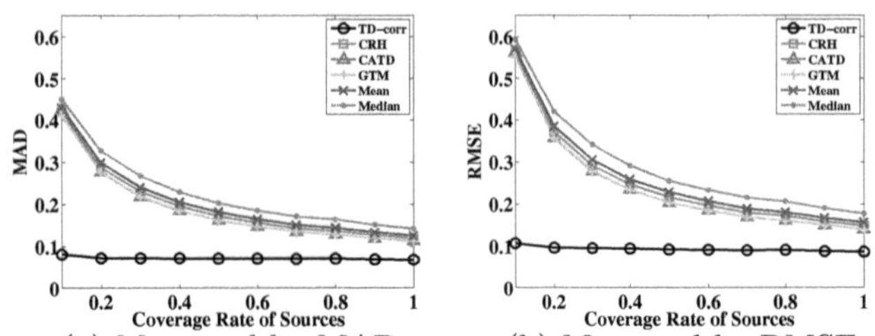

(a) Measured by MAD (b) Measured by RMSE

Figure 6: Performance Comparison on Gas Price Inference w.r.t Varying Coverage Rate

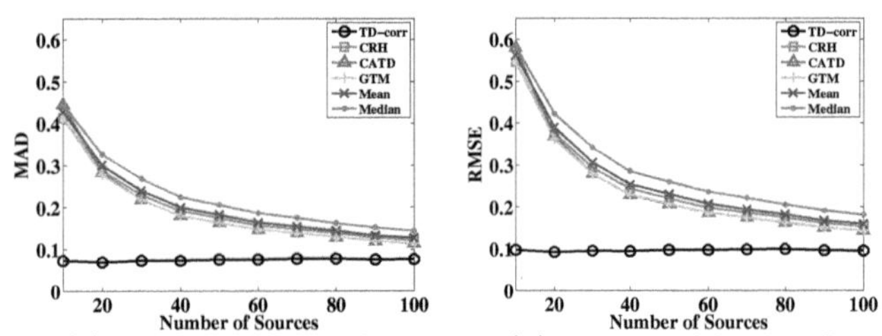

(a) Measured by MAD (b) Measured by RMSE

Figure 7: Performance w.r.t Varying Number of Users

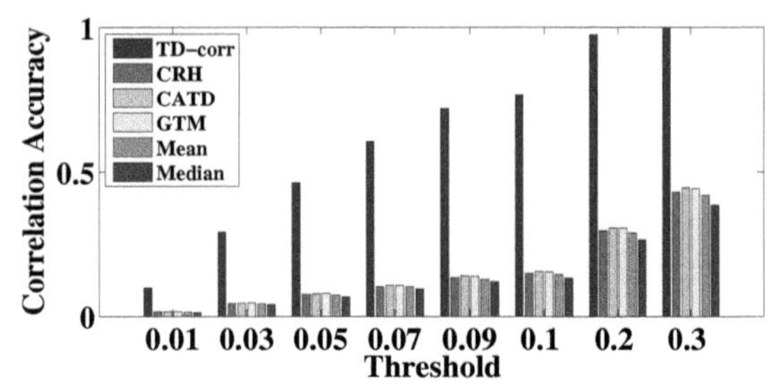

(a) Coverage Rate is 20%

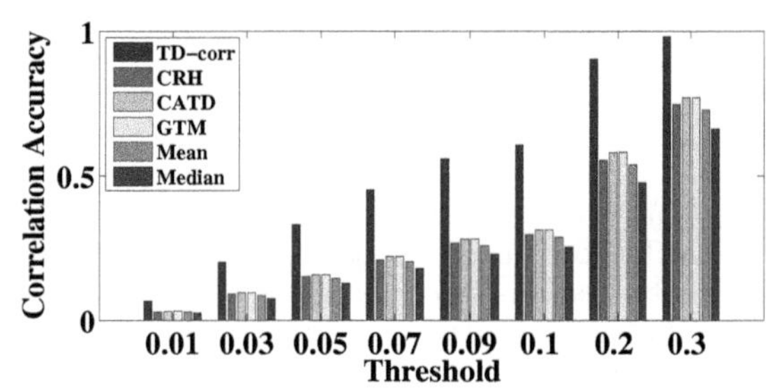

(b) Coverage Rate is 80%

Figure 8: Correlation Accuracy w.r.t Varying Threshold

ground[3], HAM weather[4], and World Weather Online[5]) for 147 locations within New York City Area. From each platform, we collect temperature forecasts of two different days as two different users, thus 6 users are formed in total. We also crawl the ground truths of hourly temperature for each location. An entity here is defined as the temperature of one location at one time. The spatial correlation is modeled using Euclidean distance with Gaussian kernel, and the temporal correlation exists among entities from the same location in consecutive time slots. The whole process of collection lasts over a month and there are 145459 entities in the dataset.

5.4.1 Experimental Results

Table 4 and Figure 9 summarize the performance of TD-corr and baselines on the weather condition estimation dataset. Similar results can be observed, compared with the experiments on the previous two datasets.

[3]http://www.wunderground.com
[4]http://www.hamweather.com
[5]http://www.worldweatheronline.com

To demonstrate the proposed approach's ability of distinguishing reliable users from unreliable ones, we compare the reliability degrees estimated by each truth discovery method. The reliability degree of a user is defined as the overall similarity between its observations and truths. The ground-truth reliability degree is calculated and compared as well. In the compared methods, different functions are adopted to calculate the reliability degree of users. For the sake of comparison, we normalize the reliability output into the range of [0,1]. Figure 10 and Figure 11 show the comparison results when coverage rates are 0.2 and 0.8 respectively. To make it clear, we demonstrate the user reliability degrees in two plots, and each of them shows the comparison between the ground truths and some of the approaches. TD-corr and ground truths are compared in Figures 10(a) and 11(a). Other baseline methods are compared in Figures 10(b) and 11(b).

We can observe that the user reliability estimated by TD-corr is very close to the user reliability derived from the ground truth. With the consideration of correlation information, the proposed TD-corr approach can better estimate the truths. Due to the intertwined process of truth and user reliability estimation, such an improved truth estima-

Table 4: Performance Comparison on Weather Condition Estimation w.r.t Varying Coverage Rate

	Coverage Rate									
	0.2		0.4		0.6		0.8		1.0	
Method	MAD	RMSE	MAD	RMSE	MAD	RMSE	MAD	RMSE	MAD	RMSE
TD-corr	**2.5081**	**3.2734**	**2.3700**	**3.0434**	**2.2984**	**2.9327**	**2.2691**	**2.8919**	**2.2420**	**2.8520**
CRH	4.0757	6.2663	3.4305	5.1666	2.8943	4.1617	2.5022	3.3352	2.2708	2.8955
CATD	4.0093	6.2208	3.3308	5.0819	2.7883	4.0444	2.4211	3.2127	2.2638	2.8598
GTM	4.7015	7.3111	3.6016	5.3953	3.0506	4.3992	2.5939	3.4938	2.2641	2.8600
Mean	4.3614	6.5426	3.9766	5.7515	3.6624	5.0880	3.4089	4.5359	3.2419	4.1882
Median	4.3418	6.5432	3.8614	5.7051	3.4252	4.9632	3.0016	4.2171	2.6409	3.4795

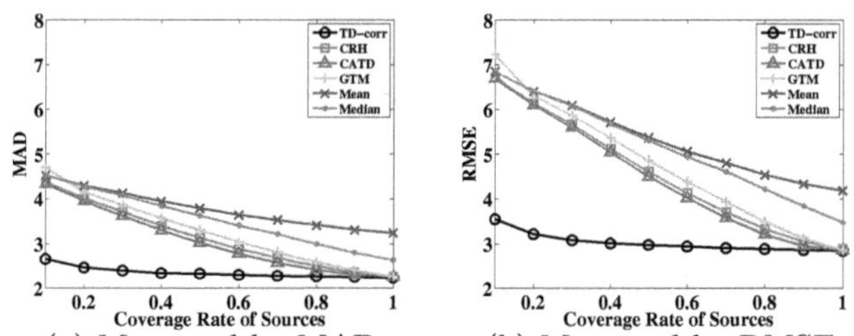

(a) Measured by MAD (b) Measured by RMSE

Figure 9: Performance Comparison on Weather Condition Estimation w.r.t Varying Coverage Rate

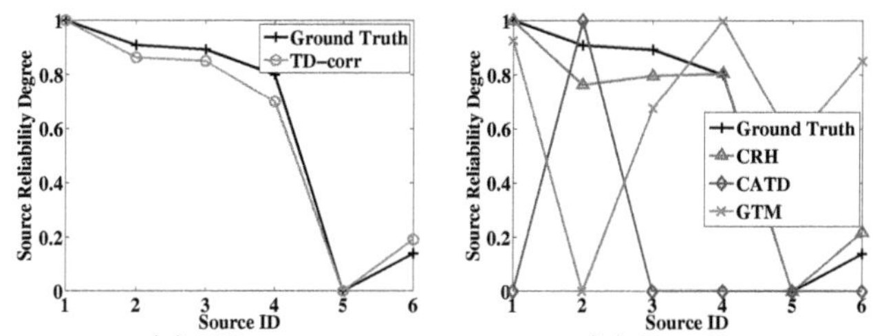

(a) TD-corr (b) Baselines

Figure 10: Comparison of User Reliability Degrees with Ground Truths (Coverage = 0.2)

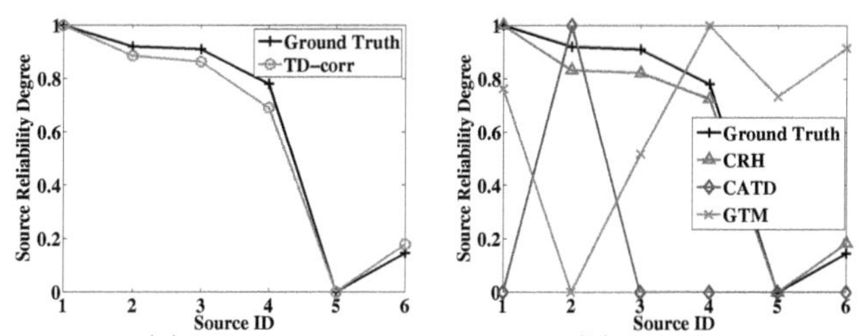

(a) TD-corr (b) Baselines

Figure 11: Comparison of User Reliability Degrees with Ground Truths (Coverage = 0.8)

tion leads to an improved estimation of user reliability. In contrast, due to the fact that the baselines do not consider the important correlation information, their truth and user reliability estimation may not be accurate, so we can observe the deviation of their estimated user reliability from that of the ground truth.

Practical convergence property of the proposed method. The proposed method converges as discussed in Section 3.4. In order to show the convergence in practice, we conduct experiments on the weather dataset and record objective function value at each iteration. As can be observed from Figure 12, the objective value decreases quickly in the first 10 iterations, then gradually reaches to a steady value. This demonstrates the convergence of the proposed method.

5.5 Efficiency Evaluation on Hadoop Cluster

Running time on hadoop cluster. As discussed in Section 4, the proposed method can be implemented based on the MapReduce model. We conduct experiments to demonstrate the running time of this parallel algorithm. Datasets are generated with different numbers of observations, varying from 10^4 to 10^8. The experiments are conducted on a 4-node Dell Hadoop cluster with Intel Xeon E5-2403 processor (4x 1.80 GHz, 48 GB RAM). Results are summarized in Table 5, which show that the running time is linear with respect to the number of observations. We calculate the Pearson product-moment correlation coefficient to further justify this. The Pearson product-moment correlation coefficient is a measure of the linear correlation between two variables. It gives a value between $+1$ and -1, where $+1$ indicates positive correlation, 0 indicates no correlation and -1 indicates negative correlation. The Pearson's correlation coefficient in Table 5 shows a strong linear correlation between the number of observations and the running time. This means that the proposed method is scalable and can be applied to large-scale data.

6. RELATED WORK

We review related work based on the following two categories.

Crowd Sensing. The research of crowd sensing [4, 6, 8, 9, 10, 13, 14, 16, 17, 18, 19, 20, 21, 22, 23, 24, 25, 32, 35, 36, 37, 38, 40, 42] has received more and more attention with the rapid development of pervasive sensors, smartphones, and network technologies. Thanks to the rich set of sensors (e.g., accelerometer, gyroscope, GPS, microphone, and camera) integrated in the mobile devices, and the pervasive WiFi and cellular networks, now people can record and share the information they perceive wherever they are and whenever they want. Recently, a variety of sensing systems have been designed for a wide spectrum of applications. Huang et al. [21] implemented a system for the search and rescue of people in emergency situations in wilderness areas. In their system, RF-based sensors, storage and processing devices are used. Eisenman et al. [14] designed a system for the cyclists to collect and share data with each other about their performance and the surrounding environment. Reddy et al. [38] designed a smartphone based platform for the cyclists to document and share routes, ride statistics, experience and etc. Mun et al. [32] proposed an application which

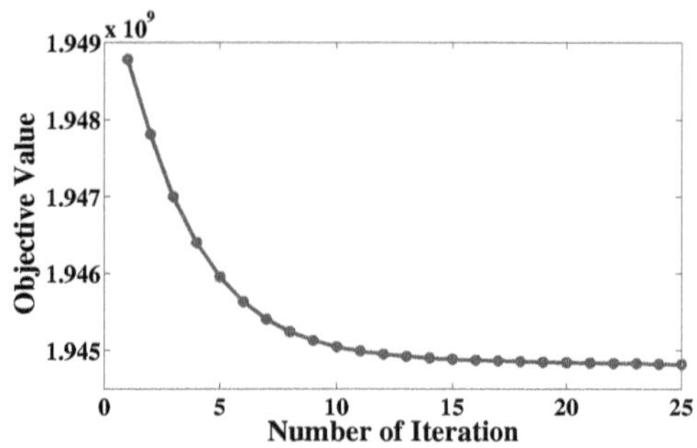

Figure 12: Convergence

Table 5: Running Time on Hadoop Cluster

# Observations	Time(s)
1×10^4	77
1×10^5	83
1×10^6	136
1×10^7	254
1×10^8	413
Pearson Correlation	0.9088

utilizes users' trajectory data to infer environmental impact and exposure. EasyTracker [4] is designed with functions that determine routes and local stops, and infer schedules with collected trajectory data. These papers focused on the design of the crowd sensing system, which is different from the task of truth discovery studied in this paper.

Truth Discovery. Truth discovery was first proposed by Yin et al. [47] as a Bayesian based approach in which the confidence of each observation is calculated as the product of the reliability of the sources that provide the observation. Later, the topic attracts much attention and methods are developed to infer both source reliabilities and true facts. Pasternack et al. [33, 34] proposed methods to incorporate prior knowledge into truth discovery. In these methods, a source "invests" its reliability on the observations it provides, and credits are collected by the confidence on its invested observations. Galland et al. [15] modeled the difficulty of getting the truths while computing source weights. Yin et al. [48] proposed a semi-supervised method which can propagate the information trustworthiness obtained from the observed ground truths. Probabilistic graphical models were adopted in [49, 50] and source selection problem was studied in [12, 39]. A maximum likelihood estimation approach was proposed by Wang et al. in [44] which adopted expectation maximization method, and it was designed for categorical data. Recently, approaches have been proposed to handle heterogeneous data types [27, 26, 41], such as categorical data and continuous data. Ma et al. [30] proposed a fine grained truth discovery model to handle users with various expertise levels on different topics. In [31], Miao et al. proposed a cloud-enabled privacy-preserving truth discovery framework for crowd sensing systems. Note that the approaches discussed in this paragraph tackle some other challenges in truth discovery but do not consider correlations among entities.

In [43], the authors considered physical correlations among entities which are modeled with the joint probability of correlated variables, and derived an expectation maximization based algorithm to infer both entities' states and sources' reliabilities. In [46], they proposed a method to capture the temporal correlations among entities, and a joint probability of any given sequence of observed values are calculated from historical data to model the temporal correlation. In [45], the authors proposed a scalable algorithm which modeled the structure of correlations as a Bayesian network. The proposed algorithm is efficient because the conditional independence property in the network is exploited. However, these approaches work on binary data and correlations, and cannot be generalized to other data types, such as continuous data. In contrast, the proposed method in this paper works on continuous data and correlations, and thus the problem setting is quite different. Li et al. [29] proposed an incremental truth discovery framework that can dynamically update object truths and source weights when the information comes sequentially. However, they only consider the temporal relations for dynamically generated data, and the proposed framework in this paper can handle any types of correlations.

7. CONCLUSIONS

In this paper, we investigate the truth discovery problem on correlated entities in crowd sensing applications. In a crowd sensing system, crowd users contribute their information about entities to the server. Since users' reliability degrees are unknown *a priori*, the observations they provide should not be trusted equally. Then how to discover the true information among the conflicting observations is a crucial task. Although some approaches have been developed to detect truths from conflicting sources, these approaches do not take the valuable information about entity correlations into account and thus cannot detect truths accurately when the coverage is low. In fact, correlations among entities widely exist and can greatly benefit the truth discovery process. In this paper, we formulate the task of truth discovery on correlated entities as an optimization problem, which models both the distance between truths and observations and the distance among truths of correlated entities. User weights are plugged into the optimization function to capture the unknown user reliability. We tackle the difficulty caused by the regularization terms added upon correlated variables. In order to solve this problem, we propose methods to partition variables into disjoint independent sets, and conduct block coordinate descent to update truths and weights iteratively. The convergence of the approach is proved. To further speed up the process, we propose a MapReduce version of the algorithm that is implemented on Hadoop cluster. We conduct experiments on three crowd sensing datasets, i.e., air quality sensing, gas price inference and weather condition estimation datasets. Results demonstrate the advantages of the proposed method in discovering true information for correlated entities over existing truth discovery approaches.

8. ACKNOWLEDGMENTS

We would like to thank the anonymous reviewers and our shepherd, Polly Huang, for their valuable comments and suggestions, which help us tremendously in improving the quality of the paper. This work was sponsored in part by US National Science Foundation under grant IIS-1319973. The views and conclusions contained in this paper are those of the authors and should not be interpreted as representing any funding agency.

9. REFERENCES

[1] Air scienctific. http://www.coilabs.com/.

[2] Thermo. http://www.thermoscientific.com.

[3] D. P. Bertsekas. *Nonlinear programming.* Athena scientific Belmont, 1999.

[4] J. Biagioni, T. Gerlich, T. Merrifield, and J. Eriksson. Easytracker: Automatic transit tracking, mapping, and arrival time prediction using smartphones. In *Proceedings of the 9th ACM Conference on Embedded Networked Sensor Systems (SenSys'11)*. ACM, 2011.

[5] D. Brélaz. New methods to color the vertices of a graph. *Commun. ACM*, 22(4):251–256, Apr. 1979.

[6] S. Chen, M. Li, K. Ren, X. Fu, and C. Qiao. Rise of the indoor crowd: Reconstruction of building interior view via mobile crowdsourcing. In *Proceedings of the 13th ACM Conference on Embedded Network Sensor Systems (SenSys'15)*, SenSys '15, 2015.

[7] Y. Cheng, X. Li, Z. Li, S. Jiang, Y. Li, J. Jia, and X. Jiang. Aircloud: A cloud-based air-quality monitoring system for everyone. In *Proceedings of the 12th ACM Conference on Embedded Network Sensor Systems (SenSys'14)*. ACM, 2014.

[8] Y. Chon, N. D. Lane, Y. Kim, F. Zhao, and H. Cha. Understanding the coverage and scalability of place-centric crowdsensing. In *Proceedings of the 2013 ACM international joint conference on Pervasive and ubiquitous computing (UbiComp'13)*, pages 3–12. ACM, 2013.

[9] Y. Chon, N. D. Lane, F. Li, H. Cha, and F. Zhao. Automatically characterizing places with opportunistic crowdsensing using smartphones. In *Proceedings of the 2012 ACM Conference on Ubiquitous Computing (UbiComp'12)*, pages 481–490. ACM, 2012.

[10] V. Coric and M. Gruteser. Crowdsensing maps of on-street parking spaces. In *Proceedings of the 9th International Conference on Distributed Computing in Sensor Systems (DCOSS'13)*, pages 115–122. IEEE, 2013.

[11] J. Dean and S. Ghemawat. Mapreduce: simplified data processing on large clusters. *Communications of the ACM*, 51(1):107–113, 2008.

[12] X. L. Dong, B. Saha, and D. Srivastava. Less is more: Selecting sources wisely for integration. *PVLDB*, 6(2):37–48, 2012.

[13] A. Dua, N. Bulusu, W.-C. Feng, and W. Hu. Towards trustworthy participatory sensing. In *Proceedings of the 4th USENIX conference on Hot topics in security (HotSec'09)*, pages 8–8. USENIX Association, 2009.

[14] S. B. Eisenman, E. Miluzzo, N. D. Lane, R. A. Peterson, G.-S. Ahn, and A. T. Campbell. Bikenet: A mobile sensing system for cyclist experience mapping. *ACM Transactions on Sensor Networks (TOSN)*, 6(1):6, 2009.

[15] A. Galland, S. Abiteboul, A. Marian, and P. Senellart. Corroborating information from disagreeing views. In *Proc. of the ACM International Conference on Web Search and Data Mining (WSDM'10)*, pages 131–140, 2010.

[16] R. K. Ganti, N. Pham, H. Ahmadi, S. Nangia, and T. F. Abdelzaher. Greengps: a participatory sensing fuel-efficient maps application. In *Proceedings of the 8th international conference on Mobile systems, applications, and services (MobiSys'10)*, pages 151–164. ACM, 2010.

[17] R. K. Ganti, F. Ye, and H. Lei. Mobile crowdsensing: current state and future challenges. *Communications Magazine, IEEE*, 49(11):32–39, 2011.

[18] S. Hu, H. Liu, L. Su, H. Wang, T. F. Abdelzaher, P. Hui, W. Zheng, Z. Xie, and J. Stankovic. Towards automatic phone-to-phone communication for vehicular networking applications. In *The 33rd IEEE International Conference on Computer Communications (INFOCOM'14)*. IEEE, 2014.

[19] S. Hu, L. Su, S. Li, S. Wang, C. Pan, S. Gu, T. Amin, H. Liu, S. Nath, R. R. Choudhury, et al. Experiences with enav: A low-power vehicular navigation system. In *The ACM International Joint Conference on Pervasive and Ubiquitous Computing (UbiComp'15)*, 2015.

[20] S. Hu, L. Su, H. Liu, H. Wang, and T. F. Abdelzaher. Smartroad: Smartphone-based crowd sensing for traffic regulator detection and identification. *ACM Transactions on Sensor Networks (TOSN)*, 11(4):55, 2015.

[21] J.-H. Huang, S. Amjad, and S. Mishra. Cenwits: a sensor-based loosely coupled search and rescue system using witnesses. In *Proceedings of the 3rd international conference on Embedded networked sensor systems (SenSys'05)*, pages 180–191. ACM, 2005.

[22] K. L. Huang, S. S. Kanhere, and W. Hu. Are you contributing trustworthy data?: the case for a reputation system in participatory sensing. In *Proceedings of the 13th ACM international conference on Modeling, analysis, and simulation of wireless and mobile systems (MSWIM'10)*, pages 14–22. ACM, 2010.

[23] W. Z. Khan, Y. Xiang, M. Y. Aalsalem, and Q. Arshad. Mobile phone sensing systems: A survey. *Communications Surveys & Tutorials, IEEE*, 15(1):402–427, 2013.

[24] N. D. Lane, Y. Chon, L. Zhou, Y. Zhang, F. Li, D. Kim, G. Ding, F. Zhao, and H. Cha. Piggyback crowdsensing (pcs): energy efficient crowdsourcing of mobile sensor data by exploiting smartphone app opportunities. In *Proceedings of the 11th ACM Conference on Embedded Networked Sensor Systems (SenSys'13)*, page 7. ACM, 2013.

[25] N. D. Lane, E. Miluzzo, H. Lu, D. Peebles, T. Choudhury, and A. T. Campbell. A survey of mobile phone sensing. *Communications Magazine, IEEE*, 48(9):140–150, 2010.

[26] Q. Li, Y. Li, J. Gao, L. Su, B. Zhao, M. Demirbas, W. Fan, and J. Han. A confidence-aware approach for truth discovery on long-tail data. *Proc. VLDB Endow.*, 8(4):425–436, 2014.

[27] Q. Li, Y. Li, J. Gao, B. Zhao, W. Fan, and J. Han. Resolving conflicts in heterogeneous data by truth discovery and source reliability estimation. In *Proc. of the 2014 ACM SIGMOD International Conference on Management of Data (SIGMOD'14)*, pages 1187–1198, 2014.

[28] Y. Li, J. Gao, C. Meng, Q. Li, L. Su, B. Zhao, W. Fan, and J. Han. A survey on truth discovery. *arXiv preprint arXiv:1505.02463*, 2015.

[29] Y. Li, Q. Li, J. Gao, L. Su, B. Zhao, W. Fan, and J. Han. On the discovery of evolving truth. In *Proceedings of the 21th ACM SIGKDD International Conference on Knowledge Discovery and Data Mining (KDD'15)*, pages 675–684. ACM, 2015.

[30] F. Ma, Y. Li, Q. Li, M. Qiu, J. Gao, S. Zhi, L. Su, B. Zhao, H. Ji, and J. Han. Faitcrowd: Fine grained truth discovery for crowdsourced data aggregation. In *Proceedings of the 21th ACM SIGKDD International Conference on Knowledge Discovery and Data Mining (KDD'15)*, pages 745–754. ACM, 2015.

[31] C. Miao, W. Jiang, L. Su, Y. Li, S. Guo, Z. Qin, H. Xiao, J. Gao, and K. Ren. Cloud-enabled privacy-preserving truth discovery in crowd sensing systems. In *Proceedings of the 13th ACM Conference on Embedded Network Sensor Systems (SenSys'15)*, SenSys '15, 2015.

[32] M. Mun, S. Reddy, K. Shilton, N. Yau, J. Burke, D. Estrin, M. Hansen, E. Howard, R. West, and P. Boda. Peir, the personal environmental impact report, as a platform for participatory sensing systems research. In *Proceedings of the 7th international conference on Mobile systems, applications, and services (MobiSys'09)*, pages 55–68. ACM, 2009.

[33] J. Pasternack and D. Roth. Knowing what to believe (when you already know something). In *Proc. of the International Conference on Computational Linguistics (COLING'10)*, pages 877–885, 2010.

[34] J. Pasternack and D. Roth. Making better informed trust decisions with generalized fact-finding. In *Proc. of the International Jont Conference on Artifical Intelligence (IJCAI'11)*, pages 2324–2329, 2011.

[35] K. K. Rachuri, C. Efstratiou, I. Leontiadis, C. Mascolo, and P. J. Rentfrow. Metis: Exploring mobile phone sensing offloading for efficiently supporting social sensing applications. In *Proceedings of the 11th International Conference on Pervasive Computing and Communications (PerCom'13)*, pages 85–93. IEEE, 2013.

[36] K. K. Rachuri, C. Mascolo, M. Musolesi, and P. J. Rentfrow. Sociablesense: exploring the trade-offs of adaptive sampling and computation offloading for social sensing. In *Proceedings of the 17th annual international conference on Mobile computing and networking (MobiCom'11)*, pages 73–84. ACM, 2011.

[37] R. K. Rana, C. T. Chou, S. S. Kanhere, N. Bulusu, and W. Hu. Ear-phone: an end-to-end participatory urban noise mapping system. In *Proceedings of the 9th ACM/IEEE International Conference on Information Processing in Sensor Networks (IPSN'10)*, pages 105–116. ACM, 2010.

[38] S. Reddy, K. Shilton, G. Denisov, C. Cenizal, D. Estrin, and M. Srivastava. Biketastic: sensing and mapping for better biking. In *Proceedings of the SIGCHI Conference on Human Factors in Computing Systems (CHI'10)*, pages 1817–1820. ACM, 2010.

[39] T. Rekatsinas, X. L. Dong, and D. Srivastava. Characterizing and selecting fresh data sources. In *Proc. of the 2014 ACM SIGMOD International Conference on Management of Data (SIGMOD'14)*, pages 919–930, 2014.

[40] F. Saremi, O. Fatemieh, H. Ahmadi, H. Wang, T. Abdelzaher, R. Ganti, H. Liu, S. Hu, S. Li, and L. Su. Experiences with greengps–fuel-efficient navigation using participatory sensing. *IEEE Transactions on Mobile Computing (IEEE TMC).*

[41] L. Su, Q. Li, S. Hu, S. Wang, J. Gao, H. Liu, T. F. Abdelzaher, J. Han, X. Liu, Y. Gao, et al. Generalized decision aggregation in distributed sensing systems. In *Proceedings of the 35th IEEE Real-Time Systems Symposium (RTSS'14)*, pages 1–10. IEEE, 2014.

[42] V. Subbaraju, A. Kumar, V. Nandakumar, S. Batra, S. Kanhere, P. De, V. Naik, D. Chakraborty, and A. MISRA. Conferencesense: A case study of sensing public gatherings using participatory smartphones. International Workshop on Pervasive Urban Crowdsensing Architecture and Applications (PUCAA'13), in conjunction with ACM Ubicomp'13, 2013.

[43] D. Wang, T. Abdelzaher, L. Kaplan, R. Ganti, S. Hu, and H. Liu. Exploitation of physical constraints for reliable social sensing. In *Proceedings of the 34th IEEE Real-Time Systems Symposium (RTSS'13)*, pages 212–223. IEEE, 2013.

[44] D. Wang, L. Kaplan, H. Le, and T. Abdelzaher. On truth discovery in social sensing: A maximum likelihood estimation approach. In *Proceedings of the 11th international conference on Information Processing in Sensor Networks (IPSN'12)*, pages 233–244. ACM, 2012.

[45] S. Wang, L. Su, S. Li, S. Hu, T. Amin, H. Wang, S. Yao, L. Kaplan, and T. Abdelzaher. Scalable social sensing of interdependent phenomena. In *Proceedings of the 14th International Conference on Information Processing in Sensor Networks (IPSN'15)*, pages 202–213. ACM, 2015.

[46] S. Wang, D. Wang, L. Su, L. Kaplan, and T. F. Abdelzaher. Towards cyber-physical systems in social spaces: The data reliability challenge. In *Proceedings of the 35th IEEE Real-Time Systems Symposium (RTSS'14)*, pages 74–85. IEEE, 2014.

[47] X. Yin, J. Han, and P. S. Yu. Truth discovery with multiple conflicting information providers on the web. *IEEE Transactions on Knowledge and Data Engineering*, 20(6):796–808, 2008.

[48] X. Yin and W. Tan. Semi-supervised truth discovery. In *Proc. of the International Conference on World Wide Web (WWW'11)*, pages 217–226, 2011.

[49] B. Zhao and J. Han. A probabilistic model for estimating real-valued truth from conflicting sources. In *Proc. of the VLDB workshop on Quality in Databases (QDB'12)*, 2012.

[50] B. Zhao, B. I. P. Rubinstein, J. Gemmell, and J. Han. A bayesian approach to discovering truth from conflicting sources for data integration. *PVLDB*, 5(6):550–561, 2012.

Cloud-Enabled Privacy-Preserving Truth Discovery in Crowd Sensing Systems

Chenglin Miao, Wenjun Jiang, Lu Su, Yaliang Li, Suxin Guo, Zhan Qin
Houping Xiao, Jing Gao, Kui Ren
Department of Computer Science and Engineering
State University of New York at Buffalo
Buffalo, New York 14260
{cmiao, wenjunji, lusu, yaliangl, suxinguo, zhanqin, houpingx, jing, kuiren}@buffalo.edu

ABSTRACT

The recent proliferation of human-carried mobile devices has given rise to the crowd sensing systems. However, the sensory data provided by individual participants are usually not reliable. To identify truthful values from the crowd sensing data, the topic of truth discovery, whose goal is to estimate user quality and infer truths through quality-aware data aggregation, has drawn significant attention. Though able to improve aggregation accuracy, existing truth discovery approaches fail to take into consideration an important issue in their design, i.e., the protection of individual users' private information. In this paper, we propose a novel cloud-enabled privacy-preserving truth discovery (PPTD) framework for crowd sensing systems, which can achieve the protection of not only users' sensory data but also their reliability scores derived by the truth discovery approaches. The key idea of the proposed framework is to perform weighted aggregation on users' encrypted data using homomorphic cryptosystem. In order to deal with large-scale data, we also propose to parallelize PPTD with MapReduce framework. Through extensive experiments on not only synthetic data but also real world crowd sensing systems, we justify the guarantee of strong privacy and high accuracy of our proposed framework.

Categories and Subject Descriptors

H.4 [**Information Systems Applications**]: Miscellaneous; K.4.1 [**Computers and Society**]: Public Policy Issues—*Privacy*

General Terms

Design, Human Factors, Security

Keywords

Crowd Sensing; Truth Discovery; Privacy; Cloud

SenSys'15, November 1–4, 2015, Seoul, South Korea.

DOI: http://dx.doi.org/10.1145/2809695.2809719.

1. INTRODUCTION

The recent proliferation of increasingly capable and affordable mobile devices (e.g., smartphones, smartwatches, smartglasses, etc.) packed with a plethora of on-board sensors (e.g., GPS, accelerometer, compass, camera, etc.) has given rise to crowd sensing, a newly-emerged sensing paradigm where the collection of sensory data are outsourced to a crowd of users participating in the sensing task. Recently, a large variety of crowd sensing systems [3–6, 12, 18–21, 28, 39–41, 45] have been developed, serving a wide spectrum of applications that have significant impact on our daily lives, including urban sensing, smart transportation, environment monitoring, localization, health-care, public opinion analysis, and many others.

However, in crowd sensing applications, the sensory data provided by individual participants are usually not reliable, due to various reasons such as poor sensor quality, lack of sensor calibration, background noise, incomplete views of observations, and even the intent to deceive. Therefore, the power of crowd sensing can be unleashed only by properly aggregating unreliable information from different participating users who inevitably submit noisy, conflicting and heterogeneous data. When aggregating crowd sensing data, it is essential to capture the difference in the quality of information among different participating users. Some users constantly provide truthful and meaningful data while others may generate biased or even fake data. In this case, traditional aggregation methods (e.g., averaging and voting) that regard all the users equally would not be able to derive accurate aggregated results.

Therefore, an ideal approach should be able to involve the probability of a user providing accurate data in the form of user weight when aggregating sensory data, and make the aggregated results close to the information provided by reliable users. The challenge here, however, is that the user reliability is usually unknown *a priori* and should be inferred from collected data. To address this challenge, the problem of *truth discovery* [29–32, 34, 35, 44, 47–50], i.e., to discover truthful facts from unreliable user information, have recently been widely studied. The common principle shared in truth discovery approaches is that a particular user will have higher weight if the data provided by him is closer to the aggregated results, and a particular user's data will be counted more in the aggregation procedure if this user has a higher weight. A variety of truth discovery approaches have been proposed to calculate user weight and aggregated results in a joint manner based on this principle.

The truth discovery approaches, though having brought significant improvement to the aggregation accuracy, fail to take into consideration an important practical issue in the design of crowd sensing systems, i.e., *the protection of user privacy*. In many crowd sensing applications, the final aggregation results can be public and beneficial to the community or society, but the data from each individual user may contain private personal information and thus should be well protected. For example, aggregating health data, such as treatment outcomes, can lead to better evaluation of new drugs or medical devices' effects, but may jeopardize the privacy of participating patients. The geotagging campaigns can provide accurate and timely localization of specific objects (e.g., litter, pothole, automated external defibrillator, etc.) by aggregating the reports of participants, however, at the risk of leaking participants' sensitive location information. Through crowd wisdom, even extremely difficult questions can be solved via aggregating the answers of a large crowd. However, personal information of individual users can be inferred from their answers.

Sometimes, user reliability is another sensitive information that should also be protected. On one hand, from user reliability information, together with his observation values, the attacker may be able to infer the personal information of the user, such as major, education level, age, gender, language, and even personality. On the other hand, in practical crowd sensing applications, the participating users usually trade their data with the system administrator for rewards, and the leakage of user reliability may lead to malicious manipulation of data price. For these reasons, in some crowd sensing applications (such as the aforementioned health data aggregation, geotagging, and crowd wisdom), user reliability should be kept private.

Therefore, it is essential to design a privacy-preserving truth discovery scheme for the crowd sensing applications where there exists variability in user reliability degrees and the privacy of users' data and reliability information is susceptible to leakage. Towards this end, we propose a *cloud-enabled privacy-preserving truth discovery* (PPTD) framework. This framework makes use of homomorphic cryptosystem [8], and can guarantee both high accuracy and strong privacy. The proposed PPTD framework works as follows. Each participating user will first send the encrypted summation of distances between his own observation values and the estimated aggregated values to the cloud server. Then, the cloud server updates users' weights in encrypted form without decrypting the received distances information, and sends the updated weight to each user. Next, each user calculates the ciphertexts of weighted data using the received encrypted weight. Finally, the final results are estimated by the cloud server based on the ciphertexts received from users. The advantage of our proposed framework is that it can accurately calculate the final aggregated results while protecting the privacy of user data, and in the meanwhile, the weight information are not disclosed to any party.

Additionally, in order to deal with massive data, we also design a parallel privacy-preserving truth discovery scheme using the MapReduce framework [10], and thus the privacy-preserving truth discovery procedure can be conducted in a parallel and distributed manner.

In summary, our contributions in this paper are:

- We propose a novel cloud-enabled privacy-preserving truth discovery framework for crowd sensing systems, which can accurately aggregate sensory data while protecting both user observation and user reliability from being disclosed.
- A parallel extension of PPTD is also designed so that the truth discovery procedure can be conducted in parallel when processing large scale crowd sensing data.
- We conduct extensive experiments on both real crowd sensing systems and synthetic data set. The results validate the claim that our proposed framework can generate accurate aggregation results while protecting the privacy of user data and weight.

In the remaining parts of this paper, we first define the problem in Section 2 and give preliminary in Section 3. Then the proposed privacy-preserving truth discovery framework and the parallel mechanism are presented in Section 4. We analyze the privacy of our proposed framework and discuss it in Section 5 and 6 respectively. In Section 7, we conduct a series of experiments to demonstrate the claims given in this paper. We discuss related work in Section 8 and conclude the paper in Section 9.

2. PROBLEM DEFINITION

In this section, we describe the problem settings of our proposed privacy-preserving truth discovery framework. Our framework contains two different types of crowd sensing parties: *cloud server* and *users*. Among them, users are the crowd participants, who perform sensing tasks with their mobile devices either voluntarily or for financial incentives, and cloud server is a platform which collects user data and conduct data aggregation. Additionally, we use *objects* to represent the entities or questions assigned by the cloud server and use *observation values* to denote the sensory readings or answers provided by crowd users. Also, the true result or answer for each task or question is represented as *ground truth* in our problem.

In practical crowd sensing systems, the security threats mainly come from the parties themselves (i.e., cloud server and users). For the sake of curiosity or financial purpose, the cloud server may try to deduce the observation and reliability values of each user. On the other hand, each user may also try to infer the information of other parties. Thus, it is of paramount importance to preserve the privacy of users' observation values. Moreover, in order to prevent any party to maliciously manipulate the data price in the scenarios where crowd users trade their data with the could server, we propose to protect the reliability value of each user from being disclosed to any party (including the user himself). Certainly, our proposed framework can be easily modified to make each user's weight known only to himself, which is discussed in detail in section 6.

We formally define the problem targeted in this paper as follows:

Suppose there are K users, denoted as $\mathcal{K} = \{1, 2, \cdots, K\}$, and a cloud server $\mathcal{S}$ that released M objects represented as $\mathcal{M} = \{1, 2, \cdots, M\}$. Let x_m^k denote the observation value provided by the k-th user for the m-th object and w_k denote the weight of the k-th user. Our goal is to let server $\mathcal{S}$ accurately estimate the ground truths $\{x_m^*\}_{m=1}^M$ for all the objects based on the information collected from users. In this procedure, each observation value (i.e., x_m^k) should not be disclosed to any party except the user who provides this value (i.e., the k-th user). Also, the weight information $\{w_k\}_{k=1}^K$ should not be disclosed to any party in the system.

To solve this problem, we propose a privacy-preserving truth discovery framework based on homomorphic cryptosystem, which enables the cloud server to conduct truth discovery on encrypted sensing data so that the private information could be effectively protected while the ground truths can be accurately estimated.

3. PRELIMINARY

Since truth discovery and homomorphic encryption technology are two important components in our proposed framework, we introduce the concepts and general procedures of them in this section.

3.1 Truth Discovery

Towards the goal of resolving conflicts in multiple noisy data sources, truth discovery has been widely studied in various domains. Although there are differences in the ways to compute user weights and estimate ground truths, the common procedure of existing truth discovery approaches can be summarized as follows. A truth discovery algorithm usually starts with a random guess of ground truths, and then iteratively conducts weight update and truth update until convergence.

Weight Update: In this step, we assume the estimated ground truth of each object is fixed. The basic idea is that a user's weight should be assigned a high value if this user provides data which is close to the estimated ground truths. Typically, the user weights are calculated as follows:

$$w_k = f(\sum_{m=1}^{M} d(x_m^k, x_m^*)) \tag{1}$$

where f is a monotonically decreasing function, and $d(\cdot)$ is the distance function which can measure the difference between users' observation values and the estimated ground truths. In this paper, we adopt the weight calculation function of CRH [30] as f due to its good practical performance:

$$w_k = \log\left(\frac{\sum_{k'=1}^{K}\sum_{m=1}^{M} d(x_m^{k'}, x_m^*)}{\sum_{m=1}^{M} d(x_m^k, x_m^*)}\right) \tag{2}$$

The distance function $d(\cdot)$ will be chosen based on the application scenarios. The proposed framework can handle various applications by plugging different functions. In this paper, we discuss two example functions for applications involving continuous or categorical data, the two most common data types in crowd sensing applications.

For the applications (e.g., environment monitoring) where the sensory data are continuous (e.g., temperature and humidity), we adopt the following normalized squared distance function:

$$d(x_m^k, x_m^*) = \frac{(x_m^k - x_m^*)^2}{std_m} \tag{3}$$

where std_m is the standard deviation of all observation values for object m. For the applications (e.g., crowd wisdom) where the data are categorical (e.g., multiple-choice answer), there are usually multiple candidate choices, and only one of them is correct. In this case, we define an observation vector $x_m^k = (0, ..., \underset{q}{1}, ..., 0)^T$ to denote that user k selects the q-th choice for object m. We then use the squared distance function to measure the difference between observation vector x_m^k and the truth vector x_m^*:

$$d(x_m^k, x_m^*) = (x_m^k - x_m^*)^T(x_m^k - x_m^*) \tag{4}$$

Truth Update: In this step, we assume the weight of each user is fixed. Then we can estimate the ground truth for the m-th object as

$$x_m^* \leftarrow \frac{\sum_{k=1}^{K} w_k \cdot x_m^k}{\sum_{k=1}^{K} w_k} \tag{5}$$

For continuous data, x_m^* represents the estimated ground truth value. But for categorical data, x_m^* is actually a probability vector in which each element represents the probability of a particular choice being the truth. The final estimation should be the choice with the largest probability in vector x_m^*.

The general truth discovery procedure can be described by Algorithm 1. The algorithm starts with randomly guessing ground truth for each object, then iteratively updates users' weights and estimated ground truths until some convergence criterion is satisfied. Usually, the convergence criterion is set depending on the requirements of specific applications. For example, it can be a threshold of the change in the estimated ground truths in two consecutive iterations.

Algorithm 1: Truth Discovery Algorithm

```
Input: Observation values from K users: {x_m^k}_{m,k=1}^{M,K}
Output: Estimated ground truths for M objects:
        {x_m^*}_{m=1}^M
Randomly initialize the ground truth for each object;
repeat
    for each user k do
        Update weight based on estimated ground truths
        (e.g., Eqn. (2));
    end
    for each object m do
        Update the estimated ground truth based on
        current weights (e.g., Eqn. (5));
    end
until Convergence criterion is satisfied;
return The estimated ground truths {x_m^*}_{m=1}^M;
```

3.2 Cryptographic Tools

3.2.1 Homomorphic Cryptographic Scheme

In our proposed privacy-preserving truth discovery framework, an additive homomorphic asymmetric cryptosystem is adopted. As widely known, there are two types of keys in the asymmetric cryptosystem: public key pk and private key sk. The public key is used to encrypt plaintext and the private key is used to decrypt the ciphertext. Considering a plaintext $m \in \mathbb{Z}_n$, where n is a large positive integer and $\mathbb{Z}_n$ is the set of integers modulo n, we denote the encryption of m as $E_{pk}(m)$. If a cryptographic scheme is said to be additive homomorphic, there should be two operators $\oplus$ and $\otimes$ which satisfy the following properties:

$$E_{pk}(m_1 + m_2) = E_{pk}(m_1) \oplus E_{pk}(m_2) \tag{6}$$

$$E_{pk}(a \cdot m_1) = a \otimes E_{pk}(m_1) \tag{7}$$

where m_1, m_2 are the plaintexts that need to be encrypted and a is a constant.

Based on the above properties, we can directly calculate the encrypted sum of plaintexts from the encryptions of them by conducting operators $\oplus$ or $\otimes$.

3.2.2 *Threshold Paillier Cryptosystem*

Although there are several additive homomorphic cryptographic schemes, we use the threshold variant of Paillier scheme [9] in our framework, because it not only has additive homomorphic properties but also satisfies the design of a threshold cryptosystem, both of which allow us to conduct secure summation on the data collected from crowd users.

In this cryptosystem, an user can encrypt the plaintext $m \in \mathbb{Z}_n$ with the public key $pk = (g, n)$ as

$$c = E_{pk}(m) = g^m r^n mod\ n^2 \tag{8}$$

where $r \in \mathbb{Z}_n^*$ ($\mathbb{Z}_n^*$ denotes the multiplicative group of invertible elements of $\mathbb{Z}_n$) is selected randomly and privately by this user. According to Equation (6), (7) and (8), the homomorphic properties of this cryptosystem can be described as

$$\begin{aligned} E_{pk}(m_1 + m_2) &= E_{pk}(m_1) \cdot E_{pk}(m_2) \\ &= g^{m_1+m_2}(r_1 r_2)^n mod\ n^2 \end{aligned} \tag{9}$$

$$E_{pk}(a \cdot m_1) = E_{pk}(m_1)^a = g^{am_1} {r_1}^{an} mod\ n^2 \tag{10}$$

where m_1, m_2 are the plaintexts which need to be encrypted, and $r_1, r_2 \in \mathbb{Z}_n^*$ are the private randoms and a is a constant.

In this paper, the (p, t)-threshold Paillier cryptosystem is adopted, in which the private key sk is divided (denoted as sk_1, sk_2, $\cdots$, sk_p) and distributed to p parties. Any single party doesn't have the complete private key. If one party wants to accurately decrypt ciphertext c, it has to cooperate with at least $t - 1$ other parties. So in the decryption step, each party $i (1 \le i \le p)$ needs to calculate the partial decryption c_i of c with private key sk_i as

$$c_i = c^{2\Delta sk_i} \tag{11}$$

where $\Delta = p!$. Then based on the combining algorithm in [9], at least t partial decryptions can be combined together to get the plaintext m.

4. PRIVACY-PRESERVING TRUTH DISCOVERY

In this section, we discuss the details of our novel privacy-preserving truth discovery (PPTD) framework.

4.1 PPTD Overview

Figure 1 shows the framework of PPTD in crowd sensing systems. Before the truth discovery procedure, we assume a semantically secure (p, t)-threshold Paillier cryptosystem has been given (e.g., established by a trusted key management center). Here p is the number of parties including both the cloud server and users, and t is the minimum number of parties needed to complete the decryption. Thus, each party in this framework has known the public encryption key $pk = (g, n)$, while the matching private decryption key has been divided and distributed to all parties (i.e., party i has got his private key share sk_i).

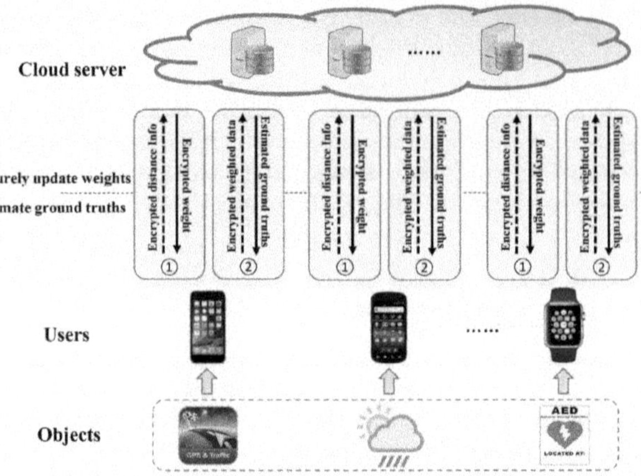

Figure 1: Privacy-preserving truth discovery framework

As shown in Fig. 1, after the objects are assigned by the cloud server, the PPTD parties will iteratively conduct the following two phases:

Phase 1: Secure Weight Update. In this phase, each user firstly calculates the distances between his observation values and the estimated ground truths provided by the cloud server according to the distance functions, then encrypts the distance information and submits the ciphertexts to the cloud server. After receiving the ciphertexts from all users, the cloud server securely updates the weight in encrypted form for each user. Then the ciphertext of updated weight is sent to each corresponding user.

Phase 2: Secure Truth Estimation. Based on the encrypted weight received from the cloud server, each user calculates the ciphertexts of weighted observation values without decrypting the weight, and then submits them to the cloud server. When the cloud server receives all the ciphertexts of weighted observation values from crowd users, it is able to estimate the ground truth for each object.

The above two phases start with a random initialization of the ground truth for each object, and are then iteratively conducted until convergence. Throughout the PPTD procedure, all the operations are conducted on encrypted data. Thus, it is ensured that the observation values of each user are known only to himself and the user weights are not disclosed to any party in the crowd sensing system.

4.2 PPTD Mechanism

In this part, we will elaborate on the mechanism of the proposed PPTD framework. Before we get into the details of the aforementioned *Secure Weight Update* and *Secure Truth Estimation* phases, we will first introduce a *Secure Sum Protocol* designed to calculate the summation of the data collected from users without disclosing them to any unintended party of the system.

4.2.1 *Secure Sum Protocol*

According to Eqn. (2) and Eqn. (5), the cloud server needs to calculate the summation of the data collected from users in order to update user weights and estimate ground truths. However, the plaintext of each user's data should not be accessible to the cloud server due to privacy concerns. To address this problem, we design a secure sum protocol based on the threshold Paillier cryptosystem [8]. As shown in Protocol 1, the proposed secure sum protocol can calculate the summation of users' data without disclosing any of them.

Protocol 1: Secure Sum Protocol

Input: The value $v_k \in \mathbb{Z}_n$ from each user $k \in \mathcal{K}$
Output: The summation $\sum_{k=1}^{K} v_k$

1. According to Eqn. (8), each user $k \in \mathcal{K}$ encrypts value v_k and sends the ciphertext $E_{pk}(v_k)$ to the cloud server $\mathcal{S}$;
2. Server $\mathcal{S}$ calculates $\mathcal{C} = E_{pk}(\sum_{k=1}^{K} v_k) = \prod_{k=1}^{K} E_{pk}(v_k)$ based on Eqn. (9);
3. Server $\mathcal{S}$ randomly selects $t-1$ users and sends $\mathcal{C}$ to them;
4. Each selected user k' calculates the partial decryption $\mathcal{C}_{k'}$ of $\mathcal{C}$ based on Eqn. (11) and sends $\mathcal{C}_{k'}$ to the cloud server;
5. Server $\mathcal{S}$ calculates its partial decryption $\mathcal{C}_{\mathcal{S}}$ and then combines it with $t-1$ other partial decryptions received from users to get the summation $\sum_{k=1}^{K} v_k$;

As we can see, in this protocol what the cloud server received from users are the encrypted values and partial decryptions. Moreover, all the calculations on the cloud server are conducted on encrypted data. What the cloud server can know at last is the summation of all the users' data, based on which each user's data can not be inferred. So the privacy of users is preserved.

4.2.2 Secure Weight Update

The first phase in our proposed framework is the secure weight update for each user. As aforementioned, the weight information needs to be updated in encrypted form in order not to be disclosed to any party. A challenge here is that, the cryptosystem we use is defined over an integer ring, but the values needed to be encrypted in our framework may not be integers. To tackle this challenge, we introduce a parameter L (a magnitude of 10) to round the fractional values. For example, the value h can be rounded by multiplying L as $\widetilde{h} = \lfloor hL \rfloor$. Here we use $\widetilde{h}$ to denote the rounded integer of h and other values in this paper will be represented in a similar way. The approximate value of h can be recovered by dividing L (i.e., $\widetilde{h}/L$).

Based on Eqn.(2), the encrypted weight can be updated as follows

$$E_{pk}(\widetilde{w}_k) = E_{pk}(\lfloor L \cdot (log(\sum_{k'=1}^{K} Dist_{k'}) - log(Dist_k)) \rfloor) \quad (12)$$

where $Dist_k = \sum_{m=1}^{M} d(x_m^k, x_m^*)$ is the summation of distances between the k-th user's observation values $\{x_m^k\}_{m=1}^M$ and the estimated ground truths $\{x_m^*\}_{m=1}^M$. As we can see, in order for the cloud server to update $E_{pk}(\widetilde{w}_k)$, it needs to collect the information about $Dist_k$ from users. This procedure can be shown in Fig. 2. For the sake of simplicity, we take the k-th user as an example in this figure.

Since the distance functions for continuous data and categorical data are different, we need to consider them separately when calculating distances. For categorical data, user k can easily calculate distances based on Eqn. (4). But for continuous data, we need to know the standard deviation std_m according to Eqn. (3), which is difficult to derive without knowing the observation values of other users. Next, we first introduce the common steps (**W1** and **W6** in Fig. 2) for all the data types to update user's weight, and then specifically discuss the calculation of std_m for continuous data (**W2**, **W3**, **W4** and **W5** in Fig. 2).

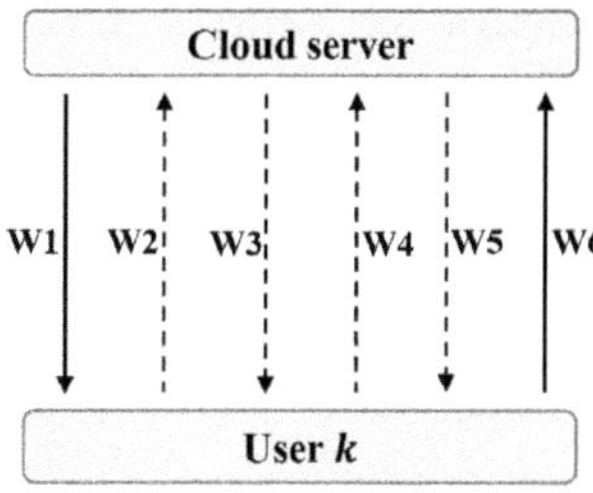

Figure 2: Secure weight update for user k

Step W1. Cloud server sends the estimated ground truths $\{x_m^*\}_{m=1}^M$ to user k. If it is the first iteration, the estimated ground truths will be randomly initialized. If it is not, the estimated ground truths are obtained from the previous iteration. When user k receives the estimated ground truths, he will first calculate two values: $Dist_k$ and $\log Dist_k$. Before the two values are submitted, user k needs to encrypt them for the purpose of privacy. For $Dist_k$, user k privately selects a random $r_{k1} \in \mathbb{Z}_n^*$, and then encrypts it as follows based on Eqn. (8).

$$E_{pk}(\widetilde{Dist_k}) = g^{\widetilde{Dist_k}} r_{k1}^n \ mod\ n^2 \quad (13)$$

Similarly for $\log Dist_k$, user k privately selects another random $r_{k2} \in \mathbb{Z}_n^*$, and encrypts it as

$$E_{pk}(\widetilde{\log Dist_k}) = g^{\widetilde{\log Dist_k}} r_{k2}^n \ mod\ n^2 \quad (14)$$

Step W6. After the encryption in above step, user k submits both $E_{pk}(\widetilde{Dist_k})$ and $E_{pk}(\widetilde{\log Dist_k})$ to the cloud server $\mathcal{S}$. Upon receiving the ciphertexts from all users, $\mathcal{S}$ calculates $sum_D = \sum_{k=1}^{K} \widetilde{Dist_k}/L$ and $\log sum_D$ based on the secure sum protocol. Then $\mathcal{S}$ encrypts $\log sum_D$ according to Eqn. (8) as

$$E_{pk}(\widetilde{\log sum_D}) = g^{\widetilde{\log sum_D}} r_{s1}^n \ mod\ n^2 \quad (15)$$

where $r_{s1} \in \mathbb{Z}_n^*$ is the private random selected by server $\mathcal{S}$. With above ciphertexts, $\mathcal{S}$ can update the encrypted weight for user k as follows based on Eqn. (9), Eqn. (10) and Eqn. (12).

$$\begin{aligned} E_{pk}(\widetilde{w}_k) &= E_{pk}(\widetilde{\log sum_D}) \cdot E_{pk}(-\widetilde{\log Dist_k}) \\ &= E_{pk}(\widetilde{\log sum_D}) \cdot E_{pk}(\widetilde{\log Dist_k})^{-1} \end{aligned} \quad (16)$$

As for continuous data, as discussed previously, the standard deviation std_m should be firstly calculated. The calculation steps are described in detail as below (these steps only need to be performed once throughout the whole truth discovery procedure).

Step W2. According to Eqn. (8), user k encrypts his observation value for object m as $E_{pk}(\widetilde{x}_m^k)$ and sends the ciphertext to the cloud server $\mathcal{S}$.

Step W3. After receiving the ciphertexts from all users, server $\mathcal{S}$ calculates $sum_x = \sum_{k=1}^{K} \widetilde{x}_m^k / L$ and $\bar{x}_m = sum_k/K$ based on the secure sum protocol, and then sends $\bar{x}_m$ to users.

Step W4. User k calculates $d_m^k = (x_m^k - \bar{x}_m)^2$ and encrypts d_m^k as $E_{pk}(\widetilde{d_m^k})$. Then k sends $E_{pk}(\widetilde{d_m^k})$ to server $\mathcal{S}$.

Step W5. When server $\mathcal{S}$ receives $E_{pk}(\widetilde{d_m^k})$ from all users, $\mathcal{S}$ calculates $sum_d = \sum_{k=1}^{K} \widetilde{d_m^k}/L$ and std_m (equals to $\sqrt{sum_d/K}$) through the secure sum protocol. Then $\mathcal{S}$ sends std_m to users.

4.2.3 *Secure Truth Estimation*

After updating user weights, the next thing is to estimate the ground truth for each object. As shown in Fig. 3, there are two major steps in this phase, which are detailed as follows.

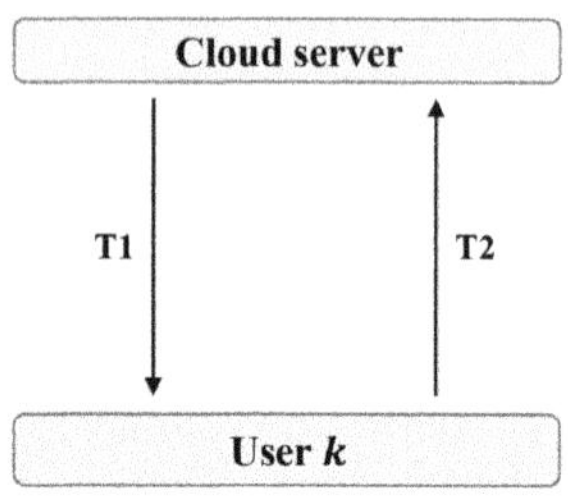

Figure 3: Secure Truth Estimation

Step T1. The cloud server sends the encrypted weight $E_{pk}(\widetilde{w}_k)$ (updated in the secure weight update phase) to user k. Then user k calculates the ciphertexts of weighted observation values based on the encrypted weight. For continuous data, user k calculates the ciphertexts according to Eqn. (10) using the following formula:

$$E_{pk}(\widetilde{w}_k \cdot \widetilde{x}_m^k) = E_{pk}(\widetilde{w}_k)^{\widetilde{x}_m^k} \quad (17)$$

For categorical data, x_m^k is a vector as described in Section 3.1, so user k needs to calculate the ciphertext for each element in this vector as follows:

$$E_{pk}(\widetilde{w}_k \cdot x_m^k(i)) = \begin{cases} E_{pk}(0) & if\ x_m^k(i) = 0 \\ E_{pk}(\widetilde{w}_k) \cdot E_{pk}(0) & if\ x_m^k(i) = 1 \end{cases} \quad (18)$$

where $x_m^k(i)$ denotes the i-th element in vector x_m^k. Please note that $E_{pk}(0)$ can be dynamically changing because every time the encryption procedure is conducted with a different random $r_k \in \mathbb{Z}_n^*$.

Step T2. After the calculation in the above step, user k submits the ciphertexts of weighted data for all the objects to the cloud server $\mathcal{S}$. When receiving ciphertexts from all the users, $\mathcal{S}$ will first calculate the numerator of Eqn. (5) as follows.

For *continuous data*, server $\mathcal{S}$ calculates the summation of weighted data (i.e., $\sum_{k=1}^{K}(\widetilde{w}_k \cdot \widetilde{x}_m^k)$) with the help of the secure sum protocol, and then derives the approximation of $\sum_{k=1}^{K}(w_k \cdot x_m^k)$ (i.e., the numerator) via dividing the summation by L^2.

For *categorical data*, we need to consider each element in the vector separately. Specifically, for the i-th element, server $\mathcal{S}$ calculates the summation of the weighted data (i.e., $\sum_{k=1}^{K}(\widetilde{w}_k \cdot x_m^k(i))$ via the secure sum protocol, and then get the approximation of $\sum_{k=1}^{K}(w_k \cdot x_m^k(i))$ (i.e., the numerator). The summations of other elements are calculated in the same way.

As the denominator of Eqn. (5), the summation of weights is also needed to estimate the ground truths. This can be easily calculated through the secure sum protocol, because $\mathcal{S}$ has already stored encrypted weights in the weight update phase. Then the ground truth for each object $m \in \mathcal{M}$ can be estimated by the cloud server based on Eqn. (5).

Please note that the ground truths estimated in this step for categorical data are probability values, which are used for updating user weights in the next iteration. The final estimation for object m should be the choice with the largest probability in vector x_m^* obtained in the final iteration.

Combining the secure weight update and secure truth estimation phases, we summarize the proposed privacy-preserving truth discovery procedure in Protocol 2. This protocol repeats the aforementioned two phases iteratively until some convergence criterion is satisfied. Then the cloud server can output the final estimated ground truth for each object.

Protocol 2: Privacy-Preserving Truth Discovery Protocol

Input: K users, M objects, observation values $\{x_m^k\}_{m,k=1}^{M,K}$ and rounding parameter L

Output: Estimated ground truths $\{x_m^*\}_{m=1}^{M}$

1 The cloud server $\mathcal{S}$ randomly initializes the ground truth for each object;

2 The cloud server $\mathcal{S}$ sends the estimated ground truths (i.e., $\{x_m^*\}_{m=1}^{M}$) and the rounding parameter L to users;

3 Each user $k \in \mathcal{K}$ calculates $Dist_k = \sum_{m=1}^{M} d(x_m^k, x_m^*)$ and gets the rounded values (i.e., $\widetilde{Dist_k}$ and $\log \widetilde{Dist_k}$) with parameter L. Then user k encrypts them as $E_{pk}(\widetilde{Dist_k})$, $E_{pk}(\log \widetilde{Dist_k})$ and sends the ciphertexts to the cloud server;

4 After receiving ciphertexts from all the users, the server $\mathcal{S}$ calculates $sum_D = \sum_{k=1}^{K} \widetilde{Dist_k}/L$ based on the secure sum protocol, then updates the encrypted weight of each user according to Eqn. (15) and Eqn. (16). Also, the updated ciphertext of weight is sent to each corresponding user;

5 When user $k \in \mathcal{K}$ receives encrypted weight from the cloud server, the user calculates ciphertexts of weighted data for continuous data and categorical data respectively according to Eqn. (17) and Eqn. (18). Then these ciphertexts are sent to the cloud server;

6 After receiving ciphertexts from all the users, the cloud server $\mathcal{S}$ estimates the ground truths $\{x_m^*\}_{m=1}^{M}$ based on step **T2**;

7 Repeat step 2~6 until the convergence criterion is satisfied and then output $\{x_m^*\}_{m=1}^{M}$;

4.3 Parallel PPTD

With the proliferation of human-carried sensing devices, an explosive increase of crowd sensing data is expected in the near future. In order to deal with such kind of massive data, we extend our proposed scheme in a parallel way using the MapReduce framework, which contains two major functions: the Map function that processes input values to generate a set of intermediate key/value pairs, and the Reduce function that merges all intermediate values associated with the same intermediate key. Here we just borrow the existing MapReduce framework, in which we do not make research contribution.

We only adapt the truth estimation phase to MapReduce framework, and there is no change in the weight update procedure. In the Map function for estimating ground truths, the input is a list of records: $(m, E_{pk}(\widetilde{w}_k \cdot \widetilde{x}_m^k), k)$, where $m \in \mathcal{M}$, $k \in \mathcal{K}$ and $E_{pk}(\widetilde{w}_k \cdot \widetilde{x}_m^k)$ is the encrypted weighted data. As shown in Algorithm 2, during the mapping process, all the input records are re-organized into key/value pairs, where the key is the ID of each object (i.e., m), and the value is the rest information. Before these key/value pairs are fed to Reducers, they will be sorted by Hadoop so that the pairs that have the same key (i.e., the same object ID m) will go to the same Reducer. In the Reducers, as seen in Algorithm 3, the truth value for each object is estimated based on step **T2** described in Section 4.2.3. Since users' weight information is also needed, we use an external file to store the encrypted weights, and all the Reducer nodes can read it. Finally, for each object a key/value pair is outputted, where the key is object ID m and the value is the estimated ground truth. The two procedures (i.e., distributed weight update and parallel truth estimation) are iteratively conducted until the whole procedure converges.

Algorithm 2: Map function for estimating truths

Input: A list of records:
$(m, E_{pk}(\widetilde{w}_k \cdot \widetilde{x}_m^k), k), m \in \mathcal{M}, k \in \mathcal{K}$
Output: A list with each element in format of
$[m, [E_{pk}(\widetilde{w}_k \cdot \widetilde{x}_m^k), k]], m \in \mathcal{M}, k \in \mathcal{K}$

output_list ← [ ];
for *each record from input* **do**
    Parse the record;
    Append *output_list* with the new record $[m, [E_{pk}(\widetilde{w}_k \cdot \widetilde{x}_m^k), k]]$;
end
return *output_list;*

Algorithm 3: Reduce function for estimating truths

Input: A list of records (sorted by object ID m):
$[m, [E_{pk}(\widetilde{w}_k \cdot \widetilde{x}_m^k), k]], m \in \mathcal{M}, k \in \mathcal{K}$
Output: A list with each element in the format of $[m, x_m^*]$

output_list ← [ ];
Read encrypted weights of crowd users from file;
Calculate the summation of weights based on the secure sum protocol;
for *all the records with the same objectID m* **do**
    Calculate the summation of weighted data through the secure sum protocol;
    Estimate ground truth x_m^* based on step **T2**;
    Append *output_list* with the new record $[m, x_m^*]$;
end
return *output_list;*

5. PRIVACY ANALYSIS

In this paper, our proposed framework is based on two assumptions: all the parties are semi-honest [33] and there is no collusion among them. The semi-honest model assumes that all the parties are honest but curious, which means they strictly follow the protocol we design, but each party will try to infer the private information of other parties based on the intermediate results he obtains during the execution of the protocol. The non-collusion model assumes the parties in our framework have no collusions, which means they will not collude with each other outside the protocol. These assumptions are reasonable in most crowd sensing scenarios, since 1) the parties want to get correct results and thus would follow the protocol for their mutual benefits, and 2) crowd users usually do not know each other, and even they know each other they are probably not willing to disclose private information to others.

As previously discussed, the security threats mainly comes from the parties themselves in practical crowd sensing systems. Thus, the goal of PPTD is to protect the observation values of each user from being disclosed to other parties, and in the meanwhile, the weight of each user should not be known by any party. Since our framework is built upon the proposed secure sum protocol, we start with the privacy analysis of this protocol.

In the secure sum protocol, the data are exchanged only between cloud server and users, and all the exchanged data are ciphertexts. Although some users obtain the ciphertext of summation $E_{pk}(\sum_{k=1}^{K} v_k)$, they cannot decrypt it because of the (p,t)-threshold Paillier cryptosystem we used and there is no collusion among users. Thus, the users will learn nothing after the execution of the protocol. Similarly, the ciphertext $E_{pk}(v_k)$ cannot be decrypted by the cloud server, and what the server can know at last is just the summation $\sum_{k=1}^{K} v_k$, based on which it cannot infer the input value v_k of each user. In this way, the privacy of each user's input value is guaranteed by this protocol.

Then we can summarize the privacy-preserving goal of our framework as Theorem 1, followed by the proof.

THEOREM 1. *Suppose $K \geq 3$ and for each object $m \in \mathcal{M}$, there are at least two users $k_1, k_2 \in \mathcal{K}$ giving different observation values (i.e., $x_m^{k_1} \neq x_m^{k_2}$). Also assume the parties are semi-honest and there is no collusion among them. Then after the execution of PPTD protocol, the observation values of each user will not be disclosed to others and the weight of each user will not be known by any party.*

PROOF. Firstly, we prove the observation values of each user will not be disclosed to others in our framework. We can achieve the goal by proving that there is not an attack algorithm, based on which one party can infer the private observation values of the users.

For the cloud server, we assume there exists an attack algorithm based on which the server can infer the observation values of user $k_1 \in \mathcal{K}$. The input of the algorithm should be the plaintexts the server knows during the privacy-preserving truth discovery procedure. These plaintexts are $\sum_{k=1}^{K} x_m^k$, $\bar{x}_m$, $\sum_{k=1}^{K} d_m^k$, std_m, $\sum_{k=1}^{K} Dist_k$, $\sum_{k=1}^{K} w_k$, $\sum_{k=1}^{K}(w_k \cdot x_m^k)$ and the estimated ground truth x_m^* for each $m \in \mathcal{M}$. Also, the cloud server knows the values K and M. According to our assumption, the server can infer the observation value $x_m^{k_1}$ $(m \in \mathcal{M})$ of user k_1 based on these input values. We also assume another user $k_2 \in \mathcal{K}$ has the observation value $x_m^{k_2}$ $(\neq x_m^{k_1})$ for the object m. Now, we exchange the observation values of k_1 and k_2, which means user k_1 has the observation value $x_m^{k_2}$ and user k_2 has the observation value $x_m^{k_1}$ for the object m after the exchange. Then, we restart the privacy-preserving truth discovery procedure. However, the plaintexts known by the server will not be changed based on our framework. That is to say, the input values of the attack algorithm will not be changed. So based on this algorithm, the cloud server would still infer the value $x_m^{k_1}$ for user k_1. However, now the observation value of user k_1 has been changed to $x_m^{k_2}$. Obviously, there is a contradiction. Therefore, such an attack algorithm does not exist and the cloud server cannot infer the observation values of users in our framework.

For each user, he can know the public values $\bar{x}_m$, std_m, x^*_m for each $m \in \mathcal{M}$ besides his private observation values based on our framework. Using the same method above, we can also prove that this user cannot infer the observation values of others.

Next, we prove the weight of each user (i.e., w_k, $k \in \mathcal{K}$) will not be disclosed to any party in our framework.

Based on the privacy-preserving truth discovery protocol, the cloud server updates the ciphertexts of the weights (i.e., $E_{pk}(w_k)$, $k \in \mathcal{K}$) instead of the plaintexts of them in each iteration. Also, the users calculate the weighted data based on the ciphertexts of weights. Based on the semi-honest and non-collusion assumptions, all the parties cannot decrypt each encrypted weight. The only plaintexts about the weights are the summations $\sum_{k=1}^{K} w_k$ and $\sum_{k=1}^{K} w_k \cdot x^k_m$, which are known by the cloud server. Since x^k_m is only known by the user, the server cannot infer w_k based on the above summations. So the weight information will not be disclosed to any party in this framework. □

6. DISCUSSIONS

Since the cryptosystem adopted here is defined over an integer ring, we use parameter L to round the fractional values to integers. During the rounding process, numerical errors are inevitably introduced. However, the accuracy of the final estimated ground truth will not be greatly affected if we select appropriate L, which is shown in Section 7.

Another issue we are concerned is missing values, which means not all the objects are observed by all the crowd users. This can be easily handled in our framework. When different users observe different subsets of the objects, we can normalize the aggregate deviations of each user by the number of his observations.

Also, to tackle the issue that some users could not respond timely after the sensing tasks are released, we can set a waiting-time threshold on the cloud server. Based on the (p, t)-threshold Paillier cryptosystem adopted in this paper, as long as at least $t - 1$ users could upload their data in time, the privacy-preserving truth discovery procedure can be completed.

Additionally, our proposed framework can be easily modified to the situation where the user weight is known only to the user himself. In this case, the weight values are updated by users themselves. In particular, during the weight update procedure, user $k \in \mathcal{K}$ just needs to submit the encrypted summation of the distances $E_{pk}(\widetilde{Dist_k})$. Then the cloud server calculates $\sum_{k=1}^{K} \widetilde{Dist_k}/L$ through the secure sum protocol. Based on this summation, each user can privately update his weight according to Eqn. (2). In the truth estimation procedure, user $k \in \mathcal{K}$ submits the ciphertexts of weighted data $\{E_{pk}(\widetilde{w_k \cdot x^k_m})\}_{m=1}^{M}$ and the encrypted weight $E_{pk}(\widetilde{w}_k)$. Then the cloud server can estimate ground truth for each object via the same method used in PPTD (step **T2**).

7. PERFORMANCE EVALUATION

In this section, we evaluate the proposed privacy-preserving truth discovery (PPTD) framework. Experiment results on both real world crowd sensing systems and synthetic data set are presented and discussed.

7.1 Experiment Setup

In this paper, we consider two different types of data: continuous data and categorical data. To evaluate the estimation accuracy of PPTD, we use following measures for the two data types:

- MAE: For continuous data, we use the mean of absolute error (MAE) to measure the mean of absolute distance between the estimated results and ground truths.
- $RMSE$: For continuous data, we also use the root of mean squared error ($RMSE$) to measure the accuracy. Compared with MAE, $RMSE$ can penalize more on the large distance and less on the small distance.
- $ErrorRate$: For categorical data, we calculate the percentage of mismatched values between estimated results and ground truths as $ErrorRate$.

The baseline approach we use in this experiment is the state-of-the-art truth discovery scheme, i.e., CRH [30], which does not take any actions to protect user privacy during the whole procedure.

A $(p, \lfloor \frac{p}{2} \rfloor)$-threshold Paillier cryptosystem is used in our experiment, and here we fix the key size as 512 (can also be set as other values according to the practical demand). Our framework was implemented in Java 1.7.0 using the Paillier Threshold Encryption Toolbox[1]. The sensing devices we use are Nexus 4 Android phones. The "cloud" is emulated by a cluster of three Intel(R) Core(TM) 3.40GHz PCs running Ubuntu 14.04, with 8GB RAM. When implementing parallel privacy-preserving truth discovery framework, we use a Dell Hadoop cluster with Intel Xeon E5-2403 processor (4x 1.80 GHz, 48 GB RAM) as the "cloud".

7.2 Experiment on Crowdsourced Indoor Floorplan Construction System

In this part, we show the experiment results on continuous data collected from a real world crowd sensing system to demonstrate the advantages of PPTD. The application is crowdsourced indoor floorplan construction [1, 2, 15], which has recently drawn much attention since many location-based services can be facilitated by it. The goal of such crowd sensing system is to automatically construct indoor floorplan from sensory data (e.g., the readings of compass, accelerometer, gyroscope, etc.) collected from smartphone users. Clearly, these sensor readings encode the private personal activities of the phone user, and thus the user may not be willing to share such data without the promise of privacy protection. For the sake of illustration, here we focus on just one task of indoor floorplan construction, namely, to estimate the distance between two particular location points in the hallway. We develop an Android App which can estimate the walking distances of a smartphone user through multiplying the user's step size by step count inferred using the in-phone accelerometer.

In our experiment, 10 volunteers are employed as smartphone users and we select 27 hallway segments in a building as the *objects*. Each party (including the cloud server and smartphone users) in this experiment holds the public key and the corresponding private key share which are produced by the cryptosystem. The ground truths of these hallway segments are obtained by measuring them manually.

[1]http://cs.utdallas.edu/dspl/cgi-bin/pailliertoolbox/

Accuracy. We first compare the accuracy of the final estimated ground truths between PPTD and the baseline approach (i.e., CRH). Since the estimation errors of PPTD are introduced by the rounding parameter L, we vary L from 10^0 to 10^6 and measure the corresponding accuracy. In the experiment, we randomly initialize the estimated ground truths, and use a threshold of the change in the estimated ground truths in two consecutive iterations as the convergence criterion. The experiment is repeated for 20 times, and we report the averaged results.

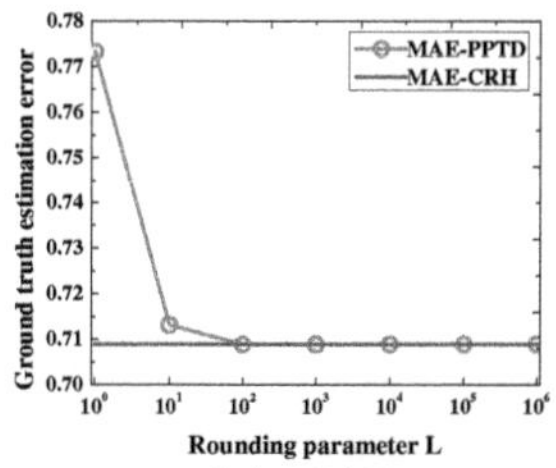

(a) MAE

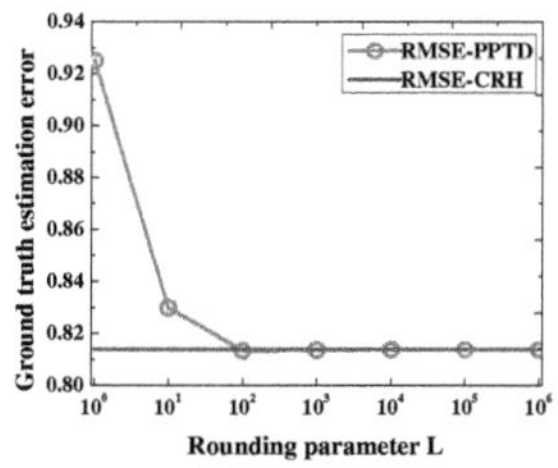

(b) RMSE

Figure 4: Ground truth estimation errors under different values of the parameter L

Figure 4 shows the ground truth estimation errors of our proposed framework and CRH under different values of the parameter L. The estimation error is measured in terms of MAE and $RMSE$, respectively. As seen in the figure, the estimation error of PPTD is almost the same as that of CRH unless the rounding parameter L is too small (i.e., 10^0 or 10^1). This is because during the rounding procedure the fractional part (i.e., decimal digits) of the original value (e.g., $L \cdot \log Dist_k$) is dropped. In this sense, the smaller the parameter L, the more decimal digits of the original value will be lost. To measure the information loss degree, we calculate the relative estimation errors of PPTD and CRH in both object truth and user weight. Here we manually decrypt user weights for the analysis purpose. In particular, we define the relative error of user weight as $||\log \mathbf{w}_c - \log \mathbf{w}_p||/||\log \mathbf{w}_c||$, where $\mathbf{w}_c$ and $\mathbf{w}_p$ are the weight vectors of all the users obtained from CRH and PPTD, respectively. Similarly, we define the relative error of the estimated ground truths as $||\log \mathbf{x}_c^* - \log \mathbf{x}_p^*||/||\log \mathbf{x}_c^*||$, where $\mathbf{x}_c^*$ and $\mathbf{x}_p^*$ are obtained from CRH and PPTD respectively. The results are shown in Fig. 5.

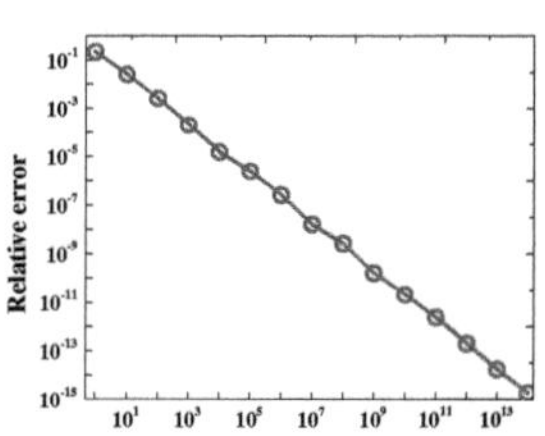

(a) Relative error of weight

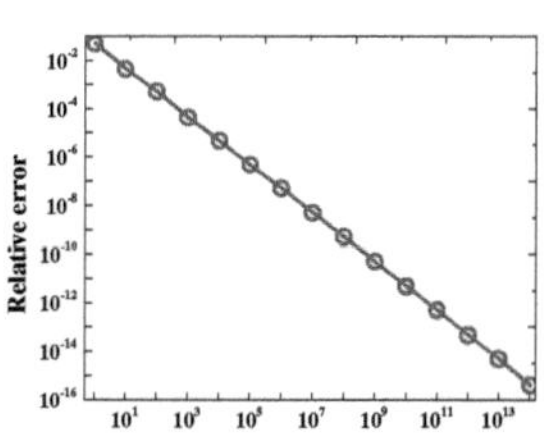

(b) Relative error of estimated truth

Figure 5: Relative errors under different values of L

As shown in Fig. 5(a) and 5(b), the relative errors in both truth and weight drop as the parameter L increases. That is to say, we do not need to worry about the estimation errors produced during the rounding procedure as long as we select a large enough parameter L.

Additionally, we evaluate the performance of PPTD under varying number of users. The number of objects is still 27, while the number of users varies from 3 to 10. We also fix the parameter L as 10^{10} and use the same convergence criterion as before. Then the experiment is repeated 20 times and the averaged results are reported.

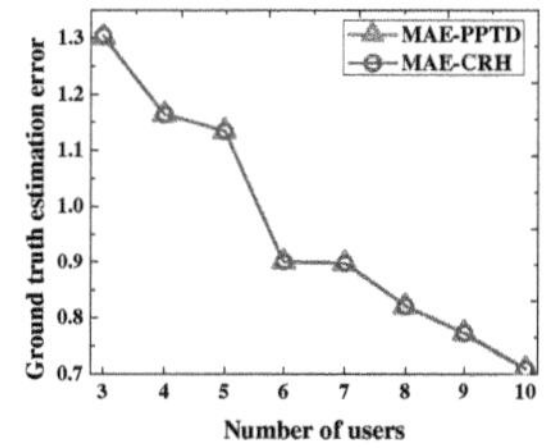

(a) MAE

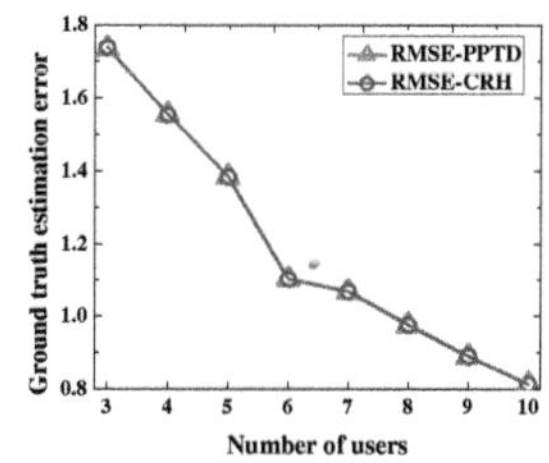

(b) RMSE

Figure 6: Ground truth estimation errors under different number of users

Figure 6(a) and 6(b) show that PPTD almost has the same estimation errors as CRH while the number of users is varying, which means that our proposed framework is robust against the change of user numbers. Also, we can see that, the estimation errors decrease with the increase of the number of users. This makes sense because it is hard to improve upon the users' individual poor observation values when the number of users that observe the same objects is small. When the number of users increases, each object is observed by more and more diversified crowd users, thus it is more and more likely to cancel out individual users' biases and errors so as to reach higher accuracy.

Convergence. Next, we show the convergence of the privacy-preserving truth discovery procedure. In this experiment, the rounding parameter L is still set as 10^{10}. Figure 7 shows the evolution of the *objective value* of the truth discovery problem, which is defined as the weighted summation of the distances between individual observations and the estimated ground truths (i.e., $\sum_{k=1}^{K} w_k \sum_{m=1}^{M} d(x_m^k, x_m^*)$). Here we repeat the experiment for 5 times with different random initialization values. As we can see, all the objective values, although under different initializations, converge quickly within just a few iterations.

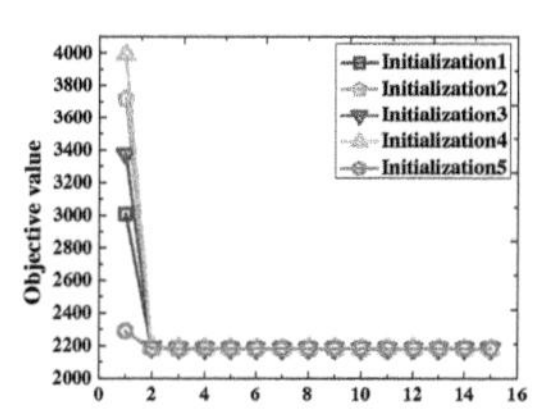

Figure 7: Convergence w.r.t Iterations

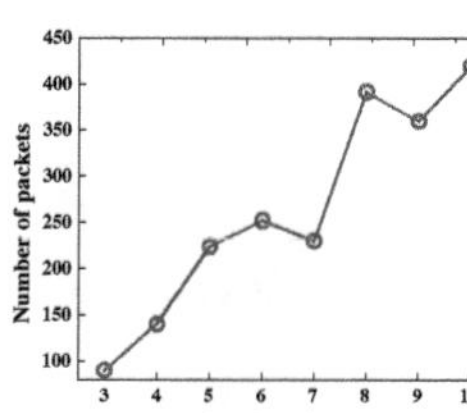

Figure 8: Communication overhead

Computational Cost. In this part, we take a look at PPTD's computational cost, which is composed of the cost on the smartphone of each user and the cost on the cloud server. Here, we also fix the rounding parameter as 10^{10}, which actually has little effect on the computational time compared with user numbers and object numbers.

On the smartphone of each user, there are two major processing procedures: 1) calculating the encrypted summation of distances, and 2) calculating the ciphertexts of weighted observation values. In this experiment, we evaluate the running time of each procedure as well as the total running time under different object numbers ranging from 3 to 27. Figure 9(a) shows the running time per iteration for the two procedures, respectively. We can see that the second procedure (i.e., calculating the ciphertexts of weighted observation values) varies more when the object number increases. Figure 9(b) gives the total time of the two procedures in each iteration. When the object number reaches 27, the total running time is only 0.039s, which is sustainable for the phone users. All the results in Fig. 9 are averaged values derived from 10 smartphones.

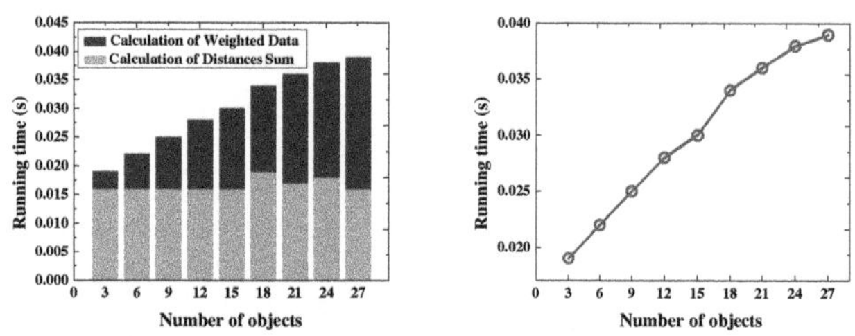

(a) Running time of each procedure (b) Total running time

Figure 9: Running time w.r.t Number of objects for continuous data on smartphone

On the cloud server, there are also two major processing procedures in each iteration: 1) updating weights, and 2) estimating ground truths. Here we evaluate the running time of each procedure, and the total running time under different object numbers as well as user numbers, respectively. From Fig. 10(a) and Fig. 11(a), we can see that most of the time is spent in updating truth for each object. That is also the reason why we need to parallelize the truth updating procedure with MapReduce framework when dealing with massive data. On the other hand, Fig. 10(b) and Fig. 11(b) demonstrate that the total running time is approximately linear with respect to both object number and the user number.

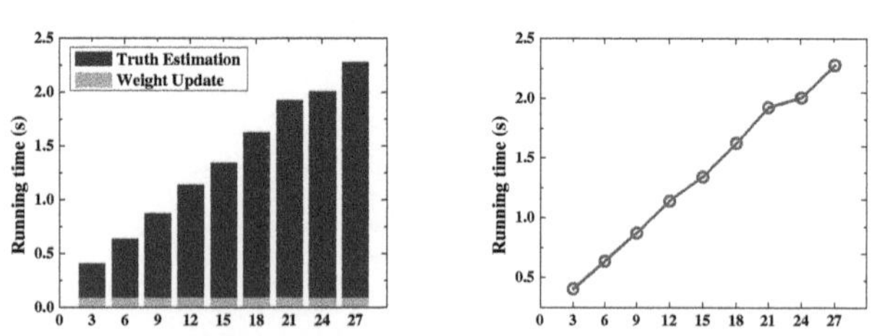

(a) Running time of each procedure (b) Total running time

Figure 10: Running time w.r.t Number of objects for continuous data on the cloud server

Communication and Energy Overhead. To evaluate the communication overhead in the privacy-preserving truth discovery procedure, we measure the number of packets ex-

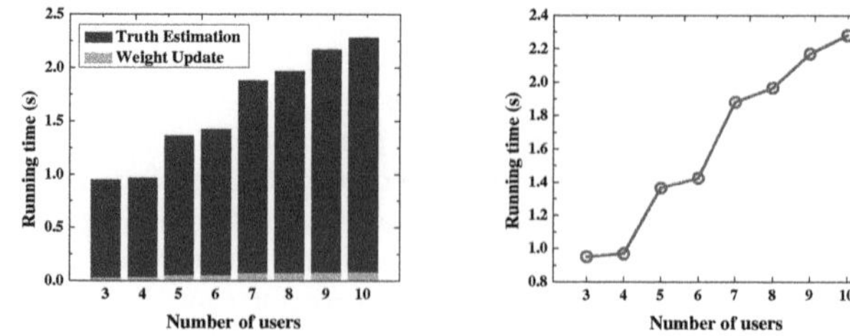

(a) Running time of each procedure (b) Total running time

Figure 11: Running time w.r.t Number of users for continuous data on the cloud server

changed between the cloud server and all the crowd users. In this experiment, we use the change of the aforementioned objective value in two consecutive iterations as the convergence criterion and the threshold is set as 0.001. Figure 8 shows the numbers of exchanged packets over all users during the whole PPTD procedure, under different user numbers (i.e., K) from 3 to 10. As seen, the overall communication overhead is roughly $O(K)$. Actually, for each user, the average number of messages needed to be exchanged with the cloud server can be roughly calculated by $6(i+1)$, where i is the number of iterations during the PPTD procedure. Considering that here we set a very conservative threshold which leads to average 6 iterations (much larger than the usual 2 or 3 iterations as shown in Fig. 7), the communication overhead is well within the realm of practicality.

The energy overhead on the smartphone of each user is mainly caused by the cipher related operations and data transmissions. For the purpose of evaluating the energy overhead, we measure the average energy consumption percentage (i.e., the energy consumed by PPTD divided by the total energy of the smartphone while it is fully charged) under different object numbers. Figure 12 shows the average energy consumption percentage in one iteration for each user. When the object number reaches 27, the energy consumption percentage is only 0.000198% for each smartphone, which is acceptable for the phone users. The results in Fig. 12 are averaged values derived from 10 smartphones in WiFi network environment.

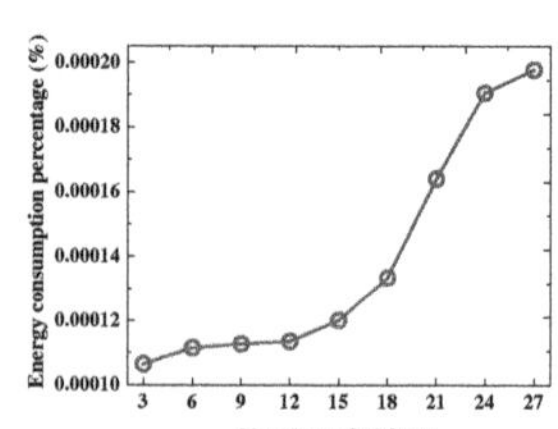

Figure 12: Energy consumption percentage on smartphone

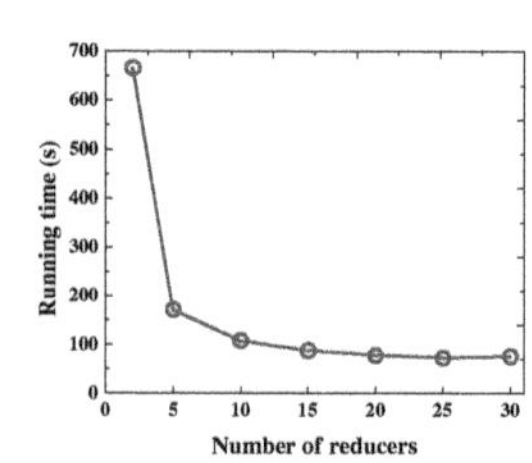

Figure 13: Running time w.r.t Number of reducers

7.3 Experiment on Crowd Wisdom System

In this part, we evaluate the performance of PPTD on categorical data provided by humans as the sensors. The experiment is conducted on a crowd wisdom system which can integrate the crowd answers and opinions towards a set of questions. We design and implement an Android App through which we can send questions and corresponding candidate answers to the crowd users. Each user who receives the questions can upload his answers to the cloud server. The cloud server can then infer the true answer for each question through aggregating the answers from different users. In order to address the concern of some users that their private personal information could be inferred from their answers, we employ PPTD upon this crowd wisdom system, encrypting user answers before they are uploaded to the cloud server. Totally, 113 volunteers are employed as smartphone users and 54 questions are sent to them with candidate answers. We use *Error Rate* as the evaluation metric and for the sake of evaluation, we have got the ground truth answer for each question.

Accuracy and Convergence. Since in this experiment, each object (i.e., question) is not observed (i.e., answered) by all the users, we use the average number of users observing each object (i.e., the ratio between the number of total answers over the number of total questions) as the tuning variable when evaluating the accuracy of PPTD. The error rates of PPTD and CRH are shown in Fig. 14(a), from which we can see that PPTD produces the same error rates as CRH at all time. Moreover, we did not show the error rates with respect to the rounding parameter L, since we find that the final aggregated results are not affected by L. This is because in this case, the negligible numerical errors introduced by L to the intermediate values are simply not large enough to change the final answers, which are categorical numbers. To evaluate the estimation error of user weights, we manually decrypt each user's weight derived by PPTD. Here we still use the relative error defined in section 7.2 to measure the errors introduced by L. The results are reported in Fig. 14(b), which show that the estimation errors can be ignored if parameter L is large enough. Additionally, we also use the threshold of the change in the estimated ground truths in two consecutive iterations as the convergence criterion, and we find both PPTD and CRH converge within two iterations.

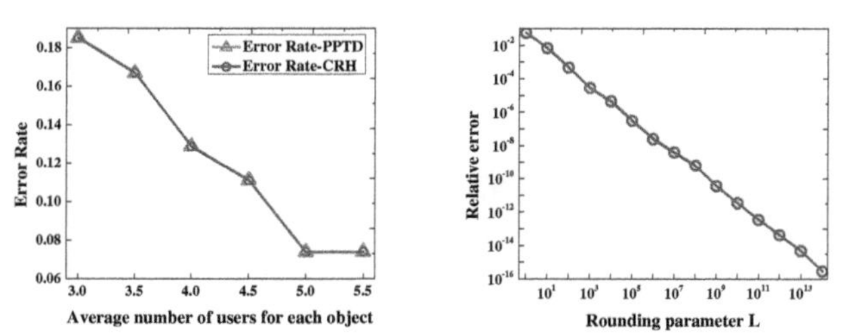

(a) Error rate (b) Relative error of weights

Figure 14: Accuracy of PPTD for categorical data

Computational Cost. Next, we evaluate PPTD's computational cost for categorical data. Similar to the experiment on continuous data, the rounding parameter L is also fixed as 10^{10} in this case. Here, we also evaluate the computational cost on user smartphone and the cloud server, respectively.

In particular, we evaluate the two major procedures on user's smartphone, and then give the total running time. In this experiment, the number of the objects observed by each user varies from 1 to 14. The results are shown in Fig. 15, from which we can see the second procedure (i.e., calculating weighted data) costs more time than the first procedure (Fig. 15(a)). This is because most of the operations in the second procedure are conducted on ciphertexts while the first procedure is mainly composed of plaintext based operations. Additionally, Fig. 15(b) shows that the largest total running time of the two procedures on user smartphone is no more than 0.45s in each iteration, which verifies the practicality of our proposed framework.

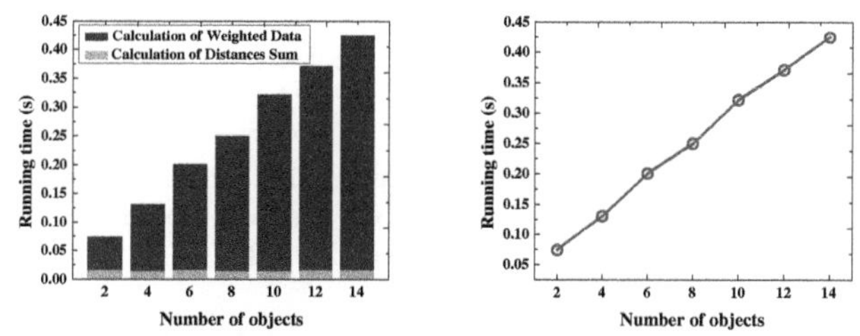

(a) Running time of each procedure (b) Total running time

Figure 15: Running time w.r.t Number of objects for categorical data on smartphone

To evaluate the computational cost on the cloud server, we vary the number of users from 13 to 113 (the corresponding number of objects varies from 20 to 54, because each question is only answered by part of the users). Figure 16 reports the running time of each procedure and the total running time in each iteration. From Fig. 16(a) we can see that the computational time of updating truths is far greater than the time of updating weights for all the scenarios, which is similar to that in the experiment for continuous data. The evaluation of total running time in each iteration can be seen in Fig. 16(b). We can see the total running time is 25.74s when the number of users is 113. This total time is reasonable, considering the number of crowd users in this experiment is ten times larger than that in the experiment for continuous data.

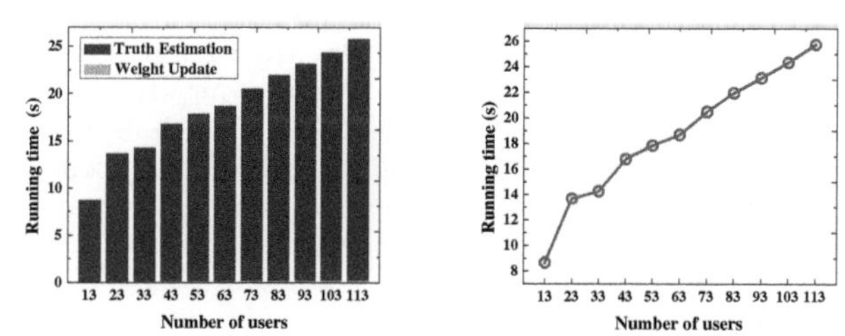

(a) Running time of each procedure (b) Total running time

Figure 16: Running time w.r.t Number of users for categorical data on the cloud server

7.4 Experiment of Parallel PPTD

From above experimental results, we can see most of the computational time on the cloud server is consumed in updating the ground truths, so we improve PPTD by adapting this procedure to MapReduce framework. In this part, the efficiency of parallel PPTD is verified. Here we use a Hadoop cluster as the cloud server. The crowd sensing system is simulated with 1000 users and 1000 objects, and the observation values are generated through adding Gaussian noise of different intensities to the ground truths. For comparison purpose, we also deploy the basic PPTD framework on the same server.

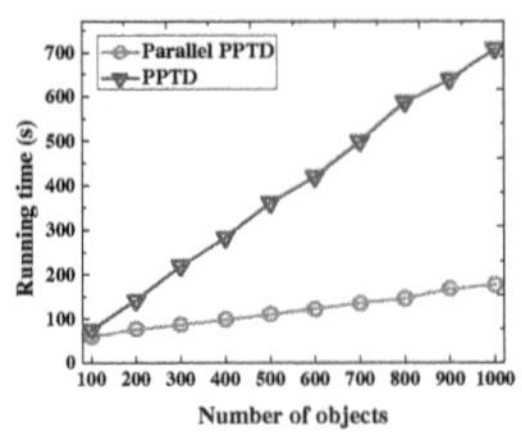

Figure 17: Running time w.r.t Number of objects for parallel PPTD

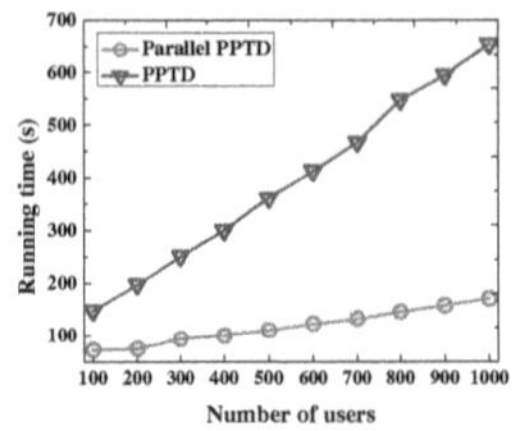

Figure 18: Running time w.r.t Number of users for parallel PPTD

When evaluating running time under different user numbers and object numbers, we adopt 10 Reducer nodes for parallel PPTD. Firstly, we fix the user number as 500 and change the object number from 100 to 1000. The running time of parallel PPTD and the basic PPTD in each iteration are shown in Fig. 17. From this figure we can see the parallel PPTD is increasingly more efficient than the basic PPTD as the number of objects goes up. When the object number reaches 1000, it takes parallel PPTD only 176.48s to complete the two procedures while the basic PPTD would have to spend 709.25s to finish the same computations. Then, we fix the object number as 500 and change the user number from 100 to 1000. Figure 18 reports the results in this case. Similar patterns can be seen. When user number reaches 1000, the parallel PPTD only spends 170.78s to finish the job, much less than the 655.38s consumed by PPTD. All the above results confirm the efficiency of parallel PPTD.

Moreover, it is important to study the effect of the node number in the Hadoop system on the performance of the proposed mechanism. In this experiment, we fix both user number and object number as 500. Figure 13 shows the running time under different number of Reducer nodes (results will be similar for the Mapper nodes). As we can see, with the increase of Reducer numbers, the running time decreases rapidly at first, and gets flattened very soon. This is because including more Reducer nodes, though improving the parallelism, will introduce more overhead (e.g., communication). Therefore, it is not true that more Reducer nodes would always lead to better performance.

8. RELATED WORK

As an effective technique to extract reliable information from crowd sensing systems, truth discovery has drawn more and more attention [29–32, 34, 35, 44, 47–50] in recent years. Representative truth discovery schemes include AccuSim [31], CRH [30], TruthFinder [50], etc. Compared with the naive averaging or voting approaches, these schemes can provide more reliable aggregated results by estimating and incorporating user reliability into the aggregation process. However, none of these schemes take actions to protect user privacy, which is a key concern in many crowd sensing systems [14].

The importance of privacy protection has long been recognized in many fields [7, 22, 36]. The representative strategies to tackle various privacy concerns include 1) anonymization [7,38,46], which removes identification information from all the interactions between the participant and other entities, 2) data perturbation [26, 27], which achieves privacy protection by adding artificial noise to the data before sharing them with others, and 3) the approaches based on cryptography or secure multi-party computation [17, 24], in which the sensitive data are encrypted and in many cases the parties need to cooperate with each other to decrypt the final results.

Recently, privacy-preserving problem is also studied with respect to crowd sensing applications. For example, [23, 42, 43] present anonymization based schemes to protect user's private information from being disclosed. Although these schemes can guarantee the users' privacy in some cases, they are not suitable for truth discovery scenarios, where instead of the anonymity of each user, what we need to preserve is the confidentiality of his observation values from which sensitive personal information (including user identity) may be inferred. Moreover, some perturbation based methods are also proposed [13,37,51]. However, it is difficult to integrate these schemes with truth discovery approaches, because the artificial noise added to each user's data would make it difficult to accurately estimate his reliability. Thus, cryptography based schemes are good choices, as they can guarantee the confidentiality of the observation values without introducing additional noise. Since some computations need to be conducted on encrypted data in truth discovery procedure, such schemes should have homomorphic properties [11]. Recently, the fully homomorphic encryption scheme [16] has drawn much attention due to the ability of taking arbitrary computations on encrypted data, but the prohibitively high computation cost makes it impractical to be used in crowd sensing applications. Although our proposed scheme is based on the traditional Paillier cryptosystem which cannot conduct arbitrary computations over encrypted data, we use it in a novel manner that well captures the specific algebra operations in truth discovery procedure without significant overhead. Additionally, paper [25] proposes a homomorphic encryption based approach to protect user privacy in crowdsourcing applications. However, it addresses a different scenario in which users can know their own reliability information. Also, paper [25] mainly focuses on categorical data. In contrast, our scheme can deal with not only categorical data but also other data types.

9. CONCLUSIONS

In this paper, we design a cloud-enabled privacy-preserving truth discovery (PPTD) framework to tackle the issue of privacy protection in crowd sensing systems. The key idea of PPTD is to perform weighted aggregation on the encrypted data of users using homomorphic cryptosystem, and iteratively conduct two phases (i.e., secure weight update and secure truth estimation) until convergence. During this procedure, both user's observation values and his reliability score are protected. In order to process large-scale data efficiently, a parallelized extension of PPTD is also proposed based on the MapReduce framework.

10. ACKNOWLEDGMENTS

We thank our shepherd Archan Misra and the anonymous reviewers for their valuable comments and suggestions. This work was sponsored in part by US National Science Foundation under grant IIS-1319973 and CNS-1262277.

11. REFERENCES

[1] S. Chen, M. Li, K. Ren, X. Fu, and C. Qiao. Rise of the indoor crowd: Reconstruction of building interior view via mobile crowdsourcing. In *Proceedings of the 13th ACM Conference on Embedded Networked Sensor Systems (Sensys'15)*, 2015.

[2] S. Chen, M. Li, K. Ren, and C. Qiao. Crowd map: Accurate reconstruction of indoor floor plans from crowdsourced sensor-rich videos. In *Proceedings of the 35th IEEE International Conference on Distributed Computing Systems (ICDCS'15)*, 2015.

[3] Y. Cheng, X. Li, Z. Li, S. Jiang, Y. Li, J. Jia, and X. Jiang. Aircloud: a cloud-based air-quality monitoring system for everyone. In *Proceedings of the 12th ACM Conference on Embedded Network Sensor Systems (Sensys'14)*, 2014.

[4] Y. Chon, Y. Kim, and H. Cha. Autonomous place naming system using opportunistic crowdsensing and knowledge from crowdsourcing. In *Proceedings of the 12th ACM/IEEE International Conference on Information Processing in Sensor Networks (IPSN'13)*, 2013.

[5] Y. Chon, N. D. Lane, Y. Kim, F. Zhao, and H. Cha. Understanding the coverage and scalability of place-centric crowdsensing. In *Proceedings of the 2013 ACM International Joint Conference on Pervasive and Ubiquitous Computing (UbiComp'13)*, 2013.

[6] Y. Chon, N. D. Lane, F. Li, H. Cha, and F. Zhao. Automatically characterizing places with opportunistic crowdsensing using smartphones. In *Proceedings of the 2012 ACM Conference on Ubiquitous Computing (UbiComp'12)*, 2012.

[7] C.-Y. Chow, M. F. Mokbel, and T. He. A privacy-preserving location monitoring system for wireless sensor networks. *IEEE Transactions on Mobile Computing*, (1):94–107, 2010.

[8] R. Cramer, I. Damgård, and J. B. Nielsen. *Multiparty computation from threshold homomorphic encryption.* Springer, 2001.

[9] I. Damgård and M. Jurik. A generalisation, a simpli. cation and some applications of paillier's probabilistic public-key system. In *Public Key Cryptography.* Springer, 2001.

[10] J. Dean and S. Ghemawat. Mapreduce: simplified data processing on large clusters. *Communications of the ACM*, 51(1):107–113, 2008.

[11] C. Fontaine and F. Galand. A survey of homomorphic encryption for nonspecialists. *EURASIP Journal on Information Security*, 2007:15, 2007.

[12] R. K. Ganti, N. Pham, H. Ahmadi, S. Nangia, and T. F. Abdelzaher. Greengps: a participatory sensing fuel-efficient maps application. In *Proceedings of the 8th ACM International Conference on Mobile Systems, Applications, and Services (MobiSys'10)*, 2010.

[13] R. K. Ganti, N. Pham, Y.-E. Tsai, and T. F. Abdelzaher. Poolview: stream privacy for grassroots participatory sensing. In *Proceedings of the 6th ACM conference on Embedded network sensor systems (Sensys'08)*, 2008.

[14] R. K. Ganti, F. Ye, and H. Lei. Mobile crowdsensing: current state and future challenges. *IEEE Communications Magazine*, 49(11):32–39, 2011.

[15] R. Gao, M. Zhao, T. Ye, F. Ye, Y. Wang, K. Bian, T. Wang, and X. Li. Jigsaw: Indoor floor plan reconstruction via mobile crowdsensing. In *Proceedings of the 20th ACM Annual International Conference on Mobile Computing and Networking (MobiCom'14)*, 2014.

[16] C. Gentry. *A fully homomorphic encryption scheme.* PhD thesis, Stanford University, 2009.

[17] O. Goldreich. Secure multi-party computation. *Manuscript. Preliminary version*, 1998.

[18] S. Hu, H. Liu, L. Su, H. Wang, T. F. Abdelzaher, P. Hui, W. Zheng, Z. Xie, J. Stankovic, et al. Towards automatic phone-to-phone communication for vehicular networking applications. In *Proceedings of the 33th Annual IEEE International Conference on Computer Communications (INFOCOM'14)*, 2014.

[19] S. Hu, L. Su, S. Li, S. Wang, C. Pan, S. Gu, T. Amin, H. Liu, S. Nath, R. R. Choudhury, et al. Experiences with enav: A low-power vehicular navigation system. In *Proceedings of the 2015 ACM Conference on Ubiquitous Computing (UbiComp'15)*, 2015.

[20] S. Hu, L. Su, H. Liu, H. Wang, and T. F. Abdelzaher. Smartroad: a crowd-sourced traffic regulator detection and identification system. In *Proceedings of the 12th ACM/IEEE International Conference on Information Processing in Sensor Networks (IPSN'13)*, 2013.

[21] S. Hu, L. Su, H. Liu, H. Wang, and T. F. Abdelzaher. Smartroad: Smartphone-based crowd sensing for traffic regulator detection and identification. *ACM Transactions on Sensor Networks (TOSN)*, 11(4):55, 2015.

[22] K. L. Huang, S. S. Kanhere, and W. Hu. Towards privacy-sensitive participatory sensing. In *Proceedings of the 7th IEEE International Conference on Pervasive Computing and Communications (PerCom 2009)*, 2009.

[23] K. L. Huang, S. S. Kanhere, and W. Hu. A privacy-preserving reputation system for participatory sensing. In *LCN*, 2012.

[24] T. Jung, X. Mao, X.-Y. Li, S.-J. Tang, W. Gong, and L. Zhang. Privacy-preserving data aggregation without secure channel: Multivariate polynomial evaluation. In *Proceedings of the 32st Annual IEEE International Conference on Computer Communications (INFOCOM'13)*, 2013.

[25] H. Kajino, H. Arai, and H. Kashima. Preserving worker privacy in crowdsourcing. *Data Mining and Knowledge Discovery*, 28(5-6):1314–1335, 2014.

[26] H. Kargupta, S. Datta, Q. Wang, and K. Sivakumar. On the privacy preserving properties of random data perturbation techniques. In *Proceedings of the third IEEE International Conference on Data Mining (ICDM'03)*, 2003.

[27] H. Kargupta, S. Datta, Q. Wang, and K. Sivakumar. Random-data perturbation techniques and privacy-preserving data mining. *Knowledge and Information Systems*, 7(4):387–414, 2005.

[28] N. D. Lane, Y. Chon, L. Zhou, Y. Zhang, F. Li, D. Kim, G. Ding, F. Zhao, and H. Cha. Piggyback crowdsensing (pcs): energy efficient crowdsourcing of mobile sensor data by exploiting smartphone app opportunities. In *Proceedings of the 11th ACM*

Conference on Embedded Networked Sensor Systems (Sensys'13), 2013.

[29] Q. Li, Y. Li, J. Gao, L. Su, B. Zhao, M. Demirbas, W. Fan, and J. Han. A confidence-aware approach for truth discovery on long-tail data. *Proceedings of the VLDB Endowment*, 8(4):425–436, 2014.

[30] Q. Li, Y. Li, J. Gao, B. Zhao, W. Fan, and J. Han. Resolving conflicts in heterogeneous data by truth discovery and source reliability estimation. In *Proceedings of the 2014 ACM SIGMOD international conference on Management of data (SIGMOD'14)*, 2014.

[31] X. Li, X. L. Dong, K. Lyons, W. Meng, and D. Srivastava. Truth finding on the deep web: is the problem solved? *Proceedings of the VLDB Endowment*, 6(2):97–108, 2012.

[32] Y. Li, Q. Li, J. Gao, L. Su, B. Zhao, W. Fan, and J. Han. On the discovery of evolving truth. In *Proceedings of the 21th ACM SIGKDD International Conference on Knowledge Discovery and Data Mining (SIGKDD'15)*, 2015.

[33] Y. Lindell and B. Pinkas. Privacy preserving data mining. In *Proceedings of the 20th Annual International Cryptology Conference (CRYPTO'00)*, 2000.

[34] F. Ma, Y. Li, Q. Li, M. Qiu, J. Gao, S. Zhi, L. Su, B. Zhao, H. Ji, and J. Han. Faitcrowd: Fine grained truth discovery for crowdsourced data aggregation. In *Proceedings of the 21th ACM SIGKDD International Conference on Knowledge Discovery and Data Mining(SIGKDD'15)*, 2015.

[35] C. Meng, W. Jiang, Y. Li, J. Gao, L. Su, H. Ding, and Y. Cheng. Truth discovery on crowd sensing of correlated entities. In *Proceedings of the 13th ACM Conference on Embedded Networked Sensor Systems (Sensys'15)*, 2015.

[36] S. Oh, T. Vu, M. Gruteser, and S. Banerjee. Phantom: Physical layer cooperation for location privacy protection. In *Proceedings of the 31st Annual IEEE International Conference on Computer Communications (INFOCOM'12)*, 2012.

[37] N. Pham, R. K. Ganti, Y. S. Uddin, S. Nath, and T. Abdelzaher. Privacy-preserving reconstruction of multidimensional data maps in vehicular participatory sensing. In *Wireless Sensor Networks*. Springer, 2010.

[38] L. Pournajaf, L. Xiong, D. A. Garcia-Ulloa, and V. Sunderam. A survey on privacy in mobile crowd sensing task management. Technical report, Technical Report TR-2014-002, Department of Mathe-matics and Computer Science, Emory University, 2014.

[39] M.-R. Ra, B. Liu, T. F. La Porta, and R. Govindan. Medusa: A programming framework for crowd-sensing applications. In *Proceedings of the 10th ACM International Conference on Mobile systems, applications, and services (MobiSys'12)*, 2012.

[40] K. K. Rachuri, C. Mascolo, M. Musolesi, and P. J. Rentfrow. Sociablesense: exploring the trade-offs of adaptive sampling and computation offloading for social sensing. In *Proceedings of the 17th Annual ACM International Conference on Mobile Computing and Networking (MobiCom'11)*, 2011.

[41] F. Saremi, O. Fatemieh, H. Ahmadi, H. Wang, T. Abdelzaher, R. Ganti, H. Liu, S. Hu, S. Li, and L. Su. Experiences with greengps–fuel-efficient navigation using participatory sensing. *IEEE Transactions on Mobile Computing (TMC)*, PP(99):1, 2015.

[42] K. Shilton. Four billion little brothers?: Privacy, mobile phones, and ubiquitous data collection. *Communications of the ACM*, 52(11):48–53, 2009.

[43] M. Shin, C. Cornelius, D. Peebles, A. Kapadia, D. Kotz, and N. Triandopoulos. Anonysense: A system for anonymous opportunistic sensing. *Pervasive and Mobile Computing*, 7(1):16–30, 2011.

[44] L. Su, Q. Li, S. Hu, S. Wang, J. Gao, H. Liu, T. F. Abdelzaher, J. Han, X. Liu, Y. Gao, et al. Generalized decision aggregation in distributed sensing systems. In *Proceedings of the 35th IEEE International Conference on Real-Time Systems Symposium (RTSS'14)*, 2014.

[45] V. Subbaraju, A. Kumar, V. Nandakumar, S. Batra, S. Kanhere, P. De, V. Naik, D. Chakraborty, and A. MISRA. Conferencesense: A case study of sensing public gatherings using participatory smartphones. In *Proceedings of the International Workshop on Pervasive Urban Crowdsensing Architecture and Applications (PUCAA'13)*, 2013.

[46] L. Sweeney. k-anonymity: A model for protecting privacy. *International Journal of Uncertainty, Fuzziness and Knowledge-Based Systems*, 10(05):557–570, 2002.

[47] D. Wang, L. Kaplan, H. Le, and T. Abdelzaher. On truth discovery in social sensing: A maximum likelihood estimation approach. In *Proceedings of the 11th ACM International Conference on Information Processing in Sensor Networks (IPSN'12)*, 2012.

[48] S. Wang, L. Su, S. Li, S. Hu, T. Amin, H. Wang, S. Yao, L. Kaplan, and T. Abdelzaher. Scalable social sensing of interdependent phenomena. In *Proceedings of the 14th ACM International Conference on Information Processing in Sensor Networks (IPSN'15)*, 2015.

[49] S. Wang, D. Wang, L. Su, L. Kaplan, and T. F. Abdelzaher. Towards cyber-physical systems in social spaces: The data reliability challenge. In *Proceedings of the 35th IEEE International Conference on Real-Time Systems Symposium (RTSS'14)*, 2014.

[50] X. Yin, J. Han, and P. S. Yu. Truth discovery with multiple conflicting information providers on the web. *IEEE Transactions on Knowledge and Data Engineering*, 20(6):796–808, 2008.

[51] F. Zhang, L. He, W. He, and X. Liu. Data perturbation with state-dependent noise for participatory sensing. In *Proceedings of the 31st Annual IEEE International Conference on Computer Communications (INFOCOM'12)*, 2012.

Talos: Encrypted Query Processing for the Internet of Things

Hossein Shafagh, Anwar Hithnawi, Andreas Dröscher
Department of Computer Science
ETH Zurich, Switzerland
{shafagh, hithnawi, drandreas}@inf.ethz.ch

Simon Duquennoy
SICS Swedish ICT
Kista, Sweden
simonduq@sics.se

Wen Hu
School of Computer Science and Engineering, UNSW
and NICTA, Sydney, Australia
wen.hu@unsw.edu.au

ABSTRACT

The Internet of Things, by digitizing the physical world, is envisioned to enable novel interaction paradigms with our surroundings. This creates new threats and leads to unprecedented security and privacy concerns. To tackle these concerns, we introduce Talos, a system that stores IoT data securely in a Cloud database while still allowing query processing over the encrypted data. We enable this by encrypting IoT data with a set of cryptographic schemes such as order-preserving and partially homomorphic encryption. In order to achieve this in constrained IoT devices, Talos relies on optimized algorithms that accelerate order-preserving and partially homomorphic encryption by 1 to 2 orders of magnitude. We assess the feasibility of Talos on low-power devices with and without cryptographic accelerators and quantify its overhead in terms of energy, computation, and latency. With a thorough evaluation of our prototype implementation, we show that Talos is a practical system that can provide a high level of security with a reasonable overhead. We envision Talos as an enabler of secure IoT applications.

Categories and Subject Descriptors

C.2.0 [**Computer-Communication Networks**]: General—*Security and Protection*

General Terms

Security, Design

Keywords

Data Security; Internet of Things; Computing on Encrypted Data; Homomorphic Encryption; Cloud Computing

1. INTRODUCTION

With the advent of the Internet of Things (IoT), there has been a rise in the number of devices empowered with sensing, actuating, and communication capabilities. These devices are typically connected to Cloud services, but are physically integrated with our living space. Hence, they deal with sensitive and private data that could be misused to infer privacy violating information. This consequently raises unique security and privacy concerns, which need to be addressed in the IoT ecosystem.

SenSys'15, November 01-04, 2015, Seoul, Republic of Korea
ACM 978-1-4503-3631-4/15/11.
http://dx.doi.org/10.1145/2809695.2809723.

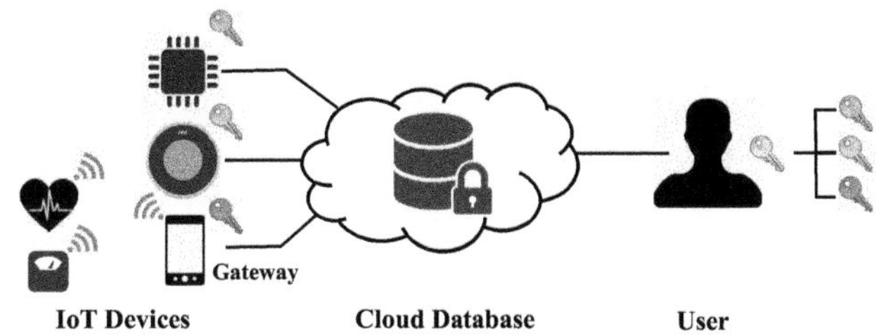

Figure 1: Talos enables protection of IoT data already at the origin. The Cloud database has no access to the encryption keys, but is able to process queries over encrypted data. All keys are derived from a master secret held by the user.

Conventional security solutions for the IoT utilize, at best, an *end-to-end* (E2E) secure channel to store IoT data on a Cloud database. A secure E2E channel protects the communication against unauthorized entities (e.g., eavesdropping and modification attacks), but leaves the data unprotected on the Cloud. Storing data in such form leaves it vulnerable to breaches [51], caused by hackers and curious administrators [1]. Moreover, financial incentives might lure our today's trusted Cloud service providers into disclosure of sensitive information derived from our data or unauthorized sharing/selling of our data [31, 39].

Encrypted Query Processing. An intuitive approach to counter such attacks is to store data in encrypted form in the Cloud database, and have all data en-/decryption performed at the user-side. This, however, is impractical, as it prevents any server-side query processing and results into undesirable application delays. To overcome this limitation, several encrypted query processing approaches [11, 17, 36, 53, 54] have been introduced in the past years. These approaches utilize cryptographic techniques (e.g., order-preserving encryption and homomorphic encryption) that allow computations to be carried out on encrypted data.

CryptDB [53] is one of the first practical systems that integrates efficient encrypted query processing into the database management system. In CryptDB, the cloud can perform traditional database queries over encrypted data and reply with the encrypted result. To achieve this, CryptDB relies on *a trusted proxy which intercepts the communication and applies en-/decryption transparent to the user.* This approach does not require any modification of the database nor the client-side and adds a modest computation overhead of 25% [53]. CryptDB is designed with web applications in mind and is not suitable for IoT application scenarios, mainly because: *(i)* it employs cryptographic schemes that are prohibitively expensive for constrained IoT devices and *(ii)* it relies on a trusted proxy, which has access to the encryption keys and plaintext information.

Talos: Encrypted Query Processing for the IoT. In this paper, we present Talos[1], an IoT data protection system which securely stores encrypted IoT data on the Cloud database, while allowing for efficient database query processing over the encrypted data (see Figure 1). In our design, we move away from CryptDB's focus on web applications only. Instead, we design a secure E2E system that stores encrypted data from IoT devices on a Cloud database, where data protection is executed at the data source. Thus, we *dispense with the role of a trusted proxy which has access to all keying material.* This allows us to address a stronger threat model, where only the end-user has access to the secret keys.

To put the use case of Talos into context, let us consider the application scenario of a health monitoring device similar to Fitbit Tracker[2] which logs heart rate, location, and timestamps. The heart rate measurements can be used to infer sensitive information about a person, such as stress, depression, and heart-related diseases. Hence, heart rate information should be protected from untrusted parties. To still allow certain computations, e.g., average, over the protected heart rate data, Talos utilizies additive homomorphic encryption (see §3.1 for the detailed descriptions of different cryptographic terms). The location is potentially also sensitive. Thus, Talos applies deterministic encryption, allowing encrypted queries correlating heart rate with location. Finally, the timestamps are encrypted with order-preserving encryption, to allow order-related searches.

One major barrier to employing cryptographic primitives on IoT devices is their resource constraints. IoT devices are inherently limited with regards to energy, memory, CPU, and bandwidth. These challenges are exacerbated with computationally heavy public-key-based cryptographic schemes, such as order-preserving and additive homomorphic encryption. Hence, we apply optimizations to these encryption schemes to make them suited towards IoT devices, yet without scarifying their level of security. Our work covers *(i)* an optimization of Paillier's additive homomorphic encryption scheme for integer data items, *(ii)* a solution enabling the elliptic curve ElGamal encryption scheme (EC-ElGamal) as an alternative additive homomorphic encryption, and *(iii)* employing an interactive order-preserving encryption scheme.

[1]In ancient Greek mythology, Talos is the protector and patron of just rulership and civil society.

[2]Fitbit Tracker Flex comprises a low-power ARM Cortex M3 Microcontroller similar to the one we based our prototype implementation on: `https://www.ifixit.com/Teardown/Fitbit+Flex+Teardown/16050`

Contributions. This paper makes the following contributions:

- Design and evaluation of Talos, a fully-implemented E2E secure system for IoT. Talos is compatible to the core CryptDB, which implements *SQL-aware encryption schemes.* We make our prototype implementation for the Contiki OS [18] publicly available[3]. Moreover, Talos is a software platform enabling additional research on data protection and could be seamlessly integrated into various IoT application scenarios.
- We propose practical solutions to enable different cryptographic primitives in constrained devices, in particular for order-preserving and homomorphic encryptions. We introduce an optimization to Paillier (additive homomorphic encryption) tailored for use with integers, and propose an effective way of mapping integers to elliptic curve points in order to enable EC-ElGamal as an alternative additive homomorphic encryption scheme.
- We demonstrate experimentally the feasibility of Talos. We quantify the performance of Talos in terms of energy, computation, communication, and latency. First, we microbenchmark the performance of the considered cryptographic primitives, both with and without hardware accelerator. Second, we quantify the overall system performance in Flocklab [20, 42], a public testbed, emulating IoT-typical scenarios.

2. OVERVIEW

We now briefly discuss background information and the security model our system addresses. Alongside, we give an overview of Talos.

We design Talos with three main actors in mind (see Figure 1): *(i)* the user who is interested in the IoT data, for instance the peak heart rate in the past month. *(ii)* the IoT devices where the data originates from. IoT devices are inherently resource limited, specifically with regards to memory. Thus, it is necessary for IoT devices to regularly offload their data into a Cloud database. In case the IoT device lacks any Internet-connectivity, the personal gateway (e.g., the smartphone for wearables) runs the Talos engine. We investigate the role of personal gateways in encrypted data processing in [59]. *(iii)* the Cloud database, which stores IoT data securely and has the ability to process queries over encrypted data. Note that IoT devices would potentially need to query the data on the Cloud to make certain actuation decisions, for instance in case of automated heating systems. However, in our current design we only consider the data producing (i.e., sensing) IoT device and address the data consuming (i.e., actuating) IoT device in future work.

IoT data consists of sensor readings (e.g., integer/float), meta-data (e.g., time, location, and identifier), and image/audio/video files. We consider text files to be significantly less represented in IoT data than in web and smartphone application data. Application developers should be aware of the sensitivity of data items and encrypt them with the adequate type of encryption. In §3, we detail the four main types of encryption and explain what functionality and security each type provides. We apply the data protection already at the IoT device, in order to reduce the attack surface and limit the need of trusted parties (see Figure 2).

[3]Talos can be downloaded from `https://github.com/hosseinsh/Talos`

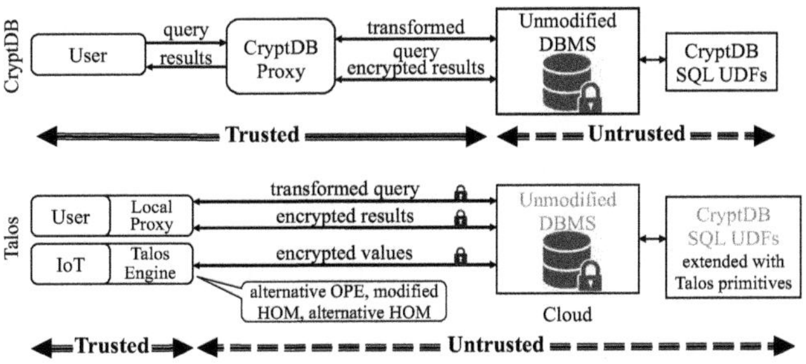

Figure 2: Talos extends CryptDB [53] to secure IoT data. Talos supersedes a trusted proxy with access to all keys. Instead, data protection is performed at IoT devices or personal gateways, e.g., smartphones.

For the Cloud database, we rely on our extended version of CryptDB [53] which is tailored towards IoT-application scenarios.

2.1 Background: CryptDB

CryptDB brings together powerful cryptographic tools, to create an encrypted query processing system targeted for database management systems (DBMS). In order to remain transparent and seamless, the en/-decryption process is performed on a trusted proxy which has access to the keying material (see upper part of Figure 2). The DBMS remains unmodified and is only extended with additional user defined functions (UDF) which perform the encrypted query processing. CryptDB addresses the threat models of honest-but-curious [48] database administrators and the concurrent compromise of the application server, proxy, and DBMS. In the latter threat, only data of logged-in users is disclosed.

CryptDB leverages the fact that most SQL-like database queries are composed of simple mathematical operations, such as equality check, order comparisons, aggregation, and joins. To allow these operations over encrypted data, known cryptographic schemes, such as order-preserving and additive homomorphic encryptions, are employed. However, only few data types need to be encrypted with these encryption schemes, to enable query executions. Hence, most data items can be protected with efficient and secure symmetric key encryptions.

For SQL-aware encryption, CryptDB defines the following main encryption types: *random* with the highest security as it provides semantic security (indistinguishability under an adaptive chosen plaintext attack), *deterministic* which reveals equality information, *order-preserving encryption* revealing order information, *additive homomorphic encryption*, enabling addition over encrypted data, and *keyword search* over encrypted texts.

We explain these encryption types in more details in §3, as we elaborate on the specific encryption schemes we employ in Talos. Specifically, for order-preserving and additive homomorphic encryptions, which are computation- and bandwidth-intensive, we explore and utilize alternative approaches to reduce overheads and render them more efficient. We intentionally do not yet support encrypted word search, as we do not yet see the use case of this scheme for IoT data.

2.2 Security Analysis

CryptDB addresses two important threat models consisting of DMBS compromise, and a more severe one including the compromise of application server, proxy, and DBMS. We not only inherit the security threat model addressed by CryptDB, but we address an even stronger database threat model, without a trusted proxy, as illustrated in the lower part of Figure 2. In addition, we address a network-based threat model. Note that IoT devices are vulnerable to physical node capture attacks. We do not address this attack specifically, however, we weaken it by utilizing a memory-protected area for key storage.

Threat 1: Cloud Database Compromise. The Cloud database provides confidentiality, i.e., secrecy of data, and no other security properties, such as integrity, correctness, or availability. The attacker is assumed to be passive, i.e., with read-only access to all database data and to the RAM of the physical machines. The attacker is however not able to modify the queries nor the encrypted data. This threat is getting increasingly important in today's Internet, with the flourishing of third party Clouds.

Unlike CryptDB, Talos is not designed to run with unmodified Web clients, but rather to facilitate an end-to-end integration with IoT devices. Therefore, we do not require a trusted proxy, thus providing stronger security than CryptDB. Talos provides the following guarantees: *(i)* at no time, the Cloud database has access to any keying material, *(ii)* during query processing, the data remain encrypted.

Note that the security of Talos is not perfect, as it reveals relationships among data items that allow for equality checks or ordering. Such data items, depending on the application scenario, are only column-wide. The remaining data items leak no further information, as long as encrypted with probabilistic encryption. Consequently, an attacker can learn the occurrence of a data item (e.g., via the histogram attack), however he can not gain access to the actual plaintext.

This data leakage could be theoretically avoided by utilizing recent advancements in theoretical cryptography (i.e., fully homomorphic cryptosystem [23]) that enable any computations over encrypted data, without revealing any information. However, these approaches are still computationally very expensive, rendering them impractical [55]. Talos is a practical system, providing strong security for most data items, while tolerating leakage of relational information for less sensitive data items.

Approach. Talos builds on the capabilities of CryptDB to allow processing of SQL-like queries over encrypted data. In addition to the CryptDB encryption schemes, we introduce a set of cryptographic primitives tailored for constrained devices. We introduce and elaborate our findings and the resulting design decisions further in a dedicated section (§3).

Moreover, Talos assumes state-of-the-art database security mechanisms to be in place. For instance, the Cloud database should additionally store encrypted backups of the database. We discuss current research approaches aiming at providing Cloud security and related cryptographic approaches in §7.

Threat 2: Network-based Attacks. This threat targets communication between the IoT device and the Cloud. This threat can be carried out by passive or active attackers, as discussed in the following. A passive attacker can launch non-intrusive eavesdropping and traffic analysis attacks. Talos addresses this threat by establishing a transport layer-based E2E secure channel between the IoT device and the

Cloud (see Figure 2). This allows to provide confidentiality, integrity protection, and authenticity of the data.

Talos utilizes weaker encryption schemes on database elements to enable encrypted query processing. With the secure E2E communication, we avert any relational data leakages, guarantee integrity protection, and authenticity of the data. An active attacker can launch a man-in-the-middle attack, to gain access to the plaintext values originated at the IoT device or make the IoT device believe it is communicating with the Cloud database (i.e., impersonation of the Cloud). Talos addresses this threat by a public-key-based authentication scheme for the E2E secure channel.

Approach. DTLS [47] provides confidentiality, authenticity, and integrity protection of communication. This is achieved by means of AES-CCM, which encrypts a given message while providing data-origin authentication and integrity protection. The main challenge with DTLS within constrained environments is the channel establishment, where the session keys are negotiated. The conventional approach is to rely on pre-shared keys. However, stronger security is obtained with the public-key-based version of DTLS. Talos applies DTLS in public-key mode with support of X.509 certificates and raw public keys, where the crypto operations could be accelerated by means of cryptographic accelerators. This way, both the IoT device and the Cloud database can authenticate each others' identity.

3. DESIGN

Encrypted query processing is an emerging research field, enabling better protection of user's private data and resolving many privacy-related issues in Cloud computing. Inspired by the recent advancements in this field, we intend to bring the benefits of encrypted query processing to the IoT domain.

3.1 Encryption Types

Encrypted query processing allows storage of encrypted data at a third party database, yet simultaneously enabling efficient search and computation over the stored encrypted data. Although it would be desirable to utilize fully homomorphic encryption [23] to allow arbitrary computations, we are yet bound to computationally feasible and efficient approaches, which enable only a subset of computations over encrypted data.

To support common SQL-like queries, it is necessary to be capable of performing equality checks and have knowledge about the order of encrypted values. However, enabling computation over encrypted data also means leaking information, i.e., any order-preserving encryption scheme will, by definition, reveal order relations. The encryption scheme is chosen per column and accounts for the intended query type, e.g., *min*, *order by*, etc. Data items that are not involved in the processing of queries are encrypted with the strongest cryptographic scheme (i.e., probabilistic encryption).

In the following, we describe the four types of encryption schemes supported in Talos.

RAND. Probabilistic or random encryption is the strongest security scheme, allowing no operation over encrypted data. This scheme is the conventional scheme, widely used in computing and storage. It has the property that the encryption of the same plaintext m results into two different ciphers c_1 and c_2 such that c_1 and c_2 are by no means related (i.e., semantically secure under a *chosen plaintext attack* (CPA)).

AES in CBC mode is a good candidate for this type of encryption. AES-CBC is a 16 Byte block-cipher encryption, producing outputs of a size multiple times of the block-size. To this end, the input is, if necessary, padded to have a modulo 16 Byte size. Efficient hardware implementations of AES encryption routines are integrated into most IoT devices. Considering the fact that IoT data typically have a smaller size than AES's block size, the Blowfish block-cipher encryption [58] with 8 Byte blocks is a good alternative, producing smaller ciphers. Blowfish was as well a candidate for AES (Rijndael was selected for the final AES), but was considered inefficient for large file sizes due to the 8 Byte block-size. We selected Blowfish among several 8 Byte block ciphers (e.g., RC5, Skipjack) due to its higher efficiency [62]. Talos employs both Blowfish and AES in CBC mode. We apply the former for data smaller than 8 Byte and the latter for data larger than 8 Byte.

DET. Deterministic encryption allows for equality checks. The encryption of the plaintext m results always into the same cipher c.

AES-ECB is a block-cipher encryption with such a property. Due to this deterministic property it is in general advised not to use ECB for encryption of large packets, as an attacker can: *(i)* change the order of the blocks or replace a block in a indistinguishable manner (i.e., substitution attack), or *(ii)* learn information about the plaintext with a histogram of repeated blocks. Therefore, for maximum security, AES-ECB should be only applied for plaintexts smaller or equal to 16 Byte. For bandwidth efficiency reasons, we employ Blowfish for plaintexts with a size smaller or equal to 8 Byte.

AES and Blowfish in CBC mode with a fixed initialization vector (IV) have the deterministic property, however due to undesirable leaks of prefix equality, they are not secure options for plaintexts larger than the block size. Therefore, we utilize AES-CMC [56] for plaintexts larger than 16 Byte, as recommended by CryptDB. AES-CMC is a tweaked combination of AES-CBC with a zero IV, where AES-CBC is applied twice on the input. The second CBC round is applied in the reverse order, i.e., from the last block to the first block. This way, the first blocks become deterministically random, and do not leak equality within a data item.

OPE. In *order-preserving encryption* (OPE) the order relationship between the plaintext inputs m_1, m_2, and m_3 is preserved after encryption, i.e.:

$$if\ m_1 \leq m_2 \leq m_3,\ then\ c_1 \leq c_2 \leq c_3 \qquad (1)$$

This way, the order information among the encrypted data items c_i is revealed, but not the actual data itself.

Order comparison is a common operation in SQL-like databases, e.g., for sorting, range checks, ranking, etc. OPE enables powerful operations and still offers relatively strong security, such that some research fields only focus on enabling secure databases or web applications by means of OPE [13,57]. One of the first provably secure OPE schemes is the approach introduced by Boldyreva et al. [9]. This

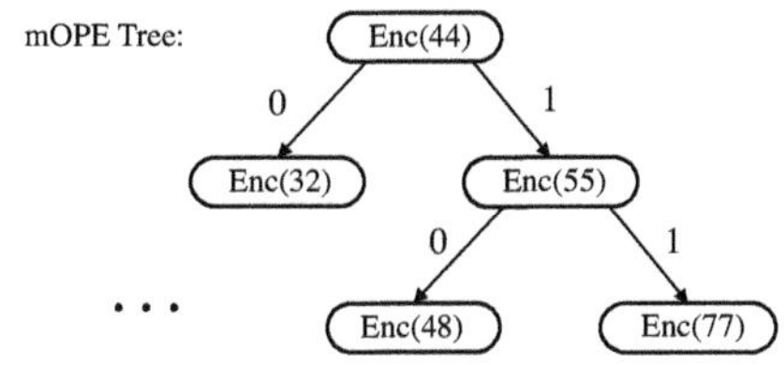

ciphertext	mOPE encoding **[path]**10..0
Enc(44)	[]10..0
Enc(32)	**[0]**10..0
Enc(55)	**[1]**10..0
Enc(48)	**[10]**10..0
Enc(77)	**[11]**10..0

Figure 3: Illustration of *mutable order-preserving encoding* (mOPE) with a balanced binary search tree. The order encoding (path to the node) is appended with a 1 and 0s, signaling the end of the encoding.

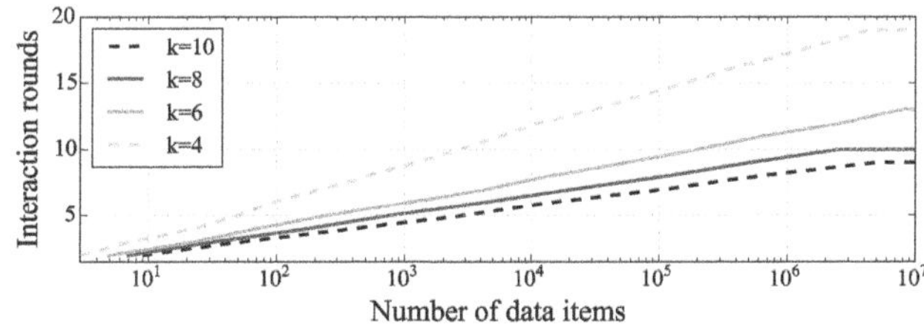

Figure 4: mOPE is an interactive approach. The number of interaction rounds depends on the current size of the database (i.e., the tree) and the parameter k of the k-ary tree in use. Talos selects k=10 in favor of fewer interaction rounds, resulting into a higher average rewrites per item in the Cloud (e.g., factor 4.7 for 10^7 items).

OPE scheme is, however, as computationally-intensive as asymmetric encryption.

In order to cope with resource constraints of IoT devices, we rely on a more recent interactive OPE approach by Popa et al. [55], which solely relies on symmetric cryptography and trades computation overhead for latency (i.e., it involves more communication). We refer to this lightweight OPE scheme, as *mutable order-preserving encoding* (mOPE) as the order encodings are mutable. Popa et al. [55] prove that mOPE fulfills the ideal security (IND-OCPA), i.e., no additional information than the order is revealed. mOPE is more secure than any other OPE approach and yet 1-2 orders of magnitude less computationally-intensive than traditional OPE schemes.

We detail the original mOPE and our optimizations to further reduce the communication overhead in §3.2.

HOM. Research on fully homomorphic cryptosystems has made significant advancements in the recent years, and been able to show that arbitrary computations on encrypted values are implementable [23]. However, the involved computations are yet prohibitively high [55] even for full-fledged devices and by far infeasible for resource constrained devices. In order to support sum and average operations over encrypted data, it is however sufficient to utilize additive homomorphic encryption schemes, such that:

$$decrypt(c_1 \circ c_2) = decrypt(c_1) + decrypt(c_2) \qquad (2)$$

Several cryptosystems exhibit homomorphic properties [21]. To start with, the textbook RSA and El-Gamal's cryptosystem are multiplicatively homomorphic. Goldwasser-Micali's (GM) [28] scheme is among the first additive homomorphic cryptosystems achieving highest security level (i.e., probabilistic public-key encryption), which inspired several later cryptosystems. Unfortunately, GM exhibits a strong drawback as its input consists of a single bit plaintext. Moreover, the expansion during encryption results into large ciphertexts (i.e., $|pq|$ bits) which, given the single bit inputs, renders this scheme impractical. Benaloh [8] introduces a generalization of GM, which supports encryption of plaintexts with higher bit-length k. This, however, comes with a higher cost of decryption. The decryption cost is dependable of k, which eliminates the gain of a higher k. The Paillier [50] cryptosystem, one of the most well-known homomorphic schemes, improves the previous schemes by reducing the degree of expansion while allowing a large k (i.e., k is equal to key-length $|pq|$). At the same time the en-/decryption costs are reasonable (i.e., exponentiation and multiplication of big numbers modulo |pq|). Efforts [37] to reduce the encryption expansion of Paillier from 2 times k have the side-effect of significantly higher computation cost.

The Paillier [50] cryptosystem is employed by CryptDB. It is, however, with regards to IoT resources, computationally intensive and results into a large ciphertext size of 256 Byte, given a key size of 1024 bit (see Table 1). In Talos, we apply a slight modification to Paillier, inspired by Ge and Zdonik [22], rendering it more efficient in terms of average bandwidth and computation per data item. Moreover, we explore the elliptic curve (EC)-ElGamal encryption scheme as an alternative additive homomorphic encryption scheme.

In §3.3, we detail our modification to the Paillier cryptossytem, our findings about EC-ElGamal, and the efficiency of each approach.

3.2 Optimized Order-Preserving Encryption

The traditional OPE by Boldyreva et al. [9] is computationally 5 orders of magnitude more intensive than symmetric encryption. mOPE [55] is a recent interactive order-preserving encryption scheme that allows us to drastically reduce this overhead. mOPE utilizes lightweight symmetric encryption and balanced search trees to preserve the order information among ciphertexts. Intuitively, mOPE derives the order relations from the structure of the tree. A tree node holds a deterministically encrypted value where the order-preserving encoding is basically the path from the root of the tree to the node, as illustrated in Figure 3. For example *encrypt*(77) has the encoding 11 concatenated with 100000 (assuming 8-bit encodings) to indicate the end of encoding. The encoding reveals that *encrypt*(77) is the largest value in this tree.

mOPE is a client-server approach. The client intends to apply mOPE on a value, while storing it in a database. The server constructs the encoding, without learning the plaintext value, and later stores the final encoding in the database. For each new value, the server only learns the relation of the new value with regards to existing ones. The protocol starts with the client sending the new ciphertext to the server, accompanied with the request to `insert`. The server starts with sending the encrypted value at the root, to learn if the new value is larger or smaller. The client decrypts the values and replies. The server traverses the tree (i.e., in worst case $\mathcal{O}(\log n)$ interactions) until it finds the right spot to insert the new value. As we show later in our evaluation in §5, the communication overhead of mOPE is lower than the computation cost of the traditional OPE.

Algorithm	Plaintext [Byte]	Ciphertext [Byte]
Blowfish-ECB	(0, 8]	8 (+ 8 RAND)
AES-ECB	(8,16]	16 (+ 16 RAND)
AES-CMC	(16, 16 + n]	16 × $\lceil \frac{n}{16} \rceil$ (+ 16 RAND)
mOPE (integer)	(0, 8]	16 (8 + 8 Byte encoding)
Paillier (1024-bit key)	(0, 128]	256
EC-ElGamal (192-bit curve)	(0, 4]	50 (2x 25* Byte EC-points)
OPE [9] (integer)	(0, 8]	16

Table 1: Plaintext-space to ciphertext-space. *EC-ElGamal's ciphertext consist of 2 EC-points, which could each be compressed to 25 Byte. In RAND, the initialization vector (IV) is added to the ciphertext.

In order to avoid long paths in the search tree, the tree needs to be rebalanced regularly. The server is able to rebalance without the help of the client, based on the order relation between nodes. However, as an encoding is based on paths in the tree, rebalancing results in mutated encodings. Hence, the name mutable OPE (mOPE). Note that the encoding is only used at the server side, to reveal ordering of encrypted data. The client does not store any encoding, as it would become obsolete after the next rebalancing.

The length of the encoding corresponds to the maximum depth of the tree, where the end of the encoding is signaled with a 10..0 padding, as depicted in Figure 3. We chose an encoding length of 64 bit and apply our previously described deterministic encryption strategy on the data items. This implies data items smaller or equal to 8 Byte are encrypted with Blowfish, data items between 8 and 16 Byte length are encrypted with AES-ECB, and data items larger than 16 Byte are encrypted with AES-CMC.

For the search tree implementation, a k-ary tree is used to achieve lower number of interactions. This way, in each interaction round, the server sends the current node containing $\leq k$ data items. The client replies with an index and an equality flag. The index refers to the index of the data item, where the new value is equal or smaller than it. The flag indicates equality of the new value to the item at the index. In the latter case, the encoding of the existing value is taken for the new value. Otherwise, the interaction continues until a leaf node is reached.

We select a 10-ary tree which offers a good trade-off between the maximum length of an interaction packet and the total number of interactions, as depicted in Figure 4. Increasing k from 4 to 10, allows us to reduce the average interaction rounds by more than half. Even though this increases the number of decryptions and comparisons per round, our results (see §5) suggest that the savings from having fewer interaction rounds outweigh this computational overhead. Note that a drawback of such tree-based interactive approach is that the worse-case number of interactions depends on the tree size. In our case the worst-case is $\mathcal{O}(\log_{10} n)$ interactions (e.g., with 10^9 existing items the worst-case is 9 rounds).

In Talos, we rely on the prototype implementation of mOPE [55] and extend it with support for UDP and IPv6. To cope with the connectionless UDP, retransmission timers on both ends reassures the termination of insert operations. More importantly, we adjusted the interaction protocol to be more concise. We transmit 2 Byte of header information appended with raw integer data (instead of ASCII representation of ciphertexts). This allows us to drastically reduce the communication overhead, up to a factor of 8. As summarized in Table 1, both OPE schemes produce final ciphertexts with the same length.

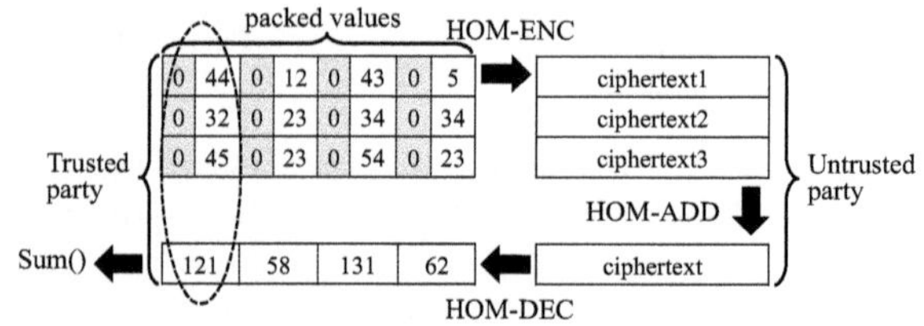

Figure 5: Illustration of our Paillier optimization. Several values are packed into one block, considered as one large number. The structure of packed values is maintained after decryption. After decryption, the sum of the final block is equal to the sum of all packed values.

3.3 Optimized Homomorphic Encryption

The Paillier cryptosystem is an additive homomorphic encryption scheme which is based on asymmetric cryptography. We briefly explain the mathematical operations involved in Paillier, in order to be able to explain how we improve its efficiency with regards to encryption expansion. The user defines the public key (n, g) and the private key d by selecting two large primes (p and q) of the same bit-length and g, a large random number modulo n:

$$n = pq, \quad d = (q-1)(p-1) \tag{3}$$

Encryption of the message m is performed as follows:

$$c = (g^m)(r^n) \bmod n^2 \tag{4}$$

where r is a large random number modulo n. Decryption of cipher c is performed as follows:

$$m = L(c^d \bmod n^2)\ \mu \bmod n \tag{5}$$

$$\text{where } L(x) = \frac{(x-1)}{n}, \quad \text{and } \mu = (L(g^d \bmod n^2))^{-1} \bmod n$$

The homomorphic addition function is defined by multiplication of the ciphers modulo n^2. Note, the ciphertext size is $2n$, i.e., for a 1024 bit key, 2048 bit (256 Byte).

In order to render Paillier more efficient, we apply a trick introduced by Ge and Zdonik [22] and illustrated in Figure 5. We use the fact that Paillier plaintext can be as large as $n =$ 1024 bits, whereas IoT data often only consists of integers. The idea is to concatenate several values to form a single larger plaintext that will be encrypted in a single Paillier operation. We leave enough space for the carry bits of each value: <space, value_1, space, value_2, ... , space, value_i>. Assuming 32-bit values and 32-bit spaces, 16 values can be packed into a ciphertext.

This way, we amortize the computation and space overhead of Paillier among several values. This approach is possible since during the homomorphic addition operation (i.e., multiplication of ciphertexts) the aligned values are summed together (see Figure 5). A user interested in the sum of a data item, now receives a ciphertext of this form: <sum_1, .. , sum_i>. After the decryption process, she can extract any sum_i and ultimately compute the total sum.

EC-ElGamal. Paillier encryption is an expensive operation on IoT devices, where it can take up to 3.1 s (discussed in §5). As an alternative additive homomorphic encryption scheme to Paillier, we present in the following EC-ElGamal in more details. EC-ElGamal's security is based on the elliptic curve discrete logarithm problem (ECDLP). This means

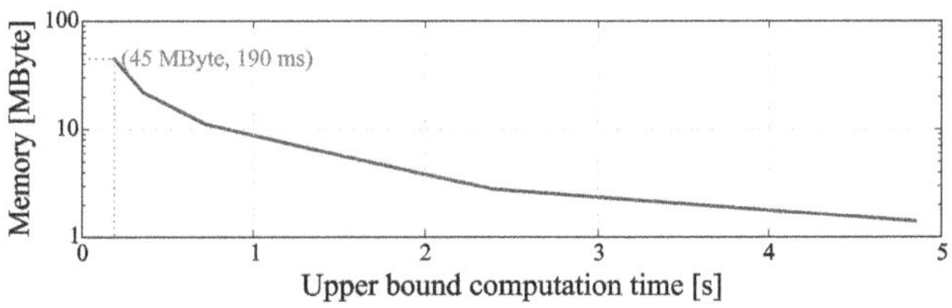

Figure 6: Memory-computation tradeoff in the Baby-Step-Giant-Step algorithm on a Google Nexus 5. Talos stores a pre-computed look-up table of 45 MByte and solves an ECDLP for an unsigned 32-bit value in maximum 190 ms with only 1 thread.

given two points P and Q on the curve, finding the scalar k such that $P = kQ$, is a hard problem. Note that the scalar multiplication kQ is calculated as k times the elliptic curve addition of Q (for more details on elliptic curve cryptography (ECC) refer to [48]). In EC-ElGamal, after defining the elliptic curve (EC) parameters such as the generator point G, the encryption of message M (a point on the curve) is defined as two points on the curve C' and C'':

$$C = (C', C''), \text{ where } C' = M + rQ,\ C'' = rG \tag{6}$$

As it is common in ECC, $Q = dG$ is the public key, d the private key, and r is a large random number. Decryption of a cipher C is performed as follows:

$$M = C' - dC'' \tag{7}$$

To perform the homomorphic addition operation, the cipher components, which are each EC-points, are added to each other (i.e., EC-point addition):

$$\begin{aligned} C_1 + C_2 &= (C_1', C_1'') + (C_2', C_2'') = \\ &(M_1 + M_2 + r_1Q + r_2Q,\ r_1G + r_2G) \\ M_{1+2} &= C_{1+2}' - dC_{1+2}'' = \\ &M_1 + M_2 + r_1Q + r_2Q - d(r_1G + r_2G) \end{aligned} \tag{8}$$

where $rdG = rQ$, since $Q = dG$.

Representation of Plaintext as EC-Point. A challenge in making practical use of EC-ElGamal is that it operates on EC-points rather than arbitrary messages. Efficiently and deterministically mapping of an arbitrary message into an elliptic curve point is an open research problem [40]. Koblitz suggests encoding of a message m into the x-coordinate of an elliptic curve [40]. This approach, however, is not homomorphic and therefore not suitable for EC-ElGamal.

We use a theoretical assumption from cryptography [48], which becomes practical in IoT scenarios, where we often deal with small integers, i.e., 32-bit. To map an integer m to an EC point M, we multiply m to a publicly known point G on the curve, i.e., $M = mG$. Such scalar EC multiplications (i.e., m times addition of G) can efficiently be performed on an IoT device. This approach is homomorphic, since

$$dec(C_1 + C_2) = M_1 + M_2 = m_1G + m_2G = (m_1 + m_2)G \tag{9}$$

At decryption time, we need to map M back to m, only with the knowledge of G. This requires solving an elliptic curve discrete logarithm problem (ECDLP). Although this is computationally infeasible for large numbers, solving it for a 32-bit integer m can be realized in a reasonable time (see Figure 6). Using the Baby-Step-Giant-Step algorithm [61],

Component	ROM [Byte]	static RAM [Byte]
Cryptographic accelerator	312	-
BigNumber operations*	2,832	-
EC operations*	1,144	-
ECDSA* + ECDH*	1,840	884
EC-ElGamal*	840	644
Paillier encryption*	712	780
mOPE client	2,322	1,396
AES (ECB, CBC, CCM)*	1,820	16
Blowfish (software)	4,548	4,168
SHA-256*	660	32
Subtotal	17,030	7,920
DTLS engine + client	16,942	7,370
Sum	33,972	15,290

Table 2: Memory size of cryptographic components of Talos on OpenMotes (considering max sizes). *All algorithms based on hardware crypto accelerator can be substituted by software implementations.

Talos is able to retrieve m from M in maximum 190 ms (benchmarked on a Google Nexus 5, a typical device where decryption takes place). To achieve an upper computation bound of 190 ms, a pre-computed look-up table of 45 MByte is necessary.

Note that this procedure does not affect the overall security: we solve the ECDLP to obtain m from M, but M itself is protected with a strong cryptography, in our case 192-bit ECC (more secure than 1024-bit RSA).

3.4 Access Control

In the following we briefly present key components of the access control mechanism adopted in Talos.

Authorization. To ensure that only authorized entities can access/add data in the Cloud database, Talos employs the OAuth2 protocol [30] to grant IoT devices authorized access to the Cloud database. In the OAuth2 protocol, the IoT device initiates a request to the Cloud. Consequently, the Cloud replies with an authentication URL, which is used to authenticate the user to the Cloud. After a successful login, the user can define the type and duration of the authorization. The next connection request from the IoT device is answered with an access token used for subsequent Cloud connections.

Key Management. Talos foresees the storage of the master secret by the user. This master secret is used to derive all the keying material used to protect the data. A PRF (Pseudo-Random Function, e.g., SHA-256) can be used to generate i deterministic keys key_i to be used by the IoT devices. For this we use a *key chaining* approach [53] that concatenates a well defined ID, e.g., column-name or data type, to the master secret (MS):

$$\text{PRF}(\text{MS}|\text{ID}_i) = key_i \tag{10}$$

The MS never leaves the user device. The derived keys are securely placed on the corresponding IoT devices.

In case *key revocation* is needed, for instance in case of disposed/compromised IoT devices, the user revokes the access token of the IoT device and re-encrypts the data in the Cloud database with a fresh key. Moreover, *data sharing* is a relevant feature that could be integrated into Talos. We are exploring data sharing for such systems in future work.

Task	current [mA]	σ
CPU idle @32 MHz	12.8	0.11
CPU active @32 MHz	20.8	0.11
AES/SHA hardware accelerator	23.6	0.13
Public-key hardware accelerator (CPU idle)	25.9	0.12
Radio Transmission (TX), CPU idle	24	-
Radio Reception (RX), CPU idle	20	-

Table 3: Current drawn during computations on OpenMotes. Given the supply voltage (2.1 V) and the duration of a task, we calculate the drawn energy: time [s] × voltage [V] × current [mA] = energy [mJ].

4. IMPLEMENTATION

We have implemented a prototype of the Talos system. Our prototype implementation consists of two main components: *(i)* The IoT component of Talos is implemented for OpenMotes[4] in the Contiki OS 2.7 [18] and *(ii)* the Cloud database component is an extended implementation of CryptDB [53]. For space reasons, we discuss only the former in more details.

OpenMotes are based on the TI CC2538 microcontroller [63], i.e., 32-bit ARM Cortex-M3[5] SoC at 32 MHz, with a public-key cryptographic accelerator running up to 250 MHz. They are equipped with 802.15.4 compliant RF transceivers, 32 kB of RAM and 512 kB of ROM.

Talos is platform independent and our findings can be applied to any other platform. We chose the OpenMote as our prototype platform, because it has a public-key cryptographic accelerator (including SHA-256) on board and due to the promising potential of 32-bit platforms in next generation embedded platforms [41,45]. Moreover, low-priced and energy-efficient cryptographic accelerators are predicted to find their ways into low-power platforms [2]. For the cryptographic accelerator, we implement generic drivers for big number arithmetic operations (utilized by RSA and Paillier) and ECC operations (utilized by ECDSA, ECDH, and EC-ElGamal). In case no cryptographic accelerator is available, these fundamental operations are provided by a software implementation. We used the crypto library Relic Toolkit [4] for this purpose.

While relying on the cryptographic accelerator Talos requires 2.4 kB of RAM and 10 kB of ROM for the crypto components. In case no cryptographic accelerator is on board, a considerable amount of memory is dedicated to Relic Toolkit. The exact memory size is dependent on several configuration parameters to optimize Relic Toolkit. It is however in the range of 8 kB of RAM and 66 kB of ROM. The breakdown of memory requirements in Talos is shown in Table 2. We use the tools `arm-none-eabi-readelf` and `arm-none-eabi-size` to perform our memory analysis on the binaries. Hereby, DTLS makes a major contribution with 7 kB of RAM and 17 kB of ROM. We measure a maximum stack size of 2 kB. It is important to mention that our memory values cannot be directly translated for 8- or 16-bit platforms, as our platform comes with 32-bit registers.

We assume hardware AES block encryption to be available (which has been integrated in most RF transceivers for more than a decade). We extend existing drivers for AES to support additional modes, such as the AES-CMC for deterministic encryption. Unfortunately, Blowfish is not supported in hardware. Our ported Blowfish implementation requires 380 Byte of RAM and 4168 Byte of ROM. For DTLS integration, we modify the tinyDTLS[6] implementation to support by demand cryptographic accelerator or software implementation (i.e., Relic Toolkit). Moreover, we extend it with a basic X.509 certificate parser.

[4]OpenMote platform: openmote.com

[5]Fitbit Tracker utilizes a microcontroller with similar capabilities.

States	Time	Energy
Public-Key Crypto (ECDSA, ECDH)	1,191.75 ms	59.1 mJ
CPU	9.46 ms	0.5 mJ
TX	47.73 ms	3.4 mJ
RX	43.46 ms	2.2 mJ
Symmetric Crypto (AES-CCM, SHA)	5.86 ms	0.48 mJ
Total (without idle)	1,232.8 ms	65.4 mJ
idle/sleep (1-2 wireless hops)	455 ms - 2 s	< 2.52 mJ

Table 4: Secure E2E channel establishment (certificate-based DTLS handshake) on the client. The number of wireless hops affects the idle time.

5. EXPERIMENTAL EVALUATION

In this section, we present the experimental evaluation of Talos on OpenMotes, representing a typical IoT device. We do not discuss the performance of the Cloud database, represented by a modified and extended version of CryptDB instance, as it is not the core of our contribution. However, we quantify the network overhead of Talos during its interaction with the Cloud database.

In the following, we first define our evaluation objectives, describe the setup, metrics, and methodology. We continue in §5.1 with a brief discussion of our results for secure E2E communication, followed by a detailed discussion of our results for encrypted data processing in §5.2.

Goals. Throughout this section, we intend to answer the following questions: *(a)* is Talos feasible on resource constrained devices? *(b)* what is the overhead of Talos in terms of computation, energy, and bandwidth? *(c)* what is the impact of the availability of cryptographic accelerators on the performance and feasibility of Talos?

Evaluation Setup. For our evaluation, we rely on Flocklab [42], a public wireless sensor network testbed. Flocklab[7] supports over the Internet communication of sensor nodes with a remote host, thus emulating IoT scenarios. Our Cloud database resides on a normal desktop connected via Internet to Flocklab nodes, with an average transmission delay of 10 ms. Our communication setup involves at least one wireless hop within Flocklab.

Metrics. We quantify the impact of Talos in terms of computation and communication overheads, and calculate the corresponding energy consumption. All tests are repeated at least 100 times, if not indicated otherwise. Standard deviation is reported only when not negligible, since it is mostly the case with CPU computation on a non-preemptive OS. Inspired by TinySec [38], we use the metrics *Byte-time* and *Byte-energy* to put computation in relation to radio transmission time and energy. In other words, we normalize our time measurements based on the transmission time of 1 Byte in 802.15.4 (i.e., 32 μs) and

[6]tinyDTLS; http://tinydtls.sourceforge.net/

[7]For our project, we extended Flocklab with OpenMotes: `flocklab.ethz.ch`

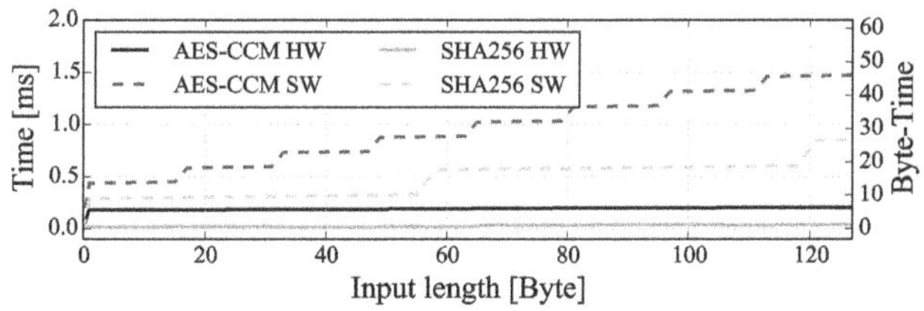

Figure 7: Secure E2E channel (AES-CCM, SHA256) with support of cryptographic accelerator (HW) compared to pure software implementation (SW).

the energy measurements based on the energy required to transmit 1 Byte on OpenMotes (i.e., 1.613 μJ). The latter is calculated as: transmission time $\times$ voltage $\times$ transmission current $= 32\ \mu s \times 2.1\ V \times 24\ mA = 1.163\ \mu J$.

Methodology. We verify the current draw in our crypto functions by utilizing a mixed signal oscilloscope, as summarized in Table 3. We then characterize the accuracy of system clocks, which we use for time measurements[8]. To this end, we use digital inputs of our oscilloscope connected to OpenMote pins to encode the start and end of events. We rely on Contiki's timer with a resolution of 30 μs and a dedicated hardware timer with an accuracy of 1 μs. We measured a maximum timer inaccuracy of 0.4%. Additionally, we leverage the energy measurement features of Flocklab during our evaluation.

5.1 Secure E2E Communication

Talos employs the certificate-based DTLS to establish a secure E2E channel. Due to space limitations, we only briefly discuss the DTLS results.

In our setup, a DTLS client from Flocklab establishes a secure channel with the Internet host. The handshake, since it involves public-key-based operations (ECDSA, ECDH), is the most expensive part of a secure E2E channel. The public-key-based operations contribute to the major part (90%) of the total energy consumption per handshake (65.4 mJ). Hence, a DTLS session should be kept alive as long as possible, for instance by means of session resumption [35]. Note, the cryptographic accelerator allows concurrent computations on the main CPU. Hence, during the long computations ideally other tasks could be scheduled.

Table 4 lists the computation time and energy costs of the different components of a handshake. The total duration of the handshake is mainly impacted by the number of the wireless hops, as indicated by the time spent in *idle* state. How much energy is drained in this state depends on the specific MAC layer in use, e.g., the level of radio duty cycling and the sleep mode.

Once the session is established and the keying material is agreed upon, a modest crypto overhead is caused by AES-CCM. AES-CCM has a performance between 31 to 55 μs for 16 to 128 Byte packets, as depicted in Figure 7. This overhead is considerably larger when using software (i.e., 293 to 1311 μs). Although the crypto accelerator draws about 13% more current, its faster execution time leads to energy savings by a factor of up to 20 for full frames (see Table 6). More importantly, the computation of AES-CCM

[8]We open-source our test interface utilizing accurate system timers (see footnote 3).

Algorithm	Input Size [Byte] 4-8	16	64	128
AES-ECB	-	0.9 μJ	1.1 μJ	1.4 μJ
-CBC	-	0.9 μJ	1.1 μJ	1.4 μJ
-CMC	-	2.1 μJ	4.8 μJ	8.5 μJ
Blowfish-ECB	1 μJ	2 μJ	8 μJ	16 μJ
Paillier	88-91 mJ	99 mJ	128 mJ	171 mJ
EC-ElGamal	11-23 mJ	46 mJ	184 mJ	368 mJ

Table 5: Energy consumption of data-protection components of Talos based on the *current* values in Table 3. Except for Blowfish, all crypto operations utilize the hardware crypto engine.

in hardware can run in parallel to the transmission of the preamble (8 symbols $\times$ 16 μs = 128 μs)

Note that the steps in Figure 7 in the software implementation are due to padding to a full block size. AES has a block size of 16 Byte, hence the steps are at 16 Byte steps. SHA has a block size of 64 Byte. The effect due to padding is optimized in the pure hardware-based modes.

Communication	Engine	Input Size [Byte] 16	64	128
AES-CCM	Hardware	8.7 μJ	9.4 μJ	10 μJ
	Relic	19.7 μJ	38.8 μJ	64 μJ

Table 6: Energy consumption of AES-CCM. The comparison to software implementation shows the energy gain of hardware accelerator.

5.2 Encrypted Data Processing

To support encrypted data processing, Talos utilizes four types of encryption. The strongest level of security is provided by probabilistic encryption (RAND), additive homomorphic encryption (HOM), followed by determinist encryption (DET), and order-preserving encoding (OPE). Each of these schemes comes with certain security-functionality tradeoffs, discussed in §3. In the following, we first discuss the performance of the individual crypto algorithms, and then elaborate on the overall system performance.

5.2.1 Microbenchmarks

We now discuss the time and energy measurements of the individual crypto algorithms, as summarized in Figure 8 and Table 5, respectively. The performance results combined with the ciphertext overheads of each algorithm (see Table 1) contributed to the design decisions in Talos.

RAND/DET. For random and deterministic encryptions, we employ various types of symmetric block cipher encryptions (AES and Blowfish). We utilize the cryptographic accelerator for AES modes, however, our Blowfish is software-based. Blowfish is known for its long initialization phase after setting the key, which in our case amounts to 12 ms, independent of the key size. Since in Talos the key is rarely changed, this overhead is acceptable. Blowfish with 23.5 μs shows a modest performance, in the same order as AES-ECB (14 μs) and AES-CBC (18 μs). Note that AES in software is by factor 3 to 10 slower, depending on plaintext size.

As shown in Figure 8(a), Blowfish, which has a blocksize of 8 Byte, quickly becomes expensive for large data. Consequently, Talos uses Blowfish for data $\leq$8 Byte. Among the different AES modes (ECB, CBC, CMC), AES-CMC has the highest overhead. This is due to the fact that

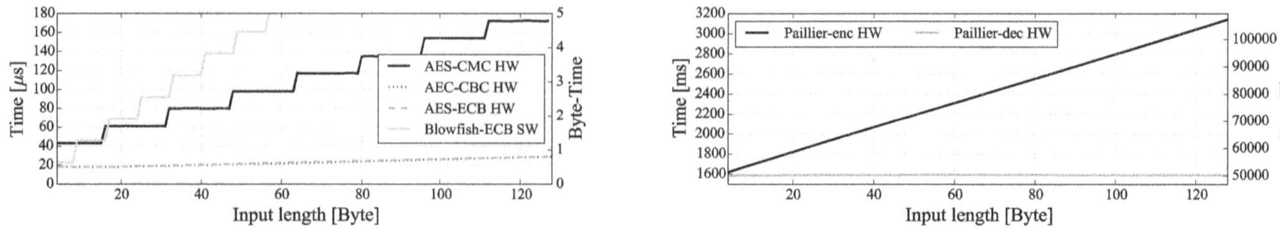

(a) Symmetric block cipher encryption, as used in random and deterministic encryption schemes. Except for Blowfish, which is implemented in software (SW), the remaining ciphers utilize the cryptographic accelerator (HW).

(b) Additive homomorphic encryption by means of Paillier utilizing the cryptographic accelerator (HW). Paillier's plaintext-size can be as large as the key size, in our case 1024 bit (128 Byte).

Figure 8: Microbenchmark of the cryptographic algorithms in Talos on a typical IoT device (i.e., OpenMote).

AES-CMC applies AES-CBC twice in order to avoid early block leakage. Talos limits the use of AES-CMC only for data ≥16 Byte.

OPE. The traditional OPE, as introduced by Boldyreva [9], relies on the hypergeometric distribution (HGD). HGD is computationally intensive and in similar orders as Paillier. Talos utilizes mOPE which is about 2 orders of magnitude more efficient than OPE. This is due to the fact that mOPE employs deterministic encryption (in our case Blowfish). Since mOPE requires interaction with the Cloud, we elaborate on its performance aspects in the following section.

HOM. Additive homomorphic encryption is the most expensive cipher in Talos. Paillier encryption starts with 1,619 ms for 4 Byte plaintext and increases linearly to 3,142 ms for 128 Byte plaintext. Decryption time is constant at 1,593 ms. Note that decryption is typically performed on more powerful devices. Paillier's performance in software is by factor 6 slower.

With EC-ElGamal we explored an alternative additive homomorphic encryption to the Paillier cryptosystem. EC-ElGamal's performance, since based on EC-points, is input-length independent. EC-ElGamal encryption takes 210 ms, whereas the decryption with 95 ms is by factor 2 faster. The 210 ms encryption time already includes a maximum upper bound of 20 ms for mapping a 32-bit value into the EC space (8-bit values require only 9 ms).

The homomorphic encryption with both Paillier and EC-ElGamal is energy intensive (see Table 5). For 4 Byte plaintext, this amounts to 88 mJ and 11.42 mJ, respectively. Note that this is equivalent to 76 and 9.8 *kB-energy*, respectively. Paillier's energy consumption in software is by factor 7.5 higher, which renders it significantly costly and not suitable for IoT.

5.2.2 System Performance

We now assess the overall performance of Talos with focus on the two schemes of order-persevering and additive homomorphic encryptions. Moreover, we discuss the impact of Talos on the lifetime of a battery-based IoT device.

mOPE. With mOPE we trade computation for communication. In §3.2, we discussed how to reduce the number of interactions in mOPE by tuning the k-ary tree to hold up to 10 values (k=10). Figure 9 depicts the total time of interactions in mOPE, based on the number of interaction rounds for k=4 and k=10. The interaction time is impacted by the transmission delay of our setup, which consists of one wireless hop.

The average roundtrip time (RTT) per interaction is higher for k=10 (68 ms) than k=4 (53 ms) because packets carry in average more elements. Similarly, the per interaction CPU time is for k=10 (314 μs) 19% higher than k=4 (264 μs). This is because in average more item decryptions are needed for the comparisons. However, in total is k=10 several times more efficient than k=4. As depicted in Figure 9, with 10^3 items in the database, mOPE with k=4 requires 9 interactions, whereas k=10 needs only 4. This is 200 ms faster than k=4. This trend continues and we experience with 10^5 items in the database 12 interactions for k=4 and only 6 interaction for k=10 (250 ms faster).

The IoT device can ideally utilize radio duty cycle techniques to reduce its energy consumption to an optimal of transmission and reception of the query and response packets of the interaction process. Assuming more than 10^5 items in the database, adding new items requires 6 interaction rounds which involves transmission and reception of 12 packets. This results into an energy consumption of 1.3 mJ. Assuming an optimistic lower bound of 1,600 ms computation time for the traditional OPE, shows that mOPE is 2 orders of magnitude more efficient than OPE.

HOM. Paillier, as discussed earlier, is computationally very expensive (encryption time is between 1.6 to 3.1 s). Its cost is prohibitive especially when compared to the encryption time of EC-ElGamal (210 ms), an alternative HOM. In order to render Paillier more efficient, we optimized it to pack several values into a single plaintext. This amortizes the expensive Paillier encryption among several values. As depicted in Figure 10, the energy per item reduces as the number of packed items increases.

EC-ElGamal, which operates on 32-bit plaintext values, consumes 11.42 mJ, and thus depicts the lower energy budget for HOM encryptions. In order to reach the same per item energy efficiency as EC-ElGamal, our optimized Paillier must pack fourteen 32-bit plaintext values. Working with 16-bit plaintext values allows to pack 32 items in one plaintext. This results in an optimal energy efficiency, by a factor 2 better than by EC-ElGamal. The possibility of packing values, however, is application scenario-dependent. In order to remain as generic as possible, we use EC-ElGamal as the default HOM for Talos.

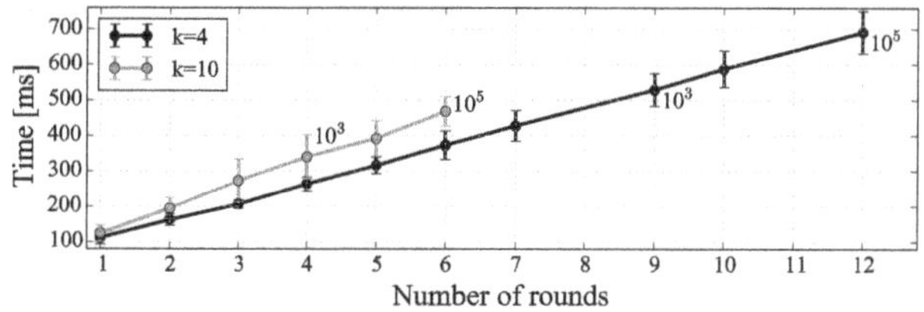

Figure 9: mOPE. Time of an insert operation based on the number of interactions for up to 10^5 items. Client is one wireless hop away from the gateway in Flocklab. Average RTT per interaction is 53 ms for k=4 and 68 ms for k=10. The per interaction CPU time is 264 μs for k=4 and 314 μs for k=10.

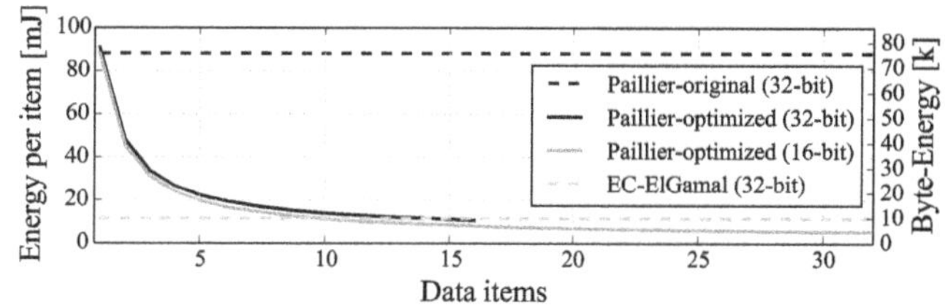

Figure 10: Additive homomorphic encryption. Our optimized Paillier is more efficient than original Paillier and can reach the efficiency of EC-ElGamal.

Energy. Talos significantly impacts the lifetime of a battery-based IoT device, specifically due to the involved crypto operations. This is an inevitable tradeoff that comes with higher security. We assume two AAA alkaline batteries with a typical capacity of 3 Wh (10.8 kJ) and a targeted lifespan of one year. This results into a daily energy budget of 29.6 J. To put this into perspective, with 20% of the daily budget (5.92 J), Talos is capable of performing: 90 DTLS handshakes, 518 EC-ElGamal based homomorphic encryptions, 5.92×10^6 random or deterministic encryptions of 32-bit values, or 5381 mOPEs (5 interactions).

Case Study. To have a better understanding about the applicability of Talos, let us again consider the application scenario of the health monitoring device which logs heart rate, location, and timestamps. As we described in §1, the logged items have different sensitivities. For instance, the heart rate measurements have the highest sensitivity, since they can be used to infer health-related information (e.g., stress, depression, or diseases). Hence, Talos protects heart rate with additive homomorphic encryption to provide semantic security and allow average and summation computations. Health monitoring devices[9] typically sample at 1 Hz (every 1 s) during sport activities and 6 times per hour otherwise. For a person with 1 h sport activity per day, this would result into a daily 3,738 data items encrypted with additive homomorphic encryption. The location, logged every 15 min, is maybe less sensitive for this person and could be encrypted with deterministic encryption, to allow encrypted queries correlating heart rate with a given location. Hereby, the timestamp for each heart rate record could be encrypted with the order-preserving encryption, to allow ordering, but not revealing the actual time.

Assuming the same underlying platform we used in our evaluation, the total daily energy cost of additive homomorphic, deterministic, and order-preserving encryptions in this scenario accounts to a total of 42.67 J per day. This would contribute to a modest 5.4% of the daily energy budget of a Fitbit device with 5 days lifetime and a lithium-polymer battery capacity of 1.2 Wh (4.32 kJ).

6. DISCUSSION

This paper provides a proof-of-concept of the potential and feasibility of building secure systems that address data privacy concerns in the IoT ecosystem. However, more research is needed to realize the full potential of Talos. Here we address some practical challenges and research points that assist in evolving Talos further.

Energy. The feasibility of Talos for IoT devices is driven by its energy efficiency. Although security comes at a price, the price should not hinder the usability of the system. We show that with a modest energy budget, Talos can be integrated on IoT devices providing strong network and data security guarantees. We achieve this by making the employed HOM and OPE schemes one order of magnitude more efficient. However, there is still potential for further optimizations, specifically for HOM, which with EC-ElGamal still accounts for a considerable amount of the energy consumption.

Hardware Accelerator. We explore the impact of hardware crypto accelerator on the feasibility of Talos. The hardware accelerator, which utilizes a separated core (running at 250 MHz), drains with 26 mA a higher current than the main core at 32 MHz (20 mA). The higher frequency and consequently lower computation time results into significant energy savings (by a factor of 2 to 20), as compared to pure software operations. More importantly, a separate core for crypto operations allows utilizing the main core for other tasks. This results into an active main core, instead of idle, as considered in our evaluation (draining a total of 33 mA for both cores). Hence, an optimal task scheduling would increase the energy efficiency of our system several times higher.

Security Analysis. Talos meets the security goals and efficiency requirements outlined in §2.2. With our efficient public-key-based E2E secure channel (DTLS), Talos defends against network-based threats. The encryption applied by Talos protects the data against curious database administrators and database compromises. Since we utilize order-preserving encryption and deterministic encryption, we allow leakage of order and equality information for less sensitive data. Sophisticated attacks could potentially misuse the gained information from this leakage. Hence, future steps should address this shortcoming of Talos.

Alternative Crypto Primitives. Recent advances in theoretical cryptography and careful optimization of crypto mechanisms allow us to build practical secure systems, such as Talos, in a novel fashion that inherently address data privacy issues through facilitating computation on encrypted data. We are currently witnessing improvements in the computational efficiency of fully homomorphic encryption [24, 25]. The already achieved improvements of

[9]Microsoft Band: `http://www.windowscentral.com/how-often-microsoft-band-checks-your-heart-rate`

6 orders of magnitude in the past decade could be further enhanced in the near future. Talos is yet bound to schemes with reasonable efficiency, however our general system design is not bound to particular schemes.

Fully Homomorphic Encryption (FHE). In Talos, we rely on additive (rather than fully) homomorphic encryption. We measured additive homomorphic encryption to be 5 orders of magnitude slower than AES, which makes it the bottleneck of our system. Hence, despite recent efforts in rendering FHE more efficient, we do not foresee FHE to be soon feasible for IoT devices. However, with GHS [25], an approach of homomorphic evaluation of AES circuit, there is hope that the benefits of FHE can find their way into IoT. GHS transforms AES ciphertexts, without access to the plaintext, into a FHE-compatible form where arbitrary computations over the hidden plaintext are possible.

7. RELATED WORK

We now discuss work related to Talos grouped in the following four categories:

E2E Security. Early efforts to bring security to WSN explored low-power cryptographic approaches [43,49], which facilitated research on secure communication protocols for IoT. Hummen et al. [35] introduce a handshake delegation scheme which allows highly constrained devices without the capability of performing public-key-based operations to still benefit from the scalability and security of public-key-based handshakes. Hu et al. [33] investigated the feasibility and advantages of hardware accelerators on low-power devices.

Privacy-Preserving Cryptography. There has been significant amount of work on cryptographic schemes [7, 10, 11, 26, 27, 44, 60] that could be utilized in privacy-preserving computations. Gentry's work [23, 24] marks a breakthrough in cryptography showing an implementable fully homomorphic encryption (FHE) scheme. Since then, his work has been incrementally enhanced up to 6 orders of magnitudes by the research community [25]. Prior to Gentry's work, the focus was on partial homomorphic encryption, where only one type of computation, such as multiplication or addition is supported [12, 14, 34].

Although FHE provides semantic security and supports at the same time arbitrary computations over encrypted data, it is not yet best suited for encrypted query processing. This is due to both its prohibitive cost and the fact that the Cloud must process all existing data in database for queries such as equality check or comparison. This is the main reason of using weaker encryption schemes such as OPE and DET to allow the database to reduce the scope of computation.

Secure multi-party computation approaches [3,32] are efficient for simple functions, however become computationally expensive for general functions. Moreover, MPC involves high interactions, large bandwidth, and coordination among the involved parties. Secure in-network processing of aggregate queries was introduced for WSNs [16, 52]. This would increase the security of approaches providing a distributed database interface for WSNs, such as TinyDB [46].

Differential privacy [19] assumes a trusted server, which obfuscates answers to avoid leaking information about data items and the query patterns.

Computation on Encrypted Data. Perrig et al. [17] introduced an efficient search over encrypted text files. This is achieved by deterministically encrypting metadata of files which are protected with strong encryption, i.e., probabilistic. Perrig et al.'s efforts paved the way for more advanced systems enabling encrypted query processing [36, 53, 54], among them CryptDB [53] which we discussed in depth in §2. Mylar [54] introduces a multi-key searchable encryption scheme, exemplified for smartphone applications. Mylar protects the content of documents and the searched words from the untrusted server.

Goldwasser et al. [15] introduce an innovative and sophisticated approach for machine learning classification over encrypted data. This approach is complementary to ours and would allow support for a wider range of data types.

Cloud Security. Commercial Cloud database services, such as Google [29], encrypt data before storage, however, the queries are still processed over plaintext data. Secure data storage is an essential measure and complementary to our approach. Utilizing a local *trusted machine* [5,6] at the database is an alternative approach to encrypted query processing. This, however, implies that the user considers the *trusted hardware* trustworthy.

8. CONCLUSION

We presented Talos, a practical secure system that provides strong communication and data security features for privacy-preserving IoT applications. Talos leverages and tailors cryptographic primitives that allow computation on encrypted data without disclosing decryption keys to the Cloud. To achieve this, we utilize optimized encryption schemes, specifically for the expensive additive homomorphic and order-preserving encryptions, accelerating them by 1 to 2 orders of magnitude.

We show the practicality and feasibility of Talos through an implementation and experimental evaluation considering both micro-benchmarking and system performance. Talos copes with the limited energy budget of constrained devices and requires a modest energy budget to provide a higher security level. Advancements in *Computing on Encrypted Data* appear to be increasingly significant to the progression of data privacy and security. Talos is the first system to address energy and computation concerns for integrating encrypted query processing into IoT systems. We anticipate that Talos will facilitate further research in this direction.

9. ACKNOWLEDGMENTS

The authors would like to express their gratitude to Raluca Ada Popa and Björn Tackmann for the insightful discussions during design phase of Talos. We thank Friedemann Mattern and Wilhelm Kleiminger for their comments on earlier versions of this paper. Moreover, we are thankful to the anonymous reviewers and our shepherd, Lu Su, for their valuable feedback. We thank Lukas Burkhalter for the support with the smartphone-related development. We would like to thank the Flocklab team, specially Roman Lim, for the support for extending Flocklab with OpenMotes. This work was partly funded by the European Commission through Nobel Grid (H2020-646184) and VINNOVA (Sweden's Innovation Agency).

10. REFERENCES

[1] A. Chen. GCreep: Google Engineer Stalked Teens, Spied on Chats, Gawker. Online: www.gawker.com/5637234, 2010.

[2] A. Perrig, J. Stankovic, and D. Wagner. Security in Wireless Sensor Networks. *Communications of the ACM*, 47(6):53–57, June 2004.

[3] Andrew C. Yao. Protocols for Secure Computations. In *Annual Symposium on Foundations of Computer Science (SFCS)*, 1982.

[4] D. F. Aranha and C. P. L. Gouvêa. RELIC is an Efficient Library for Cryptography. Online: https://github.com/relic-toolkit/relic.

[5] A. Arasu, S. Blanas, K. Eguro, R. Kaushik, D. Kossmann, R. Ramamurthy, and R. Venkatesan. Orthogonal Security with Cipherbase. In *Conference on Innovative Data Systems Research (CIDR)*, 2013.

[6] S. Bajaj and R. Sion. TrustedDB: A Trusted Hardware Based Database with Privacy and Data Confidentiality. In *ACM Special Interest Group on Management of Data (SIGMOD)*, 2011.

[7] M. Bellare, A. Boldyreva, and A. O'Neill. Deterministic and Efficiently Searchable Encryption. In *Advances in Cryptology (CRYPTO)*, 2007.

[8] J. Benaloh. *Verifiable Secret-Ballot Elections.* PhD thesis, 1988. Yale University, Department of Computer Science.

[9] A. Boldyreva, N. Chenette, Y. Lee, and A. O'Neill. Order-Preserving Symmetric Encryption. In *EUROCRYPT*, 2009.

[10] D. Boneh and M. Franklin. Identity-based Encryption from the Weil Pairing. In *Advances in Cryptology (CRYPTO)*, 2001.

[11] D. Boneh, C. Gentry, S. Halevi, F. Wang, and D. J. Wu. Private Database Queries Using Somewhat Homomorphic Encryption. In *Applied Cryptography and Network Security (ACNS)*, 2013.

[12] D. Boneh, E.-J. Goh, and K. Nissim. Evaluating 2-DNF Formulas on Ciphertexts. In *Theory of Cryptography (TCC)*, 2005.

[13] D. Boneh, K. Lewi, M. Raykova, A. Sahai, M. Zhandry, and J. Zimmerman. Semantically Secure Order-Revealing Encryption: Multi-Input Functional Encryption Without Obfuscation. In *EUROCRYPT*, 2015.

[14] D. Boneh, G. Segev, and B. Waters. Targeted Malleability: Homomorphic Encryption for Restricted Computations. In *Theoretical Computer Science Conference (ITCS)*, 2012.

[15] R. Bost, R. A. Popa, S. Tu, and S. Goldwasser. Machine Learning Classification over Encrypted Data. In *Network and Distributed System Security Symposium (NDSS)*, 2015.

[16] H. Chan, A. Perrig, and D. Song. Secure Hierarchical In-network Aggregation in Sensor Networks. In *ACM Computer and Communications Security (CCS)*, 2006.

[17] D. X. Song, D. Wagner, and A. Perrig. Practical Techniques for Searches on Encrypted Data. In *IEEE Symposium on Security and Privacy*, 2000.

[18] A. Dunkels, B. Grönvall, and T. Voigt. Contiki - a Lightweight and Flexible Operating System for Tiny Networked Sensors. In *IEEE LCN*, 2004.

[19] C. Dwork. Differential Privacy. In *International Conference on Automata, Languages and Programming (ICALP)*, 2006.

[20] ETH Zurich. FlockLab: A Testbed for Distributed, Synchronized Tracing and Profiling of Wireless Embedded Systems. Online: http://www.flocklab.ethz.ch/.

[21] C. Fontaine and F. Galand. A Survey of Homomorphic Encryption for Nonspecialists. *EURASIP Journal on Information Security*, Jan. 2007.

[22] T. Ge and S. Zdonik. Answering Aggregation Queries in a Secure System Model. In *Very Large Data Bases (VLDB)*, 2007.

[23] C. Gentry. *A Fully Homomorphic Encryption Scheme.* PhD thesis, 2009. Stanford University: AAI3382729, Advisor: Dan Boneh.

[24] C. Gentry. Fully Homomorphic Encryption Using Ideal Lattices. In *Annual ACM Symposium on Theory of Computing (STOC)*, 2009.

[25] C. Gentry, S. Halevi, and N. P. Smart. Homomorphic Evaluation of the AES Circuit. In *Advances in Cryptology (CRYPTO)*, 2012.

[26] O. Goldreich and R. Ostrovsky. Software Protection and Simulation on Oblivious RAMs. In *Journal of the ACM (JACM)*, 1996.

[27] S. Goldwasser, Y. Kalai, R. A. Popa, V. Vaikuntanathan, and N. Zeldovich. Reusable Garbled Circuits and Succinct Functional Encryption. In *Annual ACM Symposium on Theory of Computing (STOC)*, 2013.

[28] S. Goldwasser and S. Micali. Probabilistic Encryption & How to Play Mental Poker Keeping Secret All Partial Information. In *Anual ACM Symposium on Theory of Computing (STOC)*, 1982.

[29] Google Cloud Database. Security and Integration with Google Cloud. Online: https://cloud.google.com/sql/docs.

[30] D. Hardt. The OAuth 2.0 Authorization Framework. In *RFC 6749*, 2012.

[31] Haris Z. Bajwa JD and Iltifat Husain MD. Health Apps can sell your data to insurance companies, and there's nothing you can do about it. Online: http://www.imedicalapps.com/2014/08/health-apps-insurance-companies/, 2014.

[32] W. Henecka, S. Kögl, A.-R. Sadeghi, T. Schneider, and I. Wehrenberg. TASTY: Tool for Automating Secure Two-party Computations. In *ACM Computer and Communications Security (CCS)*, 2010.

[33] W. Hu, P. Corke, W. C. Shih, and L. Overs. secFleck: A Public Key Technology Platform for Wireless Sensor Networks. In *Embedded Wireless Systems and Networks (EWSN)*, 2009.

[34] Y. Hu, W. J. Martin, and B. Sunar. Enhanced Flexibility for Homomorphic Encryption Schemes via CRT. In *Applied Cryptography and Network Security (ACNS)*, 2012.

[35] R. Hummen, H. Shafagh, S. Raza, T. Voigt, and K. Wehrle. Delegation-based Authentication and Authorization for the IP-based Internet of Things. In *IEEE Sensor and Ad Hoc Communications and Networks (SECON)*, 2014.

[36] Y. H. Hwang, J. W. Seo, and I. J. Kim. Encrypted Keyword Search Mechanism Based on Bitmap Index for Personal Storage Services. In *IEEE Trust, Security and Privacy in Computing and Communications (TrustCom)*, 2014.

[37] I. Damgård and M. Jurik. A generalisation, a simplification and some applications of Pailliers probabilistic public-key system. In *Workshop on Practice and Theory in Public-Key Cryptography*, 1992.

[38] C. Karlof, N. Sastry, and D. Wagner. TinySec: A Link Layer Security Architecture for Wireless Sensor Networks. In *ACM Conference on Embedded Networked Sensor Systems (SenSys)*, 2004.

[39] Kate Kaye. FTC: Fitness Apps Can Help You Shred Calories – and Privacy. Online: `http://adage.com/article/privacy-and-regulation/ftc-signals-focus-health-fitness-data-privacy/293080/`, 2014.

[40] B. King. Mapping an Arbitrary Message to an Elliptic Curve when Defined over GF(2n). *International Journal of Network Security*, 8(2):169–176, 2009.

[41] J. Ko, K. Klues, C. Richter, W. Hofer, B. Kusy, M. Bruenig, T. Schmid, Q. Wang, P. Dutta, and A. Terzis. Low Power or High Performance? A Tradeoff Whose Time Has Come (and Nearly Gone). In *Embedded Wireless Systems and Networks (EWSN)*, 2012.

[42] R. Lim, F. Ferrari, M. Zimmerling, C. Walser, P. Sommer, and J. Beutel. FlockLab: A Testbed for Distributed, Synchronized Tracing and Profiling of Wireless Embedded Systems. In *ACM/IEEE Conference on Information Processing in Sensor Networks (IPSN)*, 2013.

[43] A. Liu and P. Ning. TinyECC: A Configurable Library for Elliptic Curve Cryptography in Wireless Sensor Networks. In *ACM/IEEE Conference on Information Processing in Sensor Networks (IPSN)*, 2008.

[44] A. Lopez-Alt, E. Tromer, and V. Vaikuntanathan. On-the-fly Multiparty Computation on the Cloud via Multikey Fully Homomorphic Encryption. In *Annual ACM Symposium on Theory of Computing (STOC)*, 2012.

[45] M. P. Andersen, and D. E. Culler. System Design Trade-Offs in a Next-Generation Embedded Wireless Platform. In *Technical Report No. UCB/EECS-2014-162*, 2014.

[46] S. Madden, M. J. Franklin, J. M. Hellerstein, and W. Hong. TinyDB: An Acquisitional Query Processing System for Sensor Networks. In *ACM Transactions on Database Systems (TODS)*, 2005.

[47] N. Modadugu and E. Rescorla. The Design and Implementation of Datagram TLS. In *Network and Distributed System Security Symposium (NDSS)*, 2004.

[48] Oded Goldreich. *Foundations of Cryptography: Volume 2, Basic Applications*. Cambridge University Press, 2004.

[49] P. Szczechowiak, L. Oliveira, M. Scott, M. Collier, and R. Dahab. NanoECC: Testing the Limits of Elliptic Curve Cryptography in Sensor Networks. In *Embedded Wireless Systems and Networks (EWSN)*, 2008.

[50] P. Paillier. Public-key Cryptosystems Based on Composite Degree Residuosity Classes. In *EUROCRYPT*, 1999.

[51] Privacy Rights Clearinghouse. Chronology of Data Breaches from 2005 to Present Date. Online: `www.privacyrights.org/data-breach`.

[52] B. Przydatek, D. Song, and A. Perrig. SIA: Secure Information Aggregation in Sensor Networks. In *ACM Conference on Embedded Networked Sensor Systems (SenSys)*, 2003.

[53] R. A. Popa, C. M. Redfield, N. Zeldovich, and H. Balakrishnan. CryptDB: Protecting Confidentiality with Encrypted Query Processing. In *ACM Symposium on Operating Systems Principles (SOSP)*, 2011.

[54] R. A. Popa, E. Stark, S. Valdez, J. Helfer, N. Zeldovich, and H. Balakrishnan. Building Web Applications on Top of Encrypted Data Using Mylar. In *USENIX Symposium on Networked Systems Design and Implementation (NSDI)*, 2014.

[55] R. A. Popa, Frank H. Li, and N. Zeldovich. An Ideal-Security Protocol for Order-Preserving Encoding. In *IEEE Symposium on Security and Privacy*, 2013.

[56] S. Halevi and P. Rogaway. A tweakable enciphering mode. In *Advances in Cryptology (CRYPTO)*, 2003.

[57] T. Sanamrad, L. Braun, D. Kossmann, and R. Venkatesan. Randomly Partitioned Encryption for Cloud Databases. In *Data and Applications Security and Privacy (DBSec)*, 2014.

[58] B. Schneier. Description of a new variable-length key, 64-bit block cipher (Blowfish). *Fast Software Encryption, Springer*, 1994.

[59] H. Shafagh, A. Hithnawi, A. Dröscher, S. Duquennoy, and W. Hu. Poster: Towards Encrypted Query Processing for the Internet of Things. In *ACM International Conference on Mobile Computing and Networking (MobiCom)*, 2015.

[60] A. Shamir. Identity-based Cryptosystems and Signature Schemes. In *Advances in Cryptology (CRYPTO)*, 1984.

[61] D. Shanks. Class Number, a Theory of Factorization, and Genera. In *Symposium Mathematical Society*, 1971.

[62] W. Stallings. *Cryptography and Network Security: Principles and Practice*. Pearson Education, 3rd edition, 2002.

[63] Texas Instruments. CC2538 System-on-Chip for 2.4-GHz IEEE 802.15.4. Online: `www.ti.com.cn/cn/lit/ug/swru319c/swru319c.pdf`, 2013.

SpinLight: A High Accuracy and Robust Light Positioning System for Indoor Applications

Bo Xie
University of Chinese Academy of Sciences
SIAT, Chinese Academy of Sciences, China
bo.xie@siat.ac.cn

Guang Tan
SIAT, Chinese Academy of Sciences
Shenzhen, China
guang.tan@siat.ac.cn

Tian He
University of Minnesota-Twin Cities
Minneapolis, MN 55455, U.S.
tianhe@cs.umn.edu

ABSTRACT

This paper presents *SpinLight*, an indoor positioning system that uses infrared LED lamps as signal transmitters, and light sensors as receivers. The main idea is to divide the space into *spatial beams* originating from the light source, and identify each beam with a unique timed sequence of light signals. This sequence is created by a coded shade that covers and rotates around the LED, blocking the light or allowing it to pass through according to pre-defined patterns. The receiver, equipped with a light sensor, is able to determine its spatial beam by detecting the light signals, followed by optimization schemes to refine its location within that beam. We present both 2D and 3D localization designs, demonstrated by a prototype implementation. Experiments show that SpinLight produces a median location error of 3.8 cm, with a 95th percentile of 6.8 cm. The receiver design is very low power and thus can operate for months to years from a button coin battery.

Categories and Subject Descriptors

C.5.3 [**COMPUTER SYSTEM IMPLEMENTATION**]: Microcomputers—*Portable devices (e.g., laptops, personal digital assistants)*

General Terms

Design, Experimentation

Keywords

Indoor positioning; Light; Sensing

1. INTRODUCTION

Fine-grained indoor localization can enable a multitude of applications. In the domain of manufacturing and warehouse management, robots with accurate location information can help to place, fetch or assemble objects. The same concept can be used for healthcare applications such as aid for the visually impaired, or as part of a home service for the elderly. In supermarkets and shopping malls, exact location of products can greatly improve the customer's shopping experience, promote targeted advertisements, and enable customer analytics [12]. In a recent survey [27], the market for location-based marketing and advertising is predicted to surpass 10 billion by 2018. To date, both the industry and academic community have made tremendous efforts to realize inexpensive, reliable, and easy-to-use location services, exploring a plethora of techniques, yet the adoption of high accuracy indoor localization is still in its infancy.

Recently, there has been an increase of interest in indoor localization using visual light communication (VLC) technologies [3, 12–14, 24, 34, 44], due to the pervasiveness of lighting infrastructure. Compared with radio frequency (RF) technologies, the propagation of light is more predictable, thus allowing more reliable location estimation using geometric models. For example, light intensity or RSS-based VLC localization has been explored in many previous studies [14, 34, 44]. Recent work shows that this approach can achieve accuracy to a half meter. The Angle of Arrival (AoA) approach [18] has also been considered for localization using smartphone cameras [3, 13].

In this paper we present a new approach to light-based localization, targeting object tracking applications and smartphone users. Apart from high accuracy, we want to achieve several goals that are important to the considered applications, and yet not completely fulfilled by prior work: (1) robustness against noise and ambient interference, (2) insensitivity to receiver orientation (provided line of sight), and (3) low energy consumption of location sensing, which is important to small-sized location tags.

In our system, called *SpinLight*, the 3D space is divided into *spatial beams* originating from the transmitter, whose coordinates are known in advance. Each beam is identified with a unique timed sequence of infrared (IR) signals. Here, we adopt infrared (IR) instead of visible light for avoiding visual disturbance to human eyes. The signal sequence is created by a hemispherical shade that covers and rotates around the LED under the drive of a programmed step motor. The shade is divided into cells by its longitude and altitude lines, and some cells are removed to allow the light to pass through. The rotation of the shade generates unique light patterns in different spatial beams. The receiver, equipped with a light sensor, is able to determine the spatial beam containing it by detecting and decoding the

SenSys'15, November 01–05, 2015, Seoul, South Korea..
© 2015 ACM. ISBN 978-1-4503-3631-4/15/11 ...$15.00.
DOI: http://dx.doi.org/10.1145/2809695.2809713.

signal pattern. With a single transmitter, the receiver can perform 2D localization, assuming a known height. An additional transmitter can be used to realize full 3D localization by creating two spatial beams whose intersection gives the receiver's location.

SpinLight features a digital-only approach in which sensors make binary decision as to the existence of a light signal. This is in contrast to existing light positioning approaches that rely on analog signals, i.e., RSS measurements. Given its digital nature, our system is significantly less affected by noise, interference, and multipath effect than RSS based systems, enjoying an order of magnitude improvement in location accuracy. Our digital approach also makes SpinLight insensitive to receiver orientation, which is shown to be a critical factor for RSS or AoA measurements and complicates receiver design [13, 14].

Very recently, there have been a few localization systems that achieve centimeter-level accuracy using RFID technology [35, 36, 43]. While these systems have the advantage of being able to work without line of sight, they fall short in several aspects, such as requiring highly dense deployment of reference tags [36], or only working for mobile objects [43]. These techniques and our design therefore have complementary functions and characteristics.

In summary, this paper makes two major contributions:

1. We propose a light positioning approach based on the idea of spatial division. Fundamentally differing from traditional methods such as RSS or AoA, this approach allows more robust localization at the receiver, with reduced requirements on receiver design and user's cooperation, and at a very low power consumption rate.
2. We present a series of optimization schemes to refine the location results of the basic design, and deal with the problem of gray areas, which are a major source of errors. Experiments show that with a single transmitter, the median location error is 3.6 cm. An additional transmitter allows 3D localization, with median accuracy of 3.8 cm. In both cases, the 95th percentiles are within 9.2 cm. The results are robust against environmental dynamics and interference.

The next section provides an overview of our system; Section 3 describes a coarse-grained localization approach; Section 4 presents optimization schemes to refine the location and deal with errors; Section 5 describes how to perform 3D localization; Section 6 presents the experimental results; Section 7 discusses several practical issues of the system; Section 8 introduces related work, and Section 9 concludes the paper.

2. SYSTEM OVERVIEW

In this section, we outline the basic design of SpinLight. The transmitter's 3D coordinates are known in advance. For simplicity, we assume that the receiver is placed on the floor plane, that is, its height $z = 0$. This assumption will be removed when we discuss 3D localization.

The transmitter device contains an IR LED chip embedded in the center of a circular base plane, which is mounted on the ceiling. Current LED chips at a few watts are quite small in size (e.g., 0.5 cm×0.5 cm), so can be approximately considered a point light source in the field. The LED chip is controlled by a microcontroller (MCU) to flash at specified

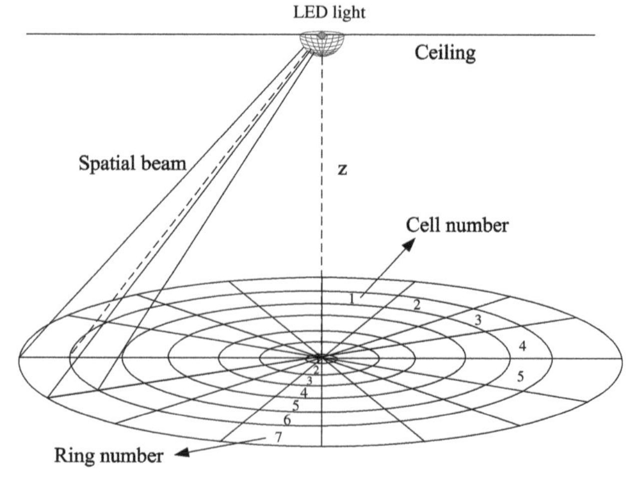

Figure 1: Spinlight overview. The system primarily comprises an IR LED lamp covered by a hemisphere shade. The shade is divided into cells that define the spatial beams. The task of the receiver is to find the beam it belongs to.

Figure 2: A shade divided into 8 s-rings, each further divided into 48 s-cells. A hollow cell represents a 1, and a closed cell 0.

rates, in order to distinguish itself from other transmitters and ambient lights in the frequency domain.

There is a hemispherical shade that covers the LED chip from below, and can rotate horizontally around the chip at a constant speed under the drive of a step motor. The shade is evenly divided to *shade rings* (or s-rings for short) and *shade cells* (s-cells) following longitude and latitude lines with pre-defined intervals, see Figure 1 for an illustration. If the shade stays still, then from the viewpoint of the light source, each s-cell is projected onto the floor, forming an area which we call a *cell.* A shade ring's projection on the floor is called a *ring.* Along with the transmitter's coordinates, the shade's radius and division parameters are also known to the receiver. The information of system configuration can be provided by a location server. Thus, assuming a known height, the receiver can calculate the layout of the projected rings and cells of a transmitter on its plane.

On the shade, some s-cells are removed to create holes, or hollow s-cells, allowing the light to pass through and form solid beams of light. These light beams generate light spots on the floor. If we label an open s-cell '1', and a closed one '0', then the arrangement of the cells creates a *coding scheme* of the shade, see Figure 2 for an example. When the shade spins around, the light beams rotate in the air, and the light spots on the floor move around in a way like the spotlight shadows on a dance floor. When a light spot sweeps across

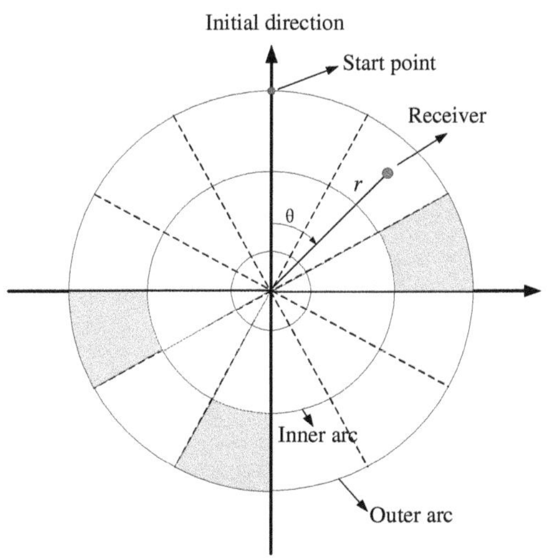

Figure 3: Projection of the coded shade.

the receiver, the light sensor will detect a window of light signal, called a *signal window*. For each s-ring, we create holes in different ways, so that receivers located in different rings can detect different flash patterns, so as to find their own rings.

Due to symmetry, receivers within different cells of the same ring will see the same sequence of signal. To differentiate the cells, we introduce a synchronization mechanism. We mark a *start point* on the upper edge of the shade, and use its angular offset clockwise from some initial direction (e.g., geographical north) to define the shade's *current direction*. Also, the LED light uses two different flash rates, and switches between the two when the shade's start point hits the initial direction. By detecting the switch of the flashing rate, the receiver knows that a new round of shade rotation begins. Thereafter, the receiver counts the number of signal windows passed to estimate its angular offset to the initial direction, called its *angle*, and determine its cell number. Section 3 describes how the receiver determines its cell number.

Identifying the receiver's cell only gives a rough location result. We propose a method to fine-tune the receiver's location. The idea is to use a specially shaped cell in each s-ring. This cell is shaped in such a way that the receiver will detect a signal window whose length is a function of the receiver's offsets to the cell's edges. With this approach, the receiver can estimate its relative position within its cell. Section 4 covers the details.

When z is unknown, position ambiguity will arise – at each height the receiver can find a spot that satisfies the timed flash pattern. In fact, there is a ray from the light source that contains infinitely many candidate positions for the receiver. In this case, we use two transmitters to create two candidate rays, whose intersection is the receiver's real position. Section 5 describes how the position is obtained.

3. 2D LOCALIZATION

In this section we first introduce the rotation control of the shade, whose main purpose is to let the receiver know when a new round of shade rotation begins, in order to calculate its angle with respect to the initial direction. We then describe the coding design and how a receiver processes the received signal to determine its cell and final location.

We focus on a 2D plane, onto which the shade is projected. Figure 3 shows an example of the projected area in the form of a polar grid, where the shade's current direction is zero. In this polar coordinate system, the receiver's location is represented by radius r and angle θ. With known 3D coordinates of the transmitter, (r, θ) can be translated to a 2D location. There are M rings, each consisting of N cells. There is a one-to-one correspondence between a cell on the floor and an s-cell on the shade. A ring consists of two circles, an *inner circle* and an *outer circle*. A cell has two arcs, one on its inner circle, called the *inner arc*, and the other on its outer circle, called the *outer arc*.

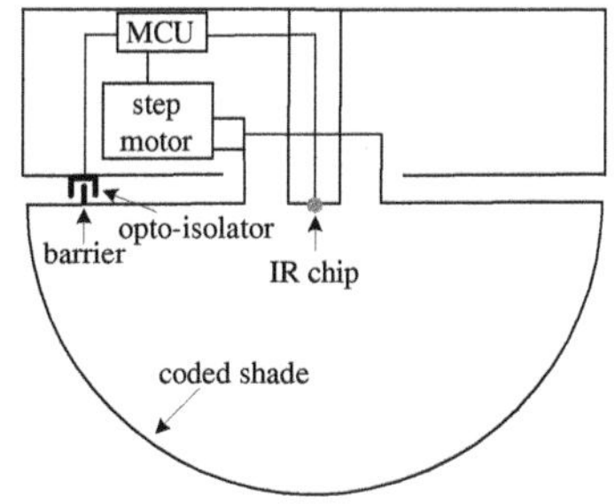

Figure 4: Structure of transmitter.

3.1 Rotation and flash control

The shade rotates horizontally around the LED chip at a constant speed in revolutions per minute (rpm). Thus, it takes the shade a constant time, called a *cell period*, to rotate the width of an s-cell. Apart from controlling the step motor, the MCU also switches on and off the light at two pre-defined frequencies. Figure 4 gives an illustration of the lamp structure. To enable the receiver to obtain its angle, an opto-isolator [21] is used. The opto-isolator is a U-shaped component, in which the IR signal is transmitted from one side to the other. We also install a small piece of plastic as a barrier on the start point of the shade. When the barrier passes through the opto-isolator, the IR light is blocked and a state change is triggered and transferred to the MCU, which then switches to another flash rate. Upon detecting a switch of flash rate, the receiver starts to count the number of cells passed, each corresponding to a signal window, to estimate its angle.

3.2 Shade coding and cell recognition

A hollow s-cell on the shade allows the light to pass through, so is labeled '1'; a closed s-cell blocks the light, so is labeled '0'. The code of each s-ring primarily comprises three parts: (1) leading bits, which help the receiver to identify the start point of the shade; (2) ring ID bits, used to identify rings; and (3) extension bits. There are also some spacing bits between the different parts.

The leading bits are simply a sequence of 1 cells, which generate a sequence of signal windows that are easy to identify. The design of the ring IDs is more complicated. Apart from being unique, it needs to tolerate errors. This requires it to encode more information. We adopt a layered structure, in which a ring ID is represented by several *macro bits*, each further represented by a number of regular bits. The

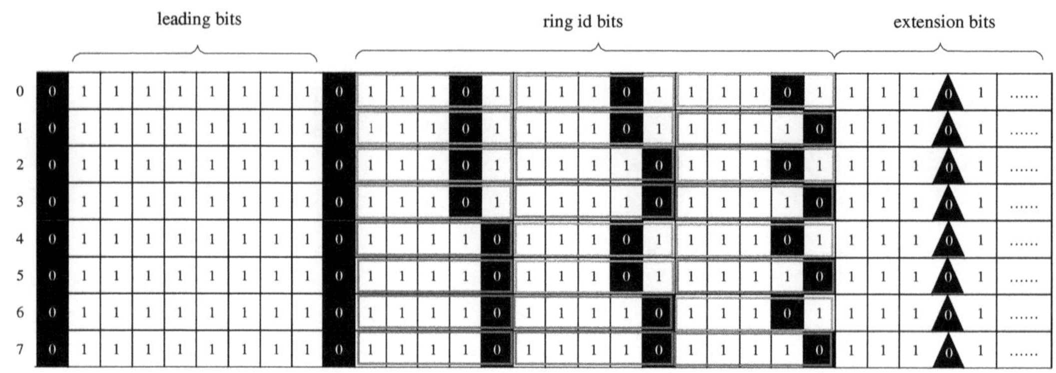

Figure 5: An example of shade code. A blue rectangle represents a macro bit **1**, and a red rectangle a macro bit **0**.

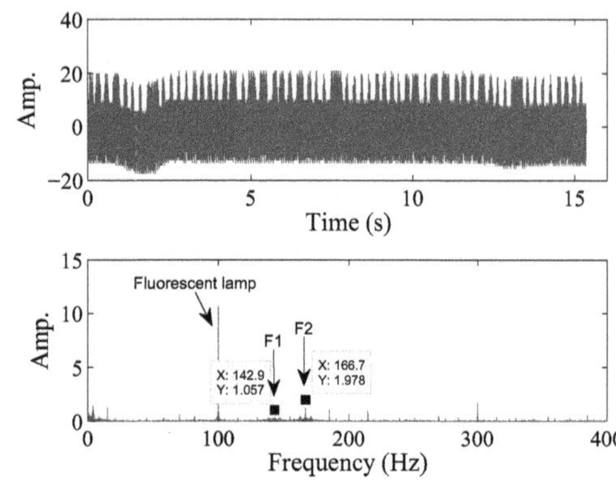

(a) Signals in time and frequency

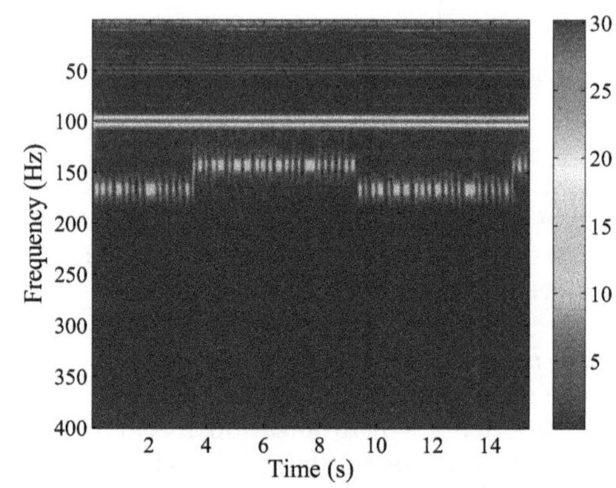

(b) Spectrogram of signals

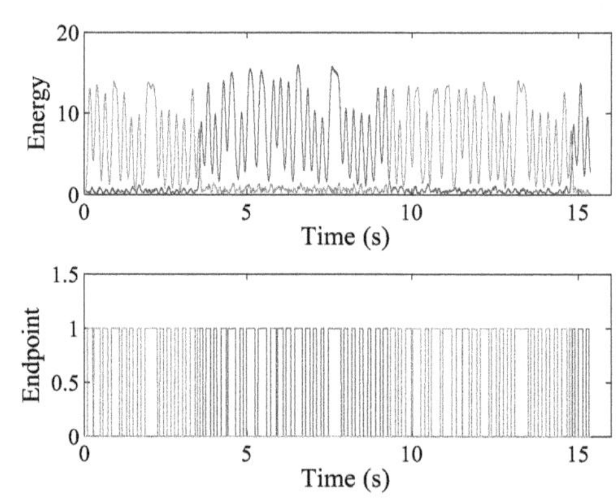

(c) Endpoint Detection

Figure 6: Signal processing for cell recognition.

extension bits are for optimizing location accuracy, and may be used for other purposes such as advanced error detection, which we leave for future study. The leading bits must be longer than a macro bit, and in the same ring, no two 0 bits are allowed to appear together. Figure 5 gives an example of shade coding, in which cells are displayed in squares for clarity. In this example, there are eight s-rings, numbered from **000** to **111**. A macro bit **0** is represented by regular bits 11101, and a macro bit **1** by 11110.

On the receiver, the received signal is a mixture of light signals from multiple sources, including possibly more than one transmitters, daylight, as well as ordinary lamps. For example, Figure 6(a) shows a sequence of signals obtained by a receiver and its frequency components. Note that the average amplitude is subtracted from the raw signal, and the fluctuation of the signal is due to interference from a person walking by while collecting the data. The transmitter uses two flash rates: 143 Hz and 167 Hz, mixed with IR from fluorescent lamps at 100 Hz. We use the wavelet transform as our signal processing tool. Figure 6(b) shows the spectrogram of the signal that contains three frequency components. A bright spot corresponds to a time interval during

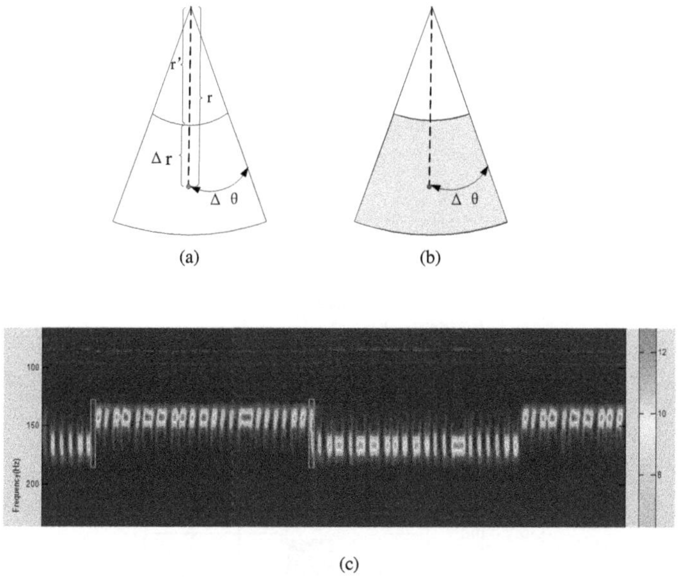

Figure 7: The receiver's location offsets, Δr and $\Delta\theta$, to its cell edges. (a) Receiver is located in a 1 cell. (b) Receiver is located in a 0 cell. (c) Wavelet spectrogram of signals used to estimate $\Delta\theta$ for a receiver initially located in a 0 cell.

which a light beam scans across the light sensor, while a gap between bright spots means a time interval during which the light is blocked. The brighter the spots, the stronger the signal. The top level is from the surrounding fluorescent lamps, which together emit IR about seven times stronger than the light from the transmitter. From the receiver's viewpoint, the sequence of bright and dark spots reflects the ring code. For example, the longest segment of consecutive bright spots represent the leading bits.

From the results of wavelet transform, we can further get the energy function of the signal, as shown in the upper panel of Figure 6(c). By filtering out irrelevant frequency components (in this case the 100 Hz one), using an endpoint detection method like those adopted in the field of speech recognition, and normalizing the energy, we can obtain the ring code shown in the lower panel of Figure 6(c). In accordance with Figure 6(b), the width of a bar is proportional to the number of 1 bits. The ring ID part directly gives the receiver's ring number, while the time interval between the first flash rate switch point and the beginning of the leading bits implies the receiver's cell number. The center of the determined cell (i.e., intersection of the cell's diagonals) is taken as the receiver's location.

4. 2D LOCALIZATION: OPTIMIZATIONS

The receiver's ring number and cell number only provide a rough estimate of its real location. To improve accuracy, one could manage to create highly dense s-cells on the shade. Suppose we want to limit the size of a (possibly distant) cell on the floor to a few centimeters, an s-cell may need a sub-millimeter level size. This will generate very blurry cell edges, because the holes are smaller than the LED chip. As a result, the receiver faces more uncertainty in detecting cells, and likely generate more errors. Moreover, a delicate construction of the shade complicates the design of the transmitter, which increases the cost. In this section we describe how to refine the location result in a software approach, and how to deal with some reliability issues arising in this process.

4.1 Fine-grained localization

To locate the receiver at a finer grain, we need to obtain its relative location to the edges of its cell. As illustrated in Figure 7(a), define $\Delta r = |r - r'|$ as the receiver's radial offset, where r is the receiver's radius, and r' the radius of its ring's inner circle. Also, define the angular offset, $\Delta\theta = |\theta - \theta'|$ as the angular distance to the side of cell that is closer to the initial direction clockwise. We label a cell '1' if its corresponding s-cell is 1, and '0' otherwise.

4.1.1 Determining $\Delta\theta$

There are two cases to deal with when determining $\Delta\theta$. First, if the receiver's location is in a 1 cell (Figure 7(a)), then the receiver is likely to see a non-integral multiple of cell periods since the shade starts a new round of rotation. Figure 6(c) gives an example in which the first bar of the blue wave is only a fraction of a regular signal window. This fraction multiplied by a cell's width in degree, that is, $360/N$, is then equal to $\Delta\theta$.

If, however, the receiver is located in a 0 cell (Figure 7(b)), then $\Delta\theta$ cannot be obtained using the above method, because the receiver will miss the light signal for an interval of $\Delta\theta$ at the beginning of a new round of rotation, and cannot know the duration of this blackout (note we do not assume clock synchronization between the transmitter and receiver). We propose a *shifted round synchronization* strategy to solve the problem. Recall that when the shade's current direction becomes zero, the MCU will instruct the LED to switch to another flash rate. In our strategy, the rate switch does not happen immediately. Instead, before switching to a certain flash rate, for example the higher one, the MCU stays one more cell period at the lower rate. Since there exist no two 0 bits together in a ring, the one-cell shift will ensure that a receiver initially located in a 0 cell will be exposed to light at the beginning of the next round of rotation, as if it were moved to the next cell clockwise in the ring. Following the method in Figure 7(a), the receiver can obtain $\Delta\theta$. Also, by detecting the pre-determined flash rate (in this case the higher one), the receiver knows it is in a shifted round of rotation, and will compensate for a cell period when calculating θ.

Figure 7(c) provides a concrete example of estimating $\Delta\theta$ for a receiver initially located in a 0 cell. The spectrogram of signal shows the two frequencies of the light, the higher frequency f_h represented by the lower level of light spots, and the lower frequency f_l by the upper level of light spots. As the shade's current direction becomes 0, an $f_h \rightarrow f_l$ switch takes place immediately. At the same time the receiver is covered by a dark (i.e., 0) cell, so will experience a blackout for a partial cell period, see the first blank rectangle in red line in Figure 7(c). From this blackout period, the receiver cannot know its relative position in the cell. Now look at the second rectangle, which represents the time of frequency change $f_l \rightarrow f_h$. With our one-cell shift strategy, the frequency change will be delayed by a cell period, allowing the receiver to be exposed to light for a partial cell period. This can be seen from the upper part of the second rectangle. The remaining cell period is left to f_h. From the split of the cell period, the receiver can obtain $\Delta\theta$.

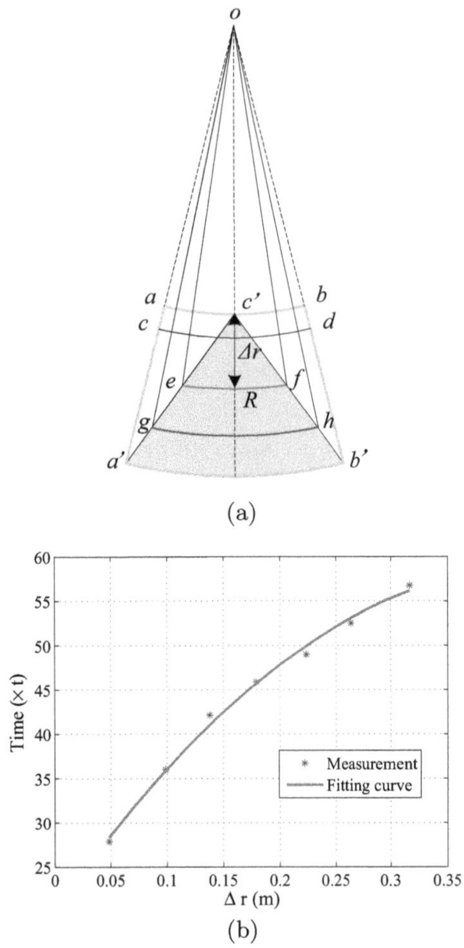

Figure 8: Illustration of the method to obtain Δr. (a) A triangle-like area in the cell $abb'a'$ that generates variable length of scan-arcs (e.g., red and blue arcs) for different Δr. (b) Measured scan-arc length in time for various Δr in a special cell, where t is the data sampling interval.

4.1.2 *Determining* Δr

For Δr, we propose a solution based on the idea of *variable window length.* Because a cell has a constant angular width, a receiver of different radius within the same cell will receive signal windows of equal length. It is this uniformity that causes the ambiguity of a receiver's radial coordinate. Figure 8 (a) shows a 1 cell, $abb'a'$, in which the two arcs ab and cd, generate signal windows of the same length, and thus are indistinguishable to a receiver on these two arcs. To solve this problem, we choose a special 1 cell on the shade, select a subarea in the shape of a spherical triangle, and close it. The spherical triangle takes the outer arc of the cell as its base side, and the middle point of the inner arc as one of its vertices. This subarea casts a shadow on the floor, see $a'b'c'$ in Figure 8 (a). Given a point with radial offset Δr in the cell, define the *scan-arc* as the intersection of this shadow area and the (0,0) centered circle passing through this point, see for example the red arc in Figure 8. The sides of $a'b'c'$ have the property that the scan-arc has monotonically increasing central angle with Δr. In Figure 8 (a), this means that $\angle eof < \angle goh$ for increasing Δr. This way, we establish a monotonic function that maps a Δr to

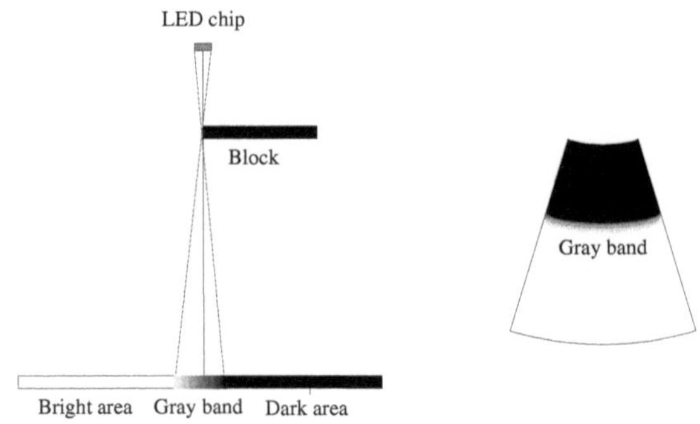

Figure 9: IR beads create gray bands between dark and bright areas.

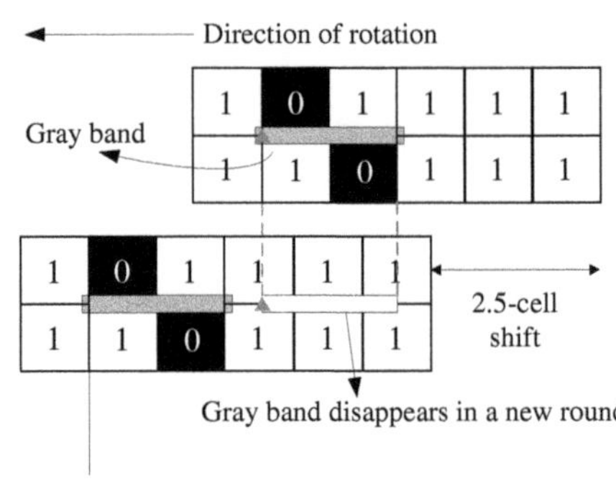

Figure 10: Avoiding gray areas by shifting 2.5 cell periods.

the angular distance of a scan-arc. When the receiver detects a signal window from this special cell, it measures the length of the scan-arc, and obtains Δr with this function.

In practice, the narrow tip of a triangular area may cause error of Δr due to the gray area problem (to be discussed in the next section). Thus, we choose to use a trapezoid-like shape, with the only difference that the tip is now an upper base. Figure 8 (b) shows the lengths of scan-arcs for various Δr measured for a special cell. We can see that the relationship between Δr and scan-arc length is highly predictable.

4.2 Dealing with gray areas

So far we have assumed that the LED offers a point source of light. In practice, however, this is not the case. The illuminating LED beads are actually embedded in a small plane with certain spacing, which will create gray bands between cells. Figure 9 shows how gray bands are formed by a non-point of light source. The gray band is an area with continuously decreasing gray degree from full darkness to full brightness. Thus, depending on the threshold value chosen for distinguishing 0 and 1, a cell's effective area may extend to a neighboring cell. In the example of Figure 9, a narrow area of the 0 cell above the geometrical border of the two cells may be seen as part of the 1 cell below, or vice versa. In these cases, we say that a cell *encroaches on* the other cell.

Gray bands can occur between cells within the same ring, or across two neighboring rings, with width much smaller than a cell's side length. The former can be coped with the shifted round synchronization method described earlier, here we consider the *cross-ring gray bands.* Such areas only

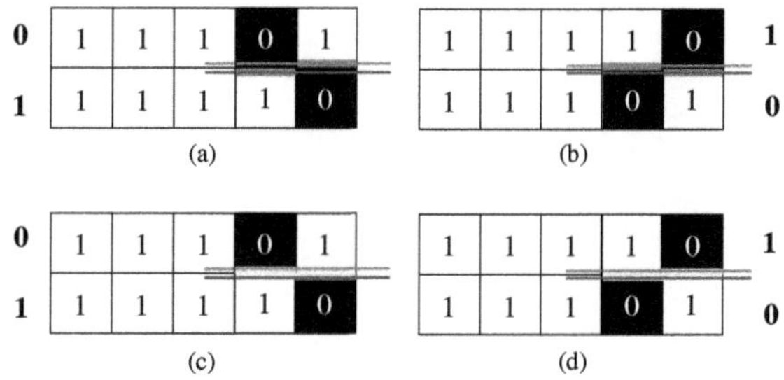

Figure 11: Erroneous cell readings due to gray bands. Red and blue lines are two examples of near-border locations where errors may occur. (a,b) Dark cells encroach on bright ones, causing erroneous reading 00. (c,d) Bright cells encroach on dark ones, causing erroneous reading 11.

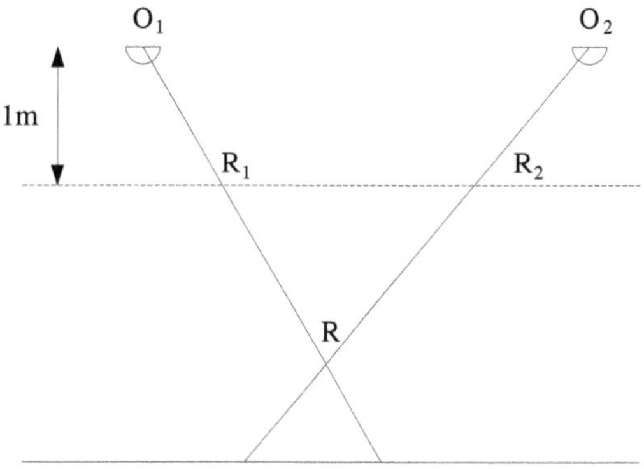

Figure 12: 3D localization with two transmitters.

occur on the border between a 1 cell and a 0 cell from two neighboring rings. In general, a receiver located in such an area may mistakenly determine the value of its cell. This leads to two potential problems for the receiver's localization: inaccurate estimation of $\Delta\theta$ and wrong determination of ring number (hence r).

Figure 10 shows a possible result of the first problem. In the figure, the receiver (red triangle) is located in the gray area between the two rings. Suppose the light signal is too weak for it to detect, then it will miss the light signal for at least two cell periods before two vertically (along radial direction) neighboring 1 cells come across. Thus the receiver cannot properly estimate $\Delta\theta$, even by shifting one cell period. Our solution for this problem is to have the shade shift two and a half cell periods instead of one, where the extra half cell period is to avoid the small gray areas around a cell's vertices. By the coding rule, no two 0 cells appear together within a ring, and any 10 and 01 cell combination must be surrounded by three consecutive 1 cells, so the 2.5 cell shift must allow an initially shadowed receiver to be exposed to the light in a new round. In our final design, the 2.5 cell shift strategy is implemented with the lower flash rate. Upon detecting the lower flash rate for a half period cell, the receiver can obtain $\Delta\theta'$, and then $\Delta\theta$ is obtained by adding the degree of 2.5 cell periods, that is $2.5 \times 360/N$, to $\Delta\theta'$.

For the second problem, we show that the potential error can be corrected with the coding rules and the triangle cells. Again, the errors can only happen between two vertically neighboring and different cells. This further means that an error can only occur between two vertically neighboring and different macro bits. Figure 11 shows the possible situations of two neighboring rings where such a situation may happen.

Suppose the 0-1 determination threshold value is set such that a 0 cell encroaches on a vertically neighboring 1 cell. Consider the example in Figure 11(a). If the receiver is located on the upper red line, then it will determine a 00 for the two cells crossed by the red line. The same goes for the lower blue line in Figure 11(a). In other words, if a 0 cell encroaches on a 1 cell, then 00 will always be determined for the last two (regular) bits of each corresponding macro bit. By the coding rules, bits 00 are illegal, so the receiver will recognize such an error. At the same time, the receiver will detect a relative wide dark band from the special cell, and thus realize it is near the border of two neighboring rings. Now look at the ring ID parts coded in macro bits, and examine the possible situations of two rings, k and $k+1$, whose ID parts may induce such an error. Let $k = \mathbf{b}_1\mathbf{b}_2\ldots\mathbf{b}_s$, where macro bit $\mathbf{b}_i \in \{\mathbf{0},\mathbf{1}\}$, then there are three cases where an increase from number k to $k+1$ will cause changes of macro bits:

1. $\mathbf{b}_1\mathbf{b}_2\ldots\mathbf{b}_{s-1}\mathbf{0}$ to $\mathbf{b}_1\mathbf{b}_2\ldots\mathbf{b}_{s-1}\mathbf{1}$, for example **0000** to **0001**,

2. $\mathbf{b}_1\mathbf{b}_2\ldots\mathbf{b}_{s-2}\mathbf{01}$ to $\mathbf{b}_1\mathbf{b}_2\ldots\mathbf{b}_{s-2}\mathbf{10}$, for example **0001** to **0010**,

3. $\mathbf{b}_1\mathbf{b}_2\ldots\mathbf{b}_{s-t-1}\mathbf{0}\mathbf{1}_1\ldots\mathbf{1}_t$ to $\mathbf{b}_1\mathbf{b}_2\ldots\mathbf{b}_{s-t-1}\mathbf{1}\mathbf{0}_1\ldots\mathbf{0}_t$, for example **0011** to **0100**

In all three cases, the two ring IDs will differ in their last few macro bits, which are aligned vertically in the code. Any pair of vertically adjacent and different macro bits will generate erroneous readings 00. Thus, the two ring IDs may generate one or more such erroneous readings. For example, if the receiver detects 00 for two consecutive macro bits, then it learns that its adjacent two rings must have **01** and **10** as their ending macro bits. More generally, from the number of consecutive macro bits that go wrong, the receiver can determine the last few macro bits of its surrounding two rings. Combining this with the other correctly recognized macro bits, the receiver is able to recover k and $k+1$.

If instead the 0-1 determination threshold value is set such that a 1 cell encroaches on a vertically neighboring 0 cell, as illustrated in Figures 11(c) and (d), then the above argument still holds except that the erroneous reading 00 becomes 11, and the receiver can find k in a similar way.

With k determined, the receiver simply takes the radius of the border circle between ring k and ring $k+1$ as its r. Combining $\Delta\theta$ obtained earlier and r it can obtain its location.

5. 3D LOCALIZATION

So far we have assumed a known height of the receiver, and obtained a 2D location. This is useful for some applications such as robot navigation [6], or object tracking on fixed height carriers. Other applications may require a full 3D location. Notice that within a 3D spatial beam generated by the cells on the lamp shade, the receiver will detect exactly the same flash pattern. Given a 2D location spot p with an assumed height, we draw a ray from the LED to

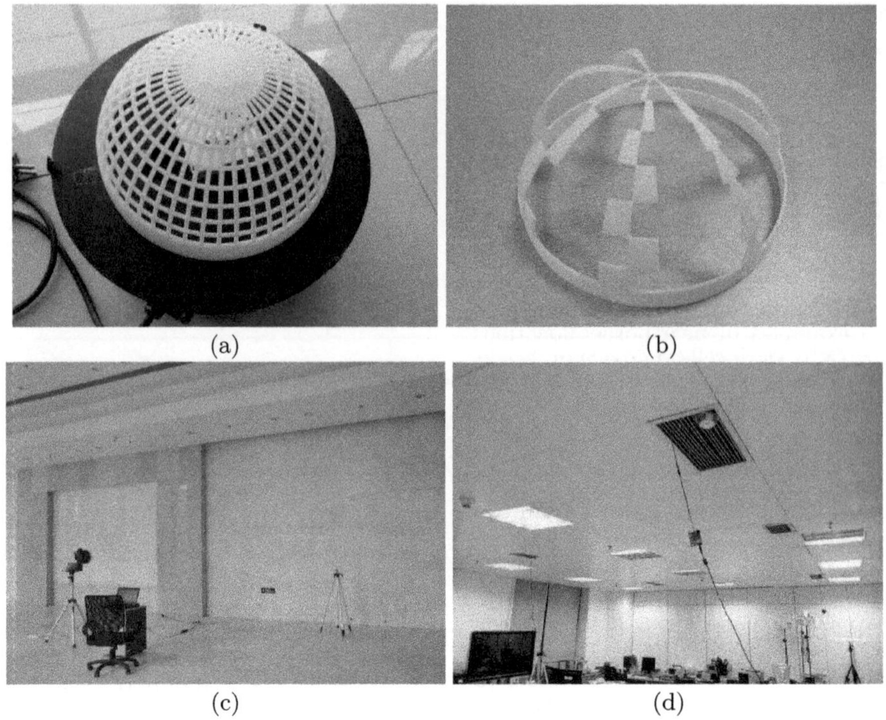

Figure 13: Experimental environments. (a) A SpinLight transmitter with a shade in its general form, (b) An example of the final shade with fixed coding, (c) Test environment for SpinLight, (d) Test environment for Epsilon, Multi-Sensor, and Weighted-Avg, where three LED lamps are mounted on the ceiling.

p, then the ray contains infinitely many points that satisfy the flash pattern constraints. Therefore, without a known height, we need at least an additional transmitter that generates another ray to solve for a 3D location. In our design, for every transmitter detected, the receiver first assumes it has a fixed height (e.g., 1 m) from the ceiling, and obtain a location, generate a ray. For multiple transmitters, the receiver finds a point that has minimum accumulative distance to all the rays using a least square method. Figure 12 provides an example in which two transmitters help the receiver at R determine its location by first finding two candidate points R_1 and R_2, creating two rays O_1R_1 and O_1R_2, whose intersection gives the receiver's location.

6. EXPERIMENTAL EVALUATION

We have implemented a prototype system of SpinLight. Figure 13(a) shows the transmitter, containing an LED chip of 3 W, covered by a 3D printed shade whose hollow cells can be covered by opaque paper to create closed cells. The used code of the shade follows Figure 5. By default, we use a single transmitter flashing at the two frequencies depicted in Figure 6. During the experiments, ordinary fluorescent lamps are turned on, which generate both visible and IR light signals at 100 Hz. For convenience of experimentation, we let the transmitter face a wall at a distance of 2.8 m to simulate a ceiling mounted lamp, see Figure 13(b). The light covers a circular area of radius 5.5 m. For 2D localization, the distance to the wall is assumed to be known to the receiver. For 3D cases, we need signal from two transmitters. This is realized by moving the transmitter to two locations 3 m apart, and collecting data separately. The raw data from the two sources are then combined before processing. Note that the environmental conditions remain the same when the transmitter works at two locations, implying that the mixed data are actually subject to stronger noise and interference than in the case of two transmitters emitting signal simultaneously.

The receiver comprises an MCU and an Intersil ISL29023 sensor [11] for light sensing, which can be configured to sense IR or visible light, and has been used in smartphones such as the Motorola XT882. For the 2D case, 131 points in the covered area are picked with uniform randomness, at which the receiver is tested. For the 3D case, we pick 59 points in the intersection area of the two lamps.

We compare five methods of light localization:

1. SpinLight-2D: the 2D version of SpinLight using a single transmitter;
2. SpinLight-3D: the 3D version of SpinLight using two transmitters;
3. Epsilon [14]: it uses the classic trilateration method based on a Lambertian RSS model, which relates light intensity with distance and angles of the signal [5].
4. Multi-sensor: in contrast to trilateration, this approach uses a single light but multiple light sensors to locate the receiver, based also on the Lambertian model. The approach is discussed in [44], simulated with manual operation in [14], and implemented in [40].
5. RSS Weighted Average (Weighted-Avg): it is an intuitive solution in which the receiver locates itself based on a weighted average of the transmitters' locations in range, where the weight is proportional to the square root of RSS;

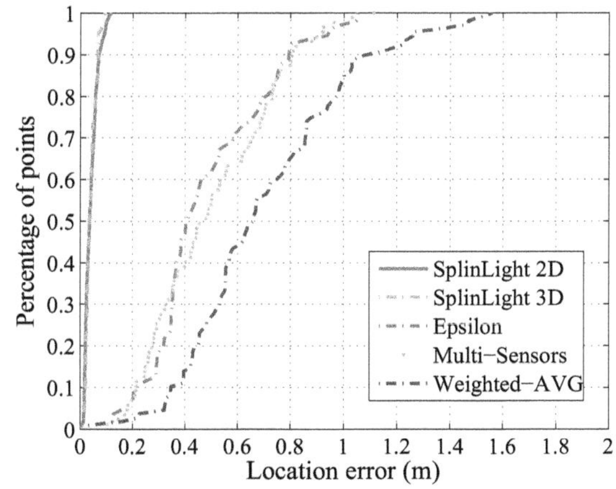

Figure 14: CDF of location error of different methods.

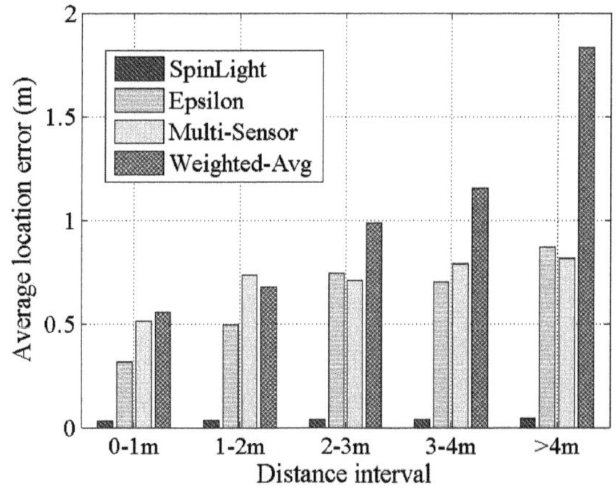

Figure 15: Location accuracy for various distance to the transmitters.

For some experiments, we will focus on 2D localization. In this case we simply use 'SpinLight' to represent 'SpinLight-2D'. For Weighted-Avg and Epsilon, we choose three IR LED lights of 8 W, and mount them onto the ceiling (Figure 13(c)). During the experiments, the receiver board is horizontally placed and the light sensor always faces upward. For Multi-sensor, we manually create multiple orientations to simulate multiple sensors, following [14].

6.1 Localization accuracy

Figure 14 presents the cumulative distribution functions (CDFs) of the different methods' location errors, and Table 1 gives some statistics of the errors. The Weighted-Avg method performs the worst, with a median error of 0.76 m, due to the coarse grained proximity detection. Epsilon and Multi-sensor produce median errors of 0.413 m and 0.481 m, respectively, which are comparable with the results in the literature. The improvements come from a more accurate RSS/AoA model, that is, the Lambertian radiation pattern. Compared with these analog signal based methods, SpinLight provides a dramatic improvement in location accuracy with a pure digital design, reducing the median error to within 0.04 m, which is an order of magnitude smaller than the errors of Epsilon and Multi-sensor. Also, it can be seen that both Epsilon and Multi-sensor have a standard deviation an order of magnitude higher than that of SpinLight, because RSS is more sensitive to noise and environmental interference.

6.2 Effect of distance

The receiver's distance to the transmitter largely determines light intensity, hence signal-noise ratio (SNR). For RSS or AoA based localization methods, a lower SNR often introduces greater error in distance or angle estimation. In this experiment, we consider the 2D case of SpinLight, and measure the receiver's distance to the transmitter's projection on the floor (or center of projections when there are multiple transmitters). The distances are divided into intervals of 1 m; for each interval, we calculate the average location error of each method. Figure 15 compares the performance of these methods. We can see that SpinLight performs stably over different distances, while the other methods generally have increasing location error for larger distances to the transmitter. For Epsilon, the location error increases by about three times from within 1 m to beyond 4 m. This is because RSS attenuates according to a square law, which implies that at a relatively large distance, the RSS becomes very small, and the same level of noise and environment interference will cause more uncertainty in distance estimate than at a small distance. The same problem exists for incident angle estimation. For Weighted-Avg, a similar trend can be found, due to the same reason as for Epsilon.

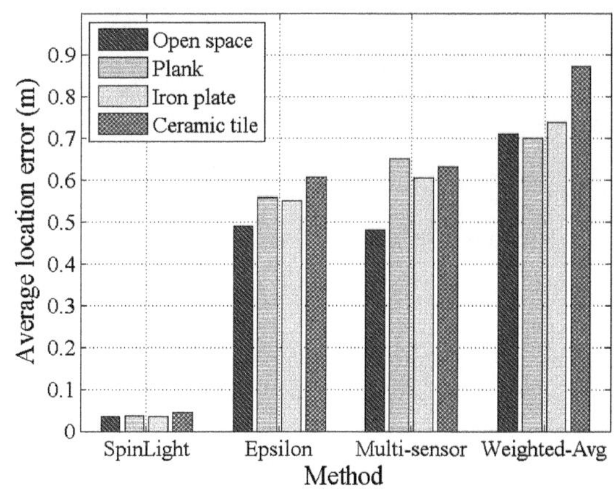

Figure 16: Effect of reflection.

6.3 Effect of reflection

We create various reflection conditions to examine the different methods' performance in more realistic settings. Objects of various types, including no object (open space), plank, non-polished iron plate, and ceramic tile, are considered. The objects are placed near the receiver and about 5 cm farther away from the transmitter, with their plane facing the light, or one of the lights in cases of multiple transmitters (as with Epsilon and Weighted-Avg). Figure 16 shows the average location error under the different conditions. It can be seen that for SpinLight, the location error is relatively stable under the different conditions, mainly be-

	Error statistics (m)					
Method	Min	Median	Mean	Max	95th Prtl	Stdev
SpinLight 2D	**0.004**	**0.036**	**0.041**	0.118	0.092	0.023
SpinLight 3D	0.016	0.038	**0.041**	**0.092**	**0.068**	**0.020**
Epsilon	0.124	0.413	0.490	1.112	0.923	0.230
Multi-sensor	0.103	0.481	0.505	1.050	0.938	0.236
Weighted-Avg	0.184	0.760	0.780	1.05	1.344	0.313

Table 1: Location error statistics of different methods.

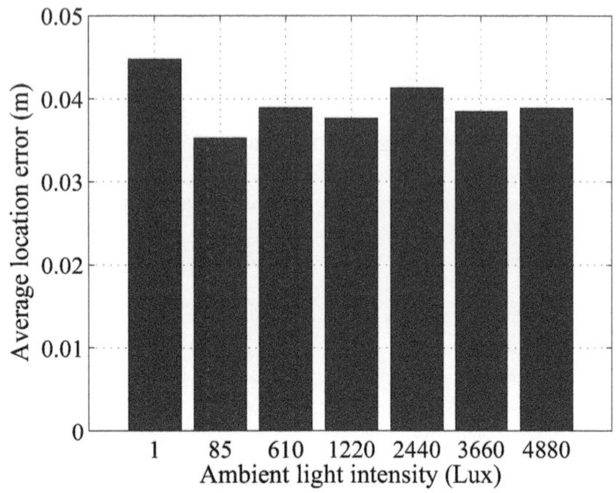

Figure 17: Effect of ambient lights.

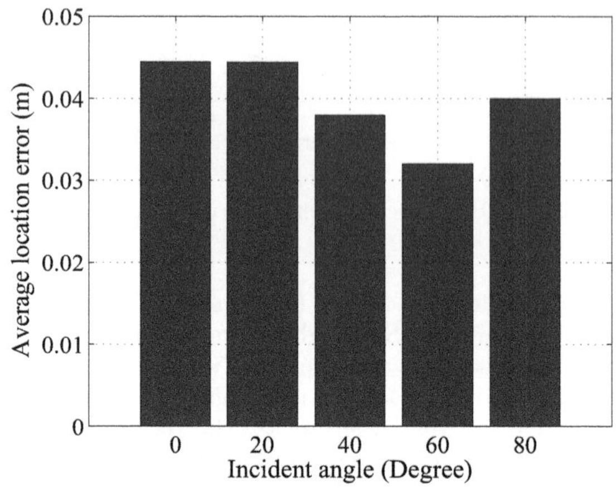

Figure 18: Effect of receiver orientation.

cause the impact of light intensity (RSS) is subdued by the binary decision in SpinLight's localization algorithm. For other methods, the location error increases quite noticeably in the presence of reflection. In particular, the ceramic tile is among the materials that have the greatest impact on location accuracy, possibly because it has a smooth surface and thus a high reflection ratio.

6.4 Effect of ambient lights

In this section we consider how a SpinLight receiver behaves under different conditions of ambient lights. We choose different places in the room at different times of the day, and select seven grades of illuminance (lux): 1, 85, 610, 1220, 2440, 3660, 4880, where 1 lux means a dark room, and 85 corresponds to a room with a few fluorescent lamps on but without daylight. The other grades represent different conditions of illuminance; for example, 4880 lux represents a location near the window on a clear day, but without direct sunlight. Figure 17 shows that for the different conditions, the average location error remains around 0.04 m, with no noticeable impact from variation of ambient lights.

6.5 Effect of orientation

A light sensor is known to be very sensitive to the incident angle of light. For RSS or AoA based localization methods, the incident angle is a key factor in the location model, and has to be carefully accounted for. Past systems use accelerometers and magnetic sensors to estimate the angle of the sensor's surface, which introduce extra errors. For example, due to magnetic interferences from metals and electronic devices, a magnetic sensor inside a building can generate errors up to tens of degrees [14, 40], which makes the location result very unreliable. We examine SpinLight's sensitivity to the receiver's orientation, by placing the receiver at a fixed location, and adjusting the incident angle from 0° (perpendicular to light) to 80°, with a 20° step size. We consider the single-transmitter, 2D case, and select 13 test points across the covered area with various distances to the center. Figure 18 shows the location error for the five incident angles at 13 test locations (colorful bars). Overall, there is no clear correlation between incident angle and location accuracy, which fluctuates between 0.03 m and 0.045 m in most cases. This indicates that SpinLight is robust against receiver orientation, thus provides more flexibility in application than RSS/AoA based solutions.

6.6 Effect of location optimizations

In Section 4, we have introduced how to use specially shaped cells and partial cell recognition to refine the location results obtained by the basic design, in which a receiver takes the center of its cell as its location. In this section we examine how these optimizations improve location accuracy. Figure 19 compares the accuracies of SpinLight with and without the optimizations. We can see the accuracy is improved by 3.9 times to 12.0 times with optimizations, depending on distance. Moreover, the larger the distance to the light source, the larger the error without optimizations. This is because the size of cells grows as the ring number increases, which makes the location obtained more coarse grained.

7. DISCUSSION

In this section we discuss a number of practical issues of the system.

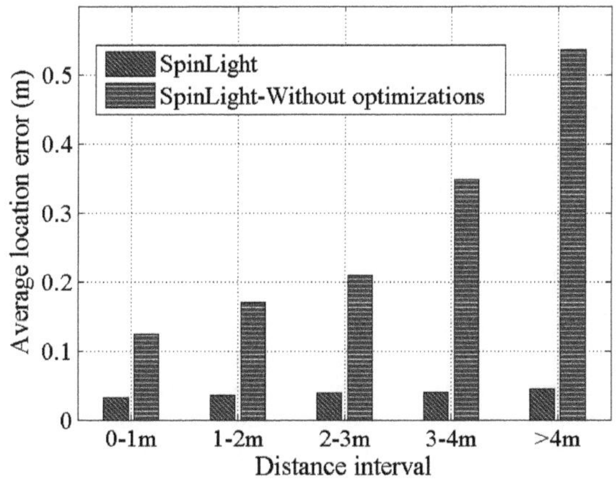

Figure 19: Effect of location optimizations.

7.1 Deployment issues and usability

In our current implementation, an LED light with only 3 W power rate covers an area of around 95 m^2. Given a higher power level (e.g., 10 W as in [14]), the coverage can potentially extend to hundreds of square meters. This obviates the need for dense deployment of transmitters. The system targets both smartphone users and passive objects localization in LOS scenarios. Today, almost all smartphones have a front-facing light sensor, which can be used by an active user for localization. Sometimes the operating system does not allow the application to sample light signals fast enough; in this case the device driver can be modified to accomplish the goal [40], or a light sensor board can be used, with connection to the phone via the audio jack [14]. For object tracking applications, we envision that a tag can be fixed to the object with exposure to light. Possible application scenarios include robot navigation in unobstructed rooms and product tracking on open assembly lines.

7.2 Localization delay

In our current prototype, the lamp shade does not run at a fast speed due to the restriction of the step motor used, so a receiver takes one to two seconds to perform localization. Here we provide an estimate of the delay in a more advanced implementation. In the worst case, the receiver needs to wait nearly two rotations to obtain its location, thus the localization delay depends on the speed of the step motor. A low cost motor for home appliances such as household electric fans can rotate at a few thousand revolutions per minute [33]. Assuming a moderate rotational speed of 600 rpm, our system would yield a 200 ms delay of localization. There is another restriction from the light sensor's sampling rate. The ISL29023 light sensor has a sampling rate between around 50 Hz to 40 KHz [11], depending on the data granularity (to which our system is not sensitive). Our experiments show that 4096 data samples per revolution produce sufficient accuracy, thus assuming a moderate sampling rate of 20 KHz, the localization delay caused by the two-round rotation is 0.4 s. It is expected that a smaller delay can be attained by optimizing the signal processing algorithm, and by choosing light sensors with a higher sampling rate. This will improve the real-time performance of the system.

7.3 Energy consumption of receiver

The light sensor used for collecting location information consumes very low power. The ISL29023 sensor, for example, consumes 0.25 mW power in normal operation [11]. This is three orders of magnitude lower than a CMOS image sensor [15], and two orders of magnitude lower than a Bluetooth Low Energy (BLE) module in active state [20]. It is even lower than an accelerometer's consumption in continuous operation [1]. For a receiver that comprises a light sensor, a processor, and a BLE module, we expect that the receiver has comparable operation time with an ordinary iBeacon tag, which lasts month to years with a coin cell battery.

8. RELATED WORK

SpinLight is motivated and inspired by research in a few lines. In this section we discuss the related work.

8.1 RF based schemes

A large class of localization techniques are based on RF, including WiFi, cellular radio [32], FM radio [9], although some employ magnetism [10] or ultrasound [7], etc. A commonly used property of RF is RSS, which is easy to obtain on standard wireless devices. However, RSS is not a reliable estimator for distance or location, as it is susceptible to indoor multipath reflections and shadowing. As a result, these solutions, be it propagation model or fingerprint based, provide only low to medium accuracy, typically to a few meters [4, 46]. Various efforts have been made to improve the accuracy. For example, physical layer information is exploited for a better distance estimation [16, 26, 39]. Another commonly used technique of RF localization is AoA [18, 19]. In recent work [41], antenna arrays are used to track RF phase to achieve sub-meter accuracy.

In the domain of RFID, both the AoA and synthetic aperture radar (SAR) approaches have been used for enhancing position accuracy. PinIt [36] leverages the multipath profiles of target tags, as well as of reference tags to generate a small position error, with a highlight on its capability to deal with non-light of sight conditions. However, PinIt requires a highly dense deployment of reference tags (e.g., with a 15 cm spacing). The techniques of PinIt is further used to enable robot navigation and object manipulation in RF-compass [35]. Tagoram [43] provides very fine-grained location for RFID tags by constructing an RF phase hologram with observations from several reader antennas. For general mobility condition, (i.e., with no a prior knowledge of the trajectory), the median position error is 12.3 cm. Tagoram assumes a moving object that simulates an antenna array, thus it does not work for stationary objects.

8.2 Light signal based schemes

Recent research on light signal based localization has been primarily carried out in the context of visual light communications (VLC). Traditional localization principles such as proximity detection, RSS, or AoA have been well explored in various respects. Rajagopal et al. [24] propose to use LED lamps as visual light landmarks by encoding information in the flash patterns of light and exploiting the rolling shutter effect of camera sensors, addressing many practical concerns. ByteLight [2] is a commercial effort that appears to follow a similar approach. For improved accuracy, RSS information, commonly derived from the Lambertian pattern [5], is used with a multilateration method to locate the receiver [42, 45, 47]. In [22], a hybrid RSS/AoA algorithm is explored for improved location accuracy. In these solutions, the receiver's RSS is sensitive to its orientation, so the receiver needs a fixed orientation (e.g., perpendicularly upward), or needs extra sensors to help rectify the RSS, in order to solve for location. Recently, Luxapose [13] uses AoA and careful image analysis to improve the accuracy to 10 cm, assuming dense deployment of LED lights and high image quality of the camera.

Some other work proposes to use optical sensors instead of cameras as receivers. As optical sensors consume much less power, this approach makes it more practical for small battery powered receivers. The Epsilon [14] system uses an optical sensor to derive RSS from at least three lamps and use the classic trilateration method to solve for location. Epsilon reports position accuracy to about a half meter. In contrast to the multi-transmitter, single receiver approach, the authors in [44] propose to use a single transmitter and multiple receivers for localization. A similar principle has been realized in [40], which offers an accuracy of 40 cm.

Using mobile light sources for positioning has been explored in some early work as well. The Lighthouse location system [25] proposes methods to generate rotating parallel light beams that scan around and help determine a receiver's distance. With three transmitters, a receiver can obtain three distance measurements, and then calculate its location. In the Spotlight system [30], the instrument for localization is an unmanned aerial vehicle, which flies over the receivers and generates encoded light signals (or events). A receiver detects the light event, records the event time sequence, and then sends it to the vehicle for location analysis. SpinLight is similar to these systems in its digital nature, but uses a different design, and works on a distinct principle of localization.

8.3 Other related work

SpinLight can also be compared with the existing work from alternative perspectives. There are some previous systems that also achieve centimeter-level accuracy, such as Active Badge [37], Bat [38], and Cricket [23]. They use a combination of ultrasound and RF sensors for localization, and are expensive and time consuming to deploy. Similar to SpinLight, the work in [19, 36, 43] also considers antenna motions, with differences in application scenarios, signal characteristics, motion style, as well as in performance objectives.

9. CONCLUSION

We have presented SpinLight, a light based localization system for indoor environments. The main innovation is its use of a rotating lamp shade to realize spatial division and coding for the environment. By detecting the flash pattern of the light signal, the receiver is able to identify the spatial beam which it belongs to, followed by optimization techniques to refine its location to a few centimeters. Compared with other light positioning systems, our design has the advantages of being less sensitive to environmental conditions and receiver orientation, and has the benefit of low power consumption. The system could be used in for example robot navigation and product assembly lines. Dead reckoning could be used to fill in the gaps of line of sight.

The transmitter in SpinLight involves a revolving shade, which may introduce instability or increase error after long periods of operation. We will investigate the impact of mechanical vibration on location accuracy, and improve the positioning algorithm to better tolerate the instability. Our future work also includes more careful signal processing for a smaller localization delay, in order to achieve real time positioning in mobile scenarios.

10. ACKNOWLEDGMENTS

We thank the anonymous reviewers for their helpful comments, and our shepherd, Koen Langendoen, whose feedback helped improve the paper and its presentation. Guang Tan was supported by NSFC under grant 61379135, Shenzhen Basic Research Funds under grant JCYJ20140610151856733, and Shenzhen Overseas High-Level Talents Innovation and Entrepreneurship Funds No. KQCX20140520154115026.

References

[1] Analog Devices, Inc. ADXL330: Small, Low Power, 3-Axis ±3g iMEMS Accelerometer (Data Sheet), 2007.

[2] ByteLight. http://www.bytelight.com/

[3] J. Armstrong, Y. A. Sekercioglu, and A. Neild. Visible light positioning: A roadmap for international standardization. *IEEE Communications Magazine*, 51(12), 2013.

[4] P. Bahl and V. N. Padmanabhan. RADAR: An Inbuilding RF-based User Location and Tracking System. In *INFOCOM*, 2000.

[5] J. R. Barry. *Wireless infrared communications*, Springer, 1994.

[6] J. Biswas and M. Veloso. Wifi localization and navigation for autonomous indoor mobile robots. In *IEEE International Conference Robotics and Automation (ICRA)*, 2010.

[7] G. Borriello, A. Liu, T. Offer, C. Palistrant, and R. Sharp. WALRUS: wireless acoustic location with room-level resolution using ultrasound. In *MobiSys*, 2005.

[8] A. Carroll and G. Heiser. An Analysis of Power Consumption in a Smartphone. *USENIX Annual Technical Conference 2010.*

[9] Y. Chen, D. Lymberopoulos, J. Liu, and B. Priyantha. FM-based indoor localization. In *ACM MobiSys*, 2012.

[10] J. Chung, M. Donahoe, I. Kim, C. Schmandt, P. Razavi, M. Wiseman. Indoor location sensing using geomagnetism. In *MobiSys*, 2011.

[11] Intersil. The ISL29023 Datasheet. July 17, 2012.

[12] A. Jovicic, J. Li, and T. Richardson. Visible light communication: Opportunities, challenges and the path to market. *IEEE Communications Magazine*, 51(12), 2013.

[13] Y.-S. Kuo, P. Pannuto, K.-J. Hsiao, and P. Dutta. Luxapose: indoor positioning with mobile phones and visible light. In *Mobicom* 2014.

[14] L. Li, P. Hu, C. Peng, G. Shen, and F. Zhao. Epsilon: A Visible Light Based Positioning System. *Proc. NSDI 2014.*

[15] R. LiKamWa, B. Priyantha, M. Philipose, L. Zhong and P. Bahl. Energy Characterization and Optimization of Image Sensing Toward Continuous Mobile Vision. *Proc. of MobiSys 2013.*

[16] A. T. Mariakakis, S. Sen, J. Lee, K.-H. Kim. SAIL: single access point-based indoor localization. In *MobiSys*, 2014.

[17] L. Ni, Y. Liu, C. Yiu, and A. Patil. LANDMARC: Indoor Location Sensing Using Active RFID. In *WINET*, 2004.

[18] D. Niculescu and B. Nath. Ad hoc positioning system (APS) using AOA. *IEEE INFOCOM*, 2003.

[19] D. Niculescu and B. Nath. Vor base stations for indoor 802.11 positioning. *ACM Mobicom*, 2004.

[20] Nordic semiconductor. *nRF8001 Product Specification 1.2.* 2013.

[21] Opto-isolator. http://en.wikipedia.org/wiki/Opto-isolator.

[22] G. B. Prince and T. D. Little. A two phase hybrid RSS/AoA algorithm for indoor device localization using visible light. In *IEEE Global Communication Conference (GLOBECOM)*, 2012.

[23] N. Priyantha, A. Chakraborty, and H. Balakrishnan. The Cricket location-support system. In *ACM MobiCom*, 2000.

[24] N. Rajagopal, P. Lazik, and A. Wowe. Visual light landmarks for mobile devices. In *IPSN*, 2014.

[25] K. Romer. The Lighthouse Location System for Smart Dust. *ACM MobiSys 2003.*

[26] S. Sen, J. Lee, K.-H. Kim, and P. Congdon. Avoiding Multipath to Revive Inbuilding WiFi Localization. In *ACM Mobisys*, 2013.

[27] G. Sterling and D. Top. Mapping the Indoor Marketing Opportunity. *Opus Research Report.*

[28] STMicroelectronics. STM32 MCU family – 32-bit Flash microcontrollers powered by ARM Cortex^{TM} – M3, May 2008.

[29] STMicroelectronics. LIS33DE datasheet, April 2009.

[30] R. Stoleru, T. He, J. A. Stankovic, D. Luebke. A High-Accuracy, Low-Cost Localization System for Wireless Sensor Networks. *ACM SenSys 2005.*

[31] S. Tarzia, P. Dinda, R. Dick, G. Memik. Indoor Localization without Infrastructure using the Acoustic Background Spectrum. In *ACM MobiSys*, 2011.

[32] A. Varshavskya, E. d. Lara, J. Hightower, A. LaMarca, V. Otsason. GSM indoor localization. *Pervasive and Mobile Computing*, 2007.

[33] Vexta PK245 technical data sheet. Velmex, Inc.

[34] VLC for location, positioning and navigation. http://visiblelightcomm.com/vlc-for-location-positioning-and-navigation/

[35] J. Wang, F. Adib, R. Knepper, D. Katabi and D. Rus. RF-Compass: Robot Object Manipulation Using RFIDs. In *ACM Mobicom*, 2013.

[36] J. Wang and D. Katabi. Dude, Where's my card?: Rfid positioning that works with multipath and non-line of sight. In *Proc. of ACM SIGCOMM*, 2013.

[37] R.Want, A. Hopper, V. Falcao, and J. Gibbons. The active badge location system. *ACM Trans. on Information Systems*, 10(1):91–102, Jan. 1992.

[38] A. Ward, A. Jones, and A. Hopper. A new location technique for the active office. *IEEE Personal Communications*, 4(5):42–47, Oct. 1997.

[39] K. Wu., J. Xiao, Y. Yi, M. Gao, and L. M. Ni. FILA: Fine-grained indoor localization. In *IEEE INFOCOM*, 2012.

[40] B. Xie, G. Tan, Y. Liu, M. Lu, K. Chen, T. He. LIPS: A Light Intensity Based Positioning System For Indoor Environments. http://arxiv.org/abs/1403.2331

[41] J. Xiong and K. Jamieson. Arraytrack: A fine-grained indoor location system. In *Usenix NSDI*, 2013.

[42] S.-H. Yang, E.-M. Jeong, D.-R. Kim, H.-S. Kim, Y.-H. Son, and S.-K. Han. Indoor three-dimensional location estimation based on LED visible light communication. *Electronics Letters*, 49(1), January 2013.

[43] L. Yang, Y. Chen, X.-Y. Li, C. Xiao, M. Li, and Y. Liu. Tagoram: Real-Time Tracking of Mobile RFID Tags to High Precision Using COTS Devices. In *Proc. of Mobicom*, 2014.

[44] S-H. Yang, E-M. Jung, S-K. Han. Indoor location estimation based on LED visible light communication using multiple optical receivers. *IEEE Communications Letters*, 17(9), Sept. 2013.

[45] M. Yoshino, S. Haruyama, and M. Nakagawa. High-accuracy positioning system using visible LED lights and image sensor. In *IEEE Radio and Wireless Symposium (RWS)*, 2008.

[46] M. Youssef and A. Agrawala. The Horus WLAN Location Determination System. In *MobiSys*, 2005.

[47] Z. Zhou, M. Kavehrad, and P. Deng. Indoor positioning algorithm using light-emitting diode visible light communications. *Optical Engineering*, 51(8), 2012.

Contour-based Trilateration for Indoor Fingerprinting Localization

Suining He Tianyang Hu S.-H. Gary Chan
Department of Computer Science and Engineering,
The Hong Kong University of Science and Technology, Hong Kong, China
{sheaa, thuab, gchan}@cse.ust.hk

ABSTRACT

Trilateration has been widely and successfully employed to locate outdoor mobile devices due to its accuracy. However, it cannot be directly applied for indoor localization due to issues such as non-line-of-sight measurement and multipath fading. Though fingerprinting overcomes these issues, its accuracy is often hampered by signal noise and the choice of similarity metric between signal vectors. We propose ***INTRI***, a novel, simple and effective ***in***door localization technique combining the strengths of ***tri***lateration and fingerprinting.

For a signal level received from an access point (AP) by the target, INTRI first forms a contour consisting of all the reference points (RPs) of the same signal level for that AP, taking into account the signal noise. The target is hence at the juncture of all the contours. With an optimization formulation following the spirit of trilateration, it then finds the target location by minimizing the distance between the position and all the contours. INTRI further uses an online algorithm based on signal correlation to efficiently calibrate heterogeneous mobile devices to achieve higher accuracy. We have implemented INTRI, and our extensive simulation and experiments in an international airport, a shopping mall and our university campus show that it outperforms recent schemes with much lower location error (often by more than 20%).

Categories and Subject Descriptors

C.2.1 [**Network Architecture and Design**]: Wireless Communication

General Terms

Design, Experimentation, System, Performance

Keywords

Indoor localization; contour-based trilateration; fingerprinting; device calibration; signal contour; linear programming.

SenSys'15, November 1–4, 2015, Seoul, South Korea..
© 2015 ACM. ISBN 978-1-4503-3631-4/15/11 ...$15.00.
DOI: http://dx.doi.org/10.1145/2809695.2809703.

1. INTRODUCTION

In traditional trilateration, a mobile device (target) first measures its distances to a number of landmarks of known location. It then estimates its position which best matches these measured distances (e.g., given by minimizing the error between the measured distances and the distances from the position to the landmarks). Such a localization technique has been widely used outdoors, with exemplary applications in GPS (Global Positioning System) and cellular positioning, where the landmarks are satellites and base stations (cell towers), respectively.

Despite of its accuracy and successful outdoor deployment, trilateration does not work well indoors because distances to landmarks cannot be estimated accurately. Such inaccuracy is mainly due to non-line-of-sight landmarks, complex indoor signal fading (due to multipath), over-simplification or parametric uncertainties in indoor propagation models, etc. Fingerprinting, on the other hand, emerges as a promising approach for indoor localization. An example is Wi-Fi fingerprinting, which is gaining popularity due to its ease of deployment without the need to install extra sensor infrastructure beyond the existing Wi-Fi network [11].

Fingerprint-based localization is usually conducted in two phases. In the first offline (survey) phase, a site survey is conducted to collect the vectors of *received signal strength indicators* (RSSIs) at known locations, the so-called "reference points" (RPs). These vectors of RSSIs are the *fingerprints* of the locations and are stored in a database. In the second online (query) phase, a user samples or measures an RSSI vector at his own position and reports it to the server (in this paper, we use "user", "mobile device" and "target" interchangeably). The server then locates the indoor user by comparing the target vector with the fingerprints using some similarity metric (such as Euclidean distance [2] between signal vectors). The target position is then estimated out of the most similar "neighbors," the set of RPs whose fingerprints closely resemble the target's RSSI.

Traditionally, the similarity metric used often treats the RSSI vector of the target as a single "entity" in comparison. This makes the neighbor selection susceptible to statistical fluctuation in signal strength and measurement noise. Due to random signals, it has been widely observed that the matching algorithm in the online phase may result in a dispersed set of neighbors (i.e., RPs which are quite distant apart in the physical space). This leads to unsatisfactory localization accuracy [11,30].

In this paper, we propose **INTRI** (**In**door **Tri**lateration using signal contours), a novel, efficient and accurate indoor

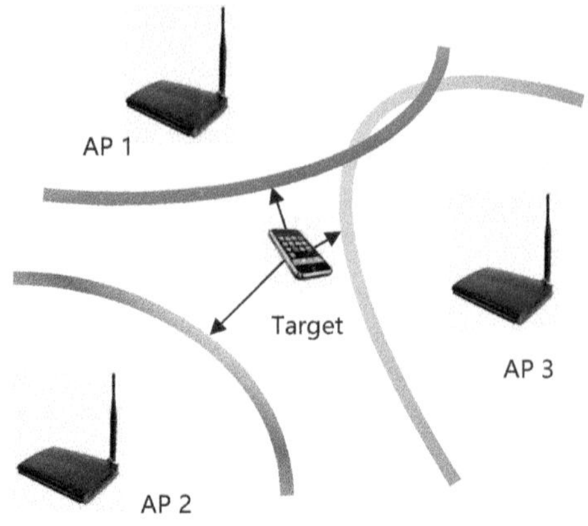

Figure 1: The basic idea of INTRI, indoor contour-based trilateration by minimizing the distance to signal contours. The contours are based on the fingerprints.

localization technique by employing the concept of trilateration in fingerprint-based environment. By treating the RSSI from each AP *individually* (instead of as a single signal vector), INTRI does not suffer from the problem of dispersed set of neighbors. It is highly robust to random signals (due to signal noise and measurement uncertainty) as it is not based on fingerprint similarity comparison.

We illustrate the basic concept of INTRI in Figure 1 with three access points (APs). Let S be the signal strength from a certain AP as measured by the target. For that AP, we can form a *contour* for S in the fingerprint region, which are the spatially distributed RPs whose signal level of the AP is S, subject to its statistical fluctuation (the figure shows a continuous contour, though in reality the signal contour consists of discrete points in space). It is clear that the target is somewhere on the contour line. Given the target's received signal vector, we can hence form the corresponding contour for each of the APs (three contours for the three APs in the figure). Following the spirit of trilateration, the target position can then be estimated by minimizing its distances to the signal contours.

INTRI integrates the highly accurate contour-based trilateration technique with indoor fingerprinting. It combines the strengths of both approaches: it does not need the positions of APs and line-of-sight (LoS) measurement, and locates the target at the junction of its measured signal levels without the dispersion problem. Though at times for concreteness our discussion in this paper is on Wi-Fi RSSI fingerprinting, INTRI is a general approach applicable to any other fingerprint signal like channel state information (CSI) [39], ZigBee [37], visible light [40] or RFID [5, 10]. It may also be a complementary module to existing sensor localization systems such as [21, 26] without modifying or adding any specialized infrastructures.

In order for INTRI to be practically deployed, we need to address the following important issues:

- *Forming contours for random signals:* Signal measurement is inherently noisy. Constructing contours needs to consider random fluctuation in order to effectively locate the target. We present how to statistically analyze the fingerprints and target RSSIs received so as to construct contours under random signals. As the target is likely to be at the region where contours meet, we discuss how to find such region.

- *Efficient contour-based localization algorithm:* We propose a novel contour-based localization algorithm based on linear programming formulation. Following the spirits of trilateration, it estimates target location with the objective to minimize the distances to the contours obtained above.

- *Adaptive online calibration for heterogeneous devices:* For the same signal, different devices may have different readings. Device readings hence need to be mapped, or "calibrated," to the corresponding signal level stored in the database so that the contours can be correctly discovered. Offline calibration for all different devices is neither efficient nor scalable. We propose an efficient and practical online scheme to calibrate devices, which adapts the target measured RSSI according to the stored fingerprints based on signal correlation. Using our efficient approach, INTRI achieves high scalability in heterogeneous devices, and robustness under noisy environment.

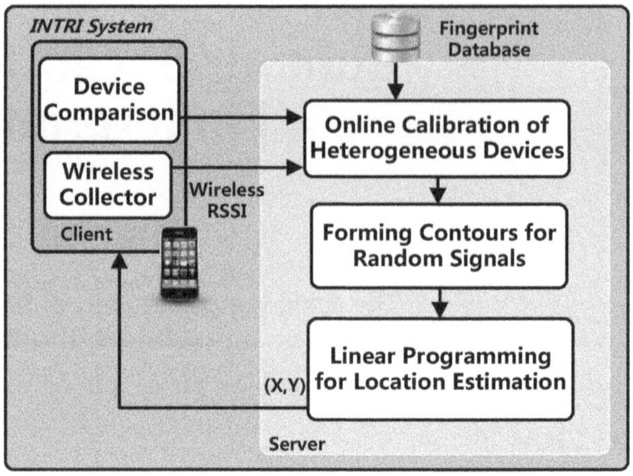

Figure 2: System framework of INTRI.

We show in Figure 2 the system framework of INTRI. The Wi-Fi fingerprint database is initialized by a site survey, storing <location, RSSI vector> pairs for each RP and vendor information of the devices used for data collection. The system is now ready for online estimation.

In the online phase, INTRI first checks the vendor information of the user's device. If that is different from the devices used for site survey, the target RSSI vector will be calibrated using the stored fingerprints. The calibrated RSSI vector is then used to construct the signal contours. Given signal contours, INTRI formulates a linear programming to jointly minimize the distances to the contours and estimates the user's position. The location is finally returned to the user's device.

We have conducted extensive simulation and large-scale experimental trials in the Hong Kong International Airport (HKIA), the Hong Kong Cyberport mall (HKCP) and our university campus (HKUST). Both simulation and experimental studies further confirm the high accuracy of INTRI.

The rest of this paper is organized as follows. After reviewing the related works in Section 2, we describe in Section 3 the construction of contours for noisy signals. Based on these contours, in Section 4 we present the linear programming formulation for localization based on the idea of trilateration. In Section 5, we propose an efficient online approach to calibrate different devices. Illustrative simulation and experimental results are presented in Sections 6 and 7, respectively. We finally conclude in Section 8.

2. RELATED WORK

We briefly discuss related works in this section. Pattern recognition techniques have been widely studied in Wi-Fi fingerprinting localization. RADAR [2] and Horus [42] are the two representative approaches. Recently more advanced techniques on pattern matching have been investigated [11–13, 22, 29]. Signal propagation model is also considered recently to derive RSSI at different locations [6, 14, 23]. EZ [6] utilizes rigid matching between signals and distances to determine the target location. More recent works like EZPerfect [31] and Modellet [23] further utilize the labeled fingerprints to derive signal propagation model and achieve higher accuracy.

In contrast to the above works, we combine the advantages of fingerprinting and trilateration approaches. We employ a geometric scheme (with spirits of trilateration) based on random fingerprint signals to constrain the target region. By formulating a novel linear programming, INTRI achieves much better localization accuracy without neighbor dispersion. INTRI is also compatible to emerging fingerprint update schemes like [4] (crowdsourcing), [5] (sensor-assisted) and [34] (crowdsourcing and model-based update) to achieve higher robustness in practical deployment.

Some other recent works leverage the temporal or spatial RSSI patterns for localization. These works consider location-dependent patterns such as the trend of RSSI sequences along corridors [33], order of RSSIs from different APs [18], or the unique existence of some Wi-Fi APs at some area [38] [20]. Once the target measures such patterns, its location is then mapped to the area. These patterns achieve promising results for constrained and narrow environment with well-defined user trajectories (like corridors or offices). To the contrary, the contours in INTRI are solely derived from fingerprints and are applicable to any indoor environment. Furthermore, INTRI does not need the positions of APs and LoS measurement, and is not based on indoor models (indoor environment may be too complex to model).

Calibrating different devices has been studied in recent works [7, 25, 28, 32]. Traditional offline calibration [32] causes extra manual efforts in real deployment and hence is not scalable. Given the target RSSI measurement, works like [7, 25, 28] utilize the deduction [25] (or ratio [28]) between AP signal values to calibrate the devices. However, large noise and fluctuation in signal levels can degrade the quality of the above calibration. Some learning-based approaches [9, 23] utilize expectation maximization to calibrate the signal difference. Different from these works, INTRI proposes a more efficient and robust scheme which maps the target signals to the signal space in fingerprint database.

To improve fingerprint localization, sensor fusion has attracted intensive attention recently. Using the smartphone inertial sensors, fusing motion information has been studied extensively to improve fingerprint-based positioning [15, 17, 36]. Peer-assisted localization has also been recently studied, making use of Wi-Fi Direct [19] and high-pitch sound [24] to measure the distance between peer devices [16] as extra position constraints. Different from above fusion approaches, INTRI solely relies on existing Wi-Fi measurement, achieving higher scalability in pervasive deployment. INTRI is also independent of these works, and is amendable to integrate with them for higher accuracy of mobile localization.

Table 1: Major symbols used in INTRI formulation.

Notation	Definition
N	Number of RPs in fingerprint database.
L	Number of APs in the site.
$\mathbf{f}_n$	Wi-Fi RSSI vector received at RP n.
f_n^l	Wi-Fi AP l's RSSI at RP n (dBm).
$\mathbf{g}$	Wi-Fi RSSI vector received at target.
g^l	Wi-Fi AP l's RSSI at target (dBm).
σ_n^l	AP l's standard deviation at RP n (dB).
σ^l	AP l's standard deviation at target (dB).
z_0	Uncertainty range parameter of contour.
$\mathbf{S}^l$	Signal contour from AP l.
$\mathbf{C}^l$	Indices of RPs on $\mathbf{S}^l$.
$\widehat{d}_l$	Pseudo distance from AP l.
D_n	Contour weight at RP n.
$\mathbf{R}$	Indices of selected RPs for LP localization.
$N^{\mathbf{R}}$	Number of RPs selected in $\mathbf{R}$.
Δ_n^l	Minimum distance between RP n and $\mathbf{S}^l$.
ω_n	Weight of RP n in target estimation.
$\mathbf{r}_n$	2-D coordinate of RP n.
$\widehat{\mathbf{x}}$	Estimated 2-D coordinate of target.

3. FORMING CONTOURS FOR RANDOM SIGNALS

In this section, we describe how to properly form the signal contours for later localization estimation (Section 4). In Section 3.1, we first present how to find the signal contour for each AP, given target random RSSIs. A contour (of an AP) consists of discrete RPs whose signal level is the same as the target's measured signal level, subject to statistical fluctuation. To achieve higher localization accuracy, the RPs visited by many contours of strong signals are preferred. Therefore, in Section 3.2 we propose a weighting scheme which is able to differentiate the importance of the RPs. The important RPs are kept while those unimportant ones (where target is unlikely at) are filtered. After the above steps, given that the target is likely to be in the "dense" region of selected RPs, we finally present in Section 3.3 how to find such region based on maximally connected components. The major symbols used in this paper are shown in Table 1.

3.1 Finding a Signal Contour

By evaluating the signal map of each given AP within the survey site, we may observe a set of RPs which share similar RSSI values subject to some statistical fluctuation. These RPs forms the signal contour for that AP. Then a target measuring a similar RSSI value is likely within a certain range from that contour. And the juncture of contours from these detected APs becomes the potential location of the target. Inspired by the above observations, we present as follows how to form the signal contours given fingerprints and target signals.

Let N and L be the total number of RPs and distinct APs detected in the whole survey site, respectively. Further let $\widetilde{F}_n^l$ be the random variable of the RSSI collected at RP n for AP l in the offline fingerprint collection, where $1 \leq n \leq N$ and $1 \leq l \leq L$. Multiple samples are collected at different time τ indexed $1, 2, \ldots, T_n^l$ for RP n and AP l, which are denoted as

$$\{f_n^l(\tau) | \tau = 1, \ldots, T_n^l, T_n^l > 1\}, \tag{1}$$

where T_n^l is the total number of samples collected. The unbiased estimate of $E(\widetilde{F}_n^l)$, denoted as $\widehat{\mu}_n^l$, is the mean of $f_n^l(\tau)$'s. The unbiased estimate on the variance of $\widetilde{F}_n^l$ is denoted as $\widehat{\sigma}^2(\widetilde{F}_n^l)$. Then $\widehat{\mu}_n^l$ and $\widehat{\sigma}^2(\widetilde{F}_n^l)$ are respectively given by

$$\widehat{\mu}_n^l = \frac{1}{T_n^l}\left(\sum_{\tau=1}^{T_n^l} f_n^l(\tau)\right), \widehat{\sigma}^2\left(\widetilde{F}_n^l\right) = \frac{1}{T_n^l - 1}\left(\sum_{\tau=1}^{T_n^l}\left(f_n^l(\tau) - \widehat{\mu}_n^l\right)^2\right). \tag{2}$$

Let f_n^l be the mean of the measured fingerprint signals (a random variable) at RP n for AP l, given by

$$f_n^l = \frac{1}{T_n^l}\sum_{\tau=1}^{T_n^l} F_n^l(\tau), \tag{3}$$

where $F_n^l(\tau)$'s are random variables distributed as $\widetilde{F}_n^l$ and $f_n^l(\tau)$'s are their realized values. Let $v(\tau)$ be a noise process independent from $f_n^l(\tau)$. Let α_n^l be a parameter determining the autocorrelation of samples. Then the signal time series can be represented as a first order autoregressive model [41],

$$f_n^l(\tau) = \alpha_n^l f_n^l(\tau - 1) + (1 - \alpha_n^l)v(\tau), \tag{4}$$

where α_n^l represents the correlation between successive samples ($0 \leq \alpha_n^l \leq 1$). For f_n^l, its expected value $\bar{f}_n^l$ and standard deviation σ_n^l [41] can be estimated as

$$\bar{f}_n^l = \widehat{\mu}_n^l, \quad \sigma_n^l = \left\{\frac{\widehat{\sigma}^2\left(\widetilde{F}_n^l\right)}{(T_n^l)^2}\left[\left(\frac{1-(\alpha_n^l)^{T_n^l}}{1-\alpha_n^l}\right)^2 + T_n^l - 1 \right.\right.$$
$$\left.\left. -(\alpha_n^l)^2\frac{1-(\alpha_n^l)^{2(T_n^l-1)}}{1-(\alpha_n^l)^2}\right]\right\}^{1/2}, \tag{5}$$

respectively. Here α_n^l can be approximated by autocorrelation coefficient with lag one [41] for the RSSI samples in Equation (1), i.e.

$$\alpha_n^l \approx \frac{\sum_{\tau=1}^{T_n^l-1}\left(f_n^l(\tau) - \widehat{\mu}_n^l\right)\left(f_n^l(\tau+1) - \widehat{\mu}_n^l\right)}{\sum_{\tau=1}^{T_n^l}\left(f_n^l(\tau) - \widehat{\mu}_n^l\right)^2}. \tag{6}$$

Such autocorrelation within sequential RSSIs may be related to the caching in Wi-Fi sampling. Wi-Fi data caching can be identified using Timing Synchronization Function (TSF) [43] of the RSSI. We can conclude that an RSSI is a cached one if its TSF is identical to another in an earlier scan result.

To illustrate that, we collect 21,000 signal vectors at 350 different locations in the HKIA with HTC One X (Android 4.3). At each location we collect 60 RSSI samples. For each AP l at an RP n, we calculate the α_n^l using Equation (6). Figure 3 shows the histograms of all α_n^l before and after cache filtering. We can see that the autocorrelation between RSSI samples decreases if we filter the cache based on TSF.

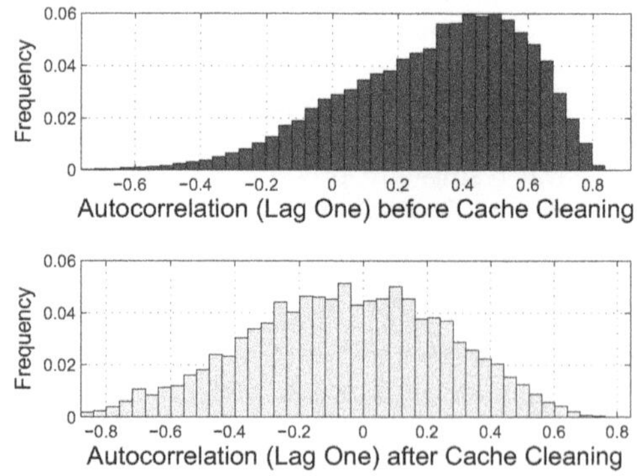

Figure 3: Lag one autocorrelation before and after cleaning Wi-Fi data cache (samples from the international airport).

Given much lower signal correlation, we can further simplify the modeling of σ_n^l [41] into

$$\sigma_n^l = \sqrt{\frac{1}{T_n^l}\widehat{\sigma}^2\left(\widetilde{F}_n^l\right)}, \tag{7}$$

However, TSF of RSSI cache is only available in the latest smartphones (supported by Android 4.2 or above). Therefore, here we implement Equations (5) and (6) to calculate σ_n^l for more general cases. Given the above, let

$$\mathbf{f}_n = [\bar{f}_n^1, \bar{f}_n^2, \ldots, \bar{f}_n^L] \tag{8}$$

be the RSSI vector (fingerprint) at RP n.

In the online query stage, denote the target measurement of AP l as g^l. We denote the RSSI vector at the target as

$$\mathbf{g} = [g^1, g^2, \ldots, g^L]. \tag{9}$$

For Equations (8) and (9), by definition, $\bar{f}_n^l = 0$ ($g^l = 0$), if AP l is not sampled at RP n (at the target).

As online g^l is also random signal, we utilize the uncertainty in offline fingerprint to characterize its variation. Specifically, let $(\sigma^l)^2$ be its variance, estimated as the mean of the variance in all the fingerprints, i.e.,

$$\left(\sigma^l\right)^2 = \frac{1}{|\mathbf{N}^l|}\left(\sum_{n\in\mathbf{N}^l}\widehat{\sigma}^2\left(\widetilde{F}_n^l\right)\right), \tag{10}$$

where $\mathbf{N}^l$ is the set of RPs detecting AP l in the site and $|\mathbf{N}^l|$ is its cardinality.

We consider the randomness in the difference between fingerprint and target RSSI, $g^l - f_n^l$ for each AP l. As g^l and f_n^l are independently measured, the variance of $g^l - f_n^l$ is therefore given by

$$\begin{aligned}\mathbb{V}(g^l - f_n^l) &= \mathbb{V}(g^l) + \mathbb{V}(f_n^l) \\ &= (\sigma^l)^2 + (\sigma_n^l)^2.\end{aligned} \tag{11}$$

A *signal contour* for AP l, denoted as $\mathbf{S}^l$, consists of a set of RPs where the target is likely within. In other words, $\mathbf{S}^l$ represents the RPs whose RSSI for AP l is likely within a certain range from g^l. Therefore, in finding the contour $\mathbf{S}^l$, we *eliminate* the RPs whose RSSI is more likely far away from the target's, i.e., if

$$\left|g^l - \bar{f}_n^l\right| > z_0\sqrt{\mathbb{V}(g^l - f_n^l)}, \ z_0 > 0, \tag{12}$$

where z_0 represents the uncertainty range. z_0 determines the sensitivity of INTRI towards the signal noise (in our experiment we will further evaluate this parameter). We hence find the signal contour for AP l as follows. Given a target RSSI g^l, we utilize Equations (11) and (12), and form the signal contour $\mathbf{S}^l$ consisting of RP $n \in \mathbf{N}^l$ such that

$$g^l - z_0\sqrt{(\sigma^l)^2 + (\sigma_n^l)^2} \leq \bar{f}_n^l \leq g^l + z_0\sqrt{(\sigma^l)^2 + (\sigma_n^l)^2}. \quad (13)$$

Given AP l, we denote the corresponding index set of RPs on contour $\mathbf{S}^l$ as $\mathbf{C}^l$, i.e.,

$$\mathbf{C}^l = \{n \in \mathbf{N}^l, \text{where } \bar{f}_n^l \text{ satisfies Equation (13)}\}. \quad (14)$$

Then we denote its cardinality as $|\mathbf{C}^l|$.

3.2 Calculation of Contour Weights

Given the found contours, an intuitive idea is to locate the target at RPs with the maximum number of contours. However, due to the indoor partitions and signal measurement uncertainty, spatially dispersed RPs may have very similar number of signal contours passing by. In this case, finding the RPs with the largest number of contours may not lead to accurate location estimation. As shown in Figure 4, a target (red diamond) measures a signal vector consisting of RSSIs from six APs, A, B, C, D, E and F. The contours of D, E and F (black circles) shift from those of A, B and C (red rectangles) due to signal fluctuation or wall partitions. Thus, the RPs in black circles may share the same number of contours as those close to target. If all these RPs are considered equally without sufficient filtering or differentiation, large location errors still exist.

Through empirical studies, we observe that the strong signals near APs provide more reliable location-dependent information than the weak ones. The stronger the RSSI, the more important the AP contour is in contributing to location estimation. This is due to the sharpness of signal strength change at the locations near the Wi-Fi APs, which differentiates RPs the most from other distant ones. Inspired by this, we consider as follows how to utilize such distinguishable RSSIs to improve location accuracy.

Take Figure 4 again as an illustration. The signals at contours of A, B and C are stronger since they are closer to the corresponding APs. If we can assign more weights on the contours with strong signals in final location decision, we can distinguish the important RPs more accurately. Thus, we propose a weighting scheme which differentiates RPs the most and finds the RPs with higher confidence. The physical intuition of the weighting scheme is based on the log-distance path loss (LDPL) model [6, 23]. We adopt it in the weighting function for signal contour differentiation, which achieves high localization accuracy.

Denote the reference power at distance d_0 as P_0^l (dBm). Let d_l be the distance between target and AP l. Then the received power at target from AP l is given by

$$g^l = P_0^l - 10\gamma^l \log_{10}\left(\frac{d_l}{d_0}\right) + X, \quad (15)$$

where γ^l denotes the decay rate of RSSI in propagation. X represents the inherent signal fluctuation and noise. Here we consider using LDPL to represent the closeness of APs for contour differentiation (not exact distance), and X has been considered separately in forming contours (Section 3.1). Based on Equation (15), we define the corresponding *pseudo distance* from AP l ($d_0 = 1$ m) as

$$\widehat{d_l} = 10^{\frac{P_0^l - g^l}{10\gamma^l}}. \quad (16)$$

Instead of indicating actual distances, we use it to represent the *confidence level* with AP signals. Specifically, the smaller $\widehat{d_l}$, the more likely the AP is nearby. Then the *contour weight* at RP n from all detected APs is defined as

$$D_n = \frac{1}{L}\sum_{l=1}^{L}\frac{1}{\widehat{d_l}}. \quad (17)$$

Using Equation (17), for each g^l at contour $\mathbf{S}^l$, we consider the potential that an AP is physically nearby. The larger D_n, the more contours of strong signals hit the RP. Such APs are more likely to be close to these RPs around the target, and we further utilize such closeness information to constrain the target region.

Then we find the RP set $\mathbf{R}$ consisting of the indices of RPs which have the highest contour weights as the potential area for final estimation, i.e.,

$$\mathbf{R} = \arg\max_n D_n. \quad (18)$$

In INTRI, we dynamically select the RPs with D_n higher than $\rho \max\{D_n\}$ ($\rho = 0.75$ in our simulation and experiment). RSSIs from an AP that is located in a region surrounded by obstacles may lead to larger γ^l than those from other APs with freer signal propagation. Here we do not assume ideal line-of-sight measurement. The external parameters (P_0^l and γ^l) in Equations (15) and (16) can be learned through gradient decent analysis over the fingerprint signals [6, 8].

To summarize, by traversing the survey site, we find the signal contours at each RP within the signal range in Equation (13), and calculate the contour weights at that RP using Equations (16) and (17). The most important RPs with strong signals will be selected to form $\mathbf{R}$.

3.3 Finding the Dense Contour Region

The selected RPs in $\mathbf{R}$ may still have "strayed RPs" due to measurement uncertainty. In Figure 5, we illustrate the spatial distribution of $\mathbf{R}$ (red rectangles), which is based on the extensive experimental observations in HKIA trials (from 1,100 target RSSI samples). We can find RPs which are physically close to each other. These RPs form a region where the target is likely at, and should be used in our localization formulation. Due to signal temporal fluctuation, some RPs (the two to the right) exist and are distant away from the target location. If included in localization, these RPs may lead to location error and unnecessary computation. Considering their spatial connectivity, we observe in Figure 5 that the RPs near the target (red diamond) form a connected component with the largest cardinality.

Based on such observation, we utilize an algorithm of finding maximally connected components, and find the region with dense contours by filtering out RPs not in the region.

We show the process of such filtering in Algorithm 1. Let $N^{\mathbf{R}}$ be the cardinality of $\mathbf{R}$. We first construct an $N^{\mathbf{R}} \times N^{\mathbf{R}}$ adjacency matrix $\mathbf{A}$, where $\mathbf{A}(i, j) = 1$ indicates that RP i and j are adjacent, and $\mathbf{A}(i, j) = 0$ otherwise (Lines 1). We set the threshold of adjacency as $\sqrt{2}$ times of the square grid width in site survey. By treating RPs in $\mathbf{R}$ as an undirected graph, we find the membership list of all connected components [35] (Lines 11 to 29). After that, we find the

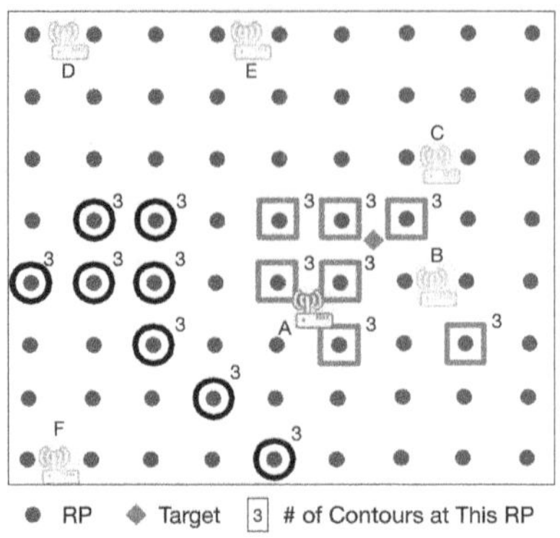

Figure 4: Illustration of differentiating signal contours.

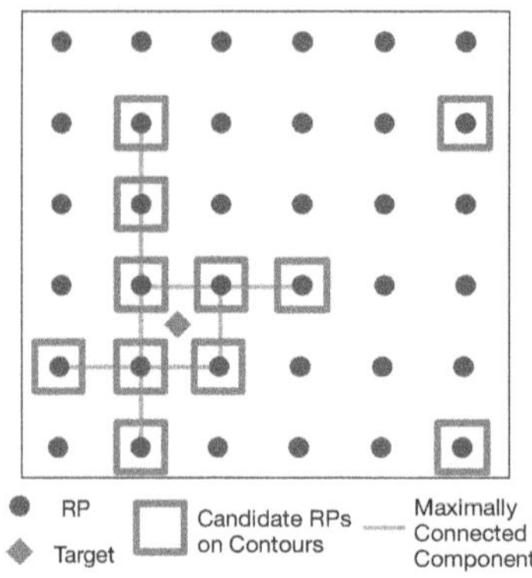

Figure 5: Illustration of maximally connected component to find the dense contour region.

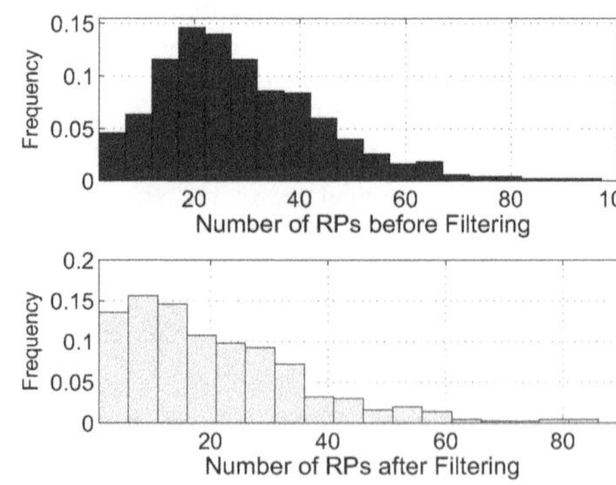

Figure 6: Histograms of $N^{\mathbf{R}}$ before and after RP filtering (the airport data).

component with the maximum number of RPs (Line 30). If multiple components have the maximum cardinality in common, we use their union for later localization.

In Figure 6, we plot the histograms of $N^{\mathbf{R}}$ from 1,100 targets in the Hong Kong International Airport before and after the proposed RP filtering. We can observe that such a scheme narrows the search scope and facilitates the final location estimation.

Algorithm 1: Finding dense contour region.

```
   Input: R: indices of selected RPs; ζ: threshold.
   Output: R: set of RPs with dense contours.
   /* Constructing Adjacency Matrix.                        */
1  A ← zeros(N^R, N^R)./* N^R × N^R matrix.                  */
2  for i ∈ {2, ..., N^R} do
3      for j ∈ {1, ..., i} do
4          if dist(i,j) ≤ ζ then
               /* Symmetric Matrix                           */
5              A(i, j) ← 1; A(j, i) ← 1;
6          end
7      end
8  end
9  isDiscovered ← zeros(N^R);
10 mem ← {};/* Set of Components                             */
11 nGp ← 0; /* Number of Components                          */
12 for n ∈ {1, ..., N^R} do
13     if !isDiscovered(n) then
14         nGp ← nGp + 1;
15         isDiscovered(n) ← 1;
16         mem[nGp].pt ← mem[nGp].pt ∪ {n};
17         ptr ← 1;
18         while ptr ≤ sizeof(mem[nGp].pt) do
               /* Find Its Neighbors.                        */
19             nbrs ← find(A(:, mem[nGp].pt(ptr)));
20             for nb ∈ {1, ..., sizeof(nbrs)} do
                   /* Connected Components                   */
21                 if !isDisovered(nbrs(nb)) then
22                     isDisovered(nbrs(nb)) ← 1;
23                     mem[nGp].pt ←
                       mem[nGp].pt ∪ {nbrs(nb)};
24                 end
25             end
26             ptr ← ptr + 1;
27         end
28     end
29 end
30 R ← MaxMembers(mem);
```

4. LINEAR PROGRAMMING FOR LOCATION ESTIMATION

In this section, we present the core formulation of INTRI. To formulate the objective function, we first define in Section 4.1 the physical (geographical) distance from an RP to signal contours. Then in Section 4.2, we formulate a linear programming based on weighted physical distances to those contours. We finally analyze the online computational complexity of INTRI in Section 4.3.

4.1 Defining Distances from an RP to Signal Contours

We are given a set of RPs where the contours locate. In the following we introduce how to utilize the signal contours as the objective for INTRI .

Recall that traditional trilateration estimates target position by minimizing the difference between the measured distances and the distances from the position to the landmarks. In our formulation, based on the same spirit, we use the distances to the constructed signal contours. As RPs on contours are discretely sampled in the survey site and a target is surrounded by RPs, we utilize in our formulation the distances from RPs in $\mathbf{R}$ to those on other contours. The RPs with small distances to other $\mathbf{S}^l$'s are likely to be the target region.

Let $\mathbf{r}_n = [x_n, y_n]$ be the coordinate of RP $n \in \mathbf{R}$. We calculate its distance from each RP m $(n \neq m)$ in $\mathbf{S}^l$, i.e.,

$$\delta^l_{nm} = \sqrt{(x_n - x^l_m)^2 + (y_n - y^l_m)^2}, \ \forall m \in \mathbf{C}_l, \qquad (19)$$

where $[x^l_m, y^l_m]$ is RP m's coordinate on signal contour l. Given all distances $\delta^l_{nm}, \forall m \in \mathbf{C}_l$, we find the minimum one, i.e.,

$$\Delta^l_n(\mathbf{g}, \mathbf{f}_n) = \min \delta^l_{nm}, \forall m \in \mathbf{C}_l, \qquad (20)$$

which represents the distance between RP n and contour l. Given above, the distances to all contours are aggregated as

$$\Delta_n = \sum_{l=1}^{L} \Delta^l_n(\mathbf{g}, \mathbf{f}_n), \qquad (21)$$

which, in other words, approximates the residual between the target estimation's distances to the landmarks and the measured distances.

By minimizing Equation (21), we minimize the distance difference and hence extend the idea of trilateration into a contour-based scheme. As the contours are derived from fingerprints and target RSSIs, we require no explicit knowledge of AP locations or LoS measurement, and therefore combine the advantages of both fingerprinting and trilateration in our formulation. In the following, we present the formulation to find the target position.

4.2 Linear Programming Formulation

Given $\mathbf{R}$ and Δ_n, we formulate the localization problem based on linear programming (LP). For each target, denote its estimated location as $\widehat{\mathbf{x}} = [\widehat{x}, \widehat{y}]$. Let ω_n be the weight assigned to $\mathbf{r}_n$ in locating the target. As the target is surrounded by the RPs in $\mathbf{R}$, its estimated position can be expressed as

$$\widehat{\mathbf{x}} = \sum_{n=1}^{N^{\mathbf{R}}} \omega_n \mathbf{r}_n, \tag{22}$$

where $\mathbf{r}_n \in \mathbf{R}$, and the weights satisfy the normalization and non-negativity, i.e.,

$$\sum_{n=1}^{N^{\mathbf{R}}} \omega_n = 1, \quad \omega_n \geq 0, \quad \forall n \in \{1, \ldots, N^{\mathbf{R}}\}. \tag{23}$$

Based on Equation (20) and (22), we extend the idea of trilateration into finding the weights which minimize the target's weighted sum of distances to all the contours, i.e.,

$$\underset{\{\omega_n\}}{\arg\min} \sum_{n=1}^{N^{\mathbf{R}}} \omega_n \Delta_n. \tag{24}$$

In real deployment, a target is far more likely to be between two neighboring RPs (or within the square grid formed by four RPs). In order to jointly consider the neighboring RPs to the target, we set a constraint over the weight ω_n at each RP, i.e.,

$$\omega_n \leq W, \; \forall n \in \{1, \ldots, N^{\mathbf{R}}\}, \tag{25}$$

where W is a dynamic parameter determined by the maximum contour weight

$$W = \frac{\max D_n}{\sum_{n=1}^{N^{\mathbf{R}}} D_n}. \tag{26}$$

Through Equations (24) and (25), we can jointly consider the physical distances (denoted as $\{\Delta_n\}$) and the contour weights (denoted as $\{D_n\}$) in our formulation.

If there are indoor wall partitions in narrow space, we can include map constraints in our basic formulation. Denote the set of map constraints as $\mathbf{E}$. For each edge $e \in \mathbf{E}$, we consider the accessible area within the map constraints as

$$a_e \widehat{x} + b_e \widehat{y} + c_e \geq 0, e \in \mathbf{E}, \tag{27}$$

where a_e, b_e and c_e are the line parameters obtained from the site map in our system initialization. The formula of map edges can be easily found using the nearest map constraints. Using the above, the localization problem can therefore be formulated as a linear programming (LP):

$$\begin{aligned} \text{Objective:} \quad & \text{Equation (24)}, \\ \text{subject to:} \quad & \text{Constraints (22), (23),} \\ & \text{(25), (26) and (27).} \end{aligned} \tag{28}$$

In other words, we opt to find the estimated position with the smallest weighted physical distances to the contours within the accessible area. INTRI returns the set of weights assigned to RPs in $\mathbf{R}$ which minimizes the distances to contours, i.e., the RPs which are closer to all contours are assigned higher weights, and vice versa.

Using some commercial optimization solver, we can solve the above LP efficiently [3]. The final solution $\{\omega_n\}$ is then used to estimate the target position according to Equation (22). We summarize INTRI in Algorithm 2.

Algorithm 2: Contour-based indoor trilateration.

Input: $\{\mathbf{r}_n\}$ and $\{\mathbf{f}_n\}$: the set of N RPs and the set of RSSI vector at each RP; $\mathbf{g}$: target RSSI vector; ζ: the threshold in determining maximally connected components; ρ: range of RPs to be selected.
Output: $\widehat{\mathbf{x}}$: estimated locations of the target.

/* Construction of Signal Contours. */
$\mathbf{C}^l \leftarrow \{\}$; /* Set of RPs with Contours. */
for $n \in \{1, \ldots, N\}$ **do**
  $D_n \leftarrow 0$;
  for $l \in \{1, \ldots, L\}$ **do**
    if $\bar{f}_n^l \geq g^l - z_0\sqrt{(\sigma^l)^2 + (\sigma_n^l)^2}$ *and* $\bar{f}_n^l \leq g^l + z_0\sqrt{(\sigma^l)^2 + (\sigma_n^l)^2}$ **then**
      $\mathbf{C}^l \leftarrow \mathbf{C}^l \cup \{n\}$; $D_n \leftarrow D_n + 10^{(g^l - P_0^l)/(10\gamma^l)}$;
    end
  end
  $D_n \leftarrow D_n / L$;
end
/* Selecting Dense Contours. */
$\mathbf{R} \leftarrow FindHighWeight(\mathbf{\Omega}, \rho, \{D_n\})$;
/* RP Filtering Using Connectivity. */
$\mathbf{R} \leftarrow FindMaxComponent(\mathbf{R}, \zeta)$;
/* Calculating Dist from Contours. */
for $n \in \{1, \ldots, N^{\mathbf{R}}\}$ **do**
  for $l \in \{1, \ldots, L\}$ **do**
    for $m \in \{1, \ldots, |\mathbf{C}^l|\}$ **do**
      $\delta_{nm}^l = \sqrt{(x_n - x_m^l)^2 + (y_n - y_m^l)^2}$;
    end
    $\Delta_n^l(\mathbf{g}, \mathbf{f}_n) = \min\{\delta_{nm}^l\}$;
  end
end
LP-based Localization Using Formulation (28);
$\widehat{\mathbf{x}} \leftarrow \sum_{n=1}^{N^{\mathbf{R}}} \omega_n \mathbf{r}_n$; /* Final Estimation. */

4.3 Complexity Analysis

We here analyze the computational complexity of INTRI:

1. *Forming contours with random signals:* Given N RPs and L APs, the complexity of finding signal contours and calculating contour weights is given by $\mathcal{O}(NL)$ (Section 3.1 and 3.2).

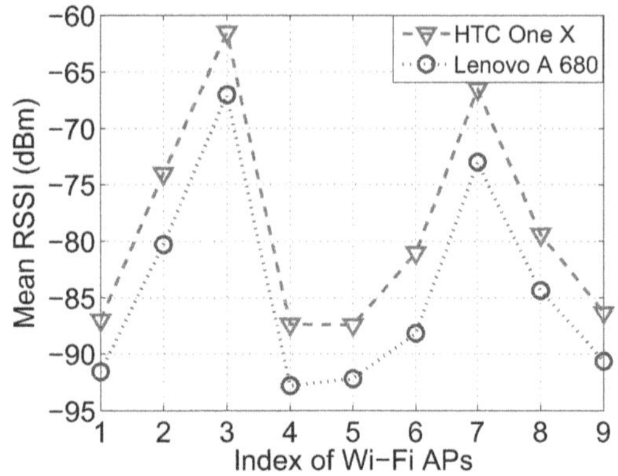

Figure 7: Device heterogeneity between two devices.

2. *Finding maximally connected components:* Given $N^{\mathbf{R}}$ selected RPs, finding the maximally connected component takes $\mathcal{O}((N^{\mathbf{R}})^2)$ [35] (Section 3.3).

3. *LP-based localization:* To prepare the objective function of LP, calculating the distances between $\mathbf{R}$ and contours takes $\mathcal{O}\left(N^{\mathbf{R}}L|\mathbf{C}^l|\right)$ (Section 4.1). In Formulation (28), there are $\mathcal{O}(N^{\mathbf{R}})$ decision variables in $\{\omega_n\}$. Thus, the LP in location estimation takes weak polynomial time, i.e., $\mathcal{O}\left((N^{\mathbf{R}})^3\right)$ [3] (Section 4.2).

To summarize, the overall online running time of INTRI is

$$\mathcal{O}\left(NL + N^{\mathbf{R}}L|\mathbf{C}^l| + \left(N^{\mathbf{R}}\right)^3\right). \quad (29)$$

After contour differentiation and finding maximally connected components, $N^{\mathbf{R}} \ll N$. Further computation reduction can be done via AP filtering and RP cluster mapping [13]. Then we can significantly reduce the number of APs and RPs. In this way, INTRI can be integrated on existing on-board LBS systems and further support mobile targets.

5. EFFICIENT ONLINE CALIBRATION FOR HETEROGENEOUS DEVICES

Due to difference in Wi-Fi network interfaces, for the same signal different smartphones may have different measurement values [14,25]. To illustrate this, we conduct an experiment and collect 1,000 RSSI samples using HTC One X and Lenovo A680, respectively. If such signal difference issue is not addressed, the contours (Section 3.1) cannot be found correctly. Figure 7 shows the similarity of signal trend between signals of the two smartphones despite the shift. Leveraging such similarity, we present an efficient algorithm to adapt to different mobile devices as follows.

In this section we consider efficient and scalable online calibration in order to reduce offline manual efforts. To this end, we map the target signals $\mathbf{g}$ to the signal space in fingerprint database. We first calculate the correlation between the target RSSI vector and that of each RP. The RPs with similar signal vectors can be leveraged for online signal calibration. The vector comparison is based on the correlation between $\mathbf{g}$ and fingerprint $\mathbf{f}_n$, i.e.,

$$corr(\mathbf{g},\mathbf{f}_n) = \frac{\sum_{l=1}^{L}\left(g^l - \bar{g}\right)\left(f_n^l - \bar{f}_n\right)}{\sqrt{\sum_{l=1}^{L}\left(g^l - \bar{g}\right)^2}\sqrt{\sum_{l=1}^{L}\left(f_n^l - \bar{f}_n\right)^2}}, \quad (30)$$

where $\bar{g} = \frac{1}{L}\sum_{l=1}^{L} g^l$ and $\bar{f}_n = \frac{1}{L}\sum_{l=1}^{L} f_n^l$. The above correlation compares relative signal trend of different APs rather than the absolute RSSI values. Based on Equation (30), we can find the RPs with similar signal trend for calibration and reduce the effect of device dependency.

To mitigate the effect of random noise, we find the top several RPs with $corr(\mathbf{g},\mathbf{f}_n) > \eta$ ($\eta = 0.95$ in our experiment) for linear calibration. For each target RSSI g^l from AP l, we find the corresponding f_n^l at RPs. Given pairs of $[g^l, f_n^l]$, we conduct the linear regression and obtain the corresponding a and b for target RSSI g^l, i.e.,

$$\widetilde{g}^l = ag^l + b. \quad (31)$$

Note that our online calibration approach is not restricted to linear model, and is general enough to apply to any other signal mapping model (e.g. [32]). Based on Equation (31) we can conduct INTRI with calibrated $\widetilde{g}^l$. Given $\mathcal{O}(L)$ APs and $\mathcal{O}(N)$ RPs, the correlation comparison takes $\mathcal{O}(NL)$. Let λ ($\lambda \ll N$) be the number of RPs whose correlation $corr(\mathbf{g},\mathbf{f}_n)$ is greater than η, and linear regression takes $\mathcal{O}(L^2\lambda^2)$. Therefore, the online computational complexity of 2-D linear regression is $\mathcal{O}(NL + L^2\lambda^2)$ [3].

6. ILLUSTRATIVE SIMULATION RESULTS

We develop a simulation environment ($100 \times 90m^2$) based on the setting of a local airport. We consider all the Wi-Fi transmitters and receivers are equipped with omni-directional antennas. The RSSI g^l (dBm) at distance d from AP l is given by the LDPL model [1]:

$$g^l = P^{TX} - L_0 - 10\gamma\log_{10}\left(\frac{d}{d_0}\right) + X, \quad (32)$$

where $X \sim \mathcal{N}(0, \sigma_{dB}^2)$ is the Gaussian measurement noise. In our simulation, we set transmission power P^{TX} 25 dBm, the path loss exponent γ 4.0, the reference path loss L_0 37.7 dBm [1] and the reference distance d_0 1 m. Based on empirical observations, if $g^l < -95$ dBm, the target cannot detect the signal of this AP and we discard this measurement.

We evaluate the performance of INTRI in terms of AP number, signal noise and survey grid size in our simulation environment. We compare INTRI with four state-of-the-art schemes:

- *EZPerfect* (EZPerf) [6,31]: a model-based Wi-Fi localization scheme which considers deriving signal propagation model from fingerprint data. Given Wi-Fi fingerprints, EZPerfect first finds the matching relationship between signals and distances from APs [6], and then locates targets with a genetic algorithm solving trilateration problem [31].

- *KL-divergence* (KL-div) [29,30]: which utilizes the Kullback-Leibler (KL) divergence distance [30] between the signal distribution at an RP and target during comparison. Then the top k RPs with the minimum KL-divergence are utilized for final estimation.

- *Weighted k-Nearest Neighbors* (WKNN) [11,12]: It computes the cosine similarity [12] between the fingerprints and the target RSSI vector. Then it finds the weighted average of k-Nearest Neighbors [11] of highest cosine similarity to estimate the target location.

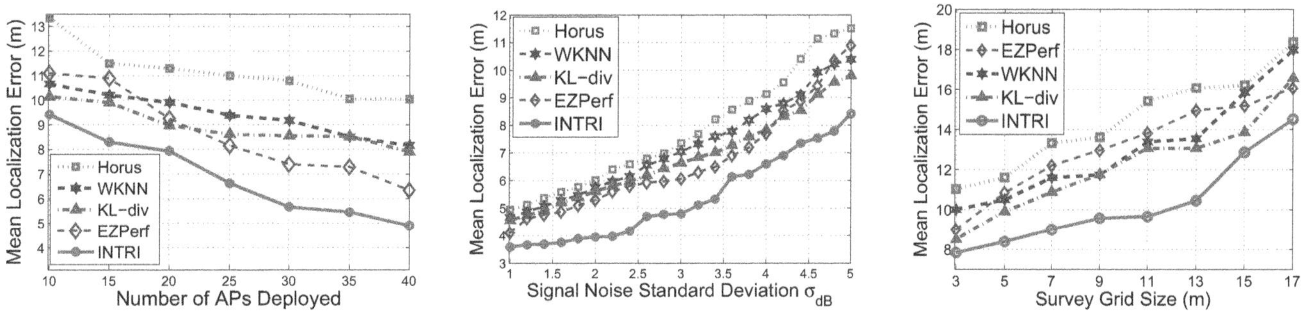

(a) (b) (c)

Figure 8: Mean errors in simulation versus (a) number of APs deployed; (b) signal measurement noise; (c) survey grid size.

- *Probabilistic algorithm* (Horus [42]): It first calculates the probability distribution of the RSSI values at each RP. Given a target RSSI vector, Horus computes the overall probability of the vector at each RP and finds the top several ones with the maximum likelihood as the target location.

Unless otherwise stated, we use following baseline parameters in simulation: 15 APs are deployed; $\sigma_{dB} = 5$ dB (Equation (32)); $k = 20$ for KL-divergence, WKNN and Horus algorithm; $z_0 = 3$ (Equation (12)); survey grid size is 5 m.

Let $\mathbf{x}_m$ be target m's true location and $\widehat{\mathbf{x}}_m$ be its estimated location. The performance metric in our experiment is the mean error (unit:m) of the estimated targets in set $\mathbf{V}$:

$$\mu_e = \frac{1}{|\mathbf{V}|} \sum_{m \in \mathbf{V}} \|\mathbf{x}_m - \widehat{\mathbf{x}}_m\|. \tag{33}$$

In Figure 8(a), we show the mean localization errors versus the number of APs. The performance of all the algorithms improves as the number of APs increases. As there are more APs deployed in the site which help differentiate the RPs, the error decreases. Compared with these traditional algorithms, INTRI achieves much lower errors under different numbers of deployed APs. It is because INTRI considers differentiating contours using contour weights, which helps distinguish the RPs and prevents dispersed estimations.

In Figure 8(b), we show the mean localization errors against the signal measurement noise (σ_{dB} in Equation (32)). Clearly, the performance of all the algorithms degrades as the noise in Wi-Fi signals increases. Signal noise leads to dispersed nearest neighbors and distance measurement error, which degrades the accuracy of traditional pattern matching algorithms and EZPerfect. Especially in different indoor environments ranging from spacious halls or narrow corridors, the signal fluctuation of fingerprints can be different. Even under large fingerprint variation, INTRI achieves much better accuracy. Different from these traditional and state-of-the-art algorithms, INTRI considers the signal variation in the contour construction. Therefore, it achieves higher robustness and localization accuracy under large signal noise.

Figure 8(c) shows the mean localization errors versus survey grid size, i.e., we vary the site survey grid width (in square shape) to change the fingerprint density, given different schemes. Accuracy suffers as grid size increases, illustrating the tradeoff between survey cost and localization accuracy. INTRI considers the signal contours in the formulation to constrain the target region. By minimizing distances to contours, INTRI prevents dispersion of nearest neighbors and achieves higher accuracy.

Figure 9: Survey site of boarding area at HKIA.

Figure 10: Survey site of HKUST campus hall.

Figure 11: Survey site of HKCP shopping mall.

7. EXPERIMENTAL EVALUATIONS

Besides simulation, we have conducted extensive experimental trials of INTRI in the Hong Kong International Airport (HKIA) (Figure 9), our university campus (HKUST) (Figure 10) and the Hong Kong Cyberport (HKCP) (Figure 11). We first present our experimental settings in Section 7.1. As the measured AP signals are different in the three sites, we discuss the comparative studies over these differences in Section 7.2. Then we illustrate the experimental results in HKIA (Section 7.3) followed by those in HKUST and HKCP (Section 7.4).

7.1 Experimental Settings

We use in our experimental studies the same state-of-the-art algorithms and comparison metrics as in Section 6. Besides, we compare the device calibration scheme in INTRI with two recent methods, signal strength difference (SSD) [25] and signal ratio (SR) [28]. SSD utilizes the differences between pairs of AP signal values as patterns. Similarly, SR calculates the ratio between pairs of AP signals as Wi-Fi fingerprints. Both methods aim at compensating the signal difference among heterogeneous devices.

In Figure 12, we show the corresponding survey floor plan of RPs and targets in HKIA. In the 10,000 m^2 site, we collect 340 RPs and 1,100 targets. We utilize HTC One X as the fingerprint collector and Lenovo A680 for target measurement. The locations of RPs are predefined on the indoor map. To balance between localization accuracy and survey cost, we use 5 m grid density in fingerprinting. At each RP, signal data is sampled from four different directions (north, west,

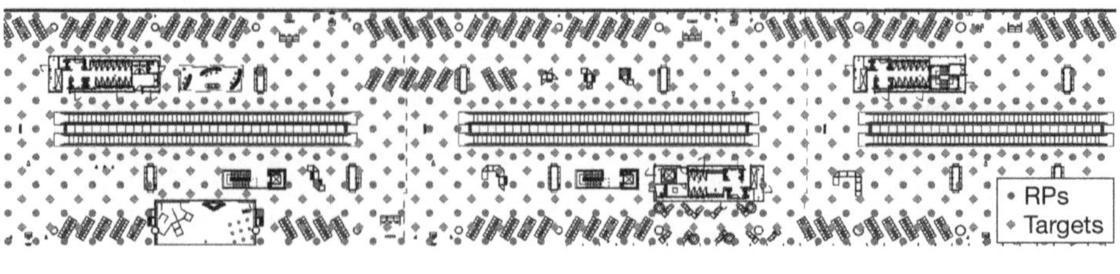

Figure 12: Indoor map of a boarding gate at the HKIA. The survey grid size is 5 m (survey conducted on July 8, 2014).

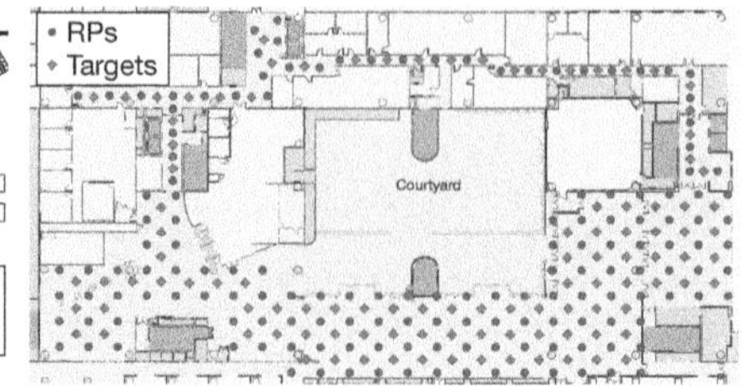

Figure 13: Hall map of HKUST campus (survey conducted on Nov. 28, 2014).

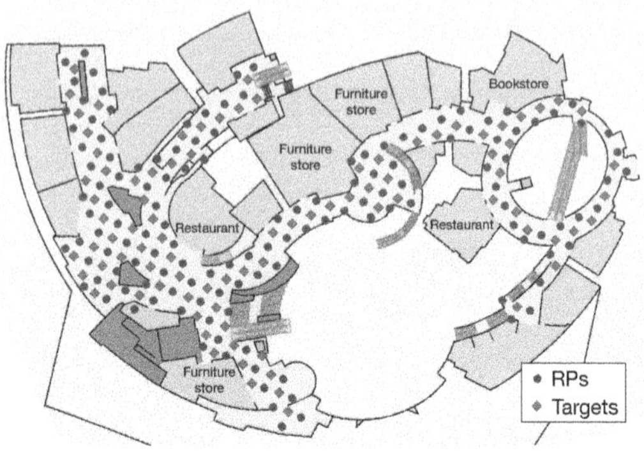

Figure 14: Indoor map of HKCP mall (survey conducted on Sept. 10, 2014).

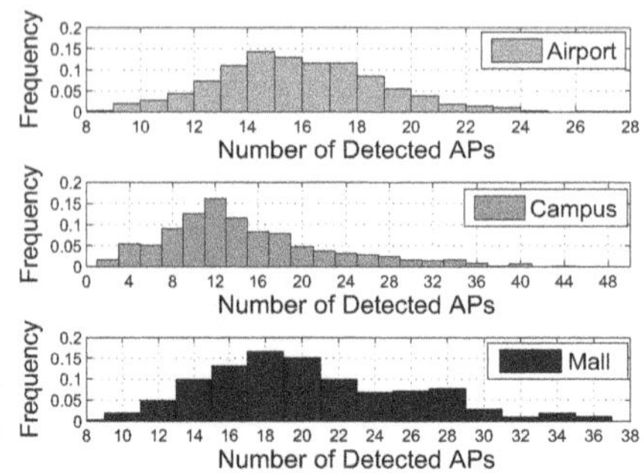

Figure 15: Histograms of detected AP number at targets in three sites.

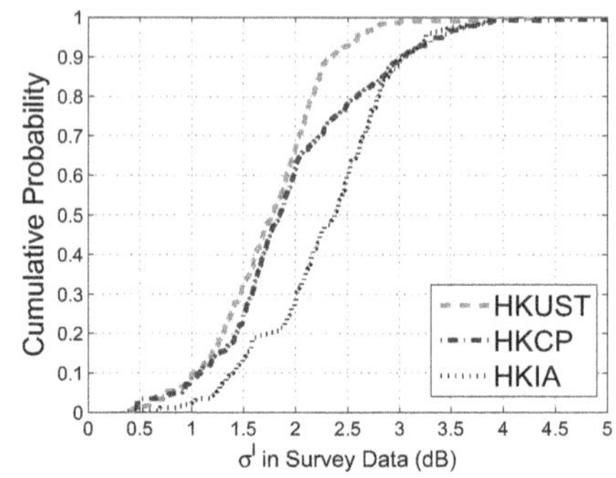

Figure 16: Average signal noise σ^l (Equation (10)) in different sites.

south and east). For each direction, 15 samples of RSSI vectors are collected. The ground truth of the target locations is also predetermined in grid form (in the testing, the surveyors find the RP or target locations from the nearest pillars, floor tiles and other noticeable indoor landmarks). Note that the data sampling is conducted with people around, and temporal fluctuation exists within the fingerprints and target signals. The time interval between samples in Wi-Fi scanning is 1 second.

Wi-Fi APs are officially pre-deployed. Thus, their number, locations and transmission power are already settled before site survey. In the data preprocessing, we filter out the mobile APs tethered by smartphones, and combine the signals of virtual APs (VAPs) [27]. Overall 360 APs are detected (each RP measures 47 APs on average). Part of these APs may be installed outside the survey site since their coverage in our site is relatively small and signals are globally weak. The target samples are collected one month later than RP collection. For schemes like KL-divergence and Horus which are device dependent, we utilize our scheme to calibrate the signals.

In the HKUST campus and the HKCP shopping mall, fingerprint collection, target sampling and data preprocessing are the same as those in the airport. Figure 13 shows the RPs and targets on campus ($100 \times 50m^2$). In campus corridor environment, we collect 250 RPs and 475 targets. Figure 14 shows the RPs and targets in the shopping mall ($150 \times 100m^2$). In the HKCP mall, we collect 680 RPs and 680 targets. In both the HKUST and HKCP, the blue dots represent RPs and the red diamonds are targets. Similar to the HKIA, we are given the officially deployed APs and we cannot manually change their settings (installation locations and TX power). In the site survey of campus corridor, overall 320 APs are detected (each RP measures 24 APs on average). In the site survey at shopping mall, overall 190 APs are detected (average 28 APs at each RP).

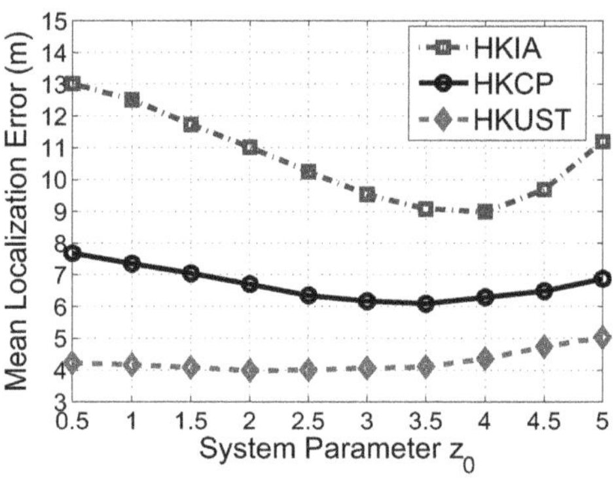

Figure 17: Mean errors versus parameter z_0 in three sites.

7.2 Comparative Studies of Different Sites

Figure 15 shows the histograms of AP number detected by targets at different sites. On average, each target can detect 16 APs on HKUST and 22 APs in HKCP. In HKIA, each target can detect 16 APs on average. Though targets in HKIA and HKUST have similar detected AP number, the survey site in HKUST is smaller and hence it has denser AP deployment. Moreover, the signal coverage of APs in our campus corridor and HKCP is constrained by the wall partitions, which helps differentiate the RPs. Therefore, we expect a better localization performance on HKUST and HKCP than in HKIA. Based on these detected APs, we evaluate the effect of different received AP numbers.

Figure 16 shows the corresponding signal noise in each survey site. We show the cumulative probability of the σ^l according to Equation (10). Clearly, we can see a smaller signal noise in HKUST and HKCP than that in HKIA. It is because the airport boarding area is large open space with

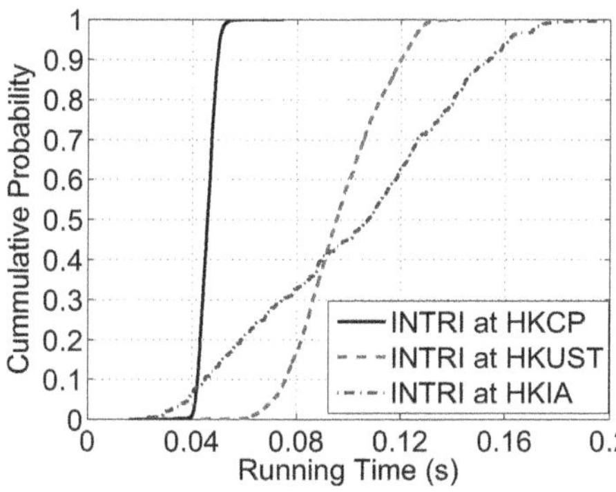

Figure 18: Cumulative probability of INTRI running time on different sites.

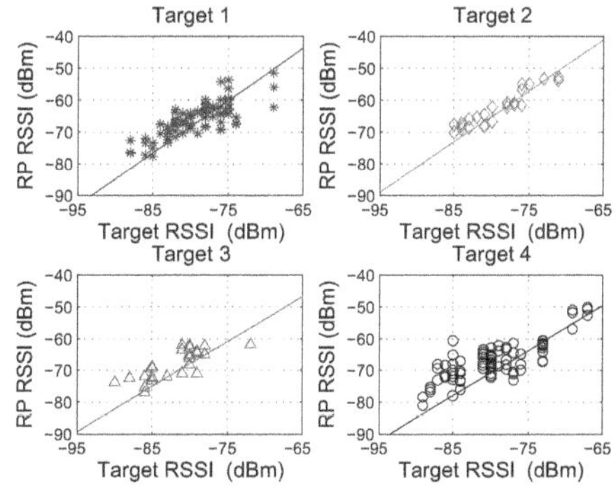

Figure 19: Calibration of target RSSI from RP signals (HKIA).

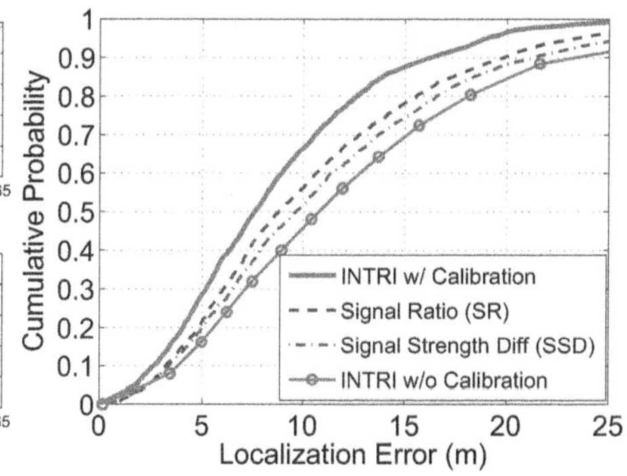

Figure 20: Performance of different device calibration methods in HKIA.

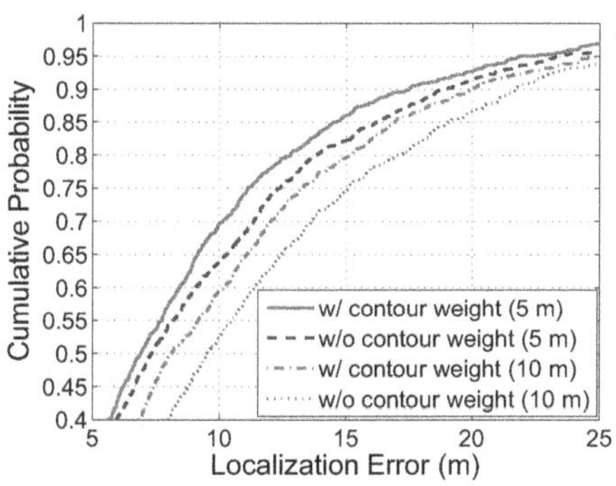

Figure 21: Performance of INTRI with and without contour weights (HKIA).

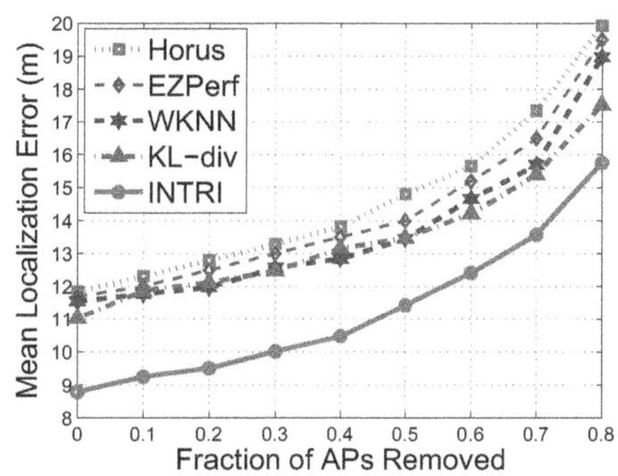

Figure 22: Mean errors versus fraction of APs removed (HKIA).

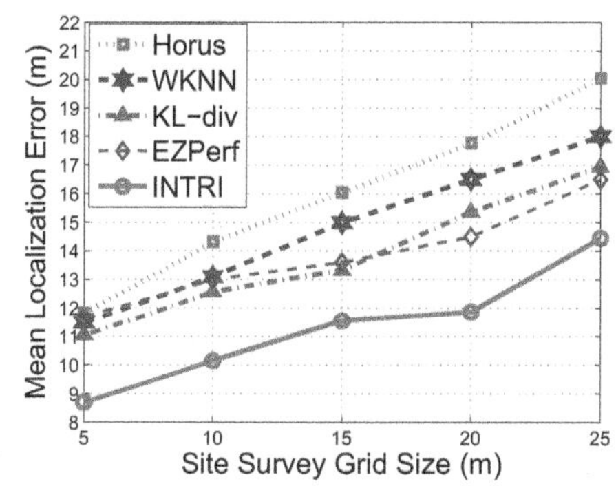

Figure 23: Mean localization errors versus site survey grid size (HKIA).

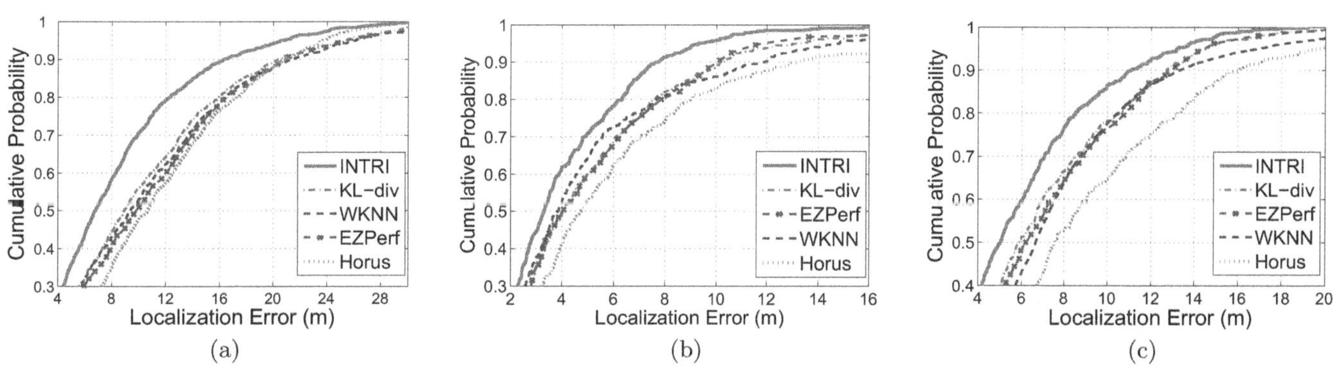

Figure 24: Cumulative probability of localization errors in (a) HKIA boarding gate; (b) HKUST campus; (c) HKCP mall.

many airline passengers, which leads to higher signal uncertainty. Based on the difference in signal noise, we adjust the parameter z_0 in Equation (12) for online localization.

Figure 17 shows the mean localization errors of INTRI in three sites given different z_0. In general, the error first decreases and then increases. This is because the localization error depends on two factors: signal noise and RP fingerprint differentiation. When z_0 is small, the tight contours cannot accommodate the large measurement uncertainty in target. Thus, the error is high. As z_0 increases, the contours can bound the target, and hence the error decreases. As z_0 further increases, the error increases because, as contours become wide, the differentiation between RPs becomes weak. Then more distant RPs are included in localization. The result shows that without sufficient RP fingerprint differentiation, wide contours would not help. Compared with HKUST and HKCP, z_0 is slightly larger in HKIA due to higher signal variance in airport (as shown in Figure 16). Thus, in our experiment, $z_0 = 4$ in HKIA, $z_0 = 3.5$ in HKCP, and $z_0 = 2.5$ on our HKUST campus.

Figure 18 shows the running time CDF of INTRI on the targets at different sites. We test INTRI on a server PC with i7 4790 (3.6GHz) CPU. It shows that at the three sites, our INTRI shows different computation time due to the difference in RP numbers and detected AP number at target side and RP side. The running time of INTRI at HKCP is much smaller than that at HKIA and HKUST. It is mainly because many of detected APs in HKCP are installed in the shop stores and have limited coverage (small contours) due to wall partitions, compared with those in HKIA and HKUST. A target can be quickly mapped to smaller areas and therefore the overall computation becomes much smaller.

7.3 International Airport Trials

Figure 19 shows the linear signal model of four different target estimations in HKIA. Target data (x-axis) are collected using Lenovo A680 while RP signals (y-axis) are from HTC One X. Based on the a and b, we obtain the calibrated signal strength, $\widetilde{g}^l$, for each given target. We can see that the linear calibration scales up the Lenovo A680 measurements (target), which matches our observation in Figure 7.

Figure 20 compares the cumulative errors of different device calibration schemes in the airport. We use uncalibrated signals in INTRI as the baseline case. The calibrated INTRI improves from the uncalibrated scheme, and also outperforms SSD and SR. It is mainly because our proposed scheme jointly considers the relative trend and the RSSI adjustment model when calibrating devices. Unlike SSD and SR, our correlation scheme mitigates the errors in signal values when INTRI calibrates target RSSI using fingerprints, which is more robust under large signal noise in the airport.

Figure 21 shows the localization error with and without differentiating the contours using HKIA data. We consider two scenarios using 5 m (default) and 10 m survey grid size. Without using contour weights, we count the number of signal contours and implement it into INTRI as the baseline case. As shown in Figure 21, simple contour counting cannot discriminate the dispersed nearest neighbors (RPs) with similar number of contours. In contrast, contour weight discriminates the fingerprints by penalizing RPs only with many weak signals. Then we mitigate the influence from the noise in the measurement. Thus, we have shown using contour weights achieves better performance than the unweighted scheme, especially under sparser survey grid size.

In Figure 22, we plot the mean localization errors of these algorithms against the number of APs used. We randomly select part of the APs detected at target side to simulate the miss of the RSSI due to crowds of people or site construction change, which generally exists in the HKIA. As the number of APs used decreases, the performance of all five algorithms degrades. INTRI is less susceptible to AP number change than other four algorithms. It is mainly because junction of contours can constrain the target in a small region and reduce the dispersed set of nearest neighbors.

Figure 23 shows the mean localization errors against the survey grid size. As the minimum grid size is five meters, columns or rows of RPs are removed to form the grid sizes with multiples of five. Clearly all five algorithms degrade as grid size increases. We can observe EZPerfect achieves slightly higher accuracy than WKNN, KL-divergence and Horus under larger grid size. It is because for EZPerfect additional distances from multiple APs constrain the target location and prevent large error. Compared with the algorithms above, INTRI has much higher localization accuracy at different grid sizes. It is because INTRI considers signal uncertainty in contours and constrains the target estimation through joint optimization. Without relying on accurate distance measurement, INTRI can still constrain the target estimation by signal contours under large grid size.

Figure 24(a) compares the cumulative errors of five algorithms in HKIA. Due to large measurement noise in the airport, WKNN's accuracy is weakened by the dispersed nearest neighbors. Horus assumes a certain distribution of signal level at each RP and therefore cannot represent real signal distribution under limited sampling. KL-divergence also requires large data sampling and dense fingerprints in signal distribution comparison. Therefore, it cannot adapt to the noisy airport environment. The large signal noise also degrades the distance accuracy of traditional trilateration in EZPerfect. In contrast to above methods, INTRI jointly considers the signal noise and distances to contours, and therefore reduces misestimation of the target.

7.4 Campus Hall & Shopping Mall Trials

Figure 24(b) and Figure 24(c) show the cumulative errors in HKUST and HKCP, respectively. Compared with the HKIA, the fingerprints and target signals in HKUST and HKCP carry less signal measurement noise. Thus, we observe the increase of localization accuracy in all the algorithms at these two sites compared with that in the airport. EZPerfect becomes slightly better than WKNN as the distance measurement becomes less noisy. Similar to Figure 24(a), INTRI achieves higher accuracy than other algorithms since it considers the signal variation in constructing contours and utilizes them to reduce the dispersed nearest neighbors. INTRI is general enough to work under different environments with markedly higher accuracy.

We also study the performance of INTRI in the HKUST and HKCP extensively. As the conclusions are qualitatively the same, for brevity we will not repeat them here.

8. CONCLUSION

Traditional trilateration has achieved much success for outdoor localization. However, it does not work well indoors due to non-line-of-sight measurement and signal fading. Fingerprinting is a promising approach for indoor localization, but its performance is vulnerable to signal noise. We propose in this work INTRI, a highly accurate algorithm which combines the advantages of both trilateration and fingerprinting to achieve much better accuracy.

Based on the spirit of trilateration, for each measured AP signal level, INTRI forms the corresponding contour, which is the set of RPs with the same signal level subject to its statistical fluctuation. The target is hence where the contour is. To estimate target's location, INTRI formulates a linear programming to minimize the distance between the location and these contours (i.e., following the spirit of trilateration). To achieve higher accuracy, INTRI addresses device heterogeneity with an efficient and scalable algorithm based on the correlation in RSSI for online signal calibration. We have conducted extensive simulation and experimental studies on INTRI in the Hong Kong International Airport, Hong Kong Cyberport mall and HKUST campus. Compared with other approaches, INTRI achieves significantly higher accuracy and robustness under signal noise (often by more than 20%).

9. ACKNOWLEDGMENTS

This work was supported, in part, by The Hong Kong R&D Center for Logistics and Supply Chain Management Enabling Technologies (ITP/034/12LP), and Hong Kong Research Grant Council (RGC) General Research Fund (610713).

10. REFERENCES

[1] N. Alsindi, R. Raulefs, and C. Teolis. *Geolocation Techniques: Principles and Applications*. Springer, 2012.

[2] P. Bahl and V. N. Padmanabhan. RADAR: An in-building RF-based user location and tracking system. In *Proc. IEEE INFOCOM*, volume 2, pages 775–784, 2000.

[3] S. P. Boyd and L. Vandenberghe. *Convex Optimization*. Cambridge University Press, 2004.

[4] K. Chang and D. Han. Crowdsourcing-based radio map update automation for Wi-Fi positioning systems. In *Proc. ACM SIGSPATIAL GeoCrowd*, pages 24–31, 2014.

[5] Y.-C. Chen, J.-R. Chiang, H.-h. Chu, P. Huang, and A. W. Tsui. Sensor-assisted Wi-Fi indoor location system for adapting to environmental dynamics. In *Proc. ACM MSWiM*, pages 118–125, 2005.

[6] K. Chintalapudi, A. Padmanabha Iyer, and V. N. Padmanabhan. Indoor localization without the pain. In *Proc. ACM MobiCom*, pages 173–184, 2010.

[7] S.-H. Fang, C.-H. Wang, S.-M. Chiou, and P. Lin. Calibration-free approaches for robust Wi-Fi positioning against device diversity: A performance comparison. In *Proc. IEEE VTC Spring*, pages 1–5, 2012.

[8] B. Ferris, D. Fox, and N. D. Lawrence. WiFi-SLAM using Gaussian process latent variable models. In *Proc. IJCAI*, pages 2480–2485, 2007.

[9] A. Goswami, L. E. Ortiz, and S. R. Das. WiGEM: A learning-based approach for indoor localization. In *Proc. ACM CoNEXT*, pages 3:1–3:12, 2011.

[10] X. Guo, D. Zhang, K. Wu, and L. Ni. MODLoc: Localizing multiple objects in dynamic indoor environment. *IEEE Trans. Parallel and Distributed Systems*, 25(11):2969–2980, Nov. 2014.

[11] D. Han, S. Jung, M. Lee, and G. Yoon. Building a practical Wi-Fi-based indoor navigation system. *IEEE Pervasive Computing*, 13(2):72–79, Apr. 2014.

[12] S. Han, C. Zhao, W. Meng, and C. Li. Cosine similarity based fingerprinting algorithm in WLAN indoor positioning against device diversity. In *Proc. IEEE ICC*, pages 4313–4317, 2015.

[13] S. He and S.-H. Chan. Sectjunction: Wi-Fi indoor localization based on junction of signal sectors. In *Proc. IEEE ICC*, pages 2605–2610, June 2014.

[14] S. He and S.-H. G. Chan. Wi-Fi fingerprint-based indoor positioning: Recent advances and comparisons. *IEEE Communications Surveys and Tutorials*, to appear.

[15] S. He, S.-H. G. Chan, L. Yu, and N. Liu. Calibration-free fusion of step counter and wireless fingerprints for indoor localization. In *Proc. ACM UbiComp*, 2015.

[16] S. He, S.-H. G. Chan, L. Yu, and N. Liu. Fusing noisy fingerprints with distance bounds for indoor localization. In *Proc. IEEE INFOCOM*, pages 2506–2514, 2015.

[17] S. Hilsenbeck, D. Bobkov, G. Schroth, R. Huitl, and E. Steinbach. Graph-based data fusion of pedometer and WiFi measurements for mobile indoor positioning. In *Proc. ACM UbiComp*, pages 147–158, 2014.

[18] Y. Jiang, Y. Xiang, X. Pan, K. Li, Q. Lv, R. P. Dick, L. Shang, and M. Hannigan. Hallway based automatic indoor floorplan construction using room fingerprints. In *Proc. ACM UbiComp*, pages 315–324, 2013.

[19] J. Jun, Y. Gu, L. Cheng, B. Lu, J. Sun, T. Zhu, and J. Niu. Social-Loc: Improving indoor localization with social sensing. In *Proc. ACM SenSys*, pages 14:1–14:14, 2013.

[20] Y. Kim, H. Shin, and H. Cha. Smartphone-based Wi-Fi pedestrian-tracking system tolerating the RSS variance problem. In *Proc. IEEE PerCom*, pages 11–19, Mar. 2012.

[21] S. Kumar, S. Gil, D. Katabi, and D. Rus. Accurate indoor localization with zero start-up cost. In *Proc. ACM MobiCom*, pages 483–494, 2014.

[22] A. Kushki, K. N. Plataniotis, and A. N. Venetsanopoulos. Kernel-based positioning in wireless local area networks. *IEEE Trans. Mobile Computing*, 6(6):689–705, 2007.

[23] L. Li, G. Shen, C. Zhao, T. Moscibroda, J.-H. Lin, and F. Zhao. Experiencing and handling the diversity in data density and environmental locality in an indoor positioning service. In *Proc. ACM MobiCom*, pages 459–470, 2014.

[24] H. Liu, J. Yang, S. Sidhom, Y. Wang, Y. Chen, and F. Ye. Accurate WiFi based localization for smartphones using peer assistance. *IEEE Trans. Mobile Computing*, 13(10):2199–2214, Oct 2014.

[25] A. Mahtab Hossain, Y. Jin, W.-S. Soh, and H. N. Van. SSD: A robust RF location fingerprint addressing mobile devices' heterogeneity. *IEEE Trans. Mobile Computing*, 12(1):65–77, Jan. 2013.

[26] A. T. Mariakakis, S. Sen, J. Lee, and K.-H. Kim. SAIL: Single access point-based indoor localization. In *Proc. ACM MobiSys*, pages 315–328, 2014.

[27] E. Martin, O. Vinyals, G. Friedland, and R. Bajcsy. Precise indoor localization using smart phones. In *Proc. ACM MM*, pages 787–790, 2010.

[28] Mikkel Baun Kjaergaard. Indoor location fingerprinting with heterogeneous clients. *Pervasive and Mobile Computing*, 7:31 – 43, 2011.

[29] P. Mirowski, D. Milioris, P. Whiting, and T. Kam Ho. Probabilistic radio-frequency fingerprinting and localization on the run. *Bell Labs Technical Journal*, 18(4):111–133, 2014.

[30] P. Mirowski, P. Whiting, H. Steck, R. Palaniappan, M. MacDonald, D. Hartmann, and T. K. Ho. Probability kernel regression for WiFi localisation. *Journal of Location Based Services*, 6(2):81–100, 2012.

[31] R. Nandakumar, K. K. Chintalapudi, and V. N. Padmanabhan. Centaur: Locating devices in an office environment. In *Proc. ACM MobiCom*, pages 281–292, 2012.

[32] J.-g. Park, D. Curtis, S. Teller, and J. Ledlie. Implications of device diversity for organic localization. In *Proc. IEEE INFOCOM*, pages 3182–3190, Apr. 2011.

[33] G. Shen, Z. Chen, P. Zhang, T. Moscibroda, and Y. Zhang. Walkie-Markie: Indoor pathway mapping made easy. In *Proc. USENIX NSDI*, pages 85–98, 2013.

[34] H. Shin, Y. Chon, Y. Kim, and H. Cha. MRI: Model-based radio interpolation for indoor

war-walking. *IEEE Trans. Mobile Computing*, 14(6):1231–1244, June 2015.

[35] S. S. Skiena. *The Algorithm Design Manual.* Springer Science & Business Media, 2008.

[36] W. Sun, J. Liu, C. Wu, Z. Yang, X. Zhang, and Y. Liu. MoLoc: On distinguishing fingerprint twins. In *Proc. IEEE ICDCS*, pages 226–235, July 2013.

[37] S.-H. Tsai, S.-Y. Lau, and P. Huang. WSN-based real-time indoor location system at the Taipei World Trade Center: Implementation, deployment, measurement, and experience. In *Proc. IEEE Sensors*, pages 1–4, Oct 2012.

[38] H. Wang, S. Sen, A. Elgohary, M. Farid, M. Youssef, and R. R. Choudhury. No need to war-drive: Unsupervised indoor localization. In *Proc. ACM MobiSys*, pages 197–210, 2012.

[39] K. Wu, J. Xiao, Y. Yi, D. Chen, X. Luo, and L. M. Ni. CSI-based indoor localization. *IEEE Trans. Parallel and Distributed Systems*, 24(7):1300–1309, Jul. 2013.

[40] Z. Yang, Z. Wang, J. Zhang, C. Huang, and Q. Zhang. Wearables can afford: Light-weight indoor positioning with visible light. In *Proc. ACM MobiSys*, pages 317–330, 2015.

[41] M. Youssef and A. Agrawala. Handling samples correlation in the Horus system. In *Proc. IEEE INFOCOM*, pages 1023–1031, 2004.

[42] M. Youssef and A. Agrawala. The Horus location determination system. *Wireless Networks*, 14(3):357–374, 2008.

[43] D. Zhou and T.-H. Lai. A compatible and scalable clock synchronization protocol in IEEE 802.11 ad hoc networks. In *Proc. ICPP*, pages 295–302, 2005.

Accurate Positioning via Cross-Modality Training

Savvas Papaioannou Hongkai Wen Zhuoling Xiao
Andrew Markham Niki Trigoni
Department of Computer Science
University of Oxford
Wolfson Building, Parks Road, Oxford, OX1 3QD, UK
e-mail: firstname.lastname@cs.ox.ac.uk

ABSTRACT

In this paper we propose a novel algorithm for tracking people in highly dynamic industrial settings, such as construction sites. We observed both short term and long term changes in the environment; people were allowed to walk in different parts of the site on different days, the field of view of fixed cameras changed over time with the addition of walls, whereas radio and magnetic maps proved unstable with the movement of large structures. To make things worse, the uniforms and helmets that people wear for safety make them very hard to distinguish visually, necessitating the use of additional sensor modalities. In order to address these challenges, we designed a positioning system that uses both anonymous and id-linked sensor measurements and explores the use of cross-modality training to deal with environment dynamics. The system is evaluated in a real construction site and is shown to outperform state of the art multi-target tracking algorithms designed to operate in relatively stable environments.

Categories and Subject Descriptors

C.3 [**Special-Purpose and Application-Based Systems**]: Real-Time and Embedded Systems

General Terms

Algorithms, Experimentation, System

Keywords

Wireless Sensor Networks; Tracking

1. INTRODUCTION

To date, the majority of positioning systems have been designed to operate within environments that have long-term stable macro-structure with potential small-scale dynamics. These assumptions allow for stable maps to be produced and gradually aged with the incorporation of minor variations.

SenSys'15, November 1–4, 2015, Seoul, South Korea.
© 2015 ACM. ISBN 978-1-4503-3631-4/15/11 ...$15.00.
DOI: http://dx.doi.org/10.1145/2809695.2809712.

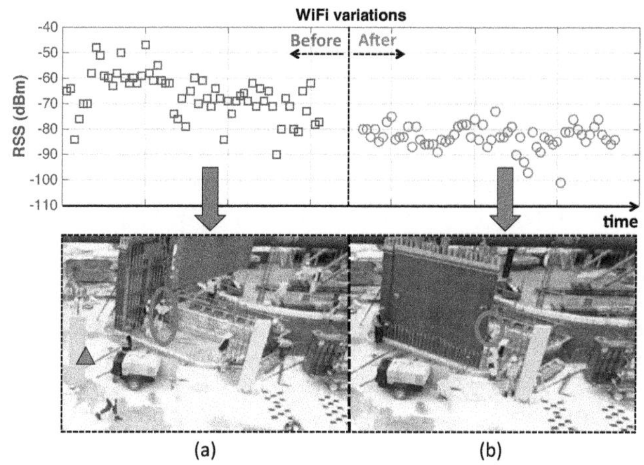

Figure 1: The WiFi signal strength received by the worker in circle is affected by the installation of a new wall (a) Before the installation, there are direct WiFi signals from the access point (shown as triangle) to the worker, (b) The worker is blocked by the new wall, which affects the propagation properties of the WiFi signals as shown in the graph above.

For example, in an indoor environment, the positions of walls and floors remain constant over time, whereas positions of furniture can change from day to day.

In this work, we tackle the problem of accurate localization in construction sites which are characterized by rapid large-scale changes in structure. For example, Fig. (1) shows the effect of a wall being installed in the middle of one of our tracking experiments. The received signal strength of a worker's smartphone from one of the access points dropped considerably after the installation of the wall, in a matter of minutes. The field of view of the camera also changed, not allowing us to directly visually track the people behind the wall. In addition to these short changes, during our experiments we observed much more significant long term changes (Fig. (2), Fig. (6)); within periods of a few weeks, the scene changed dramatically, staircases or entire floors were added, obfuscating the view to the first floors and creating additional layers where people needed to be tracked.

Currently, there is no system that allows for workers to be tracked reliably and robustly during all phases of construction. As a case in point, consider the challenges in a unified positioning system that works equally as well during deep foundation excavation through to an almost complete

Figure 2: We have conducted tracking experiments in a construction site setting: (a) the construction site on day 1, (b) the construction site on day 36, (c) floor plan of the site. The site changes rapidly from day to day, precluding the use of positioning systems which rely on stable, long-term maps.

multi-storey building. At different points in time, the performance of different techniques alters, with some improving and some degrading. The site itself changes rapidly from day to day, precluding the use of systems which rely on stable, long-term maps (e.g. WiFiSLAM) for positioning.

Our aim is to provide a system that can monitor the location of workers to indicate working hazards (e.g. red and green zones), which can be individually tailored. For example, a steel-worker has the training to operate in areas which might not yet be poured with concrete whilst forming the steel rebar. Conversely, a general construction worker should not venture into regions where steel-work has not been completed. This level of safety requires positioning precision beyond the majority of indoor positioning solutions, with desired sub-meter accuracy.

In addition, for such a positioning system to be used and adopted in the construction industry, it should be low-cost, exploit existing infrastructure and not require manual tuning and calibration. We note that a pervasive feature of construction environments is the use of site-wide closed-circuit television (CCTV) to provide security. CCTV alone is not useful for positioning, as we have to identify what each object in the video sequence actually is. This is especially challenging for low-resolution, grainy footage typically obtained from CCTV, which is unable to accurately distinguish between different people based on facial recognition. Instead however, we note that the task of identifying moving objects from a video sequence is a much easier problem. To tackle the identification problem we use devices carried by the workers which emit radio signals (WiFi/BTLE) and capture inertial measurements to assign identities to each trajectory. This is complicated by the fact that the visual detector is affected by occlusions, changing light conditions and challenges in detection when targets coalesce e.g. if workers are standing together.

We further note that when we have identified a trajectory and linked a set of visual observations with a set of radio and inertial measurements with high probability, we can then use such a trajectory to learn the parameters of all the components in the system. For example, we can learn the radio model, which can help calibrate the system for when the camera is occluded. Individuals also have different gait lengths and whilst a worker is being tracked by the high-resolution vision system, we can exploit this to learn the optimal step-length. This provides us with better measurements when a user steps behind a wall, disappearing from the camera's view. Lastly, we can also learn positions of workers that can actually be observed by a particular camera. This occlusion map is useful for filtering out impossible trajectories. In essence, we are exploiting the fact that different sensing technologies have uncorrelated failure modes to provide a robust, adaptive positioning framework. To summarize, the major contributions of this work are as follows:

1. A positioning framework explicitly designed for rapidly changing environments.
2. A technique for cross-modal sensor parameter learning.
3. A CCTV and smartphone based positioning system.
4. Extensive experiments in a real construction site.

2. PROBLEM DEFINITION

In this paper we tackle the problem of tracking people in environments equipped with one or more stationary calibrated cameras. We assume that people that desire to be tracked carry a mobile device, such as a smartphone or customized worker safety equipment, and move freely in and out of the field of view (FOV). We divide time into short time intervals, and at each time t we receive a number of camera detections of the moving objects denoted as $C_t = \{c_t^1, c_t^2, ..., c_t^j, ...\}$, $1 \leq j \leq |C_t|$. A camera detection c_t^j represents the bounding box of the j_{th} object generated by a foreground detector as shown in Fig. (4). Note that at time t we could be receiving camera detections not only from people but also from other moving objects (i.e. vehicles); false positive detections are also received due to illumination changes, shadows, etc. In order to reduce the number of false positive detections and concentrate on detecting only people we apply a head detector to the output of a foreground detector.

At time t we also receive a collection of radio measurements $R_t = \{r_t^k\}$, $1 \leq k \leq K$ where K is the total number of people with mobile devices who wish to be tracked and $r_t^k = [\text{rss}^1, ..., \text{rss}^m]_t^k$ is a vector of received signal strength (RSS) measurements of the k_{th} device from m access points. Additionally, we assume that each mobile device is equipped with an inertial measurement unit (IMU) containing an accelerometer and a magnetometer. This allows us to generate at time t a collection of inertial measurements denoted as

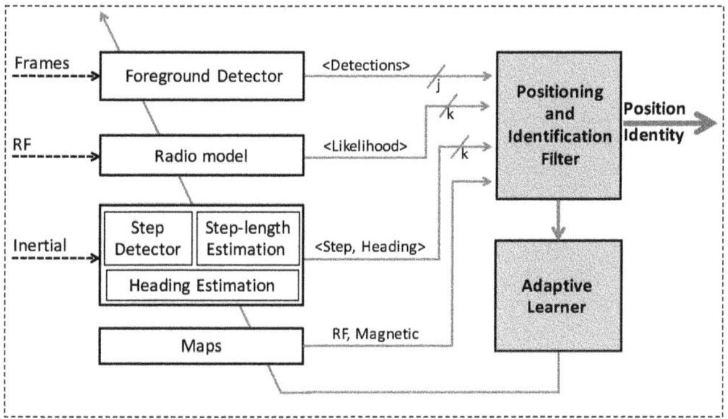

Figure 3: Overview of the proposed system architecture.

$S_t = \{s_t^k\}$ where $s_t^k = [b_t^k, d_t^k, \theta_t^k]$ is a vector that contains the step indicator, step-length and heading of the k_{th} person respectively. Each index k uniquely identifies a person and corresponds to a unique MAC address of the mobile device.

The problem to solve is the following : *Given anonymous camera detections $C_{1:t}$, id-linked radio measurements $R_{1:t}$ and id-linked inertial measurements $S_{1:t}$ estimate the trajectories of all users carrying mobile devices and moving inside the camera FOV.*

3. SYSTEM OVERVIEW

An overview of the proposed system architecture is shown in Fig. (3). The *Positioning and Identification filter* obtains anonymous camera detections, radio and inertial measurements from multiple people and is responsible for solving three problems. Firstly, it establishes the correspondences of camera detections across frames, that is, links together anonymous camera detections that correspond to the same person. Secondly, it finds the mapping between anonymous camera detections and id-linked smartphone (radio and step) measurements. Finally, it identifies and estimates the positions of multiple targets.

The *Adaptive Learner* uses the output of the filter in combination with the input observations, and performs cross-modality training. Specifically, it configures the foreground detector's internal parameters taking into account available motion measurements. In addition, it tunes the step-length estimation method by leveraging reliable camera measurements. Finally, it exploits camera measurements to learn the radio model; radio, magnetic and occlusion maps can also be learned which can be used to further improve the system's accuracy.

The remaining components of the system are existing modules which pre-process raw sensor data and transform them to camera, step and radio measurements.

4. MULTIPLE TARGET TRACKING

In this section we provide a brief overview of previous work on multiple target tracking (MTT). A more detailed description of MTT algorithms can be found in [2].

4.1 Introduction to Multiple Target Tracking

Under the general MTT setup a number of indistinguishable targets are assumed to move freely inside the field of view; they can enter and exit the FOV at random times.

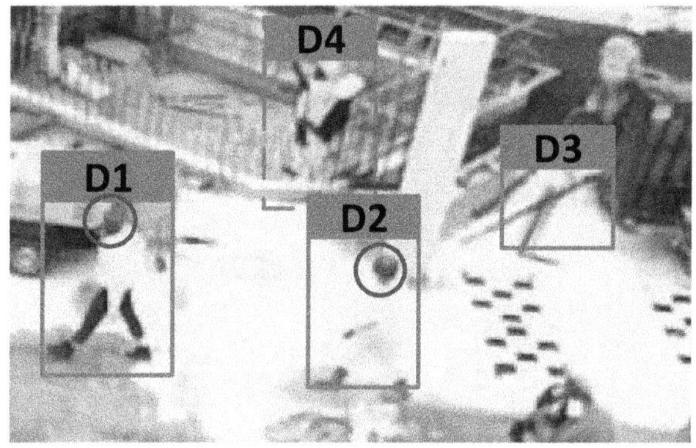

Figure 4: Camera detections generated by our system: a) people are detected correctly by a head detector applied to the output of the foreground detector (D1 and D2), b) Illumination variations create false positive detections (D3). In this case the use of the head detector allows us to discard this measurement, c) not all moving people are detected, the dotted bounding box (D4) shows a case of missing detection.

The system receives sensor data about the position of the targets periodically which are noisy, include false alarm measurements (i.e. background noise or clutter) and occur with some detection probability. Each target follows a sequence of states (e.g. positions) during its lifetime called *track*. The main objective of MTT is to collect sensor data containing multiple potential targets of interest and to then find the tracks of all targets and filter out the false alarm measurements. If the sequence of measurements associated with each target is known (i.e. id-linked measurements) then the MTT reduces to a state estimation problem (e.g. distinct Kalman/particle filters can be used to follow each target). However, when the target-to-measurements association is unknown (for example, anonymous measurements from cameras, radars and sonars are used) the data association problem must be solved in addition to state estimation. Essentially, the data association problem seeks to find which measurements correspond to each target.

MTT algorithms handle both the data-association and the state-estimation problems and they are generally divided into two categories a) *Unique-neighbor data association* and b) *All-neighbor data association*. The former methods allow at most one measurement to be used to update a given track and they usually do not permit a measurement to be used more than once. On the other hand, the all-neighbor data association methods use multiple measurements to update the track estimates. A representative algorithm from the first category is the popular multiple hypothesis tracking (MHT) algorithm [20, 1]. MHT is a deferred decision logic method which maintains multiple track hypotheses. In MHT alternative data association hypotheses are formed whenever there are measurement-to-track ambiguities. The measurement-to-track association decision is postponed until enough measurements are collected that can be used to resolve the association ambiguities. A well known all-neighbor data association method is the joint probabilistic data association (JPDA) filter [8]. JPDA approximates the posterior distribution of the targets as separate Gaussian distributions for each target. At each time step, instead of finding a single best association between measurements and tracks,

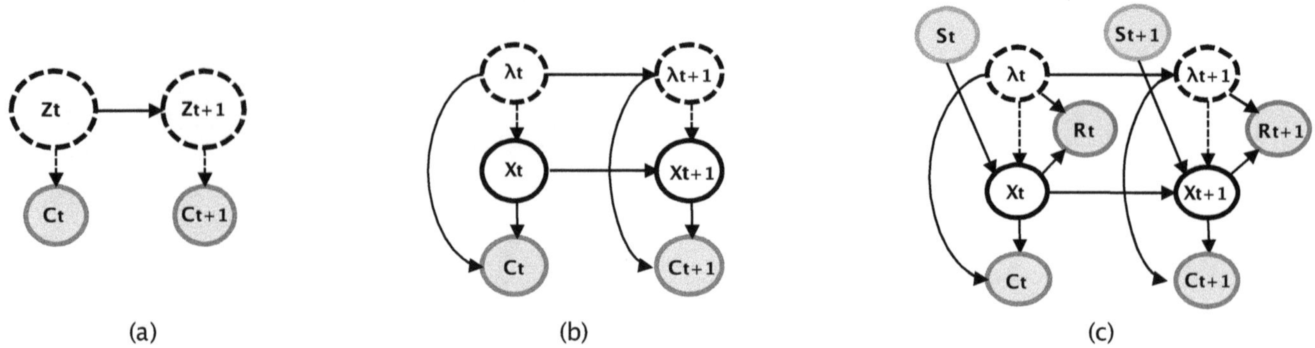

(a) (b) (c)

Figure 5: Graphical models for the multiple target tracking problem. Shaded nodes indicate observations and clear nodes indicate hidden variables. Nodes with dashed lines use particle filtering estimation. Dashed arrows indicate that the association between target states and measurements must be recovered before updating a target with a specific measurement. (a) Standard particle filter: uses sampling to estimate the joint posterior distribution of states and data associations ($P(Z_t|C_{1:t})$), (b) In Rao-Blackwellized particle filter (i.e. RBMCDA) the data-association is decoupled from the state estimation. The filter samples only from the data-associations distribution $P(\lambda_t|C_{1:t})$. The distribution of target states conditioned on the association $P(X_t|\lambda_t, C_{1:t})$ is calculated analytically. (c) Proposed approach: id-linked radio (R_t) and inertial (S_t) measurements are incorporated to RBMCDA in addition to the camera detections (C_t). The data association problem is changed compared to (a) and (b) as now we need to recover the association between id-linked measurements and tracks in addition to the anonymous measurements-to-tracks association.

JPDA enumerates all possible associations and computes association probabilities. The state of each target is then updated by every measurement with weights that depend on the association probabilities. The main disadvantage of JPDA is its tendency towards track coalescence for closely spaced targets.

Particle filters (i.e. sequential Monte Carlo methods) have also been used extensively in MTT problems [9] and are typically considered as generalizations of the MHT. Particle filters represent the data association and state posteriors as a discrete set of hypotheses (i.e. particles) and allow for non-linear state-space models.

4.2 Rao-Blackwellized Particle Filtering

In Bayesian inference, the objective is to compute the posterior distribution $P(z_{1:t}|y_{1:t})$ where $z_{1:t}$ are the hidden states at times 1 to t and $y_{1:t}$ are the received measurements up to time t. Suppose we can decompose the hidden state z_t into two parts: a root variable λ_t and a leaf variable x_t as shown below:

$$P(x_{1:t}, \lambda_{1:t}|y_{1:t}) = P(x_{1:t}|\lambda_{1:t}, y_{1:t})P(\lambda_{1:t}|y_{1:t}) \quad (1)$$

If we can compute the conditional posterior distribution $P(x_{1:t}|\lambda_{1:t}, y_{1:t})$ analytically, then we only need to sample from $P(\lambda_{1:t}|y_{1:t})$ using the particle filter. Thus, the main idea of Rao-Blackwellized particle filtering (RBPF) [6, 5] is to reduce the number of variables that are sampled by evaluating some parts of the filtering equations analytically. This reduction makes RBPF computationally more efficient than the standard particle filter, especially in high dimensional state-spaces.

The Rao-Blackwellized Monte Carlo Data Association filter (RBMCDA) [22, 23] is a sequential Monte Carlo MTT method that uses Rao-Blackwellized particle filtering (RBPF) to estimate the posterior distribution of states and data associations efficiently. More specifically, instead of using a pure particle representation of the joint posterior distribution of states and data associations (see Fig. (5a)), RBMCDA proceeds by decomposing the problem into two parts: a) estimation of the data-association posterior distribution and b) estimation of the posterior distribution of target states. The first part is estimated by particle filtering and the second part is computed analytically using Kalman filtering (Fig. (5b)). The aforementioned decomposition is possible, since in RBMCDA the dynamic and measurement model of the targets are modeled as linear Gaussian conditioned on the data association thus can be handled efficiently by the Kalman filter.

A high level overview of the RBMCDA algorithm is shown in Alg. (1). The algorithm maintains a set of N particles and each particle corresponds to a possible association of anonymous measurements (y_t) to tracks. Each particle maintains for each target its current state x_t (e.g. location) and state uncertainty (i.e. posterior distribution $p(x_t|y_{1:t})$). In the first step (line 4), a Kalman filter is used to predict the next state of a target based on its previous state ($p(x_t|y_{1:t-1})$). Then, the algorithm considers associating each anonymous measurement with each one of the targets in the particle and estimates the probability of each candidate association event (lines 5-6). The association events are modeled with the association indicator λ_t (e.g. ($\lambda_t = 0$) $\implies$ clutter association at time t, ($\lambda_t = j$) $\implies$ target j association at time t, etc). The association probability $\hat{\pi}_j$ for target j is computed from the measurement likelihood $\hat{p}(y_t|\lambda_t)$ and the prior probability of data associations $p(\lambda_t|\lambda_{t-1})$. By sampling the resulting importance distribution, the algorithm selects only one of the candidate associations (line 7) and updates the state of the respective target with the anonymous measurement (line 8). This is repeated for each anonymous measurement (e.g. for each camera detection in the camera frame). The particle's weight is then updated taking into account its previous weight and the probabilities of selected associations (line 9). Once all particles have been updated and their weights normalized (line 11), they are re-sampled based on their normalized weights (line 12). At the end of each iteration, the positions of the targets are estimated as a weighted average (i.e. mixture of Gaussians) across all particles (line 13).

Note that the algorithm above allows us to enforce data association constraints. For instance, we can express that each track is updated by at most one visual measurement, by suitably modeling association priors in line 5.

1: **Input:** N particles, a measurement vector y_t.
2: **Output:** $p(x_t, \lambda_t|y_{1:t})$: the joint distribution of target states and target-to-measurement associations at time t given measurements up to time t.
3: **for** each particle $i \in (1..N)$ **do**
4: For all targets run Kalman filter prediction step.
5: Form the importance distribution as:
For all association events j calculate the unnormalized association probabilities:
$\hat{\pi}_j^{(i)} = \hat{p}(y_t|\lambda_t^{(i)} = j, y_{1:t-1}, \lambda_{1:t-1}^{(i)})p(\lambda_t^{(i)} = j|\lambda_{1:t-1}^{(i)})$
6: Normalize the importance distribution.
7: Draw new $\lambda_t^{(i)}$ from the importance distribution.
8: Update target $\lambda_t^{(i)}$ with y_t using Kalman correction step.
9: Update particle weight.
10: **end for**
11: Normalize particle weights.
12: Resample.
13: Approximate $p(x_t, \lambda_t|y_{1:t})$ as:
$p(x_t, \lambda_t|y_{1:t}) \approx \sum_{i=1}^{N} w_t^{(i)} \delta(\lambda_t - \lambda_t^{(i)}) \mathcal{N}(x_t|M_t^{(i)}, P_t^{(i)})$
where $(M_t^{(i)}, P_t^{(i)})$ are the means and covariances of the target states of the i_{th} particle.

Algorithm 1: A high-level description of the RBMCDA filter

The existing RBMCDA algorithm is designed to work with anonymous observations. In the next section we point out how we extend it in order to exploit radio and inertial observations that are inherently linked to unique device IDs (i.e. MAC addresses).

5. PROPOSED APPROACH

We are now in a position to describe how we extend the RBMCDA framework to address the identification and tracking problem in a construction site setting. The key difference here is that we introduce id-linked observations in addition to the anonymous camera observations (Fig. (5c)). This impacts a number of steps in the algorithm above as explained in this section.

5.1 State Prediction and Update

As in the original algorithm, each particle uses a set of Kalman filters to track targets; however, in our case, we are not interested in tracking all targets within FOV; we only track people equipped with mobile devices and we continue to do so when they temporarily come out of the FOV. We extend the framework in [22, 23], in order to use id-linked observations in the prediction and correction steps of the Kalman filter. In particular, we use inertial sensor measurements to predict the next state of a person (instead of only relying on the previous state as in line 4). Furthermore, we use WiFi/BTLE and camera measurements to correct the person's state (instead of only anonymous camera measurements as in line 8).

More specifically, the target's dynamics in our system are modeled by the following linear equation:

$$x_t = F_t x_{t-1} + B_t \begin{bmatrix} d_t\ cos(\theta_t) \\ d_t\ sin(\theta_t) \end{bmatrix} + w_t \tag{2}$$

where t denotes the time index, $x_t = [x, y]^{\mathrm{T}}$ is the 2-D state vector of the target's position, F_t is the state transition matrix and the pair (d_t, θ_t) represents the target's step-length and heading respectively. Finally, B_t is a control input indicating whether a step has been taken or not and w_t is the process noise which is assumed to be normally distributed with mean zero and covariance matrix Q (i.e. $w_t \sim \mathcal{N}(0, Q)$). As we already mentioned in Section 2, our objective is to track all people that carry mobile devices. Thus, once we associate a camera measurement to a person ID (i.e. device ID) , Eqn. (2) is used as the predictive distribution of a Kalman filter to model the motion of the identified person using his/her inertial measurements.

Compared with existing techniques [19] that use heuristics to model the human motion, we will show in the evaluation section that the use of inertial measurements in our approach results in more accurate tracking. We should note here that Eqn. (2) is event-based (i.e. based on step events) and events among the different targets are inherently not synchronized. In other words, the steps of different people do not take place at the same time. However, because we need to know the predicted locations of all targets at a specific time, we process Eqn. (2) in a time-based manner. We run the prediction equation for all targets on fixed intervals (i.e. every second) and during that time we find the number of steps taken by each person and we calculate the step-length accordingly. Incomplete steps are handled by accounting only for a percentage of the step-length.

Unlike the original RBMCDA filter that only uses anonymous observations to update the target's state (line 8), in our system a measurement y_t at time t is a vector containing an anonymous location measurement (2D image coordinates transformed to the world plane via a projective transformation) from the camera system and multiple id-linked radio signal strength measurements from people's mobile devices. Thus, the state vector x_t of a target is related to the system measurements y_t according to the following model:

$$y_t = f(x_t) + v_t = \begin{bmatrix} x_t \\ \mathrm{RSS}_1\,(x_t)) \\ \mathrm{RSS}_2\,(x_t)) \\ \vdots \\ \mathrm{RSS}_m\,(x_t)) \end{bmatrix} + v_t \tag{3}$$

where f is a non-linear function that translates the state vector to the measurement domain and v_t is the measurement noise which follows a normal distribution with zero mean and covariance matrix R ($v_t \sim \mathcal{N}(0, R)$). The function RSS_i is given by:

$$\mathrm{RSS}_i(x_t) = P_i - 10 n_i log_{10} \|O_i - x_t\|_2\ ,\ i \in [1..m] \tag{4}$$

where m is the total number of WiFi/BTLE access points and $\mathrm{RSS}_i(x_t)$ is the expected signal strength at location x_t with respect to transmitter O_i. P_i is the received power at

Figure 6: Radio and magnetic maps of the construction site: (a) WiFi map obtained during the first day of the experiment showing the RSS with respect to one access-point (circle denotes the position of the AP), (b) WiFi map obtained 36 days later for the same AP which was moved from its initial location because the ground floor had to been built, (c) magnetic map on day 1, (d) magnetic map on day 36. The environment constantly changes which makes the task of localization and tracking very challenging.

the reference distance of 1 meter and n_i is the path loss exponent. In order to meet the requirements of the RBMCDA filter, i.e. calculate analytically the posterior distribution of the target states with a Kalman filter, Eqn. (3) must be linear Gaussian. The non-linearity of the measurement model in our case is handled via the unscented transformation [10]. Thus, the state estimation can be computed analytically using the unscented Kalman filter (UKF) and each particle contains a bank of UKFs; one filter for each target.

5.2 Tracking and Identification

In this section, we show how we modified the association steps in lines 5-7 to leverage id-linked measurements.

Suppose for instance that at time t we receive camera detections $C_t = \{c_t^j\}$, $1 \leq j \leq |C_t|$ and radio measurements $R_t = \{r_t^k\}$, $1 \leq k \leq K$ where K is the number of people with a mobile device. Each one of the $|C_t|$ anonymous camera detections could be one of the following three types: (a) a person with a device, (b) a person without a device or (c) clutter (e.g false camera detection caused by illumination changes). Our objective is to associate the type (a) camera detections with the correct radio measurements. In order to do that we follow the following procedure. We enumerate all possible combinations $\Omega = |C_t| \times K$ between the camera detections and the id-linked measurements and we create new measurements $y_t^i, i \in [1..\Omega]$ with the following structure:

$$y_t^i = \{c_t^m, r_t^j\},\ m \in [1..|C_t|],\ j \in [1..K] \tag{5}$$

Now, a measurement y_t^i which contains a correct association will have the following property $\text{RSS}(c_t^m) \approx r_t^j$ for the correct (m, j) pair, where RSS() is the function in Eqn. (4). In other words, if a person is detected by the camera, then his/her radio measurements (i.e. received signal strength) at that location should match the predicted radio measurements at the same location. Camera detections of type (b) and (c) would normally not exhibit the same property. As we have already mentioned the association probability is computed as the product of the measurement likelihood and association prior. The measurement likelihood of associating y_t^i with target j, $\hat{p}(y_t^i|\lambda_t = j)$ is computed as $\hat{p}(y_t^i|\lambda_t = j) = \mathcal{N}(y_t^i; \hat{y}_t, V_t)$ where $\hat{y}_t$ is the expected measurement of target j at the predicted state and V_t is the innovation covariance obtained from the UKF.

Given m simultaneous measurements within a scan the predictive distribution of data associations can be defined as an m_{th} order Markov-chain $p(\lambda_t^m|\lambda_t^{m-1}, ..., \lambda_t^1)$ which allows us to enforce certain association restrictions. In our system this predictive distribution is defined (i.e. assigns zero probability to unwanted events) so that the following conditions are met:

1. A track can be updated with at most one measurement.
2. A measurement can only be used to update at most one track.
3. An already established track (with a specific sensor ID) can only be updated with a measurement of the same sensor ID.
4. Once a camera detection is assigned to a track all other measurements which include the latter camera detection are classified as clutter.
5. A new target is not born if there is an existing target with the same sensor ID as the newborn target. This means that each particle maintains only targets with unique sensor IDs.

Some of the above restrictions can be relaxed depending on the application scenario. For instance, when two people are close to each other they can be detected as one object. In this case the 4th restriction can be relaxed in order to allow two tracks (i.e. two people with different sensor IDs) to be updated with the same camera detection.

To summarize, a particle represents states only for people carrying mobile devices - not for all people in the field of view. Inertial data of each person's device are used to predict their next state. Anonymous camera data are associated with a person's track only if they *agree* with both their inertial and radio data. Finally, we should note here that when at some time-step a particular target does not receive radio measurements then if the target is a new target the identification and creation of a new track is postponed until radio measurements are available. Otherwise, if the target is an existing target, tracking proceeds by only considering the motion model of the target (Eqn. (2)). A high-level work-flow of the proposed technique is shown in Alg. (2).

1: **Input:** N particles, camera (C_t), radio (R_t) and inertial (S_t) measurements.
2: **Output:** $p(x_t, \lambda_t|y_{1:t})$.
3: Apply Eqn. (5) to C_t and R_t to create y_t.
4: **for** each measurement $m \in (1..|y_t|)$ **do**
5: **for** each particle $i \in (1..N)$ **do**
6: For all targets in i run prediction step (Eqn. (2)).
7: Form the importance distribution and draw new association event ($\lambda_t^{(i)}$).
8: Update target $\lambda_t^{(i)}$ with m using UKF correction step. Update particle weight.
9: **end for**
10: **end for**
11: Normalize particle weights.
12: Resample.
13: Approximate $p(x_t, \lambda_t|y_{1:t})$ as in Algorithm 1

Algorithm 2: A high-level work-flow of the proposed system.

6. CROSS-MODALITY LEARNING

In this section we will show how our framework is capable of cross-modality learning, i.e. how a subset of sensor modalities is used by the *Adaptive Learner* (Fig. (3)) to train the internal parameters of the system.

6.1 Track Quality Estimation

As we have briefly mentioned in the introduction the output (i.e. track) of our *Positioning and Identification filter* can be used to learn the parameters of various internal components of our system. Once we have identified a track (i.e. we have linked a visual trajectory with radio and inertial measurements), we can use it to learn, for example, the radio propagation model since this track contains all the necessary information (i.e. location-RSS data points) for this purpose. In a similar manner we can learn radio and magnetic maps, train the foreground detector and improve the step-length estimation. All the these will be discussed in more detail later in this section. However, in order to achieve all of the above objectives, we first need to assess the quality of output tracks to make sure that they qualify for the training process. Thus, the goal of the *Track Quality*

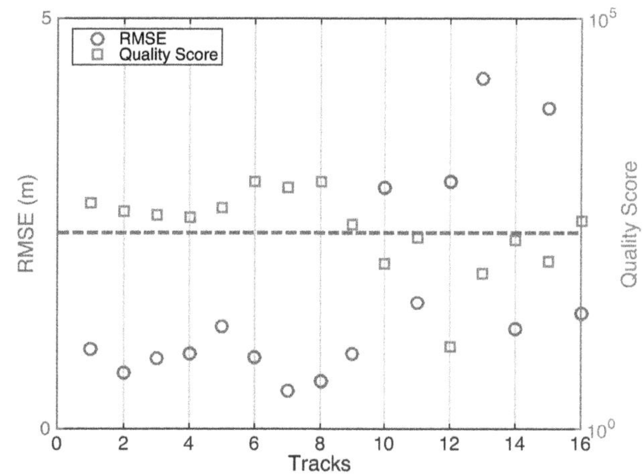

Figure 7: Track quality estimation: The figure shows the quality score of 16 tracks along with their RMSE. Tracks with quality score above the horizontal dotted line are considered qualifying and can be used for cross-modality training

Estimation phase, is to find candidate tracks which can be used for cross-modality training.

Let us assume that at time-step (or scan) t we receive m measurements $\{y_t^1, y_t^2, ..., y_t^m\}$. In addition y_t^0 is defined for each time-step to be a dummy variable indicating the possibility of a missed detection. Then the incremental quality score of a track j during this time-step is defined as:

$$\Delta L_t^j = \begin{cases} \log\left(\frac{\hat{p}(y_t^i|\lambda_t = j)p_d}{\hat{p}(y_t^i|\lambda_t = 0)}\right) & \text{, if } \exists\, i \in [1..m] \text{ s.t } \lambda_t = j \\ \log(1 - p_d) & \text{, otherwise} \end{cases}$$

where the quantity $\hat{p}(y_t^i|\lambda_t = j)$ is the likelihood of the measurement assigned to track j. The term $\hat{p}(y_t^i|\lambda_t = 0) = p(clutter)$ is the likelihood of the measurement originating from clutter which has a uniform probability density over the measurement space of volume V (i.e. $p(clutter) = V^{-1}$) and finally p_d is the probability of detection. Then, the cumulative quality score of track j is given by:

$$Q_j = \sum_{t=1}^{T} \Delta L_t^j \tag{6}$$

where T is the total length of the track. As we can see the quality score Q of a track penalizes the non-assignments due to missing detections while favoring the correct measurement-to-track associations. Fig. (7) shows that the quality score is negatively correlated with the root mean square error. Finally, in order to mark a track as a high confidence track that *qualifies* for cross-modal training its quality score is tested against a pre-determined threshold Q_{Th}. If $Q_j \geq Q_{Th}$ then the track is qualified (i.e. *high quality track*) and it can be used for cross-modality training, otherwise the track is rejected (Fig. (7)).

6.2 Foreground Detector Training

The mixture of Gaussians (MoG) [27] foreground detection which is used by our system is one of the most popular approaches for detecting moving targets from a static camera. This approach maintains a statistical representation of the background and can handle multi-modal background models and slow varying illumination changes.

In the original algorithm the history of each pixel is modeled by a mixture of K (typically 3-5) Gaussian distributions with parameters $(w_k, \mu_k, \sigma_k I)$ for the mixture weight, mean and covariance matrix of the k_{th} Gaussian component. In order to find the pixels that belong to the background, the Gaussian distributions are ordered in decreasing order according to the ratio (w_k/σ_k); background pixels exhibit higher weights and lower variances than the foreground moving pixels. The background model is obtained as $B^* = \arg\min_B \left(\sum_{k=1}^{B} w_k > P_b\right)$ where P_b is the prior probability of the background. The remaining $K - B^*$ distributions represent the foreground model.

On the arrival of a new frame each pixel is tested against the Gaussian mixture model and if a match is found the pixel is classified as a background or foreground depending on which Gaussian component it was matched with. If no match is found the pixel is classified as a foreground and it is added to the mixture model by evicting the component with the lowest weight. When a pixel is matched, the weight of that Gaussian component is updated using an exponential weighting scheme with learning rate α as $w_{t+1} = (1-\alpha)w_t + \alpha$, and the weights of all other components are changed to $w_{t+1} = (1-\alpha)w_t$. A similar procedure is used to update the mean and covariance of each component in the mixture.

The learning rate (α) controls the adaptation rate of the algorithm to changes (i.e. illumination changes, speed of incorporating static targets into the background) and is the most critical parameter of the algorithm. Fast learning rates will give greater weight to recent changes and make the algorithm more responsive to sudden changes. However, this can cause the MoG model to become quickly dominated by a single component which affects the algorithm's stability. On the other hand slow learning rates will cause a slower adaptation change which often results in pixel misclassification. Over the years many improvements have been suggested by the research community that allow for automatic initialization and better maintenance of the MoG parameters [4]. More recent techniques [26, 25] address challenges like sudden illumination variations, shadow detection and removal, automatic parameter selection, better execution time, etc .

In this section we propose a novel method for obtaining the optimum learning rate α^* of the foreground detector using the *high-quality* tracks of our filter. Suppose we are given a track $X^j_{1:T} = \{x^j_1, x^j_2, ..., x^j_T\}$ of length T where $x^j_t, t \in [1..T]$ denotes the state of the track at time t. Since, both camera and inertial measurements could have been used to estimate track $X^j_{1:T}$ then its states $x^j_t, t \in [1..T]$ are of two types: type (a) states that have been estimated using camera and inertial measurements and type (b) states that have been estimated only using inertial measurements. A high-quality track ensures that $X^j_{1:T}$ contains the right mixture of type (a) and type (b) states and thus does not deviate significantly from the ground truth trajectory. This is possible, since propagating a track by only using inertial measurements is accurate enough for short periods of time. This key property of the inertial measurements allows us to use a high quality track as if it was the ground truth trajectory to train the learning rate of the foreground detector. In other words the type (b) states of a high quality track tells us that the target is moving to specific locations and the foreground detector does not detect any target at those locations.

The quality score of tracks (Eqn. (6)) can be used to find the optimum learning rate by solving the following optimization problem: *Given a time window $\mathcal{T}$ find a learning rate α^* so that the cumulative quality score (CQS) $\sum_j Q_j$ of all high quality tracks $j \in \mathcal{T}$ is maximized.*

6.3 Optimizing the Step Length Estimation

Similar to the foreground detector training procedure, *high quality* tracks can also be used to learn the step-length model of each person being tracked. More specifically, the step-length of a user can be obtained from the universal model proposed in [21] as:

$$s = h(af_{step} + b) + c \tag{7}$$

where s is the estimated step-length, h denotes the user's height, f_{step} is the step frequency obtained from the device's accelerometer and (a, b, c) are the model parameters. The model above describes a linear relationship between step-length and step frequency weighted by the user's height.

Since the heights of people that we need to track are not known a priori every time a new track is initialized that contains a sensor ID which has not been recorded before, the step-length estimator uses Eqn. (7) to provide an initial estimate of the target's step-length. At this point the height value is set to the country's average for men of ages between 25 and 34 years old. The parameters (a, b, c) have been precomputed with a training set of 8 people of known heights using foot mounted IMUs.

As the tracking process proceeds high quality tracks are obtained periodically for each target. From these tracks the following IMU data are extracted for each step: a) step frequency, b) step start-time and c) step end-time. The start/end times of each step obtained from the IMU data are then matched to camera detections in order to obtain the position of the target during those times which are essentially the step-lengths measured from the camera system. Thus, for each target we obtain a collection of n calibration points $\{Sv^i, f^i_{step}\}^n_{i=1}$ where Sv^i is the visual step-length of the i_{th} step and f^i_{step} its frequency obtained from the IMU. The calibration set of each target is then used to train a personal step-length model of the form $Sv = w_1 f_{\text{step}} + w_0$ using the least squares fitting. Finally, the step-length estimator can switch to the trained model once the least squares goodness of fit $\left(R^2 = 1 - \frac{\text{residual sum squares}}{\text{total sum squares}}\right)$ exceeds a predefined threshold.

6.4 Radio Model/Maps Learning

High quality tracks are also being used in order to learn the parameters of the radio propagation model which our system uses as explained in Section 5. More specifically, from a high quality track $X^j_{1:T} = \{x^j_1, x^j_2, ..., x^j_T\}$ of length T, the type (a) states are extracted. Let us call a type (a) state as $\tilde{x}^j_t$; this state has been estimated using camera, radio and inertial measurements. Thus a collection of type (a) states $S = \{\tilde{x}^j_t : j \in K, t \in \mathcal{T}\}_n$ of length n where K is the total number of people with smartphones and $\mathcal{T}$ is the running time of our filter, contains n pairs of (location, RSS) measurements. Now, this collection of (location, RSS) points can be used to estimate the parameters of the log-normal radio propagation model [24] given by Eqn. (4) for each access point using least squares fitting.

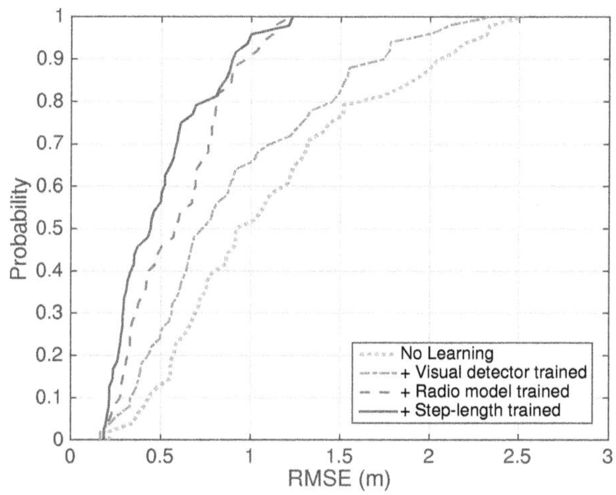

Figure 8: Cumulative distribution function of RMSE for different learning setting.

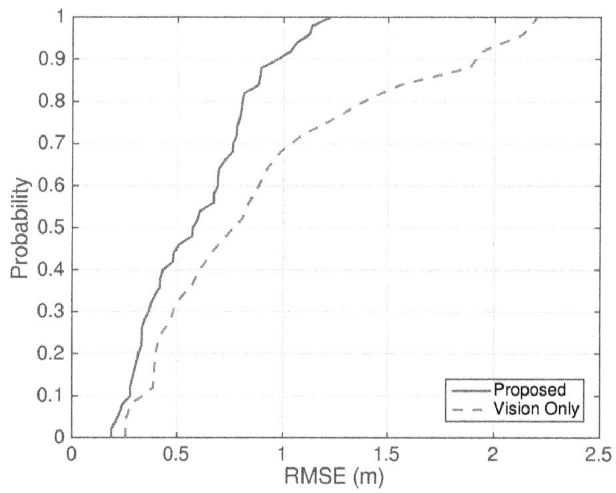

Figure 9: Accuracy comparison of the proposed approach and the original RBMCDA (vision only) algorithm.

At regular intervals we re-estimate the radio model parameters based on the most recent portion of collected data. We should note here that the parameters of the radio model are initialized empirically based on a number of studies for different environments [24].

Additionally, we can follow similar procedure to learn radio, magnetic and occlusion maps. The radio and the magnetic maps can be combined and used for localization in situations where the camera is occluded by an obstacle or they can be used in conjunction with the radio model to improve the system's accuracy. Additionally, the occlusion map, which is derived from the camera detections provides statistics about the environment (i.e. frequent visited areas, inaccessible areas, etc) which our system can use to improve its performance. For instance, suppose that a particular person is not detected by the camera during some time and our filter reverts to IMU tracking; the occlusion map can help us filter out impossible trajectories.

7. SYSTEM EVALUATION

7.1 Experimental Setup

In order to evaluate the performance of the proposed approach we have conducted two real world experiments in a construction site (Fig. (2)). In both experiments we placed two cameras with non-overlapping FOV at approximately 8 meters above the ground facing down. In the first experiment the two cameras were covering an area of approximately 11m × 9m each and in the second experiment an area of 14m × 4m each. The duration of each of the experiments was approximately 45 minutes with the cameras recording video at 30fps with a resolution of 960 × 720 px. We should also mention here that each camera was processed separately (i.e. we do not consider the multi-camera system scenario). The area of the site was outfitted with 12 WiFi and 8 BTLE access points and 5 workers were supplied with smartphone devices. The total number of people in the scene was varying from 3 to 12 as workers were entering and exiting the field of view. The objective of the experiment was to identify and track the workers who were carrying a smartphone device using camera , radio and inertial measurements. The radio measurements were obtained by their smartphones receiving WiFi and BTLE beacons at 1Hz and 10Hz respectively. The inertial measurements (i.e accelerometer and magnetometer) obtained from their smartphones had a sampling rate of 100Hz.

To obtain the ground truth of people's trajectories we followed the same approach proposed in [19]. We supplied all people to be tracked with helmets of different colors and their ground truth trajectories were obtained using a mean-shift tracker [18] to track the colored helmets. We should also note here that our approach does not make use of any appearance or color features for tracking and color features were only used to acquire accurate ground truth.

7.2 Results

The first set of experiments evaluates the tracking accuracy of our system (i.e. how well we can identify and track people with smartphone devices among all people in the FOV). Moreover, we examine what is the effect of cross-modal training on the performance of our system. Our performance metric in this experiment is the root mean square error (RMSE) between the ground-truth and the estimated trajectory. In all the experiments shown here we have used 100 particles. In addition, instead of using line 13 of Alg. (1) to estimate the filtering distribution, in each step the location of each target is estimated using the particle with the highest weight. For this test we used 30 minutes worth of data running our filter on time-windows of one minute (i.e. 1800 frames). Fig. (8) shows the error CDF over this period over all targets for different settings. More specifically, our approach achieves a 90 percentile error of 2.5m when the system is untrained, which improves to 1.8m when the foreground detector is trained. The error decreases further as the parameters of the radio propagation model are learned, achieving a 90 percentile error of 1 meter. Finally, once the optimum step-length of each person is learned the accuracy increases further to approximately 0.8 meters. As we can see the error decreases significantly once both the foreground detector and the radio model are learned. This is expected since our system requires both camera and radio measurements in order to determine the correct measurement to track association and update the target states. In the case of excessive missing camera detections, the trajectory of a tar-

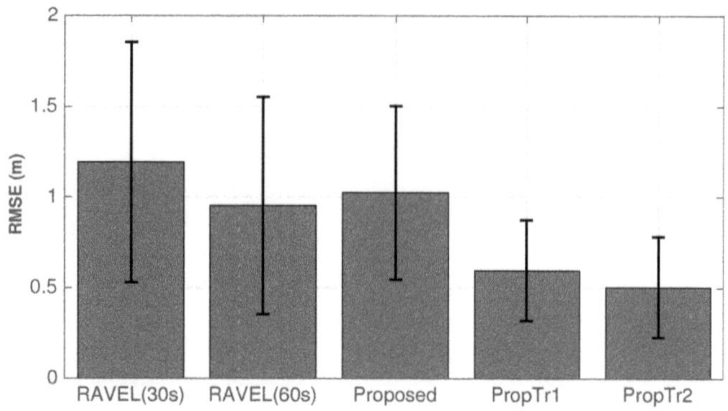

Figure 10: Tracking accuracy between the proposed approach and RAVEL. *Proposed* denotes our approach where the foreground detector and step-length model are not trained. *PropTr1* is our approach after the foreground detector has been trained and further in *PropTr2* the step-length model is also trained. *RAVEL(30s)* and *RAVEL(60s)* is the competing technique evaluated at window sizes of 30 and 60 seconds respectively.

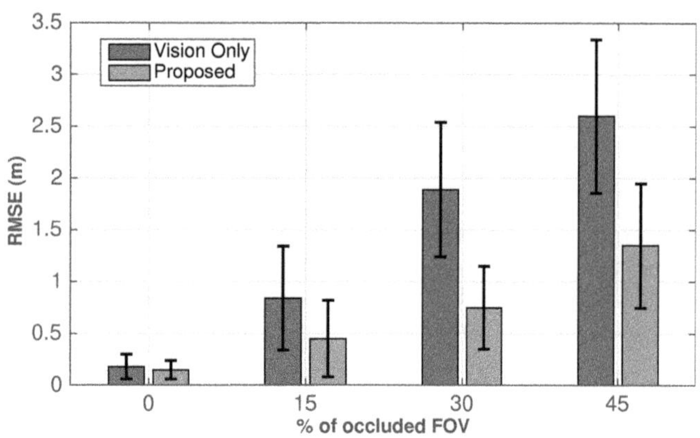

Figure 11: The figure shows the RMSE between the proposed technique and the vision-only tracking for different amounts of occlusion. The use of inertial measurements by the proposed technique improves tracking significantly in noisy scenarios.

get is estimated only by inertial measurements which is the main cause of the low accuracy. On the other hand, if the radio model was not trained, camera detections would not be able to be linked with radio measurements, which would also cause identification and tracking errors. Once the foreground detector and the radio model are trained Fig. (8) does not show any significant improvement after learning the step-length model. This is reasonable since, in this case most of the time the targets are updated with camera observations which are used to correct the predicted by the IMU states. However, from our experiments we have observed that once the camera becomes unavailable, the difference in accuracy between a trained and a universal step-length model is significant.

In our second test we compare the proposed approach with the original RBMCDA algorithm (referred to as vision-only tracker in this section) which uses only visual observations for tracking. In this test we used the same experimental setup as described in the previous paragraph. Both tech-

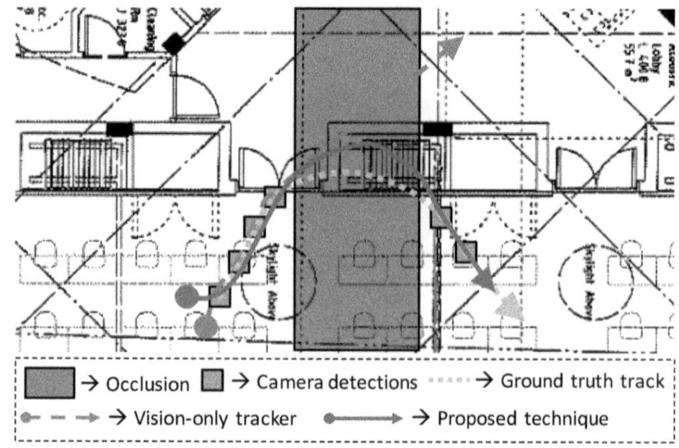

Figure 12: Illustrative example showing the difference between vision-only tracking (red line) and the proposed approach (blue line) in the presence of occlusions (gray area). In cases of prolonged missing camera detections (green squares) the constant velocity model of the vision-only tracker is not sufficient enough to maintain tracking. On the other hand the proposed technique with the aid of inertial measurements is capable of closely following the target despite the presence of long-term occlusions.

niques use the same foreground detector settings and in addition the proposed method uses a learned radio model. Fig. (9) shows the error CDF for the two methods. As we can observe the proposed technique achieves a 90 percentile error of 1 meter as opposed to vision-only tracking which has a 90 percentile error of 1.8 meters. The main source of error of the vision-only tracking is due to data association ambiguities which the proposed technique reduces significantly with the help of radio and inertial measurements. Moreover, the proposed technique supports target identification which is not possible when pure visual tracking techniques are used.

The next step is to compare our technique with the recently proposed RAVEL system [19] which is also a multiple hypothesis tracking and identification system. RAVEL which is discussed in more detail in Section 8 exploits the smoothness of motion and radio signal strength data in order to track and identify targets. Unlike our technique, RAVEL is more of a reconstruction technique (i.e. performs off-line tracking) as it requires to observe all measurements over a time window (W) in order to provide the trajectories of each target. We have tested RAVEL using time windows of sizes 30 and 60 seconds over a period of 10 minutes and we have compared it with the proposed online system. Both systems are capable of learning the radio model parameters, thus we performed these tests using the learned radio model for both systems. In Fig. (10) *RAVEL(30s)* and *RAVEL(60s)* shows the accuracy of RAVEL for window sizes of 30 and 60 seconds respectively. *Proposed* denotes the proposed system with learned radio model, *PropTr1* is the proposed system optimized one level further i.e. foreground detector training and *PropTr2* denotes the proposed approach when the step-length model is also learned. Fig. (10) shows that the average error of RAVEL decreases from 1.2m to 0.9m as we increase the window size. Our approach with a trained radio model is slightly worse than RAVEL(60). However,

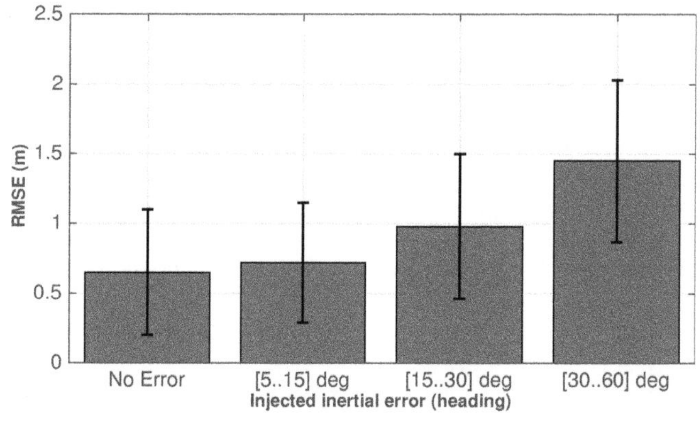

Figure 13: The RMSE of the proposed technique under different amounts of injected heading error.

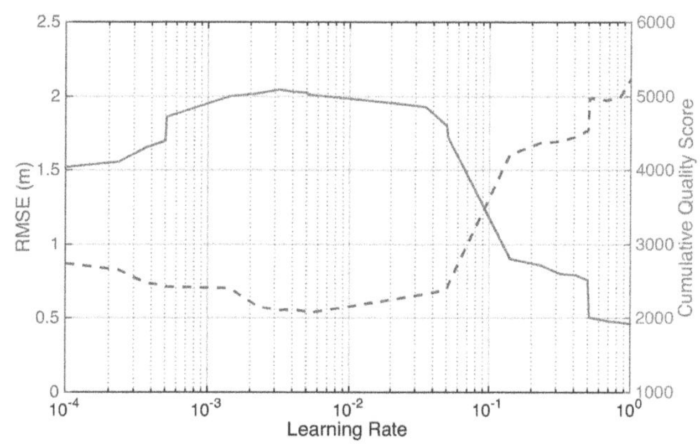

Figure 14: The figure shows the cumulative quality score (CQS) over a period of time as a function of the foreground detector learning rate (α). The optimum learning rate according to RMSE maximizes CQS, thus this metric can be used to train the foreground detector.

once our system trains the foreground detector, the average error decreases significantly and continues to decrease as the step-length model is also learned. Unlike our system, RAVEL estimates the trajectory of a target using only visual data thus it becomes easily susceptible to errors due to missing camera detections. Our system without training achieves a similar performance but in real-time.

The final set of experiments aims to demonstrate the robustness of the proposed technique. First we wanted to see how our technique performs on difficult trajectories (i.e. various amounts of occlusions and missing detections). In order to simulate occlusions we remove a specific area of the field of view (FOV) by disabling the camera detections inside that area. More specifically, we generated occlusions at random locations that occupy a rectangular area of specific size inside the FOV. Then we evaluated the accuracy of the proposed approach compared to the vision-only tracker on 50 trajectories of variable length generated from our ground truth data. Fig. (11) shows the RMSE over all trajectories between the proposed system and the vision-only tracker for different configurations of occlusions (i.e. shown as the percentage of occluded FOV). For each configuration we run the test 10 times; each time the occlusion was positioned to a different location. The two methods achieve a comparable performance when there are no occlusions. However, the proposed approach significantly outperforms the vision-only tracking in scenarios with long-term occlusions and large amounts of missing detections. In the presence of long-term occlusions the constant velocity/acceleration motion model utilized by most visual tracking techniques fails and cannot be used to reliably model the inherently complex human motion. On the other hand Fig. (11) shows that the use of inertial measurements by the proposed technique provides a more accurate model of human motion. An illustrative example is shown in Fig. (12).

Additionally in order to study how our approach can cope with variable noise from the inertial sensors we followed a similar procedure as in the previous paragraph and we generated 50 trajectories from our ground truth data. At each time-step and for each trajectory we inject a random bias error to the heading estimator. More specifically we sample a heading error uniformly from a specific range of the form $[a..b]$ *degrees* and we add it to the output of the heading estimator. By doing this we can get an idea of how our approach performs in environments with disturbed magnetic fields. Fig. (13) illustrates the results of this experiment for different amounts of injected noise. As we can see the proposed technique can cope with moderate amounts of inertial noise; achieving a sub-meter accuracy for bias up to 30 degrees.

Finally, Fig. (14) shows how our approach can find the optimum learning rate (α^*) of the foreground detector by solving the optimization problem discussed in Section 6.2. In the example above we used 5 minutes of data, running the foreground detector for different values of (α) and calculating the cumulative quality score (CQS) for that period. Our intuition is that the optimum learning rate will reduce the number of missing detections, thus increasing the number of high quality tracks as well as their quality score. This is shown in Fig. (14) where the optimum learning rates achieve a high CQS, also evident by the low RMSE.

8. BACKGROUND

A variety of positioning systems have been proposed by the research community over the past ten years. Recent surveys outlining the different techniques and their accuracies can be found in [14, 17]. In this section we will give a brief overview on the most recent positioning systems that make use of radio-, inertial- and visual- sensing (i.e. using a stationary camera) to track multiple people. The positioning systems to be described here can be divided into two categories: a) systems that combine visual and radio measurements and b) those that combine visual and inertial measurements.

Vision+Radio positioning systems: The recent Radio And Vision Enhanced Localization (RAVEL) system [19] fuses anonymous visual detections captured by a stationary camera with WiFi readings to track multiple people moving inside an area with CCTV coverage. The WiFi measurements of each person are used to add context to the trajectories obtained by the camera in order to resolve visual ambiguities (e.g. split/merge paths) and increase the accuracy of visual tracking. RAVEL operates in two phases namely tracklet generation and WiFi-aided tracklet merging. In the first phase visual detections collected over a period of time are used to form unambiguous small trajectories (i.e. tracklets). In the second phase, RAVEL uses the aforementioned tracklets to create tracklet trees for each person (i.e. probable trajectory hypotheses). Then, the WiFi measurements of each person are used to search through the tracklet tree in order to find their most likely trajectory. The most likely trajectory is the one that agrees the most with the WiFi measurements. Unlike our technique, RAVEL performs off-line tracking, i.e. the trajectory of each person is reconstructed after all camera detections and WiFi measurements for a period of time have been observed. In addition, RAVEL does not make use of inertial measurements and thus it is more susceptible to positioning errors due to missing detections (i.e. static people that become part of the background).

In a similar setting the EV-Loc system [29] estimates the position of multiple people using both WiFi and camera measurements. More specifically, EV-Loc estimates the distance of each person from a number of access points first using camera measurements and then using WiFi readings. The Hungarian algorithm [3, 12] is then used to find the best mapping between camera and WiFi measurements. After this optimization problem is solved, the camera and WiFi locations of each person are fused to form a weighted average final location. Unlike our work, EV-Loc concentrates on the problem of finding the best matching between camera and WiFi traces (i.e. the matching process is performed after the visual tracking is completed) and does not provide a general tracking framework that incorporates multiple sensor modalities.

Finally, Mandeljc et al. presented in [16, 15] a fusion scheme that extends the probabilistic occupancy map (POM) [7] with radio measurements. In the original POM framework the area of interest (i.e. the ground plane as viewed by the cameras) is divided into a number of cells forming a grid. Under this framework humans are represented as rectangles, and detections are generated using background subtraction techniques. The algorithm models each cell of the grid as random variable representing the probability of a cell being occupied by a person. Finally the goal of the algorithm is to estimate the probabilities of occupancy for each cell given binary images obtained from a background subtraction process from multiple overlapping cameras. In [16] the POM is extended so that the cell occupancy probabilities are estimated using ultra-wideband (UWB) radio sensors in addition to the cameras. Essentially, the radio measurements are anonymized and they are used to provide a prior occupancy model which is then combined with the camera occupancy model. This additional radio information increases the accuracy and robustness of the algorithm. Later in [15], the POM is extended further so that the anonymous camera detections are augmented with identity information from radio tags. The augmentation of anonymous detections with identity information is done on a frame-by-frame basis where at each time instant the optimal assignment between radio and camera locations is obtained using the Hungarian algorithm. The fusion scheme of [16, 15] was evaluated using only UWB radios which exhibit sub-meter accuracy and there is no indication of how this method will perform with radios of lower accuracy (i.e. WiFi). Although [15] seems similar to our method, it requires multiple cameras with overlapping fields of view, it does not take advantage on inertial measurements, and finally it does not possess the learning capabilities of our method.

Vision+Inertial positioning systems: Instead of using radio measurements for identification the methods in this category use inertial measurements. For instance, the system in [28] fuses motion traces obtained from one stationary camera mounted on the ceiling and facing down with motion information from wearable accelerometer nodes to uniquely identify multiple people in the FOV using their accelerometer node IDs. Background subtraction is used to detect people from the video footage and then their floor-plane acceleration is extracted by double differentiation. The camera acceleration traces are then compared against the overall body acceleration obtained from the accelerometer nodes using the Pearson's correlation coefficient. The acceleration correlation scores among all possible combinations of camera-accelerometer pairs are then used to form an assignment matrix. Finally, the assignment problem is solved using the Hungarian algorithm. The initial algorithm of [28] is extended in [11] to allow for better path disambiguation based on people's acceleration patterns by keeping track of multiple trajectory hypotheses.

More recently the OPTIMUS system [13] uses a similar approach, where inertial measurements from smartphones are used to identify visual trajectories. The algorithm uses histograms of oriented gradients (HOG) descriptors to detect people in a scene covered by one stationary camera and then optical flow is used to group consecutive detections together when there are no ambiguities forming tracklets. A track-level association procedure is then performed to merge the found tracklets and create full trajectories. At the identification stage accelerometer readings from the smartphones are converted into binary vectors that indicate the user's movement and are matched with movement vectors extracted from the visual trajectories using the Hungarian algorithm. Unlike our work, the methods described above use inertial data mostly for identification purposes; they are not used for identification and positioning. In addition, they are specifically designed having only one sensor modality in mind and thus they do not provide a general multi-sensor multi-target tracking framework.

9. CONCLUSION

In this paper we proposed a multi-modal positioning system for highly dynamic environments. We showed that it is possible to adapt Rao-Blackwellised particle filters - traditionally used to discern tracks using anonymous measurements - in order to both identify and track people being monitored by CCTV and holding mobile devices. We further showed that there is significant scope for automatically training the various sensor modalities, and this proved particularly useful in rapidly changing environments. Our experiments showed that even without training, our online approach achieves similar positioning accuracy to the existing off line RAVEL approach; with training the positioning error is decreased by a further 50%.

10. ACKNOWLEDGMENT

We would like to thank Laing O'Rourke for allowing us to conduct our experiments in their construction site and also for funding this research. We also would like to thank the anonymous reviewers and our shepherd for their valuable feedback.

11. REFERENCES

[1] S. Blackman. Multiple hypothesis tracking for multiple target tracking. *Aerospace and Electronic Systems Magazine, IEEE*, 19(1):5–18, Jan 2004.

[2] S. Blackman and R. Popoli. *Design and Analysis of Modern Tracking Systems*. Artech House radar library. Artech House, 1999.

[3] F. Bourgeois and J.-C. Lassalle. An extension of the munkres algorithm for the assignment problem to rectangular matrices. *Commun. ACM*, 14(12):802–804, Dec. 1971.

[4] T. Bouwmans, F. El Baf, and B. Vachon. Background modeling using mixture of gaussians for foreground detection-a survey. *Recent Patents on Computer Science*, 1(3):219–237, 2008.

[5] A. Doucet, N. De Freitas, and N. Gordon. *Sequential monte carlo methods in practice*. Springer-Verlag, 2001.

[6] A. Doucet, N. d. Freitas, K. P. Murphy, and S. J. Russell. Rao-blackwellised particle filtering for dynamic bayesian networks. In *Proceedings of the 16th Conference on Uncertainty in Artificial Intelligence*, UAI '00, pages 176–183, San Francisco, CA, USA, 2000. Morgan Kaufmann Publishers Inc.

[7] F. Fleuret, J. Berclaz, R. Lengagne, and P. Fua. Multicamera people tracking with a probabilistic occupancy map. *Pattern Analysis and Machine Intelligence, IEEE Transactions on*, 30(2):267–282, Feb 2008.

[8] T. E. Fortmann, Y. Bar-Shalom, and M. Scheffe. Sonar tracking of multiple targets using joint probabilistic data association. *IEEE Journal of Oceanic Engineering*, 8(3):173–184, 1983.

[9] C. Hue, J.-P. Le Cadre, and P. Perez. Tracking multiple objects with particle filtering. *Aerospace and Electronic Systems, IEEE Transactions on*, 38(3):791–812, Jul 2002.

[10] S. Julier and J. Uhlmann. Unscented filtering and nonlinear estimation. *Proceedings of the IEEE*, 92(3):401–422, Mar 2004.

[11] D. Jung, T. Teixeira, and A. Savvides. Towards cooperative localization of wearable sensors using accelerometers and cameras. In *INFOCOM, 2010 Proceedings IEEE*, pages 1–9, March 2010.

[12] H. W. Kuhn. The hungarian method for the assignment problem. *Naval research logistics quarterly*, 2(1-2):83–97, 1955.

[13] D. Lee, I. Hwang, and S. Oh. Optimus:online persistent tracking and identification of many users for smart spaces. *Machine Vision and Applications*, 25(4):901–917, 2014.

[14] D. Lymberopoulos, J. Liu, X. Yang, R. R. Choudhury, S. Sen, and V. Handzinski. Microsoft indoor localization competition: Experiences and lessons learned. *SIGMOBILE Mobile Computation and Communication Review (MC2R)*, October 2014.

[15] R. Mandeljc, S. Kovacic, M. Kristan, and J. Pers. Tracking by identification using computer vision and radio. *Sensors*, 13(1):241–273, 2012.

[16] R. Mandeljc, J. Pers, M. Kristan, and S. Kovacic. Fusion of non-visual modalities into the probabilistic occupancy map framework for person localization. In *Distributed Smart Cameras (ICDSC), 2011 Fifth ACM/IEEE International Conference on*, pages 1–6, Aug 2011.

[17] R. Mautz. *Indoor positioning technologies*. Habilitation thesis, ETH Zurich, 2012.

[18] J. Ning, L. Zhang, D. Zhang, and C. Wu. Robust mean-shift tracking with corrected background-weighted histogram. *Computer Vision, IET*, 6(1):62–69, January 2012.

[19] S. Papaioannou, H. Wen, A. Markham, and N. Trigoni. Fusion of radio and camera sensor data for accurate indoor positioning. In *Mobile Ad Hoc and Sensor Systems (MASS), 2014 IEEE 11th International Conference on*, pages 109–117, Oct 2014.

[20] D. Reid. An algorithm for tracking multiple targets. *IEEE Transactions on Automatic Control*, 24(6):843–854, 1979.

[21] V. Renaudin, M. Susi, and G. Lachapelle. Step length estimation using handheld inertial sensors. *Sensors*, 12(7):8507–8525, 2012.

[22] S. Särkkä, A. Vehtari, and J. Lampinen. Rao-blackwellized monte carlo data association for multiple target tracking. In *Proceedings of the seventh international conference on information fusion*, volume 1, pages 583–590. I, 2004.

[23] S. Särkkä, A. Vehtari, and J. Lampinen. Rao-blackwellized particle filter for multiple target tracking. *Information Fusion*, 8(1):2 – 15, 2007. Special Issue on the Seventh International Conference on Information Fusion-Part {II} Seventh International Conference on Information Fusion.

[24] S. Seidel and T. Rappaport. 914 mhz path loss prediction models for indoor wireless communications in multifloored buildings. *Antennas and Propagation, IEEE Transactions on*, 40(2):207–217, 1992.

[25] M. Shah, J. Deng, and B. Woodford. Video background modeling: recent approaches, issues and our proposed techniques. *Machine Vision and Applications*, 25(5):1105–1119, 2014.

[26] A. Sobral and A. Vacavant. A comprehensive review of background subtraction algorithms evaluated with synthetic and real videos. *Computer Vision and Image Understanding*, 122(0):4 – 21, 2014.

[27] C. Stauffer and W. Grimson. Adaptive background mixture models for real-time tracking. In *Computer Vision and Pattern Recognition, 1999. IEEE Computer Society Conference on.*, volume 2, pages –252 Vol. 2, 1999.

[28] T. Teixeira, D. Jung, G. Dublon, and A. Savvides. Identifying people in camera networks using wearable accelerometers. In *Proceedings of the 2Nd International Conference on PErvasive Technologies Related to Assistive Environments*, PETRA '09, pages 20:1–20:8, New York, NY, USA, 2009. ACM.

[29] B. Zhang, J. Teng, J. Zhu, X. Li, D. Xuan, and Y. F. Zheng. Ev-loc: Integrating electronic and visual signals for accurate localization. In *Proceedings of the Thirteenth ACM International Symposium on Mobile Ad Hoc Networking and Computing*, MobiHoc '12, pages 25–34, New York, NY, USA, 2012. ACM.

CARLOC: Precisely Tracking Automobile Position*

Yurong Jiang[†], Hang Qiu[†], Matthew McCartney[†], Gaurav Sukhatme[†],
Marco Gruteser[*], Fan Bai[‡], Donald Grimm[‡], Ramesh Govindan[†]
[†]University of Southern California
[*]Rutgers University [‡]GM Global Research & Development
{yurongji,hangqiu,mmcartn,gaurav,ramesh}@usc.edu
gruteser@winlab.rutgers.edu
{fan.bai,donald.grimm}@gm.com

ABSTRACT

Precise positioning of an automobile to within lane-level precision can enable better navigation and context-awareness. However, GPS by itself cannot provide such precision in obstructed urban environments. In this paper, we present a system called CARLOC for lane-level positioning of automobiles. CARLOC uses three key ideas in concert to improve positioning accuracy: it uses digital maps to match the vehicle to known road segments; it uses vehicular sensors to obtain odometry and bearing information; and it uses crowd-sourced location estimates of roadway landmarks that can be detected by sensors available in modern vehicles. CARLOC unifies these ideas in a probabilistic position estimation framework, widely used in robotics, called the sequential Monte Carlo method. Through extensive experiments on a real vehicle, we show that CARLOC achieves sub-meter positioning accuracy in an obstructed urban setting, an order-of-magnitude improvement over a high-end GPS device.

Categories and Subject Descriptors

J.7 [**Computers in Other Systems**]: Consumer Products; H.3.4 [**Information Storage and Retrieval**]: Systems and Software

General Terms

Design; Experimentation; Performance; Algorithms

Keywords

GPS; Map; Accuracy

1. INTRODUCTION

As mobile devices have proliferated, they have become the defacto method for estimating the position of automobiles. The built-in GPS receiver in mobile devices provides positioning for navigation, but also for context-awareness; many apps now routinely use vehicle position to suggest nearby services or points of interest. As elements of autonomous driving start to appear in commercial offerings, the accuracy of positioning vehicles will become much more important.

However, it has long been known that smartphone GPS receivers have errors on the order of 10s of meters, especially in obstructed urban environments. It is precisely in these environments, unfortunately, where accurate positioning is most necessary because of the density of services or points of interest. An order of magnitude lower positioning error of automobiles would be able to position a vehicle with up to lane-level accuracy, which will likely enable much more accurate navigation, but also more precise context-awareness in urban environments [33].

Much research (Section 5) has explored how to enhance GPS position by fusing information from other sensors such as laser-range finders and inertial sensors and from other sources, such as digital maps. Intuitively, maps can be used to constrain vehicle trajectories, inertial sensors can be used for dead reckoning when GPS is unavailable, and laser range-finders can estimate distances to landmarks in the environment, which can then be used to get a position fix.

In this paper, we explore two dimensions in this design space that can help significantly improve positioning accuracy. First, we observe that modern automobiles have hundreds of sensors that govern the operation of their internal subsystems, and some of these sensors provide odometry and heading information. These can be used to improve the efficacy of matching a car's location to a digital map, and to model its motion. Second, car sensors can also provide enough information to detect *roadway landmarks* — roadway features such as potholes or speedbumps. If these can be reliably detected, then the *position estimates of other cars at these landmarks can be used to improve a car's position estimate.*

Contributions. In this paper, we design and evaluate a system called CARLOC (Section 3) that can continuously track the precise position of a vehicle, even in highly obstructed environments. CARLOC uses a collection of techniques, some of which are inspired by prior work on robot localization, while others use existing techniques by adapt them to use car sensors, and some are novel. Specifically, CARLOC uses a non-parametric probabilistic position representation, called a *particle filter*, as a uniform framework that is able to express various forms of information fusion. CARLOC matches a car's current position estimate to a road-segment on a map. This matching, whose accuracy we improve by leveraging the availability of vehicle sensors, can be used to truncate the position uncertainty to within the nominal road width of the matched segment. CARLOC then updates the particle filter using a well-known kinematic model, but uses car sensors to accurately estimate inputs to the kinematic model.

* The first author, Yurong Jiang, was supported by Annenberg Graduate Fellowship. This material is based upon work supported by the National Science Foundation under Grant No. CNS-1330118.

SenSys'15, November 01–05, 2015, Seoul, Republic of Korea.

ACM ISBN 978-1-4503-3631-4/15/11/...$15.00.
DOI: http://dx.doi.org/10.1145/2809695.2809725 .

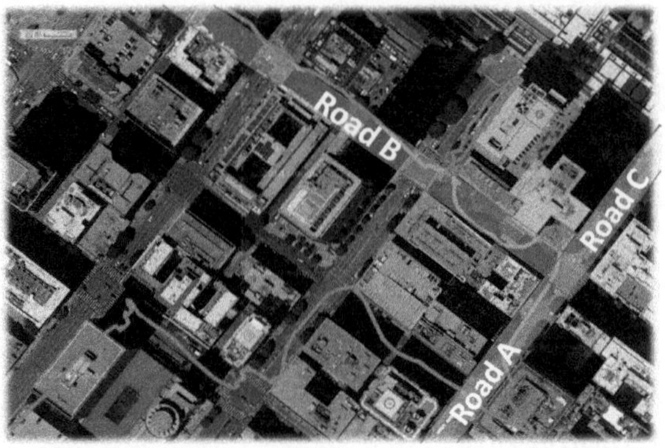

Figure 1—Portion of GPS Trace in City Downtown

A particularly novel contribution of CARLOC is the ability to enhance position estimates of a vehicle using crowd-sourced position estimates of roadway landmarks. To understand this, suppose a car hits a speed bump. If CARLOC is able to detect the speed bump, then *the car's particle filter at the instant the speed bump is encountered, is a probabilistic representation of the speed bump's position.* Suppose N cars pass over the same speed bump, the collection of all their particle filters at the speed bump represents a *crowd-sourced* collection of position estimates of the speed bump. Intuitively, one expects the distribution described by these crowd-sourced particles *to converge to the true location of the speed bump* as more and more vehicles contribute to the collection. CARLOC uses this observation and contains novel algorithms to detect three types of roadway landmarks (stop signs, speed bumps, and street corners) and to update particle filters.

Using extensive evaluations (Section 4) on roads with varying degree of satellite obstructions (and therefore various degrees of GPS availability and accuracy), we show that CARLOC has mean error of 2.7m in a highly obstructed downtown road, an order of magnitude improvement over commodity GPS, high-precision GPS receivers, differential GPS, and the closest prior work on GPS augmentation using mobile devices. In unobstructed environments, CARLOC's mean position error drops to 1.38m, while in partially obstructed environments, the mean error can vary between 1.1m and 2.2m. CARLOC's position error does not appear to depend on length of route, and a relatively small number of landmarks suffices to achieve significant accuracy. More important, each component of our design, and each optimization contributes significantly to the design.

2. BACKGROUND AND MOTIVATION

Positioning accuracy for automobiles. Over the last few years, the use of in-car navigation has increased significantly. This has been driven, in part, by the ubiquitous availability of free navigation apps on mobile devices such as smartphones and tablets. The commodity GPS receivers on these devices (that the navigation apps rely on) can be highly inaccurate in some settings. For example, Figure 1 shows GPS readings from a city downtown area, where the GPS signal reception is affected significantly by the obstructions caused by tall buildings, a well-known effect sometimes called the urban canyon effect.

To quantify the degree of error in GPS, we obtained smartphone GPS readings from nearly 200 miles of driving, on three different types of roads: *Urban roads*, e.g. a downtown road surrounded by tall buildings, *Shaded roads*, e.g. roads covered by trees, and *Opensky roads*, e.g. highway or major roads having an unobstructed view of the sky. Table 1 shows statistics for GPS errors from our traces. Although we obtain reasonably good GPS location accuracy on open sky roads, the accuracy degrades sharply on shaded and urban roads, with over 15 meters of error on average, and over 90 meters in some cases. This is consistent with other work that has observed similar errors in obstructed environments [4].

	Urban Area	Shaded Area	Opensky Area
Average Error (m)	24.3	15.3	4.7
Error STD (m)	5.5	3.2	1.6

Table 1—Measured GPS errors in three different areas

Why do we need highly accurate positioning? With these levels of inaccuracy, navigation apps may be led astray, and may give wrong turn-by-turn directions, which can lead to driver confusion. In this paper, we ask the question: *Is it possible to achieve lane-level positioning accuracy for automobiles even in highly obstructed environments?* In North America's interstate system, the nominal lane width is about 12 feet (3.6m), so our question translates to: Is it possible to achieve 3-4m accuracy, in the worst case, in obstructed environments?

Aside from more accurate (and therefore less confusing) navigation, precise positioning of vehicles can have many potential applications. Accurately positioning crowd-sourced detection of road features (e.g., potholes, rough roads etc.) can help municipalities target roadway improvements. Lane-level traffic flow analysis can help traffic agencies provision roadways; for example, an often clogged right lane might prompt the addition of a dedicated right turn lane. Moreover, insurance companies can track driver propensity to stay on fast lanes, or track violations of lane occupancy rules (e.g., on some roads, trucks are required to stay in the right lanes).

Possible Responses. One possible response is to hope that future GPS receivers will have enhanced accuracy in highly obstructed settings. As we demonstrate later, expensive GPS devices available on the market today are still susceptible to the urban canyon effect. This is not surprising, since GPS receivers will, in general, find it difficult to compensate for lack of visibility to satellites or for multipath effects.

For this reason, most prior work on precise positioning for automobiles (Section 5) has relied on information fusion: combining sensors of other modalities (like LIDAR), or other sources of information (such as digital maps), in order to augment or correct GPS readings.

Our approach. Our paper also uses this approach, but with a new twist: *we exploit the availability of sensors built-in to vehicles to improve positioning accuracy.*

Modern vehicles are equipped with several hundred physical and virtual (derived from physical) sensors on-board. These sensors provide the instantaneous internal state of all vehicular subsystems. From the industry standard CAN [26] bus and using the standard On-Board Diagnostics (OBD-II) port on cars, users can, in theory, access most of these sensors, such as: vehicle speed, steering wheel angle, throttle position, transmission lever position, and some inertial sensors [46, 25, 18]. These sensor readings are internally used to control subsystems of the vehicle, such as stability control and engine health monitoring.

While many of these sensors are proprietary, several tools [50] have been able to access these through reverse engineering. More recently, Ford and General Motors have made about 20 sensors available through their OpenXC platform and GM Developer Network respectively, so it's likely that, in the future, such information will be ubiquitously available. In collaboration with a major automotive manufacturer, we have obtained access to many internal car sensors. In this paper, we explore whether, and how, these sensors can help precisely position an automobile.

Specifically, we use in-vehicle sensors to improve positioning accuracy in two ways. First, in-vehicle sensors can provide accurate *odometry* for precise dead reckoning. By contrast, prior work has used GPS-derived speed measurements for dead reckoning. Second, in-vehicle sensors can be used to precisely identify *roadway landmarks* (a pothole, or a speed bump). In turn, *crowd-sourced* position estimates of these landmarks can be used to fix a car's position.

3. THE DESIGN OF CARLOC

In this section, we describe the design of CARLOC. We begin with an overview of the overall design, which motivates specific design challenges that are then addressed in subsequent subsections.

3.1 Overview of CARLOC

Figure 2 depicts the various components of CARLOC. At a high-level, CARLOC models the current position of the vehicle *probabilistically*: intuitively, the position of the vehicle at any point in space is associated with a specific probability. The key idea then is to *update* or *refine* this probabilistic representation using information from various sources. Then, at any given point in time, the precise position of the vehicle is obtained by *actualizing* the probabilistic representation, as described later.

One way that CARLOC updates the probabilistic representation is by using vehicle sensors to obtain distance traveled and the heading of the car. This approach, often called *dead reckoning*, is, in CARLOC, more accurate because of its use of in-built vehicular sensors. These sensors are available at frequencies ranging from 10-100Hz, so they can provide accurate estimates of distance and heading over short timescales and distances. However, vehicle sensors by themselves are insufficient: sensor errors can, over time, cause position estimates to drift significantly from the true position.

A second way to update the probabilistic representation is to periodically obtain GPS readings. These readings are associated with estimates of error, which can be used to tighten the car's position estimates. However, as shown in Section 2, GPS errors in obstructed environments can increase the car's position uncertainty.

To overcome GPS errors, one can *spatially refine* the probabilistic position estimates using digital maps. Intuitively, a car is likely to be off a roadway with a very small or near-zero probability, and map-matching algorithms [29] use this observation to refine position estimates. Car sensors provide accurate estimates of speed and turns, and these can be used to enhance existing map-matching algorithms to increase positioning accuracy.

The last component of CARLOC is based on the observation that *roadway landmarks* mark consistent positions in the environment that be exploited to refine the car's probabilistic position estimate. Consider a speed-bump on a road: if a car passes over a speedbump, it can refine its own position estimates using position estimates of *other cars when they passed over the same speedbump*. This suggests that *crowd-sourced* position estimates of roadway landmarks can be used to improve a car's position estimates. CARLOC incorporates several novel algorithms that use vehicle sensors to identify roadway landmarks.

In designing these components of CARLOC, we faced the following challenges:

- Choosing the probabilistic model for position representation, since we needed a representation that would be amenable to update and refinement from a variety of sources of information, including maps, vehicle sensors, and crowd-sourced information.

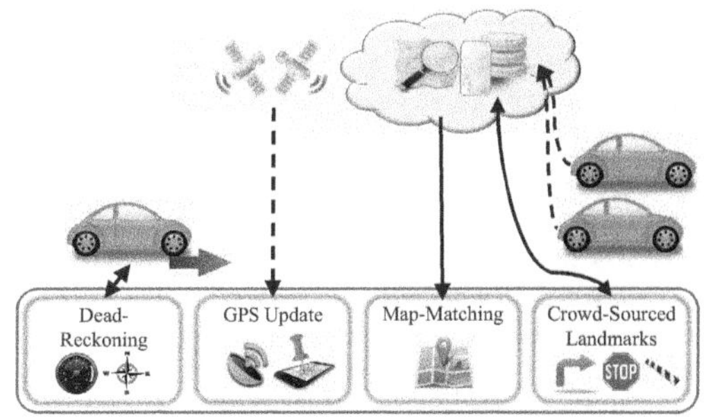

Figure 2—CARLOC Design

- Selecting a model that correctly represents GPS position uncertainty, so that the vehicle's positioning uncertainty could be appropriately updated.
- Designing a *motion model* for the vehicle that uses vehicle sensors to determine how a vehicle's position evolves over time; prior motion models have used GPS readings, but the vehicle sensors are available at much higher frequencies than GPS readings.
- Designing appropriate *map-matching* algorithms; although map-matching has been studied extensively, they rely on frequent GPS updates which can lead to matching errors in the face of significant GPS errors.
- Designing algorithms to detect landmarks from vehicle sensors, and to refine position estimates using crowd-sourced location information.

We discuss each of these challenges in the subsequent sections.

3.2 Probabilistic Representation of Position

A vehicle's position estimate has inherent uncertainty due to sensor noise. A common approach to dealing with this uncertainty is to use linearized models and assume Gaussian noise so that a Kalman filter can be applied. As prior work [12] has shown, however, vehicle positioning violates some of these assumptions; specifically, during a turn the a posteriori position distribution is non-Gaussian and non-linear filtering methods are required to solve the problem.

In this paper, we use a well-known non-parametric probabilistic model of position, based on Sequential Monte Carlo (SMC) methods. Our representation is commonly called a *particle filter* [34, 49]. A particle filter estimates the posterior density of a vehicle's position through predefined Bayesian recursion equations.

Concretely, the current position of the vehicle is represented by a set of particles. Each particle represents a probabilistic state vector, indicating the likelihood the vehicle is at this position. Thus, if we have N particles, each particle is associated with a state vector v_i (which contains its position and its orientation), and a probability or *weight* ω_i that determines the likelihood of the vehicle being in that state. At any given instant, the particle filter can be used to estimate the position of the vehicle as a weighted sum of the particles: $\frac{\Sigma_{i=1}^{N} v_i \omega_i}{\Sigma_{i=1}^{N} \omega_i}$.

This representation provides a uniform foundation for many of the kinds of fusion we are interested in. For example, vehicle odometry and bearing information can be used to update the v_i s, and the associated sensor errors can be used to update the ω_i s. Getting a GPS fix results in re-weighting the particles, and adding map constraints may require removing off-road particles from the filter. Finally, the positions of roadway landmarks can be represented as particle filters, so crowd-sourced landmark updates require merging particle filters (in a manner described later).

3.3 Map Matching

Many digital maps represent roads using *road segments* which are polyline representations of a road. Map-matching is the process of identifying the road segment corresponding to a given position. Map-matching has been used in prior work (Section 5) to improve vehicle positioning, and is in general known to be a hard problem because position errors can lead to errors in map-matching.

CARLOC builds upon a specific piece of prior work [29, 48] that models the map matching problem as a maximum likelihood path estimation on a Hidden Markov Model (HMM). In this work, the states in the HMM are the map-matched road-segments, and transitions occur when a vehicle turns from one road onto another. Given a GPS reading, one can estimate, given a model of GPS errors and using Bayes' rule, the posterior *observation probability* of the car being on a specific road segment. One can also estimate a *transition probability*; namely, at a given instant, and given a GPS reading, the probability that a transition has occurred from one road segment to another. With these observation and transition probabilities, [29] uses the Viterbi algorithm to find the maximum likelihood sequence of states (or road segments the car has traversed).

The Viterbi algorithm is fast enough that we can run map matching on a mobile device. To optimize the implementation, rather than run map-matching on every GPS update (1 per second in our implementation), we do so only when the GPS reading has deviated significantly from the last matched road segment.

CARLOC map-matching enhancements. We have modified the observation probability computations to increase its efficiency and robustness. For efficiency, we use the fact that modern GPS receivers report estimates of error: we then only search road segments that fall within these error bounds. For robustness, we avoid using GPS readings that are inconsistent with the heading (direction of motion) of the car.

Our changes to the transition probability calculations from [29] are more substantial. That work calculates transition probabilities by estimating the travel time from the last known update. One change we make is to use travel distance (as measured from car sensor readings, by integrating the instantaneous speed sensor) instead of travel time. However, travel distance isn't able to distinguish, in Figure 1, whether the car turned left from *Road A* to *Road B* or continued straight on *Road C*, since both outcomes would be equally likely.

CARLOC has additional information that can make the estimation more accurate — *car sensors that measure turns*. Specifically, using the steering wheel angle sensor, we can estimate the change in heading of the car $\Delta\theta_{j,k}$ from road segment j to road segment k. We also estimate the difference $\Delta l_{j,k}$ between the actual distance traveled and the projected distance traveled on the map (obtained by projecting GPS readings onto the road segments j and k). Using these two quantities, we can estimate the transition probability, at a given instant, of the event $\alpha_{j,k}$ of the vehicle transitioning from road segment j to road segment k from Bayes rule (M is the number of road segments considered):

$$P(\alpha_{j,k}|\Delta l_{j,k},\Delta\theta_{j,k}) = \frac{P(\alpha_{j,k}|\Delta l_{j,k})P(\alpha_{j,k}|\Delta\theta_{j,k})}{\sum_{m=1}^{M} P(\alpha_{j,m}|\Delta l_{j,m})P(\alpha_{j,m}|\Delta\theta_{j,m})} \quad (1)$$

If we assume that the difference in angle, and the difference between the projected and traveled distance are both Gaussian with zero mean and standard deviations σ_a and σ_d respectively, then this becomes:

$$P(\alpha_{j,k}|\Delta l_{j,k},\Delta\theta_{j,k}) = \frac{exp(-0.5(\frac{\Delta\theta_{j,k}}{\sigma_a})^2 - 0.5(\frac{\Delta l_{j,k}}{\sigma_d})^2)}{\sum_{m=1}^{M} exp(-0.5(\frac{\Delta\theta_{j,m}}{\sigma_a})^2 - 0.5(\frac{\Delta l_{j,l}}{\sigma_d})^2))} \quad (2)$$

Using the matched road segments. CARLOC uses the result of map-matching in three ways. First, when it starts up, CARLOC does not have a usable estimation of the vehicle's position so it projects the GPS reading onto the map-matched road segment as a position estimate.

Second, we use the map-matched road segments to filter erroneous GPS readings. Even though GPS readings come with an associated error, we have found that, especially in obstructed environments, the associated error bounds can under-estimate the actual error. To filter out these erroneous readings, we first project the GPS reading to the map-matched road-segment, then filter out readings whose projected distance to the road-segment is greater than the nominal road widths. In the map we use, Open Street Maps (OSM) [20], road segments have associated types such as residential or highway. We make conservative assumptions about the number of lanes in each type (e.g., 2 for residential and 6 for highway, in each direction), then use nominal lane width to compute road widths. If the GPS location does not fall within the road, we declare it invalid. We also use another optimization. For some roads, OSM depicts them using one road segment, for others two. If our projected GPS reading is closer to the road segment that is against the car heading, we drop that reading.

Finally, we use map-matching to update the weights on the particle filter. Intuitively, for each particle, let x be the projected distance of the particle from the outer edge of the map-matched road segment. For this calculation, we use the conservative road width estimate described in the previous paragraph. If $x > 0$ (the particle falls outside the road segment) we re-weight its probability inversely with x. Specifically, the new weight is calculated to be: $\frac{1}{\sqrt{2\pi\sigma^2}}exp(-\frac{x^2}{2\sigma^2})$, where σ is the variance of all the particles' projected distance to road segment.

3.4 Motion Model

A motion model captures how the *pose* (position and orientation) of a car (or any moving object) evolves with time. Formally, the pose consists of 5 components, 3 of which estimate position (latitude, longitude and altitude) and 2 measure orientation (heading or yaw, and pitch). In this paper, we focus on modeling motion in a 2-dimensional plane; extending to 3 dimensions is left to future work.

Changes in position and orientation can be measured using GPS, but GPS measurements have error, and are sampled relatively infrequently (once a second). Instead, CARLOC *exploits the availability of car sensors* to dead-reckon the car's pose. Dead-reckoning requires the ability to estimate *displacements* and to estimate *changes in heading*.

Estimating displacement. In theory, one can estimate displacement using the vehicle speed and acceleration and using simple kinematic equations. Thus, if x_t represents the vehicle's position vector at time t, then we can write $x_t = x_0 + v_0 t + \frac{1}{2}a_0 t^2$ where v_0 represents the velocity and a_0 the acceleration. In vehicles, the *speed sensor* can be sampled at relatively high rate (10Hz), and if we assume constant acceleration between two samples of the speed sensor, the kinematic equation to update position becomes:

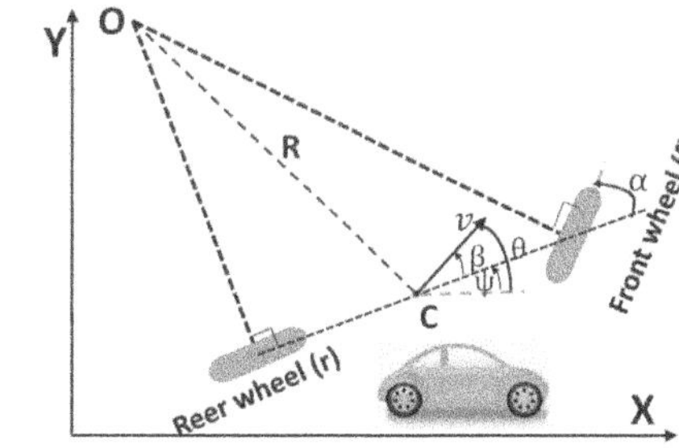

Figure 3—Kinematics of lateral vehicle motion

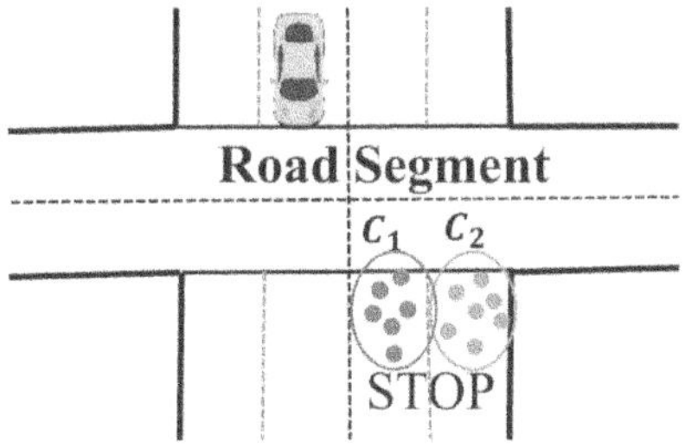

Figure 4—Multi-lane Stop Sign

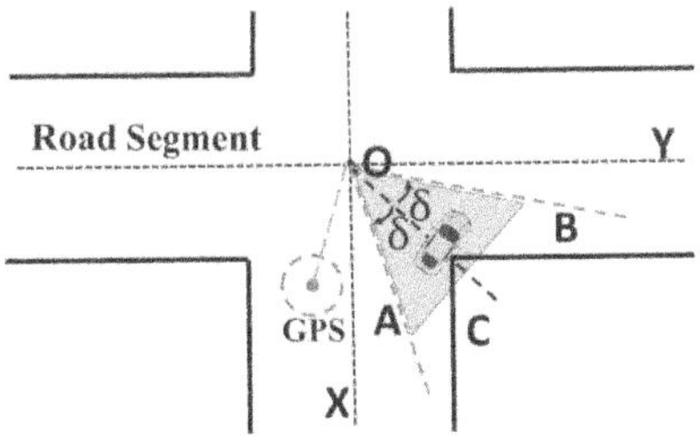

Figure 5—Street Corner Illustration

$x_t = x_{t-1} + \frac{1}{2}(v_t + v_{t-1})\Delta_t$, where Δ_t represents the sampling interval.[1]

Estimating change in heading. To estimate changes in heading, CARLOC also uses vehicle sensors. Modern vehicles expose two sensors that can help estimate changes in heading, the *steering wheel angle* and the *yaw rate* sensor. However, correctly estimating a change in heading needs to take the vehicle steering design into account. Vehicle steering follows the Ackermann geometry [1] which describes how turns are effected by steering.

A simplified version of the kinematics of lateral motion resulting from the steering system design is shown in Figure 3 [42]. In this figure, a turn angle of α on the front wheel results in an effective change in heading θ for the center of mass of the vehicle. θ consists of two components ψ and β. As [42] shows, β (the *slip angle*) can be estimated using vehicle geometry and estimates of α and ψ.

To estimate α, we use the steering wheel angle sensor reading from the vehicle and the empirical observation that there is a linear relationship between the steering wheel angle and the actual wheel angle α.

To estimate ψ, we continuously integrate the vehicle yaw rate sensor. However, we have found that errors in the yaw rate sensor can accumulate over time, so we correct for these errors by using filtered readings of GPS bearing. Our filtering uses three steps. First, we only take GPS readings that are consistent with map-matching (as described in Section 3.3). Next, we check if successive valid GPS readings are comparable to (within 10% of) the distance traveled as reported by the vehicle sensors. Finally, we check if the resulting bearing computed from the successive readings is consistent with (within 5% of) the heading change computed from the yaw rate sensors. If so, we use the GPS bearing to estimate ψ. Because the yaw rate sensor is sampled at a higher frequency than GPS, and because GPS can often be inaccurate, GPS bearing corrections occur infrequently relative to the calculations of ψ using the yaw rate sensor.

Updating the particle filter. In practice, the kinematics calculations can be affected by noise. Our particle filter representation is able to account for sensor noise as follows. Recall that each particle in the particle filter is associated with a pose vector x and a weight ω. When the vehicle moves, we update each particle's pose vector using the displacement and heading change calculations discussed above. To account for sensor noise, we assume that each particle's pose is independently affected by Gaussian noise in the speed and car sensor. We use nominal noise estimates for these sensors from the manufacturer datasheet.

[1]Rather than using a global geodetic coordinate system (e.g., latitude and longitude), we convert all poses to a local geodetic system East-North-Up (ENU [14]). This ignores the earth's curvature, but is easier to model, and has been used in the vehicular positioning literature [35, 9]. We omit the details of this conversion.

3.5 Location Update

Map-matching provides coarse location corrections by removing off-road particles. The motion model can provide fine-grain and accurate updates to particle locations but over small spatio-temporal scales. At larger time-scales, sensor errors can accumulate. As we show experimentally, these two methods alone do not achieve high positioning accuracy. So, CARLOC also uses GPS readings to update the particle filter.

Specifically, CARLOC uses GPS readings determined valid from map-matching (Section 3.3). Each GPS reading is associated with an accuracy range [6, 5] and the error distribution of GPS readings can be well approximated by a Rayleigh distribution [38]. When we obtain a valid GPS reading, we update each particle's weight according to Rayleigh distribution, based on the particle's distance to the GPS-reported location. Intuitively, particles that are far from the reported GPS location are assigned a lower weight or likelihood. When a vehicle is stopped, we might obtain multiple readings at the same location: in this case, we aggregate the error reported by those readings before re-weighting the particles.

We also apply several standard transformations to the particle filter. Recall that particles represent samples of positional probability distribution. With particle weight updates, particles need to resample occasionally to improve the probabilistic estimates. The resampling process adheres to the *Sampling Importance Re-sampling (SIR)* algorithm, by only resampling when the effective number of particles N_{eff} is less than the threshold (N_{th}). Assuming each particle has a weight of ω_i, it follows that $N_{eff} = \frac{1}{\sum \omega_i^2}$ [3, 13]. We set N_{th} to $\frac{2}{3}N$, where N is the number of particles. Moreover, an incorrect resample can cause particle diversity loss, so we also occasionally draw samples from the GPS position distribution, an approach called *sensor resetting* [31].

3.6 Crowd-sourced Landmark Positions

Given that GPS availability in obstructed urban environments is known to be poor, CARLOC uses an additional, novel positioning enhancement, *crowd-sourced landmarks*.

Suppose a car hits a speed bump. If CARLOC is able to detect the speed bump, then *the car's particle filter at the instant the speed bump is encountered is a probabilistic representation of the speed bump's position.* Suppose N cars pass over the same speed bump, the collection of all their particle filters at the speed bump represents a *crowd-sourced* collection of position estimates of the speed bump. Intuitively, one expects the distribution described by these crowd-sourced particles *to converge to the true location of the speed bump* as more and more vehicles contribute to the collection. Finally, a speed bump is an instance of a *roadway landmark*: this discussion applies to other roadway landmarks such as stop signs and street corners (at intersections).

CARLOC uses this observation to improve positioning accuracy. When a car detects a roadway landmark, it can check to see if crowd-sourced particles are available for the landmark. (These par-

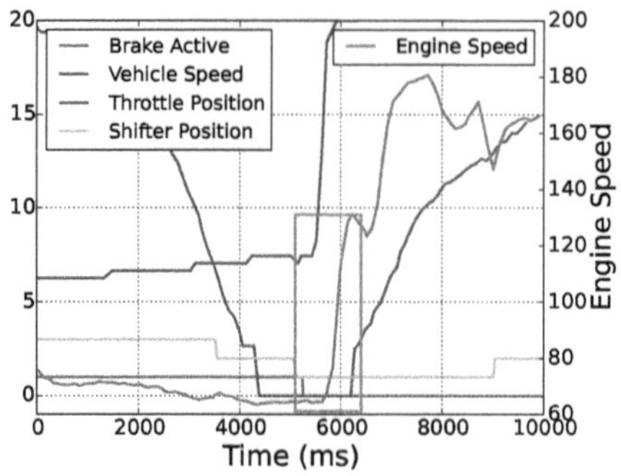

Figure 6—Stop Sign Landmark Detection

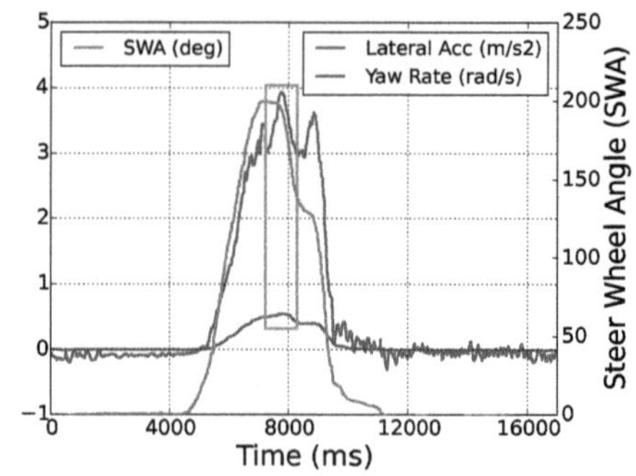

Figure 7—Street Corner Landmark Detection

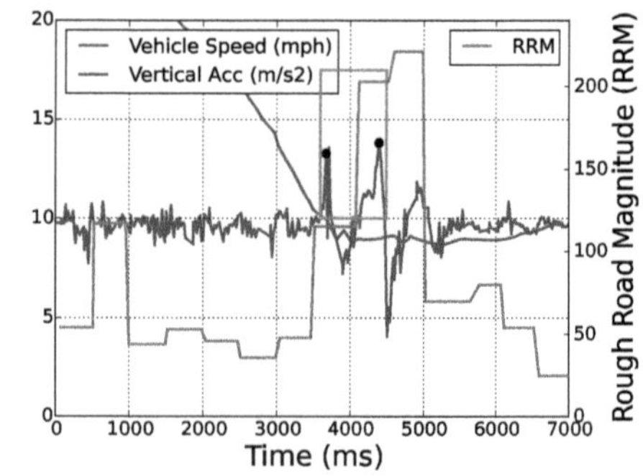

Figure 8—Speed Bump Landmark Detection

ticles can be maintained in a cloud database, and made available through a cloud service. To minimize network latency, relevant particle clouds can be pre-fetched before reaching a landmark. The detailed design of this service is beyond the scope of the paper). If they are available, the car can *resample its particle filter from the set of particles that include crowd-sourced particles* for the landmark and its own current particle filter.

This approach poses two challenges: (a) How can vehicles detect roadway landmarks? (b) How should a car's particle filter be updated using the crowd-sourced particles? We discuss answers to this question for three types of roadway landmarks below. Our detection algorithms use vehicle sensors to achieve accurate landmark detection.

Stop Signs. At a stop sign, there is usually a line drawn on the roadway surface. Drivers are supposed to stop at the line before proceeding into the intersection. Of course, not all drivers stop exactly at the line. CARLOC leverages the wisdom of the crowds: if most drivers stop at or near the line, their combined position distributions will be an accurate estimate of the average behavior of drivers when encountering a stop sign (e.g., stopping just a little before the stop sign) We make this intuition more precise below.

Detection: Our detection algorithm is based on the following observation: to leave the stop sign and enter the intersection, the driver usually releases the brake, steps on the gas pedal, as a result of which the engine speed increases, one or more gear shifts may occur, and the vehicle speed increases.

To detect this, CARLOC continuously samples the following vehicle sensors: (*Brake Active*,*Vehicle Speed*, *Throttle Position*, *Shifter Position* and *Engine Speed*). Figure 6 shows the timeseries of these sensors at a stop sign and pictorially depicts the algorithm: on the timeseries of each sensor, the algorithm applies a sliding window and attempts to discover a window that contains a brake pedal release, followed by a sharp increase in throttle position and engine speed, followed by an increase in engine speed. The particle filter **P** of the car at the time when there is a discontinuity in the vehicle speed timeseries (i.e., the time when the speed increases suddenly) marks an estimate of the location of the stop sign line. Once a car computes **P**, it can *store* **P** in a cloud service (discussed below), for later retrieval by other cars.

The precise algorithm is more complicated than this since it has to take into account many practical constraints. First, for any window that satisfies these features, we lookup the current position in an online database of stop signs [20] and our accumulated stop sign database, and only use the particle filter if it is found in the database. This eliminates false detections caused by a car stopping and then starting, say, after a delivery. This database is currently incomplete, but with time we expect its coverage to improve. For additional coverage, CARLOC uses other landmarks discussed below. Second, drivers may release the brake and roll through the stop sign, to account for which CARLOC uses a slightly larger window. Third, drivers may stop multiple times before reaching the stop sign line, since they may be queued up behind other cars. This behavior manifests itself as a sequences of detected windows, and we use the last window in the sequence. Finally, we crowd-sourcing to disambiguate traffic lights from stop signs; if some car traces don't stop at an intersection, but others do, that intersection has a traffic light, not a stop sign. We use this same technique to improve our stop sign database coverage; if every car stops near an intersection, that indicates the existence of a stop sign there.

Particle Storage and Update. When the particle filter **P** is uploaded to the cloud service, that service performs a processing step. Figure 4 shows a multi-lane road scenario, in which the cloud service can get aggregated data from cars stopping on each lane. The cloud service employs a clustering algorithm to cluster the particles based on lane width threshold; the resulting number of clusters determines the number of lanes on the road. Figure 4 shows two such clusters.

Now, suppose a car **A** wishes to update its particle filter when it reaches the stop sign. It downloads the cluster of particles closest to its current estimated position. These particles, together with its own, are then re-sampled with a probability proportional to the weight of each particle. Thus, more important particles are likely to be selected during re-sampling. These re-sampled particles then constitute the updated particle filter for **A**. In this way, if the crowd-sourced cluster of particles has converged to the actual location, the new particle filter will be closer to the car's precise position.

Street Corners. Street corners can be detected when a car performs a right turn.

Detection: At a right turn, the timeseries of the steering wheel angle sensor peaks (Figure 7). So, any maximum in the steering wheel angle (SWA) that is larger than some high threshold (90 degrees in our implementation) can indicate a street corner. We have found that this peak is fairly robust to a variety of turning behaviors. For example, even when drivers turn from the rightmost lane into the non-rightmost lane, this peak is observed.

To disambiguate other turns (for example, lane shifts at low speed which might also trigger the threshold), we correlate with two other car sensors: the lateral acceleration and the yaw rate[2] (Figure 7). During a turn, these three sensors all exhibit peaks, so CARLOC applies a sliding window to find a window in the trace that contains peaks of the three signals and then finds the average of the time of occurrence of these peaks. The particle filter of the car **P** at this time is used as an estimate of the position of the street corner and is crowd-sourced (uploaded to the cloud service). However, to disambiguate right turns at places other than intersections, we

[2]These sensors are noisy, so we use box smoothing [41] to smooth these time series.

use an online map of intersections to determine if the car's current estimated position is near an intersection; if not, **P** is not uploaded.

Particle Storage and Update: When **P** is uploaded to the cloud service, it filters outlier particles to improve accuracy. From road segment data in an online map, the location of the mid-point of the intersection can be determined, and CARLOC assumes that particles in **P** outside the shaded cone (between $\overline{OA}$ and $\overline{OB}$) in Figure 5 are unlikely to represent the car's true position, and assigns those particles very low weight.

When a car **A** reaches the street corner, it downloads the crowd-sourced particles from the cloud service and applies an update procedure identical to that for the stop sign. If a car stops before turning, then a particle update is performed only once (at the stop sign), rather than at both locations since the latter alternative could lose particle diversity (i.e., we might not have a good sample of the underlying distribution of position).

Speed Bumps. The last landmark we consider in this paper is the speed bump. CARLOC is careful to disambiguate potholes and speed bumps and uses several car sensors for this purpose.

Detection: The detection algorithm is best illustrated using Figure 8. This shows the measurements of three sensors recorded from a car traversing a speed bump: *(Rough Road Magnitude (RRM), Vehicle Speed* and inertial sensor *Vertical Acceleration).* As it approaches the bump, the car slows down and the vertical acceleration sensor exhibits a peak. These two features are used to determine a potential speed bump. CARLOC then monitors the RRM sensor and performs peak detection within a window whose scale (shown as red box) approximates the vehicle's wheelbase. If two peaks (shown in black dots) of vertical acceleration and increase of RRM are sensed, we determine a potential speed bump has been observed.

CARLOC deems the car's particle filter **P** at the first peak to be an estimate of the speed bump's location. As with other landmarks, **P** is uploaded and stored in the cloud service.

Particle storage and update. CARLOC clusters speed bump particles as it does for stop sign particles. Updating another car's particle filter follows the same re-sampling procedure as discussed above.

4. EVALUATION

In this section, we assess the performance of CARLOC in obstructed and unobstructed environments over different trip lengths, and compare its performance against other alternatives including GPS positioning from commodity GPS receivers as well as higher precision GPS receivers, and with differential GPS. Our final goal in this section is to assess the efficacy of each of the components in CARLOC: dead reckoning, map-matching, and landmark-based position augmentation.

4.1 Methodology

Experimental Setup. Our evaluations are based on multiple traces collected by two different drivers over routes with different characteristics from the perspective of a GPS receiver: *obstructed* routes in a downtown urban canyon, *unobstructed* routes with a view of the open sky at all points, and *partially-obstructed* routes with obstructed sky visibility in some locations.

The routes are all of different lengths, and of different road types (with different lane widths), as discussed below. Each trace consists of several vehicle sensor readings obtained through our car sensing platform ([18, 25]). The sensors readings we collect are already available through the CAN bus, as described earlier, and our sensor collection software can sustain continuous collection nearly 40 car sensors, of which we use only a subset.

On each route, we collect multiple traces at different times of day, which helps avoid bias caused by a specific traffic pattern. In addition, we use a subset of these traces to obtain crowd-sourced landmark positions, and evaluate the remaining traces using these crowd-sourced positions. Our results are averaged over the evaluations on these remaining traces, and we quantify the variability of our results in terms of quartiles.

Comparisons. Across all routes, we compare CARLOC performance against using a GPS receiver on a Google Nexus 5 (labeled *SPGPS* on our graphs). In addition, on some routes, we also compare against using an expensive (>$200) high-precision GPS receiver, the ublox NEO-7P GPS (*HPGPS*). Finally, we also use a companion rover receiver, the ublox LEA-6T to obtain Differential GPS (DGPS [45]) position as well as Real-Time Kinematic (RTK [43]) based positioning. It is likely that future cars may be able to incorporate these high precision receivers.

The rover receiver estimates position based on two modes [35]. The first mode returns precise location values. In its DGPS mode the rover receiver utilizes corrections from a known base station. Both modes update location at 1Hz.

Our LEA-6T rover devices use ublox firmware 7.03 and the NEO-7P devices use version 1.00. For RTK and DPGS, we use a publicly available NTRIP caster base station within 10 miles of all our experiments. We obtained access to the base station's NTRIP stream and position information through the UNAVCO consortium [53]. This station is equipped with an advanced Ashtech antenna mounted on a hilltop. On our rover devices (LEA-6T), ubx-formatted GPS measurements are captured using u-center, the ublox driver for the device with settings obtained directly from the developers of RTKLIB [54, 43].

Metrics and Ground Truth. Our measure of CARLOC performance is *positioning error* measured by distance between CARLOC's position and ground truth. Obtaining ground truth is extremely hard for positioning in some places, and we resort to three approaches.

Closed-loop routes. In our partially obstructed routes, we start the route at a well-marked location (and empty metered parking spot) and return to the same location. Our measure of accuracy then is the difference between the start position and the end position as reported by CARLOC (or any of the candidate comparison algorithms). The start position is calculated using our high-precision GPS receiver. This approach has also been used by prior work [22, 51].

High-precision GPS receiver. On our unobstructed routes, we also continuously collect readings from the high precision GPS receiver and use these as ground truth. The reported accuracy of these devices is within one meter. This method enables us to determine accuracy along the entire route instead of just at the end.

Fiducials. On our obstructed routes, as we show below, the accuracy of the high precision receiver is not sufficient. So, we resort to using *fiducials* in the environment. As we drive on the obstructed route, we stop at several easy-recognizable points (or fiducials) along the right side of the car, e.g. sidewalk ramp exit, mailbox, etc. When we stop, we record the current timestamp and take a image from the passenger side to cover the car right side road to ramp distance. We then use these images to look up Google's satellite views, pin down the points recorded in the image, and then use the location of those points (as obtained from Google Maps) as ground truth (Figure 9).

To validate our fiducial-based ground truth collection, we applied the same methodology in several locations with an unob-

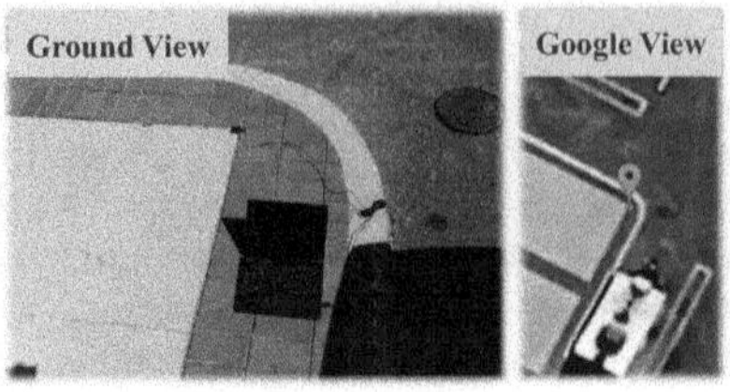

Figure 9—Static Measurement Setup

Figure 10—CARLOC and GPS Comparison in Downtown

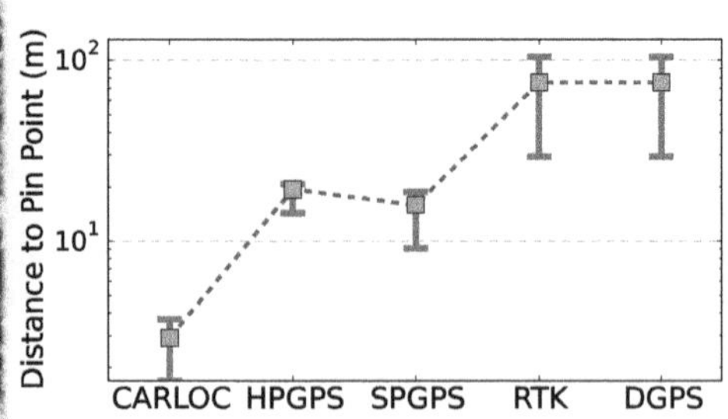

Figure 11—Map Pin Points Comparison

structed view of the sky, and at these locations we also used the high-precision reference GPS receiver to record position. We find that our pinned down points are within 1.2m of the reference receiver.

4.2 CARLOC on an Obstructed Route

Our obstructed route is a 2-mile loop in a downtown area surrounded by tall buildings (Figure 10). We collected a total of 12 traces along this loop using two different drivers at different times of day. On this route, we use only 4 landmarks: the 4 street corners shown in the figure. Of our traces, we use 8 to obtain crowd-sourced particles, and 4 to evaluate CARLOC and compare it against the high-precision GPS receiver, DGPS and RTK. As described above, we use the fiducials-based ground-truthing technique and we collected 15 different points as ground-truth.

Figure 11 shows the accuracy of each of these techniques with respect to the ground truth. The error bars represent the 25th and 75th percentile in our measurements. CARLOC has an average error of about 2.7m, with the smallest error being 0.6m as closest and the largest being 4.9m. Surprisingly, all of the alternatives have one to two orders of magnitude higher error. The high-precision receiver has an average error of 19.4m (min 7.7m, max 44m). The smartphone has an average/min/max error of 16m/1.2m/40.2m. This is slightly better than our high-precision GPS; this difference could either be within the margin of experimental error, or that smartphones have better dead-reckoning or GPS signal processing algorithms in software. Moreover, both DGPS and RTK, achieve really poor performance, with an average error of 75m, and a worst-case error of 200m.

Figure 10 depicts these results visually. In the figure on the left, it is evident that DGPS and RTK measurements span the entire area covered by the two-mile loop. In the figure on the right, the superior performance of CARLOC vis-a-vis the high-precision receiver and the smartphone are visually evident.

Why this pathological performance for the other alternatives? Clearly, both the high precision receiver and the smartphone GPS suffer from the urban canyon effect: the inability to see enough satellites affect their ability to get good position fixes. They are able to achieve reasonable performance primarily because of their use of dead reckoning filters. To understand why even the high-performance GPS receiver does not perform well, we examined the dilution of precision (DOP [30]) reported by the receiver. This measure of variability of GPS signals is much higher downtown (DTSHDOP) than along an unobstructed road with a clear view of the open sky (OSSHDOP) (Figure 12). This suggests that satellite availability and multipath effects degrade the performance of the high-performance receiver.

To further understand this performance, we discussed our findings with developers of RTKLib [43], a well-known open source software for processing GPS data which has been reported to have centimeter accuracy in many situations. As such, this forum includes many experts in GPS positioning performance. Our discussions corroborated our findings above that both DGPS and RTKLib suffer from lower satellite availability and multipath effects. It is well known that differential GPS cannot fix errors caused by differing multipath environments at the rover and basestation [10]. We have also verified that satellite availability is lower in our downtown trace (the rover receiver sees about 5 satellites) than in a trace from an unobstructed area (6-8 satellites). Finally, we notice far fewer location updates (once every 2.6s) from DGPS and RTK compared to using these on readings from an unobstructed trace (once every 1.1s). The developers of RTKlib believe these pathological errors can be improved with careful, route-specific parameter tuning, and we have left this to future work.

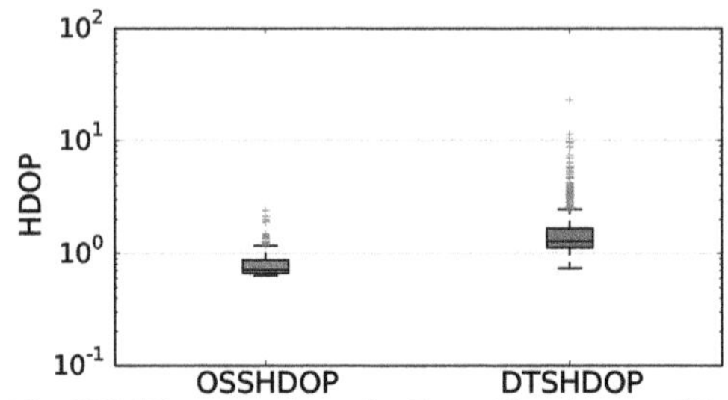

Figure 12—HDOP comparison for Open Sky Area and Downtown

4.3 CARLOC on an Unobstructed Route

We now quantify CARLOC performance along a 4.4km unobstructed route (Figure 13). Along this route, we treat the readings from the high-precision GPS receiver as ground truth, since, in this setting, its claimed accuracy is less than 1m [52]. We collected 8 traces along this route and used 5 of them to obtain crowd-sourced landmarks and 3 to evaluate accuracy. We obtained a total of 13 landmarks: 6 stop signs, 4 speed bumps and 3 street corners.

Table 2 shows CARLOC performance. When the error is computed across the entire trace (the *complete comparison*), CARLOC averages a 2.27m error with a minimum error of 0.14m and a maximum error of 4.51m. However, we believe this number is a little misleading because the high precision GPS receiver updates its position at a frequency of 1Hz, but CARLOC can track position changes every 10th of a second. So, these two readings can be off, on average by half of a tenth of a second in the worst-case. In that time, a car traveling at 45mph travels 1m, which can add to the error estimate.

To avoid this bias, Table 2 also reports error computed only at points where the car has stopped along the route (car sensors can tell us when the car has stopped). In this case (the *static comparison*), CARLOC has an average error of 1.38m and a maximum error of 2.4m. Finally, the smartphone GPS has a 3× higher worst-case error compared to CARLOC, and almost 2× higher average error.

Figure 13 pictorially depicts these results. Although the three alternatives are not visually distinguishable, the inset shows a part of the trace where the errors in the smartphone GPS are much more

	Mean (m)	Min (m)	Max (m)
Complete Comparison	2.27	0.14	4.51
Static Comparison	1.38	0.16	2.42
Smartphone GPS Comparison	4.19	0.14	15.83

Table 2—CARLOC, smartphone GPS to High-precision GPS Distance Statistics

evident: CARLOC's map matching and the motion model are able to compensate for inaccurate GPS, as a result of which it is able to much more closely follow the high-precision GPS receiver.

Figure 13—CARLOC, high-precision GPS and smartphone GPS in Open Sky Area

4.4 CARLOC on Partially-Obstructed Routes

In this section, we explore the performance of CARLOC on routes of different lengths. We also quantify the benefits of each of the components of CARLOC, and understand more closely how crowd-sourced landmarks help improve positioning.

It is hard to find unobstructed routes in metropolitan areas, so all our routes are partially obstructed. Because some of our routes are longer than our unobstructed route, it was logistically difficult to collect ground-truth using fiducials (which require significant manual effort), we used the closed-loop accuracy estimation technique described above.

Our routes range in length from 3.4km to 9.2km. For each route, we collect 15 traces, 10 of which we use for extracting crowd-sourced landmark locations, and 5 for evaluation. Along the longest of these routes, we have 19 landmarks: 5 stop signs, 10 street corners and 4 speedbumps.

Error as a function of distance. Over different distances, CARLOC is able to achieve mean error between 1.2 and 2.2m (Figure 14). The maximum errors for these 5 routes are 1.73m, 1.67m, 2.57m, 3.0m and 2.7m respectively. This is highly encouraging and suggests that lane-level precision might be achievable in most settings. Although there is a slight increase as a function of length, we believe this is largely due to difference in characteristics along the longer routes, rather than an increasing trend in CARLOC error as a function of distance. Indeed, there is no fundamental reason to believe that CARLOC error should increase with distance: any error accumulation with distance from, say the motion model would be corrected by GPS position fixes and crowd-sourced landmarks. The mean error along the longer 9.2km is slightly lower than the 7.6km trace primarily because the longer trace has two additional stop sign landmarks which improve CARLOC performance.

Contribution of different components of CARLOC. Using these traces, we are able to quantify the contribution of different components of CARLOC. Our motion model permits pure dead-reckoning (*DR*). To this, we consider the adding location updates from GPS (*DR GPS*). We also consider an alternative strategy which uses map-matching with dead-reckoning (*DR MAP*). Our final alternative strategy adds both map matching and location updates to dead-reckoning (*DR MAP GPS*).

Figure 14 shows the mean error using closed-loop error estimation for these different strategies and different route lengths.

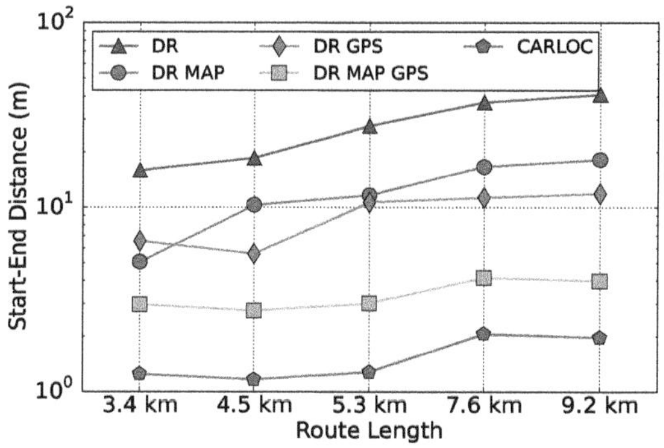

Figure 14—Different strategies' Start-End Distance

For the *DR*, we can clearly see an increase with length of trip, as expected: dead-reckoning error accumulates with distance. From the 15.9 m for 3.4 km to 40.9 m for 9.2 km trip, the errors grow almost linearly. When we add map-matching, we can see the Start-End distance for *DR MAP* drops to 10-26m. When GPS fixes are added to dead-reckoning, the errors also drop and appear to be independent of trace length. One would expect *DR GPS* to have similar error characteristics as the GPS receiver, since every position fix biases the location estimate towards the GPS position. *DR GPS* has errors of 6-10m, consistent with this expectation. Finally, with the addition of map-matching, the error of *DR MAP GPS* reduces to 3-4m across all route lengths. Finally, the addition of landmarks brings the error down to 1.2-2.2m as discussed above. These results suggest that each component plays a significant part in reducing the overall error, validating the design of CARLOC.

The Role of Landmarks. Why do landmarks perform well? How does the accuracy vary as a function of the number of landmarks along a route or the number of crowd-sourced particle filters used? [3]

How accurate are our landmarks? To measure the accuracy of our landmarks, we collected multiple traces on an unobstructed route on which we also collected measurements from our high precision GPS device (which we use as ground truth). Our route covers a total number of 9 right turns, 5 speed bumps and 4 stop signs.

We then ran our landmark detection algorithms over all traces. For each landmark in a trace, our algorithms determine the time t at which the landmark was detected (Section 3.6). In our traces, we find the nearest position reading from the high-precision GPS receiver within a small time interval Δt around t. (The high-precision GPS samples at 1Hz, which is too coarse since in 1 second the car can move several meters, so we restrict our search to a smaller window.) In our evaluations, we used 100ms for Δt for speed bumps and street corners and 300ms for stop signs, since the car stays longer at stop signs. Then, we define the *landmark error* as the difference between the estimated position of the landmark and the high-performance GPS receiver.

Figure 18 shows the statistics of landmark error for each type of landmark. The average error of three landmarks is around 2 meters. Stop signs have a minimum error of 0.6m and maximum of 2.9 m, which is encouraging. For street corners, the maximum error reaches 4m, mainly because 2 street corners are a bit obstructed, thus the results are biased by incorrect GPS readings. The minimum error can be as low as 0.3m. Speed bump errors can also reach around 4.1m, caused by a single outlier where the speed bump has a pothole just before it, which increases the error. However, the speed bump's minimum distance can reach as low as 0.15 m, which is very close to the center of the particle cloud. These results ex-

[3]We omitted the landmark detection accuracy evaluation due to space.

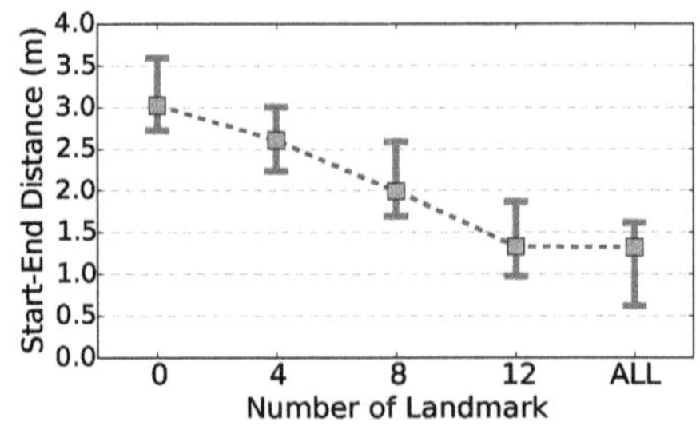

Figure 15—Start-End Distance with Number of Landmarks

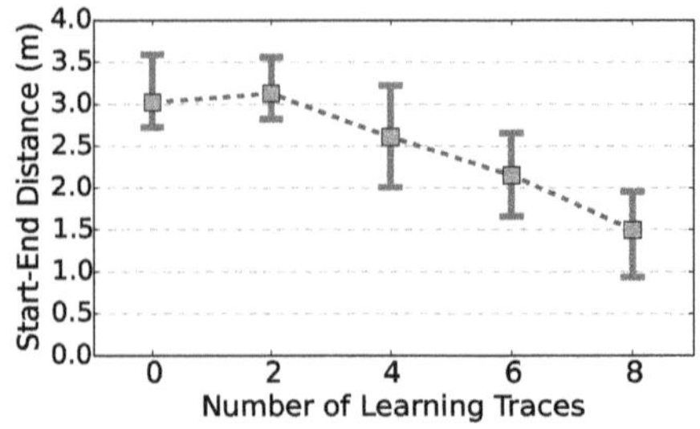

Figure 16—Start-End Distance with Number of Learning Trace

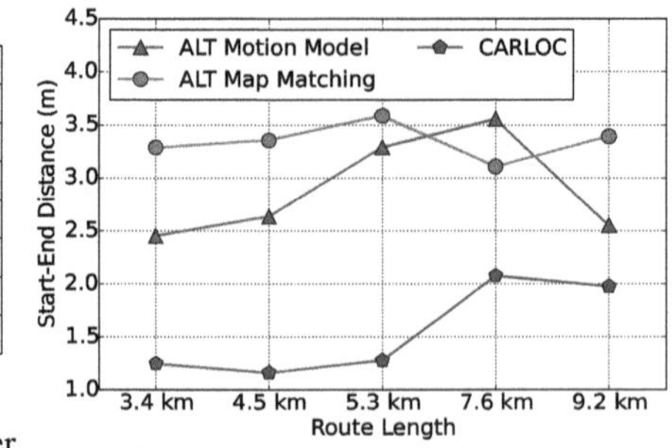

Figure 17—Map-matching and Motion Model Optimization Performance

	Precision	Recall
Stop Sign	0.89	0.95
Speed Bump	0.83	0.88
Right Turn	0.97	0.98

Table 3—Landmark Detection Accuracy

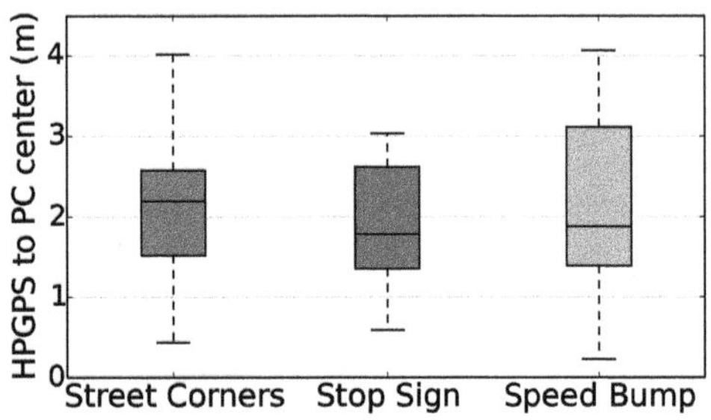

Figure 18—Landmark Error Statistics

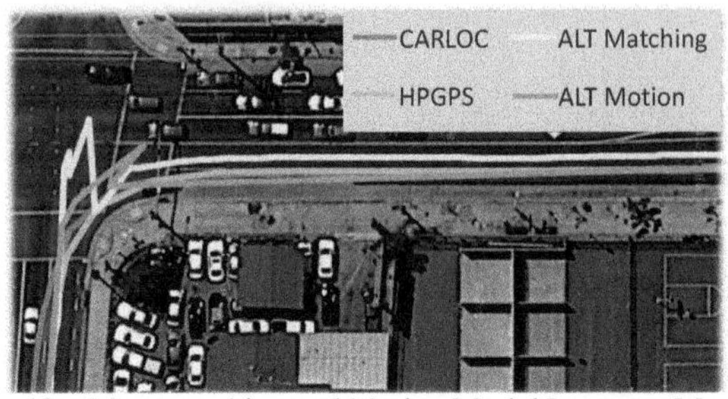

Figure 19—Map-matching and Motion Model Issues on Map View

plain why using crowd-sourced particles can improve positioning accuracy, but also indicate room for improvement in our detection algorithms.

How accurate are the landmark detection algorithms? We have described our detection algorithms in Section 3. We run our detection algorithms over all the traces we have and compare against the ground truth we collected. We summarize the precision and recall for each algorithm in Table 3. For stop sign, we apply crowd-sourcing to eliminate the outlier cases, like traffic lights. For speed bump, because of an severe pothole in our traces, our algorithm always treats it as speed bump. This brings down the overall accuracy. For right turn, we have near optimal performance. The main reason is the detection algorithm gets triggered by peak of multiple sensors, and we also apply the verification with map information, so the good accuracy performance is expected.

How many landmarks are enough? Figure 15 shows the CARLOC closed-loop error on our 5.3km loop. On this loop there are 15 landmarks, and the figure plots mean CARLOC error (and 25th and 75th percentiles) as a function of the number of landmarks used to calculate position. As expected, the error decreases as more landmarks are used in estimating position. However, beyond about 12 landmarks there is no improvement in the error, suggesting that of a relatively small number of landmarks along a route might be sufficient to achieve high accuracy.

What degree of crowd-sourcing is necessary? For the same route, Figure 16 shows the accuracy of using all 15 landmarks, but computed from an increasing number of traces. This shows what degree of crowd-sourcing is necessary. Interestingly, using 2 traces has higher error than using one trace. We found that this is because, in the second trace, the driver did not fully stop at the stop sign, inducing an error in landmark estimation. Moreover, the error drops linearly with the number of crowd sourced traces. This behavior is expected, but we don't see a flattening, suggesting that CARLOC accuracy can be improved by adding a higher degree of crowd-sourcing. We have left this to future work.

4.5 Benefits of Optimizations

CARLOC optimizes map-matching (Section 3.3) and the motion model (Section 3.4). In this section, we quantify the benefits of these optimizations.

CARLOC enhances a previously proposed map-matching algorithm [29] to include car-sensor readings that provide distance and changes in heading. The availability of these readings motivates a more sophisticated transitional probability calculation for a Hidden Markov Model, and CARLOC incorporates this. What if CARLOC had used the original transitional probability calculation? Figure 17 shows how the performance of this *ALT Map Matching* strategy performs against CARLOC for our closed-loop tests. This strategy exhibits significantly higher error between 3-3.5m across all our route lengths, suggesting that the optimization is definitely beneficial. Figure 19 illustrates one situation where the optimization helps: CARLOC is able to track the turn correctly, but *ALT Map Matching*, because its transition probability calculation does not incorporate turns, is unable to do so.

Second, CARLOC incorporates an advanced motion model that computes the slip angle β. Instead, it could have simply used heading change computed from the yaw rate (ψ in Figure 3), which would have been a coarse approximation of the slip angle. This alternative motion model, named as *ALT Motion Model*, also has higher error than CARLOC and comparable error to *ALT Map Matching* (Figure 17). The reason for this inaccuracy is also depicted in Figure 19, which shows how *ALT Motion Model* is not able to track turns.

5. RELATED WORK

We are inspired by prior work in mobile sensing based position augmentation, improved GPS-based methods, and robot localization. CARLOC sits in the unique point in the design space, with its use of vehicle sensors and crowd-sourced landmarks.

Mobile Sensing. The mobile sensing community has long explored approaches to use GPS position and other sensors to detect features on roadways (such as stop signs [7, 23] and potholes [27, 28, 57, 17, 15]). In contrast, CARLOC uses vehicle sensors to identify common roadway landmarks with the aim of improving positioning.

Closest to our work is SmartLoc [4], which estimates location and travel distance using inertial sensors on mobile devices. In obstructed environments, SmartLoc uses smartphone sensors to detect landmarks in the environment (like bridges and traffic lights), but these measurements are not crowd-sourced. CARLOC's use of vehicle sensors and crowd-sourced landmarks, together with advanced map matching, gives it an order of magnitude higher accuracy than the prior work. LaneQuest [2] uses probabilistic methods to estimate which lane a car is driving on, a qualitatively different problem than ours. LaneQuest, however, uses crowd-sourced anchors, but, unlike CARLOC, cannot leverage vehicle sensors to detect these. Similar to LaneQuest, [33] keeps track of relative location between cars, while CARLOC focuses on the problem of precisely positioning automobiles.

Several other pieces of work explore improvements to map matching: these can potentially be used to improve the accuracy of map-matching in CARLOC. Track [48] and CTrack [47] propose map-matching improvements using WiFi localization and cellular position respectively. AutoWitness [19] employs inertial sensor-based HMM and Viterbi Decoding to improve path estimation. Map-matching is just one of the components in CARLOC, and we use vehicle sensors to augment map-matching. Finally, [35] proposes fusing GPS and inertial measurements from custom hardware, and leverages DGPS for accurate vehicle position. In contrast, CARLOC does not require custom hardware, and our results show that in obstructed environments, DGPS can perform poorly.

GPS Enhancements. Much work has explored techniques to improve GPS positioning without fusion from other sensors. DGPS [45] and RTK [43, 37] use a base station and a rover receiver and are able to achieve high accuracy. More recent work has explored using DGPS [22, 21] but improving the positioning calculations; this work is able to achieve centimeter-level accuracy in unobstructed environments. Finally, a body of work has explored other improvements to DGPS and RTK [16, 44]. Unlike this class of work, CARLOC can achieve high accuracy in urban environments using a single commodity GPS receiver. High-precision GPS receivers [52] might well become available in future makes and models, but even these will require CARLOC-like fusion in obstructed or partially-obstructed urban environments.

Robot localization. Many of the techniques we use, such as the motion model and particle filters, are inspired by prior work on robot localization. Robot and vehicle localization have extensively explored fusion using information from various kinds of sensors: inertial sensors [55], stereo vision cameras [39], laser range finders [32, 11, 8, 24]. Unlike these, CARLOC explores the use of in-built vehicle sensors, and, in addition, crowd-sourcing landmark positions, in order to achieve high accuracy. Finally, other work has also explored map integration for position enhancement [40, 56, 36]; as we show, while maps and GPS can provide high accuracy, the use of crowd-sourced landmarks in CARLOC is necessary to get good results.

6. CONCLUSIONS AND FUTURE WORK

This paper presents CARLOC, a system for precisely tracking the position of an automobile. CARLOC builds upon prior work in probabilistic position estimation using map matching, but adds novel components: it uses sensors built into vehicles to augment map-matching and motion models, and crowd-sourced landmark estimates to improve positioning accuracy. CARLOC's mean error is on the order of 2m, suggesting the feasibility of lane-level positioning in the future.

Future work can explore several directions. CARLOC's motion model can be generalized to 3 dimensions to account for hilly roads. It may be possible that other alternatives like RTKLib can be tuned to achieve better performance, and it would be interesting to see how close such tuning comes to CARLOC's performance. Although CARLOC has high-accuracy and outperforms its competitors, its position tracking during turns can be improved (Figure 19). Furthermore, our current experiments are conducted with traces from 2 drivers. While our current experiments hint at the benefits of crowdsourcing, the impact of multiple drivers and cars needs further study. The landmark detection algorithms can be made more robust to different drivers' driving behaviors. CARLOC is designed to generalize to various landmarks: CARLOC can attempt to leverage additional roadway landmarks such as changes in the road surface texture, potholes, or discontinuities in lighting caused by entering a tunnel.

Finally, we propose to explore practical deployability of CARLOC. We envision this to be conceptually straightforward, since CARLOC uses in-built vehicle sensors, and needs a relatively simple cloud service for storing its particle cloud. In practice, CARLOC can be retrofitted into a car's existing navigation system as a firmware update.

7. REFERENCES

[1] Ackerman Steering Principle. http://www.rctek.com/technical/handling/ackerman_steering_principle.html.

[2] H. Aly, A. Basalamah, and M. Youssef. Lanequest: An accurate and energy-efficient lane detection system. *Proceedings of IEEE PerCom 2015*, 2015.

[3] N. Bergman. Recursive bayesian estimation: Navigation and tracking applications. dissertations no 579. *Linköping Studies in Science and Technology, SE-581*, 83, 1999.

[4] C. Bo, X.-Y. Li, T. Jung, X. Mao, Y. Tao, and L. Yao. Smartloc: Push the limit of the inertial sensor based metropolitan localization using smartphone. In *Proceedings of the 19th annual international conference on Mobile computing & networking*. ACM, 2013.

[5] J. Bornholt. *Abstractions and techniques for programming with uncertain data*. PhD thesis, Honors thesis, Australian National University, 2013.

[6] J. Bornholt, T. Mytkowicz, and K. S. McKinley. Uncertain< t>: A first-order type for uncertain data. In *Proceedings of the 19th international conference on Architectural support for programming languages and operating systems*. ACM, 2014.

[7] R. Carisi, E. Giordano, G. Pau, and M. Gerla. Enhancing in vehicle digital maps via gps crowdsourcing. In *Wireless On-Demand Network Systems and Services (WONS), 2011 Eighth International Conference on*. IEEE, 2011.

[8] F. Chausse, J. Laneurit, and R. Chapuis. Vehicle localization on a digital map using particles filtering. In *Proceedings of IEEE Intelligent Vehicles Symposium*. IEEE, 2005.

[9] P. Davidson, J. Collin, J. Raquet, and J. Takala. Application of particle filters for vehicle positioning using road maps. In *23rd International Technical Meeting of the Satellite Division of The Institute of Navigation, Portland, OR*, 2010.

[10] How Differential GPS works. http://www.trimble.com/gps_tutorial/dgps-how.aspx. 2011.

[11] M. G. Dissanayake, P. Newman, S. Clark, H. F. Durrant-Whyte, and M. Csorba. A solution to the simultaneous localization and map building (slam) problem. *IEEE Transactions on Robotics and Automation*, 2001.

[12] S. Dmitriev, A. Stepanov, B. Rivkin, and D. Koshaev. Optimal map-matching for car navigation systems. In *Proceedings of 6th International Conference on Integrated Navigation Systems, St. Petersburg*. DTIC Document, 1999.

[13] A. Doucet. On sequential simulation-based methods for bayesian filtering. 1998.

[14] East-North-Up Coordinates System. http://www.navipedia.net/index.php/Transformations_between_ECEF_and_ENU_coordinates.

[15] J. Eriksson, L. Girod, B. Hull, R. Newton, S. Madden, and H. Balakrishnan. The pothole patrol: Using a mobile sensor network for road surface monitoring. In *Proceedings of the 6th International Conference on Mobile Systems, Applications, and Services*, MobiSys '08. ACM, 2008.

[16] J. Farrell and T. Givargis. Differential gps reference station algorithm-design and analysis. *IEEE Transactions on Control Systems Technology*, 2000.

[17] D. Festa, D. Mongelli, V. Astarita, and P. Giorgi. First results of a new methodology for the identification of road surface anomalies. In *Proceedings of IEEE International Conference on Service Operations and Logistics, and Informatics (SOLI)*, 2013.

[18] T. Flach, N. Mishra, L. Pedrosa, C. Riesz, and R. Govindan. Carma: towards personalized automotive tuning. In *Proceedings of the 9th ACM Conference on Embedded Networked Sensor Systems*. ACM, 2011.

[19] S. Guha, K. Plarre, D. Lissner, S. Mitra, B. Krishna, P. Dutta, and S. Kumar. Autowitness: Locating and tracking stolen property while tolerating gps and radio outages. In *Proceedings of the 8th ACM Conference on Embedded Networked Sensor Systems*, SenSys '10, pages 29–42. ACM, 2010.

[20] M. Haklay and P. Weber. Openstreetmap: User-generated street maps. *Pervasive Computing*, 2008.

[21] W. Hedgecock, M. Maroti, A. Ledeczi, P. Volgyesi, and R. Banalagay. Accurate real-time relative localization using single-frequency gps. In *Proceedings of the 12th ACM Conference on Embedded Network Sensor Systems*. ACM, 2014.

[22] W. Hedgecock, M. Maroti, J. Sallai, P. Volgyesi, and A. Ledeczi. High-accuracy differential tracking of low-cost gps receivers. In *Proceeding of the 11th annual international conference on Mobile systems, applications, and services*. ACM, 2013.

[23] S. Hu, L. Su, H. Liu, H. Wang, and T. F. Abdelzaher. Smartroad: a crowd-sourced traffic regulator detection and identification system. In *Information Processing in Sensor Networks (IPSN), 2013 ACM/IEEE International Conference on*, pages 331–332. IEEE, 2013.

[24] A. S. Huang and S. Teller. Probabilistic lane estimation using basis curves. Robotics: Science and Systems (RSS), 2010.

[25] Y. Jiang, H. Qiu, M. McCartney, W. G. Halfond, F. Bai, D. Grimm, and R. Govindan. Carlog: a platform for flexible and efficient automotive sensing. In *Proceedings of the 12th ACM Conference on Embedded Network Sensor Systems*. ACM, 2014.

[26] K. H. Johansson, M. Törngren, and L. Nielsen. Vehicle applications of controller area network. In *Handbook of networked and embedded control systems*. Springer, 2005.

[27] J. Karuppuswamy, V. Selvaraj, M. M. Ganesh, and E. L. Hall. Detection and avoidance of simulated potholes in autonomous vehicle navigation in an unstructured enviornment. In *Proceedings of Intelligent Robots and Computer Vision XIX: Algorithms, Techniques, and Active Vision*, volume 4197, 2000.

[28] C. Koch and I. Brilakis. Pothole detection in asphalt pavement images. *Adv. Eng. Inform.*, 25(3), 2011.

[29] J. Krumm, E. Horvitz, and J. Letchner. Map matching with travel time constraints. Technical report, SAE Technical Paper, 2007.

[30] R. B. Langley. Dilution of precision. *GPS world*, 10(5):52–59, 1999.

[31] S. Lenser and M. Veloso. Sensor resetting localization for poorly modelled mobile robots. In *Proceedings of IEEE International Conference on Robotics and Automation (ICRA'00)*. IEEE, 2000.

[32] J. Levinson, M. Montemerlo, and S. Thrun. Map-based precision vehicle localization in urban environments. In *Robotics: Science and Systems*, volume 4, page 1. Citeseer, 2007.

[33] D. Li, T. Bansal, Z. Lu, and P. Sinha. Marvel: multiple antenna based relative vehicle localizer. In *Proceedings of the 18th annual international conference on Mobile computing and networking*, pages 245–256. ACM, 2012.

[34] J. S. Liu and R. Chen. Sequential monte carlo methods for dynamic systems. *Journal of the American statistical association*, 1998.

[35] E. D. Martí, D. Martín, J. García, A. De La Escalera, J. M. Molina, and J. M. Armingol. Context-aided sensor fusion for enhanced urban navigation. *Sensors*, 2012.

[36] P. Merriaux, Y. Dupuis, P. Vasseur, and X. Savatier. Wheel odometry-based car localization and tracking on vectorial map. In *Intelligent Transportation Systems (ITSC), 2014 IEEE 17th International Conference on*, pages 1890–1891. IEEE, 2014.

[37] T. D. of Transportation. TxDOT survey manual - GPS RTK surveying. http://onlinemanuals.txdot.gov/txdotmanuals/ess/gps_rtk_surveying.htm. April 2011.

[38] A. Papoulis and S. U. Pillai. *Probability, random variables, and stochastic processes*. Tata McGraw-Hill Education, 2002.

[39] I. Parra, M. Sotelo, D. F. Llorca, and C. Fernández. Visual odometry for accurate vehicle localization-an assistant for gps based navigation. In *17th International Intelligent Transportation Systems World Congress*, pages 1–6, 2010.

[40] A. U. Peker, O. Tosun, and T. Acarman. Particle filter vehicle localization and map-matching using map topology. In *IEEE Intelligent Vehicles Symposium (IV)*. IEEE, 2011.

[41] L. Qi, D. Sun, and G. Zhou. A new look at smoothing newton methods for nonlinear complementarity problems and box constrained variational inequalities. *Mathematical Programming*, 2000.

[42] R. Rajamani. *Vehicle dynamics and control*. Springer Science & Business Media, 2011.

[43] RTKLIB: An open source program package for GNSS positioning. http://www.rtklib.com/. 2011.

[44] E. M. d. Souza, J. F. G. Monico, and A. Pagamisse. Gps satellite kinematic relative positioning: analyzing and improving the functional mathematical model using wavelets. *Mathematical Problems in Engineering*, 2009.

[45] R. I. Technologies. What is differential GPS. http://www.roseindia.net/technology/gps/what-is-Differential-GPS.shtml. February 2008.

[46] The OpenXC Platform. http://openxcplatform.com.

[47] A. Thiagarajan, L. Ravindranath, H. Balakrishnan, S. Madden, L. Girod, et al. Accurate, low-energy trajectory mapping for mobile devices. In *NSDI*, 2011.

[48] A. Thiagarajan, L. Ravindranath, K. LaCurts, S. Madden, H. Balakrishnan, S. Toledo, and J. Eriksson. Vtrack: accurate, energy-aware road traffic delay estimation using mobile phones. In *Proceedings of the 7th ACM Conference on Embedded Networked Sensor Systems*, pages 85–98. ACM, 2009.

[49] S. Thrun. Particle filters in robotics. In *Proceedings of the Eighteenth conference on Uncertainty in artificial intelligence*, pages 511–518. Morgan Kaufmann Publishers Inc., 2002.

[50] Torque Pro . https://play.google.com/store/apps/details?id=org.prowl.torque&hl=en.

[51] R. Triebel, P. Pfaff, and W. Burgard. Multi-level surface maps for outdoor terrain mapping and loop closing. In *IEEE/RSJ International Conference on Intelligent Robots and Systems*. IEEE, 2006.

[52] Ublox Chips. http://www.ublox.com/en/.

[53] UNAVCO consortium. http://www.unavco.org/instrumentation/networks/status/pbo/overview/.

[54] B. Wiśniewski, K. Bruniecki, and M. Moszyński. Evaluation of rtklib's positioning accuracy usingn low-cost gnss receiver and asg-eupos. *TransNav: International Journal on Marine Navigation and Safety of Sea Transportation*, 7(1), 2013.

[55] O. J. Woodman. An introduction to inertial navigation. *University of Cambridge, Computer Laboratory, Tech. Rep. UCAMCL-TR-696*, 2007.

[56] M. Yu. *Improved positioning of land vehicle in ITS using digital map and other accessory information*. PhD thesis, The Hong Kong Polytechnic University, 2006.

[57] X. Yu and E. Salari. Pavement pothole detection and severity measurement using laser imaging. In *Proceedings of IEEE International Conference on Electro/Information Technology (EIT)*, 2011.

Bolt: A Stateful Processor Interconnect

Felix Sutton, Marco Zimmerling, Reto Da Forno, Roman Lim, Tonio Gsell,
Georgia Giannopoulou, Federico Ferrari, Jan Beutel, and Lothar Thiele
Computer Engineering and Networks Laboratory
ETH Zurich, Switzerland
{firstname.lastname}@tik.ee.ethz.ch

ABSTRACT

The wireless sensor network community is currently undergoing a platform paradigm shift, moving away from classical single-processor motes toward heterogeneous multi-processor architectures. These emerging platforms promise efficient concurrent processing with energy-proportional system performance. The use of shared interconnects and shared memory for inter-processor communication, however, causes interference in the time, power, and clock domains, which prevents designers from fully harnessing these benefits. We thus designed BOLT, the first ultra-low-power processor interconnect for the compositional construction of heterogeneous wireless embedded platforms. This paper presents the architectural blueprint for interconnecting two independent processors, while enabling asynchronous inter-processor communication with predictable run-time behavior. We detail a prototype implementation of BOLT, and apply formal methods to analytically derive bounds on the execution time of its message passing operations. Experiments with a custom-built dual-processor platform show that our BOLT prototype incurs a negligible power overhead relative to state-of-the-art platforms, offers predictable message passing with empirical bounds that match the analytical ones to within a few clock cycles, and achieves a high throughput of up to 3.3 Mbps.

Categories and Subject Descriptors

C.1.2 [**Computer Systems Organization**]: Multiprocessors—*interconnection architectures*; C.3 [**Computer Systems Organization**]: Special-Purpose and Application-Based System—*real-time and embedded systems*

General Terms

Design, Experimentation, Performance

Keywords

Cyber-physical systems; multi-processor; processor interconnect; predictability; composability; resource interference

SenSys'15, November 1–4, 2015, Seoul, South Korea.
© 2015 ACM. ISBN 978-1-4503-3631-4/15/11 ...$15.00.
DOI: http://dx.doi.org/10.1145/2809695.2809706.

1. INTRODUCTION

In the early days of sensor networks, platforms featuring a single 8- or 16-bit microcontroller (MCU), such as Mica [25] and Telos [43], spawned the development of a wide range of *sense-and-send* applications. These platforms offered modest computing resources well matched to the demands of low-rate sensing of temperature, humidity, light, etc. Low-power operation was achieved by interleaving sensing, data processing, and communication tasks and by judiciously managing the power state of hardware components.

Challenges. Although this design approach has been extensively followed to demonstrate the feasibility of wireless sensing applications, through our own experiences in designing, developing, and maintaining large-scale sensor network installations we have encountered recurring patterns that impede the construction and reliability of wireless embedded systems. We have observed that the engineering effort in realizing such systems is labor-intensive with respect to the design, test, and diagnosis of hardware and software components. While difficult to quantify, we argue that these practical complexities lead to implementations that are often unreliable, not readily adaptable to changing requirements, exhibit long development cycles, and are over-dimensioned to satisfy performance targets. This leads us to pose the following question: *Why is it difficult to design such systems?*

A careful analysis of existing wireless device architectures, in conjunction with a survey of the state of the art in the embedded systems design literature, reveals that the main problem is rooted in the *interference of hardware and software components in the time, power, and clock domains.*

One may think that simple sense-and-send applications do not suffer from this problem. However, also in these scenarios several tasks must be executed concurrently: reading sensors, processing data, transmitting packets, etc. *Sense-and-react* applications (*e.g.*, in cyber-physical systems [49]) additionally feature control and actuation tasks. These concurrent tasks interfere when they compete for shared resources such as clock cycles, memory, and peripherals. While labor-intensive engineering may partially handle such resource interference in highly deterministic scenarios, this approach is not only unsustainable in the long term but also ineffective if tasks are triggered by unpredictable events (*e.g.*, in surveillance or tracking scenarios [3]). Further, as the system load increases, the effects of resource interference increasingly affect the timing behavior of individual tasks, which in turn adversely impacts overall system performance. When incorporating power management techniques additional complexity is added to the system, further exacerbating the problem.

Contribution. To address the above challenges, we advocate a disruptive approach to the construction of future wireless embedded platforms. We propose the functional separation of tasks onto a multi-processor architecture whereby the tasks interact through asynchronous message passing using a processor interconnect with predictable timing characteristics. *Predictability* of the interconnect entails that passing a message takes a known, bounded time irrespective of the attached processors. As a result, the proposed architecture decouples processors in the time, power, and clock domains, facilitating the composable construction of customized platforms. *Composability* not only gives the system designer the flexibility to select hardware and software components satisfying the needs of the application, but also ensures that their interconnection does not change the properties of the integrated parts [27]. Furthermore, predictability of the message passing interface is essential to meeting the performance requirements imposed by certain application domains or wireless standards with tight latency constraints.

This paper presents BOLT, the first processor interconnect that enables the composable construction of ultra-low-power wireless embedded systems. BOLT provides predictable asynchronous communication between two arbitrary processors, and thus decouples the processors in the time, power, and clock domains. BOLT sits between both processors and hides all complexities associated with handling asynchronous message transfers from system developers. Two message queues, one for each direction, with first-in-first-out (FIFO) semantics form the core of this stateful interconnect. A signaling protocol allows for concurrent message reads and writes on both queues, and indicates when there is at least one message ready to be read out from a queue and when a queue is empty. The two message queues as well as all internal state reside in non-volatile memory, thus preserving the state of BOLT independent of the power states of the two processors. BOLT requires only a minimal software interface with well-defined semantics and predictable timing to be implemented on either processor. This concept of a stateful interconnect allows designers to choose arbitrary off-the-shelf or custom processors and "bolt" them together to create a customized dual-processor platform while avoiding resource interference.

We make the following contributions in this paper:

- Sec. 3 presents the design of BOLT.
- Sec. 4 validates our design by detailing a prototype implementation of BOLT on a state-of-the-art low-power MCU.
- Sec. 5 uses formal methods to derive bounds on the worst-case execution time of BOLT's message passing operations.
- Sec. 6 details BOLT's interface and how it should be used.

Using our BOLT prototype, we have built a heterogeneous dual-processor platform consisting of a 32-bit ARM Cortex-M4 and a 16-bit TI system on chip (SoC). Extensive experiments with this platform in Sec. 7 demonstrate the following: *(i)* BOLT achieves power decoupling while incurring negligible power overhead with a current drain of 430 nA during periods of inactivity; *(ii)* the execution times of message passing operations exhibit empirical bounds that match the analytical bounds to within a few clock cycles; *(iii)* BOLT provides a high throughput of 1.5–3.3 Mbps for inter-processor messages that are 16–128 bytes in length; and *(iv)* BOLT enables the smooth concurrent execution of event-triggered sensing and wireless communication—a scenario that is complex, labor-intensive, and error-prone to implement on current platforms. BOLT is available at `http://bolt.ethz.ch`.

2. BACKGROUND AND RELATED WORK

This section discusses the needs of low-power wireless embedded applications, the corresponding requirements on software components and hardware platforms, and the problem of resource interference in state-of-the-art architectures.

2.1 Classical Mote Architectures

In the early days of sensor networks, there was substantial interest in new hardware and software architectures for sensor nodes. These so-called *motes* typically provide the interface to sensors, and process and communicate data. Different hardware platforms have been developed both in industry and academia, exploring different points of the design space to match the demands of certain application domains (see, for example, Cricket [45], Mica [25], Telos [43], Iris [12], EYES [26], SunSPOT 9 [42], BTnode rev.3 [9], and TinyNode [13]). Attempts towards adaptivity at run-time often leverage multiple resources of the same type with different properties, for example, multi-radio platforms like BTnode rev.3 [9] or Opal [30] and the concept of wake-up radio [47]. Both the architectures and the design principles focused on finding the right trade-off between energy efficiency and the application-driven computing and communication requirements, interfaces to sensors, integration of state-of-the-art radios, small form factors, and autonomous operation [29].

2.2 Changing Requirements

Over the years the field of distributed low-power wireless embedded systems has matured to a point where now serious applications of societal and economic importance are within reach, such as the Internet of Things (IoT), industrial process control and supervision, environmental and structural monitoring, smart logistics, personalized medicine, home automation, and traffic control. In many of these applications, measurements are precious and must not be lost [52], so data must arrive reliably and in real-time [23, 46], responses are safety-critical [17], sensors are relatively expensive, and deployment and maintenance of a network is labor-intensive and costly. Thus, it is inevitable that distributed low-power wireless embedded systems become a high-quality infrastructure with known and predictable properties.

The requirements for successful hard- and software architectures in these domains are also much better understood than in the early days of SmartDust [31]. Developing software for heavily resource constrained hardware platforms is known to be highly labor-intensive due to the tight coupling between functional and non-functional properties on the one hand and detailed hardware properties on the other. Despite advances in model-based design techniques, specific models of computation, intensive distributed testing and verification cycles, distributed low-power systems are still error-prone. To make matters worse, the final installations are often embedded into hostile environments that are unknown at design time and exhibit dynamically changing properties.

The application domains differ substantially in their requirements and hence a single platform does not suite them all with respect to computational, communication, and memory resources, available energy budget, and degree of integration [5]. Nevertheless, we can identify two common trends.

- *Increasing resource demand.* The program and data memory required to implement even seemingly simple functionality has grown significantly. Similar observations hold for the required computational resources that very often cannot be fulfilled by the simple 8- or 16-bit MCUs that were employed in the first generation of motes.

- *Need for adaptability.* Application tasks such as communication, sensing, actuation, and computation are highly dependent on the occurrence of events (*e.g.*, on sensor and radio interfaces) and the availability of energy. The same holds for the associated modes of operation such as radio states, MCU power modes, duty cycle, and clock speeds.

One of the early attempts to increase the amount of available resources was the Imote2 [39], at the cost of high sleep currents limiting its use in energy-constrained settings. More recently, there are new MCU generations appearing on the market that combine low sleep currents, short wake-up times, and rich peripherals with a relatively high compute power, such as the ARM Cortex-M family [6] used in products from NXP, STMicroelectronics, Silabs, Freescale, and Atmel. But their appearance only solves part of the problem inherent to classical mote architectures: highly adaptive and event-triggered application tasks with widely varying resource requirements interfere on shared resources, thus violating the principles of modularity and separation of concern.

To illustrate this *resource interference* problem, let us consider an application that requires high-rate sampling of sensors, for example, acoustic sensors in a structural monitoring application [52]. Due to the fact that the single processing resource, the MCU, also needs to handle time-critical events from the wireless communication component, the computational power may not be sufficient and interference between tasks is inevitable. As a second example, suppose an application requires a node to react timely to events, for example, to quickly perform an actuation or to localize signal sources depending on the pairwise differences in the arrival of events at different nodes. Again, limited resources and interference on the single computing resource lead to unpredictable behavior in such adaptive scenarios. This kind of resource interference can only partly be hidden by software abstraction layers (*e.g.*, provided by TinyOS [37] and Contiki [14]), often leading to fragile, monolithic, and over-provisioned systems that are tedious to design, implement, debug, and maintain.

As a result, already early on in the history of sensor networks, modular architectures have been proposed that allow designers to seamlessly compose a node architecture from components that match the target application domain.

2.3 Modular Multi-processor Architectures

Early solutions to remove some of the deficiencies as described above have been the construction of modular architectures that can be adapted to the need of various application domains, including the 4-layer modular architecture in [44], the MIT Media Lab modular platform [8], the stackable architecture [41], and Epic [15]. In all of these designs, components communicate via a shared bus or a set of shared standard interconnects such as UART, I2C, SPI, and 1-wire. New shared interconnects like M-bus [35] have been specifically designed for ultra-low-power connectivity.

The need for heterogeneous systems consisting of multiple, possibly heterogeneous components that dynamically match resources to the specific task at run-time (*e.g.*, sleep modes, clock options, voltage scaling, component shut down) to allow for highly adaptive applications has been recognized by other communities as well, especially in the area of mobile communications. As a consequence, we increasingly see designs combining heterogeneous resources for ultra-low-power applications, such as the LPC4300 [40] from NXP, and the VF3xxR and MKW2xDx [21] from Freescale. All these designs use bus-based interconnects or shared-memory communication between the components. One notable exception is the TI F28M3x series [50], which is expressly designed for application domains requiring safety certifications. Instead of relying exclusively on shared resources for communication, it contains a FIFO buffer for conflict-free communication at the cost of not being aimed for ultra-low-power operation.

It has been recognized that whenever multiple resources communicate, the use of shared busses and shared memory seriously hampers modularity [32]. The major obstacle for application domains with high dependability and safety requirements, such as automotive and avionics, to adopt multi-core and multi-resource platforms is the inevitable interference on shared resources [34]. Thus, there is currently no accepted path to certification, which requires guarantees on correct timing and function [51].

The main consequences of using shared memory or busses for communication among components are the following:

- *Coupling of power and clock domains.* To reach the goal of energy-proportional performance, where the energy consumed grows with the amount of useful task execution performed, systems use different power and clock domains. However, a shared bus couples these domains and requires tight coordination of power and clock management. As a result, the principles of separation of concerns and isolation of independent functionalities are violated, and power management requires interaction with many hardware and software layers [5]. As a rule, unnecessary interference and dependencies introduced on the hardware layer can rarely be decoupled by means of higher-level software constructs.
- *Interference in the time domain.* Using shared memory, constructs like semaphores and locks allow for mutually exclusive access to shared resources. However, they also make the timing of activities on one resource dependent on that of activities on another, seriously violating composability and the possibility of independent design. In other words, engineering must be re-done system-wide for each newly designed task. Similarly, the bus as a shared communication medium causes timing interference, leading to highly pessimistic timing bounds (*e.g.*, when using protocols like first-come-first-serve, fixed priority, round-robin) or inefficient communication (*e.g.*, when using partitioned protocols like TDMA, time-triggered architecture [33]).

Due to these deficiencies, alternatives like distributed memory, asynchronous message passing, and queue-based communication are all well understood in their underlying concepts and widely used in distributed systems, multi-processor systems, and networks on chip (NoC)[28, 22]. However, they have not yet been thoroughly investigated in ultra-low-power wireless embedded systems. This paper aims to fill this gap.

3. BOLT DESIGN

We introduce Bolt, a new processor interconnect for ultra-low-power wireless embedded systems. By providing bidirectional asynchronous message passing with predictable message transfer times, Bolt is a key building block for the communication between components on emerging dual-processor platforms to support ultra-low-power applications with high dependability requirements and stringent timing constraints. Bolt simplifies the design of such applications by completely eliminating or at least limiting the interference among differ-

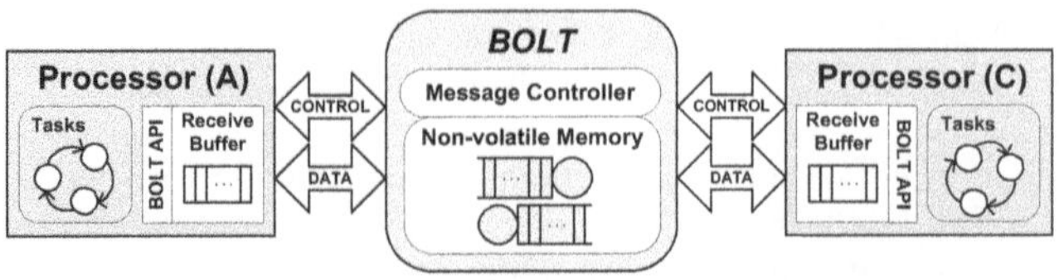

Figure 1: Overview of Bolt processor interconnect. By providing predictable bidirectional asynchronous message passing between processors A and C, Bolt decouples them in time, power, and clock domains.

ent hardware and software components on shared resources. As such, BOLT promotes a radical paradigm shift toward the *composable* construction and *predictable* operation of heterogeneous ultra-low-power wireless embedded platforms.

3.1 Overview

As depicted in Fig. 1, BOLT is a piece of integrated hardware and software that sits between two processors A and C. BOLT lets A and C asynchronously exchange messages while executing within their own time, power, and clock domains. This entails in particular that each processor can independently write messages into BOLT or read messages out of BOLT. We design and implement BOLT in such a way that the execution time of these read and write operations can be tightly bounded. Based on these bounds, we conceive a well-defined software interface by which each processor accesses BOLT in a non-blocking manner to exchange messages of variable length and possibly with different priorities.

The unique properties of BOLT allow for composable system designs. That is, a designer can choose any two commercially available processors and existing software artifacts and integrate them to create a customized platform that satisfies the application needs, *without changing the properties of the integrated parts.* These parts can be separately designed, implemented, and validated, thus leading to modular systems that are easier to develop, understand, and maintain.

Key to achieving these beneficial properties is to tackle the problem of interference between different hardware and software components on shared resources. To solve this problem, we take a disruptive approach in BOLT that is guided by the following established embedded systems design principles [24, 48]: *(i)* try to avoid interference; *(ii)* if interference is unavoidable, try to tightly bound it; and *(iii)* specify an interface with formally verified and predictable properties.

We describe next how to apply principles *(i)* and *(ii)* to the design of BOLT. Since principle *(iii)* depends on a concrete implementation of BOLT (see Sec. 4) and a formal analysis of its timing properties (see Sec. 5), we discuss the interface by which the processors access BOLT in Sec. 6. While the basic concept can be extended to more than two processors, we stick to the dual-processor case for illustration purposes and its immediate applicability to the separation of concurrent application (A) and communication (C) tasks.

3.2 Architecture

BOLT adopts asynchronous message passing to avoid interference between processors A and C wherever possible, as per design principle *(i)*. Thus, BOLT decouples processors A and C in the time, power, and clock domains.

- *Time.* Processors A and C interact with BOLT over dedicated *control* and *data channels*, as illustrated in Fig. 1. Using these channels, messages can be asynchronously transferred between each processor and BOLT, irrespective of the state of the other processor. Due to this and by buffering messages until they are read out, BOLT effectively decouples A and C in time.
- *Power.* BOLT stores undelivered messages and all internal state in non-volatile memory. Thus, it also decouples the two processors in power, enabling independent power management of A and C over a maximum dynamic range, including deep sleep and power off modes. BOLT can also retain its own state and undelivered messages after a complete power failure, which may suddenly occur, for example, in energy harvesting settings.
- *Clock.* Finally, there exist implementation choices for the data channel that allow A and C to select and adjust their clock frequencies, decoupling them in the clock domain.

To achieve these properties, the control and data channel between BOLT and the attached processors must be serviced by independent hardware blocks, thus enabling simultaneous message requests and message transfers from either processor. To support independent bidirectional message transfers, BOLT stores undelivered messages in two *FIFO queues*, as illustrated in Fig. 1. One queue is for messages written into BOLT by A and read out by C, while the other queue is for messages written by C and read by A.

BOLT's *message controller* manages the state of the message queues and the operation of the control and data channels. The message controller consists of software and hardware components. The latter can be realized on a multitude of hardware options, ranging from general-purpose MCUs to field-programmable gate arrays (FPGAs). A concrete message transfer is initiated asynchronously by one of the processors over the control channel, prior to the actual message transfer over the data channel.

Control channel. Operating the control channel means coordinating data channel access for message transfers and indicating the availability of messages to the target processor. The signaling sequence of the control channel, as described in Sec. 4, ensures that each processor can initiate message transfers without causing inter-processor interference in the power and clock domains. Indeed, each processor is free to trigger a read or write operation at any moment in time over the control channel, and transfer the message over the data channel without interfering with the concurrent execution of the other processor.

For example, at the end of a write operation, BOLT uses the control channel to inform the target processor that there is now a pending message. It is then up to the discretion of the target processor when to inspect the control channel and when to initiate a read operation. Whenever the target processor is not busy performing local operations, it can read the message from BOLT using its dedicated control and data channels irrespective of the state of the other processor.

By the same token, the power management of one processor is independent of the messaging operations invoked by the other processor. That is, one processor may, for example, choose to reside in a deep sleep mode for a given period of time as determined by its duty cycle, and is not explicitly woken up by the arrival of a message buffered in BOLT.

Data channel. The actual message transfer between a processor and BOLT occurs over a bidirectional data bus that supports master/slave operation. Two popular examples of standardized busses supporting master/slave operation are SPI and I2C. Each interconnected processor is the master

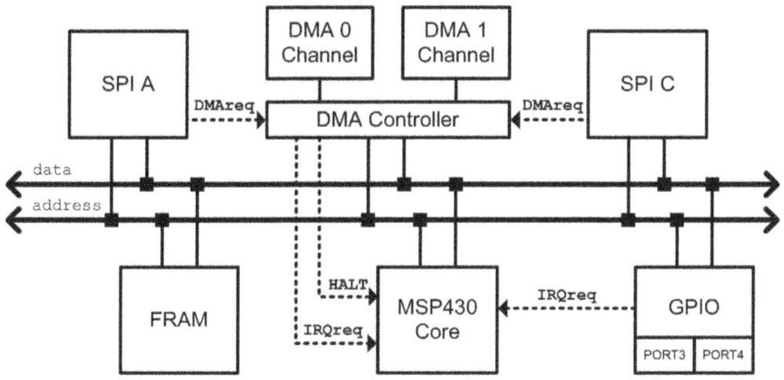

Figure 2: Simplified hardware block diagram of the MCU used in our prototype implementation of Bolt.

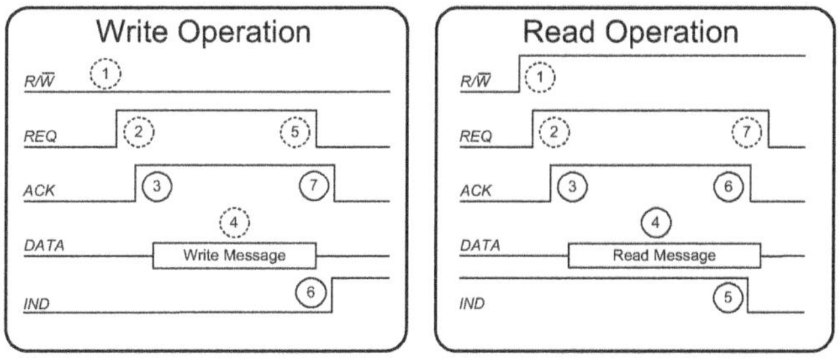

Figure 3: Signal sequences for write and read operations. The signals numbered with solid circles are driven by Bolt, while those numbered with dashed circles are driven by the interconnected processor.

of its dedicated data channel; that is, it provides the clock required to transfer each bit over the bus, while Bolt is always the slave. This ensures that each processor can transfer messages using its own independent clock frequency, thereby decoupling both processors in the clock domain.

Bounding unavoidable interference. Our architectural design decisions described thus far effectively avoid any interference between processors A and C in the power and clock domains. In the time domain, however, A and C may interfere. Since message transfers are asynchronous, it is possible that A and C simultaneously request a message operation on the *same* queue: one processor wants to read a message, while the other processor wants to write a message. This situation creates unavoidable interference at the message controller, because two processors compete for access to the same message queue (*i.e.*, a shared resource).

Following design principle *(ii)*, we intend to tightly bound the execution time of read and write operations despite this kind of resource interference. To this end, our design and implementation of Bolt strives to reduce as much as possible the hardware and software complexity of the message controller. By consequently following this guideline, we are able to accurately model the message controller and to determine tight bounds on the execution time of read and write operations using a model checker, as described in Sec. 5.

We acknowledge that if a message queue is full, a processor will not be granted access to write a message into Bolt, thereby blocking the write operation. We address this problem through the concept of virtual queues and appropriate buffer dimensioning, as discussed in Sec. 6.

4. BOLT IMPLEMENTATION

To demonstrate the viability of our design, we implement a Bolt prototype using the 16-bit TI MSP430FR5969 MCU running at an 8 MHz clock frequency. This particular MCU is well-suited due to its ultra-low power dissipation in sleep mode, the availability of built-in non-volatile storage in the form of ferro-electric random access memory (FRAM), an abundance of built-in peripherals, and its commercial availability at low cost. We next detail the hardware architecture of the MSP430FR5969, followed by a description of Bolt's software state machine that executes on top of it.

4.1 Hardware Architecture

Fig. 2 depicts a simplified hardware block diagram of the MSP430FR5969 including its built-in peripherals. The MCU is based on a Von Neumann architecture, where the core accesses program and data memory using a shared bus. The core, the FRAM, and all peripherals are attached to a shared 16-bit data bus and a 20-bit address bus. All program code, message data structures, and run-time variables are stored in the non-volatile FRAM of size 64KB. The instruction processing of the core may be interrupted by either the general-purpose input/output (GPIO) module or the direct memory access (DMA) controller using auto-vectored interrupt processing, whereby each peripheral interrupt is processed according to fixed priorities. The priorities are defined in hardware such that the DMA controller has a higher interrupt priority than the GPIO module.

The GPIO module has two ports, namely PORT3 and PORT4, each of which supports several input/output (I/O) lines. An I/O line can be individually configured to initiate an interrupt on either a rising or a falling-edge. If an interrupt condition is detected on either port, the GPIO module will inform the core through an interrupt request *IRQreq*. In the case of simultaneous interrupt conditions, hardware prioritization ensures that the interrupt service routine (ISR) associated with PORT3 is executed before that of PORT4.

The MCU provides two independent SPI hardware modules, namely SPI A and SPI C. The byte-wise transfer between the SPI receive buffer and the FRAM is coordinated by dedicated DMA channels, that is, DMA0 for SPI A and DMA1 for SPI C. The DMA controller manages the bus arbitration and interrupt priority, with DMA0 having a higher priority than DMA1. When an SPI module has received or transmitted a byte, a hardware trigger is signaled to the DMA controller *DMAreq* to initiate a memory transfer (*e.g.*, to store the received byte to FRAM or to fetch the next byte to transmit from FRAM). Before the DMA controller can perform such memory transfers, it must seize control of the shared bus from the core. The DMA controller initiates this takeover by halting the core through a hardware-driven request *HALT*. The core is allowed to complete the current clock cycle before it is halted, thus relinquishing its control of the address and data bus. The byte transfer between SPI and FRAM takes precisely two clock cycles, after which the halt request is cleared by the DMA controller and the core resumes operation as bus master on the next clock cycle. Once a fixed number of bytes has been transferred, as determined by the DMA's software configuration, the DMA controller will inform the core using an interrupt request.

Control channel. A dedicated GPIO port is used to implement the control channel toward each interconnected processor. Specifically, PORT3 is assigned to processor A, while PORT4 is assigned to processor C. We adapt a four-phase handshake protocol [38] to provide coordinated access for reading or writing a message over the data channel, as il-

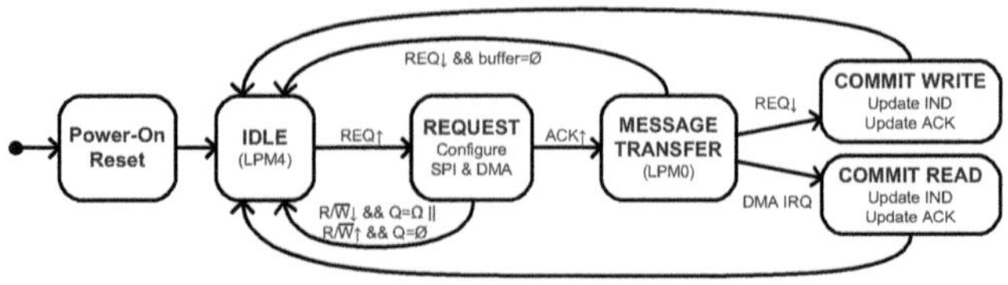

Figure 4: Bolt software state machine.

lustrated in Fig. 3. The control channel consists of the four lines $R/\overline{W}$, REQ, ACK, and IND. The $R/\overline{W}$ line defines the requested operation as either a message read or a message write. The REQ line is used by the interconnected processor to request the specified message operation, while the ACK line is used by BOLT to grant a message transfer over the corresponding data channel. If BOLT's message queues are empty or full, access to the data channel will not be granted for a read or a write operation, respectively. BOLT indicates to a processor when there is at least one message available to read using a dedicated IND line. The IND line is updated at the completion of every message operation.

Data channel. A dedicated SPI module is used to transfer messages between BOLT and each interconnected processor. BOLT configures both SPI modules in slave mode, thus decoupling each interconnected processor with respect to their clock domains. Dedicated DMA channels facilitate fast message transfers between each SPI module and the message data structures stored in FRAM.

4.2 Software State Machine

Fig. 4 shows BOLT's software state machine executing on the MSP430FR5969. Once the hardware is powered on, execution starts in a Power-On-Reset state where all state variables and message queues are initialized. If a queue contains undelivered messages, the IND line is asserted accordingly. The two REQ lines are configured as interrupt wake-up sources. The MCU is put into deep sleep (LPM4), while all other hardware blocks are turned off. The MCU remains in deep sleep until a read or write operation is initiated.

When either processor initiates a read or write operation by setting the $R/\overline{W}$ line and raising the REQ line, the associated IRQ wakes the MCU from deep sleep. Once the core is awake, the GPIO ISR will first determine the requested mode of operation and configure the corresponding SPI module and DMA channel for message transfer before updating the ACK line accordingly. The MCU will then enter a low-power mode (LPM0) with the core turned off, while the DMA and SPI modules remain active.

The completion of a message transfer is also processed by an ISR. However, depending on the message operation, either the GPIO or DMA ISR will be invoked. If the operation is a write, the falling edge of the REQ line signals the end of the message, thereby invoking the GPIO ISR. If the operation is a read, the DMA controller will trigger an interrupt toward the core. The ISR will update the internal data structures, update the ACK and IND lines, and disable the associated SPI and DMA peripherals. If there is an on-going message transfer involving the alternate processor, the MCU will return to the LPM0 sleep mode; otherwise it will return to the LPM4 deep sleep mode.

5. FORMAL TIMING ANALYSIS

As discussed in Sec. 3, two of BOLT's key design principles are to avoid resource interference wherever possible, and if interference is unavoidable, try to tightly bound it. Upper bounds on the interference on shared resources may be found using extensive measurements in a simulation environment or on an actual implementation of the system. However, this approach is extremely time-consuming and often infeasible in practice due to the number of possible combinations of input parameters and initial states of the system that need to be explored. An alternative approach, and one that has been well-studied in the embedded systems community, is to use formal methods such as model checking [7]. Through the construction of an accurate model of the system, one can apply rigorous mathematical tools to analytically derive safe bounds on interfering resources. We leverage such formal methods in verifying the timing predictability and functional correctness properties of BOLT.

In particular, we show next that BOLT has tightly bounded worst-case execution times for read and write operations, and that the physical interface operates according to its specification. We start by identifying the relevant hardware and software components of the BOLT prototype, and construct a model of their interactions using a network of timed automata [4]. We then parametrize the model based on our prototype and formally verify the timing and functional properties of BOLT using the Uppaal model checker [36].

5.1 Model Checking

The challenge in constructing a model of our BOLT prototype is capturing the complexity of several time-dependent and interacting state machines each of which has their own independent clock domain. In particular, processor A and C initiate message operations within their own clock domain, while the BOLT MCU responds to these operations using its own clock. Furthermore, contention between the execution of GPIO and DMA ISRs need to be formally modeled.

As a solution to this challenge we propose to model all interactions as timed automata and to extend each automaton with an independent clock variable. This technique is based on the theory developed in [4], where networks of time-dependent state machines interact through synchronization channels. This formalism allows us to model the complex interactions between BOLT and the interconnected processors by incrementing all clock variables synchronously.

We use Uppaal, a popular toolbox for the modeling, simulation, and verification of timed automata networks [36]. We construct a run-time model of our BOLT prototype and its interactions with two interconnected processors. The run-time model consists of four interacting timed automata:

- the processor automaton
- the BOLT software state machine automaton
- the GPIO port automaton
- the DMA channel automaton

In the following, we introduce the behavior modeled by each automaton. Due to space constraints, we limit detailed explanations to the BOLT software state machine automaton.

5.1.1 *Processor Automaton*

The processor automaton represents the expected signaling sequence of a read or write operation, according to the specification in Sec. 3. There are two instances of this automaton, one for each interconnected processor, each with its own clock variable. The type of operation (*i.e.*, read, write, or no-operation) and the time instant at which an operation is started are specified as non-deterministic transi-

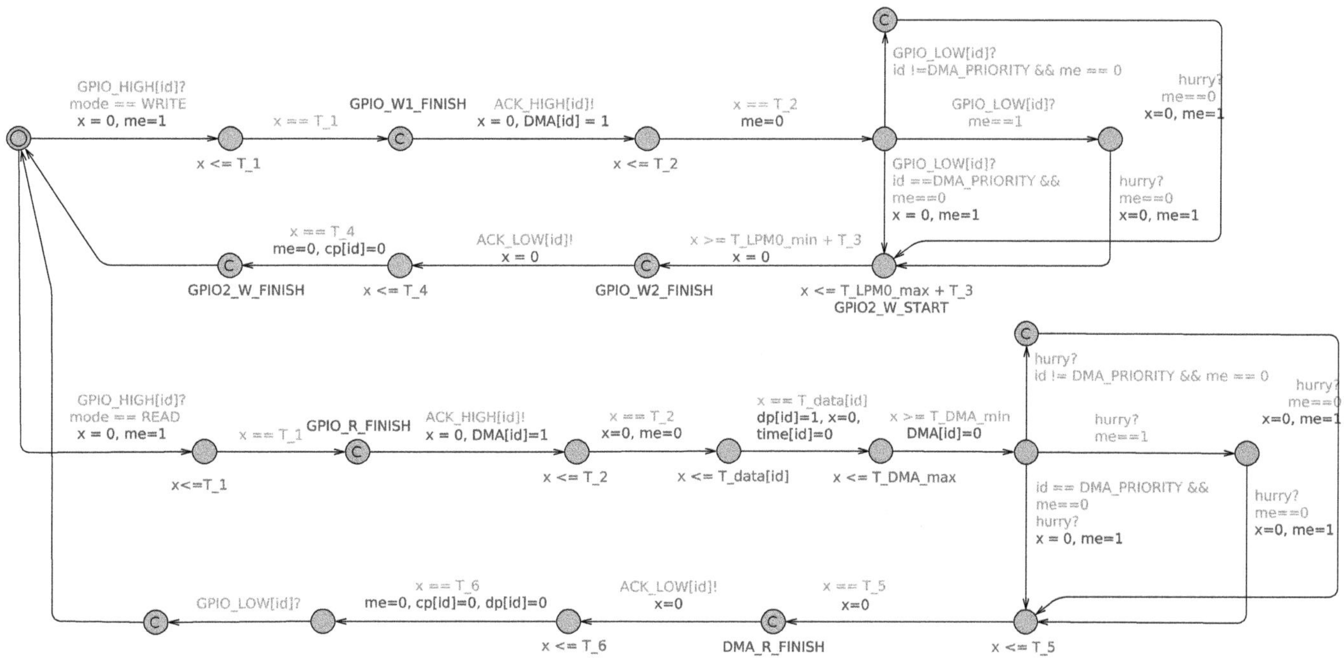

Figure 5: Timed automaton modeling the Bolt software state machine of Fig. 4 within the Uppaal toolbox.

tions. This level of non-determinism ensures that we indeed capture the worst-case timing operation of BOLT. Note that during verification, the Uppaal model checker will exhaustively explore all feasible scenarios and concurrent activities.

5.1.2 Bolt Software State Machine Automaton

The BOLT software state machine automaton represents the software execution of the BOLT message controller. The automaton, shown in Fig. 5, uses features like state invariants and transition guards provided by Uppaal [36] to model the execution time of each GPIO and DMA ISR.

Variable transition times, such as the wake-up time from the LPM0 low-power mode of the core, are incorporated into the automata by limiting the invariant to at most the maximum delay, while relaxing the guard to at least the minimum delay. In this way, the Uppaal tool is free to choose an arbitrary delay within the specified bounds and can explore all possible transitions. The execution of either GPIO and DMA ISRs is protected by a binary semaphore in the software state machine. This ensures that only one ISR can be executing at any moment in time. The prioritization of the ISR execution is defined by the GPIO port automaton.

5.1.3 GPIO Port Automaton

The purpose of the GPIO automaton is to model the hardware prioritization between the two GPIO ports. The final state machine model of BOLT contains two GPIO automaton instances, one for each processor port. They model the detailed protocol interactions and the case of simultaneous message requests by the two connected processors. The corresponding priority-based arbitration is taken into account as well as the fact that the GPIO port has lower hardware priority than the DMA controller; that is, if a DMA interrupt is pending, the GPIO port automaton will ensure the DMA ISR acquires the semaphore first. Another important behavior modeled by this automaton is the time to wake-up from LPM4. We use global state variables to ensure the wake-up time is bypassed when there are ongoing operations.

5.1.4 DMA Channel Automaton

Once a GPIO port has taken the binary semaphore, the execution time of the ISR may be extended due to a DMA memory transfer between the SPI peripheral bus and the FRAM. The DMA channel automaton ensures that the hardware prioritization between each DMA channel is adhered to. As described in Sec. 4.1, when there is a byte to transfer between the SPI and the FRAM, the DMA controller stalls the MCU for two clock cycles. We model this using Uppaal's stop-watch feature [11], whereby a timed automaton can stop the clock of another automaton. This feature enables each DMA channel to stop the clock associated with the BOLT automaton for precisely two clock cycles before allowing it to resume. In this way, we precisely capture the interactions described for the MSP430FR5969 in Sec. 4.

5.1.5 Complete System Model

Table 1 lists the number of states, transitions, and clock variables of the individual timed automata templates. The complete system model comprises of nine automaton instances: two processor automata (for processors A and C), two BOLT software state machines, two GPIO port automata, two DMA channel automata, and one supplementary automaton that enforces the urgent selection of specific transitions in the network of timed automata. The resulting model of the complete system consists of 125 states, 165 transitions, 8 clock variables, and 15 synchronization channels.

Table 1: Timed automata in the Bolt system model

Automaton	#States	#Transitions	#Clocks
Processor	14	13	1
BOLT software	24	28	1
GPIO port	19	32	1
DMA channel	5	9	1

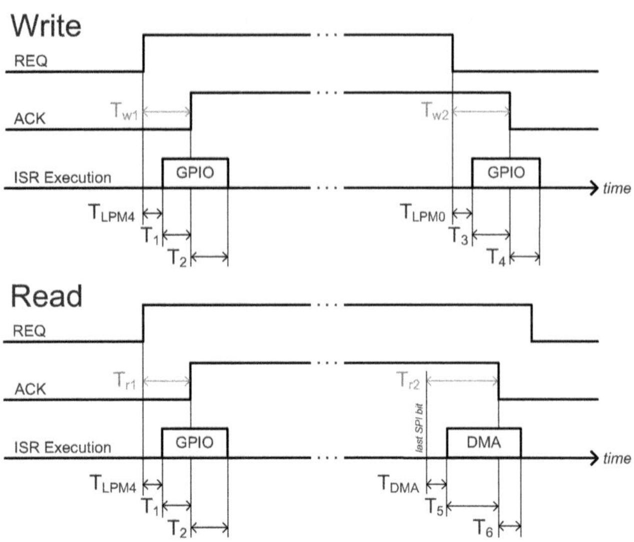

Figure 6: GPIO and DMA interrupt service routine execution with respect to read and write operations.

5.2 Timing Parameter Characterization

The timed automata templates model the high-level hardware/software operation of BOLT, parametrized using low-level timing parameters. We now describe the methodology we use to obtain safe bounds on these quantities.

Fig. 6 shows the execution of the GPIO and DMA ISRs with respect to the *REQ* and *ACK* lines for both read and write operations. To determine the specific worst-case delays in terms of clock cycles of the MSP430FR5969, we first need to investigate two important issues: *(i)* unbalanced ISR execution time, and *(ii)* non-deterministic hardware delays.

Since the GPIO and DMA ISRs must always determine which of the two processors is to be serviced, conditional statements are needed to select the desired control flow, resulting in the ISRs exhibiting port-specific execution times. By inserting the appropriate number of no-operation instructions into the ISR assembly code, we ensure that the GPIO and DMA ISRs execute a constant number of clock cycles, irrespective of which processor triggers the interrupt.

The next problem to address is the MCU's delay in waking up from the low-power sleep modes, denoted by T_{LPM4} and T_{LPM0}, and the time it takes from signaling a DMA interrupt until the beginning of an interrupt context, denoted by T_{DMA}. Typically, these hardware-specific delays are specified in the datasheet of the MCU as being deterministic. However, detailed measurements on our BOLT prototype with a logic analyzer show that the particular delays concerned are in fact non-deterministic within a small bounded range. Fig. 7 shows the histograms of the measured delays expressed in clock cycles of the MSP430FR5969 MCU.

With the measured upper and lower bounds of the timing delays, as listed and defined in Table 2, the formal system model is fully parameterized. The timed automata model can now be used to determine the worst-case timing bounds on the complex run-time dynamics of BOLT.

5.3 Timing Predictability Analysis

To find the worst-case execution time for read and write sequences, that is, T_{r1}, T_{r2}, T_{w1} and T_{w2} as annotated in Fig. 6 and defined in Table 2, we extend the Uppaal model in three ways. First, we add an additional global clock variable to support the construction of verification queries using a common time base. Second, we modify the processor automaton such that the Uppaal model checker can non-deterministically select the type of operation (*i.e.*, read, write, or no-operation) performed by each processor instance. Third, we introduce a delay at the beginning of each operation and allow the model checker to non-deterministically select the delay of each operation. By selecting an appropriate upper bound for the delay (*e.g.*, double the expected duration of a single operation), it is assured that all possible singular and simultaneous operations, with all possible relative timing offsets, are explored with clock cycle resolution.

We determine the worst-case execution times by submitting queries to the Uppaal model checker. Specifically, we query the existence of a global time value that exceeds a given threshold X for a specific BOLT instance and state. We apply binary search to find the minimum threshold X that satisfies the query. Table 3 shows the worst-case execution times for singular read and write as well as simultaneous read and write operations as derived from the Uppaal model.

We now use these values to determine the worst-case execution time for any BOLT operation, irrespective of the type of operation performed. We define the worst-case execution time of the request phase $T_{request}$ and the commit phase T_{commit} in terms of the maximum execution time of read and write sequences as defined in Fig. 6. The worst-case execution times are defined by the following expressions:

$$T_{request} = \max(T_{r1}, T_{w1})$$
$$T_{commit} = \max(T_{r2}, T_{w2})$$

Table 4 summarizes the results for each GPIO port instance. As expected, the request phase execution time dif-

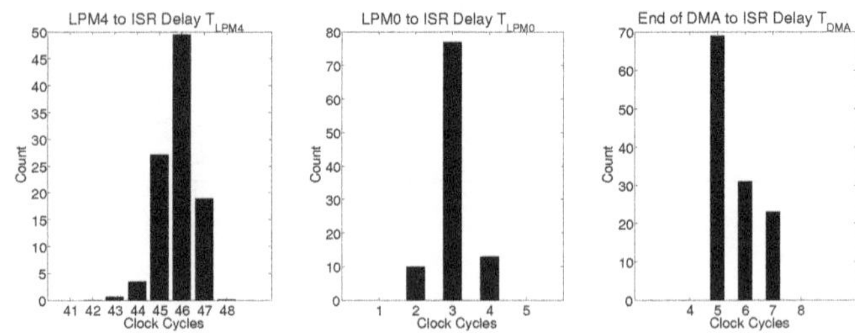

Figure 7: Histogram of wake-up delays T_{LPM4}, T_{LPM0}, and DMA interrupt delay T_{DMA} in MCU clock cycles.

Table 2: Measured timing parameters of the system model in MCU clock cycles as annotated in Fig. 6

Parameter	Description
$T_{LPM4} \in [41,48]$	Wake-up from LPM4 until beginning of ISR execution
$T_1 = 172$	Start of GPIO ISR until rising edge of the *ACK* line
$T_2 = 48$	Rising edge of the *ACK* line until the end of the GPIO ISR
$T_{LPM0} \in [2,4]$	Wake-up from LPM0 until beginning of ISR execution
$T_3 = 149$	Start of the GPIO ISR until falling edge of the *ACK* line
$T_4 = 58$	Falling edge of the *ACK* line until the end of the GPIO ISR
$T_5 = 117$	Start of the DMA ISR until the falling edge of the *ACK* line
$T_6 = 59$	Falling edge of the *ACK* line until the end of the DMA ISR
$T_{DMA} \in [5, 7]$	Last bit on the SPI bus until the beginning of the ISR execution

Table 3: Analytically determined worst-case execution times for singular reads and writes and simultaneous read & write operations in MCU clock cycles

	Write		Read		Read & Write			
	T_{w1}	T_{w2}	T_{r1}	T_{r2}	T_{w1}	T_{w2}	T_{r1}	T_{r2}
PORT3	220	153	220	124	418	397	418	357
PORT4	220	153	220	124	466	397	466	357

Table 4: Worst-case execution times in MCU clock cycles for request and commit phases, irrespective of whether Bolt executes a read or a write operation

	$T_{request}$	T_{commit}
PORT3	418	397
PORT4	466	397

fers between the two GPIO ports due to different priorities. The execution time of the commit phase is identical for both GPIO ports, since the DMA controller halts the core for the same number of clock cycles under the worst-case scenario.

5.4 Functional Correctness

We define functional correctness of BOLT in terms of the asynchronous signaling sequence defined in Sec. 3. Given a valid input signal sequence, BOLT should always provide a correct output sequence. In terms of the developed timed automata model, the formal validity of BOLT's functional correctness is assessed based on the existence or absence of a deadlock. Here, a deadlock denotes a state in which no edge transition can be executed by any automaton in the system model, that is, the system "stalls." After verifying the absence of such a deadlock in the developed model by submitting an appropriate query to the Uppaal model checker, we can conclude that the model developed does not exhibit a state sequence leading to a deadlock.

6. BUILDING APPLICATIONS WITH BOLT

The stateful processor interconnect provided by BOLT is a stepping stone toward building highly reliable, resource-efficient, and timing-critical wireless embedded applications. BOLT concentrates on contributing a communication mechanism with well-defined semantics and known timing properties. We now describe the interfaces as well as the necessary implications for a successful integration with BOLT.

6.1 Interface Specification

The complexity of real-world wireless sensing applications implies that multiple message types, coupled with the possibility for prioritization between message types, may be required. For example, messages containing protocol data may be considered low priority, while messages containing protocol control information may be considered high priority.

In the case of only a single message priority, the problem of non-blocking writes required by our asynchronous message passing scheme can be solved by correctly dimensioning the available buffer space based on the expected read and write dynamics associated with the application domain.

If instead multiple message priorities are needed, the problem becomes significantly more complex. We thus introduce an abstraction called *virtual queues* to reduce the problem to the single priority-based message flow problem. We consider a virtual queuing system, as shown in Fig. 8. Messages of priority i are written into a queue of length B_i, and are

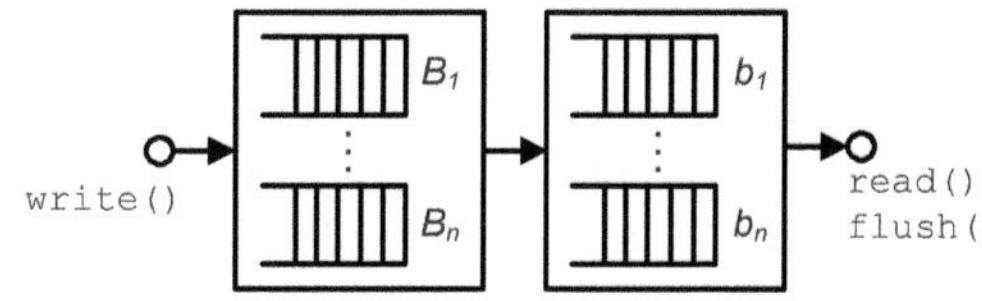

Figure 8: Message passing through virtual queues.

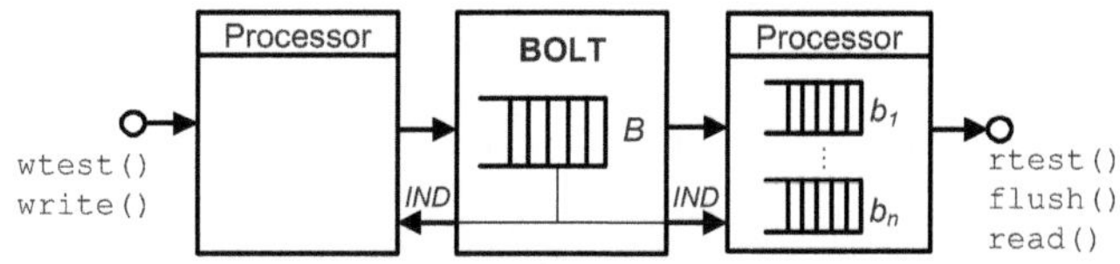

Figure 9: Realization of virtual queues using Bolt.

read from a separate queue of length b_i. We define the rate at which all messages in queue B_i are transferred into queue b_i as the *flush rate*. Under this construction, it is possible to compute the queue lengths B_i and b_i for each priority i under the assumption of a minimum flush rate.

Fig. 9 shows how the virtual queue abstraction is mapped onto a concrete message queue in BOLT. The length of the BOLT message queue B must be greater than or equal to the aggregate queue sizes of all prioritized queues, $B \geq \sum_{i=1}^{n} B_i$, while the receive buffer must be at least as large as all prioritized queues, that is, $b_i \geq B_i$ for all message priorities i.

Virtual queues make it possible for a single processor to handle more than one input queue, *e.g.*, in the case where BOLT is extended to more than two processors. With an appropriately dimensioned flush rate, the virtual queue abstraction coupled with an aggregate *IND* line, *i.e.*, representing the availability of a message in any of the pending message queues, BOLT facilitates non-blocking message operations. If more than one thread having data dependencies executes on a single processor, asynchronous batch processing [10] may be applied to guarantee timing constraints. However, if more than one thread performing BOLT message operations executes on a single processor, a non-preemptive round-robin scheduler may be employed to ensure non-blocking message operations with predictable timing behavior.

6.2 Application Programming Interface

BOLT provides a simple application programming interface (API) as shown in Table 5 (see also Fig. 9). Besides `read` and `write`, it includes the three additional functions `rtest`, `wtest` and `flush`. The following preconditions must be met by each interconnected processor when using BOLT.

- There must be space for at least one message in BOLT before `write` is called.
- There must be at least one message pending in the receive buffer before `read` is called.
- There must be no buffer overflow of the receive buffer.

The first precondition is satisfied by maintaining a local variable on each attached processor that stores the number of free messages in BOLT. This variable is initialized when the *IND* line is low, is decremented by one at each `write` invocation, and is accessed using the `wtest` function. It follows that `wtest` must return a positive integer before a `write` is invoked. The second precondition is satisfied by storing a counter for the number of messages available in the receive buffer for each message priority i. A `read` therefore can only be invoked if `rtest` returns a positive integer for a specified priority level. The last precondition is satisfied by

Table 5: Bolt application programming interface

Function	Description
`msg_t* read(int i)`	Read a message of priority i from receive buffer
`void write(msg_t *m, int i)`	Write a message of priority i into BOLT
`int rtest(int i)`	Return number of messages of priority i in receive buffer
`int wtest(int i)`	Return number of free spaces in BOLT available for messages of priority i
`void flush(void)`	Read all messages from BOLT into receive buffer

invoking **`flush`** at a rate no greater than that determined by a queue buffer size analysis.

If a message queue is empty upon a read request or the message queue is full upon a write request, the BOLT state machine will not raise the *ACK* line in response to the raising of the *REQ* line. Instead, the BOLT state machine will safely return to an idle state and wait for the next request, while the requesting processor may stall indefinitely waiting for the *ACK* line. Nevertheless, the BOLT API ensures that an interconnected processor can perform a non-blocking read or write operation. This is done by monitoring the state of the *IND* line, maintaining local message counters, and appropriately executing the **`wtest`**, **`rtest`** and **`flush`** functions.

6.3 Message Consistency

In a real-world system, the loss of power or the reset of a processor can lead to a loss of state. While the issue of reconstructing state or managing erroneous state (*e.g.*, after a reboot) is left to higher layers, BOLT ensures that the messages it maintains are consistent. Specifically, the architecture and interfaces of BOLT guarantee functional correctness of the processor interconnect in case of a spontaneous loss of power. This is achieved by storing both the BOLT message queues and all associated state in non-volatile memory, which will persist through a loss of power. Furthermore, the BOLT state machine ensures that partially read messages are not removed from the message queue, while partially written messages are removed from the message queue. This behavior ensures that undelivered messages can always be safely retrieved from BOLT when power is re-established.

7. EVALUATION

This section evaluates the performance of our BOLT prototype using extensive experiments with a custom-built dual-processor platform. First, we focus on a single BOLT instance and characterize its operation in terms of power decoupling, power overhead, timing predictability, and message throughput. Then, we demonstrate the benefits of BOLT in a typical event-triggered wireless sensing scenario.

7.1 Custom-built Dual-processor Platform

Fig. 10 shows a custom-built heterogeneous dual-processor platform, where BOLT interconnects two state-of-the-art processors with different computing capabilities and power dissipation: a 32-bit STM ARM Cortex-M4 STM32F303VCT6 running at 72 MHz and a 16-bit TI CC430F5137 SoC running at 20 MHz. We constructed this platform by connecting

Figure 10: Custom-built heterogeneous dual-processor platform used in the experiments. The Bolt prototype interconnects a 32-bit ARM Cortex-M4 (left) with a 16-bit TI CC430 SoC (right).

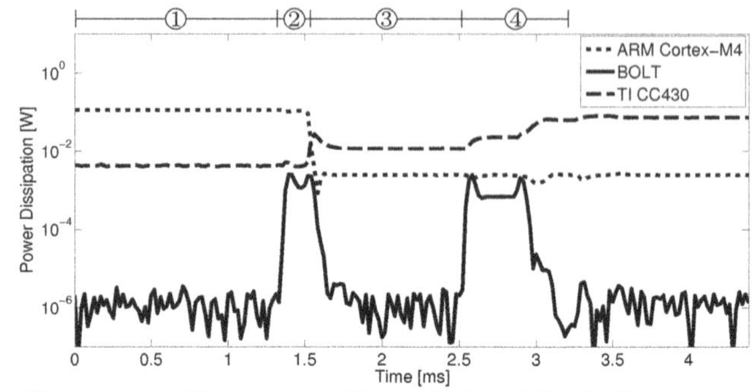

Figure 11: Power profiles of the ARM Cortex-M4, the TI CC430, and our Bolt prototype.

BOLT's control (4 I/O lines) and data (3-wire SPI bus) channels to each processor, and developing a small software module for each processor that implements the read and write operations as described in Sec. 4.1. We use this platform in the following experiments.

7.2 Power Decoupling

We start by illustrating how BOLT decouples two processors in the power domain. To this end, we perform an example execution with the dual-processor platform, using an Agilent N6705A DC power analyzer to measure the current of our BOLT prototype, the Cortex-M4, and the CC430 at a supply voltage of 3.0 V and a sampling rate of 48 kHz.

Execution. Fig. 11 shows the power dissipation of the three cores over a period of 4.5 ms. We can distinguish four phases.

In *phase* ①, BOLT and the CC430 reside in a low-power sleep mode, while the Cortex-M4 collects sensor measurements by periodically sampling its built-in analog-to-digital converter (ADC). BOLT dissipates approximately 1.3 μW.

In *phase* ②, once enough samples are collected, the Cortex-M4 writes a single message into BOLT using an SPI frequency of 4 MHz. When the Cortex-M4 initiates the write operation, BOLT goes from deep sleep into active mode, where it dissipates about 1.1 mW. At the end of the write operation, BOLT asserts the *IND* line to indicate to the CC430 that a message is pending and then returns to deep sleep.

At the beginning of *phase* ③, the CC430 wakes up, initializes its wireless transceiver, and waits until the communication channel is available. During this time, the Cortex-M4 and BOLT both reside in energy-saving sleep modes.

In *phase* ④, the CC430 reads the pending message from BOLT using a 2 MHz SPI clock and proceeds to transmit the contents of the message over its wireless radio.

Finding. The above execution shows that BOLT decouples two processors in the power domain. Indeed, each processor is free to locally decide when to enter or awake from a sleep mode, irrespective of the current power state and activity of the alternate processor and BOLT itself. This enables optimal power management over a maximum dynamic range.

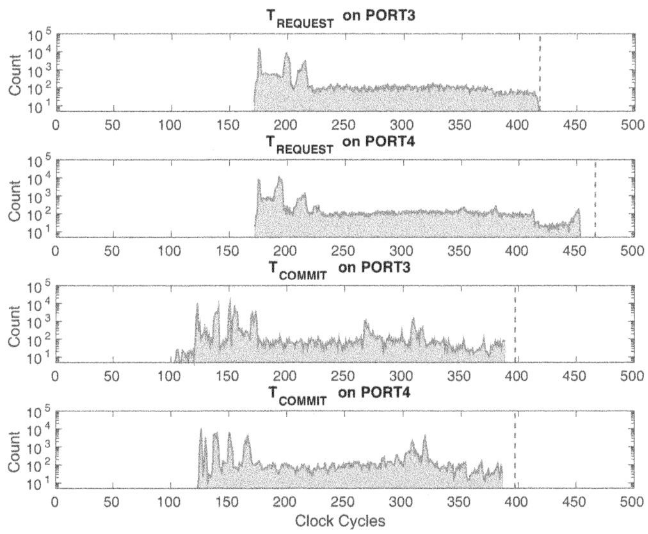

Figure 12: Histograms of the execution times of request and commit phases for concurrent message operations by two interconnected processors. Vertical dashed lines indicate the upper bounds from Table 4 determined with the Uppaal model checker.

7.3 Power Overhead

Using power measurements from the previous experiment, we quantify the power overhead of our BOLT prototype.

Results. When BOLT does not perform reads or writes, its power dissipation of 1.3 μW is less than state-of-the-art low-dropout voltage regulators, and, in our setup, several orders of magnitude lower than the sleep modes of both interconnected state-of-the-art processors, as visible in Fig. 11. Furthermore, BOLT's *active* power dissipation of 1.1 mW is comparable to the *sleep mode* power dissipation of the Cortex-M4. We thus conclude that BOLT incurs a negligible power overhead in a dual-processor platform design.

7.4 Timing Predictability

In a second experiment, we empirically verify the analytical bounds on the execution time of read and write operations determined by the Uppaal model checker in Sec. 5.

Setting. The time to complete a read or a write operation depends on the time to transfer the message over the SPI bus and the time BOLT needs to execute its interrupt-driven state machine according to the request and commit phases of the asynchronous interface, as detailed in Sec. 4. While the message transfer time is given by the message length and the SPI frequency, the duration of the request and commit phases, $T_{request}$ and T_{commit}, are non-deterministic due to interference on the same message queue in case of simultaneous accesses by both interconnected processors.

We accurately measure $T_{request}$ and T_{commit} on our BOLT prototype using a logic analyzer sampling at 25 MHz, while the Cortex-M4 and the CC430 perform concurrent message operations. We configure each processor to write a fixed number of messages into BOLT, before reading out all pending messages. The Cortex-M4 writes 48-byte messages and the CC430 writes 24-byte messages, resulting in equal message transfer times over the SPI busses. In total, 100,000 simultaneous message operations are performed, using a randomized waiting time between successive message operations to stress-test BOLT and to generate different access patterns.

Table 6: Maximum queue size and average throughput of Bolt prototype for different message lengths

Message length [bytes]	16	32	48	64	128
Max. messages per queue	1075	568	380	290	148
Avg. throughput [Mbps]	1.5	2.1	2.5	2.8	3.3

Results. Fig. 12 shows historgrams of $T_{request}$ and T_{commit} measured for the Cortex-M4 attached to PORT3 and the CC430 attached to PORT4. We see the analytical bounds are extremely tight: they are at most 12 clock cycles greater than the worst-case execution times we measured. This can be attributed to our quest for simplicity in the design and implementation of BOLT as well as our accurate modeling.

Further, in accordance with the model, the worst-case execution time of the request phase, $T_{request}$, is slightly longer on PORT4 than on PORT3 (48 MCU clock cycles), because of the interrupt prioritization of PORT3 over PORT4. Instead, the worst-case execution time of the commit phase, T_{commit}, is approximately equal for both ports. This is due to the fact that DMA memory transfers performed during the commit phase, as described in Sec. 5.3, halt the MCU for an equal number of clock cycles for each DMA channel.

In summary, the results demonstrate that our BOLT prototype exhibits timing-predictable read and write operations, satisfying a key requirement for enabling composability.

7.5 Message Throughput

Next, we quantify the maximum message throughput supported by our BOLT prototype.

Setting. We determine the throughput by measuring the time to write a sequence of messages into BOLT at a SPI frequency of 4 MHz. Specifically, we let the Cortex-M4 write 1000 messages into BOLT, and measure the message transfer time with a logic analyzer. We consider write operations as they take longer than read operations: a message can be read 29 MCU clock cycles faster than it can be written.

Results. Table 6 shows the maximum queue size (number of messages that fit into a queue) and the average throughput for different message lengths. We see that the throughput increases with the message length, supporting up to a maximum of 3.3 Mbps for 128-byte messages. Assuming the available memory in BOLT is evenly allocated to both FIFO message queues, the number of messages that can be stored into each queue is inversely proportional to the message size, allowing up to 1075 16-byte messages to be stored. Thus, by choosing a suitable message length, BOLT can support applications with high inter-processor communication demands.

7.6 Use Case: Event-triggered Sensing

In a final experiment, we demonstrate the benefits of BOLT in a typical event-triggered wireless sensing scenario.

Scenario. The application demands resource-constrained embedded devices to handle unpredictable *sensor events* originating from a physical process, while simultaneously servicing the wireless network interface to report those events over the radio. Upon the occurrence of an event, a device starts to acquire ADC samples to classify the event, and constructs a message containing all metadata associated with the event. The time between event detection and the first ADC sample should be as short as possible so as to maximize the number of samples that contain useful data about the event. To report events and coordinate their operation, devices run a low-power wireless communication protocol.

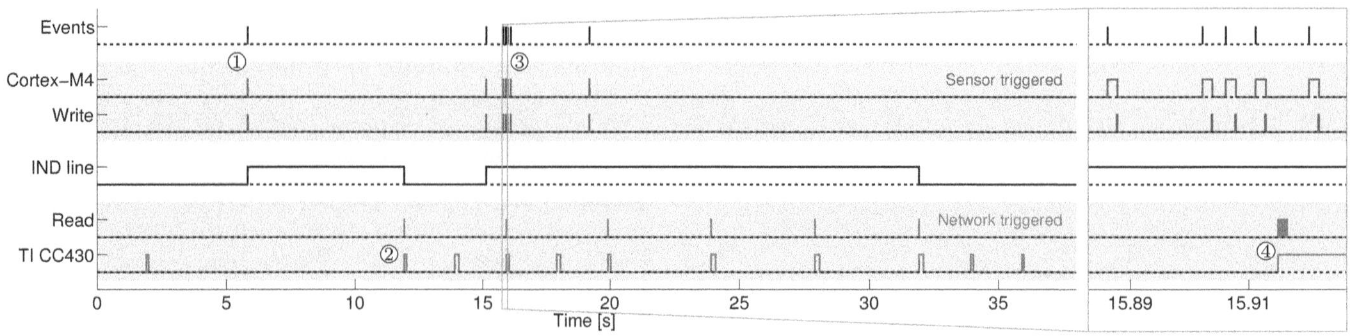

Figure 13: Signal trace extracted from an example event-triggered wireless sensing application using Bolt.

Given the timing constraints inherent to many protocols and standards, such as scheduled wake-ups [16, 18] and communication slots [1, 2], devices execute subject to hard real-time deadlines. During periods of inactivity, devices reside in a low-power sleep mode to meet the application's lifetime goal.

Without Bolt. Realizing this application based on a single-processor platform would lead to resource interferences whenever sensing and networking events must be handled at the same time, resulting in degraded performance or even erroneous behavior. By contrast, partitioning sensing and networking tasks onto two different processors improves a device's capability to handle both types of events in a timely manner. However, using a shared memory or a shared bus for inter-processor communication would entail a tight coupling of the two processors in the time, power, and clock domains, with all the drawbacks discussed in Sec. 2.

With Bolt. Using BOLT as the interconnect avoids these issues and provides maximum flexibility in selecting appropriate processors for each task, for example, the Cortex-M4 as a capable application processor and the CC430 as a ultra-low-power communication processor. Furthermore, software implementation and re-use are simplified, processors can independently switch power modes while exchanging messages within guaranteed timing bounds, and the overall system becomes significantly more robust and easier to maintain.

The costs of BOLT relative to directly connecting two processors via I/O lines and a SPI bus is application-specific and difficult to quantify. Besides the additional cost of the MCU, there is an increase in the overall hardware surface area; our BOLT prototype requires 49 mm^2 plus support circuitry. The total power dissipation of the platform increases by 1.3 μW during periods of no message exchange. Each message transfer consumes about 350 nJ assuming 128-byte messages at a 4 MHz SPI frequency, while the message throughput reduces by about 17 % compared to an optimally configured SPI bus and under the best-case assumption that both processors are always ready to service the SPI to read and write messages. In our view, the benefits of BOLT far outweight these costs.

Bolt in action. We implemented the above application on our custom-built dual-processor platform. The CC430 runs the Low-power Wireless Bus (LWB) [19], a communication protocol that uses fast and highly reliable Glossy floods [20] to transmit packets among nodes in a multi-hop network.

Fig. 13 shows a representative execution trace illustrating the interaction of the two processors through BOLT. The top three rows show the arrival of sensor events, the servicing of sensor events, and the writing of event messages into BOLT by the Cortex-M4. The fourth row indicates the state of BOLT's *IND* line towards the CC430. The last two rows show the reading of event messages from BOLT and the processing of network-triggered events by the CC430.

Looking at the first and the last row, we see that sensor events occur randomly and possibly in bursts, while network events occur periodically with the period changing according to the required communication bandwidth.

By inspecting the active phases of both processors, we see that BOLT allows them to act independently of each other. For example, at time ①, a sensor event triggers the Cortex-M4 to wake up from sleep mode and to write a new message into BOLT. The *IND* line indicates a pending message to the CC430. This message is then asynchronously requested from BOLT by the CC430 at time ②, where it starts to interact with the network as determined by LWB's communication schedule [19]. The independent handling of sensor and network events ensures task deadlines are adhered to, even in cases of heavy event bursts as visible at time ③ in Fig. 13.

As shown in Sec. 5.3, the time to perform message operations with BOLT can be tightly bounded. In this use case, this property enables the communication processor to read a sequence of pending messages just before they are sent over the radio via Glossy at time ④, thereby limiting the number of wake-up cycles performed by the communication processor, and thus reducing the platform's energy footprint.

8. CONCLUSIONS

In this paper, we focus on the resource interference problem in today's wireless embedded platforms. We argue that to address this problem, a multi-processor architecture built around an interconnect offering asynchronous message passing with guaranteed message transfer times is needed. Based on this idea, we design and implement BOLT, a stateful interconnect for ultra-low-power wireless embedded systems. We show how our BOLT prototype avoids interference in the power and clock domains, while exhibiting tight bounds on unavoidable interference in the time domain between two interconnected processors. Evaluation using a custom-built heterogeneous dual-processor platform shows that BOLT can fully decouple the interconnected processors while providing high-throughput, timing-predictable inter-processor communication at a negligible power overhead. We thus maintain that the architectural blueprint provided by BOLT is an important building block for the composable construction of next-generation wireless embedded platforms.

Acknowledgments. We thank Luca Mottola, the anonymous reviewers, and our shepherd Jie Liu for valuable feedback. This work was scientifically evaluated by the SNSF and financed by the Swiss Confederation and Nano-Tera.ch.

9. REFERENCES

[1] HART communication foundation. `http://en.hartcomm.org/main_article/wirelesshart.html`.

[2] IEEE 802.15.4e Wireless Standard - Amendment 1: MAC sublayer. `http://standards.ieee.org/findstds/standard/802.15.4e-2012.html`.

[3] T. Abdelzaher, B. Blum, Q. Cao, Y. Chen, D. Evans, J. George, S. George, L. Gu, T. He, S. Krishnamurthy, L. Luo, S. Son, J. Stankovic, R. Stoleru, and A. Wood. EnviroTrack: Towards an Environmental Computing Paradigm for Distributed Sensor Networks. In *Proceedings of the IEEE International Conference on Distributed Computing Systems (ICDCS)*, 2004.

[4] R. Alur and D. L. Dill. A theory of timed automata. *Theoretical Computer Science*, 1994.

[5] M. P. Andersen and D. E. Culler. System design trade-offs in a next-generation embedded wireless platform. Technical Report Technical Report No. UCB/EECS-2014-162, University of California at Berkeley, 2014.

[6] ARM. Cortex-M Series. `http://www.arm.com/products/processors/cortex-m/`.

[7] C. Baier and J.-P. Katoen. *Principles of model checking*. MIT Press Cambridge, 2008.

[8] A. Y. Benbasat and J. A. Paradiso. A compact modular wireless sensor platform. In *Proceedings of the 4th International Symposium on Information Processing in Sensor Networks (IPSN)*. IEEE Press, 2005.

[9] J. Beutel, M. Dyer, M. Hinz, L. Meier, and M. Ringwald. Next-generation prototyping of sensor networks. In *Proceedings of the 2nd International Conference on Embedded Networked Sensor Systems (SenSys)*. ACM, 2004.

[10] Q. Cao, D. Wang, T. Abdelzaher, B. Priyantha, J. Liu, and F. Zhao. Energy-optimal batching periods for asynchronous multistage data processing on sensor nodes: foundations and an mPlatform case study. In *Proceedings of the 16th IEEE Real-Time and Embedded Technology and Applications Symposium (RTAS)*, 2010.

[11] F. Cassez and K. Larsen. The impressive power of stopwatches. In *CONCUR 2000 - Concurrency Theory*. Springer, 2000.

[12] Crossbow Technology. `http://www.xbow.com`.

[13] H. Dubois-Ferrière, L. Fabre, R. Meier, and P. Metrailler. Tinynode: a comprehensive platform for wireless sensor network applications. In *Proceedings of the 5th International Conference on Information Processing in Sensor Networks (IPSN)*. ACM, 2006.

[14] A. Dunkels, B. Grönvall, and T. Voigt. Contiki – a lightweight and flexible operating system for tiny networked sensors. In *Local Computer Networks*, 2004.

[15] P. Dutta and D. Culler. Epic: An open mote platform for application-driven design. In *Proceedings of the 7th International Conference on Information Processing in Sensor Networks (IPSN)*. IEEE, 2008.

[16] P. Dutta, S. Dawson-Haggerty, Y. Chen, C.-J. M. Liang, and A. Terzis. Design and evaluation of a versatile and efficient receiver-initiated link layer for low-power wireless. In *Proceedings of the 8th ACM Conference on Embedded Networked Sensor Systems (SenSys)*, 2010.

[17] P. Dutta, M. Grimmer, A. Arora, S. Bibyk, and D. Culler. Design of a wireless sensor network platform for detecting rare, random, and ephemeral events. In *Proceedings of the 4th International Symposium on Information Processing in Sensor Networks (IPSN)*, 2005.

[18] A. El-Hoiydi and J.-D. Decotignie. WiseMAC: An ultra low power MAC protocol for multi-hop wireless sensor networks. In *ALGOSENSORS*, 2004.

[19] F. Ferrari, M. Zimmerling, L. Mottola, and L. Thiele. Low-power wireless bus. In *Proceedings of the 10th ACM Conference on Embedded Network Sensor Systems (SenSys)*, 2012.

[20] F. Ferrari, M. Zimmerling, L. Thiele, and O. Saukh. Efficient network flooding and time synchronization with Glossy. In *Proceedings of the 10th ACM/IEEE International Conference on Information Processing in Sensor Networks (IPSN)*, 2011.

[21] Freescale. VF3xxR and MKW2xDx Series. `http://www.freescale.com`.

[22] A. Hansson, K. Goossens, M. Bekooij, and J. Huisken. CoMPSoC: A template for composable and predictable multi-processor system on chips. *ACM Transactions on Design Automation of Electronic Systems (TODAES)*, 2009.

[23] W. P. M. H. Heemels, K. H. Johansson, and P. Tabuada. An introduction to event-triggered and self-triggered control. In *Proceedings of the IEEE 51st Annual Conference on Decision and Control*, 2012.

[24] T. A. Henzinger and J. Sifakis. The discipline of embedded systems design. *Computer*, 2007.

[25] J. L. Hill and D. Culler. Mica: A wireless platform for deeply embedded networks. *IEEE Micro*, 2002.

[26] L. F. Hoesel, S. Dulman, P. J. Havinga, and H. J. Kip. Design of a low-power testbed for wireless sensor networks and verification. Technical report, University of Twente, Centre for Telematics and Information Technology (CTIT), 2003.

[27] A. Jantsch. Models of computation for networks on chip. In *Proceedings of the 6th International Conference on Application of Concurrency to System Design (ACSD)*, 2006.

[28] A. Jantsch and H. Tenhunen. *Networks on chip*. Springer, 2003.

[29] M. Johnson, M. Healy, P. van de Ven, M. J. Hayes, J. Nelson, T. Newe, and E. Lewis. A comparative review of wireless sensor network mote technologies. In *IEEE Sensors*, 2009.

[30] R. Jurdak, K. Klues, B. Kusy, C. Richter, K. Langendoen, and M. Brunig. Opal: A multiradio platform for high throughput wireless sensor networks. *IEEE Embedded Systems Letters*, 2011.

[31] J. M. Kahn, R. H. Katz, and K. S. J. Pister. Next century challenges: mobile networking for Smart Dust. In *Proceedings of the 5th Annual ACM/IEEE International Conference on Mobile Computing and Networking (MobiCom)*. ACM Press, 1999.

[32] H. Kim, D. de Niz, B. Andersson, M. Klein, O. Mutlu, and R. Rajkumar. Bounding memory interference delay in COTS-based multi-core systems. In *Proceedings of the 20th IEEE Real-Time and*

Embedded Technology and Applications Symposium (RTAS), 2014.

[33] H. Kopetz and G. Bauer. The time-triggered architecture. *Proceedings of the IEEE*, 2003.

[34] O. Kotaba, J. Nowotsch, M. Paulitsch, S. M. Petters, and H. Theiling. Multicore in real-time systems–temporal isolation challenges due to shared resources. In *Proceedings of Workshop on Industry-Driven Approaches for Cost-effective Certification of Safety-Critical, Mixed-Criticality Systems*, 2013.

[35] Y.-s. Kuo, P. Pannuto, G. Kim, Z. Foo, I. Lee, B. Kempke, P. Dutta, D. Blaauw, and Y. Lee. MBus: A 17.5pJ/bit/chip portable interconnect bus for millimeter-scale sensor systems with 8nW standby power. In *Proceedings of the IEEE Custom Integrated Circuits Conference*, 2014.

[36] K. G. Larsen, P. Pettersson, and W. Yi. Uppaal in a nutshell. *International Journal on Software Tools for Technology Transfer*, 1997.

[37] P. Levis, S. Madden, J. Polastre, R. Szewczyk, K. Whitehouse, A. Woo, D. Gay, J. Hill, M. Welsh, E. Brewer, et al. Tinyos: An operating system for sensor networks. In *Ambient Intelligence*. Springer, 2005.

[38] C. J. Myers. *Asynchronous Circuit Design*. John Wiley & Sons, 2001.

[39] L. Nachman, J. Huang, J. Shahabdeen, R. Adler, and R. Kling. Imote2: Serious computation at the edge. In *Wireless Communications and Mobile Computing Conference*. IEEE, 2008.

[40] NXP Semiconductors. Cortex-M4 MCUs with Cortex-M0 Co-Processors. `http://www.nxp.com/products/microcontrollers/core/cortex_m0_m4f/`.

[41] B. O'Flynn, S. Bellis, K. Delaney, J. Barton, S. C. O'Mathuna, A. M. Barroso, J. Benson, U. Roedig, and C. Sreenan. The development of a novel minaturized modular platform for wireless sensor networks. In *Proceesdings of the 4th International Symposium on Information Processing in Sensor Networks (IPSN)*. IEEE, 2005.

[42] Oracle Labs. SunSPOT. `http://www.sunspotworld.com`.

[43] J. Polastre, R. Szewczyk, and D. Culler. Telos: Enabling ultra-low power wireless research. In *Proceedings of the 4th International Symposium on Information Processing in Sensor Networks (IPSN)*, 2005.

[44] J. Portilla, A. De Castro, E. De La Torre, and T. Riesgo. A modular architecture for nodes in wireless sensor networks. *Universal Computer Science*, 2006.

[45] N. B. Priyantha, A. Chakraborty, and H. Balakrishnan. The cricket location-support system. In *Proceedings of the 6th Annual International Conference on Mobile Computing and Networking (MobiCom)*. ACM, 2000.

[46] A. Rowe, D. Goel, and R. Rajkumar. FireFly Mosaic: A vision-enabled wireless sensor networking system. In *Proceedings of the 28th IEEE International Real-time Systems Symposium (RTSS)*, 2007.

[47] E. Shih, P. Bahl, and M. J. Sinclair. Wake on wireless: an event driven energy saving strategy for battery operated devices. In *Proceedings of the 8th Annual International Conference on Mobile Computing and Networking (MobiCom)*. ACM, 2002.

[48] J. Sifakis. Rigorous system design. *Foundations and Trends® in Electronic Design Automation*, 6(EPFL-ARTICLE-185999), 2012.

[49] J. Stankovic, I. Lee, A. Mok, and R. Rajkumar. Opportunities and obligations for physical computing systems. *Computer*, 2005.

[50] Texas Instruments. F28M3x Series. `http://www.ti.com/lsds/ti/microcontrollers_16-bit_32-bit/c2000_performance/control_automation/f28m3x/products.page`.

[51] R. Wilhelm, D. Grund, J. Reineke, M. Schlickling, M. Pister, and C. Ferdinand. Memory hierarchies, pipelines, and buses for future architectures in time-critical embedded systems. *IEEE Transactions on Computer-Aided Design of Integrated Circuits and Systems*, 2009.

[52] N. Xu, S. Rangwala, K. K. Chintalapudi, D. Ganesan, A. Broad, R. Govindan, and D. Estrin. A wireless sensor network for structural monitoring. In *Proceedings of the 2nd International Conference on Embedded Networked Sensor Systems (SenSys)*. ACM, 2004.

MarketNet: An Asymmetric Transmission Power-based Wireless System for Managing e-Price Tags in Markets

Hyung-Sin Kim
Department of ECE and INMC
Seoul National University
hskim@netlab.snu.ac.kr

Hosoo Cho
Department of ECE and INMC
Seoul National University
hscho@netlab.snu.ac.kr

Myung-Sup Lee
Department of ECE and INMC
Seoul National University
mslee@netlab.snu.ac.kr

Jeongyeup Paek
School of Computer Science and Engineering
Chung-Ang University
jpaek@cau.ac.kr

JeongGil Ko
Department of Software Convergence Technology
Ajou Univerisity
jgko@ajou.ac.kr

Saewoong Bahk
Department of ECE and INMC
Seoul National University
sbahk@snu.ac.kr

ABSTRACT

Updating price tags in a large-scale market is a recurrent task, still performed manually in most markets. Given that human-errors can easily lead to customer complaints and accounting inaccuracies, the ability to autonomously reconfigure price tags can be of significant benefit. With the introduction of low-power display techniques such as electronic-ink, applications of enabling electronic, wirelessly reconfigurable price tags show potential for future deployment. In this work, we examine networking architectures that can be applied in such scenarios. Through a series of preliminary pilot studies in an actual supermarket, we show that the performance of existing protocols are *not* ready to overcome the unique challenges of busy market environments. We identify underlying technical challenges and propose *MarketNet*, an asymmetric transmission power-based system designed for densely populated, obstacle-rich, downwards traffic-oriented environments. We evaluate *MarketNet* in a large indoor market visited by 5000+ customers per day. Our results show that *MarketNet* addresses the challenges of the target application and environment, while achieving higher packet delivery performance with noticeably lower radio duty-cycles than existing protocols such as RPL and SHDP.

Categories and Subject Descriptors

C.2.1 [**Computer-Communication Networks**]: Network Architecture and Design—*Wireless communication*
; C.3 [**Special-Purpose and Application-Based Systems**]: Real-time and embedded systems

General Terms

Design, Experimentation, Measurement, Performance

SenSys'15, November 1–4, 2015, Seoul, South Korea..
© 2015 ACM. ISBN 978-1-4503-3631-4/15/11 ...$15.00.
DOI: http://dx.doi.org/10.1145/2809695.2809717.

Keywords

Wireless sensor networks, network architecture, routing protocol, low-power lossy network, RPL

1. INTRODUCTION

Low-power embedded wireless sensor networking technologies, with their ease of deployment and ubiquitous connectivity, have the potential to empower a number of real-world applications [17, 27, 28, 29, 32]. Many of these are designed around our everyday environments to simplify routine tasks that are straightforward, repetitive, and both time- and labor-intensive. Some applications, such as electronic price tagging in markets, are near commercialization, and a number of systems have been developed using various wireless technologies [5, 33]. Furthermore, technologies such as electronic ink for low-power displays have further catalyzed the potential deployment in these application domains.

Specifically, given that prices can change frequently in busy markets (e.g., due to changes in competitor prices or product freshness), updating price tags in a large-scale market is a tedious and error-prone task, still performed manually in most markets. For example, our collaborators and a number of previous work indicate that for items such as fresh grocery, on average, the prices change up to eight times a day. Given a large number of items carried in large-sized markets, manually updating prices not only incurs significant labor, but can increase customer complaints and accounting inaccuracies due to frequent human errors [5].

Despite electronic price tagging being an interesting application for low-power embedded systems, as a research community, we are still far from understanding the real wireless channel characteristics in such human-active and obstacle-present environments. Furthermore, while these electronic tags should be reconfigured wirelessly, we still lack knowledge on how these environments challenge existing wireless networking protocols. For example, it is unclear (practically) whether the use of multihop networking benefits or harms the application-level performance, or whether an alternate architecture such as asymmetric transmission power-based networks is a better fit in such scenarios.

In this work, we incorporate real-world networking constraints by taking a practical approach and design a prototype system for wireless electronic price tagging applica-

Figure 1: Our experimental market environment: a crowded indoor market with a size of 90×60 meters, >10k types of items, and >5000 customers per day.

tions. Specifically, our design and implementation addresses (1) low and fair energy consumption at price tag nodes, (2) automatic repeat request (ARQ)-based reliability considerations with minimal operational overhead and (3) optimizing downstream wireless communication for e-price tag updates.

Based on a literature survey of pre-existing networking protocols that suit our purpose, our design follows an asymmetric transmission power network architecture in which a basestation node can reach individual price tags via single hop (using high-power transmission), while the price tags transmit data to the basestation over multiple hop links (using low-power radios). To verify this intuition, we exploit the single-hop downlink protocol (SHDP) [13] and perform a preliminary deployment using low-power embedded networking platforms. The prototype system covers an urban, crowded large-scale indoor market place of dimension 90×60 meters which displays 10k+ items and is visited by over 5000 customers per day (Figure 1). We also compare this with RPL, the IETF standard IPv6 routing protocol for low-power and lossy networks [4], over the same deployment. From this preliminary pilot study we identify additional system-level design goals that address challenges of crowded indoor market environments. Chief among them, we find that large crowded markets exhibit bursty loss patterns, and external noise sources and active human movements heavily impact the link-level performance of wireless systems. With these findings, we design *MarketNet*, a system to address such unique challenges of a busy market.

We then evaluate *MarketNet* in two different real-world environments. First, we construct a 30-node indoor testbed to validate our proposed system architecture. Following initial validation, we move to the target market environment to confirm that real-world channel conditions are effectively mitigated by *MarketNet*. We also use RPL and SHDP-based networks for benchmark comparison. From these deployments and experimental evaluations, our results show that *MarketNet* adapts well to real-world wireless channels, and shows performances that match the best of the two other compared networking protocols while maintaining a radio duty-cycle of about half of those protocols in most cases.

Specifically, the contributions of this work are four-fold.

- First, we introduce application-level requirements and technical challenges in designing an electronic price-tag system for indoor markets, collected from a series of interviews with store managers.
- Second, we empirically measure the performance of various networking protocols in a real-world crowded indoor market place and identify performance issues and challenges that limit their effectiveness.
- Third, with the application requirements and real-world challenges at the basis, we present a set of key ideas that include a high transmission power root, a network-wide superframe architecture, and uplink period partitioning to design *MarketNet* for wireless electronic price-tagging in large crowded market environments.
- Lastly, we validate the performance of *MarketNet* under various environments including a large, real-world indoor market with 10k+ items and 5000+ customer base. Our results show that asymmetric transmission power-based tagging performs well under real-world channel conditions.

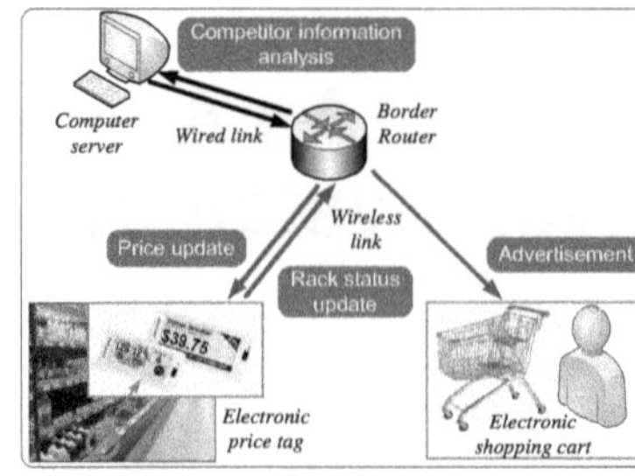

Figure 2: Application scenario for our wirelessly reconfigurable electronic price tagging system, consisting of a wireless-enabled central server and end devices such as price tags and shopping carts.

This paper is structured as follows. In Section 2 we introduce our application scenario and its requirements. We also discuss candidate network architectures for our application. Next, Section 3 presents results from our initial pilot deployment of a wireless price tagging system in an indoor market. We also perform experiments to better understand wireless channel environments of crowded markets and identify additional practical design issues. Section 4 introduces details on *MarketNet*, and we present testbed as well as real market deployment results in Section 5. In Section 6 we position our work among prior work, and conclude the work with discussions and a summary in Section 7 and Section 8.

2. ELECTRONIC PRICE TAGGING SYSTEMS

This section motivates the electronic price tagging application and describes its technical challenges. We present potential networking options for designing these systems and describe the basis for a preliminary pilot study in an urban indoor market environment.

2.1 Target Application: Wirelessly Re-configurable Electronic Price Tagging

Our work aims to design a low-power wireless system with the goal of providing a remotely reconfigurable price tagging system for large, indoor market environments as pictured in Figure 1. Specifically, we target to design a system where a large number of wireless-enabled e-ink-based price tags are used to present product prices, and additional sensors on each tag are used to track the supply level of each item for alerts when the rack becomes empty. In this application, a wireless-enabled central server manages and updates the price tags for all items in the market, and generates reports to the store manager (or related personnel) of rack statuses. Furthermore, we envision to include screen-mounted mobile shopping carts to the application to provide customers with discounts and promotions.

We conducted interviews with market managers and they indicated that price updates happen frequently (e.g., ~8 times a day for some products). Prices are updated with respect to the products' freshness (e.g., meat, bread, produce) or due to real-time pricing of competing markets. Figure 2 illustrates this target application scenario. Currently, price updating occurs manually and customer complaints due to incorrect prices are one of the major challenges in large-scale markets. As a result, automating this process and providing additional profit seeking opportunities (e.g., real-time promotions on shopping carts) can benefit the market and improve the quality of service for the customers.

For this target application, our work began with a series of interviews with market managers where we gathered a set of application level requirements as below.

- **Downstream-focused Network Traffic:** For electronic price tagging, a majority of the traffic will be price updates that occur several times a day, along with promotional information updates for shopping carts from a central server. Most of the upstream traffic from tags to the server are acknowledgments and rack status updates. Overall, bottlenecks are more likely to arise in the downstream direction.
- **Mass-scale and Real-time Price / Status Updates:** For updating price tags, multiple products may require reconfiguration, or the promotion information on many carts may require simultaneous updates. Therefore, the system should effectively support mass-scale updates, specifically at least 100 products per minute, as indicated by market managers (and also in previous work [5]). Furthermore, managers requested that the system makes price updates within 10 seconds after updating the server.
- **Maintaining Low-power Non-root Nodes:** While the root node's energy consumption is less of an issue, for the system to be practically useful, the lifetime of the price tags' and shopping carts' radio modules should last for >3 months[1]. For energy efficiency, an e-ink-based display is preferred over LCD, and radio duty-cycling is a must.
- **Data Reliability:** Market managers selected reliability of product price updates as the highest priority system requirement. A system for electronic price tagging should assure that the prices are reliably updated with minimal transmission overhead.

2.2 Network Architecture Options for Electronic Price Tagging

For the application requirements identified above, there are several candidate solutions that we can adopt when designing a wireless system for our target application. We explore the possibilities by introducing two networking architecture paradigms; first, a homogeneous (symmetric) transmission power-based network (*HPN*), and second, an asymmetric (heterogeneous) transmission power network (*APN*).

[1]While a 3 month deployment may seem short for a WSN node (considering systems deployed in outdoor environments), our surveys show that this is within tolerable range for the market managing staff. Achieving a longer lifetime would be beneficial, but, we surveyed the staff for a minimum lifetime that the they could tolerate given the hardware constraints of our system. Note that, the sales items on the shelves need to be re-stocked manually by employees several times a day. Therefore, replacing a pair of AA batteries every 3 months adds only minimal extra labor. Thus, this is still a several orders-of-magnitude improvement to current practice with paper tags.

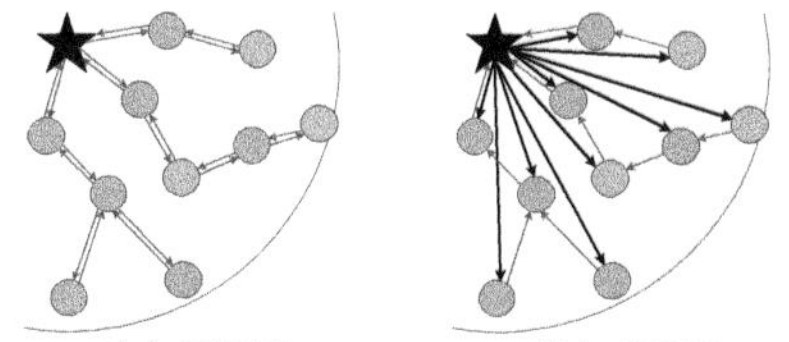

(a) HPN (b) APN

Figure 3: Network architecture of HPN and APN.

The first approach of configuring a network with homogeneous transmission power is a popular network architecture used in many wireless systems. In such systems, all nodes in the network use identical transmission power, except for cases where adaptive transmission power control schemes are applied [18, 21]. Multi-hop networking protocols rely on this homogeneity to compute link quality metrics for determining the route a packet should take [4, 9]. In RPL, a standard IETF IPv6 routing protocol for low-power and resource-limited platforms, a destination oriented directed acyclic graph (DODAG) is constructed towards a root, and this DODAG is used for both collection and downstream traffic patterns [4]. RPL can be layered on top of low-power MAC protocols such as low-power listening (LPL) [23]. By deploying low-power nodes in the market and connecting them using RPL and LPL, we can construct a low-power IPv6 multi-hop network supporting price reconfigurations upon request over the Internet.

The second networking paradigm utilizes asymmetric and heterogeneous transmission power-based networks (APNs). Specifically, given that a central node (e.g., gateway or basestation) is typically connected to a wall-powered device with no energy limitations, this node can utilize a higher-power radio to broadcast its messages via single-hop (or a reduced number of hops). We illustrate these approaches in Figure 3. Notice that in APNs, the gateway node has the capability to deliver downstream messages via direct connections, while upstream traffic follows a multihop architecture, similar to HPNs. The benefit of this second approach is in the efficient delivery of downstream price updates, with non-root nodes still maintaining a low-power profile. For upwards traffic, APNs may utilize RPL+LPL protocols to achieve energy efficient packet delivery.

We choose the single hop downlink protocol (SHDP) [13] to effectively exploit the asymmetry of the second approach. SHDP supports downstream traffic using local acknowledgments (ACKs), neighbor forwarding, and reduced neighbor contention to achieve reliable downstream packet delivery while allowing non-root nodes to perform low-power operations. In SHDP, due to the differences in transmission power, the destination node (i.e., a low-power node) is not required to send ACK packets to the root directly. Instead, SHDP achieves reliability by allowing the destination and its neighbors to exchange ACK packets "locally". Following this, the neighbors forward any missing packets opportunistically to account for transmission failures. Running SHDP on top of LPL helps to achieve a low-power network of many small-sized price tags with a central PC-connected gateway reconfiguring the entire network using (near) single hop links (at most two hops using local forwarding). The challenge here lies in ensuring that data is delivered to all nodes while obeying transmission power constraints imposed by regulatory organizations (e.g., FCC). While downward communication occurs via single-hop, upstream routes use RPL routes.

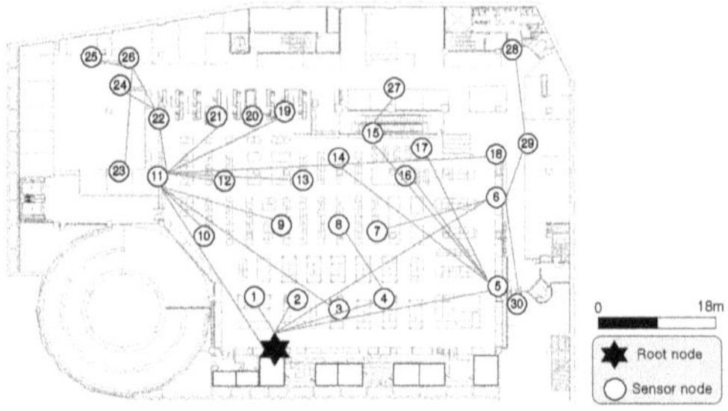

Figure 4: Topology map of our 30 node market environment with a snapshot of RPL routes.

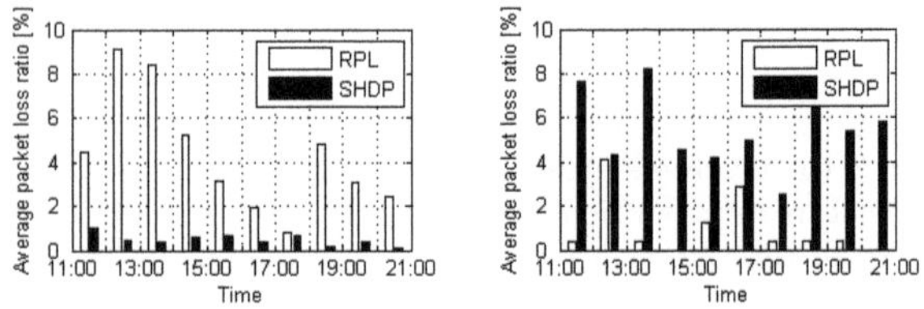

(a) Per hour packet loss ratio (downlink)

(b) Per hour packet loss ratio (uplink)

Figure 5: Packet loss ratio of RPL and SHDP for uplink and downlink traffic. SHDP shows a lower loss rate for downlink traffic, while RPL outperforms on uplink packet delivery performance.

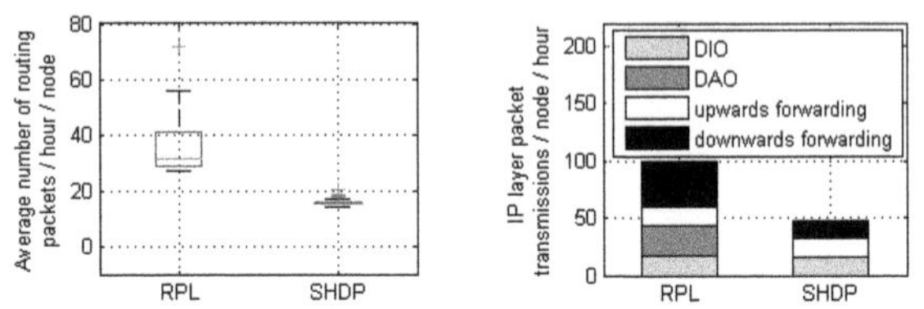

(a) Routing overhead distribution of each node

(b) Average transmission overhead per node per hour

Figure 6: Transmission overhead of RPL and SHDP. SHDP provides lower overhead by suppressing DAO messages and multihop forwarding.

Using these architectures, we implemented two prototype network systems, one with RPL and the other with SHDP. In the following section, we present results from a series of pilot deployments in a real-world large-scale indoor market.

3. PRELIMINARY PILOT STUDIES

Using the two candidate network architectures, we perform a preliminary pilot study in an urban indoor market environment. Figure 4 shows the topology deployed at a single floor market with an area of 90m×60m. The goal of this study is to confirm whether the two aforementioned systems perform well in real environments, and further identify what characteristics of these channel environments challenge the performance of our two candidate network architectures.

3.1 Performance of Pre-existing Protocols

We start our preliminary performance testing in the market using 30 low-power nodes representing reprogrammable price tags, and one basestation node. We use TelosB [24] clone devices as the low-power nodes, and also for the root node in the HPN experiment. For the APN experiments, we use the MTM-CM3300MSP node as the high-power root, which is similar to a TelosB with a 10 dB power amplifier. The low-power nodes use a transmission power of -15 dBm while the high-power root uses 10 dBm. Each node (including the root) has an antenna of 5 dB gain. We consider a downward traffic-focused scenario where the interval of packet generation (IP packets with 20 byte payload) to and from each node are 90 and 450 seconds, respectively. Given our topology, from the basestation's perspective, this corresponds to sending one downwards packet every three seconds, and receiving one upwards packet every 15 seconds. With this configuration, we use RPL (on top of LPL) as a representative low-power multihop routing protocol (HPN), and SHDP (on top of LPL) to validate the performance of APN. We set the sleep interval of underlying LPL as 2 seconds, and RPL produced a 4-hop network in our topology.

Figure 5 presents the packet loss trends for downlink and uplink traffic when using RPL- and SHDP-based networks for 10 hours (11AM - 9PM). For downlink, SHDP outperforms RPL mainly due to the fact that RPL, to begin with, was not designed to provide optimized downwards routes. Rather, RPL typically achieves downwards routing using the reverse of the upwards routes, despite the asymmetry of wireless links [30]. In RPL, the routes are adjusted only by the children nodes; thus, if the parent experiences severe downlink packet loss, it takes a while for the parent to inform children of its status. Furthermore, control packet losses further delay these route updates. Thus, RPL results in high packet loss when focusing more on downwards traffic than upwards traffic in dynamic channel environments. On the other hand, SHDP uses higher power for downlink transmissions and local retransmissions to assure the reliability as well as to support two-hop nodes.

Nevertheless, for uplink, RPL outperforms SHDP despite SHDP constructing uplink routes using RPL. This is due to the interference caused by the high-power downward transmissions in SHDP. Specifically, uplink packets face communication challenges from the root's downwards transmissions, leading to high SHDP packet loss. Nodes distant from the root are more significantly affected by this interference since they are outside the root's clear channel assessment (CCA) range. Unfortunately, this cannot be resolved by simply provisioning new upward routes since the high-power transmission covers the entire network.

Figure 6(a) and Figure 6(b) plot the per hour routing overhead of each low-power node and their average transmission overhead at the IP layer, respectively. From Figure 6(a) we notice that the routing overhead of SHDP is approximately 52% lower than RPL. While SHDP uses RPL for its upwards routes, we see this reduction due to the fact that SHDP suppresses destination advertisement object (DAO) messages, which are periodically issued at each non-root node to initiate downwards RPL routes. Furthermore, Figure 6(b), where we present a breakdown of packet transmissions, shows that SHDP results in lower transmission overhead by removing multi-hop forwarding for downwards transmissions and minimizing route control packets.

Finally, Figure 7 shows the distribution of duty-cycle of each node, including the total radio-on time not only for its transmissions but also for reception, overhearing, and LPL idle listening. It shows that SHDP achieves a lower duty-cycle than RPL (i.e., 30% lower on average, and 66% lower

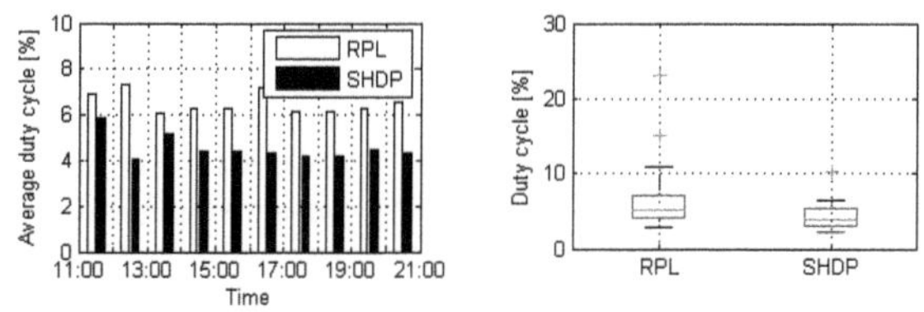

(a) Average per hour duty-cycle (b) Distribution of duty-cycles of each node

Figure 7: Duty-cycle of RPL and SHDP. SHDP improves duty-cycle performance due to lower transmission overhead.

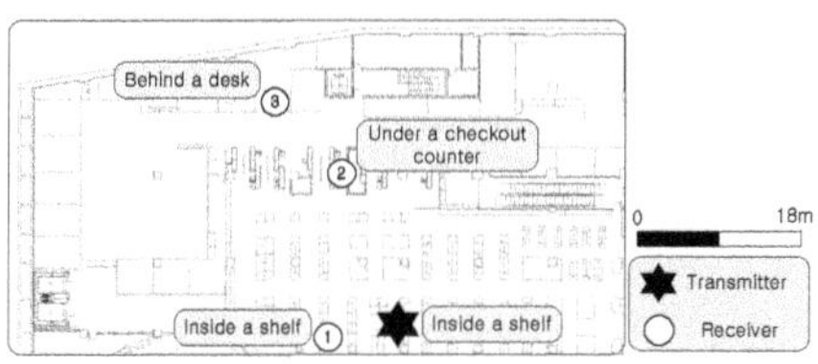

Figure 8: Link testing topology.

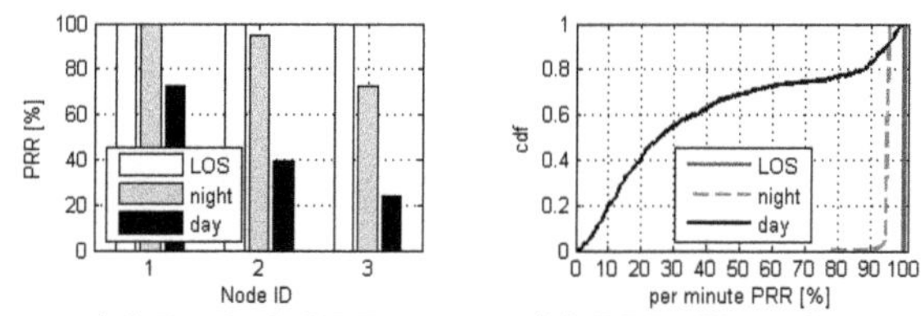

(a) Per-link PRR (b) PRR CDF of link 2

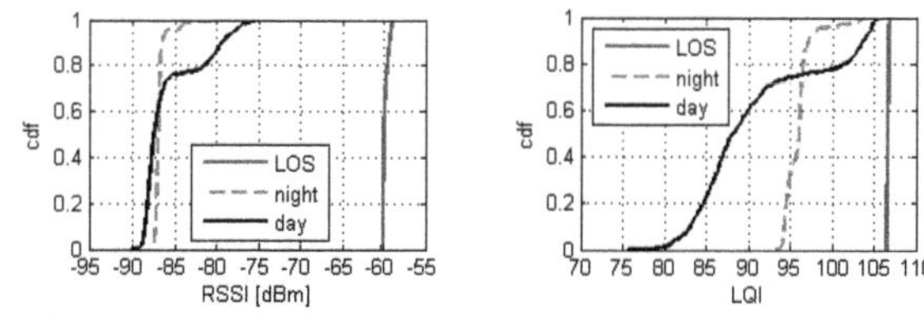

(c) RSSI CDF of link 2 (d) LQI CDF of link 2

Figure 9: Link characteristics of our indoor market environment for channel 26. Packet delivery performance degrades due to the effect of metal shelves and human activities during the day-time.

for the worst performing node), which is due to the reduction in transmission overhead for each non-root node.

Overall, our preliminary studies show that RPL- and SHDP-based networks each possess their own advantages and disadvantages. While RPL provides reliable upward performance, SHDP operates exceptionally well for downwards traffic and improves the energy consumption by reducing the transmission overhead. With these results in mind, we emphasize once again that our target application asks for effective *downwards* traffic delivery. Nevertheless, it is also important that upwards delivery is reliable, given that messages such as rack status updates and application layer acknowledgments are carried via upwards packets.

3.2 Channel Characteristics of a Crowded Indoor Market Environment

To better understand the wireless conditions in our target environment and also effectively address the limitations of RPL- or SHDP-based networks, we performed an additional study to investigate channel environments in various dimensions. For this, we set up a testing environment as in Figure 8. We install three receivers with a single transmitter broadcasting packets of 72 bytes (MAC payload) at an inter-packet interval (IPI) of 50 msec with 0 dBm transmission power. We select the receivers' locations so that we capture various aspects of the market including active human movements, RF propagation over metal shelves and long-distance communications. Unless specified, we take our measurements on IEEE 802.15.4 channel 26, which, in the U.S., is free from WiFi. For reference, we conducted another line-of-sight (LOS) experiment, where each link has the same distance as the market, but in a different environment[2].

Figure 9 presents various link-performance metrics from this experiment. First, Figure 9(a) presents the per-link packet reception ratio (PRR) both for the day-time (noon-10PM) and night-time (11PM-9AM). By comparing the PRR of LOS and market night-time cases, we observe that the metal shelves carrying items have impact on RF signal propagation, by lowering the night-time PRR of link 2 and 3 compared to the LOS PRR of the same distance. On the other hand, by comparing the PRR of the day- and night-times, we can deduce the impact of human activities, which also heavily impacts packet delivery performance.

To understand the impact of human activities further, we analyze the characteristics of link 2 in detail, where the receiver is located at one of the most crowded areas in the market. Figures 9(b), 9(c) and 9(d) plot the cumulative density function (CDF) of the per-minute PRR, received signal strength indicator (RSSI) and link quality indicator (LQI) of link 2 for LOS, day- and night-times. These figures show that all performance metrics in the market are significantly worse than the LOS case: suggesting that an urban market introduces a challenging wireless environment. Combining Figures 9(a) and 9(b) shows that, not only is the average PRR for the day simply lower than the night, the per-minute PRR patterns are widely spread. This suggests that the day-time PRR varies heavily with dynamic channel conditions. The fact that per-minute PRR during the night is mostly >95% serves as evidence that day-time human movements not only degrades the average packet delivery performance, but also gives heavy impact to the link's dynamics. Other metrics such as RSSI and LQI show a similar trend, in which the values are much more dynamic during the day.

It is meaningful to point out that the average RSSI is higher during the day than the night despite its low PRR in Figure 9(c). We explain this using Figure 10, where we plot the channel noise in the market sampled at 1 KHz. Notice here that there is a substantial amount of noise on channel 26, comparable enough to channel 17, which actively interferes with WiFi traffic. After some investigation, we identified that there was a significant amount of WiFi traffic on channel 26 as well, which is authorized in South Korea, where our experiments were conducted. Therefore, active WiFi on channel 26 caused the day-time background noise levels to increase. While many sensor networking protocols utilize RSSI as an easy-to-gather, low-complexity, and robust networking metric [8], our results imply that using RSSI in our target environment is not a good design choice in selecting high quality links.

[2]We omit the picture of this deployment due to the lack of space.

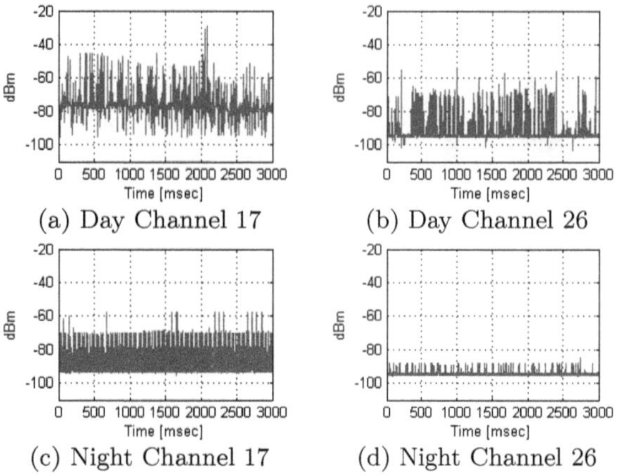

(a) Day Channel 17 (b) Day Channel 26 (c) Night Channel 17 (d) Night Channel 26

Figure 10: 1 KHz RSSI sampling traces. The country we test in allows for WiFi traffic on channel 26, causing noise spikes during the day.

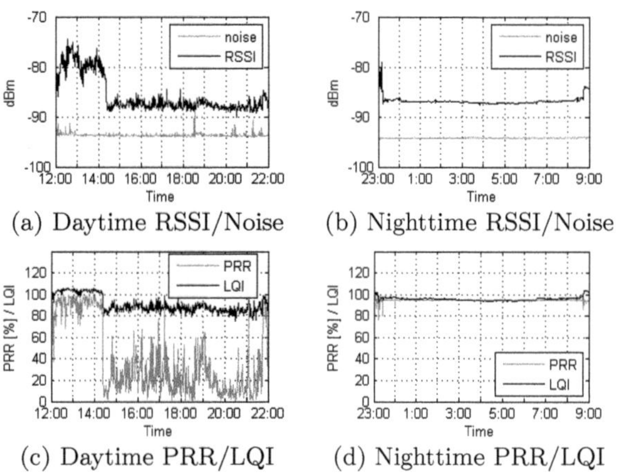

(a) Daytime RSSI/Noise (b) Nighttime RSSI/Noise (c) Daytime PRR/LQI (d) Nighttime PRR/LQI

Figure 11: Characteristics of link 2 over time for channel 26. Human activities cause links fluctuation on both short and long term perspectives.

We can see similar phenomena in Figures 11(a) and 11(b) as well, where we plot the per-minute average RSSI and noise floor levels of link 2 for 10 hours during the day- and night-times, respectively. The long term measurement plots provide us with a longitude perspective of the short-term noise sampling presented in Figure 10. Here, we make another interesting observation. The sudden decrease in RSSI during the day (between 2PM and 3PM) was caused from the filling in of items (i.e., water bottles) on the shelves at which the transmitter was located. Once items were refilled, the RSSI level dropped and this lower RSSI was continuously maintained throughout the day. As Figure 11(c) shows, this same artifact impacted the LQI and PRR performances as well. Likewise, our target environment introduces many man-made hard-to-predict challenges (similar to those reported in [12][31]), which are unique to the indoor market environment, causing the wireless links to fluctuate on both short- and long-term perspectives.

Lastly, we examine the packet loss patterns of link 2 by analyzing the conditional packet delivery function (CPDF) in Figure 12. The CPDF (introduced in [19]) corresponds to the probability of a packet being successfully received after n consecutive failures or successes. Negative numbers represent consecutive successes, while positive numbers represent consecutive failures. For example, $CPDF(20)$ is the probability of a successful delivery after 20 consecutive failures on the link. Likewise, $CPDF(-20)$ is the probability of a successful reception after 20 consecutive successful receptions. Therefore, the CPDF is a good measure of link burtiness and the channel coherence time.

Figure 12(a) through 12(g) sequentially plot the per hour CPDF of link 2 from 3PM to 10PM, after the refilling event occurred at the rack near the transmitter between 2PM and 3PM. We can first notice from the non-uniformity of the CPDF plots that links in the market environment are heavily bursty. Furthermore, since the length of the CPDF's negative (e.g, left) tail represents the maximum number of consecutive successes (or maximum time duration of good link quality, when combined with IPI), we can see here that the link burstiness varies over time. We conjecture that this was an impact of human movement activities, and to validate this we present the correlation between the negative tail length (i.e., maximum consecutive successes per hour) and human movements (manually collected on the link between the transmitter and receiver node 2) in Figure 12(h). Here we validate the fact that the positive burstiness decreases with an increasing number of customers, naturally suggesting that human activities impact the link burstiness

In addition, using Figure 13, where we plot the 1 KHz noise sampling traces for when a near-by microwave oven is active, we noticed that the microwave oven, frequently used to provide samples of cooked food at several points in the market, impacted the burstiness of the wireless links [34].

3.3 Technical Issues to Overcome

Based on the above observations, we summarize unique technical challenges of the market environment as below:

- **Human Movements and Market Activity:** Human activity is one of the main reasons for link dynamics during the day. Specifically, the impact of human movements prevents the links from making successful transmissions for long durations. Furthermore, the impact of typical market activity, such as the use of the microwave oven, causes market's link conditions to continuously fluctuate. These issues create the need for a robust networking layer.
- **Metal racks and items:** Metal racks and their items impact the link characteristics in two ways. First, they become an obstacle for RF signals. Second, the item stock status cause long term fluctuation on the link quality.
- **Noise Statistics:** Unlike the U.S., our market environment is not free from WiFi interference even on IEEE 802.15.4 channel 26. The interference problem is difficult to overcome by simply identifying alternative routes since the impact of other radios is prevalent in most cases.

4. ADDRESSING THE CHALLENGES WITH MarketNet

The lessons from Section 3 suggest that constructing a two-way multihop network of symmetric transmission power links (with RPL) provides 'reasonable' performance for our target environment, but is not ideal in terms of overhead and downwards packet delivery reliability. On the other hand, an APN provides satisfactory downlink performance, but fails in providing satisfactory uplink performance due to the

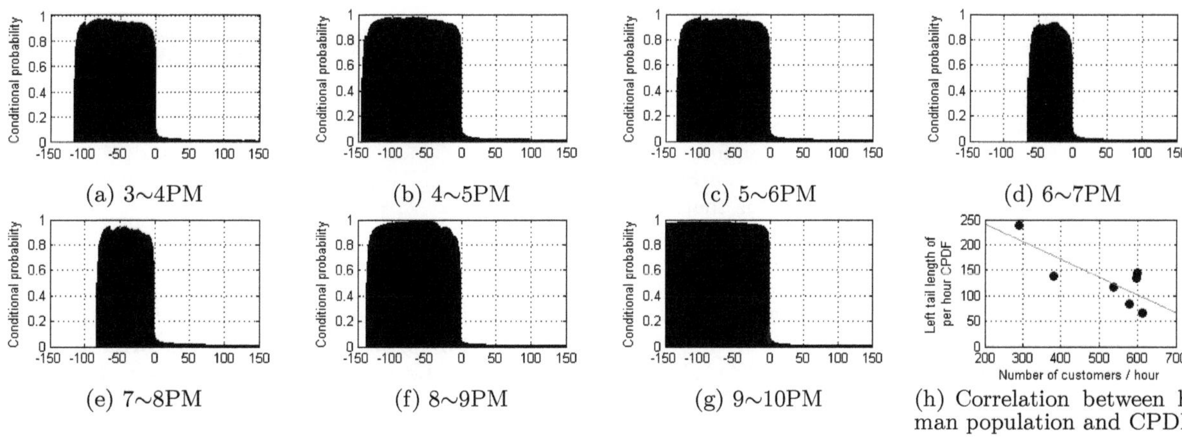

(a) 3∼4PM (b) 4∼5PM (c) 5∼6PM (d) 6∼7PM

(e) 7∼8PM (f) 8∼9PM (g) 9∼10PM (h) Correlation between human population and CPDF

Figure 12: Per hour conditional packet delivery function (CPDF) for different hours during the day, along with the negative tail (or left tail) lengths' correlation with human population.

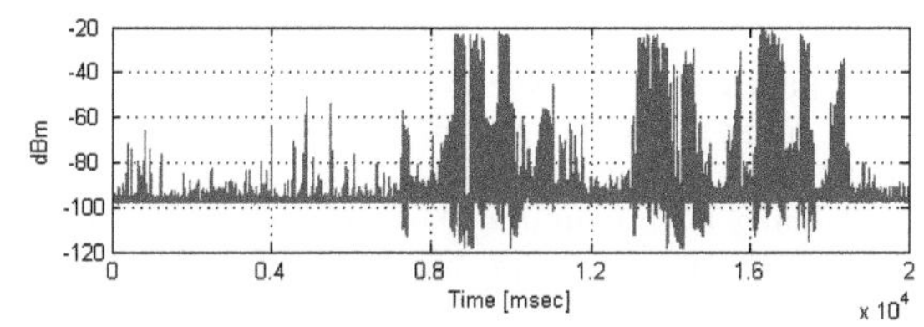

Figure 13: 1 KHz RSSI sampling on channel 26, performed near a microwave oven. Microwave oven is another major factor of link quality fluctuation.

contention and interference occurring near the high-power transmitting basestation. Given these characteristics, we now design a more suitable solution for our application.

In doing so, we take the observation that our application heavily relies on satisfactory downwards packet delivery performance (e.g., price updates). Therefore we borrow some of the concepts proposed in SHDP in enabling APN-based systems to design *MarketNet*. Specifically, *MarketNet* puts RPL at its basis in order to provide end-to-end multihop IPv6 routing, but it is a complete re-design of RPL with the concept of APNs that adopts the advantages of both RPL and SHDP. As our results will later show, *MarketNet* enhances the performance over both RPL and SHDP in our target environment of interest.

The main issue with SHDP-based APN is that it faces high contention and interference near the basestation due to its high-power transmission. In order to compensate for the increased interference range of the root, the APN should provide an end-to-end latency significantly shorter than the one-hop latency of the HPN. Naturally, as the work in [13] also shows, APNs reduces this latency by design. However, reducing the latency to be below that of one-hop packet transmission latency of HPN is non-trivial; thus, this suggests that we need to significantly redesign and improve SHDP to achieve reliable upward packet delivery.

4.1 MarketNet System Design

Our approach to minimize the end-to-end latency of downward packets in an APN combines the high transmission power at the root to achieve single hop downwards packet delivery with the *network-wide time synchronization*. Specifically, *MarketNet* synchronizes all nodes in the network with the high transmission power root and exploits a network-wide superframe architecture. This allows all low-power nodes in *MarketNet* to wake-up and sleep their radios simultaneously. Compared to LPL, which requires half of the sleep interval, on average, for one hop packet delivery (due to the uncertain neighbors' wake-up schedules), our superframe-based scheme significantly reduces the packet delivery latency to only a packet length while reserving more time for upward packets and radio sleep. Furthermore, the superframe dedicates and separates transmission periods for the root and individual low-power nodes using time division duplex, which protects low-power nodes from the root's high power transmission interference. Lastly, the reduction in packet transmission time allows nodes to maintain very short radio active periods to improve their energy efficiency.

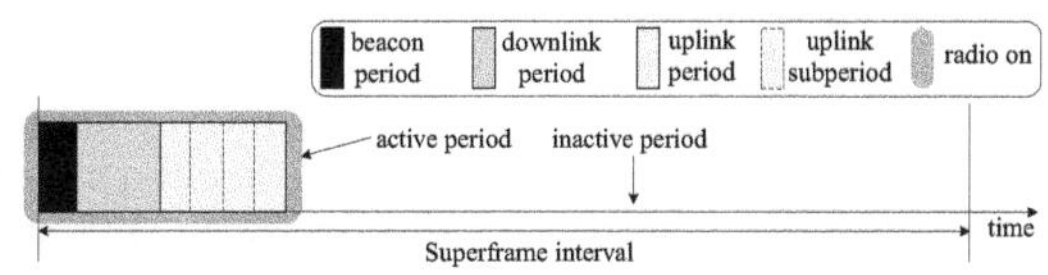

Figure 14: Superframe structure of *MarketNet*. Downlink and uplink transmission periods are designated using a beacon message sent by the root.

4.2 Network-wide Superframe Architecture

This section describes *MarketNet*'s superframe architecture in detail, including the basic superframe operations, uplink period partitioning, and initial synchronization.

4.2.1 Basic Operation

Figure 14 illustrates *MarketNet*'s network-wide superframe structure. A superframe consists of an inactive period and an active period, where the active period is further divided into the beacon, downlink, and uplink periods. At the start of a beacon period, the root broadcasts a *regular beacon* frame with high transmission power, which contains three types of information: (1) A *beacon timer* which is the time interval until the next regular beacon transmission (i.e., start of the next superframe), (2) next downlink period duration, and (3) next uplink period duration.

A non-root node wakes up just before the start of the agreed upon beacon period and receives the next incoming (expected) beacon frame. Using the information in the beacon, a non-root node configures its downlink, uplink and idle durations. Given that these event times are controlled centrally at a single point, a positive side effect is that the duty-cycle (and in turn the lifetime) can be easily estimated and controlled at the central server. Furthermore, although the downlink period starts directly after the beacon reception, the periodic nature of the beacon interval allows the non-root nodes to wake up accurately at a level of reasonable synchronization, despite missing several beacon messages. While many time synchronization schemes exist (e.g. FTSP [22]), we take a simple approach since our application requirements are at millisecond-level accuracy.

When nodes enter the downlink period, only the root is allowed to transmit. All other nodes simply receive packets and transmit ACKs when required in between transmissions. Our current design of *MarketNet* makes multiple unicast IPv6 packet transmissions to individual nodes from the root instead of transmitting batches of downwards messages via multicast. We take such a design choice due to three reasons. First, we try to reduce the implementation complexity at the low-power non-root nodes (e.g., avoid complex multicast addressing). Second, unicast message transmission would mean that the entire network is idle except the destination node that transmits its ACK packet for the downwards message; therefore, minimizing the contention during ACK transmissions and avoids ACK-explosion. Third, the aggregation of price update messages can cause additional latency at the central server. Nevertheless, we foresee the issue of aggregating messages and making multicast transmissions as an interesting future work.

MarketNet includes a best-effort retransmission scheme to increase the reliability of data delivery using a predefined maximum number of retransmissions. In APNs, while the root's transmission successfully reaches the destination, the ACK cannot reach the root over single-hop. To provide reliable delivery in such cases, *MarketNet* utilizes "local ACK packets" rather than end-to-end ACKs, and borrows the neighbor forwarding scheme in SHDP [13]. Specifically, neighbor nodes of the destination confirm the downward packet delivery on behalf of the root by overhearing both the data and ACK packets. If an ACK is not overheard, neighboring nodes locally retransmit the overheard downlink packet to the destination during the following uplink period. Once the downlink duration ends, the uplink period starts for its pre-defined duration (as specified in the beacon) so that low-power nodes can send their messages or perform neighbor forwarding. Following this, the superframe specifies an idle period for the nodes to turn off their radios until the next beacon reception.

4.2.2 Uplink Period Partitioning

Unlike the beacon-enabled mode in the IEEE 802.15.4 standard which requires each cluster head to have an independent superframe duration (i.e., wake-up at different times) for mitigating inter-cluster interference [11], *MarketNet* allows all low-power nodes to share a single superframe since it has a root enabled to cover the entire target area using high-power transmissions. This naturally brings reduced implementation complexity and a common wake-up schedule for messages such as RPL control messages. However, such operations can cause congestion as multiple nodes compete for channel access within a limited uplink duration.

To alleviate this problem, as Figure 14 shows, we partition the uplink period into several sub-periods so that each is just long enough to transmit one packet assuming a maximum IEEE 802.15.4 frame length. The intuition behind this partitioning is to combine the benefits of CSMA with a TDMA-based approach. Specifically, a node that intends to send packets selects a sub-period (at random) and suppresses its packets unless they are at the beginning of this sub-period *and* its CCA succeeds. This constraint helps reduce the number of contenders on the channel [14]. Furthermore, *MarketNet* uses priority-based random backoff as a function of the queue occupancy to allow congested nodes to utilize relatively more sub-periods in the uplink period.

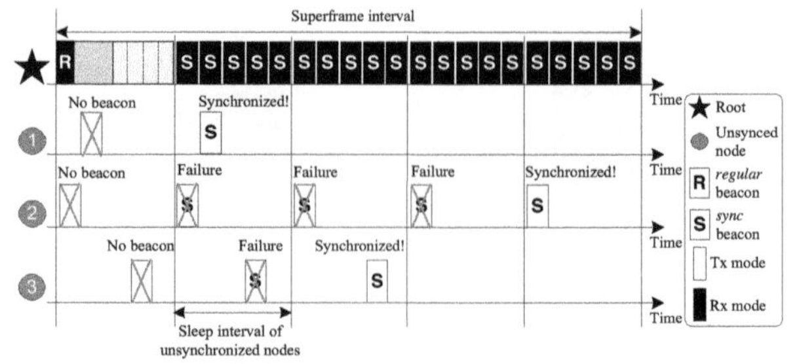

Figure 15: An example of *MarketNet*'s initial synchronization procedure. The root broadcasts sync beacons in the inactive period for new (unsynchronized) nodes to join the superframe architecture.

4.2.3 Initial Synchronization

While the method above is effective once the entire network is synchronized, there are a couple more considerations to make when the network is not fully synchronized or when a new node joins the system. Failing to do so will cause a node to continuously miss the beacons that advertise transmission schedules.

To this end, as we show in Figure 15, an unsynchronized node wakes up periodically and monitors the wireless medium, similar to LPL operations. In the mean time, during the idle times in the aforementioned superframe while the low-power nodes are sleeping, the root broadcasts *sync beacons* continuously, which contains only the start time of the next *regular beacon*. Once an unsynchronized or newly joined node hears this message, it also enters radio sleep mode until the next beacon interval. This scheme allows nodes to maintain their low-power sleep cycles while quickly joining the synchronized network. To achieve reliable *sync beacon* delivery, we set the initial sleep interval of unsynchronized nodes to be much smaller than the superframe interval. This allows new nodes to put multiple efforts for picking up the *sync beacon* message, resulting in robust synchronization under dynamic link conditions.

Lastly, the high-power root does not transmit a *sync beacon* for every inactive period but only at a larger periodical intervals (e.g., 100 superframe intervals). This prevents the procedure from monopolizing the wireless medium. Since all nodes in each network use a single superframe and the *sync-beacon* occupies the channel only shortly, *MarketNet* can construct a larger network consisting of multiple roots.

4.3 IPv6 and Routing Layers in MarketNet

4.3.1 Neighbor Forwarding Suppression

From the preliminary evaluations of SHDP, we noticed that even when a destination node successfully receives a downward packet from the root, the ACK delivery towards its neighbors could fail due to natural link dynamics, such as external channel noise in our environment (Figure 10). This unreliable ACK delivery results in unnecessary local packet retransmissions, which lowers the nodes' energy efficiency. The unnecessary local retransmission also comes from high node densities, since each node has many neighbor nodes.

Since inefficient neighbor forwarding causes uplink period contention, *MarketNet* implements a scheme where a destination's neighbor node will *probabilistically* suppress downward packet forwarding based on the expected number of neighbors of the destination node. Assuming that we aim to deliver a missing downward packet to the destination with N neighbors with a successful delivery probability denoted as P_{succ}, each neighbor node suppresses its transmissions with probability of P_{supp}, determined by

$$P_{supp} = (1 - P_{succ})^{\alpha/N} \quad (1)$$

where α is a predefined parameter which balances reliability and transmission overhead. With increasing α, each node aggressively participates in neighbor forwarding, which impacts the reliability positively (more retransmissions) at first, and negatively (more packet drops due to congestion) after some point. This neighbor retransmission suppression allows for best-effort downlink packet delivery with minimal traffic overhead in dynamic channel conditions. To distribute the neighbor count N to the neighboring nodes, we include this information in the routing beacon messages used for multihop routing (as an optional field in the RPL DODAG Information Object (DIO) messages).

4.3.2 DIO Transmission Interval Adjustment

RPL uses DIO messages for route advertisement to construct multihop routes to the root, and the trickle timer is used to control the DIO transmission interval [4, 20]. This allows RPL to achieve both low overhead and fast route recovery. For this purpose, the trickle timer initializes the DIO interval to be small, and doubles the timer after each DIO transmission until a maximum value (e.g., 256 msec and 262 sec in TinyRPL, respectively [15]) is reached.

However in *MarketNet*, if the DIO transmission interval is smaller than the superframe interval, severe contention can occur during the uplink period, given that multiple DIOs can be stacked at the packet queue during the inactive period. Through our preliminary studies, we observed that *MarketNet* suffers from DIO collisions during the initial phases since all nodes transmit DIOs at the minimum interval when joining the network. To overcome this issue, we configure the initial DIO transmission interval as the superframe interval in *MarketNet*. This cross-layer approach allows *MarketNet* to quickly construct and recover its base routing topology without causing congestion from DIO transmissions.

5. SYSTEM EVALUATION

We now present empirical evaluations of *MarketNet* using an indoor testbed and a market environment as in Section 3.

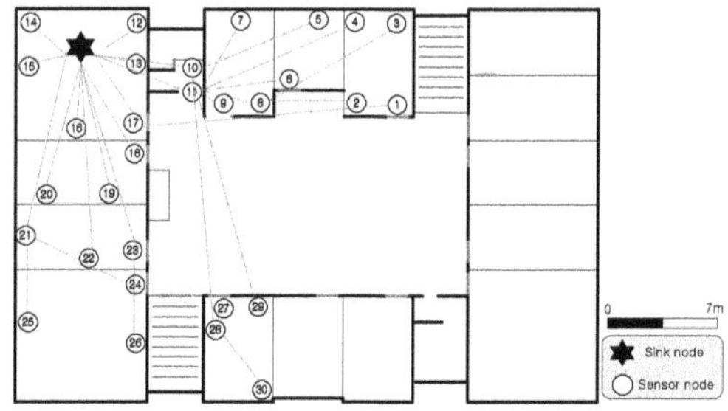

Figure 16: Topology map of indoor 30-node testbed with a snapshot of RPL's routing paths.

5.1 Testbed Evaluations

Figure 16 presents the topology of our testbed where a total of 31 nodes were deployed on a single floor office with one node acting as the root of the network, resulting in a 4-hop network. Using this testbed, we first present results for the packet loss rate, duty-cycle and networking overhead for varying sleep intervals.

In this experiment, we generate periodic uplink packets (from the low-power nodes to the root) at an interval of 450 seconds, while sending downlink packets (from the root to low-power nodes) at an interval of 90 seconds (i.e., traffic rate of 3 seconds/packet at the root). We select such a balance between the two types of traffic based on an interview with market mangers. Furthermore, for RPL and SHDP, we vary the sleep intervals of the underlying LPL operations to be 0.5, 1, 2 and 2.5 seconds so that the LPL interval is below the traffic rate of 3 seconds/packet at the root. We empirically set $\alpha = 2$ for *MarketNet* to minimize transmission overhead while providing reliable downward packet delivery.

We use a superframe interval of 6 seconds for *MarketNet*, and the downlink and uplink transmission durations are configured to be 90 and 120 msec, respectively, allowing for a steady 5.79 seconds of radio off time per superframe interval. We select these values for two major reasons. First, our goal was to achieve at least 3 months lifetime for our price tags on two AA batteries based on the interviews with the market managers. Given that a typical AA battery has a capacity of 900 mAh, and calculating for ~60 mW of active power consumption on our nodes, our target duty-cycle was 3.5% or lower. Secondly, from our literature survey which suggested a price update throughput of over 5000 messages per hour [5], our target downlink throughput is 100 packets per minute. This requires for at least a 90 msec downlink period each 6 seconds. The uplink period duration was configured to allow sufficient time for forwarding the given uplink traffic (for all low-power nodes) over multiple hops.

As a result, as Figure 17(c) shows, this configuration leads to achieving a radio duty-cycle of 3.5% for all low-power nodes in *MarketNet*. In contrast, the radio duty-cycles of RPL and SHDP converge at a higher value due to the transmission inefficiency and networking overhead (Figure 17(d)) while maintaining the same level of reliability as *MarketNet*. If we configure the LPL sleep interval of RPL and SHDP higher hoping to improve the duty-cycle, nodes would not be able to handle the given traffic and the duty-cycle will further increase. We note that *MarketNet*'s superframe architecture allows us to further adjust its radio duty-cycle with respect to the energy consumption of the e-price tags' sensors and display units to match the target lifetime.

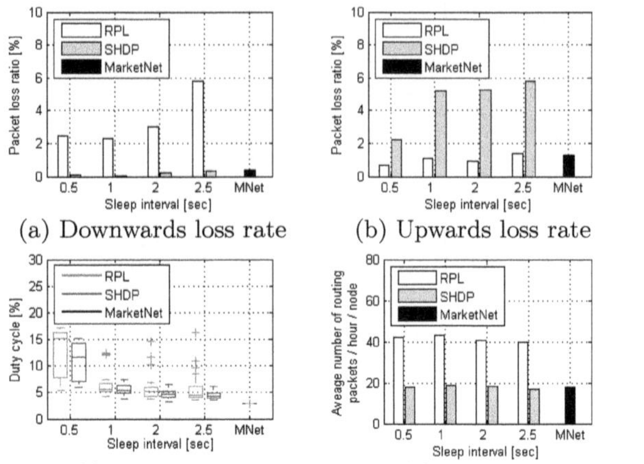

(a) Downwards loss rate (b) Upwards loss rate

(c) Duty-cycle (d) Overhead

Figure 17: Loss-rate and radio duty-cycle results from the testbed for varying sleep intervals and *MarketNet*. *MarketNet* provides the lowest networking overhead and duty-cycles.

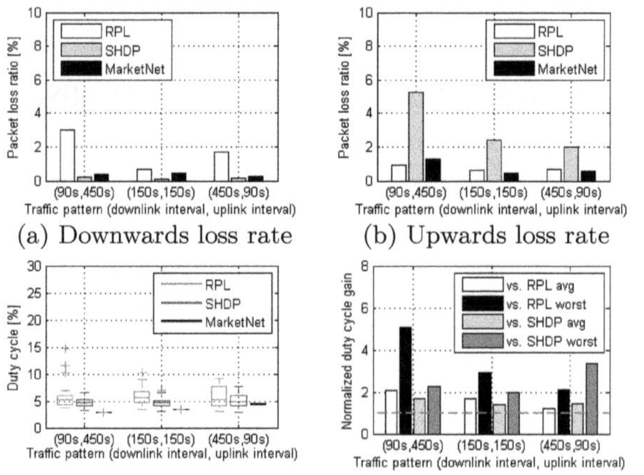

(a) Downwards loss rate (b) Upwards loss rate

(c) Duty-cycle (d) Normalized duty-cycle

Figure 18: Loss-rate and duty-cycle results from the testbed for varying uplink and downlink traffic interval patterns. *MarketNet* shows the lowest packet loss and duty-cycles.

We can see from Figures 17(a) and 17(b) that *MarketNet* shows reduced uplink packet loss ratios compared to the other two protocols. Especially, compared to SHDP, we noticed that the explicit separation of uplink and downlink packets allows the upwards packet delivery performance to match that of RPL. Given that RPL is used as its basis, this is the most ideal performance for *MarketNet*.

On a different perspective, we vary the uplink and downlink traffic intervals (i.e., [90sec, 450sec], [150sec, 150sec] and [450sec, 90sec]), while maintaining an LPL sleep interval of 2 seconds. Under such conditions, Figures 18(a) and 18(b) show that the performance of *MarketNet* takes the best of RPL and SHDP for both uplink and downlink traffic. The benefits of reduced radio duty-cycle also holds in this experiment as we plot in Figures 18(c) and 18(d). Figure 18(d) plots the normalized duty-cycles of RPL and SHDP against the duty-cycle of *MarketNet*. In many cases, the duty-cycle of *MarketNet* outperforms others by two-fold.

Finally, on the testbed, we examine the impact of utilizing uplink partitioning (c.f., Section 4.2.2) using Figures 19(a) and 19(b). Here, we compare the performance of *MarketNet* with and without uplink partitioning. These experiments were performed during the night-time to focus solely on the effect of congestion. The results show that uplink partitioning improves both link layer ETX and uplink packet delivery performance. The improvement becomes more significant with increasing uplink traffic, which confirms that our uplink partitioning scheme reduces packet collisions by designating slots for the nodes' transmissions.

Overall the results from the testbed suggest that *MarketNet*, on an operational perspective, successfully addresses the performance limitations of RPL and SHDP.

5.2 Market Deployments

For evaluating *MarketNet* in the market, we deploy nodes identically to our preliminary measurements in Section 3 (c.f., Figure 4). Furthermore, we select the same set of networking parameters as in the testbed experiments (e.g. LPL sleep interval of 2 seconds). While experiments were not performed simultaneously (i.e., 11AM-9PM on different days),

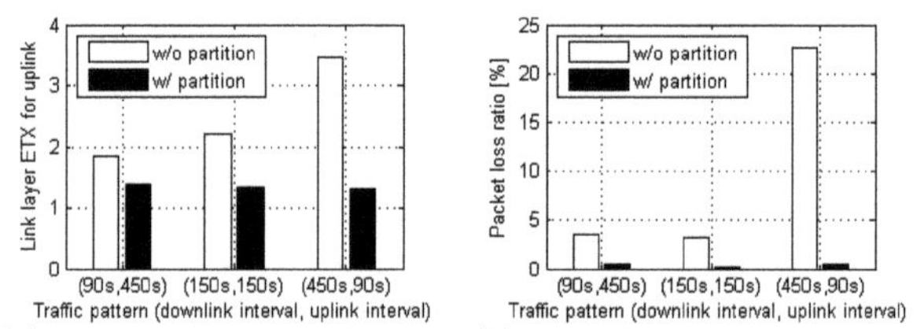

(a) Link layer ETX for uplink. (b) Uplink packet loss ratio.

Figure 19: Impact of uplink partitioning. Uplink partitioning minimizes both the per-link ETX and packet loss ratios for uplink traffic by separating transmission slots.

which could lead to inconsistent results due to potential interference from other systems and differences in WiFi activities over different wireless channels, we confirmed that for the three days of testing (e.g., one for each system), the number of market customers were roughly similar.

We first present the packet loss ratio for uplink and downlink traffic in Figures 20(a) and 20(b), respectively. We noticed that *MarketNet* maintains reliable ($< 1\%$) downlink packet delivery regardless of the number of customers during the day, as SHDP does. In contrast, the downlink performance of RPL fluctuates mostly due to dynamic channel conditions during busy times, especially due to human activities. During these periods, link qualities may change frequently, but RPL's route changes cannot keep pace with the link fluctuations. Therefore, even if a RPL node changes its route with respect to the fluctuations, without frequent DAO updates, the parent node is unaware of changes, leading to non-optimal path selection and packet losses for downward traffic. On the other hand, uplink performances of all three protocols vary as time passes due to unstable low-power links in dynamic environments as discussed in Section 3.2, where SHDP provides the worst performance.

Specifically, the main reason behind the slightly better performance of RPL in some cases compared to *MarketNet* is owing to LPL used under RPL. A link layer transmission

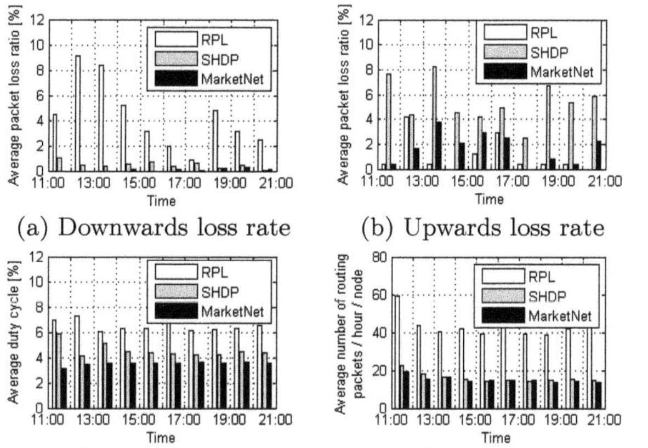

(a) Downwards loss rate (b) Upwards loss rate

(c) Duty-cycle (d) Overhead

Figure 20: Network performance over 10-hour period for RPL, SHDP and *MarketNet* in the market environment. While the real market environment introduces an additional level of fluctuation over time, the performance trends of *MarketNet* match our testbed results.

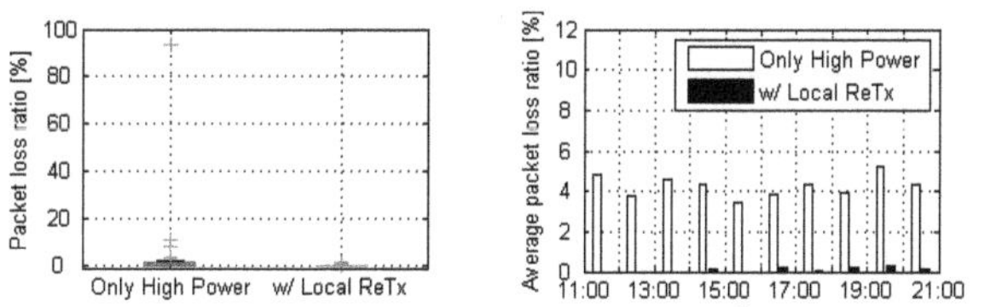

(a) Loss rate of each node. (b) Loss rate vs. time.

Figure 21: Downwards loss rate of *MarketNet* with and without neighbor forwarding scheme. Neighbor forwarding significantly improves reliability when transmission of high power root suffers from link dynamics or path loss.

of LPL involves a set of repetitive transmissions for a sleep interval, which produces a dense retransmission effect. With retransmissions at the link and LPL layers, RPL holds a higher chance of delivering packets in dynamic channel conditions. Furthermore, since RPL also uses DAO messages to determine link qualities, it has a higher chance of selecting higher quality links compared to SHDP and *MarketNet*. Nevertheless, Figure 20(c) shows that *MarketNet* achieves the lowest duty-cycle by sacrificing such retransmissions and removing DAO overhead (as plotted in Figure 20(d)).

We analyze the performance of high power transmissions in *MarketNet* using Figures 21(a) and 21(b). Firstly, high power root successfully transmits 95% of downwards packets via single hop. However, direct downward transmissions suffer from unfair reliability among nodes due to different path loss, which leads to 93.23% of loss rate for the worst node (i.e., node 25) as shown in Figure 21(a). Furthermore, Figure 21(b) shows that link dynamics impact the performance of high power transmission, which causes unstable reliability in the time domain. These observations confirm that neighbor forwarding (i.e., local retransmission) is necessary to achieve reliable downward packet delivery in *MarketNet*.

We now look deep into the performance of the three protocols, especially on the packet transmission perspective at

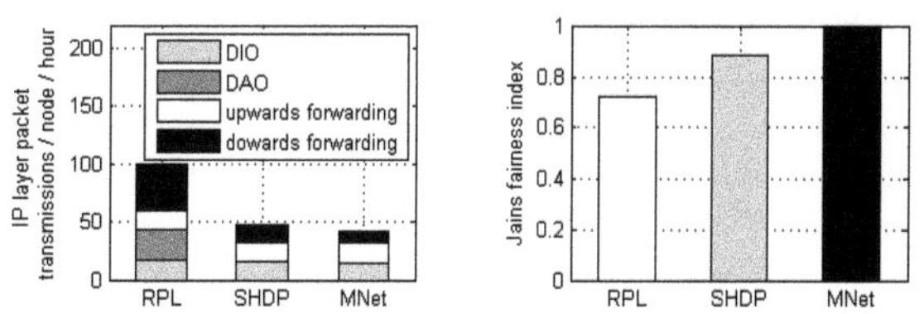

(a) Transmission breakdown (b) Duty-cycle fairness

Figure 22: Transmission overhead and duty-cycle fairness in the market for RPL, SHDP and *MarketNet*. The reduction in transmission overhead is due to the suppression of DAO transmissions and packet forwarding for downwards delivery. Furthermore, *MarketNet* shows a fair duty-cycle performance among the deployed nodes.

the low-power nodes using Figure 22(a). The number of DIO packets used to maintain the base multihop topology is almost identical, implying that the overall network stability of the systems is similar despite testing them on three different days. By suppressing DAO transmissions, SHDP and *MarketNet* successfully reduce the traffic overhead on low-power nodes. Furthermore, SHDP and *MarketNet* allows low-power nodes to forward downlink packets only when they detect failure of high-power transmissions, which noticeably reduces the frequency of downward forwarding.

Lastly, Figure 22(b) plots the Jain's Fairness Index for the radio duty-cycle of low-power nodes in the network. We see that the use of superframes and synchronized wake-ups lead the nodes in *MarketNet* to achieve a fair duty-cycle. On the other hand, the multihop packet forwarding participation forces RPL to show the lowest fairness in terms of duty-cycle distribution among nodes. The low and fair duty-cycle of *MarketNet* synchronizes the lifetime of all low-power nodes. It also minimizes the need for irregular human intervention, compared to RPL and SHDP, where some nodes deplete their batteries earlier than the others.

Comprehensively, our evaluations show that the performance of *MarketNet* takes the positive ends of both RPL and SHDP in several ways. Compared to RPL, *MarketNet* significantly improves downlink performance with much lower transmission overhead. Compared to SHDP, *MarketNet* provides greatly improved uplink performance. Most importantly, *MarketNet*'s network-wide synchronization allows nodes to enjoy a longer and fairer lifetime.

In our evaluations, we compare *MarketNet* with RPL because, given that is considered to be the *de-facto* standard IPv6 routing protocol for low-power and lossy networks. As alternative comparisons, recently proposed networking protocols such as ORPL [3] or LWB [6] can also be considered. Nevertheless, ORPL in which nodes in the network "anycast" messages through the RPL DODAG, the fairness between the nodes and routing overhead cannot outperform RPL. Moreover, the anycast overhead of ORPL can lead to sacrificing the radio duty-cycle for improved packet delivery performance over RPL. As for LWB in which the Glossy protocol [7] is used as it basis, we believe it could potentially be a candidate protocol that can be compared to *MarketNet* to see their respective advantages and disadvantages. We leave this as an interesting future work.

6. RELATED WORK

Electronic price tagging in large-sized markets has gained interest for several years, and a number of systems have been developed around various wireless networking technologies. Yu et al. [33] discusses the implementation of the Electronic Intelligent Tag (EIT) system on wireless sensor networks for intelligent management of supermarkets. EIT is an electronic display device that replaces the traditional paper price tag. It also provides a way to distribute frequent and effective promotional activities. Although the paper proposes an architecture and design, it does not provide details of the implementation nor performance evaluations. Furthermore the authors do not discuss wireless communication challenges of the environment as we present in Section 3.2. The work closest to ours is the electronic price label (EPL) system [5], which provides a similar electronic replacement for paper labels. The EPL system features two-way communication between a controller and electronic price labels to ensure price accuracy and reliability. Nevertheless, the evaluation of EPL does not consider variability of wireless link characteristics in real-world market environments.

A number of works have investigated the performance of RPL [4] and IEEE 802.15.4 in various network configurations. Ko et al. experimentally evaluated the performance of RPL and 6LoWPAN using TinyOS [16] and showed that the performance is similar to the widely used collection tree protocol (CTP) [9], while benefiting from an IPv6-based architecture. Ancillotti et al. and Bressan et al. studied the performance of RPL in the context of smart grids. The former proposed a cross-layering design for RPL which provides enhanced link estimation and efficient management of neighbor tables [1]. The latter discussed the deployment of a smart monitoring system using LLNs and performed RPL simulations for a smart grid scenario [2]. As simulation studies, the results do not incorporate wireless channel characteristics of the real-world. Gungor et al. measured IEEE 802.15.4 link qualities in real power grid environments and discussed associated opportunities and challenges [10]. Their work was limited to the link layer and did not consider the routing or application layer performance.

7. DISCUSSIONS

The purpose of this work was to propose a suitable networking solution for e-price tagging applications given their system-level requirements. We summarize some interesting future research directions and discussions below.

- There is always a possibility that a single root and its associated APN cannot cover the entire market environment as a single network. In such cases, the use of multiple roots, interconnected in a tiered architecture would be more suitable [26]. In such cases, each root can use a orthogonal superframe with other root nodes either in the time or frequency domain to avoid interference. *MarketNet* allows for this extension to take place easily, but the exploration of practical and systematic issues regarding such deployments is left as future work.
- While *MarketNet* achieves 99.9% and 98.3% data delivery reliability for downlink and uplink traffic (98.7% and 93.8% for the worst nodes), respectively, for some markets, this may not be enough. For guaranteed reliable transport, standard TCP or other reliable protocols such as RCRT [25] can be employed on top of *MarketNet* to complete the price updating procedures.
- Although we test the performance of *MarketNet* using 30 nodes, in practice, price tags are more densely deployed in urban markets. (e.g., +10k tags in our test field). *MarketNet* addresses this challenge using its uplink period partitioning and neighbor forwarding suppression. While we explore the initial steps to form a networked system for the market environment, at-scale testing an how we can resolve any systematic issues in the deployments remains as an important next step of research.
- Optimally provisioning an e-Price tag network given a store layout by performing offline analysis and then placing the devices would be an interesting direction for future research as well. While we do not explore this direction in the scope of this work, we conjecture that this will be a challenging approach given the dynamics of the wireless environment within the market.

The key points of our work are in proposing the use of asymmetric (heterogeneous) transmission power to achieve both (1) downlink reliability and (2) low-power end devices for battery operation. In other words, if we increase the transmission power of the end devices to form a single-hop topology, this would sacrifice the nodes' energy efficiency. On the other hand, reducing the root's transmission power and forming a symmetric multihop topology, would reduce the downlink reliability as in the RPL experiments. Our goal is to achieve the best of both worlds, given the constraints introduced from our devices and the application itself.

8. CONCLUSION

For over a decade, many wireless systems have been designed to automate routine tasks that were previously performed manually. Our work builds on past works by showing how low-power wireless systems can help improve a busy market environment using electronic, wirelessly reconfigurable price tags. This work started with a critical examination of existing networking architectures that could potentially be used for such applications. We performed experiments to gather empirical data and gauge how real-world wireless environments impact their performance. Furthermore, we present *MarketNet*, which addresses the challenges of the application and environments, then evaluate *MarketNet* through a deployment in an actual market. We envision that by addressing additional systematic and deployment-specific challenges, and combining such experiences with the *MarketNet* network architecture, we will be able to enhance *MarketNet*'s practical utility in busy market environments.

Acknowledgments

We would like to thank the reviewers for their insightful comments and Prof. Bhaskar Krishnamachari for his efforts in shepherding the paper. This work was supported in part by a grant to Bio-Mimetic Robot Research Center Funded by Defense Acquisition Program Administration and by Agency for Defense Development (UD130070ID), and in part by Basic Science Research Program through the National Research Foundation of Korea (NRF) funded by the Ministry of Education (NRF-2014R1A1A2056626).

9. REFERENCES

[1] E. Ancillotti, R. Bruno, and M. Conti. Reliable data delivery with the ietf routing protocol for low-power

and lossy networks. *IEEE Transactions on Industrial Informatics*, 10(3):1864–1877, Aug. 2014.

[2] N. Bressan, L. Bazzaco, N. Bui, P. Casari, L. Vangelista, and M. Zorzi. The deployment of a smart monitoring system using wireless sensor and actuator networks. In *IEEE International Conference on Smart Grid Communications (SmartGridComm)*, pages 49–54, Oct. 2010.

[3] S. Duquennoy, O. Landsiedel, and T. Voigt. Let the tree bloom: Scalable opportunistic routing with orpl. In *Proceedings of the 11th ACM Conference on Embedded Networked Sensor Systems*, SenSys '13, 2013.

[4] T. W. Ed., P. T. Ed., A. Brandt, J. Hui, R. Kelsey, P. Levis, K. Pister, R. Struik, J. Vasseur, and R. Alexander. RPL: IPv6 Routing Protocol for Low-Power and Lossy Networks. *RFC 6550*, Mar. 2012.

[5] J. G. Evans, R. A. Shober, S. A. Wilkus, and G. A. Wright. A low-cost radio for an electronic price label system. *Bell Labs Technical Journal*, 1(2):203–215, 1996.

[6] F. Ferrari, M. Zimmerling, L. Mottola, and L. Thiele. Low-Power Wireless Bus. In *Proceedings of SenSys*, Toronto, Canada, November 2012.

[7] F. Ferrari, M. Zimmerling, L. Thiele, and O. Saukh. Efficient network flooding and time synchronization with glossy. In *Proceedings of IPSN*, 2011.

[8] R. Fonseca, O. Gnawali, K. Jamieson, and P. Levis. Four-Bit Wireless Link Estimation. In *Proceedings of the sixth workshop on Hot Topics in Networks (HotNets)*, Nov. 2007.

[9] O. Gnawali, R. Fonseca, K. Jamieson, D. Moss, and P. Levis. Collection Tree Protocol. In *ACM SenSys*, pages 1–14, 2009.

[10] V. Gungor, B. Lu, and G. Hancke. Opportunities and challenges of wireless sensor networks in smart grid. *IEEE Transactions on Industrial Electronics*, 57(10):3557–3564, Oct. 2010.

[11] IEEE Standard for Information technology – Telecommunications and information exchange between systems – Local and metropolitan area networks. Specific requirements – Part 15.4: Wireless Medium Access Control (MAC) and Physical Layer (PHY) Specifications for Low-Rate Wireless Personal Area Networks (LR-WPANs). Available at `http://www.ieee802.org/15/pub/TG4.html`, May 2003.

[12] A. Kara and H. L. Bertoni. Effect of people moving near short-range indoor propagation links at 2.45 ghz. *Communications and Networks, Journal of*, 8(3):286–289, Sept 2006.

[13] H.-S. Kim, Y.-J. Choi, and S. Bahk. Elimination of multi-hop transmission from downlink in low power and lossy networks. In *IEEE International Conference on Communications (ICC)*, pages 305–310, 2014.

[14] T.-H. Kim, J.-S. Han, H.-S. Kim, and Y.-H. Lee. Alleviation of contention collision in ieee 802.15.4 networks. In *Wireless Communications and Networking Conference (WCNC), 2013 IEEE*, pages 65–70, Apr. 2013.

[15] J. Ko, S. Dawson-Haggerty, D. E. Culler, J. W. Hui, P. Levis, and A. Terzis. Connecting Low-power and Lossy Networks to the Internet. *IEEE Communications Magazine*, 49(4):96 –101, Apr. 2011.

[16] J. Ko, S. Dawson-Haggerty, O. Gnawali, D. Culler, and A. Terzis. Evaluating the Performance of RPL and 6LoWPAN in TinyOS. In *Proceedings of the Workshop on Extending the Internet to Low power and Lossy Networks (IP+SN'11)*, Apr. 2011.

[17] J. Ko, J. Lim, Y. Chen, R. Musaloiu-E., A. Terzis, G. Masson, T. Gao, W. Destler, L. Selavo, and R. Dutton. MEDiSN: Medical Emergency Detection in Sensor Networks. *ACM Transactions on Embedded Computing Systems (TECS), Special Issue on Wireless Health Systems*, 2010.

[18] J. Ko and A. Terzis. Power control for mobile sensor networks: An experimental approach. In *Sensor Mesh and Ad Hoc Communications and Networks (SECON), 2010 7th Annual IEEE Communications Society Conference on*, pages 1–9, 2010.

[19] H. Lee, A. Cerpa, and P. Levis. Improving Wireless Simulation Through Noise Modeling. In *Proceedings of the Sixth International Conference on Information Processing in Wireless Sensor Networks (IPSN'07)*, 2007.

[20] P. Levis, T. H. Clausen, J. Hui, O. Gnawali, and J. Ko. The Trickle Algorithm. *RFC 6206*, Mar. 2011.

[21] S. Lin, J. Zhang, G. Zhou, L. Gu, J. A. Stankovic, and T. He. ATPC: Adaptive Transmission Power Control for Wireless Sensor Networks. In *Proceedings of the 4th ACM Conference on Embedded Network Sensor Systems*, (SenSys'06), Nov. 2006.

[22] M. Marot, B. Kusy, G. Simon, and A. Ledeczi. The flooding time synchronization protocol. In *Proceedings of the 2nd ACM Conference on Embedded Network Sensor Systems*, (SenSys'04), pages 39–49, Nov. 2004.

[23] D. Moss, J. Hui, and K. Klues. Low power listening. *TinyOS TEP 105.*

[24] Moteiv Corporation. Tmote Sky. Available at `http://www.moteiv.com/products/tmotesky.php`.

[25] J. Paek and R. Govindan. RCRT: Rate-controlled Reliable Transport Protocol for Wireless Sensor Networks. *ACM Transactions on Sensor Networks*, 7(3):20:1–20:45, Oct. 2010.

[26] J. Paek, B. Greenstein, O. Gnawali, K.-Y. Jang, A. Joki, M. Vieira, J. Hicks, D. Estrin, R. Govindan, and E. Kohler. The Tenet Architecture for Tiered Sensor Networks. *ACM Transactions on Sensor Networks*, 6(4):34:1–34:44, July 2010.

[27] J. Paek, J. Hicks, S. Coe, and R. Govindan. Image-Based Environmental Monitoring Sensor Application Using an Embedded Wireless Sensor Network. *Sensors*, 14(9):15981–16002, 2014.

[28] R. Szewczyk, A. Mainwaring, J. Anderson, and D. Culler. An Analysis of a Large Scale Habitat Monitoring Application. In *Proceedings of the 2nd ACM Conference on Embedded Network Sensor Systems*, (SenSys'04), Nov. 2004.

[29] G. Tolle, J. Polastre, R. Szewczyk, N. Turner, K. Tu, P. Buonadonna, S. Burgess, D. Gay, W. Hong, T. Dawson, and D. Culler. A Macroscope in the Redwoods. In *Proceedings of the 3rd ACM Conference*

on Embedded Network Sensor Systems, (SenSys'05), Nov. 2005.

[30] A. Woo, T. Tong, and D. Culler. Taming the underlying challenges of reliable multihop routing in sensor networks. In *Proceedings of the 1st ACM Conference on Embedded Network Sensor Systems*, (SenSys'03), pages 14–27, Nov. 2003.

[31] T. A. Wysocki. Characterization of the indoor radio propagation channel at 2.4 GHz. pages 84–90, 2000.

[32] N. Xu, S. Rangwala, K. K. Chintalapudi, D. Ganesan, A. Broad, R. Govindan, and D. Estrin. A Wireless Sensor Network for Structural Monitoring. In *Proceedings of the 2nd ACM Conference on Embedded Network Sensor Systems*, (SenSys'04), Nov. 2004.

[33] K. Yu, Z. Xie, J. Qian, and G. Jin. The implementation of electronic intelligent tag system based on wireless sensor network. communications and network. *Communications and Network*, 5:39 – 43, 2013.

[34] X. Zheng, Z. Cao, J. Wang, Y. He, and Y. Liu. Zisense: Towards interference resilient duty cycling in wireless sensor networks. In *Proceedings of the 12th ACM Conference on Embedded Network Sensor Systems*, (SenSys'14), pages 119–133, Nov. 2014.

DrunkWalk: Collaborative and Adaptive Planning for Navigation of Micro-Aerial Sensor Swarms

Xinlei Chen
Carnegie Mellon University
Pittsburgh, PA, USA
xinlei.chen@sv.cmu.edu

Aveek Purohit
Carnegie Mellon University
Pittsburgh, PA, USA
imaveek@gmail.com

Carlos Ruiz Dominguez
Carnegie Mellon University
Pittsburgh, PA, USA
carlos.ruiz.dominguez@sv.cmu.edu

Stefano Carpin
UC Merced
Merced, CA, USA
scarpin@ucmerced.edu

Pei Zhang
Carnegie Mellon University
Pittsburgh, PA, USA
peizhang@cmu.edu

ABSTRACT

Micro-aerial vehicle (MAV) swarms are a new class of mobile sensor networks with many applications, including search and rescue, urban surveillance, radiation monitoring, etc. These sensing applications require autonomously navigating a high number of low-cost, low-complexity MAV sensor nodes in hazardous environments. The lack of preexisting localization infrastructure and the limited sensing, computing, and communication abilities of individual nodes makes it challenging for nodes to autonomously navigate to suitable preassigned locations.

In this paper, we present a collaborative and adaptive algorithm for resource-constrained MAV nodes to quickly and efficiently navigate to preassigned locations. Using radio fingerprints between flying and landed MAVs acting as radio beacons, the algorithm detects intersections in trajectories of mobile nodes. The algorithm combines noisy dead-reckoning measurements from multiple MAVs at detected intersections to improve the accuracy of the MAVs' location estimations. In addition, the algorithm plans intersecting trajectories of MAV nodes to aid the location estimation and provide desired performance in terms of timeliness and accuracy of navigation. We evaluate the performance of our algorithm through a real testbed implementation and large-scale physical feature based simulations. Our results show that, compared to existing autonomous navigation strategies, our algorithm achieves up to 6× reduction in location estimation errors, and as much as 3× improvement in navigation success rate under the given time and accuracy constraints.

SenSys'15, November 1–4, 2015, Seoul, South Korea..

DOI: http://dx.doi.org/10.1145/2809695.2809724

Categories and Subject Descriptors

C.2 [**Computer-Communication Networks**]: Distributed Systems—*Distributed applications*; I.2 [**Artificial Intelligence**]: Distributed Artificial Intelligence—*Multiagent systems*

Keywords

Mobile Sensor Networks; Micro-Aerial Vehicle; Swarm

1. INTRODUCTION

In many hostile, dangerous, or otherwise inaccessible environments (such as urban search and rescue, environmental monitoring, surveillance, etc.), situational awareness is needed. However, in these dangerous scenarios, manual deployment of sensors is often not feasible.

In such scenarios, autonomously navigating MAV swarms to a set of goal locations, in accordance with the needs of domain experts, can provide significant benefit. Further, utilizing a large number of low-cost, low-complexity mobile sensor nodes, as opposed to using a limited number of sophisticated robots, can be more cost effective and provide increased robustness through redundancy. In addition, small lightweight mobile sensor nodes provide greater safety as the effects of their collisions with the objects or persons in the indoor environment are inconsequential.

MAV swarms are an emerging class of networked mobile systems with widespread applications in such domains. These swarms consist of miniature aerial sensor nodes with limited individual sensing, computing and communication capabilities [1, 2]. Initial work in the operation of MAVs has focused on outdoor or highly instrumented environments that rely on external sensors to control individual devices [3, 4]. However, such centralized sensing approaches are hampered in indoor environments by obstructions (walls, furniture, etc.). At the same time, reliance on sensing infrastructure implies requirement for a large deployment of support sensors covering all the locations that a MAV may visit [5]. Thus these approaches are only applicable in pre-surveyed locations.

This paper presents DrunkWalk, a technique for cooperative and adaptive navigation of swarms of micro-aerial sensors in environments not formerly preconditioned for operation. The key focus behind this networked MAV swarm research is to rely on collaboration to overcome limitations of individual nodes and efficiently achieve system-wide sensing objectives.

In DrunkWalk, the MAV swarm self-establishes a temporary infrastructure of a few landed MAV's acting as radio beacons. Using radio signature or fingerprints from beacon nodes, the algorithm detects intersections in trajectories of exploring mobile MAV nodes. The algorithm combines noisy dead-reckoning measurements from multiple MAVs at the detected intersections to improve the accuracy of the MAVs' location estimates. Most importantly, the algorithm adaptively plans trajectories of MAV nodes according to the certainty of their location estimations – directing movement to improve location estimates when certainty is low, and directing MAV to the goal location when certainty of location estimates is high. The adaptive strategy enables DrunkWalk to improve the location estimation accuracy and success rate of navigation under given time and accuracy constraints.

The main contributions of this paper are:

- An adaptive planning algorithm for navigation that enables the swarm to collaboratively achieve up to 6× reduction in location estimation errors, and as much as 3× improvement in navigation success rate under the given time and accuracy constraints.
- A planning algorithm that determines the quality of location estimations and uses it to adaptively plan node motion.
- Real MAV testbed experiments and large scale physical feature based simulations using radio signatures collected from the physical world and empirically determined sensor noise models validating our assumptions.

The rest of this paper is organized as follows. Section 2 gives a high level overview of the architecture and operation of the system. Section 3 gives a detailed technical description of the various algorithms presented in the paper. Section 4 evaluates and analyzes the system through extensive simulations and validates assumptions through MAV testbed experiments. Further discussion of some extra system details are stated in Section 5. In Section 6, we describe related work and discuss the state-of-the-art infrastructure-free navigation techniques in context of MAV swarm deployment. Finally, we draw conclusions and summarize our contributions in Section 7.

2. OVERVIEW

Potential MAV swarm sensing applications will require mobile sensors to autonomously navigate to desired locations in operating environments with no localization infrastructure. In this paper, we address the problem of how a network of mobile sensors can be navigated to pre-determined positions under time and accuracy constraints.

2.1 Operation & Architecture

The system begins operation with a swarm of MAV's being introduced into the operating environments. We make the assumption that a coarse map of the building is available and can be utilized by domain experts to pre-determine suitable placement of sensors. This is a valid assumption in most scenarios, as emergency response personnel have access to the rough floor-plans of buildings through city registries, and thanks to increased availability of indoor maps tailored to location based services (e.g., indoor Google maps).

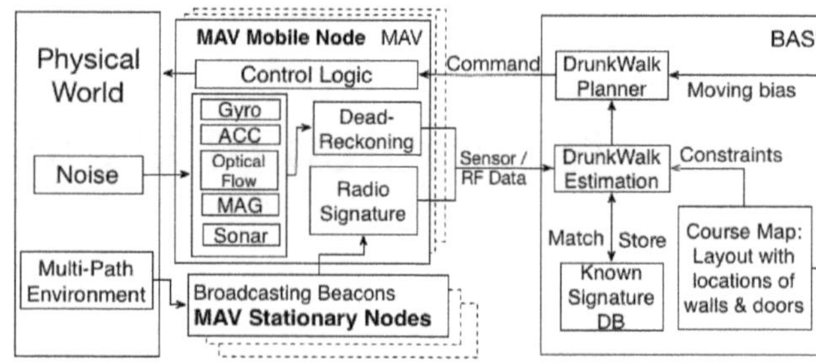

Figure 1: The figure shows the architecture of our navigation system. The mobile MAV nodes send dead-reckoning sensor data and radio signatures to a base station. The base runs the DrunkWalk estimation and planning algorithm and issues movement commands to individual MAV nodes.

The proposed system has 3 major operational phases: setup, estimation and planning (the latter two proceed in conjunction):

- **Setup:** The system autonomously establishes a transient infrastructure of stationary MAV nodes acting as wireless beacons. These nodes land upon being introduced into the area and remain stationary during the process. The objective of the stationary nodes is to enable mobile MAV nodes to obtain radio signatures or fingerprints of locations traversed on their paths. These nodes use a simple dispersion algorithm [6, 7] that lets them spread out in the environment *without any estimation of their location.*
- **Estimation:** The system then desires to estimate the locations of nodes in order to guide them to their goal locations. To realize this, the system first uses dead reckoning sensors such as an optical flow velocity sensor and magnetometer (in our test MAV platform) to get a rough estimate of the motion path of mobile nodes. Second, the system uses radio fingerprints, collected by mobile nodes from the self-established wireless beacons, to determine *snapshot points*, i.e. location points that were previously visited by other nodes or by itself. Finally, the system uses the snapshot points to combine location estimates from multiple nodes and collaboratively improve location estimations of the entire swarm.
- **Planning:** Having estimated locations, the system plans paths for each node that 1) leads to subsequent goal positions and 2) improves location estimation accuracy. The quality of the planned path depends greatly on the accuracy of the initial location estimate of nodes. A bad location estimate will render any attempt to plan a deterministic path useless – *when the nodes don't know where they are, they cannot plan a correct path to their destination.*

Our system thus considers the quality of location estimation in planning node paths. The path planner commands nodes movement such that they increase the number of snapshot points and potentially improve location estimates when the quality of their estimates is likely to be low. On the other hand, when the location estimates are likely to be more accurate, the planner uses the map to direct them to their designated goal locations.

Figure 1 shows the architecture of the system. Through dispersion algorithm, the system deploys **Stationary MAV Nodes** that act as wireless beacons. **Mobile MAV Nodes** explore and obtain dead-reckoning measurements from their on-board sensors and radio RF-signatures from the stationary beacons. The mobile nodes relay this to a **Base**. The Base stores a database of known radio signatures (**Signature DB**) that is used to determine snapshot point in node paths and apply corrections to their dead-reckoning estimates. The corrected location estimates are used by the Base in conjunction with a coarse map (indoor layout with location of walls and doors) of the environment to command the subsequent movements of MAV nodes.

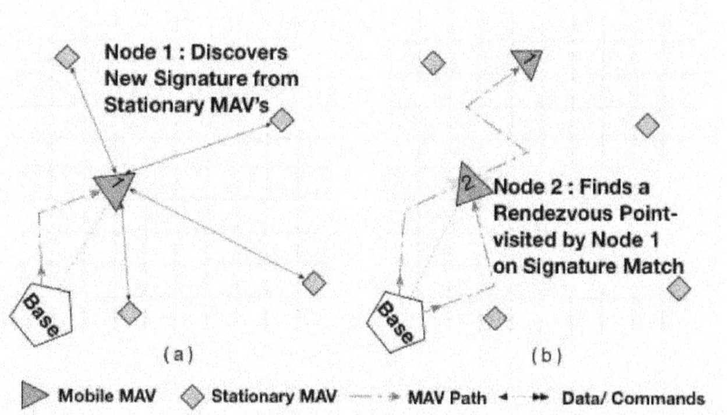

Figure 2: The figure shows the process of determining snapshot points. (a) Node 1 moves and obtains a radio signature from stationary MAV. This is entered into the the Base Signature DB as new signature. (b) When Node 2 visits the same location, its collected radio signature matches existing signature and a correction can be performed at the Base.

2.2 Improving Location Estimation Through Swarms

The core idea behind our estimation approach is to use relatively large number of mobile sensors in the swarm to collaboratively reduce the error. This is achieved by detecting when nodes move over the same space in the environment and combining their individual location estimations at these points. Errors in dead reckoning measurements are mainly due to noise in inertial sensors that are independent across nodes and time [8]. Thus, combining estimates from multiple nodes and propagating corrections to them improves their location estimations. Figure 2 illustrates the on-line process of determining snapshot point from radio measurements.

2.2.1 Determining Snapshot Points

The location estimation requires a node to be able to determine when it visits a location previously visited by itself or by another nodes - *a snapshot*. The snapshot point provides the opportunity to combine estimations from multiple independent mobile nodes and improve location estimations.

The system determines a snapshot point using radio fingerprints collected by mobile nodes from the self-established beacon nodes. The radio fingerprints are collected in an *online* fashion, i.e., the nodes discover fingerprints as they explore the space. These fingerprints are sent to the Base and matched with a database of previously discovered signatures. If the signature matches an existing signature in the database (decided by a cosine distance and a threshold), the point is classified as a snapshot point and a correction can be applied to the current location estimation. If the signature does not match any existing signatures, it is added to the database as a new entry.

2.2.2 Combining Estimates at Snapshot Points

The process of combining location estimations must be performed carefully. The naive approach would be to take the average of all location estimates for a particular snapshot point. However, this approach does not consider the nature of the underlying distribution of noise in location estimations that often does not follow a normal distribution especially in indoor environments.

Combining estimations is a chicken and egg problem that requires a snapshot point to estimate and update its own location from visiting mobile nodes, and subsequently, use the updated location to correct the estimates of the visiting mobile nodes.

To achieve this, we employ a particle filter based approach. A particle filter [9] is a Bayesian estimation method to estimate system state based on multiple noisy sensor measurements. We use a particle filter to track the position and orientation of each mobile node. Similarly, we use a particle filter to track the position of each snapshot point as it is discovered and visited by the MAV nodes. Every visit to a snapshot point by a mobile node results in the the mobile node *correcting* the estimation of the particles of the snapshot point, which in turn *corrects* the estimations of the particles of the mobile node. The various estimation algorithms are described in detail in Section 3.

2.3 Adaptive Path Planning

We described how a snapshot point between the paths of nodes can be utilized to improve location estimates. Planning paths is thus the second chicken and egg problem encountered in navigation. Better location estimates are needed by nodes to navigate to predetermined regions quickly. However, at the same time, achieving better location estimations may require nodes to take detours (to find snapshot points) costing time and energy. The planning component of our system seeks to make a suitable trade-off between these aspects of navigation.

2.3.1 DrunkWalk

In order to reach the goal regions, we use an indoor layout with location of walls and doors of the environment. It should be noted that the algorithm does not require high quality maps with information of the position of obstacles. Such rough maps are generally available or easy to obtain in most application scenarios.

The rough map enables us to bias the direction of node movement towards predetermined goal regions, if the current location of the node in the map can be reasonably determined. However, due to noisy sensors, the location of individual nodes cannot always be estimated correctly, which makes it difficult to consistently plan correct paths. The system attempts to solve this by operating in two modes:

- **Exploration:** In this mode, the MAV node attempts to seek snapshot points that can potentially improve the location estimates of the MAV node. This is executed when the quality of location estimations (determined by the entropy of the tracking particle filter distribution) is low.
- **Navigation:** In this mode, the MAV node attempts to follow the direction of the bias from the graph using the estimated location from the DrunkWalk algorithm. This is executed when the quality of location estimates is high.

It is easy to see that the performance of the navigation step depends on the outcome of exploration step. However, the exploration step requires extra use of resources that increases the time of navigation. Therefore, the DrunkWalk algorithm seeks to optimize this trade-off by adaptively switching between these two modes.

3. DESCRIPTION

This section provides a detailed description of the major components of our proposed system. First, this section describes how the location and orientation of the MAVs and the positions of the signatures are estimated over time using a set of particle filters. A separate particle filter is associated to each MAV in the team and each RF-signature being localized in space. Therefore, particles estimating the position and orientation of the MAVs include the components c_x, c_y, c_ϕ, whereas particles estimating the location of the signatures include components s_x, s_y for the position. As described in Section 2, a base station exchanges information with the MAVs (commands and measurements) and maintains a database of known signatures (see Figure 1). Due to the limited on-board computational power on the MAV, our current implementation performs all computations in the base.

3.1 Particle Filter Background

A particle filter is a Bayesian estimation method using a finite number of elements (so called *particles*) to represent a non-parametric probability density. It was introduced in the fifties [10] and became popular in robotics in the last two decades [9].

As a specific implementation of a more general recursive Bayes filter under the Markov assumption, it requires assumption of availability of two probabilistic models, namely the state evolution model (often called motion model in mobile or robotic applications) and the measurement model. Assuming the unknown state to be estimated at time t is indicated by x_t, the state evolution model provides

$$p(x_t|x_{t-1}, u_t) \quad (1)$$

where u_t is the known command given to the system at time t. The measurement model, instead, is given by

$$p(z_t|x_t) \quad (2)$$

where z_t is the measurement at time t. Due to the Markov assumption, x_t is conditionally independent from x_k with $k < t-1$ once x_{t-1} is known. Similarly, given x_t, the measurement z_t is conditionally independent from any other variable. Note that one does not need to commit to specific distributions in Eq. 1 and Eq. 2, e.g., they do not have to be Gaussian distributions. The generic algorithm to propagate a posterior using a particle filter is given in Algorithm 1, where we mostly follow the notation presented in [9]. The algorithm starts with a set of M particles $\mathcal{X}$ estimating the posterior of x_{t-1}, i.e., the state x at time $t-1$. Given the latest command u_t and measurement z_t, it produces a new set of M particles providing an updated posterior estimate for x at time t. The ith particle in $\mathcal{X}_t$, $x_t^{[i]}$, represents the ith possible hypothesis about the state at time t. Algorithm 1 shows the generic particle filter algorithm. The first *for* loop creates a new set of M particles sampling the motion model from the set of existing particles, while the second *for* loop implements the so-called *importance resampling*. The set of particles provides a discrete approximation for the posterior.

Data: $\mathcal{X}_{t-1}, u_t, z_t$
Result: $\mathcal{X}_t$
1 $\mathcal{X} \leftarrow \emptyset$;
2 $\mathcal{X}_t \leftarrow \emptyset$;
3 **for** $i \leftarrow 1$ **to** M **do**
4 $\quad x_t^{[i]} \leftarrow$ sample $\sim p(x_t|x_{t-1}^{[i]}, u_t)$;
5 $\quad w_t^{[i]} \leftarrow p(z_t|x_t^{[i]})$;
6 $\quad \mathcal{X} \leftarrow \mathcal{X} \cup \{< x_t^{[i]}, w_t^{[i]} >\}$;
7 **end**
8 **for** $i \leftarrow 1$ **to** M **do**
9 $\quad$ draw j with probability $\alpha\, w_t^{[j]}$;
10 $\quad \mathcal{X}_t \leftarrow \mathcal{X}_t \cup \{x_t^{[j]}\}$;
11 **end**

Algorithm 1: Generic particle filter algorithm

3.2 MAV Location Tracking

In this subsection, we show how the generic particle filter estimator can be specialized to estimate the location of the MAVs. To reduce the computational complexity, rather than implementing a centralized particle filter jointly estimating the location of all the MAVs, we associate a particle filter to each MAV. Assuming there are N_M MAVs involved in the navigation task, the system then creates and updates N_M particle filters. Each filter is initialized with $M = 100$ particles uniformly distributed in the area. All computations take place on the base station.

3.2.1 Prediction from Motion Models

For the prediction step, it is necessary to use a generative law to implement the particle creation in line 4 of Algorithm 1. To this end, we use equations similar to the ones given in [7]. Let the command at time t be $u_t = (v_t, \omega_t)$, where v_t is the translational velocity and ω_t is the rotational velocity. Note that the control system always generates commands in which only one of the two components is different from 0, i.e., the MAV either translates or rotates, but does not make both movements at the same time. Then, a new particle is generated as

$$\begin{pmatrix} c_x \\ c_y \\ c_\phi \end{pmatrix}_t^{[i]} = \begin{pmatrix} c_x \\ c_y \\ c_\phi \end{pmatrix}_{t-1}^{[i]} + \delta t \begin{pmatrix} v_t \cos(c_{\phi}{}_{t-1}^{[i]}) \\ v_t \sin(c_{\phi}{}_{t-1}^{[i]}) \\ \omega_t \end{pmatrix} \quad (3)$$

where δt is the time interval between two commands. The correctness of the equation follows form the assumption that only one of v_t and ω_t can be different from 0. Noise is added to the translational and rotational velocities as per the empirically obtained actuation noise models $p(n_v)$ and $p(n_\omega)$ from our test MAV platform, but can be specified as per the specific sensor or MAV platform used. Thus, $v_t^{[i]}$ and $\omega_t^{[i]}$ are obtained as:

$$v_t^{[i]} = v_t + n_v^{[i]}\ ,\ n_v^{[i]}\ is\ drawn\ from\ p(n_v) \quad (4)$$

$$\omega_t^{[i]} = \omega_t + n_\omega^{[i]}\ ,\ n_\omega^{[i]}\ is\ drawn\ from\ p(n_\omega) \quad (5)$$

where v_t and ω_t are the nominal commands. In our simulations, according to [7], $p(n_v)$ and $p(n_\omega)$ are specified as normal distributions with $\mu = 0$ and σ is expressed as a percentage of the value of v_t or ω_t.

3.2.2 Correction from Measurements

The correction step hinges on the weights assigned to the particles (line 5 in Algorithm 1). Each MAV is equipped with a magnetometer sensor returning a measurement for its heading. Moreover, RF-signature snapshot provides another measurement. These two measurements are asynchronous in the sense that, while the on-board heading sensor can be queried after each command is executed, signature matching occurs only when revisiting a location associated with a known signature. In the following, we therefore separately describe, how the two different weights are computed, given that they are generated and used (via resampling) in separate stages.

The heading measurement is straightforward to integrate. According to former experimental measures [11], the nominal heading returned by the sensor is affected by Gaussian noise with a known variance σ^2 ($\sigma = 40$ degrees to be precise). Therefore, for the heading weight we set

$$p(z_t|x_t) = f_{\mathcal{N},\sigma^2}(z_t - c_{\phi}{}_t^{[i]}) \quad (6)$$

where $f_{\mathcal{N},\sigma^2}$ is the density probability of a Gaussian with 0 mean and variance σ^2, and the argument $z_t - c_{\phi}{}_t^{[i]}$ is normalized to account for the 2π period.

The process is substantially different for RF-signature snapshot points. In this case, rather than computing $p(z_t|x_t)$, we determine $w_t^{[i]}$ through a two steps process. 1) When a signature is measured, the first step is to communicate with the known signatures database to determine whether the signature is new or has been encountered already (either by the same MAVs or a different one). If the database determines the signature is new, the MAV does not perform the second step and does not compute weights (however, the signature is stored in the database and a new particle filter is created; see section 3.3 for details.) 2) On the contrary, if the database determines that a signature snapshot points is taking place, the second step starts. First, on the database side, the particle filter estimating the position of the signature being revisited is updated (see section 3.3 for details.) After the RF-signature particle filter has been updated, each particle in the MAV particle filter is assigned a weight as follows. A GMM is created starting from the particles in the signature being matched. Such GMM is a bidimensional probability density function with the following equation:

$$f_{GMM}(x, y) = \frac{1}{M}\sum_{i=1}^{M} f_{\mathcal{N},\Sigma}^{i}(x, y) \quad (7)$$

where $f_{\mathcal{N},\Sigma}^{i}$ is a bidimensional Gaussian distribution with mean $\mu = [s_x^{[i]}\ s_y^{[i]}]^T$ and covariance matrix Σ (a diagonal matrix with value 2 on the main diagonal). Then, each particle is assigned the weight

$$w_t^{[i]} \leftarrow f_{GMM}(c_{x}{}_t^{[i]}, c_{y}{}_t^{[i]}). \quad (8)$$

After all weights have been computed, resampling can take place as described in Algorithm 1.

3.2.3 Adding Particles Using Coarse Map

Due to the unavoidable errors in the estimation process, we implemented an additional step to counter the formerly mentioned particle depletion problem. After the new set $\mathcal{X}_t$ has been created, we determine the location with the highest number of particles. Let v_d be this location, and let N be the set of neighbor nodes according to the coarse map. Then, the 25 particles with the lowest weight are discarded and replaced by an equal number of particles generated using a random distribution over the space associated with the nodes in N. The rationale behind this step is to generate particles to recover errors due to the erroneous determination that a transition from a room to the next effectively took place.

3.3 Particle Filter for Snapshot Points

We now describe how the spatial location of the signatures can be estimated using a set of particle filters. For the MAVs case, we do not compute a centralized estimation, but we rather associate a filter with each signature to be tracked. This estimation process has two main differences with the position and orientation estimation for the MAVs. First, the number of signature locations to be estimated is not known upfront. So new filters need to be created on-the-fly when a new signature to be localized is identified. Second, signatures do not move. Therefore the estimation process does not include a prediction step, only a correction step. As for the MAVs, each filter includes 100 particles.

3.3.1 Initialization from MAV Particles

As described in the previous subsection, a new signature is generated when the known signatures database receives a query from one of the MAVs with an RF-signature that cannot be matched to any of the formerly discovered ones. In this case, a new entry in the database is created and a new particles filter is instantiated. The initial set of particles for this new filter is copied from the particles of the vehicle that discovered the feature, while discarding the component related to heading because it is irrelevant for the signature estimation process.

3.3.2 Correction from MAV Particle Filter

Correction happens when a MAV queries signature database with a signature that can be matched with one of the entries already discovered. In this case, Algorithm 1 is executed for the signature filter, with the exception of line 4, because no prediction takes place. The weight for $w_t^{[i]}$ for the ith particle is computed as follows. First, the position of the MAV that generated the snapshot point is determined by taking the average of its particles. Note that this average is implicitly weighted, because through the resampling process, particles with higher weight will be included more often in the particle set (see line 9 in Algorithm 1). As a result, they will be counted multiple times when computing the average. Let $\overline{x}$ be the computed average position of the MAV generating the match, and let $s_{t-1}^{[i]}$ be the position of the ith particle in the signature particle filter at time $t-1$, and let $d_i = \left\| \overline{x} - s_{t-1}^{[i]} \right\|_2$ be the Euclidean distance between the expected position of the MAV and the particle. The weight of each particle at time t is then defined as

$$w_t^{[i]} = F_{d,\delta}(d+K) - F_{d,\delta}(d-K) \tag{9}$$

where $F_{d,\delta}$ is the cumulative density function of a Gaussian distribution with mean d and variance δ. This formula is based on our experimental testbed showing that revisits are correctly detected when the displacement between the original and the new position is within K meters. The specific values for δ and K depend on the number of anchors and are further described in Section 4.5.3. Once weights have been computed, correction for the estimate of the signature particle filter can then take place through resampling, as described in Algorithm 1.

3.3.3 Database of Fingerprints

In order to help location estimation correction with snapshot points after each movement, the system maintains a database of fingerprints. A fingerprint at a specific location is a set of RSSI values from different stationary nodes measured by the MAV and stored in a dictionary data structure. When the node arrives at a new location, it calculates the cosine similarity between the newly discovered fingerprint and the fingerprints stored in the database. A pre-defined threshold T_{sig} is used to decide whether it is a new or known fingerprint.

3.4 DrunkWalk Planning

In this section, we describe how the system plans the paths of MAV nodes with location estimates of varying quality in order to deploy quickly. Figure 3 shows a flowchart of the planning algorithm.

3.4.1 Coarse Map

The system uses the layout with location of walls and doors of the environment to extract a coarse map. The doors are usually selected as the destination where we navigate the MAVs.

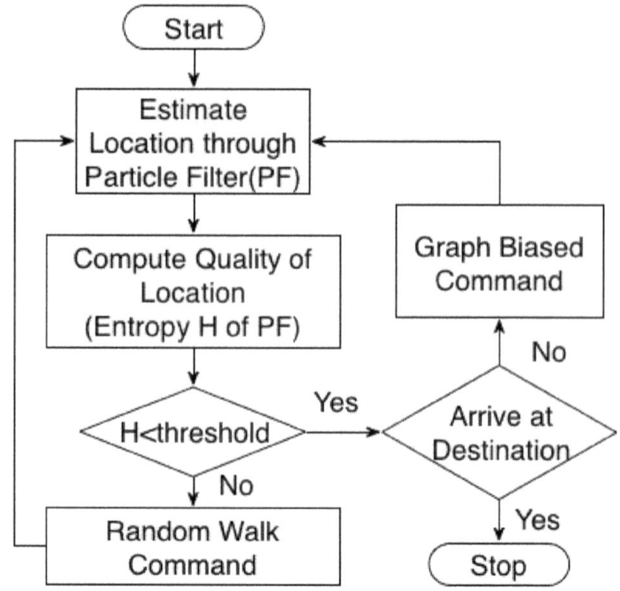

Figure 3: The figure shows the flowchart of the DrunkWalk planning algorithm. The planner adaptively changes between random walk and graph biased movement based on the entropy of particle filters tracking respective MAV nodes.

The coarse map makes very few assumptions about the quality of the map but provides a way to bias the motion of MAV nodes towards designated locations.

3.4.2 Entropy as Quality of Location Estimates

The entropy of a random variable x can be defined as the expected information that the value of x carries. In the discrete case, it is given by

$$H(x) = E[-\log_2 p(x)] \tag{10}$$

which represents the number of bits required to encode using an optimal encoding, assuming that $p(x)$ is the probability of observing x. The entropy can therefore be used as an indication of the uncertainty of the estimate of a particle filter. The lower the entropy the better the certainty of the location estimate is, and vice versa. For the particle filter, we calculate the entropy [9] of the weights at time t as

$$H_t = -\sum_{i=1}^{M} w_t^{[i]} \log_2 w_t^{[i]}. \tag{11}$$

3.4.3 Exploration

When the entropy of the particle filter is high (> threshold T_H), the system seeks to primarily improve the location estimates. The intuition here is that with an incorrect estimation of current location, using the bias from the graph is likely to be incorrect. This also results in cases where the

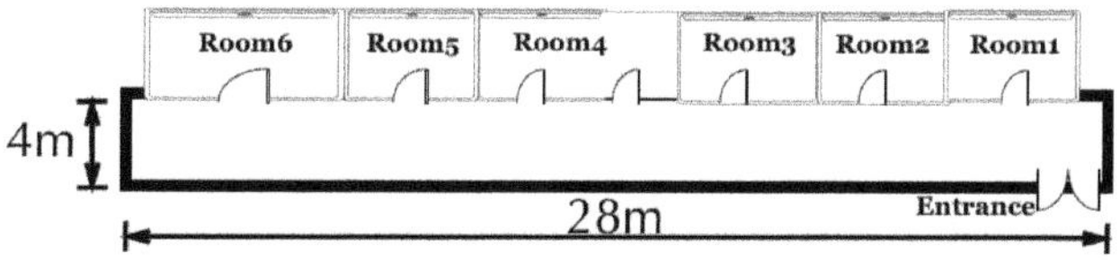

Figure 4: The figure shows the floor plan of 6 rooms with a hallway used for physical feature based simulation and real testbed experiments. The MAVs start from the entrance of the building and are navigated to different goal areas.

MAV may get stuck and can potentially perform worse than a purely random deployment strategy.

With this in mind, the planner employs a random walk strategy to direct the motion of MAV nodes. With random walk, the likelihood of nodes discovering snapshot points increases and so does the likelihood of improving their location estimates. This is referred to as the exploration step.

3.4.4 Navigation

Correspondingly, when the uncertainty of location estimates is low ($H_t < T_H$), the planner commands the nodes to follow the bias indicated by the coarse map. With a more accurate location, likelihood of nodes following the bias and then reaching the intended destination increases.

A key point in choosing the directional bias from the graph is that it is sampled based on the distribution of particles in the node's particle filter. For example, consider a node with 20 particles indicating its position as room 1 and therefore requiring the node to go north-west to exit the room, while 80 particles indicate the node is in room 2 and must move south. In this case, the planner samples the movement direction according to the distribution of particles over the nodes of the graph, i.e., the node has a 20% chance of being commanded to move north-west and a 80% chance of receiving a south command.

3.4.5 Collision Recovery Strategy

MAV platforms have very limited sensing capability and often do not employ sophisticated obstacle detection sensors. Proposed MAV platforms [1] rely on their low weight and often use collisions themselves to discover obstacles. However, a strategy is needed in dealing with collision so as to prevent MAV nodes from being stuck and enable them to back off from corners and crevices and seek out openings. This is especially useful when location estimates are inaccurate. The planner employs a random exponential back-off strategy, where nodes move in randomly chosen direction (uniformly from a discrete number of directions) for a time duration that increases exponentially with the number of recent collisions. This is implemented by keeping a counter for collisions in a certain time-window. The counter is decremented with time if no new collisions are encountered.

4. EVALUATION

In this section, we evaluate the performance of our system in planning MAVs paths through physical feature based simulation and real experiments on a MAV testbed. Both simulation and real experiments are conducted in a building with

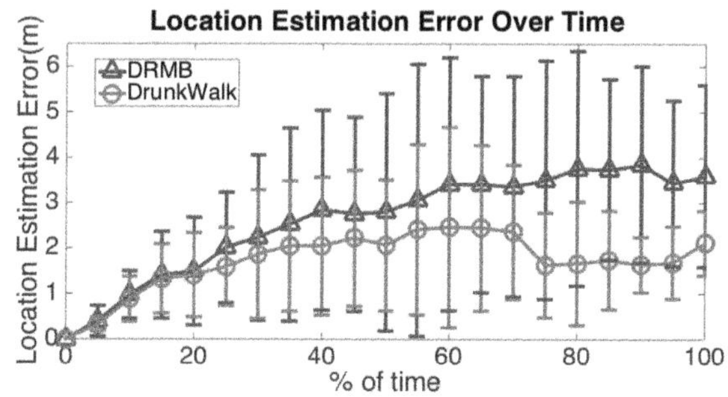

Figure 5: The figure shows the average and standard deviation of location estimation errors at different flying duration heading for the near destination using DrunkWalk and DRMB from 5 experiments. Drunkwalk achieves around 2m location estimation errors on average and 1-1.5m standard deviation.

multiple rooms connected with a hallway as shown in Figure 4. The MAVs start from the entrance and are navigated to different goal areas (rooms).

The evaluation focuses on the following aspects:

- Characterizing the performance of the system in terms of 1) navigation duration and 2) average accuracy of location estimations in comparison to existing navigation approach.
- Testing the robustness of the system with changing parameters, such as number of stationary MAV nodes, noise of sensors, and radio fingerprint accuracy.
- Validating the assumptions of the simulation experiments through real MAV testbed experiments.

For both testbed experiments and simulation, we compare our DrunkWalk algorithm to another online navigation strategy that does not require any location infrastructure. We briefly describe it below:

- **Dead-Reckoning with Map Bias (DRMB):** Dead-reckoning with Map Bias is an infrastructure-free technique used to estimate a node's location in unknown environments [12]. This method uses measurements from motion sensors, optical flow and gyroscope, to estimate the change in position of the node. Having an estimate of location, we then use the map to bias the direction of the node's movement similar to DrunkWalk.

4.1 Testbed Experiment Setup

To validate our system in a realistic setting, we implement our algorithm on a server and the SensorFly [1] [13] MAV testbed. The SensorFly platform used in our test has an 8-bit 16Mhz AVR AtMega128rfa1 micro-controller, a 3-axis accelerometer, a 3-axis gyroscope, a 2-axis optical flow velocity sensor, a 3-axis magnetometers, a ultrasonic altitude sensor and a XBee radio [14]. The platform has a flight time of 6-10 minutes. The SensorFly nodes are capable of translational and rotational motion directed by on-board PID control algorithms utilizing feedback from the on-board sensors.

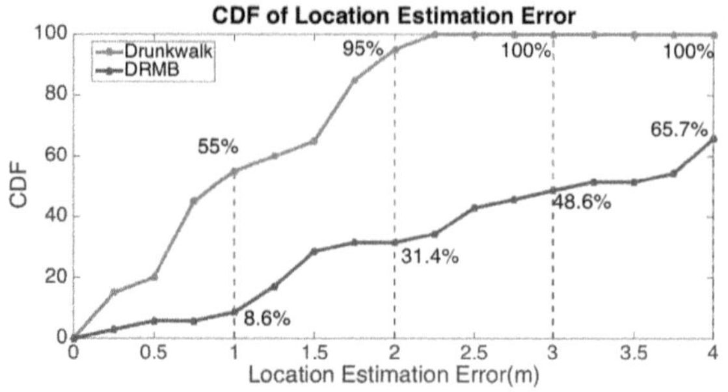

Figure 6: The figure shows the cumulative distribution function (CDF) of location estimation errors to arrive at near destination using both DrunkWalk and DRMB from a typical run.

In our setup, we manually fly 8 MAVs on a $4m \times 28m$ arena shown in Figure 4. Six nodes are allowed to disperse and deploy as beacons at initialization, while 2 nodes fly to seek out the destinations. The nodes are introduced to the rooms at the entrance and navigated to 3 kinds of goal destinations: near destination (room 2), medium destination (right door of room 4) and far destination (room 5). In addition, a laser range finder is used to track the location of the nodes as ground truth.

4.2 Testbed Experiment Results

We utilize the MAV testbed to illustrate the location estimation errors from short to long distances to compare performances and robustness of DrunkWalk with that of DRMB.

Figure 5 compares the performance and robustness of DrunkWalk and DRMB at different phases of navigation duration. We plot the average and standard deviation of location estimation errors from 5 experiments at different % of navigation duration. It is noted that we stop the experiments at 600 seconds even if the drones do not arrive at the destination since this is the typical flying time of SensorFly node. At the first 20% of the navigation duration, DrunkWalk performs similarly as DRMB due to lack of snapshot points to correct location estimation errors. After this initial period, DrunkWalk's snapshot point correction maintained location estimation errors within the range of 1.5m to 2m. In contrast, the error of DRMB kept accumulating to larger than 3m. This is because multiple measurements at snapshot points can correct the location estimation errors in DrunkWalk. In addition, after 30% of the navigation time, the standard deviation of DrunkWalk location estimation is also 30% – 60% smaller than DRMB approach. This shows DrunkWalk is more reliable than DRMB.

Figure 6 shows cumulative distribution function (CDF) of location estimation errors using DrunkWalk and DRMB from a typical experiment. In DrunkWalk, corrections from snapshot points help keep errors within 2.5 meters. In comparison, location estimation error of DRMB remains unbounded. More than 50% of the time, DRMB has more than 3 meters error, compared to less than 1 meter error for DrunkWalk.

To illustrate the performance of DrunkWalk and DRMB for medium and far destinations, we use Figures 7 and 8 to show single run experiment results. We further evaluate them through simulated results in section 4.3. Note that

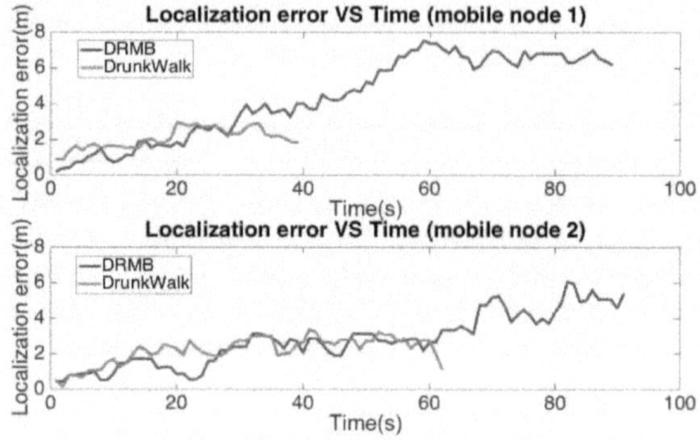

Figure 7: The figure shows the location estimation error over time using DrunkWalk and DRMB to the medium destinations. Mobile nodes with DrunkWalk arrive at the destination earlier than those with DRMB due to their capability to limit the location estimation errors.

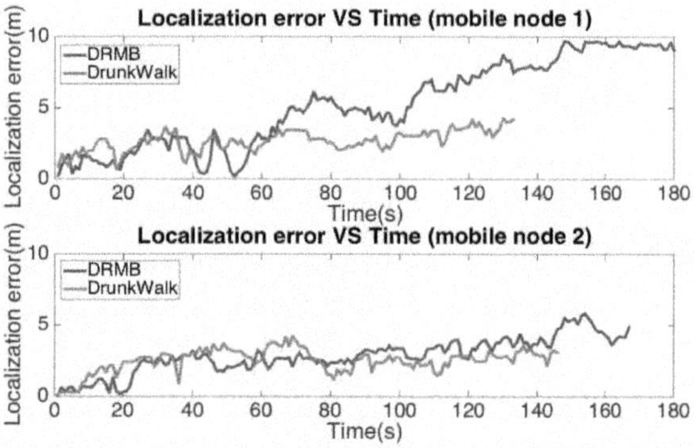

Figure 8: The figure shows the location estimation error over time using DrunkWalk and DRMB to the far destinations. It is noted that we do not plot all the data for mobile node 1 since it fails to arrive at the destination before the battery was exhausted (600 seconds).

besides the node using DRMB in the upper plot in Figure 8, the lines end when nodes reach their destination. The mobile node 1 failed to arrive at the far destination before 600 seconds when the battery was exhausted.

For both medium and far destinations, in the first 20 seconds, similar to navigation to near destination, DrunkWalk has similar location estimation errors with DRMB. After this initial period, adequate snapshot points help DrunkWalk to limit the location estimation errors while the error of DRMB keeps accumulating. This shows that multiple measurements at snapshot points in DrunkWalk do help limit location estimation errors. The higher location estimation accuracy from DrunkWalk leads to shorter (around 50%) navigation duration. It should be also noted that when using DRMB, mobile node 1 fails to arrive at the far destination before the battery died (600 seconds) while mobile node 2 arrives at the destination in around 170 seconds. This shows the unreliability of DRMB. On the other hand, both mobile node 1 and 2 with DrunkWalk arrive at the medium and far destination within similar durations. This shows the stability of DrunkWalk with the help of snapshot points.

4.3 Physical Feature Based Simulation Environment

We implemented a MAV simulation environment [15] for the SensorFly MAV indoor sensor swarm to evaluate our planning algorithms at large scale. The simulator includes a realistic physical arena, as well as sensor noise models, MAV mobility models and indoor radio signature collected from the testbed described earlier.

For our evaluations, we configure the simulator as follows:

- **Arena** – We use a multi-room indoor scenario shown in Figure 4, where nodes are required to autonomously navigate to different goal areas. We collect the radio fingerprint from the real arena and feed them into the simulation platform to evaluate our system. This represents a typical indoor apartment scenario where such systems may be deployed in search and rescue applications. For more complex maps, we concatenate on portions of the map in figure 4.
- **Node Sensors** – The sensor nodes in the simulation are modeled after the SensorFly [1] MAV platform, which is also used in our testbed experiments described in section 4.1. Each node has a XBee 802.15.4 radio and Dead-Reckoning sensors – a gyroscope, an optical flow velocity sensor and an ultrasonic altitude measurement sensor. Noise models are obtained through empirical measurements on the testbed MAV platform.
- **Node Mobility** – The MAV nodes can turn by a commanded angle and move for a commanded time and velocity. We set the velocity to 1.0 m/s in accordance with the testbed MAV parameters. The velocity of course varies in accordance with the noisiness of the optical flow sensor, that provides feedback to each MAV's control algorithm.
- **Simulation Time-steps** – The simulation time-step is chosen as $1sec$ that enables nodes to cover a distance of $0.8m$ to $1.2m$ in one simulation tick.
- **Radio** – The simulation supports estimating received signal strength (RSS) measurements between two nodes. The RSS is collected in the real scenario.
- **Destination** – We adopt the far destination (room 6) as the destination for simulation since this is the hardest situation which shows the baseline of the system performance and robustness.

All experiments were performed 25 times with 10 MAVs (6 stationary nodes and 4 mobile nodes) to evaluate both the performance and robustness of the system. We run the simulation for a time period of 600 seconds ($\tilde{1}0$ minutes) corresponding to the typical battery life of current generation MAV nodes.

4.4 System Performance

This section evaluates our system performance under different destination constraints and time limitations. A successful navigation is achieved when the node can be navigated to the destination within the given accuracy and time limitation. For example, if the destination coordinate is (4 meters, 5 meters), the required accuracy is 1 meter and time limit is 90 seconds, a successful navigation means that the mobile node can arrive within the range of 1 meter from (4 meters, 5 meters) within 90 seconds.

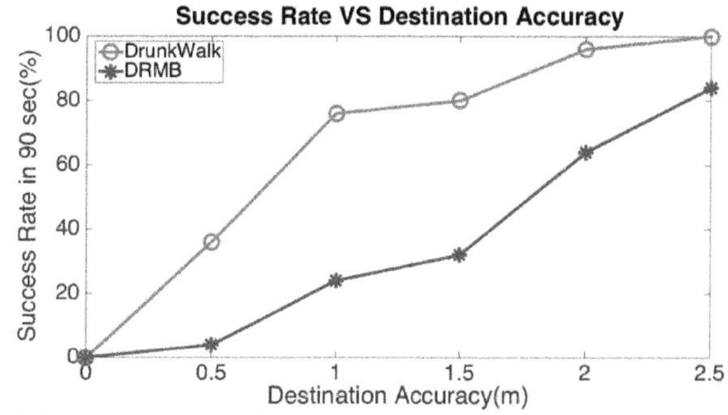

Figure 9: The figure shows the navigation success rate under different destination accuracy constraints within 90 seconds for DrunkWalk and DRMB.

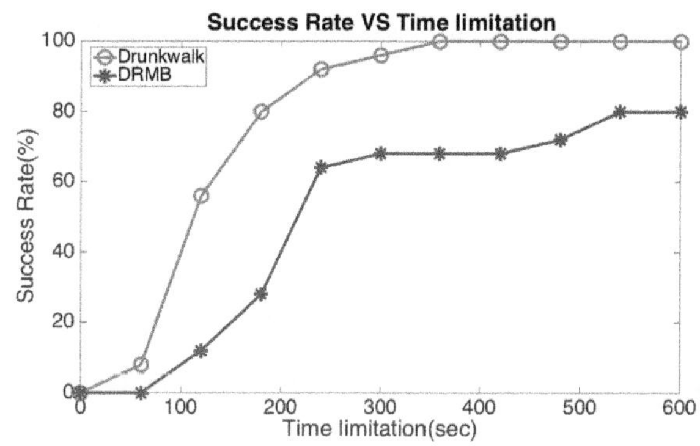

Figure 10: The figure shows the success rate as a function of time limitation under 0.5m destination accuracy constraint, using DrunkWalk and DRMB alone.

Figure 9 shows the navigation success rate as a function of destination accuracy constraints within 90 seconds using DrunkWalk and DRMB. When the destination accuracy is strict (0.5 meter), DrunkWalk achieves acceptable success rate of around 40% while DRMB shows less than 5%. This means that, under very strict destination accuracy constraint, DRMB cannot achieve the accuracy within the time limitation. while DrunkWalk can still work with the help of snapshot points. For less constrained destination accuracy (1 meter to 2 meters), DrunkWalk shows consistently 30% to 40% higher success rate than DRMB. Futhermore, DrunkWalk achieves 100% success rate for even looser destination accuracy constraint (2.5m) while DRMB can also get 84% success rate. This is expected since above 2.5 meter range is more than one half of the hallway width (4.0 meters), where even with high location estimation errors, the mobile node can still arrive at the destinations simply by following the walls.

Figure 10 plots the success rate as a function of time limitation for both DrunkWalk and DRMB under a 0.5m destination accuracy constraint. Under a strict time limitation constraint (60 seconds), even DrunkWalk only achieved 8% success rate since it is not able to get enough snapshot points to get accurate location estimation on the way to the destination. When the time limitations are released (120 seconds to 300 seconds), DrunkWalk shows 30% to 50% higher success rate than DRMB. This is because DrunkWalk has enough time to get snapshot points to correct the location

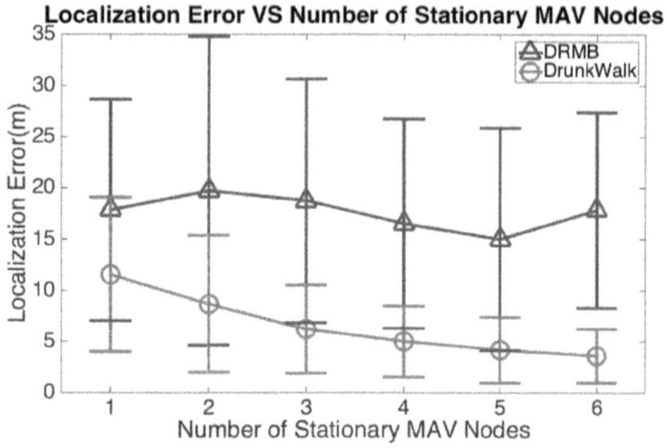

Figure 11: The figure shows the location estimation error with varying number of stationary MAV nodes using DrunkWalk and DRMB. DrunkWalk has an obvious decreasing trend when the number of stationary MAV nodes increases. It is noted that DRMB does not use stationary MAV and its performance variance in the figure is due to noise from sensors.

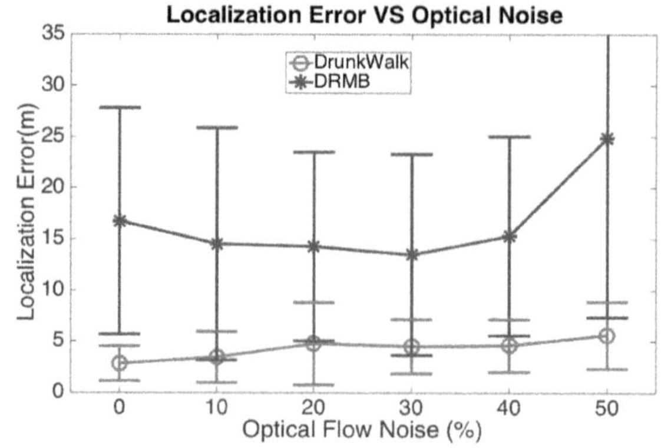

Figure 12: The figure shows location estimation error as a function of optical flow noise using DrunkWalk estimation and DRMB alone. The noise per sensor is modeled as a normal distribution with varying standard deviation. The plot shows that DrunkWalk is able to correct the DRMB error and maintain low standard deviation.

estimation errors, while the error of DRMB keeps accumulating. After 300 seconds, DrunkWalk achieves 100% success rate, while the success rate of DRMB becomes stable yet still below 80%. This means that even with loose time constraints, DrunkWalk still gets more than 20% higher success rate than DRMB.

4.5 System Robustness

In this section, we evaluate the robustness of our system by examining the location estimation errors under different system setups of both DrunkWalk and DRMB.

4.5.1 Number of Stationary MAV Nodes

Figure 11 shows the location estimation errors for different numbers of stationary MAV nodes, where Drunkwalk achieves 1.5× to 6× reduction for average and 1.5× to 4× reduction for standard deviation compared to DRMB. This shows its better capability and reliability to limit location estimation error. This can be attributed to improvement on matching snapshot with larger number of stationary nodes broadcasting beacons. We can also see the decreasing trend for both average and standard deviation in Drunkwalk when the number of stationary nodes increase, which means that increasing the number of stationary nodes do help enhance performance.

4.5.2 Navigational Sensor Noise

The noise in motion measurements due to Dead-Reckoning sensors is an important parameter in determining the eventual performance of the algorithm. Different MAV platforms and operating environments might have different amount of noise in their motion measurements, making it useful to analyze the performance of the algorithm for varying levels of sensor noise. For our simulations, in agreement with empirical measurements on our MAV platform, we model noise as a normal distribution with a standard deviation proportional to the sensor measurement [7], [11]. For the optical flow velocity sensor, a noise corresponding to a normal distribution with 0 mean and standard deviation of 20% of the measured velocity value was added. For the magnetometer,

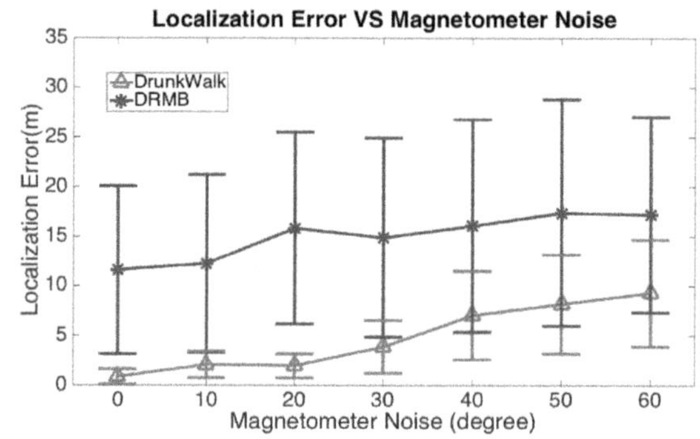

Figure 13: The figure shows location estimation error as a function of magnetometer noise using DrunkWalk estimation and dead reckoning alone. The noise per sensor is modeled as a normal distribution with varying standard deviation. The plot shows that DrunkWalk is able to correct the DRMB error and maintain low standard deviation.

a 30° noise corresponds to a normal distribution with 0° mean and standard deviation of 30°. The resultant noise in DRMB location can be computed as per the motion update equation [7], [11]. We apply sensor noise to both DRMB and DrunkWalk estimates.

Figure 12 and 13 show the location estimation error in DRMB and DrunkWalk for 10 nodes at various sensor noise levels. In Figure 12, with optical flow noise level increasing from 0 to 50%, the average location estimation error of DrunkWalk increases from 2.5m - 5.5m while that of DRMB goes up very quickly to around 25 meters. The error increase is limited due to the corrections from the multiple measurements at the same snapshot points. In Figure 13, a faster increasing trend (from 0.5 to 7.5 meters) is observed with the magnetometer noise increase. In addition, similar increasing trends are observed for both DrunkWalk and DRMB. This indicates that high noise from magnetometer weakens the correction capability on location estimation errors. However, during

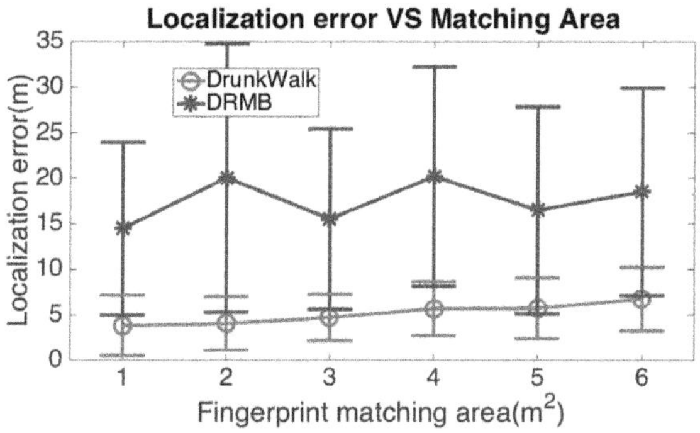

Figure 14: The figure shows location estimation error as a function of signature matching area for DrunkWalk and DRMB. To be noticed, DRMB does not work with stationary MAV and noise from sensors cause the performance variance.

operation, raw magnetometer noise can be mitigated by gyroscope data.

4.5.3 Radio Fingerprint Accuracy

Location estimation error depends on the resolution to identify snapshot on the node paths. This is accomplished by using radio signature from stationary MAV nodes deployed at the beginning. When a radio signature collected by a node at a certain location is similar to a fingerprint in the database, the system classifies it as snapshot and performs the correction of location estimates. Thus, the performance of DrunkWalk depends on the resolution of the fingerprints matching, i.e., the area or distance within which two radio fingerprints can be reliably classified as being at the same location. If the criteria is too loose, incorrect points may be matched together, which leads to few snapshot points.

Figure 14 shows location estimation error as a function of signature matching area for DrunkWalk and DRMB for 10 nodes. We observe that DrunkWalk offers an improvement of over 3× compared to DRMB even for a poor matching resolution of $6m^2$. In case of MAV navigation, where the low-cost of nodes makes it possible to deploy a relatively large number of beacon nodes and attain high fingerprint accuracies of around $1m^2$, DrunkWalk provides a much larger reduction in error.

5. DISCUSSION

Several aspects of DrunkWalk planning algorithm warrant further discussion and could probably lead to extensions to DrunkWalk.

5.1 Parameter Tuning

We now describe how some key parameters affect the system performance and give some guidance on tuning them.

We model all the sensor and noise distributions according to real tests either by ourselves or from related work [7], [11]. After we got these values, we use them in our simulation platform and the real system.

The signature matching resolution is affected by four parameters: number of stationary nodes, K and δ in Equation 9, and T_{sig} in section 3.3.3. Just as trilateration [16], we need at least 3 stationary nodes to estimate x and y location. However, due to the noise from radios, we need more stationary beacons. In our experiments, we found 6 seems to give good results. In order to tune K and δ in Equation 9 and the threshold T_{sig} for matching signatures, we refer to our previous work [7]. After we decide the value of K, we should set up the sample rate for snapshot points higher than K/2 per sample according to the Nyquist-Shannon sampling theorem [17] to ensure recover the radio map.

Another parameter, T_H in section 3.4.3 affects the adaptive planning strategy. The range of entropy is from 0 to log(N), where N is the number of particles. How we set T_H depends on how we hope to bias our planning strategy. If we set T_H close to 0, that means we bias more to random walk. If we set the T_H close to log(N), that means we prefer to trusting the location estimation more and bias more to follow the coarse map.

Moreover, the reader can refer to [18] for guidance to set up the number of particles . In our system, we adopt 100 particles for both motion tracking and snapshot points.

5.2 Different Layout Geometry

DrunkWalk can deal with more complicated layout geometry and should achieve similar performance, although it is only tested and simulated in a layout shown in Figure 4. The multiple rooms connected with a hallway in Figure 4 can be decomposed into basic unit for complicated layout geometry. For a different layout geometry, we can regard it as a concatenation of these basic units and set up a series of intermediate destinations to help the drones arrive at the final destinations. E.g. for those multiple interconnected rooms with no hall layout, it is similar to the situation with only room 1, room 2 and the hallway in Figure 4. In this case, we regard the hallway as a loose room interconnected with room 1 and room 2. In addition, by sensing the sudden change in altitude and using a floor altitude look-up table, DrunkWalk could also deal with multiple floor conditions.

5.3 Message Overhead

In our system, message overhead is composed of three parts: 1) Stationary drones broadcasting messages to flying drones for RSSI measurements takes 1 bytes for each message. Each stationary drones broadcast messages 10 times per second. 2) Flying drones report the RSSI values, heading information and some other status information to the server every second. The corresponding message size is 20 bytes for each flying drone. 3) The link from server sending different command messages to different flying drones every second. The overhead of the command message takes 14 bytes. In real systems, due to the collision, the real overhead is often higher than the above value.

6. RELATED WORK

Works related to DrunkWalk maily fall into three domains: sensor networks, robotics and mobile computing.

The sensor network domain has a number of works on deploying and navigating mobile sensors [19, 20, 21, 22]. Howard et al. [23, 24] present techniques for mobile sensor network deployment in an unknown environment. Their approach constructs fields such that each node is repelled by both obstacles and by other nodes, enabling the network to spread itself throughout the environment. Similarly, Batalin et al. [25] present a deployment algorithm for robot teams without access to maps or location. The robots are assumed to be equipped with vision sensors and range finders and select a direction away from all their immediate sensed neighbors and move in that direction. The algorithm does not require communication between nodes but also does not allow nodes to be deployed at designated locations. The domain experts have no control over the emergent deployment locations of the nodes.

The problem addressed in this paper can also be seen as an instance of the Simultaneous Localization And Mapping (SLAM) problem that has been extensively studied in the area of robotics [9, 26, 27, 28]. In fact, in the system we described multiple MAVs try to localize themselves while at the same time trying to acquire a representation of the spatial distribution of the radio signatures. In recent years there have been copious research in SLAM using either methods based on Kalman filters [29, 30, 31, 32] or particle filters [33, 34, 35, 36]. Both approaches, however, have been mostly applied to solve instance of the SLAM problem where mobile agents are equipped with sensors returning distances (e.g., laser range finders, or sonars) or cameras (either monocular or stereo). Therefore, the ultimate objective of these solutions to the SLAM problem was to map physical entities located in the environment, like walls, obstacles, etc. Methods based on Kalman filters are not applicable for the scenario we consider because we are dealing with multimodal, nonparametric probability distributions. Therefore, we opt for a solution based on particle filters.

Approaches based on explicit perception and processing of radio signals have been mostly aimed at implementing localization systems with the underlying assumption that radio signals were preliminarily collected off line to build so-called *map signals* [37, 38, 39, 40]. A recent paper by Twigg et al. [41] discusses a system where a robot autonomously discovers the area within which connectivity with an assigned WiFi base station is ensured. Their solution, however, solves only the mapping side of the problem because the robot is equipped with a laser range finder solving the localization problem. In other words, RSS readings are mapped to the physical space exploiting the availability of a different sensor providing reliable localization.

For people carrying mobile devices, SLAM-like approaches have recently been proposed that fuse WiFi-based RSS and motion sensor data to simultaneously build a sensor map of the environment and locate the user within this map. e.g. radio fingerprint maps [42, 43, 44, 45], or organic landmark maps [46, 47]. These approaches focus on the location estimation part of an orthogonal problem, where the motion of users cannot be controlled and hence, does not involve motion planning or deployment. Purohit et al. [7] present a system for infrastructure-free single room *sweep* coverage with MAV sensor swarms. Their approach, however, does not involve the concept of location estimation and navigation and does not support navigating nodes to pre-assigned destinations.

To the best of our knowledge, this paper presents the first attempt to solve a SLAM problem using a swarm of MAVs that combines location estimation and adaptively planning to improve the success rate and accuracy of navigation.

7. CONCLUSION

This paper presents a system for collaborative and adaptive planning of resource-constrained MAV sensing swarms to quickly and efficiently navigate to preassigned locations. The system uses collaboration between nodes of the swarm to overcome the sensing and computational limitations of MAV nodes, and the challenging operating environments. We comprehensively evaluate the system through large-scale simulations and real MAV testbed experiments showing that DrunkWalk achieves up to 6× reduction in location estimation errors, and as much as 3× improvement in navigation success rate under the given time and accuracy constraints.

8. ACKNOWLEDGEMENTS

We would like to thank our shepherd Prof. Akos Ledeczi and the anonymous reviewers for their insightful and constructive comments. This research was supported by Intel, Nokia, NSF under the grant CNS1135874 and CNS1149611, and DARPA under the grant D11AP00265. The 4th author Stefano Carpin is partially supported by the Army Research Lab under contract MAST-CNC-15-4-4. Any opinions, findings, and conclusions or recommendations expressed in these materials are those of the author and should not be interpreted as representing the official policies, either expressly or implied, of the funding agencies of the U.S. Government.

9. REFERENCES

[1] A Purohit, Zheng Sun, F Mokaya, and Pei Zhang. SensorFly: Controlled-mobile sensing platform for indoor emergency response applications. In *Proceeding of the 10th International Conference on Information Processing in Sensor Networks (IPSN)*, pages 223–234, 2011.

[2] Robert J. Wood. The First Takeoff of a Biologically Inspired At-Scale Robotic Insect. *IEEE transactions on robotics*, 24(2):341–347, 2008.

[3] Karthik Dantu, Bryan Kate, Jason Waterman, Peter Bailis, and Matt Welsh. Programming micro-aerial vehicle swarms with karma. In *Proceedings of the 9th ACM Conference on Embedded Networked Sensor Systems*, SenSys '11, pages 121–134, New York, NY, USA, 2011. ACM.

[4] Matthew Turpin, Nathan Michael, and Vijay Kumar. Trajectory design and control for aggressive formation flight with quadrotors. *Autonomous Robots*, 33(1-2):143–156, February 2012.

[5] S. Shen, N. Michael, and V. Kumar. Vision-based autonomous navigation in complex environments with a quadrotor. In *iros*, Tokyo, Japan, nov 2013.

[6] Ryan Morlok and Maria Gini. Dispersing robots in an unknown environment. In *7th International Symposium on Distributed Autonomous Robotic Systems (DARS)*, 2004.

[7] Aveek Purohit, Zheng Sun, and Pei Zhang. Sugarmap: Location-less coverage for micro-aerial sensing swarms. In *Proceedings of the 12th International Conference on*

Information Processing in Sensor Networks, IPSN '13, pages 253–264, New York, NY, USA, 2013. ACM.

[8] I. Constandache, R.R. Choudhury, and I. Rhee. Towards mobile phone localization without war-driving. In *INFOCOM, 2010 Proceedings IEEE*, pages 1–9, 2010.

[9] S. Thrun, W. Burgard, and D. Fox. *Probabilistic Robotics*. MIT Press, 2006.

[10] A. Doucet, J.F.G. de Freitas, and N.J. Gordon, editors. *Sequential Monte Carlo methods in practice*. Springer-Verlag, 2001.

[11] Zheng Sun, Aveek Purohit, Shijia Pan, Frank Mokaya, Raja Bose, and Pei Zhang. Polaris: Getting accurate indoor orientations for mobile devices using ubiquitous visual patterns on ceilings. In *Proceedings of the Twelfth Workshop on Mobile Computing Systems & Applications*, HotMobile '12, pages 14:1–14:6, New York, NY, USA, 2012. ACM.

[12] Johann Borenstein, Liqiang Feng, and H. R. Everett. *Navigating Mobile Robots: Systems and Techniques*. A. K. Peters, Ltd., Natick, MA, USA, 1996.

[13] Aveek Purohit, Pei Zhang, Brian M Sadler, and Stefano Carpin. Deployment of swarms of micro-aerial vehicles: from theory to practice. In *Robotics and Automation (ICRA), 2014 IEEE International Conference on*, pages 5408–5413. IEEE, 2014.

[14] Digi International. XBee Multipoint RF Modules Datasheet, 2009.

[15] A Purohit and Pei Zhang. Controlled-mobile sensing simulator for indoor fire monitoring. In *Wireless Communications and Mobile Computing Conference (IWCMC), 2011 7th International*, pages 1124–1129, 2011.

[16] Dimitris E Manolakis. Efficient solution and performance analysis of 3-d position estimation by trilateration. *Aerospace and Electronic Systems, IEEE Transactions on*, 32(4):1239–1248, 1996.

[17] Abdul J Jerri. The shannon sampling theorem: Its various extensions and applications: A tutorial review. *Proceedings of the IEEE*, 65(11):1565–1596, 1977.

[18] M Sanjeev Arulampalam, Simon Maskell, Neil Gordon, and Tim Clapp. A tutorial on particle filters for online nonlinear/non-gaussian bayesian tracking. *Signal Processing, IEEE Transactions on*, 50(2):174–188, 2002.

[19] Maxim A Batalin and Gaurav S Sukhatme. Coverage, exploration, and deployment by a mobile robot and communication network. In *Information Processing in Sensor Networks*, pages 376–391. Springer, 2003.

[20] Maxim A Batalin and Gaurav S Sukhatme. Coverage, exploration and deployment by a mobile robot and communication network. *Telecommunication Systems*, 26(2-4):181–196, 2004.

[21] Ting Liu, Christopher M Sadler, Pei Zhang, and Margaret Martonosi. Implementing software on resource-constrained mobile sensors: Experiences with impala and zebranet. In *Proceedings of the 2nd international conference on Mobile systems, applications, and services*, pages 256–269. ACM, 2004.

[22] Yong Wang, Pei Zhang, Ting Liu, Chris Sadler, and Margaret Martonosi. Movement data traces from princeton zebranet deployments. *CRAWDAD Database*, 129, 2007.

[23] Andrew Howard, Maja J. Matarić, and Gaurav S. Sukhatme. An Incremental Self-Deployment Algorithm for Mobile Sensor Networks. *Autonomous Robots*, 13(2):113–126, September 2002.

[24] Andrew Howard, Maja J Matarić, and Gaurav S Sukhatme. Mobile sensor network deployment using potential fields: A distributed, scalable solution to the area coverage problem. In *Distributed Autonomous Robotic Systems 5*, pages 299–308. Springer, 2002.

[25] Gaurav S. Sukhatme Maxim A. Batalin. Spreading Out: A Local Approach to Multi-robot Coverage. *Proceedings of the 6th International Symposium on Distributed Autonomous Robotics System*, 2002.

[26] Wolfram Burgard, Cyrill Stachniss, Giorgio Grisetti, Bastian Steder, Rainer Kummerle, Christian Dornhege, Michael Ruhnke, Alexander Kleiner, and Juan D Tardós. A comparison of slam algorithms based on a graph of relations. In *Intelligent Robots and Systems, 2009. IROS 2009. IEEE/RSJ International Conference on*, pages 2089–2095. IEEE, 2009.

[27] Denis Chekhlov, Mark Pupilli, Walterio Mayol-Cuevas, and Andrew Calway. Real-time and robust monocular slam using predictive multi-resolution descriptors. In *Advances in Visual Computing*, pages 276–285. Springer, 2006.

[28] Austin I Eliazar and Ronald Parr. Dp-slam 2.0. In *Robotics and Automation, 2004. Proceedings. ICRA'04. 2004 IEEE International Conference on*, volume 2, pages 1314–1320. IEEE, 2004.

[29] Tim Bailey, Juan Nieto, Jose Guivant, Michael Stevens, and Eduardo Nebot. Consistency of the ekf-slam algorithm. In *Intelligent Robots and Systems, 2006 IEEE/RSJ International Conference on*, pages 3562–3568. IEEE, 2006.

[30] G. Dissanayake, P. Newman, S. Clark, H.F. Durrant-Whyte, and M. Csorba. A solution to the simultaneous localisation and map building (SLAM) problem. *IEEE Transactions of Robotics and Automation*, 17(3):229–241, 2001.

[31] Guoquan P Huang, Anastasios I Mourikis, and Stergios I Roumeliotis. Analysis and improvement of the consistency of extended kalman filter based slam. In *Robotics and Automation, 2008. ICRA 2008. IEEE International Conference on*, pages 473–479. IEEE, 2008.

[32] Shoudong Huang and Gamini Dissanayake. Convergence and consistency analysis for extended kalman filter based slam. *Robotics, IEEE Transactions on*, 23(5):1036–1049, 2007.

[33] Giorgio Grisetti, Cyrill Stachniss, and Wolfram Burgard. Improving grid-based slam with rao-blackwellized particle filters by adaptive proposals and selective resampling. In *Robotics and Automation, 2005. ICRA 2005. Proceedings of the 2005 IEEE International Conference on*, pages 2432–2437. IEEE, 2005.

[34] G. Grisetti, C. Stachniss, and W. Burgard. Improved techniques for grid mapping with Rao-Blackwellized particle filters. *IEEE Transactions on Robotics*, 23(1):36–46, 2007.

[35] Giorgio Grisetti, Gian Diego Tipaldi, Cyrill Stachniss, Wolfram Burgard, and Daniele Nardi. Fast and accurate slam with rao–blackwellized particle filters. *Robotics and Autonomous Systems*, 55(1):30–38, 2007.

[36] Andrew Howard. Multi-robot simultaneous localization and mapping using particle filters. *The International Journal of Robotics Research*, 25(12):1243–1256, 2006.

[37] P. Bahl and V. Padmanabhan. RADAR: An in-building RF-based user location and tracking system. In *IEEE Int. Conference on Computer Communications*, pages 775–784, 2000.

[38] A. Ladd, K. Bekris, A. Rudys, D. Wallach, and L. Kavraki. On the feasibility of using wireless ethernet for indoor localization. *IEEE Transactions on Robotics and Automation*, 20(3):555–559, 2004.

[39] Moustafa Youssef and Ashok Agrawala. The horus wlan location determination system. In *Proceedings of the 3rd international conference on Mobile systems, applications, and services*, pages 205–218. ACM, 2005.

[40] S. Zickler and M. Veloso. RSS-based relative localization and tethering for moving robots in unknown environments. In *IEEE Int. Conference on Robotics and Automation*, pages 5466–5471, 2010.

[41] J. Twigg, J. Fink, P.L. Yu, and B.M. Sadler. Efficient base station connectivity area discovery. *International Journal of Robotics Research*, 2013.

[42] Brian Ferris, Dieter Fox, and Neil Lawrence. Wifi-slam using gaussian process latent variable models. In *Proceedings of the 20th International Joint Conference on Artifical Intelligence*, IJCAI'07, pages 2480–2485, San Francisco, CA, USA, 2007. Morgan Kaufmann Publishers Inc.

[43] Mikkel Baun Kjærgaard. A taxonomy for radio location fingerprinting. In *Location-and Context-Awareness*, pages 139–156. Springer, 2007.

[44] Guobin Shen, Zhuo Chen, Peichao Zhang, Thomas Moscibroda, and Yongguang Zhang. Walkie-markie: Indoor pathway mapping made easy. In *Proceedings of the 10th USENIX Conference on Networked Systems Design and Implementation*, nsdi'13, pages 85–98, Berkeley, CA, USA, 2013. USENIX Association.

[45] Jie Yin, Qiang Yang, and Lionel M Ni. Learning adaptive temporal radio maps for signal-strength-based location estimation. *Mobile Computing, IEEE Transactions on*, 7(7):869–883, 2008.

[46] He Wang, Souvik Sen, Ahmed Elgohary, Moustafa Farid, Moustafa Youssef, and Romit Roy Choudhury. No need to war-drive: Unsupervised indoor localization. In *Proceedings of the 10th International Conference on Mobile Systems, Applications, and Services*, MobiSys '12, pages 197–210, New York, NY, USA, 2012. ACM.

[47] Aveek Purohit, Zheng Sun, Shijia Pan, and Pei Zhang. Sugartrail: Indoor navigation in retail environments without surveys and maps. In *Sensor, Mesh and Ad Hoc Communications and Networks (SECON), 2013 10th Annual IEEE Communications Society Conference on*, pages 300–308. IEEE, 2013.

Sensing Ambient Light for User Experience-Oriented Color Scheme Adaptation on Smartphone Displays

Jiadi Yu, Jiaming Zhao
Department of Computer Science and Engineering
Shanghai Jiao Tong University
{jiadiyu, jmzhao}@sjtu.edu.cn

Yingying Chen
Department of Electrical and Computer Engineering
Stevens Institute of Technology
yingying.chen@stevens.edu

Jie Yang
Department of Computer Science
Florida State University
jie.yang@cs.fsu.edu

ABSTRACT

With the rapid development of information technology, mobile devices have exhibited increasing popularity in recent years. To support the anytime-anywhere service model of mobile devices, one important problem related to the screen display arises when using these devices (e.g., smartphone and tablet) under various lighting conditions. On one hand, it is hard for users to see the display clearly under strong lighting conditions (e.g., sunlight). On the other hand, the screen appears dazzling under weak lighting conditions. This problem related to the mobile device display can significantly degrade user experience and undermine the successful deployment of the anytime-anywhere mobile service model. Existing solutions mainly focus on the automatic adjustment of brightness level under different light conditions. We show that merely utilizing brightness level to solve the display problem is not enough to maintain the user experience under both strong and weak lighting scenarios through experimenting with over 200 volunteers. In this work, we take a different approach by investigating automatic color scheme adjustment to improve user experience. We find that *Readability*, *Comfort level* and *Similarity* are major factors that contribute to user experience. In recognizing these problems, we propose a system, ColorVert, which utilizes the DKL color space to adaptively transform color schemes by sensing ambient light to improve user experience under various lighting scenarios. Our experimental evaluation with over 200 precipitants and various mobile devices demonstrates that ColorVert is more effective in both maintaining as well as improving user experience compared with the existing automatic brightness adjustment system.

Categories and Subject Descriptors

H.5.2 [**INFORMATION INTERFACES AND PRESENTATION**]: User Interfaces—*Input devices and strategies*

SenSys'15, November 1–4, 2015, Seoul, South Korea..
 ISBN 978-1-4503-3631-4/15/11 ...$15.00.
DOI: http://dx.doi.org/10.1145/2809695.2809709 .

General Terms

Design, Experimentation, Human Factors

Keywords

Smartphone display; color scheme; user experience; sensing ambient light

1. INTRODUCTION

Mobile devices such as smartphones and tablets have received increasing popularity over the recent years and blended into our daily lives. In particular, equipped with high resolution screens and various web browsers, modern mobile devices have become one of the major sources for web surfing. According to the survey on the Internet, 250 million smartphones were sold in the 3rd quarter of 2013 alone[1]. Compared with traditional desktops or laptops, one important problem related to the screen display is surfaced when using these devices under different lighting conditions for supporting the anytime-anywhere mobile service model. That is, the user experience of screen reading is strongly associated with ambient environments, among them the most important factor is the lighting conditions. On one hand, under strong lighting conditions (e.g., sunlight), some text colors are washed off by the strong light and become undistinguishable from the background color, rendering unreadability. On the other hand, the dazzling screen often makes our eyes uncomfortable at night. Thus, to ensure the successful deployment of the anytime-anywhere mobile service model, it is highly desirable to develop a scheme that can adaptively adjust the way the screen displays the content based on the dynamic ambient environments.

Existing studies on improving smartphone user experience under different light conditions mostly focus on the adjustment of the brightness level. For example, Android and iOS have automatic brightness adjustment system, which can change the brightness level of the screen according to the light strength. And there are subsequent studies to improve such systems by capturing more precise light strength [2]. However, these solutions are far from satisfactory as users remain suffering under both strong and weak lighting conditions even if the highest brightness level is applied. Thus, merely adjusting the brightness level of the device screen cannot solve the problem completely. In this paper, we take a different viewpoint by developing adaptive color scheme adjustment to maintain and improve user experience under different light conditions. Although there exist some work to improve user experience by adjusting color saturation of images and videos[3] or enhancing image contrast[4, 5] according to ambient light, it is hard for these solutions to achieve the high readability for texts under different light conditions. Most of the studies related to color scheme transformation [6] [7], however, only focus on the energy consumption of different color schemes rather than the user experience.

Since 84% of users utilize their smartphones for web surfing[8], we focus our study on web browsers. Although the user experience of mobile devices has gained much attention, existing work has not concerned the impact of the webpage color scheme to user experience. We first set out to investigate the main factors that contribute to user experience when using smartphones. Through an extensive study of over 200 volunteers and the analysis of webpage color schemes, we find that the user experience is mainly determined by *Readability, Comfort level* and *Similarity between the transformed color scheme and the original one.* We further propose ColorVert, which improves user experience by adaptively adjusting the color scheme of web pages based on sensed ambient light under dynamic environments. Specifically, ColorVert applies a novel color transformation algorithm to calculate the optimal color scheme under both strong (e.g., direct strong sunlight) as well as weak lighting conditions based on ambient light sensing. Our prototype implementation of ColorVert on Android-based smartphones and tablets verifies the feasibility of using ColorVert in real environments. Based on the feedback from over 200 volunteers, our system could effectively improve user experience compared with the existing brightness adjustment system. Although our work only focuses on dealing with web browsers, we believe the proposed color transform adaptation approach could be easily extended to handle other smartphone tasks using screen displays.

We highlight our main contributions as follows:

- We empirically investigate the impact factors on user experience when using mobile device under different lighting conditions with over 200 volunteers. The important finding is that the user experience is mainly determined by the readability, comfort level and similarity between the transformed color scheme and the original one.
- We develop a dynamic color scheme adaptation system for smartphone web browsers, namely ColorVert, which can adaptively transform color scheme of webpages to maintain and improve user experience through sensing ambient environments.
- We implement ColorVert on four types of Android devices including smartphones and tablets with different screen sizes. Our prototype of ColorVert shows that our system is light weight and is feasible to use in real-world scenarios.
- We conduct extensive experiments with over 200 volunteers to evaluate the performance of ColorVert. The results of users' feedback confirm that our ColorVert system is effective in improving user experience under both strong and weak lighting conditions.

The rest of this paper is organized as follows. We give an in-depth motivation study in Section 2. Section 3 and Section 4 presents the design details and color transformation algorithm of the ColorVert system respectively. In Section 5, we evaluate the performance of ColorVert and analyze the results. Related work is reviewed in Section 6. Finally, we give conclusive remarks in Section 7.

2. MOTIVATION STUDY

We first provide the background on readability and comfort level of the smartphone screen. Then through the investigation of the existing automatic brightness adjustment system on smartphones and the color scheme of webpages, we find the reason of user experience degradation under both strong and weak lighting conditions. Finally, from the results of user preference survey, we discover main factors that affect user experience.

2.1 Preliminaries

We first introduce the background of the smartphone screen readability and comfort level.

2.1.1 The measurement of Readability

Photometry is the science about the measurement of visible light in terms of its perceived brightness to human vision. The most important physical quantity given in photometry is luminance[9]. Luminance(cd/m^2) describes the amount of light passes through a particular area with a given angle.

Given the smartphone is equipped with OLED displays, there is an effective way to calculate the luminance of screen. Since OLED consists of three kinds of light emitting diode, the total spectral power distribution is the addition of those light sources, specified by an (R,G,B) tuple in the RGB color space. We can first calculate the relative luminance [9][10] of a color, defined as $Y = 0.2126R + 0.7152G + 0.0722B$, where Y is the relative luminance, with its value normalized to 1 for a given white point (when R=G=B=1). We can observe from the formula that green light contributes the most to the luminance, while blue light contributes the least.

Further, we are not only concerning about the luminance of a certain object, but also its luminance difference compared with another object, i.e. the Luminance Contrast:

$$Contrast\% = \frac{|L_1 - L_2|}{max(L_1, L_2)} \cdot 100\%, \quad (1)$$

where L_1 and L_2 are the respective luminance of the objects.

Based on the above information, Relative Visual Performance (RVP) model is introduced to measure the readability[11][12]. It is measured by the speed and accuracy with which a visual task is performed. Specifically, RVP is measured using Reaction Time (RT) which defines as the interval between the onset of the stimulus and the response by humans. Human can reach different RT values given a set of different characteristics of the stimulus. RVP is formally defined by:

$$RVP\% = \frac{RT_0}{RT} \cdot 100\%, \quad (2)$$

where RT_0 is the smallest reaction time a person can achieve, given the best lighting condition and stimulus characteristics. RT is the reaction time of a certain condition. A bigger RVP value indicates we spend less time to get the information of the stimulus and results in a better readability condition, whereas a smaller RVP value means less readability. Usually, a RVP value greater than 80% implies good readability [13][14][11].

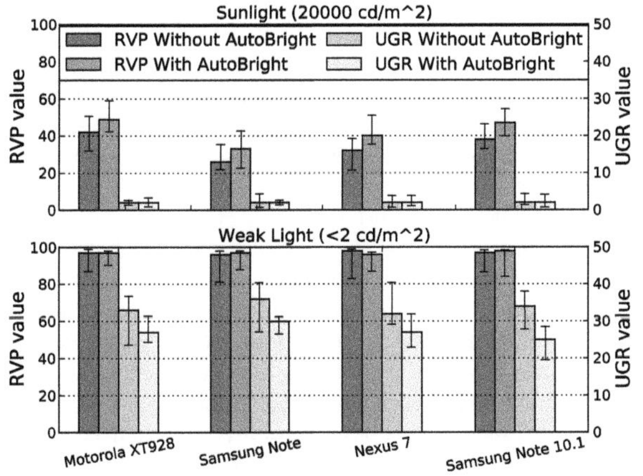

Figure 1: Influence of automatic brightness control on RVP and UGR.

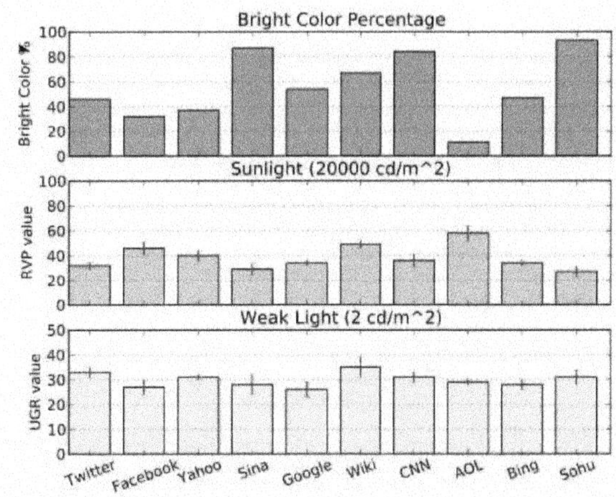

Figure 2: Bright color ratio, RVP and UGR value of different webpages.

2.1.2 The measurement of Comfort Level

When the difference of luminance level between the target and the environment becomes too large, our eyes feel uncomfortable when looking at a target. To evaluate the comfort level, we use the standard metric provided by International Commission on Illumination, the Unified Glare Rating (UGR)[15][16].

$$UGR = 8log\frac{0.25}{L_b}\sum_n(\frac{L_n^2\omega_n}{p_n^2}), \quad (3)$$

where L_b is the ambient luminance, L_n is the luminance of each light source n, ω_n is the solid angle of the light source seen from the observer and p_n is the Guth position index, which depends on the distance from the line of sight of the viewer. By using the UGR, we could analyze the impact of the light emitted by the screen of the smartphone on our eyes. Normally, the standard office lighting has $UGR \leq 19$. A UGR value larger than 25 may make our eyes uncomfortable[15].

2.2 Investigating Existing Automatic Brightness Adjustment System

Since we cannot see the screen clearly under strong lighting conditions and feel the screen is too dazzling at night, many smartphone operating systems (Android and iOS for example) perform automatic brightness control, which dynamically adjusts the smartphone brightness level based on the ambient light strength. In this section, we show that the automatic brightness adjustment system has limited improvement on user experience under strong and weak lighting conditions.

Table 1: The details about the volunteers.

Sex	Age	Under Sunlight	Under Night	Total
Male	20-30	32	21	99
	30-50	25	12	
	over 50	6	3	
Female	20-30	40	21	107
	30-50	18	17	
	over 50	7	4	
Total		128	78	206

2.2.1 User Experience under Strong Lighting Condition

Since the strong light reflected by the smartphone screen can decrease the luminance contrast and wash off the color of texts, it is often hard for us to see the words clearly. As existing work employs automatic brightness adjustment system to improve user experience, we investigate its effectiveness under direct strong light (sunlight) of $20000cd/m^2$ with four kinds of mobile devices: Motorola XT928 with a 4.5' screen, Samsung Galaxy Note with a 5.3' screen, Nexus7 with a 7' screen and Galaxy Note with a 10.1' screen. We implement the tool Psychopy[17] on smartphones to set up experiments to measure the RVP and UGR value of webpages. For Samsung Galaxy Note smartphones, besides automatic brightness adjustment system, we also apply the adapt display mode [3] on our experiments, which is able to automatically adjust color saturation according to ambient light.

To measure RVP value via the Equation 2, the smallest reaction time (RT_0) can be calculated from the formula in [11][12]. For Reaction Time (RT), we do experiments the similar as [11][12]. We recruit 206 volunteers of different ages randomly on college campus. For 128 of them, smartphones are placed under direct sunlight with ambient luminance around $20000cd/m^2$ measured by light sensor. For the other people, smartphones are placed at night where ambient luminance is less than $2cd/m^2$. The details about the volunteers is shown on Table.1. During each trial in the experiment, a webpage is displayed on the screen of smartphones, after a brief, random time delay, and each volunteer is asked to touch the screen as soon as they detect the newly displayed webpage. The time between webpage onset and response is recorded as the RT for that trial. The webpages are selected from the sites most frequently visited by users. After the experiment, each volunteer has a block of RTs for all displayed webpages, and then we are able to calculate their RVP values for the webpages. Moreover, the UGR value of each displayed webpage can be calculated from the Equation 3 according to [15][16].

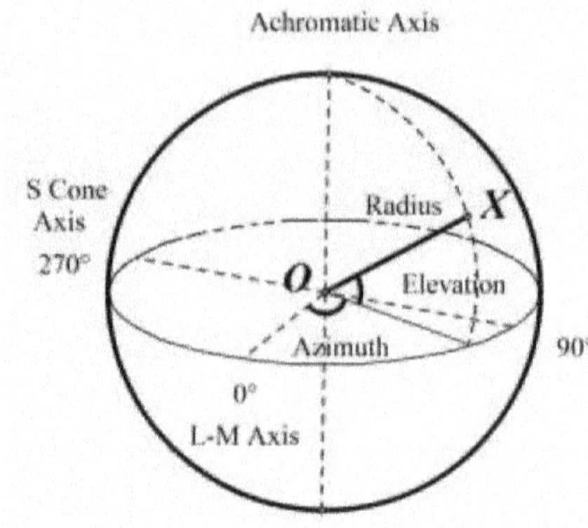

Figure 3: DKL Color Space.

The results are shown in the upper half of Fig.1. From the figure, we can see that, under strong lighting condition, although the UGR value is low enough to keep a good comfort level, the automatic brightness adjustment system only slightly improve the RVP value, which is still too low to achieve a satisfactory readability level (i.e., the RVP value is much less than 80%). The adapt display mode of Samsung Galaxy Note do not much contribute to improve readability level for webpages.

2.2.2 *User Experience under Weak Lighting Condition*

When ambient light strength is weak, as the ambient luminance L_b in Equation 3 decreases, the UGR value increases sharply. A large UGR value would degrade the comfort level for reading. Although the automatic brightness adjustment system could reduce the luminance level of the screen, the results are still far from satisfactory. We perform similar experiments when the ambient light strength is low. From the experiment results shown in the bottom half of Fig.1, the UGR value is still very large (i.e., UGR >19), which results in low comfort level. Moreover, under weak lighting condition, the RVP value is high enough for good readability.

The reason of the large UGR value is that most of the webpages use white or other bright colors as background. Even though the overall luminance level of the screen is reduced, a bright background color still keeps L_n at a high level, which results in low comfort level.

2.3 Studying the Relationship between Color Schemes and User Experience

Since existing brightness adjustment system is not good enough to satisfy user, we study another aspect, *color scheme*, which has significant impact on user experience. In order to understand the relationship between color schemes and user experience, we conduct a survey on the color schemes of some popular webpages. We randomly select 1000 webpages from popular websites such as Google, CNN, etc. It is noticed that most webpages use bright colors in many places in order to attract the attention of user. According to our survey results in Fig.2, 84% of the words on the CNN are light grey and blue, 54% of the words on Google search results page are sky blue and red. Because a lot of webpages utilize bright color scheme, their readability or comfort level are seriously undermined under both strong or weak lighting conditions.

On one hand, under strong lighting conditions, the bright color on the webpages results in the low RVP value. As is shown in the middle part of Fig.2, for most webpages under study, RVP values are under 40%, whereas good readability has RVP value larger than 80%. To fully understand the impact of color on user experience, we introduce the DKL (Derrington, Krauskopf and Lennie) color space[18], which is based on the Macleod and Boynton chromaticity diagram. The DKL color space is shown in Fig.3. DKL uses three axis to describe the color space: S-cone axis, L-M axis, and achromatic axis. For any given plane that is perpendicular to the achromatic axis, all colors on the plane have the same luminance value, i.e., luminance contrast is zero. The biggest plane which intersect the achromatic axis at center is called Isoluminant Plane. Every color is represented in the 3-dimensional space, i.e., (α,h,r), using spherical coordinates that specify the elevation(α) from the isoluminant plane, the azimuth(h) that stands for the hue, and the radius(r) that is the fraction of the maximal modulations along the cardinal axes of the space. By using the DKL color space, we can easily distinguish the luminance effect from the color effect. It is thus convenient for us to analyze the effect of colors on user experience. For a bright color scheme, both foreground and background colors are located in the upper half of the DKL sphere, whose contrast is low, resulting in a low RVP value (i.e., poor readability).

On the other hand, under weak lighting conditions, the bright colors on the webpages cause the high value of UGR, which degrade the comfort level when reading. Our experiment about the bright colors' influence on comfort level is shown in the bottom part of Fig.2. The UGR value is measured when the ambient luminance is less than $2cd/m^2$. It can be seen that for most of the bright colors, UGR value is around 30, which is larger than level of comfortable reading. The reason of the large UGR value is that bright colors keep L_n in Equation 3 at a high level.

2.4 User Preference Investigation

From our above analysis, the existing automatic brightness adjustment system is far from satisfaction of user experience under both strong and weak lighting conditions. Meanwhile, we find user experience has a strong relationship with color schemes. We thus can transform the color scheme of webpages to achieve a better user experience. In the study, the 206 volunteers mentioned in Section 2.2 are shown the same static webpages on smartphones with a series of color schemes. For 128 of them, smartphones are placed under direct sunlight with ambient luminance around $20000cd/m^2$ measured by light sensor. For the other people, smartphones are placed at night where ambient luminance is less than $2cd/m^2$. The volunteers are asked to score each web page by 1 to 10 with our grading system, in which the level one indicates that the color scheme results in the lowest user experience and the level increases as the user experience improves. We select webpages from the sites most frequently viewed by user, and for each webpage we present 3 color schemes:

- **Original**, remain the original color scheme of webpages with existing automatic brightness adjustment system.
- **Inversion**, replace all colors with their inversion color. Since most of the webpages use bright colors for back-

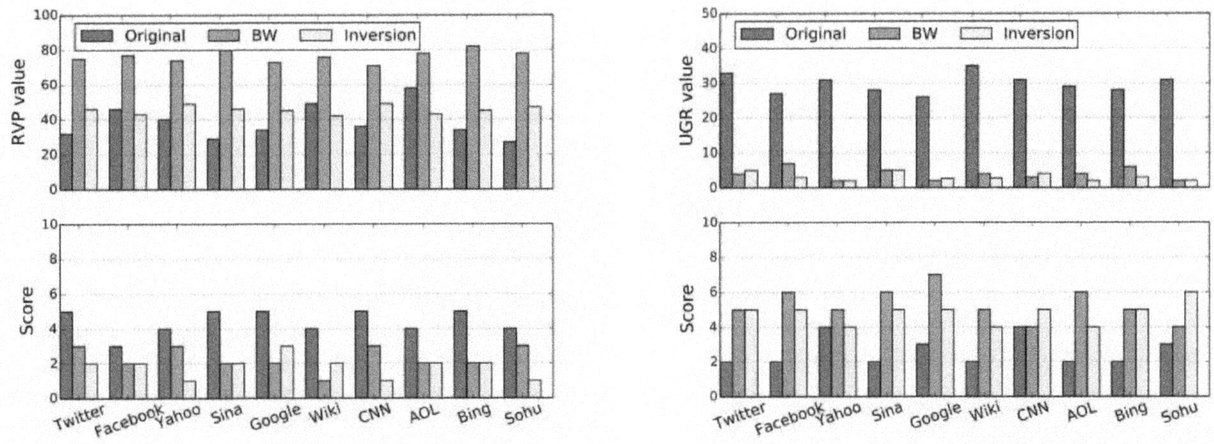

(a) strong light (b) weak light

Figure 4: User preference of different color schemes.

ground and foregrounds, use inversion can increase RVP value and decrease UGR value.

- **Black-White**, for Black-White color scheme. Under strong lighting condition, the RVP value can reach the maximum when we use white for background and black for foreground. Under weak lighting condition, the UGR value can be significantly decreased when we use black for background and white for words.

All transformations are applied to foregrounds and background. The average scoring results and the RVP value under strong ambient light are shown in Fig.4(a), whereas the average scoring results and UGR value under weak ambient light are shown in Fig.4(b). From the scores given by users, we obtain important user feedbacks. Under strong lighting conditions, the Original and Inversion color schemes cannot meet users' requirement on readability, i.e., RVP values are low. Although the Black-White scheme can achieve the highest RVP value among those transformation methods, the scores given by users are very low. This is because a Black-White scheme is dull to users. Therefore, a high RVP value alone can not satisfy users. Moreover, although RVP values are low for the original color scheme, users give a relative high preference score for it. The reason is that users are used to the original color scheme of a webpage and if the color scheme is not similar to the original one, users may feel the webpage is strange and unsatisfactory. Thus, users prefer the webpage to be similar to the original one. Under weak lighting conditions, users prefer the color scheme with a lower UGR value, like Black-White or Inversion color scheme. This is because a lower UGR value means a better comfort level, which contributes to user experience improvement.

According to the analysis above, we find that the automatic brightness adjustment system is not satisfactory and color schemes have significant impact on user experience. User experience thus can be improved by transforming color schemes. In particular, we notice that user prefer color schemes with a high RVP value under strong lighting condition and a low UGR value under weak lighting condition. In addition, users prefer color schemes which are similar to the original one.

3. COLORVERT DESIGN

In order to build an efficient color scheme adaptation system, we devise a new system, ColorVert, that improves user experience by dynamically adjusting the color scheme of webpages based on the light strength sensed at the light sensor on smartphones. The workflow of ColorVert is shown in Fig.5. There are three major units in our system: *Dynamic Sensing Unit*, *Transforming Unit*, *Execution Unit*. Firstly, a Sensing Unit senses the changes of ambient light strength. When ColorVert captures the change of light strength, it will trigger the Transforming Unit where the optimal color scheme for the present webpage will be calculated. Secondly, Transforming Unit gathers useful information about the webpage such as font size and colors from the web browser engine. Based on ambient light strength and the webpage information, the Color Transformation Algorithm is employed to generate the best substitute color for both the background and foregrounds of the webpage. Finally, the Executing Unit receives the output of the algorithm and applies the new color scheme to display on the smartphone screen.

Dynamic Sensing: ColorVert can sense ambient environments and calculate the optimal color transformation scheme accordingly. Light sensor in smartphones can sense light events, which happens when ambient light strength has significant change. When ColorVert captures the change of light strength, it will trigger the Transforming Unit where the optimal color scheme for the present webpage will be calculated. Since the light strength change leads to the change of RVP and UGR value, it is possible that readability and comfort level are degraded. ColorVert thus needs to calculate the optimal color scheme once the change of light strength happens.

Transforming: After ColorVert senses ambient environments, the Transforming Unit first collects information from both the light sensor and the web browser, such as the ambient light strength, original color scheme and font size of the webpage. Based on the collected information, ColorVert

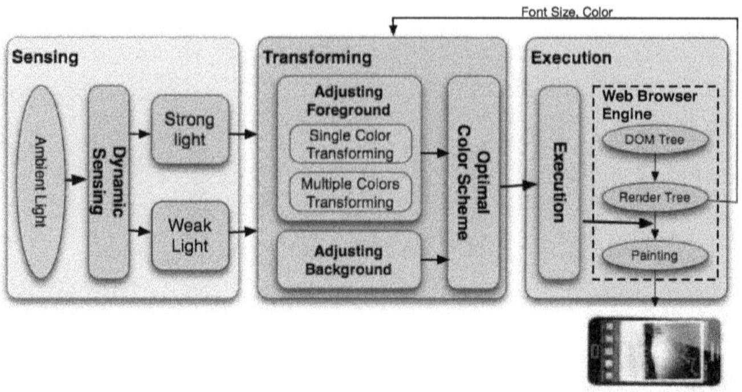

Figure 5: ColorVert design model.

employs Color Transforming Algorithm to calculate the optimal color scheme for foreground and background respectively. Considering the contrast between foreground and background color of webpages, the algorithm calculates the optimal color scheme of foreground and background respectively. Specifically, the color scheme transforming algorithm considers user readability, the comfort level and the similarity between transformed color scheme and original color scheme. The calculated optimal color scheme thus can significantly improve user experience. The detailed algorithm is introduced in Section 4.

Execution: The final step is to apply the optimal color scheme to Web Browser. Considering the working flow of the Web Browser Engine, after a webpage is successfully downloaded, the Web Browser Engine first begin to parse the file and construct a DOM tree. DOM tree contains the styling information together with visual instructions in the HTML and CSS. Then, the DOM tree is used to construct a Render Tree. Finally, a Painting stage traverses the Render Tree and paints each node by calling a series of Library functions.

ColorVert is executed at the painting stage of the Web Browser, after the Render Tree of a webpage is constructed. During the painting stage, ColorVert changes the interface between Web Browser Engine and Library functions to substitute the original color scheme with our optimal color scheme. Thus the painting functions paint the render tree nodes with the specified colors.

4. COLOR SCHEME TRANSFORMING ALGORITHM

In this section, we present the color transformation algorithms, which are used to calculate the optimal color scheme in Transforming Unit. The optimal color scheme can significantly improve user experience.

4.1 Criteria Construction

According to our analysis in Section 2, user experience is mainly determined by the following factors: RVP value (i.e., readability) for strong lighting conditions, UGR value (i.e., comfort level) for weak lighting conditions and Similarity between the original and transformed webpage.

1)RVP value: The mechanism of deciding RVP value is complex. In our experiment, we find that there are mainly three factors affect RVP value: *Luminance Contrast*, *Color Hue Difference* and *Font Size*.

Luminance Contrast: In Section 2, we illustrate how to calculate the actual luminance contrast and RVP value. All colors on a plane of the DKL color space have the same luminance value. The luminance contrast is the distance of two planes. In order to exclude the effect of color hue, we select a pair of foreground and background color from the achromatic axis in Fig.3 (i.e., $(90^0, 0, r)$) to study the relationship between the luminance contrast and RVP value. The font size of words is fixed at 13px. We observe the words and record RVP values under different luminance contrast levels between the foreground and background color (i.e., different the r value). The results are shown in Fig.6 that RVP is up to 80% when luminance contrast is equal to θ. It can be seen that when luminance contrast is bigger than θ, there is no significant change in RVP value as luminance contrast increases, while when the luminance contrast is less than θ, the RVP value decreases dramatically as luminance contrast decreases. Therefore, when luminance contrast is bigger than a certain value θ, the RVP value can satisfy the requirement of readability.

Color Hue Difference: Besides luminance contrast, the color hue can also affect RVP value. In order to exclude the effect of the luminance contrast, we select a pair of foreground and background colors from the isoluminant plane (i.e., $(0, h, r)$ in the DKL color space, where h is the color hue and r specifies the radius). The color hue difference of a color pair is defined as $|h_1 - h_2|$, where h_1 is the color hue of the foreground color and h_2 is the background color hue. First we discuss the impact of r on RVP value. In this experiment, we fix h_1 at 0 degree and h_2 varies from 0° to 360°. As the experiment results shown on the upper half of Fig.7, RVP value is the highest when the color hue difference is equal to 180°, i.e. $|h_1 - h_2| = 180^o$. The results also show that the bigger the r value, the higher the RVP value, where $r = 1$ indicates that the color is on the surface of the DKL color sphere. Next, we discuss the impact of h_1 on RVP value. We set h_1 as a series of values $(0^o, 60^o, \ldots, 300^o)$. $|h_1 - h_2|$ varies from 0° to 360° and r is fixed at 1. The results are presented on the bottom half of Fig.7. The results show that as long as the color hue difference of the color pair remains the same, RVP value is similar among different color hue h_1. This indicates the color hue itself does not affect RVP value, what matters is only the color hue difference between the foreground and background.

Font Size: A bigger font size can make the words more clear and improve user experience in reading. Font size is usually specified in CSS, with the unit px. Most words in the ordinary webpages are within the range of 10-25px. We fix the color hue difference at 180^0 to discuss the relationship between the font size and RVP value. The experiment results are shown in Fig.8. We can see that the change in font size results in the change of θ, i.e., the bigger the font size, the smaller the luminance contrast constraint θ.

2) UGR value: Under weak lighting conditions, we can improve user experience by decreasing UGR value. From the Equation 3, UGR value can be decreased by reducing the total luminance of the screen L_n.

3) Similarity: Similarity is another important factor that contributes to user experience. In order to evaluate the Similarity of a transformed color with the original one, we define the distance of two colors, color a and b, as the spherical distance of two points in the DKL space, repre-

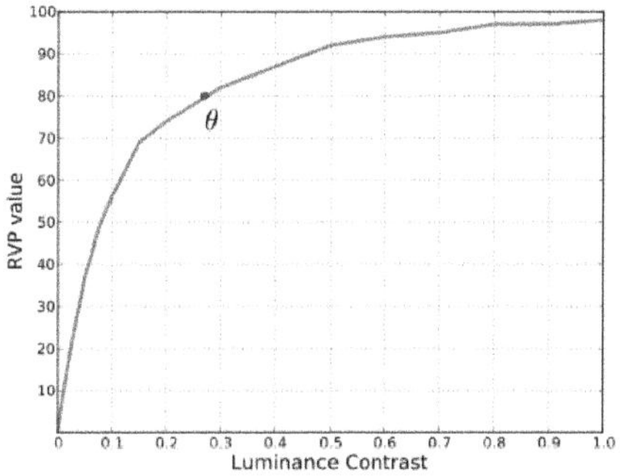

Figure 6: Relationship between the luminance contrast and RVP value.

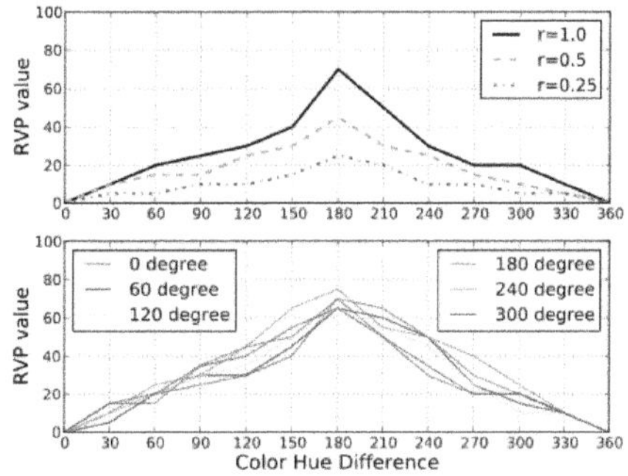

Figure 7: Relationship between the color hue and RVP value.

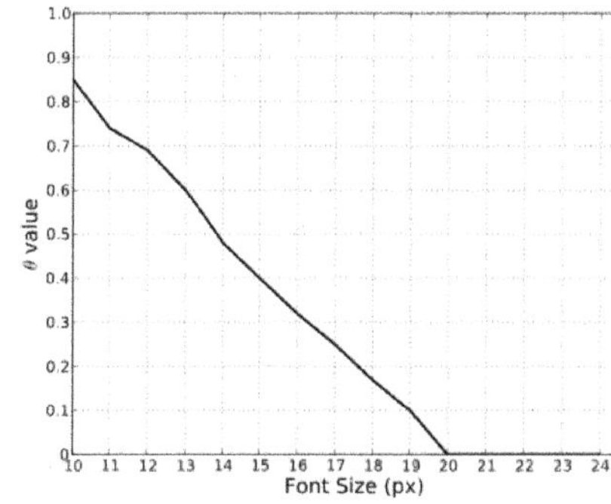

Figure 8: Relationship between the font size and RVP value.

sented as *distance*(a, b). The smaller *distance*(a, b) implies a higher similarity.

4.2 Color Transformation under Strong Lighting Condition

In this section, we discuss the color transformation algorithm under strong lighting conditions based on the criteria above. Given a webpage include foreground colors $(x_1, x_2, \ldots, x_n)$ and a background color y, we aim to find an optimal color scheme that consists of foreground color $(x'_1, x'_2, \ldots, x'_n)$ and an uniform background color y'.

4.2.1 *Foreground Color Transformation*

The foreground of a webpage is its various words that contain different information. Firstly, we design an optimal substitution for a single color words. Since a webpage is normally composed of words with different colors, we need to further deal with the problem of multiple foreground colors. With the criterion constructed, we determine the available color pairs for foreground and background. Based on the criteria discussed in Section 4.1, when performing color transformation, we need to consider the following constraints:

- We should keep the luminance contrast of the foreground and background above θ.
- Color pairs of foreground and background should be located on the surface of the sphere ($r = 1$), and their color hue difference should be 180°.

Since the bright color texts are easier to be washed off by the strong light, we select the foreground colors from the bottom half of the sphere (i.e., dark colors) in the DKL color space. In order to meet the the luminance contrast and color hue constraints of the foreground and background, the upper half of the sphere is selected for background. We then can calculate the *Available Area*, i.e., the colors in those areas can meet the constraints of the foreground and background. It is shown in shaded areas (surface spherical crowns) in Fig.9. Also, the font size results in the change of the shading area. When the font size becomes bigger, the available area also becomes bigger, and vice versa.

Single Color: Considering the available area, our transformation method for a single color x is quite straightforward. We just need to find out a color x'_1 in the available area which has the highest similarity with the original color. Fig.9 shows our transformation method. In order to keep the similarity, the h value of the original color x_1 is fixed. Firstly, we increase the r value of the x_1 to x_1^*. Then, we decrease the α value of x_1^* until it goes into the available area. Finally, x'_1 is selected as new word color, and the other half of the color pair y_1 as background color. So for a single color, we could effectively find a color pair that is optimal.

Multiple Colors: Most of popular webpages usually have multiple bright colors on a single webpage. If each color is transformed using the method above, it is possible that color collision could occur. Color collision means two or more different colors in the original webpage are transformed to the same color. To illustrate this, we refer to Fig.9, which shows a bright color x_1 is transformed to x'_1 on a webpage. Suppose that the original color scheme of the webpage also include the color x'_1, or there is another color x_2 which is also transformed to x'_1 by the method above, a color collision occurs. Usually, in webpages, different word colors are used to represent different kinds of information. If the color collision occurs, it is hard for users to distinguish them and understand what kind of information they are representing. Therefore, it is necessary to eliminate the color collision.

To avoid color collision, we first extend our definition of Similarity: similarity is not only associated with the distance between two colors, but also associated with their relative weight that is the percentage of a given foreground color. The color with a higher percentage, i.e., bigger weight, has a larger impact on the similarity. So we use the weighted distance to evaluate the similarity of two color schemes. We assume that the original color scheme includes color $(x_1, x_2, \ldots, x_n)$, and the new color scheme includes color $(x'_1, x'_2, \ldots, x'_n)$ after transformation. w_i in $(w_1, w_2, \ldots, w_n)$ represents the weight of the corresponding color. If x_i is already located in the available area before transformation, then we do not change x_i and let $x'_i = x_i$. The similarity can be defined as:

$$\frac{1}{WeightedDistance} = \frac{1}{\sum_{i=1}^{n} w_i \times distance(x_i, x'_i)}. \tag{4}$$

A smaller weighted distance indicates the color scheme is more similar to the original one.

Further, we introduce a constrain to our transformation method, that is

$$\{\forall x'_i, x'_j | distance(x'_i, x'_j) > \beta, i \neq j\}, \tag{5}$$

where β is a parameter that describes the color distance that can distinguish two kinds of colors. This constraint guaran-

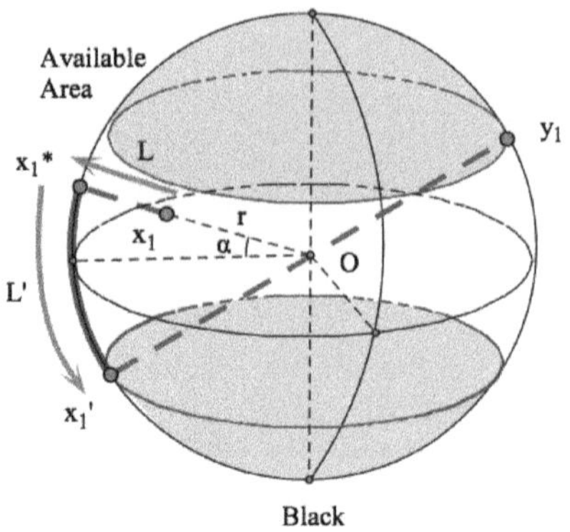

Figure 9: Transformation method for single foreground color under strong lighting conditions.

tees that any two colors in the new color scheme must be separated for a certain distance, so that any two word colors could be easily distinguished. In order to guarantee the constraint, we set collision areas, which represent the sets of points that have distances less than β with any already selected color. We select a color from *remaining available area* (that is, *available area* − *collision area*) with the largest similarity (i.e., $min(WeightedDistance)$). Apparently, in order to maintain the largest similarity, the color selected should be on the boundary of the remaining available area.

With the two equations above, we could calculate the optimal color scheme for multiple foreground colors. The algorithm is described in Algorithm 1. Since a color with a bigger weight should have a higher transformation priority according to the Equation 4, we first sort all the colors according to their weights. Then the first *for* loop can find out all the colors that do not need to transform and then update the remaining available area accordingly. In the second *for* loop, we deal with colors that need to change, i.e., select a color with the largest similarity from the remaining available area. Suppose that we totally maintain k points on the boundary of the remaining available area, the complexity of the loop is $O(nk)$. However, considering that there are usually only a few kinds of colors in a webpage, k is much larger than n, so the total complexity of the algorithm is $O(k)$.

4.2.2 Background Color Transformation

Above work allows us to find an optimal color scheme for a given webpage with many foreground colors. We can always find an optimal background color for a foreground color, e.g., if x'_1 in Fig.9 is selected as foreground color, the other half of the color pair y_1 is selected as background color. This is because it can guarantee Color Hue constraints, i.e.,

$$|h_{foreground} - h_{background}| = 180^o. \quad (6)$$

Thus, many background colors will be selected for multiple foreground colors. However, users are used to a uniform background in a webpage for all foreground colors. So we present a background calculation algorithm to find an optimal uniform background color as follows.

We assume that $(y'_1, y'_2, \ldots, y'_n)$ are the background colors for multiple foreground colors. (x'_i, y'_i) is a color pair that meet our all constraints. Assume the color y' is the optimal background color for the whole webpage, we should select a

Algorithm 1 FOREGROUND COLOR TRANSFORMATION

Require: A set of foreground colors $(x_1, x_2, \ldots, x_n)$ in a webpage and their respective weight $(w_1, w_2, \ldots, w_n)$ and font size $(f_1, f_2, \ldots, f_n)$.
Ensure: The approximate optimal foreground colors $(x'_1, x'_2, \ldots, x'_n)$ which can meet our constraint in Equation 5 and maximize the similarity in Equation 4.
Sort $(x_1, x_2, \ldots, x_n)$ according to their weight so that their weight is in a decreasing order.
Initialize the similarity sum of the colors as $\mathcal{S}$
Initialize the collision area as $\mathcal{C}$
for $i = 1 \rightarrow n$ **do**
    Calculate the Available Area $\mathcal{A}_i$ to the font size f_i
    if Color x_i is already in its available area **then**
        Let $x'_i = x_i$
        Let x'_i as centre, β as radius, draw sphere SP_i
        Update the collision area as $\mathcal{C} = \mathcal{C} \cup SP_i$
    end if
end for
for $i = 1 \rightarrow n$ **do**
    if Color x_i is not in its available area $\mathcal{A}_i$ **then**
        $\mathcal{A}_i = \mathcal{A}_i - \mathcal{C}$
        From the boundary of $\mathcal{A}_i$ select the color x'_i which can minimize $distance(x_i, x'_i)$
        Let x'_i as centre, β as radius, draw sphere SP_i
        Update collision area as $\mathcal{C} = \mathcal{C} \cup SP_i$
        Update $\mathcal{S} = \mathcal{S} + w_i \times distance(x_i, x'_i)$
    end if
end for

color that is the closest to all color $(y'_1, y'_2, \ldots, y'_n)$ as y', i.e., minimal weighted distance:

$$min(\sum_{i=1}^{n} w_i \times distance(y', y'_i)). \quad (7)$$

Thus, from Equation 7, we can calculate a color y' as the optimal uniform background color.

4.3 Color Transformation under Weak Lighting Conditions

In this section, we discuss the color transformation algorithm under weak lighting conditions. When we use our smartphones at night, the luminance of ambient light L_b is very low. A slightly increasing of L_n in Equation 3 thus could rise the UGR value sharply, which makes our eye uncomfortable. In order to reduce the value of UGR, we should try to reduce the luminance of our smartphone screen, i.e., L_n.

4.3.1 Background Color Transformation

Since the background color occupies most of the screen and contributes to most of the luminance, it is important to first find a background color with a low luminance level. Taking this fact into consideration, black is the best color to use as background at night, because its luminance is zero, which is in accordance with the luminance level of the ambient environment. Black color can significantly reduce the UGR value and makes our eyes quickly adapt to the display screen, so user experience is improved.

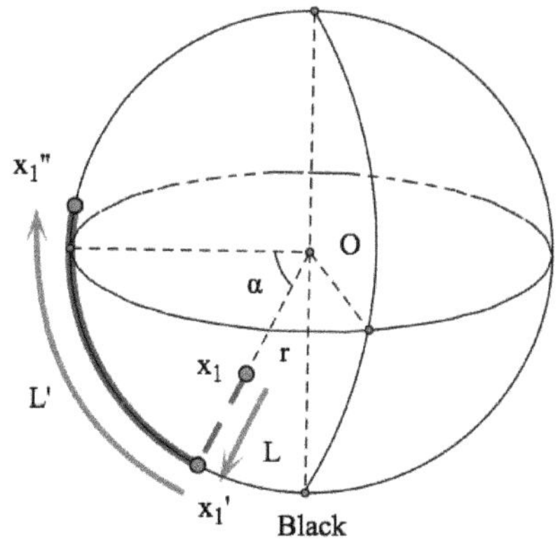

Figure 10: Transformation method for single foreground color under weak lighting conditions.

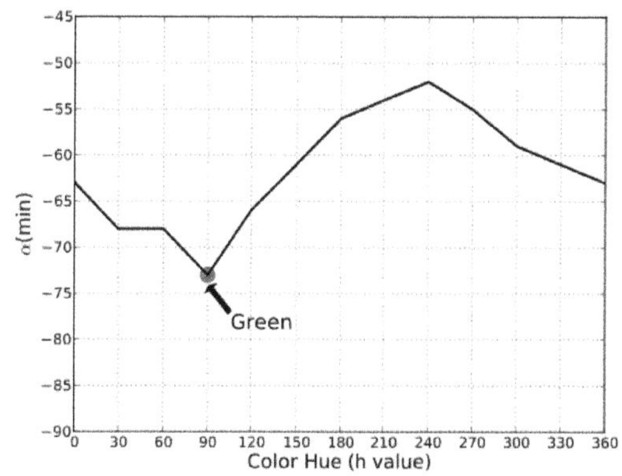

Figure 11: Color hue difference and their minimum α value.

4.3.2 *Foreground Color Transformation*

For foreground, we need to consider color transform algorithm for single color and multiple colors. There are some constraints that we need to take into consideration for the foreground color transformation under weak lighting conditions.

- Readability of a webpage: we should make sure that the RVP value is above a certain value χ.
- Similarity between the original color and transformed color: the new color should be selected from the same hue axis of the DKL color space, i.e., $h = h'$.

Single Color: Given the criteria above, we first focus on RVP requirement. RVP can be improved by increasing the luminance contrast. Fig.10 shows our transformation method. If there is a foreground color x_1 with $RVP_{x_1} < \chi$, we first move the color x_1 along the line L. If RVP value requirement cannot be satisfied when it reach x_1', we continue moving the color alone the arc L' by increasing the α value of the color till we find a color x_1'' with $RVP_{x_1''} \geq \chi$. For any foreground color x_i with $RVP_{x_i} \geq \chi$, we do not transform the color.

We further discuss the transformation method for an achromatic color. Achromatic colors, especially black, usually occupy a large percent of total words in a webpage. Since achromatic colors do not belong to a certain color hue, it could be moved in any directions. Thus, we need to find out a certain direction, i.e., a certain color hue that could meet the requirement of RVP value as well as maintaining the lowest luminance. An experiment is performed in order to find the optimal color hue. In our experiment, we select black as background of the webpage and $x(\alpha, h, r)$ for foreground. According to the results presented in Fig.7, we fix $r = 1$ and let h equals to a series of values. For each value of h, color set $(\alpha, h, 1)$ is a longitude on the surface of the sphere. Then from $\alpha = -90^o$, we gradually increase the value of α, until the RVP value of the word exceeds the requirement χ. The results are shown in Fig.11. Firstly, the color we select meets the RVP requirement. So according to our experiment above, for each color hue h_i, we guarantee that $\alpha \geq \alpha_{i_{min}}$ (α is the minimum that can meet our RVP value requirement). Secondly, we should keep UGR value as low as possible. Since α represents the luminance of a certain color, the bigger the α is, the higher luminance the color has. To keep the lowest possible UGR, we should select the color hue with a smallest $\alpha_{i_{min}}$, which is green (h= 90°) according to the experiment results. Therefore, under weak lighting conditions, green can meet RVP value requirement with the lowest α and is the best substitution for achromatic colors.

Multiple Colors: For multiple colors, it is possible that conflict can occur when performing color transformation. We already discuss the solution to color conflict under strong lighting conditions on Section 4.2. Similarly methods are applied under weak lighting conditions.

5. EVALUATION

In this section, we first present the prototype implementation of ColorVert and then we evaluate ColorVert under both strong and weak lighting conditions respectively. After that, we discuss the transformation time and overhead of ColorVert.

5.1 Prototype Implementation

We implement ColorVert as an Android App and install it on four mobile devices with different CPU frequency and screen size, i.e., Motorola XT928 with a 4.5' screen and a 1.2GHz dual core CPU, Samsung Galaxy Note with 5.3' screen and a 1.4GHz dual core CPU, Nexus 7 with a 7' screen and a 1.3GHz quad core CPU, Galaxy Note 10.1 tablet with a 10.1' screen and a 1.4GHz quad core. ColorVert senses the light strength condition by using the light sensor embedded on the mobile devices. According to the light sensor's reading, ColorVert calculates the optimal color scheme and executes it on the mobile devices. Fig.12 and Fig.13 show two examples of the original and transformed webpages performed by ColorVert under strong lighting conditions with various lighting strengths. We observe that in the transformed webpages bright colors become darker as the strength of the sunlight increases, while the similarity of the two webpages is preserved before and after applying ColorVert. We then present two examples of transformed webpages performed by the inversion color scheme and ColorVert respectively in Fig.14 and Fig.15 under weak lighting conditions. We find that although the background color of both schemes is adapted to black so that UGR value is reduced, the foreground colors from ColorVert are more comfortable to users than those from the inversion scheme.

(a) original (b) $20000cd/m^2$ (c) $30000cd/m^2$ (d) $40000cd/m^2$

Figure 12: Example 1 of applying the ColorVert prototype under strong lighting conditions.

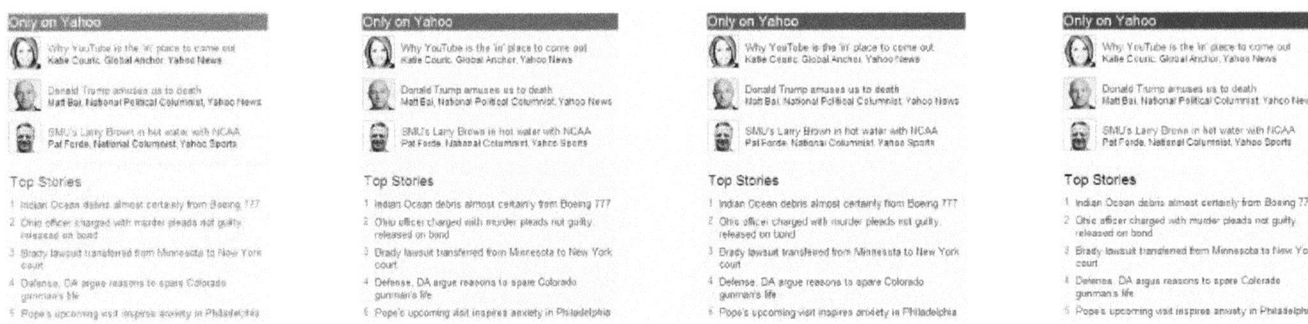

(a) original (b) $20000cd/m^2$ (c) $30000cd/m^2$ (d) $40000cd/m^2$

Figure 13: Example 2 of applying the ColorVert prototype under strong lighting conditions.

(a) inversion (b) colorvert

Figure 14: Example 1 of applying Inversion and ColorVert schemes under weak lighting conditions.

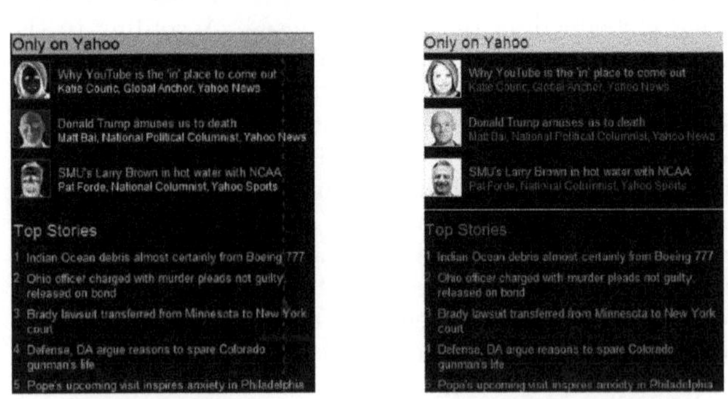

(a) inversion (b) colorvert

Figure 15: Example 2 of applying Inversion and ColorVert schemes under weak lighting conditions.

5.2 Impact on User Experience of ColorVert

In order to evaluate the effectiveness of ColorVert, we first request those 206 volunteers mentioned in Section 2 to grade the user experience for some popular webpages which are transformed by ColorVert on Motorola XT928, with an ambient light strength of around $20000cd/m^2$ for strong lighting conditions (sunlight) and around $2cd/m^2$ for weak lighting conditions (at night). With each webpage, users are shown with both the original with auto-brightness adjustment(**Original**) and the transformed webpage(**ColorVert**) simultaneously on two Motorola XT928 phones and they are not aware of which one is the transformed one. The results of the survey are shown in Fig.16. For each webpage, two bars on the left show the RVP value and user experience score of the strong sunlight respectively while the two bars on the right show the UGR value and user experience score of the weak light respectively. From Fig.16 we can observe that with ColorVert, RVP values are improved to around 70% under strong lighting conditions, which is sufficient for satisfying reading experience. User experience scores are also significantly improved under strong lighting conditions. Moreover, under weak lighting conditions, although UGR values are decreased with a small decline compared with the inversion color scheme, the better comfort level and similarity help ColorVert a lot to achieve a higher score of users' feedback. From our study, we observe that the preserved similarity and the improved readability and comfort level contribute to the user experience improvement.

Next, we evaluate the performance of our system under different light strengths by using different smartphones. We randomly select 100 webpages and use four different mobile devices to display these webpages. Fig.17(a) shows our

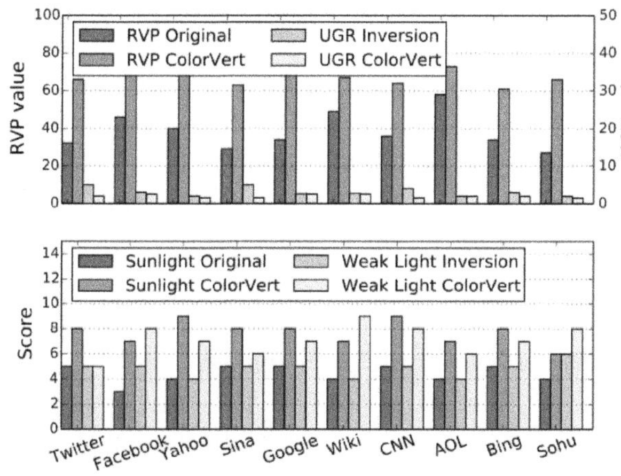

Figure 16: RVP, UGR and user experience score of ColorVert.

results under strong lighting conditions, in which sunlight strength varies between $15000 - 30000cd/m^2$. $RVP\ Ratio$ is the ratio between RVP value of the optimal color scheme and original one, i.e.,

$$RVP\ Ratio = \frac{ColorVert\ RVP}{Original\ RVP}. \tag{8}$$

It can be seen from the figure that as sunlight strength increases, the RVP Ratio rises, which indicates that ColorVert effectively prevents RVP value from sharp decreasing under strong lighting conditions. Also, we set up another experiment to evaluate the impact of different screen sizes on ColorVert. ColorVert is applied to the four devices stated above and we require volunteers to score the color scheme. We present the average user experience score in the bottom half of Fig.17(a). From the figure, ColorVert improves user experience on all four kinds of devices. And there are little difference of the user feedback for different screen sizes.

For weak lighting conditions, we perform similar experiments which restrict the ambient light luminance in the range of $0 - 100cd/m^2$ and calculate the UGR Ratio, which is defined as

$$UGR\ Ratio = \frac{ColorVert\ UGR}{Inversion\ UGR}. \tag{9}$$

Fig.17(b) shows the results. It can be seen that the UGR Ratio decreases as lighting strength goes down, which indicates that ColorVert can reduce the UGR value under weak lighting conditions. User experience survey under weak lighting conditions shows similar results as those of strong lighting conditions.

Therefore, our color transformation model can achieve a good user experience across different webpages and mobile devices for both sunlight and weak lighting conditions.

5.3 Transformation Time

Transformation time is another critical issue that concerns our system. User experience would be severely degraded if the transformation time cannot keep up with the occurrence of different kinds of events. We set up our system on four mobile devices, and further set their CPU frequency to certain levels. Then we randomly select 100 webpages and open them on four devices with different CPU frequencies under

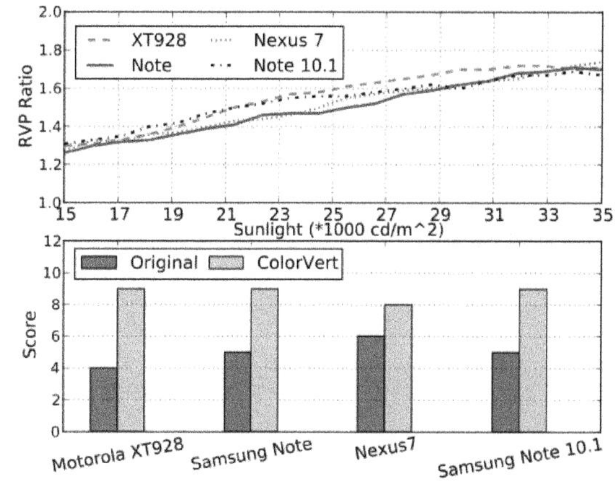

(a) strong light

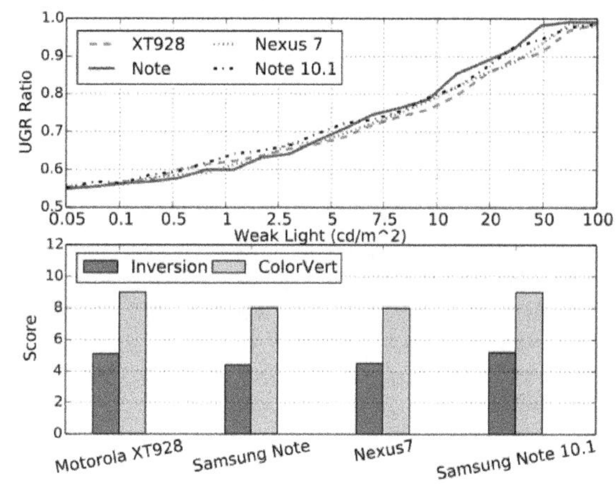

(b) weak light

Figure 17: UGR, RVP ratio and user experience score of different devices.

both strong and weak lighting conditions. In order to extract the time of color transformation, webpages are first saved on our mobile devices to avoid the interference from network connection. We record both the time consumed to load a webpage with and without our system and calculate their average time difference. Based on the trace collected, Fig.18 plots CDF of the color transformation time of ColorVert. It can be seen from the Fig.18 that for Motorola XT928 which uses 1GHz CPU frequency, about 90% of the ColorVert transformation time are within 25ms. Other devices show similar results. These results are very encouraging as they demonstrate the transformation time is very short, which is not noticeable by users. Also, we could see from the Fig.18 that CPU frequency almost has little effect on the performance of our system. Therefore, the delay caused by our system is acceptable in daily use and will not cause user experience degradation.

5.4 Overhead Analysis

Although Sensing Unit monitors the user and light event in real time and recalculate the optimal color scheme according to the events, the overhead of our system is negligible. Firstly, when there is no event occurs, our system does not perform any calculation. Secondly, we have taken various of

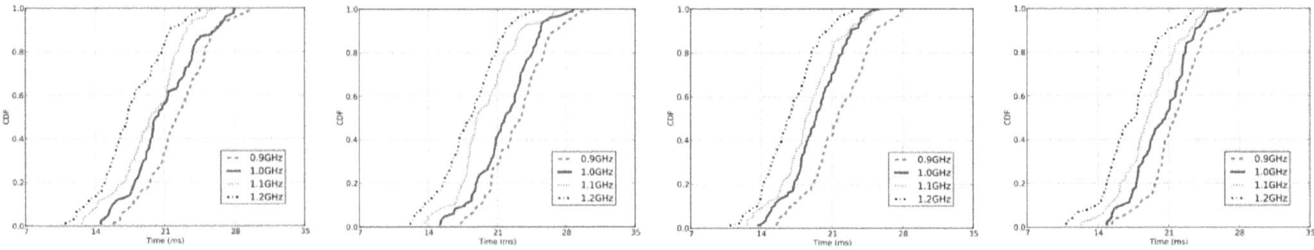

(a) Motorola XT928 (b) Samsung Galaxy Note (c) Nexus 7 (d) Samsung Galaxy Tab

Figure 18: CDF of average transform speed of ColorVert on different devices.

methods to decrease the occurrence frequency of both sensing light and human-screen interactions to further lessen the overhead. Also, total recalculation has a complexity of $O(k)$ and Fast Transformation only performs a linear transformation. So that only a few computation is need to calculate our optimal color scheme. As a result, our system is lightweight and the overhead could be negligible.

6. RELATED WORK

In this section, we review the existing work that related to our research. Modern mobile devices have introduced the automatic brightness adjustment system[19], which could change screen brightness level with ambient light. There are subsequent studies aimed at improving the performance of automatic brightness adjustment system[2] to improve user experience. However, they only focus on the luminance level of the screen without taking the color scheme into consideration, which is insufficient under very strong and weak lightning conditions.

With the explosive growth of smartphone usage, there are some researches about color scheme for smartphone displays to improve user experience under strong and weak lightning conditions. [20] present a theoretical basis to adjust use-preferred color temperature for smart-phone displays under various illuminant condition, but [20] do not consider readability and similarity that contribute to user experience, and do not propose any adaptive color scheme solution. Although there exist some work to improve user experience by adjusting color saturation[3] or contrast[4, 5] according to ambient light, they focus on images and videos display which is hard to achieve higher readability for texts. Moreover, [21] shows long-wavelength light affects visual performance under weak lightning conditions, but they do not discuss relationship between foreground and background color.

Moreover, researchers are interested in smartphone screen color scheme adaptation. Focused on saving the energy, [6] can adjust the color scheme of webpages to reduce the power consumption of smartphones. [7] constructs a predictive model for mobile systems and [22] uses a multi-objective optimization to find the most energy efficient color scheme. However, the purpose of these work is to improve energy efficiency while sacrifices user experience. The work[23] proposes a frame rate adaptation system, which considers both energy efficiency and user experience. However, it does not refer to the adaptive color adjustment for improving user experience. Also, there are some existing studies that try to adjust webpages for smartphone screens[24][25]. However, they aim at fitting the webpage into the small smartphone screen without considering the effect of ambient light on user experience.

Although the user experience of mobile devices has gained much attention, existing work has not concerned the impact of the webpage color scheme to user experience. Our work is different from the previous studies in that we explore the relationship between color and user experience, then design ColorVert, which can adaptively adjust the color scheme to improve user experience.

7. CONCLUSION

In this paper, we address the problem on the readability of mobile device screen display under dynamic lighting conditions. Through analyzing the color schemes on mobile device displays, we find that merely applying bright colors results in user experience degradation under both strong and weak lighting conditions. Furthermore, after running experiments with over 200 volunteers, we find that readability, comfort level and similarity are major factors that contribute to user experience when reading mobile device screens. We develop an adaptive color scheme transformation system, ColorVert, which senses the ambient light conditions and utilizes our proposed color transformation algorithm to adaptively calculate the optimal color scheme under both strong and weak lighting conditions. We prototype ColorVert on several types of smartphones and tablets. Extensive experiment results with over 200 participants demonstrate the effectiveness of the ColorVert design compared with the existing automatic brightness adjustment system. The prototype implementation shows that ColorVert is feasible to be applied in real-world scenarios for maintaining and improving user experience under various lighting conditions.

Although our work only focuses on dealing with plain text of web browsers, we believe the proposed color transform adaptation approach could be easily extended to handle other smartphone tasks with plain text using screen displays. In the future, we will extend our user experience-oriented color scheme on display of images, video and embedded text.

Acknowledgement

Research was sponsored by National Science Foundation CNS1217387, SES1450091, NSFC 61170238, NSFC 61373157, 973 Program 2014CB340303, Changjiang Scholar and Innovative Research Team in University (IRT1158, PCSIRT) China.

8. REFERENCES

[1] venturebeat.com, "Smartphone sales pass 250m in q3." [Online]. Available: http://venturebeat.com/2013/10/28/smartphone-sales-pass-250m-in-q3-and-samsung-grew/

[2] T.-Y. Ma, C.-Y. Lin, S.-W. Hsu, C.-W. Hu, and T.-W. Hou, "Automatic brightness control of the handheld device display with low illumination," in *Computer Science and Automation Engineering (CSAE), 2012 IEEE International Conference on*, vol. 2.

[3] The best smartphone display (it's not who you think). [Online]. Available: http://gizmodo.com/the-best-smartphone-display-its-not-who-you-think/

[4] Y. Monobe, H. Yamashita, T. Kurosawa, and H. Kotera, "Fadeless image projection preserving local contrast under ambient light," *Color and Imaging Conference*, vol. 2004, no. 1, pp. 130–135(6), 2004.

[5] T. O. Aydin, K. Myszkowski, and H.-P. Seidel, "Predicting display visibility under dynamically changing lighting conditions," *Computer Graphics Forum*, vol. 28, pp. 173–182, 2009.

[6] M. Dong and L. Zhong, "Chameleon: a color-adaptive web browser for mobile oled displays," *Mobile Computing, IEEE Transactions on*, vol. 11, no. 5.

[7] Y. Wen, Z. Liu, W. Shi, Y. Jiang, A. M. Cheng, and K. Le, "Energy efficient hybrid display and predictive models for embedded and mobile systems," in *Proceedings of the 2012 international conference on Compilers, architectures and synthesis for embedded systems.*

[8] anhosting.com, "How many people use smartphones to browse websites?" [Online]. Available: http://www.anhosting.com/blog/2012/11/how-many-people-use-smartphones-to-browse-websites/

[9] H. L. M. H. K. Hammond, "The metric system in illuminating engineering," in *Radiometry and Photometry.*

[10] M. Stokes, M. Anderson, S. Chandrasekar, and R. Motta, "A standard default color space for the internet-srgb," *Microsoft and Hewlett-Packard Joint Report*, 1996.

[11] M. S. Rea and M. J. Ouellette, "Visual performance using reaction times," *Lighting Research and Technology*, vol. 20, no. 4, pp. 139–153, 1988.

[12] M. S. Rea and M. J. Ouellette, "Relative visual performance: A basis for application," *Lighting Research and Technology*, vol. 23, no. 3, pp. 135–144, 1991.

[13] S. Plainis and I. Murray, "Neurophysiological interpretation of human visual reaction times: effect of contrast, spatial frequency and luminance," *Neuropsychologia*, vol. 38, no. 12.

[14] B. M. O.DONELL, J. F. Barraza, and E. M. Colombo, "The effect of chromatic and luminance information on reaction times," *Visual neuroscience*, vol. 27, no. 3, p. 119, 2010.

[15] CIE, "Discomfort glare in interior lighting," in *Discomfort Glare in Interior Lighting.*

[16] CIE, "Calculation and presentation of unified glare rating tables for indoor lighting luminaires."

[17] J. W. Peirce, "Psychopy psychophysics software in python," *Journal of neuroscience methods*, vol. 162, no. 1.

[18] D. I. MacLeod and R. M. Boynton, "Chromaticity diagram showing cone excitation by stimuli of equal luminance," *JOSA*, vol. 69, no. 8, pp. 1183–1186, 1979.

[19] C. S. Bell, "Automatic brightness control for displays," Apr. 19 2011, uS Patent 7,928,955.

[20] K. Choi and H.-J. Suk, "User-preferred color temperature adjustment for smartphone display under varying illuminants," *Optical Engineering*, vol. 53, pp. 061 708–061 708, 2014.

[21] R. Mantiuk, A. G. Rempel, and W. Heidrich, "Display considerations for night and low-illumination viewing," in *Proceedings of the 6th Symposium on Applied Perception in Graphics and Visualization.*

[22] S. Singh, D. Katiyar, M. Theodorou, S. Prasad, U. Mishra, R. Bhaskar, K. Pandey, O. Verma, A. Mishra *et al.*, "Nutritional and morphological attributes of stay green vis-à-vis go-brown sorghum cultivars at different stages of maturity." *Indian Journal of Animal Sciences*, vol. 79, no. 4.

[23] H. Han, J. Yu, H. Zhu, Y. Chen, J. Yang, G. Xue, Y. Zhu, and M. Li, "E 3: energy-efficient engine for frame rate adaptation on smartphones," in *Proceedings of the 11th ACM Conference on Embedded Networked Sensor Systems*, 2013, p. 15.

[24] M. Jones, G. Marsden, N. Mohd-Nasir, K. Boone, and G. Buchanan, "Improving web interaction on small displays," *Computer Networks*, vol. 31, no. 11.

[25] N. Bila, T. Ronda, I. Mohomed, K. N. Truong, and E. de Lara, "Pagetailor: reusable end-user customization for the mobile web," in *Proceedings of the 5th international conference on Mobile systems, applications and services.*

cETX: Incorporating Spatiotemporal Correlation for Better Wireless Networking

Song Min Kim Shuai Wang Tian He

Department of Computer Science and Engineering
University of Minnesota

{ksong, shuaiw, tianhe}@cs.umn.edu

ABSTRACT

In this work, we experimentally observe the existence of spatiotemporal correlation among adjacent wireless links within short time intervals. Such an observation calls attention to potential errors in existing popular metrics built upon the assumption of link independence. Specifically we propose cETX (correlated ETX), a generalized metric, to compensate for estimation errors suffered by the widely-adopted ETX in the presence of correlated interference. To the best of our knowledge, this is the first work to introduce a unified metric embracing both temporal and spatiotemporal correlations. The highlight of the cETX metric is its broad applicability and effectiveness. Evaluations on ZigBee (802.15.4) and Wi-Fi (802.11b/g/n) testbeds deployed in a lab, corridor, and on a bridge reveal that: Simply replacing ETX with cETX (i) cuts down the error by 70.2% and 62.1%, respectively, and (ii) saves averages of 22% and 37% communication cost in three unicast [4, 13, 17] and nine broadcast protocols [7, 18, 23, 24, 27, 30, 40] at the price of only 0.7% additional overhead.

Categories and Subject Descriptors

C.2.1 [**Network Architecture and Design**]: Wireless communications

Keywords

Wireless routing; Route metrics; Energy efficiency

1. INTRODUCTION

Wireless links are unreliable and prone to losses due to noise and interference [16, 19, 35, 36, 42]. To effectively utilize these unreliable wireless links, research calls for metrics that can accurately estimate the qualities of individual links as well as end-to-end paths. Among the extensive volume of admirable studies dealing with routing under lossy links [8, 11, 41], expected transmission count (ETX) [11] is the most popular for its generality and effectiveness, and has been cited over 3,000 times according to Google Scholar.

SenSys'15, November 1–4, 2015, Seoul, South Korea.
© 2015 ACM. ISBN 978-1-4503-3631-4/15/11 ...$15.00.
DOI: http://dx.doi.org/10.1145/2809695.2809704.

Our further studies on link characteristics, however, reveal that ETX suffers from a few limitations. First, recent work on the temporal property of wireless links [10, 32] shows that transmissions over a link within a short time interval are highly dependent, indicating the existence of temporal correlation among transmissions. This property is not taken into account in the design of the ETX metric, imposing a limitation on its ability to reflect the true link quality. This is because ETX is defined as the inverse of packet reception ratio (PRR). This value is in fact the mean of the geometric random variable with independent trials, indicating that ETX is implicitly built on the independence assumption among transmissions.

Another link characteristic enlightened by current work ([28, 33]) is the existence of a reception correlation among the receivers of broadcast packets due to cross-network interference and correlated shadowing. Simply put, the receptions of broadcast packets at adjacent nodes are correlated at the same time instant, indicating spatial correlation. In this work, we observe that spatial correlation interplays with temporal correlation to exhibit reception correlation at consecutive links. In other words, there exists spatiotemporal correlation, i.e., the packet reception of a link is dependent on the recent reception at preceding links along a path. Since existing metrics including ETX are hop-by-hop designs, they fail to take spatiotemporal correlation into account.

In this paper, we reveal why ETX cannot represent the true quality of links in the face of temporal and spatiotemporal correlation. To address this issue, we design an enhanced version of ETX, called correlated ETX (cETX) that explores the phenomena to reflect the true performance of links and paths more precisely compared to ETX. In detail, we provide a unified metric embracing both temporal and spatiotemporal correlation factors. While keeping the intuitive idea of ETX intact (i.e., explicitly quantifying expected number of transmissions), our metric selects better links and paths that leads to less transmissions, thus achieving energy savings. In summary, our contributions are as follows:

- We experimentally reveal the phenomenon of spatiotemporal correlation and its potential impact on routing designs.
- We propose a new metric – cETX, capable of capturing temporal and spatiotemporal properties of wireless links. To the best of our knowledge, this is the first work to embed the two effects into a unified metric.
- We demonstrate how to incorporate cETX into (i) classical shortest path unicast algorithms and (ii) clas-

sical/collaborative broadcast algorithms, while maintaining the unicast path optimality and minimizing network-wide broadcast overhead distributively.

- We compare the accuracy of cETX and ETX through ZigBee and Wi-Fi testbed experiments, and via analysis on the Roofnet [3] trace to demonstrate error reduction of 70.2%, 62.1%, and 33.2%, respectively.
- We experimentally validate the applicability and effectiveness of cETX by replacing ETX with cETX in three unicast and nine broadcast protocols utilizing diverse network structures. cETX cuts down averages of 22% and 37% communication cost at the price of only 0.7% additional overhead via parameter piggybacking.

The paper is organized as follows. Section 2 motivates the work. Section 3 follows with the underlying model and reasoning. Section 4 and Section 5 present the design and implementation of cETX, where its applications are introduced in Section 6. Section 7 evaluates cETX, followed by in-situ deployment demonstration in Section 8. We summarize related work in Section 9 and conclude in Section 10.

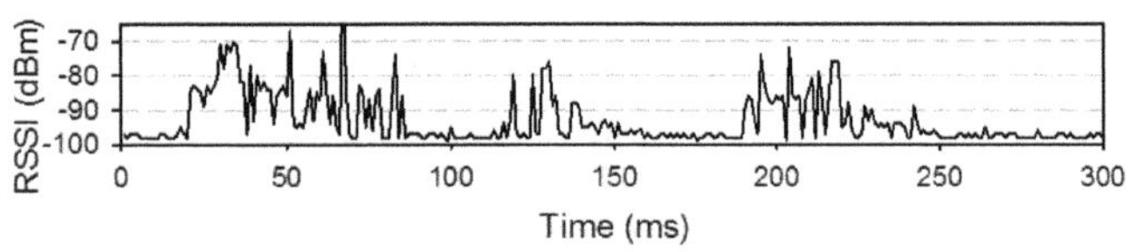

Figure 1: Interference Burst

2. MOTIVATION

Spatiotemporal correlation occurs with the interference and shadowing spanning through multiple links and last for a duration of multiple packets. Figure 1 shows the interference captured under an office environment where many of the spike bursts last over tens of milliseconds. The captured signal strength ranges from -70 to -90dBm, a level of typical Wi-Fi signals. In sum, the observed interference from Wi-Fi is not only explosive, but also strong enough to simultaneously affect multiple low-power 802.15.4 links, suggesting that it is one of the causes of spatiotemporal correlation.

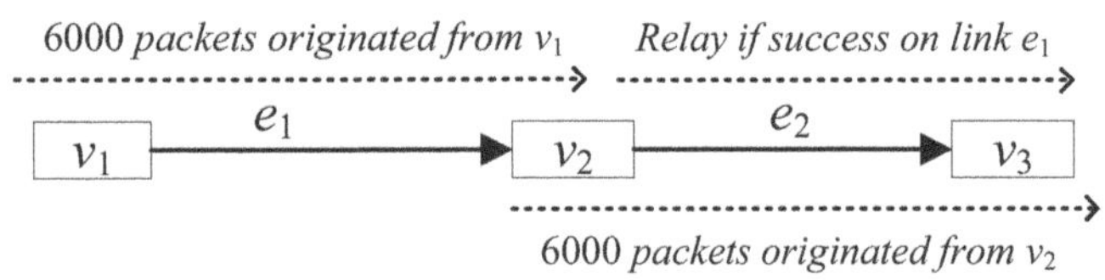

Figure 2: Experiment Topology

2.1 Spatiotemporal Correlation Revealed

We experimentally validate the phenomenon of spatiotemporal correlation in practice, among consecutive wireless links along a path. A simple two-hop network is formed as shown in Figure 2, operating on 802.15.4 channel 12 with a transmission power of -25dBm. Ten such networks are deployed for statistical significance. In each network, two cases are tested. **Case #1:** Node v_1 transmits 6000 packets to v_2. Upon successfully receiving a packet, v_2 *relays* the packet to v_3 five times, each after 2, 8, 14, 20, and 26*ms* delay. **Case #2:** Node v_2 transmits 6000 packets generated by itself to v_3. Please note that, in case #1, transmission over link e_2 only occurs upon success on e_1. Therefore the reception success probability on e_2 in this case is conditional, given the success on preceding link e_1. On the other hand, the success probability over e_2 in case #2 is considered marginal, as it is irrelevant to e_1.

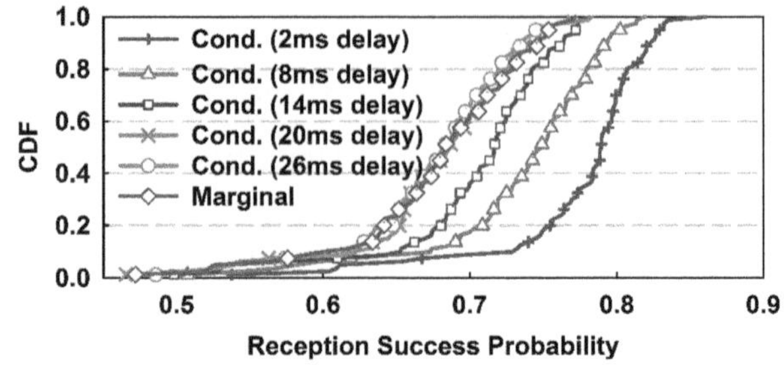

Figure 3: Validating spatiotemporal correlation: whenever v_2 successfully receives a packet from v_1 it *relays* the packet five times to v_3 with different delays after reception. Thus, the success ratio of the relayed packets are *conditional* to the success of the transmission from v_1 to v_2, whereas the packets originated at v_2 are *marginal*.

Figure 3 shows the experiment results of e_2's reception success probabilities, where conditional curves are obtained from case #1, and the marginal is from case #2. There exists a significant difference between the conditional probability with 2*ms* delay and the marginal probability. This supports the existence of spatiotemporal (positive) correlation between e_1 and e_2. That is, success on the preceding link (e_1) strongly implies success on the following link (e_2). Moreover, 20 and 26*ms* curves nearly overlap with the marginal curve, indicating spatiotemporal correlation fades away after 20*ms*. To conclude, the experiment result gives us a simple but effective design guidance: We can increase the chance of a successful reception of a packet by simply relaying it within a short time interval, e.g., within 20*ms* in our experiment.

Link1:	*F*	*S*	*S*	*F*	*S*	*F*	*F*	*S*	*F*	*S*
Link2:	*F*	*F*	*F*	*S*	*S*	*S*	*F*	*F*	*S*	*S*
	t_0	t_1	t_2	t_3	t_4	t_5	t_6	t_7	t_8	t_9

Figure 4: Temporal correlation effect: Despite the same reception ratios, bursty failure in Link2 demands 1.9 transmissions where Link1 requires 1.6.

2.2 Impact of Temporal Correlation

We illustrate the effect of temporal correlation via a simple example in Figure 4. In the history of ten transmissions of two links, S and F represent transmission success and failure. Since both links experience five S and five F, ETX indicates that the two links have equal performance, i.e., 10/5=2 expected transmissions. However, the true average transmissions are not equal. Let's consider the case where we start transmitting at t_0. On Link1, the transmission succeeds at t_1 which causes two transmissions (i.e., fail at t_0, success at t_1). It costs four on Link2 as it succeeds at t_3 after three failures. Similarly, when we start the transmission at t_1, Link1 succeeds in a single transmission, while Link2 requires three.

When the start of a transmission occurs with equal probabilities across $t_0 - t_9$, we obtain the true average number of transmissions by repeating the above process up to t_9 and taking the average. This yields $(2 + 1 + \cdots + 1)/10 = 1.6$ and $(4 + 3 + \cdots + 1)/10 = 1.9$ for Link1 and Link2, indicating that Link1 is indeed a better link, despite their equal ETX. The performance difference of the two links can be described via conditional probability of failure followed by success, i.e, $Pr(S^n|F^{n-1})$ for $1 \leq n \leq 9$. This represents the link's ability to recover from failures. Thus, larger value indicate better performance. The values are 0.8 and 0.4 for Link1 and Link2, which confirms our argument.

Figure 5: Temporal Correlation in real trace forces two links with similar reception ratios to exhibit different demands of 2.05 and 2.98 transmissions.

The observation is further verified on the real traces in Figure 5, collected from two pairs of MICAz nodes. Each trace from two links holds a record of 10^3 packet transmissions. Black bars indicate failures while whites indicate successes. The packet reception ratios of Link3 and Link4 are 0.49 and 0.5, leading to approximately the same ETX of 2 for both links. However, the difference in the true average transmissions is quite large; 2.05 and 2.98 for Link3 and Link4, respectively. This is due to the consecutive failure chunks demonstrated in Link4; it is less able to recover from the failure than Link3. This difference again can be represented by the conditional probability. The values of $Pr(S^n|F^{n-1})$ are 0.49 and 0.29 for Link3 and Link4.

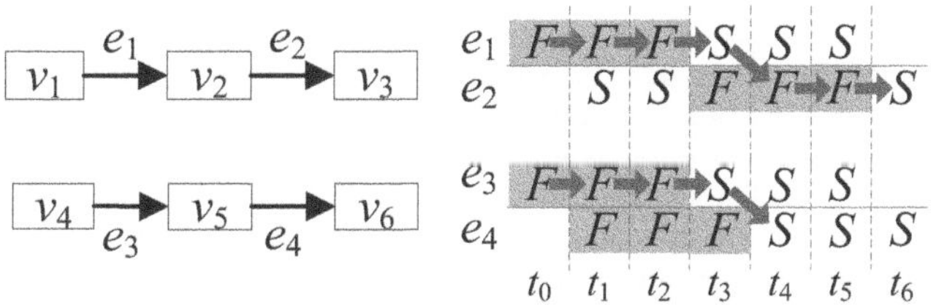

Figure 6: Higher spatiotemporal correlation in consecutive links allows a better chance of success on the succeeding link following the link proceeding it. Marked with arrows, the number of transmissions for an end-to-end delivery is therefore smaller for the lower path.

2.3 Impact of Spatiotemporal Correlation

In Figure 6, we use two two-hop paths to show how spatiotemporal correlation affects the network performance that ETX fails to capture. The packet reception ratios of every link in the figure, e_1-e_4, are equally 1/2. This yields ETX value of $2 + 2 = 4$ for both upper and lower paths. However, the links in the lower path, e_3 and e_4, are more positively correlated to each other than those (e_1 and e_2) in the upper path. Starting with the upper path, suppose that node v_1 has a packet to deliver to node v_3 and starts sending at time t_0. The packet successfully reaches v_2 after four transmissions (i.e. F→F→F→S). The transmission on e_2 starts at t_4 but succeeds at t_6, consuming three transmissions (F→F→S). Therefore, end-to-end delivery in the upper path consumes a total of seven transmissions. This forwarding flow is demonstrated in Figure 6 as arrows. Similarly, we can easily see that the lower path requires five transmissions. This indicates that the lower path performs better than the upper path, despite their equivalence in the ETX values.

This example suggests that spatiotemporal correlation can improve the network performance. That is, when consecutive links in a path are strongly (positively) correlated, forwarding a packet shortly after receiving it from the preceding link has a high chance of successful receptions in the following link. Therefore, spatiotemporal correlation should be considered for an accurate performance measurement in multi-hop scenarios. To do so, we represent the degree of spatiotemporal correlation with conditional probability, i.e., $Pr(S_i^n|S_{i-1}^{n-1})$ at arbitrary time t_n when e_{i-1} precedes e_i. To verify, the conditional probability in this example yields $0.33 = Pr(S_2^n|S_1^{n-1}) < Pr(S_4^n|S_3^{n-1}) = 1$, correctly reflecting the relative performance of the two paths under spatiotemporal correlation.

3. DESIGN BACKGROUND

In this section, we first present the model that lays the foundation of our design. Then, we provide empirical evidences and analysis on the suitability of such a model for our purpose of capturing correlation.

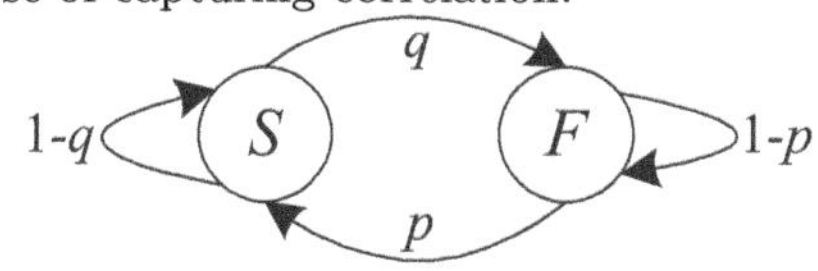

Figure 7: Gilbert Model

3.1 Underlying Model

This section presents the underlying model to help understand our design presented in the next section. Recall in section 2 we showed that both temporal and spatiotemporal correlations can be quantified by conditional probabilities. A simple way of modeling with conditional probabilities is the Markov representation. Our design starts off from the *Gilbert Model* [15] in Figure 7, a famous channel model based on two state Markov chain. In the model, S indicates error-free state, while F is when the channel is erroneous. The state transition probabilities are denoted as p and q. That is, by letting $Pr(F^n)$ and $Pr(S^{n-1})$ denote the probabilities of being at states F and S at times t_n and t_{n-1} respectively, then $p = Pr(S^n|F^{n-1})$. Similarly, $q = Pr(F^n|S^{n-1})$. Moreover, steady state probabilities of the two states are computed as

$$\pi_S = \frac{p}{p+q}, \pi_F = \frac{q}{p+q} \tag{1}$$

where they indicate the chance of being at the corresponding state at an arbitrary time instant regardless of the initial state, after a sufficient number of state transitions. We follow this model to represent status of a single link.That is, a transmission over the link succeeds if and only if the link is in state S, while fails in state F. This lets transition probabilities, p and q, to indicate temporal correlation within the link. Extending the model to capture spatiotemporal correlation will be discussed later in Section 4.

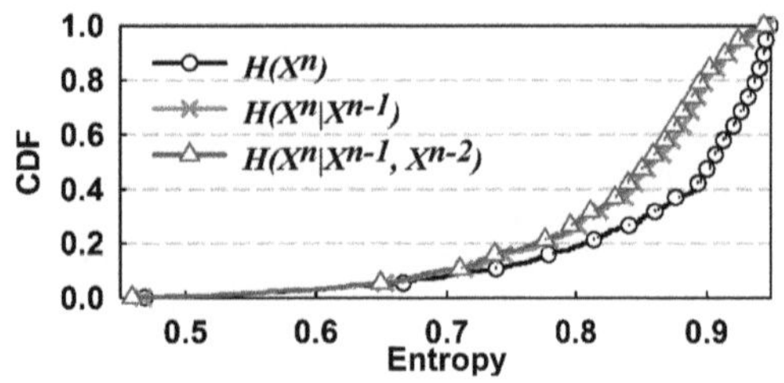

(a) Under Temporal Correlation

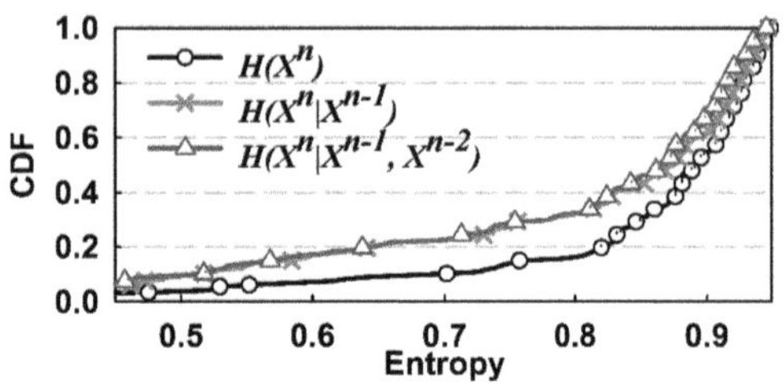

(b) Under Spatiotemporal Correlation

Figure 8: Residual entropies in both (a) and (b) suggest that estimation on correlated links can benefit from 1st order Markov chain design, while a higher order model is not necessary.

3.2 Validity of 1st Order Markov Design

Our design is based on the Gilbert Model which is a first-order Markov model. In other words, the design benefits from the success/failure information obtained from the previous transmission to infer success of the following transmission. This raises a natural follow-up question: Can we even better estimate the success/failure of the next transmission, given the information on the last two, or even three transmissions? In other words, will a higher order Markov model help to further improve the quality of estimation? To this end, we analyze experimental data to show that the first order Markov model is the right choice; adopting higher order models will not make noticeable differences, while imposing additional complexity to the design and computation.

We achieve this by applying the concept of *entropy* from the information theory, which quantifies the uncertainty within a random variable as number of bits. Higher bit indicates higher uncertainty, which leads to lower estimation quality. Let X^n be a bernoulli random variable indicating reception success or failure at an arbitrary time instant, t_n. Then, the entropy within X^n is denoted as $H(X^n)$, indicating the marginal entropy. We further let X^{n-1} and X^{n-2} indicate reception success or failure at t_{n-1} and t_{n-2}, respectively (i.e., one and two time instants preceding X^n). Then, the conditional entropy expresses the amount of uncertainty in X^n when the value of X^{n-1} or both X^{n-1} and X^{n-2} are known, denoted as $H(X^n|X^{n-1})$ and $H(X^n|X^{n-1}, X^{n-2})$. For brevity entropy computations are given in Appendix A.

Since success or failure can be expressed in a single bit, the maximum uncertainty is 1, when we do not have any clue on success or failure. Conversely, the uncertainty of 0 is when it can be perfectly estimated. Figure 8 shows marginal and conditional entropies in the face of two correlations. Figure 8(a) was obtained from experimental data of 5×10^5 consecutive packets over 50 links with packet interval of $6ms$, where experiment in Figure 8(b) was done similarly to that in Section 2.1. While achieving the entropy of 0 is impossible due to natural randomness in links caused by shadowing and multipath fading, two clear observations can be made from the figures: (i) The gaps between conditional and marginal entropies indicate that the knowledge on previous transmission is helpful in estimating the success or failure of the following transmission, again verifying the existence of spatiotemporal and temporal correlations. (ii) $H(X^n|X^{n-1})$ and $H(X^n|X^{n-1}, X^{n-2})$ are very close in both figures, suggesting 1st order is as good as higher order design in the estimation quality, despite its lower complexity. This supports the effectiveness and sufficiency of our 1st order Markov-based design.

4. MAIN DESIGN

Based on the observations in the previous section we design cETX on top of the Gilbert Model. However, this model is only capable of representing the status of a single link. This means that the model is not enough to express spatiotemporal correlation, which is a relationship across multiple links. In this section, we address this issue by proposing an extended model, from which our metric cETX is derived.

4.1 Design Overview

As an extension of ETX, cETX inherits the main idea of ETX to represent link quality by the expected number of transmissions. It is shown later in this section that cETX also retains the additive property of ETX, such that the path cost is simply the sum of cETX. Nevertheless, unlike ETX which assumes the packet receptions are independent, we take both temporal and spatiotemporal correlations into account to more accurately estimate the link/path cost. In fact, cETX is a generalized version of ETX, extended to incorporate knowledge on any degree of correlation into the link/path cost. For example, cETX simply reduces to ETX when there is no correlation among links.

4.2 Extended Gilbert Model

We propose an extended representation of the Gilbert Model for a few distinctive features that the original model does not possess. Specifically, it enables (i) the straightforward model extension to multi-hop scenarios, (ii) tracking the packet forwarding status to allow the computation of cETX directly from the model, and (iii) capturing spatiotemporal correlation among consecutive links in a path.

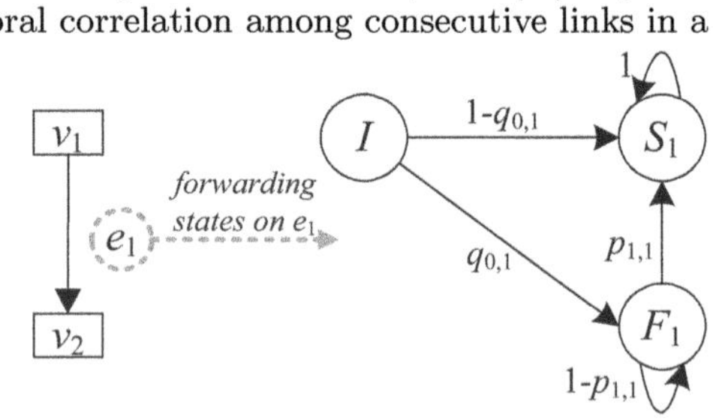

Figure 9: A single-hop network (left) and the corresponding extended Gilbert Model representation (right). The model enables direct computation of our metric as well as straight-forward adaption to multi-hop scenario.

The Extended Gilbert Model describes the forwarding status of each packet in the form of 1st order Markov chain. For ease of understanding we start from a single-hop network and its corresponding model depicted in Figure 9. The three states, S_1, F_1, and I, express packet forwarding on e_1. States S_1 and F_1 indicate the success and failure of the transmission over e_1, while I stands for the initial state indicating that the transmission has not yet taken place. Then, the packet forwarding process on the model follows intuitive steps: starting from state I, a transition to either S_1 or F_1 occurs depending on the transmission success or failure. Upon failures, retransmission attempts are made to transit from F_1 to S_1, until S_1 is reached.

From the definition of state I, it is clear that its initial probability is 1. Now let us describe the transition probability introduced in the model. Keeping notations consistent to the previous sections, let S_1^n and F_1^{n-1} denote the transmission success and failure over e_1 at time t_n and t_{n-1}, respectively. Then, $p_{1,1}$ denotes the probability of a successful transmission after a failure in the previous time instant, $p_{1,1} = Pr(S_1^n|F_1^{n-1})$. Note that the subscript $_{1,1}$ used in $p_{1,1}$ denotes these two transmissions occur on the same link, e_1. Essentially $p_{1,1}$ represents the temporal correlation between consecutive transmissions within e_1. On the contrary, $q_{0,1}$ simply indicates the probability of failure in the initial transmission over e_1. Zero in the subscript implies that no previous transmission exists. Because we do not retransmit a packet that has already been received, the transition probability from S_1 to any other state is 0. In other words, the forwarding process over link e_1 terminates once S_1 has been reached.

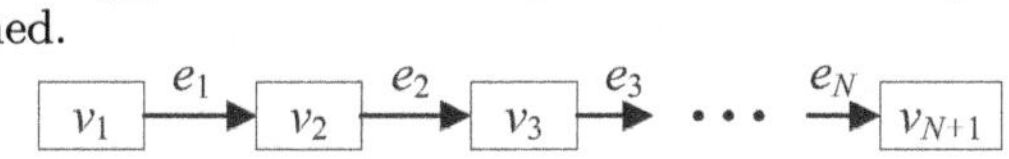

Figure 10: N-hop Linear Network

4.3 Multi-hop Gilbert Model

In the previous section we proposed the extended Gilbert Model for a single-hop network. We now further expand the model to a multi-hop scenario depicted in Figure 10.

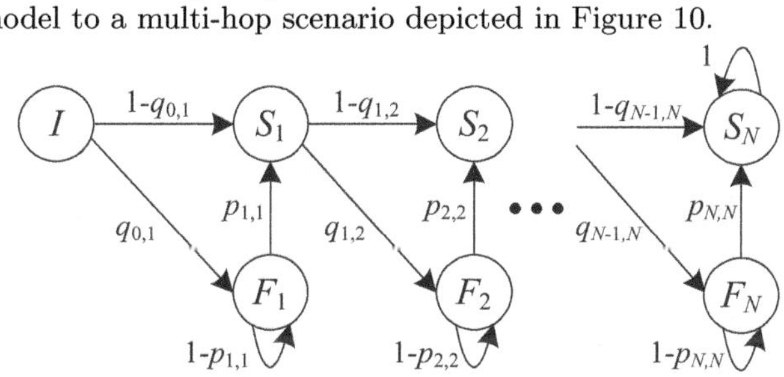

Figure 11: N-hop Gilbert Model

The multi-hop Gilbert Model for the corresponding network is given in Figure 11, where it is an extension from the model in Figure 9 to express multiple links. As shown in the figure, the extension is as simple as adding a pair of S and F states per link. Then, the spatiotemporal parameter is introduced between consecutive links. In the multi-hop path once a successful transmission takes place in the preceding link, an immediate transmission follows in the next link. For instance, v_2 starts its transmission over e_2 shortly after the transmission success from v_1 to v_2 over e_1. The dependency between these two consecutive events is spatiotemporal correlation, which can be represented as $q_{1,2} = Pr(F_2^n|S_1^{n-1})$ where the subscript $_{1,2}$ on $q_{1,2}$ denotes that success at previous time t_{n-1} occurred on e_1, where the following failure was on e_2. Generally, spatiotemporal dependency is considered between any two consecutive links, indicated as $q_{i-1,i}$ for $2 \leq i \leq N$ in the multi-hop Gilbert Model. Clearly the multi-hop model captures both temporal and spatiotemporal correlation via p and q parameters.

4.4 cETX Computation

We now show how our metric cETX can be computed from the multi-hop model in Figure 11. Note that cETX over a link is defined as the estimated number of transmissions to deliver a packet over the link. Suppose we want to compute cETX for an arbitrary link, $cETX_{e_i}$. Transmission on e_i starts on state S_{i-1}, and ends when S_i has been reached (I and S_1 for e_1). Since the state transition occurs for every transmission, the cETX_{e_i} value equals the expected number of transitions to reach state S_i from S_{i-1}. This is often referred to as the expected first passage time in Markov chain theory, which can be computed as follows:

$$cETX_{e_i} = 1 + q_{i-1,i} \times \frac{1}{p_{i,i}} \tag{2}$$

The equation can be intuitively understood by referring to our model. The first term in Eq.(2), i.e., 1, indicates the initial transmission which is mandatory. The second term indicates the product of the initial transmission failure probability, i.e., $q_{i-1,i}$, and the expected number of transmissions under the failure of the initial transmission, i.e., $\frac{1}{p_{i,i}}$. Therefore, the equation simply implies that a low cETX value is achievable where there are two conditions: (i) a small chance of the failure in the initial transmission, and (ii) a high chance of recovering from the failure in case the initial transmission fails.

Special Case: Eq.(2) shows that cETX is a function of spatiotemporal ($q_{i-1,i}$) and temporal ($p_{i,i}$) correlation parameters. However, the initial link e_1 is a special case as there is no link preceding it. In other words, e_1 has no link to be spatiotemporally correlated to it. Therefore $q_{0,1}$ is expressed sorely in terms of temporal correlation parameters, $p_{1,1}$ and $q_{1,1}$, to be the steady state probability of F_1. Please note that $q_{1,1}$ is found in the original Gilbert Model (q in Figure 7). Borrowing the steady state probability in Eq.(1) and rewriting with our notations, we have

$$q_{0,1} = \frac{q_{1,1}}{p_{1,1} + q_{1,1}} \tag{3}$$

The rationale behind this equation is as follows. The first transmission on the initial link is triggered at an arbitrary time instant, whenever the sender has a packet to transmit. This indicates that we need to estimate the link state at time t_n without the knowledge of the state at t_{n-1}. In this case, our best estimate becomes the steady state probability of S_1, which is simply the ratio of the time e_1 spent in S_1. Now, we can finally obtain $cETX_{e_1}$ by plugging in Eq.(3) to Eq.(2).

$$cETX_{e_1} = 1 + \frac{q_{1,1}}{(p_{1,1} + q_{1,1}) \cdot p_{1,1}} \tag{4}$$

Path cETX: Our metric retains the additive property of ETX, indicating that path cETX is the sum of link cETXs in the path. This serves as the key that allows us to find the optimal path with cETX with appropriate modifications to traditional shortest path algorithms, which will be discussed in later part of the paper. For a proof on the additive property, let us again consider the network and its model in Figures 10 and 11, where $cETX_E$ represents the cETX of the entire N-hop path. Then, $cETX_E$ is the expected first passage time from state I to S_N. Let the first passage time from state I to S_1 be denoted by a random variable Y_1, from S_1 to S_2 as Y_2, and so on until Y_N. Then, by definition $cETX_E$ is the expected value of the sum of all Y_i, i.e., $cETX_E = E[\Sigma_{i=1}^N Y_i]$. Due to the linearity of expectation and since $cETX_{e_i} = E[Y_i]$, we have

$$cETX_E = \sum_{i=1}^{n} cETX_{e_i} \tag{5}$$

Hence the additive property holds. We also note that cETX is indeed a generalized version of ETX, and it simply reduces to ETX under independent packet receptions. Proof on the relationship between cETX and ETX under different degrees of correlations is given in Appendix B.

5. IMPLEMENTATION ISSUES

This section describes how to obtain the parameters p and q for cETX computation, and shows *burst probing* enables precisely measuring the true performances of wireless links.

	t_0	t_1	t_2	t_3	t_4	t_5	t_6	t_7	t_8	t_9	t_{10}	t_{11}
e_1	F	F	S	F	S	F	F	S	S	F	F	S
e_2	F	F	F	F	S	F	F	S	S	S	S	S

Figure 12: Parameter Computation Example

5.1 Parameter Computation

Among the parameters required by our design, those related to temporal correlation within a link are p and q. We again use S_n and F_n to denote the transmission success and failure at t_n. Let us compute the p and q values for e_2 in Figure 12. Maximum likely estimation for these parameters can be obtained simply by counting the number of transitions between success and failure, which turns out to be $p_{2,2} = Pr(S_2^n|F_2^{n-1}) = 1/3$ and $q_{2,2} = Pr(F_2^n|S_2^{n-1}) = 1/5$ for $0 < n \leq 11$. Similarly, the spatiotemporal correlation parameter when e_1 precedes e_2 is also computed as $q_{1,2} = Pr(F_2^n|S_1^{n-1}) = 1/2$.

5.2 Measurement in Practice

Probing refers to the technique of transmitting a small number of packets to support some fundamental functions including link quality measurement and neighbor discovery. Thus probes are commonly utilized in various state-of-the-art link metrics [10, 14, 25, 26]. Specifically, they adopt the classical periodic probing, where a single probe message is broadcast every fixed interval. However this mechanism suffers from limitations in measuring link performances; We observe that immediate retransmissions and relays induce a stream of packets within a short time interval to impose correlations between transmissions, which cannot be captured by periodic probes. To address this issue, we propose burst probing, where a batch of consecutive probes are sent at a short time interval. In the meantime, to keep the overhead at a reasonable level, the interval between probe bursts is set such that the number of probe packets per unit time is kept the same as that of periodic probing. This ensures the equivalent amount of overhead when cETX replaces ETX.

Unlike temporal parameters, measuring the spatiotemporal parameter via probing incurs additional overhead. This is because the spatiotemporal parameter for a link needs to be measured for every preceding link. To avoid such overhead, we obtain spatiotemporal parameters via the normal data traffic. Recall that the spatiotemporal correlation parameter is simply the failing probability of the initial transmission, just after the packet is received from the preceding link. This statistic can be easily collected; whenever a node receives a data packet, it records the preceding link, as well as the transmission success/failure of the initial transmission. This information is piggybacked on probes to be broadcast to its neighbors. To sum up, cETX assumes spatiotemporal independence under data traffic volume insufficient to obtain spatiotemporal parameter, where the accuracy of cETX nevertheless exceeds that of ETX due to the consideration of temporal correlation. Spatiotemporal correlation is reflected as the traffic increases, where multiple data flows in the network offer cETX with more opportunity to select better routes considering spatiotemporal correlation.

5.3 Overhead under Link Dynamics

We run an experiment to compare the link estimation performances of cETX and ETX in relation to the overhead they induce. To summarize, our result indicates estimation error for cETX is only 1/3 of ETX, at the cost of only 0.7% additional overhead. Experimental details are as follows: Burst probing in cETX occurs every 40s, where five consecutive probes are sent each time. ETX sends one probe every 8s. Both probing schemes induce overhead of 1/8 probe per second, indicating a fair comparison. To further maintain fairness, both metrics use the history of up to 90 probes, the value suggested by ETX [11]. In other words, when there is a data packet to be forwarded (every 10s in our case), both metrics use the history of the last 90 probes to estimate the number of (re)transmissions until a successful delivery. Then, the estimations are compared to the number of transmissions that actually occurs, to verify their accuracies. The 80-minute experiment consists of 11 MICAz nodes, v_1 through v_{11}. One node (v_1) serves as the sender while all others are receivers.

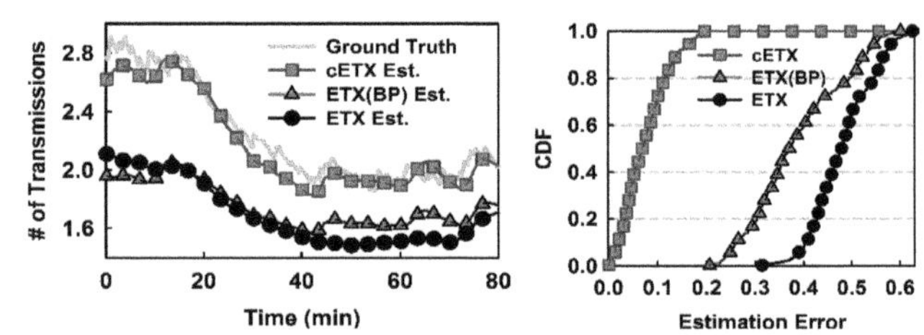

(a) Estimation under dynamics (b) Error distribution

Figure 13: Link estimation with cETX closely reflects the actual value (i.e., the ground truth) while ETX is rather optimistic. This is because cETX accounts for bursty losses which ETX fails to capture.

Figure 13(a) shows the result on a link between v_1 and v_8. The ground truth indicates the actual number of transmissions, while other curves are estimations based on probe history. Furthermore, Figure 13(b) exhibits the distribution of the estimation error (i.e., the absolute difference from the ground truth). We note that there are two versions of ETX in the figure, where one is the original ETX with periodic probing and the other is the modified ETX with burst probing. From the figures, we find that the estimate of cETX is far better than both versions of ETX. The average estimation error of cETX, ETX with burst probing, and original ETX in all ten links are 0.16, 0.42, and 0.48. The performance of ETX with burst probing sits in between cETX and the original ETX because it benefits from burst probing which mimics the data (re)transmission scenario, but it fails to accurately capture the correlation within. We note that the degree of cETX's advantage in accuracy applies to the link metrics built on top of ETX, such as 4B [14].

The overhead incurred by probes is approximately 3.2% of the total energy consumed. Since probing is adopted in the majority of the link metrics, its overhead should be amortized. On the other hand, exclusive overhead introduced by our design is the extra information piggybacked on probe packets. This takes up a tiny portion of about 0.7% of the total energy consumption.

5.4 Compatibility with Different MAC

The generality of cETX allows it to be applied to networks running various MAC protocols. This is because (i) both contention-based [9, 29, 43] and reservation-based [31, 44] MACs adopt a quick-retransmission policy for lost packet, which incurs temporally correlated, consecutive loss captured by cETX. For example CSMA commonly serves as the basis function for contention-based MACs, where the retransmission for a lost packet is made after a short duration of ACK timeout – 864us and 372us for ZigBee [39] and Wi-Fi [38], respectively. (ii) Spatiotemporal correlation captured via data traffic in cETX naturally reflects the forwarding scheme adopted by the network. That is, the corresponding degree of spatiotemporal correlation is captured regardless of immediate or delayed (e.g., duty cycled networks) packet forwarding. Immediate forwarding is likely to exhibit spatiotemporal correlation. On the other hand, when the delay is sufficiently large, cETX reflects the independence between consecutive links (i.e., no spatiotemporal correlation) where cETX still remains more accurate than ETX due to its consideration on temporal correlation.

6. UNICAST/BROADCAST OVER CETX

Replacing the popular metric of ETX, cETX can be generically applied to many protocols. This section presents how optimality is maintained in unicast protocols, followed by the benefit to broadcast schemes.

6.1 Application to Unicast

When spatiotemporal correlation is considered, the cETX value of a link is dependent on the preceding link. In this section we demonstrate via an example, how optimal shortest path can be found in a distributed manner using distance vector with two-hop information.

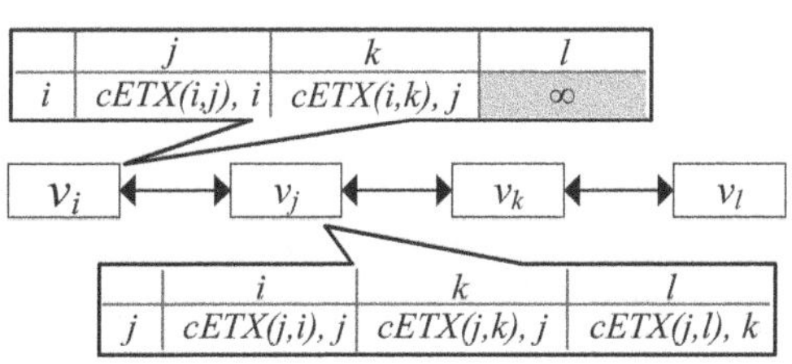

Figure 14: cETX in Unicast – Example Scenario

Let us consider a simple four-node network in Figure 14, where $cETX(i,j)$ indicates cETX from node v_i to v_j. Initially, nodes attain local information about their two-hop neighbors by exchanging information between one-hop neighbors. Then the problem becomes: How cETX beyond two hops can be obtained through further iterative exchanges. That is, how the gray box in v_i's distance vector (i.e., $cETX(i,l)$) can be found. First, we note that $cETX(i,l) \neq cETX(i,j) + cETX(j,l)$, as $cETX(j,l)$ does not reflect the effect of correlation among the link between v_i and v_j and the link between v_j and v_k. Instead, $cETX(i,l)$ can be obtained via the below relationship:

$$cETX(i,l) = cETX(i,k) + cETX(j,l) - cETX(j,k)$$

where last the term, $cETX(j,k)$, is the cost of link between v_j and v_k *not considering* the correlation with the link between v_i and v_j (i.e., the special case in Section 4.4). Referring back to Figure 14, the above equation implies that v_i can obtain $cETX(i,l)$ via exchange of distance vector with its direct neighbor, v_j. In fact, the equation can be generally applied to finding cETX to any multiple hops (i.e., v_l of any hop distance from v_i), given that v_j and v_k are one and two-hop neighbors to v_i.

The case of convergecast: Support of unicast, the most fundamental data delivery mechanism, indicates cETX's applicability to a wide range of protocols whom unicast serves as their basis operation. Convergecast is one example, which consists of unicasts whose destinations are the sink. In convergecast the impact of spatiotemporal correlation is determined by immediate or delayed forwarding, where cETX inherently covers both the cases via its unicast support.

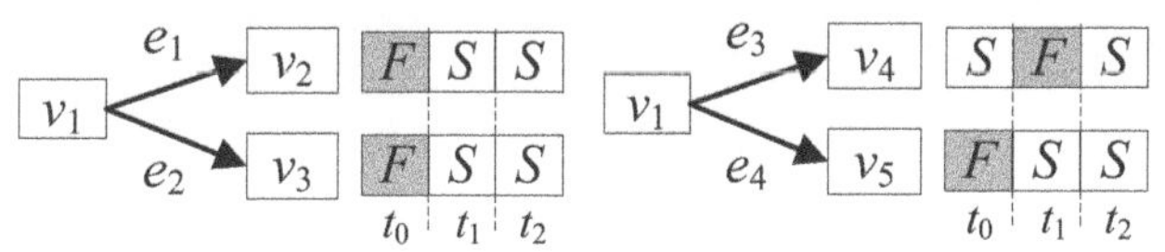

(a) Positively correlated (b) Negatively correlated

Figure 15: Benefit of cETX in broadcast: (a) and (b) require 1.25 and 1.66 transmissions to deliver 2 packets to both receivers. Performance improves when receivers are positively correlated, which can be captured by cETX.

6.2 Application to Broadcast

This section presents how cETX can help improve the performance of broadcast protocols. First, let's consider the positively correlated case in Figure 15(a). If v_1 starts broadcast at t_0, the two receivers will both receive the second packet at t_1, causing two transmissions to deliver the packet to both receivers. If the broadcast starts at t_1, the two receivers immediately receive the packet, indicating that a single transmission is consumed. Similarly, at t_3, only one transmission is required. Therefore, an average of $(2+1+1)/3 = 1.25$ transmissions are needed for the network in Figure 15(a), while it is $(2+2+1)/3 = 1.66$ in Figure 15(b). Here we calculate the expected number of transmissions – $E(T)$ for a source node to reliably broadcast one packet to all the receivers with the consideration of temporal and spatial correlation using cETX. Without loss of generality, we assume that the link quality of the N receivers satisfies $Pr(S_1^n) \geq Pr(S_2^n) \geq \ldots \geq Pr(S_N^n)$. Since the node with a better link receives most of the packets earlier than the node with a worse link [37], we have

$$\begin{aligned} E(T) &= \frac{1}{Pr(S_1^n)} + \sum_{i=2}^{N} \frac{Pr(F_i^n | S_{i-1}^n)}{Pr(S_i^n)} \\ &= \sum_{i=1}^{N} cETX_{e_i} - N + 1 \end{aligned} \tag{6}$$

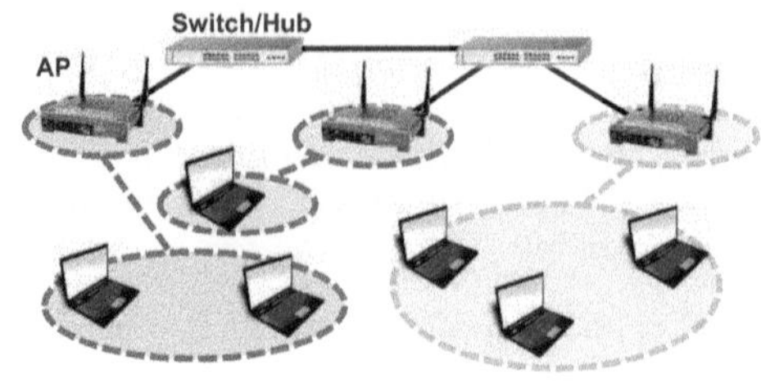

Figure 16: Collaborative broadcast in Wi-Fi. APs connected via wires cooperatively deliver data to all the users (laptops). Dotted circles indicate user groups assigned to APs. In cETX a group consists of highly correlated users.

This lets cETX to be integrated within various broadcast protocols by selecting forwarder which minimizes $E(T)$.

Eq.(6) can be further applied to a novel communication paradigm for Wi-Fi networks, demonstrated in Figure 16. In collaborative broadcast multiple APs connected via wires share the same data to collaboratively deliver it to all users. Grouping and assigning users to APs are done via Eq.(6). Both ordinary and collaborative broadcasts are further described and evaluated in the next section.

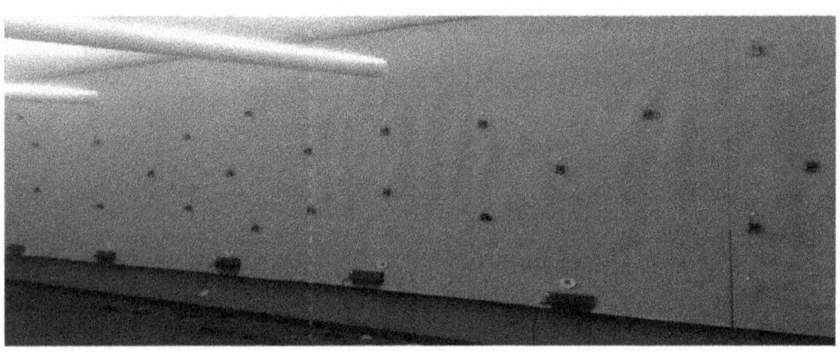

(a) ZigBee (lab)

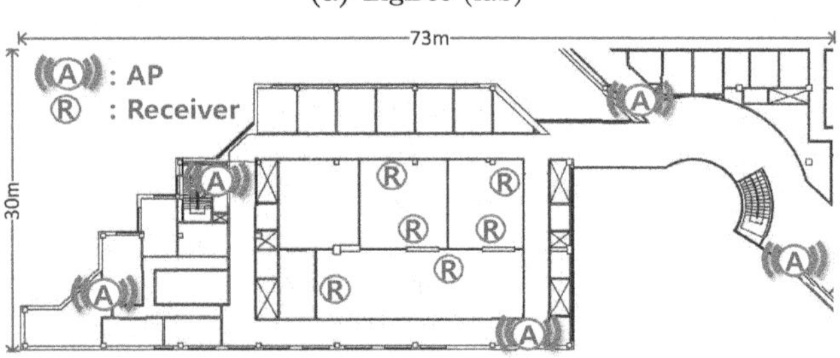

(b) Wi-Fi (university building)

Figure 17: ZigBee and Wi-Fi Testbeds

7. TESTBED EXPERIMENTATION

In this section we show that our design can be universally applied to various wireless technologies under different scenarios: We evaluate the performance of cETX in indoor testbeds on ZigBee (802.15.4) and Wi-Fi (802.11) platforms, under unicast and broadcast scenarios with twelve protocols.

7.1 Baseline

Various representative studies in unicast and broadcast domains are implemented for cETX evaluation.

• **Unicast**: We adopt cETX in three representative unicast routing protocols. **(i) LQSR** [13]: Extends the DSR [20] protocol by taking unreliable links into account. **(ii) srcRR** [4]: Similar to LQSR, but without path switching to improve network robustness. **(iii) OLSR** [17]: Routing is executed only through a subset of nodes (i.e, Multi Point Relays) to reduce the control overhead. The three protocols offer different degrees of freedom in path selection to affect the benefit of cETX.

• **Broadcast**: We integrate cETX to nine classical broadcast protocols with diverse underlying network structures, showing the wide applicability of cETX. **(i) tree based**: C-Tree [7], **(ii) cluster based**: forwarding node cluster (Cluster) [40], **(iii) Multi-Point Relay**: MPR [30], **(iv) pruning based**: Self Pruning (SP [24]), Dominating Pruning (DP [24]), Partial Dominating Pruning (PDP [27]), and Total Dominating Pruning (TDP [27]), **(v) RNG based**: RNG relay subset (RNG [18]), and finally, **(vi) network coding based broadcast protocols**: CODEB [23].

7.2 Performance Metrics

The following performance metrics are adopted through our evaluation.

• **Number of Transmissions**: The average number of (re)transmissions to deliver one packet to the destination. Less number of transmissions indicate energy savings.

• **End-to-End Delivery Delay**: The average latency for a packet to be delivered to the destination.

• **End-to-End Delivery Ratio**: The success probability of a packet delivered end-to-end. That is, the number of (re)transmissions in each link in a path do not exceed the retransmission limit.

7.3 Experiment Setup

Experimental results in this section are obtained from two physical testbeds, ZigBee and Wi-Fi, with below settings.

• **ZigBee**: We randomly deploy 22 MICAz motes running TinyOS as shown in Figure 17(a). Transmission power is set to be -25dBm to ensure multi-hop network, up to 5 hops. Node placement is kept the same for all evaluated metrics for fairness. Experiment for each metric lasts for two hours, during which an end-to-end packet delivery is made every four seconds, for a total of 1,800 deliveries per metric. CSMA is performed for each (re)transmission with random delay, where the average interval between retransmissions is approximately $6ms$. We limit the maximum number of retransmissions for each packet to be 7 (unless otherwise stated) following most practical systems to safeguard networks from being overwhelmed by retransmissions and collisions. Lastly, time stamps and sequence numbers of the delivered packets are logged in the nodes' flash, and uploaded to a PC at the end of the experiment.

• **Wi-Fi**: Depicted in Figure 17(b), five APs are installed in the corners of the floor, where we use laptops with the `Lorcon2` packet injection library [2] to play the role of AP generating downstream traffic. It is a reasonable approach since laptops/PCs are frequently used as APs in practice via software AP [1]. Six receivers are placed in three different rooms, separated by concrete walls. Although mainly 802.11g on channel 6 is used for its popularity, analyses later in the section implies a similar benefit in 802.11b and 802.11n as well. A total of 10^5 packet transmissions are made in 40 minutes, with the power of 20dBm. Links with packet reception ratios from 10% to 95% are observed, where we commonly apply EWMA (Exponential Weighted Moving Average) on every metric. Control overhead of different probing (i.e., burst probing in cETX and ETX(BP), and periodic probing in ETX) is kept consistent for fairness.

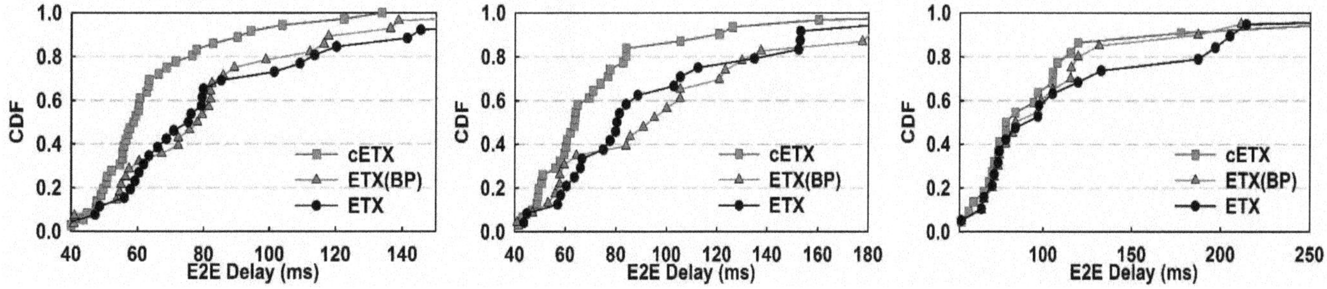

(a) LQSR (b) srcRR (c) OLSR

Figure 19: End-to-End Delay: cETX reduces the delay from 10.7% to 26.7% compared to ETX, where the improvement is achieved by the wiser route selection. LQSR allows the highest degree of freedom in the path selection, thus benefits most from cETX.

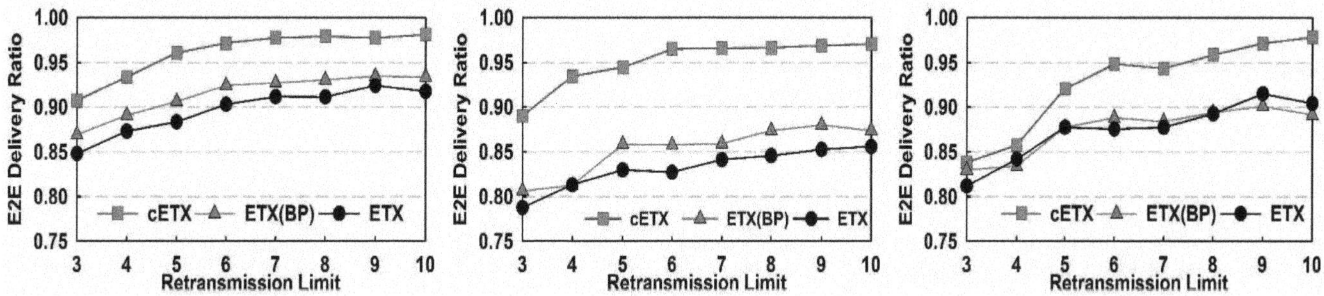

(a) LQSR (b) srcRR (c) OLSR

Figure 20: End-to-End Delivery Ratio: cETX tends to select links without burst failures, that are safer from exceeding the retransmission limit. This naturally leads to a higher delivery ratio compared to ETX.

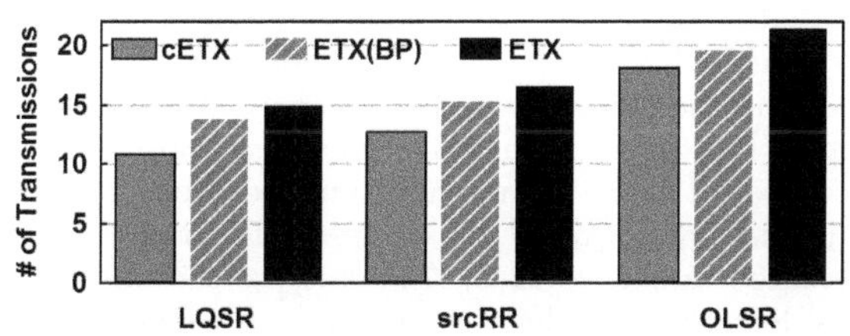

Figure 18: cETX saves 27.8%, 24.1%, and 15.8% of transmissions for LQSR, srcRR, and OLSR, compared to ETX.

7.4 Unicast

Figure 18 depicts the performance of cETX on unicast, obtained from the ZigBee testbed in Figure 17(a). Compared to ETX, cETX saves 27.8%, 24.1%, and 15.8% of transmissions for LQSR, srcRR, and OLSR. This demonstrates that cETX makes wiser routing decisions than ETX. Compared to ETX(BP), the percentage of savings becomes 21.6%, 17.5%, and 7.7%. This is because ETX(BP) benefits from burst probing for a slight performance enhancement over the original ETX. Furthermore, the advantage of cETX is the largest for LQSR and smallest for OLSR. The reason for this lies in the number of paths to choose from. While LQSR grants the most freedom in selecting paths, srcRR and OLSR restrict the frequent path switch to avoid high control overhead. Especially, OLSR only allows paths with MPR (Multi Point Relay) nodes. Figure 19 shows the end-to-end delay of metrics in the three protocols. cETX again exhibits the best performance, where the average reduction in delay ranged from 10.7% to 26.7%. Again LQSR obtains the biggest performance improvement due to the largest selection of paths.

• **Impact of Retransmission Limit:** Now we vary the limitation in the number of retransmissions from 3 to 10 and investigate its effect on the performance. Packet in delivery is dropped whenever the number of transmissions in a single link exceeds the limit, indicating failure in the end-to-end delivery. Note that exceeding the limit requires a link exhibiting continuous failures, which cETX precisely avoids to select. On the other hand, ETX blindly selects paths without considering this issue, leading to a worse delivery ratio. As shown in Figure 20, regardless of protocol cETX consistently achieves delivery ratios of over 94% for retransmission limit of 7 or higher.

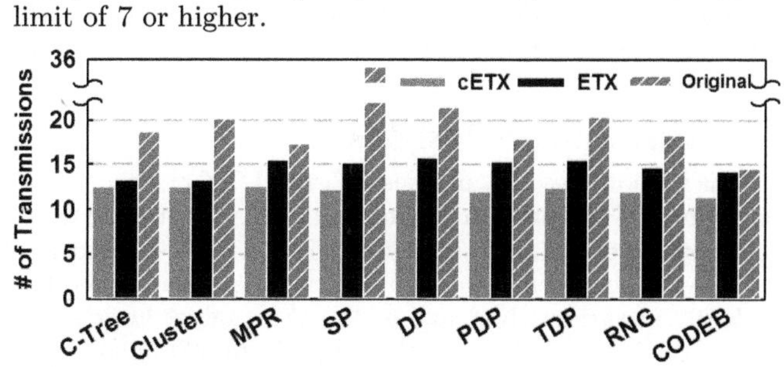

Figure 21: The Performance in Broadcast: cETX saves an average of 37% transmissions in nine broadcast protocols.

7.5 Broadcast

The experimental results on nine classical reliable broadcast protocols, tested on ZigBee testbed, are shown in Fig-

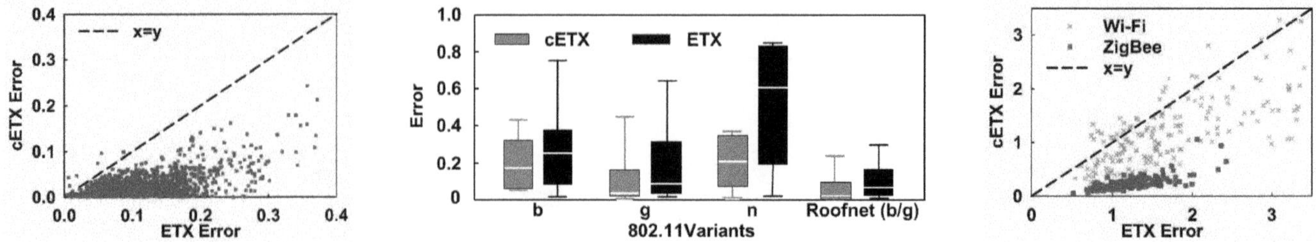

(a) Unicast (ZigBee) (b) Unicast (Wi-Fi) (c) Broadcast

Figure 22: Interpretation error is notably lower in cETX. In unicast cETX error is less than half of ETX. The performance of ETX rapidly drops in 802.11n where the fast transmission rate induces a high temporal correlation among consecutive transmissions. Roofnet shows the smallest error due to the outdoor environment with low degree of wireless interference. Under broadcast cETX reduces the error by 72.3% and 21.5% on ZigBee and Wi-Fi, respectively.

ure 21. On average, the protocols need 20.5 transmissions to guarantee delivery of a packet to the entire network, while the number becomes 14.7 and 12.2 for ETX and cETX. Knowing that CODEB saves 31.6% of transmissions compared to the schemes without network coding, our design makes a further 21.4% improvement upon CODEB due to following reasons: a low link correlation may cause the nodes in a cluster to lose different packets, causing more retransmissions. With the consideration on spatial and temporal correlations, the protocols benefit from cETX to select forwarders with the minimum transmission cost (i.e., $min(\frac{E(T)}{N})$), thus forming clusters with high correlations.

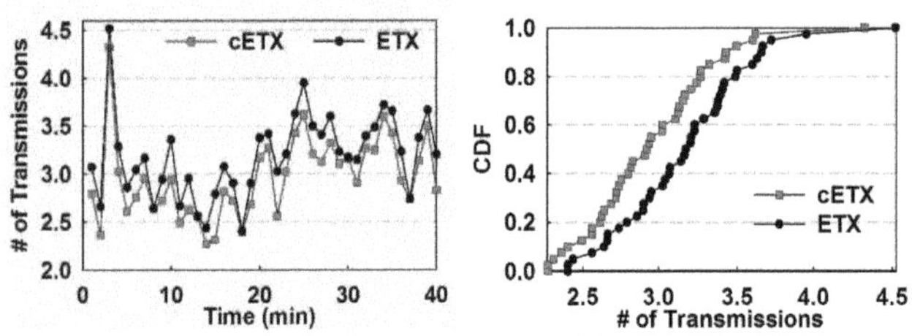

(a) Number of Transmissions (b) Distribution

Figure 23: In (a) cETX consistently reduces number of broadcasts compared to ETX, indicating energy savings. This is shown as distribution in (b).

Figure 23 shows the improvement achieved for collaborative broadcast on Wi-Fi testbed depicted in Figure 17(b). Five APs collaboratively deliver 10^5 packets to all six receivers. As cETX allows grouping highly correlated receivers to minimize retransmissions, its transmission cost is consistently less than or equal to that of ETX. The reduction can be as large as 34.1%.

7.6 Performance Insights

This section provides analysis on *why* cETX performs better than ETX. Results on ZigBee platform are obtained from the 11-node experiment in Section 5.3. For Wi-Fi, experiments with six receivers and 2×10^5 packets are analyzed for each 802.11 variant: b, g, and n. We also analyze large-scale public Wi-Fi traces (5.6×10^5 packets from 560 links) from the MIT's Roofnet project [3] to validate the generality of our design.

•Interpretation accuracy in unicast: We first show the metrics' abilities to accurately interpret the probe reception history. That is, given the history, we observe how precisely a metric captures the performance of the corresponding link. This is done by comparing ETX and cETX values to the true value, introduced in Section 2.2. We use *error* as the measure of interpretation quality, which is the absolute difference between the metric and the true value. The result on ZigBee platform is depicted in Figure 22(a). Error for cETX is less than that of ETX for most of the time, where it is 70.2% less on average. This is because ETX fails to capture highly correlated burst failures. This trend continues to Wi-Fi in Figure 22(b) regardless of its variants; ETX errors exceed those of cETX by 45.1%, 84.7%, and 160.3% in 802.11b, g, and n. Analysis on the Roofnet trace, which is a mixture of 802.11b and g, indicate the error is 49.6% larger in ETX. We note that error in Roofnet trace is generally smaller compared to our experiments; Roofnet is measured in outdoor deployment, where the degree of interference (i.e., the main cause of burst failures) is limited.

•Interpretation accuracy in broadcast: In both traditional and collaborative broadcasts, multiple receivers form a cluster in which members receive the packets from the designated sender. (i.e., APs) A smart grouping of receivers and assigning them with the right sender play a key role in determining the efficiency of the network. With the consideration of link correlation, cETX shows an improved accuracy compared to ETX in computing the expected number of transmissions required for a cluster for a given sender, as presented in Figure 22(c). Similarly to the unicast case, error is defined to be the absolute value of the difference of the true value and the values computed by cETX and ETX. The figure shows adopting cETX reduces the error by up to 67.6% in Wi-Fi where in ZigBee it is as high as 91.4%. This is because multiple low-power ZigBee links can easily be victims of cross-network interferences, inducing correlation among links. On average, cETX reduces the error by 21.5% and 75.3% in Wi-Fi and ZigBee, respectively. This advantage provides a rational explanation of the transmission (i.e., energy) saving achieved in the broadcast protocols shown earlier in the section.

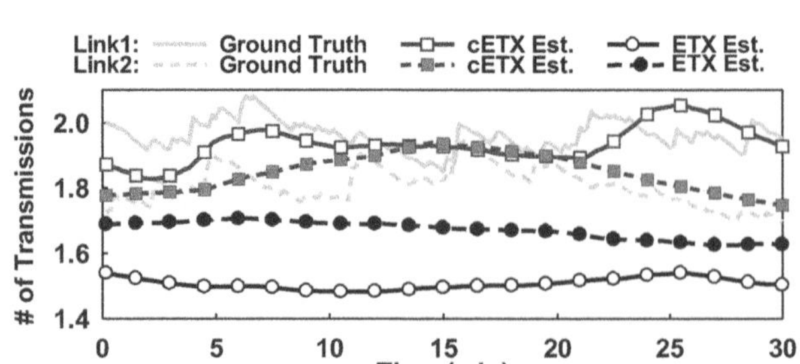

Figure 24: Unlike ETX, cETX accurately estimates the ground truth, where the quality of Link2 is either better or at least similar to that of Link1.

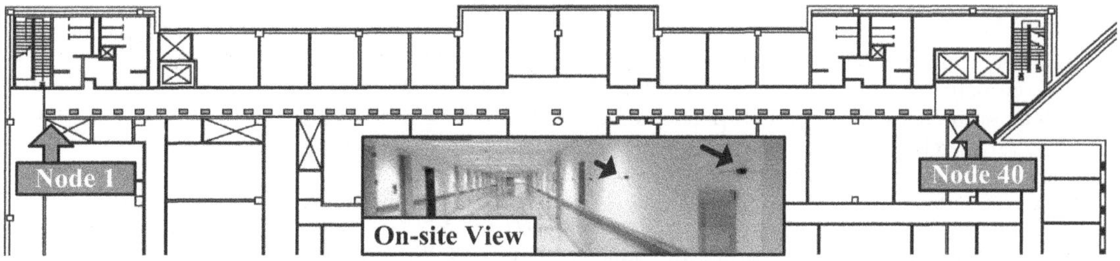

(a) Corridor

(b) Bridge

Figure 25: Indoor (corridor) and outdoor (bridge) experiment setup. On each site 40 MICAz nodes are linearly deployed every 1.8m, for 70m. In the corridor nodes were attached to the wall, 1.8m above the floor, while on the bridge they were deployed on the steel fence of height 1.5m. The corridor is within a university building with heavy Wi-Fi traffic.

•**Estimation accuracy and route selection:** An inaccurate interpretation leads to an imprecise link quality estimation and further, a sub-optimal route selection. We show how this occurs in practice via Figure 24, showing the estimated and real number of transmissions on two distinct links for 30 minutes. The figure conveys two ideas: (i) cETX estimation is more precise and thus (ii) cETX makes better routing decision. When making a selection between links 1 and 2, ETX suggests link 1 should be chosen over link 2, due to the lower ETX value. However, the ground truth indicates otherwise, i.e., link 2 always has a better or similar (at 17th min) performance than link 1. cETX is free from this problem, explaining the performance gain obtained in the unicast and broadcast algorithms in the earlier parts of the section.

8. IN-SITU DEPLOYMENT

In this section we conduct experiments under practical indoor and outdoor settings, in the aim to give a better understanding on the impact of our design in real-world applications. Forty MICAz nodes are deployed in a corridor in a university building and on a bridge crossing a river – common sites for popular applications including tracking and maintenance/safety monitoring – as shown in Figure 25. Nodes are deployed every 1.8m spanning 70m end to end. The transmission power is set to be -15dBm to assure multiple neighbors, where each node roughly has 10-12 neighbors (i.e, 5-6 neighbors to the node's right and left). Other parameters are kept the same as previous experiments. A thousand end-to-end (i.e., from node 1 to 40) packet deliveries are made, via LQSR embedding either ETX or cETX.

Results on delivery delay, shown in Figure 26(a), suggests that cETX's performance gain is more significant in the corridor (21.5% reduction) than on the bridge (8.9% reduction). This is due to the degree of wireless interference; In the university building hundreds of Wi-Fi users are connected to over fifty Wi-Fi access points, creating excessive amount of wireless interference. This causes burst failures in the experiment, forcing ETX to select poorly performing paths suffering from long delivery delays well above 1 second. Similar observation can be made in Figure 26(b). The average number of transmissions are 28.8 and 36.9 for cETX and ETX in the corridor, respectively, indicating 21.9% reduction. Due to the same reason as in the delay case, smaller degree of reduction (9%) is observed on the bridge, compared to what is achieved in the corridor.

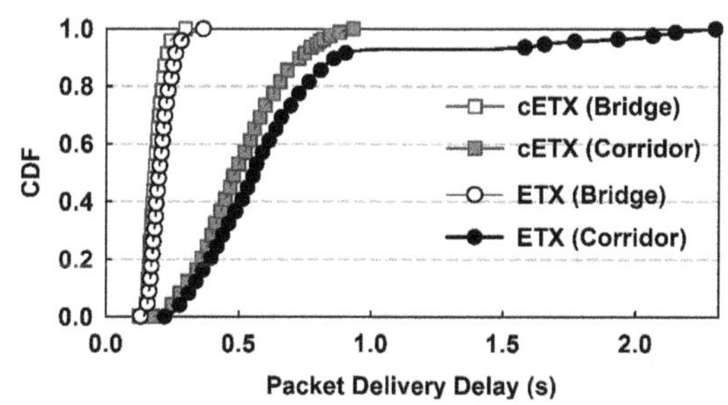

(a) Delay distribution

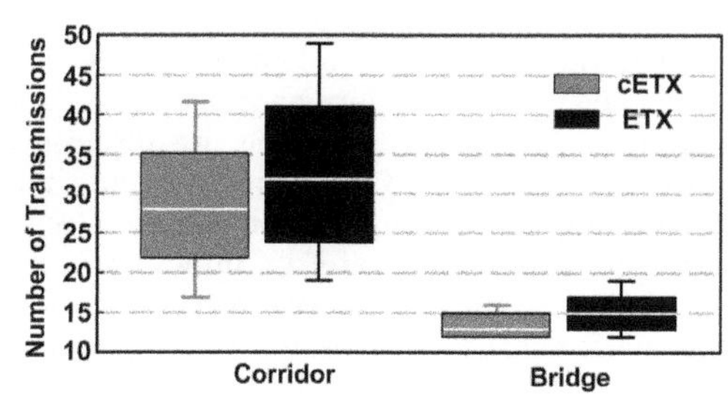

(b) Number of transmissions

Figure 26: In-situ results for 10^3 packet deliveries.

9. RELATED WORK

Our work is built on top of two phenomena addressed in separate studies, namely, temporal and spatiotemporal correlation. We briefly summarize how the two phenomena have been studied so far in relation to our work.

The impact of temporal correlation in ZigBee network, as well as in Wi-Fi, has been demonstrated clearly via extensive measurements and analyses in [34], where the authors propose a metric to quantify the degree of correlation. Furthermore, the works including BRE [6], 4C [25], and TALENT [26] exploit short-term dynamics based on packet overhearing to utilize intermittent and burst links. In RNP [10] and mETX [22], temporal properties of links were considered in routing, by counting consecutive failures and taking the variance of failure probability, respectively. However, the works in this category pays little or no attention to correlation across different links.

The comprehensive study on packet-level spatial correlation in [33] suggests a metric to predict performances of diversity-based protocols based on the intensity of correlation. To date, the phenomenon has been exploited in a wide range of wireless domains including ZigBee [45], Wi-Fi [33], and cellular networks [26]. For instance, it was utilized in network coding for efficient multicast [21] and broadcast [5]. Furthermore, Spatial correlation was studied in the presence of constructive interference to achieve fast data dissemination [12]. In this work we consider spatiotemporal correlation, which expands the effect of spatial correlation to the time domain. The unified design allows us to improve the unicast performance as well as the broadcast performance. In addition, the previous studies focus on particular protocol designs, while this work provides a generalized form of the widely-adopted ETX. Our work can broadly improve a wide range of protocols.

10. CONCLUSION

Our empirical study on temporal and spatiotemporal correlations in packet receptions shed light on the possibility of further improvement in network performance. In this work, we reveal that the most widely adopted link metric, ETX, fails to reflect the true link performance due to the ignorance of correlations. To address this issue, we propose cETX, a generalized version of ETX capturing not only temporal correlation but also spatiotemporal correlation. Because our design keeps the intuitive idea of ETX intact, we can simply replace ETX with cETX in existing protocols to obtain better routing performance. Our evaluations on both ZigBee and Wi-Fi testbeds demonstrate that cETX cuts down the metric error by 75.8% and 62.1%, and saves 22% and 37% communication cost for three unicast and nine broadcast protocols with only 0.7% additional overhead.

A. ENTROPY COMPUTATION

Introduced in the *information theory*, entropy defines the the amount of uncertainty contained in a random variable. Let X^n be a bernoulli random variable indicating reception success or failure at time instant t_n. Then $H(X^n)$ represents the entropy within X^n, where it is computed as

$$H(X^n) = -\sum_{x^n \in \{succ, fail\}} Pr(x^n) log_2 Pr(x^n) \qquad (7)$$

which is a marginal entropy as it only considers one random variable, without any given conditions. Furthermore, let X^{n-1} and X^{n-2} be bernoulli random variables for reception success or failure at one and two time instants prior to X^n. Then, the conditional entropy is the degree of uncertainty in X^n, when the value of X^{n-1} or both X^{n-1} and X^{n-2} are known a priori, denoted as $H(X^n|X^{n-1})$ and $H(X^n|X^{n-1}, X^{n-2})$. The conditional entropies are found by the following equations.

$$\begin{aligned} H(X^n|X^{n-1}) &= H(X^n, X^{n-1}) - H(X^{n-1}) \\ H(X^n|X^{n-1}, X^{n-2}) &= H(X^n, X^{n-1}, X^{n-2}) \\ &\quad - H(X^n|X^{n-1}) - H(X^{n-2}) \end{aligned}$$

where the joint entropies, $H(X^n, X^{n-1})$ and $H(X^n, X^{n-1}, X^{n-2})$, are computed similarly to Eq.(7). That is, by replacing the marginal probability $Pr(x^n)$ by joint probabilities, $Pr(x^n, x^{n-1})$ and $Pr(x^n, x^{n-1}, x^{n-2})$.

B. THE PROPERTIES OF CETX

In this appendix we provide the relationship between cETX and ETX, under various degrees of correlations.

• **Under independence:** cETX is a generalized version of ETX, where cETX simply reduces to ETX when packet receptions are independent. For simplicity, we omit the subscript for the following parts of the section. For an arbitrary link, spatiotemporal independence turns $cETX$ from Eq.(2) to the form of Eq.(4). Then, when transmissions are temporally independent,

$$Pr(S^n|F^{n-1}) = Pr(S^n|S^{n-1})$$

which leads to $p + q = 1$. By plugging in this condition within Eq.(4), we have

$$cETX = \frac{p+q}{p} = \frac{1}{Pr(S^n)} = ETX$$

where we used Eq.(3) and the rationale behind it. Thus, cETX is equivalent to ETX when transmissions are independent.

• **Effect of correlation:** Here we show how cETX is determined in relation to the correlation. For clarity, in direct comparison to ETX, we use cETX in Eq.(4). When link faces failure burst, the following condition holds:

$$Pr(F^n|F^{n-1}) > Pr(F^n|S^{n-1})$$

We thus have $p + q < 1$. Plugging in the condition within Eq.(4), we obtain

$$cETX = \frac{q}{(p+q) \cdot p} + 1 > \frac{q}{p} + 1 = ETX$$

Therefore, cETX is larger than ETX when the link experiences burst failure. In other words, ETX normally underestimates the transmission cost because of the ignorance of correlations.

ACKNOWLEDGEMENT

This work was supported in part by the National Science Foundation under grants CNS-0845994 and CNS-1444021. We sincerely thank our shepherd Dr. Luca Mottola and the reviewers for their valuable comments and feedback.

11. REFERENCES

[1] Hostapd. `http://hostap.epitest.fi/hostapd/`.

[2] Lorcon wireless packet injection lib. `https://code.google.com/p/lorcon/`.

[3] Mit roofnet. `http://pdos.csail.mit.edu/roofnet/doku.php?id=publications#sigcomm_traces/`.

[4] D. Aguayo, J. Bicket, and R. Morris. Srcrr: A high throughput routing protocol for 802.11 mesh networks. In *Ph.D. Diss, MIT*, 2004.

[5] S. M. I. Alam, S. Sultana, Y. C. Hu, and S. Fahmy. Link correlation and network coding in broadcast protocols for wireless sensor networks. In *SECON*, 2012.

[6] M. H. Alizai, O. Landsiedel, J. A. B. Link, S. Götz, and K. Wehrle. Bursty traffic over bursty links. In *SenSys*, 2009.

[7] K. Alzoubi, P. Wan, and O. Frieder. New distributed algorithm for connected dominating set in wireless ad hoc networks. In *Hawaii Int. Conf. System Sciences*, 2002.

[8] R. Banirazi, E. A. Jonckheere, and B. Krishnamachari. Heat-diffusion: Pareto optimal dynamic routing for time-varying wireless networks. In *INFOCOM*, 2014.

[9] M. Buettner, G. V. Yee, E. Anderson, and R. Han. X-mac: a short preamble mac protocol for duty-cycled wireless sensor networks. In *SenSys*, 2006.

[10] A. Cerpa, J. L. Wong, M. Potkonjak, and D. Estrin. Temporal properties of low power wireless links: Modeling and implications on multi-hop routing. In *MobiHoc*, 2005.

[11] D. S. J. De Couto, D. Aguayo, J. Bicket, and R. Morris. A high-throughput path metric for multi-hop wireless routing. In *MobiCom*, 2003.

[12] M. Doddavenkatappa, M. C. Chan, and B. Leong. Splash: Fast data dissemination with constructive interference in wireless sensor networks. In *nsdi*, 2013.

[13] R. Draves, J. Padhye, and B. Zill. Routing in multi-radio, multi-hop wireless mesh networks. In *MobiCom*, 2004.

[14] R. Fonseca, O. Gnawali, K. Jamieson, and P. Levis. Four-bit wireless link estimation. In *HotNets*, 2007.

[15] E. N. Gilbert. Capacity of a burst-noise channel. *Bell System Technical Journal*, 39(2), 1960.

[16] P. Guo, J. Cao, K. Zhang, and X. Liu. Enhancing zigbee throughput under wifi interference using real-time adaptive coding. In *INFOCOM*, 2014.

[17] P. Jacquet, P. Muhlethaler, T. Clausen, A. Laouiti, A. Qayyum, and L. Viennot. Optimized link state routing protocol for ad hoc networks. In *IEEE INMIC*, 2001.

[18] J.Cartigny, F. Ingelrest, and D. Simplot. Rng relay subset flooding protocols in mobile ad hoc networks. *International Journal of Foundations of Computer Science*, 2003.

[19] S. Ji, R. Beyah, and Z. Cai. Snapshot/continuous data collection capacity for large-scale probabilistic wireless sensor networks. In *Infocom*, 2012.

[20] D. B. Johnson and D. A. Maltz. Dynamic source routing in ad hoc wireless networks. In *Mobile Computing*, 1996.

[21] A. Khreishah, I. M. Khalil, and J. Wu. Distributed network coding-based opportunistic routing for multicast. In *MobiHoc*, 2012.

[22] C. E. Koksal and H. Balakrishnan. Quality-aware routing metrics for time-varying wireless mesh networks. *IEEE Journal on Selected Areas in Communications*, 24(11), 2006.

[23] E. L. Li, R. Ramjee, M. M. Buddhikot, and S. C. Miller. Network coding-based broadcast in mobile ad-hoc networks. In *INFOCOM*, 2007.

[24] H. Lim and C. Kim. Flooding in wireless ad hoc networks. In *Computer Communications Journal*, 2001.

[25] T. Liu and A. Cerpa. Foresee (4c): Wireless link prediction using link features. In *IPSN*, 2011.

[26] T. Liu and A. Cerpa. Talent: Temporal adaptive link estimator with no training. In *SenSys*, 2012.

[27] W. Lou and J. Wu. On reducing broadcast redundancy in ad hoc wireless networks. *IEEE Transactions on Mobile Computing*, 2002.

[28] S. Pattem, B. Krishnamachari, and R. Govindan. The impact of spatial correlation on routing with compression in wireless sensor networks. *ACM TOSN*, 2008.

[29] J. Polastre, J. Hill, and D. Culler. Versatile low power media access for wireless sensor networks. In *SenSys*, 2004.

[30] A. Qayyum, L. Viennot, and A. Laouiti. Multipoint relaying for flooding broadcast messages in mobile wireless networks. In *HICSS*, 2002.

[31] I. Rhee, A. Warrier, M. Aia, and J. Min. Z-mac: A hybrid mac for wireless sensor networks. In *SenSys*, 2005.

[32] K. Srinivasan, P. Dutta, A. Tavakoli, and P. Levis. An empirical study of low-power wireless. *ACM TOSN*, 6(2), 2010.

[33] K. Srinivasan, M. Jain, J. I. Choi, T. Azim, E. S. Kim, P. Levis, and B. Krishnamachari. The kappa factor: Inferring protocol performance using inter-link reception correlation. In *MobiCom*, 2010.

[34] K. Srinivasan, M. A. Kazandjieva, S. Agarwal, and P. Levis. The beta-factor: Measuring wireless link burstiness. In *SenSys*, 2008.

[35] J. Tang, G. Xue, C. Chandler, and W. Zhang. Interference-aware routing in multihop wireless networks using directional antennas. In *INFOCOM*, 2005.

[36] P.-J. Wan, Z. Wang, H. Du, S. C.-H. Huang, and Z. Wan. First-fit scheduling for beaconing in multihop wireless networks. In *INFOCOM*, 2010.

[37] S. Wang, S. M. Kim, Y. Liu, G. Tan, and T. He. Corlayer: A transparent link correlation layer for energy efficient broadcast. In *MobiCom*, 2013.

[38] Wireless LAN Working Group. Ieee standard part 11: Wireless lan medium access control (mac) and physical layer (phy) specifications. *IEEE Std 802.11-2012 (Revision of IEEE Std 802.11-2007)*, pages 1–2793, March 2012.

[39] Wireless Personal Area Network (WPAN) Working Group. Ieee standard part 15.4: Low-rate wireless personal area networks (lr-wpans). *IEEE Std 802.15.4-2011 (Revision of IEEE Std 802.15.4-2006)*, pages 1–314, Sept 2011.

[40] J. Wu and W. Lou. Forward-node-set-based broadcast in clustered mobile ad hoc networks. In *Wireless Comm. and Mobile Comp.*, 2003.

[41] J. Wu, M. Lu, and F. Li. Utility-based opportunistic routing in multi-hop wireless networks. In *ICDCS*, 2008.

[42] G. Xing, M. Li, H. Luo, and X. Jia. Dynamic multiresolution data dissemination in wireless sensor networks. *IEEE Trans. Mob. Comput.*, 2009.

[43] W. Ye, J. Heidemann, and D. Estrin. Medium access control with coordinated, adaptive sleeping for wireless sensor networks. *IEEE/ACM Transactions on Networking*, 2003.

[44] W. Ye, F. Silva, and J. Heidemann. Ultra-low duty cycle mac with scheduled channel polling. In *SenSys*, 2006.

[45] G. G. J. B. T. G. Zhiwei Zhao, Wei Dong and C. Chen. Modeling link correlation in low-power wireless networks. In *INFOCOM*, 2015.

Orchestra: Robust Mesh Networks Through Autonomously Scheduled TSCH

Simon Duquenney[1]
simonduq@sics.se

Beshr Al Nahas[2]
beshr@chalmers.se

Olaf Landsiedel[2]
olafl@chalmers.se

Thomas Watteyne[3]
thomas.watteyne@inria.fr

[1]SICS Swedish ICT, Sweden
[2]Chalmers University of Technology, Sweden
[3]Inria, France

ABSTRACT

Time slotted operation is a well-proven approach to achieve highly-reliable low-power networking through scheduling and channel hopping. It is, however, difficult to apply time slotting to dynamic networks as envisioned in the Internet of Things. Commonly, these applications do not have predefined periodic traffic patterns and nodes can be added or removed dynamically.

This paper addresses the challenge of bringing TSCH (Time Slotted Channel Hopping MAC) to such dynamic networks. We focus on low-power IPv6 and RPL networks, and introduce Orchestra. In Orchestra, nodes autonomously compute their own, local schedules. They maintain multiple schedules, each allocated to a particular traffic plane (application, routing, MAC), and updated automatically as the topology evolves. Orchestra (re)computes local schedules without signaling overhead, and does not require any central or distributed scheduler. Instead, it relies on the existing network stack information to maintain the schedules. This scheme allows Orchestra to build non-deterministic networks while exploiting the robustness of TSCH.

We demonstrate the practicality of Orchestra and quantify its benefits through extensive evaluation in two testbeds, on two hardware platforms. Orchestra reduces, or even eliminates, network contention. In long running experiments of up to 72 h we show that Orchestra achieves end-to-end delivery ratios of over 99.99%. Compared to RPL in asynchronous low-power listening networks, Orchestra improves reliability by two orders of magnitude, while achieving a similar latency-energy balance.

Categories and Subject Descriptors

C.2.1 [**Network Architecture and Design**]: Wireless Communication

Keywords

TSCH, RPL, Scheduling, Wireless Sensor Network

SenSys'15, November 1–4, 2015, Seoul, South Korea..

ACM 978-1-4503-3631-4/15/11 ...$15.00.
DOI: http://dx.doi.org/10.1145/2809695.2809714.

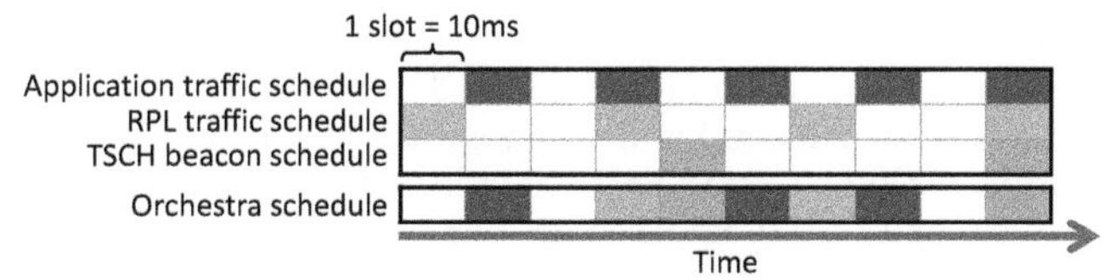

Figure 1: In Orchestra, several schedules repeat at different periods (here 2, 3, and 5), with slots allocated to specific traffic planes (resp. Application, RPL, TSCH). Slots are skipped whenever overlapped by a slot in a higher priority schedule (priority increasing from top to bottom in the figure).

1. INTRODUCTION

Context. As the Internet of Things (IoT) is emerging, there is an increasing need for low-power communication solutions that are both flexible (*i.e.*, are easy to use and able to to satisfy a variety of often dynamic application requirements) and robust (*i.e.*, work reliably). Example applications range from smart homes to smart cities, including wearable consumer devices. In these scenarios, short-range, low-power mesh networking is envisioned as a candidate technology to achieve both energy-efficiency and reliable large-scale operation.

Challenge. Flexibility and reliability are opposing goals. Asynchronous low-power mesh networks (including low-power IPv6) are flexible and support non-deterministic applications, but are best-effort. State-of-the art solutions have loss rates in the range of one percent [15, 19, 21, 11]. In the absence of end-to-end reliability, i.e., transport layer re-transmissions, such a loss rate is too high for most applications. With end-to-end reliability, losses trigger costly re-transmissions which often come in burst and result in jittery performance. At the other end of the spectrum, deterministic networks running TDMA and scheduled traffic can achieve 2 or 3 orders of magnitude fewer losses (*i.e.*, up to one loss per 10.000 packets or more) [8, 2, 37, 12, 28]. We investigate how to achieve such high level of reliability in non-deterministic scenarios.

Approach and Distinction. In this paper, we make a case for autonomous TSCH (Time Slotted Channel Hopping [1]) scheduling in non-deterministic low-power RPL and IPv6 networks. We show that even though it requires global synchronization, TSCH is practical in sparse traffic scenarios, and helps achieve high reliability in networks running a distributed routing protocol such as RPL [40]. The key challenge we address is that of creating TSCH schedules without hindering any of the flexibility of RPL networks and matching the requirements of non-deterministic applications. Orchestra achieves this with local, autonomous scheduling, and requires neither a centralized nor a distributed scheduler.

This is radically different from traditional TSCH scheduling solutions such as WirelessHART [14] and ISA100.11a [17], which rely on a centralized scheduling entity. This is also different from the standards being developed in the IETF 6TiSCH working group [33], which employ schedule negotiation between neighbor nodes.

In Orchestra, nodes employ simple periodic schedules and update the schedules automatically and instantly as the routing topology evolves. A TSCH schedule in Orchestra consists of a set of over-provisioned communication slots dedicated each to a specific communication plane: MAC, routing and application (as illustrated in Figure 1). As a result, Orchestra allows building a generic, flexible, low-power routing backbone using RPL while benefiting from the robustness of TSCH. Our schedules allow to reduce contention drastically, or even eliminate it altogether in certain cases.

Results. We implement Orchestra and TSCH in Contiki [10], and experiment in two testbeds with 98 and 25 nodes, each with a different hardware platform. In total, our evaluation bases on 219 individual experiments, up to 72 hours long, and a total of 1,178,601 UDP packets routed from source to destination. We show that Orchestra enables autonomous TSCH scheduling in RPL networks, and achieves end-to-end delivery ratios over 99.99%. This is an improvement of 1 or 2 orders of magnitude over state-of-the-art asynchronous solutions such as RPL with ContikiMAC. We show that Orchestra achieves this strong reliability while keeping energy and latency close to the state of the art.

Contribution. The main contribution of this paper is Orchestra, a system that allows TSCH nodes to maintain their schedules autonomously, driven by the state of the routing protocol. Orchestra operates without a centralized scheduler, and without inter-node schedule negotiation nor path reservation. We demonstrate experimentally that Orchestra is practical, scalable, and achieves end-to-end loss rates two orders of magnitude below low-power listening.

Outline. The remainder of this paper is organized as follows. §2 gives necessary background on TSCH and RPL, before introducing the basic concepts of Orchestra. §3 characterizes the potential benefits of TSCH as an alternative to asynchronous MAC layers. §4 discusses the design of Orchestra and §5 details implementation aspects. §6 discusses the results of our thorough experimental evaluation in two different testbeds as well as in controlled simulation. We discuss related work in §7 and conclude in §8.

2. OVERVIEW

This section introduces necessary background and gives a brief overview of our system, Orchestra.

2.1 TSCH

The IEEE802.15.4e-2012 [1] standard defines a number of MAC protocols for IEEE802.15.4. In this paper, we focus on TSCH (Time Slotted Channel Hopping), which inherits from WirelessHART and ISA100.11a.

TSCH nodes form a globally synchronized low-power mesh network. Nodes may join the network after hearing an Enhanced Beacon (EB) from another node. Time synchronization trickles from the PAN coordinator down to leaf nodes along a Directed Acyclic Graph (DAG) structure. Time is cut into timeslots; timeslots are grouped into one or more slotframes. A timeslot, typically 10 ms long, is long enough for a node to send a frame and for the receiver to acknowledge it. A TSCH schedule indicates to a node what to do in each timeslot: transmit, receive or sleep. A timeslot in a slotframe is identified by its time offset (when in the slotframe it occurs), its channel offset (denoting the frequency to communicate on), and a set of properties: whether it is to be used for transmission, reception, time synchronization, etc. Slots can be dedicated or shared, *i.e.*, contention-free or contention-based with CSMA back-off.

TSCH networks use channel hopping: the same slot in the schedule translates into a different frequency at each iteration of the slotframe. The result is that successive packets exchanged between neighbor nodes are communicated at different frequencies. In case a transmission fails because of external interference or multi-path fading, its retransmission happens on a different frequency, often with a better probability of succeeding than using the same frequency again [37].

How the communication schedule in the TSCH network is built and maintained is out of the scope of the established standards. The traditional way to scheduling (used in WirelessHART, ISA100.11a, and one of the modes in 6TiSCH) is to use a centralized entity which gathers information from the network, computes a schedule centrally, and disseminates routes and schedules to the nodes. Since late 2013, the IETF 6TiSCH working group is defining mechanisms to support decentralized scheduling. In this approach, a node negotiates with its neighbor to add/remove a slot to their local schedule.

2.2 RPL

RPL [40] is the routing protocol for low-power IPv6 networks standardized by the IETF ROLL working group. It is an oriented distance-vector routing protocol that organizes nodes in a Destination-Oriented DAG (DODAG) structure. The DODAG is rooted at the border router node (Internet access point). Each node is attached a *rank*, *i.e.*, its distance to the root using some cost function (*e.g.*, the ETX metric).

A node sends a packet towards the root by forwarding it to a neighbor node with a smaller rank. Routing from the root to one of the nodes is done by using the reverse links. In this paper, we focus on the *storing mode* of RPL: each node maintains a routing table towards its routing children, *i.e.*, the nodes further away from the root than itself. RPL uses unicast and broadcast signaling messages; namely, DIO (to disseminate the metrics), DIS (to request DODAG information) and DAO (to disseminate routes) messages. Routing from any node to another is done by first routing *up* to a common ancestor (along decreasing ranks), then *down* to the destination (following the routing tables).

2.3 Orchestra in a Nutshell

This paper introduces Orchestra, a new approach to scheduling in TSCH+RPL networks[1]. Orchestra is radically different from existing scheduling solutions in that it does not involve any extra central entity, negotiation, signaling, nor multi-hop path reservation among nodes. In-

[1]The approach developed in this paper is general enough to be applied to other scheduled MAC layers and any routing protocol. The focus of this paper is on TSCH and RPL.

stead, nodes maintain their own schedule locally and autonomously, based on their RPL neighbors and parents. As a result, Orchestra makes TSCH as flexible as asynchronous MAC layers, and able to support random-access traffic.

An Orchestra schedule contains different slotframes of different lengths. Each slotframe is dedicated to a particular type of traffic: TSCH beacons, RPL signaling traffic or application data. Nodes select slots using scheduling rules which reduces contention drastically, or in certain cases eliminates contention (see §4.2). This makes Orchestra particularly appealing for low-power IPv6 scenarios where different applications generate event-based data, without any predefined (*e.g.*, periodic) traffic pattern.

A concrete example Orchestra schedule contains:

- A dedicated broadcast slot from every node to its children for TSCH beacons, repeating every X slots;
- A slot common for all nodes in the network for broadcast+unicast for RPL signaling (DIO, DIS, DAO), repeating every Y slots;
- A dedicated unicast slot from every node to its RPL preferred parent, repeating every Z' slots;
- *N* dedicated unicast slots from every node to each of its children, repeating every Z" slots.

Orchestra uses slotframe lengths which are mutually prime, ensuring the slots overlap each other evenly, without unintended synchronization effects. The key is that we select the time and channel offset of the every slot as a function of the sender's or the receiver's identifier (MAC address or a unique network node ID). Depending on the scheduling rules, Orchestra can either attain very low levels of contention, or operate contention-free.

3. A CASE FOR TSCH IN LOW-POWER MESH

Before moving to the detailed design of Orchestra, we discuss and characterize the potential benefits of TSCH over asynchronous solutions.

Cost of Global Synchronization. TDMA protocols are often regarded as impractical in random-access or sparse traffic scenarios, because of the overhead of global synchronization. In TSCH, nodes keep synchronized to one or several time sources, re-adjusting their clock whenever receiving a data of acknowledgment packet from it. In IEEE802.15.4, the maximum clock drift allowed is 40 ppm (parts per million), *i.e.*, max 80 ppm among two nodes. Assuming a guard time of ± 1 ms (the default value in TSCH), a node needs to re-synchronize to its time source neighbor every 12.5 s. Resynchronizing involves sending a short data packet, and receiving a short acknowledgment, which accounts for around 6 ms of radio on-time. Under these assumptions, resynchronization results in an additional radio duty cycle of $6\ ms/12.5\ s = 0.048\%$.

In practice, this baseline cost can be pushed even lower. In our testbeds (see §6.1) we measured an average drift between nodes in the range of 10–20 ppm, way below the 80 ppm assumed above. It is possible, in addition, to have nodes characterize their drift at runtime and adjust their clock dynamically, further reducing the cost of synchronization [4].

The numbers above show that synchronization can be obtained at a very low cost, in fact insignificant when compared to the typical duty cycle of mesh networks, in the order of

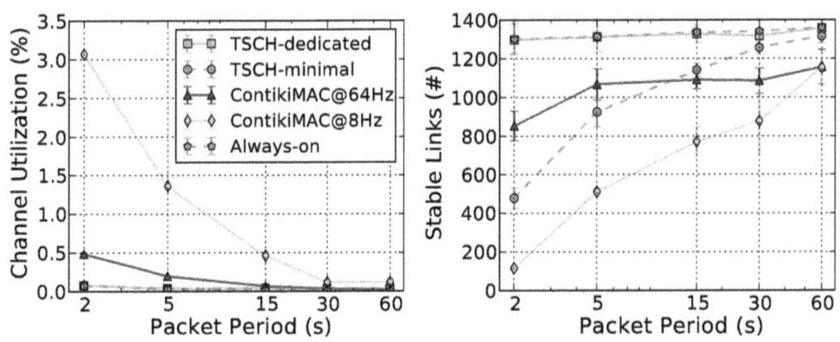

(a) Channel utilization (b) Total number of stable links

Figure 2: Periodic Broadcast Probing Experiment. ContikiMAC has much higher channel utilization than TSCH and *Always-on*, resulting in fewer stable links as high traffic loads. TSCH with dedicated slots, being completely contention-free, yields performance similar to the baseline *Always-on*.

percent or tens of a percent [15, 19, 21, 11] (*e.g.*, ContikiMAC in its default settings has a 0.6 % baseline duty cycle [9]). We therefore argue that TSCH is practical even in sparse traffic scenarios.

Scheduled vs. Asynchronous. We run an initial set of experiments to characterize link properties when using different MAC layers. We use the Indriya testbed [6], containing 98 TelosB nodes. We implement TSCH for the Contiki OS, and compare TSCH against ContikiMAC and the *Always-on* MAC, where nodes listen all the time and transmit using CSMA (Contiki's Nullrdc+Csma with link-layer ACK). The latter two are contention-based, asynchronous MAC layers. ContikiMAC [9] is a state-of-the-art low-power listening protocol that builds upon well established mechanisms [23, 16] described next. In ContikiMAC, nodes transmit their packet repeatedly for one period (*e.g.*, 125 ms) until the receiver wakes up and acknowledges it. Nodes are loosely synchronized through a phase-lock mechanism, which reduces strobe length towards already known neighbors. Although *Always-on* is generally impractical in low-power scenarios, we include it as a baseline approach.

In the experiment, every node transmits a broadcast packet at a given period with added jitter, and all packet receptions are logged. We use 3 different asynchronous MAC layers: *Always-on*, ContikiMAC at 8 Hz (default setting, wakeup period of 125 ms), ContikiMAC at 64 Hz (wakeup period of 15.6 ms). We use 2 different configurations for TSCH: TSCH-minimal, based on the 6TiSCH minimal configuration [35], where every node has a single shared communication slot for any traffic (here we use a slotframe of 1 slot, *i.e.*, all slots are active), and TSCH-dedicated where we use the nodes' unique node ID in the testbed to allocate a dedicated transmission slot to every node, ruling out all contention. For fairness with *Always-on* and ContikiMAC, and to focus on scheduling rather than channel hopping, we run TSCH on a single channel (channel 26, among the best channels in Indriya) in this specific experiment.

Figure 2 summarizes the results of this experiment. We look at two metrics. First, channel utilization is the average portion of time spent by a node with its radio transmitting. Second, the number of stable links, refers to the total number of links with PRR (Packet Reception Rate) above 90%.

ContikiMAC leads to high channel utilization with packet strobing, *i.e.*, up to 3% per node, which, in the 98 node testbed, corresponds to on average 3 nodes transmitting at any point in time. In comparison, TSCH and *Always-on* nodes have a channel utilization below 0.08%, a 37× factor improvement. This results in lower contention, and in turn a higher number of stable links.

Channel Hopping. An essential benefit of TSCH is its channel hopping nature. Channel hopping is known to effectively combat external interference and multi-path fading [38, 37], thereby increasing channel capacity and reducing the energy spent in packet retransmissions. Channel hopping can achieve similar benefits in asynchronous MACs, but at the cost of extra synchronization overhead [32, 24].

Orchestra aims at making TSCH as flexible as asynchronous MACs, while enjoying reduced contention (through scheduling) and robustness (through channel hopping).

4. Orchestra DESIGN

We introduce Orchestra, a system for routing-aware, autonomous slot allocation in random-access TSCH networks.

4.1 Big Picture

In Orchestra, nodes adapt their schedule by exploiting information from the RPL topology, and following a set of *scheduling rules*. This results in periodic activity patterns, with slotframes and slots assigned to different traffic planes such as TSCH beacons, RPL signaling, or application data.

Network Bootstrap. When switched on, a node joins the TSCH network by listening until it receives a Enchanced Beacon (EB), either from the PAN coordinator or another node. After synchronizing to that EB, the node runs Orchestra. A viable Orchestra setup requires slots for sending and receiving packets to/from any neighbor. This emulates an always-on link to all neighbors, allowing RPL nodes to discover their neighbors and build a topology.

TSCH-RPL Topology Mapping. Orchestra consistently uses the node's RPL preferred parent as its TSCH time source neighbor[2]. As the RPL topology evolves and parent switches occur, nodes update their TSCH time source accordingly. This yields a loop-free timing structure (a tree in this case), taking advantage of RPL's built-in loop avoidance mechanism. Furthermore, we use the RPL rank as TSCH join priority, as defined in the 6TiSCH architecture [33]. Doing so, we also take advantage of the RPL mechanisms for gradient convergence and stability. In case a node loses synchronization, it also leaves the RPL network, ensuring a clean slate bootstrap after re-joining.

TSCH Time Synchronization. TSCH time synchronization happens on any packet (or ACK) from the time source neighbor. In Orchestra, time synchronization happens primarily through periodic TSCH and RPL beacon transmission. This is efficient as a single broadcast message allows all children to update their clocks. Whenever a node has not communicated with its time source neighbor for a given duration (we use 12 s), it sends a unicast keep-alive message. The packet is re-sent until acknowledged, and re-synchronization is done by using the timing information embedded in the IEEE802.15.4e enhanced ACK.

[2]Note TSCH supports multiple time sources, but in our current design, Orchestra sticks to a single time source.

Routing-aware Scheduling. Throughout the network lifetime, Orchestra installs and updates TSCH schedules by using information from the routing layer. RPL runs unmodified, with slots being set up automatically as the topology evolves, ensuring network connectivity and allowing upper layers to run transparently. A basic example is where Orchestra maintains a dedicated slot for parent to child communication, repeating at a fixed period (*e.g.*, 1 s), at a time offset and channel offset selected from the parent's unique node ID. Whenever a child switches parent, it updates its slot to match the new parent's node ID.

4.2 Scheduling

Orchestra runs deployment-specific scheduling rules that describes how to maintain TSCH slotframes and slots as a function of the routing topology.

4.2.1 Orchestra Slots

We identify four main types of slots in Orchestra: common shared slots, receiver-based shared slots, sender-based shared slots, and sender-based dedicated slots. Orchestra are dynamically mapped at runtime into 0, 1, or multiple TSCH slots. The different types of Orchestra slots are illustrated in Figure 3, in a 4-node network (Figure 3a) and showing only the slots for child-to-parent traffic.

Common Shared Orchestra Slots (CS). CS Orchestra slots consist in one shared slot used by all nodes in the network for both Rx (reception) and Tx (transmission), as illustrated in Figure 3b. The slot is installed at fixed coordinates (time and channel offset), resulting in a behavior similar to slotted ALOHA. This emulates an always-on link, allowing RPL to discover neighbors and run seamlessly. Note that TSCH uses an exponential back-off to resolve contention in shared slots, triggered whenever a unicast transmission is unacknowledged.

Receiver-based Shared Orchestra Slots (RBS). RBS are assigned for communication between two neighbors, at coordinates (time and channel offset) derived from properties of the receiver. At every node, a RBS Orchestra slot results in one Rx slot (coordinates based on the node), and one Tx slot per neighbor (coordinates based on the neighbor). To calculate slot coordinates, one can use a hash of the node's MAC address, modulo the slotframe length, or exploit unique node identifiers when available.

A typical example is for child-to-parent communication: nodes listen for any traffic in one slot, and children maintain a transmit slot towards their parent. As nodes switch parent, they update their transmit slot autonomously. Because several nodes may install slots towards the same receiver, contention may arise in such slots. For instance in Figure 3c, #3 and #4 contend to send to their parent #2, using standard TSCH back-off.

Sender-based Shared Orchestra Slots (SBS). SBS are similar to RBS, except that the slot coordinates are obtained from properties of the sender node rather than the receiver. At every node, a SBS Orchestra slot results in one Rx slot per neighbor (coordinates based on the neighbor) and a single Tx slot (coordinates based on sender node). This results in higher energy consumption than RBS (Tx slots cost nothing when there is no traffic, whereas Rx slots always require a wakeup), but can also help decrease contention by avoiding per-receiver slot assignement.

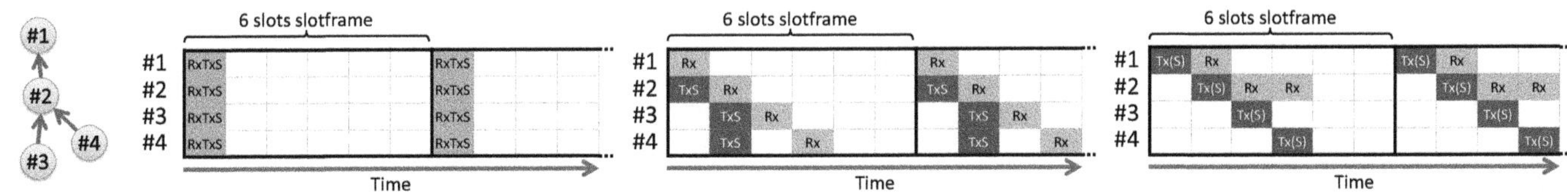

(a) Topology (b) Common Shared Slot (c) Receiver-based Shared Slot (d) Sender-based (Shared) Slot

Figure 3: Illustration of the different Orchestra slot types, in a 4-node network, showing child-to-parent slots. Slot properties are also shown: Reception (Rx), Transition (Tx), Shared (S). In common shared slots, all nodes wakeup up simultaneously to receive or transmit in a contention-based manner. In receiver-based slots, nodes have their own receive slot (here based on node ID), and their children contend when sending to them. In sender-based slots, nodes have their own transmit slot, and their parent wakes up to receive from them.

For instance, for child-to-parent communication, nodes have one fixed Tx slot, and parents maintain a Rx slot for each of their children. Whenever switching parent, the child does not need to update its transmit slot, but the old parent must remove a listen slot and the new parent install a new one. In Figure 3d, #2 has two listen slots, one for each of its children #3 and #4. Here again, contentions are resolved with the back-off from standard TSCH shared slots.

Sender-based Dedicated Orchestra Slots (SBD). In a slotframe long enough to accommodate unique transmit slots to every node, and assuming unique node identifiers are available, contention-free communication is possible. Orchestra achieves contention-free communication with SBD, which are similar to SBS except they use dedicated TSCH slots instead of shared. Note that with TSCH dedicated slots, lost packets are re-sent without a back-off (using the next slot towards the same neighbor). Unique node IDs can be hard-coded at deployment time, or obtained at runtime from a network manager.

4.2.2 Orchestra Slotframes

Orchestra manages several slotframes at every node, each of which is assigned to a particular traffic plane, *e.g.*, TSCH beaconing, routing traffic, application. Slotframes consist of a set of slots, with properties defined by simple scheduling rules. The slotframes repeat at periods that are mutually prime, ensuring they cycle independently. In case slots from different slotframes overlap, the slot in the highest priority slotframe takes precedence[3].

The length of a slotframe introduces a trade-off in traffic capacity, network latency and energy consumption.

Traffic Capacity. Shorter slotframes have their slots repeat more often, resulting in higher traffic capacity. Orchestra's approach is to over-provision TSCH in order to support non-deterministic traffic, and the slotframe length is the primary way to control the amount of over-provisioning for a given traffic plane.

Network Latency. The per-hop latency on a given traffic plane is basically proportional to the length of the slotframe for this particular traffic plane.

[3]Note that this is a slight departure from the standard TSCH slotframe priority rules, where *Tx* slots take precedence over other slots independent of slotframe handles. This departure is not strictly required but makes Orchestra slot interaction easier to comprehend.

Energy Consumption. Similarly, the shorter the slotframe, the more often nodes have to wake up to listen or transmit, resulting in higher energy baseline.

4.2.3 Scheduling Rules

Orchestra maintains its schedules using simple *scheduling rules*, described in this section. Scheduling rules are a set of TSCH slotframes and slots enhanced with a number of Orchestra-specific properties. Some of the slotframe and slot properties are per IEEE802.15.4e (labeled *std*), other include extensions to standard properties (*ext*), or are introduced by Orchestra (*new*).

The properties of an Orchestra slotframe S are:

Handle *(std).* A unique positive integer for both identification and priority. The smaller it is, the higher the priority.

Length *(ext).* The number of slots in the slotframe. Must be mutually prime with all other slotframe lengths in the network.

Traffic Filter *(new).* The traffic plane the slotframe is intended for. Filters packet properties (*e.g.*, *unicast*, *broadcast*) and protocols (*e.g.*, *TSCH*, *RPL*).

Slotframes are made of Orchestra slots, each mapped into 0, 1 or multiple TSCH slots depending on the current TSCH and RPL state. An Orchestra slot can for instance be reserved for communication with all TSCH time sources, RPL children, or the current RPL preferred parent. The properties of a slot are:

Neighbors *(new).* The neighbor or set of neighbors the Orchestra slot is to be instantiated for, such as the RPL preferred parent or all RPL children. The resulting TSCH slots are updated automatically whenever changes occur in the TSCH or RPL state.

Coordinates *(ext).* The time and channel offset within the slotframe. Can either be fixed or a variable such as a node ID a hash of the neighbor MAC address.

Options *(std).* Standard TSCH options. Includes: *Rx* (reception), *Tx* (transmission), *S* (shared), defining what the slot can be used for, and if it is shared or dedicated.

Although today the Orchestra rules are statically programmed in the nodes, one could design a CoAP-based management interface to define new rules at runtime. Once the slotframes and slots are installed, Orchestra executes TSCH according to standard IEEE802.15.4e, except for transmit slots. For transmit slots, in addition to matching the packet and slot address fields, Orchestra checks the packet against the traffic filter of the current slot's slotframe.

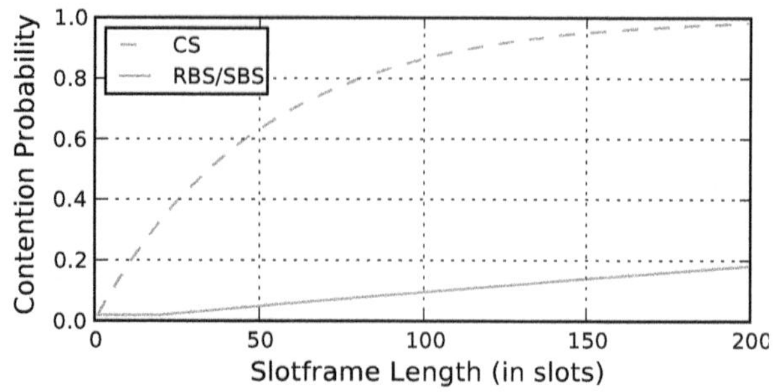

Figure 4: Analytical contention probability for CS slots vs. RBS and SBS slots, for 20-node clique and a traffic load of one packet per 500 ms. RBS and SBS do not eliminate contention but reduce it drastically. SBD are not in the figure as they are contention-free.

4.3 Performance Analysis

This section analyzes the contention rates obtained with different types of Orchestra slots. It then formulates guarantees on the frequency of overlap among different slotframes, and derives bounds for the nodes' radio duty cycle.

4.3.1 *Contention Rate*

Orchestra slots repeat at a constant period to serve a particular traffic plane. This is a behavior equivalent to slotted ALOHA for each traffic plane. In slotted ALOHA, the probability for any transmission to face contention is [41]:

$$p(cont_{slottedALOHA}) = 1 - e^{-T} \quad (1)$$

Where T is the average traffic load on the slot, with traffic following a Poisson distribution. For instance, if there is on average one packet sent every two slot, $T = \frac{1}{2}$.

Let us consider a simple case with a network of N nodes, all connected to each other (a clique). In a setup with one slotframe of length L with a single CS slot, the load on every slot is $T \times L$, and the contention probability is:

$$p(cont_{CS}) = 1 - e^{-TL} \quad (2)$$

In a case with RBS or SBS slots, the traffic is spread over all slots in the slotframe. If the slotframe is longer than or equal to the network size, the traffic is spread evenly across all nodes, decreasing the traffic load by a factor N. Otherwise, all slots are shared equally among nodes, decreasing the traffic load by a factor of only L. As a result, the contention probability is:

$$p(cont_{RBS}) = p(cont_{SBS}) = \begin{cases} 1 - e^{-\frac{TL}{N}} & \text{if } L \geq N \\ 1 - e^{-T} & \text{otherwise.} \end{cases} \quad (3)$$

Finally, sender-based dedicated slots (SBD) are by design contention-free:

$$p(cont_{SBD}) = 0 \quad (4)$$

Figure 4 shows $p(cont_{CS})$, $p(cont_{RBS})$ and $p(cont_{SBS})$ for a 20-node network, with an overall traffic load of one packet per 500 ms and 10 ms slots ($T = \frac{1}{50}$). In all cases, contention increases for longer slotframe as a result of sparser slot repetition. At any slotframe length, RBS and SBS decrease the level of contention by an important factor. They are therefore advisable in any scenario where a common rendez-vous slot is not required.

4.3.2 *Slotframe Overlap*

Every slotframe repeats with at a given period (its length in slots). Let B_{slots} be the number of slots in slotframe B of length B_{len}. Let $coll_B$ denote the event of a given slot colliding with any slot in B. The probability for any slot to collide with B is:

$$p(coll_B) = \frac{1}{B_{len}/B_{slots}} \quad (5)$$

When such slot collision occur, the slot from the slotframe with smaller handle takes precedence, all other slots are skipped. We denote SF the set of all slotframes in the system. The probability for A (handle denoted as A_h) to be skipped due to a slot collision with any other slotframe is:

$$p(skip_A) = 1 - \left(\prod_{\forall B \in SF,\ B_h < A_h} 1 - p(coll_{A,B}) \right) \quad (6)$$

4.3.3 *Duty Cycle Bounds*

Let $rxMinDc$ be the radio duty cycle of a *Rx* slot when no communication occurs, defined as $rxMinDc = \frac{rxGuardTime}{slotLength}$ where $rxGuardTime$ denotes the TSCH *Rx* guard time and $slotLength$ the TSCH slot duration. $A_{dcRxBase}$ is the listening cost of slotframe A, in the absence of communication:

$$A_{dcRxBase} = (1 - p(skip_A)) \times \frac{A_{rxSlots} \times rxMinDc}{A_{len}} \quad (7)$$

Here, $A_{rxSlots}$ is the number of slots with *Rx* flag in slotframe A.

In the absence of data to send, a node does not switch on its radio in transmit slots. Therefore, the lower bound duty cycle of slotframe A is $A_{dcLower} = A_{dcRxBase}$.

Because of reception guard times, *Rx* slots result in a maximum duty cycle (denoted $rxMaxDc$) higher than *Tx* slots (denoted $txMaxDc$). The upper bound duty cycle is reached when a full-sized packet is received (resp. sent) at every *Rx* slot (resp. *Tx*-only slot):

$$A_{dcUpper} = (1 - p(skip_A)) \times \frac{A_{rxSlots} \times rxMaxDc + A_{txOnlySlots} \times txMaxDc}{A_{len}} \quad (8)$$

Where $A_{txOnlySlots}$ is the number of slots in slotframe A with *Tx* flag but not *Rx* flag.

The system-wide lower and upper bound duty cycle are denoted respectively $dcLower = \sum_{\forall A \in SF} A_{dcLower}$ and $dcUpper = \sum_{\forall A \in SF} A_{dcUpper}$.

4.4 Example Orchestra Schedules

We introduce a number of example Orchestra setups used throughout the paper for discussion and evaluation.

4.4.1 *6TiSCH Minimal Schedule*

A simple example is the schedule defined by the 6TiSCH minimal configuration [35]. It consists of a single slotframe with a single common shared (CS) slot. This configuration is a very practical one, as it establishes basic connectivity between every node, for any traffic type. However, all slots are shared in the entire network, resulting in a purely contention-based scenario. We refer to such a setup as *TSCH-min-X*, where X is the length of the slotframe.

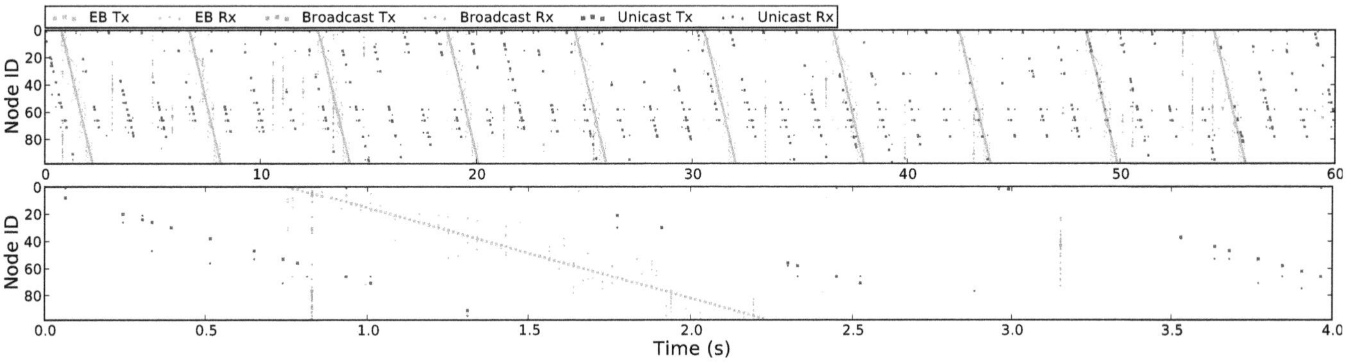

Figure 5: A 60 minutes slice of Orchestra running in Indriya (top) and a zoomed view on 4 seconds (bottom). The EB and unicast slotframes result in diagonal lines of activity as they contain a single *Tx* slot each, with time offset equal to node ID. The broadcast slotframe has a single common shared slot at time offset 0, and therefore results in vertical lines, as all nodes are listening simultaneously. All slotframes repeat with a different periodicity. The duty cycle is 0.47%.

4.4.2 Setup with Receiver-based Unicast Slots

We describe a more advanced setup made of three slotframes, including one receiver-based slotframe for unicast. We refer to such a setup as *TSCH-RB-X-Y-Z*, where X, Y, Z are the length of the three slotframes S0, S1, S2.

EB Slotframe. The first slotframe (S0) is dedicated to EB (TSCH Enhanced Beacon) transmissions, used for TSCH association and child-parent synchronization. The slotframe is longer than the number of nodes in the network, and consists of one sender-based dedicated (SBD) slot. As a result, every node has one Tx slot, and one Rx slot to listen for EBs from its time source. All transmissions in S0 are contention-free. We use $X = 397$ slots as a default length for S0.

Broadcast Slotframe. We add a slotframe (S1) with one common shared (CS) slot for RPL broadcast messages. As described in §4.3, S1 periodically collides with S0, as the latter has a higher priority. We use $Y = 31$ slots as a default length for S1. The probability for this slot to collide with S0 and be skipped is:

$$p(skip_{S1}) = 1-(1-p(coll_{S0})) = \frac{1}{S0_{len}/S0_{slots}} \approx 0.005 \quad (9)$$

Receiver-based Unicast Slotframe. We finally add a slotframe (S2) for unicast traffic with the RPL parent and all children, through a receiver-based shared (RBS) slot. In this setup, every node wakes up at a time offset derived from its own MAC address, listening for incoming traffic. We assign time offset $hash(MAC)\%Z$ to every node, where Z is the slotframe length. The probability for any slot in S2 to be skipped due to a collision with either of the previously described slotframes is:

$$p(skip_{S2}) = 1 - (1 - p(coll_{S0})) \times (1 - p(coll_{S1}))) \approx 0.037 \quad (10)$$

Which means that unicast transmissions to a given neighbor will occur with a 96.3% probability, and be postponed to the next slot otherwise.

4.4.3 Setup with Sender-based Unicast Slots

We introduce a variation of the setup above, where unicast transmissions take place in a sender-based shared (SBS) slot. S0 and S1 are the same as for TSCH-RB, but S2 is modified to use SBS instead of RBS. We refer to this setup as *TSCH-SB-X-Y-Z*, where X, Y, Z are the length of S0, S1, and S2.

In this setup, every sender has a transmit slot assigned in S2, and every node listens to their RPL parent and children's slot. The main benefit of TSCH-SB is that it reduces contention in comparison to TSCH-RB where all transmissions to a given node take place in the same slot. The downside is a higher energy baseline, as nodes need to wake up and listen at each of their or parents and children's slots. In scenarios where all nodes have a unique ID, and where the slotframe length Z is greater than the network size, one can ensure contention-free transmissions, and replace the shared *Tx* slot with a dedicated one.

Figure 5 shows Orchestra running with this setup with unicast slotframe of 101 slots (TSCH-SB-101) on the Indriya testbed's 98 TelosB nodes (*c.f.*, §6.1). In this specific run, we use the testbed node IDs to define the time offsets, resulting in cascaded transmissions. The figure shows the periodic transmissions of EBs (orange, cascaded), broadcast slots (green, all nodes aligned for contention-based communication) and unicast (blue, cascaded).

5. SYSTEM INTEGRATION

We discuss here a number of modifications we applied to Contiki's RPL implementation in order to gear it towards high reliability, and we introduce our implementation of TSCH and Orchestra.

Reliable RPL. Because we are aiming for high reliability, and to make sure TSCH nodes always have a reachable time source neighbor, we fine-tune RPL as follows.

First, we noticed that the ETX metric builds best-effort rather than reliable routes. For instance, a 56% PRR hop (ETX=1.8) is considered better than two perfect hops (ETX=1+1=2). When reliability matters, the latter should be clearly preferred. We use the squared ETX value as the link's cost in order to favor good links while preserving the gradient nature of RPL.

Second, we have to make RPL less aggressive in switching parents to avoid switching to a neighbor with which we do not have good statistics yet. To this end, we implement a simple probing mechanism: every node transmits a unicast probe to its best or second best parent at a given interval (we use 4 min in this paper's experiments). This allows a node to maintain up-to-date link estimates, ensuring that it always has some knowledge about the link quality to its backup (second best) parent. We also use the RSSI from received DIOs to calculate an initial estimate of the ETX towards the sender of this DIO.

Third, we noticed that, although RPL manages to repair routing loops eventually, a number of packets is always dropped in the process. To avoid this, we add a mechanism where, whenever a routing loop is detected, the receiver node transmits a unicast DIO message to the sender, thereby forcing the immediate update of both nodes' routing state.

We found that these enhancements greatly improve the end-to-end delivery ratio, not only with TSCH and Orchestra but also with asynchronous MAC layers (*e.g.*, up to 99.8% delivery with ContikiMAC+RPL data collection, the best results we are aware of in the literature).

Implementation. We implement[4] TSCH and Orchestra for the Contiki OS. This implementation supports two platforms, both evaluated in the next section: TelosB (MSP430, 10kB RAM, 48kB flash, external CC2420 radio) and NXP JN5168 (SoC with 32-bit RISC CPU, 32kB RAM, 256kB flash, 802.15.4 radio) [25]. In both implementations, all TSCH operations are governed by a timer interrupt (32kHz clock for TelosB, 16MHz for JN5168), and radio interrupts are disabled. TSCH is entirely responsible for managing the radio and reading out data whenever appropriate, as well as for generating and parsing IEEE802.15.4e enhanced ACKs and beacons. Runtime schedule modifications are done as follows: first wait for the end of the current slot, disable TSCH, proceed during next slot, resume TSCH operation.

TSCH (with Orchestra TSCH-min setup and queue space for 16 packets), when compiled for TelosB, has a memory footprint of 10kB flash and 2kB RAM. Due to the limited memory available on the TelosB, we were unable to run RPL with support for downwards routing in addition to TSCH, only upwards traffic is supported. All available Contiki RPL features are supported on the JN5168.

6. EVALUATION

In this section, we first present extensive experiments in two different testbeds, demonstrating Orchestra's superiority against state-of-the-art asynchronous MAC layers in reducing contention and achieving high reliability. Second, we run simulations to compare against a centralized scheduler, where we quantify the cost in latency and energy of our autonomous scheduling approach, and demonstrate Orchestra's adaptability to varying link conditions. Table 1 summarizes our testbed evaluation results.

6.1 Setup

Simulation and Testbeds. We use three different environments. First, we run experiments in the Indriya testbed [6], featuring 98 TelosB nodes in a three-floor office building in Singapore. We use node #2, on the top floor, as root of the network. An experiment in Indriya lasts 1h, repeated between 3 and 10 times. Results shown are averages with standard deviation.

Second, to overcome the memory restrictions of the TelosB platform, we use a testbed (JN-IoT) of 25 JN5168 nodes deployed in an office building. We use node #1, in a corner, as root. Results on the JN-IoT testbed are from a single experiment for each configuration, each experiment lasting between 16h and 72h. The results we report are gathered through a total of 219 testbed experiments and we routed 1,178,601 UDP packets from source to destination.

[4]The code is available at `https://github.com/simonduq/orchestra`.

Testbed	Traffic	Protocol	PDR [%] (loss rate)
Indriya Nodes: TelosB Size: 98 nodes ∅ hops: 4.2 ∅ density: 16	*Upwards* 60s interval	*Always-on*	99.91 (1 / 1139)
		ContikiMAC-64	99.8 (1 / 482)
		ContikiMAC-8	99.0 (1 / 98)
		TSCH-min-3	99.87 (1 / 779)
		TSCH-min-5	99.2 (1 / 127)
		TSCH-RB-7	99.996 (1 / 27,044)
		TSCH-SB-7	99.996 (1 / 25,450)
		TSCH-SB-47	99.997 (1 / 35,700)
JN-IoT Nodes: JN5168 Size: 25 nodes ∅ hops: 3 ∅ density: 13	*Upwards* 30s interval	*Always-on*	99.97 (1 / 2893)
		TSCH-min-5	99.86 (1 / 715)
		TSCH-SB-29	99.991 (1 / 11,160)
	Down-up 50s interval	*Always-on*	99.92 (1 / 1152)
		TSCH-min-5	99.85 (1 / 674)
		TSCH-SB-29	99.98 (1 / 5607)

Table 1: Testbed experiments summary. Orchestra TSCH-RB and TSCH-SB consistently achieve the lowest loss rates, outperforming the low-power alternative ContikiMAC by two orders of magnitude. Through contention avoidance and channel hopping, Orchestra also beats the *Always-on* MAC, with 4 to 35 times fewer losses.

Third, to compare Orchestra against static scheduling with full control on the network conditions, we use Cooja, Contiki's network simulator. Cooja emulates TelosB nodes running compiled MSP430 firmware. Cooja allows us to have full control over network conditions and emulates varying connectivity in a repeatable manner.

Protocols. We use Orchestra with all three configurations from §4.4. We compare Orchestra against a centralized, static scheduler (described in §6.6) and the asynchronous MAC layers *Always-on* and ContikiMAC at 8Hz and 64Hz (*c.f.*, §3). All protocols use a maximum of 8 retransmissions per hop, and a maximum of 16 packets in the queue. As for the TSCH slot timing, on TelosB, we use 15 ms slots and a guard time of ±0.6 ms. On JN5168, we use 10 ms slots and a ±0.25 ms guard time. Finally, we run *Always-on* and ContikiMAC over the best channel available, 26, and TSCH over the four best channels: 15, 20, 25, 26.

Application Scenarios. We run two different application scenarios: *upwards* routing and *down-up* routing. In *upwards*, nodes transmit a packet to the network root at a given average interval, with added jitter to emulate non-deterministic traffic. This is done with RPL downwards routing disabled. In *down-up*, the network root picks a node in the network at random and transmits a request to it. The destination answers immediately by sending a response back. This is a classic traffic pattern in IoT scenarios, *e.g.*, in RESTful architectures with CoAP. In all cases but centralized scheduling, nodes run RPL, 6LoWPAN, and all application traffic is raw UDP with a 16 bytes payload. The first 15 minutes of every run are always excluded, to allow the network to form and RPL to converge to a stable topology.

Metrics. The three main metrics we focus on are the end-to-end packet delivery ratio (PDR), end-to-end latency, and radio duty cycle. The PDR is the portion of packets sent at the application layer which make it to their final destination, possibly over multiple hops. The end-to-end latency

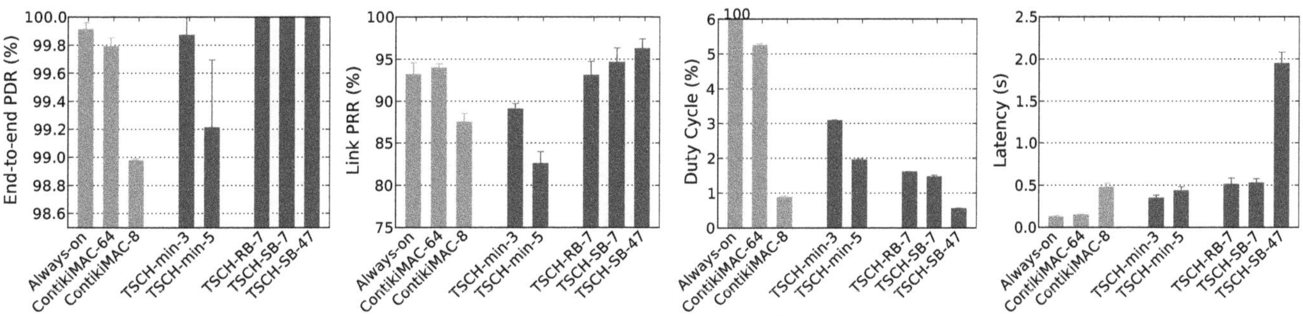

(a) (End-to-end) PDR (b) Unicast PRR (c) Duty Cycle (d) Latency

Figure 6: *Upwards* Experiments in Indriya. Orchestra results in the highest delivery ratios, here between 99.996% and 99.997%. This is partly explained by higher link PRR, reaching as high as 97%, in comparison with ContikiMAC's 94% (twice as many losses in the latter case). ContikiMAC, however, offers the best latency-energy balance. Note that the y-axis of the PDR and PRR plots does not begin a zero.

is measured between the initial application's intention to send a packet and its reception at the final destination. The duty cycle is the portion of time spent with the radio on (either transmitting, listening or receiving), and is used as a platform-independent measure of energy consumption. In addition, we look at the link packet reception rate (PRR), which the per-hop, per-transmission attempt success rate.

6.2 Comparison with Asynchronous MACs

We run Orchestra, *Always-on* and ContikiMAC in Indriya, with *upwards* traffic generated at every node at an average 60 s interval. Figure 6 summarizes our results.

All Orchestra configurations achieve the highest PDRs, above 99.99%, *i.e.*, less than one end-to-end loss per 10k packets or 10^{-4} loss rate. The best asynchronous results are with *Always-on*, reaching a PDR of 99.9% *i.e.*, a loss rate of 10^{-3}, one order of magnitude behind Orchestra. ContikiMAC is an other order of magnitude below, with 99% or a loss rate of 10^{-2}.

Figure 6b shows the MAC success rate, *i.e.*, the link quality achieved by each protocol. For all protocols, there is a clear correlation between link quality and end-to-end PDR, which means the overall performance is mostly limited by medium access (rather than routing or queue drops). Orchestra achieves the highest MAC success rates, *e.g.*, 97% with TSCH-SB-47 against 93% for *Always-on*. We attribute this mostly to Orchestra's ability to reduce contentions. TSCH-min, which is fully contention-based, results in the lowest success rates.

ContikiMAC obtains a loss rate which is two orders of magnitude above Orchestra, but achieves the best latency-energy balance. For instance, ContikiMAC@8Hz yields a 0.5s latency for duty cycle of 0.8%, while TSCH-SB-7 has a duty cycle of 1.4% for the same latency. *Always-on* results by design in 100% duty cycle, and also achieves the lowest latency results, as nodes never have to wait for their neighbor to wake up before sending.

6.3 Contention Control and Scalability

One of the main goals of Orchestra is to reduce contention through scheduling, in order to increase link success rate and overall reliability. A limitation, however, is that Orchestra achieves this by having slotframes with a fixed size, and

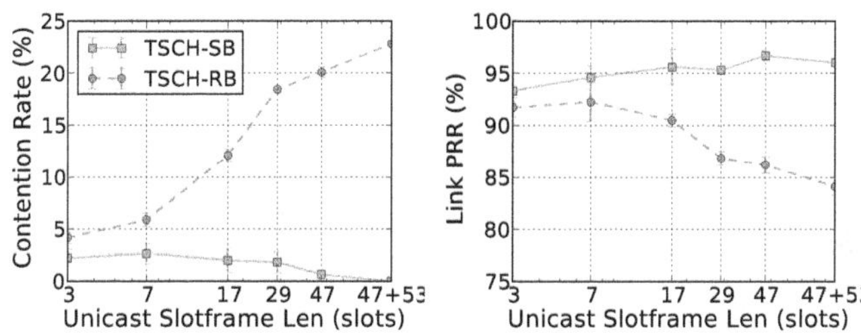

(a) Contention Rate (b) Unicast PRR

Figure 7: With TSCH-SB, longer slotframes translate to more available timeslots and less contention. With 47+53 slots, the network is contention-free. Lower values result in a contention rate below 3%. TSCH-RB suffers from longer slotframes, due to increased pressure on the nodes' *Rx* slots. Note that the y-axis of the PRR plot does not begin a zero.

spreading out nodes across all slots in the slotframe. This might cause network capacity and scalability issues. We investigate this by varying the unicast slotframe length in TSCH-RB and TSCH-SB. We argue that varying the slotframe for a fixed number of nodes (Indriya's 98 nodes) produces an effect similar to increasing traffic load or network size for a fixed slotframe; this allows us to get insights on Orchestra's network capacity and scalability.

Figure 7 shows our results with TSCH-RB-3 to TSCH-RB-47 and TSCH-SB-3 to TSCH-SB-47 (receiver-based and sender-based shared slots). We also introduce an extra case, TSCH-RB-47+53 and TSCH-SB-47+53, where two unicast slotframes are used, with size 47 and 53. This increases the number of different unicast slots to 100, more than the network size. In this particular case, we use the nodes' unique ID to allocate a unique slot to each. TSCH-SB-47+53 is therefore guaranteed to be fully contention-free (sender-based dedicated slots).

Figure 7a shows that, as predicted by our analytical model in §4.3.1, the contention rate for TSCH-RB increases at larger slotframes. TSCH-SB shows much lower contention rates, and with the opposite trend: it performs at its best with longer slotframes to eventually reach no contention at

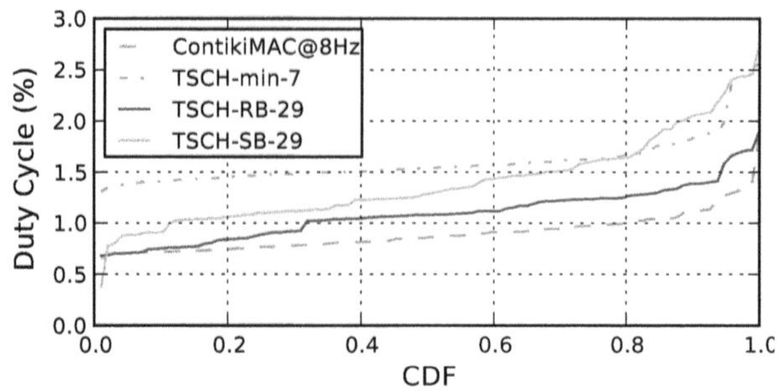

Figure 8: Orchestra's sender-based schedules (TSCH-SB) have the drawback of producing less evenly distributed duty cycles among nodes, compared to ContikiMAC, TSCH-min, or TSCH-RB.

all in the 47+53 case. With slotframes of length 3 to 29, contentions remain roughly constant, in the 2–3% range. Such low contention rates result in high link PRR, above 95% in most cases (Figure 7b). We attribute TSCH-SB's superiority in here in handling contention to its sender-based nature. Receiver-based slots are more likely to cause contention, where all transmissions to a given node take place in the same slot. This is not captured by our analytical model from §4.3.1, which considers clique networks only (in a clique, transmissions from/to any node may collide).

6.4 Energy Distribution and Bounds

Figure 8 shows how different Orchestra configurations affect the distribution of radio duty cycle among nodes. For each configuration, we pick parameters leading to comparable duty cycles, *i.e.*, with all nodes between 0.3% and 3%. A first observation is that TSCH-SB results in less evenly-balanced radio duty cycles than TSCH-RB. This can be attributed to the varying number of unicast *Rx* slots in this *upwards* traffic scenario. TSCH-SB requires one such slot for every child, whereas in TSCH-RB nodes have a single unicast *Rx* slot.

Table 2 shows the minimum and maxium per-node radio duty cycle, as measured during all experiments, against the theoretical bounds defined in §4.3. For all configurations, including ContikiMAC, we find the theoretical lower bounds to be accurate. Deriving accurate upper bounds proves more difficult. For ContikiMAC, which is asynchronous, the upper bound is the case where a node transmits broadcasts continuously, which can lead to a duty cycle as high as 88%. With TSCH-SB-29 we also get a very high maximum value of 31%, which corresponds to the case where a node uses all of its 29 unicast slots for listening to its children. TSCH-min-7 and TSCH-RB-29, due to their more predictable schedules, allow us to derive more realistic and usable upper bounds, both under 1.75× the maximum measured.

To summarize, in scenarios where energy consumption must be bounded, Orchestra can produce schedules that guarantee no node will have its radio turned on more than *e.g.*, 3% of the time.

6.5 Orchestra in IoT Scenarios

We now move to the JN-IoT testbed, and run both *upwards* and *down-up* traffic experiments. Because ContikiMAC is not ported to the JN5168 platform, we only run *Always-on* and TSCH. We use the TSCH-min-5 and TSCH-SB-29 configurations. In the latter, as we have a unicast slotframe of size greater than the network size, we use the node's unique ID to derive contention-free slots. The results are shown in Table 1.

	Duty Cycle (%)			
	Experiments		Theoretical	
	Min	Max	Min	Max
Contikmac@8Hz	0.66	1.89	0.6	88
TSCH-min-7	1.30	2.56	1.14	4.48
TSCH-RB-29	0.68	1.90	0.54	3.00
TSCH-SB-29	0.38	2.75	0.28	31.19

Table 2: Measured and theoretical min and max duty cycle. Lower bounds are predicted accurately in all cases, but upper bounds with ContikiMAC or TSCH-SB are very pessimistic.

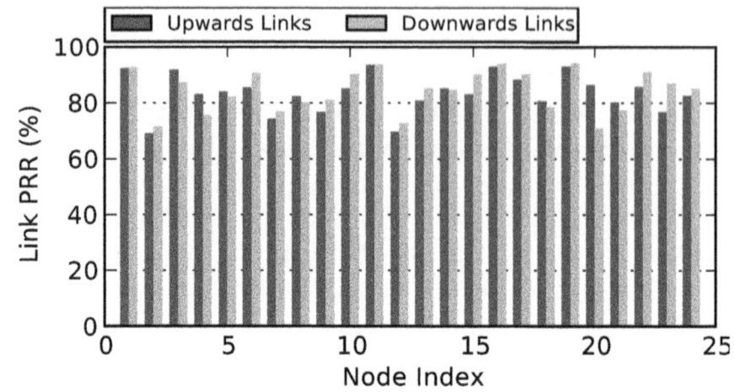

Figure 9: *Down-up* experiment in the JN-IoT testbed: per-node link PRR. All links are usable both ways, albeit not perfectly symmetric.

In general, the PDRs in JN-IoT are lower than in Indriya. This is due to differences in physical topologies and deployment sites. In particular, we noticed significant fluctuations in link quality during workdays when compared to nights, to an extent much greater than in Indriya.

In both *upwards* and *down-up* experiments, TSCH-SB-29 achieves the highest PDRs: about 4× fewer losses than with the *Always-on* MAC and 10× fewer than TSCH-min-5. For all three configurations (*Always-on*, TSCH-min-5, TSCH-SB-29), the results when involving downwards routing are worse than in the *upwards* scenario. We attribute this to inherent properties of RPL rather than TSCH or Orchestra.

In RPL, the topology is optimized towards the root, and downward traffic is merely enabled by reusing links in the reverse direction, with no guarantee on link quality. Figure 9 shows, for every node, the average link PRR when routing up (from the node) or down (towards the node). Although links are mostly symmetric, there are a few notable exceptions, such as node 20 with an average PRR of 86% up, 71% down. In the TSCH-SB-29 experiment, out of 258k packets sent in 72h, 46 were lost, 35 of them while going downwards, 11 while going upwards. Half of the downwards losses are attributed to link losses (in part due to link asymmetry), others are due to temporary RPL inconsistencies (loops or outdated routes following topology updates).

Overall, this series of experiment in the JN-IoT testbed demonstrates that Orchestra can run reliably on different hardware platforms and networks, as well as with more challenging traffic patterns.

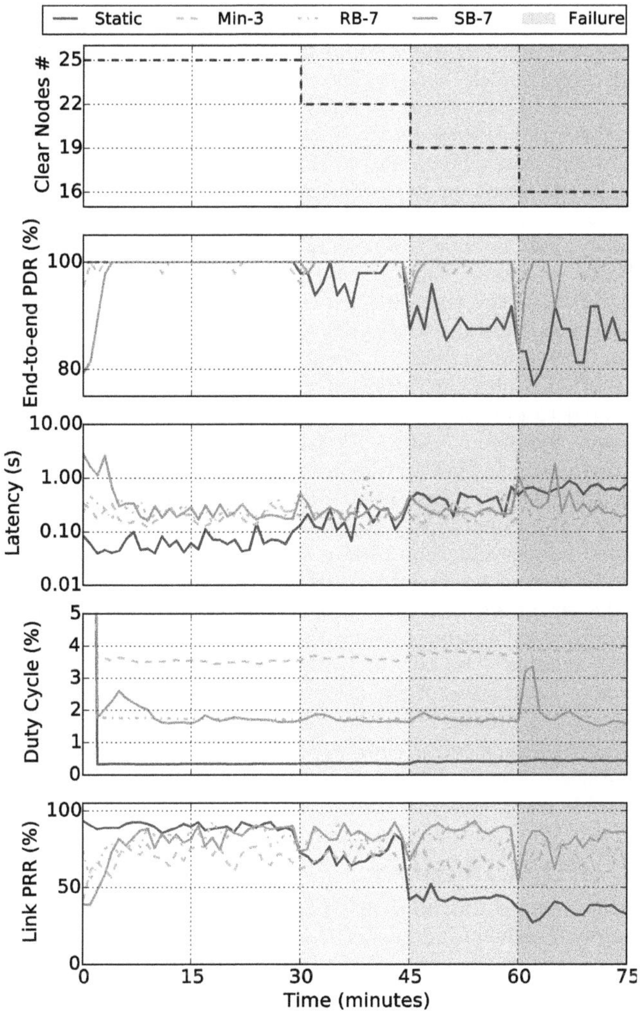

Figure 10: Orchestra compared to a simple static schedule. From minute 30 onward, we inject link failures on three random nodes every 15 minutes. Orchestra quickly adapts to these changes while the static schedule suffers despite retransmission slots. Note that the y-axis of the node count and the PDR plots does not begin a zero.

6.6 Comparison with Static Scheduling

The goal of this section is to evaluate the overhead of using Orchestra with RPL when compared to a centralized, static scheduler, and at the same time show the flexibility of Orchestra with RPL in reacting to network dynamics.

As a benchmark, we implement a simple offline scheduler inspired by the work of Pöttner et al. [28]. The scheduler takes PRR measurements for every link as input, computes their routing metric – it uses squared ETX, as in Orchestra, to favor good links – and uses Dijkstra to compute the shortest path from each node to the sink. Routes are built to support data-collection traffic only, at a pre-defined interval (30 s in our experiments). For each route, we compute a static TSCH schedule of transmissions throughout the network. Routes are scheduled redundantly to allow for retransmissions. Note that this is a simple scheduler, with no runtime re-configuration nor multi-path transmissions.

For this particular evaluation, we utilize Cooja/MSPSim simulations in order to fully control the conditions of the experiments. We configure the wireless links in the model to reflect the links quality we measured in the JN-IoT testbed. It should be noted, however, that this wireless link model in Cooja exhibits uniformly distributed losses which are not realistic in bursty low-power networks. Nonetheless, we argue that it is sufficient for this particular experiment.

In order to simulate network dynamics, we tune down the reception probability of three randomly chosen nodes to 0.1× their initial PRR *i.e.*, the affected nodes can still transmit as before, but are 10× more likely to drop incoming data packets. We repeat this every 15 minutes, choosing another three nodes without recovering the previously attenuated nodes. This is done exactly in the same order for the different experimental setups. We run the experiments for 75 minutes in Cooja, and start introducing failures only after 30 min to demonstrate a baseline of stable conditions.

We compare the static schedule (denoted as *Static*) to the following three configurations of Orchestra: TSCH-min-3, TSCH-RB-7, TSCH-SB-7. Figure 10 shows the results for each setup. First of all, when the network is stable (until minute 30), we notice the extremely low cost of *Static*. Compared to Orchestra, *Static* yields a 4 to 8× lower duty cycle (TSCH-SB-7 and TSCH-Min-3) and 10× lower latency. We attribute these to the schedules and routes in *Static*, which are (1) dimensioned to the traffic load (2) optimized to minimize latency along the network shortest path (3) and built offline involving no neighbor discovery and routing protocol at runtime. In terms of end-to-end PDR, both solutions perform exceptionally well, with the exception that Orchestra needs a little bit of startup time (about 5 minutes in this particular setup) to find good links and stabilize, while *Static* comes pre-configured with the best links and schedules.

Second, we examine the results after injecting network reception failures (minute 30 and onward): *Static* directly decreases in terms of performance, because it does not adjust to topology changes. With Orchestra, however, the PDR drops temporarily each 15 minutes and then RPL quickly finds new routes and recovers.

Overall, Orchestra reacts quickly to changes in network connectivity, but compared to a schedule built centrally for a specific topology and traffic pattern, it has a significant overhead in both latency and energy.

7. RELATED WORK

We review related work in three categories: (1) scheduled MAC and routing, (2) asynchronous, low-power routing and (3) synchronous transmissions.

Scheduled MAC and Routing. The idea of synchronizing nodes and channel hopping to combat multi-path fading and external interference is established in many technologies, including Bluetooth and cellular systems. It was brought to low-power wireless networking through a proprietary protocol called Time Synchronized Mesh Protocol (TSMP). Early promising results [8] pushed the core technology of TSMP to be standardized as WirelessHART [14], ISA100.11a [17] and IEEE802.15.4e [1].

In a WirelessHART network, a central entity computes the communication schedule based on application requirements and on information it gathers about network connectivity. The schedule is injected into the network and continuously updated throughout the lifetime of the network [18]. In static networks with predictable traffic patterns, commercial TSCH-like networks such as WirelessHART or SmartMesh IP [36] offer very high reliability (published results include 99.999% on a 49 node industrial deployment [8], 99.95% on a 15-node testbed [28]), and a decade of battery lifetime [39]. Note that the centralized scheduling algorithms are not part of the standards and much attention has been given to scheduling theory in the context of TSCH networks [27, 30, 31, 44].

In scenarios where the network topology and traffic patterns are not fixed, decentralized scheduling is applicable. Tinka et al. [34] present, to the best of our knowledge, the first paper to propose and demonstrate a decentralized scheduling solution for TSCH networks. A common shared slot is used for neighbor discovery and for negotiating the addition of dedicated slots. This work motivated further approaches [26, 43, 22]. For example, Morell et al. [22] take schedule negotiation one step further and propose multi-hop reservation through label switching. Focusing on very low data-rates and not limiting itself to TSCH, Dozer [2] employs distributing scheduling for energy-efficient routing. Its goal of high energy efficiency leads to significantly higher latency when compared to Orchestra. For example, experiments report an average latency of 30 s and a PDR of 98.5% at a radio duty-cycle of 0.2% for a testbed of 90 nodes [12]. To the best of our knowledge, Orchestra is the first distributed solution which does not require negotiation between nodes.

In October 2013, the IETF created the 6TiSCH working group, which standardizes how to use an IPv6-enabled upper stack on top of IEEE802.15.4e TSCH. 6TiSCH specifies a number of mechanisms to manage the TSCH schedule [33]. It defines a CoAP-based management protocol which can be used for central scheduling, and a protocol for neighbor nodes to negotiate distributed scheduling. 6TiSCH, however, leaves it to the implementer to decide which scheduling approaches fit best. Orchestra could be considered a third scheduling option for 6TiSCH networks.

Asynchronous, Low-power Routing. At the other end of the spectrum, asynchronous, low-power routing enables dynamic applications and transparently allows nodes to join and leave. However, its packet loss can be up to several percent: For example, CTP reports delivery ratios between 94% and 99.9% in data collection depending on the network size and topology [15]. Recent approaches such as ORW [21], ORPL [11] and BFC [29] improve in terms of energy efficiency and – in part – latency over CTP but still have an average PDR of roughly 99%. Moreover, these do not employ scheduling and channel hopping; thus, they cannot avoid external interference, multi-path fading, or contention as efficiently as Orchestra. EM-MAC [32] and MiCMAC [24] integrate channel hopping into asynchronous, low-power routing. As a result, they increase reliability, especially in the presence of external interference, but channel hopping with the loosely synchronized operation leads to an extra overhead in terms of latency and radio duty-cycle [24].

Synchronous Transmissions. A recent direction in low-power wireless networks is synchronous transmissions: Glossy [13] provides fast and efficient network flooding by precisely timing transmissions: it ensures that a receiver successfully receives even in the presence of multiple, concurrent transmissions – of the same packet – by exploiting constructive interference and capture effect. LWB [12] provides data collection and dissemination primitives on top of Glossy. In LWB, a central scheduler dynamically injects collection and dissemination schedules based on the traffic requests of the individual nodes. Chaos [20] combines synchronous transmission and in-network processing to provide fast, reliable, and energy efficient data collection and processing. Others show fast data dissemination [7, 5] and point-to-point routing [3, 42] based on synchronous transmissions. Approaches based on synchronous transmissions report very high reliability, low latency, and energy efficiency. For example, Glossy reports a reliability of more than 99.99%. However, synchronous transmissions always need one central entity to control and initiate the synchronous transmissions. Moreover, they – inherently – have a high channel utilization and are often limited in terms of generality such as being restricted to periodic traffic. Orchestra, in contrast, provides general purpose routing with RPL and IPv6.

Summary. Orchestra differs from previous TSCH scheduling approaches in that nodes compute their own schedule locally and autonomously, based on routing-layer information. Thus, it does not require any central entity nor communication among nodes to reserve schedules and paths. This makes it as flexible and application-independent as non-scheduled asynchronous solutions. Orchestra is significantly more reliable – by two orders of magnitude in our experiments – than state-of-the-art asynchronous low-power routing while achieving a similar latency-energy balance. Compared to synchronous transmissions, Orchestra has the advantage to support random-access traffic, which makes it suitable for non-deterministic low-power IPv6 applications.

8. CONCLUSION

This paper introduces Orchestra, a solution for autonomous scheduling of TSCH in RPL networks. Orchestra runs without any central scheduling entity nor negotiation, and supports low-power random-access traffic. The key idea is to provision a set of slots for different traffic planes, and to define the slots in such a way that they can be automatically installed/removed as the RPL topology evolves.

We implement Orchestra in Contiki and conduct an extensive evaluation in simulation and on two different testbeds. We demonstrate the practicality of Orchestra and its ability to consistently achieve the highest delivery ratio, while striking an interesting latency-energy balance.

As part of future work, we plan to investigate how to optimize time synchronization, reduce energy consumption further, and explore management solutions for 6TiSCH to enable runtime reconfiguration of Orchestra.

Acknowledgments

We would like to thank the CIR Lab in Singapore for providing the Indriya testbed, and Amy L. Murphy, our shepherd, for her insightful comments. This work was partly supported by the distributed environment Ecare@Home funded by the Swedish Knowledge Foundation 2015-2019, the EIT Digital RICH Activity, and VINNOVA (Sweden's Innovation Agency).

9. REFERENCES

[1] 802.15.4e Task Group. 802.15.4e-2012: IEEE Standard for Local and metropolitan area networks–Part 15.4: Low-Rate Wireless Personal Area Networks

(LR-WPANs) Amendment 1: MAC sublayer, 16 April 2012.

[2] N. Burri, P. V. Rickenbach, and R. Wattenhofer. Dozer: Ultra-Low Power Data Gathering in Sensor Networks. In *Proceedings of the Conference on Information Processing in Sensor Networks (ACM/IEEE IPSN)*, 2007.

[3] D. Carlson, M. Chang, A. Terzis, Y. Chen, and O. Gnawali. Forwarder selection in multi-transmitter networks. In *Proceedings of the Conference Distributed Computing in Sensor Systems (DCOSS)*, 2013.

[4] T. Chang, T. Watteyne, K. Pister, and Q. Wang. Adaptive synchronization in multi-hop tsch networks. *Comput. Netw.*, 76(C):165–176, Jan. 2015.

[5] M. Doddavenkatappa and M. C. Chan. P3: A practical packet pipeline using synchronous transmissions for wireless sensor networks. In *Proceedings of the Conference on Information Processing in Sensor Networks (ACM/IEEE IPSN)*, 2014.

[6] M. Doddavenkatappa, M. C. Chan, and A. Ananda. Indriya: A Low-Cost, 3D Wireless Sensor Network Testbed. In *Proceedings of the Conference on Testbeds and Research Infrastructures for the Development of Networks & Communities (TridentCom)*, 2011.

[7] M. Doddavenkatappa, M. C. Chan, and B. Leong. Splash: Fast data dissemination with constructive interference in wireless sensor networks. In *Proceedings of the Symposium on Networked Systems Design & Implementation (USENIX NSDI)*, 2013.

[8] L. Doherty, W. Lindsay, and J. Simon. Channel-Specific Wireless Sensor Network Path Data. In *Proceedings of the 16th International Conference on Computer Communications and Networks (ICCCN)*, pages 89–94, Turtle Bay Resort, Honolulu, Hawaii, USA, 13-16 August 2007. IEEE.

[9] A. Dunkels. The ContikiMAC Radio Duty Cycling Protocol. Technical Report T2011:13, Swedish Institute of Computer Science, 2011.

[10] A. Dunkels, B. Gronvall, and T. Voigt. Contiki - A Lightweight and Flexible Operating System for Tiny Networked Sensors. In *Proceedings of the Conference on Local Computer Networks (IEEE LCN)*, 2004.

[11] S. Duquennoy, O. Landsiedel, and T. Voigt. Let the Tree Bloom: Scalable Opportunistic Routing with ORPL. In *Proceedings of the International Conference on Embedded Networked Sensor Systems (ACM SenSys 2013)*, Rome, Italy, Nov. 2013.

[12] F. Ferrari, M. Zimmerling, L. Mottola, and L. Thiele. Low-Power Wireless Bus. In *Proceedings of the Conference on Embedded Networked Sensor Systems (ACM SenSys)*, 2012.

[13] F. Ferrari, M. Zimmerling, L. Thiele, and O. Saukh. Efficient Network Flooding and Time Synchronization with Glossy. In *Proceedings of the Conference on Information Processing in Sensor Networks (ACM/IEEE IPSN)*, 2011.

[14] H. C. Foundation. WirelessHART Specification 75: TDMA Data-Link Layer, 2008. HCF_SPEC-75.

[15] O. Gnawali, R. Fonseca, K. Jamieson, D. Moss, and P. Levis. Collection Tree Protocol. In *Proceedings of the Conference on Embedded Networked Sensor Systems (ACM SenSys)*, 2009.

[16] J. W. Hui and D. E. Culler. Ip is dead, long live ip for wireless sensor networks. In *Proceedings of the Conference on Embedded Networked Sensor Systems (ACM SenSys)*, 2008.

[17] ISA. ISA-100.11a-2011 – Wireless Systems for Industrial Automation: Process Control and Related Applications, 2011.

[18] A. N. Kim, F. Hekland, S. Petersen, and P. Doyle. When HART goes wireless: Understanding and implementing the WirelessHART standard. In *ETFA*, pages 899–907. IEEE, 2008.

[19] J. Ko, J. Eriksson, N. Tsiftes, S. Dawson-Haggerty, J.-P. Vasseur, M. Durvy, A. Terzis, A. Dunkels, and D. Culler. Industry: Beyond Interoperability: Pushing the Performance of Sensor Network IP Stacks. In *Proceedings of the 9th ACM Conference on Embedded Networked Sensor Systems*, SenSys '11, pages 1–11, New York, NY, USA, 2011. ACM.

[20] O. Landsiedel, F. Ferrari, and M. Zimmerling. Chaos: Versatile and Efficient All-to-All Data Sharing and In-Network Processing at Scale. In *Proceedings of the Conference on Embedded Networked Sensor Systems (ACM SenSys)*, 2013.

[21] O. Landsiedel, E. Ghadimi, S. Duquennoy, and M. Johansson. Low Power, Low Delay: Opportunistic Routing meets Duty Cycling. In *Proceedings of the Conference on Information Processing in Sensor Networks (ACM/IEEE IPSN)*, 2012.

[22] A. Morell, X. Vilajosana, J. L. Vicario, and T. Watteyne. Label switching over IEEE802.15.4e networks. *Transactions on Emerging Telecommunications Technologies*, 24(5):458–475, Aug. 2013.

[23] D. Moss and P. Levis. BoX-MACs: Exploiting Physical and Link Layer Boundaries in Low-Power Networking. Technical Report SING-08-00, Stanford, 2008.

[24] B. A. Nahas, S. Duquennoy, V. Iyer, and T. Voigt. Low-Power Listening Goes Multi-Channel. In *Proceedings of the International Conference on Distributed Computing in Sensor Systems (IEEE DCOSS 2014)*, Marina Del Rey, CA, USA, May 2014.

[25] NXP Laboratories UK Ltd. *Data Sheet: JN516x IEEE802.15.4 Wireless Microcontroller*, 2013.

[26] M. R. Palattella, N. Accettura, M. Dohler, L. A. Grieco, and G. Boggia. Traffic Aware Scheduling Algorithm for reliable low-power multi-hop IEEE 802.15.4e networks. In *PIMRC*, pages 327–332. IEEE, 2012.

[27] M. R. Palattella, N. Accettura, L. A. Grieco, G. Boggia, M. Dohler, and T. Engel. On Optimal Scheduling in Duty-Cycled Industrial IoT Applications using IEEE802.15.4e TSCH. *IEEE Sensors Journal*, 13(10):3655 – 3666, Oct. 2013. doi:10.1109/JSEN.2013.2266417.

[28] W.-B. Pöttner, H. Seidel, J. Brown, U. Roedig, and L. Wolf. Constructing Schedules for Time-Critical Data Delivery in Wireless Sensor Networks. *ACM Trans. Sen. Netw.*, 10(3):44:1–44:31, May 2014.

[29] D. Puccinelli, S. Giordano, M. Zuniga, and P. J. Marrón. Broadcast-free collection protocol. In *Proceedings of the 10th ACM Conference on Embedded*

Network Sensor Systems, SenSys '12, pages 29–42, New York, NY, USA, 2012. ACM.

[30] A. Saifullah, P. B. Tiwari, B. Li, C. Lu, and Y. Chen. Accounting for Failures in Delay Analysis for WirelessHART Networks, 2012.

[31] A. Saifullah, Y. Xu, C. Lu, and Y. Chen. Real-Time Scheduling for WirelessHART Networks. In *Real-Time Systems Symposium (RTSS), 2010 IEEE 31st*, pages 150–159, Nov 2010.

[32] L. Tang, Y. Sun, O. Gurewitz, and D. B. Johnson. Em-mac: A dynamic multichannel energy-efficient mac protocol for wireless sensor networks. In *Proceedings of the Twelfth ACM International Symposium on Mobile Ad Hoc Networking and Computing*, MobiHoc '11, pages 23:1–23:11, New York, NY, USA, 2011. ACM.

[33] X. Thubert (Ed.), T. Watteyne, R. Struik, and M. Richardson. An Architecture for IPv6 over the TSCH mode of IEEE 802.15.4e - draft-ietf-6tisch-architecture-06, Mar. 2015. IETF Draft.

[34] A. Tinka, T. Watteyne, K. S. J. Pister, and A. M. Bayen. A Decentralized Scheduling Algorithm for Time Synchronized Channel Hopping. *EAI Endorsed Transactions on Mobile Communications and Applications*, 11(1), 9 2011.

[35] X. Vilajosana (Ed.) and K. Pister. Minimal 6TiSCH Configuration - draft-ietf-6tisch-minimal-06, Mar. 2015. IETF Draft.

[36] T. Watteyne, L. Doherty, J. Simon, and K. Pister. Technical Overview of SmartMesh IP. In *Proceedings of the 2013 Seventh International Conference on Innovative Mobile and Internet Services in Ubiquitous Computing*, IMIS '13, pages 547–551, Washington, DC, USA, 2013. IEEE Computer Society.

[37] T. Watteyne, S. Lanzisera, A. Mehta, and K. Pister. Mitigating Multipath Fading through Channel Hopping in Wireless Sensor Networks. In *Communications (ICC), 2010 IEEE International Conference on*, pages 1–5, May 2010.

[38] T. Watteyne, A. Mehta, and K. Pister. Reliability Through Frequency Diversity: Why Channel Hopping Makes Sense. In *Proceedings of the 6th ACM Symposium on Performance Evaluation of Wireless Ad Hoc, Sensor, and Ubiquitous Networks*, PE-WASUN '09, pages 116–123, New York, NY, USA, 2009. ACM.

[39] T. Watteyne, J. Weiss, L. Doherty, and J. Simon. Industrial IEEE802.15.4e Networks: Performance and Trade-offs. In *Proceedings of IEEE International Conference on Communications (ICC), Internet of Things Symposium*, London, UK, June 2015.

[40] T. Winter (Ed.), P. Thubert (Ed.), and RPL Author Team. RPL: IPv6 Routing Protocol for Low power and Lossy Networks, Mar. 2012. RFC 6550.

[41] Y.-C.Jenq. On the stability of slotted aloha systems. *Communications, IEEE Transactions on*, 28(11):1936–1939, Nov 1980.

[42] D. Yuan, M. Riecker, and M. Hollick. Making 'Glossy' Networks Sparkle: Exploiting Concurrent Transmissions for Energy Efficient, Reliable, Ultra-Low Latency Communication in Wireless Control Networks. In *Proceedings of the European Conference on Wireless Sensor Networks (EWSN)*, 2014.

[43] P. Zand, A. Dilo, and P. Havinga. D-MSR: A Distributed Network Management Scheme for Real-Time Monitoring and Process Control Applications in Wireless Industrial Automation. *Sensors*, 13(7):8239–8284, 2013.

[44] H. Zhang, P. Soldati, and M. Johansson. Optimal Link Scheduling and Channel Assignment for Convergecast in Linear wirelessHART Networks. In *Proceedings of the 7th International Conference on Modeling and Optimization in Mobile, Ad Hoc, and Wireless Networks*, WiOPT'09, pages 82–89, Piscataway, NJ, USA, 2009. IEEE Press.

Directional Transmissions and Receptions for High-throughput Bulk Forwarding in Wireless Sensor Networks

Ambuj Varshney
Uppsala University, Sweden
ambuj.varshney@it.uu.se

Luca Mottola
Politecnico di Milano, Italy and
SICS Swedish ICT, Sweden
luca@sics.se

Mats Carlsson
SICS Swedish ICT, Sweden
matsc@sics.se

Thiemo Voigt
Uppsala University, Sweden
SICS Swedish ICT, Sweden
thiemo@sics.se

ABSTRACT

We present DPT: a wireless sensor network protocol for bulk traffic that uniquely leverages electronically switchable directional (ESD) antennas. Bulk traffic is found in several scenarios and supporting protocols based on standard antenna technology abound. ESD antennas may improve performance in these scenarios; for example, by reducing channel contention as the antenna can steer the radiated energy only towards the intended receivers, and by extending the communication range at no additional energy cost. The corresponding protocol support, however, is largely missing. DPT addresses precisely this issue. First, while the network is quiescent, we collect link metrics across all possible antenna configurations. We use this information to formulate a constraint satisfaction problem (CSP) that allows us to find *two multi-hop disjoint paths* connecting source and sink, along with the corresponding antenna configurations. Domain-specific heuristics we conceive ameliorate the processing demands in solving the CSP, improving scalability. Second, the routing configuration we obtain is injected back into the network. During the actual bulk transfer, the source funnels data through the two paths by quickly alternating between them. Packet forwarding occurs deterministically at every hop. This allows the source to implicitly "clock" the entire pipeline, sparing the need of proactively synchronizing the transmissions across the two paths. Our results, obtained in a real testbed using 802.15.4-compliant radios and custom ESD antennas we built, indicate that DPT approaches the maximum throughput supported by the link layer, peaking at 214 kbit/s in the settings we test.

SenSys'15, November 1–4, 2015, Seoul, South Korea..
ACM 978-1-4503-3631-4/15/11.
DOI: http://dx.doi.org/10.1145/2809695.2809720 .

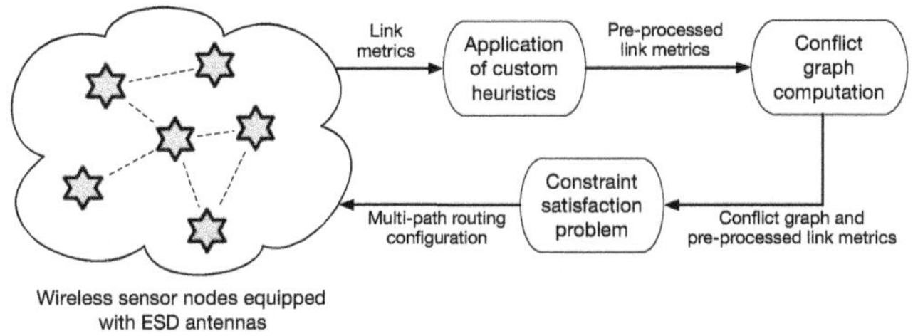

Figure 1: DPT operation.

Categories and Subject Descriptors

C.2.1 [**Network Architecture and Design**]: Wireless Communication

Keywords

Directional antennas, Bulk data transmissions, Wireless sensor networks, Electronically controlled antennas

1. INTRODUCTION

Bulk traffic is arguably a frequent pattern in wireless sensor networks (WSNs), often found in scenarios such as structural health monitoring [4, 27, 36], wildlife monitoring [13] and volcano monitoring [47]. In these scenarios, tens of resource-constrained sensor nodes quietly monitor some event of interest. Upon recognizing such an event, they gather large amounts of data; for example, high-frequency acceleration samples, which are then sent over multiple hops to a powerful sink node for further processing.

Challenges. The literature includes several WSN protocols to support the bulk traffic pattern [9, 39]. Most of them are, however, based on omni-directional antennas, that is, transmissions are thought to spread the radiated energy equally in every direction. Differently, electronically switchable directional (ESD) antennas can concentrate the radiated energy only in given directions [21], using a software control to determine the direction of maximum antenna gain on a per-packet basis. This allows one to reduce channel contention by directing the antenna only towards the intended receivers and to increase the communication range with no impact on energy consumption. This antenna technology recently proved to be viable also for WSN devices [34]: antennas like the one we use in this work can indeed meet the relevant energy and form factor constraints.

In principle, the features of ESD antennas would make them ideal to support bulk traffic. The reality, however, is that network designers are unable to reap the benefits of ESD antennas for bulk traffic because of the lack of protocol support. Existing solutions [9, 39] are indeed unsuited to operate with ESD antennas, as they simply do not consider antenna directionality. As a result, they cannot work outright without undergoing significant changes in their design.

Conceiving multi-hop wireless protocols using ESD antennas is challenging. For example, these antennas introduce additional complexity in topology construction and maintenance because of the large number of antenna configurations possible between nodes. Existing work using directional antennas, on the other hand, typically target traffic patterns other than those germane to WSNs, and are often limited to one-hop configurations [30, 31, 33]. The few attempts in WSNs are, however, limited to using directional antennas only when transmitting [32], hence missing out on part of the benefits brought by this antenna technology.

Moreover, when forwarding data over multiple hops, intra-path and inter-path interference significantly affects the attainable throughput [26]. Existing approaches to avoid intra-path interference use wireless channel diversity [35, 39] or separate interfering flows in time [26]. The former approaches are limited by the availability of interference-free channels, which are in fact difficult to identify in the increasingly crowded radio environments where WSNs are deployed [49]. Time-multiplexing the flows, on the other hand, is typically detrimental to the overall throughput.

Contribution. To tackle these challenges, we design DPT (Directional Pipelined Transmission): a multi-hop wireless protocol we expressly conceive to support bulk traffic using ESD antennas. At the core of DPT is the use of multiple disjoint paths for multi-hop routing and a custom approach to synchronize packet transmissions all the way up to the data sink. The protocol operation unfolds in several distinct steps, shown in Figure 1:

1. While the system is quiescent; for example, whenever nodes monitor their sensors awaiting an event [47], we gather link metrics for all possible antenna configurations. As soon as we probe every antenna configuration for a node, thus having complete information for a given device, these metrics are communicated to the sink. This process repeats periodically.

2. Upon a request of bulk transfer from any of the nodes, the sink first applies domain-specific heuristics to filter out link metrics likely immaterial to determining the routing configuration; next, it uses the processed link metrics to derive a model of the network as a function of antenna configurations and to determine the *conflict graph*. The latter identifies the packet transmissions that would interfere with each other in the absence of capture effect [29].

3. The link metrics and conflict graph are input to a constraint satisfaction problem (CSP) to identify a routing configuration with two node- and link-disjoint paths. Such configuration minimizes the overall cost of the routes according to the chosen link metric. The domain-specific heuristics we apply at the previous step ease the processing demands in solving the specific problem instance at the sink, improving scalability.

4. We inject the solution returned by the CSP solver into the network, including the node-by-node paths and the corresponding antenna configurations. The source funnels data through the two paths by alternating between them, as shown in Figure 2. Along each path, we make packet forwarding occur within deterministic latencies [35]. As a result, each path is implicitly "clocked" by the source when injecting the packet. The sink operates opposite to the source, and alternates the receiving antenna configuration between the two downstream nodes. This works only if the two paths differ by an even number of hops, which we give as an additional constraint to the CSP solver.

The advantages of our solution are several: *i)* unlike the state of the art, it makes full use of directional transmission on *both* the transmitter and receiver end, harvesting the most benefits from ESD antennas; *ii)* it does not require multiple wireless channels to operate, which are increasingly hard to identify in many settings; and *iii)* it spares the need for a separate time-synchronization protocol to schedule transmissions, reducing the overhead.

These advantages materialize in a performance near the maximum throughput possible over the link-layer technology we use. Our results indicate that DPT can send bulk data at a maximum throughput of 214 Kbit/s and at a mean throughput of 203 Kbit/s, with a minimum packet reception rate of 90%. This performance holds as long as the state of the network at the time of collecting the link metrics remains comparable to that at the time of performing the bulk transfer, which is expected to be the case in most of the target application scenarios [4, 13, 27, 36, 47]. In such scenarios, indeed, links are stable over periods of hours [46]. Nonetheless, we also investigate how DPT's performance changes whenever these conditions do not hold.

The paper proceeds as follows. We discuss related work in Section 2. Section 3 presents DPT's design, whereas implementation details are briefly discussed in Section 4. Section 5 presents our experimental evaluation. Before concluding, we place DPT's performance in the perspective of existing literature on bulk transfer protocols in Section 6,

2. BACKGROUND

We present background material to provide a foundation for the remainder of the paper.

2.1 Applications and Protocols

Applications characterized by bulk traffic include structural health monitoring [4, 27, 36], wildlife monitoring [13], and volcano monitoring [47]. In these scenarios, the need for high-throughput bulk transfers extends beyond the mere necessity of delivering data, as the protocol efficiency may also affect the data quality. For instance, Werner et al. [47] report that communicating to the sink a single volcanic event, which alone generates around 50 Kbytes of data per sensor node, may take so long to prevent the detection of many back-to-back seismic events.

When deploying these applications, the system is typically partitioned into a dense sensing network and a sparse backbone of forwarding nodes [2]. The latter are equipped

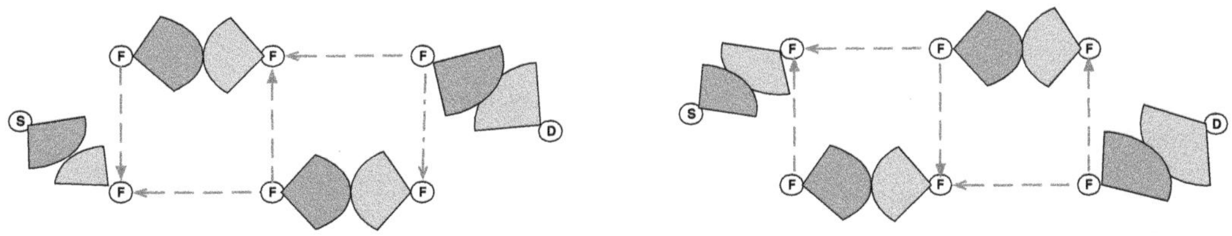

(a) Even-numbered transmissions

(b) Odd-numbered transmissions

Figure 2: DPT: transmissions occur in parallel over the two paths at non-interfering links. *The nodes change antenna orientation based on which of the two paths is active. S indicates the source node, D indicates the sink, and F nodes are forwarding. Dashed arrows indicate possible interference at the receiving end. Darker (red) arcs indicate directional transmissions, lighter arcs (blue) are directional receptions.*

with external omni-directional antennas and power amplifiers, which allow them to cover hundred(s) of meters in a single hop, thus reducing the overall number of hops within the forwarding backbone [38]. Precisely because of this, the use of ESD antennas is appealing in these scenarios, in that they can increase communication range at the same energy cost, sparing the need for energy-consuming power amplifiers. In addition, the ability to reduce contention on the wireless channel might further reduce energy consumption by increasing the reliability of the individual transmissions.

Among existing bulk traffic protocols, many employ various forms of packet scheduling often combined with conditional immediate transmission (CIT) [35]: a forwarding mechanism that achieves high end-to-end throughput. For example, Flush [26] achieves a throughput of 4.8 Kbit/s by controlling the rate of transmissions to ensure packets on the same path do not interfere. PIP [39] uses CIT and multiple channels to reach a throughput of roughly 58.4 Kbit/s. Burst forwarding [12] shows lower throughput than PIP, but uses radio duty cycling and hence gains in energy efficiency. Zhang et al. use CIT and optimal scheduling to reach a throughput of up to 202.4 Kbit/s [48]. Chen et al. develop a collection protocol that uses multiple channels and multiple paths [5]. P3 [9] uses CIT, multiple channels, and synchronous transmissions [17] to forward packets using a subset of the nodes identified from global topology information.

In contrast to DPT, these approaches are all based on omni-directional antennas and may require multiple channels to operate. The latter is also a requirement for multi-radio platforms [14]. Given the crowded radio spectrum [49], this may become an issue: it will be increasingly difficult to identify multiple interference-free channels, and yet if only one of them is interfered, the whole protocol operation may suffer. For example, Doddavenkatappa et al. state "(if) one of the channels used in a pipeline is bad, the pipeline stalls and throughput degrades significantly" [9].

2.2 Directional Antennas

Directional antennas that can dynamically direct transmissions such as switched and adaptive beamforming are widely employed in cellular and ad-hoc networks. A significant body of work exists in this field [8]. Recent examples include the work by Arslan et al. who design an efficient WiMax beamformer antenna and implement real prototypes [1] as well as works on adaptive beamforming for indoor wireless LANs [7]. Liu et al. design a wireless network whose access points (AP) use phased array directional antennas to achieve high throughput in dense, indoor environments [30]. They further develop a distributed protocol called SPEED and demonstrate in a testbed with directional antennas that it can lead to capacity improvement [31]. Along the same lines, Ramanathan et al. implement and evaluate a complete system solution for ad-hoc networks [40]. These kinds of antennas, however, are not suitable for sensor network applications; for example, because of physical size constraints.

Existing literature investigating the use of ESD antennas in sensor networks can be roughly divided into two categories, focusing on the design of either antenna prototypes or network protocols. The former works demonstrate the viability of ESD antennas, showing that current technology can meet the requirements of form factor and energy consumption. However, these works rarely assess the impact of the prototypes on the network performance. Specifically, Giorgetti et al. [19] assess the improvements in link performance with a prototype designed by combining four patch antennas. Viani et al. [44] present a design based on parasitic elements, and analyze its ability to reduce interference and to support localization. Parasitic elements are a common choice to reduce cost and size [7] and are also used by Nilsson [34] in the design of SPIDA, the specific ESD antenna we employ, further described in Section 4.

In the second category, protocols are often designed based on idealized antenna models that are rarely evaluated with real hardware [20, 41]. An exception is Felemban et al. [15], who also present a testbed evaluation of their neighbor discovery protocol. We use a modified version of this protocol to collect link metrics when the network is quiescent. Other works focus on specific network services considered in isolation, such as neighbor discovery [43] and MAC [16]. Mottola et al. demonstrate how slight modifications to an existing collection protocol designed for omni-directional antennas can lead to significant performance improvements using ESD antennas [32]. They use simulations based on an empirical link-layer model of the SPIDA antenna.

Overall, our work complements the existing literature by tackling the problem of employing ESD antennas for bulk traffic, an area where dedicated solutions are missing.

3. DPT: DIRECTIONAL PIPELINED TRANSMISSION

First, we provide an overview of the protocol operation. Next, we describe how we gather the necessary link metrics and how we pre-process them by applying custom heuristics to aid scalability. Then, we illustrate the CSP formulation [18] we use to identify the packet routes.We conclude by describing how the identified routing configurations reach the WSN nodes, and then used for bulk transmissions.

3.1 Overview

We adopt a centralized approach. Target applications usually feature a powerful sink to process the sensed data [38], which we leverage also to identify the routing configuration.

Many wireless sensor network applications requiring support for bulk transfers also feature large periods of inactivity between sensing cycles; for example, as in volcano monitoring [47]. As we describe in Section 3.2, we take advantage of such inactive periods to probe the wireless links across all possible antenna configurations. This step outputs a link metric depending on the given antenna configurations. For example, if an antenna features k possible directions of maximum gain, every link is in principle characterized by k^2 metrics, corresponding to every transmitter-receiver antenna configuration. However, due to directional transmissions and receptions, many of these combinations are unfeasible, since the nodes can only communicate when the sender and the receiver antenna lobes sufficiently overlap. We then funnel the link metrics to the sink. We use subsequent rapid floods with the antennas in omni-directional mode to this end, as in existing work [9].

Section 3.3 describes how the sink pre-processes the link metrics. First, the sink applies dedicated heuristics to simplify this information before using them to establish the routing paths. Indeed, we experimentally verify that out of the feasible transmitter-receiver antenna configurations, only a small portion is typically part of an efficient routing configuration. The remaining link metrics can be disregarded without significantly affecting the overall efficiency, yet greatly easing the processing demands at the sink, thus improving scalability. Next, the sink determines possibly interfering links, that is, pairs of links and corresponding antenna configurations that—if used simultaneously—would cause the transmissions to collide without the capture effect to possibly redress the situation [29]. We call this information *conflict graph.*

As described in Section 3.4, the link metrics and conflict graph are then fed as input to a CSP solver, which determines the two non-interfering paths based on a CSP formulation of the routing problem. This includes, among the stated constraints, the conditions that allow the two paths to be both link- and node-disjoint, as well as the restrictions on the difference in the length of the two paths. In principle, our approach would also work for more than two disjoint paths, but that would not provide further improvements, because: *i)* two paths are already sufficient to approach the maximum throughput supported by the link-layer, *ii)* at the source, packets cannot be generated faster than this. In a sense, with DPT it is the source's ability to quickly inject packets in the pipelines that becomes the limitation.

The solution the CSP solver returns is then injected back to the network, where every node configures its directional antenna accordingly. We use subsequent network floods [17] with antennas set in omni-directional configuration to communicate these data to the nodes. As we illustrate in Section 3.5, at this point the source can start funneling data through the two paths, alternating the upstream node with the corresponding antenna configuration. Transmissions along the two paths will then occur in parallel until they join at the sink, which switches the receiving antenna configuration by alternating between the two downstream nodes.

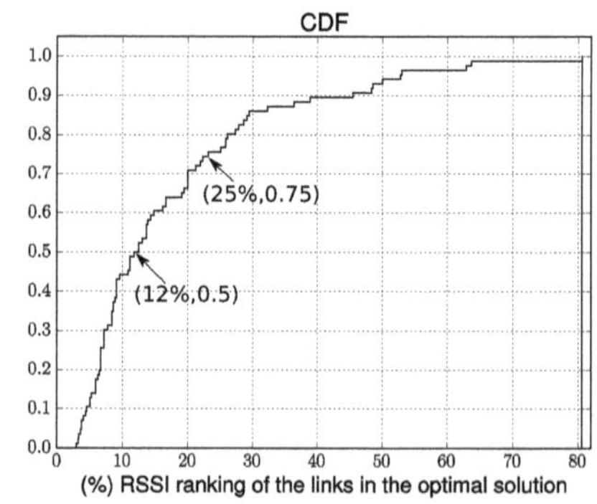

Figure 3: Ranking of antenna configurations based on RSSI values against whether the antenna configuration becomes part of an optimal solution. *Notably, 75% of the antenna configurations in an optimal solution lie within the top 25% antenna configurations, according to RSSI values, for the same link.*

3.2 Collecting Link Metrics

To provide the input to determine the two node- and link-disjoint paths, we need to gather the link metrics. Compared to networks with omni-directional antennas, the procedure to do so changes in the presence of ESD antennas. In principle, we need to probe every links for every possible antenna configuration.

To this end, we use a neighbor discovery protocol that employs a token-based approach, similar to SAND [15]. The token is released by the sink. A node holding the token performs the neighbor discovery by sending HELLO messages along every possible antenna configuration. The neighbors send replies in a time-slotted manner. Once a node finishes neighbor discovery, the collected link metrics are sent to the sink. We repeat the procedure across the entire network until a node requests a bulk transfer.

For every transmitter-receiver antenna configuration, as link metrics we estimate the packet delivery rate (PDR), as well as the mean signal strength (RSSI) of the received packets, as returned by the radio chip. To determine the PDR, we send a fixed number of REPLY messages along each antenna configuration in response to a single HELLO message. The PDR is used as a link metric to find disjoint paths with highest reliability. Differently, the RSSI values are used to identify transmissions that would collide if scheduled simultaneously, which is eventually represented as the conflict graph.

For every node, the sink attempts a round of neighbor discovery for a maximum number of times, by regenerating the token upon expiration of a timer. Beyond the maximum number of retries, the sink considers a node as failed and proceeds with the next one.

3.3 Pre-processing Link Metrics

In response to a request from a source to perform a bulk transfer, the sink pre-processes the collected link metrics before triggering the CSP solver. In doing so, the sink considers the last hour of link metric data, based on evidence found in the literature on the link dynamics in the scenarios we target [46]. This pre-processing includes two steps.

Applying heuristics. Based on experimental evidence, we recognize that not all the feasible transmitter-receiver antenna configurations are to be considered by the CSP solver.

We rather observe that only a small fraction of such antenna configurations tend to become part of the optimal solution, and that this fraction is identifiable beforehand.

Figure 3 verifies this observation, based on a dataset we collect from real-world experiments, further illustrated in Section 5. We obtain the chart by considering any two nodes connected by a link in the optimal solution, and by ordering the antenna configurations between these nodes according to the RSSI value. The X axis therefore indicates the percentage of antenna configurations with highest RSSI value out of all antenna configurations for a link. The Y axis plots the cumulative distribution function (CDF) of such antenna configurations in the optimal solutions, that is, what fraction of optimal solutions includes the corresponding percentage of antenna configurations with highest RSSI value.

The key insight from Figure 3 is that 75% of the antenna configurations for a link that is part of an optimal solution lie among the 25% antenna configurations with highest RSSI values for the same link. Further, we observe that almost half of the antenna configurations for a link that is part of an optimal solution lie within the 12% antenna configurations with highest RSSI values for the same link.

In essence, the plot tells us that the antenna configurations ultimately part of an optimal solution are likely those with highest RSSI, whereas antenna configurations corresponding to medium or low RSSI are rarely included. Based on this observation, we develop two heuristics to filter out likely immaterial antenna configurations. This reduces the size of the problem's input, speeding up the execution of the CSP solver and hence improving scalability.

One possibility is to only keep the M antenna configurations with highest RSSI. We call this heuristic *top M configurations*. For example, if between two given nodes we initially find 20 feasible antenna configurations and $M = 5$, we only keep the 5 highest RSSI antenna configurations and discard all others. The value of M is experimentally derived from the same dataset used to create Figure 3. This approach should be especially effective for many outdoor scenarios where nodes are kept in line of sight, as in many of the applications we target [13, 47]. In these scenarios, the antenna orientation directed straight towards the receiver typically results in the highest signal strength [37].

Another possibility is to filter out antenna configurations only between the node pairs with a large number of feasible antenna configurations, so not to remove antenna configurations between nodes that enjoy fewer choices. To this end, we first compute the average number of feasible antenna configurations between any pair of nodes. Then, across the nodes with more feasible configurations than the average, we keep only the N% best configurations, based on RSSI values. We call this heuristic *weighted top N%*.

For both heuristics we quantitatively measure, in Section 5, both the speed-up in processing time to identify a solution to the routing problem and their impact on a solution's optimality. Indeed, both heuristics do not guarantee to retain an antenna configuration that would be included in the optimal solution. Running the risk of removing a useful antenna configuration is, however, the cost to pay for increased scalability in solving the CSP.

Computing the conflict graph. Notions akin to our conflict graph are widely used in wireless networks to identify interfering links [25, 30, 31]. In this work, we compute a form of conflict graph from the link metrics output by either heuristic. We check, for every link in the network and associated antenna configurations, the RSSI value corresponding to every potentially concurrent transmission towards a common receiver r. If two links and associated antenna configurations are found to yield RSSI values whose difference is below a threshold T_c, the links and their antenna configurations are added to the conflict graph. We use T_c to determine whether capture effect [29] takes place and thereby either packet would be correctly received nonetheless.

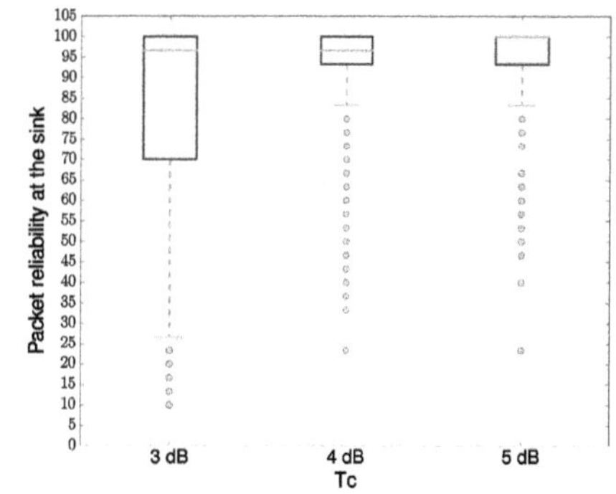

Figure 4: Packet reliability at the sink for different values of T_c. *In the box plot, the top gray horizontal bar represents the median and the lower gray horizontal bar the minimum (excluding outliers) while the circles represent the outliers. The upper hinge of the box represents the 75 percentile, and the lower hinge represents the 25 percentile. A setting close to the co-channel interference tolerance level leads to high variance and low efficiency.*

The key question is how to set T_c. Using CC2420 radios, T_c is found to be around 3 dB for single transmissions, which equals the co-channel interference tolerance level of the radio chip [6]. However, RSSI values may vary over time also with directional antennas [45]. Setting T_c exactly to 3 dB when computing the conflict graph—which must remain valid for the duration of the bulk transfer—might lead to packet corruption, as the RSSI values of concurrent transmissions may temporarily fall below the radio's co-channel interference tolerance level.

Figure 4 provides evidence of this phenomenon, based on an excerpt of the real-world experiments we discuss in Section 5. The chart shows that, as T_c increases, the system performs increasingly better in terms of packet reliability at the sink. Moreover, the variance between different experiments also decreases as T_c increases, as higher values of T_c offer added resilience to RSSI fluctuations. Care must be taken, however, in increasing the value of T_c. An excessively high value may needlessly reduce the solution space, excluding the use of links that would rather correctly operate simultaneously because of capture effect.

To complicate matters, we also observe that some of the links can be interfered by more than one concurrent transmission. In these situations, the combined signal strength of the interfering transmissions also increases, possibly requiring a further increase in T_c. To address this issue, we may adjust T_c as a function of how many links are possibly interfering, or modify the formulation of the CSP to prevent the concurrent use of links possibly interfered by more than one transmission. Both approaches, however, would increase the complexity of the processing at the sink and be detrimental to overall scalability.

Because of the considerations above, we set $T_c = 6$ dB and use this setting for the evaluation in Section 5. The evidence we collect in our experimental setting demonstrates that this configuration strikes a good balance between resilience to RSSI fluctuations, also in the presence of multiple interfering links, and the reduction of the solution space.

3.4 Optimization problem

Given the pre-processed link metrics and the conflict graph, we formulate the routing problem as a Constraint Satisfaction Problem (CSP) and attempt to optimally solve it.

We model the network as a digraph. The node set $\mathcal{N}$ is composed of the sensor nodes with designated source node $o \in \mathcal{N}$ and sink node $d \in \mathcal{N}$. Let $\mathcal{C}$ denote the configuration set of the transmitter antenna of every node (except the sink) as well as of the receiver antenna of every node (except the source). In our experiments, $|\mathcal{C}|= 6$, that is, for any given link, there are 36 combined configurations.

We set $w_{i,j,t,r}$ to be inversely proportional to the packet delivery rate on link (i, j) with antenna configuration (t, r), and use an infinite cost for antenna configurations with insufficient connectivity. We model the conflict graph as a set $\mathcal{F}$ of tuples $\langle i, j, t, r, i', j', t', r' \rangle$ where $i, j, i', j' \in \mathcal{N}$ and $t, r, t', r' \in \mathcal{C}$, denoting that link (i, j) with combined configuration (t, r) is in conflict with link (i', j') with combined configuration (t', r') if used at the same time.

Our goal is to find a disjoint path route from the source to the sink at minimal cost subject to specific constraints. Our CSP model uses the following decision variables, where $i \in \mathcal{N}$ and $p \in [1, 2]$ distinguishes the path:

$S_{i,p} \in \mathcal{N}$: successor of node i on path p, if i is on path p, otherwise i.

$T_{i,p} \in \mathcal{C}$: transmitter configuration of node i on path p, if i is on path p, otherwise 1.

$R_{i,p} \in \mathcal{C}$: receiver configuration of node i on path p, if i is on path p, otherwise 1.

$D_{i,p} \in \mathbb{N}$: distance in hops, at most $|\mathcal{N}|-1$, from the source to node i on path p, if i is on path p, otherwise 0.

We are to find an assignment to these variables that minimizes the overall cost of the routing configuration, which is a function of the S, T, R variables:

$$\text{Minimize} \sum_{i \in \mathcal{N}\setminus\{d\}, p \in [1,2]} w_{i,S_{i,p},T_{i,p},R_{S_{i,p},p}} \tag{1}$$

Whether the solution is admissible depends on the following constraints:

C1: There should be two link- and node-disjoint paths from the source to the sink.

C2: We must *not simultaneously* use pairs of links in the conflict graph.

C3: The length of the paths must differ by an even number.

Constraint **C1** guarantees that each node and each link is only part of one path while constraint **C2** ensures that concurrent transmissions do not collide destructively. Note that, however, constraint **C2** does not prevent the solution from using links in the conflict graph at different times. This is intentional, in that it fosters higher parallelism throughout the two source-sink paths. On the other hand, without constraint **C3**, packets from the two disjoint paths would arrive simultaneously at the sink and collide. We now explain how the above constraints are modeled in our CSP.

Constraint **C1** is modeled by (2–7) in the following. In doing so, we use the successor representation of paths, as defined for $S_{i,p}$ variables. By using the convention that *i)* the path must originate from the source (2); *ii)* the source is the successor of the sink (3); and *iii)* any node that does not take part in a given path is its own successor, we have the necessary condition that both sets of successors are permutations of $\mathcal{N}$ (4). Such permutation conditions are propagated very efficiently by CSP solvers. Link-and node-disjointness are straightforward to express (5). Equation (6) and (7) prevent cycles, by ensuring that all $D_{i,p}$ values are valid.

$$S_{o,1} \neq o \neq S_{o,2} \tag{2}$$

$$S_{d,1} = S_{d,2} = o \tag{3}$$

$$\{S_{i,1} \mid i \in \mathcal{N}\} = \{S_{i,2e} \mid i \in \mathcal{N}\} = \mathcal{N} \tag{4}$$

$$\forall i \in \mathcal{N} \setminus \{o, d\} : S_{i,1} = i \lor S_{i,2} = i \tag{5}$$

$$D_{o,1} = D_{o,2} = 0 \tag{6}$$

$$\forall i \in \mathcal{N} \setminus \{d\}, \forall p \in [1, 2] : \quad D_{i,p} = \begin{cases} 0, & \text{if } S_{i,p} = i \\ D_{S_{i,p},p} - 1, & \text{otherwise} \end{cases} \tag{7}$$

Constraint **C2** is modeled by (8), which needs to be transformed into a form suitable for the CSP solver, because the solver has no efficient way of expressing that a tuple is a member of the set. Thus, in a pre-solving phase, we transform (8) into an and-or-tree with equalities $x = v$ at the nodes, where x is a decision variable and v is an integer:

$$\begin{aligned} &\forall i, j \in \mathcal{N} \setminus \{d\}, p, q \in [1, 2] : \\ &(D_{i,p} + D_{j,q} + p + q) \bmod 2 = 0 \implies \\ &\langle i, S_{i,p}, T_{i,p}, R_{S_{i,p}}, j, S_{j,q}, T_{j,q}, R_{S_{j,q}} \rangle \notin \mathcal{F} \end{aligned} \tag{8}$$

Constraint **C3** is straightforward to express:

$$(D_{d,1} + D_{d,2}) \bmod 2 = 0 \tag{9}$$

Finally, as is often the case in combinatorial optimization, the problem contains an obvious symmetry: any solution can be transformed to an equivalent solution by swapping the two paths. To avoid this useless degree of freedom, we break the symmetry with (10):

$$S_{s,1} < S_{s,2} \tag{10}$$

By using only a subset of the constraints, it is straightforward to get the optimal solution for a single path with the corresponding antenna configurations.

3.5 Bulk Transfer

Once the CSP solver identifies a solution to the routing problem, we encode the individual node and antenna configurations in dedicated control packets, which we inject into the network using rapid network floods [17] with the antennas in omni-directional mode. By doing so, every node

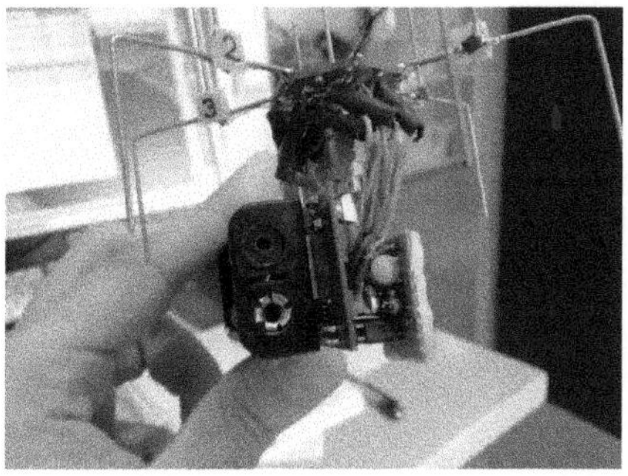

Figure 5: The ESD antenna we use in our experiments. *The antenna is integrated with a standard TMote Sky node. Contiki drivers allow to control the direction of maximum gain in software.*

on either path knows what is the receiving/transmitting antenna configuration as well as the identity of the upstream node, and prepares for the bulk transfer. We use a similar packet to trigger the actual bulk transfer at the source.

As hinted before, the source alternates between the two upstream nodes, funnelling data along either path. By doing so, the source implicitly "clocks" the entire pipeline: from now on, the forwarding transmissions at the intermediate nodes proceed with deterministic latency, using techniques similar to CIT [35]. At the sink, we apply the opposite mechanism, and alternate the antenna configurations between the two downstream nodes to receive data from either path[1].

As the bulk transfer proceeds, DPT continues to operate efficiently as long as the network state reflects the link metrics used to determine the two disjoint paths. Although this is expected to be the case in most of the applications we target [4, 13, 27, 36, 47]—where link qualities are observed to be stable over periods of hours [46]—we design a simple mechanism to find out whenever such conditions cease to hold and a routing reconfiguration is necessary.

Specifically, we allocate one byte per hop in the packet header to store RSSI information. At the intermediate forwarding nodes, we append the RSSI of the received packet before forwarding the packet further. On receiving the packet at the sink, we inspect the RSSI information collected at all hops along the forwarding path. The sink can then compare this information with that used earlier to determine the routing paths. In case of a significant mismatch, the sink temporarily stops the bulk transfer, re-initiates the process of collecting link metrics, computes a new optimal solution to the same CSP given the new input data, and resumes the transfer.

4. PROTOTYPE

We create a hardware/software prototype of DPT including custom-built ESD antennas. We use the prototype to perform a real-world evaluation, reported in Section 5.

Antenna. We use an ESD antenna similar to the one of Nilsson [34, 50], connected to a standard TMote Sky node that features a CC2420 radio [6]. The antenna has six parasitic elements surrounding a quarter wavelength monopole antenna. As a result of this design, the antenna gain varies as an offset circle from -4 to +7 dB in the horizontal plane. The six parasitic elements can be individually grounded or isolated using a software control. When all the parasitic elements are isolated, the antenna operates in omni-directional mode. If all the parasitic elements except one are grounded, the direction of the maximum antenna gain is towards the isolated element. This results in six directional configurations of the antenna, plus the omni-directional mode. The change of the direction of maximum gain happens within a few microseconds.

Contiki drivers allow a programmer to control the grounding or isolation of individual parasitic elements via software. The resulting antenna prototype is comparable to state-of-the-art dynamically steerable antennas available for WSNs [7, 19, 44]. We construct a number of these antennas for our experiments.

DPT implementation. We implement DPT on top of Contiki [11], along with a technique similar to CIT [35]. To further improve the throughput, we pipeline packet transmissions on the nodes. When we start to receive a packet and the start of frame delimiter (SFD) pin goes high, we send an already buffered packet from the microcontroller's memory to the radio transmit buffer. As we finish receiving the packet and the SFD pin goes down, we immediately strobe the radio to transmit the packet we transferred to the radio transmit buffer in the meantime. As the radio prepares the packet for transmission, we change the antenna direction towards the upstream node.

We use fixed-size packets for pipelined transmissions, which enables fast and deterministic-time forwarding of the packet as well as ensures that we can meet the timing requirements for the capture effect. This requires that concurrent packet transmissions start within $160us$ of each other [28]. While the packet is being transmitted over the air, we copy the previously received packet from the radio's receive buffer to the microcontroller's memory. These techniques are also used by other high-throughput bulk transfer protocols [9, 39].

At the source node, when forwarding packets over the disjoint paths, we ensure that the packets are sent back-to-back with minimal delay. This is required to improve the throughput since the delay that occurs when loading packets into the radio transmit buffer at the source is lost once and for all, as it cannot be gained back. For this, we employ a technique similar to Glossy [17] to quickly load a packet at the source: as soon as we finish transmitting a packet, we immediately strobe the radio for the next transmission over the disjoint path. While the radio calibrates and begins the transmission of the preamble, we load the packet to be transmitted. As transmitting is slower than packet loading over the SPI bus that connects the radio to the microcontroller on the TMote Sky, we do not cause buffer under-runs.

The target applications can tolerate some packet loss [13, 47]. Thus, in our current implementation, we do not use link-layer acknowledgments, which improves the end-to-end throughput. If needed, one can send negative acknowledgments after the bulk transfer finished to retrieve lost packets from the source, as done in Flush [26].

CSP solver. We use MiniZinc 2.0 to solve the CSP. The process includes two phases: the flattening [18] of the MiniZinc model to a FlatZinc program, and the solving of the FlatZinc program. Flattening expands all quantified expres-

[1]In the case of paths of unequal lengths, packets on the shorter path start to arrive earlier than on the longer path, as the pipeline in the latter needs more time to fill up. In this case, we only start to alternate antenna configuration at the sink once we have received a number of packets from the shorter path equal to the difference in the number of hops.

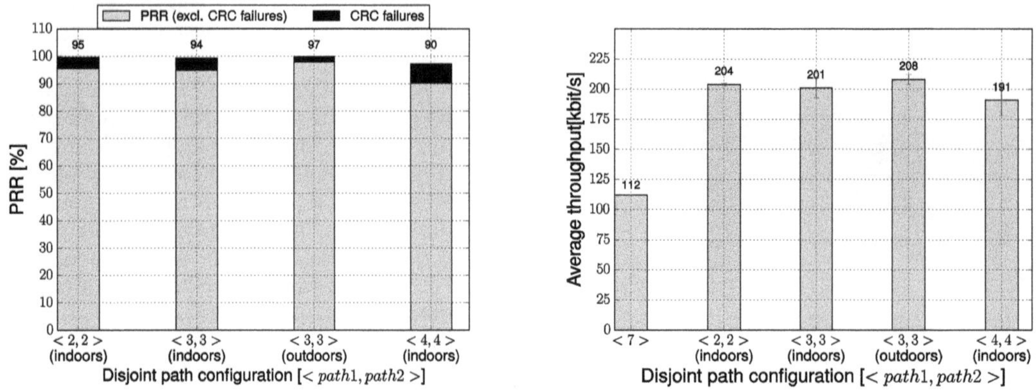

(a) PRR (b) Throughput

Figure 6: PRR and throughput for paths of equal length. *DPT achieves a PRR above 90% and a maximum throughput of 214 Kbit/s, close to the theoretical maximum. The number of hops between source and sink have little impact on the performance.*

sions, nested logical expressions, and macros into a sequence of variable declarations and constraints. In Section 5, we report the processing times for the two phases separately. The flattening phase still presents room for improvements: increasing its efficiency is largely a matter of effective engineering. In contrast, the solving phase is difficult to further optimize, as the problem is inherently NP-hard.

5. EVALUATION

This section presents the experimental results we collect by running DPT in real-world testbeds we build, considered the absence of public testbed infrastructures featuring ESD antennas. Overall, our results indicate that:

- DPT approaches the maximum throughput allowed by the underlying link layer in most of the settings we test, reaching a maximum performance of 214 kbit/s;
- the routing configuration output by the solver remains usable, that is, the conflict graph still applies, much longer than the duration of a typical bulk transfer;
- our custom heuristics more than halve the solving times at the sink, with negligible impact on the optimality of the obtained solution;
- in most scenarios, particularly with a larger number of nodes, disjoint paths can be determined with high probability, confirming the feasibility of our approach.

The remainder of this section illustrates the details leading to the aforementioned results. Section 5.1 reports on the performance of DPT in throughput and packet reception rate (PRR). We study the effect on the link dynamics on our approach in Section 5.2, whereas Section 5.3 analyzes the efficiency of the solving process at the sink. Finally, Section 5.4 offers some considerations on how often disjoint paths do exist in a general network. Complementing this discussion, Section 6 places DPT's performance in the larger perspective of existing literature on bulk transfer protocols.

Testbeds. We run experiments in a 32 sqm office environment as well as in an 80 sqm outdoor area in front of our institution's main building. The office environment features a complex radio setting, with metallic objects in the corners and in the ceiling. Other interfering wireless networks, such as WiFi, Bluetooth, and appliances operating in the ISM 2.4 GHz band, are also abundantly present. This environment is harsh compared to that of our target applications, whose characteristics are better approximated by the cleaner radio environment we find outdoors. The results we report next for the office environment thus represent a worst case.

Table 1: The number of different routing configurations we observe in our experiments. *We use $\langle a, b\rangle$ to denote path 1 of length a and path 2 of length b.*

<2,2>	<3,3>	<4,4>	<4,2>	<5,3>
3	9	5	3	3

In both testbeds, we deploy up to twelve WSN nodes equipped with our ESD antennas. To create a multi-hop settings, we set the radio transmit power to -25 dBm. We use 802.15.4 channel 15, as it is the least interfered channel in the office environment. In the indoor experiments, we place the nodes randomly and differently for each experiment run, but always approximately one meter above the ground. In the case of outdoor experiments, the nodes are again randomly placed in a different way for every experiment run, approximately half a meter above the ground and in line of sight of each other.

5.1 Bulk Transfer Performance

We first analyze whether we achieve our primary goal, that is, achieving high-throughput bulk transfer.

Settings and metrics. Given a random placement of the nodes, we collect link metrics for about an hour and then trigger a bulk transfer of 350 Kbytes, using 123 bytes packets. Out of the 123 bytes, 1 byte is used to store the length of the packet, 2 bytes for the 802.15.4 frame check sequence field, and 5 bytes for control information. The remaining 115 bytes constitute the application payload. To calculate the throughput we consider all the application data transmitted within the duration of a bulk transmission, as done in related work [9, 39].

In our setup, and even more in real applications, it is difficult to control or to predict the shape of the routing solution output by the CSP solver. The experiments we run yield, as a result, different routing configurations with different frequencies. Table 1 summarizes how many occurrences of which routing configuration we observe in our experiments. The results include configurations where the disjoint paths have equal or different lengths. We analyze these separately, to understand the influence of the routing configuration on

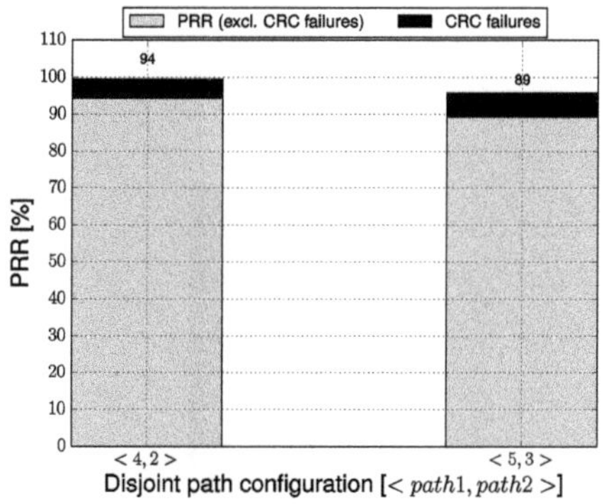

Figure 7: PRR for paths of unequal length. *Paths of different lengths do not cause synchronization problems, as the performance remains similar to the case of equal length paths, shown in Figure 6(a). Similar considerations apply to throughput as well.*

the synchronization along the parallel paths. We also investigate the impact of lossy links.

We take throughput and PRR as performance metrics, similar to existing literature on bulk transfer protocols [9, 39]. At the sink and at all intermediate nodes, we measure these quantities by keeping track of sequence numbers embedded within the packets, whether the received packet is corrupt, and the time when we start to receive the first and the last packet in each experiment. When computing both metrics, we exclude corrupted packets from the statistics, which then cover only useful application data even though approaches for recovering packets with bit-errors exist [22].

Equal length paths. Figure 6 shows DPT's performance in throughput and PRR for different disjoint path configurations of equal length. For both metrics, an increasing number of hops has little impact on the performance. This provides evidence of the scalability of our approach against the depth of the network.

Figure 6(a) shows that in most settings, DPT receives packets with a PRR above 90%. We also observe that a small percentage of packets have CRC failures. This is likely due to external interference from other wireless devices in the office environment, as the fraction of packets with CRC failures is comparatively higher than in the outdoor setting. Considered the intense levels of interference in the office environment, nonetheless, we can maintain that their impact on DPT's performance is arguably limited.

Figure 6(b) shows the mean and maximum throughput we measure in our experiments. Our results demonstrate that DPT achieves a maximum throughput of 214 Kbit/s, approximating the maximum link-layer throughput [35]. As we mentioned, the source cannot generate packets faster than said maximum. Because of this, DPT's performance, as well as that of any other bulk transfer protocol based on the same radio technology, is upper-bound by the source's ability to generate packets.

As a reference, Figure 6(b) also includes the throughput we achieve by operating DPT over a single path. As one would indeed expect in case the synchronization across the two paths would be accurate, the throughput when using two paths is almost twice that of the single path.

Unequal length paths. Figure 7 shows DPT's performance in throughput and PRR in case the routing configuration includes paths of different length. The plot demonstrates that DPT achieves a PRR above 90% in this case as well. Worth noticing is also that the PRR of the configuration with six nodes ($\langle 4,2\rangle$) is similar to the PRR of the configuration with the same number of nodes but equal length paths ($\langle 3,3\rangle$ in Figure 6(a)). The same holds for the configuration with eight nodes in Figure 7 ($\langle 5,3\rangle$) compared to the configuration with the same number of nodes and equal length paths ($\langle 4,4\rangle$ in Figure 6(a)). These observations provide evidence that even with disjoint paths of unequal length, the fast deterministic packet forwarding keeps the jitter at the forwarding nodes to the minimum and avoids synchronization problems that would lead to colliding transmissions. The same considerations apply to the throughput performance, which we do not show for brevity.

Lossy links. While the CSP solver finds the optimal disjoint paths, it is still possible that one of them includes a lossy link. The reason for this could simply be that there is indeed no better path available. To understand how this occurrence may affect the performance, we intentionally make one of the links drop packets randomly. Specifically, we consider two given disjoint paths: $source \rightarrow 1 \rightarrow 2 \rightarrow 3 \rightarrow sink$ and $source \rightarrow 4 \rightarrow 5 \rightarrow 6 \rightarrow sink$, and make node 5 drop 25% of the packets—chosen randomly—when it forwards packets to node 6.

Figure 8 shows the results of this experiment. Figure 8(a) shows the PRR on a per-node basis. As expected, the PRR at node 6 is lower than at other intermediate nodes, because of the losses on the link connecting node 5 to node 6. In turn, this affects the PRR at the sink. Similar considerations apply to the throughput figures, as Figure 8(b) demonstrates. These results show that the presence of a lossy link affects the performance in an appreciable manner.

We acknowledge this limitation of DPT, essentially caused by the absence of redundancy in the routing configuration. Nevertheless, there are ways to redress the situation. One possibility, for example, is to implement a local repair mechanism that, upon recognizing a lossy link, attempts to locally change the routing configuration based on inputs provided by the CSP solver, such as alternative upstream nodes that can be output together with the optimal solution.

5.2 Link Dynamics

In this experiment we investigate the effect of link dynamics. To this end, we collect the link metrics over a period of more than 24 hours in our indoor office environment on a working day using 10 ESD antennas. We process the link metrics over the past hour and compute the solution to the multi-path routing problem.

The results indicate that the optimal solution changes quite rapidly after it has been obtained, in particular during daytime when people move and more interference is present. This is expected in an indoor environment. Nevertheless, more important for DPT is the timescale at which the solution obtained remains *usable*, since this determines if we can successfully complete a bulk transfer. A solution is usable as long as the transmissions which happen simultaneously can leverage the capture effect on a given receiver, and thus do not collide. This holds true if the difference in the RSSI measures of all pairs of involved links, with given antenna configurations, are still above the threshold T_c.

To investigate this aspect, we choose an upper bound for the times it takes to solve the CSP, inject the solution into the network, and trigger the source to start the bulk trans-

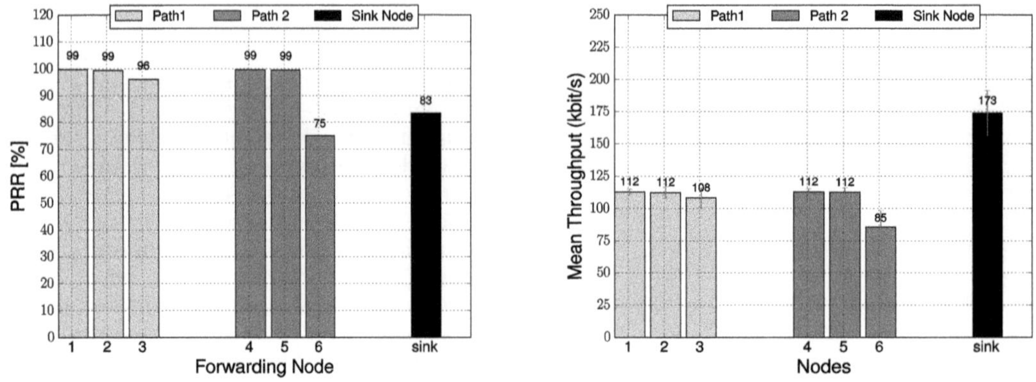

(a) PRR (b) Throughput

Figure 8: Throughput and PRR in the presence of a lossy link, in a configuration with eight nodes. *To emulate a bad link, 25% of the packets are dropped randomly as they are forwarded from node 5 to node 6. The lossy link significantly affects the PRR and throughput.*

Heuristic	Running time improvement (%)	No solution/ Sub-optimal	β (avg)
Top M=5	57.09	2/2	57
Top M=10	34.37	0/0	81
Weighted top N=25%	44.33	0/0	76

Table 2: The performance of different heuristics in running times and impact on a solution's optimality. *We indicate under "No solution/Sub-optimal" the number of times when no solution or a sub-optimal solution is found. A sub-optimal solution has a higher cost than the optimal solution according to Equation (1). Both heuristics provide drastic improvements in running time, whereas only using* top M *with* $M = 5$ *we observe an effect on the optimality of the routing configuration.*

fer as described in Section 3.5. We select a conservative upper bounds of 5 minutes. Thus, we shift the collected link-metrics by an interval of 5 minutes and compute the solution at every such interval over the entire period of 24 hours. For each such solution, we investigate at which time scale the solution is still usable.

Results. Figure 10 depicts the result of the experiment. The figure indicates that the routing solutions found are usable during the duration of a typical bulk transfer. Further, it shows that for almost 50% of the solutions the disjoint path remains usable for a time period larger than 50 minutes, which suggests that in many cases the collection of links metrics can proceed leisurely.

5.3 CSP Solving

We study the efficiency of the solving process at the sink. First, we measure the running times without applying the heuristics of Section 3.3. We consider these figures as a baseline. Next, we measure the improvements brought by the heuristics against the impact in terms of optimality of the obtained routing configurations.

All measurements are taken using MiniZinc 2.0 on an Intel Core i7 at 3.5 GHz with 16 Gbytes of RAM running OS X 10.10.2. As input, we use the link metrics collected in thirteen real-world experiments among those used to understand the bulk transfer performance, reported in Section 5.1. This data set, albeit not vast, represents very diverse scenarios in terms of shape and characteristics of the network topology. We thus maintain that the results we describe next are already conducive to valuable observations.

Results. Figure 9 depicts the results we collect. Based on our data set, the running times without applying any heuristics, are not prohibitive, yet still significant. Moreover, as discussed in Section 4, the process consists of two distinct phases, namely the flattening of the CSP formulation, and the solving itself. The flattening step greatly dominates the total running time—by orders of magnitude—despite the solving step being NP-hard, whereas the flattening step is not. This crucially indicates that the largest room for improvement is in the flattening step.

Confronted with these results, we devise the heuristics illustrated in Section 3.3 to reduce the *size* of the CSP input to the flattening step, aiming at lowering the overall running times. Figure 9 confirms that this strategy is indeed effective. The running times are often more than halved compared to the baseline. The gains also appear more marked at larger scales. In particular, for 12 nodes, *top M* with $M = 5$, that is, by keeping only the five strongest antenna configurations according to RSSI values between a pair of nodes, we can reduce the solving time to 58 seconds: a 66% improvement over the baseline.

When applying the heuristics, however, we may mistakenly filter out links that would be included in the optimal solution if they were available to the CSP solver. In turn, this would inevitably result in a sub-optimal output by the CSP solver. To understand this trade-off, we consider the difference in the value of the objective function in our CSP formulation, specified in Equation (1).

Moreover, even if two solutions have the same overall cost, they may still differ in the links or antenna configurations employed. To this end, we defined a metric β as the percentage of links and corresponding antenna configurations found in both solutions. In a sense, β indicates the extent of topological overlapping between two solutions; thus, $\beta = 100\%$ if two routing configurations are identical, whereas $\beta = 0\%$ if two solutions are different in all links or antenna configurations.

Table 2 presents the average results across all network topologies we test. The numbers indicate that our heuristics

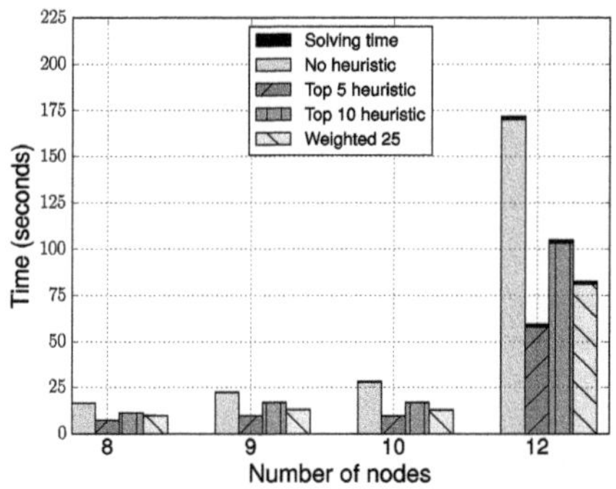

Figure 9: Running times of the solving process at the sink. *The flattening step dominates the solving times. The heuristics reduce the running times by more than half, with greater improvements with more nodes.*

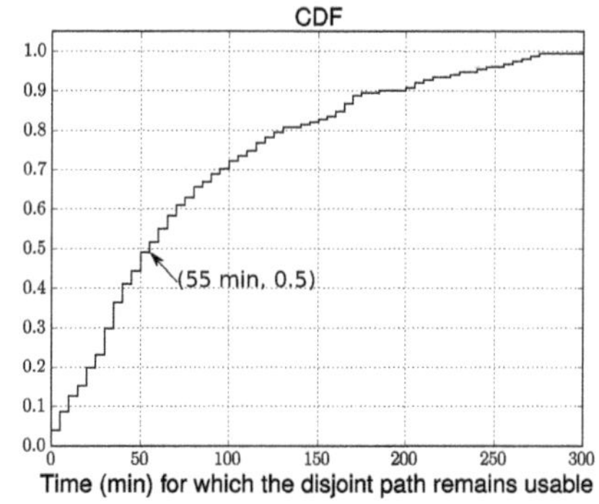

Figure 10: The timescale at which the disjoint path remains usable. *For over 50% of the solutions the disjoint path is usable for over 55 minutes.*

do reduce the running times at the sink, but sometimes at the cost of sub-optimal routing configurations. For example, using *top M* with $M = 5$, we reduce the running times by 57%, on average. However, the optimality of the solution is partly affected: in two instances out of thirteen, the solution is sub-optimal, that is, Equation (1) evaluates to a higher value. Moreover, in other two instances, MiniZinc cannot find a solution, likely because the heuristic removes a link that is fundamental to identify the disjoint paths.

Increasing M to 10 reduces the improvement in running times to around 34%, but does *not* affect the optimality of the solution. Indeed, the cost returned by MiniZinc by solving Equation (1) is exactly the same with and without using *top M*. Interestingly, the routing configuration is not identical. As β equals 81, we conclude that some links or antenna configurations differ. Applying *weighted top N%* with $N = 25\%$ leads to similar conclusions, with better improvements in running time compared to *top M* with $M = 10$.

In conclusion, we argue that both heuristics are useful to the practical applicability of DPT. Crucially, both offer tunable parameters that designers may use as a knob to explore the trade-off between running times at the sink and optimality of the routing configuration.

5.4 Feasibility

DPT operates by forwarding packets over two node- and link-disjoint paths. A natural question is then to test how likely it is to find two such paths between a source and a sink in a general network. To find an answer, we use a synthetic network model generator we implement. This allows us to quickly test a sizable number of network topologies.

Our tool generates the network model by randomly distributing a configurable number of nodes over a limited area as follows. We place the initial node completely random. After placing a node, we place the next one at a distance from the previous node that follows a Gaussian distribution with a mean roughly three quarters of the communication range when our ESD antenna is set to omni-directional mode. Following the idea of the Poisson Disc distribution, we also enforce a minimum distance between the new node and all previously placed nodes.

When all nodes are distributed in the area, we compute the physical distance between each pair of nodes and assign it an omni-directional RSSI value based on the log-distance path loss model, using a path loss exponent of two, typical of free space [23, 42]. Given a directional antenna configuration for the two nodes, we manipulate the omni-directional RSSI based on empirical values that we have gathered during our experiments. For the antenna configurations in the direction of maximum gain, we increase the directional RSSI compared to the omni-directional value, and vice versa in the opposite antenna direction. Based on this network model, we construct the conflict graph and input it to the solver, as if the link metrics were collected from a real network. The solver then searches for the optimal solution to CSP formulation in Section 3.4.

Results. We check networks of 12 and 18 nodes. For these networks, disjoint paths form in more than 60% and 80% of the 50 simulations, respectively. The evidence shows that the 1-hop neighbors of the sink and of the source are crucial. If these do not offer sufficient options to form the two node- and link-disjoint paths, finding a solution to the CSP becomes difficult. On the other hand, if the network is sufficiently dense, there are typically more than enough options in the more central parts of the network.

While these results are based on random placement, real deployments rarely consist of randomly-scattered nodes. Nodes are rather placed carefully to cover the events of interest and/or to obtain a well-connected network [38]. In this regard, we believe that existing tools for pre-deployment, such as Scale [3] and Trident [24], can be fruitfully employed to ensure that disjoint paths can be formed in most cases; for example, by also checking how the network topology changes by switching to a different radio channel. The fallback solution, always available with DPT, is to use just one path.

6. DISCUSSION

An experimental comparison of DPT against existing protocols for bulk transmissions, such as P3 [9] or PIP [39], is hardly feasible. These protocols are indeed developed and evaluated on testbeds with omni-directional antennas. They would then need significant redesigns to work with ESD antennas. Moreover, even if such re-designs were possible, the protocol logic would fundamentally mismatch the antenna operation. In simpler terms, it would be a case of "fitting a square peg into a round hole".

What we can do, however, is to place DPT's performance into the larger perspective of the state of the art, as reported in the relevant literature. We discuss this on two accounts: throughput and energy consumption.

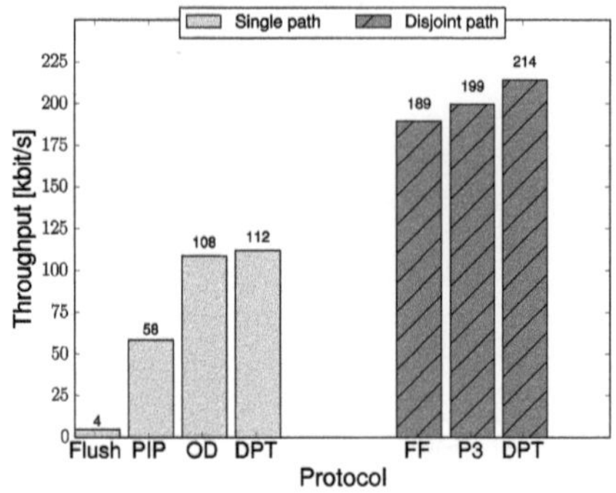

Figure 11: Maximum throughput of DPT and existing bulk transfer protocols. *The performance figures for the latter are taken from literature. The absolute numbers suggest that DPT outperforms existing protocols in terms of maximum performance, while using only one channel.*

Throughput. Figure 11 reports the maximum throughput figures for DPT and existing bulk transfer protocols, as found in the literature.

The left part of the chart shows the throughput of DPT and of other bulk transfer protocols when operating on a single path. The highest throughput found in the literature using this configuration is that of Österlind and Dunkels [35], indicated as OD, who achieve 108.8 kbit/s. This is 97% of the upper bound with 802.15.4 radios over single paths and multiple hops [35][2]. Flush [26] is considerably slower with a throughput of only 4.8 kbit/s. By using a custom TDMA mechanism, multiple channels, and CIT, PIP [39] achieves a throughput of 58.4 kbit/s, which corresponds to 52% of the upper bound. DPT, on the other hand, achieves a throughput slightly higher than that of Österlind and Dunkels. The reason for this is that switching radio channel, as they do, takes slightly more time than reconfiguring our ESD antenna, hence the higher throughput.

Using multiple paths, as in the protocols on the right part of Figure 11, the source can inject packets into the network as quickly as possible. Hence, the maximum throughput can approach the theoretical radio bandwidth, barring any processing delay between consecutive packets. With this configuration, the highest throughput reported in the literature is that of P3 [9], which attains 199.68 kbit/s. Ekbatanifard et al.'s FastForward [14] leverages a dual-radio platform, which in some sense also uses two paths. With this technique, they achieve a throughput of 189.6 kbit/s. Our approach achieves a maximum throughput of 214 kbit/s, hence markedly higher than existing protocols.

Energy consumption. Table 6 reports the energy consumed by DPT, P3, and PIP in a bulk transfer of 100 Kbytes across 4 hops, as found in the literature for the latter two.

In these settings, these protocols differ in throughput and number of nodes required for the transfer. For example, DPT's two disjoint paths require together eight nodes, while PIP uses five nodes on a single path. P3 makes use of a modified form of Glossy floods [17], which results in employing way more nodes than both PIP and DPT. In a 4 hops setting, P3 uses approximately 26 nodes [9].

[2]The upper bound of 112.5 kbit/s is simply half of the theoretical radio bandwidth, due to the half-duplex operation.

Metric	DPT	P3	PIP
throughput (kbit/s)	203	199	58
nodes employed	8	26	5
per-node energy (mJ)	236.5	241.2	810
network-wide energy (mJ)	1891.6	6271.1	4050
energy ratio to DPT	1	3.32	2.14

Table 3: Energy consumption for transferring 100 Kbytes of data over 4 hops using DPT and existing bulk transfer protocols. *The performance figures for the latter are taken from literature. DPT outperforms both P3 and PIP in network-wide energy consumption.*

All three protocols, nonetheless, keep the radio always on during a bulk transfer. By making the established assumption of a 60 mW power consumption when the radio is turned on [10], DPT and P3 would enjoy a lower per-node energy consumption compared to PIP. This is essentially because, due to higher throughput, the bulk transfer takes less time in DPT and P3, roughly 4 seconds for 100 Kbytes of data.

On a network-wide scale, however, P3's use of Glossy floods is detrimental to the overall energy figures. By employing more nodes than DPT for the same bulk transfer, a system running P3 would consume more than three times the energy. This is essentially the price to pay for the added resilience provided by Glossy floods. As for the network-wide energy consumption of PIP, this is still more than twice that of DPT. This time, the result is due to the larger latency to complete the transfer, which forces nodes to keep their radios on much longer.

Note that, as in P3 and PIP, we do not consider the energy cost to acquire the topology information necessary to setup the bulk transfer, as in P3, or to establish the multi-hop path from source to sink in a distributed fashion, as in PIP. Essentially, the problem of topology discovery is orthogonal to that of achieving energy-efficient high throughput, and dedicated solutions are needed.

7. CONCLUSION

Directional antennas reduce contention while extending the communication range. In this paper, we use these features to devise DPT, the first high-throughput bulk transfer protocol that leverages ESD antennas. We transmit data over two multi-hop disjoint paths that we find by solving a CSP formulation of the routing problem at hand. Our results, obtained in a testbed using 802.15.4 radios and ESD antennas, indicate that DPT achieves a maximum throughput of 214 kbit/s, close to the maximum supported by the link layer, in the settings we test.

Acknowledgements

This work was partly supported by the Swedish Research Council, VINNOVA, SSF, and the Technological Cluster Project "Zero-energy Buildings in Smart Urban Districts" (EEB) of the Italian Ministry for University and Research.

8. REFERENCES

[1] M. Y. Arslan, K. Sundaresan, S. V. Krishnamurthy, and S. Rangarajan. Design and implementation of an integrated beamformer and uplink scheduler for ofdma femtocells. In *13th ACM International Symposium on Mobile Ad Hoc Networking and Computing*, MOBIHOC '12, pages 215–224, 2012.

[2] M. Buevich, D. Schnitzer, T. Escalada, A. Jacquiau-Chamski, and A. Rowe. Fine-grained remote monitoring, control and pre-paid electrical service in rural microgrids. In *13th International Symposium on Information Processing in Sensor Networks*, IPSN '14, pages 1–12, 2014.

[3] A. Cerpa, N. Busek, and D. Estrin. Scale: A tool for simple connectivity assessment in lossy environments. Technical report, Center for Embedded Network Sensing, 2003.

[4] K. Chebrolu, B. Raman, N. Mishra, P. K. Valiveti, and R. Kumar. Brimon: A sensor network system for railway bridge monitoring. In *6th International Conference on Mobile Systems, Applications, and Services*, MOBISYS '08, pages 2–14, 2008.

[5] Y. Chen, P. H. Gomes, and B. Krishnamachari. Multi-channel data collection for throughput maximization in wireless sensor networks. In *11th IEEE International Conference on Mobile Ad Hoc and Sensor Systems*, MASS '14, pages 443–451, 2014.

[6] Chipcon AS. *CC2420 datasheet - 2.4 GHz IEEE 802.15.4 / ZigBee-Ready RF Transceiver (Rev. B)*.

[7] R. Choudhury, T. Ueda, J. Bordim, and N. Vaidya. Beamnet: An ad hoc network testbed using beamforming antennas. In *Vehicular Technology Conference*, 2005.

[8] H. Dai, K.-W. Ng, M. Li, and M.-Y. Wu. An overview of using directional antennas in wireless networks. *International Journal of Communication Systems*, 26(4):413–448, 2013.

[9] M. Doddavenkatappa and M. C. Chan. P3: A practical packet pipeline using synchronous transmissions for wireless sensor networks. In *13th International Symposium on Information Processing in Sensor Networks*, IPSN '14, pages 203–214, 2014.

[10] A. Dunkels, J. Eriksson, N. Finne, and N. Tsiftes. Powertrace: Network-level power profiling for low-power wireless networks. Technical Report T2011:05, SICS Swedish ICT, Mar. 2011.

[11] A. Dunkels, B. Gronvall, and T. Voigt. Contiki - a lightweight and flexible operating system for tiny networked sensors. In *Proceedings of the 29th Annual IEEE International Conference on Local Computer Networks*, LCN '04, pages 455–462, 2004.

[12] S. Duquennoy, F. Österlind, and A. Dunkels. Lossy links, low power, high throughput. In *9th ACM Conference on Embedded Networked Sensor Systems*, SENSYS '11, pages 12–25, 2011.

[13] V. Dyo, S. A. Ellwood, D. W. Macdonald, A. Markham, C. Mascolo, B. Pásztor, S. Scellato, N. Trigoni, R. Wohlers, and K. Yousef. Evolution and sustainability of a wildlife monitoring sensor network. In *8th ACM Conference on Embedded Networked Sensor Systems*, SENSYS '10, pages 127–140, 2010.

[14] G. Ekbatanifard, P. Sommer, B. Kusy, V. Iyer, and K. Langendoen. Fastforward: High-throughput dual-radio streaming. In *Proceedings of the 10th International Conference on Mobile Ad-Hoc and Sensor Systems*, MASS '13, pages 209–213, 2013.

[15] E. Felemban, R. Murawski, E. Ekici, S. Park, K. Lee, J. Park, and Z. Hameed. Sand: Sectored-antenna neighbor discovery protocol for wireless networks. In *7th Annual IEEE Communications Society Conference on Sensor Mesh and Ad Hoc Communications and Networks*, SECON '10, pages 1–9, 2010.

[16] E. Felemban, S. Vural, R. Murawski, E. Ekici, K. Lee, Y. Moon, and S. Park. Samac: A cross-layer communication protocol for sensor networks with sectored antennas. *IEEE Transactions on Mobile Computing*, 9(8):1072–1088, Aug. 2010.

[17] F. Ferrari, M. Zimmerling, L. Thiele, and O. Saukh. Efficient network flooding and time synchronization with glossy. In *Proceedings of the 10th International Conference on Information Processing in Sensor Networks*, IPSN '11, pages 73–84, 2011.

[18] T. Feydy, Z. Somogyi, and P. Stuckey. Half reification and flattening. In *Principles and Practice of Constraint Programming CP 2011*, volume 6876 of *Lecture Notes in Computer Science*, pages 286–301. Springer Berlin Heidelberg, 2011.

[19] G. Giorgetti, A. Cidronali, S. Gupta, and G. Manes. Exploiting low-cost directional antennas in 2.4 ghz ieee 802.15.4 wireless sensor networks. In *European Microwave Week*, 2007.

[20] H. Gossain, T. Joshi, C. D. M. Cordeiro, and D. P. Agrawal. Drp: An efficient directional routing protocol for mobile ad hoc networks. *IEEE Trans. on Parallel & Distributed Systems*, 17(12):1438–1541, 2006.

[21] R. C. Hansen. *Electrically small, superdirective, and superconducting antennas*. John Wiley & Sons, 2006.

[22] F. Hermans, H. Wennerström, L. Mcnamara, C. Rohner, and P. Gunningberg. All is not lost: Understanding and exploiting packet corruption in outdoor sensor networks. In *11th European Conference on Wireless Sensor Networks - Volume 8354*, EWSN 2014, pages 116–132, 2014.

[23] S. L. Howard, C. Schlegel, and K. Iniewski. Error control coding in low-power wireless sensor networks: When is ecc energy-efficient? *EURASIP Journal on Wireless Communications and Networking*, 2006(2):29–29, 2006.

[24] T. Istomin, R. Marfievici, A. L. Murphy, and G. P. Picco. Trident: In-field connectivity assessment for wireless sensor networks. In *ExtremeCom*, 2014.

[25] K. Jain, J. Padhye, V. N. Padmanabhan, and L. Qiu. Impact of interference on multi-hop wireless network performance. In *9th Annual International Conference on Mobile Computing and Networking*, MOBICOM '03, pages 66–80, 2003.

[26] S. Kim, R. Fonseca, P. Dutta, A. Tavakoli, D. Culler, P. Levis, S. Shenker, and I. Stoica. Flush: A reliable bulk transport protocol for multihop wireless networks. In *5th International Conference on Embedded Networked Sensor Systems*, SENSYS '07, pages 351–365, 2007.

[27] S. Kim, S. Pakzad, D. Culler, J. Demmel, G. Fenves, S. Glaser, and M. Turon. Health monitoring of civil infrastructures using wireless sensor networks. In *6th International Conference on Information Processing in Sensor Networks*, IPSN '07, pages 254–263, 2007.

[28] O. Landsiedel, F. Ferrari, and M. Zimmerling. Chaos: Versatile and efficient all-to-all data sharing and in-network processing at scale. In *11th ACM Conference on Embedded Networked Sensor Systems*, SENSYS '13, pages 1:1–1:14, 2013.

[29] K. Leentvaar and J. Flint. The capture effect in fm receivers. *IEEE Transactions on Communications*, 24(5):531–539, 1976.

[30] X. Liu, A. Sheth, M. Kaminsky, K. Papagiannaki, S. Seshan, and P. Steenkiste. Dirc: Increasing indoor wireless capacity using directional antennas. *SIGCOMM Comput. Commun. Rev.*, 39(4):171–182, Aug. 2009.

[31] X. Liu, A. Sheth, M. Kaminsky, K. Papagiannaki, S. Seshan, and P. Steenkiste. Pushing the envelope of indoor wireless spatial reuse using directional access points and clients. In *16th International Conference on Mobile Computing and Networking*, MOBICOM '10, pages 209–220, 2010.

[32] L. Mottola, T. Voigt, and G. Picco. Electronically-switched directional antennas for wireless sensor networks: A full-stack evaluation. In *10th IEEE Communications Society Conference on Sensor, Mesh and Ad Hoc Communications and Networks*, SECON '13, pages 176–184, 2013.

[33] V. Navda, A. P. Subramanian, K. Dhanasekaran, A. Timm-Giel, and S. Das. Mobisteer: Using steerable beam directional antenna for vehicular network access. In *5th International Conference on Mobile Systems, Applications and Services*, MOBISYS '07, pages 192–205, 2007.

[34] M. Nilsson. Directional antennas for wireless sensor networks. In *Proc. 9th Scandinavian Workshop on Wireless Adhoc Networks (Adhoc'09)*, 2009.

[35] Österlind F. and Dunkels A. Approaching the maximum 802.15.4 multi-hop throughput. In *5th ACM Workshop on Embedded Networked Sensors*, EMNETS '08, 2008.

[36] J. Paek, K. Chintalapudi, R. Govindan, J. Caffrey, and S. Masri. A wireless sensor network for structural health monitoring: Performance and experience. In *2nd IEEE Workshop on Embedded Networked Sensors*, EMNETS '05, pages 1–9, 2005.

[37] B. Raman and K. Chebrolu. Design and evaluation of a new mac protocol for long-distance 802.11 mesh networks. In *11th Annual International Conference on Mobile Computing and Networking*, MOBICOM '05, pages 156–169, 2005.

[38] B. Raman and K. Chebrolu. Censor networks: A critique of "sensor networks" from a systems perspective. *SIGCOMM Comput. Commun. Rev.*, 38(3):75–78, July 2008.

[39] B. Raman, K. Chebrolu, S. Bijwe, and V. Gabale. Pip: A connection-oriented, multi-hop, multi-channel tdma-based mac for high throughput bulk transfer. In *8th ACM Conference on Embedded Networked Sensor Systems*, SENSYS '10, pages 15–28, 2010.

[40] R. Ramanathan, J. Redi, C. Santivanez, D. Wiggins, and S. Polit. Ad hoc networking with directional antennas: a complete system solution. *IEEE Journal on Selected Areas in Communications*, 23(3):496–506, 2005.

[41] S. Roy, D. Saha, S. Bandyopadhyay, T. Ueda, and S. Tanaka. A network-aware mac and routing protocol for effective load balancing in ad hoc wireless networks with directional antenna. In *4th ACM International Symposium on Mobile Ad Hoc Networking and Computing*, MOBIHOC '03, pages 88–97, 2003.

[42] N. Scholastica. Pathloss prediction model of a wireless sensor network in an indoor environment. *International Journal of Advanced Research in Electrical, Electronics and Instrumentation Engineering*, 3(9), 2014.

[43] S. Vasudevan, J. Kurose, and D. Towsley. On neighbor discovery in wireless networks with directional antennas. In *IEEE 24th Annual Joint Conference of the IEEE Computer and Communications Societies.*, INFOCOM '05, pages 2502–2512 vol. 4, 2005.

[44] F. Viani, L. Lizzi, M. Donelli, D. Pregnolato, G. Oliveri, and A. Massa. Exploitation of Parasitic Smart Antennas in Wireless Sensor Networks. *Journal of Electromagnetic Waves and Applications*, 24(7):993–1003, 2010.

[45] T. Voigt, L. Mottola, and K. Hewage. Understanding link dynamics in wireless sensor networks with dynamically steerable directional antennas. In *10th European Conference on Wireless Sensor Networks*, EWSN'13, pages 115–130, 2013.

[46] H. Wennerstrom, F. Hermans, O. Rensfelt, C. Rohner, and L.-A. Norden. A long-term study of correlations between meteorological conditions and 802.15.4 link performance. In *10th IEEE Communications Society Conference on Sensor, Mesh and Ad Hoc Communications and Networks*, SECON '13, pages 221–229, 2013.

[47] G. Werner-Allen, K. Lorincz, J. Johnson, J. Lees, and M. Welsh. Fidelity and yield in a volcano monitoring sensor network. In *7th Symposium on Operating Systems Design and Implementation*, OSDI '06, pages 381–396, 2006.

[48] H. Zhang, F. Osterlind, P. Soldati, T. Voigt, and M. Johansson. Rapid convergecast on commodity hardware: Performance limits and optimal policies. In *7th IEEE Communications Society Conference on Sensor Mesh and Ad Hoc Communications and Networks*, SECON '10, pages 1–9, 2010.

[49] G. Zhou, J. A. Stankovic, and S. H. Son. Crowded spectrum in wireless sensor networks. In *3rd IEEE Workshop on Embedded Networked Sensors*, EMNETS '06, 2006.

[50] E. Öström, L. Mottola, and T. Voigt. Evaluation of an electronically switched directional antenna for real-world low-power wireless networks. In *Real-World Wireless Sensor Networks*, Lecture Notes in Computer Science, pages 113–125. Springer Berlin Heidelberg, 2010.

When Pipelines Meet Fountain: Fast Data Dissemination in Wireless Sensor Networks

Wan Du, Jansen Christian Liando, Huanle Zhang, Mo Li
School of Computer Engineering, Nanyang Technological University, Singapore
{duwan, cjansen, Huanle.Zhang, limo}@ntu.edu.sg

Abstract

This paper presents *Pando*, a completely contention-free data dissemination protocol for wireless sensor networks. Pando encodes data by Fountain codes and disseminates the rateless stream of encoded packets along the fast and parallel pipelines built on constructive interference and channel diversity. Since every encoded packet contains innovative information to the original data object, Pando avoids duplicate retransmissions and fully exploits the wireless broadcast effect in data dissemination. To transform Pando into a practical system, we devise several techniques, including the integration of Fountain coding with the timing-critical operations of constructive interference and pipelining, a silence-based feedback scheme for the one-way pipelined dissemination, and packet-level adaptation of network density and channel diversity. Based on these techniques, Pando can accomplish the data dissemination process entirely over the fast and parallel pipelines. We implement Pando in Contiki and for TelosB sensor motes. We evaluate Pando's performance with various settings on two large-scale open testbeds, Indriya and Flocklab. Our experimental results show that Pando can provide 100% reliability and reduce the dissemination time of the state-of-the-art by 3.5×.

Categories and Subject Descriptors

C.2.1 [**Network Architecture and Design**]: Wireless communication; C.2.2 [**Network Protocols**]: Protocol architecture

Keywords

Wireless sensor networks; Data dissemination; Fountain codes; Constructive interference

1. INTRODUCTION

Data dissemination reliably diffuses a bulk of data to all the nodes in a wireless sensor network. It provides a fundamental service for many applications, like on-the-air reprogramming [27,39] and application updating [2]. One important metric of data dissemination for these applications is reliability, which is measured by the proportion of the data received at each node over the data to be disseminated. To provide high reliability, traditional data dissemination protocols [17–19, 22, 28, 30, 36, 40] flood data packets over multiple hops with contention-based access control protocols like CSMA/CA, which suffers long backoff delay and severely limits the channel spatial reuse. Recent advance in physical-layer cooperative broadcasting [43] allows multiple synchronized transmissions constructively add on each other. Multiple senders can thus transmit the same packet simultaneously and the constructively interfered transmissions can be successfully decoded at the receivers. Glossy [13] builds upon this principle and experimentally demonstrates that constructive interference can remove unnecessary channel contention and improve the flooding performance. Another work, PIP [38], exercises multi-channel communication and enables adjacent links in a multi-hop path to operate concurrently. Based on Glossy and PIP, Splash [7] enables data dissemination over the fast and parallel pipelines by combining constructive interference and pipelining, thereby significantly improving the channel utilization.

The combination of constructive interference and pipelining, however, represents a challenge to the reliability of data dissemination. Due to the varied quality of different channels at different nodes [5,52] and the unreliability of constructive interference when the number of concurrent transmitters or the packet size is large [7,50], the packet reception rate at different nodes in a network may vary significantly. As a result, the same data object needs to be disseminated in multiple rounds to recover specific packets missing at few nodes. To achieve high reliability, Splash requires three rounds of data dissemination and employs contention-based local recovery after three rounds of pipelined data dissemination. Splash suffers from the long tail problem, where the dissemination time for achieving 100% reliability is orders of magnitude longer than the time needed for 80% reliability.

This paper presents *Pando*, a completely contention-free data dissemination protocol, which tackles the long tail problem in data dissemination of constructive interference and pipelining. Pando introduces randomness in the disseminated packets and fully exploits the wireless broadcast effect. It encodes data with Fountain codes [34] and continuously pumps the rateless stream of encoded data into the network. Since every encoded packet contains innovative information for the original data, receivers become insensitive to the loss of individual packets. Pando avoids the overhead of

SenSys'15, November 1–4, 2015, Seoul, South Korea..

DOI: http://dx.doi.org/10.1145/2809695.2809721.

re-disseminating the entire data object in rounds. The dissemination process is terminated once all nodes in the network accumulate sufficient encoded packets and successfully recover the original data. Pando accomplishes the dissemination process entirely over the contention-free pipelines. Thus, it can fully use the network resource and asymptotically approach the network capacity.

Transforming the idea behind Pando into a practical system is challenging for at least two reasons. First, the encoding and decoding of packets using Fountain codes need to be integrated into the timing-critical operations of constructive interference and pipelining. Incautious design of the Fountain decoder will lead to uncertainty in data transmission, which may impair the synchronization of constructive interference and paralyze the pipelined data dissemination. Second, a stop condition of the data dissemination has to be set and conveyed to the source. The data dissemination should be terminated once all nodes recover the original data object. The source stops pumping packets into the network and the relaying nodes stop forwarding packets to their lower layer. In the pipelined data dissemination, however, all nodes are either receiving packets from their upper layer or relaying the received packets to their lower layer all the time. No explicit feedback channels can be used to convey the acknowledgements from all nodes to the source.

By tackling the above challenges, we make the following three contributions.

1. We design a radio-driven coding scheme where the computation of Fountain encoding and decoding is accommodated into the intervals between the timing-critical operations of highly-synchronized constructive interference and pipelining. Fountain coding and transmission controls are tailored to guarantee a deterministic software delay, which is essential to limit the time offset of concurrent transmissions within 0.5 μs (the synchronization requirement for generating constructive interference with high probability [13]). By parallelizing data coding and transmissions, we also avoid adding coding latency in dissemination time.

2. We devise a novel feedback approach in the one-way pipelines to timely acknowledge the successful recovery of the data object and stop the dissemination process. We leverage the silence of channels to aggregate and convey the acknowledgements from the leaf nodes to the source. The feedback process is carefully integrated with the pipelined data dissemination to guarantee the reliability of data dissemination. The threshold of channel silence is adapted dynamically according to the ambient noise and interference. Packet loss is also considered to eliminate its impact on data dissemination and feedback delivery.

3. We apply packet-level adaptation of channel diversity and network density to boost the dissemination efficiency. By adapting the channel allocation and the number of concurrent transmitters for every packet, all nodes experience cycled channel assignments and better wireless diversity. This avoids few poorly-performing nodes to hinder the entire pipelines. We design a set of techniques to incorporate the adaptation operations into the feedback process and pipelined data dissemination, such as scheduled silence of leaf nodes, fast channel switching and failure recovery.

We implement Pando in Contiki and evaluate its performance on Indriya [6] and Flocklab [31], two large-scale testbeds for wireless sensor networks. In our experiments, Pando is able to successfully disseminate a data file of 32 kBytes over a network of up to 6 hops within 6 seconds. We compare Pando with state-of-the-art data dissemination protocols, Splash [7] and Deluge [19], over various network configurations. Our experimental results suggest that Pando reduces the average dissemination time of Splash by 3.5×, corresponding to a reduction factor of 32.7× over Deluge.

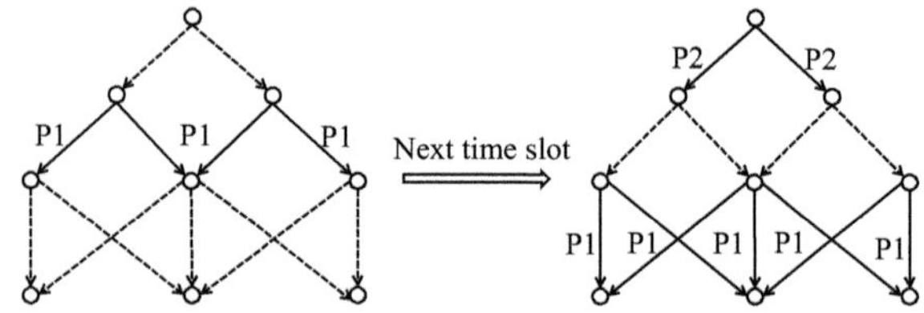

Figure 1: The pipelined tree built on constructive interference and pipelining. 'P1' and 'P2' represent the first packet and the second packet respectively.

2. MOTIVATION

The goal of data dissemination is to deliver a bulk of data (e.g., an executable file or an application updating profile) to all the nodes in a network. Any packet loss may make the received data useless. Reliability and dissemination time are thus two key performance metrics for data dissemination. To achieve high reliability, previous protocols, like Deluge [19] and ReXOR [8], transmit the data object hop by hop with explicit acknowledgements and retransmissions. The network resources are significantly underutilized in such a way due to high multiple access overhead and low spatial reuse. For instance, two transmissions can occur concurrently only if they are apart from each other for at least three hops [19]. By leveraging constructive interference, Glossy [13] allows multiple nodes to simultaneously transmit one packet without backoff or spatial multiplexing. The spatial reuse is further improved by enabling multiple layers transmitting concurrently on distinct channels [38]. Therefore, the data dissemination time could be essentially reduced by combining constructive interference and pipelining [7].

In this section, we experimentally study the data dissemination enabled by constructive interference and pipelining, and reveal its long-tail problem. We also demonstrate the gain and challenges of incorporating Fountain coding into the pipelined data dissemination.

2.1 Constructive interference and pipelining

Based on constructive interference and pipelining, a tree topology is built, as depicted in Figure 1. One packet is forwarded simultaneously by all nodes at a same layer which interfere constructively with each other; meanwhile, multiple packets can be transmitted concurrently by different layers that make use of distinct channels. In each time slot (corresponding to the transmission time of one packet), all received packets are disseminated one-hop further from the upper layers (closer to the source) to the lower layers. In this paper, for the nodes at the same layer, we refer the nodes at their upper layer as their parent nodes and the nodes at the lower layer as their child nodes.

In the pipelined tree, the channel quality varies at different nodes [5, 52] and constructive interference becomes unreliable if the number of concurrent transmitters is large [50]. As a result, some packets may not be received by several nodes, and the data dissemination is not reliable. To the

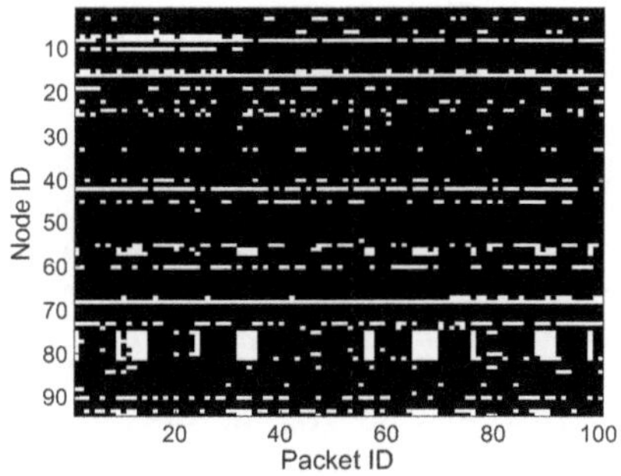

(a) **First round (85% reliability).**

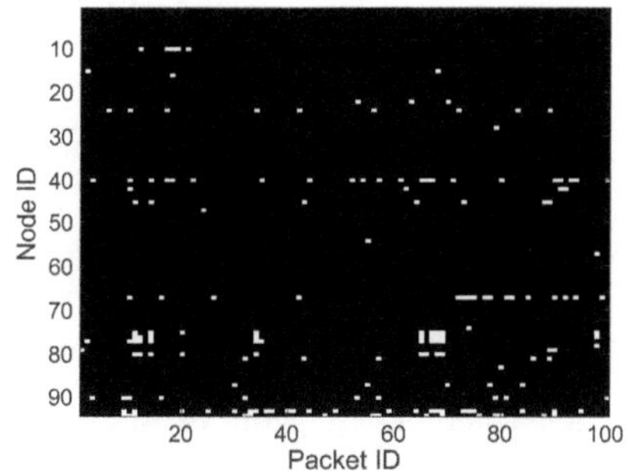

(b) **Second round (96.8% reliability).**

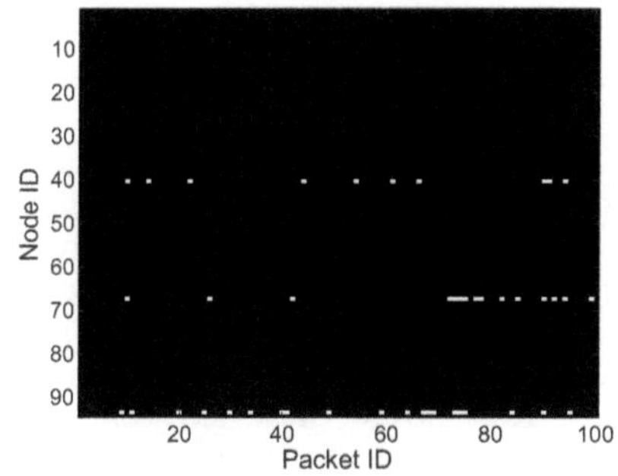

(c) **Third round (99% reliability).**

Figure 2: The packet reception performance of every node after each round in Splash. One black point represents that the packet is correctly received by the relative node. One white point refers to a packet loss. Due to the space limitation, only the first 100 packets (instead of all 500 packets) in each round are presented.

best of our knowledge, Splash [7] is the latest data dissemination protocol that combines constructive interference and pipelining. It disseminates the data object multiple times and relies on a local recovery phase to achieve high reliability. In the first two rounds, it disseminates the same data object twice. In the third round, 500 XOR-encoded packets are disseminated. Every encoded packet is the linear combination of 20 randomly-selected original packets. When a node receives an encoded packet, it can recover a missing original packet only if it has received 19 original packets which were used to generate that encoded packet. After the dissemination over the fast pipelines, a local recovery phase is performed. Nodes request the missing packets from their neighbors using CSMA/CA-based multiple access.

2.2 The long-tail problem

We conducted a series of experiments with Splash [7] on Indriya [6], the same testbed used in [7]. A data object of 32 kBytes (i.e., 500 packets of 64-byte payload) is disseminated in each experiment. Figure 2 depicts a snapshot example of the packet reception for every node after each round. Figure 2a demonstrates that the network reliability is high (85%) after the first round although the packet reception rate varies for different nodes. The network reliability is calculated as the average reliability of all nodes in the network. From Figure 2a to Figure 2b, the second round only increases the reliability from 85% to 96.8%. It is inefficient to repeatedly disseminate *the whole data object* to *all nodes*. On average, for one node, 76.2% of its received packets are duplicate. Figure 2c shows that the reliability improvement of XOR coding is limited (from 96.8% to 99%). 97.8% of the XOR packets cannot contribute to the recovery of original data. The empirical design of Splash (e.g., 500 XOR-encoded packets) deviates from the best setting which requires an optimal number of XOR packets according to the reception of the first two rounds.

Figure 3 depicts the network reliability progress of Splash. It reveals that the long tail problem is severe in Splash. The total dissemination time of Splash for achieving 100% reliability is more than 10× larger than the time for achieving 75.9% reliability in the first round. Two obvious reasons can be found in Figure 3. Compared with the first round, the last two rounds provide limited contributions to the reliability progress. The contention-based local recovery (i.e., more than 13 seconds) is time-consuming. As reported in [7], the local recovery phase is much longer than the total transmission time of three dissemination rounds.

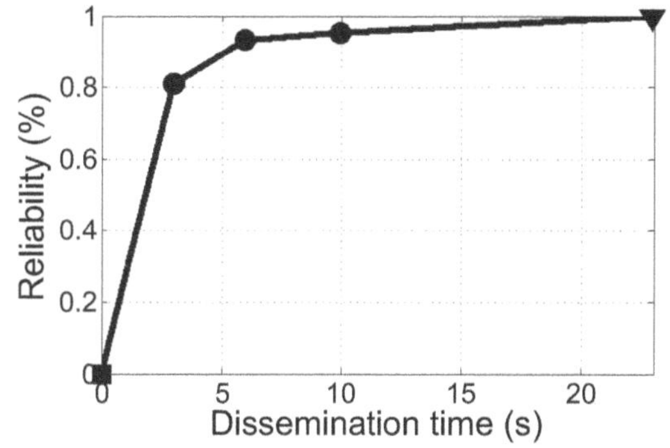

Figure 3: Network reliability of Splash at some specific time points. The end of 3 dissemination rounds is indicated by circle markers. The local recovery phase is from the end of the third round till the last node correctly receives the data object.

2.3 Fountain coding in data dissemination

To address the long-tail problem in data dissemination, we use Fountain codes to introduce randomness in the disseminated packets. We disseminate the Fountain-encoded packets along the fast and parallel pipelines. Every encoded packet is a linear combination of several randomly-selected original packets. Regardless of which packets one node has received, every encoded packet provides innovative information to the recovery of the original data. Instead of the identity of individual packets, the number of received packets becomes the key factor that determines the reliable reception of a data object. When a node accumulates sufficient amount of encoded packets, it recovers the original data by simple linear determinant calculation.

By incorporating Fountain coding into the pipelined data dissemination, duplicate retransmissions are avoided and the network capacity can be asymptotically approached as rateless-encoded packets are disseminated over the fast and parallel pipelines. For example, if we replace the data packets in the same trace of the above experiment (Section 2.2) with Fountain-encoded packets, we can achieve 100% network reliability by just disseminating 1132 encoded packets, thereby reducing the dissemination time of Splash by *7.2*×.

Although Fountain codes have been implemented in some previous data dissemination protocols [17, 18, 40], they all use Fountain codes to improve the performance of single-hop transmissions. The integration of Fountain coding with pipelined data dissemination is challenging. The highly-synchronized operations of constructive interference and pipelining can be easily paralyzed by incautious design of Fountain coding. During the dissemination, all nodes (except the source) are either receiving or transmitting on the downlinks. They do not have any time to decode a packet or send an acknowledgement to their parent node. In a naive way of Fountain-enabled data dissemination, the source first disseminates a certain number of encoded packets and all nodes begin to decode after the dissemination. The decoding time is comparable with the dissemination time. To achieve 100% reliability, a local recovery phase has to be performed or the source must know the decoding result of every node. It is troublesome to collect the feedback from all nodes using CSMA/CA-based multiple access and multi-hop routing. After the feedback collection, the source has to resume the data dissemination if any nodes have not received sufficient packets. Such a loop may have to be performed multiple times. The above simple solution cannot eliminate the overhead of multiple access and defies the goal of constructive interference and pipelining.

3. PANDO

Pando works as a service middleware in the protocol stack to provide fast and reliable data dissemination. A wake-up protocol (details in Section 4) is developed to trigger data dissemination, when general network activities (e.g., data collection or duty cycling) are being performed in sensor networks. During the data dissemination process, the general network activities are temporarily suspended, and the sensor mote resources (e.g., CPU and radio) are in active mode. Since Pando's dissemination is fast (6 seconds to disseminate a file of 32 kBytes across a network of 31 nodes), Pando has negligible impact on other network activities. Compared with existing data dissemination protocols that use much longer time for data dissemination, Pando essentially reduces the energy consumption of individual nodes and prolongs the network lifetime.

In this section, after a preliminary analysis of Fountain codes, we introduce three techniques that are used to make Pando into a practical system. The Fountain coding in Pando is radio-driven. The coding computation is accommodated into the CPU idle intervals of transmission operations; at the same time, the integration is carefully tailored to guarantee the strict synchronization of constructive interference and pipelining (Section 3.2). A silence-based feedback scheme is developed for the one-way pipelines to promptly terminate the source and complete the dissemination process (Section 3.3). Packet-level adaptation of network density and channel diversity is adopted to boost the performance of constructive interference and pipelining (Section 3.4).

3.1 Preliminaries on Fountain codes

Fountain codes, like LT codes [33] and random linear codes [34], encode a data object of k packets, $\{X_1, X_2, \cdots, X_k\}$, into a rateless stream of encoded packets, $\{Y_1, Y_2, \cdots\}$. One encoded packet is generated by linearly combining a certain number of randomly-selected original packets. Once a node correctly receives m ($m \geq k$) encoded packets, it can recover the original data using the Gaussian Elimination (GE) or Belief Propagation (BP) decoding algorithm. The coding efficiency is calculated as k/m.

Although Pando is not limited to any specific Fountain codes, in our current implementation, we choose LT codes in consideration of its succinct design (i.e., low computation overhead). Every encoded packet of LT codes is calculated by performing XOR operations of d packets that are randomly chosen from k original packets, where $d = 1, 2, \ldots, k$. For an encoded packet $Y_i, 1 < i < \infty$, the degree d is determined by a distribution $\rho(d) = P_d$, where P_d is the probability that d original packets are selected to encode Y_i. The default robust Soliton degree distribution produces low coding efficiency for the applications of sensor networks with small number of packets. We implement an optimized degree distribution proposed in SYNAPSE++ [40], which produces high coding efficiency for small data objects. Like in the previous work [10], we use a best seed of the random number generator. It produces the lowest decoding overhead and avoids the time consumption of random number generation in the decoding process. Although the random linear codes may provide higher coding efficiency, its computation overhead is high. It generates encoded packets using modular multiplication in Galois Field (GF) 2^8, which is time-consuming to execute compared with XOR operations.

3.2 Radio-driven coding scheme

We perform the encoding and decoding of LT codes along with the timing-critical communication operations of highly-synchronized constructive interference and pipelining. Since the microcontroller is mostly in idle mode while the radio is receiving or transmitting, the microcontroller can execute the coding computation in parallel with the transmissions performed by the radio hardware. The goal of our design is to find the largest idle intervals of the microcontroller for Fountain coding, under the precondition of controlling the synchronization offset between the concurrent transmissions of constructive interference within 0.5 μs. Thus, we need to guarantee that the generated idle CPU intervals are constant and the coding computation occupies deterministic time.

Constant intervals of idle CPU. We generate two large constant idle intervals in the operations of constructive interference and pipelining based on two observations. First, the time to read/write one byte from/into the radio through the Serial Peripheral Interface (SPI) bus (e.g., 5.75 μs for general low-power microcontrollers) is much shorter than the latency of transmitting/receiving one byte by the radio hardware (i.e., 32 μs for IEEE 802.15.4-compliant transceivers). Second, although the operations of constructive interference and pipelining are timing-critical, they only need to execute a few CPU commands at some important time points, e.g., sending commands to set the radio to the right state when an interruption is received. Therefore, after reading/writing one packet from/into the radio and executing the commands, the microcontroller goes into idle mode for a long time that can be used for Fountain encoding and decoding.

We design Pando on top of the flooding protocol in Glossy [13] and the pipelining of PIP [38]. In Glossy, hardware interrupts are used to implicitly synchronize the concurrent transmissions. When multiple nodes receive a packet simultaneously, they detect the interrupt for the end of the reception at the same time. Based on the interrupt, their microcontrollers immediately set their radios to TX mode and write the data into the TX buffer of the radios. They then enter idle mode till the end of the transmission. After the transmission, the microcontrollers also detect an interrupt and set the radios to RX mode to receive the next packet. They go into idle mode for a long duration before the end of the reception. Since the transmission time and the operations of constructive interference are predefined, the idle interval is constant for every packet transmission.

To make sure that the coding computation in the constant idle interval and the following hardware interrupt do not impact each other, a guard interval, corresponding to the transmission time of 8 bytes, is added before the end of each interval. Based on the guard interval, the coding procedure can save its context before the hardware interrupt and resume its operation in the next idle interval. A timer is set at the beginning of the idle interval. It expires when the radio begins to receive the last 8th byte. The microcontroller saves the decoding context when the timer expires.

Deterministic coding time. To be safely inserted into the constant idle intervals, the coding computation should be decomposable and each decomposed piece should occupy deterministic time. We begin to decode once two encoded packets are received. New received packets can be added into the decoding process incrementally. Upon receiving a packet from its parent nodes, a node has two time slots to decode that packet before the next packet is received. In these two slots, the node transmits that packet to its child nodes and receives the new packet from its parent nodes respectively. During the transmission and reception performed by the radio hardware, the microcontroller tries to complete the decoding of the received packet in its idle intervals.

The Accumulative Gaussian Elimination (AGE) algorithm [10] is used for incremental decoding. Although the BP algorithm is less computationally expensive, AGE provides higher coding efficiency (e.g., a coding efficiency of 89% for a data object of 16 original packets). AGE transforms the top-left square submatrix of the coefficient matrix into an identity matrix when few packets are received. As new packets are received, AGE extends the submatrix gradually. The original data is recovered when the size of the submatrix becomes equal to the number of original packets.

At the end of each idle interval, the decoding algorithm saves the context by recoding the decoding results and the intermediate variables, including the size of the submatrix, the coefficient matrix and the calculated results of data packets. The decoding computation occupies deterministic time which ends before the guard interval. In our implementation, the context saving costs at most 64 μs, which is much smaller than the guard interval (256 μs for IEEE 802.15.4 radios). The encoding can also be performed incrementally. The computation of encoding one packet is much less than the decoding of one packet, and thus nodes are able to generate one encoded packet every two time slots.

Timing process. Figure 4 presents the key timeline of Pando. When the microcontroller receives an interrupt for the end of a transmission (the SFD pin is set to low), it immediately sets the radio to the RX mode by sending two commands (i.e., channel setting and RXON) to the radio. After calibration (192 μs), the radio is ready to receive any incoming signals. When a node receives the first two bytes (Glossy header for synchronization) of a packet, instead of reading the following bytes one by one as Glossy, it begins to decode the previously-received encoded packet

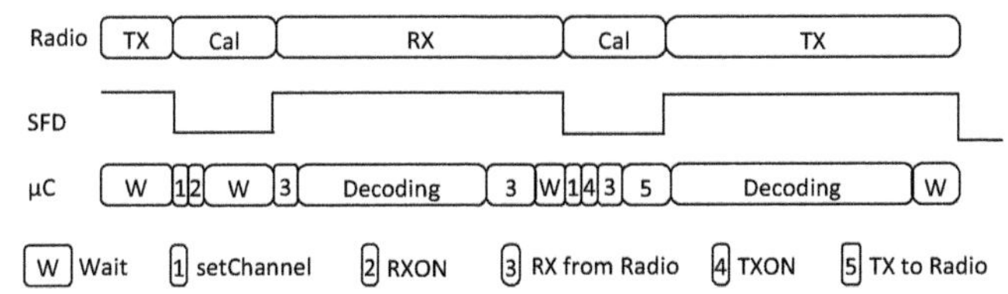

Figure 4: State transition of the radio and the microcontroller in Pando.

for a certain duration (e.g., 1688 μs in our implementation). It then resumes reading the received data from the radio and switches to waiting state during the guard interval.

By detecting an interrupt for the end of a packet reception (the SFD pin is set to low), the microcontroller sets the sending channel and sends a TXON command. After that, it reads the last eight bytes of the received packet from the RX buffer of the radio and writes the whole received packet to the TX buffer of the radio. Then, the microcontroller is able to perform Fountain coding before the radio begins to transmit the last eight bytes.

Results. We have implemented the radio-driven coding scheme in Contiki for TelosB sensor motes, a typical sensor mote type that has been widely used in current sensor network deployments. A TelosB sensor mote includes a TI CC2420 radio which supports the IEEE 802.15.4 standard. The packet size in Pando is set to 73 bytes, including 64-byte payload, 7-byte MAC header and 2-byte footer. Except the 8-byte guard interval, the transmission time of the first 65 bytes is 2080 μs. It only takes 392 μs to read these bytes from the radio into the microcontroller via the SPI bus. Therefore, the microcontroller has 1688 μs for decoding during the reception of one packet. In the same principle, the microcontroller has a similar idle interval when the radio is transmitting.

Pando can be implemented on any hardware platforms that support constructive interference. Glossy [13] successfully demonstrated the feasibility of realizing constructive interference on IEEE 802.15.4-compliant hardware platforms. All the parameters of Pando, including RX/TX data rate, calibration interval and SPI transmission speed, are set according to the IEEE 802.15.4 standard. We do not need to tune these parameters for different hardware platforms.

3.3 Silence-based feedback scheme

As the source continuously pumps the rateless encoded packets into the network, Pando approaches 100% reliability automatically over the fast and parallel pipelines. Based on the radio-driven coding approach, all nodes can successfully decode the received packets when they are disseminating data packets. To promptly terminate the source and complete the dissemination process, every node needs to send an acknowledgement to the source when it correctly recovers the original data object. In the pipelined data dissemination, however, nodes are either receiving new packets from their parent nodes or relaying the received packets to their child nodes. The acknowledgement transmission of one node should not impact its role as a forwarder or the synchronized transmissions of other nodes. A feedback scheme is needed to convey the acknowledgement of every node to the source during the data dissemination process.

A silence-based feedback scheme is devised for the one-way parallel pipelines. With this feedback scheme, the acknowledgement of every node is delivered from the lower layers, merged at the relay node, and finally reaches the source. When a node succeeds in decoding, it can generate the Fountain encoded packets by itself using the recovered packets and continue transmitting the encoded packets to its child nodes without receiving new packets from its parent nodes. The successful nodes can thus monitor the transmission of their child nodes in the RX slots. In addition, the nodes at upper layers are likely to recover the original data earlier than the nodes at lower layers, since all packets are forwarded from the source to the lower layers. Therefore, the nodes at upper layers are likely to be ready for detecting the feedback before their child nodes succeed in decoding.

In Pando, a leaf node stops transmitting when it successfully recovers the original data. Its parent nodes (i.e., relay nodes) can detect such silence by measuring the Received Signal Strength Indicator (RSSI) value on the sending channel of that leaf node. A relay node terminates transmitting, when all its child nodes become silent, corresponding to a RSSI value lower than a threshold ($RSSI_{threshold}$). The silence of a relay node indicates that both itself and its child nodes have successfully recovered the original data object. In such a way, the acknowledgements from all child nodes are aggregated at that relay node. The fused feedback can be further conveyed to the source across the network.

In our experiments using the above feedback scheme, some nodes stop working, because the transmissions are always triggered by the lower layer and the time offset among the concurrent transmissions increases. We solve this problem by requiring the relay nodes to synchronize back with their parent nodes periodically. Since the dissemination is triggered from the source, the downlink packets have more precise synchronization information and are used to calibrate the relay nodes. In our current implementation, nodes listen to the feedback channel only in the odd RX slots.

As an example, Figure 5 demonstrates the dissemination process of a 16-packet data object in Pando. The encoded packets are disseminated from the source to the other nodes layer by layer. Every node needs 17 encoded packets (one extra packet is the coding overhead) to recover the original data. In this example, we assume no packet loss occurs. All nodes correctly recover the original data object when the 17th packet is received. When the leaf nodes at the third layer receive the 17th packet, after two time slots, they succeed in decoding and stop transmitting. The relay nodes at the second layer detect the channel silence in their 19th RX slot and terminate their dissemination. The fused feedback of silence is captured by the nodes at the first layer in their 21st RX slot and finally reaches the source. The whole dissemination process is terminated after the 21st RX slot of the source. Figure 5 shows that the silenced-based feedback scheme is efficient. Along the path, the relay nodes only need 1 or 3 slots to forward the aggregated feedback to their parent nodes. In this example of three-hop network, five slots (13.6 ms) are sufficient for the feedback aggregation and delivery after the last leaf node succeeds in decoding.

False negative of channel silence. Due to ambient noise or interference from nearby devices using the same frequency band, a node may not be able to detect the channel silence, when all its child nodes succeed in decoding and stop transmitting. To eliminate the false negative of channel silence, we dynamically adapt the RSSI threshold of channel silence ($RSSI_{threshold}$) according to the noise and interference condition. Between the wake-up protocol and the data dissemination, we leave 10 time slots, during which all nodes measure the RSSI of free channels (denoted as $RSSI_{silence}$). During data dissemination, when a node successfully receives a packet, it measures the channel RSSI and updates the RSSI value of successful packet reception (denoted as $RSSI_{rx}$). In our experiments on two large-scale testbeds deployed in both indoor and outdoor environments, $RSSI_{rx}$ is always larger than $RSSI_{silence}$. We set $RSSI_{threshold}$ as $(RSSI_{silence} + RSSI_{rx})/2$. If some noise or interference appears, $RSSI_{rx}$ increases and $RSSI_{threshold}$ becomes thus large. When the child nodes are not transmitting, with such a high $RSSI_{threshold}$, the channel is measured as silent even in the appearance of noise or interference.

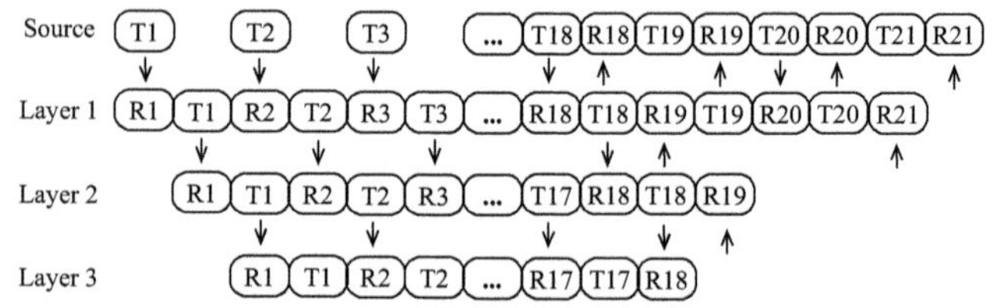

Figure 5: Dissemination process of a 16-packet data object in Pando. 'T1' refers to the first TX slot. 'R1' represents the first RX slot. The arrow indicates the signal transmission direction.

False positive of channel silence. When a node fails to receive a packet, it cannot forward that packet. Its parent node may interpret this silence as successful decoding. To filter out such false silence, every node only infers that all its child nodes have completed the reception when M consecutive silent slots are detected. In practical, M is small based on two facts. First, even if a node cannot transmit, its parent node is likely to detect a high RSSI by the signal from the other child nodes at the same layer. Second, it is rare that a node cannot receive the packet from its parent node consecutively, especially when our packet-level adaptation of network density and channel allocation is applied. In our implementation, M is set to 3, which can filter out all false silences in a large-scale sensor network that is densely deployed in a building. We will show in Section 5 that the overhead of the feedback process is small compared with the significant improvement of data dissemination efficiency.

3.4 Packet-level adaptation of channel diversity and network density

In pipelined data dissemination, some nodes may have poor packet reception due to bad channel quality or unreliable constructive interference. Some channels may be lossy at some node locations because of ambient noise or interference from other nodes or devices. The bad channel can be replaced by exchanging the assigned channel among nodes. On the other hand, constructive interference may not work well at some nodes as the synchronization offset is high. The performance of these nodes can be improved by changing the set of concurrent transmitters, since constructive interference is likely to be strong for a small number of concurrent transmitters [50] and the capture effect occurs at some locations of concurrent transmitters [13]. With capture effect, a radio is able to receive one signal despite the interference from other transmitters, when the signal is stronger and arrives earlier than the interference [24].

Splash [7] changes the channel allocation and network density after each dissemination round. Such round-level adaptation, however, cannot effectively adapt to the channel variations. Few poorly-performing nodes may hinder the entire pipelines for a whole round. Moreover, every node can only experiences three different channels at most in the three dissemination rounds respectively.

By applying Fountain codes in data dissemination, Pando enables packet-level adaptation of channel allocation and network density. Pando allocates every packet with a specific channel and changes the number of concurrent transmitters for every packet transmission. Nodes set their RX/TX channel according to the packets they are going to receive or transmit. Packet-level adaptation can only be enabled in the data dissemination of Fountain-encoded packets. As the encoded packets are independent to each other, the loss of an individual packet caused by unreliable constructive interference or bad channel at some nodes can be immediately compensated by the following packets disseminated with different channels and network densities. Compared with round-level adaptation, Pando avoids that some poorly-performing nodes hinder the dissemination process for a long time. Moreover, every node circularly experiences all available channels which fully exploits the wireless diversity.

A set of techniques are designed to incorporate the adaptation operations into the pipelined data dissemination and the silence-based feedback process. In order not to impact the synchronized transmissions of constructive interference and pipelining, channel switching is divided into two steps, i.e., calculating which channel to use for the next packet and setting the channel in the radio. The first step is executed in the idle interval of the microcontroller and the last step introduces constant software delay. A recovery mechanism is adopted to address the failure caused by packet losses. The transmissions of leaf nodes are scheduled according to the feedback scheme.

Channel diversity. Figure 6 presents the data dissemination process of packet-level channel allocation. Every packet is assigned with a unique channel. Four channels (i.e., Channel 15, 20, 25, 26 in the IEEE 802.15.4 standard) that experience light link correlations [5] are used circularly. At the beginning, all nodes in the network are set to a default channel to receive the first packet. After forwarding the received packet to their child nodes, they immediately switch to the channel allocated for the next packet. When the previous packets are being forwarded by the relay nodes, a new packet is released by the source. The minimum distance between two packets using a same channel is at least eight hops, which are large enough to avoid the intra-path interference in typical sensor networks [38].

Channel switching is performed at the end of each transmission. To ensure that it produces deterministic software delay, as shown in Figure 4, channel switching is enabled by sending two commands (i.e., channel setting and RXON) to the radio immediately when the SFD interrupt for the end of transmission is detected. The channel of the next packet is calculated according to the sequence number of the last received packet. The computation is short (addition of two integers) and performed before the microcontroller goes to waiting state during the guard interval. It does not cause any software delay to channel switching.

If a node misses a packet because the signal is not detected or the CRC checking fails, it stays at the same channel and

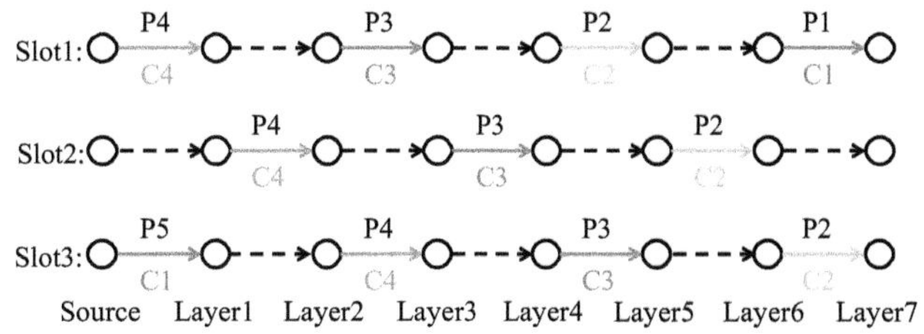

Figure 6: Packet-level channel allocation. 'P1' represents the first packet. 'C1' indicates the first channel. From slot 1 to slot 2, all the packets in the network are forwarded one hop further by the nodes of different layers with distinct channels.

tries to overhear that packet transmitted by the other nodes at the same layer. Before the overhearing, the node starts a RX timer to record a time slot. If the overhearing fails, it can still switch the channel to the new coming packet from the parent nodes in time. When multiple packets are missing consecutively, the node is also able to set to the right channel by counting the slot sequence using the RX timer. The slot sequence is calibrated frequently when a packet is received. The racing problem occurs if a node begins to receive after its parent nodes transmit. Such misalignment becomes worse as more time slots pass. To solve the racing problem, the RX timer is set slightly shorter than a time slot. In our implementation, nodes switch to the next channel 50 μs earlier than the start time of the next transmission.

Network density. In Pando, although leaf nodes do not have any child nodes, they transmit the received packets to enable the overhearing of the nodes at the same layer. The transmissions of leaf nodes do not impose any overhead to the data dissemination time, since they use a unique channel and happen at the same time with other transmissions.

To adapt the network density at packet level, the leaf nodes transmit a received packet only when the sequence number of that packet is even. For the received packets with odd sequence number, the leaf nodes do not transmit them. Because more than 50% of nodes in a data collection tree are leaf nodes [7], disabling the transmissions of leaf nodes for odd packets can significantly reduce the number of concurrent transmitters. In addition, if a node does not receive an even packet correctly, it does not transmit either. Since the set of successful receivers varies for each packet, the set of concurrent transmitters also changes for the following transmission of that packet. Therefore, the network density is altered for every packet and the reliability of constructive interference is improved.

The leaf nodes do not transmit in the time slots of odd packets. When considering the feedback scheme, these silent slots may be wrongly detected as successful decoding by the parent nodes. Our integrated design of the network density adaptation and the feedback scheme avoids such misunderstanding. In the time slots of odd packets when the leaf nodes are not transmitting, the parent nodes are receiving packets from the upper layer and do not listen to their child nodes for feedback detection. As in Figure 5, the leaf nodes only transmit in their even TX slots, corresponding to the odd RX slots of their parent nodes, in which the parent nodes listen to the feedback from the leaf nodes. Therefore, the silence of leaf nodes in the time slots of odd packets does not impact the feedback process.

4. IMPLEMENTATION

We implement Pando on TelosB sensor motes with Contiki operating system. In this section, we introduce some technical details which enable the Pando implementation.

Wake-up protocol of Pando. To incorporate Pando's data dissemination with the general network activities of sensor networks, before the dissemination of a data object, the source first broadcasts a start command across the network multiple times. The reception probability of such a short command (4 bytes) over a multi-hop sensor network of constructive interference is more than 99.99% for 6 retransmissions [13]. In our implementation, the start command is disseminated 20 times and it only takes tens of milliseconds in the fast and parallel pipelines. After the dissemination of the start command and the silent interval of 10 time slots, the source begins to transmit the first encoded packet.

The general applications of sensor networks usually work on a single channel. The channel 26 of the IEEE 802.15.4 standard is widely adopted in real deployments of sensor networks, because it is not overlapping with the channels of Wi-Fi (see http://www.wi-fi.org/) [45]. We disseminate the start command on channel 26 (the default channel in Pando). The start command includes information about the data object size. All nodes resume the previous network activities (e.g., data collection or duty cycling), when they complete the data dissemination and the feedback delivery.

Page-based dissemination. We divide the data object (e.g., 32 kBytes) into small pages (e.g., 2 kBytes in our current implementation) and disseminate the pages sequentially due to the memory constraints of wireless sensor motes (e.g., 10-kByte RAM memory on TelosB). The source begins to disseminate a new page when the current page has been correctly received by all nodes. The source knows the dissemination of one page has terminated thank to the silence-based feedback scheme. When a node succeeds in decoding and completes its feedback task, it switches to the default channel and waits for the packets of the next page. If the dissemination of the current page is not completed, the successful nodes may receive some packets from some other nodes that are still transmitting packets. They check the sequence number of the received packets. If it is larger than the last packet they received, they infer that the packets are from the current page; otherwise, they start the dissemination of a new page.

State machine of nodes. Figure 7 illustrates the state machine of the nodes in Pando. The bold arrows indicate how a node performs in an ideal case. At first, all nodes receive packets from their upper layer and immediately relay the packets to their lower layer. When a node successfully recovers the original data, it performs the following four operations sequentially: receiving a packet from its parent node, forwarding that packet to its child nodes, listening to its child nodes, and transmitting a self-generated encoded packet to its child nodes. It switches to the next page when it detects that all its child nodes are silent. Upon the completion of one page, the source starts a new page or terminates the whole dissemination process.

We introduce several failure recovery mechanisms to cope with packet losses. As described in Section 3.4, if a packet from the upper layer is corrupted, the node stays in the same channel and tries to receive that packet from the other nodes at the same layer. After that, the node switches to the next channel for the coming packet from its upper layer.

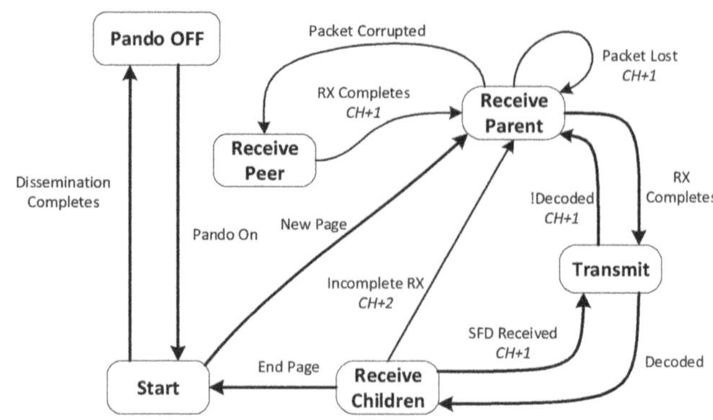

Figure 7: Node state machine in Pando.

If no SFD interrupts are detected on the feedback channel, the node loses synchronization and goes back to listen to its parent node by setting the channel accordingly. The node follows the right circulation of channels by using a RX timer to count the dissemination slots.

5. EVALUATION

We conduct a series of experiments on two large-scale open testbeds of wireless sensor networks, Indriya [6] and Flocklab [31]. Both testbeds deploy sensor motes inside a building and operate on 2.4 GHz. Indriya currently has 99 TelosB sensor motes with dense deployment. In Flocklab, 31 Tmote Sky sensor motes are sparsely deployed with low network density and some sensors are installed outdoors. The packet size is set to 64 bytes for most of the experiments and the data object is 32 kBytes (i.e., 500 packets).

We execute Pando while a conventional data collection protocols (e.g., CTP [15] for TinyOS and Contiki Collect [21] for Contiki) is running. Pando builds the pipelined tree based on the topology information provided by Contiki Collect. Every node only needs to know its hop count, and the ID of its parent node and its child nodes. Since data collection is a general application of sensor networks, a hierarchical tree is usually maintained throughout the network lifetime. Therefore, the construction of pipelined tree imposes negligible overhead on Pando's data dissemination.

Protocols. In our experiments, we compare Pando with Deluge [19] and Splash [7], of which we could find the source code. They are two state-of-the-art data dissemination protocols. Deluge is the first reliable data dissemination protocol developed in 2004. Many protocols have been devised in the last decade to improve its performance, such as MC-Deluge [53], Rateless Deluge [17] and MT-Deluge [14]. They all disseminate a data object in small pages hop by hop using a handshake mechanism and CSMA/CA-based multiple access. In 2013, Splash is designed to partially eliminate the contention overhead using constructive interference and pipelining. It is the latest data dissemination protocol with the best reported performance. For the other data dissemination protocols that we cannot find the source code, we compare Pando with them by literature studies.

Metrics. We evaluate the data dissemination protocols using four metrics: reliability, dissemination time, energy consumption and memory cost. Pando's dissemination time is measured from the start of protocol (e.g., transmission of the start command) to the termination of the source. Since Splash has no explicit termination time, we monitor

Table 1: Dissemination time (second) on Indriya[1].

Test #	Size (hops)	Pando	Splash	Splash w/o encoding
1	7	9.7	40.2	22.3
2	8	13.3	40.4	22.5
3	9	10.4	39.4	21.6
4	8	12.4	39.7	21.9
5	7	11.0	40.8	22.9
Average	8	11.4	40.1	22.3

Table 2: Dissemination time (second) on Flocklab.

Test #	Size (hops)	Pando	Splash	Splash w/o encoding	Deluge (2 kBytes)
1	6	5.7	36.4	18.4	481.4
2	5	4.3	36.3	18.3	471.7
3	9	7.7	36.4	18.4	481.4
4	6	6.4	36.3	18.3	481.4
5	5	4.4	36.5	18.6	466.9
Average	6	5.7	36.5	18.7	476.6

the traces of all nodes and calculate the dissemination time as the last node correctly receives the data object.

5.1 Performance comparison

Table 1 and Table 2 show the dissemination time of three protocols on Flocklab and Indriya respectively. For each experiment, we run Deluge, Splash and Pando separately. For each protocol, five tests are conducted with different locations of the source node. Each run lasts 30 minutes. For Deluge and Splash, the data dissemination ends when the last node correctly recovers the original data. For Pando, it ends when the source receives the feedback and stops transmitting. Before the data dissemination, Splash needs to first generate the XOR-encoded packets for the third round. Splash spends about 18 seconds to encode 500 XORed packets on TelosB with TI MSP430 microcontroller. In Table 1 and Table 2, we also present the dissemination time of Splash without encoding in which the time spent on encoding is not included in the dissemination time of Splash.

The experiment results reveal that all three protocols can achieve 100% network reliability. It takes Pando 11.4 seconds and 5.7 seconds to disseminate a file of 32 kBytes on Indriya and Flocklab respectively. Splash needs about 40.1 seconds and 36.5 seconds. Pando reduces the dissemination time of Splash by an average factor of 3.5 and 6.4 on Indriya and Flocklab, corresponding to 71.6% or 84% reduction respectively. Even not considering the encoding time in Splash, the reduction factor achieved by Pando over Splash is 2.0 and 3.3 on Indriya and Flocklab. Pando fully utilizes the parallel pipelines during the entire dissemination process and the Fountain-coding computation in Pando does not add any overhead on the dissemination time.

Deluge has two versions: TinyOS's DelugeT2 and Contiki's Deluge. We use Contiki's Deluge, because it is difficult to execute TinyOS's DelugeT2 on remote testbeds which requires to run some tools on the machine connected to the source node. In our experiments on Flocklab, Contiki's Deluge spends 476.6 seconds to disseminate 2 kBytes, corresponding to 7625.6 seconds for 32 kBytes. Pando reduces the dissemination time of Deluge by 1337.8×. Since the implementation of Deluge in Contiki is less efficient than DelugeT2, we calculate the reduction factor over Deluge based on the result of DelugeT2 (524 seconds) reported in [7]. The authors in [7] did the experiments on Indriya with 139 sensor nodes. At present, only 99 sensor nodes are available on Indriya. The dissemination time of DelugeT2 on current Indriya is approximated as 373.2 seconds (i.e., $524 * 99/139$ seconds). The reduction factor over DelugeT2 achieved by Splash and Pando is 9.3 and 32.7 respectively. Splash has improved the performance of Deluge significantly. Pando further improves the gain of Splash by 3.5×.

[1]We encountered several technical problems for running Contiki's Deluge on the remote testbed Indriya. The experiments of Contiki's Deluge succeeded on Flocklab and the results in Table 2 show that the dissemination time of Contiki's Deluge is orders of magnitude larger than Pando.

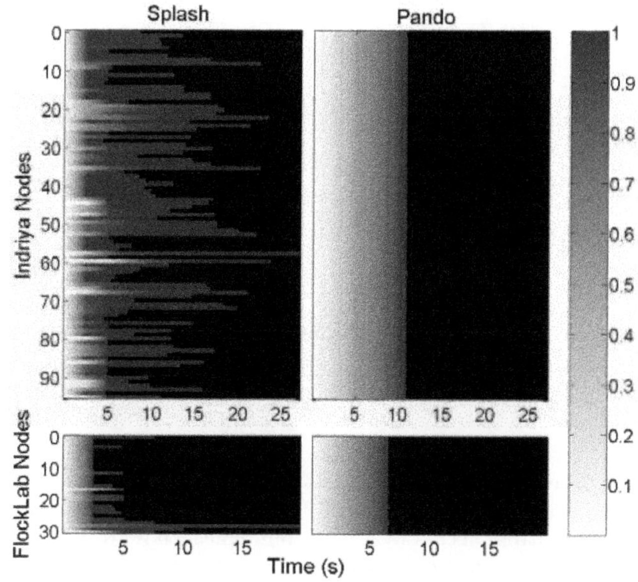

Figure 8: Reliability of individual nodes achieved by Pando and Splash on Indriya and Flocklab.

For the experiment results on Flocklab in Table 2, Pando produces higher improvement to the previous two protocols than the results on Indriya, since the sensor motes of Flocklab are more sparsely deployed and constructive interference performs better with small number of concurrent transmitters. Comparing Table 1 and Table 2, we also find that the gain of constructive interference and pipelining is huge. From Flocklab to Indriya, although the number of sensor nodes increases more than 2×, the dissemination time of both Pando and Splash only increases less than 1×. Based on constructive interference, the delivery of one packet from one layer of multiple nodes to another layer can be completed by just one transmission. With pipelining, the transmissions on different layers can occur simultaneously. Pando makes the gain of constructive interference and pipelining bloom in data dissemination, since it completes the entire data dissemination process over the fast parallel pipelines.

Reliability of individual node. Figure 8 demonstrates the reliability of individual nodes. The encoding overhead is not included in the dissemination time of Splash. The dissemination time of all protocols is when all nodes achieve 100% reliability. It is the time that the last node (the last row) turns to black. On Flocklab, Pando completes the data dissemination within 5.7 seconds when the source receives the aggregated acknowledgement from all nodes in the last page dissemination. Splash's data dissemination ends at

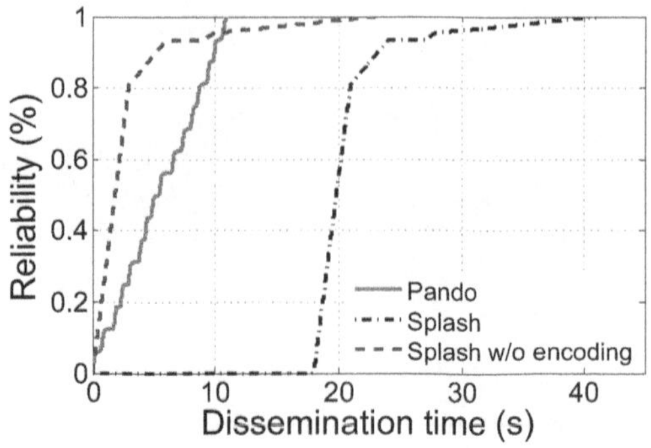

Figure 9: Network reliability progress on Indriya.

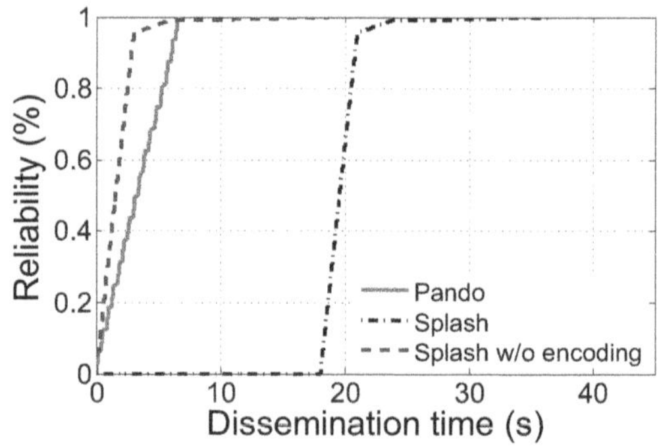

Figure 10: Network reliability progress on FlockLab.

18.7 seconds when the last node successfully receives the data object. The dissemination speed of Pando is 3.3× faster than Splash. Pando completely eliminates the contention-based multiple access overhead, but Splash has to disseminate the data object multiple times and rely on the local recovery to achieve 100%. Moreover, in Pando, all nodes present a similar progress rate. The packet reception rate is more uniformly distributed across all the nodes, since the network density and channel allocation are adapted for every packet transmission.

Reliability progress. Figure 9 and Figure 10 depict the progress of the average network reliability achieved by Splash and Pando on Indriya and Flocklab respectively. The experiment results reveal that Splash has high XOR encoding overhead and long tail problem. Pando completes the data dissemination even before the end of encoding of Splash. Even if we do not count the encoding time in the data dissemination time for Splash (i.e., Splash w/o encoding), it still has the long-tail problem. Pando eliminates the long-tail problem in pipelined data dissemination and reduces the dissemination time of Splash by 2.0× and 3.3× on Indriya and Flocklab respectively. Although the reliability progress rate of Pando is lower than Splash (i.e., Splash w/o encoding) in the first round due to the feedback collection in the page-based data dissemination, Pando achieves much shorter dissemination time than Splash and the network reliability of Pando progresses smoothly for the dissemination of each data page. Pando is able to asymptotically approach the optimal dissemination time and adapt to different network deployments and dynamic link conditions.

Energy consumption. The nodes in wireless sensor networks are typically working in the duty-cycled mode, which reduces their energy consumption by setting them in low-power state periodically. The dissemination in the duty-cycled mode is extremely time-consuming due to the long-preamble transmissions [11]. Therefore, current data dissemination protocols [7, 14, 17–19, 40] keep the hardware resources on sensor motes (e.g., microcontroller and radio) in active state during the data dissemination process. During the dissemination, the power consumption of Pando is the same as the previous protocols, since all of them keep the nodes in active mode. Therefore, compared with the previous protocols, benefitting from a shorter dissemination time, Pando reduces the energy consumption of individual nodes by the same reduction factor as the dissemination time.

The Fountain coding in Pando is performed during the idle intervals of the microcontroller and does not impose any extra energy consumption. The default design of Splash or the other data dissemination protocols do not exploit the idle interval of the microcontroller or set the microcontroller to a power-saving mode during such idle intervals. Even if we enable Splash to sleep during the idle intervals of the microcontroller, the saving energy is very limited, because the energy consumption of sensor motes is dominated by the transceiver and the transceiver is transmitting or receiving packets during the whole data dissemination process. For example, the power consumption of the transceiver on TelosB is 69 mW (23mA*3V), which is much larger than the power consumption of the microcontroller, i.e., 5.4 mW (1.8mA*3V). Using the experiment traces in the above experiments, if we set the microcontroller to a power-saving mode (e.g., 0.002mA) during the idle intervals for Splash, only 5.2% energy could be saved. It is small, compared with the energy saving gain of Pando over Splash (69.5%).

Memory cost. Pando uses 6.24 kBytes of RAM, 32 kBytes of data flash memory, and 31.49 kBytes of ROM (program flash memory). TelosB is composed of 10 kBytes of RAM, 1 MBytes of data flash memory, and 48 kBytes of ROM. Pando uses about 2.24 kBytes of RAM to store the received packets of current page. Without temporarily storing of encoded packets in the flash memory, Pando minimizes the data memory cost and significantly reduces the number of data flash memory access. Splash has to store the received packets in the data flash memory and read them into RAM for post-processing after the 3 dissemination rounds.

Comparison with other protocols. We compare Pando with other data dissemination protocols by referring to their performance reported in their papers [8, 9, 14, 17, 22, 53]. All the previous protocols compare their performance with Deluge [19], the first reliable data dissemination protocol for wireless sensor networks. Based on the result reported in the papers of these protocols (i.e., reduction factor of dissemination time over Deluge), we can calculate the relative gain of Pando over other existing protocols.

Table 3 tabulates the reduction factor of dissemination time produced by the previous data dissemination protocols and Pando over Deluge. The protocols developed before Splash can only provide a reduction factor around 1.6 (maximum 2.4) over Deluge, because they all are based on the contention-based multiple access. Pando and Splash are orders of magnitude faster than Deluge, since they are based on constructive interference and pipelining. By fully exploiting the fast and parallel pipelines as well as the packet-level adaptation of network density and channel diversity, Pando asymptotically approaches the network capacity and reduces the dissemination time of Splash by more than 3.5×.

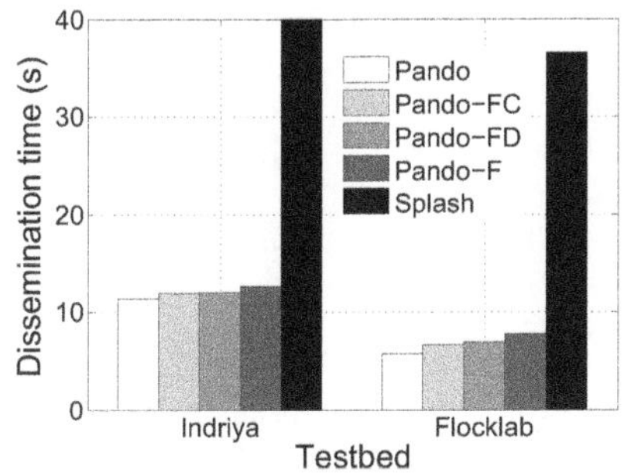

Figure 11: Contribution of individual techniques in Pando.

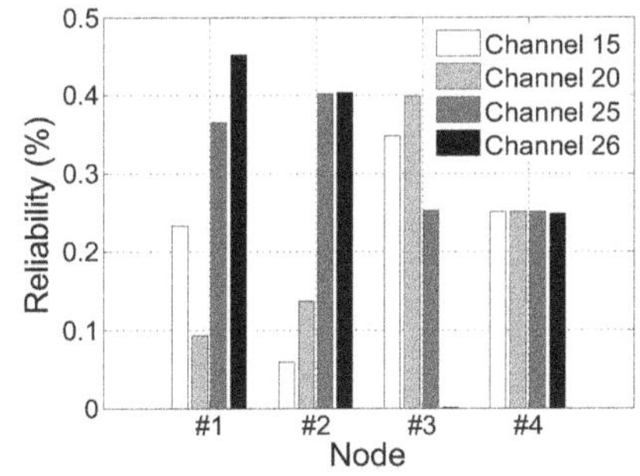

Figure 12: Channel quality experienced by four nodes of Indriya.

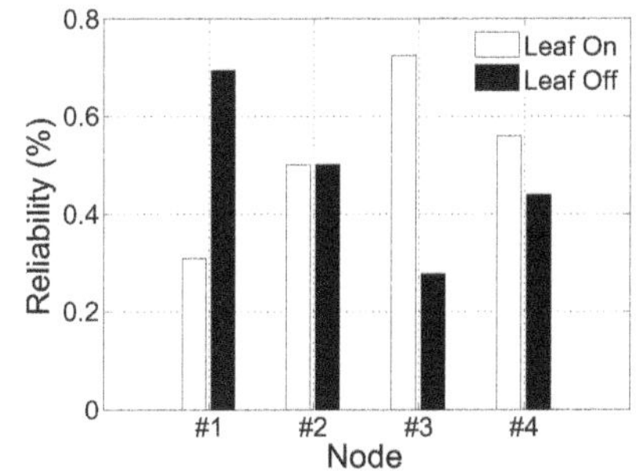

Figure 13: Network density experienced by four nodes of Indriya.

Table 3: Reduction factor of dissemination time over Deluge achieved by the existing data dissemination protocols in wireless sensor networks.

Protocols	Number of nodes	Data size (KB)	Reduction factor
MNP [22](2005)	100	5	1.21
MC-Deluge [53](2005)	25	24.3	1.60
Rateless Deluge [17](2008)	20	0.7	1.47
ReXOR [8](2011)	16	4	1.53
ECD [9](2011)	25	10	1.44
MT-Deluge [14](2011)	20	0.7	2.42
SYREN [1](2013)	21	0.5	1.6
Splash [7](2013)	139	32	9.3
Pando	99	32	32.7

5.2 Contribution of individual techniques

To further analyze the gain of Pando, we execute Pando in several versions, in which the individual techniques of Pando are enabled separately. The results are shown in Figure 11. In Pando-F, the packet-level adaptation of both network density and channel diversity is disabled. The performance gain of Pando-F mainly comes from the Fountain coding. In Pando-FC, besides Fountain coding, we also enable the packet-level adaptation of channel diversity. Similarly, in Pando-FD, the packet-level adaptation of network density is enabled. Pando in Figure 11 represents the full version of Pando with all techniques.

Fountain codes. According to Figure 11, Pando-F can reduce the dissemination time of Splash by 3.2× and 4.7× on Indriya and Flocklab respectively. The fundamental gain of Pando comes from the integration of Fountain codes with the pipelined data dissemination. To tailor LT coding into the highly-synchronized communication on the resource constrained sensor motes, we disseminate the data object in small pages, which introduce some overhead due to the feedback collection for each page. In our current implementation, we adopt a page size of 32 packets. The gain of Pando can be further improved by enlarging the page size with more powerful hardware.

Packet-level adaptation of channel diversity. By comparing the results of Pando-FC with Splash in Figure 11, we find that Pando with Fountain codes and packet-level adaptation of channel diversity can improve the reduction factor of dissemination time over Splash to 3.4 and 5.5 on Indriya and Flocklab respectively. Besides the improvement achieved by Fountain coding, the packet-level adaptation of channel diversity can further enhance the performance of Pando-F by 5.6% and 14.3% on Indriya and Flocklab.

Figure 12 shows the contribution of each channel to the reliability of four different nodes on Indriya. Different channels have different performance at different locations. Channel 26 contributes ignorable increase of reliability at the location of node 3. It may be caused by the interference from the other nodes or devices. Figure 12 fully demonstrates the diverse performance of the four available channels at different nodes, and suggests the necessity of packet-level channel diversity. By changing the channel allocation at packet-level, every node in the network experiences the four channels equally and circularly. The packet reception becomes more uniform across different nodes. Therefore, Pando maximizes the performance of Fountain codes in data dissemination, as it does not have to spend much time to deliver some packets to few poorly-performing nodes.

Packet-level adaptation of network density. As shown in Figure 11, the packet-level adaptation of network density of Pando-FD reduces the dissemination time of Pando-F by 4.8% and 10.4% respectively on Indriya and Flocklab. Figure 13 presents the contributions of two different network densities (determined by whether the leaf nodes transmit) for four different nodes of Indriya. The performance of concurrent transmissions is related to the node locations. Some nodes work well when the neighboring leaf nodes participate in the concurrent transmissions; the others may benefit more for a small number of concurrent transmitters. With packet-level adaptation of network density, Pando makes the reception performance of individual nodes more uniformly distributed across the network.

Packet-level adaptation of channel diversity and network density. According to the experiment results in Figure 11, Pando reduces the dissemination time of Pando-F by 9.5% and 26.0% on Indriya and Flocklab respectively. The dissemination time of Pando is 5.7 seconds on Flocklab and the dissemination time of Pando-F is 7.7 seconds. Such significant improvement demonstrates that the packet-level adaptation of channel diversity and network density is necessary for the Fountain-enabled data dissemination of constructive interference and pipelining.

Silence-based feedback. For the dissemination of one page, Pando needs an average of 276.4 ms and 135.0 ms to deliver the feedback information from the last successful node to the source on Indriya and Flocklab respectively. The number of consecutive silent slots M is set to 3 on Indriya, since the nodes of Indriya are more densely deployed and more packet losses occur. M is set to 2 on Flocklab for more efficient feedback collection. On both testbeds, there are no

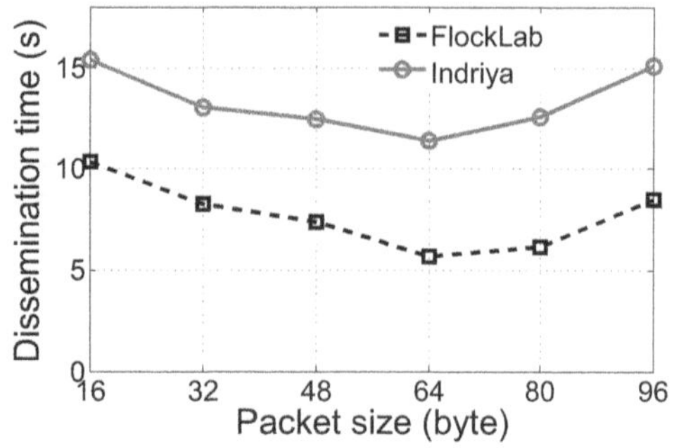

Figure 14: Performance for different payload sizes.

nodes that mistakenly stop their dissemination because of false channel silence. For the data object of 32 kBytes, the feedback delivery in Pando takes 4.4 seconds and 2.2 seconds in total on Indriya and Flocklab respectively. Although this amount of time is not directly used for disseminating the data packets, it is necessary to start the dissemination of a new data page and terminate the whole dissemination process. Even including the feedback time, Pando's dissemination time is still less than Splash by 28.7 seconds and 30.8 seconds on Indriya and Flocklab respectively.

In our experiments, we observe that the dynamic adaption of channel silence threshold $RSSI_{threshold}$ can well prevent the false negative of silence detection. The $RSSI_{threshold}$ could be from -91 dBm to -78 dBm for different nodes. For the node with a threshold of -78 dBm, it can detect a silence channel even the noise or interference is as large as -78 dBm. For the node with a threshold of -91 dBm, the noise and interference at its location are small, and it can successfully receive a packet with a signal of -89 dBm.

5.3 Effect of packet size

Figure 14 examines the performance of Pando with different packet sizes. The best performance of Pando comes with a moderate size of data packet, i.e., 64 bytes. When the packet size is small, the preamble of the physical and MAC layer introduces high percentage of overhead and occupies a large portion of the dissemination time. When the packet size is large, the performance of constructive interference decreases. From Figure 14, we see that the optimal packet size is 64 bytes for both testbeds. Although the performance of Pando depends on the best setting of packet size, the optimal setting does not change across testbeds with different densities and scales.

6. RELATED WORK

In-field deployments of wireless sensor networks normally require remotely wireless reprogramming [23, 26, 27, 35, 41, 46]. Content dissemination is also needed in other wireless networks, like vehicular networks [25] and social networks [29]. A variety of data dissemination protocols have been developed based on different techniques in the last decade. The best next-hop forwarder is selected by investigating its program version [19, 28], the information of its neighbors [22] or its link quality [9]. The frequency of advertisement messages in Deluge is adjusted according to the network density [3]. The link correlation [1, 47, 48, 54] and opportunistic forwarding [16] are considered in flooding. The multi-channel scheme is used to improve the spatial reuse [30]. A backbone subnetwork is built to deliver data to the other nodes based on a minimum connected dominating set [36,49]. The delay constraint is taken into account in [20]. Selective dissemination is studied in [37, 42]. A data-centric data dissemination scheme is proposed in [4]. The above protocols disseminate data hop by hop using CSMA/CA or TDMA, which limits the spatial reuse and imposes heavy overhead of multiple access.

The multiple access overhead is addressed by capture effect for flooding in wireless multi-hop networks [24,32,44,51]. However, the performance of capture effect decreases when many nodes are transmitting simultaneously [32]. Many practical works, e.g., A-MAC [11], Glossy [13] and LWB [12], experimentally show that the reliability of constructive interference is high. However, the payload size of the transmitted packets in these works is small (i.e., 8 or 15 bytes). For the dissemination of a large data object, long payload size (e.g., 64 bytes) should be used. According to the experiments in [7], also confirmed by our experiments, constructive interference becomes unreliable for large packet size. Meanwhile, PIP [38] constructs a fast data delivery pipeline using multiple channels. Splash [7] partially eliminates the multiple access overhead in data dissemination by combining constructive interference and pipelining.

Fountain codes [34] have been widely used to improve the broadcasting efficiency. The light-weight fountain transmission is first realized by LT codes [33]. SYNAPSE++ [40] leverages LT codes to enhance the broadcasting efficiency of Deluge [19] in each hop. DLT [10] use LT codes to improve the networking performance of wireless sensors. Network coding schemes, like random linear codes and XOR coding, are also adopted to improve the single-hop broadcasting efficiency in wireless sensor networks [8, 17, 18]. The above protocols based on Fountain codes or network coding, however, are designed for single-hop transmissions with explicit acknowledgement.

7. CONCLUSION

This paper presents *Pando*, a completely contention-free data dissemination protocol for wireless sensor networks. By integrating Fountain codes with constructive interference and pipelining, Pando is able to continuously disseminate rateless encoded packets over the parallel pipelines. Three techniques, including radio-driven encoding and decoding, silence-based feedback scheme and packet-level adaptation of network density and channel diversity, are developed to transform Pando into a practical system, which asymptotically approaches the network capacity. Experiment results demonstrate that Pando can provide 100% reliability and significantly outperform the previous data dissemination protocols in dissemination time and energy consumption.

8. ACKNOWLEDGMENTS

We thank our shepherd Prof. Silvia Santini and the anonymous reviewers for their valuable suggestions and feedback. We also thank the kind help and support offered by the Indriya testbed team led by Prof. Mun Choon Chan from NUS and the Flocklab testbed team led by Dr. Jan Beutel and Prof. Lothar Thiele from ETH Zurich. This work is supported by Singapore MOE AcRF Tier 2 MOE2012-T2-1-070 and NTU Nanyang Assistant Professorship (NAP) grant M4080738.020.

9. REFERENCES

[1] S. Alam, S. Sultana, Y. C. Hu, and S. Fahmy. SYREN: Synergistic link correlation-aware and network coding-based dissemination in wireless sensor networks. In *IEEE MASCOTS*, pages 485–494, 2013.

[2] A. Boulis, C.-C. Han, and M. B. Srivastava. Design and implementation of a framework for efficient and programmable sensor networks. In *ACM MobiSys*, pages 187–200, 2003.

[3] S. Cho, H. Shin, S. Han, H. Cha, and R. Ha. Density-adaptive network reprogramming protocol for wireless sensor networks. *Wireless Communications and Mobile Computing*, 10(6):857–874, 2010.

[4] M. Ditzel and K. Langendoen. D3: Data-centric data dissemination in wireless sensor networks. In *The European Conference on Wireless Technology*, pages 185–188, 2005.

[5] M. Doddavenkatappa and M. C. Chan. P3: a practical packet pipeline using synchronous transmissions for wireless sensor networks. In *ACM/IEEE IPSN*, pages 203–214, 2014.

[6] M. Doddavenkatappa, M. C. Chan, and A. L. Ananda. Indriya: A low-cost, 3d wireless sensor network testbed. In *TRIDENTCOM*, 2011.

[7] M. Doddavenkatappa, M. C. Chan, and B. Leong. Splash: Fast data dissemination with constructive interference in wireless sensor networks. In *USENIX NSDI*, pages 269–282, 2013.

[8] W. Dong, C. Chen, X. Liu, J. Bu, and Y. Gao. A lightweight and density-aware reprogramming protocol for wireless sensor networks. *IEEE Transactions on Mobile Computing*, pages 1403–1415, 2011.

[9] W. Dong, Y. Liu, C. Wang, X. Liu, C. Chen, and J. Bu. Link quality aware code dissemination in wireless sensor networks. In *IEEE ICNP*, pages 89–98, 2011.

[10] W. Du, Z. Li, J. C. Liando, and M. Li. From rateless to distanceless: Enabling sparse sensor network deployment in large areas. In *ACM SenSys*, pages 134–147, 2014.

[11] P. Dutta, S. Dawson-Haggerty, Y. Chen, C.-J. M. Liang, and A. Terzis. Design and evaluation of a versatile and efficient receiver-initiated link layer for low-power wireless. In *ACM SenSys*, pages 1–14, 2010.

[12] F. Ferrari, M. Zimmerling, L. Mottola, and L. Thiele. Low-power wireless bus. In *ACM SenSys*, pages 1–14, 2012.

[13] F. Ferrari, M. Zimmerling, L. Thiele, and O. Saukh. Efficient network flooding and time synchronization with glossy. In *ACM/IEEE IPSN*, pages 73–84, 2011.

[14] Y. Gao, J. Bu, W. Dong, C. Chen, L. Rao, and X. Liu. Exploiting concurrency for efficient dissemination in wireless sensor networks. *IEEE Transactions on Parallel and Distributed Systems*, pages 691–700, 2013.

[15] O. Gnawali, R. Fonseca, K. Jamieson, D. Moss, and P. Levis. Collection tree protocol. In *ACM SenSys*, pages 1–14, 2009.

[16] S. Guo, Y. Gu, B. Jiang, and T. He. Opportunistic flooding in low-duty-cycle wireless sensor networks with unreliable links. In *ACM MobiCom*, pages 133–144, 2009.

[17] A. Hagedorn, D. Starobinski, and A. Trachtenberg. Rateless Deluge: Over-the-air programming of wireless sensor networks using random linear codes. In *ACM/IEEE IPSN*, 2008.

[18] I.-H. Hou, Y.-E. Tsai, T. F. Abdelzaher, and I. Gupta. AdapCode: Adaptive network coding for code updates in wireless sensor networks. In *IEEE INFOCOM*, 2008.

[19] J. W. Hui and D. Culler. The dynamic behavior of a data dissemination protocol for network programming at scale. In *ACM Sensys*, pages 81–94, 2004.

[20] H. S. Kim, T. F. Abdelzaher, and W. H. Kwon. Dynamic delay-constrained minimum-energy dissemination in wireless sensor networks. *ACM Transactions on Embedded Computing Systems*, 4(3):679–706, 2005.

[21] J. Ko, J. Eriksson, N. Tsiftes, S. Dawson-Haggerty, J.-P. Vasseur, M. Durvy, A. Terzis, A. Dunkels, and D. Culler. Industry: beyond interoperability: pushing the performance of sensor network ip stacks. In *ACM SenSys*, pages 1–11, 2011.

[22] S. S. Kulkarni and L. Wang. MNP: Multihop network reprogramming service for sensor networks. In *IEEE ICDCS*, pages 7–16, 2005.

[23] T.-t. T. Lai, Y.-h. T. Chen, H.-h. Chu, and P. Huang. Pipeprobe: mapping hidden water pipelines. In *ACM SenSys*, pages 375–376, 2009.

[24] O. Landsiedel, F. Ferrari, and M. Zimmerling. Chaos: Versatile and efficient all-to-all data sharing and in-network processing at scale. In *ACM SenSys*, pages 1:1–1:14, 2013.

[25] I. Leontiadis, P. Costa, and C. Mascolo. Persistent content-based information dissemination in hybrid vehicular networks. In *IEEE PerCom*, pages 1–10, 2009.

[26] I. Leontiadis, C. Efstratiou, C. Mascolo, and J. Crowcroft. Senshare: Transforming sensor networks into multi-application sensing infrastructures. In *EWSN*, pages 65–81, 2012.

[27] P. Levis, D. Gay, and D. Culler. Active sensor networks. In *USENIX NSDI*, pages 343–356, 2005.

[28] P. Levis, N. Patel, D. Culler, and S. Shenker. Trickle: A self regulating algorithm for code propagation and maintenance in wireless sensor networks. In *USENIX NSDI*, pages 15–28, 2004.

[29] S. Li, L. Su, Y. Suleimenov, H. Liu, T. Abdelzaher, and G. Chen. Centaur: Dynamic message dissemination over online social networks. In *ICCCN*, pages 1–8, 2014.

[30] C.-J. M. Liang, R. Musăloiu-e, and A. Terzis. Typhoon: A reliable data dissemination protocol for wireless sensor networks. In *EWSN*, pages 268–285. Springer, 2008.

[31] R. Lim, F. Ferrari, M. Zimmerling, C. Walser, P. Sommer, and J. Beutel. Flocklab: A testbed for distributed, synchronized tracing and profiling of wireless embedded systems. In *ACM/IEEE IPSN*, pages 153–166, 2013.

[32] J. Lu and K. Whitehouse. Flash flooding: Exploiting the capture effect for rapid flooding in wireless sensor networks. In *IEEE INFOCOM*, pages 2491–2499, 2009.

[33] M. Luby. LT codes. In *IEEE FOCS*, pages 271–280, 2002.

[34] D. J. MacKay. Fountain codes. *IEE Proceedings-Communications*, pages 1062–1068, 2005.
[35] L. Mottola, G. P. Picco, M. Ceriotti, S. Gună, and A. L. Murphy. Not all wireless sensor networks are created equal: A comparative study on tunnels. *ACM Transactions on Sensor Networks*, 7(2):1–33, 2010.
[36] V. Naik, A. Arora, P. Sinha, and H. Zhang. Sprinkler: A reliable and energy efficient data dissemination service for wireless embedded devices. In *IEEE RTSS*, pages 777–789, 2005.
[37] B. Pásztor, L. Mottola, C. Mascolo, G. P. Picco, S. Ellwood, and D. Macdonald. Selective reprogramming of mobile sensor networks through social community detection. In *EWSN*, pages 178–193, 2010.
[38] B. Raman, K. Chebrolu, S. Bijwe, and V. Gabale. PIP: A connection-oriented, multi-hop, multi-channel tdma-based mac for high throughput bulk transfer. In *ACM Sensys*, pages 15–28, 2010.
[39] N. Reijers and K. Langendoen. Efficient code distribution in wireless sensor networks. In *ACM WSNA*, pages 60–67, 2003.
[40] M. Rossi, N. Bui, G. Zanca, L. Stabellini, R. Crepaldi, and M. Zorzi. SYNAPSE++: code dissemination in wireless sensor networks using fountain codes. *IEEE Transactions on Mobile Computing*, pages 1749–1765, 2010.
[41] S. Santini, B. Ostermaier, and A. Vitaletti. First experiences using wireless sensor networks for noise pollution monitoring. In *Proceedings of ACM REALWSN*, pages 61–65, 2008.
[42] M. Sathiamoorthy, K. R. Moghadam, B. Krishnamachari, and F. Bai. Helper node allocation strategies for content dissemination in intermittently connected mobile networks. In *IEEE SECON*, pages 55–63, 2014.
[43] B. Sirkeci-Mergen, A. Scaglione, and G. Mergen. Asymptotic analysis of multistage cooperative broadcast in wireless networks. *IEEE Transactions on Information Theory*, pages 2531–2550, 2006.
[44] D. Son, B. Krishnamachari, and J. Heidemann. Experimental study of concurrent transmission in wireless sensor networks. In *ACM SenSys*, pages 237–250, 2006.
[45] K. Srinivasan, M. Jain, J. I. Choi, T. Azim, E. S. Kim, P. Levis, and B. Krishnamachari. The κ factor: Inferring protocol performance using inter-link reception correlation. In *ACM MobiCom*, pages 317–328, 2010.
[46] I. Stoianov, L. Nachman, S. Madden, T. Tokmouline, and M. Csail. PIPENET: A wireless sensor network for pipeline monitoring. In *ACM/IEEE IPSN*, pages 264–273, 2007.
[47] T. Zhu, Z. Zhong, T. He and Z.-L. Zhang. Exploring link correlation for efficient flooding in wireless sensor networks. In *USENIX NSDI*, 2010.
[48] S. Wang, S. M. Kim, Y. Liu, G. Tan, and T. He. CorLayer: a transparent link correlation layer for energy efficient broadcast. In *ACM MobiCom*, pages 51–62, 2013.
[49] S. Wang, G. Tan, Y. Liu, H. Jiang, and T. He. Coding opportunity aware backbone metrics for broadcast in wireless networks. *IEEE Transactions on Parallel and Distributed Systems*, 25(8):1999–2009, 2014.
[50] Y. Wang, Y. He, X. Mao, Y. Liu, and X.-Y. Li. Exploiting constructive interference for scalable flooding in wireless networks. *IEEE/ACM Transactions on Networking*, pages 1880–1889, 2013.
[51] K. Whitehouse, A. Woo, F. Jiang, J. Polastre, and D. Culler. Exploiting the capture effect for collision detection and recovery. In *IEEE EmNetS-II*, pages 45–52, 2005.
[52] Y. Wu, J. Stankovic, T. He, S. Lin, et al. Realistic and efficient multi-channel communications in wireless sensor networks. In *INFOCOM*, 2008.
[53] W. Xiao and D. Starobinski. Poster abstract: Exploiting multi-channel diversity to speed up over-the-air programming of wireless sensor networks. In *ACM SenSys*, pages 292–293. ACM, 2005.
[54] Z. Zhao, W. Dong, J. Bu, Y. Gu, and C. Chen. Link correlation aware data dissemination in wireless sensor networks. *IEEE Transactions on Industrial Electronics*, 2015.

Poster Abstract: Robust and Efficient Sensor-assisted Face Recognition System on Smart Glass

Weitao Xu†, Yiran Shen‡, Neil Bergmann†, Wen Hu†‡
† School of Information Technology and Electrical Engineering, University of Queensland, Australia
‡ Singapore-MIT Alliance for Research and Technology,Singapore
†‡ School of Computer Science and Engineering, University of New South Wales, Australia
{w.xu3,n.bergmann}@uq.edu.edu†
{yiran}@smart.mit.edu‡
{wen.hu}@unsw.edu.au†‡

ABSTRACT

Face recognition is one of the most popular research problems on various platforms. New research issues arise when it comes to resource constrained devices, such as smart glasses, due to the overwhelming computation and energy requirements of the accurate face recognition methods. In this paper, we have prototyped a robust and efficient sensor-assisted face recognition system on smart glasses by exploring the power of multimodal sensors including the camera and Inertial Measurement Unit (IMU) sensors. Evaluation shows that the prototyped system is up to 10% more accurate than the state-of-the-art face recognition methods while its computational cost is in the same order as an efficient benchmark method (e.g., Eigenface).

Categories and Subject Descriptors

H.4 [**Information Systems Applications**]: Miscellaneous

General Terms

Algorithms, Design, Experimentation, Performance

Keywords

Face recognition; Smart glass; Sparse representation

1. INTRODUCTION

Face recognition has emerged as an active research area with numerous applications over the past decades. The possibility of using wearable devices to help people recognize people is becoming the focus of research with the advent of smart glasses such as Google Glass. In this work, we aim to develop a robust and efficient *in-situ* face recognition system on smartglasses. Face recognition has been well researched in the computer vision community, yet there remains much work to be done on mobile devices. As discussed in [2], most of the advanced face recognition methods fail on mobile devices because of the tension between high computation requirements and resource constraints.

To overcome the limitations and facilitate the useful information provided by smart glasses, this work prototypes a novel sensor-assisted face recognition system which runs locally on smart glasses by exploiting both the camera and sensors on smart glasses to improve the recognition accuracy and reduce the energy consumption. The system recognizes the identities based on face image sequences collected from different view angles and utilizes the IMU sensors to improve its efficiency. Fig. 1 provides a brief overview of the prototyped system, which is simple and intuitive.

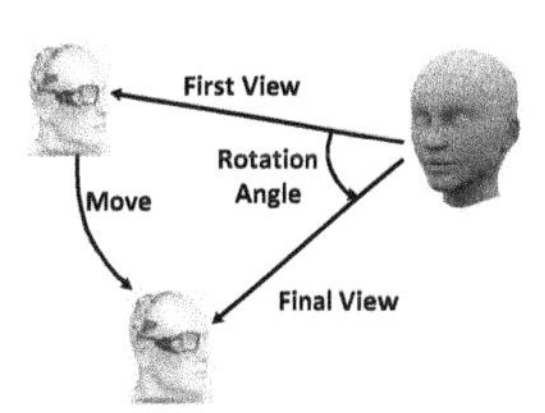

Figure 1: System Overview

2. SYSTEM ARCHITECTURE

The system starts capturing face images when the user starts to take a few steps around the subject. During movement, The angle information of the face images are estimated by the IMU sensors embedded on the smart glasses. The images and the associated angle labels are recorded and stored for further processing. After user stops recording face images, the optimal subset of the frames is chosen via the sampling optimization algorithm by exploring the information from multimodal sensors. Finally, the MVSRC is applied on the samples to obtain the classification result.

2.1 MVSRC

We propose a novel face recognition algorithm called Multiview Sparse Representation based Classification (MVSRC) by combining the mobile nature of smartglasses. The key assumption behind MVSRC is that face images obtained from different view angles tend to have a high agreement on the sparse representations because each of the face images from

SenSys'15, November 01-04, 2015, Seoul, Republic of Korea
ACM 978-1-4503-3631-4/15/11.
DOI: http://dx.doi.org/10.1145/2809695.2817873 .

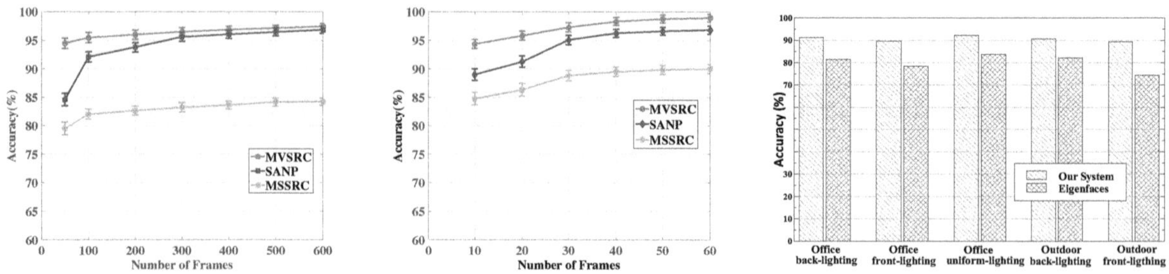

(a) MVSRC: Honda/UCSD dataset (b) MVSRC: Private dataset (c) User Study

Figure 2: Evaluation results

the same person should be linearly represented by the same class in the dictionary. Suppose we have acquired a set of M feasible face images from the camera. We can obtain a set of estimated coefficients vectors $\hat{X} = \{\hat{x}_1, \hat{x}_2, ..., \hat{x}_M\}$ by solving the ℓ_1 optimization problem as in [2]. The new sparse representation model can be expressed as:

$$\hat{x}_{sum} = \sum_{m=1}^{M} \alpha_m \hat{x}_m \quad (1)$$

where α_m is the weight assigned to $\hat{x}_m$ based on the *Sparsity Concentration Index* (SCI) defined as:

$$SCI(\hat{x}_m) = \frac{K \cdot max_j \|\delta_j(\hat{x}_m)\|_1 / \|\hat{x}_m\|_1 - 1}{K - 1} \in [0, 1] \quad (2)$$

The new model exploits the sparsity information of the multi-view face images.

2.2 Optimized Sampling Strategy

Considering the computation and energy consumption issues of the smart glasses, applying MVSRC straightforwardly on all of the M face images obtained is not a desirable choice because it requires M ℓ_1 optimizations. Moreover, a large amount of redundant information exists among the adjacent frames as the face images with similar view angles contain large overlaps. To find the best sampling strategy, we propose to optimize the downsampling on the face images set with a predefined energy budget. The energy budget E_b is preset and we aim to find the optimal subset Ω_s of the face images set I to achieve the highest recognition accuracy A_c by solving the optimization problem below:

$$\Omega_s = \arg\max_{\Omega} A_c \quad \text{s.t. } E_{total} \leq E_b, \Omega \subseteq I \quad (3)$$

where Ω is one of the arbitrary subsets of I and E_{total} is the total energy consumption for face recognition. To solve Eq 3, we propose to use IMU sensors to estimate the angles of multi-view face images and then find Ω_s by a novel Support Vector Regression (SVR) model.

3. EVALUATION

In the first experiment, we compare MVSRC with two state-of-the-art face recognition methods, namely, SANP and MSSRC on two face datasets: the Honda/UCSD video dataset [1] and a private dataset collected by smartglass. In this experiment, we vary the maximum number of images that are used to perform classification and compute the accuracy of different methods. From the results in Fig. 2, we can see that MVSRC achieves the best recognition accuracy compared with SANP and MSSRC. The performance gap between MVSRC and SANP is up to 10% and 5% on the two datasets respectively.

The prototype of the system is implemented on Vuzix M100 Smart Glass and the programming language is JAVA, we use JNI to wrap C++ libraries. We recruited 15 volunteers (5 users and 10 subjects) for user study and evaluate the performance of the prototype for recognizing identities in several real-world environments. In this experiment, each subject has 30 face images for training. For comparison purpose, we also implement the OpenCV face recognition methods on the smart glass. We evaluate the recognition accuracy and resource consumption of our prototype and OpenCV methods (Eigenfaces).

As we can see in Fig. 2(c), our prototyped system is very stable under different lighting conditions. It outperforms Eigenfaces significantly in every experimental category and is up to 10% more accurate than Eigenfaces. From the system overhead shown in Tab. 1, we find that the resource consumption of the system is comparable to Eigenfaces.

Table 1: System overhead

Statistic	Our System	Eigenfaces
Computation Time	516-582ms	247-331ms
Energy Consumption	506-535mJ	316-410mJ
Memory Usage	55-64MB	30-40 MB

4. CONCLUSION

In this paper, we explore the capability of smartglasses and propose a novel face recognition system which utilizes the power of multimodal sensors. Evaluations demonstrate that our system is both accurate and efficient compared to the state-of-the-arts.

5. REFERENCES

[1] K.-C. Lee, J. Ho, M.-H. Yang, and D. Kriegman. Video-based face recognition using probabilistic appearance manifolds. In *CVPR*, pages I–313. IEEE, 2003.

[2] Y. Shen, W. Hu, M. Yang, B. Wei, S. Lucey, and C. T. Chou. Face recognition on smartphones via optimised sparse representation classification. In *IPSN '14*, pages 237–248. IEEE Press, 2014.

Shonabondhu: A Sensing Middleware to Handle Flash Flood

Nova Ahmed
ECE
North South University
Dhaka, Bangladesh
nova.ahmed@northsouth.edu

Mahmudur Rahman Khan
ECE
North South University
Dhaka, Bangladesh

Minhaz Ahmed Syrus
ECE
North South University
Dhaka, Bangladesh

ABSTRACT
We present a distributed custom developed low cost sensing middleware named Shonabondhu that is able to handle flash flood in developing countries like Bangladesh.

Categories and Subject Descriptors
C.2.4 [**Distributed Systems**]:Distributed Applications.

General Terms
Performance, Design, Experimentation.

Keywords
Flash Flood, Middleware, Sensor based System, Distributed Sensor Middleware, Solution for Natural Disaster in Bangladesh

1. INTRODUCTION
I could save my cattle if I had just half an hour of time.

All the fisheries industry is gone due to flash flood.

I have nothing!

These are not excerpts from newspaper articles; these are real world scenario in a village of Bangladesh where flash flood is one of the most severe problems. Flash Flood occurs when the river water level rises rapidly within a short period of time (often, within 2 hours water level can rise as high as few meters) mainly caused by sudden heavy rainfall in locality. It is a major problem in many different countries like Bangladesh, India, China, Nepal, Malaysia, Philippines and many other countries [1, 2, 3].The problem is challenging from computing perspective where the region based water level measurement is not the only indicator to detect an eminent flood – it depends on the physically distributed river network along with weather and seasonal information requiring a distributed system that is able to learn and act in real time.

There have been an array of research studies that consider water level sensing, monitoring and /or prediction and offer valid system support for deployment of such system. E. A. Bashar et al. [4] have worked on water monitoring system deployed at Honduras, a river in Massachusetts using a predictive sensor environment; Ivan Stonianov et al. [5] used sensor network to monitor Boston Sewer Commission Data, Jirapon Sunkpho et al. [6] uses real time flood monitoring system deployed at Thammarat a Southern province of Thailand; Danny Hughes et al. [7] uses sensor based system to study flood monitoring system on the River Ribble in North West England. The major difference lies in the problem scopes. In the cases of previously conducted studies – a single river and river bank is studied. Our water monitoring system must include various locations that are geographically distant..

We have proposed a middleware system named Shonabondhu which contributes to real time flood information handling and dissemination along with long term data analysis and prediction. It consists of servers which are assigned a gradient information as a function of its current state in terms of local water level, rainfall along with historical information for that region regarding that particular time of year called gradient servers.

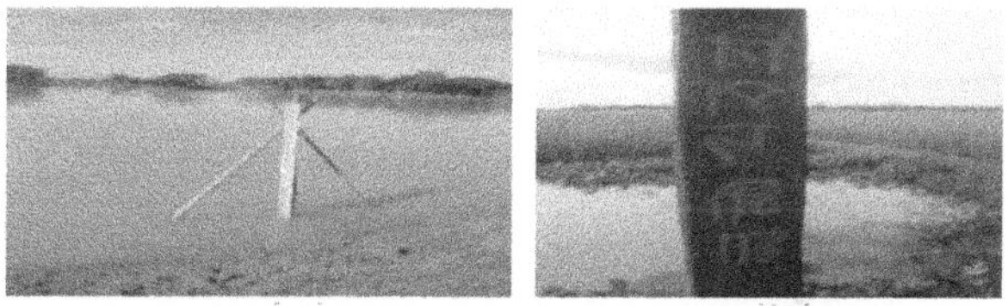

Figure 1. Manual Flood Water Measurement

2. Flash Flood
Flash flood refers to a phenomenon where water level raises rapidly within a short period of time caused by sudden incident of heavy rainfall-a major problem in many countries such as India, China, Nepal, Malaysia, Philippines and many other countries [2,7]. We have focused our attention to flash flood problem in Bangladesh. The current water monitoring system is primitive and manual where the water level is periodically checked by people against an installed water level measurement stick as can be seen in Figure 1.The person in charge makes a phone call to the central office which is logged by an office on a three hour interval. Often water level rises are not recorded as it rises up during the night when water level is not measured.

3. ARCHITECTURE IMPLEMENTATION
Shonabondhu System works in three different planes as can be seen in the schematic presented in Figure 2 – the first plane consist of Server/Servers residing in Cloud and is responsible for long term data forecasting which impacts strategic planning and making long term decisions regarding flood and flood affected areas; the second plane consists of the distributed local servers known as Gradient Servers which use real time decision making and forecasting at local points based on its gradient information

SenSys'15, November 1–4, 2015, Seoul, South Korea.
ACM 978-1-4503-3631-4/15/11.
DOI: http://dx.doi.org/10.1145/2809695.2817874

calculated by local water level, rainfall level, time and expected water level; the third plane is responsible for real time monitoring and consists of water level sensors deployed at various localities.

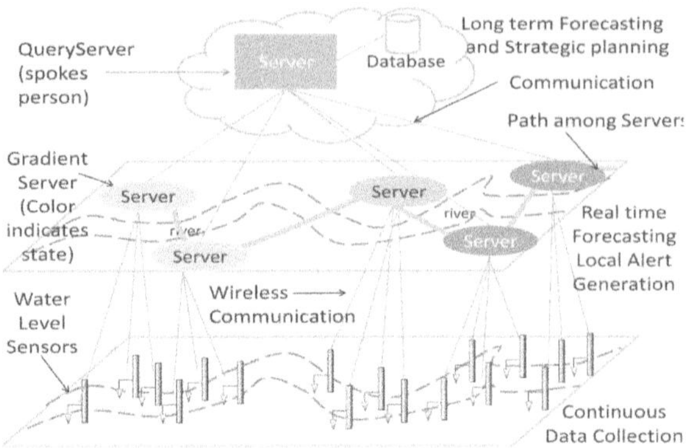

Figure 2. System Architecture

The *query server* is responsible for handling the user level queries during monsoon season. It is responsible for aggregated data collection and long term data analysis so that corresponding strategic decisions can be made during off season.

Gradient servers are distributed multithreaded servers placed at various physical locations. The servers communicate among themselves using their gradient information which is a function of its current water level, rainfall, time and expected water level. The servers are responsible for making local forecasting of data and work proactively to alert other servers along the physical vicinity so that advanced alert messages can be generated

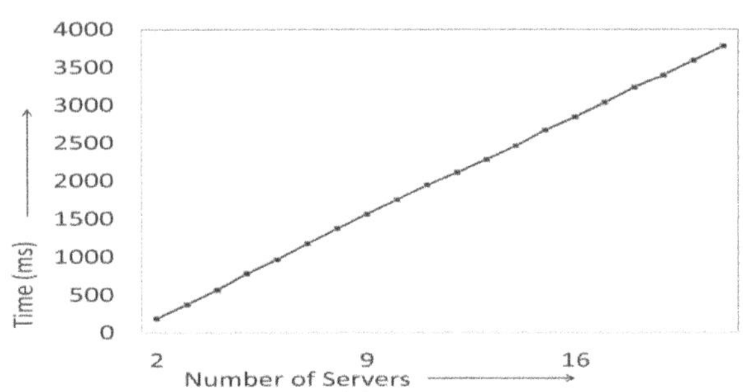

Figure 3. Scalability Study

Our Flow based communication across the Gradient nodes is conducted by sensing emulated sensor data packet transformation. As can be seen in Figure 3, the system is scalable across the increase of gradient nodes, showing linear rise of communication overhead.

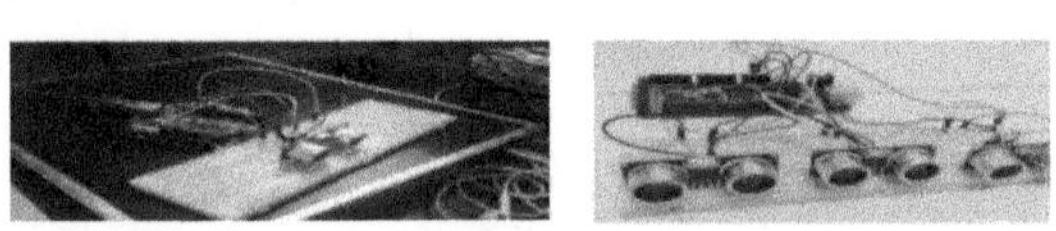

Figure 4. Ultrasonic Sensor used in System

At the lowest plane of our architecture, we have abundance of *sensors near the river banks*. There are several kinds of water level sensors available under limited cost (we are focused to provide a lower cost solution considering the economic situation of our country). We have considered ultrasonic sensors which uses the reflection of a signal to find out the distance of an object and liquid level sensor using optical devices which uses optoschmitt trigger to detect the level of water [8] and we have used a cluster of three sensors for better accuracy as can be seen in Figure 4. The sensors have the factory specification of reading maximum range of 4000 cm and Minimum range of 2 cm having measuring angle of 15 degrees.

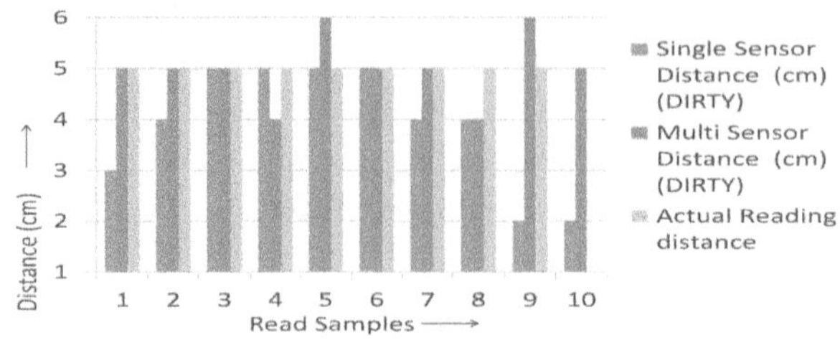

Figure 5. Comparison of single sensor, cluster sensor with respect. to actual readings

The cluster of sensors are able to perform with higher accuracy compared to a single sensor as can be seen in Figure 5 – the result is conducted in river water mentioned as Dirty water as opposed to clear water tests in laboratory.

4. CONCLUSION

We have presented a middleware named Shonabondhu which uses distributed sensor system and other environmental factors to estimate flash flood situation in Bangladesh. Our experiments show promises in terms of low cost sensing and scalability.

5. REFERENCES

[1] Danny Hughes et al.. Exploiting extreme hetegeneity in a Flood Warning Scenario using the GridKit Middleware. In *Proceedings of the 5th International Workshop on Middleware Tools, Services and Run-Time Support for Sensor Networks*, 29-34.

[2] List of Flash Flood, Web link: http://en.wikipedia.org/wiki/List_of_flash_floods (Last accessed on March, 2014)

[3] Nova Ahmed. Gradient Sensor Middleware System design for Flash Flood prone River banks in Bangladesh. Grace Hopper Celebration for Women in Computing, 2013.

[4] Elizabeth A. et al. 2008. Model-based monitoring for early warning flood detection. In *Proceedings of the 6th ACM conference on Embedded network sensor systems*, 295-308.

[5] Ivan Staoianov et al. Sensor Networks for monitoring water supply and sewer systems: Lessons from Boston. 2006. In *Eight Annual Water Distribution Systems Analysis Symposium (*WSDA), Ohio, USA.

[6] Jirapon Sunkpho et al. 2011. Real-time flood monitoring and warning system. In *Songklanakarin Journal of Science and Technology (SJST)*.33(2), 227-235, Mar-Apr. 2011.

[7] Danny Hughes et al.. Exploiting extreme hetegeneity in a Flood Warning Scenario using the GridKit Middleware. In *Proceedings of the 5th International Workshop on Middleware Tools, Services and Run-Time Support for Sensor Networks*

[8] Ultrasonic Rangile Module, Weblink: http://www.micropik.com/PDF/HCSR04.pdf (Last accessed on March, 2014).

Poster: Exact All-terminal Reliability Analysis of Bounded-degree Networks with Tutte Polynomials

Jae-Hyun Park*
School of Computer Science and Engineering
Chung-Ang University, 84 Heukseok-Ro, Dongjak-Ku
Seoul 156-756, Republic of Korea
hyunie@cau.ac.kr

ABSTRACT

The reliability of the Internet of Things is critical because the services of it will be concerned with real life, although the low cost may limit the number of links of each computer. In this paper, we analyze the all-terminal reliability of wireless regular graphs of which the number of links of each node is bounded. We derive the exact reliability polynomials for four regular graphs that are important candidates. The reliability polynomials are directly derived from the Tutte polynomial, which is the seminal work of the algebraic graph theory. To make the Tutte polynomials for graphs, we use the fastest program that was recently developed. As a result, we found that the torus graph of width three or more is the most reliable bounded degree network.

Categories and Subject Descriptors

C.2.1 [**Computer-communication Networks**]: Network Architecture and Design—*Network topology, Wireless communication*; C.4 [**Performance of Systems**]: Reliability, availability, and serviceability; G.3 [**Probability and Statistics**]: Reliability and life testing

General Terms

Reliability

Keywords

Reliability analysis; Reliability polynomial; Tutte polynomial; Bounded-degree network; Resource-constrained network; Internet of Things

1. INTRODUCTION

A popular open-source electronics platform Arduino is easy to use by providing affordable hardware and simple application programming interface (API). It is possible to implement the desired functionality at a lower cost. For example the Arduino Uno, for which we need to pay only $35, is already being used as a controller for the do-it-yourself (DIY), an artistic effect, or the Internet of Things.

However, Arduino provides a bounded number of communication links. For example, the Arduino Uno provides only one hardware universal asynchronous receiver/transmitter (UART) of the Atmega 328 controller for serial communication, and also provides at most three software-emulated UARTs. Besides, Atmega 2560 controller of Arduino Mega has four hardware UARTs for serial communication. If we pay the cost of twice, we can use four hardware ports at maximum.

The reliability of the Internet of Things is really important because it will be embedded into a physical system that concerned with real life. For example, when it is used for a security system at home, the networks should provide virtually uninterrupted service. It is also used to manage some constructions such as building, bridge, or freeway, or is used to manage the containers carrying meat products or seafood products. For these cases, the networks may become regular graphs like grid since the structure of the constructions is regularly shaped.

To find the most reliable network of which link resource is constrained, we analyze the reliability of the regular networks of which each node communicates with other nodes through only four links. We found that the torus graph of which the width is greater than or equal to three is the most reliable.

The all-terminal reliability is ideal to measure the reliability of the Internet of Things, because a computer in a network can connect to all other computers even through the lossy (or faded) wireless channel. For example, a sensory computer may send a command to any actuator computer to execute an action if it recognizes some patterns from sensory data.

The all-terminal reliability of the graph is represented by the reliability polynomial [2]. To derive the reliability polynomial, we should enumerate the number of survived network configurations. Recently, it was found that the exact reliability polynomial can be directly derived from the Tutte polynomial, that is the seminal result of the algebraic graph theory. We enumerate the number of the configurations of normally operating network by using the Tutte polynomial, so we make the exact reliability polynomials to analyze the reliability of graphs, including the torus graph, the Harary graph, the grid graph, and the multiple-rings graph.

*Corresponding author: Jae-Hyun Park (Tel.: +82 2 820 5310; Fax: +82 2 823 5301; http://cau.ac.kr/~jaehpark).

SenSys'15, November 1–4, 2015, Seoul, Republic of Korea.
ACM 978-1-4503-3631-4/15/11.
DOI: http://dx.doi.org/10.1145/2809695.2817875.

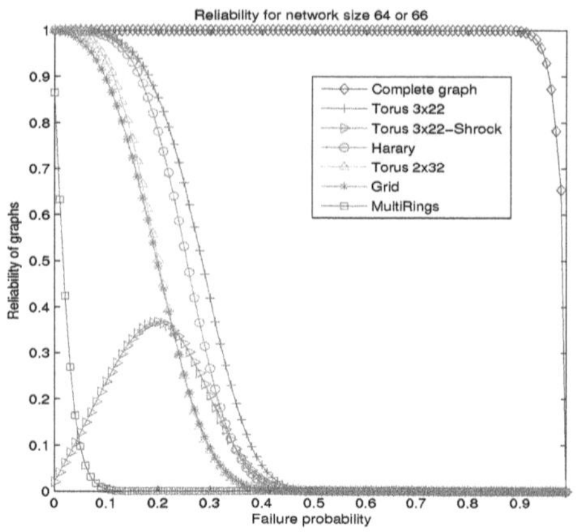

Figure 1: Reliability for the regular graphs

2. RELIABILITY POLYNOMIALS

We assume nodes are perfect and links fail independently with the identical probability ζ, while $\rho = 1-\zeta$ is the probability that a link normally operates. We assume that the nodes are invulnerable, because each node contains a simple controller with a little memory that can be recovered by resetting it when a fault occurs. We assume the communication modules for wireless links are vulnerable because wireless links are significantly more prone to failures or are even lossy.

The all terminal reliability polynomial $R(G, \rho)$ is defined as the probability that there is an operating communication path between any two nodes in the network. The contribution to $R(G, \rho)$ arise from the sum of the number of connected spanning subgraphs of G. A spanning tree is a subgraph containing N nodes, $N-1$ edges, and no cycles. Here a spanning subgraph is a subgraph $G' = (V, E')$ with $E' \subseteq E$.

We denote a connected spanning subgraph as $H = (V, E_H)$. Each contribution to $R(G, \rho)$ is weighted by a factor $\rho^{|E_H|}$ reflecting the probability that the $|E_H|$ edges are normally operating, multiplied by a factor $(1-\rho)^{|E|-|E_H|}$ reflecting the probability that the edges in the complement set $\{e \in E; e \notin E_H\}$ of cardinality $|E|-|E_H|$ are faulty. The reliability polynomial is $R(G, \rho) = \sum_{H \subseteq G} \rho^{|E_H|}(1-\rho)^{|E|-|E_H|}$ [2].

The reliability polynomial $R(G, \rho)$ can be also expressed in terms of the Tutte polynomial $T(G, x, y)$ as [2]

$$R(G, \rho) = \rho^{|V|-1}(1-\rho)^{|E|-|V|+1} T(G, 1, \frac{1}{1-\rho}) ,$$

where the Tutte polynomial of a graph $G = (V, E)$ is a two-variable polynomial defined as follows [3]:

$$T(G, x, y) = \begin{cases} 1 & E(G) = \emptyset \\ xT(G/e, x, y), & e \text{ is a bridge} \\ yT(G-e, x, y) & e \text{ is a loop} \\ T(G/e, x, y) + T(G-e, x, y) & \text{otherwise.} \end{cases}$$

Recently, a fast algorithm has been developed based on the idea of caching intermediate graphs and their Tutte polynomials and that of using graph isomorphism to avoid unnecessary re-computation of branches of the computation tree, and that of employing several heuristics [3]. We use this algorithm to calculate the Tutte polynomials for getting the reliability polynomials for larger size graphs. The reliability polynomial of 3×11 torus graph is:

$$\begin{aligned} R(Torus_{3\times 11}, \zeta) = (\zeta - 1)^{32} \cdot (&8822951714960\zeta^{34} \\ &+ 46244516348824\zeta^{33} + 127608027653898\zeta^{32} \\ &+ 245654843548510\zeta^{31} + 369192337673060\zeta^{30} \\ &+ 459832643126868\zeta^{29} + 492253388276122\zeta^{28} \\ &+ 463999212467582\zeta^{27} + 391702607807808\zeta^{26} \\ &+ 299843193183622\zeta^{25} + 210079966240760\zeta^{24} \\ &+ 135688059189900\zeta^{23} + 81243363437998\zeta^{22} \\ &+ 45291630557690\zeta^{21} + 23588813290911\zeta^{20} \\ &+ 11507400682426\zeta^{19} + 5268067612874\zeta^{18} \\ &+ 2266039929384\zeta^{17} + 916414610749\zeta^{16} \\ &+ 348426657524\zeta^{15} + 124455336357\zeta^{14} \\ &+ 41701831534\zeta^{13} + 13077217436\zeta^{12} \\ &+ 3825009180\zeta^{11} + 1038766465\zeta^{10} + 260337440\zeta^{9} \\ &+ 59735940\zeta^{8} + 12419044\zeta^{7} + 2307239\zeta^{6} + 375936\zeta^{5} \\ &+ 52327\zeta^{4} + 5984\zeta^{3} + 528\zeta^{2} + 32\zeta + 1) \end{aligned}$$

where ζ $(= 1-\rho)$ is the probability that fault occurs at a link.

The exact calculation of the reliability polynomials for a few graphs including the complete graph and the lattice strips of width two were presented by S. Chang and R. Shrock [2]. Chang and Shrock had also approximated the Tutte polynomial of the lattice graphs of width three, which was given at Appendix A.5 of [1]. However, as shown in Fig.1, the approximation does not incorrectly estimate the reliability of the torus graphs.

As shown in Fig.1, if the network size is 66, and if the link failure probability ζ is 0.3, in terms of the all-terminal reliability, the torus graph is better than the Harary graph by 0.156 or 15.6 percent.

3. CONCLUSIONS

We found that the torus graph of width three or more is the most reliable graph among the four degree regular graphs. The all-terminal reliability of the torus network is better than that of the Harary graph by 0.156 or 15.6 percent when the network size is 66 and the link failure probability ζ is 0.3.

4. REFERENCES

[1] S.-C. Chang and R. Shrock. Exact potts model partition functions on wider arbitrary-length strips of the square lattice. *Physica A: Statistical Mechanics and its Applications*, 296(1):234–288, 2001.

[2] S.-C. Chang and R. Shrock. Reliability polynomials and their asymptotic limits for families of graphs. *Journal of Statistical Physics*, 112(5-6):1019–1077, 2003.

[3] G. Haggard, D. J. Pearce, and G. Royle. Computing Tutte polynomials. *ACM Trans. Math. Softw.*, 37(3):24:1–24:17, Sept. 2010.

Poster Abstract : Accurate Vehicle Detection in Intelligent Transportation Systems (ITS) using Wireless Magnetic Sensors

Fawad Ahmad
University of Engineering and Technology
Peshawar, Pakistan
fawad.ahmad@outlook.com

Sahibzada Ali Mahmud
Sarhad University of Science and IT
Peshawar, Pakistan
mahmud.ee@suit.edu.pk

ABSTRACT

Wireless Sensor Networks (WSN) have emerged as a suitable solution for real-time vehicle data collection in many ITS applications. We propose the use of magnetometers in conjunction with WSN for real-time vehicle data collection. Magnetometers when used as sensor nodes offer advantages over other vehicle sensing technologies that include cost-effectiveness, energy efficiency, resistance to changes in environmental conditions, ease of re-deployment and flexibility. In this paper we present our prototype of a wireless magnetic sensor, algorithms for vehicle detection, vehicle speed estimation and vehicle length estimation and quantify their performance. Results from field evaluations prove the feasibility of our proposed solution for accurate vehicle data collection

Categories and Subject Descriptors

J.2 [**Computer Application**]: Physical Sciences and Engineering—*Engineering*

Keywords

Intelligent Transportation Systems (ITS); Wireless Magnetic Sensors; Vehicle Detection

1. INTRODUCTION

A number of methodologies have been employed for vehicle data collection, each with it's own advantages and limitations, the most established being magnetic induction loops. Inductive loops are expensive in terms of cost and energy consumption, they require pavement cuts for installation thus reducing pavement life and their maintenance also requires lane closure. On the other hand, magnetometers are cost-effective, energy-efficient, re-deployable, resistant to changes in environmental conditions and do not need maintenance. In [1], [2], [3], [4] and [5], magnetometers have been used for vehicle detection. In [2], a wireless magnetic sensor node was used for vehicle detection, speed estimation and vehicle classification achieving accuracies of 98 % , 90 % and 80 % respectively.

SenSys'15, November 1–4, 2015, Seoul, South Korea..
ACM 978-1-4503-3631-4/15/11.
DOI: http://dx.doi.org/10.1145/2809695.2817876 .

In this paper we present a prototype of our developed wireless magnetic sensor, three novel algorithms for vehicle detection, velocity estimation and vehicle length estimation. From field evaluations, we prove that the sensor node detects vehicles with 100% accuracy, estimates velocity with 94% and lengths 90% accuracy, more than those achieved in [2].

2. PROPOSED SOLUTION

In this section we present our prototype for vehicle data collection along with the proposed algorithms. The wireless sensor network used in this architecture consists of an end-device and a central data-logger. The data-logger consists of a single wireless transceiver based on IEEE 802.15.4. The magnetic sensor node consists of three main components:

1. Three-axis magnetometer.
2. Microcontroller (32-bit MCU).
3. Wireless Transceiver (IEEE 802.15.4).

The three-axis magnetometer samples the Earth's magnetic field at a specific frequency. The sampled data is supplied to the MCU periodically which processes it according to our signal processing algorithms to extract the vehicle count, vehicle speed and vehicle length from the raw data. The processed data is sent to the wireless transceiver which then forwards it to the central data-logger through the IEEE 802.15.4 protocol.

2.1 Vehicle Detection Algorithm

The flow chart for the vehicle detection algorithm is given in Figure 1. The application starts by configuring the sampling rate, gain and mode of the magnetometer. Once the magnetometer is configured it starts supplying the MCU data at a fixed sampling rate. Let the time interval between two consecutive samples of the magnetometer be, T_s, the distance covered by a vehicle in one T_s be d_s, the length of the vehicle be $L_{vehicle}$. The probability of detecting a vehicle in S samples is dependent upon:

$$\therefore \quad P(D) \propto L_{vehicle}, S, \frac{1}{d_s}$$

2.2 Velocity and Length Estimation Algorithms

To estimate the velocity of a vehicle we propose a solution that involves only a single magnetometer. The velocity of a vehicle with length $L_{vehicle}$ detected by a magnetometer in N samples, with a sampling rate f such that the length of the magnetometer is considered zero, we have

$$V_{vehicle} = \frac{L_{vehicle}}{d_s} = \frac{L_{vehicle}}{N * T_s} = \frac{L_{vehicle} * f}{N}$$

$$L_{vehicle} = \frac{N * V_{vehicle}}{f} = N * V_{vehicle} * T_s$$

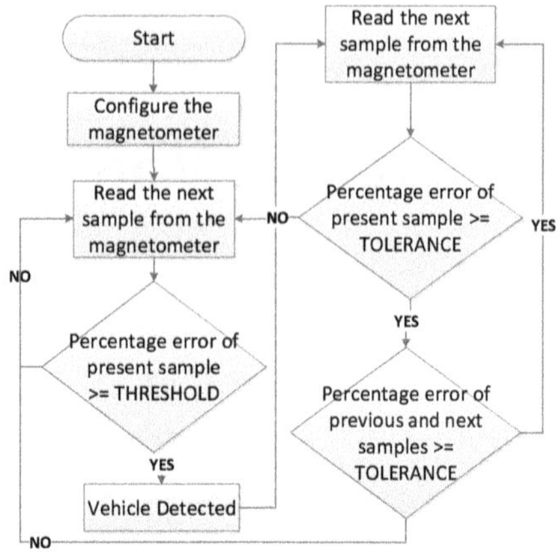

Figure 1: Vehicle Detection Algorithm

3. PERFORMANCE EVALUATION

To evaluate the feasibility of using a wireless magnetic sensor node for vehicle data collection, we conducted some real-time tests in a parking lot and on a highway, with the z-axis of the magnetometer cutting the direction of motion of the vehicles. The parameters and some results obtained from the real-time tests are summarized in Table 1. From Table 1, we can see that the disturbance along z-axis is more as compared to the other axes. The motion of the vehicle is also registered along the other two axes due to the large amount of ferric material in the vehicle and the fringing magnetic field. However, using the x-axis and y-axis of the magnetometer for vehicle detection can lead to erroneous results in multiple lane scenarios. After rigorous field experiments, we came up with a few conclusions:

- The magnitude of the disturbance will be greatest along that axis of the magnetometer which cuts the motion of the vehicle (z-axis in our experiments).
- The number of disturbance samples will be greatest for the axis parallel to the direction of motion.
- Due to the large amount of ferric material in the engine, the highest peak registered by any vehicle will be in its frontal region.

In the next set of field tests, we performed the field evaluations of the three proposed algorithms. A total of 50 vehicles including sedans, hatchbacks and station wagons were passed over the magnetic sensor to test the vehicle detection algorithm. The results from the tests proved that the accuracy of our proposed solution for vehicle detection with a sampling rate of 15 Hz was 100% as compared to the 98% achieved in [2] with a sampling rate of 128 Hz. The THRESHOLD and TOLERANCE values for the algorithm were determined by running simulations in MATLAB, attaining an accuracy of 100% for vehicle detection.

For the field evaluations of our velocity estimation algorithm we used a single magnetic sensor node. From our evaluations, we found that if the actual vehicle length was supplied to the velocity estimation algorithm, then the accuracy was more as compared to the case when an average vehicle length was used for all vehicles. Another observation was that increasing the sampling rate yielded more detection samples, thus increasing the accuracy. The accuracy achieved, using the exact vehicle lengths, was 94 % as compared to 90% in [2]. The drawback of increasing the sampling rate of the magnetometer is that the energy consumption of the sensor node increases which is undesirable especially if the sensors are battery operated.

Parameter	Value
Sampling Rate	15 Hz
Number of Vehicles	24
Vehicle Detections	24
Speed of Vehicles	1 km/hr - 120 km/hr
Sensitive Axis	Z-Axis
Z-Axis Disturbance	275%
X and Y-Axis Disturbance	65%

Table 1: Parameters for Evaluation in Parking Lot

In a given scenario when all vehicles are traveling at a constant speed $V_{vehicle}$, we can estimate the length $L_{vehicle}$ of the vehicle. We computed the length of 10 vehicles and compared them with their actual lengths. The average accuracy obtained from the results is 89 %. We can further increase the accuracy by increasing the sampling rate of the magnetometer; however as discussed in the previous section, that results in greater energy consumption.

4. CONCLUSION

In this demo paper we presented a solution for accurate vehicle detection in ITS using wireless magnetic sensors with advantages like low energy consumption, wireless connectivity, high accuracy, cost-effectiveness and minimal maintenance. We presented the design of our proposed prototype for a wireless magnetic sensor as well as three algorithms for vehicle detection, velocity estimation and vehicle length estimation. The performance evaluation of the wireless magnetic sensor and vehicle detection algorithms in the field proved that our proposed solution could achieve an accuracy of 100 % in vehicle detection, 94% in velocity estimation with a single sensor and 90% accuracy in length estimation. To extend our work we plan on conducting field evaluations for extended time periods on busy roads in order to quantify the performance of the algorithms in terms of accuracy and energy efficiency. We also plan on incorporating the ability to classify vehicles on the basis of vehicle size using the sampling rate, width and height of the detected pulse.

5. REFERENCES

[1] M. J. Caruso, T. Bratland, C. H. Smith, and R. Schneider. A new perspective on magnetic field sensing. *SENSORS-PETERBOROUGH-*, 15:34–47, 1998.

[2] S. Cheung, S. Coleri, B. Dundar, S. Ganesh, C.-W. Tan, and P. Varaiya. Traffic measurement and vehicle classification with single magnetic sensor. *Transportation research record: journal of the transportation research board*, (1917):173–181, 2005.

[3] J. J. Ding, S.-Y. Cheung, C.-W. Tan, and P. Varaiya. Signal processing of sensor node data for vehicle detection. In *Intelligent Transportation Systems, 2004. Proceedings. The 7th International IEEE Conference on*, pages 70–75. IEEE, 2004.

[4] A. Haoui, R. Kavaler, and P. Varaiya. Wireless magnetic sensors for traffic surveillance. *Transportation Research Part C: Emerging Technologies*, 16(3):294–306, 2008.

[5] E. Sifuentes, O. Casas, and R. Pallas-Areny. Wireless magnetic sensor node for vehicle detection with optical wake-up. *Sensors Journal, IEEE*, 11(8):1669–1676, 2011.

Poster: Power Spectrum Analysis of Reflected Waves with Ultrasonic Sensors Indicates "What the Target is"

Takanori Komatsu
Meiji University
4-21-1 Nakano, Tokyo 1648525, JAPAN
tkomat@meiji.ac.jp

Jun-ichi Akita
Kanazawa University
Kakuma, Kanazawa 9201192, JAPAN
akita@is.t.kanazawa-u.ac.jp

ABSTRACT
We consider that ultrasonic waves can be used not only for measuring the distance to a target but also for comprehending what the target is simultaneously. We assumed that the physical characteristics of a target object (especially, surface information) are embedded in the power spectrum structure of the ultrasonic waves reflected from the target. The results of our investigation to analyze the characteristics of the power spectrum structure of waves reflected from various kinds of target materials showed whether target objects are soft and deformable or hard and undeformable.

Categories and Subject Descriptors
H.5.m. [**Information interfaces and presentation**] (e.g., HCI): Miscellaneous; H.5.2 [**User Interfaces**] (D.2.2, H.1.2, I.3.6) Input devices and strategies (e.g., mouse, touchscreen)

General Terms
Measurement.

Keywords
Ultrasonic; reflected waves; power spectrum; total harmonic distortion.

1. INTRODUCTION
Distance-sensing methodologies that work in a non-contact manner have been proposed in various studies, and ultrasonic waves are commonly used for various kinds of applications, such as range finders for robots [1,2], medical inspection [3,4], fish detection [5,6], and non-destructive inspection [7,8,9]. These methodologies are used to determine the distance to a target object by measuring the arrival time of the reflected ultrasonic waves.

We then assumed that certain information especially surface information of the target is embedded in the reflected ultrasonic waves that are utilized for distance-sensing. To confirm this assumption, we transmitted ultrasonic waves to various kinds of objects and measured the reflected ultrasonic waves. We then investigated whether certain attributes of reflected waves can represent physical characteristics (surface information) of an object or not.

SenSys '15, November 1–4, 2015, Seoul, South Korea.
ACM 978-1-4503-3631-4/15/11.
DOI: http://dx.doi.org/10.1145/2809695.2817877

We assumed that the power spectrum structure of the reflected waves contains the physical characteristics of a target object. We then focused on two characteristics, differential total harmonic distortion (THD_N) and primary signal to noise ratio (S_1NR). We then define THD_N as the differences of THD and THD+N in [dB] to eliminate the factors of harmonics as follows.

$$THD_N = THD - (THD + N)$$
$$= \frac{\sqrt{V_2^2 + V_3^2 + \cdots V_n^2}}{V_1} - \frac{\sqrt{V_2^2 + V_3^2 + \cdots V_n^2 + N^2}}{V_1}$$

Here, V_1 is the voltage swing of the primary factor, and V_i is the voltage swing of the factor whose frequency is a multiple of the *i*th by the primary factor. THD represents the distortion of a wave, while THD+N does the distortion of the wave with factors other than the harmonics taken into account. So THD_N is a measurement that represents the ratio of the primary factor to other factors except for the harmonics. In addition, we define a novel measurement for comprehending the power spectrum characteristics of a reflected ultrasonic wave, the primary signal to noise ratio (S_1NR), as defined below.

$$S_1NR = \frac{V_1^2}{P_{total}}$$

Here, P_{total} is the power of the whole received wave, defined as the sum of the square of all the factors' voltage swings. Note that S_1NR is defined as the square of V_1 divided by the power to adjust the unit dimension.

These measures represent the relationship of the primary factor to other factors that are expected to contain information on the physical characteristics of a target object, such as whether it is hard or soft.

2. EXPERIMENT
We measured the THD_N and S_1NR of reflected ultrasonic waves from various kinds of objects. We prepared 13 different materials as target objects, shown in Table 1. These objects were selected because they are typical daily items. The shape of these objects was almost a square, with roughly 300 [mm] on each side.

The transmitting ultrasonic signal of a 40 [kHz] sinusoidal wave is generated by a micro controller (Cypress, CY8C24123) and drives the ultrasonic transducer (SPL, UL1612MPR) by using an amplifier (Liner Technology, LT1632) with a high-current drive capability at a voltage swing of 20 [Vp-p]. Note that the half-power angular of the transducer is 50 [deg]. An ultrasonic wave reflected from a target object is received by an ultrasonic microphone (Knowles Electronics, SPM0404UD5), which is sensitive up to 65 [kHz], and amplified by ×1,000 by an operational amplifier (National Semiconductor, LM358) to capture the PC-controlled digital oscilloscope (Pico Technology,

Picoscope2205A) for calculating its power spectrum. The gap between the transmitting transducer and the receiver was set at 100 [mm]. Figure 1 shows the set-up of equipment and object (left) and actual experimental scene (right).

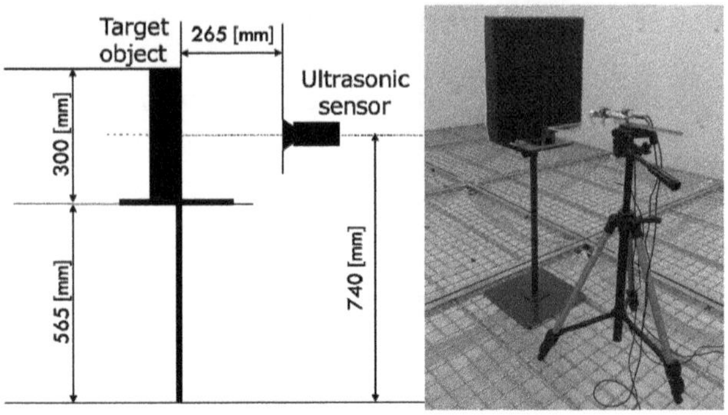

Figure 1. (left) Set-up of equipment and object, (right) In action (object: acoustic absorption material).

3. RESULTS

We measured the THD_N and S_1NR twice for each object. The average measured values of THD_N and S_1NR are listed in Tables 1. The order of measuring the object was the same as the numbering shown in the left column of this table. Tables 1 shows that the objects that showed smaller values of THD_N and S_1NR were the (2) bath mat, (5) sponge, (1) acoustic absorption material, and (6) handy mop, which are soft and deformable materials, while the objects with larger values were the (4) Styrofoam, (3) steel sheet, (12) cork board, and (10) plywood, which are hard and undeformable materials. As the result of our investigation, we found that the measured values of THD_N and S_1NR clearly represented one of the physical characteristics of the objects; that is, whether a target was soft and deformable or hard and undeformable.

Table 1. Measured Average THD_N [dBc] and S_1NR [V^2/M]

No.	Object	**THD_N**	**S_1NR**
1	Acoustic absorption	-9.56	2.43
2	Bath mat	-10.47	2.29
3	Steel sheet	-2.79	5.11
4	Styrofoam	-2.34	5.61
5	Sponge	-10.08	2.34
6	Handy mop	-8.13	2.54
7	Plastic mat	-4.98	3.68
8	Artificial grass	-5.59	3.66
9	Vibration absorber	-4.29	2.98
10	Plywood	-3.63	4.63
11	Acrylic board	-4.03	3.64
12	Cork board	-2.91	4.98
13	Polypropylene film	-2.71	4.91

4. DISCUSSIONS AND CONCLUSION

The results of our investigation clearly showed that objects that are soft and deformable showed lower THD_N and S_1NR values, while those that are hard and undeformable had higher values. Eventually, this investigation revealed that our assumption was confirmed. Future investigation is indispensably required to comprehend in detail the meanings of the THD_N and S_1NR values, respectively.

In our investigation, in parallel with measuring the power spectrum structure of the reflected waves, we measured the arrival time of these waves in order to measure the distance to the target object, and we could confirm that this measurement had the same quality as traditional ultrasonic distance sensors, e.g., about 265 mm, as shown on the left of Figure 1. Among these two measurements (one for power spectrum and the other for arrival time), one measurement does not interfere with the other measurement, and vice versa, so our proposed measurement simply augmented the function of traditional ultrasonic sensors. We believe that our framework could have an impact on current user interface technologies.

5. REFERENCES

[1] Crowley, J. L. 1989. World modeling and position estimation for a mobile robot using ultrasonic ranging, In Proceedings of *1989 IEEE International Conference on Robotics and Automation*, Vol. 2, pp. 674 – 680.

[2] Vandorpe, J., Van Brussel, H., and Xu, H. 1996. Exact dynamic map building for a mobile robot using geometrical primitives produced by a 2D range finder, In Proceedings of *1996 IEEE International Conference on Robotics and Automation*, Vol. 1, pp. 901 – 908.

[3] Bartrum, R. J., Crow, H. C., and Foote, R. T. 1977. Ultrasonic and Radiographic Cholecystography, *The New England Journal of Medicine 296*, 538 – 541.

[4] Sarvazyan, A. P., Rudenko, O. V., Swanson, S. D., Fowlkes, J. B., and Emelianov, S. Y. 1998. Shear wave elasticity imaging: a new ultrasonic technology of medical diagnostics, *Ultrasound in Medicine & Biology 24*, 9, 1419 – 1435.

[5] MacLennan, D. N. 1990. Acoustical measurement of fish abundance, *Journal of Acoustic Society of America 87*, 1 – 15.

[6] Simmonds, E. J., Williamson, N. J., Gelotto, F., and Aglen, A. 1992. *Acoustic survey design and analysis procedure: A comprehensive review of current practice*, ICES Cooperative Research Report No. 187 (International Council for the Exploration of the Sea, Denmark, 1992).

[7] Blitz, J., and Simpson, G. 1996. *Ultrasonic methods for non-destructive testing*, Chapman & Hall, London: UK.

[8] Drinkwater, B. W. and Wilcox, P. D. 2006. Ultrasonic arrays for non-destructive evaluation: A review, *NDT & E International 39*, 7, 525 – 541.

[9] Pagodinas, D. 2003. Ultrasonic signal processing methods for detection of defects in composite materials, NDT.net *8, 7*, http://www.ndt.net/article/v08n07/pagodin/pagodin.htm

Poster Abstract: An Online Approach for Gait Recognition on Smart Glasses

Yiran Shen†, Chengwen Luo‡, Weitao Xu⋆, Wen Hu‡
†Singapore-MIT Alliance for Research and Technology, Singapore
‡School of Computer Science and Engineering, University of New South Wales, Australia
⋆School of Information Technology and Electrical Engineering, University of Queensland, Australia

ABSTRACT

With the fast development and increasing population of the wearable devices involves in our daily life, the security of the privacy information on those devices is attracting significant attentions. One of the possible solution is to enable the devices to recognise the real owner with authentication system. Biometrics recognition is popular used for authentication systems. The biometrics used including faces, fingerprints, gait cycles and etc. Using gait cycles as the criteria for identities recognition is superior than other biometrics as the gait information can be collected by the IMU sensors which are most popular embedded on portable devices and they cannot be reproduced by the invaders. We propose, Securitas, the continuous authentication system exploits the information from IMU sensors on the smart glasses to distinguish different wearers.

1. INTRODUCTION

Wearable computing applications are booming after recent introduction of high profile products such as Google Glass, Apple Watch and FitBit wristhand. Smart glasses have attracted significant attentions since the first commercialised prototype of Google Glass was introduced in 2013. Then the new version of Google Glass and a number of new smart glasses were released such as GlassUp AR, Vuzix M100, Microsoft Hololense and etc. The new technology provides tremendous opportunities to improve industry, energy and resource consumption, agriculture, business productivity, and our health. However it also has substantially potential risk. Information such as our daily routines and activities and our health data has substantially commercial value and it is highly likely that this will be targeted by hackers in the future in the same way that credit card information is now.

Wearable computing devices such as smart glasses typically have inexpensive multiple modality sensors such as inertial measurement units (IMUs) on-board. In this work, we aim for a *step-change* in classifying on-board sensor observations on smart glasses for the purpose of biometrics authentication of wearers. Due to the small form factor of wearable devices, traditional authentication methods such as passwords do not offer good user experience because of the need for screen and keyboard, and are not appropriate. Therefore, research communities have started to investigate methods for wearer authentication based on *bioimpedance* measurements from the wearer's wrist [2], and gait analysis based on shoes [1] or hips [3] mounted IMU sensors. Gait analysis based on IMUs is preferable for the authentication on wearable devices because almost all of the smart wearable devices feature IMUs; other biometrics sensors such as fingerprint, iris or bioimpedance sensors are not popular equipped; authentication system based on predefined gestures are sometimes intrusive and will interrupt the activities of the users. Gait recognition is based on the pattern of walking steps which is non-intrusive and walking is one of the most frequent activities of users when using smart glasses.

To address these challenges, we propose a novel gait recognition method that enables the highly accurate authenticity and can be run *in-situ* on smart glasses. We build a continuous authentication system based on the proposed gait recognition method which exploits the information of the most common activities when using smart glasses, i.e., walking. Different from the traditional *entry* authentication system, the continuous authentication system runs implicitly in background and try to detect suspicious users. When a suspect is detected, the device will be locked and prompt message to request for further authentication such as password, gestures or other *entry* authentication methods.

(a) Google Glass

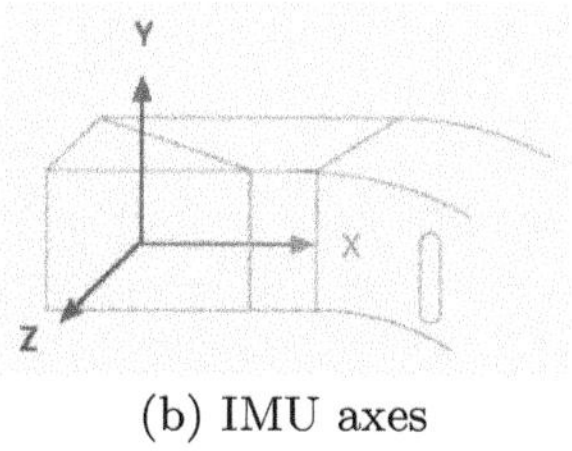

(b) IMU axes

Figure 1: The axes of the IMU sensors on Google Glass

Current commercilised smart glasses (e.g., Google Glass) are used for system implementation. The gait recognition is based on the information extracted from the IMU sensors

SenSys'15, November 1–4, 2015, Seoul, South Korea..
ACM 978-1-4503-3631-4/15/11.
DOI: http://dx.doi.org/10.1145/2809695.2817878 .

(accelerometer and gyroscope) in 6 degrees of freedom. The sensors locations and coordinates are shown in Figure 1.

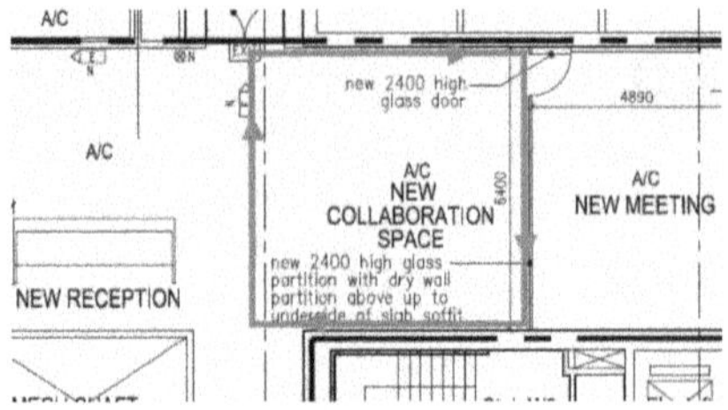

Figure 2: The floor map of the experiment environment

We conducted the two days experiment to collect the suitable dataset. The second day experiment is conducted after one week of the first day experiment to include more dynamics in the dataset. During the data collecting session, the subject is asked to wear Google Glass while walking along the specific route in clockwise (or counterclockwise) as shown in Figure 2. The data generated by the IMUs (accelerometer and gyroscope) and its corresponding timestamps are recorded.

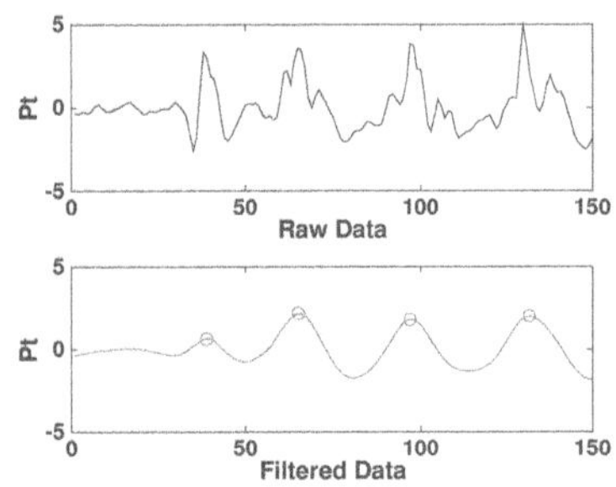

Figure 3: Sensor data before and after low pass filter

The collected data is deteriorated by noises as shown on the top of Figure 3. To recognise the gait information of different wearers, the step cycles need to be separated accurately by finding the local maximums of the sequential data. The local maximums are revealed on the bottom of Figure 3 after we applied butterworth low pass filter on the noisy data. Then the steps are separated according to the locations of the local maximums.

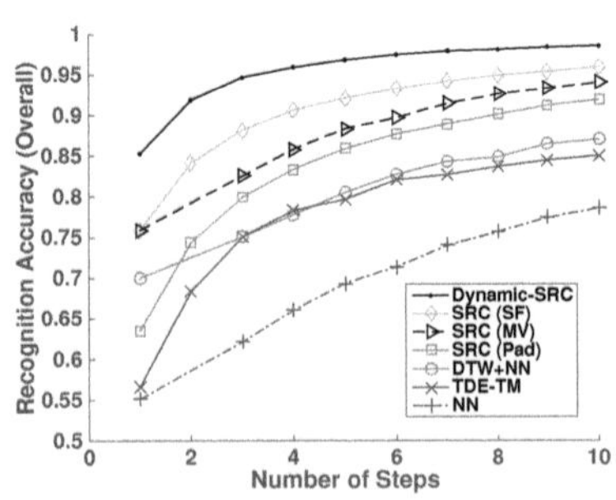

Figure 4: Comparison of recognition accuracy

After the step cycles are extracted, our proposed method, Dynamic-SRC, is applied to recognise the identities of the wearers. We also implement other state-of-the-art gait recognition approaches as comparisons. The results in Figure 4 show that our proposed approach outperforms its peers significantly.

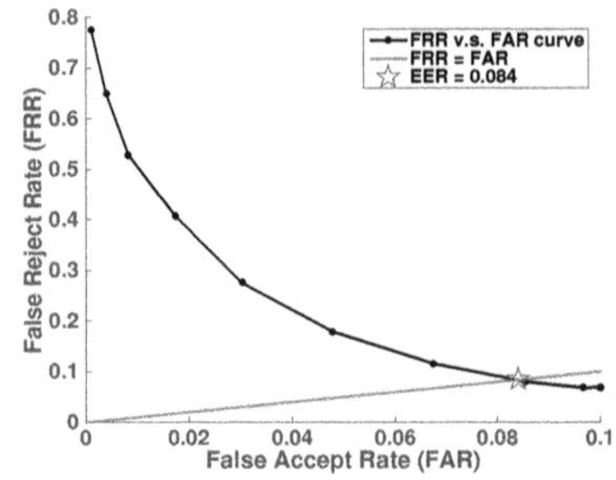

Figure 5: The performance of authentication system

Basing on Dynamic-SRC, we implement a continuous authentication system on Google Glass to recognise the wearers. As the results shown in Figure 5, the new system produces an EER (Equal Error Rate) as low as 0.08 which indicates a promising authentication performance.

We also evaluate the resource consumption of the authentication system. Table 1 presents the detailed resource consumption (computation and energy) of the authentication system on Google Glass. The computation time and energy consumption are computed by averaging the results from 30 authentication attempts. The energy consumption is profiled by $E = PT$, where P is the average power and T is the runtime of the profiled component. The average power $P = Current \times Voltage$, where the $Current$ and $Voltage$ of the battery is obtained via Android APIs.

Table 1: Resource consumption of the authentication system on Google Glasses

	Computation Time	Energy Consumptio
Step Detection	620 ms	173 mJ
Data Interpolation	29 ms	8.1 mJ
ℓ_1-Homotopy	659 ms	183.9 mJ
DTW Residual	213 ms	59.4 mJ
Total	4, 001 ms	1, 116 mJ
Average Response Time	901 ms	N.A.

2. REFERENCES

[1] S. Bamberg, A. Benbasat, D. Scarborough, D. Krebs, and J. Paradiso. Gait analysis using a shoe-integrated wireless sensor system. *Information Technology in Biomedicine, IEEE Transactions on*, 12(4):413–423, July 2008.

[2] C. Cornelius, R. Peterson, J. Skinner, R. Halter, and D. Kotz. A wearable system that knows who wears it. In *Proceedings of the 12th annual international conference on Mobile systems, applications, and services*, pages 55–67. ACM, 2014.

[3] M. B. Crouse, K. Chen, and H. Kung. Gait recognition using encodings with flexible similarity measures.

Poster: L^3: Vehicle Lane-Level Localization on Highways Using Smartphones

Zhichen Wu, Jianda Li, Jiadi Yu, Yanmin Zhu
Department of Computer Science and Engineering, Shanghai Jiao Tong University
800 Dongchuan Road, Shanghai, China
{jerry_wzc, lijianda, jiadiyu, yzhu}@sjtu.edu.cn

ABSTRACT

When road-level localization cannot satisfy people's need for convenience and safety driving, lane-level localization becomes a corner stone. In this paper, we propose a vehicle *Lane-Level Localization* (L^3) system, which utilizes smartphone sensors to real-time locate the vehicle on lane-level on highways. The system is based on the observation that each type of lane change has its unique pattern on the vehicle's lateral acceleration. Extensive experiments demonstrate that L^3 is both accurate and robust in real driving environments.

Categories and Subject Descriptors

C.3 [**Special-Purpose and Application-Based Systems**]: [real-time and embedded systems]

Keywords

Lane-level localization, lane change, smartphone sensors, lateral acceleration

1. INTRODUCTION

With the development of traffic networks, the demand for lane-level localization becomes urgent. It can solve many traffic problems, such as driving safety issue, navigator precision, and lane-level road condition monitoring. Existing work on vehicle lane-level tracking mostly depends on pre-deployed infrastructures and additional hardwares.

In this paper, we consider a sensing approach, which only uses smartphone sensors to realize vehicle lane-level localization on highways. The basic idea is to track vehicles on lane-level by sensing lane change behaviors. Under the assumption that a vehicle gets on highways from the outermost lane, the lane after any lane change can be inferred.

We first investigate the readings from smartphone sensors to depict each kind of lane change. Through empirical studies of the driving traces collected from real driving environments, we find that each kind of lane change has its unique pattern on readings from accelerometers on x-axis. Based on these patterns, we propose a vehicle *Lane-Level Localization* (L^3) system, which utilizes smartphone sensors to identify lane change behaviors and track vehicles on lane-level.

The advantage of our system, L^3, is that it realizes lane-level localization by sensing the unique patterns in natural driving conditions through simple smartphone sensors. Furthermore, L^3 is easy to implement and computational on standard smartphone platforms. Our extensive experiments in real driving environments validate the accuracy and the feasibility of our system.

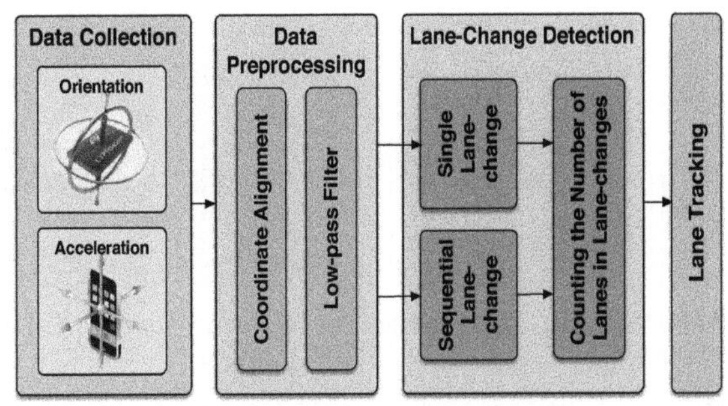

Figure 1: Work flow of L^3.

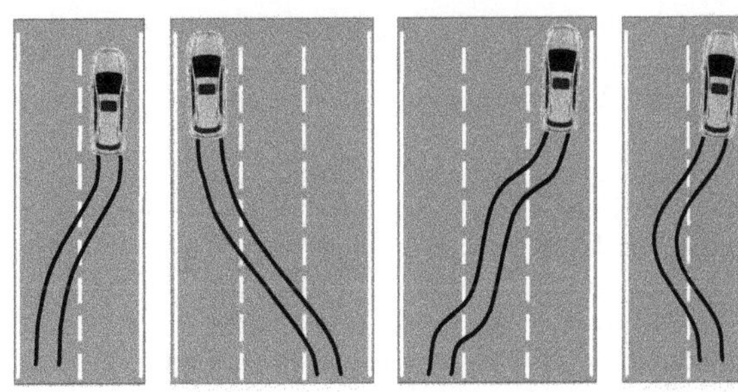

(a) (b) (c) (d)

Figure 2: Lane Change Models

2. SYSTEM DESIGN

The work flow of L^3 is illustrated in Figure 1. There are four sub-tasks, which are *Data Collection, Data Preprocessing, Lane Change Detection* and *Lane Tracking.*

In *Data Collection*, lateral acceleration and velocity are real-time read from accelerometers and GPS in smartphones.

In *Data Preprocessing*, *Coordinate Alignment*[1][2] is used to align the coordinates of a smartphone and a vehicle, and *Low-Pass Filter*[3] is used to reduce the roughness of roads.

SenSys'15, November 1–4, 2015, Seoul, South Korea..
ACM 978-1-4503-3631-4/15/11.
DOI: http://dx.doi.org/10.1145/2809695.2817879.

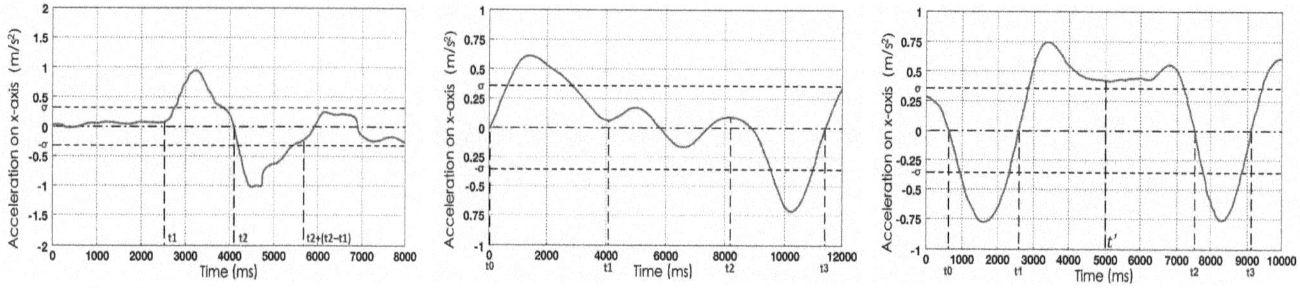

(a) Single lane-change. (b) Syntropy sequential lane-change. (c) Entypy sequential lane-change.

Figure 3: Wave of lateral acceleration in lane changes

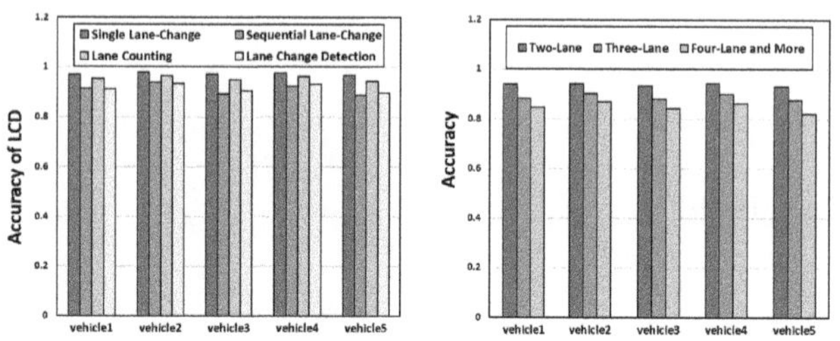

(a) Accuracies of lane change detections. (b) Highways with different lane numbers.

Figure 4: Performance of L^3 on five vehicles.

Lane Change Detection is performed to detect all kinds of lane change based on its patterns on the vehicle's lateral acceleration. The components of *Lane Change Detection* are as follow.

1. Single Lane-Change Detection: Single lane-changes, as shown in Figure 2(a) and 2(b), are lane changes which can be either leftward or rightward and are not limited to the neighbor lane. The lateral acceleration pattern can be both up-to-down or down-to-up sinusoids. For example, a rightward single lane-change is shown in Figure 2(a) and it has the pattern in Figure 3(a).

2. Sequential Lane-Change Detection: Sequential lane-changes, as shown in Figure 2(c) and 2(d), are combination of several lane changes in a short time. In ***Syntropy Sequential Lane-Change***, lane changes happen in the same direction. A syntropy sequential lane-change which consists of two rightward lane changes is shown in Figure 2(c) and its wave of lateral acceleration is two semi-waves separated by a blank, as shown in Figure 3(b). In ***Entypy Sequential Lane-Change***, lane changes happen in the reverse direction. An entypy sequential lane-change which consists of a leftward and a rightward lane changes is shown in Figure 2(d) and its wave of lateral acceleration is a down-to-up-to-down sinusoid, as shown in Figure 3(c), which also has the following character:

$$\int_{t_0}^{t_1} a(t)dt + \int_{t_2}^{t_3} a(t)dt \approx - \int_{t_1}^{t_2} a(t)dt, \quad (1)$$

where the *ith* semi-wave starts at t_{i-1} and ends at t_i.

3. Counting the Number of Lanes: After a lane change is detected, our system counts the number of lanes the vehicle crosses. By integral the lateral velocity over time, the lateral displacement of the vehicle can be calculated. And by dividing the lateral displacement by the width of the lane, the system can obtain exactly how many lanes it crosses.

For each component in *Lane Change Detection*, specific algorithms are designed so that lane changes can be detected both qualitatively and quantitatively.

In *Lane Tracking*, a Gaussian Distribution is applied to represent the probability density of lane identification. The lane with the highest probability is taken as the current lane of the vehicle.

3. EVALUATION

To evaluate the generality and the robustness of L^3, we conduct experiments in real driving environments using five pairs of smartphones and vehicles equipped with DVRs for 5 months, during which all the daily driving on highways is recorded.

Figure 4(a) shows the accuracies of lane change detections on five vehicles. On average, the accuracies of single lane-change detection, sequential lane-change detection, and lane counting are 97.08%, 91.02%, and 95.3% respectively. And the average accuracy of lane change detection is 91.49%.

Figure 4(b) shows the accuracies of L^3 on highways of different numbers of lanes. On average, the accuracies on highways with two-lane, three-lane, and four-and-more-lane highways are 93.7%, 88.7%, and 84.6% respectively. And the average accuracy of L^3 is 86.94%.

4. CONCLUSION

In this paper, we address the problem of vehicle tracking on lane-level in order to improve driving safety and convenience. In order to realize the lane-level localization on highways, we propose a lane-level localization system, L^3, to detect lane change behaviors through their unique patterns on readings from smartphone sensors and then track vehicles on lane-level through a Gausian Distribution method. The key insight is that natural driving conditions present unique features and can be exploited to enable accurate real-time lane-level localization. Our extensive experiments show that L^3 can perform with an average accuracy of 86.94%.

5. REFERENCES

[1] Y. Wang, J. Yang, H. Liu, Y. Chen, and et al. Sensing vehicle dynamics for determining driver phone use. In ACM MobiSys, 2013.

[2] H. Han, J. Yu, H. Zhu, Y. Chen, and et al. Senspeed: sensing driving conditions to estimate vehicle speed in urban environments. In IEEE INFOCOM, 2014.

[3] Y. Wang, J. Yang, Y. Chen, H. Liu, and et al. Tracking human queues using single-point signal monitoring. In ACM MobiSys, 2014.

Poster Abstract: Asynchronous Acoustic Localization using Commercial Devices

Jongtack Jung, Kangho Kim, Woonghee Lee and Hwangnam Kim
School of Electrical Engineering, Korea University ,Seoul, Korea
{skylover89, mybalam2k, tgorevenge, hnkim}@korea.ac.kr

ABSTRACT

In this paper, we design and implement an asynchronous multi-device acoustic localization system. Although the relative position and distance can be useful to many applications such as drone swarming, not much research has been conducted on the field. As synchronizing multiple devices can be difficult or even impossible with certain hardware, we devised an asynchronous algorithm that provides a high accuracy ranging and localization. A high performance ranging and localization technique that uses a relatively minor source, sound, can provide a new set of characteristics. Our proposed algorithm can work on most commercial devices that have acoustic capabilities.

Categories and Subject Descriptors

H.5.5 [**Information Interfaces and Presentation (e.g., HCI)**]: Sound and Music Computing

Keywords

Acoustic Ranging, Synchronization, Localization

1. INTRODUCTION

We present an acoustic indoor localization system without synchronization techniques. The proposed system estimates the relative position of a device by measuring the distance between the devices with the time of flight (ToF) of the sound. The ToF of the sound is not accurately obtainable due to following reasons: device synchronization, clock misalignment, and improper signal detection. To accurately measure the range with decimeter precision, the clock skew needs to be less than 300 μs. When the device instructs the speaker to emit a sound and microphone to record, it takes a while to process the instructions for commodity hardware. The misalignment can be as long as 100 ms with the best smartphones, which is 30 meters in distance. Lastly, the detection of the time of arrival can be instable, because of physical phenomena such as multi-path effect [1]. We propose an asynchronous multi-device acoustic localization which does not require a synchronization among the devices, overcoming the stated problems.

SenSys'15, November 1–4, 2015, Seoul, South Korea..
ACM 978-1-4503-3631-4/15/11.
DOI: http://dx.doi.org/10.1145/2809695.2817880 .

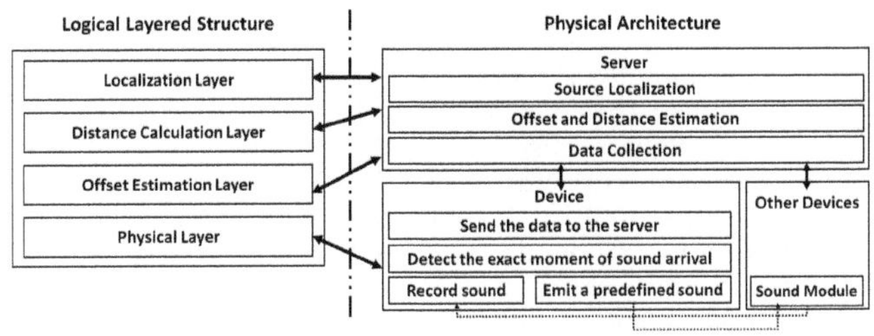

Figure 1 – The logical/physical architecture of the system: the alignment of logical and physical architecture is drawn on the figure with arrows.

Figure 2 – Odroid XU hardware prototype: the Odroid device is equipped with a microphone an a speaker.

2. SYSTEM DESIGN

There are largely four parts composing the system: signal detection, offset estimation, distance calculation, and localization. The categorization builds a type of layered structure, as shown in Figure 1. The physical operations are also shown in Figure 1. All devices start recording, and a second later, each device emits a sweep sound. The moments of arrival of all sweep sounds are detected by all devices, and the information is sent to the server where the information is processed through the logical layers.

Hardware Design. We developed a prototype hardware module with Odroid XU, as well as smartphones such as Vega No.6, Galaxy Nexus, and Galaxy S3. The Odroid hardware is instable, causing poorer performance than the smartphones. We believe the cause of the instable input is the instable power input to the microphone, which results in very noisy data. Yet, we included the prototype for our experiments to examine the performance of our system in poorer condition.

Physical Layer. Physical layer oversees all physical transactions: the emission and detection of the signal. Synchronization among the devices is not assumed, so all moments

Table 1 – The delay matrix: after pair-wise entry subtraction based on the assumptions. Only the delay components remain.

Send \ Recv	Device 1	Device 2	Device 3	...	Device n
Device 1	R_1+S_1	R_2+S_1 $-(R_1+S_2)$	R_3+S_1 $-(R_1+S_3)$		R_n+S_1 $-(R_1+S_n)$
Device 2	-	R_2+S_2	R_3+S_2 $-(R_2+S_3)$		R_n+S_2 $-(R_2+S_n)$
Device 3	-	-	R_3+S_3		R_n+S_3 $-(R_3+S_n)$
⋮					
Device n	-	-	-		R_n+S_n

of arrival detection are only of the device itself. The system tries to look for the first peak for signal detection. Our system requires the knowledge of the distances among the devices to calculate offsets, and the distances can only be found when the traveling sound is of a direct path. We assume that the multipath signal cannot be much larger because the signal has bounced off one or more surfaces. Thus, we find the first peak that is larger than a certain fraction of the largest peak. A heuristic algorithm that runs on the offset estimation layer finds the best fitting fraction value.

Offset Estimation Layer. The offset estimation layer finds the time offset among the sounds. The detected signals can be expressed as Table 1 with an assumption that $T_{AB} = T_{BA}$. After setting an arbitrary variable (e.g. R_1) to 0, the set of delay offsets can be calculated with a system of equations, with respect to the variable.

Distance Calculation Layer. The distance calculation layer accepts n sets of delays, decides which ones are genuine, computes the result. Distance calculation layer validates multiple sets of equations from the offset estimation layer and finds the best fitting answer. Each set of equations from offset estimation layer is a solvable system of equations. The answer of the system is the values of R and S, thus when all R and S are found the detected values can be translated to propagation delays. The propagation delays are the distances in different unit. As a result, a set of equations gives a matrix of propagation delays.

Localization Layer. In the localization layer, the distance and offset information is used to find the localized object. There are two localization methods: time of arrival (ToA) localization and time difference of arrival (TDoA) localization [2]. ToA localization is used when the localized device has a pair of a speaker and a microphone, while TDoA localization is used when the device only uses either a speaker or a microphone.

3. EVALUATION

Experiments presented have been carried out in 10 m x 16 m room. The room has a few obstacles with a slightly leveled floor: the very back of the room is roughly 1 m higher than the very front. The entire set of experiments has been carried out indoors, because acoustic ranging is better carried out outdoors as demonstrated in [3].

4. CONCLUSION

We have implemented the system using cheap commodity hardware, compared to other systems that normally require

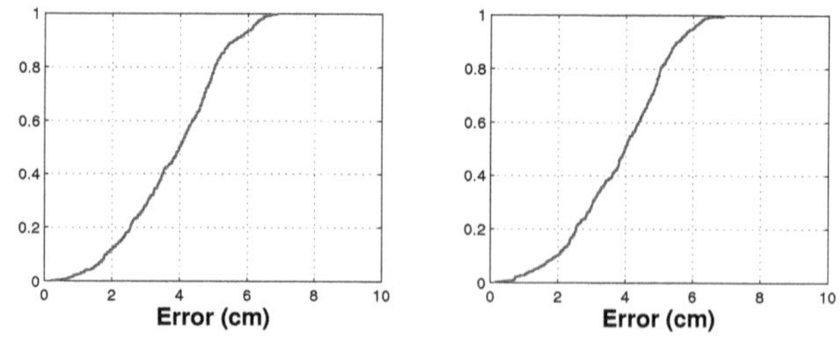

((a)) 4 anchors ((b)) 3 anchors

Figure 3 – ToA error

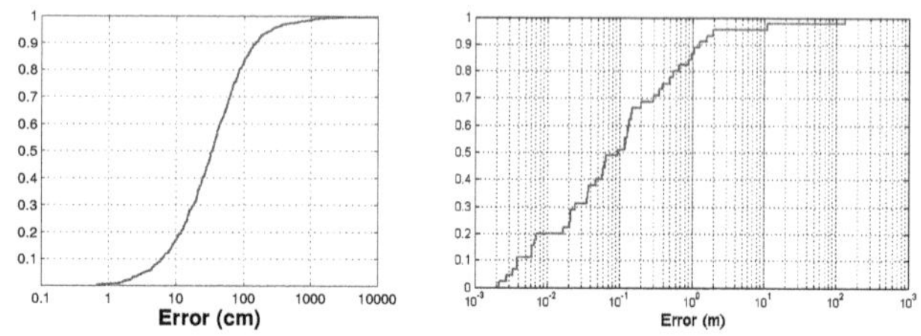

((a)) 4 anchors ((b)) Smartphone only

Figure 4 – TDoA error

extremely expensive hardware for synchronization. The limited range of our system can be overcome with a larger deployment of more anchors, especially with low cost hardware. With low cost hardware and high accuracy, we expect our proposed system can be applied to wider range of applications.

Acknowledgements

This work was supported by Samsung Research Funding Center of Samsung Electronics under Project Number SRFC-IT1401-09.

5. REFERENCES

[1] Badiey, M., Katsnelson, B. G., Lin, Y.-T., and Lynch, J. F. Acoustic multipath arrivals in the horizontal plane due to approaching nonlinear internal waves. *The Journal of the Acoustical Society of America 129*, 4 (2011), EL141–EL147.

[2] Kaune, R. Accuracy studies for tdoa and toa localization. In *Information Fusion (FUSION), 2012 15th International Conference on* (2012), IEEE, pp. 408–415.

[3] Peng, C., Shen, G., Zhang, Y., Li, Y., and Tan, K. Beepbeep: A high accuracy acoustic ranging system using cots mobile devices. In *SenSys '07, November 6-9, 2007, Sydney, Australia* (2007).

Poster: ParkGauge: Gauging the Congestion Level of Parking Garages with Crowdsensed Parking Characteristics

Jim Cherian[1] Jun Luo[1] Hongliang Guo[1] Shen-Shyang Ho[1] Richard Wisbrun[2]
School of Computer Engineering, Nanyang Technological University, Singapore[1]
Traffic Management, Traffic Assistance, BMW Group, Germany[2]
{jcherian, junluo, guohl, ssho}@ntu.edu.sg[1] richard.wisbrun@bmw.de[2]

ABSTRACT

Finding available parking spaces in dense urban areas is a globally recognized issue in urban mobility. Whereas prior studies have focused on outdoor/street parking, we target at (indoor) parking garages where the infrastructure supports (e.g., GPS and Wi-Fi) assumed by existing proposals are unavailable and counting vehicles by crowdsensing is difficult. To this end, we present ParkGauge as a system gauging the congestion level of parking garages; it infers (coarse-grained) parking occupancy from crowdsensed parking characteristics instead of counting the parked vehicles. ParkGauge adopts mostly low-power sensors in the driver's smartphone to determine driving states, contexts and temporal parking characteristics of a garage, including time-to-park and time-in-cruising/queuing. Mining such data collected from a crowd of drivers at various garages yields a good measure of their congestion levels and provide recommendations (in real-time) to drivers coming to these venues.

1. INTRODUCTION

Dense urban areas worldwide face high demand on parking infrastructure especially in mega-cities. While on-street parking has led to serious traffic congestion, multi-storeyed *car parks* (aka, *parking garages*), which are the major urban parking facilities for mega-cities, can also produce serious on-road congestion because of long queues of vehicles waiting to enter them. This is because their occupancy is not made available to drivers who could be otherwise guided towards less congested venues. Existing infrastructure-based systems require sensors and/or beacons at parking lots or on vehicles, making them expensive and not very scalable. Recent infrastructure-free works such as ParkSense [4] and PocketParker [3] have demonstrated crowdsensing for parking occupancy detection, however they focus on outdoor parking and are not able to get assistance from Wi-Fi and/or GPS mostly unavailable to indoor parking garages. Inertial sensing has been widely used for transportation mode detection (e.g., [2, 5, 1]), but it is very hard to infer occupancy information from direct inertial sensor readings: they may suggest driving states such as braking or turning, but such events seem unrelated to parking occupancy unless we use certain inference mechanisms and establish their connections.

We propose ParkGauge as a system to gauge the congestion level (or coarse-grained occupancy) of parking garages in urban areas. In order to apply infrastructure-free inertial sensing for this purpose, ParkGauge innovates in using (temporal sequences of) driving states (e.g., braking and turning) to infer temporal parking characteristics (e.g., time-to-park) that are in turn exploited to deduce garage occupancies. To the best of our knowledge, ParkGauge is the first crowdsensing system exploiting temporal information to indicate parking occupancy for indoor parking garages.

Unlike existing crowdsensing-based parking systems, ParkGauge does not require a "crowd" for sensing individual parking garages. A small amount of sensing data acquired from each parking garage is sufficient, whereas the "crowd" is needed only to enhance coverage across a large urban area.

2. SYSTEM OVERVIEW AND DESIGN

ParkGauge runs as an application in a driver's smartphone that can be docked in a standing position during driving and to be taken along with the driver upon completing a parking. The architecture of ParkGauge has a 4-layer presentation shown in Figure 1, so that connections between the seemingly unrelated sensing data and our gauging objectives can be made through a multi-stage inference. It uses the accelerometer and gyroscope to detect driving-relevant phone status, and a *Hidden Markov model* (HMM) to infer hidden *driving state* from observable phone status. Barometer is used to detect floor changes, and geo-fencing to trigger parking arrival detection. The (temporal) sequence of *driving states* are classified to *driving contexts*, which help to derive temporal parking characteristics such as time-to-park. This can be used to generate useful information presentable to drivers, such as coarse-grained occupancy (inferred by regression) and accurate Expected Time of Arrival (ETA).

3. EXPERIMENTS AND EVALUATION

We have implemented ParkGauge as an Android application, along with a back-end server. While the model learning procedure is done offline in the server using the collected datasets, all the online detections are performed on ParkGauge application, which periodically reports data to the server. Experiments were performed in parking garages at-

SenSys'15, November 01-04, 2015, Seoul, Republic of Korea
ACM 978-1-4503-3631-4/15/11.
DOI: http://dx.doi.org/10.1145/2809695.2817881.

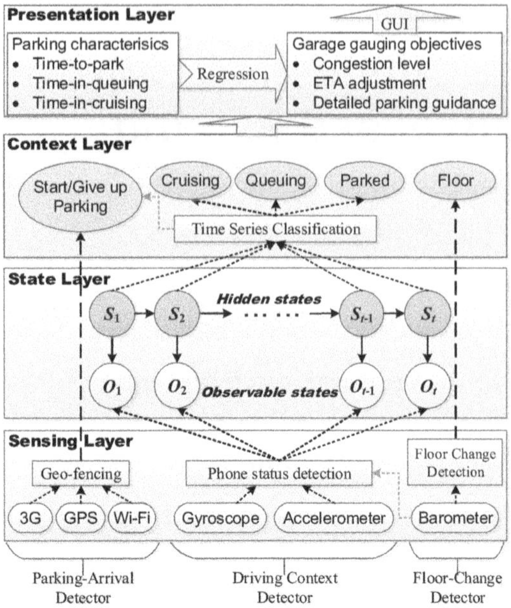

Figure 1: System architecture of ParkGauge.

tached to shopping malls, during which more than 100 traces were collected, including 46 self-parking sessions.

3.1 Inferring Driving States and Contexts

To demonstrate the inferred driving states and contexts, we use the raw sensor readings plotted in Figure 2 from a 4.5 minute long parking trial during a peak hour at a shopping mall. The vehicle arrived at an almost fully occupied garage, so it faced a queue at the entrance, and spent time in cruising to find a parking lot even after getting three levels down.

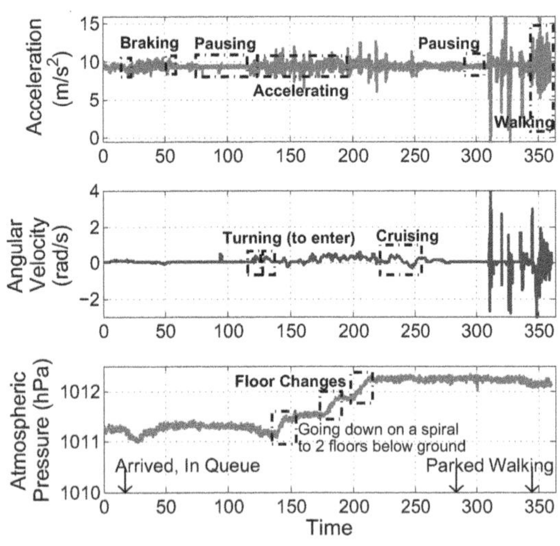

Figure 2: Raw data trace from a parking trial

3.2 Accuracy of time-to-park Estimation

As shown in Figure 3(a), the errors in estimating time-to-park may range from 5s to around 30s. Most errors are around the mean of 18s. Given that the normal values of time-to-park are in the order of minutes (or tens of minutes in the worst case), we deem this performance very accurate.

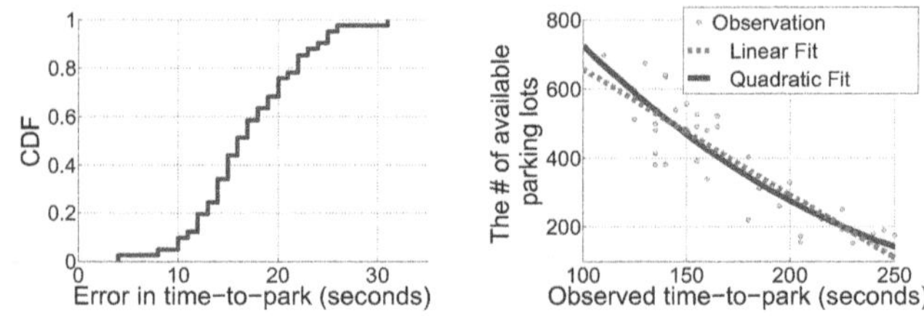

Figure 3: (a) CDF for the estimation errors of time-to-park. (b) Fitting the relation between parking occupancy and time-to-park through regression.

3.3 Gauging Parking Occupancy

We use regression to recover the relation between occupancy and time-to-park based on the collected data. We only show one set of results from a popular shopping mall in Figure 3(b); the experiments were done from 10:00am to 16:00pm. We perform both linear and quadratic regression on the data, and the results are very close to each other. For simplicity, we use the linear regression results to map an estimated time-to-park to occupancy, and store such a mapping in the server for individual parking garages. When a user queries a location, ParkGauge retrieves the estimated *time-to-parks* from nearby parking garages along with their corresponding mapping. It then computes the occupancies locally and displays it both numerically and graphically. The user may also choose to view the *time-to-parks* directly and feel the level of difficulty in finding a parking lot.

4. CONCLUSION AND DISCUSSIONS

ParkGauge innovates in using inertial sensing data (from low-power sensors) to gauge temporal characteristics and infer a coarse-grained occupancy of parking garages and this is demonstrated through extensive experiments. Our current implementation requires the smartphone to be docked in a standing position, but this can be addressed by existing phone attitude estimation algorithms. Finally, we strongly believe that the idea behind ParkGauge can be extended also to outdoor parking and other occupancy detection scenarios.

5. REFERENCES

[1] S. Hemminki, P. Nurmi, and S. Tarkoma. Accelerometer-based Transportation Mode Detection on Smartphones. In *Proc. of the 11th ACM SenSys*, page 13, 2013.

[2] P. Mohan, V. N. Padmanabhan, and R. Ramjee. Nericell: Rich Monitoring of Road and Traffic Conditions using Mobile Smartphones. In *Proc. of the 6th ACM SenSys*, pages 323–336. ACM, 2008.

[3] A. Nandugudi, T. Ki, C. Nuessle, and G. Challen. PocketParker: Pocketsourcing Parking Lot Availability. In *Proc. of the 2014 ACM UbiComp*, pages 963–973, 2014.

[4] S. Nawaz, C. Efstratiou, and C. Mascolo. ParkSense: A Smartphone Based Sensing System for On-Street Parking. In *Proc. of the 19th ACM MobiCom*, pages 75–86, 2013.

[5] S. Reddy, M. Mun, J. Burke, D. Estrin, M. Hansen, and M. Srivastava. Using Mobile Phones to Determine Transportation Modes. *ACM Trans. on Sensor Networks*, 6(2):13, 2010.

Poster Abstract: Non-invasive Human Activity Monitoring using a Low-cost Doppler Sensor and an RF Link

Yang Zhao
Distributed Intelligent Systems Lab
GE Global Research
Niskayuna, New York USA
yang.zhao@ge.com

Ting Yu
Computer Vision Lab
GE Global Research
Niskayuna, New York USA
yut@ge.com

Jeffrey Ashe
Biomedical and Electronic Systems Lab
GE Global Research
Niskayuna, New York USA
ashe@ge.com

ABSTRACT

This paper presents a non-invasive human activity monitoring system with a low-cost Doppler sensor and a pair of radio frequency (RF) sensors. This radio-based system combines the strengths of two sensing modalities: fine granularity from a Doppler sensor and large sensing coverage from an RF link. The system is capable of detecting subtle human motion such as breathing, as well as walking in a large area. We deploy the system and perform experiments in a 5.5 m by 7.5 m room to classify four activities. Experimental results show that the average classification rate is 90%, 31% more accurate than a single Doppler system.

Categories and Subject Descriptors

C.3 [**Special-purpose and application-based systems**]: Real-time and embedded systems, Signal processing systems

General Terms

Design, Experimentation, Measurement

Keywords

Activity recognition, Doppler, Radio frequency

1. INTRODUCTION

Human activity monitoring is a very important topic in many applications such as security, remote monitoring for elder care, and demand controlled ventilation and lighting for smart facility. In this work, we focus on monitoring vital signs and common activities for hospitalized patients.

Traditional activity monitoring methods use sensor tags such as inertial measurement unit (IMU), or fingertip attached to human body to monitor their activities. However, these systems and methods require user cooperation, and often cause discomfort to users. Computer vision-based methods provide a non-cooperative way of human activity monitoring, but they suffer from the privacy issue, which limits their use in many applications.

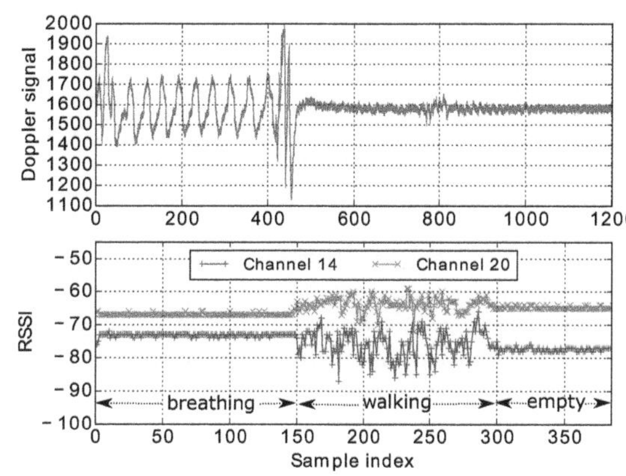

Figure 1: Doppler and RSSI time series from different activities.

As RF sensors and networks become more pervasive, radio-based methods are becoming a promising way of detecting, locating people [1], and even recognizing human activity [3]. In this paper, we investigate radio-based tag-free human activity monitoring. We design a low-cost low-power Doppler sensor modified from a commercial-off-the-shelf (COTS) range-controlled radar [2] to monitor a person's motion within its field of view. To solve the limited detection range problem of the Doppler sensor, we integrate a pair of COTS RF sensors to cover a large area. By integrating two radio sensing modalities, the system is capable of recognizing human activity with both high accuracy and large coverage in a non-invasive way.

2. METHOD AND SYSTEM

The Doppler sensor is modified from a commercial Doppler motion sensor originally designed for home security. The hardware modification is made such that the Doppler sensor is sensitive enough to detect subtle motion due to breathing and heart beat [2]. The Doppler sensor operates at 5.8 GHz, and we set the sampling rate to be ten Hz. We use two TI CC2531 radios to create an RF link. We use a wireless basestation and a time division multiple access (TDMA) protocol to collect received signal strength indicator (RSSI) between two radios from 16 frequency channels at 2.4 GHz

SenSys'15, November 1–4, 2015, Seoul, South Korea..
ACM 978-1-4503-3631-4/15/11.
DOI: http://dx.doi.org/10.1145/2809695.2817882.

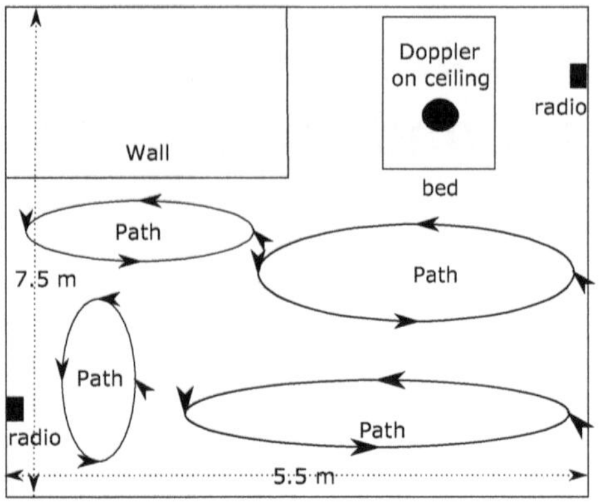

Figure 2: Experimental testbed layout.

ISM band [1]. The sampling rate is set to be three Hz on each channel. We connect the output of the Doppler sensor and the basestation to a single board computer, on which we perform data acquisition, data fusion and activity classification.

The Doppler signal and the RSSI on an RF link are complimentary with respect to sensing human motion. We can see this from the example shown in Fig 1. When a person is breathing in bed, the Doppler signal clearly shows the periodic pattern of the respiration motion. However, the RSSI time series do not show such pattern due to their coarse granularity. When a person is walking in the room, the Doppler sensor cannot always capture the motion: the signal has high variation when the person is close to the sensor (Doppler sample index from 780 to 810), but the variation is negligible when the person walks far away from the sensor. Theoretically, the Doppler sensor has a range loss inversely proportional to range to the fourth power ($1/R^4$), while the one-way radio communication range loss is inversely proportional to range squared ($1/R^2$) in the free space. Fig 1 clearly shows that the RSSI measurements from two frequency channels are both highly variable when a person is walking in the room.

For our patient monitoring application, we classify the following four activities: 1) breathing in bed, 2) turning in bed, 3) walking in room, and 4) no vital signs (empty bed and room). In the classification, we choose the Doppler features used in [2], such as: the mean and standard deviation of the Doppler signal, the peak frequency of the Doppler power spectral density (PSD). In addition, we use two more features: the averaged variance of RSSI over all frequency channels, and the variance of the PSD peak frequencies (each peak frequency is from a short-time window divided from the Doppler signal). After we use these features from the Doppler signal and RSSI to build a feature vector, we use support vector machine (SVM) with a radial basis function kernel to classify four human activity states.

3. EXPERIMENTS AND RESULTS

We perform experiments in a 5.5 m by 7.5 m mock hospital room with an adjustable hospital bed. We deploy the Doppler sensor on a ceiling-mounted rail above the bed, and we plug two radio nodes to the power outlets on the walls. The experimental layout is shown in Fig 2. Note that the Doppler sensor may be deployed at a different location and angle to cover a relatively larger area, but it cannot cover the entire room based on our measurements.

	breathing	turning	walking	empty
breathing	7	3	0	0
turning	0	10	0	0
walking	0	0	10	0
empty	0	1	0	9

Table 1: Confusion matrix from SVM (ten tests for each activity).

We recruit two human subjects to perform ten tests (each occurs for two minutes) for each of the four activities. For the breathing in bed activity, we ask them to breathe normally in bed with three orientations facing upwards, right and left. For the turning in bed case, human subjects turn their bodies from one side to the other randomly in bed. They also walk along different paths at different locations in the room, as shown in Fig 2. Note that we do not perform individual training for walking at each location, or breathing with each orientation. Instead, we can use walking at certain locations as training data to test walking at other locations. Compared with the recent activity recognition work [3], our system removes the location-dependent training requirement. That is, our system does not need to perform extensive training for each user orientation or each possible location in a room.

We use leave-one-out cross validation method to evaluate the performance of our system. The confusion matrix from our 40 tests is shown in Table 1. The average classification rate is 90%. If only the Doppler sensor is used, the classification rate is 55%. We deploy two RF nodes at three other locations, and we achieve 31% performance improvement on average, compared with the single Doppler system.

4. CONCLUSIONS AND FUTURE WORK

We design a low-cost activity monitoring system by combining a Doppler sensor with a pair of RF communication nodes. The integrated sensing system is capable of classifying four human activity states with high accuracy. One important future topic is to explore other ways of deploying the Doppler sensor and the RF radios. We plan to investigate more features from the RSSI and Doppler signal. We also plan to perform experiments with more human subjects, and investigate more machine learning algorithms in the future.

5. REFERENCES

[1] M. Bocca, O. Kaltiokallio, N. Patwari, and S. Venkatasubramanian. Multiple target tracking with RF sensor networks. *IEEE Transactions on Mobile Computing*, 2013.

[2] C. Graichen, J. Ashe, M. Ganesh, and L. Yu. Unobtrusive vital signs monitoring with range-controlled radar. In *IEEE Signal Processing in Medicine and Biology Symposium (SPMB)*, 2012.

[3] B. Wei, W. Hu, M. Yang, and C. T. Chou. Radio-based device-free activity recognition with radio frequency interference. In *International Conference on Information Processing in Sensor Networks (IPSN)*, 2015.

Poster : A Medium Access Control Protocol for Full-duplex Wireless Information and Power Transfer

Shiho Kodera
Graduate School of Informatics, Shizuoka University
kodera@aurum.cs.inf.shizuoka.ac.jp

Yoshiaki Narusue
Graduate School of Information Science and Technology, The University of Tokyo
narusue@akg.t.u-tokyo.ac.jp

Yoshihiro Kawahara
Graduate School of Information Science and Technology, The University of Tokyo
kawahara@akg.t.u-tokyo.ac.jp

Takashi Watanabe
Graduate School of Information Science and Technology, Osaka University
watanabe@ist.osaka-u.ac.jp

Shunsuke Saruwatari
Graduate School of Informatics, Shizuoka University
saru@inf.shizuoka.ac.jp

ABSTRACT

Full-duplex wireless information and power transfer allows the implementation of wireless sensor networks without batteries. In a full-duplex wireless network, an access point and sensor nodes transmit information and power signals simultaneously. However, this simultaneous transmission leads to a collision problem. To solve this collision problem, we propose a media access control (MAC) protocol, namely the Full-Duplex Simultaneous Wireless Information and Power Transfer Medium Access Control (FD-SWIPT MAC) protocol, for full-duplex wireless information and power transfer. The evaluation results show that the proposed FD-SWIPT MAC protocol outperforms other MAC protocols.

Categories and Subject Descriptors

C.2.2 [**Computer Communication Networks**]: Network Protocols—*Medium Access Control Protocols*

General Terms

Design; Performance

Keywords

Wireless full-duplexing; information and power transfer; sensor networks; medium access control protocols

1. INTRODUCTION

Wireless sensor networks with capabilities of information sensing, computation, and wireless communication allow the acquisition of high-definition data in the physical world. However, sensor networks have a power supply problem. The current sensor networks are driven by a primary or secondary battery, which needs to be either replaced or recharged.

Sensys '15, Seoul South Korea
ACM 978-1-4503-3631-4/15/11.
DOI: http://dx.doi.org/10.1145/2809695.2817883 .

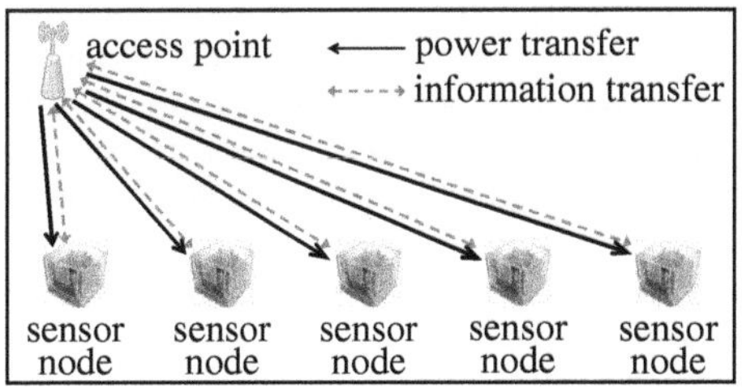

Figure 1: Our final objective

2. FULL-DUPLEX WIRELESS INFORMATION AND POWER TRANSFER

To solve the limitations of using a battery, we exploit full-duplex wireless networks for simultaneous transmission of data and power signals. Figure 1 shows our final objective. The access point and sensor nodes transmit data through bidirectional communication. The access point also transmits the power signals to the sensor nodes.

Our system is mainly applied to the sensors in a machine. Many machines such as vehicles, vending machines, ATMs, and printers have a number of sensors. There is a demand for simultaneous wireless transmission of data and power because of its design flexibility and low maintenance costs. The data and power signals are transmitted in the same frequency band in full-duplex wireless networks [1] for efficient use of the radio spectrum, where the access point receives data while canceling the power signals which the access point is sending.

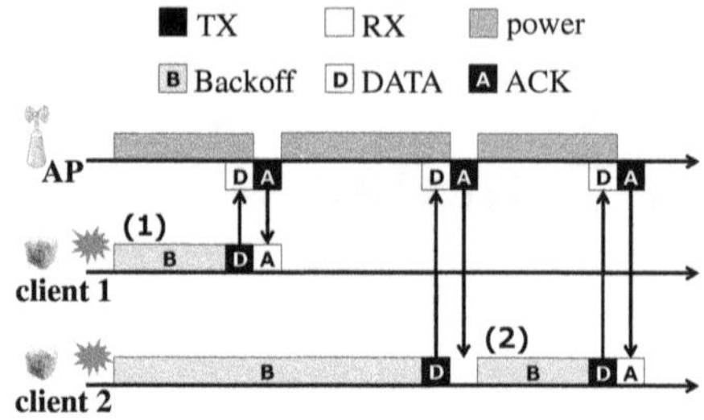

Figure 2: FD-SWIPT MAC protocol

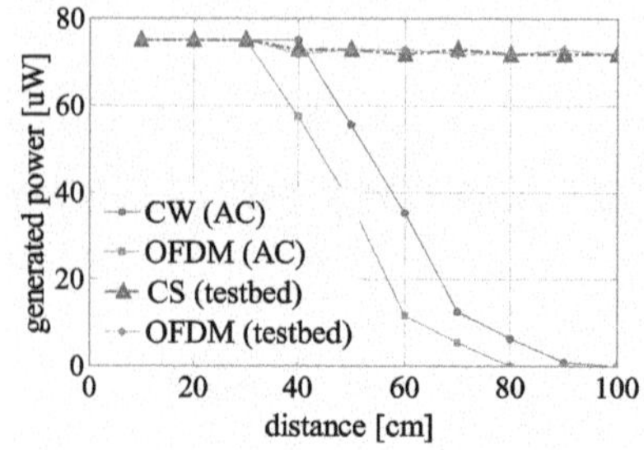

Figure 3: Power generation vs. the distance between AP and SN

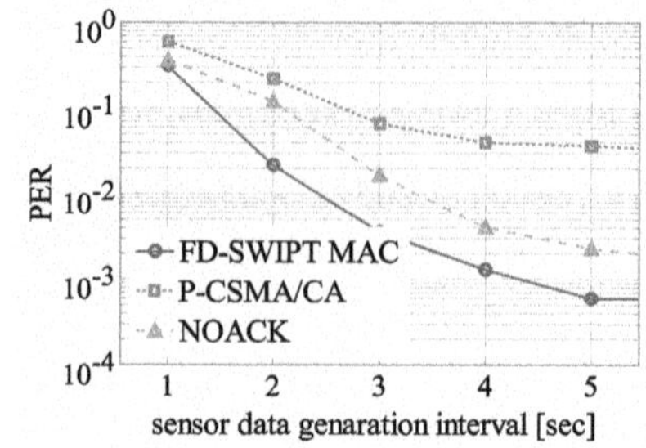

Figure 4: Comparison of MAC protocols

3. FD-SWIPT MAC PROTOCOL

The support of physical layer is not sufficient for full-duplex wireless data and power transfer. The access point and sensor nodes cannot use conventional CSMA/CA, which is a MAC layer in IEEE 802.11 or IEEE 802.15.4. The conventional CSMA/CA waits for a random backoff time to avoid collisions before sending a frame. At the end of the backoff time, the sensor node senses the presence of a carrier wave from other nodes. If no carrier waves are detected, the sensor node starts transmitting the frame. If a carrier wave is detected, the sensor node waits for a random backoff time again. If conventional CSMA/CA is used for the simultaneous transmission of data and power signals, sensor nodes will not be able to transmit any frame because the access point continuously sends power signals which will be detected by the sensor nodes as carrier waves.

To solve the problem in conventional CSMA/CA, we propose the FD-SWIPT MAC protocol, which avoids collisions without sensing the carrier wave in collaboration with an access point. Figure 2 shows the basic operation of our proposed FD-SWIPT MAC protocol. FD-SWIPT MAC protocol waits for a random backoff time when arriving a new frame (Figure 2-1), which is the same as the conventional CSMA/CA. At the end of the random backoff time, the FD-SWIPT MAC protocol sends the frame without sensing the carrier, unlike conventional CSMA/CA. The access point can receive the frame because the access point has wireless full-duplex capability. After receiving the frame, the access point stops transmitting the power signal, and sends an ACK frame to the sensor node. If the sensor node cannot receive the ACK frame, the sensor node waits for a random backoff time and re-sends the frame (Figure 2-2).

4. PRELIMINARY EXPERIMENT

For evaluating the MAC protocol described in section 3, we conducted a testbed experiment to determine the amount energy that can be transferred by radio. The testbed was a 1 m×1 m×1 m hexahedron constructed with twenty 30 mm×30 mm aluminous structural members and TG joints. Six aluminous panels were attached to the hexahedron and a radio was encased in the hexahedron. We measured the amount of power generated while changing the distance between an access point and the rectenna. We used Mango Communications WARP v3 as an access point. The output transmission power was 20.3 dBm. The access point sent a continuous wave or 20 MHz OFDM signals.

Figure 3 shows the experimental results. The horizontal axis represents the distance [cm] between the access point and the rectenna, and the vertical axis represents the amount of power generated [μW]. The experimental results show that the amount of power generated is almost 0 in the anechoic chamber (AC) although it is 75 μW in the testbed, which is approximately equal to the amount of power generated when the distance is 10 cm.

5. EVALUATION

We evaluated three MAC protocols through computer simulations and experimental analysis described in section 4. We measured the frame error rate of each node at each interval for generating sensor data [sec]. The number of sensor nodes was 100 and power generated was 75.0 μW. The number of re-transmissions and repetitive transmissions required was 5. The power consumption of each node was 57.4 mW while transmitting, 65.0 mW while receiving, and 0 mW while sleeping for reference CC2420 using MICAz and TelosB.

We compare three protocols, i.e., CSMA/CA, NO ACK and the proposed FD-SWIPT MAC protocol. CSMA/CA treats power signals as a frame, where a power frame and data frames compete to acquire a shared medium, and does not assume full-duplex communication. NO ACK repeats random backoff and sends a frame without sensing the carrier for a fixed number of times.

Figure 4 shows the simulation results. The horizontal axis represents the sensor data generation interval [sec] and the vertical axis represents the frame error rate. From Figure 4, it can be seen that the FD-SWIPT MAC protocol has the best performance among the three MAC protocols.

6. CONCLUSION

In this paper, we proposed a MAC protocol for the simultaneous transmission of data and power signals. The evaluation through experiments and computer simulations show that our protocol has the best performance.

7. ACKNOWLEDGEMENTS

This work was supported by SCOPE (Strategic Information and Communications R&D Promotion Programme) of Ministry of Internal Affairs and Communications, Japan.

8. REFERENCES

[1] Bharadia, D., McMilin, E., and Katti, S. Full duplex radios. In *Proceedings of the ACM SIGCOMM 2013* (August 2013), 375–386.

Poster Paper: Maximizing Renewable Energy Usage in Buildings using Smart Energy Switching Platform

Qasim Khalid, Naveed Arshad
Department of Computer Science
SBASSE, LUMS, Pakistan
{qasim.khalid, naveedarshad}@lums.edu.pk

Jahangir Ikram
Department of Electrical Engineering
SBASSE, LUMS, Pakistan
{jikram}@lums.edu.pk

Categories and Subject Descriptors

H.4 [**Information Systems Applications**]: Miscellaneous; J.7 [**Computer Applications**]: Computer in Other Systems—*Command and control*

General Terms

Optimization, Algorithm, Hybrid Solar PV System

Keywords

solar PV optimization, hybrid renewable energy system, fine-grained clustering, smart switch

1. INTRODUCTION

Solar energy is slated to be an important energy source for reducing dependence in fossil fuels. Past few years have seen unprecedented deployments of solar energy in many countries of the developed world. However, solar energy uptake in developing countries is rather slow. This is particularly true for solar energy installations on buildings. Since buildings consume more than 40% of energy, it is important that greener buildings are encouraged through on-site production of renewable energy [2]. However, limited possibility of energy buyback programs in developing countries is one of the reason for less solar deployments. Also, in some countries the electricity infrastructure is so fragile that energy buyback programs at smaller scale are not feasible. Therefore, if the building owners like to go green then huge battery banks are needed to make the best use of solar energy. But battery banks add quite a bit of cost to the overall solar energy infrastructure in buildings. This extra upfont and maintenance cost is one of the reasons that hampers the growth of solar on buildings.

Hybrid solar energy systems are used when energy buyback programs are available [1]. In this work we make a case that traditional hybrid solar energy deployments are not feasible for places without energy buyback programs. Instead we propose an idea of a solar energy system for buildings that is somewhere between hybrid and off-grid solar energy systems.

Hybrid Solar Energy Systems make the coupling of the solar energy and grid energy at the main electricity distribution point of a building. This model of energy distribution works best when the grid is stable and energy buyback programs are available. In absence of the option of putting the energy back on the grid one would like the buildings to maximally utilize the solar energy. But the hybrid solar energy systems, while costing a fortune, do not utilize the maximum available solar energy. This is because the hybrid inverters charge the batteries from grid energy at night and when the batteries are fully charged in the morning the solar energy available is only utilized to run the needs of the buildings during daytime. Thus, the batteries are not charged from the solar energy, hence, maximum solar energy is not utilized. Also, the energy needs of buildings are not consistent with the solar insolation curve and about 30-50% solar energy is not utilized. Furthermore, there are other problems with the inverters that make them less efficient for places without energy buybacks. To this end in this work, we present a Smart Energy Switching Platform (SESP) that takes the coupling of the solar power and energy from the grid at device level for more fine grained utilization of solar energy. Our initial results show a reduction of about 42% in upfront and maintenance cost of SESP when compared with hybrid solar energy systems for the same building.

SenSys'15, November 1–4, 2015, Seoul, Republic of Korea
ACM 978-1-4503-3631-4/15/11.
http://dx.doi.org/10.1145/2809695.2817884.

2. APPROACH AND ARCHITECTURE

Figure 1 shows the architecture of SESP. Selected devices in the building are connected with two sources of energy i.e. solar and grid using a Smart Switch. Smart Switch is placed with a single electrical device or a cluster of devices to control the source of energy. Smart Switches sense the live energy usage of devices. This live energy information is communicated to a Central Coordinator using Zigbee communication module. The central controller also receives live information on real-time solar energy production. State of charge in the batteries is also reported to the central controller. Energy information from the respective smart switches, information on solar energy production and the state of charge in the batteries are used for making the switch of a cluster between solar or grid energy based using user-defined preferences. User may set priorities on the state of charge in the batteries, or priorities on running clusters on solar or grid energy. Based on these priorities, SESP tries to maximize the usage of solar energy amongst the device clusters. SESP also has a weather forecaster that predicts the solar insolation of the next day and the next few hours using publicly available weather information[3].

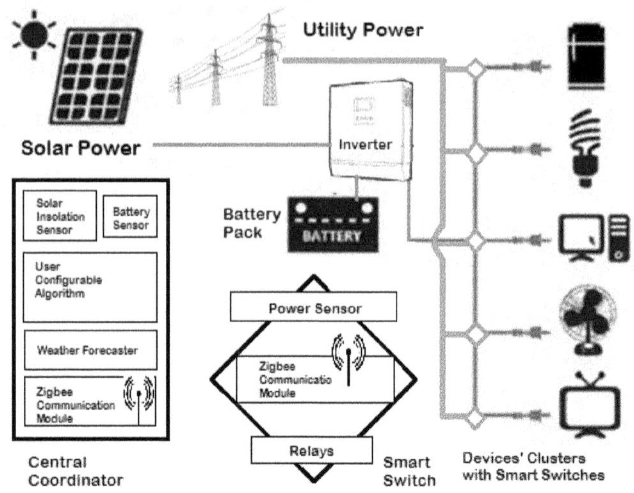

Figure 1: Smart Energy Switching Platform. (Diamond symbols are Smart Switches where energy from solar and energy from the grid is coupled)

In its default state, the SESP works in the following manner: At sunrise the system starts sensing the solar energy production. Central controller keeps a sorted list energy usage information from all clusters. As soon as the solar energy production is enough to switch the least energy consuming cluster its energy source is shifted to solar. The Central Coordinator sends a control signal to a Smart Switch to change the source of energy for the cluster. Based on a user-defined time interval the central controller checks the solar energy production and tries to match with a combination of clusters to maximally utilize the solar energy. Also the central controller keeps enough buffer in the batteries to meet any shortfall solar energy production for a brief time period.

3. PRELIMINARY RESULTS

Figure 2a shows the result of SESP on a sunny day in a building with six clusters of varying profiles. In this figure, one can note that as soon as the solar energy is available at sunrise one or more clusters are shifted to solar energy. After a given time interval a new set of clusters are shifted to solar energy. This process continues until sunset. The solar energy usage is almost exactly the same as the solar insolation curve. Thus, at the end of the day the efficiency of solar energy production in this particular building is more than 97% of the available solar insolation. Figure 2b shows the same building with patchy sunlight. On this particular day the solar energy efficiency is more than 94%.

To summarize the SESP is able to bring the cost of the system down by about 42% even after adding the cost of Smart Switches and related electric wiring. Further the payback period of a solar energy system is down from nine to to seven years. This reduction in cost and payback period is possible by reducing the number of batteries required in the system which in turn reduces the maintenance cost of the system. Also, using SESP one does not need expensive MPPT Hybrid Inverters and can use the PWM Off-grid inverters which are available in half the price.

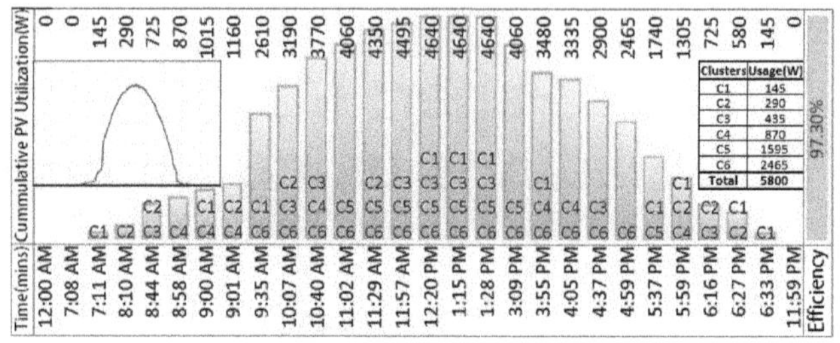

(a) Sunny

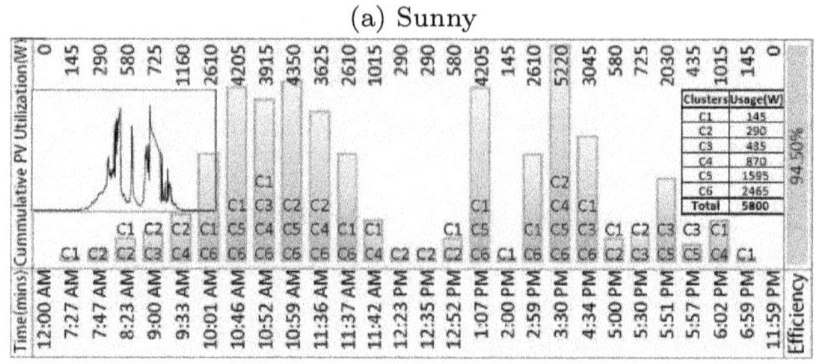

(b) Both Sunny Cloudy

Figure 2: SESP Solar Energy Utilization on a sunny day and in a day with partial overcast

4. CONCLUSION AND FUTURE WORK

SESP provides an alternate model for solar energy utilization at places where energy buyback programs such as net-metering or feed-in tariffs are not available. The design of SESP is deliberately kept simple to encourage its usage in developing countries. Moreover, one can install SESP with only two Smart Switches. By doing this, cost of the system will be reduce even further.

One possible future direction is to extend this system at neighborhood scale. Since some buildings have minimal energy needs during weekends and holidays the energy could be utilized in neighborhood buildings by making an energy co-op. Presently the system uses a simple bin-packing algorithm. However, for scalability this needs to be updated with a more sophisticated and scalable algorithm.

Another possible direction is to improve the algorithm to cater for planning power load shedding during the daytime. The battery needs to have enough storage to keep the high priority clusters energized during such outages. Another more challenging improvement in the algorithm is to plan for unplanned outages of varying durations.

Yet another direction is to cater varying power profiles of the clusters. Presently we are assuming the power profiles of the clusters to be constant. However, in reality power profiles vary all the time.

5. REFERENCES

[1] O. Erdinc and M. Uzunoglu. Optimum design of hybrid renewable energy systems: Overview of different approaches. *Renewable and Sustainable Energy Reviews*, 16(3):1412 – 1425, 2012.

[2] L. Perez-Lombard, J. Ortiz, and C. Pout. A review on buildings energy consumption information. *Energy and Buildings*, 40(3):394 – 398, 2008.

[3] N. Sharma, J. Gummeson, D. Irwin, and P. Shenoy. Cloudy computing: Leveraging weather forecasts in energy harvesting sensor systems. In *Sensor Mesh and Ad Hoc Communications and Networks (SECON), 2010 7th Annual IEEE Communications Society Conference on*, pages 1–9. IEEE, 2010.

Poster Abstract: A Dynamically Switchable Scheduling System in Wireless Sensor Networks

Yoshiki Komachi*, Jin Nakazawa†, Hideyuki Tokuda†
Graduate School of Media and Governance*, Faculty of Environment and Information Studies†
Keio University
ysk@ht.sfc.keio.ac.jp, jin@ht.sfc.keio.ac.jp, hxt@ht.sfc.keio.ac.jp

ABSTRACT

Operating Systems (OS) in wireless sensor nodes can be classified into event-driven systems or multithreaded systems. Most event-driven systems, such as TinyOS, drive down power consumption although context switching for real-time processing is not available. Among multithreaded systems, non-preemptive systems, such as Protothreads [2] in Contiki [1], often have lack of real-time processing capability. In Protothreads, if a higher-priority task was posted while a lower-priority task has been running, the lower-priority task cannot be preempted. Thus, one challenge is that without changing the semantics of Protothreads, how the system can be preemptive as well as lowering the power consumption for real-time tasks such as target tracking.

In this paper, we propose a dynamically switchable scheduling system for operating systems using Protothreads where events with time constraint have occurred. This system enables to trigger interruption, to process real-time tasks preferentially when real-time events occurred, and to save energy by executing tasks except real-time tasks as a standard event-driven system. Exeprimental results show that latency in Contiki is reduced by about 75% in the best case and is kept constant with power efficiency.

Categories and Subject Descriptors

D.4.7 [**Operating Systems**]: Organization and Design—*Real-time systems and embedded systems*; D.4.1 [**Operating Systems**]: Process Management—*Scheduling*

Keywords

Real-Time Processing; Low Power Consumption

1. INTRODUCTION

Along with cheaper and high performanced sensor nodes, Wireless Sensor Networks (WSN) are widely used in various application domains. There are various types of applications adapted to WSN, such as habitat monitoring, health monitoring, and target tracking. In target tracking applications, specific tasks (e.g., an task for detection of targets) must be processed with power efficiency as well as in real-time.

Operating Systems in wireless sensor nodes can be classified into event-driven systems or multithreaded systems. Not based on preemption, event-driven systems are built with low energy consumption. However, on event-driven systems, it is difficult to develop various applications and tasks are not processed in real-time. On the contrary to event-driven systems, most multithreaded systems which handle preemptive multitasking support real-time processing. Nevertheless, context switching makes multithreaded systems' power consumption higher.

Nano-RK [3], a multithreaded system in WSN, supports fixed-priority preemptive multitasking. This system enables hard and soft real-time processing by different two scheduling algorithms. In standard multithreaded systems (e.g., Nano-RK), variables' values are kept by being stored states of registers if interruption has occurred. The values are read again, and the processing is resumed after execution of the currently executed task was completed. Besides regular processing, these extra processing for context switching needs extra power. Therefore, power consumption of multithreaded systems is higher than other event-driven systems.

In Contiki, an event-driven system, Protothreads enables switching between tasks as same as other multithreaded systems, and processes will be executed if events are received. Events are inserted into an queue when the events occurred, and the events are kept in the queue until the events are accepted in First In First Out (FIFO) order. Unlike standard multithreaded systems, in Contiki using Protothreads, utilization of CPU will be abandoned by return values, which enables keeping power consumption lower. In case of switching between tasks, timers are not used for interruption in current Protothreads. Tasks are inserted into the queue when the timer's counts were larger than current time. The task that manages the timers is periodically executed, its priority is equal to the other tasks' priority.

2. PROBLEMS

There are tradeoffs between low power consumption and real-time processing. This is because event-driven systems are designed on the assumption that tasks are not interrupted, and context switching by saving states of registers needs much energy in multithreaded systems. However, both keeping power consumption lower under normal conditions and real-time processing in case of occurrence of real-

SenSys'15, November 1–4, 2015, Seoul, Republic of Korea.
ACM 978-1-4503-3631-4/15/11.
DOI: http://dx.doi.org/10.1145/2809695.2817885.

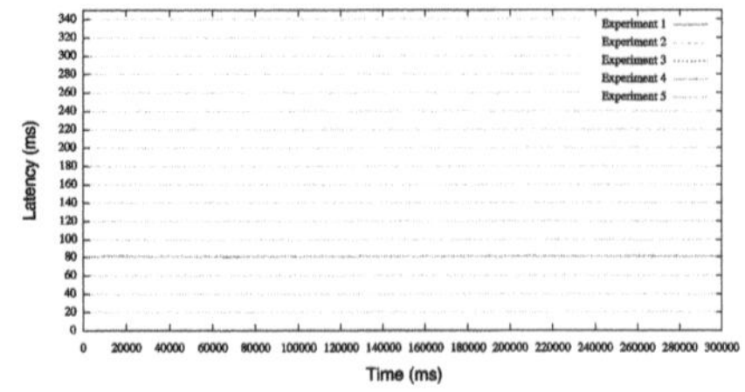

Figure 1: Latency in Our System

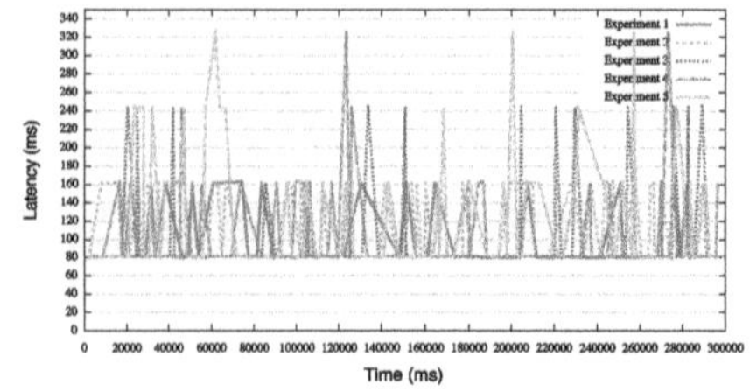

Figure 2: Latency in Contiki

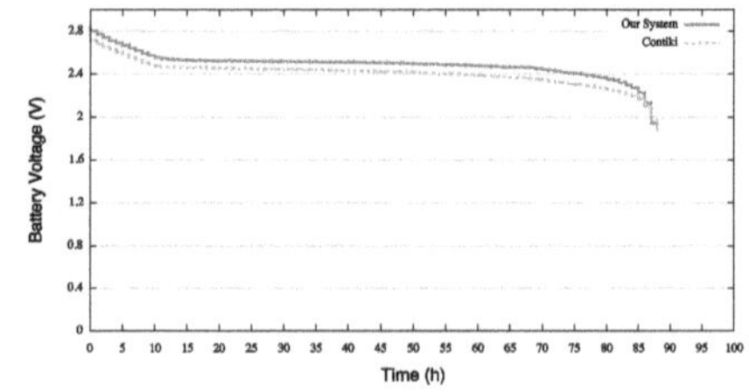

Figure 3: Power Consumption

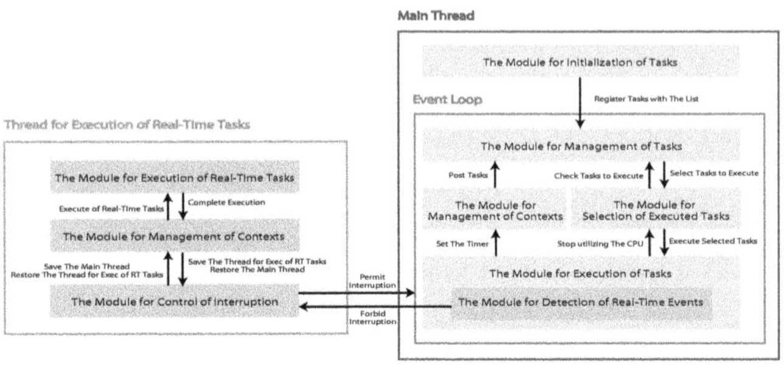

Figure 4: System Architecture

time events are needed in the specific situations (e.g., target tracking).

Although Protothreads implemented on the event-driven system enables switching between tasks, this system is unable to interrupt an executed task, to switch to higher-priority tasks, and to execute these tasks when these tasks wait for execution. This is because the scheduler will not be executed unless an executed task issues a return instruction.

3. DESIGN AND IMPLEMENTATION

Our system consists of many event handlers and an event loop. The event loop waits for the arrival of events, and an event handler correlated with the event would be executed. During execution of the event loop, an executed task is interrupted, and the current thread is switched to a real-time thread when real-time event was issued. Execution of the event loop is resumed again after execution of the real-time task was finished. Our system enables switching between tasks by Protothreads for general events except real-time events. Figure 4 shows system architecture of our system.

Our system based on Contiki 2.6 is implemented on MicaZ, which has an Atmel AVR Atmega 128 8-bit microcontroller and a 4-Kbyte static RAM.

4. EVALUATION

4.1 Evaluation Environment

We evaluate the latency, time from occurrence of real-time events to being executed intended tasks, by increasing the number of tasks and an incidence of events little by little. In this evaluation, Cooja, a simulator designed for Contiki on virtual machines, are used.

In order to evaluate power consumption, an application that randomly sends current battery voltage as real-time events to the base station is deployed to MicaZ.

4.2 Discussion

In Contiki, if events waiting for execution have been already inserted at the moment of real-time events' occurence, high latency could be observed. This is because events are inserted in FIFO order. Against Contiki, when real-time events were issued, our system enables real-time tasks to be executed by interruption of current execution if a current task are being executed. This leads to lower latency.

According to Figure 1, the time from issue to execution is constant although our system needs as much as 80ms to execute real-time tasks. In wireless sensor nodes, since radio modules require the highest power, refraining from utilizing wireless communication per a unit leads to lower power consumption. Our system enables radio to be turned on periodically, which results in realization of power saving. Figure 3 shows that our system is comparable to Contiki in power consumption in spite of making Contiki preemptible.

In standard multithreaded systems, as each task has each priority, both interruption and context switching are needed whenever tasks which have higher priority than an executed task wait for execution. In our system, since general tasks except real-time tasks are handled like event-driven systems, the number of both interruption and context switching can be reduced.

5. CONCLUSIONS

Under normal conditions, in our system as the event-driven system, event handlers associated with occurred events are executed. When real-time events occurred, a current task is interrupted, and execution of the interrupted task will be resumed as soon as execution of the real-time task is completed. As a result of experiments, our system enables real-time tasks to be executed within 82ms, which is about 25% of the execution latency of Contiki. Furthermore, latency is kept constant without drastically increasing in power consumption.

6. REFERENCES

[1] A. Dunkels, B. GrÃűnvall, and T. Voigt. Contiki - a lightweight and flexible operating system for tiny networked sensors, 2004.

[2] A. Dunkels, O. Schmidt, T. Voigt, and M. Ali. Protothreads: Simplifying event-driven programming of memory-constrained embedded systems. In *In Proc. 2006 SenSys*, pages 29–42. ACM Press, 2006.

[3] A. Eswaran, A. Rowe, and R. Rajkumar. Nano-rk: an energy-aware resource-centric rtos for sensor networks. In *Real-Time Systems Symposium, 2005. RTSS 2005. 26th IEEE International*, pages 10–pp. IEEE, 2005.

Poster Abstract: Solar-Powered Adaptive Street Lighting Evaluated with Real Traffic and Sunlight Data

Sei Ping Lau, Alex S. Weddell, Neil M. White, Geoff V. Merrett
Electronics and Computer Science
University of Southampton
{spl1g11, asw, nmw, gvm}@ecs.soton.ac.uk

ABSTRACT

Street lighting is an important resource; it has been shown to reduce crime, improve road safety, and increase economic activity. These benefits, however, come with a cost: an annual emission of 64 million tonnes of CO_2. Solar-powered street lighting is attractive for its use of renewable energy and its ease of installation (particularly in off-grid applications), but sizing and control is a non-trivial task. This paper describes TALiSMaN-Green, a traffic-aware street lighting scheme which takes account of road users as well as the available energy to dynamically adjust lighting levels. Simulations using real traffic and sunlight data illustrate that solar-powered streetlights can be managed to deliver consistent usefulness throughout the night.

Categories and Subject Descriptors

J.M [**Computer Applications**]: Miscellaneous

Keywords

Energy prediction; street lighting

1. INTRODUCTION

In our previous work, we proposed TALiSMaN, a scheme for dynamically managing streetlight brightness using a distributed network of road-user sensors [2]. The scheme considers the lighting needs of motorists and pedestrians by dynamically setting lighting levels while also trying to minimize energy consumption. The decentralized scheme works wirelessly, with each streetlight transmitting to its neighbors when it senses a road user in its vicinity; the surrounding streetlights then set their light levels appropriately. Simulation results indicate an ability to reduce the energy consumption of streetlights by 45-98% (depending on traffic volume) without affecting usefulness.

Solar-powered streetlights have the potential of offering lighting to off-grid areas (e.g. rural locations), but pose the added complication of having a finite supply of energy at the beginning of each night. When TALiSMaN is used with solar-powered streetlights, if enough solar energy was not harvested during the day, the battery becomes suddenly depleted at which point the light is turned off. TALiSMaN-Green [2] was developed to address this. Energy demand and streetlight operational hours are predicted using machine learning. The scheme (Figure 1) uses these predictions, along with the charge status of the battery, to condition the brightness level requested by TALiSMaN to ensure it continues operation (at reduced brightness) until morning.

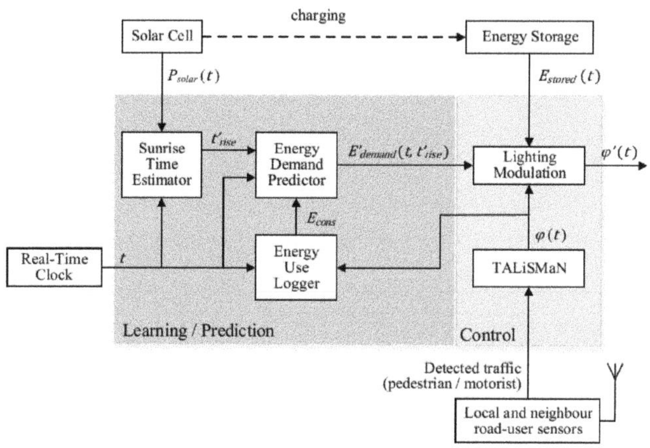

Figure 1: The TALiSMaN-Green control scheme.

While TALiSMaN-Green was shown to be effective, its evaluation made some two approximations: 1) road users were modeled using synthetic data estimated from abstract and under-sampled estimates of vehicle traffic, and 2) harvested solar energy was modeled assuming a constant initial battery charge on every evening and on every streetlight. As the success of TALiSMaN-Green depends on the effectiveness of the machine learning algorithms, these approximations may be unrepresentative of real performance. Here, we present the results of evaluating TALiSMaN-Green with real traffic and solar data.

2. EVALUATING TALISMAN-GREEN

TALiSMaN-Green was evaluated using StreetlightSim[1], a simulation environment which couples OMNeT++ network simulation with road user simulation. To model traffic, real

[1]The StreetlightSim tool is available to download from `http://www.streetlightsim.ecs.soton.ac.uk/`

SenSys'15, November 1–4, 2015, Seoul, Republic of Korea.
ACM 978-1-4503-3631-4/15/11.
DOI: http://dx.doi.org/10.1145/2809695.2817886.

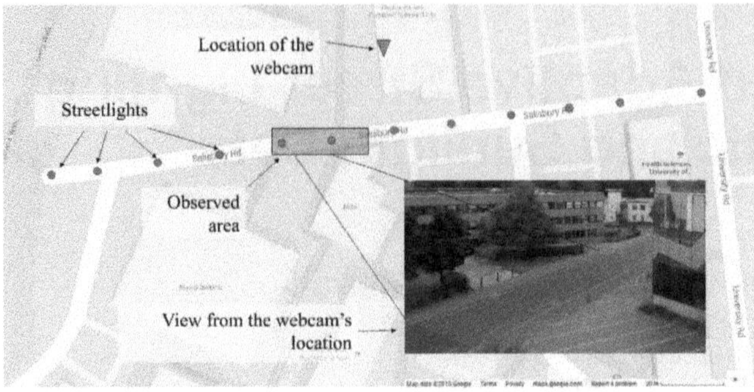

Figure 2: Data collection set-up and evaluation scenario.

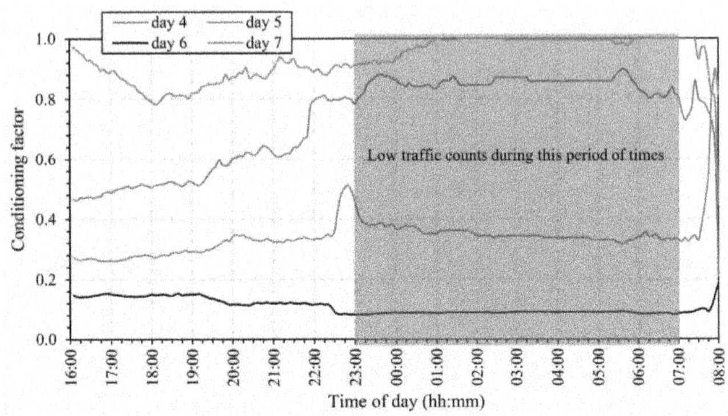

Figure 3: Conditioning factor for a single streetlight across several days of the evaluation period.

data was collected over a continuous six-week period in late winter 2015. A camera was placed in a window overlooking the road (Figure 2), and the video processed [3]. To model harvested energy, real solar radiation data [1] was used from a similar six-week winter period to estimate how much energy could be harvested on each day. To vary the amount of energy harvested by each streetlight (representing local spatial variation in sunlight, e.g. due to shadowing), a random attenuation factor was applied. Solar panel and batteries were sized to enable all-night operation with TALiSMaN, assuming average sunlight levels for a typical winter day.

3. RESULTS

Figure 3 shows the conditioning factor for a streetlight on several days of the test (a factor of 1.0 represents normal TALiSMaN operation, whereas <1.0 represents additional throttling of the brightness to manage the night's energy budget). Each day, variations in available solar energy mean the streetlight's batteries get charged to different levels; this results in a different initial conditioning factor every day. A gradual adjustment of the conditioning factor can be seen: this is normal operation, as the scheme acts to predict likely energy use and continually revise the conditioning factor in response to observed behavior. As Figure 4 shows, the streetlights only become depleted a few minutes before the 8am sunrise; this contrasts with conventional TALiSMaN, where 50% of the streetlights are depleted by 22:00. Figure 5 shows the usefulness of street lighting: TALiSMaN-Green's remains consistent throughout the night, while conventional TALiSMaN's drops significantly.

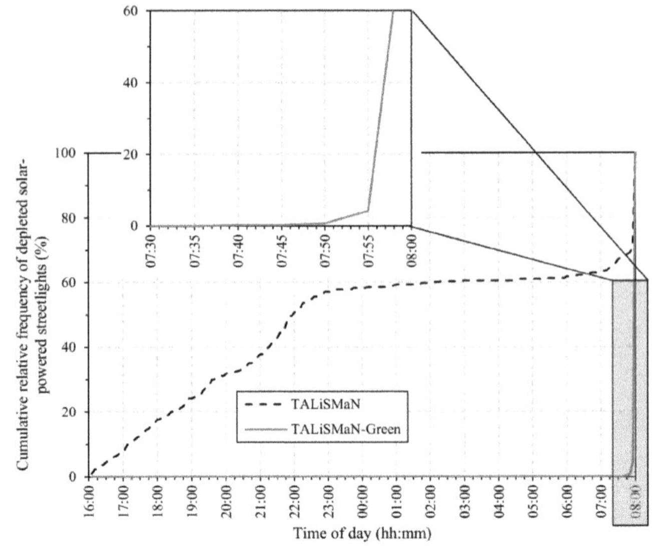

Figure 4: Proportion of solar-powered street lights which are not operational (because they have depleted batteries).

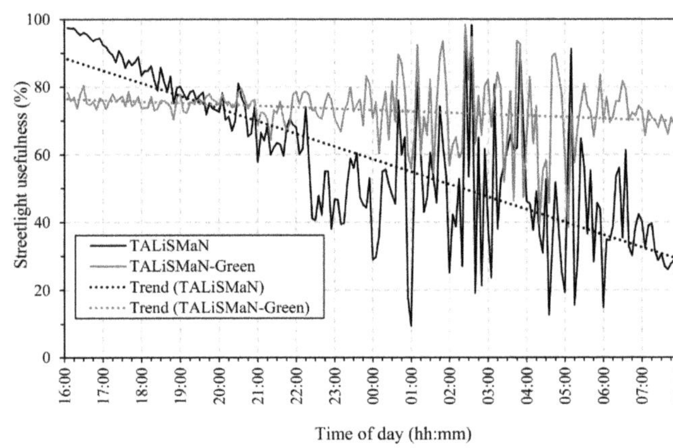

Figure 5: Mean streetlight usefulness experienced by users.

4. CONCLUSIONS

The effectiveness of TALiSMaN-Green has been evaluated using real sunlight and road traffic data, and has been shown to manage the operation of solar-powered streetlights to maintain consistent usefulness throughout the night.

5. REFERENCES

[1] A. Andreas and S. Wilcox. Solar radiation monitoring station (sorms) humboldt state university, 2007. [Online] `http://dx.doi.org/10.5439/1052559`.

[2] S. P. Lau, A. S. Weddell, G. V. Merrett, and N. White. Energy-neutral solar-powered street lighting with predictive and adaptive behaviour. In *ENSsys '14 Proceedings of the 2nd International Workshop on Energy Neutral Sensing Systems*, pages 13–18. ACM, November 2014.

[3] A. Sobral. Vehicle detection, tracking and counting, 2012. [Online] `https://www.behance.net/andrewssobral`.

Poster Abstract: Enspect—Simplifying the Design of Energy Harvesting Systems

Nick F. Tinsley, Stuart T. Witts, Jacob M. R. Ansell, Emily Barnes,
Simeon M. Jenkins, Dhanushan Raveendran, Geoff V. Merrett, Alex S. Weddell
Electronics and Computer Science
University of Southampton
{ntinsley, switts, jansell, ebarnes, sjenkins, draveendran, gvm, asw}@ecs.soton.ac.uk

ABSTRACT

The design of sensing systems powered from energy harvesting can be complex. Design decisions are required concerning the properties and parameters of energy harvesting, conversion, and storage devices. The quantity and properties of environmental energy are typically both temporally and spatially variant, while the current consumption of the load electronics also changes dynamically. In this paper we describe Enspect, an open-source hardware/software tool which simplifies the design of energy harvesting sensing systems by assisting in the specification of harvesting and storage devices. It does this by enabling the long-term collection of data on energy availability, and modeling and simulating the performance of a complete system.

Categories and Subject Descriptors

B.8.2 [**Hardware**]: Performance and ReliabilityPerformance Analysis and Design Aids

Keywords

Design tools, Energy harvesting, Modeling

1. INTRODUCTION

Energy harvesting offers a variety of attractive features to wireless sensing devices [1] but, due to significant differences in deployment environments and application requirements, every new system is typically completely redesigned. This is necessitated by the interdependencies between parts of the system, ranging from the spatial and temporal variation exhibited by different environmental energy sources, the multidimensional parameter space of energy harvesters and circuits, and the requirements of different applications.

Existing tools can capture data on energy availability from a single energy harvesting source. Ekho [2] captures data on the performance of a photovoltaic (PV) cell and allows it to be later replayed, while [3] is a portable device which measures the spectral composition of light and predicts available power from different PV cell chemistries. However, system designers may be unsure which energy harvester is most appropriate for a certain load and application; e.g. they may be considering either PV cells or thermoelectric generators (TEGs), or perhaps plan to use a combination of harvesters.

Here, we present Enspect, an open source[1] tool comprised of two parts: (1) a logger which collects long-term in-situ data on environmental energy availability from a variety of sources, and (2) analysis software that models the performance of a complete system to evaluate component choices.

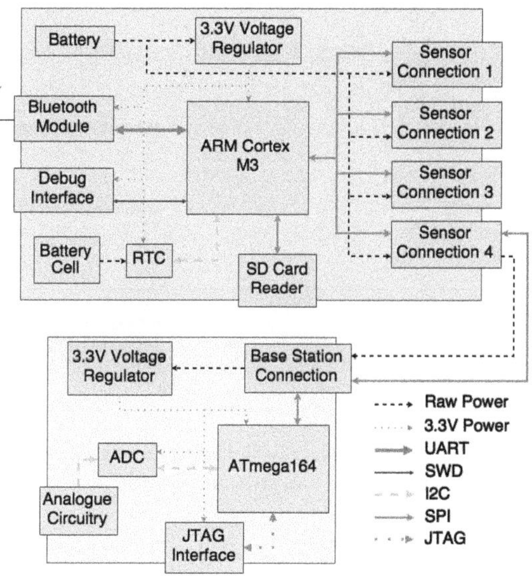

Figure 1: Block diagram of Enspect's data collection unit (DCU) and sensor module.

2. ENSPECT

To enable data on environmental energy availability to be collected, Enspect's Data Collection Unit (DCU), shown in Figure 1, can interface with up to four independent sensor modules. These may be used to evaluate different types of energy source (e.g. light and temperature difference), or the availability of energy in multiple nearby locations or different orientations. In the example shown, the PV sensor modules is capable of logging light intensity as well as its coarse spectral composition (RGB + infra-red). Intelligence

[1]Obtain schematics, embedded software, and PC analysis software from `http://www.enspect.ecs.soton.ac.uk`

SenSys'15, November 1–4, 2015, Seoul, Republic of Korea.
ACM 978-1-4503-3631-4/15/11.
DOI: http://dx.doi.org/10.1145/2809695.2817887.

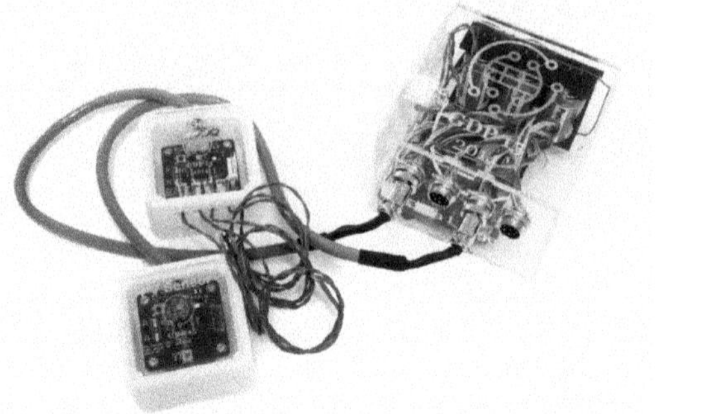

Figure 2: Enspect DCU with PV and TEG sensor modules.

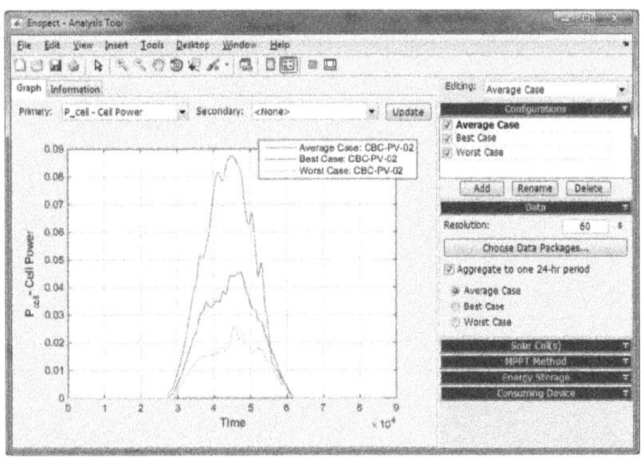

Figure 3: Analysis tool, predicting PV cell power output from average, best, and worst case data.

is devolved to these modules, with processing taking place on the on-board microcontroller to minimize the amount of traffic to the DCU; typically modules will report their readings at 2 Hz, but this can be reconfigured in software. The system is plug-and-play: it will recognize the sensor modules connected and configure itself appropriately. It can be configured over Bluetooth, and logs data to an SD card. The system has a minimum 24 hour operating lifetime. Figure 2 shows the DCU with two sensor modules (PV and TEG).

The MATLAB analysis software (Figure 3) takes data obtained by the DCU and models system performance. It uses models of energy harvester performance, which can be derived from datasheets or empirical measurements, and allows the system design to be manipulated to observe the effect of various component choices. For example, it allows various techniques for maximum power point tracking to be evaluated, as well as enabling the capacity of the energy storage device (battery) to be adjusted. The software is modular so its components can be exchanged.

The tool introduces the concept of a power 'surplus' and 'deficit'; a surplus is when the battery is full and harvested energy is wasted; a deficit is when the battery is empty and cannot provide power to the load. If a system experiences both surplus and deficit, it indicates under-sized energy storage. If it only exhibits a deficit, it may be due to the harvester being under-sized. Figure 4 shows a complete system simulation, with a duty-cycled sensor node powered from a PV harvester: (a) with an under-sized battery (exhibiting surplus and deficit); (b) with an appropriately-sized battery.

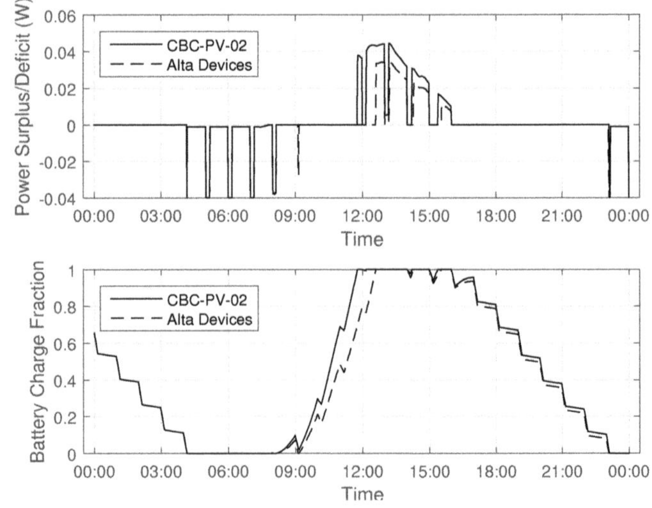

(a) Under-sized battery

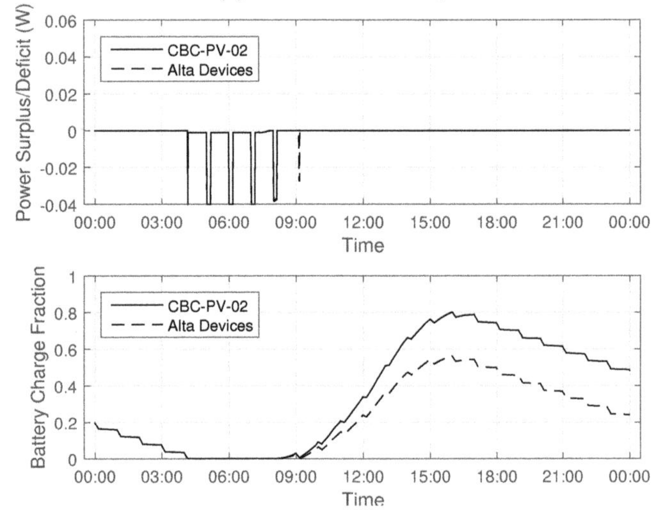

(b) Appropriately-sized battery

Figure 4: Simulation of system, with two battery capacities.

3. CONCLUSIONS

Enspect simplifies the development of energy harvesting systems. It allows long-term data to be collected, and allows decisions to be made on the design of an energy harvesting system. By illustrating the charge state of the system, and using energy surplus and deficit concepts, the robust design of energy harvesting systems has become more intuitive.

4. REFERENCES

[1] S. Beeby and N. White. *Energy Harvesting for Autonomous Systems.* Smart Materials, Structures, and Systems Series. Artech House, 2014.

[2] J. Hester, T. Scott, and J. Sorber. Ekho: Realistic and repeatable experimentation for tiny energy-harvesting sensors. In *Proc ACM SenSys'14*, pages 1–15, New York, NY, USA, 2014. ACM.

[3] J. Sarik *et al.* More than meets the eye - a portable measurement unit for characterizing light energy availability. In *Global Conf. Signal and Information Processing*, pages 387–390, Dec 2013.

Poster Abstract: MICO: Model-Based Irrigation Control Optimization

Daniel A. Winkler Robert Wang Francois Blanchette*

Miguel Á. Carreira-Perpiñán Alberto E. Cerpa

Electrical Engineering and Computer Science
*Applied Mathematics
University of California, Merced
{dwinkler2,rwang6,fblanchette,mcarreira-perpinan,acerpa}@ucmerced.edu

ABSTRACT

Lawns, both public and private, make up the largest irrigated crop in North America by surface area. Although there have been improvements in sprinkler head technology and weather assimilation, state-of-the-art irrigation systems do nothing to adjust for heterogeneous terrain or varying lawn environments. In this work, a computationally lightweight soil moisture movement model is developed, which allows the computation of optimal irrigation valve scheduling using standard optimization techniques. A prototype sprinkler head is produced with the ability to sense local soil moisture conditions, wirelessly communicate, and independently actuate based on the optimal schedule centrally computed. This prototype is then deployed to control two parallel irrigation systems covering a total of more than 10,000 ft^2 for a duration of 5 weeks. It is shown that lawn health can be maintained by using the topography of the space to take advantage of runoff to provide improved coverage while using an average of 23.4% less water. We also show that the initial capital and operating costs of our system could be amortized by our water savings in 13 months while maintaining and/or improving quality of irrigation and lawn health.

Categories and Subject Descriptors

J.7 [**Computers In Other Systems**]: Command & control; C.3 [**Special-Purpose and Application-Based Systems**]: Real-time and embedded systems

Keywords

Irrigation; Monitoring; Control

1. INTRODUCTION AND MOTIVATION

As the western United States suffers its fourth year of a historical drought, coming on the heels of a similar drought in the south-east United States, resources have become widely available to promote efficient use of freshwater. In spite of this, lawn (turf) irrigation systems continue to operate inefficiently. As turf makes up North America's largest irrigated crop by surface area [1], improved efficiency will help to alleviate the freshwater shortages the nation is experiencing.

Efficient watering is critical to the health of the turf and surrounding environment. Insufficient irrigation will cause turf to lose its healthy look, and eventually cause plant death. Generally, groundskeepers and homeowners prevent this by over-irrigating, but over time this can lead to root rot, soil instability, and in extreme cases the leeching of harmful chemicals into the groundwater, as examined in [3].

In this work, we identify the cause of these issues to be an incorrect amount of irrigation applied to the soil surface and create an irrigation system that benefits from two main contributions. The first is the development of a sprinkler node with the ability to sense its environment using a soil moisture sensor, actuate independently based on a centrally-computed schedule, and communicate wirelessly with sister nodes in the environment. The second contribution is the development of a computationally-efficient moisture movement model that incorporates the fundamental sources of water movement in an irrigated environment, which is used in coordination with an optimization framework to determine optimal valve scheduling for the distributed sprinkler nodes. Using this model-driven approach, we are able to provide more precise irrigation control to turf areas, and demonstrate over a five-week deployment that quality of service can be improved, while reducing system water consumption.

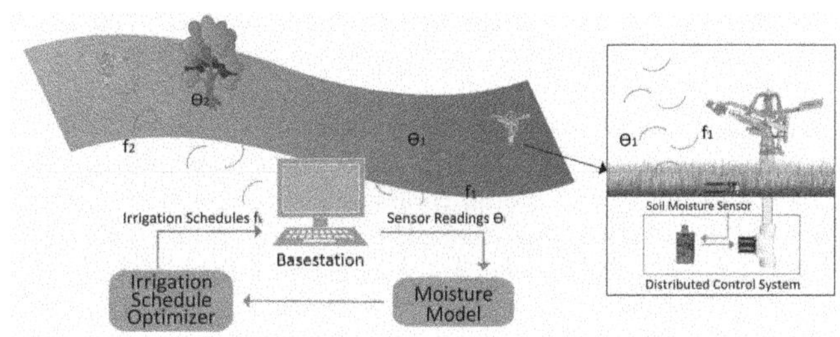

Figure 1: MICO System Architecture Overview

2. SYSTEM OVERVIEW

The MICO system architecture can be seen in Figure 1. The MICO nodes are integrated into the irrigation system's

SenSys'15, November 1–4, 2015, Seoul, South Korea..
ACM 978-1-4503-3631-4/15/11.
DOI: http://dx.doi.org/10.1145/2809695.2817888.

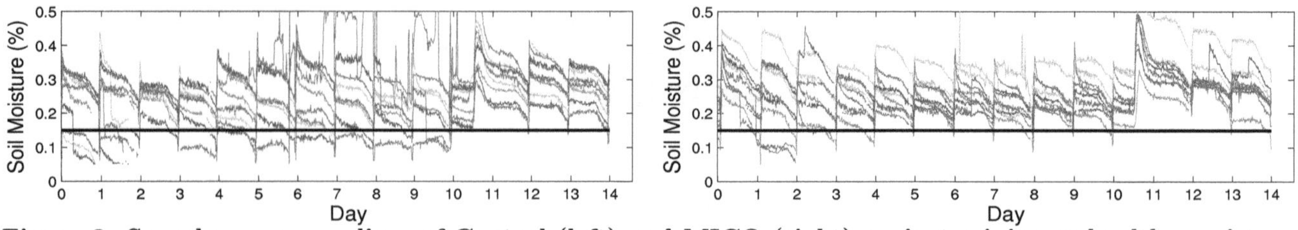

Figure 2: Sample sensor readings of Control (left) and MICO (right) against minimum healthy moisture

architecture, each equipped with a soil moisture sensor, a solenoid to control water flow to the attached sprinkler, and a tmote sky for radio communication. To react to environmental conditions, soil moisture data is collected by each MICO node in the space and routed to the *Basestation*, interfacing between the 802.15.4 network and another communication medium, such as an ethernet or 4g network.

Under a set of valve schedules, the *Moisture Model* is used to calculate movement of moisture across the surface and through the sub-surface. Sensitive to diffusion, gravity, and soil physics, it determines where water travels after being distributed by sprinklers. However, a discretized moisture movement model may consist of millions of variables and take minutes to solve one problem. As an optimizer may need to evaluate the model thousands of times to converge on a solution, we approximate the model as a linear system to make optimization practical. Once discretized in time and space for numerical evaluation, the model is fed into the *Irrigation Schedule Optimizer* to be converted into a constrained optimization problem. With current sensor readings as initial conditions and a minimum saturation level as a goal state, the *Irrigation Schedule Optimizer* solves the problem to determine an activation schedule for each MICO node in the space that provides sufficient moisture to all turf in the space while minimizing system water consumption.

Computed schedules are then disseminated by the *Basestation* through the wireless sensor network to their respective MICO node. Once received, the *Distributed Control System* then steps through the received schedule and routes power to the attached solenoid to activate the sprinkler.

3. CASE STUDY: LIVE DEPLOYMENT

As all-inclusive models for our application have not been researched, we must deploy an irrigation system that can compare our control modifications to existing systems. Ideally, existing irrigation infrastructure can be used to test our control strategies. However, we found that the granularity of irrigation control on our campus was poor, with regions spanning over 10,000 ft^2 actuated by a single valve. As such, we chose to deploy our own parallel infrastructure to run our experiments. We developed two identical irrigation systems, 70'x70' each, each with 9 MICO nodes uniformly distributed across each. One system uses the control schedules used by the university (Control), and the other uses the control schedules generated by the *Irrigation Schedule Optimizer.* As the two side-by-side irrigation systems have identical topography, lawn type, and irrigation infrastructure, any differences in water consumption and service quality can be attributed to the schedules run by each.

4. EXPERIMENTAL RESULTS

4.1 Quality of Service

To determine if the MICO system maintains lawn health, we compare sensor readings from both systems to the volumetric water content threshold known as the permanent wilting point (θ_{pwp}), where the soil becomes too dry for the plant to extract moisture. Sustained moisture below θ_{pwp} will result in wilting and death of the plant. θ_{pwp} is generally found to be between 10-15% [2], so we assign θ_{pwp} to be a conservative 15%. Figure 2 shows the sensor readings from each of the 9 sprinkler nodes from Control and MICO systems compared to the minimum moisture threshold θ_{pwp}. Across the deployment, the Control system spends a combined 1362 hours beneath θ_{pwp}, in comparison to 417 hours with the MICO system. Although this shows MICO is not perfect, the reduced time spent with insufficient moisture demonstrates that more precise watering strategies by modeling the environment and system can provide an improved quality of service, despite using less water.

4.2 Water Consumption Analysis

Throughout the deployment, actuation was closely monitored to keep track of the total on-time for each sprinkler in both systems. This actuation time is used to calculate each system's total water consumption, based on each sprinkler's regulated flow rate. The water consumption from the Control system is representative of the schedules used by campus groundskeepers. In comparison, the water consumption of the experimental system is found to reduce water consumption over the Control by 9-38% each day, with an average of 23.4% water savings over the span of the deployment.

5. CONCLUSIONS

In this work, we created a computationally-light irrigation moisture movement model that can be analyzed using standard optimization techniques to determine optimal valve scheduling based on environmental conditions and irrigation system. We then develop a prototype sprinkler head with soil moisture sensing, actuation, and wireless communication capability to determine system efficiency improvements with higher granularity of control. These sprinkler nodes are then deployed to irrigate an area of turf covering 10,000ft^2 for 5 weeks. Analysis of the data collected shows that, although the MICO system consumed 23.4% less water, the lawn sustained unhealthy moisture levels 3.23$\times$ less than with the Control system, demonstrating an improved quality of service over standard irrigation systems. As a system, MICO is estimated to pay for itself in $\sim$13 months based on water savings alone.

6. REFERENCES

[1] Looking for lawns. http://earthobservatory.nasa.gov/Features/Lawn/printall.php.
[2] Permanent wilting point. http://nrcca.cals.cornell.edu/soil/CA2/CA0212.1-3.php.
[3] T. Harter and J. R. Lund. Addressing nitrate in california's drinking water. 2012.

Poster Abstract: CARLOC: Precisely Tracking Automobile Position

Yurong Jiang[†], Hang Qiu[†], Matthew McCartney[†], Gaurav Sukhatme[†],
Marco Gruteser[*], Fan Bai[‡], Donald Grimm[‡], Ramesh Govindan[†]
[†]University of Southern California
[*]Rutgers University [‡]GM Global Research & Development
{yurongji,hangqiu,mmcartn,gaurav,ramesh}@usc.edu
gruteser@winlab.rutgers.edu
{fan.bai,donald.grimm}@gm.com

ABSTRACT

Precise positioning of an automobile to within lane-level precision can enable better navigation and context-awareness. However, GPS by itself cannot provide such precision in obstructed urban environments. In this paper, we present a system called CARLOC for lane-level positioning of automobiles. CARLOC uses three key ideas in concert to improve positioning accuracy: it uses digital maps to match the vehicle to known road segments; it uses vehicular sensors to obtain odometry and bearing information; and it uses crowd-sourced location estimates of roadway landmarks that can be detected by sensors available in modern vehicles. CARLOC unifies these ideas in a probabilistic position estimation framework, widely used in robotics, called the sequential Monte Carlo method. Through extensive experiments on a real vehicle, we show that CARLOC achieves sub-meter positioning accuracy in an obstructed urban setting, an order-of-magnitude improvement over a high-end GPS device.

1. INTRODUCTION

As mobile devices have proliferated, they have become the de-facto method for estimating the position of automobiles. The built-in GPS receiver in mobile devices provides positioning for navigation, but also for context-awareness; many apps now routinely use vehicle position to suggest nearby services or points of interest. As elements of autonomous driving start to appear in commercial offerings, the accuracy of positioning vehicles will become much more important.

However, it has long been known that smartphone GPS receivers have errors on the order of 10s of meters, especially in obstructed urban environments. It is precisely in these environments, unfortunately, where accurate positioning is most necessary because of the density of services or points of interest. An order of magnitude lower positioning error of automobiles would be able to position a vehicle with up to lane-level accuracy, which will likely enable much more accurate navigation, but also more precise context-awareness in urban environments [4].

SenSys'15, November 01–04, 2015, Seoul, Republic of Korea.
ACM 9978-1-4503-3631-4/15/11.
DOI: http://dx.doi.org/10.1145/2809695.2817889 .

We explore two dimensions in this design space that can help significantly improve positioning accuracy. First, we observe that modern automobiles have hundreds of sensors that govern the operation of their internal subsystems, and some of these sensors provide odometry and heading information. These can be used to improve the efficacy of matching a car's location to a digital map, and to model its motion. Second, car sensors can also provide enough information to detect *roadway landmarks* — roadway features such as potholes or speedbumps. If these can be reliably detected, then the *position estimates of other cars at these landmarks can be used to improve a car's position estimate.*

We design and evaluate a system called CARLOC that can continuously track the precise position of a vehicle, even in highly obstructed environments. CARLOC uses a collection of techniques, some of which are inspired by prior work on robot localization. Specifically, CARLOC uses a non-parametric probabilistic position representation, called a *particle filter*, as a uniform framework that is able to express various forms of information fusion. CARLOC matches a car's current position estimate to a road-segment on a map. CARLOC then updates the particle filter with a relatively simple kinematic model, but uses car sensors to accurately estimate inputs to the kinematic model. Finally, CARLOC enhances position estimates by using crowd-sourced position estimates of roadway landmarks. CARLOC utilizes novel algorithms to detect roadway landmarks and update the particle filters based on those crowd-sourced landmarks.

2. THE DESIGN OF CARLOC

Figure 1 depicts the various components of CARLOC. At a high-level, CARLOC models the current position of the vehicle *probabilistically*: intuitively, the position of the vehicle at any point in space is associated with a specific probability. The key idea then is to *update* or *refine* this probabilistic representation using information from various sources. Then, at any given point in time, the precise position of the vehicle is obtained by *actualizing* the probabilistic representation, as described later.

One way that CARLOC updates the probabilistic representation is by using vehicle sensors to obtain distance traveled and the heading of the car. This approach, often called *dead reckoning*, is, in CARLOC more accurate because of its use of in-built vehicular sensors. These sensors are available at frequencies ranging from 10 100Hz, so they can provide accurate estimates of distance and heading over short timescales and distances. However, vehicle sensors by themselves are insufficient: sensor errors can, over time, cause position estimates to drift significantly from the true position.

A second way to update the probabilistic representation is to periodically obtain GPS readings. These readings are associated with

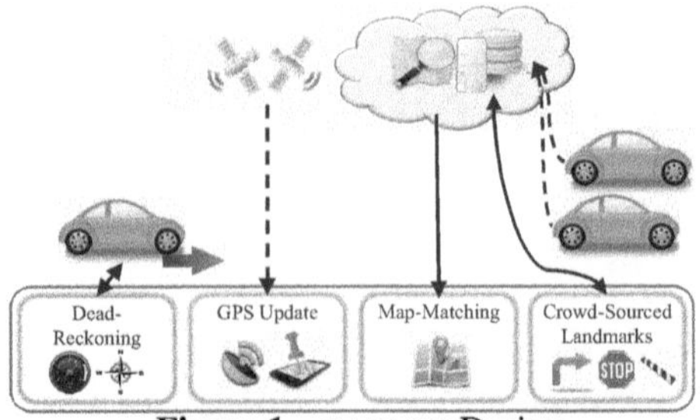

Figure 1—CARLOC Design

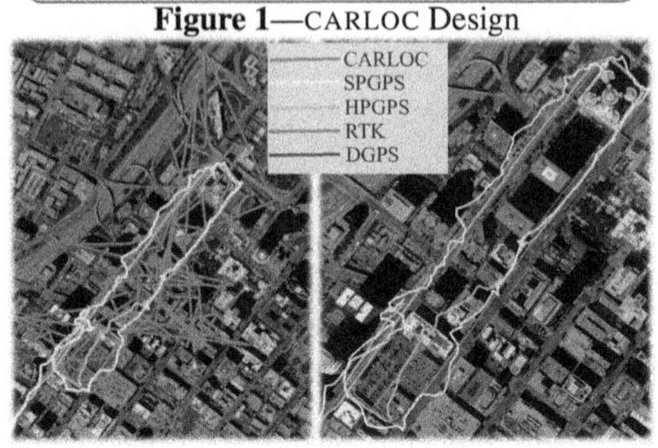

Figure 2—CARLOC and GPS Comparison in Downtown

estimates of error, which can be used to tighten the car's position estimates. GPS errors in obstructed environments can increase the car's position uncertainty.

To overcome GPS errors, one can *spatially refine* the probabilistic position estimates using digital maps. Intuitively, a car is likely to be off a roadway with a very small or near-zero probability, and map-matching algorithms [3] use this observation to refine position estimates. On the other hand, inertial sensors can speed up map-matching process by identifying condition changes. For example, detecting turn from inertial sensor will let CARLOC switch the matched road segment immediately. Thus, CARLOC's access to car sensors can help improve accuracy of its map-matching algorithms. More description of our map-matching algorithm can be found in the full paper.

The last component of CARLOC is based on the observation that *roadway landmarks* mark consistent positions in the environment that be exploited to refine the car's probabilistic position estimate. Consider a speed-bump on a road: if a car passes over a speedbump, it can refine its own position estimates using position estimates of *other cars when they passed over the same speedbump*. This suggests that *crowd-sourced* position estimates of roadway landmarks can be used to improve a car's position estimates. CARLOC incorporates several novel algorithms that use vehicle sensors to identify roadway landmarks. In current design, CARLOC detects 3 roadway landmarks *Stop Sign*, *Street Corner* and *Speed Bump*. The detailed landmark detection algorithms are discussed in the full paper.

3. EVALUATION

We conducted experiments with 2 drivers driving over routes with different characteristics from the perspective of a GPS receiver. Across all routes, we compare CARLOC performance against using a GPS receiver on a Google Nexus 5 (labeled *SPGPS* on our graphs). In addition, on some routes, we also compare against using an expensive (>\$200) high-precision GPS receiver, the ublox NEO-7P GPS (*HPGPS*). Finally, we also use a companion rover receiver, the ublox LEA-6T to obtain Differential GPS (DGPS [6]) position as well as Real-Time Kinematic (RTK [5]) based positioning. Our measure of CARLOC performance is *positioning error* measured by distance between CARLOC's position and ground truth. We use three types of ground truth based on experiment setup: *Closed-loop routes* , *High-precision GPS receiver* and *Google Maps*. More details are described in the full paper.

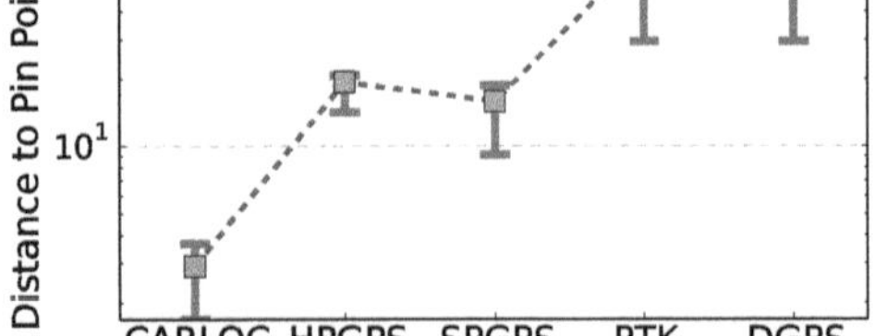

Figure 3—Map Pin Points Comparison

CARLOC on an Obstructed Route Our obstructed route is a 2-mile loop in a downtown area surrounded by tall buildings (Figure 2). CARLOC and compare it against the high-precision GPS receiver, DGPS and RTK. We use the Google Maps based ground-truthing technique and we collected 15 different points as ground-truth. More description is in the full paper. Figure 3 shows CARLOC has an average error of about 2.7m, with the smallest error being 0.6m as closest and the largest being 4.9m. Surprisingly, all of the alternatives have one to two orders of magnitude higher error. Figure 2 depicts these results visually. In the figure on the left, it is evident that DGPS and RTK measurements span the entire area covered by the two-mile loop. In the figure on the right, the superior performance of CARLOC vis-a-vis the high-precision receiver and the smartphone are visually evident.

More results for two other conditions *Un-obstructed route* and *Partially Obstructed route* are discussed in detail in full paper.

4. FUTURE WORK

Our current experiments hint at the benefits of crowdsourcing, but the impact of multiple drivers and cars would require significant study. Especially the landmark detection algorithms can be made more robust to different drivers' driving behaviors. Moreover, our CARLOC framework is designed to generalize to various landmarks. CARLOC can attempt to leverage additional roadway landmarks such as changes in the road surface texture, potholes, or discontinuities in lighting caused by entering a tunnel

5. REFERENCES

[1] T. Flach, N. Mishra, L. Pedrosa, C. Riesz, and R. Govindan. Carma: towards personalized automotive tuning. In *Proceedings of the 9th ACM Conference on Embedded Networked Sensor Systems*. ACM, 2011.

[2] Y. Jiang, H. Qiu, M. McCartney, W. G. Halfond, F. Bai, D. Grimm, and R. Govindan. Carlog: a platform for flexible and efficient automotive sensing. In *Proceedings of the 12th ACM Conference on Embedded Network Sensor Systems*. ACM, 2014.

[3] J. Krumm, E. Horvitz, and J. Letchner. Map matching with travel time constraints. Technical report, SAE Technical Paper, 2007.

[4] D. Li, T. Bansal, Z. Lu, and P. Sinha. Marvel: multiple antenna based relative vehicle localizer. In *Proceedings of the 18th annual international conference on Mobile computing and networking*, pages 245–256. ACM, 2012.

[5] RTKLIB: An open source program package for GNSS positioning. http://www.rtklib.com/. 2011.

[6] R. I. Technologies. What is differential GPS. http://www.roseindia.net/technology/gps/what-is-Differential-GPS.shtml. February 2008.

[7] Ublox Chips. http://www.ublox.com/en/.

Poster Abstract: A Low-Power Sensing Method Using Linux Kernel on Android Devices

Masaru Takagi
The University of Tokyo
7-3-1 Hongo, Bunkyo
Tokyo, Japan
takagi@akg.t.u-tokyo.ac.jp

Yoshihiro Kawahara
The University of Tokyo
7-3-1 Hongo, Bunkyo
Tokyo, Japan
kawahara@akg.t.u-tokyo.ac.jp

Tohru Asami
The University of Tokyo
7-3-1 Hongo, Bunkyo
Tokyo, Japan
asami@akg.t.u-tokyo.ac.jp

ABSTRACT

According to the statistics, people upgrade smartphones at every two years, which means tremendous number of phones will be left unused. In this paper, we propose a method to use Android-based smartphones as wireless sensors for environmental monitoring. Although the idea of using smartphones as a wireless sensor sounds naive, the previous approaches were un-practical because of its limited battery life. In this paper, we exploit the Linux kernel boot mode on Android devices to extend the battery life drastically. Unlike normal mode, power consumption in the kernel mode is minimum but still it is possible to access to all the sensors in principle. In this paper, we measure the power consumption of Nexus5 while booting, running and shutting down Android OS / Linux kernel and estimate the battery life assuming a duty cycle. The results show that utilizing the Linux kernel can extend the battery life up to 10.9 times when the sensing interval is 3 minutes.

Categories and Subject Descriptors

H.4 [**Information Systems Applications**]: General

General Terms

Measurement, Performance

Keywords

Smartphone Sensing, Battery Life

1. SMARTPHONE SENSING

The rapid spread of Android smartphones equipped with high quality sensors has encouraged many researchers to consider the utilization of smartphones as sensor devices[3].

Android OS supports many types of built-in sensors such as temperature, humidity, accelerometer and gyro sensor,

SenSys '15, November 01-04, 2015, Seoul, Republic of Korea
ACM 978-1-4503-3631-4/15/11.
http://dx.doi.org/10.1145/2809695.2817890

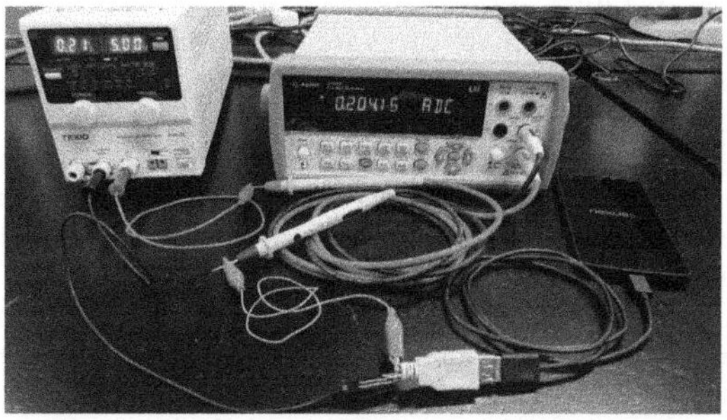

Figure 1: Power measurement of Nexus5

and can applied for many purposes. In addition, Android devices natively support LTE/3G network connections. Mobile Virtual Network Operators (MVNOs) offer LTE/3G connections at less than $3 per month even in Japan and lots of used smartphones are distributed on online auction less than $80. Moreover, most Android-based smartphones sold in Asia region comes with waterproof housing. Thus, the utilization of "used" smartphones for sensing is much more reasonable choice than developing a new sensing hardware using microcontrollers.

DSP.Ear[1] utilizes the co-processors and reduces the power consumption of voice recognition. Piggyback CrowdSensing [2] lowers the energy overhead by exploiting the opportunities in which the user of the device uses the target sensor device or the network interface. These researches implicitly assume that the target devices are used in daily life and routinely charged by the user. Thus these approaches are not suitable for environmental monitoring without commercial power supply. The biggest challenge is how to reduce the power consumption and extend its battery life.

To tackle with this issue, we propose to utilize the Linux kernel mode on Android devices without booting the Android OS. This operation mode is typically found when the handset is switched-off but connected to a charger. Linux kernel has several boot scripts, such as `init.rc`, executed during the boot process. By registering the sensing tasks to this script, we can set off a sensing task by just switching on the Android device.

2. POWER MEASUREMENT

To estimate how much the battery life can be stretched, we measured the power consumption of Nexus5 while booting, running and shutting down Android OS and the coun-

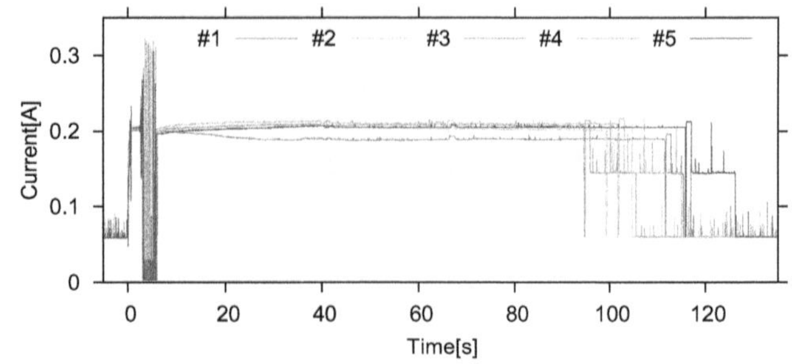

Figure 2: Transition of current while booting Android OS on Nexus5

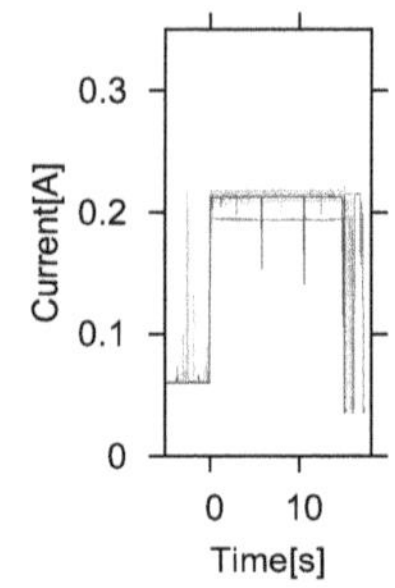

Figure 3: while shutting down

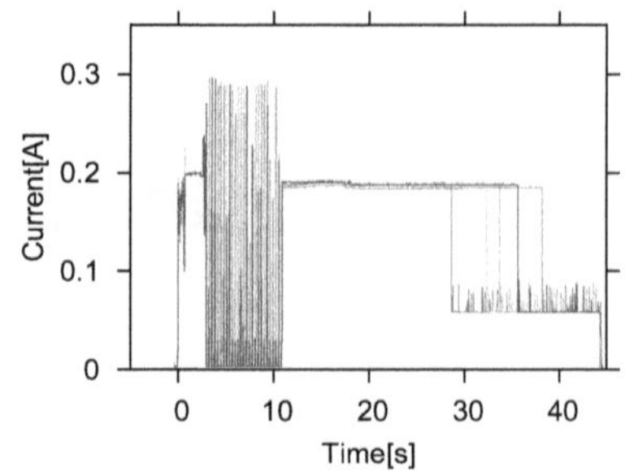

Figure 4: Transition of current while booting Linux kernel

terparts of Linux kernel. In order to boot only Linux kernel, we utilized the battery charge mode of AOSP ROM for Nexus5, which appears only when the device is switched off and connected to a charger. In the experiments, we supplied Nexus5 with the power from a stabilized power source equipment and measured the current with the multi-meter, Agilent 34410A. We conducted 5 measurements for each condition and drew graphs in different colors (#1∼#5).

Figure 2 shows the transition of the current while booting the Android OS. It took 44 seconds in average before the broadcast intent delivered, which notifies the completion of the boot process, but took 120 seconds in average before the current became stable around 0.06A. During the boot process, the device consumed 85.2J in average.

Figure 3 shows the current while shutting down the Android OS. It took 15 seconds in average before the current became stable and 12.5J of energy consumed in total.

Figure 4 shows the current while booting the Linux kernel alone. It took only 11 seconds in average and the current became stable around 0.06A in 34 seconds. Total power consumed during the boot process was 21.2J in average. The shut down process of the Linux kernel is short enough and we can ignore its effect to the battery life.

3. BATTERY LIFE ESTIMATION

We then estimated the battery life in the practical scenario based on the result of the power measurement. In this scenario, we switch on the device, measure the temperature and shut down the device once every n hour. We also assume the following four conditions. First, it takes 2 seconds to measure the temperature. Second, the additional power consumption of the temperature sensor is negligible, because Android devices always monitor the temperature of its battery, CPU and so on. Third, the capacity of the battery is 2300mAh, which is the same number as Nexus5. Finally, given that it takes around 1 year for the battery to be completely discharged naturally, the power consumption while the device is switched off is $2300mAh \times 3.8V \div (365 \times 24h) \simeq 1mW$.

In case of using Android OS, the device consumes 27.0J for booting, 1.5J while sensing, 12.5J for shutting down and $3.6n$J while suspending. Total energy per cycle is $(3.6n + 41.0)$J (The red bars in Figure 5). On the other hand, in case of using the Linux kernel only, the device consumes 2.5J for booting, 1.1J while sensing, and $3.6n$J while suspending. Total energy per cycle becomes $(3.6n+3.6)$J (The blue bars in Figure 5). The gray line in Figure 5 shows the battery life in case keeping on the Android OS.

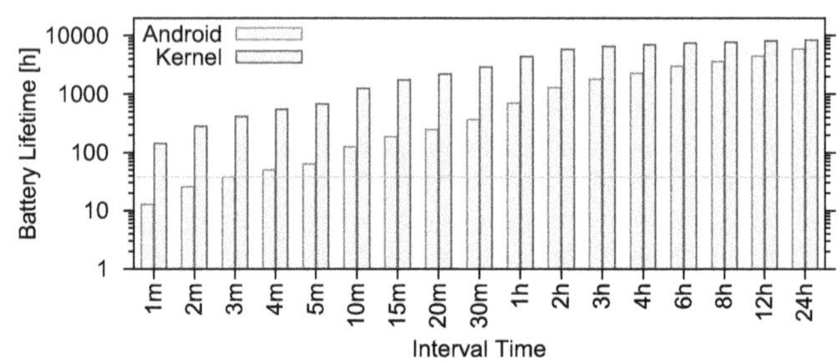

Figure 5: Estimated battery life for each duty cycle

All in all, the shorter the cycle length is, the more the battery life improves. When the cycle length is 3 minutes, utilization of the Linux kernel can extend the battery life 10.9 times. If we set the cycle length up as 1 hour, the battery life will become about half a year.

4. CONCLUSION

In this paper, we proposed to utilize the Linux kernel on Android devices without booting the Android OS. According to our results, we can extend the battery life up to 10.9 times longer than before. As part of future work, we are going to transplant the `RTCWAKE` function from Linux distributions for desktop devices in order to schedule the next boot.

5. REFERENCES

[1] P. Georgiev, N. D. Lane, K. K. Rachuri, and C. Mascolo. Dsp.ear: Leveraging co-processor support for continuous audio sensing on smartphones. In *Proceedings of the 12th ACM Conference on Embedded Network Sensor Systems*, SenSys '14, pages 295–309, New York, NY, USA, 2014. ACM.

[2] N. D. Lane, Y. Chon, L. Zhou, Y. Zhang, F. Li, D. Kim, G. Ding, F. Zhao, and H. Cha. Piggyback crowdsensing (pcs): Energy efficient crowdsourcing of mobile sensor data by exploiting smartphone app opportunities. In *Proceedings of the 11th ACM Conference on Embedded Networked Sensor Systems*, SenSys '13, pages 7:1–7:14, New York, NY, USA, 2013. ACM.

[3] M.-R. Ra, B. Liu, T. F. La Porta, and R. Govindan. Medusa: A programming framework for crowd-sensing applications. In *Proceedings of the 10th International Conference on Mobile Systems, Applications, and Services*, MobiSys '12, pages 337–350, New York, NY, USA, 2012. ACM.

Poster Abstract: An Indoor-Outdoor Navigation Service for Subway Transportation Systems

Xiaoqiang Teng, Deke Guo, Xiaolei Zhou, Zhong Liu
National University of Defense Technology, China
{tengxiaoqiang13,guodeke,xiaolei.nudt}@gmail.com,{liuzhong}@nudt.edu.cn

ABSTRACT

The proliferation of mobile computing has prompted navigation to be one of the most attractive and promising applications. Conventional designs of navigation systems mainly focus either indoor or outdoor navigation. However, people have a strong need for navigation from a large open indoor environment to an outdoor destination in real life. In this poster, we present a joint navigation system, named *ioNavi*. It can enable passengers to easily deploy indoor-outdoor navigation service for subway transportation systems in a crowdsourcing way, without comprehensive indoor localization systems. Any self-motivated passenger records and shares its individual walking trace and associated rich set of sensor readings, from a location inside a subway station to an uncertain outdoor destination within a given range, such as one kilometer. *ioNavi* further extracts navigation traces from shared individual traces, each of which is not necessary to be accurate and useful. A subsequent following user achieves indoor-outdoor navigation services by tracking a recommended navigation trace.

1. INTRODUCTION

Navigation services are highly attractive for each passenger to obtain the most convenient and shortest walking path from an indoor position inside a subway station to a nearby outdoor destination (e.g., a shopping mall) for subway transportation systems. This essential requirement, however, is not easy to be satisfied due to the following reasons. First, such subway stations suffer complicated indoor structures, especially for those interchange stations. Second, the passengers are unaware of the situation around each exit entrance of a subway station, especially when some exit entrances are on the road to other indoor buildings. The lack of necessary indoor-outdoor navigation not only brings a lot of trouble for the passengers but also considerably decreases the efficiency of subway transportation system.

Conventional methods are to make each passenger learn from the posted map, which provides coarse outdoor situation information around the subway station. The map information, however, is insufficient to meet the navigation demand for most passengers. Moreover, it is non-trivial for passengers to find an appropriate navigation path quickly and accurately by looking at the map, especially for users with no sense of direction. Although mobile device applications, such as Subway Navigation [1], are recently developed, they just integrate existing map information inside subway station into mobile devices. Thus, they also cannot realize the indoor-outdoor navigation automatically. Moreover, conventional designs of navigation systems mainly focus either indoor or outdoor navigation [2], no matter the joint navigation system from indoor to outdoor.

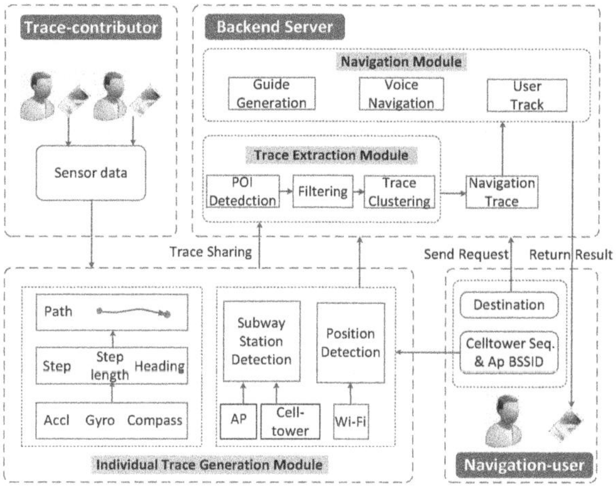

Figure 1: System architecture

In this poster, a joint navigation system is proposed, *ioNavi*, which can be easily deployed in a crowdsourcing way without the support of comprehensive indoor localization systems. The *ioNavi* consists of three major components (Fig.1). (1) Each of trace-contributors makes its mobile device automatically record the walking trace and rich set of sensing data along the trace, from its indoor beginning point to an outdoor destination. A self-motivated contributor will report its individual walking traces to a backend server for upcoming usages. (2) The backend server continuously collects and processes such inaccurate individual traces, so as to derive more available navigation traces and expand the navigation area in both indoor and outdoor area. (3) A navigation-user will achieve a recommended navigation trace according to its coarse indoor position and an outdoor destination. Meanwhile, the user also contributes its actual walking trace and associated sensing data to the backend server.

SenSys '15, November 01-04, 2015, Seoul, Republic of Korea
ACM 978-1-4503-3631-4/15/11.
DOI: http://dx.doi.org/10.1145/2809695.2817891.

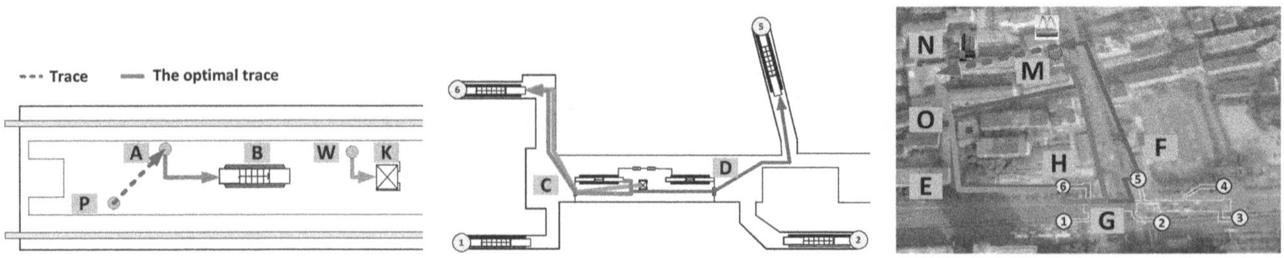

(a) Traces on floor one (b) Traces on floor two (c) Outdoor traces

Figure 2: Traces from subway station positions to outdoor destinations.

2. CHALLENGES AND TECHNIQUES

The implementation of system, however, entails substantial challenges which require practical solutions to cope with.

First, users should start with detecting whether or not they locate in a subway station and which subway station before executing the *ioNavi*. In the case of a wrong detection of the subway station, each shared trace is not only unusable but also consumes unnecessary energy due to record the trace via a mobile device. Moreover, such wrong traces will directly misguide the following users. In this work, motivated by the fact that each subway station has been covered by distinguishing Access Points (AP) and signal strength of the cell-towers, we design a dedicated method for using such identifiable metrics to detect the subway station. Thus, users trigger the *ioNavi* only when necessary.

Second, although users instantly report their indoor-outdoor traces to the backend server, such individual traces could not be directly shared with the following users. The root cause is the lack of accurate locations and measurements during the indoor-outdoor traces and the fact that the observed walking traces sometimes cannot reflect the planed traces due to the interference of the crowd. Accordingly, the backend server has to extract useful traces from mass of disorganized traces. In this work, we combine the point of interest detection, dead reckoning, and trace clustering to realize the trace extraction by the backend server.

Finally, a user may naturally find multiple traces from the backend server. The challenge is how can the backend server derive and recommend an optimal trace with the shortest walking distance. In this work, we utilize both historical knowledge and the latest information to accurately derive the optimal trace for each navigation request. On the contrary, it is possible that none of extracted trace of the backend server involves the current position of a user. To solve this problem, we recommend the trace, whose starting point is closest to the current position of the user. After the end of navigation, the user also contributes its actual walking trace and associated sensing data to the backend server. That is, each navigation-user can further act as a trace-contributor.

3. PERFORMANCE EVALUATION

Evaluation methodology and scenarios. The *ioNavi* prototype is implemented on different android phones, including Galaxy S4, MI3, and Nubia Z5. All of such mobile phones are equipped with the inertial sensors (accelerometers, compasses, and gyroscopes), light sensor, Wi-Fi module, GPS module, and GSM module. In this poster, we conduct the experiments from the *Yingbin Road* station and expand to the whole subway line 2 in Changsha, China.

Navigation Performance. Four contributed traces are considered from the indoor position A in the *Yingbin Road* station to the outdoor destination M (*McDonald's*). As shown in Fig.2, there exist three blue traces and one red trace from A to M. The red trace is the optimal one.

Five volunteers participate in this experiment. Note that, they are not aware of the traces at the beginning, and only know that the destination is *McDonald's*. The navigation performance is evaluated under three situations.

There exist many traces from the user's starting point to the destination. There exist four traces from A to M in Fig.2. The red trace is the optimal one among them in terms of the walking distance and time. In this experiment, they start with inputting the destination as the *McDonald's*. Then, *ioNavi* returns the recommended walking traces to their mobile phones. We find that all of users can successfully reach the destination along the provided trace. This experiment confirms that *ioNavi* can recommend an optimal navigation trace, when there exist many traces from the user's starting point to the destination.

None of shared traces starts at the user's current position but at least one shared trace ends at the user's destination. As shown in Fig.2, none of those shared traces starts at the P and ends at the destination M. After any volunteer queries the *McDonald's*, the system returns a blue dash trace from P to A as the first stage and another trace from the A to the destination M. According to such two stage traces, all volunteers can successfully reach the destination M.

None of shared traces meets the user's navigation requirement, but the user's starting point and destination point are involved by some shared traces. In Fig.2, the trace-contributor shared two traces, $A \rightarrow M$ and $W \rightarrow N$ (green line). In our experiment, *ioNavi* navigates volunteers walking from A to N. Obviously, none of shared traces meets such navigation requirements. However, *ioNavi* can derive out a new trace, which can guide volunteers successfully reach the destination, i.e., $A \rightarrow B \rightarrow C \rightarrow H \rightarrow E \rightarrow O \rightarrow N$.

4. ACKNOWLEDGMENTS

This work is supported in part by the Preliminary Research Funding of National University of Defense Technology under grant NO.ZDYYJCYJ20140601.

5. REFERENCES

[1] Subway navigation.
`http://play.google.com/Subway_Navigation`.

[2] Y. Zheng, G. Shen, L. Li, C. Zhao, M. Li, and F. Zhao. Travi-navi: self-deployable indoor navigation system. In *Proceedings of ACM MobiCom*, pages 471–482, 2014.

Poster: Data-Centric Task Scheduling for Battleship Island Monitoring

Kotomi Kuroki
Shizuoka University
kuroki@aurum.cs.inf.shizuoka.ac.jp

Shiho Kodera
Shizuoka University
kodera@aurum.cs.inf.shizuoka.ac.jp

Narito Kurata
National University Corporation Tsukuba University of Technology
kurata@a.tsukuba-tech.ac.jp

Takuji Hamamoto
Tokyo City University
thama@tcu.ac.jp

Shunsuke Saruwatari
Shizuoka University
saru@inf.shizuoka.ac.jp

ABSTRACT

This paper presents our results of the acquisition of actual data of collapsing buildings, as part of our work on the Battleship Island monitoring project [1]. Our Battleship Island monitoring system performs its task by acquiring data of images, sounds, and acceleration of collapsing buildings. The system is powered by solar energy. To enable the efficient use of solar-powered energy, this paper proposes a data-centric task scheduling system which consists of the DC-LQ (Data Centric LQ-Tracker) and BLB scheduling (battery-level based scheduling). An evaluation using computer simulation shows that data-centric task scheduling outperforms conventional task scheduling.

Categories and Subject Descriptors

C.4 [**Computer Systems Organization**]: Performance of Systems

General Terms

Design

Keywords

Battleship Island monitoring; task scheduling; energy harvesting

1. BATTLESHIP ISLAND MONITORING

In theory, the structural health monitoring work is nearing completion. However, in practice, our knowledge of the collapse of buildings, such as during the Great Hanshin earthquake, is insufficient, because collapses resulting from events such as these are rare events. To acquire actual data of collapsing buildings, such as images, sounds, and acceleration,

SenSys'15, November 1–4, 2015, Seoul, South Korea
ACM 978-1-4503-3631-4/15/11.
DOI: http://dx.doi.org/10.1145/2809695.2817892 .

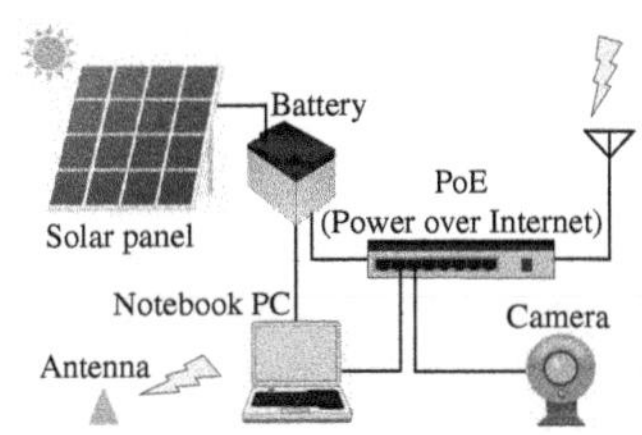

Figure 1: Monitoring system

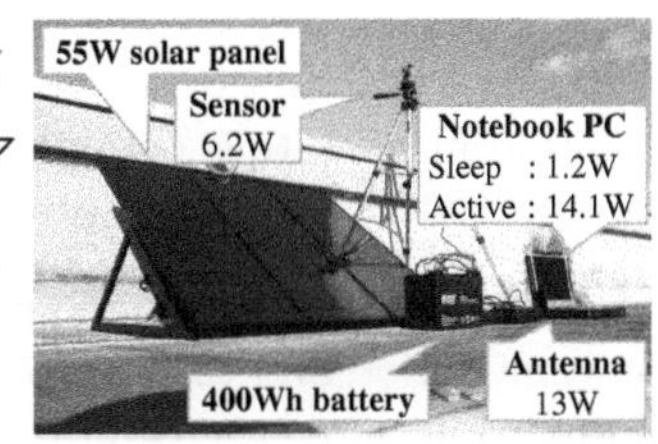

Figure 2: Prototype system

we decided to focus on Battleship Island. Battleship Island is a unique environment in the world because there are many buildings which are collapsing as a result of aging.

This paper is the first report of a Battleship Island monitoring system. On Battleship Island, buildings are monitored by a system that uses solar power and collects and transmits data by wireless communication because of the complete absence of a power supply and network on the island. Figure 1 shows the structure diagram of the monitoring system implemented on Battleship Island. Figure 2 shows an image of the prototype system, including the power generation and the power consumption devices. The monitoring system we implemented on the island consists of a Coleman PVS-55W solar panel which supplies 55 [W], a 400 [Wh] battery for energy storage, a TOUGHBOOK CF-195W1ACS notebook, and a Speed USB STICK U01 as wireless communication device. The sensors and U01 connect to the computer via USB. The measurements indicated that the computer consumes about 1.2 [W] in its sleep mode, and about 14.1 [W] when it is active. In addition, the acquisition of sensor data consumes 6.2 [W], whereas data transmission to the mainland by wireless communication consumes 13 [W].

2. TASK SCHEDULING FOR BATTLESHIP ISLAND MONITORING

The monitoring system on Battleship Island uses sensor nodes to acquire and transmit the data they collect. However, data acquisition and subsequent transmission using the limited energy provided by a solar panel is problematic. The problem was addressed by ensuring the monitoring system satisfies three requirements: to schedule multiple tasks such as sensing and transmission, to maximize the amount of sensor data, and to minimize the worst data loss time, which is the maximum value of data loss time involving periods during which the sensors are not acquiring data.

3. DATA-CENTRIC SCHEDULING

This paper proposes a data-centric task scheduling system which aims to maximize the amount of sensor data, while, at the same time, minimizing the worst data loss time and its variance. Our scheduling is based on DC-LQ and BLB scheduling. DC-LQ determines the sensing period and the sleep period of a sensor node, whereas BLB scheduling determines which task the sensor node performs in accordance with remaining battery power when the sensor node starts.

3.1 DC-LQ

DC-LQ determines the duration of the sensing and sleep periods based on a duty cycle such that the variance of sleep periods is low. In this work, we define the duty cycle as the rate of an operating period to every one period of sensing and sleeping in the repeating cycle of periods. The operating period is the sum of the start-up time and the sensing period. For example, the duty cycle becomes 0.9 if the operating period and the sleeping period are 27 minutes and 3 minutes in a cycle, respectively. To determine the duty cycle, DC-LQ uses LQ-Tracker[2] to dynamically control the duty cycle for the sensor network system using energy harvesting. It determines the duty cycle by using control theory based on the target and the current battery levels. However, the sleep period varies depending on the duty cycle, because LQ-Tracker uses a fixed time to determine one duty cycle. Thus, the fluctuation of the sleep period increases the worst data loss time.

To solve this problem in LQ-Tracker, we programmed DC-LQ to adjust the duration of one cycle to stabilize the sleep period. In turn, this presented the problem of how to determine the sleep period. Therefore, DC-LQ determines the sleep period based on past measurements thereby reducing the worst data loss time.

First, DC-LQ determines the duty cycle by LQ-Tracker when a sensor node restarts from sleep mode. Then, DC-LQ calculates the sleep period based on the duty cycle. The sleep period T_{sleep} [sec] is represented by equation (1).

$$T_{\text{sleep}} = \begin{cases} T_{\text{cycle}}(1-D) & (First) \\ T'_{\text{sleep}} + \alpha(T_{\text{cycle}}(1-D) - T'_{\text{sleep}}) & (Other) \end{cases} \quad (1)$$

T_{cycle} [sec] is the predetermined time to be used as a reference for one cycle, and D indicates the duty cycle determined by LQ-Tracker. α is a constant which shows the amount of variance allowed in sleep periods and α has a value between 0 and 1. The initial sleep period is based on the duty cycle and T_{cycle}, which represents one cycle. Second and later, T_{sleep} [sec] is the result of adding the previous sleep period T'_{sleep} [sec] and new sleep period to the new duty cycle. After DC-LQ determines the sleep period by equation (1), DC-LQ determines a sensing period, T_{sence} [sec], based on the sleep period and the duty cycle. T_{sence} is determined by equation (2).

$$T_{\text{sense}} = \frac{T_{\text{sleep}} D}{1-D} - T_{\text{wake}} \quad (2)$$

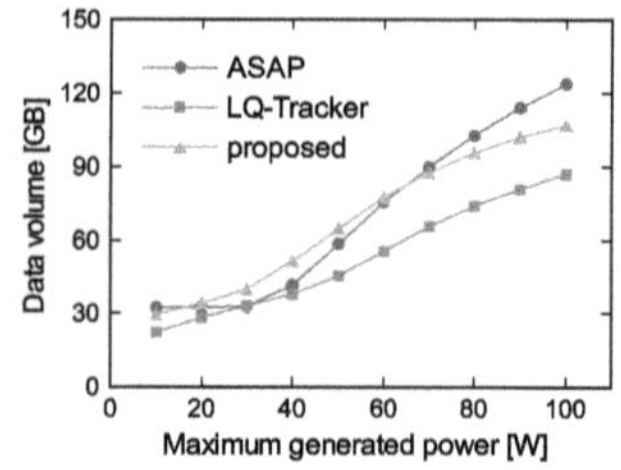

Figure 3: Amount of sensor data

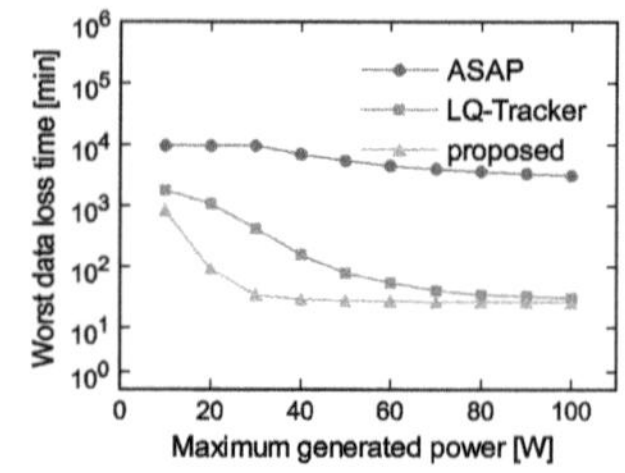

Figure 4: Worst data loss time

T_{wake} [sec] is the system-specific time for starting a sensor node. T_{sence} is the result of subtracting the starting time of a sensor node from the time during which the sensor node is not sleeping.

3.2 BLB Scheduling

BLB scheduling determines the task priorities of the sensor node when it restarts from sleep mode. The highest priority task is performed in any case; on the other hand, the lowest priority task is performed only when sufficient energy is available. In the Battleship Island monitoring project, it is not important to collect data in real time. Therefore, BLB scheduling determines the highest priority tasks to be DC-LQ and sensing data, and the lowest priority task to be data transmission.

4. EVALUATION

The efficacy of the proposed method was confirmed by evaluating the amount of sensor data and the worst data loss time by computer simulation. In addition, the relative performance of the proposed method was evaluated by comparing the following three approaches, ASAP (As Soon As Possible), LQ-Tracker, and the proposed method. Figure 3 shows the amount of sensor data that is collected in the case of maximum generated power. We can see that the proposed method consistently achieves about 1.3 times the amount of sensor data of LQ-Tracker. Figure 4 shows the worst data loss time for maximum generated power. We can see that the proposed method achieves significant reduction of the worst data loss time compared with the ASAP approach.

5. CONCLUSION

In this paper, we have proposed DC-LQ in combination with BLB scheduling as a data-centric task scheduling method for Battleship Island monitoring. The system is currently running on Battleship Island.

6. ACKNOWLEDGEMENTS

This work was supported by JSPS KAKENHI Grant Number 26289194. We thank the Nagasaki City world heritage promotion room and Akihiro Tomioka of Japan Aviation Electronics for their support.

7. REFERENCES

[1] Battleship island monitoring. `http://sarulab.inf.shizuoka.ac.jp/battleship/`.

[2] C. M. Vigorito, D. Ganesan, and A. G. Barto. Adaptive control of duty cycling in energy-harvesting wireless sensor networks. In *IEEE SECON*, pages 21–30, 2007.

Poster Abstract: Fair Scheduling for Energy Harvesting WSN in Smart City

Kai Li
The Singapore University of Technology and Design, Singapore
kai_li@sutd.edu.sg

Chau Yuen
The Singapore University of Technology and Design, Singapore
yuenchau@sutd.edu.sg

Sanjay Jha
The University of New South Wales
Sydney, Australia
sanjay@cse.unsw.edu.au

ABSTRACT

We consider the problem of data collection from a large-scale energy harvesting sensors in smart city. We study a novel scheduling optimisation model for WSN with Wireless Power Transfer (WPT), that maximises the amount of collected data under constraints of radio link quality and WPT efficiency, while ensuring a fair data reception. A WPT-WSN testbed is built and preliminary results show that the WPT efficiency is jointly affected by distance between WPT transmitter and receiver, and their antenna orientation.

1. MOTIVATION

For WSN in smart city, the scheduling strategy is required to dynamically prioritise data transmissions from a large number of sensors (several hundreds) and provision resources such that collected data are maximised [1, 2, 3]. Especially, for wearable sensors on human body, they typically have low residual energy levels after being outdoor for an extended period and limited bandwidth due to their weight and size limitations. With energy harvesting capability (*i.e.,* Wireless Power Transfer (WPT)), the sensor node can be charged by a WPT transmitter. A number of considerations make the data collection non-trivial. First, WPT efficiency of the node is low if it is far from the WPT transmitter (large-scale channel fading) or has antenna orientation bias (shown in Section 3). It is thus critical to collect more data from those nodes before their residual energy is exhausted. Second, the wireless link quality of data transmission between each node and base station (BS) may vary with time. Having a node transmit during instances when the channel quality is poor is likely to result in packet reception errors, which in turn would require retransmissions and thus increased energy expenditure. Third, data should be downloaded from the nodes in a fair way. In particular, the amount of data collected from each node should be greater than a certain application-specific threshold. This is important to maximise the accuracy of data analysis, e.g., in the context of mobility modelling and population characteristics for human sensing in smart city.

SenSys'15, November 01–04, 2015, Seoul, Republic of Korea.
ACM 978-1-4503-3631-4/15/11.
DOI: http://dx.doi.org/10.1145/2809695.2817893 .

We study an optimisation model for Fair Scheduling with WPT (FS-WPT) to maximise data collection in a large-scale WSN with WPT. FS-WPT schedules the data collection based on both the link quality and the harvested energy from WPT. This enables the nodes with the lowest energy reserves and the best chance of achieving successful transmissions to transfer their data first. Moreover, FS-WPT addresses fairness criteria so that a specific number of data is received from each node. For performance evaluation, we consider the scheduling problem in the context of real-world applications, such as smart city or smart building [4, 5], where the network consists of hundreds of nodes. The data of sensor node is offloaded to the BS, meanwhile, the sensor node harvests energy from a wireless charger using WPT. Specifically, data transmission and energy harvesting work in different frequency bands so that the channel of WPT is uncorrelated with data communication channel. FS-WPT is application-agnostic and hence applicable to a wide variety of large-scale energy harvesting wireless sensing scenarios. Our first contribution in this work is the design of communication frame structure of FS-WPT for the energy harvesting WSN. Our second contribution is an implementation of a WPT-WSN testbed, and we empirically study the link behaviour for better understanding of the WPT characteristics. The results of this paper are significant because they provide invaluable information for correcting the scheduling model and system in future research.

2. COMMUNICATION FRAME STRUCTURE

We implement an extended frame structure to our work [6] for scheduling optimisation with WPT. We utilise a 2-stage communication model, with random channel access period (RCAP) followed by scheduled data transmission period (SDTP) (shown in Figure 1). The two periods interchange periodically and are synchronised by the BS. The purpose of the RCAP is to collect information about sensor nodes, including their current link quality, the amount of available data, and the energy harvested from WPT. The BS calculates a transmission schedule at the end of RCAP and broadcast to all the nodes. Based on the transmission schedule, the sensor node only transmits data packets during its scheduled time in SDTP to prevent interference.

3. EXPERIMENTS ON WPT-WSN TESTBED

In this section, we present the implementation of our testbed and preliminary experimental results of WPT efficiency.

The sensor node is equipped with a rechargeable battery, a WPT receiver and a RFBee transceiver. A POWERCAST

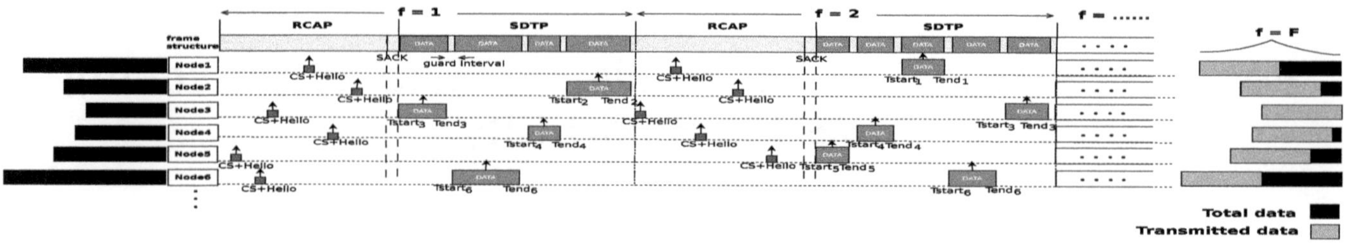

Figure 1: The timing relationship. f is frame sequence and F denotes total number of frames. $Tstart_i$ and $Tend_i$ stand for the starting and ending time of node i's data transmission respectively. The nodes with different data amounts compete for the channel in RCAP and they are scheduled to transmit data in SDTP.

WPT transmitter transfers power wirelessly to the WPT receiver (a P2110 powerharvesting board with a 1 dBi omnidirectional antenna) to charge the node's battery. Since WPT is carried out in the 915 MHz band while the sensor node communicates in the 2.4 GHz band, our testbed achieves simultaneous wireless communication and power transfer. The hardware setup is shown in Figure 2.

Figure 2: The implementation of WPT-WSN testbed.

In the first experiment, we measure the WPT efficiency with different distance between the WPT transmitter and receiver. Due to the radiation exposure protection, the distance has to be further than $20cm$. The sampling rate is fixed at 1 samples/s. As shown in Figure 3, the effective amount of energy harvested by the sensor node decreases with increase in the distance.

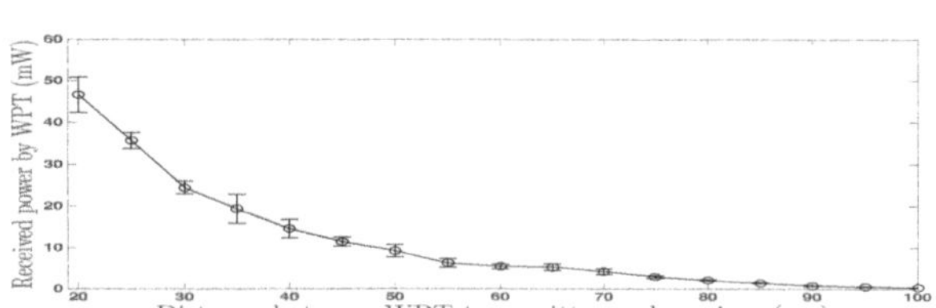

Figure 3: Received power of WPT receiver on the sensor node for varying distances. The error bars show the standard deviation over 250 samples.

Next, we conduct an experiment with different WPT receiver antenna orientation. Each orientation has 1000 samples. Figure 4 shows that antenna orientation affects the received power at the WPT receiver. The distance between WPT transmitter and receiver is fixed at $55cm$. Zero degree rotation means that the two antennas are directly facing each other. When the antenna orientation is at 90 and 270 degrees (two antennas are orthogonal to each other), the node harvests the lowest energy from the WPT transmitter.

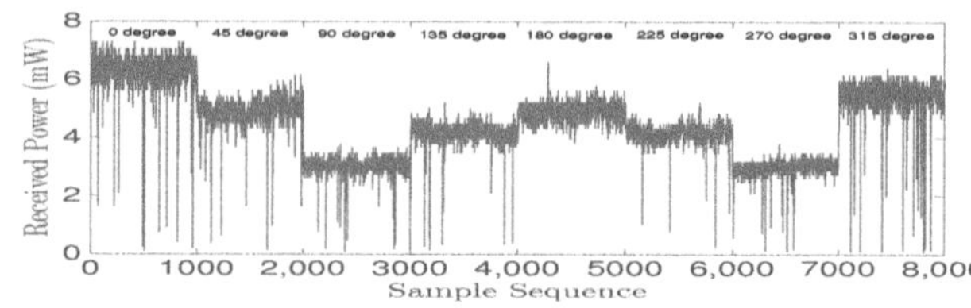

Figure 4: Received power on the sensor node for varying antenna orientation of the WPT receiver.

4. FUTURE WORK

Based on the two experiments discussed in the previous section, we observe that the WPT efficiency is one of key factors for the scheduling model. Therefore, FS-WPT is proposed to prioritise the nodes for scheduling based on a ratio of the link quality and harvested energy. For future work, we will implement FS-WPT on our WPT-WSN testbed and evaluate the performance for the fair data reception.

Acknowledgement

This research is supported by the MND Research Fund Sustainable Urban Living Grant.

5. REFERENCES

[1] J. Zhang, C. Yuen, and C.-K. Wen, "Large-system analysis of ergodic sum-rate in wireless-powered mimo communication network," in *SECON Workshops*. IEEE, 2014, pp. 57–61.

[2] X. Chen, C. Yuen, and Z. Zhang, "Wireless energy and information transfer tradeoff for limited-feedback multiantenna systems with energy beamforming," *IEEE Trans. Veh. Technol.*, vol. 63, no. 1, pp. 407–412, 2014.

[3] P. Subendran, S. K. Viswanath, C. Yuen, and C. S. Veerappan, "Adaptive transmission for self-sustainable energy harvesting wireless sensor network," in *ICFCNA*. IET, 2014, pp. 1–5.

[4] A. Zanella, N. Bui, A. P. Castellani, L. Vangelista, and M. Zorzi, "Internet of things for smart cities," *IEEE Internet of Things Journal*, 2014.

[5] Z. Wan, Y. Tan, and C. Yuen, "Review on energy harvesting and energy management for sustainable wireless sensor networks," in *ICCT*. IEEE, 2011, pp. 362–367.

[6] K. Li, B. Kusy, R. Jurdak, A. Ignjatovic, S. S. Kanhere, and S. Jha, "κ-FSOM: Fair link scheduling optimization for energy-aware data collection in mobile sensor networks." in *EWSN*. Springer, 2014, pp. 17–33.

Poster: Coordination of Wireless Sensor Networks using Visible Light

Ambuj Varshney
Uppsala University, Sweden
ambuj.varshney@it.uu.se

Luca Mottola
Politecnico di Milano, Italy and
SICS Swedish ICT, Sweden
luca@sics.se

Thiemo Voigt
Uppsala University, Sweden
SICS Swedish ICT, Sweden
thiemo@sics.se

ABSTRACT

Wireless sensor networks are often deployed indoors where artificial lighting is present. Indoor lighting is increasingly being composed of Light Emitting Diodes (LEDs) that offer the ability to precisely control the intensity and the frequency of the light carrier. This can be used to coordinate wireless sensor networks (WSN). The periodic variations in the light intensity can synchronise the clocks on the sensor nodes, while the ability to modulate the light carrier enables the transmission of control information like channel assignment or transmission schedules. We present Guidelight, a simple mechanism that uses controlled fluctuations in the light intensity to coordinate sensor nodes. Guidelight can wake-up or time synchronise sensor nodes or even send small bits of control information to them. All of these have separate dedicated solutions in WSN. Guidelight aims to provide a single solution to all these problems. Our initial experiments demonstrate the ability of Guidelight to trigger sensor nodes. We demonstrate Guidelight is able to trigger sensor nodes selectively at a mean error of 21 μs.

1. INTRODUCTION

Many WSN applications are deployed indoors in the presence of artificial lighting. In an indoor environment artificial lighting is increasingly composed of LEDs. LED bulbs' ability to encode information in the illumination discretely is appealing to many applications. Indoor localisation is one such application that has benefited greatly. The state of the art localisation techniques using Visible Light Communication (VLC) achieve sub-meter precision [2] while they are nonintrusive and only use the existing lighting infrastructure. However, the benefits of using VLC in other WSN applications are still largely unexplored.

Achieving coordination among sensor nodes is important to most WSN applications. This could be, e.g., for channel assignment to avoid interference [1], or to synchronise local clocks on sensor nodes [4] or to wake up sensor nodes in a synchronous manner. All of these have been extensively studied and dedicated protocols exist. However, these dedicated protocols makes it difficult to use them together in an application. Further, the exchange of control messages over radio spectrum in these protocols has high overhead [4]. VLC could be one possible solution to this problem. The existing efforts to use light for coordination have been limited to time synchronisation where the natural flicker in fluorescent lighting has been used to calibrate clocks on the sensor nodes [3]. This is limited by the natural frequency of the light, which restricts the achievable accuracy and also makes it impossible to send any control information.

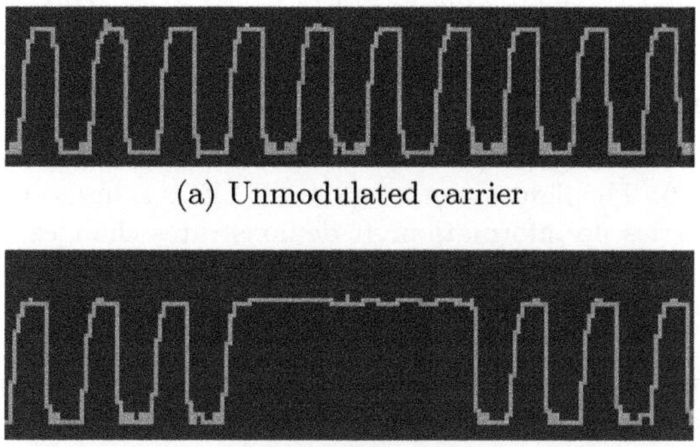

(a) Unmodulated carrier

(b) Trigger signal

Figure 1: Light intensity changes observed using a photodiode. *PWM of frequency 5 KHz provides an unmodulated light carrier. We embed a period of 700 μs of constant amplitude as a trigger. The period is small enough to avoid noticeable flicker to human eyes.*

The frequency of light intensity changes of LED light bulbs can be easily changed from a few KHz to MHz. This allows for fine-grained time synchronisation depending on the needs of the application. Further, the light could be modulated to embed small bits of control information. This makes it possible to send information such as channel assignment or transmission schedules to the deployed sensor nodes. Most sensor node platforms already have an onboard light sensor which can receive this control and synchronisation information. We explore this potential with Guidelight, a solution that uses VLC to control WSNs.

2. MECHANISM

The key idea behind VLC is that if the frequency of light intensity change is sufficiently high, it is not noticeable to the human eye. However, these intensity changes can be tracked by sampling the light sensor fast enough. Guidelight exploits this idea for its operation. Commercial off the shelf LEDs provide dimming support using a Pulse Width Modulation (PWM) signal. The frequency of the signal is

SenSys'15, November 1–4, 2015, Seoul, South Korea..
ACM 978-1-4503-3631-4/15/11.
DOI: http://dx.doi.org/10.1145/2809695.2817894.

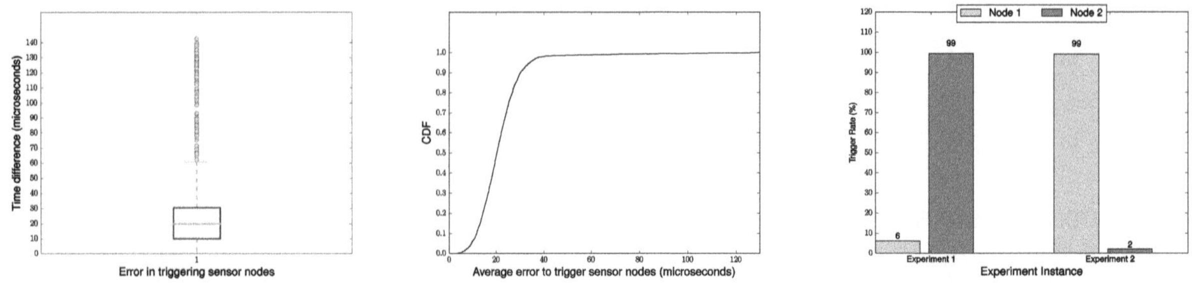

(a) Error (b) Mean error (c) Selective Trigger

Figure 2: Guidelight is able to selectively trigger sensor nodes. *(a) Represents the box plot of error in triggering sensor nodes. In the box plot, the middle gray horizontal bar represents the median and the top gray horizontal bar the maximum (excluding outliers) while the circles represent the outliers. The upper hinge of the box represents the 75 percentile, and the lower hinge represents the 25 percentile. The nodes are triggered at a median error of 20 μs. (b) Represents the CDF of the mean error to trigger five sensor nodes. The nodes are triggered over 90 % of the times with an mean error of 30 μs (c) The bar represents the trigger rate for sensor nodes. Guidelight can selectively trigger sensor nodes with high accuracy.*

usually kept higher than a few KHz to avoid unease to humans [2]. The light emanating out off LEDs is unmodulated and carries no information. It demonstrates changes in the intensity with a period similar to the PWM signal. For example, in our experiments we drive the LED with a PWM signal of frequency 5 KHz which results in light intensity fluctuations as in Figure 1(a). Guidelight introduces within this unmodulated carrier a short period of controlled light fluctuations divergent from the periodic pattern of the PWM signal. This fluctuation could be either a modulated carrier with small bits of control information or a period of constant light intensity acting as trigger/wakeup signal for the sensor nodes. The exact nature and length of this period depends on the application needs and the processing capabilities of the sensor node. In our experiments, we introduce a period of constant illumination as shown in Figure 1(b). The length of the period acts as an address of group of nodes sharing similar application characteristics which need to be triggered synchronously. The period of constant intensity also helps to trigger the nodes synchronously as it has lower processing overhead compared to decoding a modulated carrier.

3. EXPERIMENTS

Basic experiment. In this experiment, we investigate the effectiveness of the trigger mechanism. We keep five Tmote sky nodes within the illumination range of a high intensity LED. The LED is rated at 5 W and a brightness of 1200 cd. The nodes are kept at a distance of half a meter away from the LED. We manage the LED with a MOSFET switch controlled by an Intel Edison unit that generates a PWM signal at a frequency of 5 KHz. In this signal, we introduce a period of constant illumination lasting 600 μs as trigger at an interval of 500 ms. The sensor nodes keep track of the changes in the light intensity. As soon as the sensor nodes detect the trigger they set a designated General Purpose Input/Output (GPIO) port of the microcontroller to the high state. We collect timing data for over 1800 *seconds* using a logic analyser. We measure the error as the time difference between the first node to be triggered and the remaining nodes. Figures 2 (a) and (b) show the result of our experiment. The results indicate that the sensor nodes are triggered at a median error of 20 μs with the minimum error being 0.04 μs and the maximum error (excluding outliers) being 60 μs. Figure 2(b) shows that the mean error of five sensor nodes being triggered is less than 32 μs for over 90% of the time. We believe this can be decreased further by reducing the jitter in the ADC sampling process.

Selective triggering. In this experiment, we investigate if we can selectively trigger sensor nodes based on distinct trigger patterns. We use the same setup as in the earlier experiment, though using only two sensor nodes. We program each node to respond to a different trigger. *Node 1* responds to a trigger of 900 μs and *node 2* responds to a trigger of 500 μs. We run two instances of the experiment. In the first instance, we embed a trigger of 500 μs in the light carrier, while in the second instance we embed a trigger of 900 μs. As in the basic experiments, the sensor nodes respond to the trigger by setting the designated GPIO port to high state. We run each experiment for 600 *seconds* and capture the timing data. As performance metric, we measure the *Trigger Rate (TR)*. To calculate the TR we find the number of times a sensor node was triggered during an experiment and the total number of triggers that were sent. Figure 2(c) shows the result of our experiment. The results indicate that the sensor nodes can be selectively triggered with high accuracy. The minimum possible time difference between two different triggers depends upon the frequency of the carrier and the choice of the trigger pattern.

4. FUTURE WORK

We are further working to improve Guidelight aiming to reduce error in triggering of sensor nodes. We are also looking into modulation schemes to embed information into the trigger. In future work we will combine Guidelight with a wake-up circuit similar to the one described by Rajagopal et al. [5] to reduce energy costs.

5. REFERENCES

[1] V. Iyer et al. Detecting and avoiding multiple sources of interference in the 2.4 ghz spectrum. In *EWSN 2015*.

[2] L. Li et al. Epsilon: A visible light based positioning system. In *NSDI 2014*.

[3] Z. Li et al. Flight: Clock calibration using fluorescent lighting. In *ACM Mobicom 2012*.

[4] M. Maróti et al. The flooding time synchronization protocol. In *ACM SenSys 2004*.

[5] N. Rajagopal et al. Hybrid visible light communication for cameras and low-power embedded devices. In *VLCS 2014*.

Poster: Exploring the Need for Sensor Learning and Collaboration in IoT-based Parking Systems

Yu Huang‡, Dian-Xuan Wu‡*, Chuang-Wen You‡, Chi-Ling Yang‡*, Seng-Yong Lau†, Kai-Lung Hua*, Wen-Huang Cheng[II], Yi-Ling Chen†, Jane Yung-Jen Hsu‡
‡Intel-NTU CCC Center, National Taiwan Univ., Taipei, Taiwan
*Dept. of Computer Science & Information Eng., National Taiwan Univ. of Science & Technology, Taipei, Taiwan
†Dept. of Electrical Eng., National Taiwan Univ., Taipei, Taiwan
[II]Research Center for Information Technology, Academia Sinica, Taipei, Taiwan
b02902084@ntu.edu.tw, m10315014@mail.ntust.edu.tw, cwyou@ntu.edu.tw, b10115016@mail.ntust.edu.tw, sylau@ntu.edu.tw, hua@mail.ntust.edu.tw, whcheng@citi.sinica.edu.tw, yiling@arbor.ee.ntu.edu.tw, yjhsu@csie.ntu.edu.tw

ABSTRACT

The need to find parking contributes to road congestion and leads to unnecessary fuel consumption. Of all emerging parking systems, Internet-of-Things (IoT)-based systems have demonstrated the feasibility of real-time delivery of parking availability using magnetic sensors. However, existing magnetic-based methods are prone to false positives caused by electromagnetic fields emitted from surrounding electric facilities. In this study, we conducted a 3-month data collection in a parking area. We identified the need to introduce learning and collaboration into the design of our detection algorithm which recognizes learned patterns associated with car arrivals or departures, and to filter out unreliable events based on spatial and temporal features.

Categories and Subject Descriptors

H.4.m [**Information Systems Applications**]: Miscellaneous.

General Terms

Design, Experimentation

Keywords

Smart parking; Internet of Things (IoT); magnetic sensing.

1. INTRODUCTION

The information of parking slot availability is critical to efficiently locate empty parking slots [1]. To this end, existing outdoor parking systems have been designed based on wireless sensors (or the Internet of Things (IoT)) [2], cameras [3], etc., among which IoT-based systems developed by Streetline Inc.[1] or in the SFpark project[2] have been deployed in North America and European cities. However, interference from electromagnetic fields emitted by electric facilities on the street such as overhead trolley lines [2] often leads to false positives and thus degraded accuracy. Moreover, the diversity of car models also complicates parameter tuning for detection algorithms. These challenges limit current magnetic-based methods to around 90 percent accuracy [2].

In this study, we explored the problem by collecting and analyzing sensor data associated with *transient events* (car arrivals and departures). On reviewing these data, we see a need for learning and collaboration in the design of a detection algorithm which recognizes learned patterns associated with transient events and filters out unreliable events based on spatial and temporal characteristics for higher accuracy.

[1]Streetline, `http://www.streetline.com`
[2]SFpark, `http://sfpark.org`

SenSys '15, November 01-04, 2015, Seoul, Republic of Korea
ACM 978-1-4503-3631-4/15/11.
http://dx.doi.org/10.1145/2809695.2817895.

2. DEFICIENCIES IN EXISTING MAGNETIC-BASED DETECTION METHODS

Existing magnetic-based detection methods identify parking events by recognizing fixed sets of changing patterns, or significant value changes based on threshold-based methods. Typically, a change pattern of the magnetic field over one axis of a transient event is consisted of two parts, including (1) a moving phase in which drivers maneuver their cars to properly park or depart; and (2) a stopping phase, in which drivers stop the engine and leave their cars. To identify deficiencies in existing magnetic-based detection, in our pilot data collection we deployed two parking sensors in the center of two adjacent parking slots. We collected parking data for a total of 104 days (about 3 months) and 16 different vehicle models. These methods fail in the following scenarios.

Unexpected patterns caused by different car models: Given the diversity of car models, magnetic field changes caused by arrivals (departures) vary with the car design. Fig. 1(a) shows the data collected for an idling Mercedes Benz E200 Kompressor. Due to the magnetic field generated by electric components of its Kompressor engine, the resultant reading observed in each axis fluctuated in the stopping phase, especially along the z axis. Further, the readings jumped when the engine was stopped because the magnetic disturbances caused by the engine disappeared.

On the other hand, a magnetic-based detection algorithm can be confused by other cases with insignificant differences between the magnetic field readings prior to and after the moving phase. Fig. 1(b) shows the readings along three

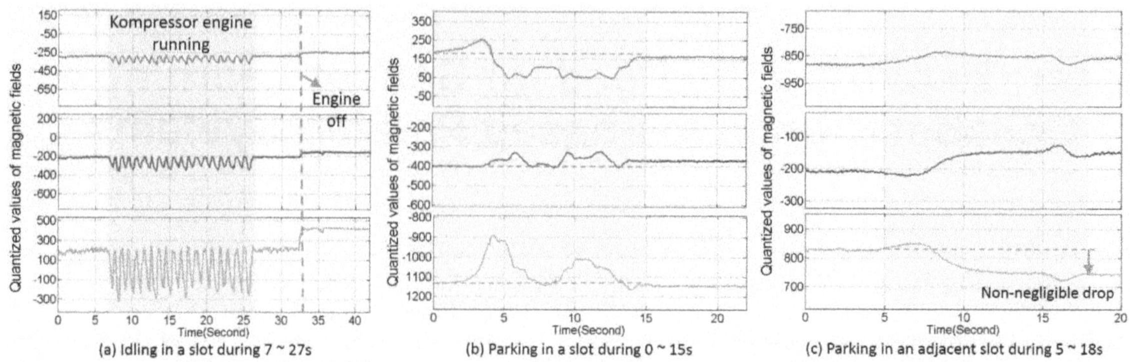

Figure 1: Collected readings of a magnetic sensor in three scenarios.

axes while a Toyota Camry was parking. Such small differences force the detection algorithm to rely only on changes in magnitude during the moving phase, which exhibit a pattern different from that in Fig. 1(a). If we measure only moving-phase changes in magnitude without learning to discriminate these two patterns, we register false positives (or false negatives) for Fig. 1(a) (or (b)).

Adjacent interference when parking in nearby slots: Parking slots are usually aligned in rows on either side of a parking aisle in a dedicated area. A car parking in a slot interferes with the magnetic fields measured in both adjacent slots. Fig. 1(c) shows such interference from a car parking in an adjacent slot. Of the three axes, the z-axis changes are non-negligible and could be comparable to or larger than that associated with a normal transient event, e.g., the z-axis change in Fig. 1(b).

We seek to correctly identify all transient events (such as that in Fig. 1(b)) while not incorrectly detecting unseen patterns (Fig. 1(a)) or interference caused by adjacent car arrivals or departures (Fig. 1(c)) as transient events. Instead of solely measuring change magnitudes, the system must learn change patterns associated with real transient events. The implications drawn from this pilot data collection influenced the design of our system described below.

3. SYSTEM OVERVIEW

The proposed system detects transient events with a buried parking node centered in each parking slot. Each node is equipped with a low-power microcontroller and a high-resolution magnetic sensor. By collecting offline the changes in the earth's magnetic field and training a discriminative model to identify transient events, the system uses the local sensor to predict potential transient events using machine learning techniques (i.e., *local event classification*). Potential transient events are wirelessly sent through gateways back to a backend server to globally determine final transient events based on their spatial and temporal characteristics (i.e., *global event filtering*).

Local event classification: To recognize the change patterns of potential transient events, we extract feature segments using a sliding window (empirical-determined 10-second duration, with 50% overlap). We define features to capture the car model (e.g., size/components of different models) and parking behavior (moving speed when forward/backward parking, etc.) statistics embedded in each segment. For each segment, we extract statistical features as an input vector to classify segments as either transient or non-transient using a support vector machine (SVM) [4].

Global event filtering: Global event filtering exploits temporal and spatial correlations to collectively identify real transient events from all potential ones. Since transient events are classified using an SVM, we estimate their reliability with its value proportional to the distance from the SVM classification boundary [4]. Given the reliability information associated with updates of potential events, we can define spatial and temporal rules (e.g., if potential events occur simultaneously in two adjacent slots, use the more reliable one) to identify real transient events.

4. PRELIMINARY STUDY

To evaluate the accuracy of the local event classification, we segmented the set of magnetic data described in Sec. 2 into 239 (538) transient (non-transient) segments. All segments were divided into training and testing sets. We trained discriminative parking models on the training segments and evaluated the accuracy on each test segment. The resulting *accuracy* defined as the number of correctly-recognized segments divided by the number of all segments in the (manually-labelled) ground-truth data set was 97.81%. We are currently developing a system prototype and conducting experiments to validate the system.

5. ACKNOWLEDGEMENTS

This work was supported in part by the Ministry of Science and Technology, National Taiwan University, and Intel Corporation under Grants MOST 103-2911-I-002-001, NTU-ICRP-104R7501, and NTU-ICRP-104R7501-1.

6. REFERENCES

[1] Accelerating sustainability: Demonstrating the benefits of transportation technology. `http://digitalenergysolutions.org/dotAsset/933052fc-0c81-43cf-a061-6f76a44459d6.pdf`.

[2] The learning curve of smart parking. `http://www.nytimes.com/2012/12/23/technology/smart-parking-has-a-learning-curve-too.html`.

[3] K. Blumer, H. R. Halaseh, M. U. Ahsan, H. Dong, and N. Mavridis. Cost-effective single-camera multi-car parking monitoring and vacancy detection towards real-world parking statistics and real-time reporting. In *Proc. ICONIP 2012 - Volume Part V*, pages 506–515. Springer-Verlag, 2012.

[4] C.-C. Chang and C.-J. Lin. Libsvm: A library for support vector machines. *ACM Trans. Intell. Syst. Technol.*, 2(3):27:1–27:27, May 2011.

Poster Abstract: Toward Efficient and Secure Code Dissemination Protocol for the Internet of Things

Jun young Kim, Wen Hu, Sanjay Jha
School of Computer Science and Engineering
UNSW Australia
{junyoungkim,wen.hu,sanjay}@cse.unsw.edu.au

Hossein Shafagh
Department of Computer Science
ETH Zurich, Switzerland
shafagh@inf.ethz.ch

Mohamed Ali Kaafar
National ICT Australia
dali.kaafar@nicta.com.au

ABSTRACT

Current Wireless Sensor Networks (WSNs) approaches do not provide an efficient and secure code dissemination function due to emerging issues of IoT applications. In this work, we adopt a multicast approach instead of the existing end-to-end or epidemic approaches. In order to enable the multicast approach, we propose an efficient/robust group key distribution scheme. We will evaluate and quantify the performance of our prototype implementation in a public testbed, while emulating several practical IoT settings, and show our security measures against known attack models.

1. MOTIVATION

Securely updating remotely deployed nodes, commonly referred to as code dissemination is a necessary function for the ongoing success of the IoT. Thread group[1] depicts a good use-case example, which is organized by major IT companies such as ARM, Qualcomm, and Samsung. The main goal of this IoT project is to securely connect/manage a large number (+250) of various devices in home networks. Since the vision is to run even battery-powered devices for years, low-power and secure over-the-air update is a necessary and essential functionality. Communication and computation are two premium resources for the energy friendly design, as radio activities and security operations consume the major share of energy on constrained devices. Unfortunately, existing code dissemination solutions for WSNs exhibit poor efficiency in the context of the IoT due to several emerging IoT issues [6], such as:

- **Heterogeneity**: It is challenging to design a framework that can manage various types of devices. In order to support the heterogeneity with existing solutions, applications coherently become more complex and suffer from performance degradation.
- **Mobility**: Having a coherent and stable view of the network topology is a significant factor for managing IoT applications. Mobility related dynamics make this process difficult and result into inefficiencies.
- **Connectivity**: IoT applications naturally come with the Internet connection capability, which results in exposure to a wider types of adversaries. It is desirable to identify these emerging threats, and be able to quickly provide efficient solutions.

Existing over-the-air (re)programming protocols for WSNs are based on the epidemic communication [5] which assumes homogenous sensor nodes in the network with all nodes participating in the (re)programming process. Given the multitude of systems in an IoT network, the epidemic approach would require non-target nodes to participate in the propagation resulting in unnecessary cryptographic operations and additional packet forwarding overhead. In this paper, we adopt a multicast communication approach, where only target nodes involved in the code-image update actively take part in the process.

In order to enable a secure multicast, we rely on secure group key distribution among dynamic set of target nodes. However, existing group key distribution schemes may not be suitable for IoT deployments since they assume known/fixed group sizes, unscalable overhead, or neighbor pairings. For example, End-to-End (E2E) schemes exhibit high communication overhead, Pairwise schemes require neighbor pairing, and Pre-Shared-Key (PSK) solutions cannot support key revocation. Although Broadcast Encryption (BE) [3] exhibits excellent distinctions, most BEs are k-resiliency systems, where $k+1$ exposed keys can collude to generate shared secrets. Since IoT nodes are vulnerable to physical node capture attack, where adversaries compromise nodes to extract pre-installed keys, achieving a full or higher collusion resistance requires infeasible communication/storage overhead.

2. OUR APPROACH

We investigated several Public key cryptographic-based Broadcast Encryption schemes (PBE) (see Table 1) to address the collusion issue of BE schemes. Based on our initial study, we propose to use BGW_t [1], which results in additional storage but improves overall communication/computation efficiency with following benefits:

1. **The shortest ciphertext size**: Shorter or fixed size ciphertext can improve the communication overhead for the group key distribution. BGW_t achieves the shortest ciphertext size of $O(1)$, but trades off linear storage to store all other nodes' public keys.

[1] `http://threadgroup.org/`

SenSys'15, November 1–4, 2015, Seoul, South Korea..
ACM 978-1-4503-3631-4/15/11.
DOI: http://dx.doi.org/10.1145/2809695.2817896.

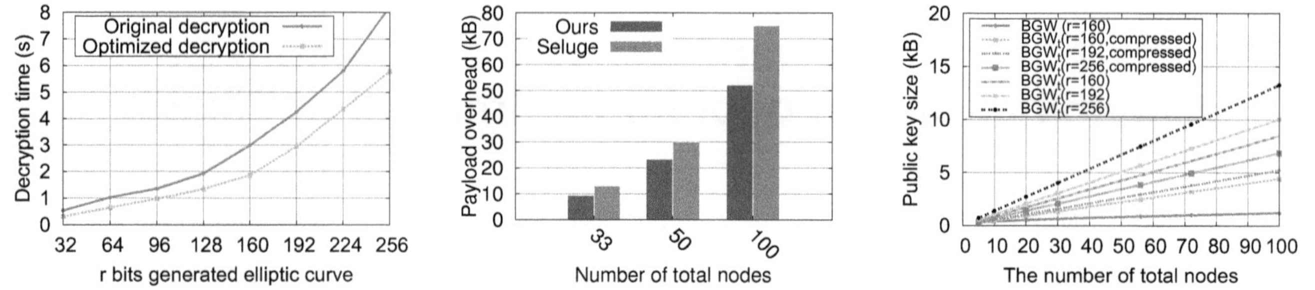

(a) Our group key decryption time before/after optimization.
(b) Key distribution overhead comparison between our approach and Seluge.
(c) Our storage overhead is linear, but feasible in practical settings

Figure 1: Initial evaluation results of our prototype implementation.

	←Key/ciphertext size→			Complexity	
	Public	Private	Ciphertext	λ_E	λ_D
Trivial	$O(n)$	$O(1)$	$O(t)$	$O(t)$	$O(1)$
Delerablée$_1$ [2]	$O(n)$	$O(1)$	$O(r)$	$O(r^2)$	$O(r)$
Delerablée$_2$ [2]	$O(n)$	$O(n)$	$O(1)$	$O(r^2)$	$O(r^2)$
BGW [1]	$O(\sqrt{n})$	$O(1)$	$O(\sqrt{n})$	$O(\sqrt{n})$	$O(\sqrt{n})$
BGW_t [1]	$O(n)$	$O(1)$	$O(1)$	$O(n)$	$O(1)$

Table 1: Comparison of our short listed PBEs [2] in an n-node network targeting arbitrary t nodes, r non-target nodes. Note that λ_E denotes encryption complexity, λ_D denotes decryption complexity.

2. **Lower decryption complexity**: On a dissemination protocol, encryption is performed at the level of a resource-rich server while decryption is performed at the level of constrained nodes. Lower decryption complexity can enhance the energy consumption.

3. **Fixed size private key**: BGW_t has $O(1)$ private key size and the key can be stored in a tamper resistant storage to effectively mitigate physical attacks.

4. **Key revocation efficiency**: Key revocation is necessary when a key is lost or a node is compromised. The majority of BE schemes requires linear or logarithmic overhead for the key revocation process. However, our revocation process only requires updating one ciphertext regardless of the number of revoked keys.

5. **Dynamic targeting**: PBEs including BGW_t can dynamically change the target group.

Once we securely distribute a group key to arbitrary targets, we leverage the key for further security requirements.

3. EARLY RESULTS

We implement our node side BGW_t on the Openmote platform[2]. Although the group key decryption is only required once per dissemination session, it is still computationally expensive. To address this, we optimize our node side BGW_t implementation with elliptic curve optimization techniques by means of the pre-computation technique that Boneh et al. [1] suggested for an efficient implementation. Fig. 1(a) shows the optimized group key decryption (e.g., from 2982 ms to 1864 ms in 160 bits generated curves).

We show the efficiency gain of our key distribution overhead compared to Seluge [4], a state-of-the-art epidemic approach. Fig. 1(b) depicts our approach's superior key distribution and performance in medium sized networks. The efficiency gain gap between ours and Seluge is proportional to the size of the network since Seluge's key establishment overhead depends on the number of neighboring nodes. This gap will be wider in dense networks such as home IoT applications. We plan to present the propagation gain for bulk data transfer. We expect our approach to improve all aspects from Seluge such as group key distribution, code propagation, security, collusion resistance, and key revocation, except pre-key-installation overhead. Although our storage overhead is linear, it is feasible in practical settings as it is quantified in Fig. 1(c). For instance, 4.4 kB storage is required in a 100 node network with 160 bits generated elliptic curves.

[2] `http://www.openmote.com/`

4. CONCLUSION

In this project, we propose a secure code dissemination protocol to address emerging IoT issues. Initial results suggest that our approach is more efficient and robust compared to existing WSNs solutions. We will evaluate the performance of our prototype implementation in a public testbed.

5. ACKNOWLEDGMENT

This work is partially supported by Australian Research Council Discovery grant DP150100564.

6. REFERENCES

[1] D. Boneh, C. Gentry, and B. Waters. Collusion resistant broadcast encryption with short ciphertexts and private keys. In *Advances in Cryptology–CRYPTO 2005*, pages 258–275, 2005.

[2] C. Delerablée, P. Paillier, and D. Pointcheval. Fully collusion secure dynamic broadcast encryption with constant-size ciphertexts or decryption keys. In *Pairing*, pages 39–59. 2007.

[3] A. Fiat and M. Naor. Broadcast encryption. In *Advances in Cryptology-CRYPTO*, pages 480–491, 1994.

[4] S. Hyun, P. Ning, A. Liu, and W. Du. Seluge: Secure and dos-resistant code dissemination in wireless sensor networks. In *ACM/IEEE IPSN*, 2008.

[5] P. A. Levis, N. Patel, D. Culler, and S. Shenker. *Trickle: A self regulating algorithm for code propagation and maintenance in wireless sensor networks.* Computer Science Division, University of California, 2003.

[6] M. Zorzi, A. Gluhak, S. Lange, and A. Bassi. From today's intranet of things to a future internet of things: a wireless-and mobility-related view. *Wireless Communications, IEEE*, 17(6):44–51, 2010.

Poster Abstract: CountryRoads: Large-Scale Nationwide Ridesharing System

Weiwei Jiang
Department of Electronic Engineering
Tsinghua University
jww13@mails.tsinghua.edu.cn

Chunxiao Jiang
Department of Electronic Engineering
Tsinghua University
jchx@tsinghua.edu.cn

Pei Zhang
Department of Electrical and Computer Engineering
Carnegie Mellon University
peizhang@sv.cmu.edu.cn

Lin Zhang
Department of Electronic Engineering
Tsinghua University
linzhang@tsinghua.edu.cn

ABSTRACT

The Chinese Spring Festival travel season (Chunyun) has been called the largest annual human migration in the world with approximately 3.6 billion trips in 2014. Understandably, all forms of transportation are stressed at or near saturation during this period and many people, especially lower-income individuals fail to get to their destinations.

We present CountryRoads, a ridesharing system to address the transportation shortage during Chunyun. The CountryRoads system collects users' route information, and matches drivers and passengers as an online bipartite matching problem based on the proximity of the passenger's origin and destination and the route of the driver. The system is evaluated during four Chunyun periods from 2012 to 2015 with up to 17272 users and forms 4777 ridesharing tuples in 2015.

1. INTRODUCTION

The Spring Festival travel season (also known as the Chunyun period) in China, when billions of people go back home to unite with their family, happens every year.During this period, the demand for public transportation (railway, road and air) far exceeds their regular capacity. Due to this, many lower-income individuals fail to obtain a ticket home or have very limited choices. At the same time, more travelers choose to drive private cars for the home-going trip during Chunyun period. However, personal vehicle trips in general typically have low occupancy. This is only exasperated during the Chunyun period due to the case where workers often work away from their family, and have to drive back alone.

In recent years, ridesharing service has been proposed to improve traffic efficiency. The service generally relies on self-organization of travelers that have similar itineraries and time schedules so that they could travel together [1, 2, 3]. Furthermore, many recent work have explored using mobile devices to facilitate pairing riders so that real-time on-demand ride service could be provided [4, 5, 6].

These approaches become less efficient as scale increases in both distance and participants. We present CountryRoads, a scalable ridesharing system that matches the drivers who are willing to share their spare seats with passengers who fail to get a ticket of public transportation. We let the users report as much as possible their personal information to gain trust from their counterpart so as to increase the chance for a successful match. After getting users' information, CountryRoads conducts an online matching algorithm to search the matching scheme between the drivers and the passengers and sends the matching results to them. Finally, the pair will arrange specifications associated with the trip.

SenSys'15, November 1–4, 2015, Seoul, South Korea..
ACM 978-1-4503-3631-4/15/11.
DOI: http://dx.doi.org/10.1145/2809695.2817897 .

2. SYSTEM OVERVIEW

The system structure of CountryRoads is shown in Figure 1. It is consisted of three modules: the sensing module, the matching module and the notification module. In the *sensing module*, we use the SMS platform, the website and the smart phone application to collect user's route information and personal information. In the *matching module*, the system conducts a centralized online algorithm using the route information. In the *notification module*, the matching result is sent to users by SMS once generated.

2.1 Sensing Module

The "sensors" we use in CountryRoads relies on human sensors that include SMS platform, website and smart phone application. The users report their route information and personal information through these platforms. The first challenge is that our sensors lack the ability of proactive sensing and some users may not want to report their personal information due to privacy consideration. We alleviate this problem by partnering with the China Central Television (CCTV), as well as other government partners to increase credibility.

In addition, we demonstrate that by giving higher priority to those users with more information in the matching process, we could encourage more users to provide their personal information to increase trust from the driver and increase likelihood of a successful pairing.

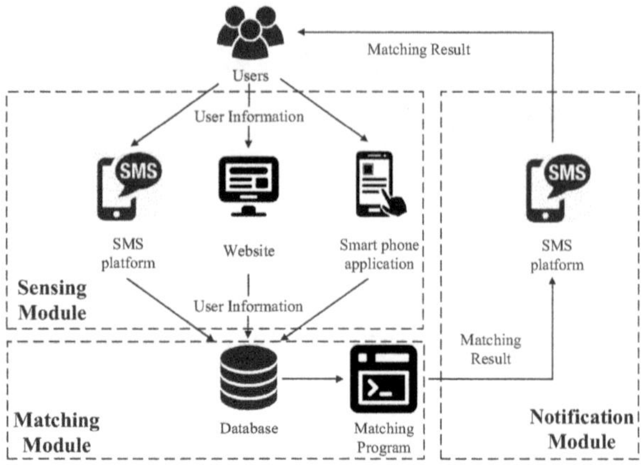

Figure 1: System structure of CountryRoads.

2.2 Matching Module

Matching module pairs up the drivers and the passengers. We formulate this problem as an online bipartite matching problem. The weight of the edge between a driver and a passenger represents the utility of them being matched. We use four features to estimate the utility: (1) Origin deviation ΔO: the distance between the origin cities; (2) Destination deviation ΔD: the distance between the destination cities; (3) Detour distance *Detour*: the extra distance the driver has to travel if he go to pick up the passenger and drop off the passenger before arriving his own destination; (4)Departure date deviation ΔT: the date difference between the departure dates.

We adopt a utility estimation with the following form

$$U_d(p) = U_p(d) = \frac{1}{1 + e^{(\alpha\Delta O + \beta\Delta D + \gamma Detour + \delta\Delta T)/\text{driver's mileage}}},$$

where $\alpha, \beta, \gamma, \delta$ are parameters and *driver's mileage* is used to eliminate the variation between trips with different mileages.

To make a tradeoff between stability and efficiency and deal with the dynamic setting, we use an online algorithm as follows:

Online Stable Matching: The matching is performed periodically every T minutes. In each round, the matching is formed by a greedy mechanism, using only edges with weight greater or equal to a threshold τ. The greedy mechanism constructs a matching by adding the highest weight one after another, until there are no more unmatched pairs with an edge between them.

We claim that Online Stable Matching satisfies stability in the following theorem:

Theorem 2.1. *Online Stable Matching yields a stable matching in any given round.*

2.3 Notification Module

The main function of the notification module is to notify the users who are matched in the matching module once the matching result is generated so that they could contact with each other and plan the trip as soon as possible. Specifically, for each ridesharing tuple the matching module generates, CountryRoads sends a text message to the driver and the passenger respectively, which contains the counterpart's name and phone number. Finally, the pair will arrange details offline.

3. SYSTEM DEPLOYMENT

CountryRoads was launched in 2012 with very limited public media advertising and the matching process was conducted manually, which only formed about 100 tuples. In 2013 and 2014. We began to promote CountryRoads on website and in television (including CCTV) and built a SMS platform to communicate with the users. The matching process was based on the names of origins and destinations.

With the previous three years' attempts, we further developed and improved CountryRoads in 2015 by using our online stable matching algorithm. In 2015, we collected 9,787 passenger routes and 7,485 driver routes within a time period of 25 days from January 25 to February 18, which was the day before Chinese New Year. In total, we formed 4,777 ridesharing tuples in 2015 and we interviewed 1013 tuples afterwards to check whether they succeeded to travel together. Our finding was that among the 1013 tuples, 235 tuples managed to travel together. Our main results of deploying CountryRoads in 2015 Spring Festival travel season are summarized in Table 1.

Table 1: Main results of deploying CountryRoads in 2015 Spring Festival travel season

Start date	January 25, 2015
End date	February 18, 2015
Duration	25 days
Number of drivers	7,485
Number of passengers	9,787
Number of ridesharing tuples	4,777
Adopt ratio (estimated)	23.20%

We found in our survey the main reason of unsuccessful pairing was that the passenger got a train ticket. However the survey also mentioned that many users were relieved to have a backup.

4. REFERENCES

[1] Brian Caulfield. Estimating the environmental benefits of ride-sharing: A case study of dublin. *Transportation Research Part D: Transport and Environment*, 14(7):527 – 531, 2009.

[2] Pengfei Gong and Wenquan Li. Urban traffic demand control based on carpooling: A case of nanjing. In *Remote Sensing, Environment and Transportation Engineering (RSETE), 2011 International Conference on*, pages 1863–1866, June 2011.

[3] Niels Agatz, Alan Erera, Martin Savelsbergh, and Xing Wang. Optimization for dynamic ride-sharing: A review. *European Journal of Operational Research*, 223(2):295 – 303, 2012.

[4] Nelson D Chan and Susan A Shaheen. Ridesharing in north america: Past, present, and future. *Transport Reviews*, 32(1):93–112, 2012.

[5] Lyft. `http://www.lyft.com`. [Online; accessed September 6, 2015].

[6] Uber. `http://www.uber.com`. [Online; accessed September 6, 2015].

Poster: Were You in the Cafe Yesterday? Location Proof Generation & Verification for Mobile Users

Chitra Javali*†, Girish Revadigar*†, Wen Hu*, and Sanjay Jha*
{chitraj,girishr,wenh,sanjay}@cse.unsw.edu.au

*School of Computer Science & Engineering, UNSW Australia, Sydney, AUSTRALIA
†National ICT Australia (NICTA), Australian Technology Park, Sydney, AUSTRALIA

ABSTRACT

In recent years, Location Based Services (LBS) and related applications are gaining popularity for providing access to the resources. LBS can either increase or decrease the access privileges of the users based on their location. Current mobile devices lack the intelligence to prove their location when requested. In this paper, we propose our novel solution for generating location proof for mobile users leveraging unique wireless characteristics and verification of the location claim by application services.

1. INTRODUCTION

Location based services are applications which provide access to the existing users based on their location. For instance, in a health-care system, the authorized personnel e.g., doctors may be allowed to access the complete information/records of a patient if they are in hospital, and may have limited access to the records if they are at other locations. The doctor needs to prove his/her location to the Location Based Service (LBS) in order to get additional privileges. Similarly, in a bank or organisation, access to sensitive data and resources may be provided only if the officials are present in the particular building. LBS also extends to other services e.g., a coffee shop offering incentives to frequently visiting customers, etc.. In all the above listed applications it is important for the user to prove his/her location to the services without being dishonest.

In this paper, we aim to provide location proof to a user who intends to claim benefits based on the location. Note that our scheme does not aim to find the precise location of the user i.e., localisation, rather we propose location proof generation and verification scheme which proves the presence of the user within an area of interested region at a particular time. Location tag generation by an entity e.g., Access Point, and regeneration and verification of the location tag by another entity, say Verifier, is a very challenging task. The process must be highly secure so that the adversary must not be able to replicate the location tag, nor the tag be reused by a User to claim benefits at any other time. Our protocol is information theoretically secure as it employs fuzzy vault technique, initially proposed in [3]. Our proposed solution leverages the existing wireless network infrastructure e.g., Wi-Fi, together with Wi-Fi capable devices such as smart-phones, PDAs etc.

SenSys'15, November 01–04, 2015, Seoul, Republic of Korea
ACM 978-1-4503-3631-4/15/11.
DOI: http://dx.doi.org/10.1145/2809695.2817898.

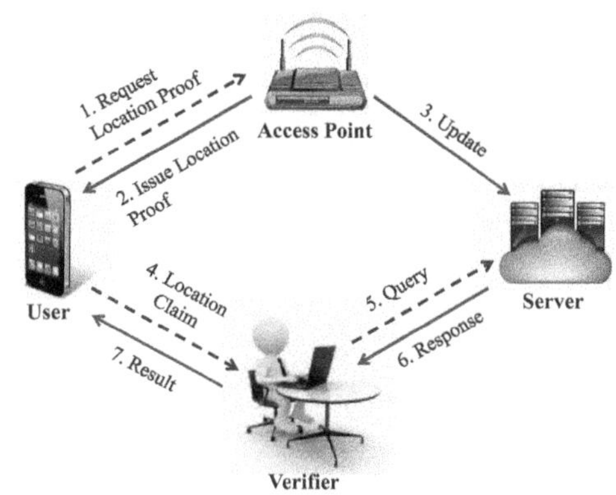

Figure 1: Message flow between the four entities of our proposed system model.

Location claim and verification has been studied in prior work [5]. However, a major drawback is that they do not specify the details of the way a location tag is generated. Echo protocol [6] securely verifies the location claims of the users with number of nodes i.e., verifiers. However, each of the verifier must measure the time with some precision. Researchers in [4] have proposed proximity testing between two adjacent nodes on social network, however, it does not verify the location provided by either of the users.

Our contributions: (i) We propose a novel information theoretically secure location tag generation and verification mechanism for mobile users to claim their location in LBS. (ii) Our solution exploits wireless channel characteristics and does not require any user interaction and is independent of user activity. (iii) We conduct an extensive set of experiments in real indoor environment with commercially available off-the-shelf devices and our results reveal that the location proof cannot be replicated by any adversary even if present in the vicinity of the legitimate user/devices. We believe that we are the first to leverage the unique spatio temporal wireless characteristics i.e., channel state information (CSI) to provide location proof for LBS.

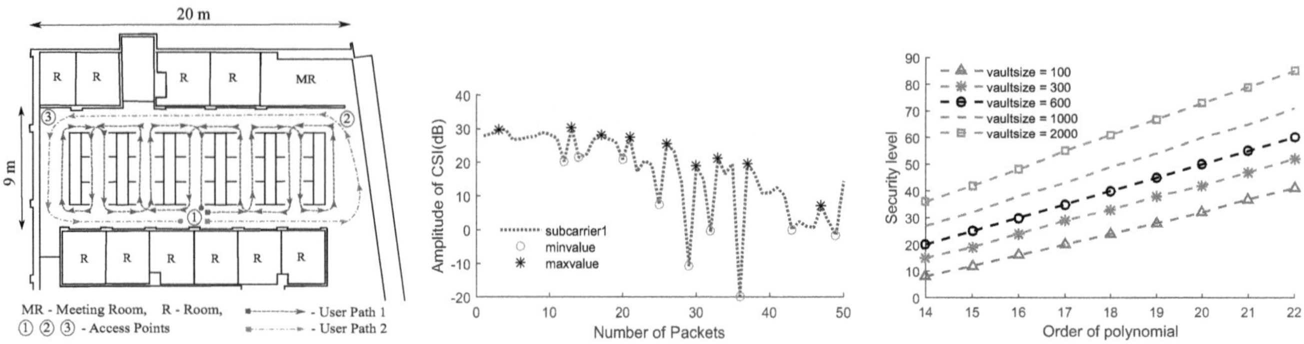

(a) Floor plan for experimental set-up (b) Selected maximum and minimum values for a subcarrier (c) Security level (bits) vs. Order of polynomial

Figure 2: Floor plan for experimental set-up and evaluation results.

2. PROTOCOL AND EVALUATION

Our system model consists of four entities viz., User, Access Point (AP), Server and Verifier. The message flow between the four entities is as shown in Fig. 1. We assume that the AP and Verifier are honest and trusted where as the Server is honest but curious to know the location tag and the User is authenticated.

Proposed protocol: (i) User sends a request, $Req \parallel ID_{user}$ to the AP for location proof, ID_{user} is a unique identity provided by Verifier to an existing User. (ii) The AP sends an acknowledgement, $ACK \parallel ID_{AP}$ to the User and begins to capture the packets sent by the User to extract CSI. (iii) As there are 30 subcarriers in a single stream of CSI, the AP randomly picks subcarriers and detects the maximum and minimum values of the signal in a specific window size. This process is repeated till the number of maximum and minimum values is equal to the degree k of polynomial $p(x)$ which is constructed such that the coefficients of the polynomial are the elements of *locn_tag*. The concatenation of all maximum and minimum values forms a *locn_tag*. The corresponding distinct x co-ordinates of maximum and minimum values of the signal constitute set $\mathcal{A}$ of size t, where $t \geqslant k$. AP computes the polynomial projections $p(\mathcal{A})$ giving $\mathcal{P}$. (iv) As any adversary or User must not be able to tamper the *locn_tag*, a number of random points $\mathcal{C}$ are added to the projections. More the number of $\mathcal{C}$, higher is the security. (v) AP now constructs the vault $\mathcal{V} = \mathcal{P} \cup \mathcal{C}$. The AP sends the location proof, $Locn\_proof = \{m, MAC(locn\_tag, m)\}$ to the User, where $\{m = \mathcal{V} \parallel Nonce \parallel ID_{user} \parallel ID_{AP} \parallel T_{stamp}\}$ and MAC is a secure hash algorithm.

AP also constructs a set $\mathcal{B}$ of size t such that $\mathcal{A} \cap \mathcal{B} > k+1$ and submits $\{\mathcal{B} \parallel ID_{user} \parallel ID_{AP} \parallel T_{stamp}\}$ to the Server. During location claim, the User provides *Locn_proof* to the Verifier. The Verifier then extracts ID_{user}, T_{stamp} and ID_{AP} from message m and submits to the Server. The Server provides the corresponding $\mathcal{B}$ to the Verifier. The Verifier reconstructs the $locn\_tag'$ from $\mathcal{V}$ by employing Lagrange interpolation. If $MAC(locn\_tag, m) == MAC(locn\_tag', m)$, the Verifier sends a success result to the User.

Experimental Evaluation: Fig. 2a shows the floor plan and set-up used for our experiments. Laptops equipped with Intel 5300 NIC were used as APs to extract CSI from the packets [2]. The packets from a Nexus4 mobile device were captured on 3 antennas of APs. The User followed the two paths 20 times for each AP. Fig. 2b shows the selected maximum and minimum values for a window size = 50 for one of the subcarrier. In order to determine the security of $\mathcal{V}$, the order of $p(x)$ was varied. From Fig. 2c we observe that the security of the vault increases with increase in polynomial order and also size of $\mathcal{V}$, for a constant $t = 22$. Depending on the application and the security level required, more number of random points can be added to the projections. For most applications 85-bit security offers good cryptographic security [3]. The location tag can be generated periodically based on the application requirement. Our protocol is secure against replay attack, collusion attack and the generated *locn_tag* is non-transferable as we employ secure hash algorithm. Additionally, device fingerprinting mechanisms [1] can be used to distinguish between different mobile devices to prevent the above mentioned attacks.

3. CONCLUSION

In this paper we have proposed a novel information theoretically secure location proof generation and verification protocol for mobile users. Our protocol does not require any additional infrastructure and can be implemented by employing commercially available off-the-shelf devices. Our experimental results prove that our protocol offers good cryptographic security. We would like to investigate different solutions for preventing collusion attack in our future work.

4. ACKNOWLEDGEMENT

This work is partially supported by Australian Research Council Discovery grant DP150100564.

5. REFERENCES

[1] V. Brik, S. Banerjee, M. Gruteser, and S. Oh. Wireless device identification with radiometric signatures. In *MobiCom*, 2008.

[2] D. Halperin, W. Hu, A. Sheth, and D. Wetherall. Predictable 802.11 packet delivery from wireless channel measurements. In *SIGCOMM*, 2010.

[3] A. Juels and M. Sudan. A fuzzy vault scheme. *Des. Codes Cryptography*, 38(2):237–257, 2006.

[4] A. Narayanan, N. Thiagarajan, M. Lakhani, M. Hamburg, and D. Boneh. Location privacy via private proximity testing. In *NDSS*, 2011.

[5] S. Saroiu and A. Wolman. Enabling new mobile applications with location proofs. In *HotMobile*, 2009.

[6] N. Sastry, U. Shankar, and D. Wagner. Secure verification of location claims. In *Wise*, 2003.

Poster Abstract — Context-aware Adaptation Mechanism for Smart Resources: A RGBD Sensor Case Study

Eduardo Munera
emunera@ai2.upv.es

Jose-Luis Poza-Luján
jopolu@ai2.upv.es

Juan-Luis Posadas-Yagüe
jposadas@ai2.upv.es

Manuel Muñoz
mmunoz@ai2.upv.es

Juan Fco. Blanes Noguera
pblanes@ai2.upv.es

Institute of Control Systems and Industrial Computing. Universitat Politècnica de València
Valencia, Spain, +34 96387700

ABSTRACT

In Distributed Control Systems (DCS) the distribution of sensor data needs to be optimized in order to reduce the client process redundancy, i.e.: same sensor data processing in different clients. This paper presents an implementation of Embedded Networked Sensors as Smart Resources that allows to access to high-level information abstracting the user from low level mechanisms. The distributed services provided by Smart Resources implement self-aware adaptation mechanisms in order to suit the performance to the context. Information integrity must be also ensured during this adaptation. The Smart Resource implementation is based on a RGBD sensor. Through a set of experiments is evaluated the performance of the reconfiguration and adaptation mechanisms and detailed the influence of the data integrity according to the provided service.

Categories and Subject Descriptors

I.2.9 [**Robotics**]: Sensors. I.2.10 [**Vision and Scene Understanding**]: 3D/stereo scene analysis. I.4.8 [**Scene Analysis**]: Object recognition.

General Terms

Algorithms; Sensors performance; Reliability; Experimentation.

Keywords

Cyber-physical systems; RGBD camera; Distributed systems; Smart resources; Smart devices; Adaptive systems; Quality of Context; Quality of Service.

1. INTRODUCTION

Nowadays, distributed sensors are evolving to provide processed information avoiding the clients to execute process algorithms and consequently decreasing their load. The smart device paradigm defines an intelligent sensor, which provides preprocessed sensorial data. When, besides, an adequate level of abstraction for accessing transparently to smart devices information is provided, they can be known as Smart Resources [1]. In some critical applications Smart Resources should ensure some specific service requirements in spite of internal constrains, as for example CPU load. These service requirements can be specified with the quality of context (QoC) [2] and quality of service (QoS) [3] parameters. Main objectives are: to present the implementation of a Smart Resource based on a RGBD camera as one of the most widely used sensors for automated and robotics systems [4], evaluate its dynamical to the system requirements, and check the reliability of the information and the data integrity. For this reason some experiments will detail the influence of the context adaptation mechanisms into the trustworthiness of a RGBD recognition service.

SenSys'15, November 1–4, 2015, Seoul, South Korea.
ACM 978-1-4503-3631-4/15/11.
DOI: http://dx.doi.org/10.1145/2809695.2817899

2. SMART RESOURCE: RGBD SENSOR

The development of Smart Resources allows reusability of sensor applications in DCS tasks by providing high-level information through distributed services and Smart Resource architecture is depicted in Figure 1. The information is accessed by the distributed network which implements QoS mechanisms. Smart Resources base their execution on the Smart Devices, which implement a Control Kernel Middleware (CKM) [5], for providing real-time and QoC mechanisms for the execution context evaluation. The RGBD Smart Resource is designed to deal with visual and depth information to offer environment features information. Data is processed by the execution and composition of processes in the Smart Plugin Topology (SPT) [5]. Self-aware and context evaluation mechanisms improve the plugin execution performance based on the QoS and QoC measures [5]. By the specification of Service Requirements (SR) and Quality Requirements (QR) a Task Configuration Module (TCM) will select the more appropriate execution profile according to the current quality measures [6]. The result of this implementation is shown in Figure 2.

3. EXPERIMENTS AND RESULTS

Experiments will test the adaptation performance and the influence in the recognition accuracy. A variable number of clients will apply for different services of the RGBD smart resource. Every client connection and disconnection event will produce changes in the quality values, i.e.: increasing CPU load, which can trigger some quality alarms as shown in Figure 3.a. As a result, the TCM will dynamically adapt the active execution profile. This adaptation will lead to decrease (or augment) the image resolution used by the process plugin as is depicted in Figure 3.b. The same experiment will be repeated 100 times.

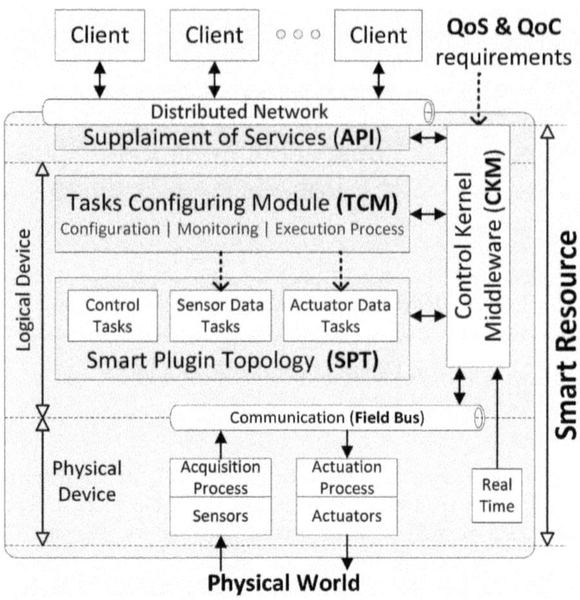

Figure 1. Smart Resource: Components and relations.

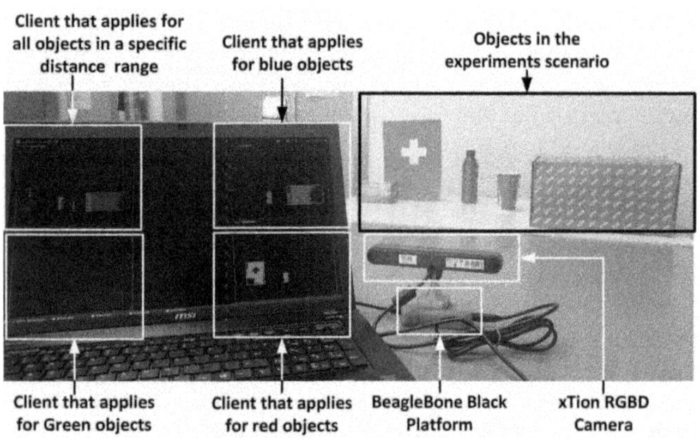

Figure 2. Infrastructure used in the experiments.

During each one it will be annotated the perception fails (not to detect an environment element) and the recognition fails (not to recognize one detected element) in order to establish the mean of all the executions. Analyzing the results, Table 1 summarizes the perception and recognition fails in each profile, as Figure 4 shows the evolution of the accumulated error for each profile along the experiments. As conclusion, any client that applies for an adaptive resolution service must be aware of a possible decrease in the information reliability. As a result, Smart Resource services will guarantee best data reliability and trustworthiness without offering flexible adaptation mechanisms, while non-critical services will suit the execution context by adapting the information rate or the process load although the data uncertainty rises. Therefore user can choose the most adequate type of services according to the criticality of the implementing tasks.

4. ACKNOWLEDGMENTS

Work supported by the Spanish Science and Innovation Ministry MICINN: CICYT project M2C2: "Codiseño de sistemas de control con criticidad mixta basado en misiones" TIN2014-56158-C4-4-P and PAID (Polytechnic University of Valencia): UPV-PAID-FPI-2013.

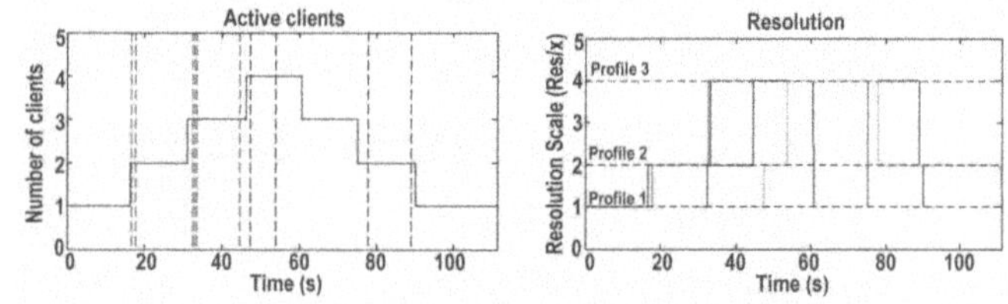

(a) (b)

Figure 3. (a) Number of active clients and quality events. (b) Active profile for each client.

Table 1. Table of accumulate errors.

Scenarios	Profile 1	Profile 2	Profile 3
Perception Fails %	0.0060	0.0230	0.2740
Recognition Fails %	0.0000	0.1752	0.0130
False Positive %	0.0020	0.0000	0.0000
Total Error %	0.0027	0.0661	0.0957

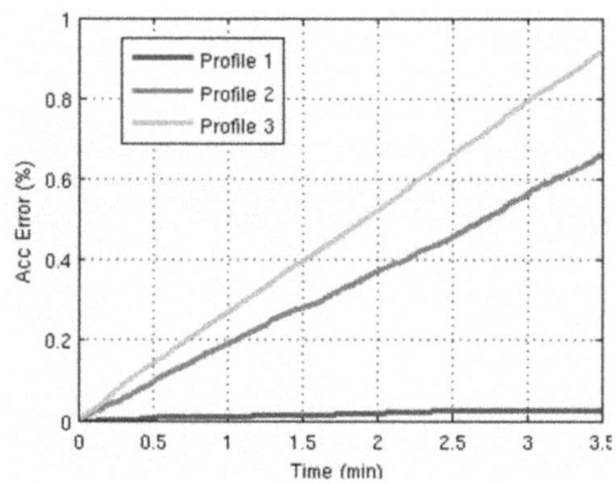

Figure 4. Infrastructure used in the experiments.

5. REFERENCES

[1] E. Munera, M. Muñoz Alcobendas, J.-L. Posadas-Yagüe, J.-L. Poza-Luján, and J. F. Blanes Noguera. Smart resource integration for robot navigation on a control kerned middleware based system. International Journal of Imaging and Robotics, 15(4):117-129, 2015.

[2] T. Buchholz, A. Ku¨pper, and M. Schiffers. Quality of context: What it is and why we need it. In Proceedings of the workshop of the HP OpenView University Association, volume 2003, 2003.

[3] C. Aurrecoechea, A. T. Campbell, and L. Hauw. A survey of qos architectures. Multimedia systems, 6(3):138–151, 1998.

[4] N. Silberman, D. Hoiem, P. Kohli, and R. Fergus. Indoor segmentation and support inference from rgbd images. In Computer Vision–ECCV 2012, pages 746–760. Springer, 2012.

[5] P. Albertos, A. Crespo, and J. Simó. Control kernel: A key concept in embedded control systems. In 4th IFAC Symposium on Mechatronic Systems, 2006.

[6] E Munera, JL Poza-Lujan, JL Posadas-Yagüe, JE Simó-Ten, JF Blanes Noguera. Dynamic Reconfiguration of a RGBD Sensor Based on QoS and QoC Requirements in Distributed Systems. Sensors, 15(8), 18080-18101, 2015.

Poster Abstract: Drone Can Find Lost Smartphones

Sunyong Kim*, Yohan Kim*, Sun Young Park†, Ryangsoo Kim*, Hyuk Lim*

*School of Information and Communications

†Physics Concentration, College

Gwangju Institute of Science and Technology (GIST)

Gwangju 61005, Republic of Korea

Email: hlim@gist.ac.kr

ABSTRACT

In this paper, we propose a single-drone-based localization for radio frequency (RF) sources in an outdoor environment. For fast and accurate localization, we propose a dynamic trajectory planning scheme, which guides the RF scanning drone toward a direction minimizing the geometric dilution of precision (GDOP) in order to minimize the uncertainty of location estimation for target RF sources.

1. INTRODUCTION

In an emergency scenario such as rescuing people who are in natural disaster or with injury in an isolated place, a mobile flying device (a.k.a., drone) can be used for localizing the people in need if they have a radio frequency (RF) device transmitting RF signals. While an RF device is transmitting RF signals, a drone can detect the signals and measure the signal strength at several different points. With the signal strength measurements stamped with a sampling position, the drone can locate the RF signal source. This approach can be applied to various applications such as finding victims in natural disaster, lost smartphones, missing children in public area, and rogue wireless access points.

The most closely related work is wireless sensor network localization with mobile landmarks in [2, 1]. In [1], three deterministic trajectories for mobile landmarks were evaluated in terms of the localization accuracy. They have studied the tradeoff relationship between the localization accuracy and the trajectory resolution. In [2], five deterministic trajectories were evaluated for an in-building disaster scenario. While most related work focused on the localization performance evaluation with static and predetermined paths for mobile landmarks, our work considers a dynamic path planning for drone-based localization.

2. DRONE-BASED LOCALIZATION

We consider a drone-based localization scenario, in which a single drone measures multiple RSSI (received signal strength indicator) samples from a target device and computes the target position. The unknown location of a target device is given by $\boldsymbol{\theta}_t = [x_t, y_t, z_t]$. Along a trajectory, a drone measures RSSI samples, and the location for the i-th RSSI measurement (i.e., RSSI_i) is denoted as $\boldsymbol{\theta}_i = [x_i, y_i, z_i]$. Using RSSI_i, the distance between the target device and the measurement location is obtained by

$$\hat{d}_i = 10^{\frac{\beta - RSSI_i}{10 \cdot \alpha}} \text{ [m]}, \tag{1}$$

where α is a path loss exponent, and β [dBm] is a reference RSSI value measured at a reference distance.

Under the assumption that the path loss model is unknown, the parameters, α and β in (1) should be estimated as well as the target position. The localization with unknown path loss model can be formulated as an optimization problem that minimizes the sum of squared errors between the Euclidean distance with the coordinates ($\boldsymbol{\theta}_t$ and $\boldsymbol{\theta}_i$) and the estimated distance in (1) as follows:

$$\begin{aligned} \underset{\boldsymbol{\theta}_t, \alpha, \beta}{\text{minimize}} \quad & \sum_{i=1}^{M} (d_E(\boldsymbol{\theta}_t, \boldsymbol{\theta}_i) - \hat{d}_i)^2 \\ \text{subject to} \quad & \alpha \geq 2, \end{aligned} \tag{2}$$

where $d_E(\cdot)$ is the Euclidean distance, and M is the number of RSSI samples.

SenSys'15, November 1–4, 2015, Seoul, Republic of Korea.
ACM 978-1-4503-3631-4/15/11.
http://dx.doi.org/10.1145/2809695.2817900.

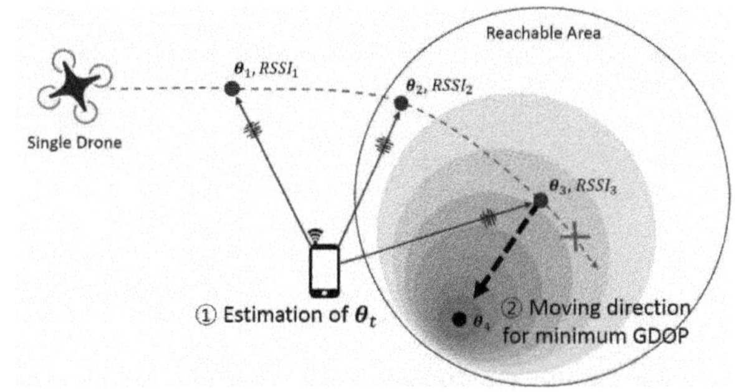

Figure 1: Example of trajectory planning scheme based on GDOP

3. TRAJECTORY PLANNING

We propose a trajectory planning scheme to guide an RF scanning drone toward a direction that minimizes the geometric dilution of precision (GDOP) [3] for more accurate localization as illustrated in Fig. 1. In satellite navigation systems, GDOP specifies the effect of the geometry of satellites on the position error of a target device. A large

GDOP indicates there exists a high uncertainty of the target position estimate due to the geometry of satellites. In a drone-based localization, it is also possible to determine GDOP by geographical positions where the drone gets the RSSI samples.

Let $\mathbf{G}$ denote a geometry matrix as follows:

$$\mathbf{G} = \begin{bmatrix} \frac{(x_1-\hat{x}_t)}{R_1} & \frac{(y_1-\hat{y}_t)}{R_1} & \frac{(z_1-\hat{z}_t)}{R_1} & -1 \\ \frac{(x_2-\hat{x}_t)}{R_2} & \frac{(y_2-\hat{y}_t)}{R_2} & \frac{(z_2-\hat{z}_t)}{R_2} & -1 \\ \vdots & \vdots & \vdots & \vdots \\ \frac{(x_{i+1}-\hat{x}_t)}{R_{i+1}} & \frac{(y_{i+1}-\hat{y}_t)}{R_{i+1}} & \frac{(z_{i+1}-\hat{z}_t)}{R_{i+1}} & -1 \end{bmatrix}, \quad (3)$$

where $R_{i+1} = d_E(\boldsymbol{\theta}_{i+1}, \hat{\boldsymbol{\theta}}_t)$. Note that $\hat{\boldsymbol{\theta}}_t$ is the estimated target location in (2), and $\boldsymbol{\theta}_{i+1}$ is the drone location to be determined for the next $(i+1)$-th measurement. Using $\mathbf{G}$, we obtain a matrix $\mathbf{Q}$ as

$$\mathbf{Q} = (\mathbf{G}^T\mathbf{G})^{-1} = \begin{bmatrix} \sigma_x^2 & \sigma_{xy} & \sigma_{xz} & \sigma_{xt} \\ \sigma_{xy} & \sigma_y^2 & \sigma_{yz} & \sigma_{yt} \\ \sigma_{xz} & \sigma_{yz} & \sigma_z^2 & \sigma_{zt} \\ \sigma_{xt} & \sigma_{yt} & \sigma_{zt} & \sigma_t^2 \end{bmatrix}. \quad (4)$$

Then, GDOP is given by GDOP $= \sqrt{\sigma_x^2 + \sigma_y^2 + \sigma_z^2 + \sigma_t^2}$, which is a function of $\boldsymbol{\theta}_{i+1}$.

Because smaller GDOP achieves more accurate localization, the drone location for the next $(i+1)$-th measurement can be determined by an optimization problem that minimizes GDOP as follows:

$$\begin{aligned} \underset{\boldsymbol{\theta}_{i+1}}{\text{minimize}} \quad & \text{GDOP} \\ \text{subject to} \quad & d_E(\boldsymbol{\theta}_{i+1}, \boldsymbol{\theta}_i) \leq c, \end{aligned} \quad (5)$$

where c is the maximum distance that the drone can reach within a certain interval. Once the optimal point $\boldsymbol{\theta}^*_{i+1}$ is determined in (5), the drone is set to fly to the direction of $\boldsymbol{\theta}^*_{i+1}$. As shown in Fig. 1, a drone captures a certain number of RF samples and estimates a target position $\hat{\boldsymbol{\theta}}_t$ by (2). With $\hat{\boldsymbol{\theta}}_t$, it computes $\boldsymbol{\theta}^*_{i+1}$ by (5) and changes its moving direction toward $\boldsymbol{\theta}^*_{i+1}$. As the drone captures more RF samples at the locations with smaller GDOP, the estimated target location is repeatedly updated and is to be more accurate.

4. EXPERIMENTS AND RESULTS

We consider a drone-based RF source localization scenario in which a drone equipped with an RF signal sniffer scans a 2.4 GHz RF spectrum and localizes the RF signal source in a 150×50-m ground area. We installed a Beagle-Bone-Black embedded board equipped with a wireless module and a GPS module to an off-the-shelf drone as shown in Fig. 2. Kismet software was used to capture the RF signals from a target device. The target device was configured to send a beacon signal at every 5 seconds. We compared the proposed trajectory scheme with two other schemes, i) a predetermined whole-area scanning pattern trajectory from the top/left to bottom/right corner , and ii) a naive scheme to make the drone continuously head to the estimated target position.

Figure 3 shows the position errors with respect to the number of RF samples for three different trajectories. In Fig. 3, the position error for the fixed area-scanning trajectory becomes smaller up to 6 RF samples, but thereafter

Figure 2: Drone-based RF source localization system

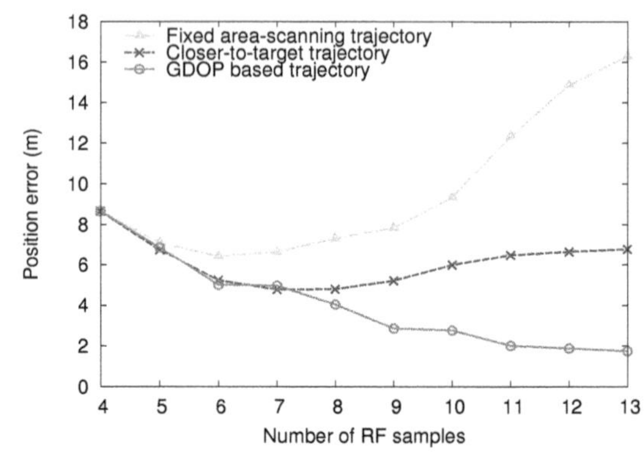

Figure 3: Position error with respect to RF samples

rapidly increases as the number of RF samples the drone captured increases. This is due to that many RF samples captured at a long distance from the target were used for localization, and these samples were more susceptible to RF noises and fading. For the closer-to-target trajectory, the position error was the same as that of the proposed scheme up to 7 samples. However, it slightly increased and leveled off. The reason is that once the target position was estimated with the first several samples, the drone flied to the position and remained stationary at the same position even though the initial estimate is not accurate. On the contrary, the proposed scheme achieved the lowest position error, and remarkably it showed that the position error continuously decreased as the drone captured more RF samples because it effectively reduced the uncertainty of the estimated target location by moving to the position that minimizes GDOP.

5. ACKNOWLEDGMENTS

This work was supported in part by EWRC at GIST, originally funded by DAPA and ADD.

6. REFERENCES

[1] D. Koutsonikolas, S. M. Das, and Y. C. Hu. Path planning of mobile landmarks for localization in wireless sensor networks. *Computer Communications*, 30(13):2577–2592, 2007.

[2] O. Artemenko, et al. How different trajectories of moving beacons influence the localization of nodes in disaster scenarios using wireless communication. In *IEEE WPMC 2014*, 367–372, 2014.

[3] E. Swanson. Geometric dilution of precision. *Navigation*, 25(4):425–429, 1978.

Poster Abstract: Communicating "in the Air"– Studying the Impact of UAVs on Sensor Network Data Collection

Hoon Jeong, Changwon Lee, Jaehong Ryu, Byeong-Cheol Choi and JeongGil Ko*
Electronics and Telecommunications Research Institute, Daejeon, Korea
*Department of Software Convergence Technology, Ajou University, Suwon, Korea

ABSTRACT

The commercialization of cheap unmanned aerial vehicles (UAVs) is starting to change the way we, as sensor network system designers, think of data collection. Specifically, UAVs provide a third dimension of mobile data collection as we can now traverse the sky with minimal obstacles, rather than rovering the ground with wheeled robots. However, despite UAVs or drones being an interesting platform with the potential to change sensor network deployment topologies, little do we understand on how data collection will perform "in the air". In this work we present a preliminary empirical study on the performance of aerial data collection using an IEEE 802.15.4 radio-equipped drone connecting itself to sensor nodes positioned on the ground. Our results show that a drone-based data collection platform outperforms that of an "at ground-level" data collection unit, despite being at identical distances. Based on this study, we identify the increased data collection height and "easy-to-achieve" line-of-sight as key features that make this possible.

1. INTRODUCTION

For more than a decade, researchers and the industry have put effort to deploy low-power wireless sensors networks in various extreme environments. As a way to effectively deliver data from distant locations, multihop networking protocols were widely used to forward data over multiple hops and over wide geographical regions.

Another approach to collect data over wide regions and distant locations is to utilize robotic mobile data collection platforms [1]. Typically operating with wheels, the trajectory planning of these devices and ad-hocly configuring a collection protocol suitable for these mobile data collectors has also been an interesting research topic to many. Specifically, given that even in this case, data collection still remains on a two-dimensional plane, most of the research in this domain focused on achieving low-cost and fast routing performance along with optimizing the traveling routes to maximize the efficiency of the system. Despite such efforts, the fact that ground-level mobile platforms performed less effective in obstacle-rich environments (e.g., forests) made practical deployments of these devices difficult.

More recently, we have witnessed the commercialization of unmanned aerial vehicles (UAVs) in various forms. Typically, denoted as "drones" or "quadcoptors", these aerial devices open a new opportunity to diversify sensor network data collection platforms [2, 3]. However, while we roughly understand that the third-dimensional factor in system deployments, "height" can bring positive impact to the radio connectivity or the packet delivery performance itself, as a research community, we are still in the early stages of understanding how impactful and effective a drone can be for our systems. This work is a first step in answering this question. We introduce UAVs as a potential platform for data collection and discuss briefly about some benefits that such a system architecture can bring. Furthermore, we perform a pilot study for understanding these benefits by deploying a small sensor network in the woods near ETRI in Daejeon Korea. The nodes in this network are configured to report packets towards a data collection unit located at various positions on an adjacent road. Using two types of data collection platforms, one mobile unit at ground-level (e.g., ~2m above the ground) and a drone, we present preliminary data collection performance results.

SenSys'15, November 1–4, 2015, Seoul, Republic of Korea
ACM 978-1-4503-3631-4/15/11
http://dx.doi.org/10.1145/2809695.2817901.

2. SYSTEM ARCHITECTURE

Many researchers agree that UAVs can be a new way of interacting with a pre-deployed sensor network as a mobile data collector. Especially for harsh environment deployments, in which human or ground-level platforms have difficulties in physically accessing, UAVs or drones can simplify the data collection process. We now briefly summarize some of the system-level benefits a UAV-based sensor data collection system architecture.

- **Improved Line-of-Sight (LOS) Connectivity:** The fact that drones use height as part of their movement trajectory opens the possibility to better achieve LOS in many harsh deployment conditions.
- **Simplified Trajectory Configurations:** By performing movements in the air, a UAV faces less obstacles compared to ground-level mobile data collecting platforms.
- **Improved Energy Efficiency for Sensor Nodes:** By obtaining the sensor data via single hop, rather than constructing a multihop network, low-power nodes can perform aggressive radio duty-cycling.

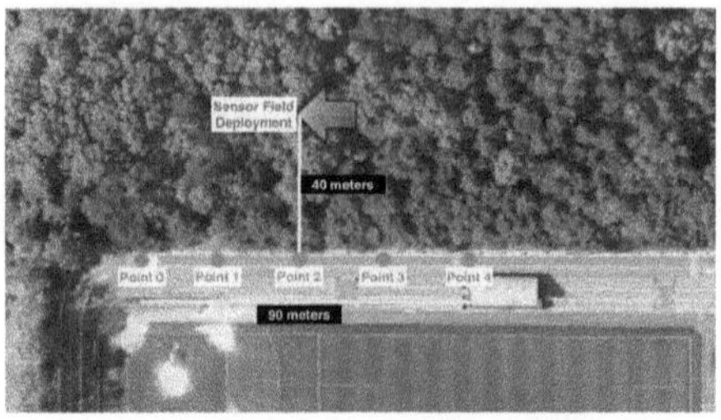

(a) Map of deployment field

(b) Sensor field installation in the woods

(c) TMote Sky installation on drone

(d) Wireless communicating drone in the sky

Figure 1: Pictures taken from our pilot deployment of a drone-based data collection network.

For showcasing the impact of UAVs on ground-level sensor network data collection we construct a testing environment as in Figure 1. We set up a sensor network in the woods ~40m apart from the nearest road, where a ground-level mobile rover can perform data collection. Here, the trees and the geographical characteristics of the woods bother the sensor network nodes to form an LOS link to the road. In this configuration, we set a ground-level data collection rover with a communication platform installed ~2m above the ground to collect data at five different data points and also perform data collection with a drone at ~10m and ~15m altitudes. We use a TelosB device with its on-board antenna and send periodic data from the sensor network in the woods at a rate of 10 packets/sec. The goal of this sample deployment was to confirm the impact of utilizing a UAV for sensor network data collection from a harsh environment. While for the setting in our experiments we can think of utilizing a multihop network, in more extreme cases a multihop network (or a relay network) can lead to a single point of failure; thus, utilizing a UAV can be a beneficial option.

3. EVALUATION

As we see in Figure 2, where we plot the packet reception ratio (PRR) of incoming packets at each data collection point, the PRR observed with the UAV outperforms the PRR of the ground-level rover for all locations. This is mainly an impact of the height that UAVs introduce, which

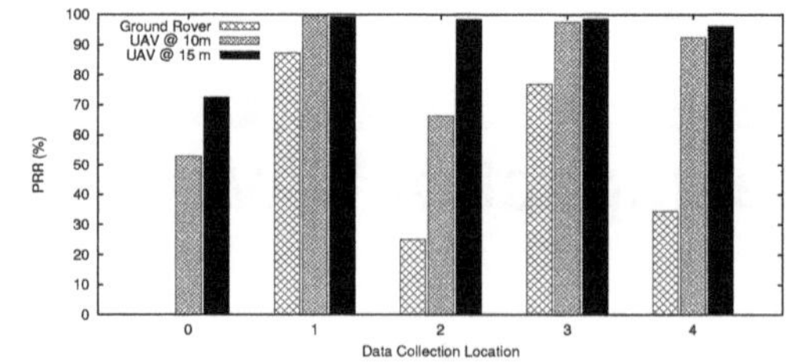

Figure 2: PRR at different data collection points.

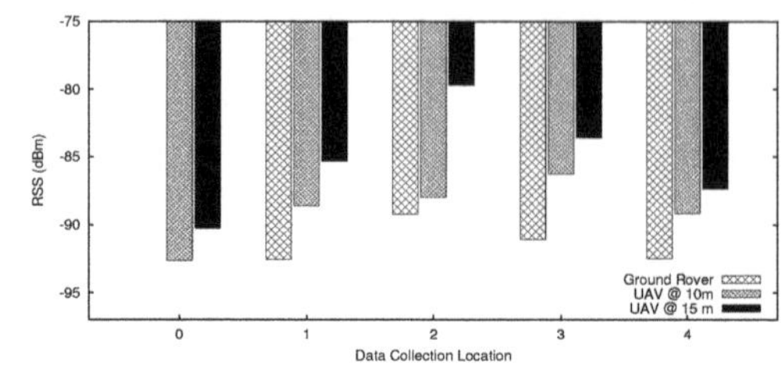

Figure 3: RSS at different data collection points.

naturally reduces the amount of obstacles that the RF signals face as they are transmitted over the wireless medium. We can also see that an even higher configuration (e.g., 15m compared to 10m) shows a slightly better performance for some location while not dominant itself.

In terms of the received signal strength (RSS) in Figure 3, we can also see a similar trend in which the UAV-based experiments show an improved RSS performance in all cases. These results, together can serve as evidence that utilizing UAVs can benefit the data collection performance by overcoming harsh environmental factors using the height factor.

4. SUMMARY

In this work we show an experimental validation on the impact of UAVs for sensor network data collection. We identify system-level advantages that UAVs can bring for data collection scenarios in harsh-environment sensor network deployments and show this effectiveness using a preliminary empirical pilot deployment. Our results show that the height benefits and freedom to select a aerial trajectory can allow the UAV to act as a effective data collection unit for ground-level sensor network deployments.

Acknowledgments

This work was supported by the Basic Research Project (Development of an integrated early detection system of landslides based on real-time monitoring) of KIGAM funded by the MSIP, Korea.

5. REFERENCES

[1] Y.K. Leow and Ying Shang. Mobile robot tracking in wireless sensor networks. In *ICNSC*, April 2010.

[2] Steven K. Teh, Luis Mejias, Peter Corke, and Wen Hu. Experiments in Integrating Autonomous Uninhabited Aerial Vehicles(UAVs) and Wireless Sensor Networks. In *Australasian Conference on Robotics and Automation*, 2008.

[3] Joaao Valente, David Sanz, Antonio Barrientos, Jaime del Cerro, Angela Ribeiro, and Claudio Rossi. An air-ground wireless sensor network for crop monitoring. *Sensors*, 11, 2011.

Poster Abstract: Model Predictive Control with Real-time Occupancy Detection

Alex Beltran and Alberto E. Cerpa
Electrical Engineering and Computer Science
University of California, Merced
{abeltran2,acerpa}@andes.ucmerced.edu

ABSTRACT

Buildings are responsible for more than 40% of US primary energy consumption. Of that, nearly 50% goes to heating, ventilation and air-conditioning (HVAC) systems. Savings made in HVAC systems therefore have a major impact in energy consumption and are of critical importance. We present a model predictive control framework (MPC) for smart building control. The framework has several components, including (a) occupancy sensing in real-time, (b) occupancy prediction models based on historical occupancy data, (c) thermodynamic building models, (d) weather forecasting data, and (e) a model predictive control optimization that tries to minimize monetary costs in energy use while maintaining quality comfort bounds for the building's users. We tested the system in a real building with over 40 workers, and we show that we could obtain monetary savings of more than 50% without sacrificing user comfort.

Categories and Subject Descriptors

J.7 [**Computers In Other Systems**]: Command & control; C.3 [**Special-Purpose and Application-Based Systems**]: Real-time and embedded systems

Keywords

Building, Monitoring, Control

1. INTRODUCTION

Smart sustainable buildings represent a major paradigm shift. According to the US Department of Energy, buildings account for nearly 40% of US primary energy consumption in 2010, 72% of which is electrical energy. Of this total, 50% of the energy consumed in buildings is used for heating,ventilation, and air-conditioning (HVAC) systems [1]. It is also projected that in the next 25 years gas usage will increase annually by 1% in commercial buildings [2]. Any energy reduction not only impacts cost associated with conditioning the building, but also lowers carbon emissions. Due to this potential for savings, conditioning buildings while minimizing energy usage and keeping occupants comfortable has been a topic of interest in research.

In commercial buildings, one source of inefficiency is empty or partially filled rooms in the conditioning zones. We leverage a sensor network approach in our system with MPC to provide both adequate conditioning of a zone while minimizing energy usage. In our experiments, we show that the combination of occupancy detection, occupancy prediction, and MPC saves more energy than MPC alone.

SenSys'15, November 1–4, 2015, Seoul, South Korea..
ACM 978-1-4503-3631-4/15/11.
DOI: http://dx.doi.org/10.1145/2809695.2817902.

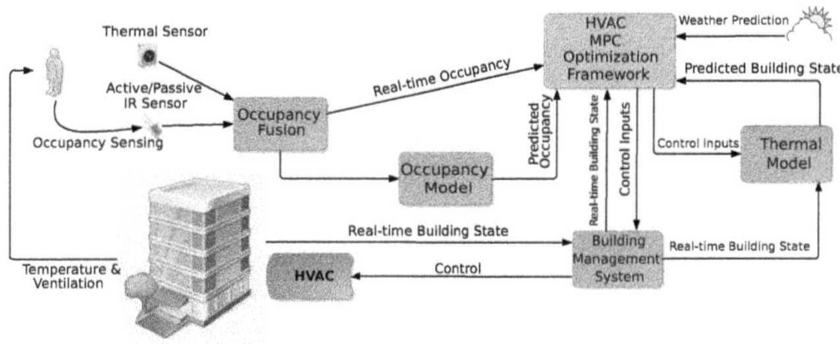

Figure 1: Architecture of our system

2. SYSTEM ARCHITECTURE

Figure 1 shows the system architecture overview that is described in the following modules. Realtime building state (i.e. sensor data) from the building is collected by the Building Management System (BMS) upon request of the HVAC MPC Optimizer. The data collected comes from sensors that are standard in buildings such as thermostats, flow and temperature sensors throughout the building's ducts and zones controlled by the HVAC system. This data is then provided to both the MPC Optimizer and the Thermal Model Module. The MPC Optimizer also provides different control inputs to the building's Thermal Model, such that it can predict building behavior for different time horizons. We use thermal-array sensors to observe real time occupancy and pass these values to Occupancy Model Module. This module predicts the number of occupants in each zone of the building. This prediction is also sent to our MPC Optimizer. Additionally, we use local weather forecast to gather the outdoor temperature, which affects the thermodynamics of the zone.

Occupancy Detection: Occupancy detection is done using a thermal sensor node developed by [3]. The node uses an infrared thermal array sensor and a passive infrared sensor (PIR). The thermal array has a 8x8 resolution with a $3m \times 3m$ field of view. When the PIR sensor detects no movement for 10 minutes the sensor node takes a snapshot of the infrared thermal sensor and uses this sample as the

Zone	Type	Electricity	Gas	Total
Zone 1-5	Baseline	\$98,721	\$83,441	\$182,163
Zone 1-5	MPC Occ.	\$51,287.58	\$35,343.90	\$86,631
Zone 6-7	Baseline	\$47,945	\$23,693	\$71,638
Zone 6-7	MPC No Occ.	\$32,938	\$13,760	\$46,698

Table 1: Projected Cost

background. When an occupant enters the room, we sample with the infrared thermal sensor to get new temperature readings, and use background subtraction to identify the presence of a person. Using the PIR as a trigger for the thermal sensor extends the battery life of the node. We gather a set of training data and use an artificial neural network for classification.

Occupancy Prediction: In our system we use a Blended Markov Chain [4] for prediction. The temporal transitions to a new state depends only on the current occupancy state and the time. These multiple temporal matrices are then blended together and renormalized to prevent states without exits. This permits us to predict the occupancy given the current state and pre-condition zones accordingly.

Model Predictive Control: The HVAC system we modeled is a single duct central cooling AHU with terminal reheat. In order to model the thermodynamics of a zone, we use a resistive-capacitive system where each zone is considered a capacitor and interactions between zones are resistors. The capacity of the zone is how much air of a different temperature it takes to raise or lower the temperature. Resistance takes into consideration the heat transfer between zones. This model is constrained by physical constraints of the HVAC system and the occupancy comfort constraints. It is optimized to minimize monetary cost using the predicted state over the next hour.

3. EXPERIMENTAL EVALUATION

Our experiments were conducted in University of California, Merced during the early spring with approval from the Institutional Review Board (IRB). In Merced, the average high temperature in spring is $67°F$ and average low temperature is $41°F$. We chose a single floor office space with a square footage of $5750ft^2$. This building contains 40 workers that occupy the building between 6:00am and 2:00am.

In our evaluation we have three main comparison points. The first is the baseline method of control, which is what is normally used in the building. This strategy has a fixed conditioning schedule between 6am until 2am the following day. The second control strategy uses MPC without occupancy information. This strategy uses the MPC framework in two zones and assumes a fix schedule between 6am in the morning and until 2am the following morning. The final strategy uses MPC with occupancy detection and prediction. Both MPC methods are evaluated at the same time for 3 work weeks. The cost of running these three control strategies are projected onto the building for the year and are shown in Table 1. Comparing the totals in Table 1, we see that using MPC alone provides 35% additional savings compared to the baselien and using MPC with occupancy provides 52% savings. Although both tests result in significant savings, using MPC with occupancy provides an additional 17% savings. Overall in the experiment we save 48% compared to the baseline strategy used in our campus. This additional savings show that it is beneficial to include occupancy detection and prediction when using a MPC strategy.

Figure 2 is a close up of the zone dynamics using our MPC with occupancy strategy of a single day for Zone 1,

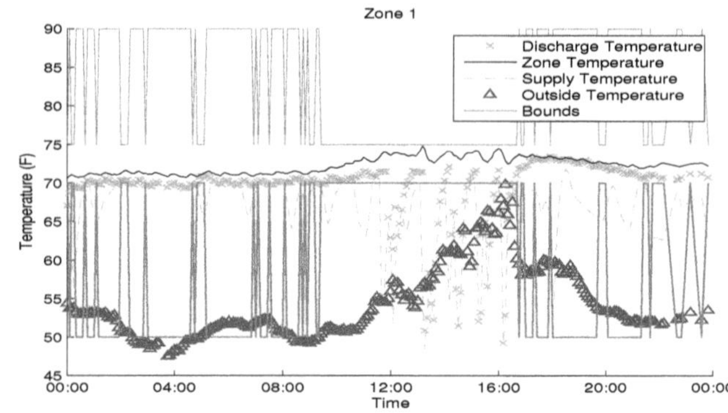

Figure 2: Zone temperature dynamics w/ MPC and Occ.

the break room. Comfort bounds are set between $70°F$ and $75°F$ and are broaden to $50°F$ and $90°F$ when the zone is unoccupied. In Figure 2, there are dips in the supply temperature which is the temperature provided to all zones. The discharge temperature is the air temperature provided to each zone, i.e. the air temperature after being heated in a terminal reheat system. If very little air flow is supplied to the zone, the zone temperature will change only slightly, while if a larger air flow is directed to the zone, the zone temperature will change more radically based on the air mix between the current zone and discharge air. We can see that in the afternoon around 12:00 until 16:00 there is an increase in load due to occupants. To compensate for this load, the system uses cool outside air instead of spending energy cooling down hot re-circulated air. During the evening, our system keeps the temperature near the occupied comfort bound due to previous occupancy patterns by the late night custodial staff. The supply temperature is significantly higher than the outside temperature, therefore that means there is a large amount of recirculated air in the zone. Near the end of the day there is little flow going into the room so the discharge temperature is approximately the same as the zone temperature.

4. SUMMARY AND FUTURE WORK

Model Predictive Control (MPC) is a proven method of controlling a building based on predicted conditions of the building, occupants, and weather. A majority of the work conducted in this field has been done to provide efficient models with the assumption that building is occupied during a fixed period of time. We show that by using MPC we can achieve savings of 35% and gain an additional 14% savings by using occupancy detection and an occupancy prediction model. Overall our system was able to save an additional 48% energy when compared to the current strategy used the building we tested in. Additional work is necessary to compare our MPC strategy to other sensor based strategies.

5. REFERENCES

[1] 2010 building energy data book. U.S. Dept. of Energy.

[2] Annual energy outlook 2014 with projections to 2040, 2014.

[3] A. Beltran, V. L. Erickson, and A. E. Cerpa. Thermosense: Occupancy thermal based sensing for HVAC control. In *BuildSys'13*, pages 11:1–11:8, Rome, Province of Rome, Italy, 2013. ACM.

[4] V. L. Erickson, M. Á. Carreira-Perpiñán, and A. E. Cerpa. OBSERVE: Occupancy-based system for efficient reduction of HVAC energy. In *IPSN'11*.

Poster: Towards Robust Reprogrammability for Wireless Sensors

Nicole Tobias, Connor Bolton, Josiah Hester, Lanny Sitanayah, Jacob Sorber
School of Computing
Clemson University
{rtobias, mcbolto, jhester, lsitana, jsorber}@clemson.edu

ABSTRACT

Embedded systems that are wirelessly reprogrammed can be rendered useless by certain programming errors, excessive power consumption, or misconfigurations in the hardware. These types of situations can leave a device in a state that compromises its programmability, often rendering the device useless. Existing attempts to address the problem of robust wireless reprogramming have all been software-based solutions, that are vulnerable to certain errors, such as memory corruption, can corrupt the recovery programs. We propose a hardware-based solution to wireless reprogramming, physically separating the programmer and target device. This separation limits the propagation of errors, and ensures the device will always be recoverable. In this poster we will present the design and an early prototype of our approach — an ultra-low-power, low-cost hardware solution to ensure recovery from fatal errors and reprogrammability in wireless systems. This poster discusses the current system design, initial results, and system analysis from our current prototype. We also present future and ongoing directions, as well as key research questions. This work was funded by National Science Foundation grants CNS-1314342 and CNS-1453607. Any opinions, findings, and conclusions or recommendations expressed in this material are those of the authors and do not necessarily reflect the views of the National Science Foundation.

Categories and Subject Descriptors

C.3 [**Special-Purpose and Application-Based Systems**]: Microprocessor/microcomputer applications

General Terms

Hardware, Embedded Systems, Wireless Networks

Keywords

Hardware Approach, Wireless Reprogramming, Robust Reprogramming, Low-Power, Embedded System

SenSys '15, November 01-04, 2015, Seoul, Republic of Korea
ACM 978-1-4503-3631-4/15/11.
http://dx.doi.org/10.1145/2809695.2817903

1. INTRODUCTION

Robust wireless reprogramming and seamless recovery from different classes of program errors are a must for a wireless system to have reliable data and a long lifetime. In the past decade, wireless sensor networks have become very prominent in many academic and industrial data acquisition applications. These networks must collect reliable and useful data for accurate analysis to take place. At times, these sensor nodes are deployed with logical errors in their application code. These errors can affect the reliability of the device by rendering data meaningless and hindering its ability to be reprogrammed wirelessly. Human intervention is sometimes required; however, manual recovery of a sensor node is a costly, time intensive, and often impossible process.

Enabling robust reprogramming of a wireless sensor network is a challenging task. Prior approaches to disseminating code updates to a network have been exclusively software-only solutions. A variety of software-based techniques, such as Deluge [2], Rateless Deluge [1], Stream [3], SYNAPSE++ [4], Trigger [5], attempt to address this issue. These techniques present some shortcomings in the presence of certain memory errors that can potentially overwrite portions of restorative code and are limiting in situations where the target device has intermittent power.

Software-only approaches can be rendered inoperable in the presence of certain classes of program errors. For example, if the current program running on the sensor misconfigures the radio, consumes too much energy, or overwrites the recovery program itself, the device may not be available for reprogramming. Programs that misuse memory can overwrite or corrupt portions of memory that are being used by the wireless network and possibly render sensor data meaningless.

We present a novel hardware-based approach to enable the wireless retasking of a sensor device in spite of software and configuration errors introduced by programmers. Our approach uses an ultra-low-power coprocessor that is physically separate from the primary application processor. The coprocessor will monitor the processing, communication, and energy consumption of the application processor to facilitate error analysis and enable robust reprogramming.

2. THE SYSTEM OVERVIEW

In contrast to previous systems, our approach is primarily a hardware-based solution that enables more robust reprogramming than prior techniques. This system uses a coprocessor to monitor and reprogram a devices main application processor. This allows for two physically separate computing

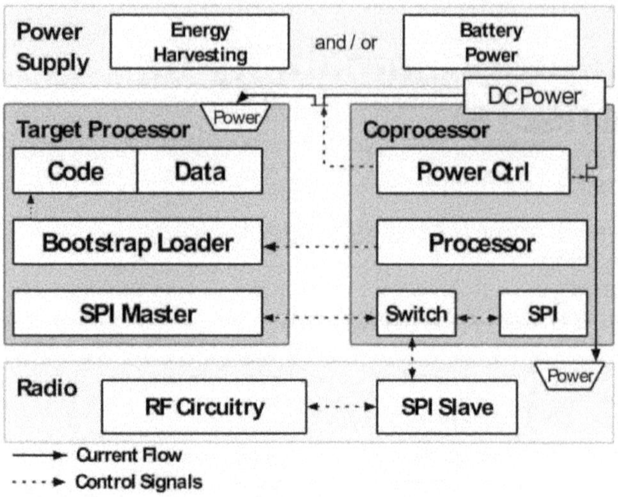

Figure 1: This figure shows the high level view of the system.

environments to be utilized for storing recovery programs such that one processor's potential memory errors cannot tamper with the coprocessor's stored restoration image. By using a design that physically separates the recovery program from the target program, the coprocessor cannot be affected by the target program. This is beneficial in scenarios where program errors that overwrite memory on the main application processor are now incapable of overwriting the recovery programs that reside in the coprocessor's memory. This means that the target device will always be able to be reprogrammed and restored in the presence of errors that limited the existing techniques as well as the ones that they still address.

This system is being designed with three goals in mind. We hope the hardware-based approach of this system will provide the following benefits to a wireless sensor:

- Reliable reprogramming
- Robust recovery/fault tolerant system
- Low cost, low power, and a small footprint

The coprocessor stores a recovery image that can be used in the event of target device failure. This recovery image will return the target device to an acceptable state. The coprocessor is positioned in such a way that it is able to observe all communication between the main processor and the device's radio, allowing it to monitor incoming and outgoing communications and changes made to the radio's configuration. Figure 1 shows how the coprocessor monitors the target device.

When the user wishes to reprogram the system, they will define a special packet, called a *restoration packet*, and send it over the radio to signal the need/want to reprogram the application processor. Once the coprocessor recognizes that a restoration packet has been sent, it will restore the main processor to a preset state so that it can accept and install new code updates reliably.

3. POSTER DESCRIPTION

This poster will present this on-going project and an overview of the current system. We will describe the designs and future implementation of both the hardware and software of our system. Goals and challenges, as described in the previous section, and initial results from our current work will also be presented.

4. CONCLUSIONS & FUTURE WORK

Wirelessly reprogrammed devices and systems will continue to have massive impact on future data collection and dissemination in both academic and industrial research for years to come. To ensure that these systems have a long lifetime and can continue to collect data reliably, they must be able to seamlessly recover from various program error cases and be kept in a state that can accept new programs/tasks throughout the system's continuance. Due to the physical separation of the coprocessor from the application processor, the coprocessor can reliably reprogram the target device regardless of error symptoms resulting from memory corruption, power consumption, and other system errors of the target device. Its ultra-low-power consumption can be optimized to work with devices that are power conservative in nature, such as energy-harvesting sensors.

Long-term monitoring of a low-power system would require the coprocessor device to come online only to assist reprogramming when necessary. Future directions of interest are to expand the current features of our system to also be used in scenarios of remote debugging as well as system recovery. The coprocessor should detect errors, if present, and return useful error information. Both current and future implementations of wireless device networks could benefit from such a low-power, low-cost, robust reprogramming system in many ways.

5. REFERENCES

[1] A. Hagedorn, D. Starobinski, and A. Trachtenberg. Rateless deluge: Over-the-air programming of wireless sensor networks using random linear codes. In *Proceedings of the 7th international conference on Information processing in sensor networks*, pages 457–466. IEEE Computer Society, 2008.

[2] J. W. Hui and D. Culler. The dynamic behavior of a data dissemination protocol for network programming at scale. In *Proceedings of the 2nd international conference on Embedded networked sensor systems*, pages 81–94. ACM, 2004.

[3] R. K. Panta, I. Khalil, and S. Bagchi. Stream: Low overhead wireless reprogramming for sensor networks. In *INFOCOM 2007. 26th IEEE International Conference on Computer Communications. IEEE*, pages 928–936. IEEE, 2007.

[4] M. Rossi, N. Bui, G. Zanca, L. Stabellini, R. Crepaldi, and M. Zorzi. Synapse++: code dissemination in wireless sensor networks using fountain codes. *Mobile Computing, IEEE Transactions on*, 9(12):1749–1765, 2010.

[5] R. Tompkins, T. B. Jones, R. E. Nertney, C. E. Smith, and P. Gilfeather-Crowley. Reconfiguration and management in wireless sensor networks. In *Sensors Applications Symposium (SAS), 2011 IEEE*, pages 39–44. IEEE, 2011.

Poster Abstract: Energy Optimization Framework in Wireless Sensor Network

Niloufar P. Esfahani

Alberto E. Cerpa

Electrical Engineering and Computer Science
University of California, Merced
{nesfahani,acerpa}@ucmerced.edu

ABSTRACT

We present a holistic architecture for energy management in sensor networks. Our architecture is based on a model-driven approach which attempts to (a) establish functional relationships across different components of the software stack and the interrelated parameters based on empirical data, (b) use the maximum sensor value and time-synchronization errors acceptable by the users of the sensor network application as input to establish minimum quality of service requirements, and (c) optimize the parameter values of all the software modules within the node's application stack to minimize total energy consumption for each sensor node. We explore the trade-offs of the design space by using a non-trivial application that includes sensing, time synchronization and routing modules and show that when using our architecture, we can provide energy savings in the average of 37% to 76% while still maintaining quality of service both in terms of the expected sensing and time-synchronization errors. We further show that even when using modules that perform *significantly* better than others with default values (e.g. ORW $\gg$ CTP), we can still reduce overall energy consumption by properly adjusting the parameters of lowest performance modules and provide energy savings in the average of 30% to 43%.

Categories and Subject Descriptors

C.2.1 [**Network Architecture and Design**]: Wireless communication; C.4 [**PERFORMANCE OF SYSTEMS**]: Performance attributes

Keywords

Component, Energy, Optimization

1. INTRODUCTION

There have been many efforts geared towards improving energy efficiency of different components of the system including data sampling, query processing, radio communication and processor duty cycling. However, these individual components may not be flexible to adapt to changing network and application dynamics. Perhaps more importantly,

SenSys'15, November 1–4, 2015, Seoul, South Korea..
ACM 978-1-4503-3631-4/15/11.
DOI: http://dx.doi.org/10.1145/2809695.2817904 .

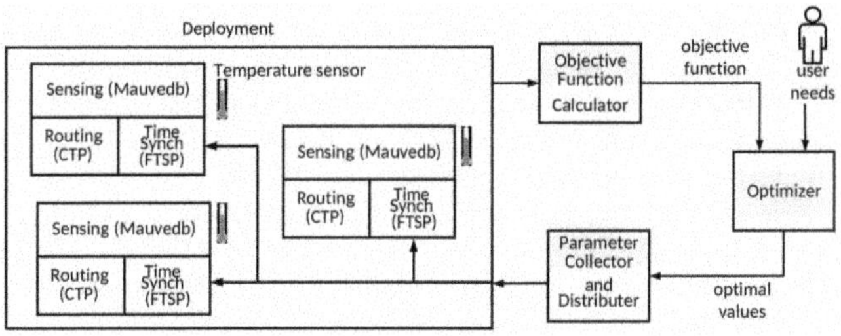

Figure 1: System Architecture

each component is designed to optimize energy consumption from a component-centric point of view, without considering the inter-relationships among the different components in the sensor stack. We take a fresh look at this problem by considering the energy trade-offs caused by the use of multiple components simultaneously, and provide a framework that optimizes the overall system energy consumption in a holistic way, based on the inter-relationships among components and the user constraints that bound the expected application quality of service.

In many applications, most of the energy consumption of wireless sensor networks comes from radio communication. In our work, we use the number of packet transmissions (TX) as a proxy that approximates energy consumption[1]. Our goal in this work is to reduce the number of packet transmissions (TX) while maintaining quality of service constraints based on user input. We do this by finding functional parametrized relationships based on empirical data among the different components of the sensor software stack, and minimize the TX based on user constraints. Our goal is to find the optimal parameters that allows minimization of the system energy consumption.

2. SYSTEM ARCHITECTURE

We have used a non-trivial application consisting of three core components: time synchronization, sensing and routing modules. These components are representative of multiple data collection sensor network applications and provide a good sample of the design space. We use FTSP [4] for time synchronization between different nodes, and CTP [2] for multi-hop radio communication. The sensing application is similar to MAUVEDB [1]. Sensor nodes sense an environmental parameter (e.g. temperature) over time, and build their own temperature model. Each node builds a simple linear regression model between the temperature and time, and calculates the best fit. If the difference between a value

[1]We plan to incorporate radio duty-cycling and actual energy measurements in future work

sensed by the node and the model prediction is larger than a specific threshold defined by the user, then the application forwards the outlier data sample towards the sink, and the node recalculates the temperature model. While a sensor node could send every sample value for maximum accuracy, there is a trade-off between the number of transmissions required (and their energy usage), and the accuracy that can be achieved. By optimizing only for the required user's accuracy needed, we can minimize the overall energy consumption. Similarly, time synchronization accuracy and data error thresholds can be manually-defined by the user, to ensure that minimum application requirements are met while energy is minimized.

Figure 1 shows the overall system architecture. By deploying the application over different sensor nodes, and using arbitrary empirical data for different parameters of the system (e.g. beacon frequency, sampling frequency, time synchronization rate, and error threshold) in acceptable ranges to see how they affect the packet transmissions (TX), we calculate the relationships between them for different modules. TX is tracked for each module in the application including specialized transmissions for time synchronization, beaconing for route discovery, and transmitted data packets for sensing application in each component. As an example, by increasing beacon frequency, more beacon packets are transmitted to maintain the routes (TX in routing component increases), but the improved links make fewer data packet transmissions necessary in sensing application (TX in sensing component decreases). This trade-off in the objective function is an example of why we need to obtain the optimal values in the system. The *Objective Function Calculator* module then sums up these usage statistics and calculate the objective function in linear and non-linear formats (linear and non-linear relationships between TX and related parameters). Once calculated, the objective function along with user-defined constraints are sent to the *Optimizer* module, which calculates optimal values of operation. Parameters are then given to the *Parameter Collector and Distributor* module, which disseminates them to all sensing nodes.

3. EXPERIMENTAL EVALUATION

In our analysis, we determine how the inclusion of our optimized operation parameters affect the amount of radio transmissions that occur, as well of the merits of choosing a linear or non-linear objective function. In order to test how good are the linear and non-linear objective function approximations derived above, we run a 20 minute experiment where we test the number of total transmission packets by using the parameters obtained by each, constrained by different maximum time error and data error thresholds specified by the user. Our experiment consists of a wireless network testbed, consisting of 57 sensor nodes, distributed through a building. Across all time error constraints from 0.5 to 3μs, we see an average of 37% packet reduction using linear objective function parameters, and an average of 47% reduction across a data error range of 1% to 10%. For non-linear objective function we see an average of 76% packet reduction across all time error constraints and in the average of 64% reduction across data error constraints. This is substantial improvement and the user-defined constraints provided to the optimizer ensures that the quality of service of the sensing, time synchronization, and routing are all maintained.

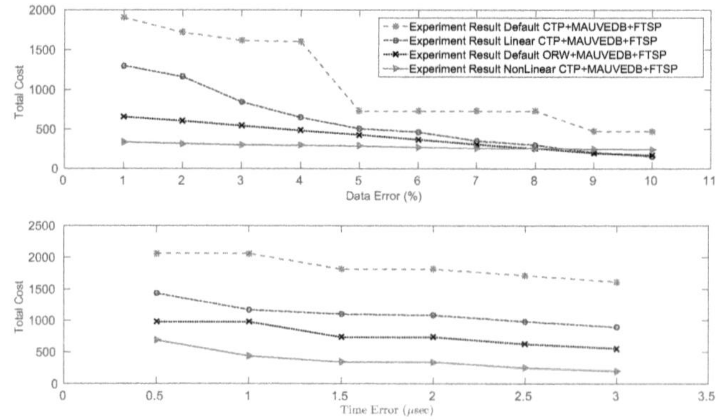

Figure 2: Comparing results of using ORW with CTP as user specified threshold of a) data error changes (top), b) time error changes (bottom)

Another commonly-used data collection communication protocol is ORW [3]. Although similar to CTP in purpose, more advanced duty-cycling allows it to use less energy. We chose to compare the standard ORW network usage to CTP using our optimization framework, as shown in Figure 2. The x axis in Figures 2a and 2b represents the user-defined maximum threshold for data and time error, respectively, and the y axis represents the "cost" of the strategy, in packet transmissions. As shown, in default operation and even using parameters determined by the linear objective function, CTP sends significantly more packets to maintain the same quality of service with ORW. However, by using parameters determined by the non-linear objective function, it is shown to greatly reduce packet transmissions, allowing our application with CTP to reduce packet transmissions from 50% to 10% (average 30%) over a data error range of 1 to 8% (ORW is better than our application for the data error from 8% to 10%), and from 30% to 64% when changing the maximum time error from 0.5 to 3μs (average 43%). Our preliminary results show that application efficiency can be greatly improved by performing local optimization.

4. CONCLUSIONS

We have presented an architecture for energy management of the wireless sensor nodes in a holistic manner. Our framework is based on a model-driven approach which has 3 steps: 1) Calculating functional relationships among different components and their parameters. 2) Considering the user constraints. 3) Building an objective function based on the functional relationships among components and optimizing based on user constraints. We obtain energy savings in the average of 37% to 76% compared to the components default values. We also show that even when using ORW, which performs better than CTP, we can still reduce overall energy consumption by using the proper parameters and provide energy savings in the average of 30% to 43%.

5. REFERENCES

[1] A. Deshpande and S. Madden. Mauvedb: Supporting model-based user views in database systems. SIGMOD '06, pages 73–84, New York, NY, USA, 2006. ACM.

[2] O. Gnawali, R. Fonseca, K. Jamieson, D. Moss, and P. Levis. Collection tree protocol. SenSys '09, pages 1–14, New York, NY, USA, 2009. ACM.

[3] O. Landsiedel, E. Ghadimi, S. Duquennoy, and M. Johansson. Low power, low delay: Opportunistic routing meets duty cycling. IPSN '12, pages 185–196, New York, NY, USA, 2012. ACM.

[4] M. Maróti, B. Kusy, G. Simon, and A. Lédeczi. The flooding time synchronization protocol. SenSys '04, pages 39–49, New York, NY, USA, 2004. ACM.

Poster Abstract: Cross-Layer Optimization for Low-power Wireless Coexistence

Anwar Hithnawi, Su Li, Hossein Shafagh
Department of Computer Science
ETH Zurich, Switzerland
{hithnawi, lisu, shafagh}@inf.ethz.ch

Simon Duquennoy
SICS Swedish ICT
Kista, Sweden
simonduq@sics.se

James Gross
School of Electrical Engineering
KTH Stockholm, Sweden
james.gross@ee.kth.se

ABSTRACT

We present a system that leverages physical layer features to combat *Cross-Technology Interference* (CTI) in low-power wireless networks. Our system incorporates: *(i)* a lightweight interference detection mechanism for low-power radios that recognizes the type of interference in the received signal, *(ii)* a lightweight error detection mechanism to estimate and characterize error patterns within interfered packets, and *(iii)* a CTI-aware protocol that dynamically adapts transmission and recovery mode to the current interference patterns. We implement a prototype of our system for the low-power IEEE 802.15.4 in software defined radios (SDR). Our early results of the system components demonstrate that we can achieve a high accuracy in error detection and interference type identification. Moreover, we observed a significant performance improvement compared to the standard 802.15.4 systems without interference-awareness.

Categories and Subject Descriptors

C.2.1 [**Computer Communication Networks**]: Network Architecture and Design—*Wireless communication*

Keywords

Low-power Wireless; Coexistence; CTI; Cross-Layer Design

1. INTRODUCTION

Embedded computing devices are increasingly integrated in objects and environments surrounding us, paving the way for the Internet of Things' vision of digitizing the physical world. These devices utilize low-power sensors and RF transceivers for a range of performance-sensitive applications, such as health systems, general monitoring and tracking, home automation, etc. Emerging low-power wireless technologies (e.g., BLE, 802.15.4, and backscatter) are expected to endure interference from other radio technologies. The CTI problem is exacerbated for these networks [1], where energy and complexity constraints prohibit the use of sophisticated interference suppression and cancellation techniques that are finding their ways into unconstrained wireless systems [4, 5]. CTI has not been adequately addressed in low-power wireless networks. This is mainly because diagnosing the type of interference in received signal is non-trivial. Current low-power networks treat CTI as collision, hence, perform exponential backoff and continuously defer their transmission. With the existing power asymmetry in the unlicensed bands, such handling imposes significant coexistence problems, where high-power interferers can completely starve low-power technologies.

SenSys'15, November 01-04, 2015, Seoul, Republic of Korea
ACM 978-1-4503-3631-4/15/11.
http://dx.doi.org/10.1145/2809695.2817905

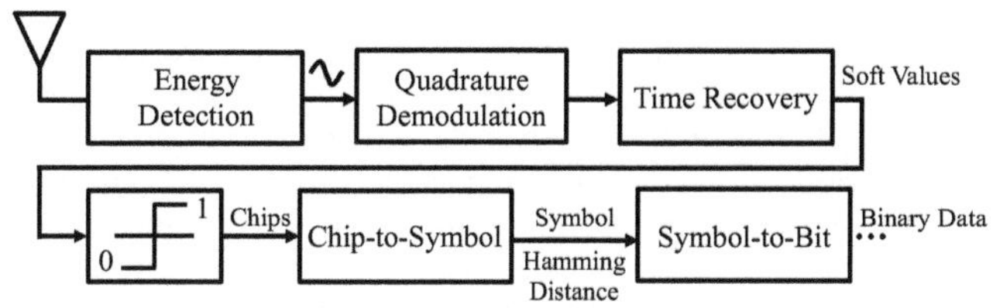

Figure 1: Considered physical layer hints at the 802.15.4 receiver.

Approach In this project, we thoroughly investigate how to best exploit physical layer (PHY) information in low-power radios and consequently make insightful adaptation decisions when subject to CTI. In particular, we focus on discerning *Intra-* and *Cross-Technology Interference*, estimating, localizing, and recovering errors. We propose a reactive and adaptive recovery scheme, which observes error characteristics harnessed from PHY hints to adjust the recovery settings. The recovery mechanism primarily runs an adaptive coding which derives optimal coding redundancy based on the observed error meta-data for different CTI patterns. For packets received with long error bursts which are beyond adaptive coding recovery capabilities, our diversity combining-based packet merging recovery is applied.

2. SCOPE AND DESIGN

With our system we present a cross-layer solution that allows low-power wireless nodes to communicate in interfered environments by getting the most out of received signals. In the following, we briefly highlight relevant aspects and components of our system.

Physical Layer Hints: When an interfered signal is received, besides standard processing, such as demodulation, chip-to-symbol mapping, and delivering decoded symbols to data-link layer, physical layer also accommodates further hints that can be exploited to boost the performance of wireless systems. In our design, we leverage distinctive features of the 802.15.4 PHY such as, uniform signal amplitude and the unique signal shaping, to discern *Intra-* and *Cross-Technology Interference* and to estimate the confidence of received symbols in interfered packets (see Figure 1). We

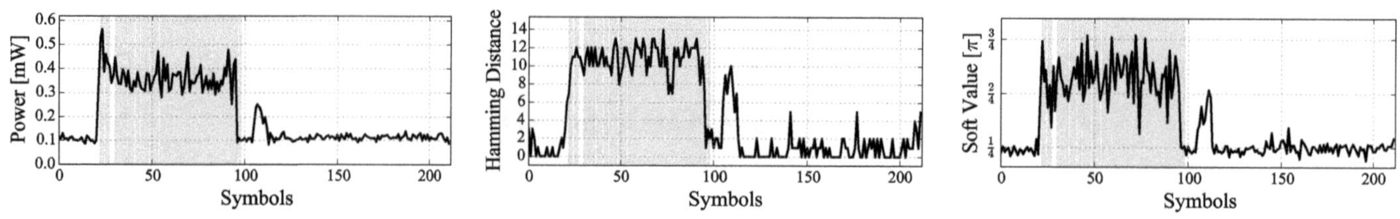

(a) Power. (b) Hamming distance. (c) Soft values.

Figure 2: Considered PHY hints in the presence of interference. The gray area indicates erroneous symbols.

consider the following PHY hints (see Figure 2): *(a) Signal Power:* when two signals interfere, their energies add up. Therefore interfered segments of the received signal experience larger power than the rest of the signal. The interfered segment of the signal exhibits lower SINR, thus experiences a higher error rate. *(b) Hamming Distance:* in the 802.15.4 PHY, symbols are spread to a 32-chip codeword ahead of transmission. The de-spreading is performed by mapping the received codeword to the symbol with the highest correlation. The distance between the input and output codewords of the chip-to-symbol mapper can serve as a direct indicator for the confidence of symbol decoding. *(c) Demodulation Soft Values: Soft Values* (SV) of demodulated bits are float numbers output by the demodulator. The binary demodulated bits are retrieved after passing the soft values through a binary slicer. However, besides the bit value, SV also contains the confidence information about the demodulation [3], and serves as indicator on the similarity between the received signal and ideal signal shape.

Interference Type Identification. We exploit variations in SV for interference type detection. The core idea is to inspect the modulation and signature shape of the interfered signal, which is reflected on the soft values. In case the signal shape is similar to the ideal shape this would translate into smaller variations to the ideal soft value. Note that when subject to *Intra-Technology Interference*, the baseband signal passed to the quadrature demodulator eventually is a 802.15.4 signal (i.e., OQPSK with half sine shaped). Hence, the quadrature demodulator output will be close to the ideal soft value. In contrast with CTI, the baseband signal passed to the quadrature demodulator is of different shape and this consequently reflects on the demodulator output being distanced from the ideal output.

Error Estimation and Localization. The previously mentioned PHY hints expose statistical differences between interfered and non-interfered symbols, which render them suitable candidates to detect erroneous symbols. However, designing practical symbol error detection algorithms based on these PHY hints with acceptable false positive and false negative rates is challenging. We propose an error estimation algorithm that jointly uses the number of unmatched bits of decoding results and received signal power.

CTI-aware Protocol. Our system recovers from a variety of interference patterns. The receiver estimates errors in interfered packets. The derived error meta-data is then used to choose a suitable recovery mechanism; currently alternating between two primary recovery mechanisms: *(a)* adaptive FEC to deal with transient interference with errors limited to few bytes, and *(b)* diversity combining-based packet merging to recover bursty errors. For such bursty error patterns, we expect diversity combining to decrease the ratio of erroneous symbols to a level where FEC can fully recover the packet. Our diversity combining is based on *Maximum Ratio Combining* (MRC) [2].

3. PRELIMINARY RESULTS

Prototype Implementation. We build a prototype of our system using SDR (i.e., USRP N210 and GnuRadio).

Experimental Setup. We expose an 802.15.4 link to the following four interfering technologies: 802.11, 802.15.4, wireless camera, microwave oven, and Bluetooth. Our traces include the complex signal of 35875 corrupted packets by interference.

Results. Now we discuss the early results of our performance evaluation of interference type diagnosing and error estimation mechanisms. We estimate the effectiveness of our interference type identification scheme in detecting the occurrence of *Intra-* and *Cross-Technology Interference.* For low SINR, we can identify the type of interference with high accuracy. In case of *Intra-Technology Interference* and very low SINR, the capture effect takes place. Thus, the interference signal can be accurately demodulated and this is reflected into lower variations of the soft values. Therefore, we can achieve high detection accuracy in these ranges. However, the accuracy decreases when the interference becomes weaker. Our symbol error estimation approach yields a stable performance with a precision and recall of 82% and 92%, respectively. The average achieved accuracy is 94.3% $\pm$ 2.4. Moreover initial experiments indicate a significant performance improvement on a system-level performance compared to 802.15.4 systems without interference-awareness.

4. FUTURE WORK

We propose a cross-layer solution that allows low-power wireless links to develop a better cognition of the CTI patterns in the channel. We harness physical layer information to allow a better estimation, detection, and recovery of interference. We will show the practically, adaptability, and performance of our system through an enhanced prototype implementation and thorough evaluation considering both micro-benchmarking and system performance.

5. REFERENCES

[1] A. Hithnawi, H. Shafagh, S. Duquennoy. TIIM: Technology-Independent Interference Mitigation for Low-power Wireless Networks. In *ACM IPSN*, 2015.

[2] D.G. Brennan. Linear Diversity Combining Techniques. *Institute of Radio Engineers (IRE)*, 46(1):1075–1102, 1959.

[3] G. Woo, P. Kheradpour, D. Shen, D. Katabi. Beyond the Bits: Cooperative Packet Recovery Using Physical Layer Information. In *ACM MobiCom*, 2007.

[4] S. Gollakota, F. Adib, D. Katabi, S. Seshan. Clearing the RF Smog: Making 802.11n Robust to Cross-technology Interference. In *ACM SIGCOMM*, 2011.

[5] S. Hong, S. Katti. DOF: A Local Wireless Information Plane. In *ACM SIGCOMM*, 2011.

Demo: KAIHUI: Towards Quantifying Activeness of Meeting Using Smartphones

Akira Yoneoka
Aoyama Gakuin Univ., Japan
yone@rcl-aoyama.jp

Yanan Wang
The Univ. of Electro-Communications, Japan
wang@ni.is.uec.ac.jp

Niwat Thepvilojanapong
Mie University, Japan
wat@net.info.mie-u.ac.jp

Itaru Usami
Aoyama Gakuin Univ., Japan
itaru@rcl-aoyama.jp

Yoshito Tobe
Aoyama Gakuin Univ., Japan
yoshito-tobe@rcl-aoyama.jp

ABSTRACT

Meetings are considered to be indispensable for decision making of groups, and thus efficiency is required for meetings. However, it is difficult to discuss the efficiency of meeting in a quantitative way. Based on this background, we define metrics to quantify the meeting activity and we implement a system to evaluate the metrics called KAIHUI. A smartphone is used as a KAIHUI client to record meeting audio. Then a KAIHUI server analyzes and calculates activeness according to the proposed metrics. In this demonstration, we show the basic operations of KAIHUI using a smartphone.

Categories and Subject Descriptors

H.4 [**Information Systems Applications**]: Miscellaneous; D.2.8 [**Software Engineering**]: Metrics—*complexity measures, performance measures*

General Terms

Theory

Keywords

Meeting activeness, activeness evaluation, mediation, facilitation, domination, smartphone application

1. INTRODUCTION

Recent advance of Internet technology and its proliferation lead to various means of communication. However, face-to-face meeting is necessary and suitable for some situations such as brainstorming, problem solving and idea exchanging meetings. In fact, many organizations still depend on regular meetings to accomplish their goals.

SenSys '15 Jung-gu, Seoul, South Korea
ACM 978-1-4503-3631-4/15/11.
DOI: http://dx.doi.org/10.1145/2809695.2817846 .

Meeting-aided system and protocol have been developed in the past [1]. Nevertheless, such systems did not provide quality or activeness of meeting. Thus we do not have a clue to improve the quality of meeting. The outcome of a meeting highly depends on activities and behavior of attendees. There are several kinds of meeting's attendees, i.e., someone is talkative and likely to speak most of the meeting period while someone favors to be a good listener. Both kinds of attendees are not favored for brainstorming meetings which ask for contribution from all attendees. Therefore, quantitative analysis of meeting's attendees are necessary to improve meeting performance.

This work aims to quantify activeness of meeting from voice data recorded by a smartphone. Hence we define activeness metrics from different points of attendees' behavior and their interactions. In particular, we consider three issues: (i) how long an attendee speaks, (ii) how often an attendee speaks, and (iii) how a speaker gives a turn to other attendees. To study the proposed metrics, we design and implement a system called KAIHUI. KAIHUI employs a client-server model, where a client smartphone is used to record voice data and a server is responsible for speech processing and activeness analysis. If the activeness is expressed as quantitative values, we can give each attendee advice to improve the quality and activeness of meetings based on the metrics.

In this demo abstract, we describe the metrics for measuring meeting activeness and a brief of our demonstration.

2. ACTIVENESS METRICS

We consider *active meeting* is a meeting that all or most of attendees actively discuss the meeting's topics and meeting leader's opinions are responded by attendees. Thus we define three metrics for evaluating activeness of meeting.

2.1 Metric I: Meeting Equality

Generally, longer period of speaking in comparison with silent and total meeting periods indicates better participation of an attendee. However, if an attendee actively discusses the meeting's topic during the meeting while most of other attendees stay silent, it may be difficult to judge the meeting as an active one. Therefore, we define *meeting equality* to evaluate whether all attendees join and discuss the meeting's topic in a fair manner.

Let t_i $(i = 1, 2, \ldots, K)$ be total speaking period of attendee i, where K is the total number of attendees. A ratio of speaking period is defined as total speaking period of an attendee divided by speaking period of all attendees (Eq. 1).

$$P_i^E = \frac{t_i}{\sum_i^K t_i}. \tag{1}$$

The fairness of participation is defined according to the entropy of information theory. If the speaking periods of all attendees are equal, the fairness of participation is the maximum value. On the other hand, the fairness of participation is the minimum value (0) if the discussion is monopolized by an attendee for the whole meeting. However, the maximum value depends on the number of attendees thus normalization of the metric is necessary. Therefore, the equality of discussion (Equality) is defined in Eq. 2.

$$\text{Equality} = \frac{H(E)}{\arg\max_K H(E)} \times 100, \tag{2}$$

$$\text{where } H(E) = -\sum_i^K P_i^E \log_2 P_i^E. \tag{3}$$

2.2 Metric II: Meeting Domination

Dominant behavior is a key determinant in the formation of a group's social structure, and consequently group dynamics. Dominance is also a necessary characteristic of a successful mediator who balances participation and derives consensus for better performance. Hence we include domination as one of activeness metrics.

An attendee is considered to be a dominator if the frequency of her/his speaking is above the average speaking frequency of all attendees. The *meeting domination* is defined as a normalized number of dominators in comparison with the total number of attendees.

Let q_i $(i = 1, 2, \ldots, K)$ be speaking frequency, i.e., the number of turns, of an attendee i. A ratio of speaking frequency is the frequency of an attendee divided by the total frequency of all attendees as expressed in Eq. 4.

$$P_i^C = \frac{q_i}{\sum_i^K q_i}. \tag{4}$$

We define an average frequency as a domination threshold d, where $d = \frac{1}{K}$. An attendee is considered to be a dominator if the ratio of speaking frequency is equal to or above the domination threshold. Consequently, the domination of a meeting is defined in Eq. 5.

$$\text{Domination} = \frac{\sum_i^K N(i)}{K} \times 100, \tag{5}$$

$$\text{where } N(i) = \begin{cases} 1 & \text{if } P_i^C \geq d \\ 0 & \text{otherwise.} \end{cases} \tag{6}$$

2.3 Metric III: Meeting Mediation

Meeting's dominator or leader is a key person of an active meeting. A role of the dominator is to coordinate the meeting by giving all attendees turns to speak such that the meeting provides everybody an equal right to speak and finishes within a predetermined schedule. Thus we define a metric called *meeting mediation* to evaluate the above-mentioned role of dominator which affects the activeness of meeting. We assume state transitions of speakers is a Markov chain and dominators are determined according to the denomination threshold d. The probability of state transition from a dominator j to a speaker i is indicated by $P_{i|j}^M$. As illustrated on the left side of Fig. 1, the probabilities of transition from dominator A to speakers B and C are equal. It means dominator A provides an equal right to both speakers. On the right side of the figure, the probabilities of transition from dominator A to speakers B and C are 0.1 and 0.9, respectively. Dominator A, who lacks good facilitation in this scenario, has bias toward attendee C. As a result, we use entropy of the state transition (Eq. 7) to calculate the meeting mediation of a dominator j (Eq. 8) as follows.

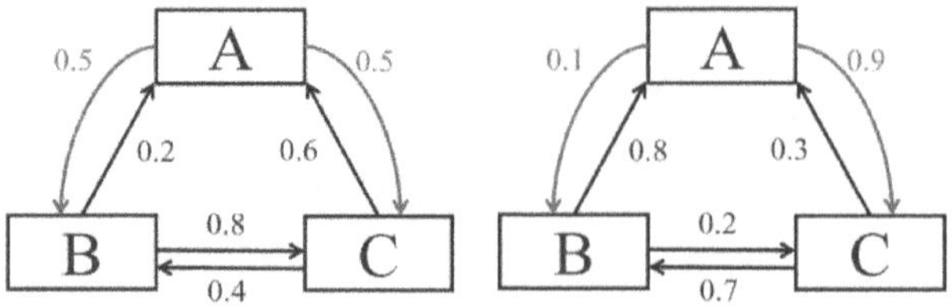

Figure 1: State transitions of speakers A, B and C.

$$H_j(M) = -\sum_{i=1, i \neq j}^{K-1} P_{i|j}^M \log_2 P_{i|j}^M. \tag{7}$$

$$\text{Mediation}_j = \frac{H_j(M)}{\arg\max_{K-1} H(M)} \times 100. \tag{8}$$

If multiple dominators exist in a meeting, the meeting mediation is an average mediation of all dominators as expressed in Eq. 9.

$$\text{Mediation} = \frac{\sum_{\forall j \in \{1,2,\ldots,K\}: P_j^C \geq d} \text{Mediation}_j}{\sum_{\forall j \in \{1,2,\ldots,K\}: P_j^C \geq d} N(j)}. \tag{9}$$

3. DEMONSTRATION

We implemented KAIHUI system on Samsung Galaxy S4 smartphones and a laptop computer. KAIHUI client on the smartphone comes with GUI to control the application. We conducted experiments can evaluated KAIHUI system and activeness metrics through seven meetings. In the demonstration, we will prepare a video to show the concept of KAIHUI and snapshots from the experiments. In addition, Interesting people can try the system at the conference venue by having a short conversation and they can see the results of activeness metrics.

4. REFERENCES

[1] C. Breslin, K. Chin, M. J. F. Gales, and K. Knill. Integrated online speaker clustering and adaptation. In *12th Annual Conference of the International Speech Communication Association (Interspeech 2011)*, pages 1085–1088, Aug. 2011.

Demo: A Hardware Platform for Separating Energy Concerns in Tiny, Intermittently-Powered Sensors

Josiah Hester, Lanny Sitanayah, Jacob Sorber
School of Computing
Clemson University
{jhester, lsitana, jsorber}@clemson.edu

ABSTRACT

Energy harvesting is an indispensable mechanism of sensor devices that operate in perpetuity. While harvesting free energy from the environment has enabled many applications, it has also spawned new problems, and new paradigms. Notably, making decisions on when to use high power sensors and external components when energy is scarce, and future supply is unpredictable. Because sensor nodes generally share a single, centralized energy store, seemingly atomic, or unrelated sensing tasks can hamper each other by drawing the supply voltage too low, and draining the energy reservoir.

This demonstration presents the United Federation of Peripherals (UFoP), a novel method of separating energy concerns in hardware by allocating dedicated energy storage (in the form of small capacitors) to specific sensor components, and charging them in a prioritized fashion with an analog front end. UFoP gives application designers a more deterministic view of energy and task scheduling, allowing them to make better informed decisions when developing sensor applications. Designers do not have to rely on crude estimates or simulations but can instead depend on in-situ analog measurements to opportunistically drive their applications.

Categories and Subject Descriptors

C.3 [**Special-Purpose and Application-Based Systems**]: Microprocessor/microcomputer applications

General Terms

Reliability, Measurement, Performance

Keywords

Energy Harvesting; Federated Energy; Task Coupling; Capacitor; Embedded System

1. FEDERATING ENERGY

Traditional sensing systems rely on a single energy source such as a battery, or super-capacitor, that powers all system components (*e.g.,* processors, sensors, radios and other peripherals) . This paradigm works well when energy reserve are large, and power failures are rare. However, for intermittently powered sensing devices [1, 2, 4–6] that live off harvested energy and die frequently, this approach can be prohibitive.

We propose a new federated approach to storing harvested energy that separates energy concerns, making it difficult for different system components to starve each other. Our approach, called UFoP (United Federation of Peripherals), uses individual per-peripheral energy stores in the form of small capacitors and low-power control circuitry to isolate and prioritize individual peripherals. Federating energy storage allows power-hungry operations to proceed without sacrificing the device's immediate ability to use other peripherals, gather new data, process incoming data, and respond to incoming stimuli. This approach also simplifies the task of programming energy-aware logic—effectively replacing complex modeling of analog circuit behaviors with simple binary decisions based on whether or not a peripheral is available.

Our initial implementation of the UFoP approach uses ultra-low-power comparators to control and prioritize the charging of individual energy stores, where the microcontroller gets the first priority. The main capacitor charges until it reaches 2.7 V, then the microcontroller turns on. When the input voltage reaches 3.1 V, the peripheral capacitors charge. Application designers can monitor these voltages to know when a peripheral becomes available.

2. SYSTEM ARCHITECTURE

Figure 1 shows a UFoP system that is integrated with two commonly used peripherals in sensing applications (*i.e.,* a sensor and a radio). The system consists of four main components: an energy harvester, charging controller, peripheral controller, and peripherals. The energy harvesting device harvests ambient energy and stores it in the first-stage capacitor. The charge controller is responsible for turning on and off the microcontroller and charging an array of peripheral capacitors. The peripheral controller turns on and off peripherals (sensor and radio), which are only available when their capacitors are charged.

Energy Harvesting: The UFoP system is powered by ambient sources. The energy harvester converts free energy from the environment (*e.g.,* solar, thermal, radio frequency (RF), and kinetic energy) into electrical energy (DC), which the harvester supplies to the rest of the system. From the harvester, the current first flows to charge first-stage capacitor that powers the microcontroller.

Charging Control: UFoP uses low-power control circuitry as charge controller to control and prioritize the charging of an array of capacitors as well as turning on and off the microcontroller. UFoP is designed with the microcontroller as a first power priority. A sensor without a microcontroller could not process data, and

SenSys'15, November 1–4, 2015, Seoul, South Korea..
ACM 978-1-4503-3631-4/15/11.
DOI: http://dx.doi.org/10.1145/2809695.2817847.

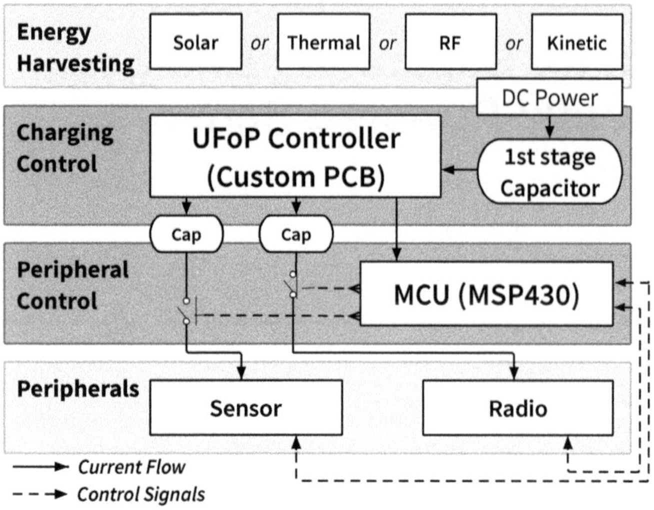

Figure 1: Overview of UFoP when integrated with a set of commonly used peripherals; a sensor, and a radio. A UFoP system is made up of four components: an energy harvester, charging controller, peripheral controller, and peripherals. The charge controller manages the charging of an array of capacitors (drawing from the first-stage capacitor) as well as turning on and off the MCU. The peripheral controller (an MSP430FR5739) gates power to the peripherals, allowing peripherals to be completely off when not in use. Peripherals and the MCU communicate independently of the charging controller.

a radio without a microcontroller would have no signal to transmit. From an implementation perspective, this is ideal since the microcontroller can then be used to control the power flow to the peripherals based on application requirements.

Peripheral Control: The peripheral controller in the UFoP system can be any ultra-low-power microcontroller. The FRAM series of MSP430 are work especially well in this function. When the first-stage capacitor capacitor charges up to 2.7 V, the microcontroller turns on. The microcontroller gates power to the peripherals, allowing peripherals to be completely off when not in use. This control communication is independent from the charging control scheme. The switches in the peripheral controller are designed to open (disconnect) when the microcontroller loses its power and turns off, *i.e.,* when the main capacitor's voltage falls below 1.8 V. This design satisfies the MSP430FR5739 supply voltage requirements, *i.e.,* 1.8 V to 3.6 V.

Peripherals: Two most commonly used peripherals in sensing applications are sensor and radio. The type of the peripherals and the tasks they perform determine the size of the capacitors used. When an application uses a lightweight sensor and a radio, the size of the capacitor for the sensor should be a lot smaller than that for the radio. If the application requires intensive data transmission, the radio's capacitor size must be large enough to support the tasks. In the UFoP system, the peripherals are only available when their dedicated capacitors are charged.

3. DEMONSTRATION DESCRIPTION

This is a demo of an associated paper presented at SenSys'15 [3] which contains a more detailed description of the system. We show the difference between a centralized energy system and a system that uses UFoP. Each system is equipped with a small solar panel, a LED flashlight is used to generate light. The availability of the MCU and each peripheral (a sensor and radio) are shown with LEDs as well as graphically on a display. This highlights the differences in each approach, and the benefits of using UFoP.

4. CONCLUSION

This demonstration presents UFoP, a federated approach to energy storage for intermittently-powered sensors. UFoP allows application developers to separate energy concerns in a system; with a dedicated energy store for each component. Sensors, radios, and other peripherals become independent of each other, allowing for simpler decision making, and guaranteed outcomes. UFoP increases availability, energy harvesting efficiency, and resiliency to programmer error.

5. ACKNOWLEDGEMENTS

The authors would like to thank the members of the PERSIST lab, for helpful discussions around UFoP deployments and experimentation.

This research is based upon work supported by the National Science Foundation under grant ACI-1212680. Any opinions, findings, and conclusions or recommendations expressed in this material are those of the authors and do not necessarily reflect the views of the National Science Foundation.

6. REFERENCES

[1] M. Gorlatova, R. Margolies, J. Sarik, G. Stanje, J. Zhu, B. Vigraham, M. Szczodrak, L. Carloni, P. Kinget, I. Kymissis, and G. Zussman. Prototyping Energy Harvesting Active Networked Tags (EnHANTs). In *Proc. 32nd IEEE Int'l Conf. Computer Communications (INFOCOM'13)*, pages 585–589, Turin, Italy, Apr. 2013. IEEE.

[2] J. Gummeson, S. S. Clark, K. Fu, and D. Ganesan. On the Limits of Effective Hybrid Micro-Energy Harvesting on Mobile CRFID Sensors. In *Proc. 8th Int'l Conf. Mobile Systems, Applications, and Services (MobiSys'10)*, pages 195–208, San Francisco, CA, USA, Jun. 2010. ACM.

[3] J. Hester, L. Sitanayah, and J. Sorber. Tragedy of the Coulombs: Federating Energy Storage for Tiny, Intermittently-Powered Sensors. In *Proc. 13th ACM Conf. Embedded Network Sensor Systems (SenSys'15)*, Seoul, Korea, Nov. 2015. ACM.

[4] A. P. Sample, D. J. Yeager, P. S. Powledge, A. V. Mamishev, and J. R. Smith. Design of an RFID-Based Battery-Free Programmable Sensing Platform. *IEEE Trans. Instrumentation and Measurement*, 57(11):2608–2615, Nov. 2008.

[5] S. Thomas, J. Teizer, and M. Reynolds. Electromagnetic Energy Harvesting for Sensing, Communication, and Actuation. In *Proc. 27th Int'l Symp. Automation and Robotics in Construction (ISARC'10)*, Bratislava, Slovakia, Jun. 2010. IAARC.

[6] Y. Yang, L. Wang, D. K. Noh, H. K. Le, and T. F. Abdelzaher. SolarStore: Enhancing Data Reliability in Solar-Powered Storage-Centric Sensor Networks. In *Proc. 7th Int'l Conf. Mobile Systems, Applications, and Services (MobiSys'09)*, pages 333–346, Krakow, Poland, Jun. 2009. ACM.

Demo Abstract: iMoon: Using Smartphones for Image-based Indoor Navigation

Jiang Dong Yu Xiao Marius Noreikis Zhonghong Ou Antti Ylä-Jääski
{jiang.dong, yu.xiao, marius.noreikis, zhonghong.ou, antti.yla-jaaski}@aalto.fi
Aalto University
Espoo, Finland

ABSTRACT

The indoor location market is growing rapidly. However, fine-grained and up-to-date indoor maps are rarely available, and the existing indoor localization and navigation services mostly require extra infrastructures to provide accurate locations. In this demonstration we show *iMoon*, an indoor navigation system that provides indoor mapping, localization and navigation services using photos and sensor data collected from widely available mobile devices. The demonstration leverages a cohesive suite of computer vision, mobile sensing, and wireless networking techniques.

1. INTRODUCTION

In this demonstration we present *iMoon*, a system that implements indoor mapping, localization and navigation services, using photos and sensor data collected from widely available mobile devices like smartphones. *iMoon* works in two phrases.

Firstly, *iMoon* builds 3D models of indoor environment from crowdsourced 2D photos using Structure-from-Motion (SfM) techniques [2, 3], and then creates navigation meshes for path planning based on the obstacle information extracted from the models. As the collected photos may not cover every corner of the space, the pedestrian path information may be partly missing from the crowdsourced 3D models. To solve this issue, *iMoon* detects user trajectories based on the collected sensor data including accelerometer and gyroscope readings, and complements the 3D models with the pedestrian paths recognized from the crowdsourced user trajectories.

Secondly, with the photo-based 3D models, *iMoon* allows users to identify their locations and facing directions with photos taken from where they are. To reduce the response delay caused by complex image processing, *iMoon* combines image-based localization with Wi-Fi fingerprinting, taking advantage of the high accuracy of image-based localization as well as the high hit-rate and low response time of Wi-Fi fingerprinting. In the navigation mode, given source and destination, *iMoon* computes navigation routes and provides guidance along a selected navigation route with textual and visual instructions. Examples can be found from Figure 1[1].

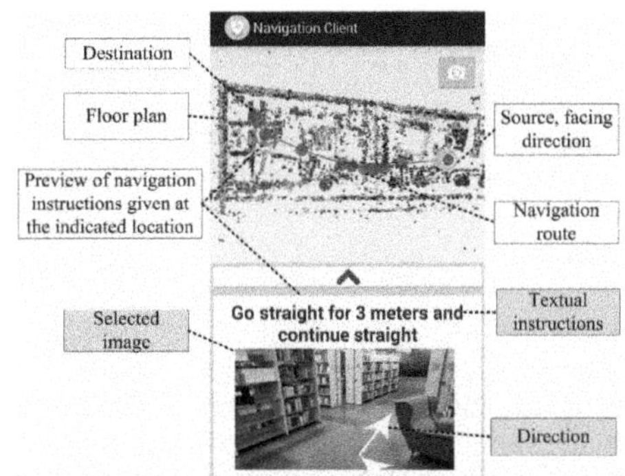

Figure 1: A screenshot of the *iMoon* Android app. The upper part includes a mini map with the color information of each 3D point reserved. The navigation route (blue line) drawn on the map includes 3 waypoints between the source and the destination. The lower part gives a preview of the navigation instructions when the user arrives at the waypoint marked by a red dotted circle. The current position and facing direction of the user (in green) are updated on the move. In addition to the textual instruction, the selected image shows the expected view, and the arrow indicates the path to take. [1]

According to the results of a small-scale field study in our department building, *iMoon* works properly, and our solution of indoor localization achieves competitive performance compared with traditional approaches: a user can be localized within 3.85 seconds on average; the location error is less than 2 meters and the facing direction error is less than 6 degrees in most cases.

2. SYSTEM OVERVIEW

As illustrated in Figure 2, *iMoon* is mainly composed of two parts: building sensor-enriched 3D models and providing locations and navigation paths based on the models.

There are 3 steps for building sensor-enriched 3D models. Firstly, 3D models are generated from crowdsourced photos. These 3D models describe the structures and objects in the scene. Navigation mesh is extracted from these 3D models. Secondly, sensor data including accelerometer

[1] A demo video of *iMoon* mobile app is available on YouTube: `https://youtu.be/sNvf7N_s59c`

SenSys'15, November 1–4, 2015, Seoul, South Korea.
ACM 978-1-4503-3631-4/15/11.
DOI: http://dx.doi.org/10.1145/2809695.2817848 .

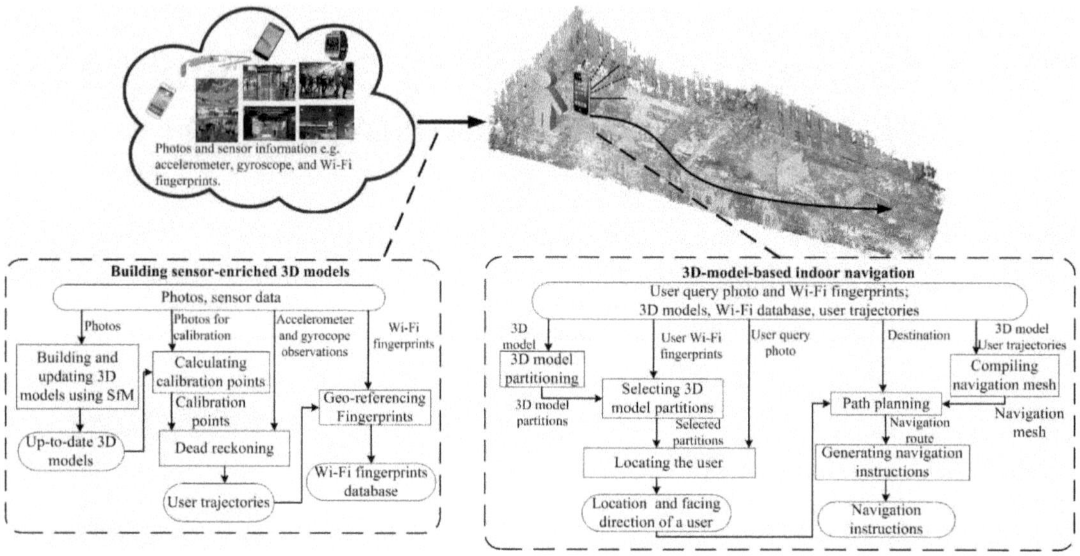

Figure 2: Overview of *iMoon*, a mobile crowdsensing-based indoor navigation system for smartphones. [1]

and gyroscope observations are used as a basis for detecting user trajectories, and the photos taken on the way are used for calibrating the trajectories. Pedestrian paths recognized from user trajectories are later integrated into the navigation mesh. Thirdly, surrounding Wi-Fi fingerprints collected along user trajectories are geo-referenced in the models.

iMoon identifies locations and facing directions using real-time photos and Wi-Fi fingerprints. With the help of SfM, a straightforward method of implementing image-based localization is by trying to register the query image to the 3D model based on feature matching. If enough matches can be found, the features provided by the query image will be added to the model, and the camera pose of the query photo will be returned, which can be considered as the location and facing direction of the user. To speed up localization, *iMoon* partitions 3D models based on feature density, and uses Wi-Fi fingerprining to select partitions efficiently. After that, a small scale image-based localization will be implemented based on the chosen partitions to acquire the accurate position and facing direction of the user.

Given source and destination, a navigation route can be calculated based on a navigation mesh. Based on the route, *iMoon* provides user-friendly navigation instructions which contains 3 components: a photo that shows the place where the given instruction is valid, a piece of text that tells the user where to go, and an arrow sign that indicates which path to take next.

3. DEMONSTRATION

In this demonstration we will show the functions of indoor localization and navigation of the *iMoon* app. As it is hard to create a complete navigation mesh of the conference site within very limited time, for demonstration purpose, we would emulate the navigation scenarios by replaying the traces of sensor data and photos collected by test users from our department building. The 3D models used for calculation would also be pre-built.

An example demonstration case is described in Figure 3a∼3d. First, the user takes a photo by tapping the camera button on the upper right of the screen. After a short while, the

(a) (b) (c) (d)

Figure 3: Screenshots that describe the steps of getting the indoor navigation route and instructions to mobile clients.

user receives an indoor map with the user's current location and moving direction marked on it. The user then clicks the destination button to choose a photo taken from the expected destination. After sending the photo to the server, a navigation route and the first navigation instruction are displayed on the screen.

4. ACKNOWLEDGMENTS

This work was supported by the Academy of Finland, grant number 278207 and 268096.

5. REFERENCES

[1] J. Dong, Y. Xiao, M. Noreikis, Z. Ou, and A. Ylä-Jääski. imoon: Using smartphones for image-based indoor navigation. In *Proceedings of SenSys '15*, Seoul, Korea.

[2] J.-M. Frahm, P. Fite-Georgel, D. Gallup, T. Johnson, R. Raguram, C. Wu, Y.-H. Jen, E. Dunn, B. Clipp, S. Lazebnik, and M. Pollefeys. Building rome on a cloudless day. In *Proc. of ECCV'10*, pages 368–381, Berlin, Heidelberg.

[3] N. Snavely, I. Simon, M. Goesele, R. Szeliski, and S. Seitz. Scene reconstruction and visualization from community photo collections. *Proc. of the IEEE*, 98(8):1370–1390, 2010.

Demo Abstract: AsthmaGuide: An Ecosystem for Asthma Monitoring and Advice

Ho-Kyeong Ra[1], Asif Salekin[2], Hee Jung Yoon[1], Jeremy Kim[2], Shahriar Nirjon[4], David J. Stone[3], Sujeong Kim[5], Jong-Myung Lee[5], Sang Hyuk Son[1], and John A. Stankovic[2]

[1]Daegu Gyeongbuk Institute of Science and Technology, [2]University of Virginia, [3]University of Virginia School of Medicine, [4]University of North Carolina at Chapel Hill, [5]Kyungpook National University School of Medicine

ABSTRACT

AsthmaGuide is a smartphone and cloud based asthma system in which a smart phone is used as a hub for collecting a comprehensive collection of information. The data, including data over time, is then displayed in a cloud web application for both patients and healthcare providers to view. AsthmaGuide also provides an advice and alarm infrastructure based on the collected data and parameters set by healthcare providers. With these components, AsthmaGuide provides a comprehensive ecosystem that allows patients to be involved in their own health and also allows doctors to provide more effective day to day care. Using real asthma patient wheezing sounds we develop a new combination of classifiers that is 96% accurate at automatically detecting wheezing. This abstract provides an overview of the design and implementation of AsthmaGuide and provides empirical evidence that AsthmaGuide is 3% – 11% more accurate in detecting wheezing sounds than standard techniques.

Categories and Subject Descriptors

H.3.4 [**Systems and Software**]: User Profiles and Alert

General Terms

Algorithm, Design, Experimentation

Keywords

Asthma Ecosystem, Environment, Advice

1. INTRODUCTION

With the integration of wireless sensor networks in hospitals and homes, healthcare providers are able to provide more accurate and personalized patient care. One group of patients that should greatly benefit from intensified daily monitoring is asthma patients. In the latest surveys by the Centers for Disease Control and Prevention, about 25 million people in the United States have asthma [2]. As of 2011, of these 25 million, 53% of these people suffered from acute asthma attacks [2]. Because there is currently no cure for asthma, the NIH states that the priority for doctors is to assess and monitor these patients as there are usually clear symptoms that indicate an oncoming asthma attack [6]. While it is obviously essential to monitor patients' lung health, per se, environmental factors can also trigger and exacerbate asthma symptoms. These environmental factors include extreme temperatures, extreme humidity or dryness, pollen, smoke, and mold [3]. The effect of these environmental factors differs from patient to patient.

Currently, there is no effective way for doctors to monitor asthma patients at home on a day to day basis. Most patients visit their doctors monthly, but once they go home there is a lack of communication between the two parties. Because the course of asthma is dependent on dynamic factors, this loss of daily information is potentially costly. There have been attempts to detect wheezing via machine learning or to make peak-flow measurements convenient [1, 7, 4, 5]. But none of these systems analyzes these factors in an integrated fashion, and they do not consider environmental factors in conjunction with lung health. Also, there are a number of asthma diary systems based on smartphones, but users typically must input all the information with little, if any, data automatically input from sensors.

In this abstract, we provide an overview of AsthmaGuide which is an asthma ecosystem that monitors asthma patients comprehensively. A smart phone is used as a hub for collecting physiological, environmental, human input, and video information. Physiological information includes lung sounds, peak flow values, and blood oxygen level. This information is then pushed to the cloud where doctors and patients can interact with this information. One feature of the cloud web application is the automatic analysis of lung sounds: they are further analyzed and classified as either normal or wheezing. Subsequently, this lung health "diary", as well as the captured environmental information, is available in essentially real time to the health care providers and patients in the form of a web application. Beyond the display of information, AsthmaGuide uses the data to provide specific patient advice. Although there are many potential asthma triggers, they are not applicable to all patients. Thus AsthmaGuide can use the data to act as a personalized coach for the patient. This system in no way replaces the doctor and we are actively working with doctors to better understand the kinds of advice that are appropriate. But

SenSys '15, November 01-04, 2015, Seoul, Republic of Korea
ACM 978-1-4503-3631-4/15/11.
http://dx.doi.org/10.1145/2809695.2817849

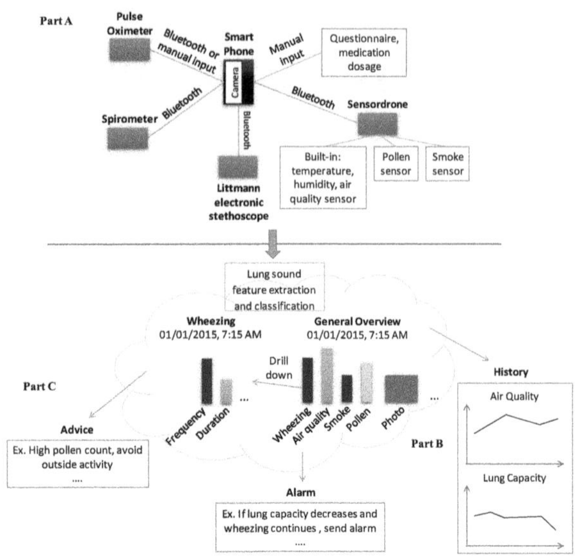

Figure 1: AsthmaGuide overview.

this automated advice can help improve patient outcomes while reducing the workload of the healthcare providers.

The contributions of this system are the following:

- AsthmaGuide which is the first comprehensive monitoring and advice system for asthma patients.
- The development of the wheezing lung sound classifier. Our classifier also uses a combination of support vector machine (SVM) and random forest classifiers, which leads to a more robust system than previous models.

2. OVERVIEW OF ASTHMAGUIDE

AsthmaGuide consists of four main components: an extensive sensor suite, the smart phone hub, the cloud web application, and the advice infrastructure. The sensor suite is where data collection occurs (Figure 1 - Part A). This data is then sent to a smart phone via a physical connection or wirelessly via Bluetooth. There are multiple sensors which can connect and transmit data to a smart phone via Bluetooth or physical connection. Patients can also take photos and/or videos of themselves with the in-phone camera, which can help healthcare providers understand their health via this built-in telemedicine modality. Some data cannot be obtained via sensors, so patients will be able to enter this information manually into the phone. Lastly, we provide a way to record patient lung sounds using a Littmann 3200 electronic stethoscope.

Once all of this data is collected, it is then pushed to the cloud where the data is stored and further analyzed (Figure 1 - Part B). The last part of our system is the advice (Figure 1 - Part C), which is based on the collected data and parameters set by healthcare providers. For example, if a patient's lung capacity decreases as dust increases, AsthmaGuide can recommend that the patient vacuum more often.

3. EVALUATION

In order to develop an accurate classifier, we focused on three types of models: C4.5 Decision Trees, Random Forest models with C4.5 trees, and SVM. The first three rows of Figure 2 show the results when using all of the features for the three types of models. The results show that of the

Classifier	Sensitivity (Wheezing Accuracy)	Specificity (Normal Accuracy)	Overall Accuracy
SVM	58/63 (92%)	15/21 (71%)	73/84 (87%)
Decision Tree (C4.5)	58/63 (90%)	18/21 (62%)	71/84 (85%)
Random Forest Classifier	60/63 (95%)	18/21 (86%)	78/84 (93%)
Combination	62/63 (94%)	19/21 (95%)	81/84 (96%)

Figure 2: Using a combination of classifiers is 3% – 11% more accurate than standard techniques.

three models, the random forest classifier performed the best with an accuracy of 93%. In order to build a more accurate classifier, next we combined the results of all three classifiers in order to take advantage of their strengths. It achieves the best result for sensitivity and specificity with a best overall accuracy of 96%.

4. DEMO SCRIPT

The objective is to demonstrate how AsthmaGuide operates and how it can allow patients to become involved in their own health and healthcare professionals to provide up-to-date care. In this demo, the user will be using a smart tablet, the AsthmaGuide sensor suite, and a Littmann electronic stethoscope. The user opens the AsthmaGuide application which prompts the user to collect lung sounds and measure lung capacity; takes a 'selfie' type picture of the user; and allows entry of his administered medication dosage from the previous day. At the same time, the sensor suite is collecting environmental data and sending it to the smart tablet. At the end of the process, the user will click on a button which sends the lung and environmental data to the cloud. Once in the cloud, the lung sounds are classified as normal or wheezing. AsthmaGuide will display the user's lung and environmental information visually on a screen.

5. ACKNOWLEDGMENTS

This work was supported, in part, by NSF grant CNS-1319302, the DGIST Research and Development Program of the Ministry of Science, ICT and Future Planning of Korea (CPS Global Center), and Institute for Information & Communications Technology Promotion (IITP) grant funded by the Korean government (MSIP) (No. B0101-15-0557, Resilient Cyber-Physical Systems Research).

References

[1] A. Alic, I. Lackovic, V. Bilas, D. Sersic, and R. Magjarevic. *A Novel Approach to Wheeze Detection*, volume 14 of *IFMBE Proceedings*. Springer Berlin Heidelberg, 2007.

[2] Centers for Disease Control and Prevention. Asthma in the us: growing every year. `http://www.cdc.gov`, 2011.

[3] Centers for Disease Control and Prevention. Common asthma triggers. `http://www.cdc.gov`, 2012.

[4] J. A. Fiz, R. Jané, A. Homs, J. Izquierdo, M. A. Garcia, and J. Morera. Detection of wheezing during maximal forced exhalation in patients with obstructed airways. *Chest Journal*, 122(1):186–191, 2002.

[5] A. Homs-Corbera, R. Jané, J. A. Fiz, and J. Morera. Algorithm for time-frequency detection and analysis of wheezes. In *IEEE Engineering in Medicine and Biology Society'*, 2000.

[6] National Heart, Lung, and Blood Institute. Asthma control keep it going. `http://www.nhlbi.nih.gov`, 2013.

[7] M. Waris, P. Helistö, S. Haltsonen, A. Saarinen, and A. Sovijärvi. A new method for automatic wheeze detection. *Chest Journal*, 122(1):33–40, 1998.

Demo Abstract: A Connection Oriented Mesh Network for Mobile Devices using Bluetooth Low Energy

Yaswanth Kumar Reddy, Praneeth Juturu, Hari Prabhat Gupta, Pramod Reddy Serikar
Shruthi Sirur, Sulekha Barak, and Bonggon Kim†
Samsung R&D Institute India-Bangalore, India and †Samsung Electronics, Suwon, South Korea
{yk.reddy,praneeth.j,harip.gupta,pramod.reddy,shruti.sirur,s.barak,bg43.kim}@samsung.com

ABSTRACT

In this demo, we present a mesh network for mobile (non static) devices using Bluetooth Low Energy (BLE). We propose a weight balancing technique to optimize the communication to the entire mesh network. The proposed mesh network has been evaluated by well-designed practical experiments to transmit the data. The preliminary results show that the BLE mesh network consumes less power and can transfer data with low latency.

Keywords

Bluetooth, Mesh, Mobile Devices, Routing.

1. INTRODUCTION

A wireless mesh network is a network topology in which each mobile device (e.g., smartphone, tablet, wearable, and laptop) can transfer the data to devices in the network. All devices in the network cooperate for sharing the data in the network. In this work, we propose a BLE Mesh Network (BMN) for mobile (non-static) devices, which is suitable for forming instant groups among mobile devices [1, 2]. The major contributions of our work are as follows:

- We propose a BMN architecture for routing the data among mobile devices. The BMN architecture does not require any modification in BLE stack.
- We develop an algorithm using Direct Acyclic Graph (DAG) for creation and maintenance of the BMN. To reduce the energy consumption and delay and increase the throughput, it uses the weight balancing technique. It uses a contingency plan to find the supplementary root device if the main root device leaves (due to mobility of the devices) the BMN.
- We developed a prototype using BLE v4.1 compatible mobile devices to check the connectivity of the proposed BMN.

2. BMN ARCHITECTURE

The BMN architecture consists application layer, mesh service layer, and BLE framework layer as shown in Figure 1. We develop the mesh service layer which includes mesh library and BLE service library.

- The BLE framework layer provides access to send and receive advertisements and establish a connected channel to exchange data. The BLE devices advertise their presence and scan to detect other BLE devices in their communication range. A connected channel is established when the device joins the BMN through any other BMN device. The connected channel is used for maintenance of BMN by exchanging the control packets.
- The mesh service layer receives raw packets from BLE framework layer via BLE service library, which are parsed using the Mesh Packet Processor. The packets are converted into different control messages or data messages and are forwarded to Mesh Node. The Mesh Node processes these messages and acts accordingly.
- When the Mesh Node receives a data message with itself as the destination, it forwards the data to the application layer. The application layer can use the received data to perform the respective operation. We used a chat application in the proposed prototype of the BMN.

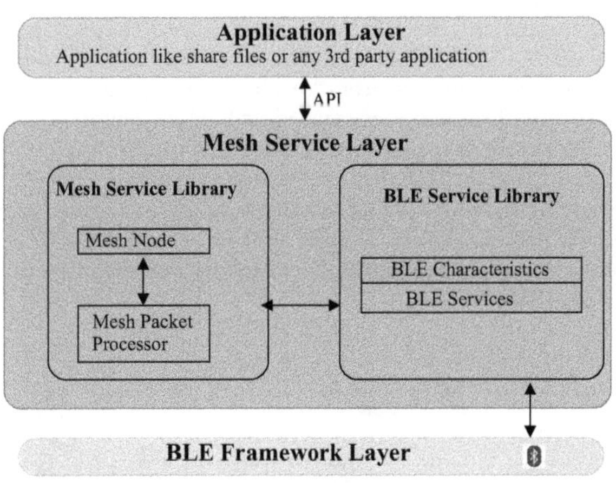

Figure 1: Overview of BLE Mesh Network (BMN) architecture.

3. DATA TRANSMISSION USING BMN

In this section, we discuss the procedure used for construction, maintenance, and optimization of the BMN.

- **BMN Formation:** Initially, all mobile devices start broadcasting a DAG Information solicitation (DIS) message for

SenSys'15, November 1-4, 2015, Seoul, South Korea.
ACM 978-1-4503-3631-4/15/11.
DOI: http://dx.doi.org/10.1145/2809695.2817850.

soliciting the DAG. A device is selected as a root of BMN and starts broadcasting a DAG information object (DIO) message as a response to DIS. Whenever the root or any connected device in BMN receives a DIS message, it broadcasts a DIO message which contains its rank. The rank of a device is based on the residual energy and the degree of the device. When a device receives DIO messages and if it is not part of the BMN, the device waits for some time for collecting more DIO messages and selects the device with lowest rank as its parent. The device establishes BLE connection with the lowest ranking device, by sending the DAO message. This lowest ranking device becomes the parent.

• **BMN Data Transmission:** The proposed BMN is suitable for mobile or static BLE devices, where any BLE device can act as a root device. In a DAG, the network is not an energy-efficient if the distance between the root and leaf devices is high. We propose a weight balancing technique using hop counts between root and its children. The source device checks its routing table and transfers the data to the next device if the destination device is present in the routing table. If the destination is not available in the routing table, the source device uses the alternate path for forwarding the data to the destination. If alternate path is also not exist, then the source device forwards the data packet to its parent device.

The whole BMN is optimized to reach the root device efficiently, which explains its importance. This behavior of root device hinders the mobility of both itself and also the BMN. To bring in mobility, we drew a contingency plan to find alternate root when the main root device leaves the BMN. Whenever a new immediate child is added to the root then it chooses one device among its children and assigns the role of alternative root. This choice is made based on the height of the subtree and number of devices in the subtree.

4. PRELIMINARY RESULTS

We implement the BMN on smartphones (Samsung Note 4, Samsung Galaxy S5, and Samsung Galaxy S6) running the Android lollipop system for chatting the text messages.

• **Latency:** Latency is measured as half the round trip time of a packet in seconds. We consider variable size of data between 1kB to 5kB. Figure 2 shows five experiments for latency. An interesting observation from this result is that the network latency is almost same in all experiments for a given value of hop counts. It indicates the stability of the proposed BMN.

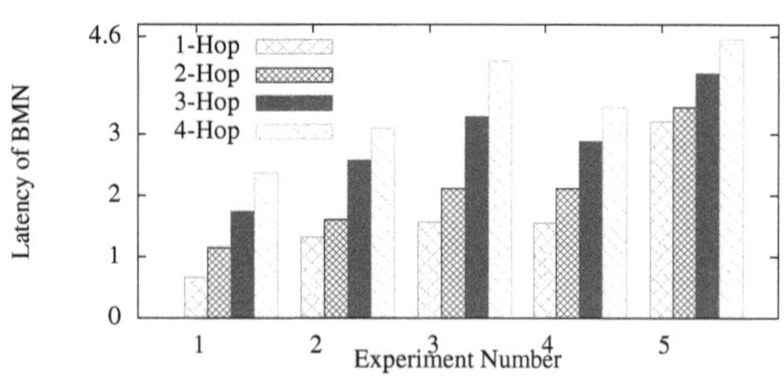

Figure 2: Experimental results for Latency of BMN.

• **Power Consumption:** We measure the power consumption using the proposed BMN. We use monsoon power monitor to measure the computational and communication energy consumption. In this experiment, the size of data is varying from 10kB to100 kB. Since, the maximum packet size in BLE is 512 kb, therefore the BMN segments the data into packets at the source. Figure 3 illustrates the power consumption of sender, relay, and receiver nodes.

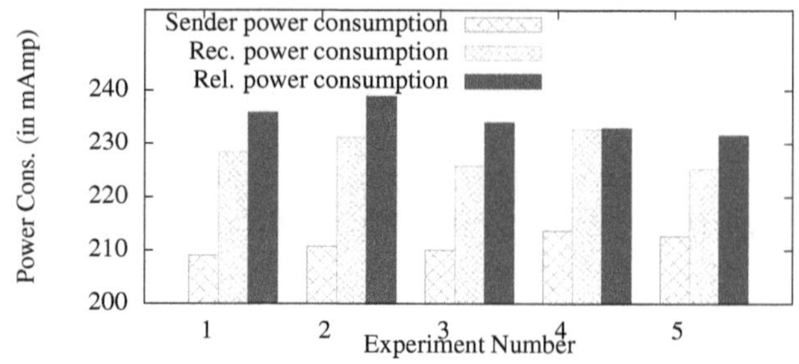

Figure 3: Experimental results for Power Consumption (in mAmp).

5. DEMONSTRATION PROPOSAL

In the on-site demonstration, conference audience will be able to operate the BMN by themselves for routing the data on Android smartphones. We will provide four Samsung smartphones, which have the BMN installed. This will allow the maximum four users at once to test out the BMN. We choose to use text messages as the input of the BMN. Figure 4 shows the Graphical User Interface (GUI) of the BMN. The attendees can also control the flashlight of the mesh devices.

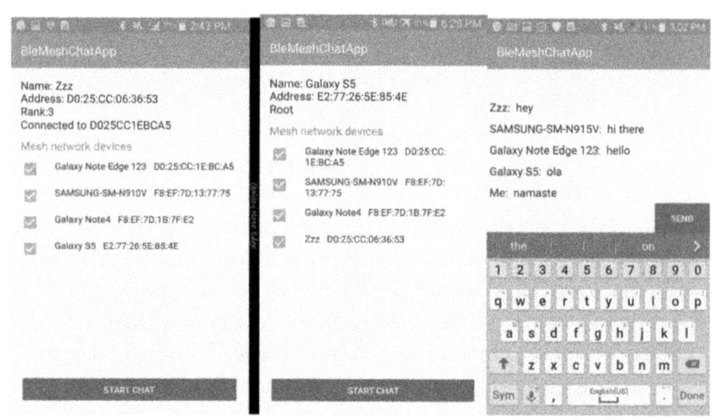

(a) (b) (c)

Figure 4: GUI of BMN for chat application. Parts (a) and (b) show the BMN devices and part (c) displaying the chat box.

6. REFERENCES

[1] S. H. Kim, P. K. Chong, and D. Kim. A location-free semi-directional-flooding technique for on-demand routing in low-rate wireless mesh networks. *IEEE Transactions on Parallel and Distributed Systems*, 25(12):3066–3075, Dec 2014.

[2] X. Zhao, J. Guo, C. T. Chou, A. Misra, and S. K. Jha. High-throughput reliable multicast in multi-hop wireless mesh networks. *IEEE Transactions on mobile computing*, 14(4):728–741, 2015.

Demo Abstract: A Smart Framework for IoT Analytic Workflow Development

Dibyanshu Jaiswal, Pubali Datta, Sounak Dey, Himadri Sekhar Paul,
Tanushyam Chattopadhyay, Avik Ghose, Abhishek Singh, Arpan Pal and Arijit Mukherjee
Innovation Labs, Kolkata
Tata Consultancy Services
{dibyanshu.jaiswal|pubali.datta|sounak.d|himadrisekhar.paul}@tcs.com
{t.chattopadhyay|avik.ghose|ab.s|arpan.pal|mukherjee.arijit}@tcs.com

ABSTRACT

Developing analytical applications for IoT based on sensor signal processing tends to be complicated as applications are executed as sequence of steps comprising of multiple alternative algorithms, including suitable feature extraction modules depending on the goal of the application. Experience shows that developers spend considerable time and effort in performing feature extraction and dimensionality reduction. In this paper we propose a framework based on a relevant case study which allows developers to drag and drop algorithms to create a workflow chain, automatically select the most relevant signal features for the particular analytic application using a training data set to generate a model and deploy the model for use. The method reduces the effort and cost of development which is deemed highly important for the analytics industry.

1. INTRODUCTION

The recent evolution of the Internet-of-Things (IoT) and the predicted volume of connected devices in the near future imply radical changes in business models mandating innovative ideas and services within and across multiple domains such as e-Governance, Health Care, Transportation and Utilities etc. However, developing such applications/services is inherently difficult and it may be unreasonable to imagine developers to be equipped with the diverse set of skills and knowledge encompassing the domain, sensor signal processing, algorithms and their usage, deployment infrastructures and more. Several recent proposals, such as [3, 4] have put forward the idea of model-driven development for IoT. Authors of [3] have proposed a separation of concerns by using knowledge models pertaining to different stakeholders to aid the application developers and in turn reduce the cost of development.

It has been seen from experience, that developers spend the most effort in choosing correct signal processing algorithms, extracting features from sensor signals and selecting the most relevant ones for analysis; and the process is entirely manual, iterative and error-prone. As part of the ongoing research on [1, 3], we have created a framework that allows the user to visually create a workflow by selecting algorithms from a repository, and automatically ranking the most relevant signal features to create a model. The model is then deployed on compute nodes to classify incoming test data and the process vastly reduces the time and effort required to create such applications.

SenSys'15, November 01-04, 2015, Seoul, Republic of Korea.
ACM 978-1-4503-3631-4/15/11.
DOI: http://dx.doi.org/10.1145/2809695.2817851.

2. SYSTEM DESIGN

The overview of the proposed demo is described in Figure 1. The framework is built around an annotated repository of crowdsourced algorithms known as *Algopedia* which contains detailed syntactic and semantic information of a large class of algorithms used in sensor signal processing for IoT applications. For a typical application, the framework allows a developer to visually create a workflow by stitching together the necessary algorithm implementations. Based on the type of input and the specific processing requirement, the developer is prompted with a selection of algorithms to choose from. Once the workflow is created, a deployable/executable model is generated by the framework (using the algorithms used in the workflow).

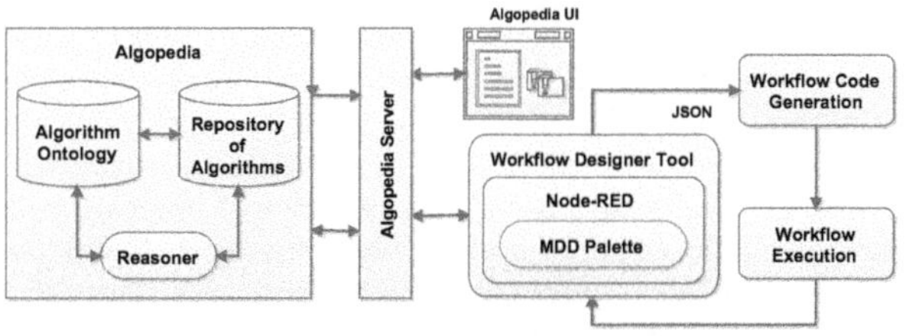

Figure 1: High level workflow for IoT Signal Processing

3. METHODOLOGY

The proposed demonstrable system, depicted in Figure 2, has two phases, namely: (i) Work-flow creation (WFC) - an one-time effort to create a working model and (ii) Work-flow execution (WFE). WFC follows typical steps for signal processing among which the most effort-intensive are *feature extraction* and *feature dimension reduction*. At this stage the

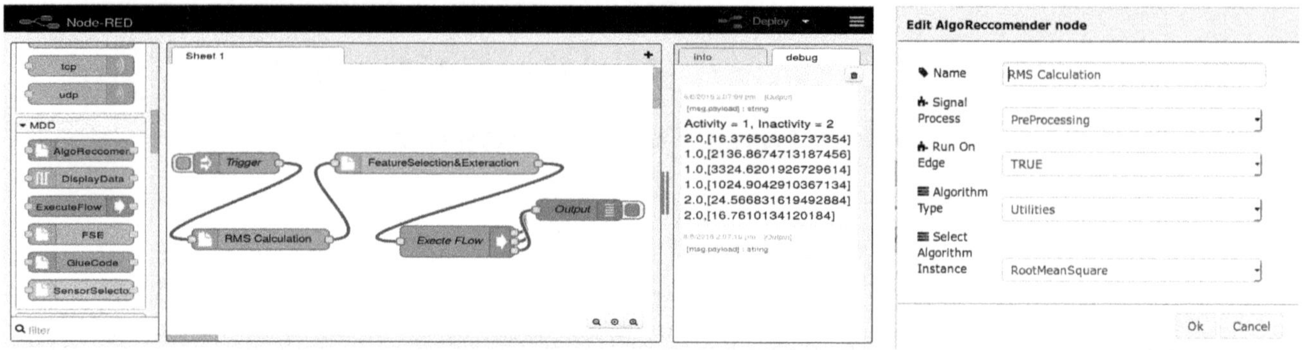

(a) Workflow creation in Node-RED (b) Algorithm Selection

Figure 2: Workflow creation and execution

system provides (i) a super-set of all features normally used in sensor signal processing from which the user can select features or opt for the novel method for automatic feature selection and dimensionality reduction, (ii) a re-usable template for sensor signal processing, (iii) a Node-RED-based interactive framework for WFC and WFE, and (iv) partitioning and deploying the work flow adaptively into cloud or edge to get optimal performance.

4. IMPLEMENTATION

Node-RED provides an easy way to define custom nodes specific to our requirement. The current setup works on Node-RED v0.10 where we have a separate palette for WFC containing nodes corresponding to the stages of signal processing workflow, such as, algorithm recommendation, feature selection and extraction and workflow execution. In the WFC phace, the nodes communicate with Algopedia via REST APIs to retrieve list of available algorithms, features etc. which are made available to the user for selection. Once the workflow is created, deployed and triggered for execution, all input/selected values from respective nodes are used to form a JSON representation of the workflow to start the WFE phase.

The WFE phase analyzes this JSON description to extract a call-graph corresponding to the workflow which is created using breadth-first traversal. The data transfer is achieved by exchanging buffers between nodes in the call-graph. The generator then creates a two top-level C-files, one for cloud execution and the other for edge (smartphones, sensor gateways etc) execution. The top-level file for edge execution contains function calls which are marked for edge, the rest goes into the top-level file for cloud execution. In the top-level files, the call graph is coded as a series of function calls as part of the `main()` function. The generator downloads all relevant function implementations from the Algopedia along with required additional libraries and creates a build description as a `makefile` through which executable modules are built - one for the cloud and another for the device itself, as shared library. The executable for the edge device is pushed to the device using the ANGELS framework [2] and the functions in the shared library can then be invoked via the ANGELS interface. The cloud executable contains these remote calls in its `main()` function body.

To validate the concept, we have experimented with two data sets among which one is an accelerometer based activity recognition data set created within our lab and the other is the benchmark MobiFall[1] data set. The proposed method can work with a recall rate of 0.9, precision value 0.97619, and F-Score 0.936548 which is significantly higher than the state of the art method with similar metric values as 0.8533, 0.9466, and 0.8974 on this dataset. The metrics were similar for the second dataset as well. In terms of workflow partitioning, by executing the pre-processing step on the edge (Sony Xperia Z-ultra, Qualcomm Snapdragon 800 quadcore cpu), we are able reduce the transferable data-size (for one minute) from 212KB to 27.1KB thereby resulting in estimated reduction of energy usage on the edge from 6.1J to 4.7J in 3G and 2.6J to 1.14J in WiFi. In terms of effort, the application was created in less than 30 minutes compared to weeks required prior to using the framework.

5. CONCLUSIONS

The prototype system described herein is an ongoing work. Going forward, we plan to include algorithm recommendation at each stage given the signal type and goal. Instead of static partitioning for execution, we intend to use energy footprint of each algorithm to decide on the partitioning point to optimize energy usage. Contextual help for each algorithm stored in the repository is another feature to be added. Considering all these, the framework will be able to provide an economic and efficient way of creating IoT analytic applications based on sensor signal processing.

References

[1] S. Dey, D. Jaiswal, R. Dasgupta, and A. Misra. A semantic sensor network (ssn) ontology based tool for semantic exploration of sensor. *Semantic Web Challenge Competition ISWC*, 2014.

[2] A. Mukherjee, H. S. Paul, S. Dey, and A. Banerjee. Angels for distributed analytics in iot. In *IEEE World Forum on Internet of Things (WF-IoT)*, pages 565–570. IEEE, 2014.

[3] A. Pal, A. Mukherjee, and P. Balamuralidhar. Model-driven development for internet of things: Towards easing the concerns of application developers. In *Internet of Things. User-Centric IoT*, pages 339–346. Springer, 2015.

[4] P. Patel and D. Cassou. Enabling high-level application development for the internet of things. *Journal of Systems and Software*, 103:62–84, 2015.

[1] MobiFall dataset is available @: `http://www.bmi.teicrete.gr/index.php/research/mobifall`

Demo: Scalable Visual Codes for Embedding Digital Data in the Physical World

Frederik Hermans
Uppsala University, Sweden
frederik.hermans@it.uu.se

Liam McNamara
SICS Swedish ICT
ljjm@sics.se

Thiemo Voigt
Uppsala University & SICS
thiemo@sics.se

ABSTRACT

Visual codes, such as QR codes, offer a low-cost alternative to RF technology when digital data needs to be embedded in objects in the physical world. However, in order to support receivers with a poor visual channel, e.g. low-resolution cameras, most visual codes are designed for low data capacity and short reading distances.

We present our work on FOCUS, a visual code that avoids earlier work's explicit trade-off between code capacity and channel quality. Rather than encoding the payload directly into individual pixels, FOCUS encodes the payload over a range of spatial frequencies. As a result, even a receiver with a very poor visual channel (e.g., a low-resolution camera, or a camera experiencing motion blur) can still partly decode a FOCUS code, because the code's low-frequency components are robust to common channel impairments. A receiver with a good channel can decode all data from the same code.

In our demo, we will present a prototype of FOCUS for smartphones and showcase how it deals with common impairments of the visual channel.

1. INTRODUCTION

To bridge the gap between the physical and the digital world, it is necessary to associate physical objects with digital data. Embedding data in physical objects enables rich, digitally assisted interactions between people and the objects around them: a sculpture in a museum provides its viewers with information about its creator; an engine part advises mechanics how it should be serviced; a projector informs a lecturer's tablet how to wirelessly connect to it.

As an alternative to RF-based solutions, visual codes, such as QR codes, offer a simple means to associate digital data with physical objects. With the proliferation of camera-equipped smartphones and wearables, people already carry a suitable receiver with them. As the quality of cameras increases, so does the capacity of their visual channel.

A fundamental challenge of visual codes arises from the heterogeneity in channels between the transmitter (i.e., the

SenSys'15, November 1–4, 2015, Seoul, South Korea.
ACM 978-1-4503-3631-4/15/11.
DOI: http://dx.doi.org/10.1145/2809695.2817852 .

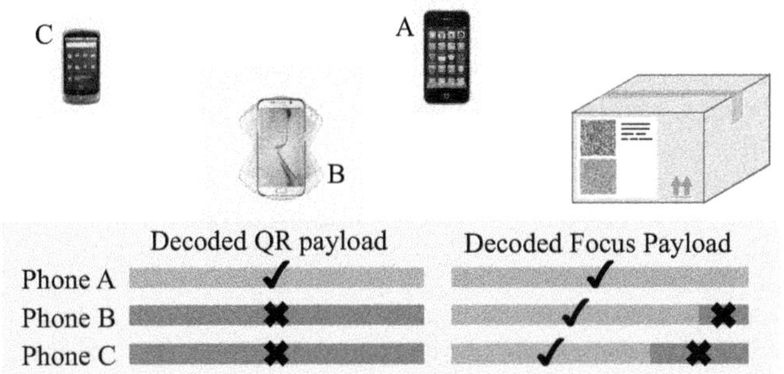

Figure 1: Smartphones at various distance try to decode a QR code and a Focus code on a parcel. In contrast to QR codes, Focus codes can still be partially decoded even at larger distances or when subject to motion blur.

displayed code) and the receiver (i.e., the camera). Consider the example from Fig. 1, where three smartphones try to retrieve data from visual codes printed on a parcel. The phones' visual channels are very different: phone A is nearby and has a high-resolution camera; phone B is experiencing motion blur; and phone C is an older model and located far away from the code. In the case of QR codes [1], only phone A would be able to retrieve the data, whereas phones B and C would not retrieve any data at all. Recently proposed visual codes offer higher capacity than QR codes [4, 6], but can only be read under very specific channel conditions (e.g., using expensive DSLR cameras or at sub-meter distances). Other work aims to support a wider range of channel conditions, but only supports low data capacity [2].

We are developing FOCUS, a new visual code that does not require earlier work's explicit trade-off between the code capacity and the required channel quality. The observation underlying FOCUS is that common impairments of the visual channel affect an image's fine details. In the frequency domain, these details are represented by high-frequency components. Therefore, rather than encoding data directly into individual pixels or small blocks of pixels, FOCUS encodes data in the frequency domain over a wide range of spatial frequencies. As a result, a receiver with a poor channel can still partially decode data from a FOCUS code by extracting the data contained in the code's low-frequency components (e.g., phone C in Fig. 1). A receiver with a good channel can decode all data contained in a code (phone A). The actual length of decoded data scales smoothly with the quality of the receiver's channel—the better the channel, the more data a receiver can decode.

2. FOCUS OVERVIEW

We briefly sketch the reasoning behind FOCUS, describe how a FOCUS code is constructed, and lay out how a receiver extracts data from a FOCUS code.

Channel impairments in frequency space. An image captured by a digital camera can be understood as a finite, real-valued 2D signal. Thus each captured image can be decomposed into a finite number of sinusoids by a Fourier transform. The sinusoids differ in their frequency: low-frequency sinusoids describe gradual changes in the image, whereas high-frequency sinusoids correspond to finer details.

Consider a camera that is perfectly aligned and focused on an LCD screen displaying an image. The camera's resolution is high enough and the camera is close enough to the screen for the effective spatial sampling rate to be equal to or greater than the Nyquist rate. In this case, the camera can perfectly capture the displayed image. Thus, if the displayed image is a visual code of any kind, all data from the code can be extracted.

Now consider the case in which the camera either is far away from the image or it only supports a low resolution. In this case, the image is captured below the Nyquist rate, i.e., the camera *undersamples* the displayed image. As a result, foldback aliasing occurs [3] and the captured image lacks details present in the displayed image. In effect, the captured image lacks the high-frequency components of the displayed image, but the low-frequency components are still correctly captured. Thus, too low a camera resolution or too a large distance between image and camera both cause the loss of high-frequency components. Similarly, consider the case in which the camera is not correctly focused on the displayed image, or in which there is motion blur from the camera or displayed image moving. In the frequency domain, these effects are similar to a low-pass filter [5]. Thus, the captured image will lack the fine details of the displayed image, while more gradual changes are preserved correctly.

Constructing a Focus code. We now outline the steps of constructing a FOCUS code for a given sequence of payload bytes. *(i)* The payload is modulated using 4-PSK, resulting in a sequence of complex symbols. *(ii)* A complex matrix is populated with the symbols following a spiral arrangement, so that symbols which represent earlier payload bytes are closer to the matrix's center. This arrangement process also ensures that the populated complex matrix is conjugate symmetric. *(iii)* The inverse Fourier transform of the complex matrix is computed. Because the matrix is conjugate symmetric, the transform is real and thus can be understood as a grayscale image. Note that elements closer to the complex matrix's center correspond to lower frequencies. Thus, due to the arrangement of complex symbols, earlier payload bytes are represented by low-frequency components in the grayscale image. *(iv)* Finally, the grayscale image is displayed on a suitable medium such as paper or screen.

Decoding a Focus code. A receiver that has captured a photo containing a code carries out the following steps. *(i)* The receiver converts the captured image to grayscale and localizes the code in the image. It then corrects the code for perspective distortion. *(ii)* The Fourier transform of the captured code is computed, yielding a complex matrix. *(iii)* The receiver extracts the complex symbols from the matrix, observing the same spiral arrangement as in the construction process. Note that if the receiver has undersampled the code (because it is too far away or due to too low camera resolution), the matrix will not contain the latter payload symbols. *(iv)* The receiver demodulates the payload symbols and validates the integrity of chunks of the reconstructed payload using checksums. Valid chunks are handed to the application layer. From our reasoning about channel impairments, it follows that latter parts of the payload are more susceptible to corruption than earlier parts.

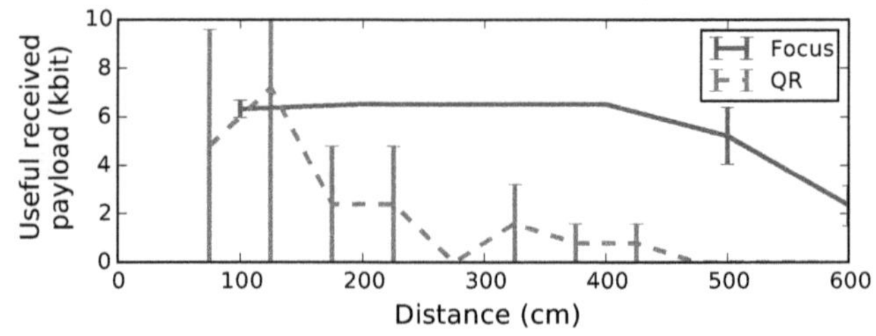

Figure 2: Number of decodable payload bits for QR codes and Focus codes over distance. Focus codes can consistently be read at larger distances.

3. INITIAL RESULTS

We are currently running experiments to investigate FOCUS's performance. Some initial results can be seen in Fig. 2, which shows how much data a receiver can decode from a FOCUS code over varying distance. In this experiment, we used a Samsung Galaxy S5 smartphone as a receiver, and codes were displayed on a LCD screen. We compared FOCUS codes to QR codes, and chose a capacity of 2048 bytes for both. The figure clearly shows how FOCUS codes can be read at larger distances and how decoding performance is much more consistent, as shown by the lower variance.

4. DEMO

In our demo, we show how our FOCUS prototype copes with different channel impairments. In particular, we will showcase FOCUS's performance on smartphones with different capabilities, ranging from older models with poor cameras to recent smartphones with high-resolution cameras and high-quality lenses. We will further demonstrate how FOCUS supports different display media by reading codes from an LCD screen and from printed paper. If physical space allows, we will also show how FOCUS's performance adapts to the distance between the reader and the code.

5. REFERENCES

[1] European Committee for Standardization. *Automatic identification and data capture techniques – QR Code 2005 bar code symbology specification: ISOi/IEC 18004-2006*. 2006.

[2] W. Hu, J. Mao, Z. Huang, Y. Xue, J. She, K. Bian, and G. Shen. Strata: Layered coding for scalable visual communication. In *ACM MobiCom 2014*.

[3] A. V. Oppenheim, A. S. Willsky, and S. H. Nawab. *Signals and Systems*. Prentice-Hall, Inc., 1996.

[4] S. D. Perli, N. Ahmed, and D. Katabi. PixNet: Interference-free Wireless Links Using LCD-camera Pairs. In *ACM MobiCom 2010*.

[5] L. G. Shapiro and G. C. Stockman. *Computer Vision*. Prentice-Hall, Inc., 2001.

[6] A. Wang, S. Ma, C. Hu, J. Huai, C. Peng, and G. Shen. Enhancing Reliability to Boost the Throughput over Screen-Camera Links. In *ACM MobiCom 2014*.

Demo Abstract: KinVocal: Detecting Agitated Vocal Events

Asif Salekin[1], Hongning Wang[2], John Stankovic[3]
University of Virginia
[1]as3df@virginia.edu, [2]hw5x@virginia.edu, [3]stankovic@virginia.edu

ABSTRACT

Many elderly who are suffering from dementia are also suffering from agitation. While most assisted living facilities and home health care situations rely upon caregivers to monitor and record agitation of their patients, the accuracy is limited because the caregiver must be present during the agitation and must record the event properly. Accurate 24-7 data would help physicians with improved diagnoses and care. To solve this problem we developed KinVocal, a system that continuously monitors and detects agitated vocal events and can be used for the elderly population suffering from dementia. KinVocal, using a novel combination of acoustic signal processing and multiple text mining techniques, automatically detects and records the 8 major vocal agitations for dementia patients as defined by the medical community. This includes: constant unwarranted request for attention or help, making verbal sexual advances, crying, screaming, laughing, cursing, speaking in repetitive sentences, and negativism. The novelty of KinVocal includes the comprehensiveness of addressing all 8 vocal events, using the text of the vocalizations only when accurate, combining text and acoustic features when necessary, and employing text mining and feature identification. A comprehensive performance evaluation includes using data from *Youtube* and movies, controlled experiments, and real in-home deployments. The results show high accuracy for all 8 vocal events.

Categories and Subject Descriptors

H.3.4 [**Systems and Software**]: User Profiles and Alert; H.5.5 [**Sound and Music Computing**]: Systems

General Terms

Algorithm, Design, Experimentation

Keywords

Vocal agitation, text mining, dementia, word sense

SenSys '15, November 01-04, 2015, Seoul, Republic of Korea
ACM 978-1-4503-3631-4/15/11.
http://dx.doi.org/10.1145/2809695.2817853

1. INTRODUCTION

The medical community has defined the the Cohen Mansfield Agitation Inventory [2] which specifies approximately 30 agitated behaviors for identifying whether a person is suffering from agitation or not. Many of these behaviors are physical such as punching or kicking. An automated system [3] already exists for monitoring and recording physical agitation behaviors. However, there is no such a system for the vocal agitation metrics of Cohen-Mansfield Inventory. In this abstract we describe KinVocal, an automated system for monitoring and recording all the vocal agitation metrics of the Cohen-Mansfield Inventory. This includes crying, screaming, laughing, cursing or verbal aggression, constant unwarranted request for attention or help, negativism, making verbal sexual advances, and talking with repetitive sentences.

Most work in acoustic signal processing for human vocal data uses either features from the signal such as pitch, energy, etc., or convert the speech to text and then use dictionaries to interpret the content of the speech. Our solution, KinVocal, divides the 8 acoustic events of Cohen-Mansfield into three equivalence classes based on the processing technique required to achieve accurate recognition of that particular event. The three classes are: use both the features of the signal and text, use only the acoustic signal features, and use only the text. Further, instead of only using dictionaries for the text we employ 3 different types of text mining techniques depending on the event being detected. This includes textual similarity, text word sense disambiguation, and repetitive sequential pattern mining. Doing this divide and conquer approach results in high accuracy at the lowest cost of processing. For example, detecting asking for help or verbal sexual advances using only textual inference or only acoustic features results in high false positives and false negatives. If we try to detect asking for help using only textual features (e.g., using similarity based text analysis and content matching), we will mistakenly falsely identify a story about helping a kid or a discussion about helping others as asking for help. On the other hand, relying only on acoustic signal processing (e.g., temporal pattern mining in the acoustic signal) cannot recognize the situation where people do not depict any specific verbal tone while asking for help, i.e., one might ask for help in a submissive tone or in a dominant tone based on his/her mood. In this case the acoustic signal alone will be insufficient due to variation of mood or tone although they correspond to the same verbal event. In another case, for crying, it is sufficient to use only acoustic features (and, in fact, there is usually no text).

The main contributions of KinVocal are:

- An automatic and comprehensive system for detecting verbal agitation based on both extending various algorithms and combining acoustic signal processing with three different text mining paradigms.
- None of the previous state of the art solutions has addressed the verbal events: asking for help and verbal sexual advances. KinVocal have shown that detection of these two vocal events depends both on the acoustic signal processing and the semantics understanding of the speech. To understand the semantics of speech we employ text data mining techniques exploring text similarity.
- Cursing is difficult to detect because many such words have multiple meanings. We have used a modified version of the adapted Lesk algorithm [1] which considers a word's sense, to detect curse words with multiple ambiguous meanings.

2. OVERVIEW OF KINVOCAL

KinVocal is an automated monitoring and recording system that detects the 8 verbal agitations of the Cohen Mansfield agitation inventory. It uses the Microsoft Kinect sensor to collect raw acoustic data. As the signal arrives, it is important to note that some noise elimination is already handled by the Kinect system. Then, once this *cleaned* data is collected, it proceeds through various stages of processing, see Figure 1, divided into three categories based on two types of signals: text and features of the raw signal. One module converts the raw signal into text. It then supplies that text to 4 other modules, i.e., those modules that are used to detect negativism, cursing, repetitive sentences which only require the text (category 1), and a combined module that addresses asking for help and verbal sexual advances which requires both the text and features of the raw signal (category 2). The raw signal only (category 3) is also sent to the module that detects crying, laughing and screaming.

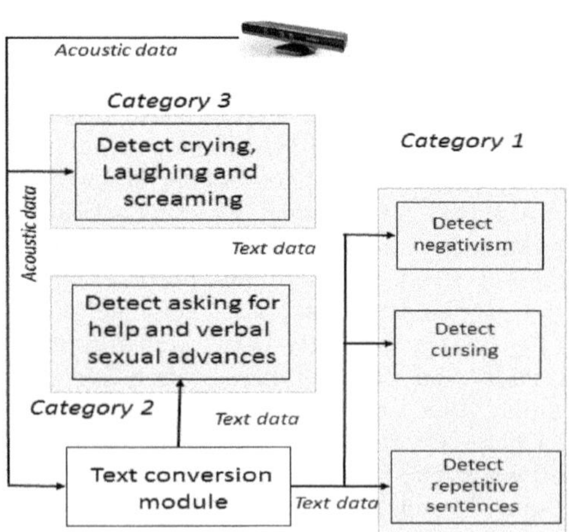

Figure 1: Block Diagram of KinVocal

3. EVALUATION

We have performed an extensive evaluation of KinVocal that includes using *Youtube*, movies, controlled experiments, and home deployments. Using a combined feature set of acoustic and textual features, KinVocal has achieved a detection accuracy of 86.62% for asking for help and a detection accuracy of 89.17% for verbal sexual advances. Also, KinVocal have detected laughing, crying and screaming using an acoustic time series approach resulting in greater than 96% accuracy. Using our modified adapted Lesk algorithm [1] we have detected cursing with 95.6% accuracy. In the future we will apply our solutions to the verbal utterances of actual dementia patients.

4. DEMO SCRIPT

The objective of the demo is to show how KinVocal monitors and detects each of the 8 verbal agitations of the Cohen-Mansfield agitation inventory. The demo will proceed in phases. First, we will list audio clips collected from *Youtube* videos or movies. This clips will then be passed through Kinect for noise removal. After noise removal, acoustic and textual features will be extracted from these audio clips. The set of clips will cover the 8 verbal agitations and a 9th situation where none of these agitations are present. Then, in the final phase of the demo, for each audio clip the 8 separate modules for each of these verbal events will take the features as input and detect whether that targeted verbal event has occurred or not.

5. ACKNOWLEDGMENTS

This work was supported, in part, by NSF grant CNS-1319302.

References

[1] S. Banerjee and T. Pedersen. An adapted lesk algorithm for word sense disambiguation using wordnet. In *Computational linguistics and intelligent text processing*, pages 136–145. Springer, 2002.

[2] J. Cohen-Mansfield. Instruction manual for the cohen-mansfield agitation inventory (cmai). *Research Institute of the Hebrew Home of Greater Washington*, 1991.

[3] S. Nirjon, C. Greenwood, C. Torres, S. Zhou, J. A. Stankovic, H. J. Yoon, H.-K. Ra, C. Basaran, T. Park, and S. H. Son. Kintense: A robust, accurate, real-time and evolving system for detecting aggressive actions from streaming 3d skeleton data. In *Pervasive Computing and Communications (PerCom), 2014 IEEE International Conference on*, pages 2–10. IEEE, 2014.

Demo: Building Reliable Wireless Embedded Platforms using the Bolt Processor Interconnect

Felix Sutton, Marco Zimmerling, Reto Da Forno, Roman Lim, Tonio Gsell,
Georgia Giannopoulou, Federico Ferrari, Jan Beutel, and Lothar Thiele
Computer Engineering and Networks Laboratory
ETH Zurich, Switzerland
{firstname.lastname}@tik.ee.ethz.ch

ABSTRACT

We demonstrate the capabilities of BOLT, an ultra-low-power processor interconnect for the composable construction of new multi-processor wireless embedded platforms. BOLT provides asynchronous bidirectional communication between two processors with predictable message transfer times. In this way, BOLT solves the resource interference problem inherent in today's wireless embedded platforms, enabling simpler and more robust system designs with minimal resource overhead. Using our BOLT prototype implemented on a state-of-the-art microcontroller, we demonstrate BOLT's composability and decoupling in time, power, and clock domains.

Categories and Subject Descriptors

C.1.2 [**Computer Systems Organization**]: Multiprocessors—*interconnection architectures*; C.3 [**Computer Systems Organization**]: Special-Purpose and Application-Based System—*real-time and embedded systems*

General Terms

Design, Experimentation, Performance

Keywords

Cyber-physical systems; multi-processor; processor interconnect; predictability; composability; resource interference

1. MOTIVATION AND DESIGN

Today's wireless embedded applications are characterized by ever-increasing resource demands, the need for run-time adaptability and energy-proportional system operation. At the same time, the employed devices must simultaneously handle several tasks ranging from sensing, actuation, data processing, wireless communications, control law computation, user interaction to power management. The prevailing solution to satisfy these conflicting design goals is the adoption of heterogeneous multi-processor architectures, such as the LPC4300 [2] from NXP and VF3xxR and MKW2xDx [1] from Freescale. These heterogeneous architectures facilitate the mapping of a single task to a single processing element, for example, the mapping of sensing and communication tasks onto dedicated processors. However, it has been recognized that whenever multiple components interact, the use of shared buses and shared memory leads to *coupling of power and clock domains* and *interference in the time domain.* Such component dependencies prevent the use of modular design techniques, therefore increasing system complexity and making the design process of multi-processor platforms a labor intensive task. In addition, multi-processor systems are often over-provisioned in order to meet runtime guarantees, thereby infringing on resource and power budgets.

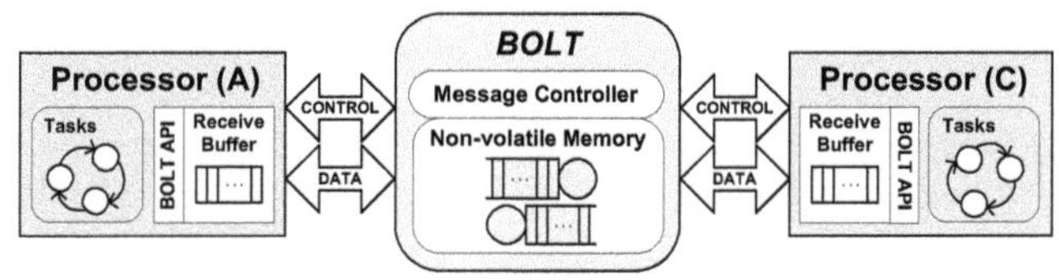

Figure 1: Bolt decouples processors *A* and *C* in time, power, and clock domains through predictable bidirectional asynchronous message passing.

To fill this gap, we have introduced BOLT [3] as a new processor interconnect providing bidirectional asynchronous message passing with predictable message transfer times. BOLT is the first architectural concept that enables the effective decoupling of two processors with respect to time, power and clock domains. BOLT is therefore a key building block for the communication between components on emerging dual-processor platforms to support low-power applications with high dependability requirements and stringent timing constraints. By completely eliminating or at least limiting the interference among different components on shared resources, BOLT simplifies the design of such applications. Consequently, the interconnected processors can schedule their tasks independently and may arbitrarily switch power modes to minimize energy consumption.

As depicted in Fig. 1, BOLT consists of integrated hardware and software that sits between two arbitrary processors *A* and *C*. We design and implement BOLT in such a way that the execution time of asynchronous message exchanges can be tightly bounded. BOLT provides a well-defined, non-blocking software interface to each attached processor. The unique properties of BOLT allow for composable system designs. That is, a designer is free to choose any two commercially available processors, build on existing software components, and integrate them to create a customized multi-

SenSys'15, November 1–4, 2015, Seoul, South Korea.
ACM 978-1-4503-3631-4/15/11.
DOI: http://dx.doi.org/10.1145/2809695.2817854.

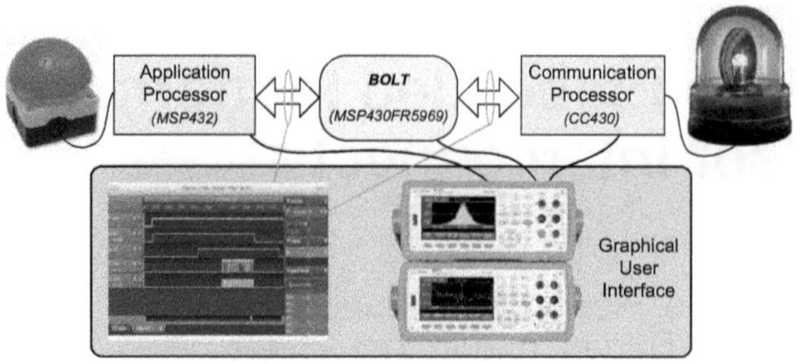

Figure 2: The demo measurement setup allows to visualize sensor events during their traversal through the Bolt architecture. Communication signals are displayed with a logic analyzer along with the power dissipation of all three processors of our prototype.

processor platform that satisfies application needs, *without changing the properties of the integrated components.* Each component can be separately designed, implemented, and validated, thus leading to modular systems with predictable timing behavior that are easier to develop, understand, and maintain.

With only 430 nA current drain during periods of inactivity, BOLT has a negligible impact on the total system power dissipation. The physical interface of BOLT consists of an SPI bus as well as additional lines for handshake signaling. A high throughput of 3.4 Mbps for messages that are 128 bytes in length can be achieved. This is only 15% less than the theoretical throughput of a standard SPI bus.

2. DEMONSTRATION

As illustrated in Fig. 2, the demonstration of BOLT leverages a multimeter and logic analyzer to visualize the power dissipation and message passing in real-time, thus giving insights into the inner workings of BOLT. Furthermore, the two main characteristics of BOLT are demonstrated: BOLT's composability and the decoupling of processors with respect to time, power and clock domains.

While any processor can be attached to BOLT, we will showcase our prototype implementation by facilitating the interconnection of two commercially available off-the-shelf evaluation platforms, namely the STM32 F3 Discovery and the Olimex MSP430-CCRF, as well as two custom development boards featuring an MSP432 application and a CC430 communication processor, as shown in Fig. 3.

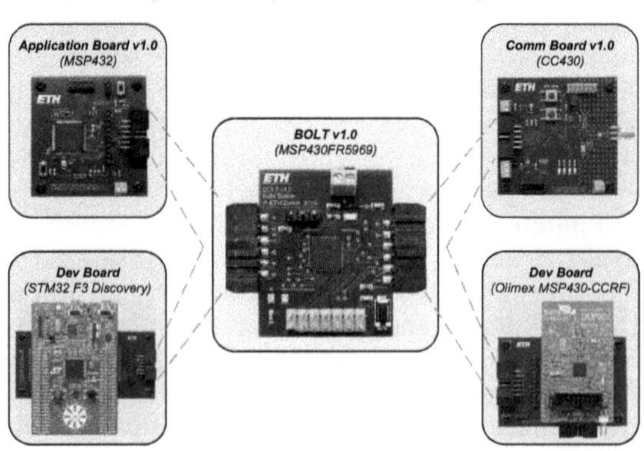

Figure 3: We demonstrate four showcase processors connectible to Bolt: MSP432, CC430, STM32 F3 Discovery and Olimex MSP430-CCRF.

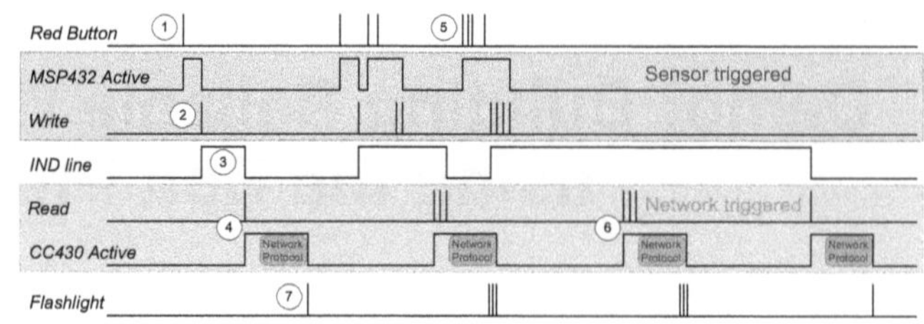

Figure 4: A signal trace from an event-triggered wireless sensing application implemented using Bolt.

In order to demonstrate BOLT's capability, we implement an event-triggered sensing application typical in many wireless sensing application scenarios. In such scenarios, resource-constrained low-power wireless sensor nodes must react to *sensor events* originating from a physical process under observation, while simultaneously reacting to *network events* originating from the wireless network. An example sequence of events and the triggered activities are shown in Fig. 4 and described in the following:

1. A sensor event is generated by pushing a button.
2. An interrupt on the application processor A triggers a wake up from deep sleep mode. After processing the sensor event, an alarm message is written to BOLT and processor A goes back to sleep mode.
3. As soon as the message has been successfully written to BOLT, the *IND* line is asserted to notify the communication processor C of the pending message.
4. Processor C reads the message queue of BOLT just before initiating the next wireless communication activity.
5. A burst of sensor events are buffered in the BOLT message queue.
6. Processor C is not impacted by the burstiness of processor A. In fact, processor C is free to choose how many messages it reads from BOLT, *i.e.*, three messages in this example. The remaining messages are read at the next scheduled communication activity on processor C.
7. Processor C reads an alarm message from BOLT, which is indicated by a flashing lamp.

While the aforementioned use case gives an intuition on what can be supported with BOLT in a very specific scenario, we believe the architectural blueprint provided by BOLT is an important building block that facilitates the construction of reliable and heterogeneous wireless embedded platforms.

Further details on BOLT are available on our website: `http://bolt.ethz.ch`.

Acknowledgements. This work was scientifically evaluated by the SNSF and financed by the Swiss Confederation and Nano-Tera.ch.

3. REFERENCES

[1] Freescale. VF3xxR and MKW2xDx Series. `http://www.freescale.com`.

[2] NXP Semiconductors. Cortex-M4 MCUs with Cortex-M0 Co-Processors. `http://www.nxp.com/products/microcontrollers/core/cortex_m0_m4f/`.

[3] F. Sutton et al. Bolt: A stateful processor interconnect. In *Proceedings of the 13th ACM Conference on Embedded Networked Sensor Systems (SenSys)*, 2015.

Demo: PowerBlade
A Low-Profile, True-Power, Plug-Through Energy Meter

Samuel DeBruin, Branden Ghena, Ye-Sheng Kuo, Prabal Dutta
Electrical Engineering and Computer Science Department
University of Michigan
Ann Arbor, MI 48109
{sdebruin, brghena, samkuo, prabal}@umich.edu

ABSTRACT

We present PowerBlade, the smallest and lowest power AC plug-load meter that measures real, reactive and apparent power, and reports this data, along with cumulative energy consumption, over an industry-standard Bluetooth Low Energy radio. Achieving this design point requires revisiting every aspect of conventional power meters: a new method of acquiring voltage; a non-invasive, planar method of current measurement; an efficient and accurate method of computing power from the voltage and current channels; a radio interface that leverages nearby smart phones to display data and report it to the cloud; and a retro power supply reimagined with vastly lower current draw, allowing extreme miniaturization. PowerBlade occupies a mere 1" by 1" footprint, offers a 1/16" profile, draws 176 mW continuously, offers 1.13% error on unity power factor loads in the 2-1200 W range and slightly worse for non-linear and reactive loads, and costs $11 in modest quantities of about 1000 units. This new design point enables affordable large-scale studies of plug-load energy usage—an area of growing national importance.

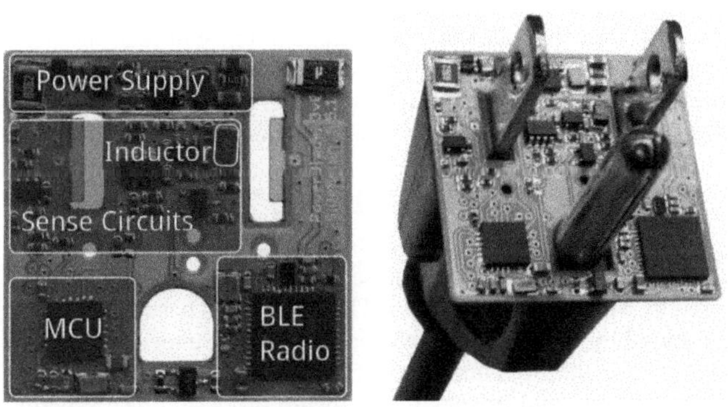

Figure 1: Front and perspective views of PowerBlade, a wireless power meter that measures real, reactive, and apparent power. PowerBlade's low profile and plug-through form factor allow it to sit inconspicuously between a plug and outlet, and its square-inch footprint saves adjacent outlets from being blocked.

SenSys'15, November 01–04, 2015, Seoul, Republic of Korea
ACM 978-1-4503-3631-4/15/11.
http://dx.doi.org/10.1145/2809695.2817855

1. INTRODUCTION

Consumers lack the tools and knowledge to actually understand their energy consumption. While the majority of building usage comes from obvious loads such as HVAC, lighting, and appliances, a remaining 20% resides in miscellaneous electrical loads (MELs) [3]. These diverse loads, from televisions and computers to vending machines and ceiling fans, represent the long-tail of electricity use. Understanding the characteristics of these loads requires insight into each device's individual consumption.

In this paper, we present PowerBlade, a new power meter design that achieves a vastly smaller form factor than prior systems. We introduce a new, essentially two-dimensional form factor, that of a plug-through power meter. PowerBlade is only 1/16 inch in depth with a 1" by 1" footprint, and metered loads are literally plugged through it and into the outlet as shown in Figure 1. Despite these size limitations, PowerBlade functions as a wireless true power meter, capable of monitoring real, reactive, and apparent power and transmitting this data in real time using Bluetooth Low Energy.

Achieving this profile requires new solutions to previously solved aspects of power meter design. Traditional AC-DC power supplies require substantial volume. Instead, PowerBlade is designed to operate at less than 6 mW average power draw, allowing it to utilize a simpler four-component supply. Traditional current sensing requires breaking the AC path in order to use a sense resistor. PowerBlade non-intrusively detects the magnetic field generated from the current passing through it. A horizontally wire-wound inductor placed parallel to the magnetic field acts as a magnetometer, allowing the current waveform to be monitored in real time.

Despite these limitations, PowerBlade is still an accurate meter. For resistive loads, like incandescent light bulbs, it remains within 1.13% of the real power measurement. Across common household loads with a range of power factors, it has an accuracy of 6.5%. Over a longer term (i.e. hours), errors in the accumulated energy measurements are comparable to popular commercial products.

PowerBlade is smaller than all previous power meters with a volume of 0.0625 in^3 and a no-load power draw of 176 mW. For comparison, Kill-A-Watt [1], a commercial system, has a volume of 14.0 in^3, and a no-load power draw of 450 mW. Academic prior work, ACme [2], has a volume of 13.7 in^3 and a no-load power draw of 100 mW. By achieving such a small form factor, PowerBlade does not block adjacent outlets, an advantage over all prior work.

We believe that PowerBlade provides a new opportunity for researchers. The plug-through form factor leads to a new way of thinking about deployments. Rather than metering every outlet in a building, PowerBlade is capable of metering every load, following the plug no matter which outlet it connects to. We believe that this will lead to new capabilities for researchers and allow a better understanding of energy consumption.

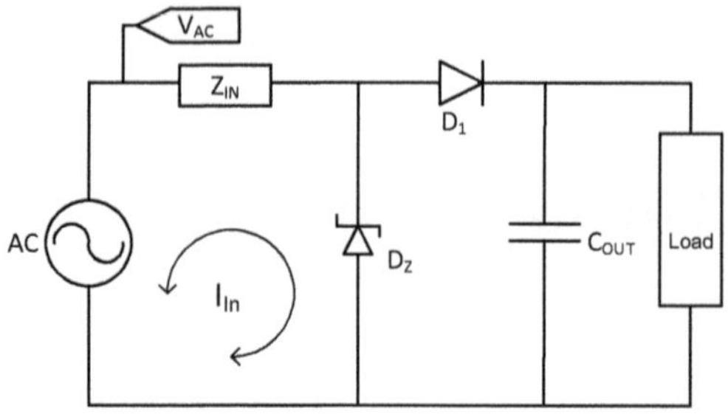

Figure 2: Zener regulated, half wave rectified power supply. Z_{IN}, either a resistor or capacitor, is used to the drop the line voltage. D_1 is a rectifying diode. C_{OUT} stores charge between each positive half cycle of the AC wave. The maximum voltage exposed to the load is the zener voltage of D_Z. This power supply design achieves an exteremely small form factor because it does not need to dissipate much power (for the resistive design) or store much charge (for the capacitive design) when the load is sufficiently low power.

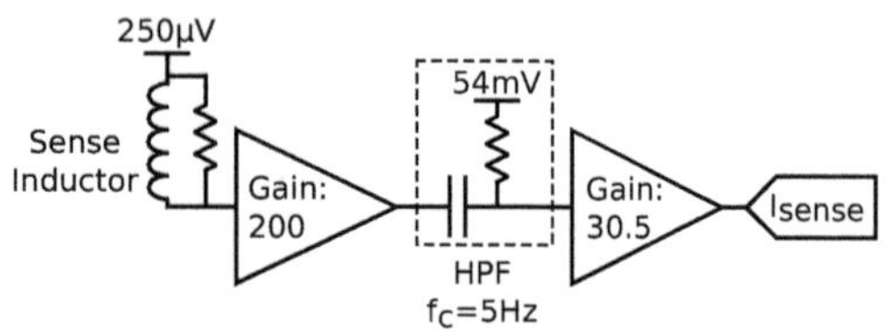

Figure 3: Current sensing circuit. A horizontally wire-wound inductor acting as a magnetometer senses the current waveform. The signal is amplified and filtered before the resulting I_{SENSE} is measured by the ADC on the MSP430.

2. OVERVIEW

In order to function as a power meter, PowerBlade has to overcome several challenges unique to its form factor. The first challenge is contact with the AC plugs. Since PowerBlade does not plug into the outlet itself, it must tap in at the device plugged through it. The PCB is designed with flexible tabs extending into the plug hole that bend and contact the load prongs.

The second challenge is the design of the power supply. While many ICs exist for AC-DC power conversion, all require large-volume components that do not meet our volume constraints. Figure 2 shows the power supply design for PowerBlade. Populating Z_{IN} with a resistor minimizes the volume required by the power supply, but introduces a static power draw of 170 mW above the 6 mW required for the MSP430 microcontroller and the nRF51822 radio to operate.

Finally, the solution for current sensing is shown in Figure 3. Using a horizontally wound inductor to sense current creates a magnetometer called a search coil [4]. Importantly, the voltage output from the coil is proportional to the change in current over time, rather than the current itself. PowerBlade integrates the signal in software after sampling it in order to recover the current waveform. The integrated current is multiplied by the sampled voltage in order to calculate power at a rate of 42 samples per AC cycle (2.52 kHz).

In order to transmit the data to users, the microcontroller transfers its power measurements over UART to a Bluetooth Low Energy radio. The radio transmits the data in broadcast advertisements, with updated measurements once per second.

To determine the accuracy of PowerBlade, we compare its measurements to a professionally calibrated benchtop power meter. Resistive loads with a unity power factor, such as incandescent lights, exhibit a sinusoidal current waveform in-phase with voltage. To evaluate PowerBlade's accuracy in this simple but common case,

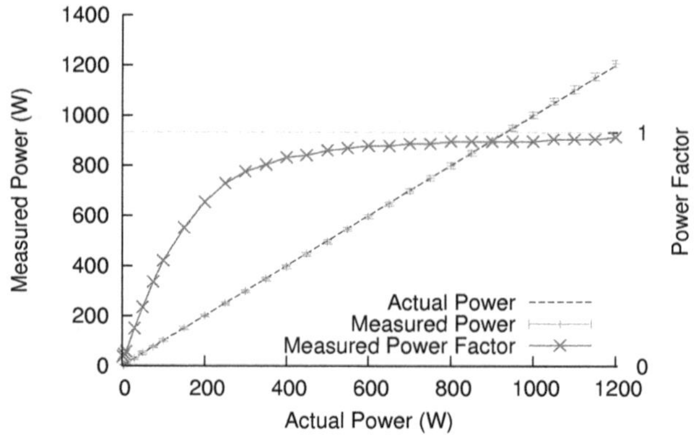

Figure 4: Metering accuracy for a variable resistive (power factor = 1) load: measured power vs actual power as well as measured power factor. The reported real power tracks accurately with ground truth. The minimum AC load for accurate metering is 2 W, and over the range from 2 W to 1200 W the accuracy in real power is 1.13%. PowerBlade's metering and reporting system is accurate over a range of resistive loads.

we use a programmable AC load with a fixed unity power factor and variable wattage. Figure 4 shows the end-to-end accuracy for a resistive load.

A video demonstrating PowerBlade and describing the design of the system is available online at https://youtu.be/oNUXhCDnHoE.

3. DEMONSTRATION

We will demonstrate PowerBlade transmitting real-time power data. In order to avoid possible issues with international AC standards, we will bring a converter that will supply 120 V at 60 Hz. We have several example loads available across a range of wattages and power factors. A smartphone application will read the measurements from PowerBlade in real time and display them to the participants. We will provide a smartphone, but the application will also be available to be installed on users' personal devices.

4. ACKNOWLEDGMENTS

This work was supported in part by TerraSwarm, one of six centers of STARnet, a Semiconductor Research Corporation program sponsored by MARCO and DARPA. This material is based upon work supported by the National Science Foundation under grant CNS-1350967, by the NSF/Intel Partnership on Cyber-Physical System (CPS) Security and Privacy under Award proposal title "Synergy: End-to-End Security for the Internet of Things, NSF proposal No. 1505684.", and by the Graduate Research Fellowship Program under grant number DGE-1256260. This work partially supported by generous gifts from Intel and Texas Instruments.

5. REFERENCES

[1] Kill-a-watt electricity use monitor. http://www.p3international.com/products/p4400.html.

[2] X. Jiang, S. Dawson-Haggerty, P. Dutta, and D. Culler. Design and implementation of a high-fidelity ac metering network. In *Information Processing in Sensor Networks, 2009. IPSN 2009. International Conference on*, pages 253–264. IEEE, 2009.

[3] S. Kwatra, J. T. Amann, and H. M. Sachs. Miscellaneous energy loads in buildings. American Council for an Energy-Efficient Economy, 2013.

[4] S. Tumanski. Induction coil sensors a review. *Measurement Science and Technology*, 18(3):R31, 2007.

Demo Abstract: Bringing Down Wires in Vehicles - Interconnecting ECUs using Wireless Connectivity

Changwon Lee, Hoon Jeong, Jaehong Ryu, Byeong-Cheol Choi and JeongGil Ko*
Electronics and Telecommunications Research Institute, Daejeon, Korea
*Department of Software Convergence Technology, Ajou University, Suwon, Korea

ABSTRACT

Most vehicles today inter-connect their electronic (sensing) components using wired communications such as CAN, Diognostic-CAN, or LIN. However, despite its simple design in connecting various automotive components, the cost and weight of installing wired connectors can increase quickly with the increasing number of electronic control units (ECUs) a vehicle supports. This work looks into the option of enabling wireless communications for intra-vehicle services, especially for less safety-critical applications. We present a wireless communication hardware platform that is used to design a vehicle's body controller / gateway device, which interconnects ECUs of heterogeneous communication mediums (e.g., CAN, LIN, etc.). We show using this demo, in which we present prototype implementations, that the latency and packet delivery performance of wireless links can be suitable for supporting various vehicular applications that relate less towards passenger safety.

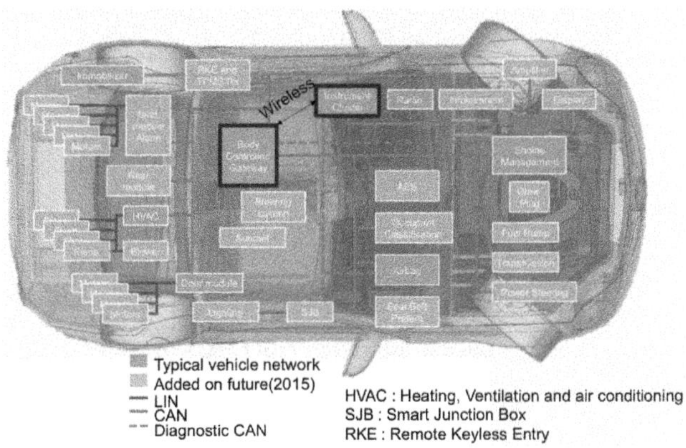

Figure 1: Diagram of a vehicle and its interconnected ECUs.

1. INTRODUCTION

Controller Area Networks (CAN) are a standard used in intra-vehicle communication applications, designed to be simple with support for priority-assisted QoS services. CAN allows for various sensors or electrical control units (ECUs) in a vehicle to easily communicate without the use of a complex routing structure [1]. In addition to CAN, standards such as Diagnostic-CAN [2] and LIN, are widely used in vehicles to connect various electronic sensing devices to a central device. To inter-connect these various communication standards, at the center of a vehicle's communication unit is a "body controller / gateway" unit (Fig 1). This gateway unit performs translation between different communication protocol and allows the sharing of data over different platforms easily. While all being simple communication methods to support, one major issue is that all these in the fact that the extension of various services can be difficult due to the overhead of the physical wiring of the devices [4].

The easy way out of this burden would be to apply wireless technologies to intra-vehicle communications. However, wireless technologies are thought to be less reliable compared to wired systems; thus, the adaptation of wireless technologies have been slow in vehicles. For safety-critical applications this has been a fairly reasonable approach. However, intra-vehicle services include not only safety-critical applications, but also less-critical applications such as info-tainment or convenience applications. If we can apply wireless connections for devices supporting such applications, we will be able to significantly reduce the installation and management costs compared to wired approaches [3].

In this demo, we suggest the use of wireless connectivity on the vehicle's "body controller / gateway" device. By attaching a wireless module to electronic units that support less critical applications, we can easily construct a point-to-point link between each sensing end point to the gateway. This will naturally reduce installation costs of ECUs and also simplify the ECU-gateway connection management.

2. SYSTEM ARCHITECTURE

In Figure 1, we illustrate a diagram of intra-vehicle connectivity of ECUs mostly in the traditional way (e.g., wired communications) and also how the connection would occur with wireless links at the "body controller / gateway". By increasing the number of wireless links, we can eventually reduce the amount of wiring harness and therefore, reduce the weight of the vehicle as well.

In order to realize this, we need to first design a hardware module that connects to the CAN transceivers and ex-

SenSys'15, November 1–4, 2015, Seoul, Republic of Korea
ACM 978-1-4503-3631-4/15/11
http://dx.doi.org/10.1145/2809695.2817856.

(a) Wireless Hardware

(b) Wireless Component Connected to an ECU via CAN

Figure 2: Picture of our wireless CAN interconnection implementation.

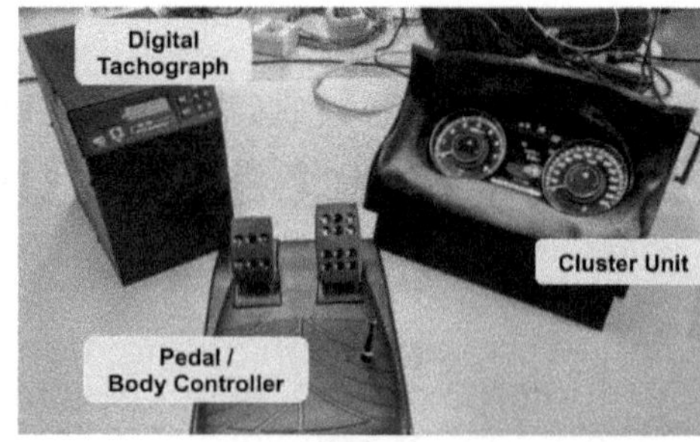

(a) Demo Hardware Setup

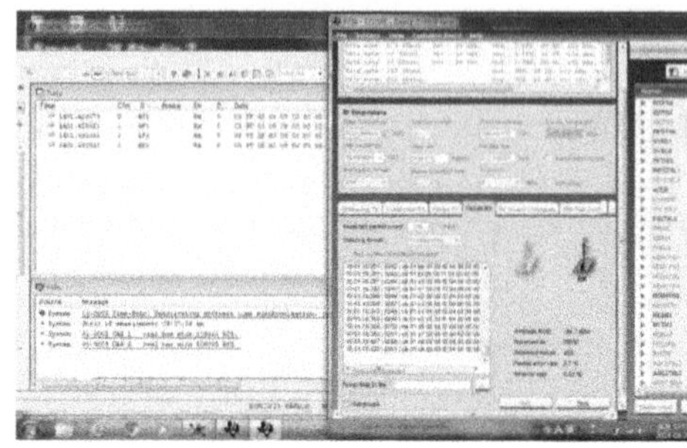

(b) Demo Screen Shot of Wireless and CANoe

Figure 3: Demo configurations.

changes messages with a distance ECU. For this, as we show in Figure 2(a), we implemented a wireless platform consisting of an ACM Cortex-M3 microcontroller with a TI CC2520 low-power radio. This platform supports direct wired connections to a local CAN unit. We plan to extend this to Diagnostic-CAN and LIN connections as well. Our platform also supports various interfaces such as JTAG and UART connections for easy extension and development. The device is powered directly through the CAN transceiver on which our platform connects to using a 3.3V voltage regulator.

Overall, once our wireless platform is fully connected with a ECU's CAN transceiver, we can design an ECU component to look as the picture in Figure 2(b), in which the originally wired connections are connected to our platform and data is sent over the wireless medium. Applications with less-critical requirements can easily substitute their current connections using our wireless module and allow ECUs at different points to wirelessly communicate.

3. DEMO DESCRIPTION

As we illustrate in Figure 3(a), our demo consists of three hardware components: a pedal with an integrated body controller as the gateway, a cluster unit, and a digital tachometer used in commercial vehicles to track and log vehicular activity. We plan to connect these hardware to a CANoe analyzer [5] and packet sniffer to present real-time analysis of the data packets being exchanged between the three platforms. Overall, using the demo system configuration in Figure 3 we plan to present the following.

- We present a working prototype of a vehicle's body controller and gateway interacting with a digital tachometer and cluster to showcase the feasibility of using wireless technologies for intra-vehicular services.
- We show that the latency and reliability of wireless connections are suitable for supporting many intra-vehicular services, which have less critical time-bounds for data delivery.

4. SUMMARY

This work presents a working prototype of a wirelessly connected intra-vehicle communication system. With wireless technology comes the opportunity to reduce the costs of installation and maintenance for various in-vehicle sensing platforms. Our demo will present the performance statistics of wireless links interacting with the CAN-standards that are used today to deliver information from various ECU devices. We will show that wirelessly connected ECUs are capable of supporting many of the non-safety-critical applications.

Acknowledgments

This work was supported by MSIP/Korea Research Council for Industrial Science and Technology under intelligent situation cognition and IoT basic technology development project.

5. REFERENCES

[1] ISO 11898-1:2003 Road vehicles – Controller area network (CAN) – Part 1: Data link layer and physical signalling.

[2] SAE J1939. Recommended Practice for a Serial Control and Communications Vehicle Network, 2013.

[3] Hsin-Mu Tsai, O.K. Tonguz, C. Saraydar, T. Talty, M. Ames, and A MacDonald. Zigbee-based intra-car wireless sensor networks: a case study. *Wireless Communications, IEEE*, 14(6):67–77, December 2007.

[4] S. Tuohy, M. Glavin, E. Jones, M. Trivedi, and L. Kilmartin. Next generation wired intra-vehicle networks, a review. In *Intelligent Vehicles Symposium (IV), 2013 IEEE*, pages 777–782, June 2013.

[5] Vector Informatik. Product Information: CANoe, 2013.

Demo Abstract: RPL over Bluetooth Low Energy

Taeseop Lee, Hyung-Sin Kim, Myung-Sup Lee, and Saewoong Bahk
Department of Electrical and Computer Engineering and INMC
Seoul National University, Seoul, Republic of Korea

E-mail: {tslee, hskim, mslee, sbahk}@netlab.snu.ac.kr

ABSTRACT

In this demo, we present interoperability between Bluetooth Low Energy (BLE) and IPv6 routing protocol for low power and lossy networks (RPL). To make the operation of RPL over BLE feasible, we design an adaptation layer between BLE and RPL, termed *ALBER*. Specifically, we develop three technical features in *ALBER* which enable BLE to be combined with RPL. First, it broadcasts RPL control messages through BLE using advertising channels with low energy consumption. Second, it updates RPL routing table considering connection management of BLE. Lastly, it estimates link quality based on round trip time of link layer ping packets to provide routing metric for RPL. We implement our *ALBER* on Linux kernel. This demo will present an operation example of RPL over BLE using *ALBER* in a small scale multi-hop topology, where each node comprises a Raspberry Pi platform and a BLE dongle.

1. INTRODUCTION

Bluetooth Low Energy (BLE) and IEEE 802.15.4 are the most popular low power and low cost wireless protocols. Recently, 6LoWPAN was designed for both to deliver IPv6 packets, which enables them to connect to larger Internet as part of Internet of Things (IoT). So far, they have been used for different applications. While IEEE 802.15.4 has been widely used in multi-hop IoT networks with IPv6 routing protocol for low power and lossy networks (RPL), BLE has supported short range (single hop range) applications such as health care and smart watch.

However, BLE is now being developed further to support multi-hop IoT networks since it has its own advantages over IEEE 802.15.4 [1]. First of all, most of today's smartphones started to be equipped with BLE rather than IEEE 802.15.4, which remarkably improved usability and accessibility of BLE. As a result, BLE has a great impact on industry and works on a lot of commercial products as wireless communication modules [3]. Furthermore, it adopts a frequency hopping mechanism to avoid wireless interference in ISM bands, and connection-based operation to reduce transmission overhead. With these advantages, interconnecting standard routing protocols such as RPL with BLE would make it a strong competitor against IEEE 802.15.4 in long range (multi-hop) IoT applications.

Although the unique technical features of BLE make it outperform IEEE 802.15.4 in many scenarios, some of them incur interoperability issues when operating RPL over (6LoWPAN over) BLE. In this abstract, we address three design issues to interconnect RPL with BLE and present our own design to resolve them, termed *ALBER* (Adaptation Layer between BLE and RPL). We implement *ALBER* on the Linux kernel. Our platform consists of Raspberry Pi for Linux device and Broadcom BCM4356ZAE for BLE module. Lastly, this demo will present a small scale operation example of RPL over BLE using *ALBER*.

SenSys'15 November 1-4, 2015, Seoul, Republic of Korea
ACM 978-1-4503-3631-4/15/11.
DOI: http://dx.doi.org/10.1145/2809695.2817857 .

2. DESIGN OF RPL OVER BLE

BLE provides two types of channels; 3 *advertising* and 37 *data* channels. *Advertising* channels are designed for device discovery and broadcast of simple data packets. When a node transmits a packet through an *advertising* channel, it does not need to have connection with its destination node. On the other hand, to transmit a packet through a *data* channel, each node should have a valid connection with its destination node. BLE establishes a connection between two neighbor nodes through handshaking procedures. Once they are connected, they are synchronized in time domain and share a periodic wake-up schedule (i.e., connection interval) to exchange packets in energy saving mode.

We consider *pros* and *cons* of using each channel type provided by BLE and design *ALBER* to utilize each channel type to transmit different types of packets. Specifically, it uses *advertising* channels to transmit RPL control messages such as DIO and DIS which are designed for device discovery at routing layer. Our intuition behind this design is that BLE needs to deliver these messages to unconnected neighbor nodes since RPL generates them to find a new parent node or send its rank information to all neighbor nodes. On the other hand, *ALBER* maps DAO and data packets into *data* channels since these packets are transmitted to each connected parent node. The channel mapping of *ALBER* enables resource constrained nodes to exchange packets consuming low energy, and to construct and recover routing topology using RPL.

However, there still remain the following three design issues to fully utilize the advantages of RPL over BLE, which are what our *ALBER* is aiming to resolve.

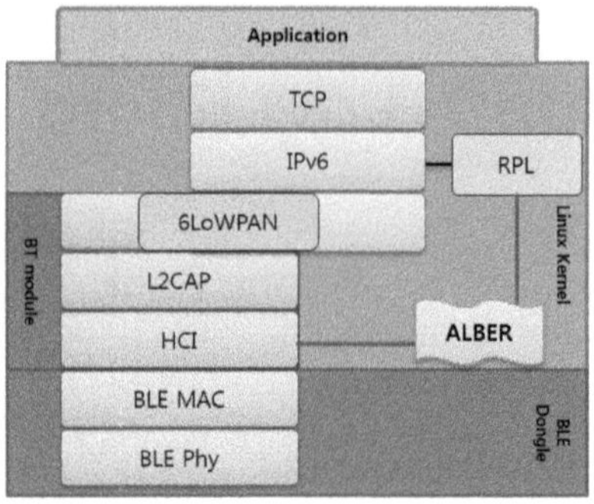

Figure 1: Protocol stack of RPL over BLE with *ALBER* on Linux kernel version 3.17.

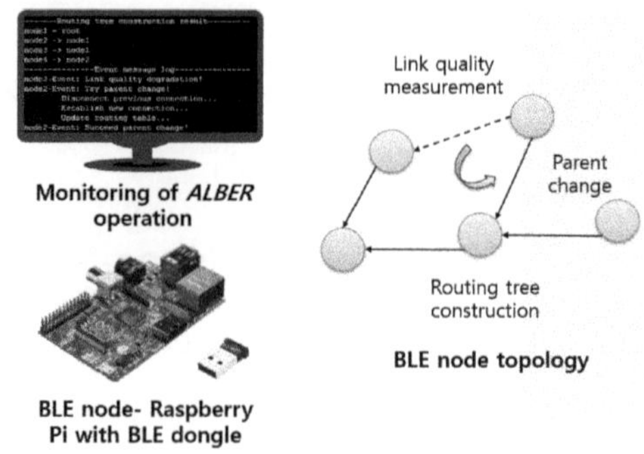

Figure 2: Our demo scenario to show the operation of RPL over BLE with *ALBER*.

- **RPL control message exchange in *advertising* channels**: Unlike *data* channel, *advertising* channels are used to deliver packets in an asynchronous manner which consists of advertising (transmitter) and scanning (receiver) mechanisms. However, it requires each node to turn on its radio module for a long time to exchange even a single packet, which results in large energy consumption. To alleviate the problem, *ALBER* includes a variant of low power listening (LPL) mechanism (sender-initiated asynchronous MAC) when using *advertising* channels, rather than applying default advertising and scanning of BLE. Thanks to duty cycling characteristics of LPL, *ALBER* significantly reduces energy consumption required for delivering RPL control messages through *advertising* channels.

- **Parent change with connection management**: RPL standard allows a node to change its parent node regardless of the underlying link layer status. Differently from IEEE 802.15.4, BLE exchanges packets through *data* channels after connection establishment, which incurs a problem of such an arbitrary parent update. Specifically, after RPL changes a parent node, all the packets targeted for the new parent start to be dropped at 6LoWPAN rather than going down to the link layer. This inefficient behavior is due to lack of a valid connection and repeats until the underlying BLE cuts off the connection with the previous parent node and establishes one with the new parent node. In contrast, we give *ALBER* the authority to accept or reject parent change request from RPL. When accepting the change request, *ALBER* first holds it and triggers a connection change of BLE. This allows RPL to have parent change and its resulting entry update in the routing table after confirming that the new connection has been established.

- **RTT-based link estimation for routing metric**: Although RPL decouples the routing metric from the main standard, the most widely used routing metric is the combination of ETX and hop distance. However, this routing metric cannot be used in RPL over BLE since BLE MAC (in Figure 1) does not provide the number of retransmissions for the upper layers. To estimate the link quality which is necessary for routing metric, *ALBER* makes each child node transmit link layer ping packets to its parent node through *data* channels and obtain the average round trip time (RTT) using an exponentially weighted moving average filter. Given that each retransmission induces a constant delay of as much as connection interval in *data* channels, we obtain ETX from measured RTT values and use it for routing metric. Our link estimation scheme has a trade-off between ping packet overhead and estimation accuracy, which needs to be controlled considering given environmental conditions.

3. IMPLEMENTATION

We have implemented *ALBER* on Linux kernel version 3.17 where 6LoWPAN for BLE and BLE host part already exist. To begin with, we implemented RPL on the Linux kernel based on Contiki RPL source code [2]. As shown in Figure 1, we placed our *ALBER* between this RPL and the host controller interface (HCI) of BLE to handle interoperability issues and implemented each function using various HCI commands and events.

As an example, we show the case of *RPL control message exchange over advertising channels.* Given that current 6LoWPAN for BLE cannot use *advertising* channels, we design RPL to transmit its control messages to *ALBER* instead of 6LoWPAN, which forces BLE to deliver them through *advertising* channels. *ALBER* achieves this channel mapping by sequentially calling *LE Set Advertising Parameters Command*, *LE Set Advertising Data Command*, and *LE Set Advertise Enable Command.*

4. DEMO SCENARIO

In our demo, we show a real time operation of *ALBER* in a small scale topology. Figure 2 depicts the specific demo scenario. We will deploy multiple BLE nodes (combination of Raspberry Pi and BLE dongle) in the conference room, which will use RPL to construct tree routing topology. We will trigger some RPL functions such as parent change by arbitrarily changing link conditions. Events that occur in *ALBER* operation will be displayed on the monitor through log messages.

5. REFERENCES

[1] Bluetooth 4.1 features & technical descriptions. Bluetooth SIG, Nov. 2013. [Online]. Available: `http://www.bluetooth.com`.

[2] Contiki RPL code for Linux. JoÃčo Pedro Taveira, Jan. 2014. [Online]. Available: `https://github.com/joaopedrotaveira/linux-rpl`.

[3] R. Heydon. *Bluetooth low energy: the developer's handbook.* Prentice Hall, 2012.

Demo Abstract: IAS: Information Analytics for Sensors

Soma Bandyopadhyay, Arijit Ukil, Chetanya Puri, Arpan Pal, Rituraj Singh, Tulika Bose
Innovation Labs, Kolkata
TATA Consultancy Services, India
{soma.bandyopadhyay, arijit.ukil, chetanya.puri, arpan.pal, singh.rituraj, tulika.bose}@tcs.com

ABSTRACT

Sensors are one of the primary building blocks of IoT. Owing to close proximity of physical world, sensors often collect sensitive information. Invariably, sensor data has rich information content. Here we propose a novel solution IAS: Information Analytics for Sensors to unlock massive potential of sensor data through information analytics and demonstrate an alerting mechanism based on criticality of sensor information. ECG anomaly detection for healthcare, unusual appliance operation detection from smart energy meter data, bad road condition as well as activity detection from accelerometer data are typical use-case scenarios. We use robust statistical and information theoretic approaches. Our approach is unsupervised and is completely sensor agnostic. This abstract provides overview of design and implementation of our tool IAS along with obtained results tested on publicly available datasets. Last but not the least, IAS validates that outliers contain most delicate information.

Categories and Subject Descriptors

H.4 [**Information Systems Applications**]: Miscellaneous

Keywords

Sensor, Sensor Dynamics, Outlier, Information, Performance

1. INTRODUCTION

Smart applications in healthcare, energy, transportation etc. carry delicate information that is mostly associated with abnormalities. Like nonstandard usage of power by households has a strong correlation with user's daily life style, privacy [7] or existence of anomalous device in their premises. Similarly in healthcare, critical information, such as discord in ECG data signifies a vital status of patient's health condition. Whereas outliers in accelerometer data indicates bad road condition, as well as detect activity of the user. An alert can be generated for all such cases. In this abstract, our proposed solution IAS-Information Analytics for Sensors (Figure 1) detects anomalous sensor signals carrying important information and measures that criticality. It is not application dependent and minimum knowledge of sensor data type is required. We address two non-trivial issues. First, we identify sensor signal dynamics, secondly derive abnormalities in sensor content signifying critical information, and measure information using similarity/dissimilarity, variation of information, entropy [6]. IAS evaluates outliers are informative. We demonstrate the efficacy of IAS using real field accelerometer, as well as ECG data.

SenSys'15, November 1–4, 2015, Seoul, South Korea..
ACM 978-1-4503-3631-4/15/11.
DOI: http://dx.doi.org/10.1145/2809695.2817858 .

2. OVERVIEW

Sensor dynamics derivation: We define sensor dynamics as extracted characteristics of the sensor signal like quasi-periodicity, stationary, non-stationary, and random. Sensor dynamics is derived by formulating suitable statistical, data distribution and information theoretic model. **Outlier class adaptation and outlier detection**: We adapt three-outlier classes [3] : point, contextual, collaborative based on derived sensor signal dynamics (Figure 2). Appropriate outlier detection algorithm belongs to adapted outlier class, for example: IAS adapts collaborative class for quasi-periodic sensor signal and uses subsequence based or clustering based outlier detection algorithm. **Information measure**: We quantify information based on entropy (Shannon and Rényi's), measure of similarity as mutual information based variation of information, dynamic time warping (DTW) based distance metric for multiple and single time series. Shannon's Entropy for a random variable X with sample space $S_x = x_i : i = 1, 2, 3, ...n : H(X) = -\sum_i p_i(X)$ $log_2 p_i(X)$. Mutual information of two random variables X and Y : $I(X;Y) = \sum_{i,j} p_{ij}(X,Y)\ log_2(\frac{p_{ij}(X,Y)}{p_i(X)p_i(Y)})$. The joint entropy, $H(X,Y) = \sum_{ij} p_{ij}(X,Y)\ log_2 p_{ij}(X,Y)$. Normalized Variation of information $D(X,Y)$ which is based on mutual information is defined as $D = 1 - \frac{I(X;Y)}{H(X,Y)}$.

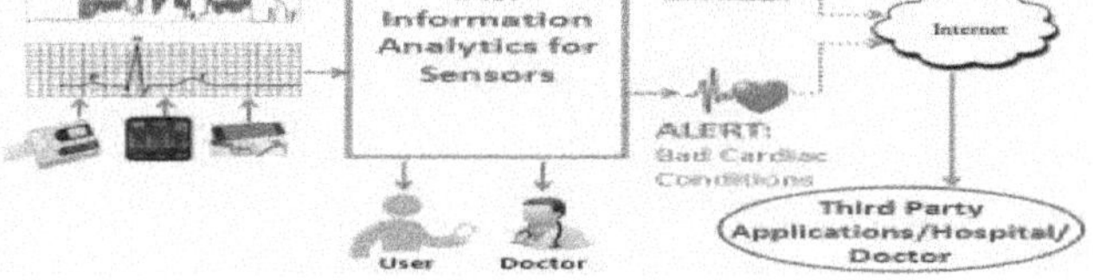

Figure 1: System View

3. EMPIRICAL EVALUATION

In this section, we demonstrate evaluation of outliers and information measure based on univariate sensor data of *type1* (Z-axis Accelerometer data [1] of reading no. '7') with synthetic anomalies and *type2* (ECG data of patient 108 [2]).

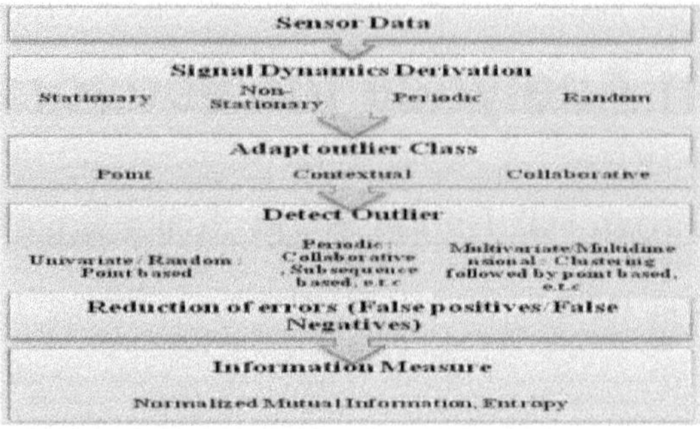

Figure 2: IAS Architecture

IAS first derives signal dynamics of sensor signals. It detects *type1* sensor data as random based on the derived statistical properties (Figure 3a) like non uniformity of mean and standard deviation, and detects *type2* sensor signal as quasi-periodic based on statistical and autocorrelation properties (Figure 3d). **Type1 sensor**: IAS adapts point based outlier detection class since derived signal dynamics of *type1* sensor is univariate random. It has chosen Thompson's Tau [5] method to detect outliers (Figure 3b) which uses normalized time series $\widehat{\mathbf{y}} = (\mathbf{y} - \mu)\backslash\sigma$ with mean, μ and standard deviation, σ and a rejection threshold $R = \dfrac{t_{\alpha\backslash 2}(n-1)}{(\sqrt{n}\sqrt{n-2+t^2_{\alpha\backslash 2}})}$ where $t_{\alpha\backslash 2}$ is critical value from Student-t distribution and n is the sample size. **Type2 sensor**: IAS adapts collaborative outlier class (Figure 3e), as derived signal dynamics of *type2* is quasi-periodic and subsequence-based outlier detection method [4] has been selected. Subsequence s of length N of time-series τ_t is discord in τ_t, which is the largest distance to its nearest non-self-match for $s \subset S$ [4]. IAS derives information of *type1* signal by calculating variation of information between normal segments and segments containing outliers, and for *type2* by calculating DTW for various subsequences (Figure 3c, 3f) showing outliers have higher information measure. **Performance Score**: For *type1* and *type2* precision, $p = 1$ and recall, $r = 1$. These are computed based on ground truth availability.

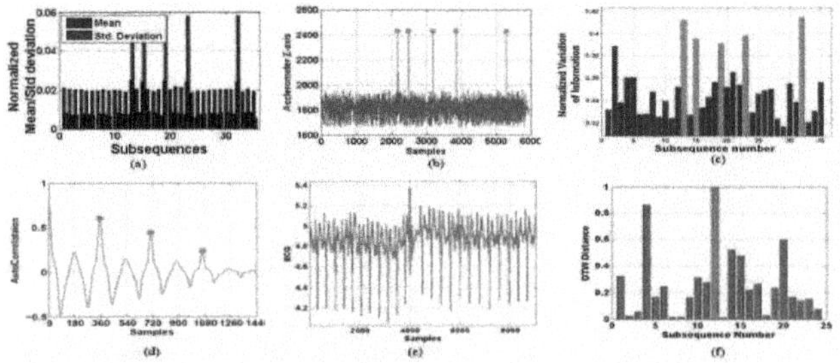

Figure 3: (a) Statistics (μ,σ^2) for different subsequences (b) Thompson's Tau based anomaly detection in *type1* data (highlighted red) (c) $D(X,Y)$ of different subsequences w.r.t each other with subsequences containing outliers (d) Quasi-Periodicity detection for *type2* (e) BFDD based anomaly detection in *type2* (highlighted red)(f) DTW distance as measure of information for *type2*, with 12th subsequence showing higher DTW score.

4. IMPLEMENTATION

A prototype of IAS is developed by using JAVA. IAS analyzes signal dynamics of various sensors and categorizes them. In the next phase, it finds the appropriate outlier detection algorithm by adapting appropriate outlier class based on sensor signal dynamics. IAS finds information measure of the sensor data based on critical information and outliers and generates alerts. IAS shows results in graphical and textual forms as 1. detected outliers, 2. various analysis like statistical, information measure, 3. performance score as True/False Positive/Negatives (TP, FP, TN, FN). Graphical representation of *type2* (ECG) signal with detected outliers (highlighted in red) in upper window and below several statistics as signal dynamics, outlier class, outlier detection type, alerts subsequence and performance measure have been shown (Figure 4). Similarly, results for *type1* data are also inferred using this system. IAS is a complete package for sensor agnostic information analytics.

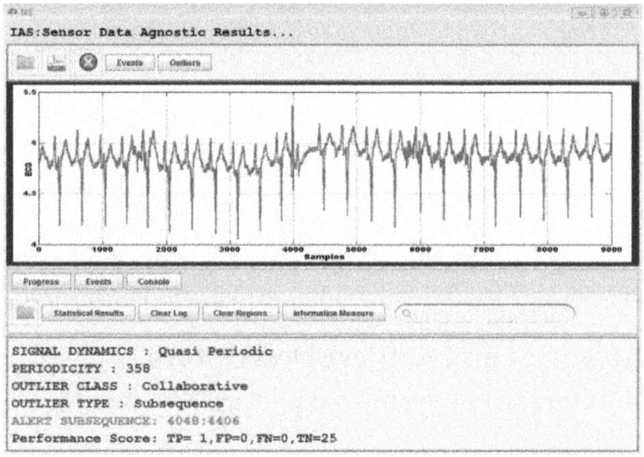

Figure 4: IAS - Displaying ECG Anomaly

5. DEMO DESCRIPTION

Objective of this demo is to present our sensor agnostic information analytics model to detect outlier, measure information content, and generate appropriate alert from abnormal information. Different sensor signals like ECG, smart meter, accelerometer would be given as input. Graphical and textual display of information analytics will be presented as outcome.

6. REFERENCES

[1] http://archive.ics.uci.edu/ml/machine-learning-databases/00287/.

[2] www.physionet.org/physiobank/database/mitdb.

[3] C. C. Aggarwal. *OUTLIER ANALYSIS*. Springer, 2013.

[4] M. C. Chuah and F. Fu. Ecg anomaly detection via time series analysis. *ACM ISPA*, pages 123–135, 2007.

[5] J. M. Cimbala. *OUTLIERS*. Penn State Univ., 2011.

[6] A. Ukil, S. Bandyopadhyay, and A. Pal. Iot privacy: To be private or not to be private. *IEEE INFOCOM*, pages 123–124, 2014.

[7] A. Ukil, S. Bandyopadhyay, and A. Pal. Spa: Smart meter privacy analyzer: Demo abstract. *ACM BuildSyS*, 2014.

Demo Abstract: Towards Recognition of Rich Non-Negative Emotions Using Daily Wearable Devices

Sinh Huynh, Rajesh Krishna Balan, Youngki Lee
School of Information Systems
Singapore Management University
{npshuynh.2014, rajesh, youngkilee}@smu.edu.sg

ABSTRACT

Recognizing user emotional states while running entertainment applications such as playing game or watching video is very important to understand and improve user experience. In this work, we designed a practical system using wearable physiological sensors including skin electrical conductivity and photoplethysmography (PPG) to recognize popular non-negative emotions that people experience when they watch videos or play games on their mobile devices. We demonstrates how our system recognizes emotional states in two phases: (1) classifying the levels of *arousal* (high or low) and *valence* (positive or neutral) at the accuracy of 94.74% and 78.95% respectively; (2) recognizing three non-negative emotions: excitement, contentment, amusement by mapping arousal and valence levels using Russel circumplex model of affect.

Categories and Subject Descriptors

J.4 [**Computer Applications**]: Social and Behavioral Sciences

Keywords

Emotion; wearable; physiological sensing; accuracy

1. INTRODUCTION

Many research studies have been conducted to recognize human emotions using speech, facial expression, gesture, or physiological signals. However, prior research work was limited in that they mainly focused on clearly distinguishable emotions (e.g., happiness, sadness, anger, neutral) [1] in well-established emotion space [2]. In this paper, we designed a specialized emotion recognition system in the context of mobile entertainment that newly focuses on three popular non-negative emotions: excitement, amusement, and contentment. The non-negative emotions are not easily separable from each other and people may feel more than one of these emotions simultaneously during game play or video watching. To recognize these emotions with potential overlap, we take an approach to classify the intensity level of each emotion instead of recognizing one specific emotion at a moment.

We notice that physiological changes such as sweat gland activity, heart activity, and circulation of blood are good indicator of emotions. Unlike the facial expression, voice, and gesture, which people can manipulate, the physiological changes are caused by the Autonomic Nervous System (ANS), which functions without conscious and voluntary control. Accordingly, it is likely that physiological signals reflect "inner" characteristics of human reaction to emotional stimuli. Our approach has advantages over other image-recognition-based methods that do not capture subtle emotions not reflected in facial expressions.

The novelty of our work lies in that we built a system to detect a richer set of non-negative emotions using non-intrusive physiological sensors. This is unique as prior work mainly focused on classifying positive and negative emotions that are easily separable. We are working towards a direction to leverage such richer emotions to automatically rate various stages and scenes of mobile games and provide natural user feedback to the mobile app developers.

2. SYSTEM OVERVIEW

The overview of the system is shown in Figure 1. Physiological signals are obtained by wearable sensors (Shimmer sensing device) and streamed to an Android mobile phone. The data processing/feature extraction block and emotion recognition block are implemented on the mobile. Notice that the outcome of emotion recognition system would be represented as dimensional emotions (e.g. high arousal, positive) [2] and intensity levels of non-negative emotions (e.g. high excitement, low contentment).

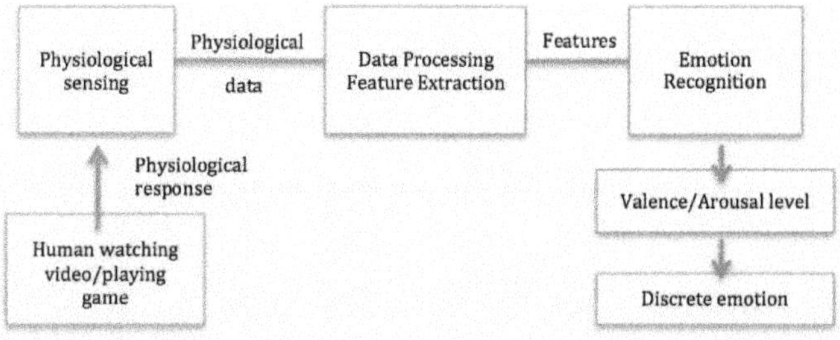

Figure 1: Emotion recognition system overview.

SenSys'15, November 1–4, 2015, Seoul, South Korea.
ACM 978-1-4503-3631-4/15/11.
http://dx.doi.org/10.1145/2809695.2817859

3. PRELIMINARY EXPERIMENTS

3.1 Experimental Setup

We conducted an experiment with 6 subjects using videos as emotion-elicitors to find the relationship between emotional states and physiological signals. After completing consent form, participants were asked to wear a Shimmer sensing device [3] to measure and record the skin conductivity and the optical heart pulse signals through the experiment. Participants were also asked to watch through a slide show on pre-prepared mobile phone. The slide show includes 7 short videos (2-4 minutes) and sell-assessment survey about the emotional experience while watching each video. The videos were selected from popular movies and Youtube clips to elicit various non-negative emotions including neutral state, excitement, amusement, and contentment. We labeled the physiological data recorded during each video based on self-assessment of participants.

3.2 Emotion Recognition

The physiological data collected from the experiment was segmented into samples corresponding to starting and ending times of each video. For the skin conductivity (SC) signals, we used a low-pass filter to remove noises. Heart rate variability (HRV, beat-to-beat interval series) is extracted from the PPG data using peak detection.

From skin conductivity and HRV series data, we extracted 35 features in various domains including statistical features in time domain, frequency domain, Poincare plot geometric statistics, and multi scale sample entropy. We used Correlation based Feature Selection to select best feature subset from the 35 features for classification model. This feature selection algorithm evaluates merit of feature subset using Pearson correlation formula, and search for the feature subset with the highest merit using Best-First-Search with maximum 5 times of consecutive non-improving loop. Because of limited size of observations, we used selected features with simple algorithms such as Naive Bayes and linear logistic to classify dimensional emotions (arousal: high/low and valence: positive/non-positive).

Table 1: Selected features for dimensional emotion classification

	Best features for classification
Arousal	Mean(SC responses), STDEV (SC), Mean(HRV entropy)
Valence	Frequency of SC Response, Low frequency (0.04-0.15hz) power of HRV, Mean(HRV entropy)

Table 2: Performance of dimensional emotion classification

	Logistic	Naive Bayes	Random Forest
Arousal	89.67%	94.75%	86.84%
Valence	76.32%	71.05%	78.95%

Using mapping rules (Table 3) adapted from Russel cirmcumplex model of affects, we can recognize three emotions excitement, amusement, and contentment at the accuracy of 76.32%, 76.32% and 78.95% respectively.

Table 3: Rules mapping dimensional emotions to discrete emotions

	High	Low
Amusement	[High arousal, Positive]	Others
Excitement	[High arousal, *]	[High arousal, *]
Contentment	[High arousal, *]	[High arousal, *]

4. DEMONSTRATION

We plan to show our demonstration in two parts. In the first part, we have prepared a video to show some observations of physiological signals recorded from our experiment. Specifically, we will replay how skin conductivity and heart rate variability changes corresponding to different emotional states. We also demonstrate the process of how emotions are recognized from the physiological data visually.

The second part is experimental demonstration in which we will allow voluntary participants to try our emotion recognition system firsthand with a Shimmer wearable sensing device and a mobile phone. Participants will first be asked to watch a video with natural scene and soothing music so that our system can get the baseline of their physiological changes. After that, they can autonomously pick some video from Youtube or our selected videos to watch on the mobile phone. Our system will show recognition outcome after each video watching session. Participants will be asked to confirm their recognized emotion including: levels of arousal and valence, intensity levels of excitement, amusement, and contentment during watching prior video. A same experimental demonstration with mobile games will also be conducted.

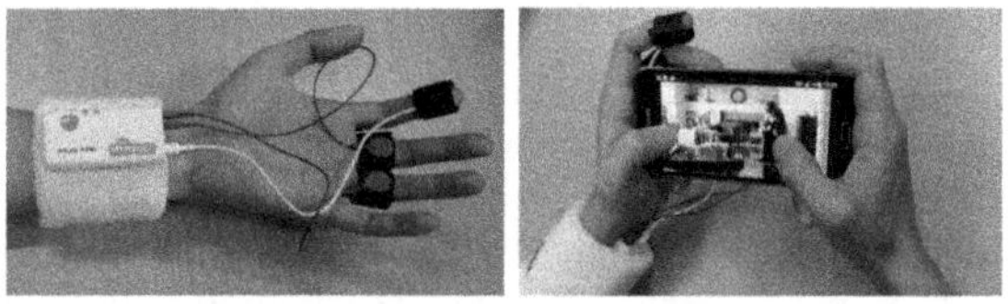

Figure 2: Participant wearing sensing device (left) and watching video on mobile (right).

5. ACKNOWLEDGEMENT

This research is supported by the National Research Foundation Singapore under its Interactive Digital Media (IDM) Strategic Research Programme.

6. REFERENCES

[1] C. L. Lisetti and F. Nasoz, "Using noninvasive wearable computers to recognize human emotions from physiological signals," *EURASIP journal on applied signal processing*, vol. 2004, pp. 1672–1687, 2004.

[2] J. A. Russell, "A circumplex model of affect.," *Journal of personality and social psychology*, vol. 39, no. 6, p. 1161, 1980.

[3] A. Burns, B. R. Greene, M. J. McGrath, T. J. O'Shea, B. Kuris, S. M. Ayer, F. Stroiescu, and V. Cionca, "Shimmer-a wireless sensor platform for noninvasive biomedical research," *Sensors Journal, IEEE*, vol. 10, no. 9, pp. 1527–1534, 2010.

Demo Abstract: Towards Global Interworking of IoT Systems - oneM2M Interworking Proxy Entities

Jaeseok Yun, Sung-Chan Choi, Nak-Myoung Sung, Jaeho Kim
Embedded Software Convergence Research Center
Korea Electronics Technology Institute
Seongnam, S. Korea
{jaeseok, csc, nmsung, jhkim}@keti.re.kr

ABSTRACT

The oneM2M global initiative has been working to standardize horizontal machine-to-machine (M2M) and the Internet of Things (IoT) service layer specifications for globally interoperable M2M/IoT solutions. However, there exist a myriad of embedded sensor systems not complying with oneM2M, such as *de facto* IoT standards (e.g., AllJoyn and IoTivity). In this paper, we present our effort in global interworking of IoT systems across multiple M2M/IoT standards, in particular, on a global scale. By implementing specialized oneM2M entities for interworking, interworking proxy entities (IPEs), we demonstrate a promise of globally interoperable IoT systems interconnected with all kinds of embedded systems.

1. INTRODUCTION

The Internet of Things (IoT) represents a technological revolution where all the objects in the world will be connected each other and comprise a huge network of networks with advances in various technical fields, including identification systems, short-range wireless communication (ZigBee, Bluetooth, WiFi), distributed sensor networks, and cellular networks and widespread use of smartphones. The IoT enables the 'things' to share their status and surrounding environments, finally providing new innovative services to people, e.g., doing daily tasks without human intervention.

Due to such IoT enabling technologies, embedded sensor network systems also facilitate Internet connectivity, and could provide data accessibility at anytime and from anywhere. However, many industry verticals rely on proprietary IoT solutions consisting of various hardware and software components to provide IoT services. For example, embedded network systems from smart home and healthcare industries would not be able to be interworked due to distinct underlying access networks or heterogeneous hardware and software systems, even though the data set shared could be used more efficiently, e.g., automated emergency call service.

SenSys'15, November 1–4, 2015, Seoul, Republic of Korea.
ACM 978-1-4503-3631-4/15/11.
http://dx.doi.org/10.1145/2809695.2817860.

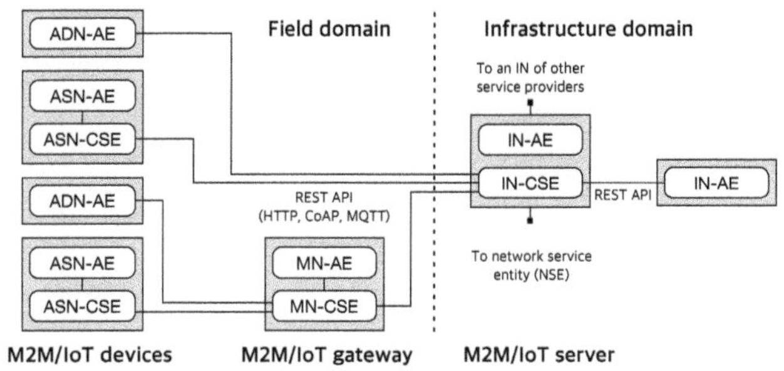

Figure 1: The oneM2M reference architecture.

The interoperability issue across IoT systems motivated the establishment of the oneM2M initiative[1]. The oneM2M is a partnership project formed by seven standards development organizations (SDOs) to standardize horizontal machine-to-machine (M2M) and IoT service layer specifications for globally interoperable M2M/IoT solutions. However, there exist another *de facto* standardization works within company alliances like AllSeen Alliance[2] and Open Interconnect Consortium[3]. Both are mainly focusing on providing developers with open-source development framework for IoT services, called AllJoyn and IoTivity, respectively. Such standards market fragmentation motivated our effort in global interworking of IoT systems across multiple IoT standards.

In this paper, we present the implementation of oneM2M interworking proxy entities (IPEs) for oneM2M systems to interwork with AllJoyn systems. The main objective of the IPE implementation is to allow IoT applications (developed complying with oneM2M) to access the AllJoyn devices (e.g., collect data and send command) via oneM2M service platforms. With the IPEs and smartphone app developed, we demonstrate service scenarios by interworking between two standards. We hope that this work will be a step towards a globally interoperable IoT ecosystem with the widespread adoption of oneM2M standards and IPEs in most industries.

2. ONEM2M STANDARDS AND IPES

Swetina *et al.* demonstrated well oneM2M standards [1]. The oneM2M architecture is based on a layered model comprising application layer, common service layer, and underlying network service layer, as shown in Fig. 1. Application

[1] http://onem2m.org/
[2] https://allseenalliance.org/
[3] http://openinterconnect.org/

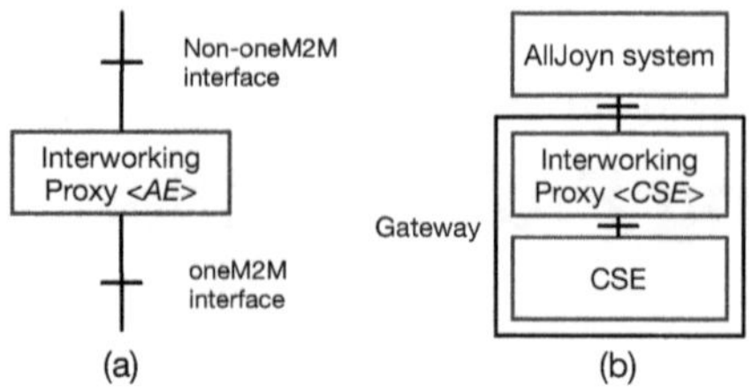

Figure 2: oneM2M IPE (a) AE and (b) CSE use.

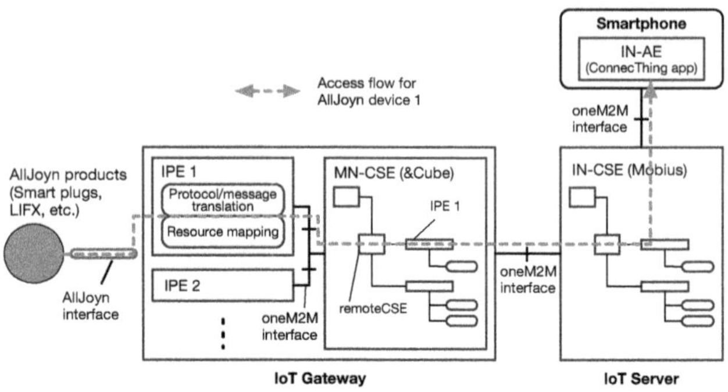

Figure 3: Interworking architecture for AllJoyn.

entity (AE) represents application services located in device, gateway, or server. Common service entity (CSE) represents an instantiation of a set of common service functions (CSFs) with which the oneM2M platform provides common services, including registration, data management and repository, device management, security, discovery, subscription and notification, etc. Network service entity (NSE) implies network services from the underlying network to be utilized by the CSEs. The oneM2M architecture divides M2M/IoT environments into two domains (infrastructure and field domain), and defines four types of nodes: infrastructure node (IN), middle node (MN), application service node (ASN), and application dedicated node (ADN).

The oneM2M defines a specialized AE, interworking proxy entity (IPE) for interworking with non-oneM2M systems as shown in Fig. 2a. Its functionalities are summarized as two main parts: supporting a non-oneM2M interface to translate non-oneM2M protocols and messages to oneM2M-specific ones, and mapping non-oneM2M data models into oneM2M resources, which are eventually exposed to oneM2M services [2]. Although oneM2M defines IPE as 'AE', we newly define the IPE for AllJoyn interworking as 'CSE' as shown in Fig. 2b. The CSE use is mainly intended to map not only data models of AllJoyn services, but also AllJoyn device information into oneM2M resource structures. Fig. 3 illustrates the overall interworking architecture for AllJoyn devices based on CSE-based IPEs, where we assumed that an IPE (e.g., IPE 1) is created for interworking with an AllJoyn device (e.g., smart plug). The IPE 1 performs protocol/message translation and then mapping AllJoyn device and service information into MN-CSE resources, which are eventually accessed by IN-AEs (e.g., ConnecThing app) via IN-CSE.

3. IMPLEMENTATION

We have implemented IN-CSE and MN-CSE using 'Mobius' and '&Cube', which are open source IoT platforms for

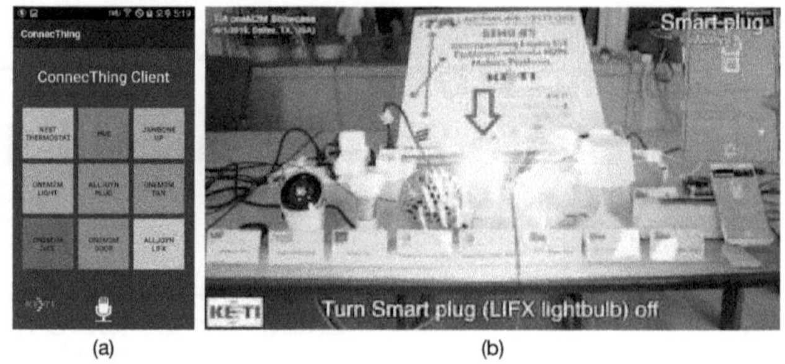

Figure 4: (a) ConnecThing app and (b) demo videos.

servers and gateways, respectively, provided by the OCEAN (Open allianCE for iot stANdards)[4]. The Mobius is running on a Red Hat Linux server, and the &Cube is installed in a Raspberry-Pi, a single-board Linux-installed computer. The IPEs are implemented as CSEs in the Pi, registered with the &Cube. For AllJoyn devices, we have chosen two types of smart plugs from Dawon DNS and PowerTech, publicly announced as AllJoyn showcase products. Finally, we have created a smartphone application (i.e., IN-AE), called ConnecThing (see Fig. 4a), which enables users to interact with the Mobius, that is, retrieve data collected by smart plugs (e.g., power consumption) or send them control commands (e.g., on or off). The ConnecThing app is implemented using representational state transfer (REST) application programming interfaces (APIs) provided by the Mobius, so any developers who are familiar with the APIs will be able to create their own applications. Fig. 4b illustrates a captured snapshot of our demo videos published on YouTube[5,6].

4. CONCLUSIONS

In this paper, we have presented our implementation work for interworking oneM2M systems with AllJoyn devices. We have implemented interworking proxy entities (IPEs) based on oneM2M common service entity (CSE), that enables users to interact with AllJoyn devices via a smartphone application, called ConnecThing. Using the IPEs and ConnecThing app, we have demonstrated interworking service scenarios between oneM2M and AllJoyn standards systems.

5. ACKNOWLEDGMENTS

This work was supported by Institute for Information & communication Technology Promotion (IITP) grant funded by the Korea government (MSIP) (No.B0184-15-1003, The Development of oneM2M Conformance Testing Tool and QoS Technology).

6. REFERENCES

[1] J. Swetina, G. Lu, P. Jacobs, F. Ennesser, and J. Song. Toward a standardized common M2M service layer platform: Introduction to oneM2M. *IEEE Wireless Comm.*, 21(3):20–26, June 2014.

[2] oneM2M. TS-0001-Functional-Architecture-V-1.6.1. Technical Specification, 2015.

[4] http://iotocean.org/

[5] https://youtu.be/FngoyncRhCM

[6] https://youtu.be/zHfIQwLBPsM

Demo Abstract: Choco - A Versatile Communication Protocol in Wireless Sensor Networks

Yuki Katsumata, Makoto Suzuki, Hiroyuki Morikawa
Research Center for Advanced Science and Technology, The University of Tokyo
4-6-1, Komaba, Meguro-ku, Tokyo, Japan
{den, makoto, mori}@mlab.t.u-tokyo.ac.jp

ABSTRACT

We present a communication protocol called Choco, which efficiently supports various traffic demands with end-to-end reliability in multi-hop Wireless Sensor Networks (WSNs). To achieve this, Choco uses fine-grained scheduling based on the insight that acknowledgements (ACKs) between ends can be delivered with little overhead using concurrent transmission. Specifically, the slot assignment is dynamically scheduled up to several times a second according to traffic loads and packet losses. We show that Choco achieves higher efficiency and reliability than ORPL+BF, which is a state-of-the-art collection protocol, for periodic traffic environments. Also, we show that in a networked imaging application, which generates burst traffic, Choco can successfully collect 5 VGA images with high efficiency from 5 nodes in approximately 168 s in an average 4.0 hop network.

1. OVERVIEW

A multi-hop WSN protocol which can efficiently support various traffic demands makes developing applications easier. This is because developers do not need to choose a suitable protocol out of many existing protocols. However, existing communication protocols support specific traffic demands. Therefore, depending on the generated traffic, different protocols and parameters must be chosen appropriately.

To tackle this issue, we are developing Choco. We focus on efficiently achieving end-to-end reliability in two major traffic demands, periodic and burst. Many applications such as environmental monitoring, structural health monitoring and networked imaging generate either or both of the traffic.

Choco is designed based on the insight that ACKs between ends can be delivered with little overhead using concurrent transmission. Choco uses synchronized slots like LWB [1], which is a collection protocol using concurrent transmission, as shown in Fig. 1. All nodes communicate according to the scheduling packets which a sink node computes and transmits. In a slot, at most one packet is transmitted by an Initiator and forwarded by Receivers with concurrent transmission. The packet is eventually delivered to the sink node.

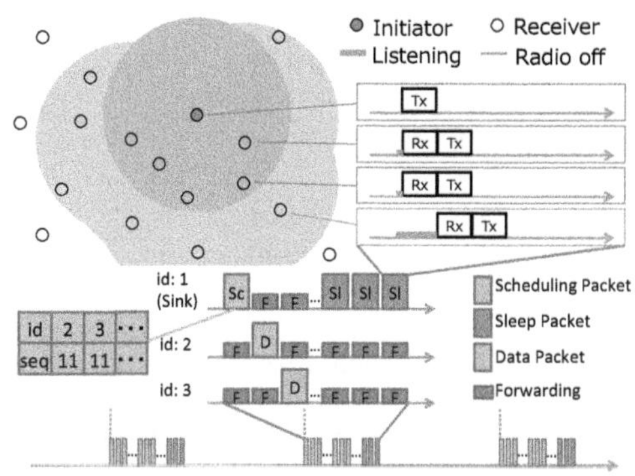

Figure 1: The overview of Choco

The differences between Choco and LWB are slot scheduling mechanisms and send buffer management. In Choco, scheduling packets designate an Initiator and sequence number of a packet to be transmitted in each of the following slots. Each designated node transmits the designated packet and deletes packets whose sequence numbers are smaller than the designated sequence number from its send buffer.

Scheduling packets are computed based on backlogs. A backlog refers to the number of packets in each node's send buffer. The sink node calculates backlogs from data packets' header, and assigns slots to the nodes whose backlogs are unknown or not zero. When backlogs of all nodes are zero, the sink node instructs all nodes to enter a sleep mode by sending sleep packets which include a wake-up time. On the wake-up time, the sink node considers all backlogs unknown.

Choco achieves end-to-end reliability for the two reasons. First, nodes retain all packets which have the possibility to be retransmitted. Second, since backlogs are not updated when a packet is lost, a sink node continues to reschedule until the successful reception or node failure detection.

Choco efficiently handles sudden traffic fluctuation without explicitly notifying traffic demands. When no traffic is generated, all nodes can sleep for a long time. When heavy traffic is generated, an additional schedule is distributed immediately after the latest transmitted schedule is exhausted.

Choco has three advantages compared to LWB. First, Choco can be applied for loss-intolerant applications since Choco provides end-to-end reliability. Second, Choco is more efficient because the number of redundant transmissions, a parameter in concurrent transmission, can be re-

SenSys'15, November 1–4, 2015, Seoul, South Korea.
ACM 978-1-4503-3631-4/15/11.
DOI: http://dx.doi.org/10.1145/2809695.2817861 .

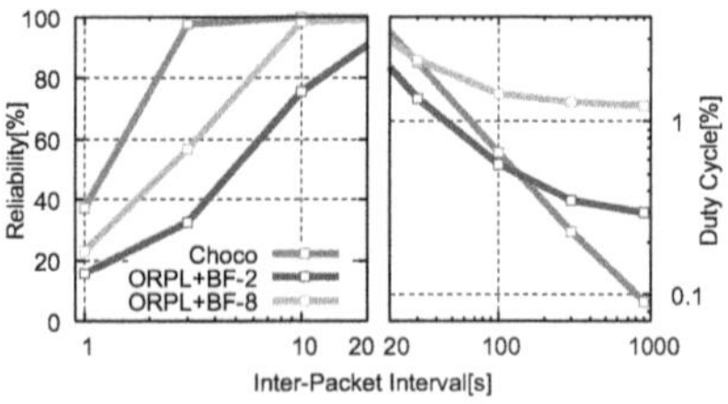

Figure 2: Summarized results (periodic traffic)

Duty Cycle[%]	IPI:1s	IPI:3s	IPI:10s	IPI:30s	IPI:100s	IPI:300s	IPI:900s
Choco	18.59	19.97	6.40	2.18	0.66	**0.23**	**0.09**
ORPL+BF-2	**7.78**	**6.87**	**4.12**	**1.35**	**0.56**	0.35	0.30
ORPL+BF-8	11.62	8.88	4.45	2.25	1.45	1.30	1.24

Reliability[%]	IPI:1s	IPI:3s	IPI:10s	IPI:30s	IPI:100s	IPI:300s	IPI:900s
Choco	**37.56**	**97.49**	**100**	**100**	**100**	**100**	**100**
ORPL+BF-2	15.91	32.84	75.45	99.71	99.93	99.91	**100**
ORPL+BF-8	23.18	56.84	98.47	99.76	**100**	**100**	**100**

Table 1: Comparison of the collection protocols (periodic traffic)

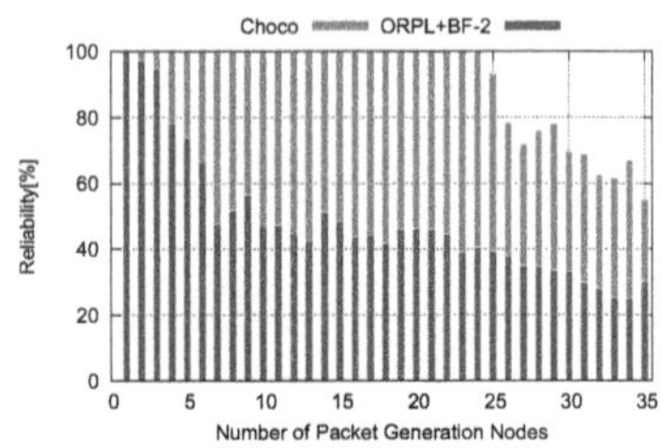

Figure 3: Number of packet generation nodes vs reliability (periodic traffic)

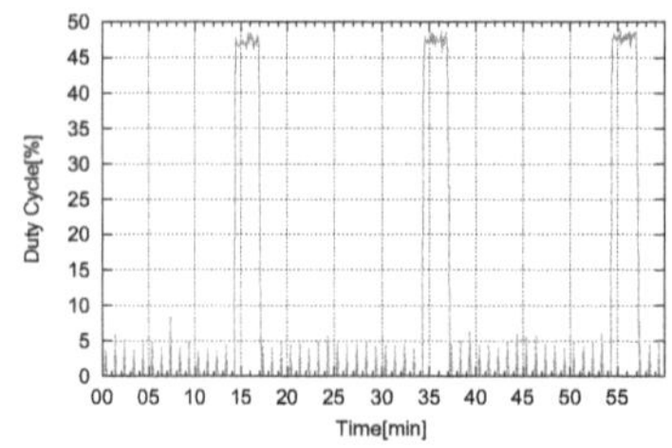

Figure 4: Duty cycle (burst traffic)

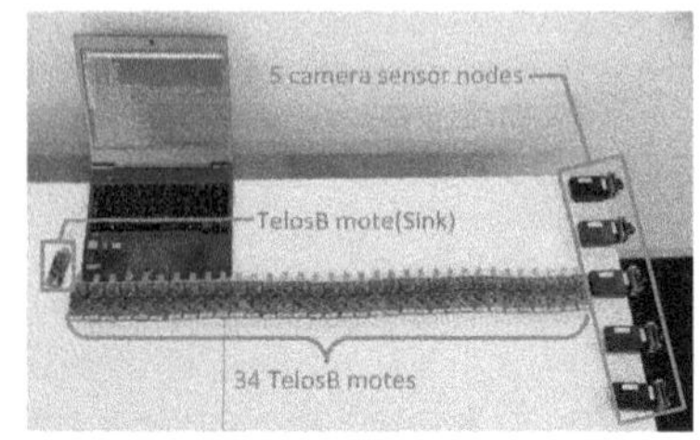

Figure 5: The demonstration layout

duced by providing 100 % reliability. The parameter is implicitly chosen in the evaluations of [1],[2] for sufficient reliability. Third, it is not necessary to report changes of traffic demands since a schedule is calculated based on backlogs.

Choco has two advantages compared to asynchronous MAC based approach such as BF [3]. First, Choco is more efficient for light traffic, because overhearing and long preambles used in LPL (Low Power Listening) do not exist in Choco. Second, Choco's reliability does not drop drastically when multiple nodes generate packets. This is because congestion does not occur in Choco owing to concurrent transmission.

2. EVALUATION

Periodic Traffic. We evaluate duty cycle and reliability of Choco, BF-2 (2 Hz LPL) and BF-8 (8 Hz LPL) with ORPL [2] as a routing protocol, using 94 nodes we are able to use on the Indriya testbed [4]. We use IEEE 802.15.4 channel 26 and transmission power of 0 dBm, and fix the payload size to 15 B. In the first experiment, the 94 nodes generate packets and we vary IPI (Inter-Packet Interval). In the second experiment, IPI is fixed to 1 s and we vary the number of packet generation nodes from 1 to 35 out of 94.

The result of the first experiment is shown in Table. 1, and the summarized result is shown in Fig. 2. Choco's efficiency is higher when the traffic is light (IPI > 300 s compared with ORPL+BF-2, IPI > 30 s compared with ORPL+BF-8). Choco's reliability is higher than or equal to that BF's in any IPI setting. When the traffic loads exceed the network capacity, Choco cannot achieve 100 % reliability because generated packets cannot be allocated to the send buffer. When LPL frequency is increased for greater reliability in BF, the minimum energy consumption also gets increased.

The result of the second experiment is shown in Fig. 3. Choco can achieve 100 % reliability when the number of packet generating nodes is less than 25. On the other hand, BF's reliability is not 100 % even when only two nodes generate packets and always lower than Choco due to congestion.

Burst Traffic. We evaluate duty cycle and throughput of Choco in a networked imaging application with 5 camera sensor nodes and 35 TelosB motes. We use IEEE 802.15.4 channel 26 and low transmission power (< -25 dBm), and fix the payload size to 74 B. Each camera sensor node generates an approximately 47 KB VGA image per 20 minutes.

Fig. 4 shows average duty cycle accross all nodes over one hour. The average duty cycle is 0.38 % for light traffic and 44.3 % for heavy traffic. 5 VGA images are collected from 5 nodes in approximately 168 s, indicating that the throughput is 1.43 KB/s, in average 4.0 hop network. This means that Choco can adapt the slot assignment according to traffic demands in the network, and shows that Choco can efficiently support burst traffic with end-to-end reliability.

3. DEMONSTRATION

In the demonstration, we will show an application which collects both periodic and burst traffic loads. The demonstration is composed of 5 camera sensor nodes, 35 TelosB motes (including a sink node) and a laptop as shown in Fig. 5. The camera sensor nodes take VGA images and generate burst traffic loads. TelosB motes periodically perform sensing of temperature, humidity and illuminance and generate periodic traffic loads. The laptop is connected to the sink node, logs the data collected from sensor nodes, and shows the performance of the network and collected images.

Acknowledgments

This work was partly supported by Council for Science, Technology and Innovation, Cross-ministerial Strategic Innovation Promotion Program, "Maintenance, Renovation, and Management of Infrastructure".

4. REFERENCES

[1] F. Ferrari, et al. Low-power wireless bus. *In Proc. of SenSys*, 2012.

[2] S. Duquennoy, et al. Let the tree bloom: Scalable opportunistic routing with orpl. *In Proc. of SenSys*, 2013.

[3] S. Duquennoy, et al. Lossy links, low power, high throughput. *In Proc. of SenSys*, 2011.

[4] M. Doddavenkatappa, et al. Indriya: A low-cost 3d wireless sensor network testbed. *In Proc. of TridentCom*, 2011.

Demo Abstract: Real-time Detection for Multiple Occupancy and Near Real-time Hogging Detection

Nguyen Huy Hoang Huy, Rajesh Krishna Balan, and Youngki Lee
School of Information Systems, Singapore Management University
nhhuy.2014@phdis.smu.edu.sg, {rajesh,youngkilee}@smu.edu.sg

ABSTRACT

In the public studying space, students sometimes hog seats. This behavior prevents others from access their needed seats, and requires man power to patrol and move stuffs from hogged seats to another place. In this paper, we present a capacitive sensor to check seat occupancy statuses in real-time (i.e. un-occupied, people occupying, and seat hogging). The device helps students to find available seats, and helps staffs to monitor seats usage remotely for better controlling over seat hogging problem without the need to patrol. Our experiment results show that the sensor can accurately detect seat occupancy. Moreover, it can clearly distinguish between human occupancy and seat hogging.

Categories and Subject Descriptors

Topic C.3 [**Special-purpose and Application-Based Systems**]: Real-time and embedded systems

Keywords

capacitive sensing; occupancy detection; hogging detection; electric field sensing; inductive proximity sensing

1. INTRODUCTION

Capacitive sensing has proven to be robust and reliable measurement technology with low power consumption. The most popular form of capacitive sensor is that used in phone screens and track-pads that take human finger capacitance as input. Prior research has focused on using capacitive sensor to controlling car's airbag system. The closest to our work is to use capacitive sensor to detection occupancy on mini bus [2]. In these prior research, the sensor was installed under chair to detect if someone was sitting on it. In our work, we use proximity capacitive sensor to detect people occupancy and seat hogging. Our goals are to solve two real-world problems related to seat availability.

The first problem is finding available seats in library or event hall. People have to move around in order to find empty seats, which cost them some efforts and may disturb other people. Using the sensor to detect seat occupancy, we can help reducing the cost of searching by showing location of empty seats. The second problem is seat hogging in library [1]. Our sensor can provide seats usage statistics, including seat hogging. This helps library's staffs to effectively monitor seat hogging problem from their desk. We can also apply the sensor in other public space like coffee shop or mall to have better facility management.

We use the capacitive sensor to detect not only people occupancy, but also seat hogging. This is different from previous works and requires dissimilar context as we discuss in next section. We achieved high detection accuracy for both people and objects.

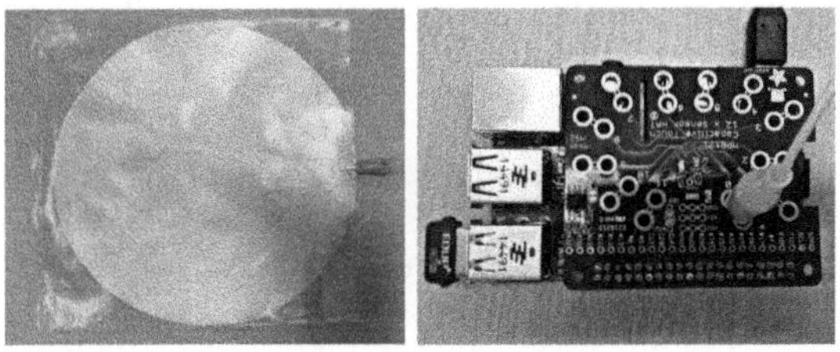

Figure 1: Two main components of our capacitive sensor, copper foil (left) and Raspberry Pi with MPR121 chip (right).

2. SENSOR DESIGN

The device used in our setup is showed in Figure 1. It consists of a Raspberry pi with capacitive touch sensor controller chip MPR121 from Freescale (www.freescale.com) to control the system and transmit data, and round shaped copper foils that act as electrodes for capacitance measurement. The sensor is powered using wall outlet.

The capacitive sensor measures changes in voltage, which is reverse proportional to capacitance.

$$V = \frac{Q}{C} = \frac{I \times T}{C} \tag{1}$$

The output result is in form of 10bit ADC (i.e. analog to digital converter). $ADC\ Counts = \frac{V \times 1024}{Vdd}$ with Vdd is constant supply voltage. Then we can calculate capacitance C knowing charge current I and charge time T

$$C = \frac{Q}{V} = \frac{I \times T}{V} = \frac{I \times T}{ADC\ counts} \times \frac{1}{Vdd \times 1024} \tag{2}$$

SenSys'15, November 1–4, 2015, Seoul, South Korea.
ACM 978-1-4503-3631-4/15/11.
http://dx.doi.org/10.1145/2809695.2817862

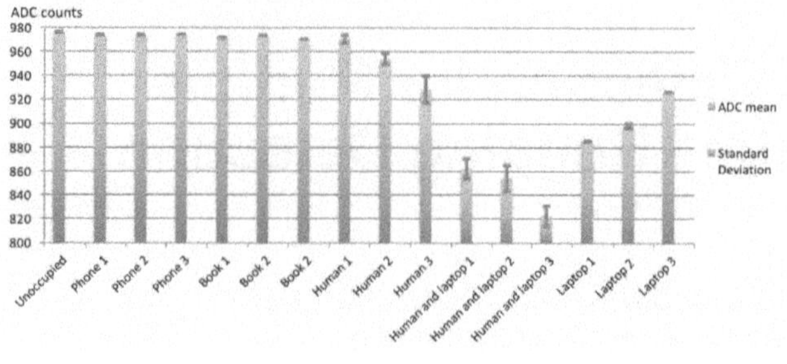

Figure 2: Measured capacitance. Blue bars are *ADC* counts (voltage) and red bars are standard deviations. Phones and books are from 960 to 980, laptops from 880 to 940, and people reach both ranges with higher standard deviation.

We setup charge current I to 50 μA and charge time per half cycle T to 1 μs to charge sensor to near upper count limit, thus maximize the sensing resolution.

It is hard to track position of non-fixed chairs which can be moved around, so we do not place sensor under chair. We place single electrode under table for each seat to detect both objects and people at the seat position. Compared to when the device is installed under chair, the principle drawback being the distance between people and the sensor, which is reverse proportional to capacitance, becomes larger and depends more on people's posture. This makes it harder to detect and distinguish people occupancy from object occupancy. We resolved the problem by fine-tuning the sensor and using *standard deviation* as people occupancy's feature. Our experiments were focused on human occupancy and objects such as laptop, book and phone that are commonly placed objects on table by students to hog the seat.

3. ANALYSIS AND DETECTION ALGORITHM

We analyzed the capacitance of object that can be putted on table. Detection result is described in Figure 2. As the result suggests, based on signal magnitude, we can easily separate objects that have low dielectric constant like phone and book from laptop. In the other hand, compared to the case when sensor is installed on chair, people sit in near proximity to the electrodes instead of directly sit on it, which causes their occupancy's capacitance reachs both book and laptop range, depending on their postures. However, variance in signal can be used as feature to differentiate human occupancy from the rest.

To identify human occupancy and object occupancy, we utilized a two-states approach;

1. First, check deviation value of output signal from baseline to detect if seat is occupied.
2. If it is then check standard deviation to differentiate people from object occupancy.

The baseline is calculated using running average algorithm on output signal, and baseline deviation is used as feature to ensures that capacitive sensor will work in any surrounding environment and can auto calibrate itself. Standard deviation is calculated on a queue of signal samples - $Standard\ deviation = sd(Queue)$. The queue is updated over time by adding new samples and remove old ones. Detection of seat hogging after people leaving has a small delay, depending on the size of sample queue. Setting the queue size at 1000 samples, it takes at most 21 seconds for object to be detected after the transition. However, people occupancy and un-occupancy state can be detected instantly.

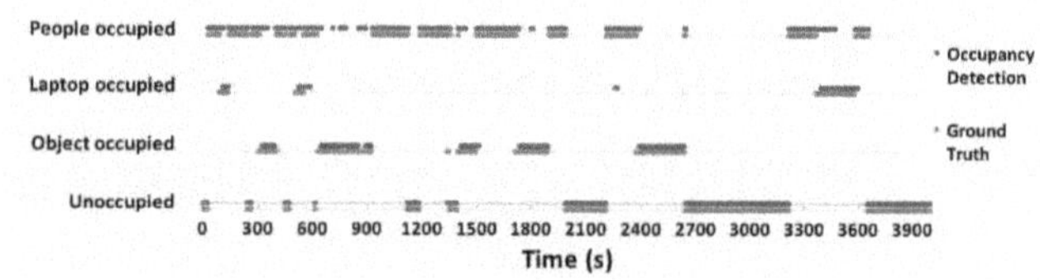

Figure 3: Occupancy detection. There are four possible states of occupancy that can be detected, including *People occupied*, *Laptop occupied*, *Object occupied* and *Un-occupied*. The green lines are detected states of capacitive sensor, and orange lines are ground truth.

Table 1: Detection performance

States	Precision	Recall
Un-Occupied	100 %	100 %
Object Occupied	97 %	100 %
Laptop Occupied	66 %	97 %
People Occupied	97 %	95 %

4. EXPERIMENT

The occupancy states of side-by-side seats are recorded by sensor, and ground truth is done by manual labeling. The detection result for the first sensor is presented in Figure 3. Detection performance of the capacitive sensor is presented in Table 1. For Un-occupied state, we got 100% precision and recall, which means the device can reliable detect if seat is occupied or not. Object and people hogging are also well detected. Accuracy drops for laptop detection due to affection of vibration when people hit the table. This slight shaking moved the laptop and raised detection error by increasing standard deviation. Possible solution for this case is increasing detection threshold for laptop case. We can also increase the queue size of signal samples to improve overal detection accuracy at expense of response time.

5. ACKNOWLEDGMENTS

This research is supported by the National Research Foundation Singapore under its Interactive Digital Media (IDM) Strategic Research Programme.

6. REFERENCES

[1] A. W. Y. LAU, E. Y. L. TAN, J. X. LEE, J. T. E. LIM, S. W. LEE, A. F. DIMIAN, Y. W. ISHAK, and V. ONG. Data from: Improve space and manpower utilisation. 2015.

[2] A. S. Zeeman, M. J. Booysen, G. Ruggeri, and B. Laganá. Capacitive seat sensors for multiple occupancy detection using a low-cost setup. In *Industrial Technology (ICIT), 2013 IEEE International Conference on*, pages 1228–1233. IEEE, 2013.

Demo: Distributed MaxRS in Wireless Sensor Networks*

Muhammed Mas-ud Hussain, Panitan Wongse-ammat, and Goce Trajcevski
Department of Electrical Engineering and Computer Science
Northwestern University
Evanston, IL 60208
{mmh683, pwa732, goce}@eecs.northwestern.edu

ABSTRACT

This work presents a distributed implementation for processing *Maximizing Range Sum* (MaxRS) query in Wireless Sensor Networks (WSN). MaxRS query is useful in many spatially-distributed event monitoring and target tracking applications. Given the location and current readings of the nodes, and a rectangle R, MaxRS finds a location of R that maximizes the sum of the readings of all the nodes covered by R. Our system performs MaxRS query in a user-specified time-interval γ and using the result obtained, attempts to maintain a certain degree of energy conservation in the WSN, based on a user-defined threshold δ. Since centralized processing of the raw readings and subsequently determining the MaxRS may incur significant communication overheads, we developed a distributed algorithm to compute MaxRS. We implemented our system in a heterogeneous WSN consisting of TelosB and SunSPOT motes, and illustrate the end-user tools: GUI for specifying required parameters, and real-time visualization of MaxRS solutions and estimated network energy consumption.

1. INTRODUCTION

Wireless Sensor Networks (WSN) represent a paradigm with broad range of practical applications, including but not limited to global-scale environmental monitoring, smart buildings and cities, medicine, agriculture, safety and hazard detection, etc. [1]. As sensor nodes are usually powered by batteries and often severely limited for recharging or replacing them, reducing the energy consumption is an ever-important topic in WSN, enabling an extension of overall network's operational lifetime [2]. While periodic sampling and transmission to a dedicated sink may be well-suited for certain applications, they may incur significant overheads in others—especially in event-based monitoring. Various works have tackled routing issues, as well as epoch-based synchronization for query processing, aggregation, and in-network algorithms to minimize communication overheads [3].

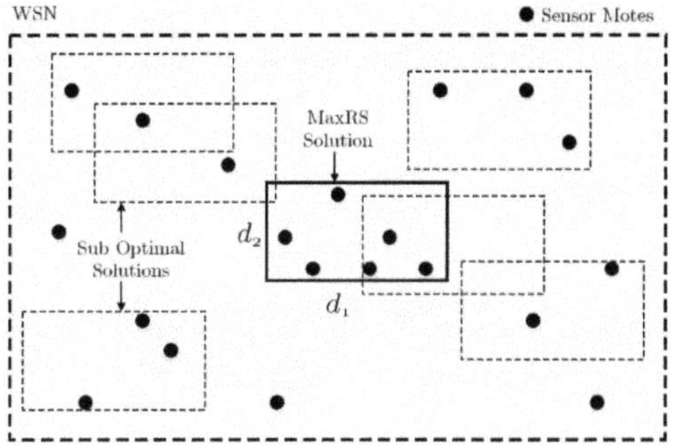

Figure 1: An example of MaxRS query in WSN.

The specific problem that we address can be described as follows. We are given a set O of *weighted objects* and a rectangle R of a specific dimension (i.e., $d_1 \times d_2$), and the *Maximizing Range Sum* (MaxRS) retrieves a location of R within the given space that maximizes the sum of the weights of all the objects covered by R. In the case of WSNs, we can think of the set of sensor nodes as the set of weighted objects. The weights of the individual sensor nodes may be set based on specific application needs, e.g., information gain (tracking an object), mote readings (event monitoring), uniform (counting), etc. An instance of the MaxRS in WSN is shown in Fig. 1, where the weights of all the sensor nodes are uniform.

MaxRS query can be used effectively for energy conservation purposes in applications such as identifying and monitoring the region with the highest density of tracked objects (e.g., gazelles); tracking the portion of the city with heaviest traffic; detecting most critical sources of forest fires (locating hotspots) and tracing their expansion routes; etc.

Our goal is to provide efficient mechanisms for: (1) Processing MaxRS query in WSN; and (2) Reducing energy consumption while maintaining its answer under dynamically changing values of the monitored phenomena. Towards this, we have developed an in-network algorithm to compute the MaxRS query, conserving the energy spent by awaking only the nodes that are within the MaxRS solution, and keeping all others asleep. We also limit the total network energy consumed in a uniformly or randomly deployed WSN to a certain degree based on a user-specified threshold by adjusting the shape of the query rectangle R accordingly. This demo paper exhibits the system that implements these

*Research supported in part by NSF grants CNS-0910952 and III 1213038, and ONR grant N00014-14-1-0215.

SenSys '15, November 1–4, 2015, Seoul, Republic of Korea.
ACM 978-1-4503-3631-4/15/11.
DOI: http://dx.doi.org/10.1145/2809695.2817863.

techniques on a network of heterogeneous motes (TelosB and SunSPOT), along with the user-interface to specify required parameters and modules for visualizing the event monitored, MaxRS results, and amount of energy consumed.

2. SYSTEM DESIGN

Two parameters in our system control how the energy efficiency is enforced:

• γ — corresponds to the time-interval of MaxRS query processing. If MaxRS is computed at time t using the current set of weights of the sensor nodes, only the nodes within the solution rectangle are kept awake between time t and $t + \gamma$. At time $t + \gamma$, MaxRS is re-computed with updated weights, and state (awake, or idle) of the nodes are changed accordingly.

• δ — denotes the target average network energy consumption. The shape of the MaxRS query rectangle is adjusted based on δ. We assume that the overall energy spent at any time is directly proportional to the number of active sensor nodes in the network. As a simple model, we assume that the whole WSN area is a $l_1 \times l_2$ meters^2 rectangle, where n sensor nodes are deployed uniformly. If k nodes total to δ energy at a time instant, then the shape of the query rectangle R would be $d_1 \times d_2$, where $d_i = \frac{k \times l_i}{n}$ $(i \in \{1, 2\})$.

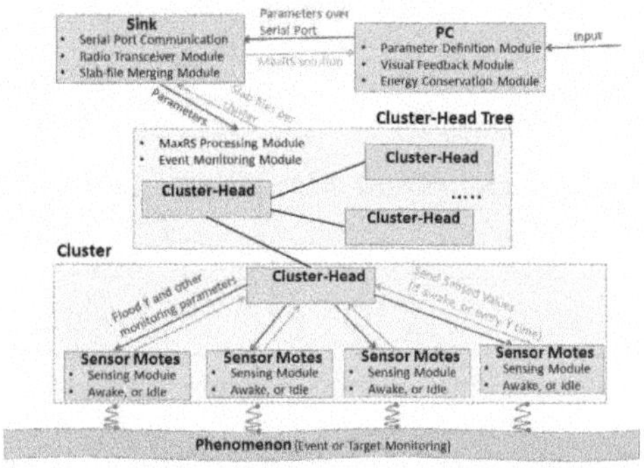

Figure 2: System Architecture.

The distributed solution for the MaxRS problem in spatial databases in [4] is the foundation of our in-network algorithm. Instead of dividing the space into m vertical slabs, we divide the space into a hierarchy of $m \times n$ grid-shaped clusters (similar to [3]), each of which has a selected cluster-head. The system architecture shown in Fig. 2 consists of the following main components:

(1) At the highest declarative level, we have the GUI that serves two main purposes: (a) Enables the users to select desired values for the required parameters; and (b) Provides a display for visualizing the boundaries of the current MaxRS solution, showing the nodes that are currently awake; the status of the monitored event (e.g., mote readings); and energy consumption in the network.

(2) The sink, connected through the serial port of the laptop: (a) Disseminates the parameters to the cluster-heads; and (b) Collects the data from the cluster-heads and performs the slab-file merging procedure described in [4].

(3) The cluster-heads form a tree-based hierarchy towards the sink. Each cluster-head calculates the slab-file information for the local cluster and coordinates the information with one of the neighboring cluster-heads to perform in-network aggregation.

(4) At the lowest level, the individual motes in each cluster conduct two simple tasks: (a) They receive related parameters from the local cluster-head; and (b) When awake, they report their readings to the local cluster-head.

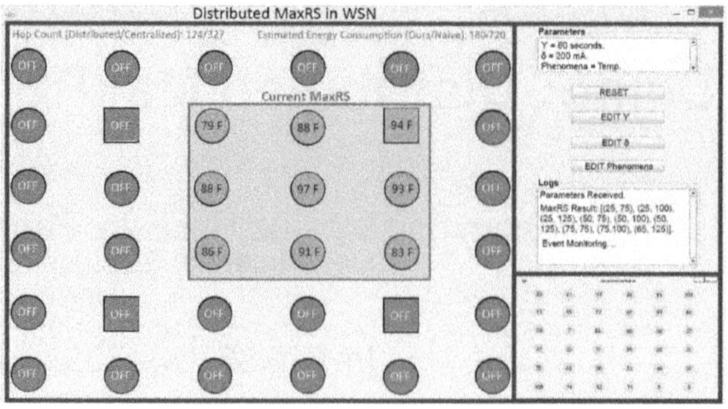

Figure 3: Graphical User Interface.

3. DEMO SPECIFICATIONS

Our demo setup will consist of an actual WSN composed of 5 SunSPOT and 32 TelosB motes, connected via the sink to a USB port of a laptop running the Java-based front-end application. The motes will be distributed uniformly, and the WSN will be organized into 4 clusters having 8 TelosB motes and 1 SunPOT (cluster-head) each. The remaining SunSPOT will be used as the sink. We will use two different phenomena for event monitoring and sensing: temperature and light. The demonstration will have two distinct parts:

P1: The first part will have the following two main phases:

Phase-1: Specification of the required parameters for energy conservation and event monitoring in the GUI, illustrating the means to control the value of: (a) γ; (b) δ; and (c) Phenomena (light, or temperature).

Phase-2: Demonstration of the real-time execution in the provided WSN based on the user-defined parameters obtained in *Phase-1*. We will display (cf. Fig. 3): (a) Current MaxRS solution; (b) Currently active motes and their readings; and (c) Effect of the values of γ and δ on (a) and (b).

P2: The second part of the demo will compare the estimated energy consumption: (a) Using MaxRS results vs. keeping all nodes awake; and (b) Centralized vs. distributed processing of MaxRS query (via total message hop count).

4. REFERENCES

[1] I. F. Akyildiz, W. Su, Y. Sankarasubramaniam, and E. Cayirci. Wireless sensor networks: a survey. *Comput. Netw.*, 38(4):393–422, Mar. 2002.

[2] G. Anastasi, M. Conti, M. Di Francesco, and A. Passarella. Energy conservation in wireless sensor networks: A survey. *Ad hoc networks*, 7(3):537–568, 2009.

[3] B. Avci, B. Zhang, M. M. Hussain, and G. Trajcevski. Evolving shapes in wireless sensor networks. In *Proceedings of the 12th ACM Conference on Embedded Network Sensor Systems*, pages 320–321. ACM, 2014.

[4] D. W. Choi, C. W. Chung, and Y. Tao. Maximizing range sum in external memory. *ACM Trans. Database Syst.*, 39(3):21:1–21:44, Oct. 2014.

Demo: Browsing the Web of Things with *Summon*

Thomas Zachariah, Joshua Adkins, and Prabal Dutta
Electrical Engineering and Computer Science Department
University of Michigan
Ann Arbor, MI 48109
{tzachari,adkinsjd,prabal}@umich.edu

Abstract

We are becoming increasingly surrounded by smart and connected devices, popularly known as the Internet of Things. The emerging user interface paradigm for many such things eschews physical buttons, knobs, and displays in favor of virtual interfaces that are downloaded from the web and rendered on remote platforms—like smartphones. However, such smartphone app-based interfaces often require tedious discovery and installation, as well as device discovery, pairing, and configuration before a user can interact with a nearby device. Requiring an explicit app install for each new device type scales poorly with device growth, and particularly hinders casual interactions with ambient devices. Instead of the high-friction, walled-garden approach now taking root, we propose *Summon*, a physical web browser that provides a seamless, scalable approach to browsing and interacting with nearby things. *Summon* leverages multiple network patterns and modern web technologies to provide users with rich device interfaces, even for devices under network or power constraints. We argue that this approach scales better and that it provides more intuitive and natural functionality for both users and developers. This demo presents the basic concept, allows others to experience our preliminary implementation, and raises several open research questions.

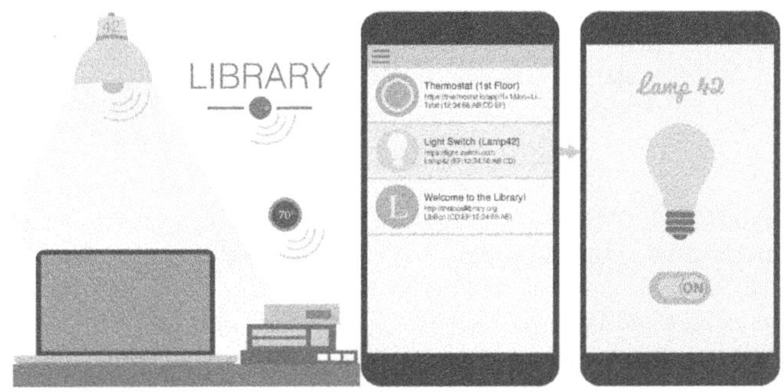

Figure 1: The *Summon* physical device browsing architecture. Peripheral devices like smart things (light bulb, thermostat) and beacons make their presence known by broadcasting information about themselves. The mobile phone *Summon* service scans the local vicinity, parses broadcast data, and displays to the user a selection of available user interfaces corresponding to the nearby devices. When a user selects an item from the list, the best possible interface for a given device is opened within the app, presenting a user interface that may interact *directly* with the device.

1. INTRODUCTION

The number of smart devices is increasing dramatically. For these devices, the paradigm for user-interaction has shifted away from on-device interfaces to richer, downloadable soft user interfaces (UIs) on remote devices like smartphones. However, requiring the involved process of app installation for every new device, as is currently prescribed in industry, is unrealistic and does not scale well. The process often requires users to have some prior knowledge of and about the devices around them, and introduces the latency, digital clutter, and privacy concerns associated with installing a native application. We need a simpler system that can enable interaction with any nearby device at any time.

Fortunately, systems are being developed to solve this problem. Google has even launched a project—the Physical Web—to support browsing the web of things without requiring users to install native applications [1]. Their system defines a protocol that devices can use to advertise information about themselves using Bluetooth Low Energy (BLE) or zero-configuration network services. Mobile phones using the system then scan for these special broadcasts, display the results to the user in a Physical Web browser, and navigate the user to either the native application or a web page referenced by the broadcast when the corresponding device result is selected. However, this system requires that both the broadcasting device and the phone maintain constant Internet connection to create an interactive user interface. This is not practical for all classes of smart devices and usage scenarios. Users need to be able to browse nearby devices and load dynamic, interactive user interfaces for devices that are not otherwise Internet connected. Moreover, devices should be able to take advantage of the reduced power and complexity of interacting using only local networking protocols.

To solve this problem, we introduce *Summon*, our physical device browser. The *Summon* architecture, like that of the Physical Web, allows smart devices to point mobile phones to rich user interfaces, as is depicted in Figure 1. Unlike the Physical Web, *Summon* defines and supports a new class of interactive user interfaces that account for the possibility of the device or phone having limited network connectivity. This new class of UIs allows *Summon* to provide users with the best user interaction experience possible for any device under whatever constraints may be at play.

SenSys'15, November 1–4, 2015, Seoul, South Korea.
ACM 978-1-4503-3631-4/15/11.
DOI: http://dx.doi.org/10.1145/2809695.2817864 .

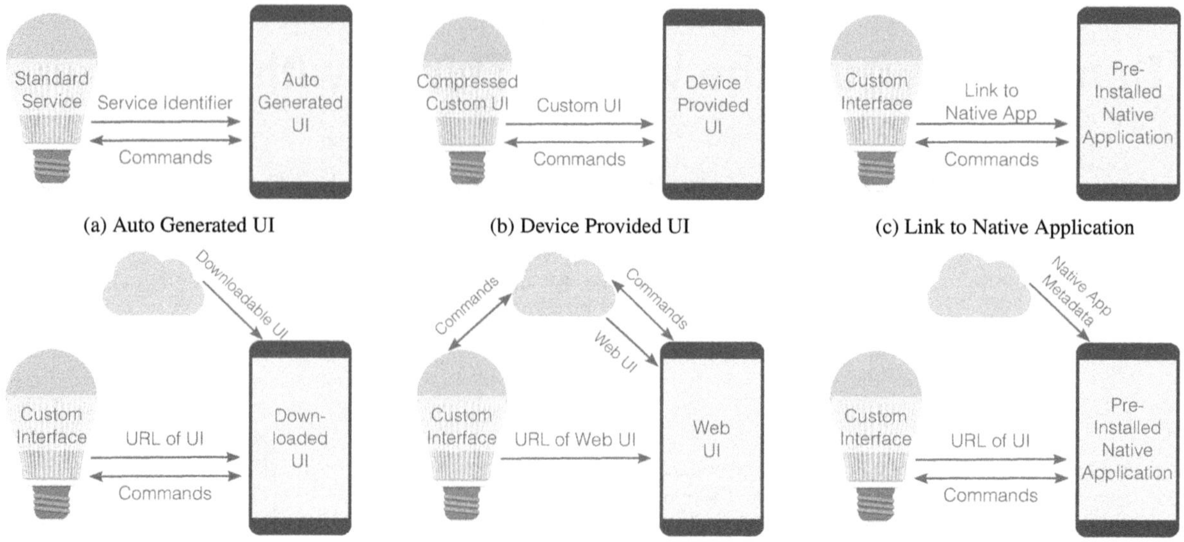

(a) Auto Generated UI (b) Device Provided UI (c) Link to Native Application

(d) Downloadable UI (e) Web UI (f) Native Application instead of Web UI

Figure 2: The different types of user interfaces that can be instantiated by *Summon*. While Physical Web only supports (c) and (e), all the user interfaces are important to a complete device browser, especially those interfaces that do not require the smart device to be connected to the Internet or the installation of a native application: (a), (b), and (d). It should also be noted that, as in (f), the device browser should give the user the richest interface possible for a given set of constraints. In (f), *Summon* starts to retrieve the downloadable UI, but checks for an installed native application as specified in the meta-data, and opens the native application instead of the downloadable UI.

2. LOADING AN INTERFACE

To achieve the goal of loading the best user interface for devices under any constraints, *Summon* defines and supports five interface types: 1) web based UIs with which devices interact entirely through the cloud, 2) native applications, 3) downloaded web-like UIs which interact directly with the device, 4) device provided web-like UIs which interact directly with the device, and 5) auto-generated UIs. The architectures for each of these UIs is shown in Figure 2. For *Summon* to load one of these UIs for a device, the device must be compatible with the *Summon* broadcasting protocol.

2.1 Broadcasting Parameters

Like Physical Web, *Summon* can receive broadcasts as Bluetooth Low Energy advertisements, or over local network service discovery protocols, mDNS and SSDP, over WiFi. As part of the broadcast parameters, the peripheral must indicate the target location from which to receive the UI. This location can be expressed as a unique identifier for a user interface hosted on the device, a package name link for a native phone application, or a URL. If the destination is a URL, for instance, it is treated as the source address for either a downloadable or web-based user interface.

2.2 Destination Resolution

An explicit goal of *Summon* is not only to provide a user with a user interface, but to provide a user with the best user interface possible given the broadcasted information. Therefore *Summon* first attempts to provide the user with a native application if one is already installed, it then attempts to load a web or web-like UI from the cloud, then attempts to load a web-like UI from the device, and on last resort, *Summon* will attempt to auto-generate a UI. *Summon* utilizes a combination of metadata at broadcasted URLs, self-identifying information held on the device, and its knowledge of the smartphone's network status to step through the possible interfaces and select the best one.

2.3 Other Design Details

Many other design decisions are necessary to fulfill the *Summon*'s goals. To achieve downloadable web-UIs that can interact directly with a device, *Summon* exposes native APIs in web-scripting languages. To allow for devices to provide UIs directly to *Summon* over BLE, *Summon* defines a Bluetooth service that specifies the retrieval of these UIs. Caching is implemented to further reduce latency and increase network independence of downloadable user interfaces, and phone services such as location and device information are exposed to allow for richer downloadable applications.

3. DEMONSTRATION

Summon will be available as a mobile application on the Android play store. Interested participants can download the application, or use our provided smartphones to interact with *Summon*-compatible peripheral devices that we have created or modified. We will configure the *Summon*-compatible peripherals such that every UI type supported by *Summon* will be on display.

We will also demonstrate the ease of using modern web tools to create user interfaces for direct interaction with devices. We will walk through the quick setup for each UI type, including steps for hosting UIs online or storing them on the device for limited connectivity scenarios. This will exhibit how *Summon* allows users to casually interact nearby devices, while providing developers a simple method for creating rich UIs for their devices.

4. ACKNOWLEDGMENTS

This material is based upon work supported by NSF under grants CNS-1239031, CNS-1350967 and CPS-1505684, and by the NSF/Intel Partnership on CPS Security and Privacy.

5. REFERENCES

[1] Google Inc. The physical web. http://www.github.com/google/physical-web.

Demo Abstract — PolyPoint: High-Precision Indoor Localization with UWB

Benjamin Kempke, Pat Pannuto, Bradford Campbell, Joshua Adkins, and Prabal Dutta
University of Michigan, Ann Arbor, MI 48109
{bpkempke,ppannuto,bradjc,adkinsjd,prabal}@umich.edu

ABSTRACT

We demonstrate PolyPoint, a high-fidelity RF-based indoor localization system that achieves 28 cm accuracy indoors and tracks a fast-moving quadcopter with only 56 cm average error. PolyPoint uses ultra-wideband signals to achieve high precision RF time-of-flight estimates between nodes. To further improve accuracy, PolyPoint exploits two forms of diversity: frequency diversity, which leverages several ultra-wideband channels to improve channel response, and antenna diversity, which adds three antennas at 120° offsets to mitigate the effects of antenna polarization and nulls. PolyPoint introduces an efficient, novel ranging protocol that maximizes these diversity sources with a minimal number of packets.

Additionally, this work introduces a new hardware platform that provides ranging and localization as a service. The minimal *TriPoint* module integrates an ultra-wideband transceiver and microcontroller with firmware that implements the PolyPoint protocol. The *TriTag* carrier board adds Bluetooth and batteries to create a complete mobile tag, and the *TriBase* anchor platform integrates a TriPoint with an Intel Edison to act as anchors for the system.

Categories and Subject Descriptors

B.0 [**Hardware**]: General; C.3 [**Special-Purpose and Application-Based Systems**]: Real-time and embedded systems

General Terms

Design, Experimentation, Measurement, Performance

Keywords

Indoor Localization, Ultra-Wideband Communications

SenSys'15, November 01–04, Seoul, Republic of Korea
ACM 978-1-4503-3631-4/15/11.
http://dx.doi.org/10.1145/2809695.2817865

1. INTRODUCTION

Global Navigation Satellite Systems (GNSS) have long been the universal gold standard for the accurate navigation of outdoor spaces. Certain systems have enabled position determination accuracy better than 10 cm. Unfortunately, these RF systems break down in indoor environments due to extreme attenuation and heavy multipath, necessitating the use of local navigation aids.

To address this, we recently introduced PolyPoint [2], a new localization system that couples the DecaWave ScenSor transceiver [1] with antenna diversity and a new, efficient ranging protocol. Utilizing antenna diversity, PolyPoint shows an order of magnitude improvement in accuracy over the use of just one antenna at each node. Furthermore, PolyPoint's ranging protocol supports the aggregation of many different range estimates across different antenna and RF channel combinations while still maintaining an update rate at tens of Hz. This demonstration builds on our original PolyPoint work. We modify the original protocol to improve robustness by spreading critical messages across multiple channels, add support for localizing multiple tags in a single space, remove the reliance on cloud-supported computation, and introduce a new, improved hardware platform that significantly improves the size, weight, and extensibility that can act as a drop-in localization module.

2. POLYPOINT OVERVIEW

PolyPoint is a localization system that uses one-way time-of-flight measurements to derive range estimates between a mobile tag and fixed-location infrastructure (anchors) to determine a tag's position. By collecting range estimates between the tag and three or more anchors, the system is able to calculate the tag's 3D position using trilateration. The mobile tag is affixed to the object to track, and position estimates are calculated in real-time.

2.1 Precision Time-of-Flight Ranging

To derive a high-precision time-of-flight range estimate between a tag and anchor, two unsynchronized nodes, requires *three* packets. The tag sends a POLL and the anchor replies with a RESP that includes turnaround time to determine the total round trip time between tag and anchor. To compensate for crystal offsets between tag and anchor, the tag sends a REF packet at a known time offset from the POLL. Comparing the sent and received timestamps for REF and POLL yield a crystal correction K. A precision range event is thus:

$$① \text{ Tag} \xrightarrow{Ref} \text{Anc} \quad ② \text{ Tag} \xrightarrow{Poll} \text{Anc} \quad ③ \text{ Anc} \xrightarrow{Resp} \text{Tag}$$

$$K = \frac{\text{Tag}_{TX\_Poll} - \text{Tag}_{TX\_Ref}}{\text{Anc}_{RX\_Poll} - \text{Anc}_{RX\_Ref}}$$

$$ToF = [(\text{Tag}_{RX\_Resp} - \text{Tag}_{TX\_Poll}) - K * (\text{Anc}_{TX\_Resp} - \text{Anc}_{RX\_Poll})]/2$$

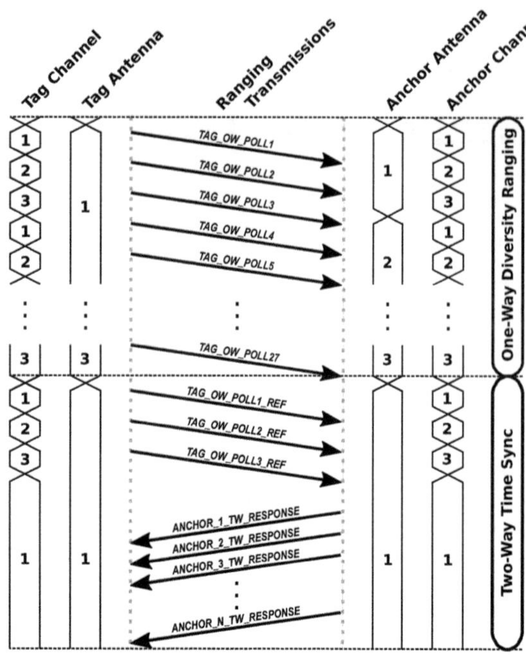

Figure 1: Ranging protocol. PolyPoint is able to leverage antenna diversity without significantly impacting position update rate. The protocol starts with a series of 27 broadcast transmissions from the tag for each combination of tag antenna, anchor antenna, and RF channel. The time-of-arrival data collected from this sequence provides information on the difference between all range estimates throughout the sequence. Finally, a two-way time-of-flight handshake is sent (on each channel for robustness) to determine the true range estimate—a total of 30 POLL messages. The offset between the first and last poll message on each channel is used to calculate the crystal frequency offset between the tag and anchor. From the first measurement, the time offset between the tag and anchor is known, leading to estimates of range for the other 26 combinations from the initial difference-based measurements.

2.2 Diversity and the PolyPoint Protocol

Ultra-wideband transceivers such as ScenSor still require the line-of-sight path to be unobstructed to produce accurate time-of-arrival measurements. In real-world scenarios, however, there are a variety of factors that can cause the line-of-sight path to be obstructed. While sufficient node density and careful placement can help avoid obstructions, differences in polarization between nodes can lead to significant attenuation of the line-of-sight path without the presence of any interfering objects. For this reason, we introduce multiple antennas at each node to mitigate the effects of polarization mismatch on ranging (and subsequently localization) error.

In a ranging event with the minimum 3 anchors and 3 antennas on each node, a naïve protocol requires $27 \times 3 \times 3 = 243$ packets. To reduce the total number of message exchanges, PolyPoint tags transmit a broadcast for each of the 27 different configurations. The difference in range estimates can be calculated at each anchor by observing the time differences between successive message receptions. A final two-way time-of-flight exchange is then performed between the tag and each anchor to account for any error in range due to clock offset. Figure 1 shows the modified two-way time-of-flight protocol used to quickly gather each of the 27 successive range estimates. For this revised protocol, 3 anchors require only $27 + 3 + 3 = 33$ packets.

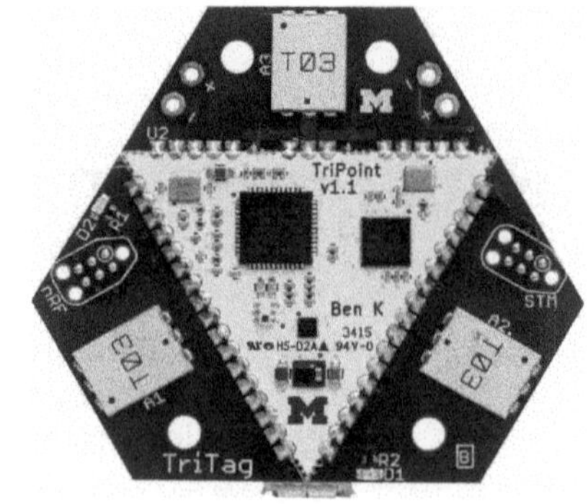

Figure 2: TriTag with onboard TriPoint module. The center triangle PCB is our new drop-on TriPoint module that integrates a UWB transceiver and microcontroller to implement the PolyPoint ranging protocol. The pictured carrier board is the TriTag, the tag to be localized, which adds batteries and Bluetooth communication with a mobile phone. The same TriPoint modules power our TriBases, an anchor solution built around the Intel Edison platform.

3. TRIPOINT LOCALIZATION MODULE

As the ranging protocol requires precise timing operations and reasonably complex radio operations, we design the *TriPoint* drop-on module which provides ranging or location as a service. TriPoint integrates the DecaWave DW1000 ScenSor UWB transceiver for ranging, a SKY13317-373LF RF switch for antenna diversity, a STM32F031G6 Cortex M0 microcontroller for protocol operation and location reporting, and on-board power regulation. Figure 2 shows the *TriTag*, a carrier board for TriPoint that adds a nRF51822 for Bluetooth communication with a mobile phone and batteries for mobile operation. The final piece of hardware is the *TriBase*, a carrier board built around the Intel Edison platform that is used as anchors for PolyPoint.

4. DEMONSTRATION

The demonstration will affix TriTags to mobile phones that report the exact location of the phone. We will also deploy a number of TriBases around the environment to act as anchors for the localization system. Users will be able to walk around the demonstration space and observe the performance of the system. We will include a handful of labeled, measured points to give users an intuition for the system accuracy. We expect to achieve sub-meter accuracy throughout the entire demonstration space. Additionally, locations will be reported to a central server that will show traces of users walking around the space on a monitor at the demonstration table.

5. ACKNOWLEDGMENTS

This work was supported in part by TerraSwarm, one of six centers of STARnet, a Semiconductor Research Corporation program sponsored by MARCO and DARPA, and by the National Defense Science and Engineering Graduate (NDSEG) Fellowship (32 CFR 168a). This work partially supported by generous gifts from Intel and Texas Instruments.

6. REFERENCES

[1] DecaWave. ScenSor DW1000. http://www.decawave.com/.

[2] B. Kempke, P. Pannuto, and P. Dutta. Polypoint: Guiding indoor quadrotors with ultra-wideband localization. In *2015 ACM Workshop on Hot Topics in Wireless*, HotWireless '15, September 2015.

Demo Abstract: Michigan's IoT Toolkit

Joshua Adkins, Bradford Campbell, Samuel DeBruin, Branden Ghena, Benjamin Kempke, Noah Klugman, Ye-sheng Kuo, Deepika Natarajan, Pat Pannuto, Thomas Zachariah, Alan Zhen, and Prabal Dutta
Electrical Engineering and Computer Science Department
University of Michigan
Ann Arbor, MI 48109
{adkinsjd,bradjc,sdebruin,brghena,bpkempke,nklugman,samkuo,dnataraj,ppannuto,tzachari,azhen,prabal}@umich.edu

ABSTRACT

Building connected, pervasive, human-facing, and responsive applications that incorporate local sensors, smartphone interactions, device actuation, and cloud-based learning—the promised features of the Internet of Things (IoT)—requires a complete suite of tools spanning both hardware and software. We present a set of these pieces, including a gateway, four hardware building blocks, multiple sensor platforms, an indoor localization system, and software for connecting users and devices. Each piece plays an integral role towards enabling applications, from facilitating rapid development of wireless smart devices to composing data streams and services from a diverse set of components. By providing layered interoperable systems, our toolkit offers cohesive support for moving beyond single-device, cloud-centric applications—typical in today's IoT landscape—and towards richer applications that incorporate multiple data streams, human interaction, cloud processing, location awareness, multiple communication protocols, historical data, access control, and on-demand user interfaces. To show how the pieces in the toolkit cooperate, we demonstrate a location-based access control application where a user's smartphone can control a room's lighting, but only from within the room. Further, data streams from the phone and nearby sensors are used to provide a constant lighting service which attempts to maintain a user-set brightness under variable external lighting conditions.

Categories and Subject Descriptors

B.4.2 [**HARDWARE**]: Input/Output and Data Communications—*Input/Output Devices*; C.3 [**COMPUTER-COMMUNICATION NETWORKS**]: Special-Purpose and Application-Based Systems

General Terms

Design, Experimentation, Measurement, Performance

Keywords

Internet of Things, Bluetooth Low-Energy, Gateway, Application Architecture, Wireless Sensing

SenSys'15, November 1–4, 2015, Seoul, Republic of Korea
ACM 978-1-4503-3631-4/15/11.
DOI: http://dx.doi.org/10.1145/2809695.2817866 .

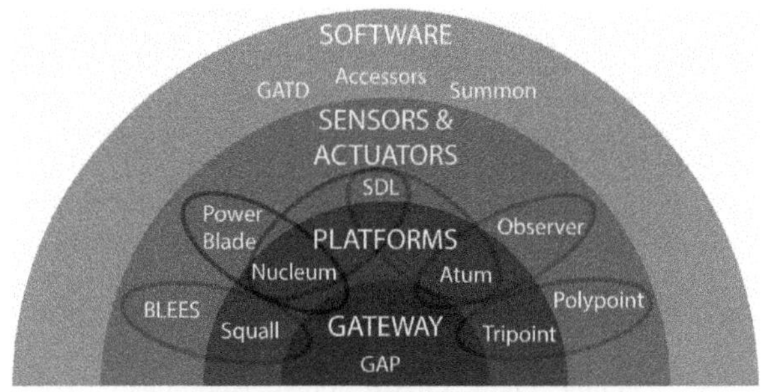

Figure 1: **The toolkit components.**

1. INTRODUCTION

As small, wireless, and low power computing integrates into more and more devices, the possibilities for dynamic applications involving people and things greatly increases. Current applications often suffer from several common pitfalls: they are limited to a single device, they rely on cloud support to connect devices and are susceptible to network failures, they require users to find, download, and install device-specific software, or they use vendor-specific APIs that limit reusability.

Our approach addresses these issues by providing software and hardware tools that explicitly facilitate local device to device communication, seamless device-to-user interactions, and data collection and processing. We provide hardware building blocks for creating new low power networked devices and sensor and actuator platforms built on top of the blocks. Further, we provide an indoor localization system that can provide real-time location updates. Figure 1 shows the layered toolkit and its components, from a gateway device to the software control layers, and Section 2 describes each piece.

We leverage our toolkit to build an office-centric application that highlights each component in the toolkit. The application allows users to read data from multiple sensors in a shared and universal smartphone application, but restricts control access to only users who are in the same room as the devices. In addition, the application simultaneously uses streaming light sensor data to provide a service that will maintain a constant lighting level as natural light changes throughout the day.

2. TOOLKIT COMPONENTS

Figure 1 overviews the suit of tools in our toolkit and Figure 2 shows the devices that are integral to building interesting Internet of Things applications. The base of this diagram is a Generic Access Point (GAP) which acts as a gateway for all of the IoT devices. GAP is a BeagleBone Black embedded Linux computer with cus-

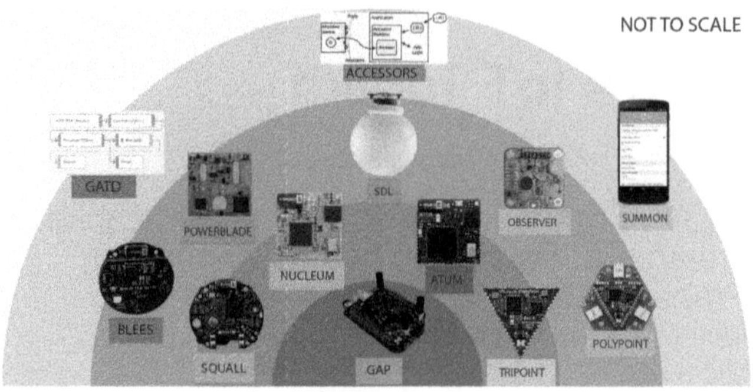

Figure 2: **Toolkit implementations.** All hardware, firmware, and software are available at https://github.com/lab11.

tom shield consisting of Bluetooth Low Energy (BLE) and IEEE 802.15.4 radios.

The next layer is a set of hardware platforms that can be used to create wireless embedded devices. Squall is a BLE tag platform that can act as a self-contained BLE beacon, or, by adding a shield on its stackable header system, a self-contained BLE sensor node. Nucleum and Atum are both solder-on modules that provide core wireless embedded functionality. Each consists of a radio (BLE and IEEE 802.15.4, respectively), a Cortex M microcontroller, a real-time clock, and non-volatile FRAM storage. Additionally, TriPoint is a solder-on support module that provides decimeter-accurate ultra-wideband (UWB) based RF ranging. Each of these platforms enables rapid prototyping of IoT sensors and actuators.

Next, our toolkit contains sensors and actuators that utilize our platforms. The Bluetooth Low Energy Environmental Sensor (BLEES) is a sensor board that stacks on top of Squall and captures temperature, humidity, pressure, acceleration and light intensity data. PowerBlade is a 1 in^2, plug through, BLE power meter [2]. Software Defined Lighting (SDL) [4] is a wall-powered lighting platform with both BLE and IEEE 802.15.4 radios and a high-power software controlled LED. Observer is an Atum-based, indoor environmental sensing platform that can sense temperature, humidity, pressure, acceleration, proximity, sound level, and light intensity, either as a stand-alone, battery-powered node, or as stack-on addition for GAP. PolyPoint [3] is an indoor RF localization system that consists of static anchors and mobile tags which utilize TriPoint modules to localize the tags.

Finally, a software layer is necessary to store data, organize communication between multiple sensors and actuators, and provide UIs for interacting with these devices. Our software tools include GATD, a service for receiving, storing, processing, and displaying streaming data; Accessors [1], a system of device interface wrappers which allow for application logic to be described and executed in a cloudlet; and Summon, a system that enables users to discover and automatically retrieve user interfaces to interact with nearby devices.

3. DEMONSTRATION

The demonstration, diagrammed in Figure 3, is an office setting where an occupant, using the Summon application on a smartphone, can scan for nearby BLEES, PowerBlade, Observer, and SDL devices and pull up a read-only UI for each. The user is also carrying a PolyPoint tag that is localizing the user, and when the user is located within a simulated room, the SDL application will be configured to permit the user to adjust the lighting. The Accessor infrastructure executes the logic for the application by listening for localization data and configuring the SDL devices with permitted users.

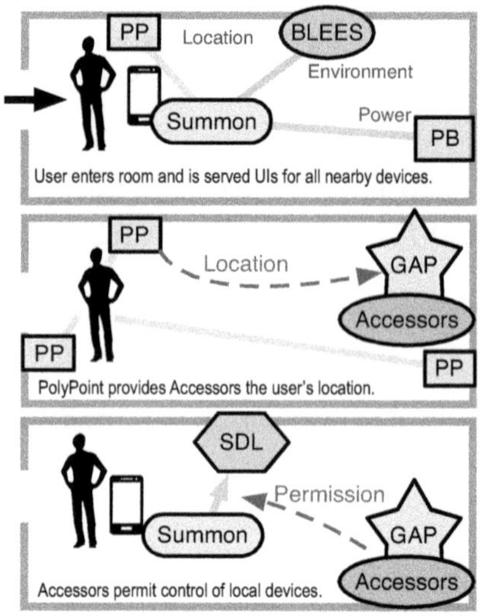

Figure 3: **Demo interaction.** When a user enters a room, PolyPoint updates the running Accessor application with the location of the user. Summon provides UIs for all BLE devices in proximity of the user, allowing the user to interact with nearby devices. Users always have read access to the devices, but when a user attempts to interact with a device, the Accessor infrastructure verifies that the user is located near the device and explicitly grants write permissions.

While the user-facing application is executing, the GAP gateway device is listening for the sensor data and forwarding the streams on to GATD. GATD archives the sensor data for observation and future processing. The data streams from the light sensors on BLEES and Observer are also fed to another Accessor based application that uses real-time lighting data to provide a "constant-lighting" service. This service can adjust the lighting in the room to keep the brightness level constant over the course of a day. This service can be enabled on the SDL devices if the user has control access based on location.

These applications demonstrate how the toolkit can provide the sensors, actuators, and infrastructure tools needed to build sophisticated applications.

4. ACKNOWLEDGMENTS

This work was supported in part by TerraSwarm, one of six centers of STARnet, a Semiconductor Research Corporation program sponsored by MARCO and DARPA, by the National Science Foundation under grant CNS-1350967, by the NSF/Intel Partnership on Cyber-Physical System (CPS) Security and Privacy under Award proposal title "Synergy: End-to-End Security for the Internet of Things, NSF proposal No. 1505684.", by the GRFP (DGE-1256260), and by ND-SEG (32 CFR 168a). This work partially supported by generous gifts from Intel and Texas Instruments.

5. REFERENCES

[1] B. Campbell, P. Pannuto, and P. Dutta. Interfacing the Internet of a trillion things. SEC'15.
[2] S. DeBruin, B. Ghena, and P. Dutta. Powerblade: A low-profile, true-power, plug-through energy meter. SenSys'15.
[3] B. Kempke, P. Pannuto, and P. Dutta. Polypoint: Guiding indoor quadrotors with ultra-wideband localization. HotWireless'15.
[4] Y.-S. Kuo, P. Pannuto, and P. Dutta. System architecture directions for a software-defined lighting infrastructure. VLCS'14.

Demo Abstract: Glimpse - Continuous, Real-Time Object Recognition on Mobile Devices

Tiffany Yu-Han Chen
MIT CSAIL
yuhan@csail.mit.edu

Lenin Ravindranath
Microsoft Research
lenin@microsoft.com

Shuo Deng
MIT CSAIL
shuodeng@csail.mit.edu

Paramvir Bahl
Microsoft Research
bahl@microsoft.com

Hari Balakrishnan
MIT CSAIL
hari@csail.mit.edu

ABSTRACT

Glimpse is a continuous, real-time object recognition system for camera-equipped mobile devices. Glimpse captures full-motion video, locates objects of interest, recognizes and labels them, and tracks them from frame to frame for the user. Because the algorithms for object recognition entail significant computation, Glimpse runs them on server machines. To achieve high accuracy, Glimpse uses an *active cache* of video frames on the mobile device. A subset of the frames in the active cache are used to track objects on the mobile, using (stale) hints about objects that arrive from the server from time to time. To reduce network bandwidth usage, Glimpse computes *trigger frames* to send to the server for recognizing and labeling.

Categories and Subject Descriptors

D.4.7 [**Operating Systems**]: Organization and Design—*Real-time systems and embedded systems; Interactive systems*

Keywords

mobile computing; wearable computing; cloud computing; caching; Google Glass

1. INTRODUCTION

Cameras of good quality are now available on almost every handheld and wearable mobile device. The high resolution of these cameras coupled with pervasive wireless connectivity makes it feasible to develop continuous, real-time object recognition applications. These applications *locate* objects in a video stream and *label* them with information associated with the objects. For example, an augmented reality application [1] that helps a user assemble furniture can pinpoint and label each piece.

To support these applications, the object recognition system must provide high *trackability*, i.e., it should be able to locate an object accurately and label it with an identifier. Achieving high trackability in real-time on mobile devices is challenging because the required computer-vision algorithms are computationally intensive and must run at the real-time rate of 30 frames per second.

For these reasons, object recognition tasks must be offloaded to more powerful servers. Offloading is a well-known idea, but in the context of continuous recognition, it must be applied with care because wireless network latencies are too high. For example, if it takes 700 milliseconds to transfer a frame and recognize its objects at a server (measured time on an LTE network), when the results arrive they will be over 20 frames old, the located object may no longer be at the reported position.

This demo introduces Glimpse, a continuous, real-time object recognition system that achieves high trackability, while reducing the amount of network bandwidth consumed relative to alternative designs. Glimpse achieves high trackability by maintaining an *active cache* of frames on the mobile device, and computing over the cached frames using the stale hints that arrive from the server to get an estimate of an object's location in the current frame. Glimpse reduces bandwidth consumption by strategically sending only certain *trigger frames* to the server to obtain object recognition hints. It sends a frame only when it is likely to produce a different answer from the local tracking.

SenSys'15, November 01-04, 2015, Seoul, South Korea.
ACM 978-1-4503-3631-4/15/11.
DOI: http://dx.doi.org/10.1145/2809695.2817867.

2. DEMONSTRATION

In this demo, we will demonstrate Glimpse with a "Follow the Celebrities" mobile application. Audiences use mobile devices or wearables to discover and track celebrity's doppelgangers nearby; the application creates an augmented reality experience by overlaying information related to the celebrity in the view of the camera. We will also demonstrate the benefit of the *active cache* design by showing the same application but without maintaining the active cache.

In addition to the interactive application, we will also display demo videos showing the benefits of Glimpse. Example videos can be viewed at `http://people.csail.mit.edu/yuhan/glimpse`.

3. REFERENCES

[1] R. Azuma. A survey of augmented reality, 1997.

Demo Abstract: Tethys – An Energy Harvesting Networked Water Flow Sensor

Holly Chiang, James Hong, Kevin Kiningham, Jiaqi Xue, Laurynas Riliskis, Philip Levis, Mark Horowitz
Stanford University
{ hchiang1, jamesh93, kkiningh, jiaqixue, riliskis, pal, horowitz}@stanford.edu

ABSTRACT
We describe Tethys, an energy-harvesting wireless water flow sensor that can monitor water use at a per-fixture level with the intention of associating water use with specific individuals. Tethys was motivated by recent efforts at Stanford University to reduce water use due to the California drought. Understanding how the university population uses water at per-person level can greatly influence policies and conservation approaches. Tethys uses Bluetooth Smart to both identify individuals as well as asynchronously upload data to the cloud for later analysis. We describe two challenges encountered in deploying Tethys: energy harvesting design and the mechanical considerations for high-pressure water at high temperatures.

Categories and Subject Descriptors
C.3 **[Special-purpose and application-based systems]**: Real-time and embedded systems

General Terms
Measurement, Experimentation, Human Factors

Keywords
Wireless Sensor Networks, Energy Harvesting, Embedded Gateway Cloud

1. INTRODUCTION
Water conservation has recently attracted a lot of attention, especially in regions impacted by drought. Individuals can conscientiously monitor their own water usage, but to reduce water usage in large organizations, such as a company or university, policies generally need to be enacted. Setting effective policies requires fine-grained knowledge of water usage patterns, and collecting large amounts of such data is hard to do with currently available water flow sensing devices. To address this, we developed Tethys.

Tethys is an embedded-gateway-cloud implementation. Energy harvesting sensors collect water flow rate and temperature data and transmit that data to nearby smartphones. The smartphones send that data to the cloud, aggregating data from all of the sensors for later data analytics. The data is securely and reliably sent through multiple different hardware and software platforms.

SenSys '15, November 01-04, 2015, Seoul, Republic of Korea
ACM 978-1-4503-3631-4/15/11.
http://dx.doi.org/10.1145/2809695.2817868

The devices were envisioned to be self-sufficient once deployed, but periodic advertising and transmission of data through Bluetooth drains the battery within a few weeks. To extend the deployment lifetime of a device, we decided to have the device implement energy harvesting. To keep the device simple, we combined the mechanisms for energy harvesting and water flow rate sensing.

Tethys devices will be installed in multiple Stanford dormitories to collect water usage data. The data will later be analyzed to determine patterns such as the impact of temperature on water usage, and water usage over time. With that knowledge policies can be designed to reduce water consumption.

2. System Design
2.1 Energy Harvesting
To harvest energy from the flow of water, we purchased electromagnetic generators commonly used to power LED showerheads. The inside of a generator rotor is lined with twelve magnets arranged in an alternating N-S-N-S pattern. The stator has nine coil windings and is placed within the rotor though separated from the rotor by the casing. Water flows into the casing through a small slit and turns the rotor before flowing back out as seen in Figure 1, generating an AC signal whose frequency is related to the flow rate. The generated signal is converted to DC through a bridge rectifier and sent through a buck converter to then charge a lithium battery.

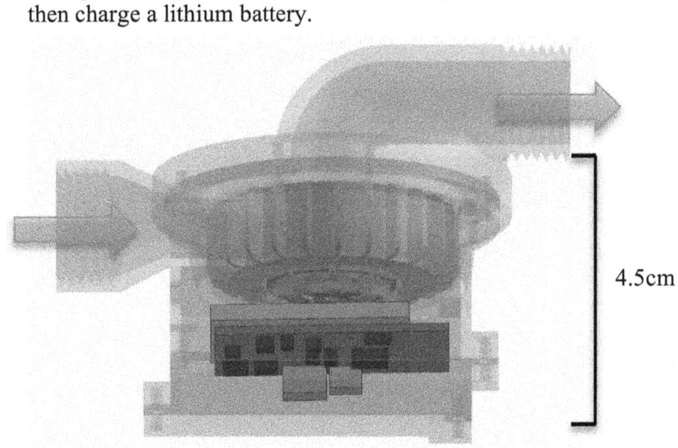

Figure 1: Device components

2.2 Energy Profile
Unlike other water flow sensing devices, Tethys stays on even when there is no water flow in order to transmit data, so the energy harvested from when the shower is on is used to power the device when the shower is off. Tethys is designed to be attached to low flow showerheads, which in the Stanford dormitories have a flow rate of 0.67 gal/min. At that flow rate, we expect to harvest

energy at the rate of 60mW. The chip uses an average of 600μW, meaning one 15 minute shower a day is enough to indefinitely power the device.

2.3 Mechanical Design

We built a casing designed to be fastened behind a showerhead or sink, as shown in Figure 2. Similar water driven electromagnetic energy harvesters used metal casings [1-2] but metal would have blocked Bluetooth so plastic was used. The parts were 3D printed, as some of the casing geometries could not be cast and 3D printing was more cost efficient at the quantities we required. The use of plastic added significant challenge to the casing design, as the water pressure had to be high enough to turn the rotor but too high a water pressure would crack the plastic. The water pressure was adjusted by changing the size and location of the entrance slit. In addition in several areas the material had to be thickened and sharp corners that were origins of cracks had to be smoothed out. Another issue was that the casing would warp and sometimes crack when hot water flowed through. The plastic material therefore needed to have a heat deflection point above the highest possible water temperature of 60°C, while also being biocompatible. To achieve both requirements the casing was 3D printed using treated ABS-like material, which has a heat deflection point of 82°C, and was afterwards coated with a thin parylene layer to make it biocompatible.

Figure 2: Deployed device

2.4 Embedded Device

Each Tethys device is programmed to take in temperature and water flow readings and send the encrypted data over BLE. A thermistor placed against the water pipe measures temperature. Water flow sensing is implemented by sending a single phase through a voltage clamp into the ADC and taking periodic measurements to calculate the voltage frequency. All sensor readings are then compressed using simple thresholding; new sensor values are only recorded if the sensor readings have a noticeable change. Every group of three sensor readings are bundled into a packet.

Encryption is implemented using an on-chip AES block. After compression, every packet is encrypted and stored in flash using OCB. Each device has a unique AES key and name which is linked into the embedded program at flash time. Additionally, the backend has a copy of each key/name pair to allow it to decrypt packets after they have been sent over the network.

2.5 Data Transmission

On the embedded device, we have a simple data characteristic that can be read by the gateway to get all sensor readings that have not yet been acknowledged by the server, along with a sequence number for each packet. The gateway is implemented in both IOS and Android as mobile applications. When the server acknowledges a packet to the gateway, the gateway writes to the data characteristic the sequence number of the last acknowledged packet. Cumulative acknowledgement is used; acknowledgement of a single packet implies acknowledgement of all previous packets. When the device receives acknowledgement for a packet from the server via a gateway, it is deleted off the device to free up space for additional sensor readings. This communication model is shown in Figure 3.

In addition to forwarding sensor values to the backend server, the gateway application attaches additional metadata such as a phone identifier and download timestamps. This information is used to provide fine-grained water consumption metrics on a user-by-user (phone-by-phone) basis as well as to provide operational metrics. The phone application is also responsible for delivering data acknowledgements from the backend server to individual sensor devices.

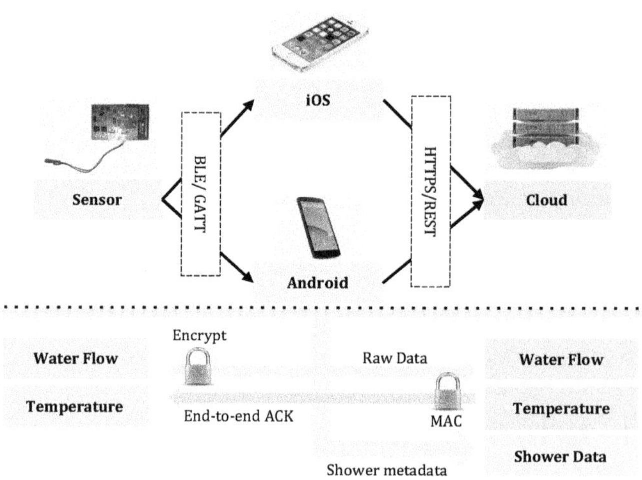

Figure 3: Communication Model

3. Demonstration

To demonstrate the performance of our device, we will have a Tethys device hooked up to a portable pump running water through a closed loop system. Water flow and temperature data will be generated and pulled from the device by nearby smartphones. The data will then be sent to the database, which we will display on a nearby laptop. Observers will be able to vary the water flow rate or temperature, and see that later reflected in the database.

4. REFERENCES

[1] P. Becker, B. Folkmer, R. Goepfert, D. Hoffmann, A. Willmann and Y. Manoli. 2013. Energy Autonomous Wireless Water Meter with Integrated Turbine Driven Energy Harvester. *Journal of Physics: Conference Series*. Vol. 476 012046 doi:10.1088/1742-6596/476/1/012046

[2] W. Hao and R. Garcia. 2014. Development of a Digital and Battery-Free Smart Flowmeter. *Energies* 2014, 7, 3695-3709; doi:10.3390/en706

Demo Abstract

ALPS - The Acoustic Location Processing System

Patrick Lazik Niranjini Rajagopal Oliver Shih Bruno Sinopoli Anthony Rowe
Electrical and Computer Engineering Department
Carnegie Mellon University
{plazik,niranjir,oshih,brunos,agr}@ece.cmu.edu

Abstract

We demonstrate *ALPS* [1], a platform that augments BLE proximity beacons with ultrasonic transmitters in a manner that allows for precise and robust indoor localization. *ALPS* uses Time-Difference-Of-Arrival (TDOA) and Time-Of-Flight (TOF) ranging to accurately localize mobile devices such as off-the-shelf smartphones and tablets in 2D space. Users inside the demo area will be able to determine their location and can directly plot it relatively to a map of the area using our app on a smartphone. Once a receiving device has determined its initial position, it can synchronize its audio clock with the transmission infrastructure to perform TOF-based localization, which provides similar position accuracy to TDOA-based localization with fewer beacons. Multilateration and trilateration processing for each device's location is offloaded onto a cloud-based solver that can provide localization as a service to *ALPS* and similar TOF/TDOA-based systems.

1 System Description

ALPS is a hybrid BLE-ultrasound system that is able to provide significantly improved ranging capabilities as compared to BLE-only beacons. The system consists of time synchronized beacons that transmit ultrasonic chirps similar to those described in [2] and [3]. These chirps are inaudible to humans, but are still detectable by modern smartphones. The phone can then use TDOA to determine ranges and to synchronize with the infrastructure (as described in [3]) so that it can directly measure TOF. *ALPS* uses BLE on each node to synchronize receivers to the transmitting infrastructure.The inclusion of BLE both simplifies the design and allows for the entire ultrasonic bandwidth to be used exclusively for ranging.

SenSys'15, November 1-4, 2015, Seoul, South Korea.
ACM 978-1-4503-3631-4/15/11.
DOI: http://dx.doi.org/10.1145/2809695.2817869

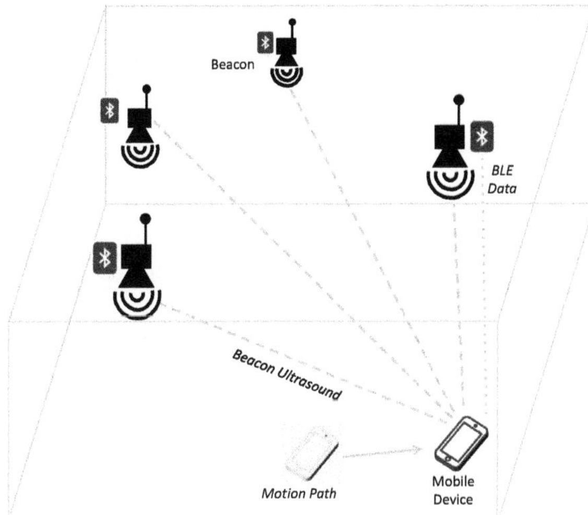

Figure 1. System overview

1.1 Architecture

A typical system setup consists of three or more *ALPS* transmitters deployed at known locations in the target area as seen in Figure 1. Placement of the transmitters is flexible, however the system performs best when the Line-Of-Sight (LOS) coverage of the transmitters is maximized. In most deployments, this would mean mounting them to the ceiling. The transmitters are time synchronized using 802.15.4 radios that listen to periodic transmissions from a master node. The timing master node can be one of the installed beacons. Once a mobile device estimates its range from four or more beacons, its position can be estimated using multilateration. *ALPS* employs a novel time synchronization technique where signals from multiple transmitters can be used to synchronize the audio sampling subsystem of each mobile device with global time. Once synchronized, the devices can perform TOF ranging. This significantly decreases the number of beacons required to cover an indoor space and improves performance in the face of obstructions.

The mobile device performs the capture and demodulation of the ultrasound signals to obtain their relative Time-Of-Arrivals (TOA) and then transmits this data via websocket to a cloud-based solver program. The solver determines the device's position via trilateration or multilateration and sends it back to the device. This architecture offloads the most processing intensive work onto a more powerful ma-

Figure 2. ALPS Beacon

chine with access to maps that can provide a faster update rate and reduced energy consumption on the resource constrained mobile device. The cloud-based solver can process the TOA data from other TOF/TDOA-based localization systems, therefore providing localization as a service.

1.2 Hardware

We demonstrate an embedded, low-power hardware platform for our transmission infrastructure. The complete hybrid ultrasound and BLE beacon is shown in Figure 2 and consists of the following main components: (1) An ultrasound transceiver board with an 802.15.4 radio (2) a BLE daughter board (3) a piezo bullet tweeter with attached omnidirectional horn and (4) a battery pack for optional battery powered operation.

1.3 Ranging

We use Time-Division-Multiple-Access (TDMA) to multiplex the transmission of our ultrasound transmitters over time and transmit ultrasonic chirps for precise ranging. Instead of encoding data using the chirps, *ALPS* relies on BLE advertisement packets in an iBeacon compatible format to signal the current TDMA time slot. This eliminates the need for a complicated and more processing intensive demodulation step on the phone and makes the ultrasound signals shorter and more likely to be detected correctly.

2 Time Synchronization

Mobile devices can be synchronized to the transmission infrastructure for performing TOF ranging instead of TDOA-based ranging. This is done by first determining the device's position using TDOA ranging and multilateration and then calculating the distance to at least one transmitter. Since the ultrasound transmissions are periodic, the beginning of the TDMA cycle can be determined based on the distance to the transmitter, the TOA of its transmission in the device's recording buffer and the time slot of the transmission. Since the device's ADC has a free running clock, we can synchronize it to the transmission cycle of the beacons by determining the sample in the recording buffer that corresponds to the

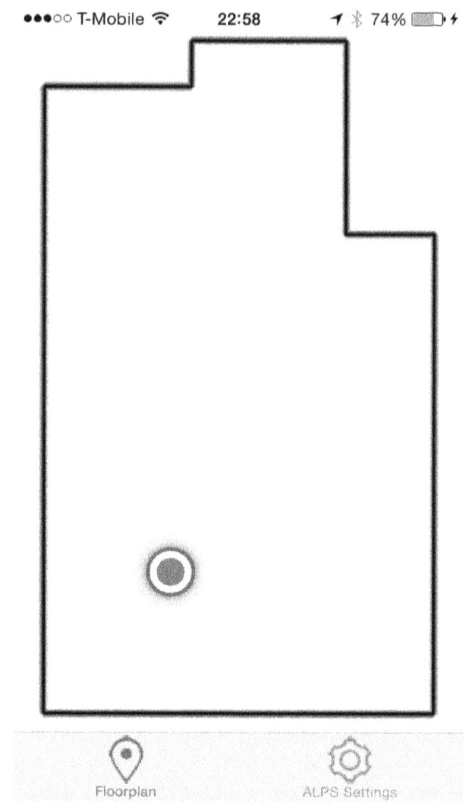

Figure 3. Screenshot of iOS localization app

beginning of the TDMA cycle. This then allows for TOF ranging to be used instead of TDOA.

3 Demonstration

We demonstrate our system by providing each user with a mobile device running an app that displays a map of the demo area and the current position of the mobile device as seen in Figure 3. The position is updated continuously as users move throughout the space. The app also displays the most recent TOA data that was obtained and whether the mobile device is synchronized to the transmission infrastructure. This will allow users to monitor which beacons were used in the last position update and experiment with how localization accuracy is impacted when beacons are selectively blocked or when the device loses synchronization.

4 References

[1] Patrick Lazik, Niranjini Rajagopal, Oliver Shih, Bruno Sinopoli, and Anthony Rowe. ALPS: A bluetooth and ultrasound platform for mapping and localization. In *Proceedings of the 13th ACM Conference on Embedded Network Sensor Systems*, SenSys '15. ACM, 2015.

[2] Patrick Lazik and Anthony Rowe. Indoor pseudo-ranging of mobile devices using ultrasonic chirps. In *Proceedings of the 10th ACM Conference on Embedded Network Sensor Systems*, SenSys '12, pages 99–112, New York, NY, USA, 2012. ACM.

[3] Patrick Lazik, Niranjini Rajagopal, Bruno Sinopoli, and Anthony Rowe. Ultrasonic time synchronization and ranging on smartphones. In *21st IEEE Real-Time and Embedded Technology and Applications Symposium*, RTAS '14, 2014.

Demo: User Support for Power Management of Continuous Sensing Applications

Chulhong Min[1], Chungkuk Yoo[1], Sangwon Choi[2], Pillsoon Park[3], Seungchul Lee[1], Changhun Lee[1], Seungpyo Choi[1], Seungwoo Kang[4], Youngki Lee[5], Inseok Hwang[6], Younghyun Ju[7], Junehwa Song[1]

[1]School of Computing, KAIST, [2]Information and Electronics Research Institute, KAIST, [3]Division of Web Science Technology, KAIST, [4]Computer Science and Engineering, KOREATECH, [5]School of Information Systems, Singapore Management University, [6]IBM Research – Austin, [7]Naver Labs

[1,3]{chulhong, ckyoo, spchoi, pillsoon.park, seungchul, changhun, spchoi, junesong}@nclab.kaist.ac.kr, [2]sangwonc@kaist.ac.kr, [4]swkang@koreatech.ac.kr, [5]youngkilee@smu.edu.sg, [6]ihwang@us.ibm.com, [7]younghyun.ju@navercorp.com

ABSTRACT

Recently, a number of continuous sensing applications have been actively proposed in research communities and commercially released in the market. However, due to their unique power characteristics, user behavior-dependent battery drain, they bring new challenges for users' power management on these applications. In this demonstration, we present a comprehensive approach to support users' power management for continuous sensing applications. First, at pre-installation time, we provide an instant, personalized power estimation of a continuous sensing application. Without exhaustive trial and error, users can decide judiciously to install a certain application or not. Second, at runtime, we provide mobility-aware battery information. With this information, users can better estimate the phone's remaining battery life based on their imminent mobility conditions and take necessary actions in advance such as carrying an additional battery or minimizing the use of applications.

Categories and Subject Descriptors

C.3 [**Special-Purpose and Application-based Systems**]: Real-time and embedded systems; H.5.m. Information interfaces and presentation (e.g., HCI): Miscellaneous.

Keywords

Smartphone; continuous sensing application; battery management; user support

1. INTRODUCTION

Recently, a variety of continuous sensing applications (hereinafter 'apps') have been actively proposed in research communities and commercially released in the market. In the background, they continuously monitor diverse user contexts such as location, physical activity, and conversation [1][4] and provide what users need right on time and place. To save energy for continuous monitoring, they often adopt context-dependent sensing pipelines. The key idea is to trigger high-power sensors selectively by low-power sensors. A common example is a location tracking app. It triggers GPS only when a user's motion is detected by power-efficient accelerometers [4]. Due to such context-dependent logic, the actual power use of continuous sensing apps largely depends on a user's physical behaviors and environmental conditions.

The contextual power consumption of continuous sensing apps brings new challenges for users' power management. First, the power impact of a continuous sensing app largely varies across different users. Thus, it is important to provide a personalized power estimation in order to help users understand the power impact of a sensing app. Second, even for an individual user, the battery drain of a sensing app depends on a user's imminent situation. Thus, while using sensing apps, users can be embarrassed due to unexpected, sudden battery drop.

In this demonstration, we present a comprehensive approach to help sensing app users manage their phone's battery. First, at pre-installation time, we provide an instant, personalized power estimation of a continuous sensing app [2]. Users can decide judiciously to install a certain app without exhaustive trial and error. Second, at runtime, we provide mobility-aware battery information. With this information, users can better estimate the phone's battery life based on their imminent mobility conditions and take necessary actions in advance such as carrying an additional battery or minimizing the use of applications.

2. POWER-IMPACT ESTIMATION AT PRE-INSTALLATION TIME

Providing an accurate, personalized power estimation of a continuous sensing app at pre-installation time is a non-trivial task. A trivial solution may involve computing the average power impact in certain, common use cases. Such estimations, however, would be inaccurate for individual users, since the power use of a sensing app varies noticeably depending on the users' physical activities, phone usage, and other environmental factors.

To take these factors into account, we devise a user-behavior aware power emulation approach. The key idea is to capture the user's physical activities and any other environmental factors, recreate this environment on a cloud-side emulator, and execute the target sensing app on the emulator to track its power use. This approach has three advantages. (1) It provides an individualized power estimation of a continuous sensing app,

SenSys '15, November 1-4, 2015, Seoul, South Korea
ACM 978-1-4503-3631-4/15/11.
DOI: http://dx.doi.org/10.1145/2809695.2817870.

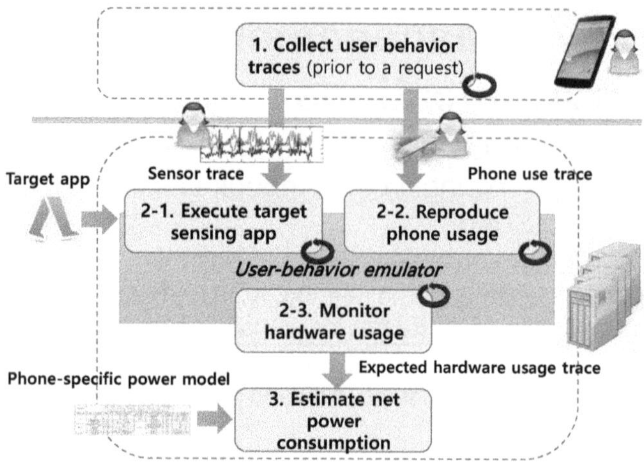

Figure 1. Overall operation for power-impact estimation

since it utilizes the user's physical sensor and phone usage data to construct an emulator environment identical to the user's personal device. (2) It estimates power use of an app without prior power profiling or knowledge of its internal logic. The emulator only requires the app's executable in order to track its hardware use, with no need of its source code. (3) It considers shared hardware use with existing apps by reproducing their resource use.

The system takes three inputs in order to provide an accurate, personalized power impact estimation of a target sensing app: a user's sensor trace, phone use trace, and the sensing app's executable. It outputs the net power increase (mW) due to the target app. The system consists of two major components, a mobile-side trace collector and a cloud-side power emulator, as depicted in Figure 1. The mobile-side trace collector runs on the user's device and is responsible for collecting the user's behavior trace: sensor traces and phone use traces. These traces are then uploaded and managed on the cloud server, which upon a power estimation request, executes its component emulator. The emulator recreates the user's environment from behavior traces, executes the target sensing app, and monitors its hardware use to provide an estimation of its power impact.

3. MONITORING OF MOBILITY-AWARE BATTERY DRAIN

We present mobility-aware battery drain information of running sensing apps in two aspects. First, we provide expected battery life for a set of mobility conditions. Figure 2(right) shows expected battery life at specific mobility conditions. It also displays the expected battery level after a specified amount of time. When the battery level is relatively high, but a long-term activity is expected, e.g., 2-hour driving, users can predict their future battery status depending on their imminent mobility condition.

Second, we provide a historical battery use summary. Figure 2(left) shows the time spent and the battery drained in standby state for each mobility conditions. This historical information is similar to the per-app battery usage that Android provides by default. When an unusual day is expected, e.g., a business trip, users can refer to the past days with similar distribution of mobility conditions.

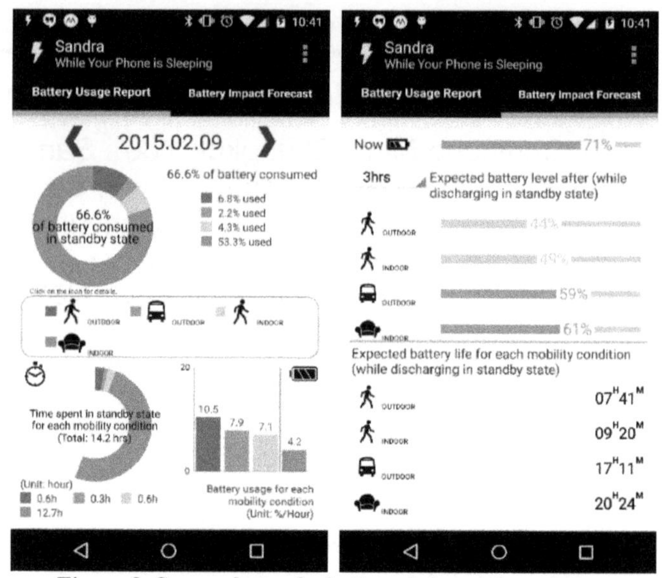

Figure 2. Screenshots of a battery information advisor

4. DEMONSTRATION

We first demonstrate the overall operation of power-impact estimation. As in Figure 1, the key operations are 1) emulating power use of a target app with given user behavior traces, 2) tracking hardware usage statistics generated by the execution of the app on the emulator, and 3) calculating the power consumption based on the hardware usage statistics. To show them effectively, we plan to build web pages and to present a short video. The web pages intuitively show the intermediate results of the internal operations. The video delivers a brief description of the system architecture and operations. We further demonstrate the current prototype of our mobility-aware battery information advisor. We plan to set up a live visualization of mobility-aware battery information, targeting commercial sensing apps. Figure 2 shows the screenshot examples.

5. ACKNOWLEDGMENTS

This work was supported by the National Research Foundation of Korea(NRF) grant funded by the Korea government(MSIP) (No. 2011-0018120).

6. REFERENCES

[1] Lee, Y., Min, C., Hwang, C., Lee, J., Hwang, I., Ju, Y., Yoo, C., Moon, M., Lee, U., and Song, J. SocioPhone: Everyday Face-to-face Interaction Monitoring Platform using Multi-phone Sensor Fusion. In *Proc. MobiSys* 2013.

[2] Min, C., Lee, Y., Yoo, C., Kang, S., Choi, S., Park, P., Hwang, I., Ju, Y., Choi, S., and Song, J. PowerForecaster: Predicting Smartphone Power Impact of Continuous Sensing Applications at Pre-installation Time. In *Proc. SenSys* 2015.

[3] Min, C., Yoo, C., Hwang, I., Kang, S., Lee, Y., Lee, S., Park, P., Lee, C., Choi, S., and Song, J. Sandra Helps You Learn: the More You Walk, the More Battery Your Phone Drains. In *Proc. UbiComp* 2015.

[4] Paek, J., Kim, J. and Govindan, R. Energy-Efficient Rate-Adaptive GPS-based Positioning for Smartphones. In *Proc. MobiSys* 2010.

Demo Abstract: Posture Correction Using Smartphone-Based Relational Intervention Model

Jaemyung Shin
KAIST
Republic of Korea
jmshin@nclab.kaist.ac.kr

Bumsoo Kang
KAIST
Republic of Korea
steve.kang@kaist.ac.kr

Jinhan Kim
KAIST
Republic of Korea
blues@kaist.ac.kr

Jina Huh
University of California, San Diego
USA
jina.huh@gmail.com

Junehwa Song
KAIST
Republic of Korea
junesong@nclab.kaist.ac.kr

Taiwoo Park
Michigan State University
USA
twp@msu.edu

ABSTRACT
Many theories and empirical research show the critical role of social relationships in shaping human behavior. Mobile and persuasive technologies present increased opportunities for affecting people's behavior. We propose the relational intervention model, which provokes a paired helper when the user performs a target behavior. In this demo, we present BeUpright, a posture-correction mobile application based on the relational intervention model.

1. INTRODUCTION
Ever-growing mobile technologies have opened up new opportunities for real-time behavior monitoring and persuasion. While the majority of research in behavior change has focused on self-administered settings, several studies have investigated how to manipulate others' behavior by employing individuals' immediate social networks [1]. We further extend this literature to investigate how an intimate, dyadic relationship can increase the efficacy of a persuasive application.

We propose the relational intervention model. The model consists of a mobile sensor device, the target user, and the helper. The helper will be provoked by the system (e.g., phone being locked) when the mobile sensor device detects that the target user is doing or has done something not in line with goal behavior. We expect that the target user will attempt to prevent the helper from experiencing provocation. These accumulated attempts will then lead to further sustained behavior change. In this demo, we present a mobile application for posture correction based on the relational intervention model.

2. RELATIONAL INTERVENTION
Figure 1 shows the process of behavior change in the relational intervention model.

1. The mobile device alerts the target user when he/she performs against a targeted behavior (e.g., bad sitting posture).
2. If the target user continues to perform against the targeted behavior, the helper's mobile phone generates an irritating event that will provoke the helper (e.g., locks smartphone for a while).
3. The helper can intervene the target user toward the target behavior to stop the irritating event.

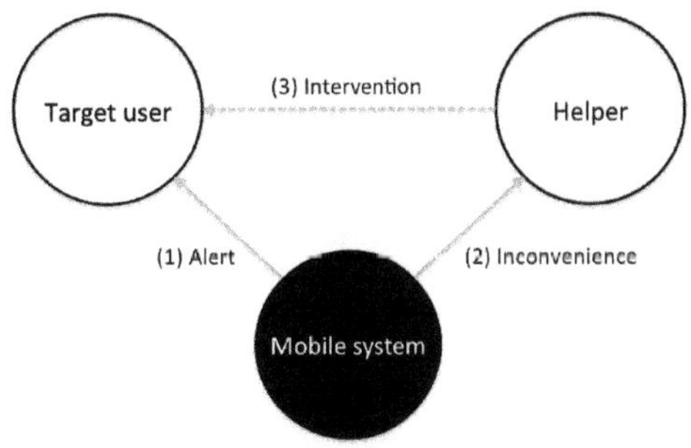

Figure 1. Conceptual diagram of relational intervention model.

We argue that the model facilitates two motivations for target users' behavior change. First, the target user wants to avoid provoking the helper with irritating events in mobile use. The target user will thus avoid ignoring the machine-generated alerts and change the target behavior. Secondly, target users will receive direct feedback from their helpers after the provocative event. The target user will be reinforced to make the association between the undesired behavior and helpers experiencing irritating events.

3. SYSTEM DESIGN
We implemented BeUpright, a mobile application to help target users keep the correct sitting posture, based on the relational intervention model (see Figure 2).

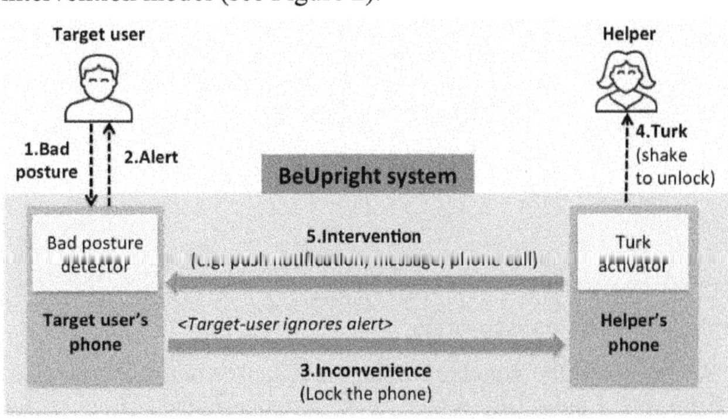

Figure 2. BeUpright System Overview.

SenSys '15, November 01-04, 2015, Seoul, Republic of Korea
ACM 978-1-4503-3631-4/15/11.
http://dx.doi.org/10.1145/2809695.2817871

3.1 Bad Sitting Posture Detection

BeUpright detects two types of bad sitting posture: *leaning backward* and *leaning forward*, the most commonly examined bad sitting postures in the literature [2]. To detect the posture of a user, BeUpright employs TI SensorTag[1], a small sensor device equipped with a variety of sensors, including a 3-D accelerometer as well as Bluetooth wireless connectivity (see Figure 3). The sensor is to be worn on the user's shirt, about one inch below the collarbone[2]. We used a small magnet to attach the sensor to a cloth.

Figure 3. Sensor for sitting posture detection.

Rather than simply assuming a single standard for the correct posture, BeUpright allows for individual posture calibration before use. Every user needs to make the app learn his/her "correct" posture during the first use, which is possible to recalibrate later.

Womersley et al. reported that leaning more than six degrees could cause lower back pain [3]. Our system classifies leaning more than six degrees from a previously calibrated correct posture as "bad" posture. To filter out temporary stretches or other unusual behavior, BeUpright alerts when a user is in his/her bad posture continuously for longer than 20 seconds.

3.2 BeUpright Application

BeUpright starts monitoring user postures after the user makes a connection between the sensor and the BeUpright application. When the target user has bad posture longer than 20 seconds, BeUpright provides an alert. If the target user does not change the posture within 10 seconds of receiving the alert, BeUpright locks the mobile phone of the target user's helper. To unlock the phone, the helper needs to shake it more than 10 times (see Figure 4a).

After the helper unlocks the phone, the helper can see the target user's face as a floating head in the main screen of the phone (see Figure 4b). If the helper drags the floating head to the outside of the screen, the system will send the target user a push notification, which lets the target user know that the helper's phone had been locked. If the helper double taps the floating head, a messaging application will appear so that the helper can intervene with the target user directly.

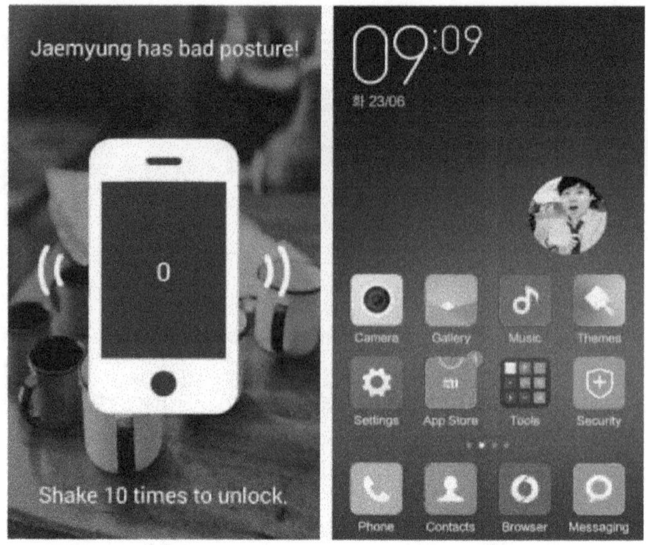

(a) (b)

Figure 4. Screenshots of BeUpright application.

4. DEMONSTRATION SETUP

We will demonstrate BeUpright with two smartphones (Google Nexus 5) and a wearable sensor (TI CC2650 SensorTag), which is to be attached about one inch below the collarbone. Two people will play the roles of target user and helper and are supposed to cooperate in achieving a shared goal (e.g., getting the highest score) in a simple mobile game (e.g., Temple Run). They will be temporarily separated and not able to see each other. The helper will be the main player of the game, and the target user will sit on an unbalanced chair that makes it hard to maintain good posture. If the target user is in a poor posture, the helper's phone will be locked for a little while, which will interfere in the helper's play. In this demo, the target user will experience the relational intervention model by trying to avoid provoking the helper with irritating events.

5. ACKNOWLEDGEMENT

This work was supported by the National Research Foundation of Korea(NRF) grant funded by the Korea government(MSIP) (No. 2011-0018120).

6. REFERENCES

[1] Chiu, M. C., Chang, S. P., Chang, Y. C., Chu, H. H., Chen, C. C. H., Hsiao, F. H., & Ko, J. C. (2009). Playful bottle: a mobile social persuasion system to motivate healthy water intake. In *Proceedings of the 11th international conference on Ubiquitous computing* (pp. 185-194).

[2] Grandjean, E., & Hünting, W. (1977). Ergonomics of posture—review of various problems of standing and sitting posture. *Applied ergonomics*, *8*(3), 135-140.

[3] Womersley, L., & May, S. (2006). Sitting posture of subjects with postural backache. *Journal of manipulative and physiological therapeutics*, *29*(3), 213-218

---

[1] http://www.ti.com/sensortag

[2] We borrowed the concept of placing a sensor under the clavicle from the Lumo lift, which is a commercialized product for posture detection.

Sophisticated Sensing on Transient Power

Josiah Hester
School of Computing
Clemson University
jhester@clemson.edu

ABSTRACT

For decades sensing systems have relied solely on battery power for execution of all activities; this has caused the focus of much research to go towards reducing energy consumption to extend the usable lifetime of a sensor. Recently, a new class of batteryless devices has arisen that promise operation in perpetuity, but often at the cost of reliability, and complexity. Programming, profiling, debugging, and building these applications is a significant challenge; designers must often be capable of implementing custom hardware to manage energy, while writing code in an environment that does not guarantee task completion. In this abstract, we motivate batteryless sensing, examine the state of the art, and propose a novel approach to programming, profiling, debugging, and building, tiny, batteryless sensors.

Categories and Subject Descriptors

C.3 [**Special-Purpose and Application-Based Systems**]: Microprocessor/microcomputer applications; D.3.2 [**Programming Languages**]: Language Classifications—*Specialized application languages*

General Terms

Measurement, Experimentation, Performance, Reliability

Keywords

Energy Harvesting; Capacitor; Federated Energy; Ekho; UFoP; Embedded System

1. INTRODUCTION

Wireless sensors use of batteries as the primary energy source has hampered their ability to be deployed for long periods of time. Batteries only have a usable lifetime of a few years if used carefully. Additionally batteries are expensive, large, and pose environmental risks when disposed—often requiring human intervention or maintenance. Because of the high costs associated with batteries, a new class of sensors emerged that instead rely on energy harvesting for all computation tasks. By replacing batteries with capacitors, these devices reduce environmental risk, can be made smaller and cheaper, and can be deployed for much longer periods of time. When sensing deployments can last on the order of decades instead of months, very long term studies of infrastructure, wildlife, and human factors become realistic.

Wireless sensing systems generally operate under the assumption that power is a stable, if limited, resource. This assumption has been challenged by batteryless platforms such as computational RFID, that are powered off small capacitors and rely on energy harvested from an RFID Reader. These devices are often only able to store enough energy for a few hundred milliseconds of work, losing memory and time when energy is not sufficient to turn on the device. Devices often operate blind, reconstructing progress from checkpoints left by a possibly long dead version of themselves. Long running tasks must be executed piecemeal across reboots using checkpointing and careful scheduling. Even *with* careful checkpointing and scheduling, sensing outcomes are never guaranteed.

Building applications resilient to inconsistent power is challenging because system designers lack the debugging tools, language support, and hardware platforms. Because of this, batteryless sensor deployments have been limited to simple programs at small scale. To move batteryless sensors beyond computational RFID and into the mainstream of traditional sensing, the developmental burden of batteryless applications must be eased.

The central thesis of this research is that batteryless devices can support long-running, sophisticated sensing applications. To test this thesis we envision building a sensing platform that transparently manages the temporal, computational, and consistency difficulties caused by flaky power, specifically we look at the following:

- Hardware solutions to managing energy storage and timekeeping between power failures (Section 2)
- Language and runtime support for computing on batteryless devices (Section 3)
- Tools which enable repeatable experimentation of batteryless devices (Section 4)

Innovating in these three areas will enable application developers to quickly and confidently prototype, test, and deploy perpetual sensing systems.

2. HARDWARE

Software solutions to managing energy and keeping time on transient power fall far short of enabling sophisticated applications. Microcontrollers draw too much energy to be able to handle energy

SenSys'15, November 1–4, 2015, Seoul, South Korea..
ACM 978-1-4503-3631-4/15/11.
DOI: http://dx.doi.org/10.1145/2809695.2822521 .

management tasks. Additionally, they cold boot too slow to keep accurate time throughout power failures. It is imperative that certain low level tasks are handled by the hardware layer to reduce the energy and time overhead as much as possible. In order to simplify development of batteryless sensing applications, we have relegated energy management, and timekeeping to the hardware layer.

Federating Energy: In most sensing systems, energy originates from a single energy store (a battery or super capacitor). This convention causes task and component coupling for capacitor based devices. This happens for the simple reasons that charging a capacitor large enough to support sensing, computation, and communication, takes longer than charging a smaller capacitor that supports just one of those functions. We have proposed UFoP (the United Federation of Peripherals) [2] as a solution to this problem; UFoP federates a device's total energy storage into multiple capacitors, each dedicated to a specific component or task.

Batteryless Timekeeping: One of the greatest challenges to batteryless computing is keeping track of time across power failures. When energy runs out, the microcontroller, volatile RAM, and all clocks are reset. This means that any previous timestamps have no meaning, since the local clock will start back at zero. Previous approaches to keeping time [3] used the data remanence properties of SRAM to measure the time since a power loss. We can extend this approach using a dedicated hardware component and an ADC for precise measurement—giving us greater configurability and precision.

3. LANGUAGE

Without language and runtime support for batteryless sensing, the hardware techniques previously described will have limited usefulness. Currently applications for batteryless sensing are highly constrained—all tasks must happen in one power cycle. This means that tasks must be simple, execute quickly, and have no dependencies, otherwise the program may not complete before a power loss. Previous work has focused on checkpointing, energy aware sensing, and scheduling; however existing approaches have too high of an overhead, or do not consider how the loss of timekeeping effects the duty cycle. We propose a language and runtime system for batteryless sensing devices that addresses these core problems. This system will be designed to track sensor data through power failures while also enabling task dependencies, and task scheduling.

Track sensor data through power failures: Application developers have no way of knowing how old data is that was gathered before a power failure, meaning that passing that data on could be a waste of energy and time. Using the hardware support for timekeeping described in Section 2, checkpointing, and application hints supplied by developers, our runtime can dynamically decide whether to use, or replace existing senor data gathered in a previous duty cycle. These automatic runtime decisions can enabling intelligent, long term gathering of sensor data despite flaky power.

Enable task dependencies, and task scheduling: Our language will enable developers to describe tasks, and their dependencies, so that sophisticated duty cycles can be created. Our runtime will take these tasks, with their real-time constraints, and attempt to make progress on them when energy is available. Application developers will not need to trim requirements so that everything can be executed in one power cycle. Instead, our language and runtime will enable longer, dependent tasks to run to completion, even if they span numerous power failures.

We envision application developers programming batteryless devices by defining a graph of tasks, connected by edges that define real time constraints, flow controls, and policy information. By separating the scheduling of tasks from the implementation details of the task, developers are free to focus on sensing outcomes and goals.

4. TOOLS

Debugging and verifying functionality in the face of flaky power presents unique challenges. Application developers need debugging tools to make the idea of perpetual batteryless sensing a reality. To address this challenge we created Ekho [1], a tool that records, and emulates energy harvesting environments. Harvested environmental energy is generally variable, scarce, and unpredictable. Using Ekho, developers can record these unpredictable Solar, RF, Kinetic, or Thermal environments, and replay these environments later. This allows developers to compare different hardware configurations, duty-cycles, sensor setups, algorithms, and much more in a realistic energy environment, pre-deployment. Using a mobile version of Ekho we developed, application designers and domain scientists can capture energy environments in difficult to reach places outside the lab, allowing for more realistic testing before a deployment.

Ekho allows us to test repeatably, and conduct rigorous experimentation with batteryless devices that was previously impossible. However, Ekho cannot guarantee that devices will work in deployment, or give line-by-line information on program and execution state. We propose a suite of extensions to Ekho that will give developers more confidence in deploying their batteryless sensors. These tools are centered around the idea of *energy aware test driven development*; specifically we look to enable breakpoint and trace based step debugging, and lay the ground work for unit testing, and code coverage metrics, for batteryless devices.

5. CONCLUSIONS

Batteryless, perpetual sensing presents unique challenges. Dealing with systems that may reboot 10-20 times a second is a difficult task. However, these devices promise to enable new realms of sensing in wildlife tracking, infrastructure, smart cities and buildings, and wearables. Before that can happen, new techniques in handling flaky power must be imagined. The central thesis of this research is that batteryless devices can support long running, sophisticated sensing applications. By constructing a specialized hardware platform, defining a language and runtime, and creating a set of tools for energy aware debugging, we can enable developers to manage the temporal, computational, and consistency difficulties caused by flaky power.

6. REFERENCES

[1] J. Hester, T. Scott, and J. Sorber. Ekho: Realistic and Repeatable Experimentation for Tiny Energy-Harvesting Sensors. In *Proc. 12th ACM Conf. Embedded Network Sensor Systems (SenSys'14)*, pages 1–15, Memphis, TN, USA, Nov. 2014. ACM.

[2] J. Hester, L. Sitanayah, and J. Sorber. Tragedy of the Coulombs: Federating Energy Storage for Tiny, Intermittently-Powered Sensors. In *Proc. 13th ACM Conf. Embedded Network Sensor Systems (SenSys'15)*, Seoul, Korea, Nov. 2015. ACM.

[3] A. Rahmati, M. Salajegheh, D. E. Holcomb, J. Sorber, W. P. Burleson, and K. Fu. Tardis: Time and remanence decay in sram to implement secure protocols on embedded devices without clocks. In *USENIX Security Symposium*, pages 221–236, 2012.

Secure and Efficient Management Architecture for the Internet of Things

Jun young Kim
School of Computer Science and Engineering, UNSW Australia
junyoungkim@cse.unsw.edu.au

ABSTRACT

The capability to securely manage embedded devices is arguably a fundamental functionality for the emerging Internet of Things (IoT). Current Wireless Sensor Networks (WSNs) approaches are not applicable directly for IoT deployments due to new challenges from emerging IoT applications. We propose to address this shortcoming and enhance the process while providing a sufficient level of security. This work proposes to design, implement and evaluate an *efficient and secure* software update/manage architecture for the IoT. We plan to conduct an extensive experimental study on a public testbed to evaluate the design tradeoff and quantify the performance of our architecture.

1. INTRODUCTION

Internet of Things (IoT) encompass a wide range of devices enabling the interconnection of the physical world to the Internet. An efficient, secure, and long-term management system is necessary, as it is studied/used in the Wireless Sensor Networks (WSNs). Since the emerging IoT applications pose a different set of characteristics, existing WSNs solutions may not work efficiently. We address these differences in terms of managing IoT applications, then provide proper solutions.

The Thread group [1] is organized by major IT companies such as ARM, Qualcomm, and Samsung. The main goal of the IoT project is to securely connect/manage a large number (+250) of various devices in home networks. Another goal is to design an energy friendly security in which, even battery powered devices can run for years. Low power and secure management functionality is a necessity to achieve the goals. In this project, communication and computation are two premium resources for the secure/energy friendly design, as radio activities and security operations consume the majority of energy on constrained devices.

2. PROBLEM DEFINITION

Managing remotely deployed sensors has been thoroughly studied in the context of WSNs. However, existing WSNs solutions exhibit poor efficiency due to a wide variety of emerging IoT issues such as mobility, heterogeneity, scale, connectivity, security and privacy, energy, and the ease of management. Among other IoT security and efficiency issues, below three are the baseline issue that make these problems challenging to solve [2]:

Heterogeneity: It is challenging to design a framework that can manage various types of devices. Existing solutions coherently become more complex and suffer from performance degradation while supporting the heterogeneity.

Mobility: Having a coherent and stable view of the network topology is a significant factor for managing IoT applications. Mobility related dynamics make this process difficult and result into inefficiency. Existing solutions experience an extreme resource degradation from constantly tracking the topology view and neighbor information.

Connectivity: IoT applications naturally include the Internet connection capability, and this results in exposure to a wider types of adversaries. It is desirable to identify these threats and provide efficient solutions.

SenSys'15, November 1–4, 2015, Seoul, South Korea..
ACM 978-1-4503-3631-4/15/11.
DOI: http://dx.doi.org/10.1145/2809695.2822522.

3. DESIGNING THE ARCHITECTURE

3.1 Secure and Efficient Code Dissemination Protocol for the IoT

Many IoT devices are launched in the market without considering security during the design phase and hence can be easily compromised [2]. This makes IoT devices an easy target for attackers. This problem will exacerbate when the number of such poorly designed, faulty, or malicious devices start to wreck havoc in future. Once deployed, IoT devices require secure code dissemination for multiple purposes such as code update, security patch, and parameter change.

3.1.1 Methodology on Group Key Distribution

Existing secure over-the-air (re)programming protocols for WSNs are based on the epidemic communication [5], which assumes homogenous sensor nodes in the network with all nodes participating in the (re)programming process. Epidemic code dissemination approaches perform efficiently and provide security in homogenous networks by exploiting *spatial multiplexing*, i.e., parallel transmissions in different parts of the network. Given the multitude of systems in an IoT network, the epidemic approach would require non-target nodes to participate in the propagation resulting in unnecessary cryptographic operations and additional packet forwarding overhead.

As an alternative for the IoT context, we explore multicast communication primitives, known to be more efficient and better suited for heterogenous nodes. In a multicast communication approach, only target nodes involved in the code-image update actively take part in the process. We can significantly reduce the communication and computation overhead compared to epidemic approaches by avoiding unnecessary computation-intensive cryptographic operations. In order to enable the secure multicast approach, a secure group key distribution is a significant pre-condition. Existing group key distribution schemes, however, assume known/fixed group sizes or neighbor pairing for efficient key distribution.

We propose to use a public key cryptography broadcast encryption scheme (BGW_t [3]), which efficiently distributes the shared group key to a dynamic number of target nodes, but results in additional storage with following benefits.
The shortest ciphertext size: Shorter or fixed size ciphertext is desirable, as it is directly proportional to the communication overhead.
Lower decryption complexity: On a dissemination protocol, encryption is performed at a resource-rich trusted server while decryption is performed at constrained nodes. BGW_t has higher encryption complexity of $O(n)$ while lower decryption complexity of $O(1)$, which enhances energy consumption/latency on the constrained nodes.
Fixed size private key: IoT nodes are vulnerable to physical node capture attack, where adversaries compromise nodes to extract pre-installed keys. BGW_t's $O(1)$ private key can be stored in the tamper resistant storage to effectively mitigate physical attacks.

3.1.2 Expected Contribution

We develop a secure over-the-air code dissemination protocol for the IoT, which adopts a multicast communication to improve the protocol efficiency in networks with heterogeneous devices. Our design process will involve the selection and implementation/optimization of a public key cryptographic broadcast encryption scheme. Then allows to distribute a fresh shared key to a dynamic number of target nodes efficiently, and provides authenticity, integrity and confidentiality to the program image update process. Our security analysis will demonstrate that our security properties are not compromised against identified adversary models. We will experimentally validate our system through a prototype IoT platform and demonstrate the efficiency in practical settings. We plan to publicly release our implementation as an open-source code.

3.1.3 Current Status

My poster submission on this work to the Sensys'15 is accepted. We are going to submit a full paper to IPSN'16.

3.2 Reliable and Secure Multicast Protocol

We addressed the open issues on the existing code dissemination approaches. Since we propose to adopt a multicast propagation for efficient code disseminate, providing reliability in the multicast protocol becomes another open problem. Based on our research, achieving a reliable multicast in the IoT environment is challenging due to the feedback implosion problem, which occurs when a large number of receivers sends feedback to the sender.

We propose to design a reliable multicast protocol by using a combination of techniques and evaluate the trade-off between communication overhead and energy to meet the application requirements.

3.2.1 Expected Contributions

Designing a practical reliable multicast protocol is a necessary task for efficient code dissemination in IoT applications. We will investigate the existing reliable multicast protocols suitable or adaptable for IoT applications, and investigate various associated mechanisms and assess their security vulnerability. This will result in a secure reliable multicast protocol for IoT applications.

3.3 Policy Management on IoT Gateways

A secure gateway which can detect mis-configurations and any policy conflict is extremely important for successful deployment of IoT at scale. Also as from the mobility and heterogeneity, the management process becomes complex and suffers from the performance degradation.

Since IoT applications consist of various network services/devices, many policies conflict to each other, which results in various performance degradation and security threats. Unfortunately, in many practical settings, the detection and resolving on-the-fly are commonly a NP-hard problem and they are categorized as different tasks.

3.3.1 Expected Contributions

To address the policy conflict detection/resolution problem, we take advantage of the distinguished modeling and reasoning capacities of Answer Set Programming (ASP) [4]. Our goal is to provide ASP solutions for reasoning over influence graphs and experimental profiles. We believe logic based algorithms can detect and resolve conflicts in predictable and reliable ways. In the end, this will enhance the policy development/management environments.

4. CONCLUSION

In this proposal, we proposed a secure and efficient management system for the emerging IoT applications. We plan to enhance the efficiency of the secure code dissemination process caused by the emerging IoT issues such as heterogeneity and mobility.

Jun young Kim received the M.Eng. degree in computer science from Hanyang University, Seoul, Korea, in 2004. After 12 years of embedded software developer career, he is currently working toward the Ph.D. degree in mid 2017 at the UNSW, Sydney, Australia supervised by Wen Hu and Sanjay Jha. His main research interest is securing the Internet of Things and Wireless Sensor Networks.

5. REFERENCES

[1] The thread group. `http://threadgroup.org/`, 2015.
[2] L. Atzori, A. Iera, and G. Morabito. The internet of things: A survey. *Computer networks*, 2010.
[3] D. Boneh, C. Gentry, and B. Waters. Collusion resistant broadcast encryption with short ciphertexts and private keys. In *CRYPTO 2005*. Springer, 2005.
[4] M. Gebser, R. Kaminski, B. Kaufmann, and T. Schaub. Answer set solving in practice. 2012.
[5] P. A. Levis, N. Patel, D. Culler, and S. Shenker. *Trickle: A self regulating algorithm for code propagation and maintenance in wireless sensor networks*. Computer Science Division, University of California, 2003.

Non Intrusive Load Monitoring: Systems, Metrics and Use Cases

Nipun Batra
Indraprastha Institute of
Information Technology
New Delhi, India
nipunb@iiitd.ac.in

ABSTRACT

Buildings across the world contribute significantly to the overall energy consumption. Targeted feedback can help occupants optimise energy consumption. In our first work we present techniques for actionable feedback across fridges and air conditioning (HVAC) units, which can save upto 25% of fridge energy and identify homes needing feedback on HVAC setpoint schedule with 84% accuracy. In our next work, we do an extensive sensor deployment in a home in Delhi, India; monitoring appliance level power, home aggregate power and other ambient parameters. Our study presents various insights unseen in the developed world, such as: frequent voltage brownouts, poor network reliability, long lasting blackouts, heavy dominance of fridge and HVAC to overall energy consumption. Our study verifies that measuring appliance level power scales poorly in cost and maintenance. Non-intrusive load monitoring (NILM) is viewed as a viable alternative where machine learning techniques are used to break down aggregate household energy consumption into contributing appliances. Despite the existence of a rich volume of literature in NILM, it remained virtually impossible to compare NILM works due to: i) lack of existence of benchmarks; ii) previous work tested on single data set; iii) inconsistent metrics. To address these challenges we developed an open source toolkit: Non-intrusive load monitoring toolkit (NILMTK), designed specifically to enable the comparison of NILM algorithms. While many new NILM techniques have been proposed in recent times, it is not clear if these can enable energy saving and whether higher accuracy translates to higher energy saving. We explore these questions in our recent work and find that existing energy disaggregation techniques do not provide power traces with sufficient fidelity to support the feedback techniques we developed in our earlier work. Our results indicate a need to revisit the metrics by which disaggregation is evaluated.

1. RESEARCH SUMMARY

Buildings across the globe contribute significantly to the overall energy consumption [4]. Previous research has shown the potential of energy saving by providing targeted energy consumption feedback to residents. We now discuss our work on providing actionable feedback based on appliance level power data.

1.1 Actionable feedback from appliance data

We focus on feedback on refrigerators and HVAC, because they contribute significantly to overall energy consumption and are available in most homes. In our first work [5], we develop a model that breaks the power trace of a refrigerator into three parts: baseline (when no one is using the fridge), defrost, and usage (energy consumption due to fridge usage). Then, we developed techniques to identify users with 1) much more energy due to fridge usage than the norm 2) much more energy due to defrost than the norm, or 3) fridges that are malfunctioning or misconfigured. We evaluated our model using a dataset with power traces from 95 refrigerators. We found that our model can break down fridge usage into its three components with only 4% error. Additionally, the three types of feedback could help users save up to 23%, 25% and 26% of their fridge energy usage, respectively. Similarly, we developed new techniques to differentiate homes with and without setback schedules on the HVAC system based on their HVAC power traces and outdoor weather patterns. This information can be used to give feedback to install a programmable thermostat. We evaluate these techniques with power traces from 58 homes and results indicate that our techniques can classify homes with 84% accuracy. Based on these results, we conclude that NILM does have the potential to provide targeted, actionable feedback that could lead to sustainable energy savings.

1.2 Residential deployment

Having found that appliance level power data can provide actionable feedback, we decided to do a dense residential deployment in a home in Delhi, India. All previous residential deployments had been done in the developed world. The philosophy behind our deployment [2] was to leave no stone unturned, whereby, we deployed 33 sensors for 73 days across a three storey home as shown in Figure 1. These sensors measured appliance level power consumption, aggregate home power consumption, utility water readings, and various ambient parameters such as temperature, light and motion. Our work highlighted the new challenges seen in the Indian settings, such as: frequent outages lasting up to 9 hours a day, voltage fluctuations upto 10 times more than that in the US, upto 25% internet packet drop in a day, heavy dominance of HVAC and fridges in overall energy (upto 50%). Our work also verified challenges in residential deployments discussed previously in the literature.

SenSys'15, November 1–4, 2015, Seoul, South Korea..
ACM 978-1-4503-3631-4/15/11.
DOI: http://dx.doi.org/2809695.2822523 .

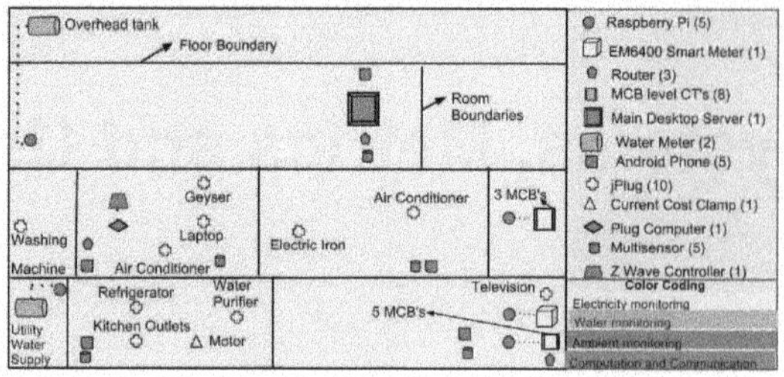

Figure 1: Home deployment schematic

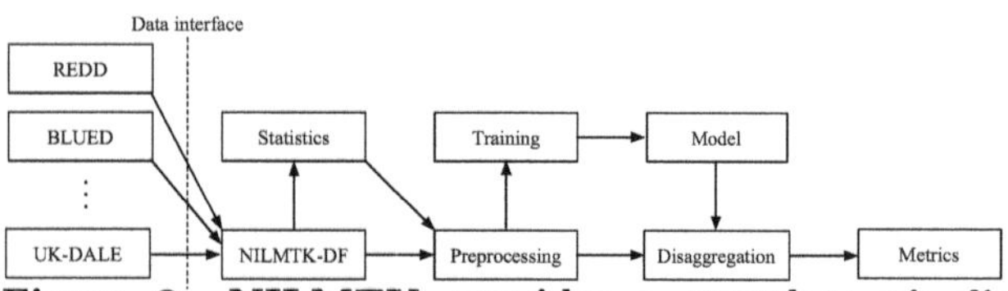

Figure 2: NILMTK provides a complete pipeline from data sets to accuracy metrics

1.3 NILMTK

Challenges in dense residential deployments severely limit scaling up potential applications requiring appliance energy data. NILM is considered a viable alternative. However, despite more than 3 decades of research in NILM, it remained virtually impossible to empirically compare different algorithms, due to: i) different data sets used, ii) the lack of reference implementations of these algorithms, and iii) the variety of accuracy metrics employed. To address these challenges, we implemented the open source NILM toolkit (NILMTK), designed specifically to enable the comparison of NILM algorithms [3]. NILMTK provides a complete pipeline from data sets to accuracy metrics (Figure 2), lowering the entry barrier for researchers to implement a new algorithm. The initial version of NILMTK provided 2 benchmark NILM algorithms (combinatorial optimisation (CO) and factorial hidden Markov model (FHMM)) and data set parsers for 6 data sets. More recently, NILMTK underwent a major rewrite allowing out-of-core operations [6] and included the seminal NILM algorithm (Hart's) and additional data sets contributed by the data set authors. The success of any such endeavour is measured by the community uptake which is evidenced by recent works which use NILMTK [7, 1, 8, 5].

1.4 New metrics to evaluate NILM

While NILMTK now enables comparison of NILM algorithms across multiple data sets, two fundamental questions remain in NILM research: can these NILM techniques actually save energy and, if so, whether higher accuracy translates into higher energy savings. Having earlier established that appliance power traces can provide specific actionable feedback, we next evaluated the feedback produced by NILM algorithms. We applied benchmark NILM algorithms provided in NILMTK and found them to give results comparable to the state-of-art on traditional NILM metrics. However, Figure 3 and 4 show that on the metrics we care about, i.e. accuracy of feedback, NILM approaches fare poorly. These results indicate a need to revisit the metrics by which disaggregation is evaluated.

2. FUTURE WORK (CLOSING THE LOOP)

Our future work spans three directions: 1) evaluate use cases where disaggregation brings in a direct value by allowing

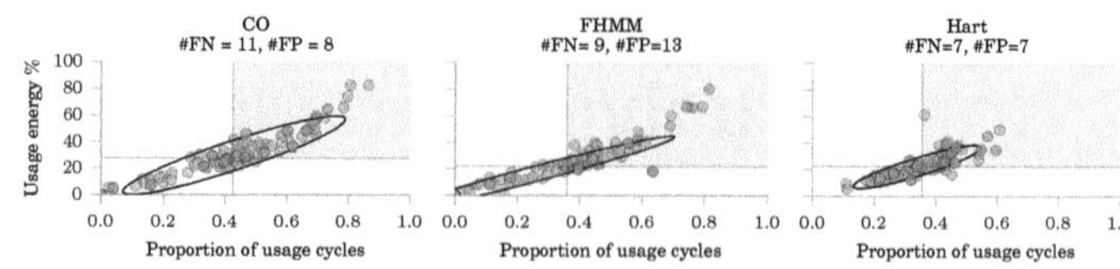

Figure 3: NILM algorithms show poor accuracy in identifying homes which need feedback for high fridge usage energy. Red dots indicate the homes which should be getting feedback based on analysis of submetered fridge data, while these algorithms would give feedback to all homes in the green region outside the elliptical boundary.

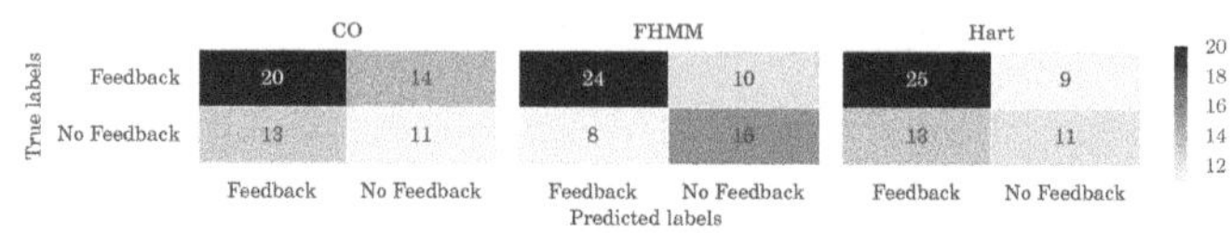

Figure 4: Classification of homes into those with setback schedules decreases from 84% with submetered power traces to 53%, 69%, and 62% respectively with power traces produced by the 3 NILM algorithms.

actionable feedback, e.g. energy apportionment; 2) improve the accuracy of existing NILM methods in context of the feedback methods we have already proposed ; and 3) evaluate these feedback methods in the wild through user studies, to understand the real world energy efficiency gains and sustenance of NILM based feedback.

3. REFERENCES

[1] J. Alcala, O. Parson, and A. Rogers. Health monitoring of elderly residents via disaggregated smart meter data and log gaussian cox processes. In *Proceedings of the second ACM International Conference on Embedded Systems For Energy-Efficient Built Environments*. ACM, 2015.

[2] N. Batra, M. Gulati, A. Singh, and M. B. Srivastava. It's Different: Insights into home energy consumption in India. In *Proceedings of the Fifth ACM Workshop on Embedded Sensing Systems for Energy-Efficiency in Buildings*, 2013.

[3] N. Batra, J. Kelly, O. Parson, H. Dutta, W. Knottenbelt, A. Rogers, A. Singh, and M. Srivastava. Nilmtk: An open source toolkit for non-intrusive load monitoring. In *Proceedings of the 5th international conference on Future energy systems*, pages 265–276. ACM, 2014.

[4] N. Batra, A. Singh, P. Singh, H. Dutta, V. Sarangan, and M. Srivastava. Data driven energy efficiency in buildings. *arXiv preprint arXiv:1404.7227*, 2014.

[5] N. Batra, A. Singh, and K. Whitehouse. If you measure it, can you improve it? exploring the value of energy disaggregation. In *Proceedings of the second ACM International Conference on Embedded Systems For Energy-Efficient Built Environments*. ACM, 2015.

[6] J. Kelly, N. Batra, O. Parson, H. Dutta, W. Knottenbelt, A. Rogers, A. Singh, and M. Srivastava. Nilmtk v0. 2: a non-intrusive load monitoring toolkit for large scale data sets: demo abstract. In *Proceedings of the 1st ACM Conference on Embedded Systems for Energy-Efficient Buildings*, pages 182–183. ACM, 2014.

[7] J. Kelly and W. Knottenbelt. Neural nilm: Deep neural networks applied to energy disaggregation. In *Proceedings of the second ACM International Conference on Embedded Systems For Energy-Efficient Built Environments*. ACM, 2015.

[8] A. U. N. SN, A. R. Lua, and R. V. Prasad. Loced: Location-aware energy disaggregation framework. In *Proceedings of the second ACM International Conference on Embedded Systems For Energy-Efficient Built Environments*. ACM, 2015.

Tackling Self Interference, Cross-Technology Interference and Channel Fading in Wireless Sensor Networks

Mohammad Mobashir
School of Computing, National University of Singapore
mobashir@comp.nus.edu.sg

ABSTRACT

Recently with a push towards "IoTification", the world foresees a sharp rise in the number of devices with wireless networking capabilities. It is inevitable to anticipate an enormous increase in both self and cross-technology interference leaving a very challenging wireless communication medium at one's disposal. Maintaining robust data transmission in this increasingly hostile 2.4GHz band without incurring significant additional energy consumption is a basic concern. Towards this end we propose a suite of protocols (Syncast and Oppcast) exploiting capture effect over multi-channels and a careful knit of spatio-temporal and channel diversity to provide robust data transmission for multiple communication paradigms (Collection and Dissemination).

Categories and Subject Descriptors

C.2.1 [**Computer-Communication Networks**]: Network Architecture and Design—*Wireless communication*

Keywords

data collection; synchronous transmissions; capture effect; spatio-temporal diversity; channel diversity

1. INTRODUCTION

When it comes to Wireless Sensor Networks, data collection and dissemination are two important services. Be it real-time urban environment monitoring (data collection) or pushing updates to already deployed devices (data dissemination), reliability is a necessity. Over the last decade, the research community has contributed enormously to make these services not only reliable but also energy efficient. However most of these efforts are either non-scalable due to severe self-interference (SI) [5] or assume the availability of sufficient channels free from cross-technology interference (CTI) [1]. In today's world these assumptions are becoming less plausible specially because of the deployments becoming denser due to "IoTification" leading to increased SI or deployments starting to move out from research labs to urban areas where CTI starts to dominate.

Recently a lot of interest has been shown to tackle CTI by successfully classifying the different sources based on fast channel sampling followed by taking necessary remedial actions. However because of extremely dynamic behavior of CTIs, channel assessment becomes exceedingly expensive since it has to be periodically repeated for the entire spectrum. Moreover protocols are usually evaluated on testbeds deployed in research labs or within academic institutions like Indriya [2] where WiFi AP (major CTI source) is configured by the organization to operate on fixed orthogonal channels (1, 6 and 11), thereby allowing ZigBee to coexist. In contrast to the above "organized" WiFi deployment, a typical urban outdoor environment is quite "unorganized" with no single CTI free ZigBee channel available to use. Thus making SI and CTI increasingly important issue to address.

SenSys'15, November 1–4, 2015, Seoul, South Korea..
ACM 978-1-4503-3631-4/15/11.
DOI: http://dx.doi.org/10.1145/2809695.2822524 .

In this research we propose a Syncast, a data dissemination protocol leveraging Synchronous transmissions [5] for speed and Capture effect over multi-channels to mitigate SI by sparsifying the network. Next we study the impact of CTI on the performance degradation of the state-of-the-art data collection protocols in an urban outdoor deployment and propose Oppcast, a robust data collection protocol for such challenging environments. Instead of complex CTI source classification and then taking corresponding remedial actions [6], our approach leverages a careful blend of spatio-temporal and channel diversities to look for transient opportunities for reliable data transmission. Oppcast deviates from previous work by eliminating the need to perform expensive link quality estimation to identify the least interfered channel. Our contributions are as follows:

- To the best of our knowledge we are the first to study the effect of Capture effect over multi-channels on synchronous transmission based protocols and used it to design Syncast which makes them scalable.
- We studied CTI in different settings and could classify the environment into "Organized" and "Unorganized" categories having different protocol requirements.
- The above observation motivated us to design Oppcast to eliminate expensive channel quality estimation and still ensure high packet reception reliability by making use of spatio-temporal and channel diversities.

The rest of the paper is organized as follows. In Section 2 and 3, we motivate the need for and present Syncast and Oppcast, followed by ongoing future work and conclusion.

2. SYNCAST

Synchronous transmission has gained popularity recently for its ability to speed up data collection and dissemination by eliminating the need for channel contention [5]. The

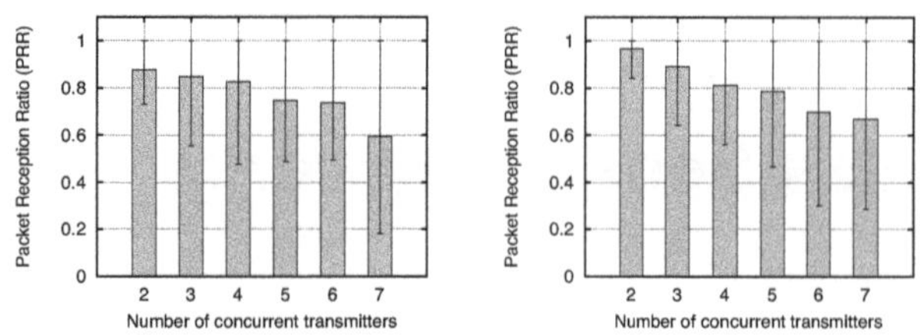

(a) Indoor Setup (b) Outdoor Setup

Figure 1: PRR vs. Number of Concurrent Transmitters for different deployments environments

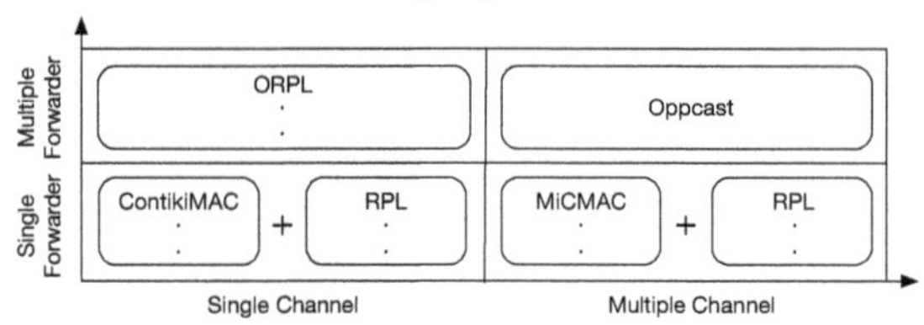

Figure 2: Positioning Oppcast among others

challenge is to maintain a synchronization accuracy of up to $0.5\mu s$ among synchronous transmitters. However due software, hardware and propagation delays synchronization error exceeds $0.5\mu s$ when the number of synchronous transmitters increases, resulting in the so-called *scalability problem* as shown in Figure 1 where on introduction of every additional concurrent transmitter, the packet reception ratio falls.

Approach: Syncast aims at scaling the synchronous transmission for large packet sizes and dense networks having large number of concurrent transmitters by exploiting capture effect to relax the timing constraint to $160\mu s$ and multi-channels to make the network sparse. Real testbed evaluation of Syncast shows consistently high reliability with up to 92% energy savings in contrast to Glossy [5] whose reliability depends on SI, CTI and packet sizes.

3. OPPCAST

Since WSN link are highly dynamic [7], link quality estimations becomes unfeasible. Most of the protocol assume that there are at least four ZigBee channels available which are orthogonal to the most commonly used WiFi channels (1, 6 and 11). In today's time with every house having wireless connectivity, this assumption is becoming less likely. From our observations, we were able to identify two environment types based on the WiFi AP deployment:

1. *Organized CTI*: Found in places like educational institutions, libraries, corporate offices, etc. where a central administration handles WiFi AP deployment. Figure 3(top) illustrates a WiFi analyzer output of one such deployment where only WiFi channel 1, 6 and 11 has been used. Indoor testbeds like Indriya is a representative example.

2. *Unorganized CTI*: Found in places lacking central control over WiFi AP deployment like shopping malls, residential complexes, etc. as illustrated in Figure 3(bottom).

Approach: A lot of research effort has been put in the past along various directions of exploiting diversities like multiple channels or multiple forwarders in isolation as illustrated in Figure 2 [1, 3, 4, 8]. Oppcast aims at providing a unified solution to exploit spatio-temporal and channel di-

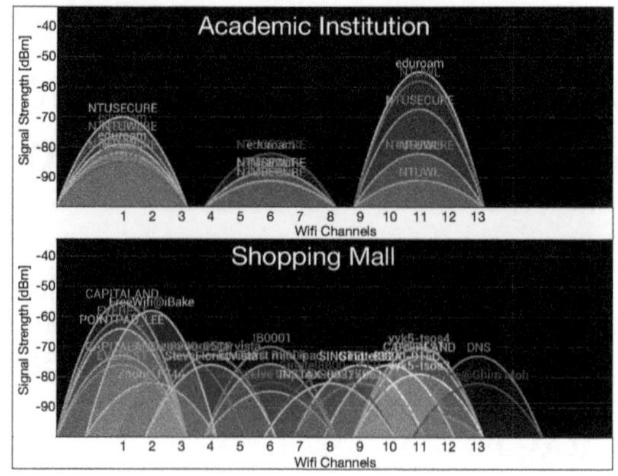

Figure 3: CTI in different deployment environments

versities to achieve robust data collection. The research is in progress and the Contiki implementation of Oppcast is being tested on both indoor and outdoor environment with preliminary results proving its robustness to CTI.

4. CONCLUSION AND FUTURE WORK

In this research we address two important challenges to wireless communication in urban outdoor environment: SI and CTI. Towards this end we proposed Syncast, a synchronous transmission based protocol for robust data dissemination exploiting capture effect over multi-channels and evaluated it on real testbed. Later we motivated the need for specialized protocols for outdoor urban environment through comparative study of different environments and proposed Oppcast, a robust data collection protocol that eliminates expensive periodic link quality estimation over multiple channels. In future we would like to study the seriousness of packet losses due to channel fading in an urban setting and try to avoid packet loss due to sudden weakening of link because shadowing from obstacles by leveraging radio as a sensor instead of additional expensive sensor deployment.

5. REFERENCES

[1] B. Al Nahas, S. Duquennoy, V. Iyer, and T. Voigt. Low-power listening goes multi-channel. In *DCOSS*. IEEE, 2014.

[2] M. Doddavenkatappa, M. C. Chan, and A. L. Ananda. Indriya: A low-cost, 3d wireless sensor network testbed. In *TridentCom*. Springer, 2012.

[3] A. Dunkels. The contikimac radio duty cycling protocol. 2011.

[4] S. Duquennoy, O. Landsiedel, and T. Voigt. Let the tree bloom: scalable opportunistic routing with orpl. In *SenSys*. ACM, 2013.

[5] F. Ferrari, M. Zimmerling, L. Thiele, and O. Saukh. Efficient network flooding and time synchronization with glossy. In *IPSN*. IEEE, 2011.

[6] A. Hithnawi, H. Shafagh, and S. Duquennoy. Tiim: technology-independent interference mitigation for low-power wireless networks. In *SenSys*. ACM, 2015.

[7] K. Srinivasan, M. A. Kazandjieva, S. Agarwal, and P. Levis. The β-factor: measuring wireless link burstiness. In *SenSys*. ACM, 2008.

[8] T. Winter. Rpl: Ipv6 routing protocol for low-power and lossy networks. 2012.

Mobile Applications Based on Smart Wearable Devices

Weitao Xu
School of Information Technology and Electrical Engineering, University of Queensland, Australia
{w.xu3}@uq.edu.edu

ABSTRACT

Ubiquity of wearable devices sparked a new set of mobile computing applications that leverage the prolific information of sensors. I will focus on two main research questions: face recognition on smart glass and gait recognition on smart watch. Face recognition is one of the most popular research problems on various platforms. New research issues arise when it comes to resource constrained devices, such as smart glasses, due to the overwhelming computation and energy requirements of the accurate face recognition methods. Biometric gait recognition refers to verifying or identifying persons by their walking style, and it provides a unobtrusive way to authenticate the user and unlock the smart watches.

1. INTRODUCTION

With recent advances in embedded computing technologies, smart wearable devices such as smartphone, smartwatch and smart glass have become increasingly popular and play significant roles in our daily lives. The pervasiveness of wearable devices sparked a set of mobile applications which leverages the information of sensors. My research will mainly focus on two questions: face recognition on smart glass and gait recognition on smart watch.

Motivation for face recognition on smart glass.

Face recognition has emerged as an active research area with numerous applications over the past decades. The possibility of using wearable devices to help people recognize people is becoming the focus of research with the advent of smart glasses such as Google Glass. Face recognition has been well researched in the computer vision community, yet there remains much work to be done on mobile devices. As discussed in [8], most of the advanced face recognition methods fail on mobile devices because of the tension between high computation requirements and resource constraints. In my research, I aim to develop a robust and efficient *in-situ* face recognition system on smartglasses.

SenSys'15, November 01-04, 2015, Seoul, Republic of Korea
ACM 978-1-4503-3631-4/15/11.
DOI: http://dx.doi.org/10.1145/2809695.2822525.

Motivation for gait recognition on smart watch.

With the pervasiveness of smart watches, much of our sensitive and private information is kept on our smartwatches. This poses great security risks to smartwatch users as the watch can be lost and stolen. Traditional authentication methods such as passwords do not offer good user experience because of the need for screen and keyboard.

Biometric gait recognition refers to verifying or identifying persons by their walking style, and it provides a unobtrusive way to authenticate the user and unlock the smart watches. Research on accelerometer-based gait recognition have shown that gait can be used to identify person [2, 5]. Motivated by this, I aim to propose a robust and efficient authentication system to recognize people when they perform normal activities in daily life. Gait recognition on smartwatch is more challenging because of the various arm motions in normal life.

2. LITERATURE REVIEW

In this section, I will discuss the related work in two aspects: face recognition on mobile devices and acclerometer-based gait recognition.

Face recognition is well researched in computer vision. It invokes new research challenges when used on smart devices. With the availability of OpenCV, many apps such as friends tagging and face unlocking have appeared on the app markets. There are three face recognition algorithms in OpenCV: EigenFaces [9], FisherFace [3] and LBPFace [1]. Although these methods can be used in real-time on smartphones, the recognition accuracies are unsatisfactory [8]. SRC [11] outperforms these three methods; however, it cannot provide consistent high recognition accuracy and is computationally intensive. To overcome its limitations, [8] proposes opti-SRC by optimizing the projection matrix to provide consistently better accuracy while solving the computation efficiency issue.

Research on accelerometer-based gait recognition was first proposed by Ailisto et al. [2] around 2005 and further developed by Gafurov et al. [5]. In the initial stages, dedicated accelerometers were used and worn on different body parts, such as lower leg [5], waist [2], hip [6], hip pocket, chest pocket and hand [10]. With the popular of smartphone, researchers have proposed several methods to authenticate users by utilizing the built-in accelerometer [7, 4].

3. RESEARCH QUESTIONS

To address the issues above, I will focus on the following research questions:

- RQ1: How can we improve the performance of face recognition system on smart glass by combining multiple views and IMU sensor data?
- RQ2: Can compressive sensing be used to improve the speed and energy efficiency of face recognition, and what is an appropriate compressive sensing sampling strategy to use?
- RQ3: How is gait recognition on smart watch affected by different activities such as normal walking, walk upstairs/downstairs, walk with texting/calling the phone, and walk with hand in jacket/pant pocket. How can gait recognition performance on smart watch be improved by leveraging the activity information?

4. PROGRESS ON FACE RECOGNITION

I have prototyped a *in-situ* face recognition system on Vuzix M100 Smart Glass. I make two contributions: I propose a Multi-view Sparse Representation based Classification (MVSRC) and propose a sampling strategy to improve the energy efficiency of MVSRC on smart glass.

4.1 MVSRC

I propose a novel face recognition algorithm called Multi-view Sparse Representation based Classification (MVSRC) by combining the mobile nature of smartglasses. The key assumption behind MVSRC is that face images obtained from different view angles tend to have a high agreement on the sparse representations because each of the face images from the same person should be linearly represented by the same class in the dictionary. Suppose I have acquired a set of M feasible face images from the camera. I can obtain a set of estimated coefficients vectors $\hat{X} = \{\hat{x}_1, \hat{x}_2, ..., \hat{x}_M\}$ by solving the ℓ_1 optimization problem as in [8]. The new sparse representation model can be expressed as:

$$\hat{x}_{sum} = \sum_{m=1}^{M} \alpha_m \hat{x}_m \quad (1)$$

where α_m is the light assigned to $\hat{x}_m$ based on the *Sparsity Concentration Index* (SCI) defined as:

$$SCI(\hat{x}_m) = \frac{K \cdot max_j \|\delta_j(\hat{x}_m)\|_1 / \|\hat{x}_m\|_1 - 1}{K - 1} \in [0, 1] \quad (2)$$

The new model exploits the sparsity information of the multi-view face images.

4.2 Optimized Sampling Strategy

Considering the computation and energy consumption issues of the smart glasses, applying MVSRC straightforwardly on all of the M face images obtained is not a desirable choice because it requires M ℓ_1 optimizations. Moreover, a large amount of redundant information exists among the adjacent frames as the face images with similar view angles contain large overlaps. To find the best sampling strategy, I propose to optimize the downsampling on the face images set with a predefined energy budget. The energy budget E_b is preset and I aim to find the optimal subset Ω_s of the face images set I to achieve the highest recognition accuracy A_c by solving the optimization problem below:

$$\Omega_s = \arg\max_{\Omega} A_c \quad \text{s.t. } E_{total} \leq E_b, \Omega \subseteq I \quad (3)$$

where Ω is one of the arbitrary subsets of I and E_{total} is the total energy consumption for face recognition. To solve Eq 3, I propose to use IMU sensors to estimate the angles of multi-view face images and then find Ω_s by a novel Support Vector Regression (SVR) model.

5. FUTURE WORK

Future work will focus on solving research question 3, i.e. gait recognition on smart watch. I will collect data from smart watch by asking participants to perform different activities (e.g. walking/running/walk upstairs) and develop methods for accurate gait recognition under various normal activities.

6. REFERENCES

[1] T. Ahonen, A. Hadid, and M. Pietikainen. Face description with local binary patterns: Application to face recognition. *PAMI*, pages 2037–2041, 2006.

[2] H. J. Ailisto, M. Lindholm, J. Mantyjarvi, E. Vildjiounaite, and S.-M. Makela. Identifying people from gait pattern with accelerometers. In *Defense and Security*, pages 7–14. International Society for Optics and Photonics, 2005.

[3] P. N. Belhumeur, J. P. Hespanha, and D. Kriegman. Eigenfaces vs. fisherfaces: Recognition using class specific linear projection. *PAMI*, pages 711–720, 1997.

[4] M. O. Derawi, C. Nickel, P. Bours, and C. Busch. Unobtrusive user-authentication on mobile phones using biometric gait recognition. In *Intelligent Information Hiding and Multimedia Signal Processing (IIH-MSP), 2010 Sixth International Conference on*, pages 306–311. IEEE, 2010.

[5] D. Gafurov, K. Helkala, and T. Søndrol. Biometric gait authentication using accelerometer sensor. *Journal of computers*, 1(7):51–59, 2006.

[6] D. Gafurov, E. Snekkenes, and T. E. Buvarp. Robustness of biometric gait authentication against impersonation attack. In *On the Move to Meaningful Internet Systems 2006: OTM 2006 Workshops*, pages 479–488. Springer, 2006.

[7] Y. Ren, Y. Chen, M. C. Chuah, and J. Yang. Smartphone based user verification leveraging gait recognition for mobile healthcare systems. In *Sensor, Mesh and Ad Hoc Communications and Networks (SECON), 2013 10th Annual IEEE Communications Society Conference on*, pages 149–157. IEEE, 2013.

[8] Y. Shen, W. Hu, M. Yang, B. Wei, S. Lucey, and C. T. Chou. Face recognition on smartphones via optimised sparse representation classification. In *IPSN '14*, pages 237–248. IEEE Press, 2014.

[9] M. Turk and A. Pentland. Eigenfaces for recognition. *Journal of cognitive neuroscience*, pages 71–86, 1991.

[10] E. Vildjiounaite, S.-M. Mäkelä, M. Lindholm, R. Riihimäki, V. Kyllönen, J. Mäntyjärvi, and H. Ailisto. Unobtrusive multimodal biometrics for ensuring privacy and information security with personal devices. In *Pervasive Computing*, pages 187–201. Springer, 2006.

[11] J. Wright, A. Yang, A. Ganesh, S. Sastry, and Y. Ma. Robust face recognition via sparse representation. *PAMI*, pages 210–227, 2009.

ENSsys 2015: 3rd International Workshop on Energy Harvesting and Energy Neutral Sensing Systems

Geoff V. Merrett
University of Southampton
Southampton, UK
gvm@ecs.soton.ac.uk

Christian Renner
University of Luebeck
Luebeck, Germany
renner@iti.uni-luebeck.de

Davide Brunelli
University of Trento
Trento, Italy
davide.brunelli@unitn.it

ABSTRACT

Complementing the topics of ACM SenSys 2015, the 3rd International Workshop on Energy Harvesting and Energy Neutral Sensing Systems (ENSsys) 2015 brings together researchers to explore the challenges, issues and opportunities in the research, design, and engineering of energy-harvesting and energy-neutral sensing systems. These are an enabling technology for future applications in smart energy, transportation, environmental monitoring and smart cities. Innovative solutions in hardware for energy scavenging, adaptive algorithms, and power management policies are needed to enable uninterrupted operation. This one-day workshop features invited and peer reviewed talks on these areas, and provides a forum for feedback, discussion and networking.

Categories and Subject Descriptors

A.0 [**Genereal Literature**]: General—*Conference proceedings*

Keywords

Energy harvesting, energy neutrality, sensing systems

1. INTRODUCTION

Complementing the topics of SenSys 2015, the International Workshop on Energy Harvesting and Energy Neutral Sensing Systems (ENSsys 2015) is now in its third edition, and brings together members of the research community to systematically explore the challenges, issues and opportunities in the research, design, and engineering of energy-harvesting and energy-neutral techniques for distributed sensing systems.

Sensing systems are one of the technological cornerstones for future applications in smart energy, future transportation, environmental monitoring and smart cities. Today, one of the major challenges of using such systems in real deployments is related to energy consumption and guaranteeing adequate lifetime. The field of energy harvesting is making significant strides, and is beginning to gain more traction in the field of sensing systems. Innovative solutions in terms of on-board hardware for energy scavenging, energy adaptive algorithms, and power management policies of the nodes in the network are the ultimate frontiers, and they open the door to unlimited and uninterrupted operation (zero-energy networks). ENSsys has solicited novel and previously unpublished technical articles describing advances in sensing systems which achieve energy neutrality through energy harvesting and ultra-aggressive power saving mechanisms. Submissions discussing practical deployments and implementation experiences were encouraged, in order to demonstrate the effectiveness of zero-energy networks.

2. TOPICS OF INTEREST

Topics of interest include, but are not limited to:

- Power management concepts, algorithms and circuits for energy harvesting sensing systems
- Middleware support and services which support interoperability between zero-energy networks
- Resource management and operating system support for energy harvesting sensing systems
- Network-wide distributed energy management (e.g. routing, adaptive duty cycling etc)
- Online measurement of energy intake and consumption
- Predicting energy intake and consumption
- Ensuring reliable operation in energy harvesting sensor systems
- Modelling, simulation and tools for effective design of future energy harvesting sensing systems
- Architectures and standards for energy-neutral sensing systems
- Internet of (battery-less) things
- Experience with real-world deployments and innovative applications

3. ENSSYS 2015 PROGRAM

ENSsys is a one day workshop, held on 01 November 2015 in conjunction with ACM SenSys in Seoul, South Korea.

SenSys'15, November 1–4, 2015, Seoul, Republic of Korea.
ACM 978-1-4503-3631-4/15/11.
DOI: http://dx.doi.org/10.1145/2809695.2809696.

3.1 Technical Programme

The day's technical programme includes:

- an invited Keynote talk from Jacob Sorber, entitled "Batteries not included: moving toward long-term sustainable sensing";
- 5x 30-minute technical presentations, followed by 10 minutes for questions, discussions and feedback;
- an interactive 'poster' session, where 3x presenters will present their work to the audience with discussion throughout.

3.2 Review Process

All papers that were submitted received three reviews from experts in the area, and were evaluated for relevance, novelty, technical contribution, and presentation. A TPC meeting was held to discuss all of the reviews, and decide upon the final technical programme.

4. WORKSHOP ORGANISERS

General Chair
Geoff V. Merrett (University of Southampton, UK)

Technical Programme Chairs
Christian Renner (University of Luebeck, Germany)
Davide Brunelli (University of Trento, Italy)

Publicity Chairs
Dong Kun Noh (Soongsil University, Korea)
Brad Campbell (University of Michigan, USA)
Alex S. Weddell (University of Southampton, UK)

Website Chair
Alberto R. Arreola (University of Southampton, UK)

Technical Programme Committee
Polly Huang (National Taiwan University, Taiwan)
Winston Seah (Victoria Uni. Wellington, New Zealand)
Guy Grebla (Google, USA)
Brad Campbell (Uni. Michigan, USA)
Vana Jelicic (University of Zagreb, Croatia)
Usman Raza (FBK Institute, Italy)
Olivier Sentieys (University of Rennes, France)
Alessandro Vinco (Tyndall Institute, Ireland)
Dora Spenza (Sapienza University of Rome, Italy)

5. ACKNOWLEDGMENTS

We would like to thank all of the authors who submitted contributions to ENSsys, and the members of the Technical Programme Committee for their excellent and timely work reviewing submissions and helping to put together an excellent technical programme.

We would also like to thank the Organising Committee for their help in the organisation and promotion of the workshop, and the SenSys 2015 Workshop Chairs for their continued support of ENSsys.

Finally, and most of all, we hope that you thoroughly enjoy this year's programme – whether you are presenting, attending, or just reading these proceedings on the ACM Digital Library.

SenSys'15 Proceedings Workshop Summary Abstract / IoT-App'15

The 2015 International Workshop on Internet of Things towards Applications

Chenren Xu
chenren@pku.edu.cn

Pei Zhang
peizhang@cmu.edu

Stephan Sigg
stephan.sigg@aalto.fi

ABSTRACT

After a very successful edition of the IoT-App workshop, its second edition is conducted in conjunction with SenSys 2015. Again, the workshop succeeded in attracting a high number of high-quality submissions. The topics of the papers submitted feature most prominently urban sensing and smart home or city. Further directions are programming concepts for IoT devices as well as advances in machine learning, particularly deep learning for IoT devices.

1. INTRODUCTION

The notion of "Internet of Things" has emerged as a last-mile solution for connecting various cyber technologies to our everyday life. It envisions a world in which the sensor devices could exist in any form factor, anywhere, in which all the sensory data will be made available to the Internet, and be readily accessible to a wide range of applications. The sensor devices are usually attached to physical objects, providing a real-time, interactive view of the physical world. Although much progress has been made at the system and sensing level, applications for these platforms are considerably lagging behind. Without compelling applications, the vision of the Internet of Things will not be realized.

The 2015 2nd International Workshop on Internet of Things towards Applications (IoT-App'15) aims to provide a forum for researchers to present thoughts and results on IoT applications. We are looking for application descriptions, development, experiences and evaluation in a wide range of domains including, but not limited to homes, offices, medical care, vehicles, transportation, supply chains and education. Particularly, we are interested in identifying new applications that are made possible by the Internet of Things, as well as new challenges these applications will pose to the design of an Internet of Things.

2. TOPICS

This years edition prominently features IoT in smart homes and cities. For instance, in [2], Meghan Clark and Prabal Dutta consider networked smart homes in the spae of technologically-mediated human interaction. They introduce an applicationcalled 'ghosting' that turns a smart connected home ino a socially connected home. In particular, they synchronise audio and lighting between two homes on a room-by-room basis so that an environment feels coinhabited by a person wo may be many miles away. The paper details the design decisions and chanllenges of such system and explores the opportunities, challenges and limitations of such 'ghosting' concept. In their discussion, they come up with further recommendations to improve the reception of such systems in a natural environment.

Suman Sankar Bhunia, Sarbani Ro and Nandini Mukherjee address in [1] a practical issue in smart cities with relation to healt-care delivery solutions. The authors build on an earlier proposed sensor-loud framework to achieve proper delivery of remote healt-care services, such as monitoring health situation from on-body sensors. Their approach to establish seamless interaction across different communication technologies involves vertical handover across 6LoWPAN, WiFi, UMTS, WiMax and other on tiny sensor nodes. This solution is able to provide uninterrupted remote health-care services in the context of Smart City.

Another aspect of Smart City, energy efficiency of smart houses with resprect to machine learning applications, is considered by Md. Sumon Shahriar and M. Sabbir Rahman in [6]. The authors exploit environmental, smart home and crowd-sourced sensor data for energy efficient applications in urban smart home scenarios. In particular, the paper discusses prediction of home energy from solar photovoltaic panels and meter data in conjunction with motion and possibly further environmental and traffic sensor data with associated human contexts. The machine learning approached preented for integrated urban sensing promise siginficant improvement in the energy budget of smart cities as a whole.

More advanced machine learning approaches, in particular, deep learning in IoT applications is considered by Nicholas D. Lane, Sourav Bhattacharya, Petko Georgiev, Claudio Forlivesi, Lorena Qendro and Fahim Kawsar in [4]. The authors discuss the challenges posed by the requirement of high accuracy inference of human behaviour and context from huge amount of noisy sensor data in complex environments and propose deep learning as a solution to this approach. They present the first measurement study of common deep learning models on representative IoT and mobile platforms. The paper details resource requirements and associated bottlenecks for deep learning models when being used to recognize categories of behaviour and context. This

SenSys'15, November 1-4, 2015, Seoul, South Korea
ACM 978-1-4503-36314/15/11.
http://dx.doi.org/10.1145/2809695.2809697.

work lays a principal foundation for the development of optimisation methods and execution environments that enable deep learning to be readily integrated into IoT and mobile systems.

A practical solution for an existing proplem in public shared spaces is discused in [3] by Nguyen Huy Hoang Huy, Nakul Gulati, Youngki Lee and Rajesh Krishna Balan. The authors track seat occupancy in a public library by means of infrared and capacitative sensors to identify hogged but not occupied seats. The paper describes lessons learned from installations with different sensor hardware and details sensor design and accuracy of results. The system was instrumented in a public library in daily use and was able to reach 100% precision and recall for occupied seats.

Finally, Laurynas Riliskis, James Hong and Philip Lewis addressed the important issue of programming IoT applications as distributed Models, Views and Controllers in [5]. In particular, they propose a novel approach for programming applications across three tiers using a distributed extension of the Model-View-Controller architecture. For this, they add a new primitive, the space, which contains properties and implementation of a particular tier. The writing of applications in this architecture affords numerous advantages such as automatic model synchronisation, data transport and energy efficiency. Their programming framework Ravel allows programming an entire embedded sensor network in a high-level language similar to the programming of web applications.

3. CONCLUSION

We are looking forward to a highly interactive, new edition of the IoT-App workshop in conjunction with Sensys 2015. Smart City and smart home are been predominant topics in this year's edition, followed by issues related to machine learning on the huge amounts of sensor data captured from IoT devices and concepts to ease programming of IoT devices in smart spaces.

4. ACKNOWLEDGMENTS

We would like to thank the people in the workshop's advisory committe, Jie Liu, Songwu Lu, Mahadev Satyanarayanan and Kaming Whitehouse for their superb support and advise. The 20 TPC members have done a great job in further raising the quality of the workshop by providing top-quality reviews. Finally, many thans to Wentai Zhang who has proven reliable and highly responsive as the web chair for the event.

5. REFERENCES

[1] S. S. Bhunia, S. Roy, and N. Mukherjee. Multi criteria assisted context aware vertical hand-over for seamless health-care services in smart city. In *Proceedings of the 2nd International workshop on Internet of Things Towards Applications (IoT-App'15)*, November 2015.

[2] M. Clark and P. Dutta. The haunted house: Networking smart homes to enable casual long-distance social interactions. In *Proceedings of the 2nd International workshop on Internet of Things Towards Applications (IoT-App'15)*, November 2015.

[3] N. H. H. Huy, N. Gulati, Y. Lee, and R. K. Balan. Real-time detection of seat occupancy & hogging. In *Proceedings of the 2nd International workshop on Internet of Things Towards Applications (IoT-App'15)*, November 2015.

[4] N. D. Lane, S. Bhattacharya, P. Georgiev, C. Forlivesi, L. Qendro, and F. Kawsar. Understanding the resource bottlenecks of deep learning on wearables, smartphones and iot devices. In *Proceedings of the 2nd International workshop on Internet of Things Towards Applications (IoT-App'15)*, November 2015.

[5] L. Riliskis, J. Hong, and P. Levis. Ravel: Programming iot applications as distributed models, views, and controllers. In *Proceedings of the 2nd International workshop on Internet of Things Towards Applications (IoT-App'15)*, November 2015.

[6] M. S. Shahriar and M. S. Rahman. Urban sensing and smart home energy optimisations: A machine learning approach. In *Proceedings of the 2nd International workshop on Internet of Things Towards Applications (IoT-App'15)*, November 2015.

Author Index

www.ingramcontent.com/pod-product-compliance
Ingram Content Group UK Ltd.
Pitfield, Milton Keynes, MK11 3LW, UK
UKHW051415290926
15471UKWH00009B/1621

9 781450 341028